THE
MANAGEMENT
CHALLENGE

THE MANAGEMENT CHALLENGE

An Introduction to Management

SECOND EDITION

JAMES M. HIGGINS

CRUMMER GRADUATE SCHOOL OF BUSINESS
ROLLINS COLLEGE

MACMILLAN PUBLISHING COMPANY
NEW YORK

MAXWELL MACMILLAN CANADA
TORONTO

MAXWELL MACMILLAN INTERNATIONAL
NEW YORK OXFORD SINGAPORE SYDNEY

Acquisitions Editor: Nina McGuffin
Development Editors: Carolyn D. Smith and Eve Kornblum
Production Supervisor: Dora Rizzuto
Production Manager: Paul Smolenski
Text Designer: Sheree Goodman
Cover Designer: Leslie Baker
Cover Illustration: Bill Bruning
Icon Illustrations: Jerry McDaniel
Photo Editor: Chris Midgol
Photo Researcher: Dallas Chang
Illustrations: York Graphic Services, Inc.

PHOTO CREDITS: Acknowledgments and credits for all photographs
appear on pages P-1 and P-2, which constitute an extension of the
copyright page.

Macmillan College Publishing Company
866 Third Avenue, New York, New York 10022

Macmillan College Publishing Company is part
of the Maxwell Communication Group of Companies.

Maxwell Macmillan Canada, Inc.
1200 Eglinton Avenue East
Suite 200
Don Mills, Ontario M3C 3N1

Library of Congress Cataloging-in-Publication Data

Higgins, James M.
    The management challenge : an introduction to management / James M.
  Higgins. — 2nd ed.
      p.   cm.
    Includes bibliographical references and index.
    ISBN 0-02-354492-9
    1. Management.   I. Title.
  HD31.H48823 1994   93-18055
  658—dc20   CIP

Printing: 1 2 3 4 5 6 7 8   Year: 4 5 6 7 8 9 0 1 2 3

This book is dedicated to Susan,
the love I've always known.

The decade of the 1990s has proved more challenging to managers than any previous decade. Only by being prepared for the challenges they face can managers hope to manage effectively.

When I began the first edition of this book in the fall of 1986, there were several good introductory management texts in the market. Several more have come into the marketplace since then. But all of these books have three shortcomings: They do not focus on the changing nature of management; they do not take a creative problem-solving perspective; and their chapters present collections of theories rather than an integrated approach to the subjects in question. *The Management Challenge* was written to address these perceived shortcomings.

This book has five key features:

1. It focuses on the changing nature of management in response to ten challenges in the internal and external managerial environments.

2. It emphasizes the problem-solving aspect of the managerial process, both for the individual manager and as part of his or her role in aiding the creative problem-solving efforts of others.

3. Various theories are integrated into models for the major subject areas; these help students understand how different approaches to management fit together.

4. The pedagogical elements of each chapter have been chosen to support the learning process. They include an opening case, learning objectives, boxed features highlighting the management challenges, discussion questions, definitions of key terms in the margins, end-of-chapter and end-of-part cases, and experiential exercises.

5. The instructor's task is facilitated by the availability of an outstanding supplements package, including an annotated instructor's edition with teaching notes in the margins. These instructional aids include overhead transparencies and videos for every chapter, plus videos for several of the case studies.

I believe that this book stands alone among management textbooks for what it offers the student and the instructor. It provides the student with a means of understanding the changing nature of management in this hectic decade. It offers the instructor the added dimension of improving his or her teaching effectiveness. A brief look at the References at the end of the book will convince the reader of the currency and academic soundness of the material presented. In addition, the book has been praised by users for its clarity, interesting themes, and overall success in conveying the wealth of information that comprises the study of management. Every effort has been made to design and illustrate the book so as to encourage the student to read further. Both the figures and the photographs were carefully chosen to closely complement the text and make the book inviting to look at.

The following sections take a closer look at the key features of *The Management Challenge* and the benefits they provide teacher and student alike.

The Changing Nature of Management

Ten challenges facing management are identified in Chapter 1 and reappear throughout the text. As they occur in each chapter, they are identified by an icon in the margin. The icons are introduced at the end of Chapter 1 along with each of the challenges. The specific challenges discussed in each chapter are listed at the beginning of the chapter. By focusing on these challenges, the student learns not only the basics of management but also how management is changing and can be expected to change further in the future.

The Problem-Solving Process

Research and experience clearly show that the primary function of a manager is to solve problems creatively and/or facilitate the creative problem-solving efforts of others, principally subordinates. *The Management Challenge* demonstrates that concept in several ways:

1. Each chapter on the functions of management is presented from the viewpoint of how a manager would make decisions.

2. Problem solving is covered early in the text, in Chapter 4, so that the student understands how the decision-making process occurs and how the presentations in the following chapters are related to the basic model of decision making.

3. At the end of most chapters—especially those discussing the functions of management (planning, leading, organizing, and controlling)—the standard decision-making model presented in Chapter 4 is displayed, incorporating the topics discussed in the chapter as they relate to the model. This helps the student understand how the material from that chapter relates to problem solving.

4. Each chapter contains a Global Management Challenge, an Ethical or Diversity Management Challenge, and a Quality or Innovation Management Challenge. Some chapters have an additional Management Challenge. These boxed features describe a problem faced by a company and the efforts it undertook to solve that problem. In most cases the organizations featured are well-known companies.

Integrative Models of the Management Functions

In many of the chapters—for example, those on problem solving, strategy, motivation, communication, leadership, human resource management, group processes, organizing, and operations management—integrative models of these processes are presented. These models reveal how the major theories and approaches discussed in the chapter fit together. They enable the student to achieve a higher level of understanding than might otherwise be possible. The chapters are not merely collections of theories, but rather offer an integrated treatment of theories.

Chapter Pedagogy

Each chapter has been carefully designed to provide students with a maximum number of learning experiences. Each chapter opens with a set of chapter objectives and a chapter outline. This is followed by a boxed opening vignette (Prologue) about a well-known company and its efforts to solve a management problem. Two opening quotations from noted management researchers, authors, and consultants help focus attention on the importance of the topics covered in the chapter. In addition, marginal notes refer back to the Prologue to demonstrate how it can be related to the points under discussion.

Each chapter closes with a summary that provides a brief review of the chapter, organized to reflect the objectives at the beginning of the chapter. Also included is a list of discussion questions, called Thinking About Management, that contains both general questions and questions on the Management Challenge features.

There are two cases at the end of each chapter. The first case (Epilogue) continues the case introduced in the Prologue and provides discussion questions. The second case (Managers at Work) features individual managers on the job and encourages students to consider their own course of action, given the same situation. In addition, an experiential exercise, Manage Yourself, helps students understand how the content of the chapter may apply to them personally.

Also contributing to the chapter pedagogy are the marginal icons used to indicate when a management challenge is being discussed in the chapter, and the marginal definitions of key terms.

New to This Edition

This second edition of *The Management Challenge* incorporates several changes in both the text and the supplements package that are designed to enhance the usefulness of the text as a teaching and learning tool while addressing the many important changes occurring in management today. Among the changes in the text are an increased focus on the global nature of management. The global chapter has been moved to the first part of the book to reflect the trend toward globalization of business. The boxed features—not only the Global Management Challenges in each chapter but others as well—highlight many global firms. In most of the chapters, a firm from Europe and a firm from the Pacific Rim are discussed either in the boxed features or in the Prologue. Two of the long cases at the end of the parts feature firms based in foreign countries.

The second edition also focuses on cultural diversity, both domestic and global, and on quality and innovation. Approximately half of the chapters contain boxed features on diversity (Diversity Management Challenge). A new chapter is devoted to quality and innovation, two managerial imperatives of the 1990s. In addition, either a Quality Management Challenge or an Innovation Management Challenge feature appears in each chapter.

Other features that are new to this edition are the Ethical Management Challenge, which appears in half of the chapters, and the Diversity Management Challenge, which appears in the other half. Also new are the marginal definitions of key terms. In addition, longer case studies have been added at the end of five of the seven parts of the book to provide an additional learning experience. Icons now identify each management challenge as it is discussed in the text, and the opening case (Prologue) is continued at the end of the chapter (Epilogue) as a way of rounding out the discussion.

Supplements

The Management Challenge is accompanied by an extensive array of supplements designed to facilitate the teaching and learning of management principles. The *Annotated Instructor's Edition* provides teaching notes for use in preparing for classroom presentations. The *Test Bank* contains more than 4000 multiple-choice, true/false, and essay questions; a *Computerized Test Bank* is also available. The *Instructor's Lecture Manual and Resource Guide* includes suggested course outlines and lecture guidelines for each chapter of the text. Also available to users of the text are transparencies, color slides, and the *All American Cheese Company software*—a simulation designed to give students a challenging and realistic introduction to the decision-making process.

The *Study Guide,* available for purchase by students, is designed to complement the instructor's lectures and help students increase their familiarity with the material discussed in the text. An outstanding feature of this guide is its application of management principles to real-world situations.

A complete visual library of videos has been compiled to accompany the second edition of *The Management Challenge.* It includes materials from a variety of manufacturing firms, service companies, and not-for-profit organizations. The videos are linked to the real-world cases discussed in the Prologue and Epilogue of each chapter of the text. Following is a list of some of the excellent videos that accompany the text:

Met Life
Apple Computers
Exxon: Cleaning Up the
   Valdez Oil Spill
Baldor: The New Baldor
   Story
American Airlines' Sabre
   System
SmithKline Beecham
Amdahl—Video Magazine

Nucor Steel
American Airlines
Morehouse College
NASA: Return to Space
Banc One: Credit Card
   Control Video
Allen-Bradley: Flexible
   Manufacturing
Steelcase: The Pyramid

Several videos are available to accompany end-of-part cases. They are:

Toyota—Think Global, Act Local
Reinventing the Chrysler Corporation
AT&T—Delight Makes the Difference
Inc. Magazine—Women in Business

Acknowledgments

No textbook is produced solely by its author. A book as complex as this one is the product of many minds. The following reviewers provided in-depth analyses of the second edition chapters at different stages of development. Their thoughtful insights are greatly appreciated.

David Blevins
University of Arkansas at Little Rock

Charna Blumberg
University of Texas at Arlington

James Cashman
University of Alabama

Norman Deunk
Central Michigan

Michael Frew
Oklahoma City University

Mary Jo Ginty
El Camino College

Nell Hartley
Robert Morris College

Richard Herden
University of Louisville

Durward Hofler
Northeastern Illinois University

Neil Humphreys
Longwood College

George Neely
Florida A & M University

Edward O'Brien
Scottsdale Community College

John Ogilvie
University of Hartford

Jim Swensen
Moorhead State University

Mary Uhl-Bien
University of Alaska, Anchorage

The following reviewers commented on the first edition chapters. Their evaluations contributed greatly to the book's success.

Benjamin L. Abramowitz
University of Central Florida

Larry G. Bailey
San Antonio College

Steven Barr
Oklahoma State University

Daniel J. Brass
Pennsylvania State University

Gene F. Burton
California State University, Fresno

Thomas M. Calero
Illinois Institute of Technology

Alan Chmura
Portland State University

Garth Coombs, Jr.
University of Colorado, Boulder

Joan G. Dahl
California State University, Northridge

Leon A. Dale
California State Polytechnic University

C. W. Dane
Oregon State University

Theodore Dumstorf
East Tennessee State University

Stanley W. Elsea
Kansas State University

Douglas Elvers
University of North Carolina, Chapel Hill

James E. Estes
University of South Carolina

Janice M. Feldbauer
Macomb Community College

Lloyd Fernald
University of Central Florida

James A. Fitzsimmons
University of Texas, Austin

David A. Gray
University of Texas, Arlington

David Grigsby
Clemson University

Gene K. Groff
Georgia State University

Eileen B. Hewitt
University of Scranton

Marvin Karlins
University of South Florida

John Vassar
Louisiana State University, Shreveport

Ann Maddox
Angelo State University

Trudy G. Verser
Western Michigan University

Jane MacKay
Texas Christian University

Douglas Vogel
University of Arizona

Solon D. Morgan
Drexel University

Louis P. White
University of Houston, Clear Lake

Daniel James Rowley
University of Northern Colorado

Many other friends, colleagues, and publishing professionals have contributed their skills and talents to the creation and revision of this book. My special thanks go to Susan Crabill, who has word-processed this manuscript through numerous drafts and shown an amazing amount of patience throughout. I would also like to express my appreciation to Sam Certo, who, as Dean of the Crummer School of Management, provided an environment in which authoring textbooks is encouraged and supported with the finest available electronic hardware and software.

The Macmillan team is to be commended for their outstanding effort. I especially want to thank Nina McGuffin, Management Editor, and Carolyn D. Smith, Senior Development Editor, for truly, without them this book would never have reached fruition. The support of Greg Burnell, Editor-in-Chief for Business and Economics, is also greatly appreciated.

I would like to thank the design and production team—Dora Rizzuto, Production Supervisor, and Patricia Smythe, Senior Designer and Art Buyer—for their patience and perseverance. The following members of the project team are also to be congratulated: Eve Kornblum, Assistant Photo Editor; Chris Migdol, Director of Photo Research; Tom Nixon, Business and Economics Sales Specialist; and Paul Smolenski, Production Manager.

Special thanks are also due to Saralyn Esh for her assistance in the writing of the Management Challenge features.

Many managers, companies, and students are described throughout the book. Most are shown striving to be better managers, and thus can serve as role models for other aspiring managers. Their efforts, too, are to be noted and commended.

James M. Higgins
Winter Park, Florida

Managing in an Ever-Changing Global Environment

77

GLOBAL MANAGEMENT CHALLENGE *Toshiba: Leaner and Meaner*
QUALITY MANAGEMENT CHALLENGE *GM Europe's Strategy of Continuous Improvement*
DIVERSITY MANAGEMENT CHALLENGE *How Companies Train Employees in Other Countries*

PART TWO

Creative Problem Solving

CHAPTER 4

The Manager as a Decision Maker and Creative Problem Solver

113

GLOBAL MANAGEMENT CHALLENGE *IKEA: The Low-Priced Alternative*
ETHICAL MANAGEMENT CHALLENGE *Levi Strauss: A Values-Driven Company*
INNOVATION MANAGEMENT CHALLENGE *3M— Masters of Innovation*

CHAPTER 5

Ethics, Social Responsibility, and the Managerial Environment

151

QUALITY MANAGEMENT CHALLENGE   *Martin Koldyke*
MANAGEMENT CHALLENGE   *Cracks in the Ivory Tower*
ETHICAL MANAGEMENT CHALLENGE
Uncommon Decency: Pacific Bell Responds to AIDS
GLOBAL MANAGEMENT CHALLENGE
Poisoning the Border

CHAPTER 8

Quantitative Methods for Problem Solving and Planning

265

GLOBAL MANAGEMENT CHALLENGE *The Finnish Parliament Applies Quantitative Methods to Energy Policy*
DIVERSITY MANAGEMENT CHALLENGE *Using Statistics to Assure Legal Compliance*
MANAGEMENT CHALLENGE *Polishing the Big Apple*
INNOVATION MANAGEMENT CHALLENGE *Football (Soccer) Match Simulations*

PART FOUR

Organizing

CHAPTER 9

The Organizing Process

309

INNOVATION MANAGEMENT CHALLENGE *Johnson & Johnson*
GLOBAL MANAGEMENT CHALLENGE *Rousing a Sleepy Giant*
ETHICAL MANAGEMENT CHALLENGE *Is Downsizing Ethical in Japan?*

CHAPTER 10

Organizational Design

351

DIVERSITY MANAGEMENT CHALLENGE
*Reorganizing Makes ABB More
Competitive*
GLOBAL MANAGEMENT CHALLENGE *Honda
Tries to Strike a Balance*
INNOVATION MANAGEMENT CHALLENGE *Rank
Xerox Restructures*

CHAPTER 11

Job Design

383

GLOBAL MANAGEMENT CHALLENGE *Nissan
Redesigns to Survive*
DIVERSITY MANAGEMENT CHALLENGE *BP's
Multicultural Teams*
QUALITY MANAGEMENT CHALLENGE
Citibank's Job Enrichment Program

CHAPTER 12

Staffing and Human Resource Management

419

DIVERSITY MANAGEMENT CHALLENGE
A Woman-Friendly Company
INNOVATION MANAGEMENT CHALLENGE
Aetna's Institute for Corporate Education
GLOBAL MANAGEMENT CHALLENGE
Personnel Management in Spain

Managing Organizational Culture, Cultural Diversity, and Change

459

INNOVATION MANAGEMENT CHALLENGE *The Creative Organizational Culture*
DIVERSITY MANAGEMENT CHALLENGE *Samsung Prepares Employees for Other Cultures*
GLOBAL MANAGEMENT CHALLENGE *Air France Must Change*

PART FIVE

Leading

Motivation and Performance

499

GLOBAL MANAGEMENT CHALLENGE *Worker Motivation at Volvo*
QUALITY MANAGEMENT CHALLENGE *Improving Quality at Whirlpool*
ETHICAL MANAGEMENT CHALLENGE *Do Some Firms Push Too Hard?*
MANAGEMENT CHALLENGE *Working in a Japanese Company*

CHAPTER   15

Group Dynamics

539

MANAGEMENT CHALLENGE   *Korea Exports Its Management Style*
GLOBAL MANAGEMENT CHALLENGE   *Rover's Teams Improve Quality*
ETHICAL MANAGEMENT CHALLENGE   *The Dow-Corning Cover-Up—A Group Think Phenomenon?*
QUALITY MANAGEMENT CHALLENGE   *A Team Cuts X-ray Processing Time*

CHAPTER   16

Leadership

577

GLOBAL MANAGEMENT CHALLENGE
Kim Woo-Choong
INNOVATION MANAGEMENT CHALLENGE
Linda Wachner Transforms Warnaco
DIVERSITY MANAGEMENT CHALLENGE
The French Manager

CHAPTER 17

Managing Communication

613

ETHICAL MANAGEMENT CHALLENGE
Citibank's Ethics Game
MANAGEMENT CHALLENGE *Improving Managers' Communication Skills*
GLOBAL MANAGEMENT CHALLENGE *Entering Japanese Markets*
QUALITY MANAGEMENT CHALLENGE *Home Depot Stresses Quality Service*

PART SIX

Controlling

CHAPTER 18

Controlling Performance: Strategic, Tactical, and Operational Control

651

ETHICAL MANAGEMENT CHALLENGE
Rothschild Bank AG
GLOBAL MANAGEMENT CHALLENGE *Problems of Control at Chernobyl*
MANAGEMENT CHALLENGE *Concurrent Control at S-K-I*
QUALITY MANAGEMENT CHALLENGE *Is There Such a Thing as Too Much Quality?*

CHAPTER   19

Management Control Systems

681

INNOVATION MANAGEMENT CHALLENGE   *The Impact of Overcontrol on Creativity*
GLOBAL MANAGEMENT CHALLENGE   *Japanese Cost Accounting Practices*
ETHICAL MANAGEMENT CHALLENGE   *Reverse Appraisal at Chrysler*

CHAPTER   20

Management Information Systems and Knowledge Management

713

GLOBAL MANAGEMENT CHALLENGE
Singapore Invests in an Information Future
QUALITY MANAGEMENT CHALLENGE   *United Uses Expert Systems to Reduce Delays at Hubs*
ETHICAL MANAGEMENT CHALLENGE   *The Ethics of Intelligence Gathering*

PART SEVEN

Contemporary Issues in Management

CHAPTER 21

Operations Management

747

ETHICAL MANAGEMENT CHALLENGE *Jack in the Box Handles a Food Poisoning Crisis*

GLOBAL MANAGEMENT CHALLENGE *ENSIDESA Integrates Computers into Manufacturing*

MANAGEMENT CHALLENGE *Fixing Broken Schedules at American Airlines*

QUALITY MANAGEMENT CHALLENGE *Samsung's Quest for Quality*

Glossary
G-1

References
R-1

Indexes
ORGANIZATION   NAME   SUBJECT
I-1

Case Studies

Experiential Exercises

THE
MANAGEMENT
CHALLENGE

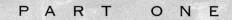

PART ONE

Introduction

Management is one of the most exciting fields of study in the business curriculum. It involves directing the organization in its efforts to be competitive and profitable. It is a dynamic endeavor carried out amid constantly changing environmental factors, both internal and external to the organization. Management must take place in all of the economic functions of the organization: marketing, operations, finance, human resources, research and development, and information management. The management process is changing as the tasks of management are increasingly transferred from managers to operative employees.

The first part of this book introduces you to the nature of management, its history, and the global perspective that is essential to management today. Chapter 1 defines management, describes its changing nature, and indicates the major challenges faced by managers; those challenges create a need for continuous improvement in management practices. Chapter 2 examines the process of management as it has been practiced over time, especially the last hundred years. Major approaches to management are reviewed from a historical perspective. Chapter 3 discusses the dynamic global business environment in which management takes place today, and the impact of that environment on the management process.

"New competitors, new technologies, and new lifestyles demand a new breed of American management."

—John A. Young,
President and CEO,
Hewlett-Packard

"We changed a lot in the 1980s, but in the next five years we'll have to change so much, it will make the last ten look like a practice run."

—Paul Allaire,
CEO, Xerox
Corporation

When you have read this chapter you should be able to:

1. Describe the management process.
2. Indicate why the management process and management styles are changing.
3. Identify and describe the three primary approaches to the study of management.
4. Describe the types of managers.
5. Discuss the universality of management.
6. List the major factors involved in both the internal and external managerial environments.
7. Discuss the question of whether management is an art or a science.
8. Describe the management matrix.
9. Indicate how and why the management process will change in the future.
10. Identify and describe the ten management challenges.

CHAPTER 1

The Changing Management Process

CHAPTER OUTLINE

Approaches to the Study of Management
MANAGEMENT FUNCTIONS
MANAGEMENT ROLES
MANAGEMENT SKILLS

Organizations and Managers
TYPES OF MANAGERS

The Universality of Management
MANAGEMENT IN FOR-PROFITS AND NOT-FOR-PROFITS
UNIVERSALITY AND DIVERSITY

The Managerial Environment
THE EXTERNAL ENVIRONMENT
THE INTERNAL ENVIRONMENT

Management: An Art or a Science?
DEVELOPING MANAGERS

The Management Matrix

The Management Challenges

The Changing Nature of Management
PRODUCTIVITY—THE BOTTOM LINE
CONCLUSION

General Electric: The Company of Tomorrow

General Electric is already the company of tomorrow. In a bold set of management actions aimed at increasing innovation and improving productivity in order to make the company more competitive, GE has set the trends that others will follow into the twenty-first century. CEO Jack Welch, long known for his strategic philosophy of buying and selling firms to gain the number 1 or number 2 position in any industry in which GE is a player, recognizes that maintaining those lofty sales and profit positions depends on improving the management approaches used throughout the company. Welch aims to increase the flow of ideas from all employees by improving the way they are managed.

Three new tools form the core of this management revolution: the workout, best practices, and process mapping. In the workout, a manager and his or her subordinates gather for a three-day retreat. Subordinates work on problems with the help of an outside facilitator; the manager does not participate in these sessions. On the third day the manager is asked to respond to solutions proposed by subordinates with a yes, a no, or a deferral for further study. (Managers are encouraged to limit the number of deferrals.) What makes the workout intriguing is that the manager's own supervisor is present on the third day, but the manager is not allowed to witness his or her reactions to the employees' suggestions. The manager faces the group of employees, and the supervisor sits behind the manager, also facing the employees. The intent is to involve employees in decision making, to solve problems, and to change managers' attitudes toward employee involvement.

In the best-practices technique, the firm compares itself with the firms that are best at performing a particular function or process. GE, for example, has compared itself with the best firms in making appliances and lightbulbs and in performing various financial functions, such as making loans. Once the comparison has been made, GE attempts to improve its performance levels by emulating the best practices of others. Significant improvements have been reported throughout GE's many businesses as a result of best-practices analyses.

In process mapping, employees complete a flowchart of a process such as making a jet engine. The flowcharts show how all the component tasks are interrelated. Employees then try to see how much time they can cut from the process. In the case of jet engines, which GE has been making for years, the firm was able to cut the manufacturing time in half through process mapping, thereby saving many millions of dollars.

What makes all these approaches work is a change in GE's corporate culture, which has become obsessed with productivity and innovation. Welch has been actively involved in the change by, among other things, attending the sessions in which the new programs were developed. He has laid out the changes he wants and has offered rewards for success. Ever ready to experiment and make things happen, Welch is confidently leading GE into the twenty-first century.

SOURCE: Thomas A. Stewart, "GE Keeps Those Ideas Coming," *Fortune* (August 12, 1991), pp. 41–49.

Management is the creative problem-solving process of planning, organizing, leading, and controlling an organization's resources so that it may achieve its mission and objectives. A manager works in an **organization,** a collection of people working in a coordinated manner to achieve a common purpose.

For hundreds of years managers have carried out these processes reasonably successfully. However, today managers throughout the world are being forced to change the way they manage. The world of work is changing dramatically, and as a result managers and the management process itself must also change.[1]

What changes must managers cope with? They include changes in society, government, technology, and the nature of competition. For example, from 1990 to 1992, the technology in the personal-computer industry resulted in a movement from laptop to notebook to palmtop PCs in a matter of months. Competition also is becoming more global. Firms may cope with these changes in a number of ways. With respect to technological changes, they may seek to get their new products to market faster. To meet the challenges of global competition, they may cut costs and open sales offices and factories in other countries. The need to adjust to these changes, combined with the growing recognition that American, Canadian, and European firms have become less competitive in world markets, has already led to significant changes in the practice of management, and more are in store. In short, now more than ever, managers are compelled to improve the way they manage.[2]

Typical of efforts to improve management practices are the dramatic changes taking place at General Electric. GE has to remain globally competitive while meeting the other challenges of the 1990s. Because of increased competition from Japanese firms in the United States and factors such as the opportunity to open new markets in Europe, GE's managers are being forced to reexamine the way they plan, organize, lead, and control. They have become more concerned with productivity, more innovative, and more participative; they not only allow, but actively encourage, their subordinates to participate in the problem-solving process, and they require higher levels of productivity and innovation.

Management: The creative problem-solving process of planning, organizing, leading, and controlling an organization's resources to achieve its mission and objectives.

Organization: A collection of people working together to achieve a common purpose.

GE's managers are being forced to reexamine the way they plan, organize, lead, and control. They have become more concerned with productivity, more innovative, and more participative; they not only allow, but actively encourage their subordinates to participate in the problem-solving process, and they require higher levels of productivity and innovation.

GE is a global firm that is on the leading edge of management change. We can learn much about what management will be like in the future by watching how GE and similar firms improve their management practices now. In this book you will find many examples drawn from the experience of firms like GE, Xerox, Hewlett-Packard, Banc One, Sony of Japan, and Thomson S.A. of France, all aimed at helping you understand where the process of management is headed.

As management continues to evolve, there will be major changes in the way managers solve problems. As at GE, much of the change will involve increased levels of participation and greater creativity. However, management is not merely undergoing evolutionary change, in which existing practices are modified; it is also experiencing revolutionary change, in which whole new approaches are being used. As Rosabeth Moss Kanter, editor of the *Harvard Business Review,* observes, "Managerial work is undergoing such enormous and rapid change that many managers are reinventing their profession as they go."[3]

A major force underlying the revolution in management is the increased use of management practices as a means of gaining a competitive edge.[4] Initiated by Japanese firms during the 1980s, this approach involves improving management through the use of programs such as workouts, best practices, and process mapping to increase productivity, spur innovation, and improve product quality. GE and other leading-edge firms have taken notice and have begun using some of these techniques. Firms and managers that fail to improve their management practices will be left behind. While good management has always played a role in a firm's competitiveness, it has only recently begun to be viewed as a competitive weapon.

Exactly where the practice of management is headed is unclear, but new approaches to management are being initiated in organizations throughout the world. These new approaches, known as the "new management," will appear at many points in this book.[5] The challenge facing managers—the management challenge—is to change the management process in the right direction at the right time to meet the demands of present and future situations. Managers need to be alert to the evolution of the management process and be willing to alter it drastically when necessary.

This chapter will focus on the management process—the functions of management, the roles expected of managers, and the skills required to be a successful manager. We will examine the types of managers and the levels of the organization at which they carry out their responsibilities. We will explore the nature of the managerial environment, both inside and outside the organization, and the question of whether management is an art or a science. We will then examine the interrelationships among the management functions and how they are related to the economic functions of a business, as revealed in the management matrix. Finally, we will describe ten challenges that are changing the managerial process and take a look at the "new management" that is emerging as a result.

Approaches to the Study of Management

Historically there have been three main approaches to the study of management. Management has been viewed as a set of functions, as a series of roles, and as the application of certain specific skills.[6] All three approaches focus on managers' behaviors, but each defines those behaviors in a different way. The functional approach suggests that managers engage in certain functions or activities to carry out their jobs. The role approach is similar, but it focuses on a different set of managerial actions. The skills approach suggests that managers must be able to apply a particular set of skills if they are to succeed at their jobs. It should be clear that none of these approaches is independent of the other two. Moreover, it is becoming increasingly clear that the functions, roles, and skills required of managers are changing.

DISCUSSION QUESTION

Do you now work or have you worked before? Describe what you see (or saw) your manager do in terms of planning, organizing, leading, controlling. Describe problem solving as your manager performed it.

Management Functions

The management process consists of several management functions or activities in which managers engage in order to achieve organizational objectives.[7] Figure 1.1 portrays two major types of management functions. **Mission functions** are activities directly associated with accomplishing an organization's mission. They include planning, organizing, leading, and controlling. These functions occur in a cyclical fashion—that is, each leads naturally to the next, as shown by the arrows in the figure. However, the cycle may be interrupted at any point—for example, by the need to reformulate plans in response to changes in the competitive environment, or by the need to reorganize to meet new cost-saving objectives. The second type of function shown in the figure is creative problem solving, the core function of management.

Mission functions: Activities directly associated with accomplishing an organization's mission. These include planning, organizing, leading, and controlling.

MISSION FUNCTIONS

As just noted, the four mission functions of management are planning, organizing, leading, and controlling. **Planning** is the process of setting objectives and determining how those objectives are to be achieved in an uncertain future.[8] In its broadest scope, planning involves the entire organization. Planning is concerned, for example, with establishing the organization's vision, mission, goals, and overall objectives and developing strategies to achieve them. In its narrowest scope, planning involves setting individual job objectives and identifying the

Planning: The process of setting objectives and determining how those objectives are to be achieved in an uncertain future.

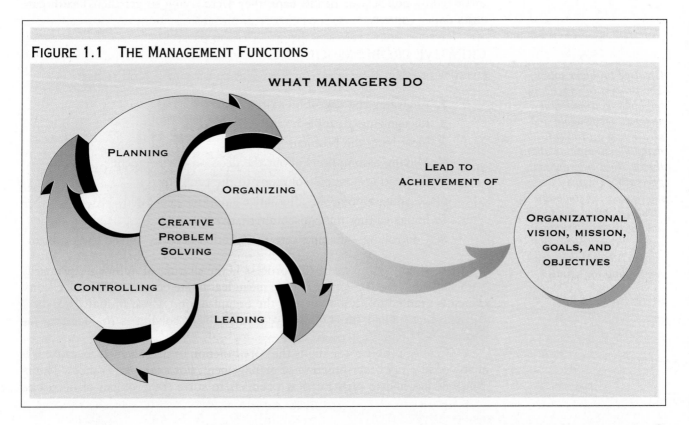

FIGURE 1.1   THE MANAGEMENT FUNCTIONS

Organizing: *The process of determining how resources are allocated and prepared to accomplish an organization's mission.*

Leading: *The process of making decisions about how to influence people's behavior and then carrying out those decisions.*

Controlling: *The process of ascertaining whether organizational objectives have been achieved and, if not, determining what actions should be taken to achieve them in the future.*

tasks required to accomplish them. Thus, when Betty Mizzell, a health services manager for Pru-Care, calculates the annual budget for her unit, she is engaging in planning.[9]

Organizing is the preparation of the resources necessary to put plans into action. It is a key step in the implementation of plans. In this process tasks are defined, personnel are assigned, and other resources are allocated. Much of organizing consists of turning specific tasks into clearly defined jobs and distributing authority among the holders of those jobs. Tasks may be organized at the level of the individual job or at the level of the department, division, or other major subunit of the organization. When workers at a Nucor specialty steel foundry prepare materials inventories according to a predetermined pattern, they are getting organized.[10] When Chevron eliminated 2,500 jobs, it too was organizing its resources.[11]

Leading is the process of making decisions about how to influence people's behavior and then carrying out those decisions. This function is often referred to as influencing, motivating, or directing. The managerial purpose of leading is to channel individuals' behavior in order to accomplish the organization's objectives. When Ken Newton, Jr., director of semiconductor procurement for Hewlett-Packard, walks around talking to his subordinates, counseling, facilitating, and building relationships, he is leading.[12]

Controlling is the process of ascertaining whether organizational objectives have been achieved and, if not, determining what actions should be taken to achieve them in the future. It is an ongoing process that consists of four steps: (1) establishing standards (more specific definitions of objectives), (2) obtaining information about performance (the extent to which standards have been met), (3) comparing the two, and (4) taking corrective or preventive action, if necessary. When Digital Equipment Corporation and Baxter International discovered that their health care expenses far exceeded budgeted amounts, they began negotiating directly with health care providers to set rates; when they established payment ceiling policies for health care, they were trying to get their health care costs under control.[13]

CREATIVE PROBLEM SOLVING

Creative problem solving is a process that consists of several steps:

Creative problem solving: *The process of practicing ongoing environmental analysis, recognizing and identifying a problem, making assumptions about the decision environment, generating creative alternatives to solve the identified problem, deciding among those alternatives, acting to implement the chosen alternative(s), and controlling for results.*

1. Analyzing the decision environment
2. Recognizing a problem
3. Identifying the problem
4. Making assumptions about the decision environment
5. Generating possible solutions to the problem
6. Deciding among the alternative solutions generated
7. Implementing the chosen alternative solution
8. Controlling—making sure the solution actually solved the problem

An increasingly vital part of this process is the sharing of authority, primarily with subordinates. (By *authority*, we mean legitimate power to make decisions, which is granted to a jobholder by the organization.) Thus, in many instances the manager's main function in creative problem solving is to facilitate the problem-solving efforts of others.

Creative problem solving is the core function of management because it is involved in every other function of management. For example, France's Thomson S.A. has had to plan for new products to solve the problem of decreased competitiveness as a result of product obsolescence,[14] and Japan's Honda recently reorganized to solve the problem of eroding competitiveness caused by high costs.[15] The centrality of problem solving has only recently become widely recognized, however, along with the importance of creativity, especially in complex situations.

ETHICS AND PROBLEM SOLVING

All of a manager's decisions should be made in an ethical manner. Managers are responsible for their decisions and are held accountable for them. In recent years, as numerous unethical practices (e.g., insider trading on Wall Street) have

> *AT GE: Managers and their subordinates meet in groups in sessions known as workouts to solve their work units' problems. In these group meetings, the manager must respond to his or her subordinates' creative problem-solving efforts. Subordinates use an outside facilitator who guides the group in its problem-solving efforts.*

ETHICAL MANAGEMENT CHALLENGE

President of Daiwa Security Forced to Resign Over Stock Scandal

It sounds a little like musical chairs, and it isn't exactly illegal in the Japanese securities industry, but it does raise some questions. When it's revealed, highly placed heads can roll.

The practice is called *tobashi*. Here's how it works: A customer agrees to buy securities at an inflated price, with the understanding that they will be repurchased within a fixed period at a slightly higher rate, to cover interest costs. The assumption is that market prices will somehow reach the inflated payment price. The securities often move among the brokerage houses as an accounting ploy, driving their face value higher with each move. However, unless market prices rise to the inflated purchase price, someone is eventually forced to account for the loss.

When Daiwa, Japan's second-largest securities house, faced losses of 85 billion yen ($640 million) early in 1992 as a result of the practice, its president, Mashahiro Dozen, was forced to resign; he was held responsible for the losses—and the questionable trading practices that caused them.

A popular executive, Dozen had served as president of Daiwa for less than three years. His departure appeared calculated to protect the firm from further damage in the *tobashi* scandal—though whether Daiwa would in fact be cleared when other Japanese firms became implicated remained uncertain.

Tobashi is one of the excesses of the easy-money "bubble economy" of the late 1980s in Japan. Some analysts expect that the effects of these excesses won't be cleared up in the financial sector until the mid-1990s.

Daiwa's largest *tobashi* customer was Tokyu Department Store, which agreed in 1991 to invest 92.2 billion yen for stocks that were actually worth about 30 billion yen. The arrangement with Daiwa ended when Daiwa couldn't take the securities off Tokyu's hands at the agreed-upon date. Through civil arbitration, Daiwa subsequently agreed to pay 80 percent of the losses that Tokyu had sustained. The repayment was costly for Daiwa. In contrast with its 1991 projection of a net profit of 50 billion yen, the unexpected *tobashi* payments resulted in a revised forecast of a 43 billion yen net loss.

SOURCE: Quentin Hardy, "Daiwa Securities' President Quits in Wake of Stock Trading Scandal," *Wall Street Journal* (March 12, 1992), p. A8.

produced negative consequences for those involved, greater emphasis has been placed on the ethical aspects of management.[16] U.S. managers are not the only ones who are being subjected to closer scrutiny. This chapter's Ethical Management Challenge explores the problems faced by one of Japan's top managers because of alleged unethical behavior. Should he have resigned?

OTHER MANAGEMENT FUNCTIONS

There are several other functions of management. Many of them can be considered part of the five principal functions just described. Among them are the following:

1. *Communicating,* or transferring information from one communicator to another. Communicating is a major function of all managers, and we will view it as part of leading.
2. *Representing,* or interacting with external constituents, often referred to as stakeholders. *Stakeholders* are groups or individuals who have a "stake" in decisions made by the organization.
3. *Staffing,* or recruiting, selecting, training, evaluating, and performing other functions related to the utilization of human resources. In this book staffing is treated as part of organizing.
4. *Negotiating,* or bargaining with various parties to reach agreements.
5. *Coordinating,* or acting to ensure understanding between members of the organization. We will treat it as part of organizing.
6. *Supervising,* or closely monitoring employee activities. Supervising may be viewed as a specialized form of management applied by first-line managers.

Some of the functions just listed typically constitute a small portion of the work of most managers, but for a few they may be very important. For example, representing is often a major function of the organization's chief executive officer (CEO) but is a minor function for most managers.

TIME SPENT ON MANAGEMENT FUNCTIONS

A landmark study of how much time managers spend on various management functions was conducted by T. A. Mahoney, T. H. Jerdee, and S. J. Carroll in the early 1960s. These researchers interviewed 452 managers from 13 companies ranging in size from 100 to more than 4,000 employees.[17] They studied several different industries, including wholesale trade, manufacturing, insurance, agriculture, public utilities, and finance. The managers included in the study ranged from first-level supervisors to chief executives.

The managers were asked how much time they spent on each of eight management functions. Table 1.1 summarizes their responses. (Note that we have linked the functions studied to the principal functions described earlier. Investigating, for example, is part of problem solving.) The numbers shown in the table are averages. In fact, the study revealed wide variances in the amount of time spent on particular functions. Among the factors influencing the amount of time spent on a function were the level of the manager, the industry, and the stage of the relevant industry or product life cycle (new, growing, mature, or declining). The study's most important finding was the amount of time spent on each function. The time spent helps verify the importance of each of the five

TABLE 1.1 Percentage of Workday Spent by Managers on Eight Management Functions

Management Function		Percentage of Workday
Functions in the Study	Closely Related to These Functions in This Book	
Planning	Planning	19.5
Investigating	Problem solving	12.6
Coordinating	Organizing	15.0
Evaluating	Controlling	12.7
Supervising	Leading	28.4
Staffing	Organizing	4.1
Negotiating	Leading	6.0
Representing	Leading	1.8

SOURCE: Adapted from T. A. Mahoney, T. H. Jerdee, and S. J. Carroll, "The Job(s) of Management," *Industrial Relations,* vol. 4, no. 2 (February 1965), p. 103.

major functions—creative problem solving, planning, organizing, leading, and controlling. (Keep in mind that managers may perform several functions simultaneously.)

Management Roles

The second approach to the study of management examines the roles that managers are expected to perform. In 1973, Henry A. Mintzberg summarized these roles in *The Nature of Managerial Work,* which has become a classic of management research. The essence of Mintzberg's theory is that the manager's activities can be divided into three categories, which are further divided into a number of specific roles.[18] Those categories and roles follow:

1. *Interpersonal relationships.* Most of the manager's time is spent interacting with others as figurehead, leader, and liaison.

2. *Information processing.* Virtually all managers must process information—they give it, receive it, and analyze it. According to Mintzberg, receiving and communicating information is the most important aspect of a manager's job. Information is vital to decision making and problem solving. The main informational roles are those of monitor, disseminator, and spokesperson.

3. *Decision making.* Ultimately managers must use the information they process to make decisions that will solve problems. Mintzberg identified four decision-making roles: entrepreneur, disturbance handler, resource allocator, and negotiator.[19]

The ten management roles identified by Mintzberg (and confirmed in subsequent studies) are listed and described in Table 1.2. Note that these roles are applicable primarily to top managers, especially chief executives. As we will see shortly, they do not necessarily apply to all levels of management.

TABLE 1.2 Mintzberg's Ten Management Roles

Role	Description	Identifiable Activities
Interpersonal		
Figurehead	Symbolic head; obliged to perform a number of routine duties of a legal or social nature	Ceremony, status, requests, solicitations
Leader	Responsible for the motivation and activation of subordinates; responsible for staffing, training and associated duties	Virtually all managerial activities involving subordinates
Liaison	Maintains self-developed network of outside contacts and informers who provide favors and information	Acknowledgements of mail, external board work, other activities involving outsiders
Informational		
Monitor	Seeks and receives a wide variety of special information (much of it current) to develop a thorough understanding of the organization and its environment; emerges as nerve center of the organization's internal and external information	Handling all mail and contacts categorized as concerned primarily with receiving information (e.g., periodical news, observational tours)
Disseminator	Transmits information received from outsiders or from subordinates to members of the organization; some information factual, some involving interpretation and integration	Forwarding mail into the organization for informational purposes, verbal contacts involving information flow to subordinates (e.g., review sessions, instant communication flows)
Spokesperson	Transmits information to outsiders on the organization's plans, policies, actions, results, and so forth; serves as expert on organization's industry	Board meetings, handling mail and contacts involving transmission of information to outsiders
Decisional		
Entrepreneur	Searches organization and its environment for opportunities and initiates "improvement projects" to bring about change; supervises design of certain projects as well	Strategy and review sessions involving initiation or design of improvement projects
Disturbance Handler	Responsible for corrective action when organization faces important, unexpected disturbances	Strategy and review involving disturbances and crises
Resource Allocator	Responsible for the allocation of organizational resources of all kinds— in effect the making or approving of all significant organizational decisions	Scheduling, requests for authorization, any activity involving budgeting and the programming of subordinates' work
Negotiator	Responsible for representing the organization at major negotiations	Negotiation

SOURCE: Adapted from Henry A. Mintzberg, *The Nature of Managerial Work* (Englewood Cliffs, N.J.: Prentice Hall, 1980), pp. 91–92.

Management Skills

The third major approach to the study of management focuses on management skills. A *skill* is an ability to translate action into results. For example, a manager who works well with people can influence them to perform at high levels of productivity. Certain skills may be innate, but managers must also be able to acquire new skills through learning and experience. Robert L. Katz has classified the essential skills of managers into three categories: technical, human, and conceptual.[20] These categories are described and illustrated in Table 1.3.

A *technical skill* is the ability to use tools, techniques, and specialized knowledge to carry out a method, process, or procedure. Almost all jobs involve technical skills of some kinds. Accountants, engineers, and professors, for example, acquire technical skills through their education and apply them in their work. Not all technical skills require preparatory education, but virtually all require some training or job experience. Thus, a salesperson may not need a college degree but must have learned how to close a sale.

Today, many managers are finding that they must learn a whole new set of technical skills. They must know about information systems, be able to use a broad range of analytical tools, and be familiar with complex technical and legal language. In addition, managers are increasingly being called upon to develop quality management programs for their units. This means that they must learn all the technical skills involved in quality management, such as statistical quality-control procedures.

Improving the quality of products and services is a major challenge facing managers in the 1990s. Many, if not most, firms recognize the need for quality improvement and are requiring their managers to learn the necessary technical skills. This chapter's Quality Management Challenge discusses quality management at one U.S. Steel plant. After you have read this feature, ask yourself why quality is so important to U.S. Steel and why it takes so long to improve product quality.

Human skills are the abilities needed to function well in interpersonal relationships. They are critical to successful management. The functional approach describes these skills in terms of leadership, and Mintzberg includes them on his list of roles in the "interpersonal" category. Thus, all three perspectives on man-

AT GE: When GE initiated a new strategy to increase productivity, its managers had to learn new skills, especially human skills, to be effective. They had to learn how to influence behaviors in more positive ways than had been used in the past.

TABLE 1.3 Essential Managerial Skills

Skill	Description	Examples
Technical	Ability to use tools, techniques, and specialized knowledge	Accountant doing an audit; engineer designing a machine
Human	Ability to work effectively in interpersonal relationships	Accounting manager supervising a group of accountants during an audit; manufacturing manager resolving conflict with a design engineer
Conceptual	Ability to see the organization as a whole and solve problems to benefit the total system	Analysis of a possible merger with another firm; analysis of employee absenteeism and turnover

SOURCE: Adapted from Robert L. Katz, "Skills of an Effective Administrator," *Harvard Business Review* (September–October 1974), p. 94.

How One Plant Prospered After Developing a Quality Management Program

When U.S. Steel's Gary Works faced quality problems serious enough to threaten the loss of customers such as General Motors and Ford in 1987—and the shutdown of the plant—a quality improvement program turned things around, almost Cinderella style. And the prince wore a hardhat.

The problem was twofold: The steel was bad and it was arriving late. Automotive customers, who bought half the plant's output, rejected 2.6 percent—the worst performance of any steel firm that year.

The solution was twofold, too. For the first half, plant managers, determined to govern best by governing least, stayed on the sidelines, allowing a small team of hourly workers to study the problems for themselves. Five steelworkers were freed from mill jobs to visit automotive customers' plants. They were generally free to change how the steel was made, stored, and shipped so that it arrived in better condition.

The other half of the solution empowered the union workers to identify problems and fix them fast, with no bureaucracy or scapegoating; they formed problem-solving teams with their customers. "We'd have instances of breakage," explained one Ford manager who uses the steel for doors and fenders, "where we'd get the managers, the engineers, the metallurgists working on it. Then the hourly guys would come in and get their heads together, and the problem would go away."

When a galvanizer found zinc flaking in steel he'd painstakingly coated against corrosion, for example, he knew immediately that the rods that trimmed zinc buildup from the steel edges must be misaligned. He went back to the mill and got them fixed. When Ford said they had to scrap the bottom sheet from each pile because of "rust," the steelworkers demonstrated that the substance could simply be wiped off; pressure had created the residue.

The team is generally credited with saving contracts and probably the plant itself, no small feat at the moment. "We used to think that workers just work and managers tell them what to do, but that's just wasting brains," said one judge in a nationwide quality-improvement competition won by the team. "These are line workers in the steel industry, supplying the auto industry. I can't think of two more battered industries. They've really pushed this idea of empowerment down where it belongs. That's the spirit of American industry that's coming back, and people don't know it."

agement identify the interpersonal function/role/skill as important. People with good human skills build trust and cooperation as they motivate, influence, or lead. The importance of these skills is becoming increasingly evident, largely because they have been applied by many international firms to increase productivity and compete more effectively with U.S. firms. Human skills are difficult to master and are becoming more so. As business is conducted on an increasingly global scale, managers are being required to learn new ways of dealing with people in foreign countries that are appropriate to their cultures—not an easy task.

When U.S. Steel's Gary Works faced serious quality problems that threatened the shutdown of the plant, the plant managers instituted a quality improvement program in which a team of steelworkers identified problems and were empowered to solve them themselves.

The grassroots input has been so well appreciated that team members now belong to their *customers'* employee-involvement teams, advising GM, for example, on avoiding problems where mirrors are bolted to doors.

The idea of giving hourly workers this kind of responsibility for the quality of the product is not a novel one, but it is not common either. At the Gary Works, it may be the wave of the future—a future that nearly didn't happen.

SOURCE: James R. Healy, "U.S. Steel Learns from Experience," *USA Today* (April 10, 1992), pp. 1B–2B.

Conceptual skills involve the ability to see the organization as a whole and to solve problems in a way that benefits the entire organization. While conceptual skills draw heavily on analytical abilities in solving problems, they also depend on the more creative and intuitive talents of the individual manager.

As noted earlier, it is becoming increasingly clear that to cope with change and other management challenges a whole new set of skills is emerging.[21] The quality management skills discussed earlier are only one example. Another set of skills involves becoming a facilitator, as opposed to a "boss." The skills it takes to work with people are different from those it takes to tell them what to do.

Organizations and Managers

As noted at the beginning of the chapter, managers do their work in organizations. There are many types of organizations and many ways of classifying them. For example, organizations may be large (IBM) or small (the local ice cream parlor). A useful way of classifying organizations is to distinguish between for-profit and not-for-profit (nonprofit) organizations. Ford Motor Company and IBM are for-profit organizations; the federal government and the United Steel Workers Union are not-for-profit organizations. We will discuss management in these two types of organizations later in the chapter.

Historically, organizations have used managers to direct the efforts of others so as to achieve the organization's objectives effectively and efficiently. **Effectiveness** refers to whether objectives are achieved. **Efficiency** describes the relative amount of resources used to obtain effectiveness. The use of excessive amounts of resources to achieve an objective may be effective, but it is not efficient. Thus, the cost of effectiveness must always be considered; if the cost of achieving objectives is too high, they may have to be abandoned.

Managers have long been responsible for planning, organizing, leading, and controlling in such a way as to ensure that the organization's objectives are achieved efficiently. A major change is occurring in many organizations, however: Management is increasingly becoming a responsibility of every individual in the organization, not just those who are formally designated as managers. In many organizations all members are managing themselves more than was generally true in the past. They are performing some of the functions of management, such as planning, not simply the tasks assigned to them as part of the organizing process.

Types of Managers

In any organization managers can be classified as either general or functional managers. In addition, managers are often classified according to their level in the organization. In this section we will briefly describe both classification systems.

GENERAL VERSUS FUNCTIONAL MANAGEMENT

A **functional manager** is responsible for a particular economic function of the organization or part of it. He or she may be concerned with some aspect of marketing, finance, operations, human resources, or information systems. Most managers are functional managers. The responsibilities of a **general manager,** in contrast, cover more than one function and often deal with all functions. General managers are normally CEOs or product or division managers.

The general manager's role is quite different from that of a functional manager. The general manager must view his or her job within the context of the total organization, a task that may be difficult for a manager who was formerly a functional manager and is predisposed to take a functional viewpoint when making decisions.

LEVELS OF MANAGEMENT

Except for the very smallest organizations, virtually all organizations have three levels of management: top, middle, and lower. (See Figure 1.2.) In large organizations there may be several layers within each of these major levels.

Effectiveness: The ability to set appropriate objectives and achieve them.

Efficiency: The relative amount of resources used to obtain effectiveness.

Functional manager: A manager who is responsible for a particular economic function of the organization or some part of it.

General manager: A manager whose responsibilties cover more than one function and often deal with all of them. General managers are normally CEOs or product or division managers.

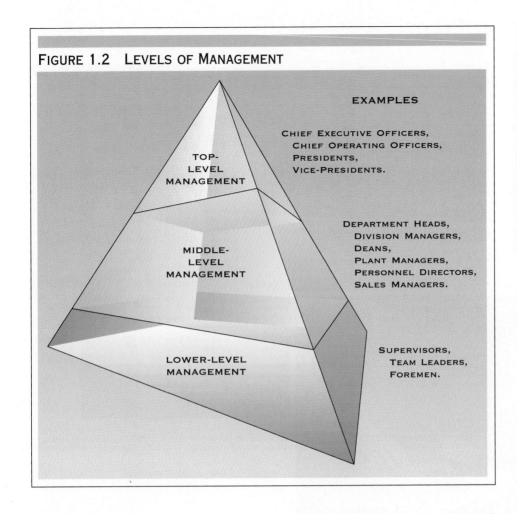

FIGURE 1.2   LEVELS OF MANAGEMENT

EXAMPLES

CHIEF EXECUTIVE OFFICERS,
CHIEF OPERATING OFFICERS,
PRESIDENTS,
VICE-PRESIDENTS.

TOP-
LEVEL
MANAGEMENT

DEPARTMENT HEADS,
DIVISION MANAGERS,
DEANS,
PLANT MANAGERS,
PERSONNEL DIRECTORS,
SALES MANAGERS.

MIDDLE-
LEVEL
MANAGEMENT

LOWER-LEVEL
MANAGEMENT

SUPERVISORS,
TEAM LEADERS,
FOREMEN.

AT GE: When GE began its efforts to change its corporate culture, it needed the commitment of all three levels of management. It also had to provide training to managers at all three levels to teach them the skills necessary to manage in the new environment.

Top Managers

Top managers include CEOs, chief operating officers, presidents, and vice-presidents. These managers direct their attention to the major issues affecting the organization. They set goals and objectives and devise strategies to achieve them. Their principal job is to scan the environment and make sure the organization is achieving its objectives. For example, John Sculley, president of Apple Computer, Inc., continually monitors Apple's environment to make sure the firm's products, prices, and distribution system meet the challenges of the competitive environment. Sculley must see to it that Apple is able to compete with IBM, Compaq, Toshiba, and other major manufacturers of personal computers.[22]

Top managers: Managers who direct their attention to the major issues affecting the organization, such as setting goals and objectives and devising strategies to meet them.

Middle Managers

Middle managers include department heads, division managers, deans, plant managers, personnel directors, and sales managers, among others. They occupy the second layer—and often the third, fourth, or fifth—of management in a large organization.

Middle managers have traditionally been thought of as critical to an organization because they translate top management's directives into instructions for lower-level management and operating employees. They have also been viewed as a crucial source of information to be used by top management in solving problems. Indeed, top managers are usually selected from the ranks of middle management.

Middle managers: Managers who occupy the second layer—and often additional layers—of management in a large organization.

MANAGERS AT DIFFERENT LEVELS OF AN ORGANIZATION FOCUS ON DIFFERENT ISSUES AND SPEND DIFFERENT AMOUNTS OF TIME ON THE VARIOUS MANAGEMENT ROLES. TOP MANAGERS FOCUS ON THE MAJOR ISSUES FACING THE ORGANIZATION, SETTING GOALS AND OBJECTIVES FOR THE ORGANIZATION AS A WHOLE. MIDDLE MANAGERS SUCH AS DEPARTMENT HEADS AND PLANT MANAGERS TRANSLATE TOP MANAGERS' DIRECTIVES INTO INSTRUCTIONS FOR LOWER-LEVEL MANAGERS AND OPERATING EMPLOYEES. LOWER LEVEL MANAGERS LIKE THIS FOREMAN IN A NISSAN PLANT ARE RESPONSIBLE FOR SUPERVISING THE ACTIVITIES OF OPERATING EMPLOYEES AS THEY IMPLEMENT THE DIRECTIVES OF UPPER MANAGEMENT.

Sometimes a manager is a top manager of one part of an organization but a middle manager from the perspective of the organization as a whole. The dean of your business school is the top manager of that school but is a middle-level manager in the college or university. The dean leads the business school but also implements the directives of the university's president or provost. Thus, a manager's level depends on the unit of the organization being analyzed.

As very large organizations attempt to become more competitive, many are reducing the number of middle managers they employ. Middle managers often process information and provide communication links between different levels of management; it is believed that this can be done more inexpensively using computerized information systems. Moreover, middle management ranks often become too large because new positions are created in order to promote lower-level managers.

Lower-Level Managers

Lower-level managers may have titles such as supervisor, team leader, or foreman. In most organizations operating employees report to lower-level managers (sometimes called front-line management). This first line of management implements the plans and directives of middle or upper management.[23] Increasingly, management at this level is using a team approach in which the manager acts as a facilitator rather than as a boss. The team manager helps the team achieve its objectives.

Lower-level managers: Managers who supervise front-line or operating employees.

Front-line management is the entry level of management. Operating employees are typically promoted to this level before moving farther up the managerial ladder. These supervisory positions are pivotal; performance here can make or break a managerial career. Normally a person who is especially good at his or her first supervisory job will be promoted to a higher level of management.

MANAGEMENT FUNCTIONS BY LEVEL[24]

Studies by Manoney, Jerdee, and Carroll and other researchers have shown that each of the four mission functions is practiced to varying degrees at different levels of management.[25] As can be seen in Figure 1.3, planning occupies much more of the time of upper-level managers than of lower-level ones. Organizing

FIGURE 1.3   MANAGEMENT FUNCTIONS BY LEVEL

	PLANNING	ORGANIZING	LEADING	CONTROLLING
TOP MANAGEMENT				
MIDDLE MANAGEMENT				
FIRST-LINE MANAGEMENT				

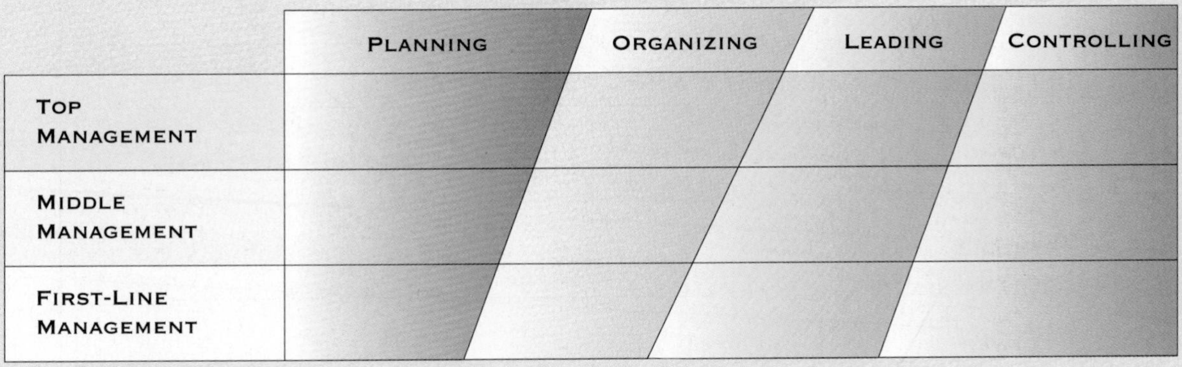

seems to occur to about the same degree at all levels. Leading and controlling are performed more at lower levels than at higher levels. Naturally, the amount of time and effort that managers devote to each of the mission functions depends on the situation. For example, if management functions are performed by all employees, the balance between the various functions performed by managers will change: Planning and leadership will require relatively more time, and organizing and controlling will require relatively less.

The studies noted here also indicate that the degree to which the management functions are practiced at each level of management varies by industry. This variance might be a result of the degree of change occurring in the industrial environment. Environments that change frequently require more planning, for example, than more stable environments. Variance in management functions by level might also result from the nature of particular industries. Some industries, such as diamond cutting, center on tasks that require close supervision; others, such as food processing, do not. Leadership practices are likely to be quite different in the two industries.

MANAGEMENT ROLES BY LEVEL

Mintzberg's list of managerial roles is based on studies of chief executives in a small number of organizations. Although Mintzberg's study was replicated (duplicated) by others with similar results,[26] the fact remains that it was carried out at the CEO level. Similar studies at other levels of management do not support Mintzberg's classifications.[27] One explanation for the differences may be that the roles of managers vary by level. At the lower and middle levels of management, for example, certain "executive" roles, such as that of figurehead, have little meaning.

MANAGEMENT SKILLS BY LEVEL

As portrayed in Figure 1.4, the skills required of managers are also thought to vary according to level. Technical skills are much more important at the lowest levels of management than at high levels, but some technical skills are needed at the upper levels. Conceptual skills are extremely important at the upper levels of management because general managers have to make broad, complex, unstructured decisions; moreover, they must deal not just with one economic function but with all of them, and they must understand how the organization operates

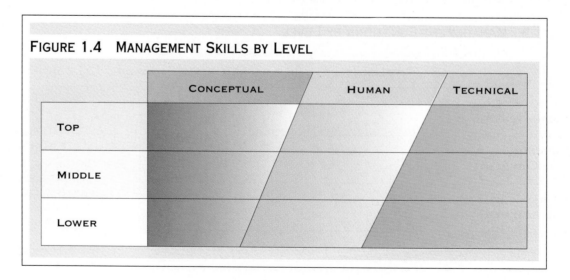

FIGURE 1.4 MANAGEMENT SKILLS BY LEVEL

	CONCEPTUAL	HUMAN	TECHNICAL
TOP			
MIDDLE			
LOWER			

within its environment. Human skills seem to be important at all three levels of management.

Researcher Virginia Boehm examined a similar set of skills by management level among managers at SOHIO. She found distinct differences among the skills required at the three levels.[28]

LINE VERSUS STAFF MANAGERS

Line managers are directly concerned with accomplishing the organization's goals; **staff managers** are in charge of units that provide support to the line units. Traditionally, marketing, operations, and finance have been viewed as line functions and virtually everything else has been considered a staff function. That view has changed somewhat as human resource management, formerly considered a staff function, has come to be viewed as critical to an organization's success. Also, some companies may consider certain functions normally viewed as staff functions to be important enough to be line functions. For example, research and development (R&D) might be considered a line function in a high-tech computer firm.

Line managers: Managers who are directly concerned with accomplishing the objectives of a particular organization.

Staff managers: Managers who are in charge of units that provide support to the line units.

The Universality of Management

In 1983, when John Sculley became president and chairman of the board of Apple Computer, Inc., the other members of the Apple board assumed that management is universal—that it can be applied to all organizations everywhere. They expected that Sculley's excellent performance as president of Pepsi-Co of America could be duplicated at Apple, with a different product in a different market using different technologies. Sculley himself, however, realized that he had to learn the specifics of the personal-computer industry before making major changes. He studied the technology, product design, and other facets of the business before he made major decisions other than those necessary to re-

When John Sculley became president and chairman of the board of Apple Computers, Inc., he studied the technology, product design, and other facets of the business before making any major decisions. He then dealt with the need to make employees more profit oriented and aware of competition.

solve immediate problems. He dealt with the need for reorganization, the need to make members of the company much more profit oriented than they had been in the past, and the need to make employees more aware of competition. However, until he had thoroughly studied the situation, he made no major product or marketing decisions.[29]

The concept of the **universality of management**—the belief that management practices are applicable to all organizations—has long been argued by experts and by managers themselves. Management probably *is* universal, but only if the manager has become familiar with the specific situation in which it must be applied. Thus, when Archie McCardell, who had been a successful executive at Xerox, assumed the presidency of International Harvester, he proceeded to make many decisions in the same way he had at Xerox. However, he failed to allow for the specifics of the situation. Having left a nonunionized environment for a unionized one, he chose to hold firm while the United Auto Workers conducted a lengthy strike against the firm. The consequence of this "problem-solving" action was bankruptcy for International Harvester.[30]

Management is universal in the sense that all managers plan, organize, lead, control, and solve problems, but the specifics of how they carry out these tasks are dictated by the situation, even within the same company. As business has become global, the universality of management has become more evident. For example, U.S. managers imitate Japanese managers and European managers imitate both U.S. and Japanese managers. Moreover, Japanese managers have adopted many techniques used in the United States and Europe. Yet in all such cases the way the techniques are applied differs because of specific factors such as cultural differences.

Management in For-Profits and Not-for-Profits

Not long ago a client from a division of a city management team explained to a consultant that several members of the division were opposed to a new management system because "it may work everywhere else, but it won't work here because we're unique."[31] This claim was partially true; although management principles can be applied to not-for-profit organizations like city governments as well as to for-profit firms like Apple or Xerox, the management process must be tailored to each situation. In the case just mentioned, it was possible to modify a basic concept known as management by objectives to meet the organization's needs.

Many people question whether management techniques and processes that work in a for-profit environment can be applied to not-for-profit organizations; however, it is possible to transfer management functions, roles, and skills from one environment to the other.[32] This is not to deny that there are significant differences between the challenges facing managers in for-profits and not-for-profits. A for-profit organization operates in a market-dominated economic situation in which customers play a major role. Not-for-profits, on the other hand, operate in more political environments in which their clients often are not the source of the funds they receive for their products and services. Various other external sources—contributors, legislators, activist groups—greatly influence the actions of managers in not-for-profit organizations.

Even within the for-profit and not-for-profit sectors there can be major differences between organizations. In the for-profit sector, for example, the environment of a manufacturing firm like U.S. Steel differs considerably from that of a service-based firm such as McDonald's. Similarly, the situation confronting a private not-for-profit organization differs significantly from that facing a public not-for-profit.[33] The Easter Seal Society must appeal to the general public; the

When New York City's Metropolitan Museum of Art began treating its operation as a business, its dependence on donations was reduced.

Federal Communications Commission must, while serving the needs of the general public, function in a highly political and bureaucratic arena.

We might ask whether the differences in management practices between for-profits and not-for-profits are greater than those between organizations within each of these categories.[34] The answer seems to be no. Management practices can be transferred from for-profits to not-for-profits, but they must be modified to fit the specifics of the situation, just as they must be modified when moving from one industry or company to another within the for-profit sector.

Many of the management success stories of recent years have occurred in the not-for-profit sector. For example, many states and cities have become known for their ability to adapt business-based management systems to their environments. Although they do not seek profits, they do seek cost savings. In North Carolina, quality circles—a participative group decision-making technique aimed at improving quality and saving money—have been employed successfully in state agencies. In the Department of Motor Vehicles, this technique resulted in annual savings of more than $50,000.[35] Similarly, the Metropolitan Museum of Art in New York City reports that once it began treating its operations like a business, it became much more successful and less in need of donations. Each year it sells hundreds of thousands of reproductions of artworks, for which it earns many millions of dollars.[36] Clearly, the fact that an organization is not-for-profit does not mean that it cannot be managed like a profit-making organization.

Universality and Diversity

We have explored whether management practices can be transferred from one company or industry to another and whether they can be applied in both for-profit and not-for-profit organizations. A related question is whether management is applicable in new and changing contexts. All but a handful of the best-known management theories and practices are based on the experiences of North American (primarily U.S.) organizations.[37] As a result, for the most part, these models and prescriptions are derived from the study of a white male management hierarchy. Only recently have women and minorities begun to enter the ranks of management in significant numbers. Moreover, almost all management models fail to recognize the effect of cultural variations on their applicability in countries other than the United States.

Within the United States, women and minorities may find that management theories and practices do not work as well for them as they might for white male managers, and white male managers may find that they do not work as well with female and minority subordinates as they do with white male subordinates. We are only beginning to understand the implications of the increased diversity of the American work environment.

Although much remains to be learned about the effects of culture on management, some progress has been made. Many American and European firms have learned how to apply management practices that were originally developed by Japanese firms, and firms in Europe and Japan are adopting many U.S. management practices. Nevertheless, throughout this book we should keep in mind that any given management practice or theory is probably based on studies of samples that are no longer fully representative of the total population of managers or workers.

The Managerial Environment

External environmental factors: *Forces external to the organization—economic/competitive, technological, political/legal, and societal.*

Internal environmental factors: *Forces internal to the organization, including people (owners, board members, general management, organized labor, nonorganized workers, informal leaders) and all other factors within the organization's boundaries (corporate culture, leadership style, organizational structure, and similar factors).*

Managers operate in extremely complex environments. They face both **external** and **internal environmental factors** that influence the way they manage. (See Figure 1.5.) The nature of the managerial environment varies with the manager's economic function and level in the organization as well as with other factors, such as whether the organization is for-profit or not-for-profit. In addition, the scope of the managerial environment is broader for general and upper-level managers than it is for functional and lower-level managers. Nevertheless, all managers must cope with both internal and external factors. For example, the manager in charge of work-in-process inventories for a modular-home manufacturer must balance the demands of the market against the demands of the production line, as well as those of the accounting department (which looks for lower inventories to reduce costs) and the sales department (which seeks higher inventories to ensure quick delivery). In short, managers are pulled in many directions by many different forces. They must always be aware of the environmental forces influencing their decisions; at the same time, they must be aware of how their decisions may affect the environment.

The External Environment

Four kinds of external forces are portrayed in Figure 1.5: economic/competitive, technological, political/legal, and societal. Each of them is made up of numerous components that have an interest in—or an impact on—the actions of the organization's management. In fact, these components often anticipate or demand certain managerial actions. For example, the federal government, a component of the political/legal environment, has passed numerous laws to provide equal employment opportunity, protect consumers, regulate the use of energy, stabilize the economy, protect the natural environment, define relationships between business and organized labor, tax businesses, and govern many other aspects of organizations' operations.

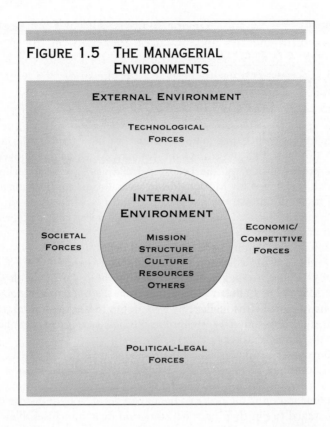

FIGURE 1.5 THE MANAGERIAL ENVIRONMENTS

EXTERNAL ENVIRONMENT

TECHNOLOGICAL FORCES

SOCIETAL FORCES

INTERNAL ENVIRONMENT

MISSION
STRUCTURE
CULTURE
RESOURCES
OTHERS

ECONOMIC/ COMPETITIVE FORCES

POLITICAL-LEGAL FORCES

Other examples of the impact of external forces can be seen in the day-to-day life of any major organization. The competitive environment is an especially potent force composed of current competitors, buyers, suppliers, substitute products, and the ever-present threat of new competitors entering the market.[38] Managers must find ways to manage the factors in the external environment—either by changing them or by adapting to them—or suffer the consequences: unachieved objectives, reduced profits, or worse—losses. This chapter's Management Challenge describes how the McDonald's Corporation has changed in order to compete better in a changing marketplace. What major changes can you identify?

The Internal Environment

Many factors within the organization affect a manager's decisions. These factors include people—owners, board members, general managers, organized labor, nonunionized workers, informal leaders, and others. They also include the organization's rules, policies, procedures, structure, strategies, culture, and resources. The manager must be able to balance the needs and requirements of all of these factors not only against each other, but also against the demands of the external environment. For example, managers must establish policies for equal employment opportunity as required by an external force—the U.S. government.

AT GE: *GE was forced by competition to change its strategies. Hence, it had to change its managers' leadership style as well. They had to become more participative, involving their subordinates in the decision process.*

Management: An Art or a Science?

Is management an art or a science? By now the answer should be obvious: It is both. For some people, skillful management seems to be a natural extension of their personalities. For most, however, management is a skill that must be

McDonald's Responds to Its Environment

Things aren't the way they used to be—even for fast-food giants in the heartland of fast food. Although, like the rest of the country, McDonald's enjoyed years of respectable profits throughout the 1980s, its U.S. sales have been declining lately. The market has changed for McDonald's in several respects: Beef consumption is down, the fast-food industry is not growing, and new arrivals are dividing and conquering the market that does exist, some with speed and price, others with better taste and nutrition.

McDonald's is fighting back with radical departures from its much revered (and frequently copied) dedication to speed and consistency. Where standardization had been almost a religion, flexibilty is now the order of the day.

CEO Michael R. Quinlan is departing from the operating system instituted and rigorously enforced by founder Ray Kroc in the 1950s, for several reasons. For one, McDonald's does only 20 percent of its business after 4 P.M. Quinlan hopes to move into the dinner market.

To lure dinner customers, where expectations are different, the menu must be expanded. More than 150 new items—from lasagna and oven-roasted chicken to eggrolls and corn on the cob—are being evaluated.

Experimentation is the order of the day in decor, too, and store owners are being encouraged to put their personal stamp on their franchises. New store formats also are being tested. Self-service franchises, small cafe-style franchises, and McDonald's on airplanes are all under consideration.

None of these moves is without risk, of course. Can service stay fast, or will the new complexity gum up the machines? If store operators have more leeway, will the McDonald's brand image be diluted? Can low prices *and* a varied menu be combined?

One aspect of the new plan is firmly in keeping with the McDonald's tradition: Technology will be a vital part of the operation. New "staging equipment" will allow parts of meals to be prepared in advance and stored for short periods. Robot machines for drinks and fries are also being tested, as well as ovens that can cook a pizza in five minutes.

When the new dinner package is ready for rollout after 1993, analysts will be watching to see if McDonald's does what it says it will to recapture market share: "Whatever it takes."

SOURCE: Lois Therrien, "McRisky," *Business Week* (October 21, 1991), pp. 114–122.

AT GE: GE's top management evidently felt that managers could be developed and that management skills could be learned. The company adopted a new set of values to which all members of the organization were expected to adhere. To manage better in this new culture, GE's managers had to undergo extensive training to acquire different skills.

learned. Many organizations fail to recognize the need to develop this skill; they simply assume that a person who has been made a manager will know how to manage. For example, one young woman complained that her company, a regional commercial bank with several billion dollars in assets, had promoted her to a management position and assumed that she would automatically know what to do. She had received no training in interpersonal or conceptual skills and only limited training in the relevant technical skills. She also had received no training in management functions or roles. This situation is all too common.[39] Not only do many managers not receive the training they need, but according to one expert, most management education neglects the subtler aspects of management, such as interpersonal relations.[40]

Developing Managers

U.S. firms that wish to develop successful managers could learn from the example of Japanese firms. Managers in major Japanese firms spend an average of at least one day a month throughout their careers learning how to manage better. In addition, at the beginning of their careers, and periodically thereafter, they participate in two- or three-week sessions of intensive management training. Japanese firms believe that managers *must* be developed; a manager's personality and leadership style cannot be changed by a one-day course but can be developed only over time and with considerable effort.

Many large American firms practice a similar approach to management development. Firms like IBM, Hewlett-Packard, and Ford train their managers with techniques similar to those used by the Japanese. The training is usually less extensive than that of Japanese managers but is repeated at intervals, often throughout the manager's career. The training received by managers in these firms depends on the function they perform and their level of management, as well as on their perceived career development needs.

The Management Matrix

The management functions—creative problem solving, planning, organizing, leading, and controlling—are applicable to each of an organization's economic functions: marketing, finance, operations, human resources, information management, and R&D. But managers must also manage the management functions. They have to plan, organize, lead, and control the planning process, for example, and the same is true for all the other functions. Thus, when Allied-Signal, Inc. reorganized its entire management structure, it first had to plan how it was going to reorganize. Then it had to organize the reorganization process, get its managers to lead the implementation of that process, and control by checking to see if the reorganization had achieved the desired results.[41] The interrelationships among economic and managerial functions can be diagrammed in the form of a matrix, as shown in Figure 1.6.

The Management Challenges

A variety of forces, or **management challenges,** are changing the nature of the management process and the functions, roles, and skills required of managers.[42] Both from within and from outside the organization, forces for change are constantly putting new pressures on managers. This has always been true, but today those forces are stronger and less familiar. In this section we will discuss the major challenges facing managers in the 1990s and their impact on managers and the management process. The ten major management challenges are listed in Figure 1.7.

Although this is an introductory text and therefore must focus on basic management theories and practices, the challenges listed in Figure 1.7 are so pervasive and important that they will appear at many points in the book. Each time one or more of them is discussed, the appropriate icon will appear in the margin. The management challenges noted in each chapter will be listed at the beginning of the chapter.

Management challenges: Forces that change the nature of the management process and the functions, roles, and skills required of managers.

FIGURE 1.6   THE MANAGEMENT MATRIX

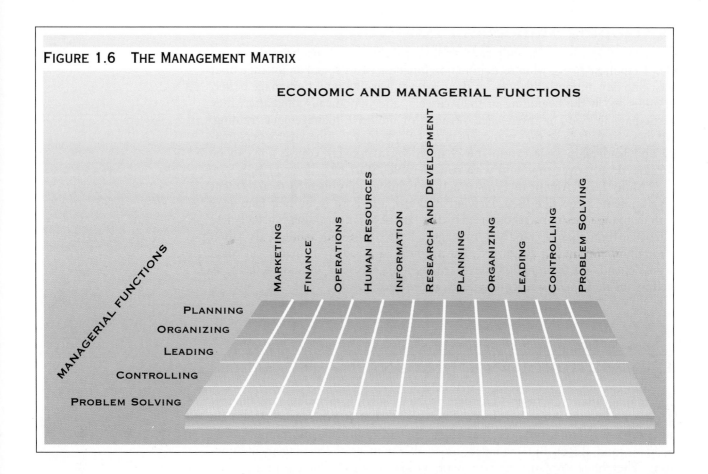

1. *Accelerating rates of change.* In his 1970 book *Future Shock,* Alvin Toffler predicted that, as we approached the twenty-first century, all aspects of life, including organizational life, would be subjected to accelerating rates of change.[43] His predictions have been borne out: Witness the collapse of the Soviet Union, the unification of Germany, the availability of color copiers and powerful laptop computers, and Japan's emerging dominance in biotechnology. Not only are changes occurring at an accelerating rate, but their magnitude is also increasing.[44]

   Managers must not only embrace change and learn how to manage it, but also ensure that all members of the organization join in this effort.[45] This is a tremendous challenge for an organization's managers, in view of most people's desire for stability and maintenance of the status quo. As Thomas J. Peters, a well-known management consultant and author, has suggested, managers must change their organizations so that they will be able to "thrive on chaos."[46] The external and internal factors affecting both individuals and organizations cannot be ignored. "Change is the order of the day. Choose it or chase it. Adapt or die," proclaimed Theodore Levitt, former editor of the *Harvard Business Review.*[47]

2. *Increasing globalization of business.* Trends like the economic integration of Europe, the probability that the Pacific Rim will be the world's most dominant economy in the next century, and

increased levels of foreign competition in most domestic economies mean that managers must develop and maintain a global perspective. The domestic market can no longer be considered sufficient to support a firm in the future. This point is so important that an entire chapter of this book is devoted to the global management challenge. In addition, each chapter contains a Global Management Challenge feature. This chapter's Global Management Challenge reviews Nestlé S.A.'s acquisition of Source Perrier S.A. as part of its strategy of global expansion. After you have read the feature, think about how the acquisition of Perrier fits into Nestlé's expansion strategy.

3. *Increasing levels of competition.* The 1990s will be the most competitive decade of this century. More and more competitors are entering both domestic and global markets. Top managers must formulate strategies to compete in markets that offer little hope of overall growth, making market share ever more critical to

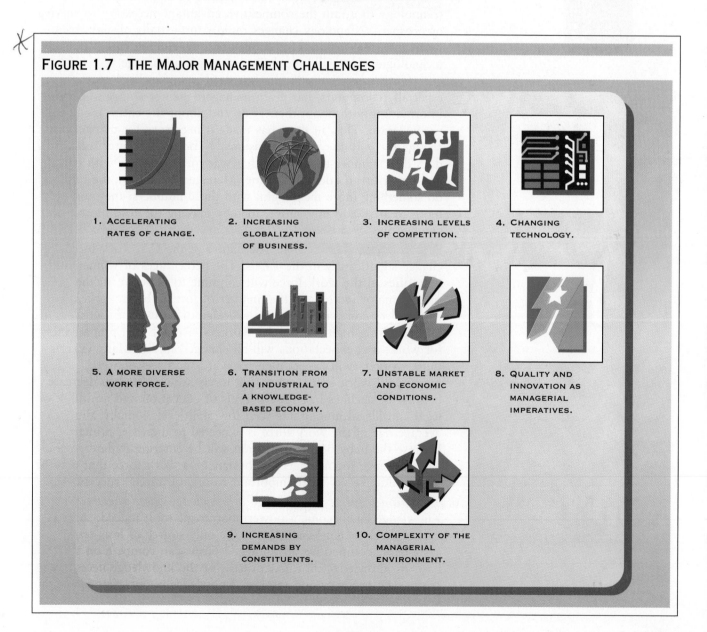

FIGURE 1.7 THE MAJOR MANAGEMENT CHALLENGES

1. ACCELERATING RATES OF CHANGE.

2. INCREASING GLOBALIZATION OF BUSINESS.

3. INCREASING LEVELS OF COMPETITION.

4. CHANGING TECHNOLOGY.

5. A MORE DIVERSE WORK FORCE.

6. TRANSITION FROM AN INDUSTRIAL TO A KNOWLEDGE-BASED ECONOMY.

7. UNSTABLE MARKET AND ECONOMIC CONDITIONS.

8. QUALITY AND INNOVATION AS MANAGERIAL IMPERATIVES.

9. INCREASING DEMANDS BY CONSTITUENTS.

10. COMPLEXITY OF THE MANAGERIAL ENVIRONMENT.

success.[48] Innovation in products, processes, marketing, and management will determine whether a firm can survive under such conditions.

When increased competition is combined with two other major challenges—the shift from an industrial to a knowledge-based economy and an anticipated shortage of labor, especially in skilled positions and the professions, accompanied by the increased demand for labor in a service-dominated economy—it becomes quite clear that managers will have to change the way they manage people.[49] In a labor-intensive economy in which labor is in short supply, workers will have higher expectations and will require more attention from management. At the same time, in order to survive, companies must eliminate many staff positions and strive to justify all positions in financial terms. Managers must "add value" to the organization's product or service if they are to be retained.[50]

4. *Changing technology.* Most firms depend in some way on technology to attain the competitive advantage necessary to survive or prosper. Technology changes rapidly in virtually all industries. Firms must be prepared for competitors developing new technologies that will give them a strategic advantage.

On the positive side, the increased use of technology, especially computers, has given managers greater ability to obtain information both about their units and about the entire organization. This, in turn, has made it necessary for managers to change the way they make decisions.[51] Today, computer software does the "number crunching" that was formerly done with pencil and paper or an adding machine. Managers now have the time to do something more meaningful with those numbers; they can be more creative and innovative, thereby making the firm more competitive.

5. *A more diverse work force.* The nature of the U.S. work force will change significantly in the 1990s. The percentages of women and minorities in the work force will continue to increase. At the same time, a major increase in the number of foreign-born workers is expected to compensate for the shortage of native-born workers in jobs requiring high skill levels. Workers' average age, preparedness for work, and expectations will all change rapidly. Many experts think workers will expect higher rewards and seek more meaningful work. Yet worker skill levels are expected to decrease because of declines in effective levels of education and an influx of legal and illegal immigrants with low skill levels. Finally, the average age of the work force is expected to increase, primarily because the baby boom generation will be entering its later years.[52] The challenge for managers is to manage a work force that may be less productive yet more important to organizational success.[53]

6. *Transition from an industrial to a knowledge-based society.* Knowledge has become a powerful strategic tool; indeed, some experts believe that knowledge is the only source of long-term, sustainable competitive advantage.[54] Firms can compete on the basis of knowledge of a new process or the knowledge necessary to create new products and services. Knowledge about customers can

Nestlé's Aggressive Acquisitions Fuel Global Ambitions

The world's largest food maker—the Swiss firm Nestlé S.A.—was a sleepy giant in the 1970s: calm, secure, and unaggressive. This is no longer true. In its efforts to stay ahead of its major competitors—the Anglo-Dutch Unilever Group and U.S.-based Philip Morris Cos., which owns Kraft-General Foods—Nestlé is no longer secure or unaggressive. Its hostile takeover of Source Perrier S.A. is a case in point.

Nestlé fought Italy's Agnelli family for more than two months in 1992 in its hostile takeover of Perrier. The duration and severity of the battle highlights the competitiveness of the food industry. The major players consistently attempt not only to eat into each other's markets, but to grow rapidly and constantly develop new products.

Nestlé had previously lacked a significant market presence in the European mineral water business. Until 1991, it viewed Perrier as an impregnable family-controlled French institution. When the family agreed to sell a large stake to the Agnellis, however, Nestlé sprang, seizing the chance to acquire Perrier's many water brands, including Contrex in France and Poland Spring in the United States.

Nestlé's first hostile takeover was in 1988, when it beat Swiss coffee and chocolate rival Jacobs Suchard in a battle for the British chocolate firm Rowntree. (Suchard was later acquired by Philip Morris.)

Helmut Maucher, Nestlé's chairman, hopes to double total sales to 100 billion Swiss francs ($66 billion) by the year 2000—not only through takeovers, but also through strategic partnerships with companies such as Coca-Cola Co. and General Mills Inc. The takeover of smaller companies, such as Perrier, is seen as one means to this end. At all the food giants, potential acquisitions are constantly under consideration.

Nestlé's expansion strategy targets ice cream, pet food, and yogurt as areas of future growth. But the world's largest food maker won't be limited to food. Acquisitions will be made in the skin-care and pharmaceutical sectors as well. Plans to gain majority control of the French cosmetics giant L'Oréal, for example, were under way even before the Perrier takeover was complete.

Maucher believes that the pace of takeovers in the global food business could be even more dramatic in the 1990s than in the 1980s—and he intends to keep up with it.

SOURCES: E. S. Browning, "Nestlé Appears to Win Battle to Acquire Source Perrier," *Wall Street Journal* (March 24, 1992), p. A13; and E. S. Browning, "Nestlé Looks to Realms Beyond Food for the Future," *Wall Street Journal* (May 12, 1992), p. B4.

also create a competitive advantage. For example, electronic data interfaces, in which customers and suppliers share data bases, result in closer relationships that help lock out competitors. Managers must learn to manage knowledge as a critical factor in success. The effective management of knowledge can lead to continuous innovation, another critical factor in organizational success.[55]

7. *Unstable market and economic conditions.* In the 1990s, U.S. firms will face an unprecedented degree of instability in market and

In the 1990s, U.S. firms will face an unprecedented degree of instability in market and economic conditions. Organizations like the Unemployed Career Network Group have been formed to try to cope with some of the consequences of economic instability.

economic conditions. Consider the savings and loan bailout program, which is expected to cost at least $500 billion at a time when federal budget deficits have reached an all-time high.[56] Consider the extremely high U.S. trade deficit, which is fueled by, among other things, lack of investment in R&D;[57] trade practices of foreign nations that are perceived as unfair by American firms;[58] continued dependence on imported oil; and past inability to compete globally on the basis of price or product quality. Consider, too, the effect of the baby boomers, who can be thought of as an "age wave" moving through the population. Managers must deal with the consequences of these and many other variables.

8. *Quality and innovation as managerial imperatives.* Managers today must learn how to improve quality within their units. High levels of product and service quality are a minimum requirement for competitiveness in this decade.[59] Consultants, researchers, and the CEOs of major firms all agree that quality is essential.[60] In addition, managers must know how to encourage innovation, not just in the creation of new or improved products and services but also in operations and other work processes, product development and marketing, and the management process.[61] In fact, quality and innovation are so important that an entire chapter of this book is devoted to them, and they appear in boxed features in many chapters.

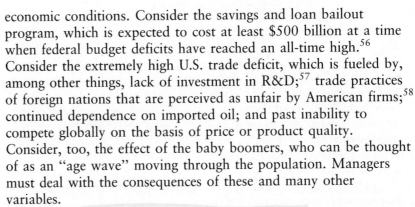

9. *Increasing demands by constituents.* In the 1990s, organizations will face increasing demands by constituents. **Constituents** are major groups affected by an organization's decisions. They may include stockholders, customers, suppliers, the general public, and competitors. Constituents' demands are likely to focus on such

issues as preservation of the natural environment, prevention of air and water pollution, reversing the depletion of the earth's ozone layer, and protection of animal rights. Constituent groups are already making vocal demands in the areas of employee health and safety, employee security during mergers and acquisitions, shareholder value, quality and service to customers (both within and outside the firm), equal employment opportunity, philanthropy, and ethical behavior. The demand for ethical behavior is especially significant. Questions of business ethics will be discussed in boxed features in each chapter, as well as in the text itself.

10. *Complexity of the managerial environment.* The rapid changes occurring in the external and internal managerial environments are increasing the overall complexity of the environment in which managers must operate. As the preceding nine challenges suggest, managers must cope with an increasing number and variety of environmental factors. Thus, the complexity of the managerial environment is itself a challenge to management as the twenty-first century approaches.

Constituents: Major groups affected by an organization's decisions.

The Changing Nature of Management

Because of the ten challenges just described, and others as well, the functions of management are undergoing dramatic changes. The kinds of changes required to meet management challenges will be discussed in detail in later chapters. Here we will briefly describe some of the most important ways in which management is expected to change.

In problem solving, more creativity will be necessary and employee participation in decision making will increase. In a sense, every employee can become a manager.[62] Employees may be asked to solve problems in a complex environment in which they plan, organize, lead, and control their own efforts to a much greater extent than they have in the past. In some cases, work teams will act almost as independent businesses.

In planning, there will be more worker participation in setting goals, more encouragement of individual entrepreneurship within the company ("intrapreneurship"), and greater use of computer simulations of actual and anticipated situations.

In organizing, there will be increased delegation of authority. Jobs will be redesigned to accommodate new technologies and make them more meaningful. The organization itself will be redesigned to give more autonomy to major subunits and eliminate middle management layers. Teamwork will become more common. Some organizations will be organized around processes, such as logistics, as opposed to functions, such as production.

In leading, growing acceptance of the concept of management as a service to the rest of the organization will lead to greater use of the technique of managing by walking around (MBWA)—facilitating, coaching, and encouraging.

In controlling, there will be increased emphasis on self-control, coupled with increased control by computers. Costs will also be watched more closely as competition intensifies.

Throughout the organization, information management will become more important and there will be demands for improvements in quality and innovation.

Productivity—The Bottom Line

Much of what management will do to meet these challenges involves increasing productivity. **Productivity** is the relationship between a firm's outputs and its inputs. The more productive a firm is, the better it can compete, especially on a global basis. If a firm is able to manage change, it can improve its productivity. If it can be a technological leader, it can also improve its productivity because it can create new products or services at lower cost. If it can improve the productivity of a diverse work force, it can become more competitive. Appropriate management of the remaining challenges—shortages of resources, demands of constituents, unstable economies and markets, and others—will also lead to increased productivity, which, in turn, will improve the firm's ability to compete.

Conclusion

Management *is* challenging. It is ever changing. It is constantly in need of fine tuning. In many companies, it needs to be completely revamped. Good managers are seldom bored; those who experience the management challenge enjoy it.

This book is based on the belief that you should not only learn about management, but also learn how managers think and go about solving problems. You will also learn how management is changing now and how it is expected to change in the future—knowledge that will help you prepare to become an effective and efficient manager.

AT GE: *GE exemplifies the company of the future. More and more authority will be granted to workers. Employees will learn to manage themselves, becoming more productive and innovative in the process.*

Summary

(Before reading this summary, look again at the objectives listed at the beginning of the chapter.)

1. Management is a creative problem-solving process that consists of planning, organizing, leading, and controlling an organization's resources to achieve its mission and objectives effectively and efficiently. It is a complex process that varies at different levels of the organization.

2. As the environment in which managers must operate has changed, there have been corresponding changes in the way managers manage and in the management process itself.

3. Management has been studied from three perspectives: as a set of functions (creative problem solving, planning, organizing, leading, controlling); as a series of roles (interpersonal, informational, decisional); and as a set of skills (technical, human, conceptual). All of these views of management are interrelated.

4. There are several ways of classifying managers. Managers differ by whether they are general managers or are responsible for a particular economic function. They also differ by the level of the organization at which they operate—top, middle, or lower. We can also distinguish between line managers, who are directly concerned with accomplishing the organization's goals, and staff managers, who are in charge of units that provide support to the line units.

5. Management is universal, but management theories and practices must be adapted to the specifics of any given situation. There may be significant differences in how managers operate in for-profit, public not-for-profit, and private not-for-profit organizations.

6. All managers must deal with forces in the external and internal managerial environments. External forces include government, technology, competition, other members of the industry, new entrants to the industry, customers, clients, substitute products, suppliers, creditors, and the economy. Internal forces include general management, other managers within the organization, informal leaders, the organization's culture, the organization's structure and strategies, and the organization's rules, policies, and procedures.

7. Management is both an art and a science. Managerial skills can be learned.

8. The management process occurs not only in each of the organization's economic functions—marketing, finance, and others—but also in the management functions themselves. The interrelationships among management and economic functions are portrayed in the management matrix.

9. The management process is changing because of several major factors in the managerial environment. The ten major management challenges are
   • Accelerating rates of change.
   • Increasing globalization of business.
   • Increasing levels of competition.
   • Changing technology.
   • A more diverse work force.
   • Transition from an industrial to a knowledge-based economy.
   • Unstable market and economic conditions.
   • Quality and innovation as managerial imperatives.
   • Increasing demands by constituents.
   • Complexity of the managerial environment.

10. Management is becoming more participative and more innovative. Every function of management is being affected by these trends.

General Questions

THINKING ABOUT MANAGEMENT

1. What is a manager? What is an organization? What does a manager do?

2. Why do organizations need managers?

3. Describe each of the functions, roles, and skills of managers. Now describe how these might differ for a nursing supervisor in charge of 50 beds in a 500-bed hospital; the president of a Women's Junior League (a volunteer service organization) with 50 members in a city with a population of 400,000; the production manager in an automobile assembly plant; and the president of a software firm with 100 employees.

4. Describe the management challenges facing the president of your college or university.

5. Describe the external and internal forces confronting the marketing manager for Apple Computer.

6. Describe how each of the factors listed in Figure 1.7 is likely to affect the product development manager in charge of creating new cars for the Pontiac Motors Division of GM. Now describe how the same factors would affect the manager of a McDonald's hamburger franchise.

Questions on the Management Challenge Features

ETHICAL MANAGEMENT CHALLENGE

1. If this event had taken place in the United States, what might have happened to the president of Daiwa Security?
2. What does your answer to the preceding question tell you about the impact of differences in cultural norms such as ethical and legal principles?

QUALITY MANAGEMENT CHALLENGE

1. Think about the quality of the products and services of the organizations for which you have worked. How could these be improved?
2. How could the quality management program at U.S. Steel's plant be transferred to an organization for which you have worked?

MANAGEMENT CHALLENGE

1. Evaluate the actions McDonald's has taken.
2. As a manager, what would you do to improve on those actions?

GLOBAL MANAGEMENT CHALLENGE

1. Does the fact that Nestlé is based in Switzerland rather than in the United States make a difference in its actions in this situation?
2. What management functions are being carried out in this situation?

E P I L O G U E

General Electric: The Company of Tomorrow

The vignette at the beginning of the chapter discussed GE's efforts to become a twenty-first-century corporation. If you were to ask managers at GE whether they enjoy managing more now than they did in the early 1980s, they would answer with an emphatic yes. Perhaps more important, their subordinates feel that they are being well managed and have opportunities for self-management that were not available to them several years ago. Viewing the GE story as a case study, answer these questions.

DISCUSSION QUESTIONS

1. What necessitated the changes in culture and management style carried out at GE?
2. How do these changes reflect the changing nature of management?
3. Identify the management challenges affecting GE in this case.
4. Indicate any other challenges that are probably affecting GE and describe their likely impact.
5. What other changes might GE's management undergo in the future?

Motivating Employees at General Mills

Linda Sampieri, vice-president for employee relations for General Mills Restaurants (Red Lobster, the Olive Garden, and others), was thinking about the changing nature of the work force. Motivation had become a major problem. She wondered what the company could do to improve the motivation of employees—cooks, waiters, hosts, dish washers. The firm's 42,000 employees were, on average, better educated than ever before, although many were less well educated. They all had much higher expectations than were typical of workers ten years ago. Further compounding Sampieri's problem was a smaller pool of potential employees.

There was an obvious need for additional training for first-level supervisors, but Sampieri was looking for something special, more innovative. Various compensation plans were being considered, and group-oriented "team programs" were also being pursued.

DISCUSSION QUESTIONS

1. What kinds of compensation programs might be tried?
2. What other kinds of motivation programs might be attempted?

Should You Be a Manager?

MANAGE YOURSELF

On the basis of what you have read in this chapter and what you know from other sources, what are the requirements of a good manager? Would you include, for example, good interpersonal skills and good conceptual skills? Complete the following list:

	Skills	Low	High
1.	Interpersonal skills		
2.	Conceptual skills		
3.	Technical skills		
4.	Planning skills		
5.	Organizing skills		
6.	Leadership skills		
7.	Controlling skills		
8.	Problem-solving skills		
9.	Quality management skills		
10.			
11.			
12.			
13.			
14.			
15.			

Rate yourself as either high or low on each factor. Should you be a manager? It's too early to tell, but you now have an idea of what's required.

"Those who cannot remember the past are condemned to repeat it."

—George Santayana

"We are the prisoners of what we know."

—Walter B. Wriston,
Former CEO,
Citicorp

CHAPTER OBJECTIVES

When you have read this chapter you should be able to:

1. Identify the five forerunners of contemporary management.

2. Indicate the principal concerns of scientific management and administrative theorists regarding the classical approaches to management.

3. Discuss the major concerns of the behavioral approach to management.

4. Describe how the management science approach attempts to improve the problem-solving process.

5. Identify the principal contributions of the systems approach to management.

6. Describe how the contingency approach functions.

7. Describe the contemporary approach.

8. Describe how critics like Thomas J. Peters have influenced management.

Learning from Management History

CHAPTER OUTLINE

Precursors of Modern Management Theory
    CLASSICAL APPROACHES
    THE BEHAVIORAL APPROACH
    THE MANAGEMENT SCIENCE APPROACH
    THE SYSTEMS APPROACH
    THE CONTINGENCY APPROACH

Contemporary Management—A Synthesis
    JAPANESE MANAGEMENT PRACTICES
    EXCELLENCE IN MANAGEMENT

Management in the Future

MANAGEMENT CHALLENGES
DISCUSSED IN THIS CHAPTER:

Accelerating rates of change.

Increasing globalization of business.

Increasing levels of competition.

Met Life: Making Sure Employees Learn from History

Metropolitan Life Insurance Company is on the leading edge in terms of work processes and management innovations. For example, it has initiated a computerized insurance application system, reducing the paperwork necessary to process applications. The application is filled out on a laptop computer; the information is then sent to headquarters either on disk or via modem transmission. Met Life's computerized information system uses an advanced local area network. All information related to claims is scanned into the network for use by claims processors and other interested parties.

Met Life's innovations don't stop at technology. When it comes to employee relations, orientation, and training and development, the firm's track record is outstanding. When it found out that its employees perceived their benefits as insufficient, it not only improved benefits but also set up a special communications program to make sure employees knew what those benefits were. The firm has since established newsletters, seminars, and videos to keep employees informed of their benefits.

With respect to training and development, the company has invested heavily in seminars, videos, and self-paced learning systems. A videotape about the company's history includes major milestones and an introduction to the organizational culture—the values stressed by the firm and its employees. The tape is used to orient new employees and is part of a series of tapes that introduce the employee to the firm, its mission, its services, its strategies, and the individual's role in relation to all of these. The company believes that its employees should share a common understanding of the firm, where it is and how it got there. The videotape format was chosen so that each manager would be able to conduct a complete orientation for his or her subordinates.

SOURCES: Susan Berger and Karen Huchendorf, "Ongoing Orientation at Metropolitan Life," *Personnel Journal* (December 1989), pp. 28–35; Elizabeth Daniele, "Met Life Uses Magic on Reps," *Insurance & Technology* (March 1991), p. 38; Catherine A. Novak, "Profiting from Diversity," *Best's Review* (March 1992), pp. 18–22, 99, 100; and "Flex Communication Pays at Met Life," *Employee Benefit Plan Review* (April 1990), pp. 26–30.

M et Life is using its past to shape its future. Its actions, when taken in the context of the quotations at the beginning of this chapter, demonstrate the importance of being aware of history and being able to learn from it without being bound by it. In management, as in many other areas of life, you need to understand what history tells you and what it does not tell you. You need to know how to use it, but you also need to know its limitations.

Managers search for patterns in the problems they face, and they tend to use learned solutions when those patterns recur. They need to know the facts about what has happened in similar situations in the past. Only when they understand the problem environment and how it developed can they fully understand the problem they are trying to solve. Experienced managers have more firsthand knowledge to draw upon than less experienced managers, but all managers can benefit from knowing the history of management. No manager has enough personal experience to deal with every problem he or she faces.

As the rate of change in our society continues to accelerate, more and more new situations will occur that are likely to resemble others that occurred in the past. This makes it possible to repeat effective solutions and avoid ineffective ones. In all of an organization's economic functions—marketing, finance, operations, human resource management, and information management—successful managers know what worked before, what didn't, and why.

As a practicing manager, you will benefit from knowing the history of management because if you heed the lessons of history, you will avoid making the same mistakes your predecessors made. You will be able to consult the appropriate sources to discover what worked and what did not. Understanding the history of management will also help you recognize when to act and when not to.[1] You will be able to identify the problems that seem to recur. By knowing how such problems have been handled in the past, you should be better able to meet the management challenges of the 1990s.

This chapter explores five forerunners of contemporary management theory: the classical, behavioral, management science, systems, and contingency approaches.[2] We review the contributions of leading experts in each of these approaches and show how each is applied today. The chapter concludes with a review of current issues, two contemporary approaches to management, and a discussion of how management may change in the future.[3]

> *AT MET LIFE: Met Life understands how important history is. It has even made a video about its history so that its employees will understand it.*

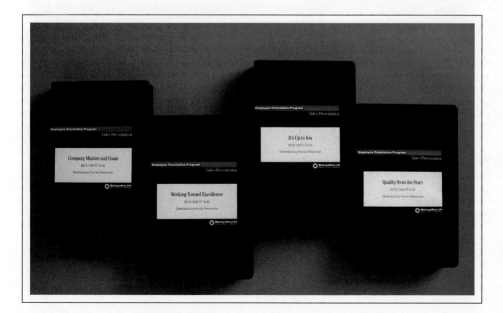

Met Life's innovations do not stop with technology. The firm has created training and development videos to orient new employees.

Precursors of Modern Management Theory

Historian Daniel A. Wren has observed that "management is as old as man."[4] But as he also pointed out, only recently has there been any scientific study of the process. One reason for this is that large business organizations have existed only since the early nineteenth century. Until the 1800s, therefore, there was no systematic development of management theory, and not until the mid-1900s did it become useful to the average manager. However, early civilizations did practice management—and in a way not very different from how it was practiced until the late nineteenth and early twentieth centuries. Table 2.1 lists major contributions to the practice of management from approximately 5000 B.C. to the late nineteenth century. To appreciate these contributions, remember that not until 1776, when Adam Smith described the benefits of the division of labor in *The Wealth of Nations*, did mass production become recognized as possible and desirable.

TABLE 2.1 The Early Evolution of Management Thought

Time Period	Contributor	Major Contributions
5000 B.C.	Sumerians	Established written records for both government and commercial use
4000–2000 B.C.	Egyptians	Employed inventory practices, sales ledgers, taxes; developed an elaborate bureaucracy for agriculture and large-scale construction, e.g., pyramids; employed full-time administrators; used forecasting and planning
4000 B.C.	Hebrews	Exception principle, departmentation; Ten Commandments; long-range planning; span of control
2000–1700 B.C.	Babylonians	Enforced law for conducting business, including standards for wages and obligations of contractors
500–200 B.C.	Greeks	Developed the work ethic; Socrates' universality of management, the beginning of the scientific method for problem solving
200 B.C.–A.D. 400	Romans	Developed a factory system for manufacturing armaments, pottery, and textiles; built roads for distribution; organized joint stock companies; used specialized labor; formed guilds; employed an authoritarian organizational structure based on function
A.D. 300–20th century	Catholic church	Decentralized hierarchical structure with centralized strategic control and policies
1300	Venetians	Established a legal framework for business and commerce
1494	Luca Pacioli	Developed the first system of double-entry bookkeeping
1776	Adam Smith	Focused on division of labor and mass production as the key to prosperity
1800	Eli Whitney	First to use interchangeable parts for mass production
1850s	Robert Owen	One of the first to recognize the importance of human resources; improved working conditions, reduced hours of work, raised minimum age of work for children
1860s–70s	Charles Babbage	Improved the efficiencies of production using mathematical problem-solving techniques; emphasized human resources

SOURCE: Based primarily on Daniel A. Wren, *The Evolution of Management Thought*, 2nd ed. (New York: Wiley, 1979), Chap. 2. Reprinted by permission of John Wiley & Sons, Ltd.

As we describe each of the major historical perspectives on management, bear in mind that management philosophies and practices reflect the society within which they exist—its culture, its values, and its needs. Moreover, the technological, social, political, and economic forces at work in any society change, and therefore management has changed over time and must continue to change.[5] Before the twentieth century, for example, the practice of management was largely authoritarian. It was based on hierarchical organizational structures similar to those developed by Egyptians, Romans, and other ancient societies with highly organized military forces. The decentralized organizational structure of the Roman Catholic church, which was imitated by most other organizations, influenced the nature of management in medieval times.[6] As Western society shifted from an agricultural to an industrial base, its leaders and scholars began to realize that traditional management approaches were unsatisfactory. What worked on a farm or in the military simply would not work in a factory. At the beginning of the twentieth century, some 150 years after the beginning of the industrial revolution and some 35 years after the beginning of industrialization in the United States, managers began to ponder the factors involved in managing and to consider alternative ways of managing.[7] It is from this point that we pursue the history of management in detail.

As an example of how management practices reflect society's values, this chapter's Diversity Management Challenge portrays how Kentucky Fried Chicken (KFC) searches for minorities and women to fill top management positions. Few firms make such an effort, and even fewer go to such lengths.

Kentucky Fried Chicken's Designate Program is a prime example of how management practices reflect society's values. Designate Bill Armstrong is market manager for the Chicago region.

Kentucky Fried Chicken

If you're serious about attracting and keeping female and minority executives, you may have to hire them fast—sometimes before a position exists.

That has been the experience at Kentucky Fried Chicken (KFC), a unit of PepsiCo Inc. that is uncommonly determined to create greater diversity in management. The KFC effort, which it calls the Designate Program, has achieved noteworthy results so far: In 1989, none of its seventeen senior U.S. managers were minority or female; by 1991, seven were.

One of the designates was Larry Drake, a ten-year veteran at Coca-Cola Co., who managed $100 million of bottler accounts. As one of Coke's highest-ranking black executives, Drake earned more than $100,000 a year, including bonuses. He had just received a master's degree in business and was aiming for a vice-presidency. Then came the offer he couldn't refuse: the title of vice-president at KFC and annual compensation of more than $150,000.

The offer did have one unusual feature, though. The position didn't yet exist. In the meantime, KFC asked him to train in the company's restaurants and learn the business from the bottom up.

This is how the Designate Program attracts other companies' seasoned managers and fresh thinkers—and achieves diversity, one of corporate America's most intractable problems. "We want to bring in the best possible people," says Kyle Craig, president of U.S. operations at KFC. "But if there are two equally qualified people, we'd clearly like to have diversity."

Classical approaches: Approaches to management developed in the early twentieth century; include scientific management and the administration and organization approach.

Classical Approaches

The **classical approaches** to management were developed early in the twentieth century. There were two major approaches: scientific management and the administration and organization approach. They focused primarily on improving work methods and formulating principles for administering and structuring organizations.

SCIENTIFIC MANAGEMENT

Scientific management: An approach to management that sought to find "the best way" to do the job. Scientific management had four underlying principles: the development of a true science of management; the scientific selection of the individual to fill each job; the scientific education and development of each employee so that he or she would be able to do the job properly; and cooperation between management and workers.

Scientific management sought to find "the one best way" to do any given job. Its leading proponent was Frederick W. Taylor, an industrial engineer whose 1911 book *The Scientific Principles of Management* revolutionized the practice of management. Other major contributors to scientific management were Henry R. Gantt and Frank and Lillian Gilbreth.

Frederick W. Taylor (1856–1915)

Frederick W. Taylor was interested in the achievement of prosperity both for the employer and for the employee.[8] Working principally with workers in heavy manufacturing industries like steel, he showed that work could be redesigned so that workers could do more. He also redesigned compensation systems so that workers *wanted* to do more. Taylor believed that by scientifically redesigning work to make it more efficient—for example, by reducing the number of motions required to perform a job—and by providing proper incentives, he could eliminate worker underachievement. Using scientific management approaches, both a company and its workers could make more money. Taylor also believed that the workers would be happier as a result. The scientific-management approach was based on four principles:

The program also aims to actively promote women and blacks into the ranks of middle management at KFC, and Designate executives help train future executives within the company.

The program finds candidates by retaining search firms owned by minorities and women, as well as firms owned by white men. Each recruiter produces one slate: all white men; all women—white and minority; or all black men. One person is hired from each search. Larry Drake was hired from a slate of seven black men, for example.

After spending some time scrubbing floors, mixing mashed potatoes, and breading onion rings, designate Drake moved on to managing clusters of restaurants and then entire markets. He's now general manager for the Midwest region, overseeing revenues of about $800 million, and is being considered for senior positions at PepsiCo's other divisions.

Since he's been at KFC, Drake has increased the odds of his acceptance in several ways. His energetic presence has earned him a reputation as a fireball. In his early weeks, he met as many of his new colleagues as possible. He called other KFC executives and invited himself into their markets for a brief visit, hoping to learn about the business and make friends at the same time. After learning that about half of his fellow senior managers ski, he even attempted the slopes. Here, however, he gives himself only mixed reviews. "It's very painful," he allows.

SOURCE: Joan E. Rigdon, "PepsiCo's KFC Scouts for Blacks and Women for Its Top Echelons," *Wall Street Journal* (November 13, 1991), pp. A1, A6.

1. The development of a true science of management
2. Scientific selection of the right individual to fill each job
3. Education and development of each employee so that he or she would be able to do his or her job properly
4. Cooperation between management and workers[9]

Taylor emphasized that all four of these principles in combination, not any one of them alone, would lead to improved productivity and increased worker satisfaction. He believed that managers should use science, not rules of thumb; that they should seek harmony, not discord; that organizations should require cooperation, not individualism; that managers should seek maximum output, not restricted output; and that each member of the organization should be developed to his or her greatest level of efficiency and prosperity.[10]

A major feature of Taylor's system was an incentive compensation plan that paid workers a piece rate for a specified amount of work and a bonus for any additional work.[11] At the time, the idea of paying people for what they did rather than for the amount of time they spent on the job was not only innovative but suspect. In fact, Taylor was summoned to testify before Congress in defense of his ideas. Unions and other groups with a vested interest in maintaining the status quo denounced many of his concepts. Nevertheless, Taylor had a major impact on the design of compensation programs, and his principles are still applied in many plants.[12] Toyota, for example, applies Taylor's principles in selecting employees.[13]

How far have we come since Taylor's time? Think of the jobs you have had. Were you paid for what you did or for simply showing up? How productive were you? Managers who want to get the most they can from workers must reward performance. They must also seek harmony and cooperation and de-

AT MET LIFE: Met Life recognized the importance of linking employee benefits to worker satisfaction. This resembles Taylor's effort to link compensation to the satisfaction of workers' needs through pay for performance, but in this case the connection is indirect.

SHOWN HERE ARE SOME OF THE EARLIEST CONTRIBUTORS TO MANAGEMENT THEORY. FREDERICK W. TAYLOR (FAR RIGHT) ORIGINATED SCIENTIFIC MANAGEMENT WITH HIS STUDIES SHOWING HOW WORK AND COMPENSATION SYSTEMS COULD BE REDESIGNED TO BENEFIT BOTH THE EMPLOYER AND THE EMPLOYEE. FRANK AND LILLIAN GILBRETH'S (TOP) MOTION AND TIME STUDIES CONTRIBUTED VALUABLE EMPIRICAL INFORMATION TO SCIENTIFIC MANAGEMENT. THE GERMAN SOCIOLOGIST MAX WEBER (LEFT), WHO COINED THE TERM *BUREAUCRACY*, WAS A MAJOR CONTRIBUTOR TO THE ADMINISTRATION AND ORGANIZATION APPROACH. ALL OF THESE THEORISTS DREW UPON THE THINKING OF ADAM SMITH, WHO DESCRIBED THE BENEFITS OF THE DIVISION OF LABOR AND THEREBY SET THE STAGE FOR THE DEVELOPMENT OF MASS PRODUCTION.

FIGURE 2.1   GANTT CHART FOR A BANK OPENING A NEW BRANCH

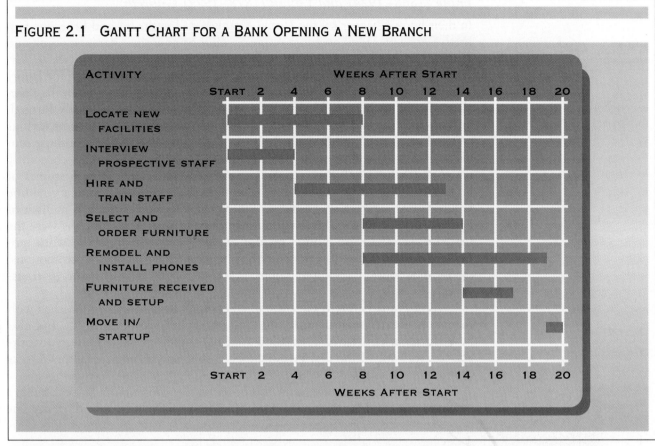

SOURCE: WILLIAM J. STEVENSON, <u>PRODUCTION-OPERATIONS MANAGEMENT</u>, 3RD ED. (HOMEWOOD, ILL.: IRWIN, 1990), P. 699.

velop their subordinates to the fullest, if they expect to solve the productivity problem. It is amazing that we face the same problems we faced eighty years ago and that they still seem to require many of the same solutions. Have we learned from history?

Henry L. Gantt (1861–1919)

One of Taylor's leading disciples was Henry L. Gantt. Gantt had worked with Taylor, and his scientific-management techniques reflect Taylor's four principles. Gantt is perhaps best known for the **Gantt chart,** a simple yet effective way to allow managers to schedule work forces across a series of tasks. Figure 2.1 shows a Gantt chart for a bank that is planning to open a new branch. Gantt charts were the forerunners of today's program evaluation review technique (PERT), a technique we will discuss in detail in Chapter 8.[14] Gantt charts also serve as the foundation for several project management software packages.[15]

Gantt chart: A simple chart that allows managers to schedule work forces across a series of tasks.

Among Gantt's other contributions were a task-and-bonus system and what he labeled "the habits of industry." Gantt felt that instead of simply developing employees' skills, supervisors should instill positive characteristics, such as industriousness and cooperation, in their subordinates. He modified Taylor's incentive system to give workers base pay plus bonuses. He was also one of the first managers to be concerned about the social responsibility of businesspeople. "The business system must accept its social responsibility and devote itself primarily to service or the community will ultimately make the attempt to take it over in order to operate it at its own interest."[16] Business philosophers and critics in the 1960s, 1970s, and 1980s have repeated these words many times.

Frank (1868–1924) and Lillian (1878–1972) Gilbreth

In their book *Cheaper by the Dozen*, Frank B. Gilbreth, Jr., and Ernestine Gilbreth Carrie provided an entertaining account of how their parents, Frank and Lillian Gilbreth, had applied scientific management in raising their twelve children.[17] However, the Gilbreths' contributions to management outside the family were also significant. While Taylor was known as the father of scientific management, the Gilbreths' forte was the study of work itself, especially through motion and time studies. Their careful studies of the work motions of various types of employees and their analysis of the time it took to perform those motions always led to increased employee productivity. The Gilbreths constantly searched for "the one best way." One of Frank Gilbreth's motion studies of bricklayers found that the number of motions necessary to lay bricks could be reduced from eighteen and a half to four. This reduction tripled the number of bricks a bricklayer could lay with no additional effort. The Gilbreths were the first researchers to use motion picture cameras and lights to study work motions; they were also the first to describe elementary human micromotions, which they labeled *therbligs* (Gilbreth spelled backward, with the *th* transposed).[18]

After Frank Gilbreth's death, Lillian Gilbreth became more concerned with the psychology of management. She studied not only work efficiency, but also how efficiency efforts, compensation systems, and other factors affected workers. She was one of the first investigators to study psychological factors in successful management.[19]

Scientific management is at the heart of the contemporary total quality management (TQM) movement. TQM focuses on job design, productivity improvement, and work methods—in short, the best way of doing a job. This

---

QUALITY MANAGEMENT CHALLENGE

AMEX Redefines Work to Obtain Total Quality

When Sarah Nolan arrived at her new post as president of AMEX Life Assurance, a subsidiary of the American Express Company based in San Rafael, California, she found business as usual. A simple change of address took two days. Sending out a new policy, ten days. Training new employees, three months. No one was embarrassed by any of this: It was typical of the industry as a whole.

Nolan didn't reform the system. She simply started over. She sent five managers representing different specialties to an empty office park and charged them with redesigning the business completely. She asked them to set it up afresh, in compliance with only three rules: Put the customer first; don't copy anything from the old system; and be ready to process applications in six months.

Nolan was putting into practice two of the basic tenets of total quality management, or TQM: willingness to see the world from the customer's point of view and eagerness to move quickly. Proponents of TQM insist that, contrary to popular opinion, speed and quality go hand in hand.

The five managers soon realized that if they were really to put the customer first, they needed to think differently about the low-level clerical workers on the front lines.

By the project's end, they had collapsed ten layers of personnel into three, each of which dealt with the public. As a result, fewer employees were needed, and

chapter's Quality Management Challenge explores how a division of American Express totally redesigned work in order to improve quality. Notice the attention that must be given to detail and the amount of change necessary for a TQM project to succeed.

ADMINISTRATION AND ORGANIZATION

During the same period that scientific management was coming to prominence, efforts were being made to discover how managers managed and how organizations were structured. Key contributors to this **administration and organization** approach were the French executive Henri Fayol; the German sociologist Max Weber, who was interested in the structure of organizations; and the Americans Mary Parker Follett, a political theorist turned business philosopher, and Chester Barnard, president of New Jersey Bell.

Administration and organization: An approach to management that focused on formulating principles for administering and structuring organizations.

Henri Fayol (1841–1925)

In 1916, Henri Fayol published a book titled *Administration Industrielle et Générale,* in which he described what he had concluded was the proper way to manage organizations and their members. Among Fayol's major contributions were a clear statement of the functions of management and a list of general management principles. He defined management as consisting of planning, organizing, commanding, coordinating, and controlling. Commanding and coordinating, when combined, are what we define as leadership. Thus, in this book, as in most others, we are essentially following Fayol's list of functions. Problem solving occurs in each of these functions. Fayol also developed a set of fourteen principles of management. These principles, which are listed in Table 2.2, specify rules for successfully managing and structuring an organization.

---

more than a third were transferred to other groups. Expenses were cut in half, and profitability increased sixfold.

The team got so focused on the idea of remembering the customer that they assigned the customer an empty chair at meetings.

Seeing through the customer's eyes can lead to major structural changes, as Nolan's experience suggests. What is required isn't achieved simply through focus groups and market research. To see through the customer's eyes, managers need to stand at the end of a long sequence of events, all of which have to mesh smoothly. If the computer is down, for example, no amount of courtesy and charm will speed things along.

In this way, each business actually comprises a chain of "internal" customers, each serving the next on behalf of the ultimate, "external" customer's satisfaction. The trick is to get everyone working together to more than satisfy this ultimate customer.

Nolan's success resulted, in part, from giving the internal customers—her managers—a real stake in the operation. "It's a staggering thing how far people will go if they own the results," she says.

Equally staggering can be the scope of the structural changes required to institute genuine TQM: substantial investments in training, consultants, and—often most difficult to achieve—attention from top management. Executives hoping for a painless ninety-day makeover don't want to hear that it will take years to correct all the things they have been doing wrong. But there's no point in exhorting workers to do better if the job isn't structured to make that possible.

SOURCE: Frank Rose, "Now Quality Means Service Too," *Fortune* (April 22, 1991), pp. 97–106.

It would be difficult to overemphasize the importance of Fayol's contributions to the practice of management. Most of Fayol's observations are relevant to most organizations today. For example, the structure of virtually all organizations is based on the division of work using highly specialized labor, whether they are making microchips or providing health care services. All organizations use the principle of authority; virtually all employ the unity-of-command concept; and all use some degree of centralization and the scalar chain of command (see Table 2.2). Moreover, we now know that most of the other principles—equity, order, stability of tenure for personnel, initiative, esprit de corps, remuneration, and discipline—can contribute to successful management. Managers seeking to solve structuring problems would do well to use many, if not most, of Fayol's basic concepts. A number of successful Japanese management practices

---

TABLE 2.2 Fayol's General Principles of Management

1. *Division of work:* This is the classic division of labor prescribed by Adam Smith. Division of labor reduces the number of tasks performed by a job unit to as few as possible. This improves efficiency and effectiveness because it allows for the simple but rapid repetition of effort.

2. *Authority and responsibility:* Authority is the right to give orders and the power to exact obedience. Responsibility accrues to those who have authority. If you have responsibility, you must also have commensurate authority. (This is the "parity principle.")

3. *Discipline:* There must be obedience and respect between a firm and its employees. For Fayol, discipline is based on respect rather than fear. Poor discipline results from poor leadership. Good discipline results from good leadership. Management and labor must agree. Management must judiciously use sanctions to ensure discipline.

4. *Unity of command:* A person should have only one manager and receive orders from only one manager.

5. *Unity of direction:* The organization, or any subunit thereof that has a single objective or purpose, should be unified by one plan and one leader.

6. *Subordination of individual interest to the general interest:* The interests of the organization as a whole should take priority over the interest of any individual or group of individuals within the organization.

7. *Remuneration of personnel:* Workers should be motivated by proper remuneration. Remuneration levels are the function of many variables, including supply of labor and condition of the economy.

8. *Centralization:* Centralization means that the manager makes the decisions. Decentralization means that subordinates help make the decisions. The degree of centralization or decentralization depends on the organization's circumstances.

9. *Scalar chain:* Managers in hierarchical organizations are part of a chain of superiors ranging from the highest authority to the lowest. Communication flows up and down the chain, but Fayol also allowed for a communication "bridge" between persons not on various dimensions of the scalar chain. The "bridge" would allow subordinates in different divisions to communicate with each other—although formally they were supposed to communicate through their bosses and through the chain of command.

10. *Order:* There is a place for everything, and everything must be in its place—people, materials, cleanliness. All factors of production must be in an appropriate structure.

11. *Equity:* Equity results from kindliness and justice and is a principle to guide employee relations.

12. *Stability of tenure for personnel:* Retaining personnel, orderly personnel planning, and timely recruitment and selection are critical to success.

13. *Initiative:* Individuals should display zeal and energy in all their efforts. Management should encourage initiative.

14. *Esprit de corps:* Esprit de corps builds harmony and unity within the firm. This harmony of high morale will be more productive than discord, which would weaken it.

SOURCE: Daniel A. Wren, *The Evolution of Management Thought* (New York: Wiley, 1979), pp. 218–221. Reprinted by permission of John Wiley & Sons, Ltd.

can be shown to be related to Fayol's principles. For example, just-in-time inventory (in which inventory arrives just in time for manufacturing) is related to the principle of order, and quality circles (groups of employees meeting to solve quality problems) are related to the principle of esprit de corps.[20]

Max Weber (1864–1920)

Max Weber was interested in improving the structure of large-scale organizations and in designing the blueprint of a structure that would help large organizations achieve their objectives; he is often referred to as the father of organization theory.[21] His major contribution to the study of management was the concept of **bureaucracy**. Weber defined bureaucracy as "the ideal or pure form of organization." His concept of bureaucracy is similar to Fayol's view of structure. Its basic elements are shown in Table 2.3.

Weber envisioned three types of legitimate authority: (1) rational, legal authority; (2) traditional authority; and (3) charismatic authority. Rational, legal authority depends on position; traditional authority on the legitimacy of the person in command; and charismatic authority on the follower's personal trust and belief in the leader.[22] According to Weber, all three forms underlie any given organizational structure.

The importance of Weber's contributions became evident in the 1940s and 1950s, when organizations around the world began to grow both in size and in complexity. As leaders began to search for ways to improve these organizations' structures, Weber's "ideal bureaucracy" became the model. At the same time, many investigators became interested in informal organizations, human relations, organizational behavior, and other factors that influence an organization's formal structure.

Bureaucracy: A form of organization characterized by division of labor, hierarchy of authority, members selected on the basis of their qualifications, and strict rules and procedures.

Mary Parker Follett (1868–1933)

Mary Parker Follett focused on relationships within an organization, especially the work group. She was instrumental in helping managers recognize the importance of the group.[23] Follett suggested that authority resided not in the power of administrators but in the situation—that is, responsibility was inherent in the functions a person performed rather than in his or her formal authority. Follett also proposed "the law of the situation," by which she meant that a person must accept a situation for what it is and try to work within it.[24]

Another of Follett's major contributions was to refine the concept of coordination. For Follett, coordination involved the sharing of responsibility by all the members of an organization and was a means of relating all the factors in a situation to each other. She felt that coordination is critical in the early stages of

---

TABLE 2.3 Characteristics of Bureaucracy

1. A division of labor in which authority and responsibility are clearly defined and legitimized.

2. A hierarchy of authority resulting in a chain of command.

3. Organizational members who are selected on the basis of their qualifications, either by examination or because of their training or education.

4. The appointment of managers and not their election (as might occur in government).

5. Managers to be paid for fixed hours and to be career oriented.

6. Managers who do not own the unit they administer.

7. Managers' conduct subject to strict rules and procedures, disciplinary actions, and controls.

SOURCE: Adapted from Max Weber, *The Theory of Social and Economic Organizations*, ed. and trans. by A. M. Henderson and Talcott Parsons (New York: Free Press, 1947), pp. 329–333. Reprinted with the permission of The Free Press, a Division of Macmillan, Inc. from *The Theory of Social and Economic Organization* by Max Weber, translated by A. M. Henderson and Talcott Parsons. Edited by Talcott Parsons, pp. 329–333. Copyright © 1947, renewed 1975 by Talcott Parsons.

an enterprise and that it is an ongoing process.[25] Follett believed that coordination achieves control because it achieves unity.

Finally, Follett was among the first management theorists to point out that leaders must have followers to be leaders and that there is a reciprocal influence between leaders and their followers. To her, however, leadership was not just a situation in which leaders have followers but, rather, one in which leaders have the ability to influence their followers.[26] This was an important distinction because it broke with the military model on which the theory of the business hierarchy had hitherto been based. A business manager does not have the absolute authority that a military officer has.

Chester Irving Barnard (1886–1961)

Chester Irving Barnard could have been a character in a Horatio Alger success story. Barnard was a poor farm boy who attended Harvard on a scholarship and later became president of New Jersey Bell and a student and teacher of the sociology of the organization. Barnard's *Functions of the Executive*, published in 1938, was many years ahead of its time. It contained many doctrines whose importance is only beginning to be fully understood. For example, Barnard identified three goals of an organization:

1. Maintaining an equilibrium of complex character (modifying a complex and ever-changing organization) in a continuously fluctuating environment of physical, biological, and social materials, elements, and forces
2. Examining the external environment and adapting to it
3. Examining and understanding the functions of executives at all levels[27]

Barnard's external focus in points 1 and 2 foreshadowed the focus on strategic planning that most organizations adopted in the 1970s. **Strategic planning** involves formulating major plans (strategies) that guide the organization in the pursuit of its major (strategic) objectives. It entails either adapting the organization to its environment or changing that environment.

Barnard's focus on the building of a cooperative system to encourage individuals to work for the good of the organization revealed similar advanced thinking. He defined the meaning of an organization as "cooperation among men which is conscious, deliberate, and purposeful."[28] He was concerned with how groups as well as individuals affected this system and how the overall organization could be maintained. He recognized that organizations are made up of subsystems, all of which contain three elements: (1) willingness to cooperate, (2) a purpose, and (3) communication.[29] Barnard believed that without members who are willing to cooperate, organizations would fail. He was also one of the first theorists to discuss the informal organization—the informal relationships that exist within the formal organization. In his view, the informal organization helps maintain communication, cohesiveness, and feelings of integrity and self-respect.[30]

Barnard is perhaps best known for his **acceptance theory of authority**. His view differs considerably from those of previous writers on the subject, except for Follett. Where Weber, for example, saw authority as flowing downward through the organizational hierarchy (a top-down approach), Barnard saw it as depending on the acceptance of authority by the subordinate (a bottom-up approach).[31] Barnard suggested that there is a "zone of indifference" within which a person will obey orders without questioning the authority of those giving them. Once an order exceeds that zone of indifference, however, the person will choose whether to accept or reject that authority.

Strategic planning: The formulation of major plans (strategies) that guide the organization in the pursuit of its major (strategic) objectives.

Acceptance theory of authority: A manager's authority is measured by the subordinate's degree of acceptance of that authority.

In 1929, the telephone operating room at the Chicago Toll Office of Illinois Bell Telephone Company was staffed by supervisors who moved around the room on roller skates to manage the 800-line switchboard.

This principle can be seen in many organizations today. People often question and even disobey their supervisor's orders. This happens, for example, when a union member refuses to obey a manager's order because "it's not in the contract, and therefore you can't make me do it." Such disobedience was also common among the American military during the Vietnam War. Many, if not most, people sometimes quietly disobey orders because the orders have exceeded their zones of indifference.

Finally, Barnard postulated three executive functions: (1) to provide a system of communication for the organization; (2) to influence people to perform at high levels; and (3) to formulate and define the organization's purpose.[32] To Barnard, the organization's creative force is its mission. He believed that executives must have a vision and should lead by example, creating cooperation where none previously existed. Barnard was one of the first writers on management to recognize that organizations must be not only effective (i.e., achieve their organizational objectives) but also efficient (i.e., use the least amount of resources to achieve those objectives). He recognized the trade-offs that could arise in attempting to achieve both effectiveness and efficiency at the same time. It might, for example, be necessary to spend massive amounts of money for advertising (thereby reducing efficiency) in order to sell more of the product (thereby increasing effectiveness).

THE LEGACY OF THE CLASSICAL APPROACHES

The classical approaches to management still provide insights into many of the problems managers face today. The scientific management approach showed that job design is critical to the efficiency and effectiveness of an organization's members. Managers should not assume that the way a job is being done is the best way. Performance can always be improved. Another insight was that managers must reward performance. The administrative concerns of the classical management approaches also have relevance today. For example, Weber's concept of bureaucracy continues to define most organizational structures. Fayol's guidelines are followed by almost all modern organizations. Barnard's view of cooperation is accepted practice. Accomplishing both effectiveness and efficiency is still an issue confronting most organizations. Managers are learning that they must strive to achieve acceptance of authority as related by both Follett and Barnard. Barnard's concerns about cooperation, strategic planning, external and internal analysis, and the need for developing systems of communication also remain relevant today.

The classical approaches have some limitations, however. The one most frequently cited is that they do not take human matters into account—that is, they do not consider how people fulfill the work roles given to them. Instead, they tend to treat worker efficiency from a mechanical viewpoint. These shortcomings were addressed to some extent by Follett and Barnard. In fact, Follett was so concerned with human factors that she is sometimes considered the founder of the human resources movement. Barnard, too, is often viewed as a founder of the behavioral approach. Barnard and Follett thus bridge the gap between the classical and behavioral approaches.

The Behavioral Approach

While Weber and Barnard were defining the concept of the organization, another approach to management—the **behavioral approach**—was being developed. Proponents of this approach were concerned with increasing productivity; they focused on understanding an organization's human element—individuals and groups and how they can be effectively and efficiently combined in a larger organization.

THE HAWTHORNE STUDIES

The focus on human factors began with a series of studies performed at the Western Electric Company's Hawthorne plant in Chicago from 1924 to 1932. The original purpose of these studies was to provide support for an advertising campaign claiming that increased electric lighting would result in higher worker productivity. The findings of the first phase of these studies, known as the illumination experiments, led investigators to examine social relationships and the work group. The **Hawthorne studies** consisted of three parts: the illumination experiments, experiments in the relay-assembly test room, and experiments in the bank wiring room.

Behavioral approach: A management approach concerned with increasing productivity by focusing on understanding the human element in an organization— individuals and groups and how they can be effectively and efficiently combined in a larger organization.

Hawthorne studies: A set of experiments that examined the effects of workers' physical environment on their productivity.

The illumination experiments at Western Electric's Hawthorne Works were based on the belief that worker fatigue, monotony, and the like were the result of improper job design and environmental conditions such as inadequate lighting or uncomfortable room temperature. Here workers in the machine shop operate under low light.

The Illumination Experiments (1924–1927)

The illumination experiments were based on the belief that worker fatigue, monotony, and the like were the result of improper job design and environmental conditions such as inadequate lighting or uncomfortable room temperature. In 1924, the National Academy of Sciences (NAS) commissioned a study of these factors at Western Electric's Hawthorne Works near Cicero, Illinois, on Chicago's west side. Two groups of workers were examined: a control group, whose illumination would *not* be varied, and a test group, whose illumination *would* be varied.

The results were surprising. Regardless of the level of light (which in one case was equivalent to moonlight), productivity increased in both the control and test groups. Unable to explain these results, the researchers began looking for other key variables, including pay, rest periods, and refreshments. Yet no matter how they manipulated the variables, the workers' productivity increased. Even after all the privileges the workers had recently earned were canceled, their productivity *still* increased. Reinstating rest pauses and refreshments led to yet another increase. The researchers were at a loss to explain the results. During the studies, which lasted until 1927, output increased from 2,400 relays to 3,000 relays per week per worker.

The Relay-Assembly Test Room Experiments

In 1927, just as the Hawthorne researchers were considering abandoning their efforts, Elton Mayo, a Harvard professor, was called in as a consultant on the studies. Mayo concluded that "a remarkable change of mental attitude in the group" explained the Hawthorne results.[33] In a sense, Mayo simply rediscovered what the nineteenth-century industrialist Robert Owen (see Table 2.1) had already suggested: Workers would perform at higher levels if managers seemed more concerned about them. The classical theorists had assumed that people always react rationally and are motivated principally by money. Environmental factors were also believed to influence productivity, but virtually no attention had been paid to the behavioral aspects of managing. In the Hawthorne studies,

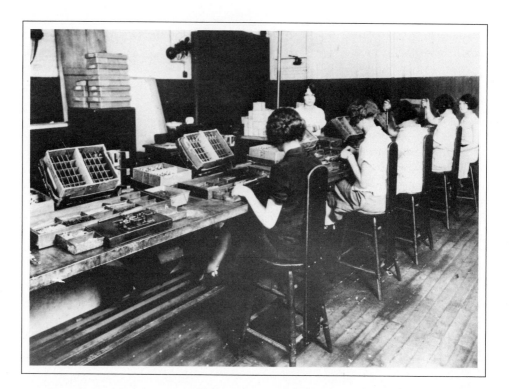

These five women were part of the relay-assembly test room experiments at the Hawthorne plant.

the special attention given to the group by the leader of the experiment, who was not viewed as a "boss" and who paid special attention to the workers' sentiments and motives, created a special relationship that led to higher productivity.[34] As a result of these studies, whenever a secondary factor in an experiment, such as the attention given the workers in the Hawthorne experiments, produces a result that could have come from the primary factor being studied—in this case, the level of lighting—the result is known as the **Hawthorne effect.**

After the experiments in the relay-assembly test room, lengthy interviews revealed that workers felt that supervisors should show concern, establish open communication with employees, and be willing to listen to employees. These experiments also uncovered the existence of informal groups—groups that are not officially designated as part of the formal organization. These informal groups were discovered as researchers sought to explain productivity levels. Interviews revealed the existence of informal group norms to which most workers adhered. The effects of such norms on worker productivity became the subject of the next phase of the study.

Hawthorne effect: *An effect produced by a secondary factor in an experiment, such as the attention given to the subjects, rather than by the factor under study.*

The Bank-Wiring-Room Experiments

The third phase of the Hawthorne study was designed to study the informal group. The bank-wiring-room experiments showed clearly that informal group norms affect productivity levels. The study revealed that the work group had a clear idea of what constituted a fair day's work and that this level of productivity was lower than management thought it should be. However, the work group also considered a certain amount of work to be the minimum that should be done. The group expected its members to do the minimum but condemned them for doing more than the maximum (i.e., a fair day's work). Those who violated the maximum were known as rate busters; those who violated the minimum were known as chiselers. Note that whereas the researcher had been an active participant in the relay-assembly test room experiment, he merely observed the bank-wiring-room group at work. As a result, group productivity in the bank wiring room tended not to change.

The primary contribution of the Hawthorne studies was to reveal the effects of behavioral factors on productivity and, in particular, on the importance of social systems within a work group. The studies clearly showed that workers' sentiments are as important as any formal requirements for the individual or group. The Hawthorne studies called for a "new mix of managerial skills—these skills were ones which were crucial to handling human situations: first, diagnostic skills and understanding new behavior; and second, interpersonal skills and counseling, motivating, leading, and communicating with workers. Technical skills alone were not enough to cope with the problems discovered at the Hawthorne works."[35] The Hawthorne studies helped shift management thought and style away from the narrow, one-sided classical view. Many managers believed that if workers' social needs were satisfied, they would perform better. Unfortunately, manipulation became a common technique for influencing workers. Managers might go out of their way to be "nice" to employees—by providing coffee and doughnuts, for example—in an attempt to increase their productivity. However, employees soon caught on to such manipulation, which often failed to achieve the desired results. So the search for a better explanation of human motivation continued.

Other issues besides those just discussed are considered part of the behavioral approach. We will encounter them in the chapters on motivation, group dynamics, and leadership.

The Management Science Approach

While the behavioral approach was gaining acceptance, other scholars were developing quantitative techniques to improve the managerial problem-solving process. These researchers initiated the management science approach to management. Like the scientific management approach, the management science approach attempted to make management decision making more rational. The **management science approach** has four primary characteristics:

1. A focus on problem solving
2. A rational orientation
3. The use of mathematical models and techniques to solve problems
4. Emphasis on the use of computers in decision support systems

Management science approach: Often called operations research or quantitative analysis; it employs mathematical techniques to solve problems.

MODELS AND TECHNIQUES

Management science, often called *operations research* or *quantitative analysis,* employs mathematical techniques to solve problems. The management science approach sprang from efforts to cope with the numerous complex problems encountered in World War II. As it turned out, the models and techniques used to solve those problems later had wide application in other business situations. Operations researchers believed that the more scientifically they could approach a problem and the more information they could use to analyze and solve it, the more likely they would be to reach a satisfactory solution. The decision would be more rational and less of a "gut reaction."

Management science: An extremely broad term encompassing virtually all the rational approaches to managerial problem solving that are based on scientific methods.

Until recently, management science has focused largely on production and planning; now, however, mathematical models and techniques and computers are being used more frequently in financial analysis, market research, personnel selection, and other decision support systems.[36] They are least successful when applied to interpersonal relations or individual human problems.

Two management researchers, Robert A. Gordon and James E. Howe, were responsible for the general belief that more rigor was needed in managerial problem solving. In 1959, Gordon and Howe prepared a report titled "Higher

Education for Business" in which they criticized business schools for not being rigorous enough.[37] Business schools responded by employing more of the management science or operations research techniques that had been developed during and after World War II. Ironically, business schools are now being criticized for focusing too much on quantitative issues and not enough on such issues as leadership, communication, and global competition. This chapter's Management Challenge discusses some of the changes being made in the business curriculum as a result of this criticism.

The Nobel prize-winning economist Herbert Simon studied how individuals make decisions in organizations from a quantitative viewpoint. He discovered that decision making is not as rational as it is generally thought to be. Simon made several observations about decision making in organizations that will be discussed in Chapter 4. His research provided an important bridge between management science and behavioral approaches.[38]

In the chapters on quantitative tools for planning and problem solving and on operations management we will highlight many of the models and techniques embodied in the management science approach. A host of tools are available to help make the problem-solving process more rational; they include simulations,

MANAGEMENT CHALLENGE

The Changing Business Curriculum

The top managers of the future will need to be able to speak a foreign language and be familiar with a foreign culture—preferably Japanese or European. They will also need to know how to negotiate and communicate, possess the appropriate social skills, provide sound leadership, be innovative and entrepreneurial, understand the global marketplace and the role of technology, and behave in an ethical manner. All of these talents are required in addition to an understanding of one's own functional area, the organization's other functional areas, and the role of strategic planning.

To accommodate these needs, MBA programs across the United States are changing, some dramatically. For example, in 1989 the University of Virginia "fundamentally altered" its curriculum, adding more political orientation and global coursework in the first year and more electives in the second year. Among other things, Virginia students learn the art of persuasion by engaging in role-playing exercises with a critical audience.

Perhaps no school has changed its business curriculum more than the University of Denver (Colorado), which has undergone a total restructuring. At Denver, the whole experience of MBA education has become more experiential, more global, and more applied. Faculty and students are required to donate ten days a year to community service. The school is experimenting with varied off-campus programs, such as a weekend "Outward Bound" excursion for faculty and students in the Rocky Mountains. The university is also making a strong effort to include ethical issues throughout its curriculum.

Similar changes may appear in undergraduate programs as well, as business schools wrestle with the changing needs of students and businesses. Business schools are also focusing more on executive education. Duke University's Fuqua School offers several such programs, including a leadership course that uses team training approaches reminiscent of boot camp. The Massachusetts Institute of

inventory control models, and statistical decision theory. These tools are especially useful in recognizing and identifying a problem and in choosing among alternative solutions.

The Systems Approach

In the 1960s and the 1970s, managers were bombarded by external environmental influences. Public-interest groups like the Sierra Club pressured managers to become more accountable for the effects of their decisions and actions on the physical environment, employee health and safety, equality of employment opportunity, and consumer protection. Business critics, management scholars, and many executives began to realize the tremendous influence of business decisions on a wide range of people outside the organization. The **systems approach** developed as a result of these concerns.

The systems approach views the organization as a system that is interdependent with other systems in its environment. An organization's environment includes the social, political, technological, and economic/competitive forces that affect it. Simply stated, systems theory maintains that everything is related

Systems approach: A management approach that views the organization as interdependent with other systems in its environment.

The top managers of the future will need to be able to speak a foreign language and be familiar with a foreign culture—preferably Japanese or European. Berlitz International found that corporations wanted cultural orientation even more than its trademark foreign-language training. In response, Berlitz quickly set up a cross-cultural division.

Technology (MIT) offers courses tailored to particular companies, and Harvard University offers an advanced management program.

SOURCES: Mary Lord, "A Harder Sell for MBA's," *U.S. News and World Report* (March 23, 1992), pp. 60–67; Jeremy Main, "Business Schools Get a Global Vision," *Fortune* (July 17, 1989), pp. 78–86; and Lyman W. Porter and Lawrence E. McKilbin, *Management Education and Development, Drift or Thrust Into the 21st Century* (New York: McGraw-Hill, 1988).

to everything else. At a time when business and its critics were having difficulty identifying the role of business in society, the systems perspective offered some insight. The interconnectedness of systems became a focal point for examining the effects of business activities. For example, DDT, a pesticide that had been widely used to protect crops, was eventually banned in the United States because of its deleterious effects on fish and birds and, ultimately, on humans. The case of DDT spurred business to consider the impacts of their decisions on other systems—not only the natural environment but also the economic system, the political system, the educational system, and consumers.

Systems theory also affected management by allowing for the conceptualization of business as an input-transformation-output system, as shown in Figure 2.2. Businesses take certain inputs—financial, human, material, informational, and technological—and transform them through operations, management, the efforts of labor, and the use of technology into outputs—products and services and financial, human, and societal consequences. Inputs often come to the organization from outside sources (materials and loans) but may also be internally generated (labor and revenues). Transformation occurs in many ways. Outputs

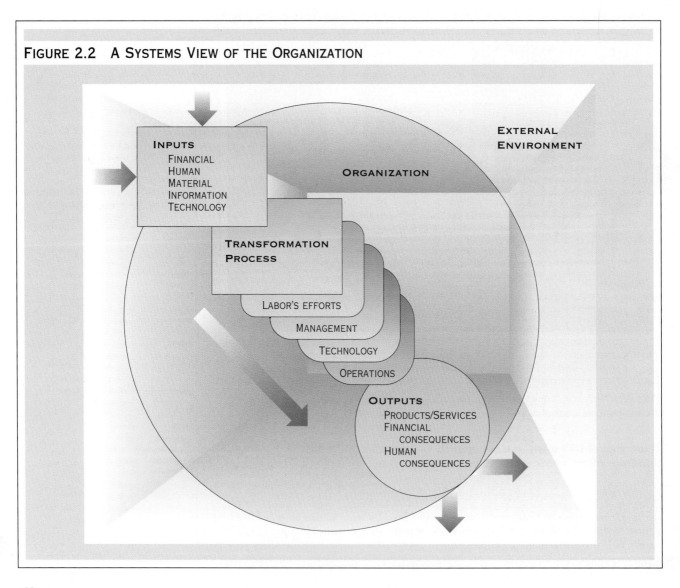

FIGURE 2.2   A SYSTEMS VIEW OF THE ORGANIZATION

are also varied, and while products and services are the principal outputs, others, such as possible harm to the environment, should not be ignored.

An important consequence of a systems approach is the recognition that business operates in a societal system and that its actions have societal consequences. From this perspective, businesses' relationships to certain entities become more apparent: For example, suppliers and creditors provide certain inputs; employees make certain transformations by performing such processes as assembling parts or processing a check; and consumers receive certain outputs—products and services.

CHARACTERISTICS OF SYSTEMS

All systems have parts or subsystems. A department, for example, is part of a company. Most subsystems, in turn, have their own subsystems (for example, the marketing system may have sales, product development, and distribution subsystems).

Systems may be open or closed. An open system interacts with its environment, whereas a closed system does not. For many years, all types of organizations—businesses and government agencies and other nonprofit organizations—operated as if they were closed systems: They failed to recognize their impacts on their stakeholders and the impacts of stakeholders on them. Today, managers increasingly recognize that businesses are open systems. When solving problems and making decisions, managers must take into account how their decisions and solutions will affect various stakeholders. This is probably the greatest lesson of systems theory. Whatever managers decide, whatever their solutions are, whatever plans they implement will affect others, and those effects must be taken into account before making or implementing a decision.

To survive and prosper, systems must have synergy.[39] **Synergy** means that the combined and coordinated actions of the parts (subsystems) of a system achieve more than all of the parts acting independently could achieve. Suppose, for example, that all of the employees of Kroger food stores set up small food stores of their own. They would not be able to achieve singly what they did collectively. As an organization, these individuals could accomplish much more because of the advantages of size, specialization of services, professional knowledge, and so on. This is what is meant by synergy.

Synergy: A condition in which the combined and coordinated actions of the parts (subsystems) of a system achieve more than all the parts could have achieved acting independently.

Ludwig von Bertalanffy is probably the best-known systems theorist.[40] Von Bertalanffy's general systems theory helped explain how organizational systems function. Von Bertalanffy was a biologist who attempted to develop a general systems theory that would fit all sciences. Although he was unable to accomplish this, his concept of steady-state equilibrium in the environment and the openness of systems to the environment became cornerstones of the systems theory of management.

Von Bertalanffy developed his ideas in the 1930s, but management did not develop a systems theory approach until the 1960s and 1970s. It then came to be viewed as a way of explaining the organization and its relationship to its environment. Management researchers Fremont E. Kast and James E. Rosenzweig extended the systems perspective to the internal functioning of the organization. They viewed an organization as a system consisting of several subsystems, including a social system, a technical system, and many others. Understanding how these subsystems work, and how they are interrelated, can help managers make better decisions because they understand the impacts of their decisions on others and vice versa.[41]

Today, management system designers use systems theory to model organizations' internal and external environments to help managers make better decisions, especially strategic ones. Many consulting firms, including the global consulting firm of McKinsey & Company, are suggesting that organizations redesign their structures to focus on the interrelatedness of components as systems designed to accomplish a few basic organizational processes.[42] Although it is too early to tell whether such proposals will gain widespread acceptance, it is clear that many organizations are becoming more systems oriented, recognizing the need to integrate subunits into the whole organization.

The Contingency Approach

Fayol and other early theorists searched for general principles of management that might be applied to all situations. However, while many of these principles worked in most situations, none could be applied to all situations. In the 1970s, it became evident that a manager's actions should be contingent on the condition of various key elements in a given situation. This led to the development of the **contingency approach.**

Contingency approach: A management approach in which the manager's actions are dependent on the conditions of various key elements in a given situation.

The first major research on contingency theory was undertaken by management researcher Fred E. Fiedler in 1967. Fiedler attempted to determine the style of leadership a manager should use in a given situation. Leadership styles have been characterized most commonly as either production oriented or people oriented.[43] Fiedler found that managers should exhibit varying degrees of concern for production and for people, depending on the quality of leader-member relations, the degree to which a task is defined, and the extent to which a manager has position power (authority stemming from the job itself).

More recently, Paul Hersey and Kenneth H. Blanchard have identified different factors on which a manager's leadership style should depend.[44] They believe that the maturity level of the subordinate work group is the key factor and that leadership style should change according to whether subordinates have low, medium, or high levels of maturity. In this context, maturity is defined as a combination of job skills and psychological maturity.

Spurred by research on contingency theory in leadership, similar research was conducted in the areas of strategic planning, personnel, and marketing. Investigators discovered that virtually all management activity is contingent on the elements of a situation.[45] A series of contingency approaches for each major function of management and for several subfunctions was worked out. In later chapters, when you study planning, organizing, leading, controlling, and even the problem-solving process itself, you will encounter various contingency models. For example:

1. In strategic planning, recommended actions are often based on the stage of the product or industry life cycle involved.
2. The design of an organization's structure must match its size, its rate of growth, environmental and technological conditions, the requirements of strategy, and the philosophy of top management.
3. In choosing a leadership style, managers should first determine the condition of several key factors, including their own personality, the personality of a particular subordinate, the dynamics of the subordinate's work group, the nature of the subordinate's job, organizational culture and structure, and other situational factors.
4. In controlling performance, the manager must recognize the purpose of the control, the measures required, the timing involved, and other variables.

Although true contingency theory would attempt to define the factors in a given situation and prescribe appropriate behavior, this becomes impossible when the potential number of elements in almost any given situation is considered. For example, Charles Hofer, who has conducted extensive research on strategic planning, has estimated that there are some 186 *million* combinations of the fifty or more key strategic planning variables.[46] Hence, for most managers, contingency theory has evolved into situational management. **Situational management** suggests that the manager must review the key factors in a situation and then determine what action to take on the basis of his or her knowledge and experience. Good managers recognize that in most situations behavior cannot be prescribed. They also recognize that some limited prescriptive models can be used to help solve problems.

The contingency theory is a problem-solving approach. It dictates that managers should consider the major elements in a situation before making a decision, whether it involves which management style to use, how to structure an organization, or a plan or a budget. They should then base their decision on their experience and knowledge, as well as on any prescribed models of actions that happen to exist for the situation.

Situational management: A review of the key factors in a situation before determining what action to take.

Contemporary Management— A Synthesis

Contemporary management is a synthesis of the five approaches to management discussed earlier, along with more recent approaches that may contribute to the improvement of management. This synthesis is illustrated in Figure 2.3. Management theorists today recognize that the management process is dynamic and that it must change as the organizational environment changes.

Contemporary management: A synthesis of traditional and contemporary approaches to management.

As Harold Koontz, a co-author of the first major text on management, observed, when they are considered separately the various approaches to management may seem "like the proverbial blind men from Hindustan (trying to figure out what an elephant is like with each touching a uniquely different part). Some specialists were describing management only through the perceptions of their specialties."[47] When the different approaches to management are combined, however, they produce a synthesis in which each contributes in some way to our view of management.

For example, scientific management provides a means for competing more effectively with foreign firms that have made major inroads in many U.S. industries and have taken complete control of some, such as the television manufacturing industry. American firms are placing renewed emphasis on job design, making products simpler, and scientifically examining the workplace to improve work functions. Automation and robotics are being applied to achieve the same ends Frederick Taylor sought at the beginning of this century.

Increased international competition has also resulted in the institutionalization of many actions that the behavioralists proposed. Chester Barnard's concern for communication and cooperation and Douglas McGregor's belief in participation to improve both effectiveness and efficiency can be seen throughout American business today. Both managers and operating employees are increasingly using management science techniques in their efforts to become more competitive and make better decisions. The amount of software available for applying those techniques is also increasing rapidly, especially in Japanese organizations, where front-line employees often have the skills to do statistical sampling. Systems theory is also being used more than ever, as organizations build complex models to evaluate the impact of their decisions on other stakeholders and, most important, on their customers and their competitors.

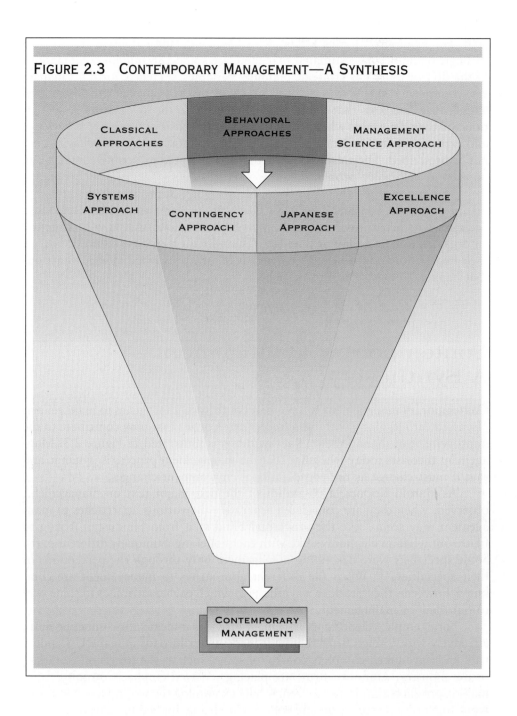

FIGURE 2.3 CONTEMPORARY MANAGEMENT—A SYNTHESIS

CLASSICAL
APPROACHES

BEHAVIORAL
APPROACHES

MANAGEMENT
SCIENCE APPROACH

SYSTEMS
APPROACH

CONTINGENCY
APPROACH

JAPANESE
APPROACH

EXCELLENCE
APPROACH

CONTEMPORARY
MANAGEMENT

Finally, more and more managers are practicing contingency theory management. They examine the variables in a problem-solving situation and then make decisions based on experience, knowledge, and any available contingency prescriptions. They no longer merely follow the traditional principles of management; rather, they apply concepts to situations.

Japanese Management Practices

Japanese management practices: A set of management practices developed by Japanese firms, focusing primarily on increasing productivity through group decision making, cooperation, and harmony.

Contemporary management has been fine tuned by the application of numerous Japanese management practices that have become extremely well known in this country. As discussed in Chapter 1, **Japanese management practices** are based on several important principles:

1. Participative management
2. Job design
3. Quantitative methods
4. Effectiveness and efficiency
5. Increasing productivity through group decision making
6. Holistic treatment of employees, who are seen as individuals rather than as interchangeable parts
7. Cooperation and harmony in the workplace[48]

When this approach, in a modified form, was applied in North American firms, it produced some notable successes.[49]

If the terms in the preceding list sound familiar, it is because they refer to the same issues that have been discussed throughout the history of American management. Indeed, they are the focal points of the five major approaches described earlier in the chapter. Many Japanese management practices actually originated in the United States.[50] For example, Douglas McGregor first articulated the emphasis on participative management, and Taylor expressed concern with job design. Barnard, Follett, and Robert Owen proposed a holistic view of the employee in the nineteenth century. American consultants, principally William Edwards Deming and Joseph Juran, brought quantitative methods to the Japanese in the 1950s. However, the group orientation of Japanese managers is a natural outgrowth of Japanese culture.

In sum, Japanese management practices embody many aspects of the five approaches to management. Japanese firms have imitated many of the more desirable aspects of American management philosophy and practices, just as U.S. firms have often imitated theirs. Japanese managers have refined some techniques and practices and pursued some that American managers chose not to pursue. These choices have been based on their applicability to Japanese culture and the needs of Japanese firms. In a similar vein, American managers must

Japanese firms have imitated many of the more desirable aspects of American management philosophy and practices, just as U.S. firms have often imitated theirs.

recognize that Japanese management practices are not totally transferable to U.S. firms; they must be adapted to American culture.[51]

Success sometimes leads to unanticipated problems. The Japanese have been so successful with their management approaches that they have come to dominate many foreign markets. As a result, other countries are considering protectionist measures to halt Japanese penetration of their markets. Responding to these protectionist actions, Akio Morita, co-founder and current chairman of Sony, has called for changes in the Japanese approach to strategy and management. This chapter's Global Management Challenge describes his proposals. Evaluate these proposals in terms of their potential influence on Japanese business activity. What is the likelihood that they will be enacted?

Excellence in Management

Thomas J. Peters and Robert H. Waterman, Jr., have added the term *excellence* to the management vocabulary. Their 1982 book *In Search of Excellence* (the best-selling business book ever) has had a profound effect on many managers and organizations.[52] Numerous corporations have instituted excellence programs in an effort to carry out the Peters and Waterman program or to achieve excellence by some other means.[53]

Peters and Waterman suggest that financially successful companies possess certain characteristics that result in excellence; these are listed in Table 2.4. This set of characteristics is based on information gathered from interviews and questionnaires and on secondary data obtained principally from thirty-three leading U.S. companies, including McDonald's, Hewlett-Packard, NCR, Eastman Kodak, IBM, 3M, Delta Airlines, and Boeing. In addition to identifying these characterisics, Peters and Waterman found that successful companies avoid management science approaches and emphasize "softer" issues such as "closeness to the customer" and the importance of innovation.[54]

Three years after the publication of *In Search of Excellence*, Peters co-

---

TABLE 2.4 Characteristics of Excellent Firms

1. *A bias for action:* They make decisions quickly; they don't suffer from "analysis-paralysis."

2. *Closeness to the customer:* They know what the customer wants, and they provide it.

3. *Autonomy and entrepreneurship (innovation):* Innovation is encouraged and the authority to innovate and take risks is given to key players.

4. *Productivity through people:* The rank and file are viewed as the root source of quality and productivity and are managed accordingly.

5. *Hands-on and value driven:* A basic philosophy of business drives the company.

6. *Sticking to the knitting:* The excellent companies are not highly diversified; they stick to one primary business.

7. *Simple form and lean staff:* Excellent companies do not have much middle management, or much support staff.

8. *Simultaneous loose-tight properties:* Excellent companies use formal control mechanisms, but individuals are expected to be very responsible, and often self-managing.

9. *Leadership—management by wandering around (MBWA):* Managers should coach, facilitate, assist, and be with their employees.

SOURCE: Thomas J. Peters and Robert H. Waterman, Jr., *In Search of Excellence* (New York: Knopf, 1985), pp. 14–16; and Thomas J. Peters and Nancy K. Austin, *Passion for Excellence* (New York: Knopf, 1985), pp. 4–7.

authored (with Nancy K. Austin) *Passion for Excellence*. The authors claimed that additional findings indicated that three characteristics from the list in Table 2.4, when combined with a particular management style, lead to excellence. This view is illustrated in Figure 2.4. The management style, MBWA (or management by walking around), involves having the manager facilitate employee performance by walking around, talking to employees, offering to remove obstacles to achievement, and obtaining resources.

In 1987, Peters wrote *Thriving on Chaos: Handbook for a Management Revolution*. In this book he identified five prescriptions for managing in the complex and turbulent environment of the future. To the elements of successful management identified in *Passion for Excellence* he added "control of the right stuff," suggesting that managers should pay more attention to strategic control and self-control and spend less time controlling unimportant factors such as minor costs. Peters also suggested that to remain excellent, companies would have to change and improve constantly.[55]

The "excellence" characteristics identified by Peters and Waterman are

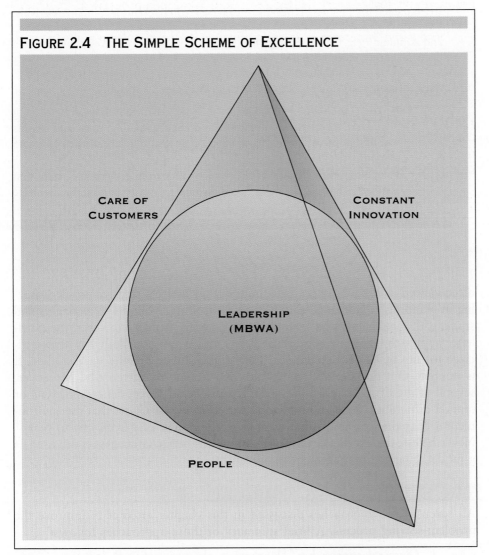

FIGURE 2.4   THE SIMPLE SCHEME OF EXCELLENCE

CARE OF CUSTOMERS

CONSTANT INNOVATION

LEADERSHIP (MBWA)

PEOPLE

SOURCE: THOMAS J. PETERS AND NANCY K. AUSTIN, <u>PASSION FOR EXCELLENCE</u>.
(NEW YORK: KNOPF, 1985) P.5. COPYRIGHT © 1985 BY THOMAS J. PETERS AND NANCY K. AUSTIN.
REPRINTED BY PERMISSION OF RANDOM HOUSE, INC.

Sony's Morita Calls for New Japanese Management Paradigm

It comes from an unexpected quarter—inside the ranks of Japanese management. Perhaps from one of the most unexpected quarters—the chairman of Sony, Akio Morita. The message? Japanese business practices are unfair in a global context, and management must change. Managers should eschew the fierce and single-minded competitiveness that helped create the second-largest economy in the world and move toward the accepted practices of the international community, particularly Europe and the United States.

Morita sees Japanese management as a victim of its own success. Considering their nation to be in the process of rebuilding for the past five years or more, managers have paid their workers less, taken slimmer profit margins, and paid stockholders smaller dividends than is common abroad. While these practices have strengthened the Japanese economy, they have created resentment in Japan's rivals. They also represent a sacrifice of the interests of Japanese employees, shareholders, and communities. The time has come, Morita says, to stop viewing business as a burden-sharing enterprise and start looking at it as *reward* sharing.

Morita's argument, which shocked the business world when it appeared in the February 1992 issue of *Bungei Shunju*, cites several specifics:

- Japanese price-setting practices are unique. The idea of first setting a target price that meets the competition and then assigning costs and profits within that price constitutes an invasion or a strangulation when exported abroad.

- The government's policy of encouraging industrial growth has meant that companies have had to target their resources toward meeting the challenge

---

often viewed as *the* way to manage. Indeed, they address creative problem solving in planning, organizing, leading, and controlling. Millions of managers and students of management have read the "excellence" books. However, the excellence approach has some critics. The Peters and Waterman study has been criticized for not being very systematic: Only successful companies were studied. It is possible that unsuccessful companies had similar characteristics. Moreover, several of the firms included in the study subsequently experienced financial or market difficulties. Peters himself admits in *Thriving on Chaos* that the environment is changing so rapidly that what is excellent may vary from year to year.[56] Nevertheless, the **excellence approach,** in which these characteristics are used as a model, changed management significantly.

Excellence approach to management: An approach in which characteristics of excellent firms are used as models for other firms.

The Synthesis—A Summary

All seven of the approaches discussed in this chapter attempt to improve the problem-solving process. A brief summary of those approaches follows:

1. *Classical approaches.* The three goals were rational decision making, better job design, and improved productivity.

of local competition. Profits were typically reinvested in R&D and equipment or allotted toward internal reserves, rather than being shared.

- Suppliers may also have been pressured. In return for the stability of long-term relationships, manufacturers have often taken control over matters such as delivery deadlines and prices.
- The community as a whole has been ignored. In contrast with the average corporate donation in the United States of 1.55 percent in 1989, for example, Japanese companies donated only 0.33 percent.

Although these conditions allow Japan to compete effectively in foreign markets, tolerance of these practices is reaching its limit, Morita warns. He advises reform in several areas:

More holidays and fewer work hours

Fairer compensation for a better "quality of life"

Higher dividend payout ratios

Fairer partnerships with suppliers

Greater contributions to the local community

Protection of the environment and conservation of resources

Japan needs to compete according to the same rules as the rest of the world, Morita observes. "By ridding the United States and Europe of fear, Japan could be recognized as a true partner in coping with global issues."

Not surprisingly, in Japanese business circles Morita's remarks were met with considerable skepticism. Takeshi Nagano, chairman of Mitsubishi Materials Corporation, said: "Japan's hourly wages are the highest in the world. What Morita said is wrong."

SOURCE: Akio Morita, "Why Japan Must Change," *Fortune* (March 9, 1992), pp. 66–67.

2. *The behavioral approach.* Key concerns were how to motivate, lead, communicate, achieve cooperation, and raise productivity through participative management.

3. *Scientific management.* The goal was to make decision making more logical and analytical.

4. *The systems approach.* The major issue was to ensure that managerial decisions take into account the organization's environment in terms of inputs, transformation processes, and outputs.

5. *Contingency management.* The manager needs to consider all the major elements of a situation before making a decision.

6. *Japanese management practices.* Major concerns include employee participation in decision making, group problem solving, and the use of quantitative methods.

7. *Excellence in management.* The principal focus is on how to improve management in order to make companies more "excellent."

A close look at the preceding seven approaches reveals several common themes:

1. Improving the rationality of decision making
2. Achieving effectiveness and efficiency, especially through job design
3. Proper use of human resources, especially in terms of manager-subordinate relationships
4. The organization's interactions with its environment, especially regarding strategic planning and social responsibility
5. Factors to be considered in making decisions
6. The extent to which subordinates should participate in making decisions

The blending of the seven approaches to create a synthesis can be compared to randomly distributing seven different-colored marbles in a clear vase. Distinct colors are noticeable on close inspection, but from a distance only a single color is seen. The management process as described in this book draws from each of the various approaches. At first you will note the distinctive features of each, but over time they will blend. There is, however, no consensus on a single system, nor is there a unified management theory. Moreover, management is constantly changing; as a result, additional approaches will evolve. At present, a **new management** is emerging, an approach consisting of several new concepts and ideas. We mentioned earlier, for example, that McKinney and Company suggests that organizations be designed around processes rather than functions. Basic changes in strategic planning, innovation, and other forms of organizational design have also been suggested, and the management of knowledge has been identified as vital to management in the future. It is too soon to tell which, if any, of these ideas will dominate. Each will be discussed in more detail in later chapters.[57]

This book takes the view that we can learn a lot from management history, but because we often do not, we must relearn what we already knew. The same issues that emerged as focal points in the development of each of the seven major approaches remain issues today. However, while the issues seem to be the same, the answers change. One of the major changes occurring in organizations today is that they are studying the successes and failures of firms other than their own, seeking to improve by learning what has worked in the past and what has not. This openness helps to avoid repeating the mistakes of others.[58]

New management: An evolving set of new approaches to management.

AT MET LIFE: *Met Life learned from its history, from the history of its industry, and from the history of management. It did not repeat the mistakes others had made in the past.*

Management in the Future

In the future, as new approaches to management emerge, the contemporary synthesis will be fine-tuned and perhaps even revolutionized. There is no shortage of new approaches.[59] For example, the need to become more competitive in the global marketplace has spurred organizations to institute management systems characterized by greater cooperation, participation, and delegation. Chester Barnard recognized the need for these changes more than fifty years ago and Douglas McGregor reaffirmed it in the 1950s.

Thomas J. Peters is fond of saying that virtually any management approach would have been successful for U.S. business organizations after World War II because of the huge pent-up demand for goods. Peters believes that the true test of management problem solving is meeting competition. Increased competition has revealed that traditional and classical management practices are inappropriate. As he points out in *Thriving on Chaos,* managers must now learn to thrive on the massive changes occurring in our society.[60] However, in addition to accelerating change, managers face many other challenges, as discussed in Chapter 1. As a consequence, in the 1990s, management will be characterized by greater emphasis on empowerment, integrated management through sophisticated information systems, innovative thinking, quality, flexibility, global perspectives, organizational learning, an orientation toward processes, multicultural adaptation, a focus on customer needs, and speed in problem solving.[61]

Summary

(Before reading this summary, look again at the objectives listed at the beginning of the chapter.)

1. There are five principal approaches to management thought: classical, behavioral, management science, systems, and contingency.

2. Scientific-management theorists may be described as searching for "the one best way." Administrative theorists were attempting to determine universal rules for structuring the organization and engaging in the management process.

3. The behavioral approach focuses on the human element: individuals and groups and their interactions in organizations. Communication, cooperation, trust, and delegation of authority are critical components of this approach.

4. The management science approach attempts to use quantitative techniques to improve the analytical nature and the rationality of decision-making and problem-solving processes.

5. The systems approach views the organization as a transformer of inputs into outputs and focuses on the interdependency of the organization with stakeholders both in the external environment and within the organization. It helped make managers aware of the impact of their decisions in such areas as the natural environment and employee health and safety.

6. The contingency theory suggests that a manager must consider all elements in any situation and arrive at a decision that balances all of their requirements.

7. Contemporary management is a dynamic synthesis of the five earlier approaches, in addition to Japanese management practices and the excellence approach.

8. Thomas J. Peters and other critics of the management process have caused managers to examine their management practices. Many organizations and managers are questioning past practices and changing the way they manage. They are using the prescriptions set forth by Peters and others to meet the challenges of a rapidly changing environment.

General Questions

1. Show how each of the seven approaches to management discussed in this chapter has contributed to the following managerial themes. (Not all approaches have been described as contributing to each theme. What position do you think theorists in each approach might have taken on each?)
   a. Increasing rationality in decision making
   b. Effectiveness and efficiency
   c. Using human resources
   d. The relationship of the organization to its environment
   e. Factors to consider in solving problems in any managerial situation
   f. The extent to which subordinates should participate in making decisions

2. Identify the contributions to management of each of the following individuals: Frederick W. Taylor, Henry Gantt, Frank and Lillian Gilbreth, Henri Fayol, Mary Parker Follett, Max Weber, Chester Barnard, Elton Mayo, Herbert Simon, Ludwig von Bertalanffy, Kenneth Boulding, Thomas J. Peters, and Robert H. Waterman, Jr.

3. Is scientific management applicable today? Why?

4. Is Weber's ideal of bureaucracy still valid? What are its strengths and weaknesses?

5. Relate Fayol's fourteen principles of management to a college and to the dean of a college.

6. If you were the manager of a grocery store, how could you use management science techniques?

7. Describe your class as an open system.

8. Describe your instructor as a contingency manager. How well does he or she use the contingency approach to manage the class?

9. Draw a model that represents a synthesis of the five major approaches to management. It can be any shape or form and can contain any number of components, but it must show how the five approaches blend into one.

10. Describe the key components of management in the 1990s.

Questions on the Management Challenge Features

DIVERSITY MANAGEMENT CHALLENGE

1. What does Larry Drake do to assure his personal success?

2. Describe the PepsiCo designate program and how it achieves the goal of greater multiculturalism in top management.

QUALITY MANAGEMENT CHALLENGE

1. How does AMEX's action fit into scientific management?

2. How does AMEX's action differ from what might be done in a manufacturing organization?

MANAGEMENT CHALLENGE

1. How have the management challenges affected business school curriculums?

2. How has the business curriculum changed at your school? How should it change?

GLOBAL MANAGEMENT CHALLENGE

1. How likely are Morita's suggestions to be accepted in Japan? Why?

2. What changes in Japanese management and business practices are likely to occur? (This question requires general knowledge of the changes occurring in Japan.)

E P I L O G U E

Met Life: Making Sure Employees Learn from History

Recently Met Life has begun to include cultural-diversity issues in its orientation program. It is also attempting to attract minority applicants as part of an effort to improve its service to black, Hispanic, and Asian-American customers. Met Life managers now have a complete set of videotapes and packaged materials to provide orientation and development for new and current employees.

DISCUSSION QUESTIONS

1. Why would a firm want its employees to be familiar with its history?

2. Why would a firm make an effort to have employees understand its culture?

3. How might employees be "trapped" by Met Life's history if they were not aware of it?

Florida Informanagement Services (FIS)

FIS is a data-transaction, information-processing company that serves savings banks throughout Florida and adjoining states. It is in the unique position of being owned by most of its users, who created the organization for the purpose of supplying information-processing services. Competitive forces in the industry are pressuring the firm to diversify, but its owners are very reluctant to give their approval to anything that would increase their data costs, even for a short period.

In the spring of 1986, FIS held its annual strategic planning conference. The company's top managers and an outside facilitator spent two exhausting days formulating the six or seven major strategic issues the organization was to work on during the next year. Among them were studies to be performed on possible candidates for acquisition and analyses of other businesses the firm might wish to enter.

About three months after the planning conference, the group met with the planning facilitator again to discuss the progress that had been made in carrying out the plans. At that point not much had happened, but the group agreed to meet once a month to evaluate progress, assign responsibilities, and set priorities.

Harry Shuman, president of FIS, and Bob LaHair, chief operations officer, pondered the situation they faced. It was the spring of 1987, and they had failed to do much about their strategic plans. As had often happened in the past, they had carried out the operational aspects of their plans without difficulty but had never gotten around to the strategic aspects. They both felt that they needed to take the initiative and get the ball rolling, but they were not quite sure how to go about it.

DISCUSSION QUESTIONS

1. How has this firm been trapped by what it already knows?
2. Why is it easier for a firm like this to carry out operations than to implement strategies?
3. How should Shuman solve this problem?

The Management History Crossword Puzzle

MANAGE YOURSELF

How well do you remember the contributions of each of the giants of management history? Complete the following puzzle to find out.

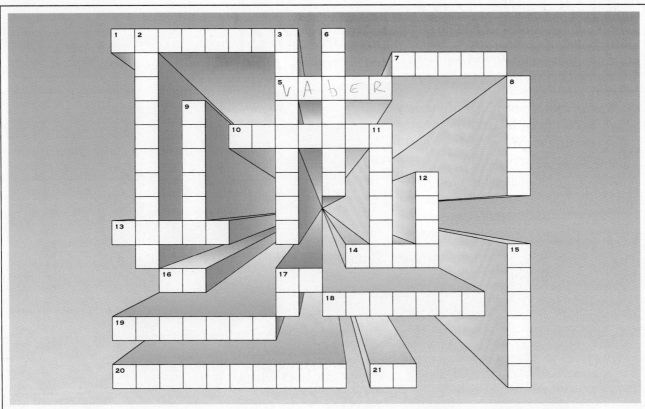

ACROSS

1. PIONEERED MOTION STUDY
5. DESCRIBED BUREAUCRACY
7. FATHER OF MODERN MANAGEMENT
10. FIRST CLASS MAN (ASK YOUR INSTRUCTOR)
13. A PLANNING AND CONTROL CHART IS NAMED AFTER HIM
14. AUTHOR OF MANAGEMENT HISTORY BOOK
16. 19—, THE YEAR OF FRANK GILBRETH'S DEATH
17. NUMBER OF CHILDREN IN THE GILBRETH FAMILY
18. POINTED OUT IMPORTANCE OF "RECIPROCAL INFLUENCE"
19. ACCEPTANCE THEORY
20. DO MORE THAN A FAIR DAY'S WORK
21. NUMBER OF FAYOL'S PRINCIPLES

DOWN

2. 18TH CENTURY REVOLUTION
3. SERIES OF STUDIES CONDUCTED FROM 1924 TO 1932
6. EARLY USERS OF DEPARTMENTATION (MISP INTL)
8. ITEM (SINGULAR) PRODUCED BY ASSEMBLY OPERATORS IN STUDIES REFERENCED IN #4 ABOVE
9. FAYOL'S _____ DE CORPS
11. FATHER OF SCIENTIFIC MANAGEMENT
12. RAISED MINIMUM AGE OF WORK FOR CHILDREN (IN A TABLE)
15. A MODERN APPROACH TO MANAGEMENT (SINGULAR)
17. 19—, THE YEAR OF FRED TAYLOR'S DEATH

SOURCE: ADAPTED FROM ARTHUR G. BEDEIAN, MANAGEMENT, 2ND ED. (CHICAGO: DRYDEN, 1989), P. 63.

MRS. M. O. ADEPOJU
(DISTRIBUTOR FOR COCA-COLA)
COW MARKET BODIJA IBADAN.

Enjoy
Coca-Cola
Coke

"Our government has done a very poor job of bilateral negotiation on trade. We've got to get Japan to accept reciprocity."
—Edward Hennessy, Jr.,
CEO,
Allied-Signode Corporation

"Clearly, Japan has replaced the United States as the world's financial leader."
—R. Taggart Murphy,
Chase Manhattan Asia
Limited

Managing in an Ever-Changing Global Environment

CHAPTER OBJECTIVES

When you have read this chapter you should be able to:

1. Describe what is meant by the globalization of business and give some examples of its occurrence.

2. Identify the triad of key markets and the size of each.

3. Discuss the Japanese as competitors.

4. Review the strengths of the "Four Tigers" of the Pacific Rim.

5. Describe what has happened as a result of the Europe 1992 initiative and its possible impacts on North American firms.

6. Discuss the implications of East-West integration.

7. Describe how managers should manage in a global environment, identifying the impacts of economic, political/legal, sociocultural, and technological forces.

8. Describe the difficulties involved in applying management practices used in one country to management situations in another.

9. Identify the various stages of strategic activity in global businesses.

10. Describe the typical macro organizational structures of global corporations.

11. Describe leadership in global situations.

12. Describe control in global situations.

13. Identify the unique problems of managing a multinational corporation.

MANAGEMENT CHALLENGES DISCUSSED IN THIS CHAPTER:

 Increasing globalization of business.

 Changing technology.

 A more diverse work force.

 Quality and innovation as managerial imperatives.

 Increasing demands by constituents.

Apple Computer: Global Competitor par Excellence

It's difficult to label any firm as competitively excellent these days. Circumstances change so rapidly that unless a firm is right on the leading edge of technology, strategy, innovation, and management, it isn't likely to remain excellent very long. However, one company seems to have managed its way to competitive excellence. Apple Computer Incorporated has made the right moves at the right time. It has not merely kept abreast of technology, but led it. It has followed the right strategy, and its entire strategy is based on innovation. Finally, its management style gives employees, even the lowest-level employees, decision-making power, something most experts agree is absolutely essential to success in the 1990s. Strategically, in addition to focusing on innovation and technology, Apple has moved to become a truly global player, attacking its competitors in their home markets. In Japan, for example, it gained a significant share of the personal-computer market in the early 1990s (from 1 to 6 percent in three years), thereby becoming almost a cult phenomenon. It has marketed not only its products, but its image: It sponsers concerts by singers like Janet Jackson, as well as golf tournaments (which are very popular in Japan), and sells Apple tee shirts, mugs, and other paraphernalia.

Apple learned how to market its products and image in Japan, after almost ten years without success, largely because it hired Shigechika Takeuchi away from Toshiba to run its Japanese operation. It has forged alliances with Sony, which manufactures its notebook PC; with Sharp, which makes Newton, Apple's electronic organizer; and with Toshiba, which manufactures Apple's new multimedia Macintosh, featuring video, text, and sound.

Apple has also forged a major alliance with IBM in which the former archrivals have agreed to share hardware (from IBM) and software (from Apple). They have entered into joint ventures to produce a whole new type of operating software, to create a "Power PC" that will allow Apple to use IBM's powerful new RISC technology, to develop a supergadget that will have multimedia capabilities and a new version of UNIX, and to improve the compatibility of IBM and Apple machines. This alliance will help both companies compete globally, but it is especially important for Apple, which felt that it could not afford the R&D necessary for these projects.

Apple has always been strong in Europe, where it has the lion's share of the market. About 25 percent of its revenues come from its European operations. However, smaller concerns, such as Dell Computers Inc., are cutting into Apple's European market share. Part of Apple's success in Europe is attributable to the European market's tendency to lag behind the U.S. market in terms of new product introductions and marketing strategies. Forty percent of all personal computers in European institutions of higher learning are Macintoshes, helping to assure Apple of a strong user base as students from those institutions enter business firms.

SOURCES: Steve Gibson, "PDA's Killer: Breakthrough Technology or the Next Hula Hoop?" *Infoworld* (July 27, 1992), p. 34; Neil Gross and Kathy Rebello, "Apple: Japan Can't Say No," *Business Week* (June 29, 1992), pp. 32–33; Robert D. Hof and Deidre A. Depke, "An Alliance Made in PC Heaven," *Business Week* (June 24, 1991), p. 42; Andrew Kupfer, "Apple's Plan to Survive and Grow," *Fortune* (May 4, 1992), pp. 68–72; Steven Levy, "Talkin' Macintosh Blues," *Macworld* (September 1992), pp. 75–78; Richard Pastore, "Apple's Savior Across the Sea," *Computerworld* (August 6, 1990), pp. 83, 89; Stuart Rock, "Apple's Hectic Teenage Years," *Director* (September 1990), pp. 42–46; Lee The, "Apple Near Deal for IS," *Datamation* (July 15, 1992), pp. 46–60; Liza Weiman and Tom Moran, "Newton: A Step Toward the Future," *Macworld* (August 1992), pp. 129–131.

The single most significant global economic event since the formation of OPEC occurred in 1992, when the twelve nations of the European Economic Community (EEC) became one market. The ramifications of this event for companies in countries all around the world, but especially for those in Europe, the United States, Canada, and Japan, are significant and could prove to be tumultuous. Large companies like Apple Computer have recognized the need to become global players, to form alliances, and to be active participants in the Japanese and European markets. Firms like IBM, Ford, and GM are already entrenched in Europe but have taken further action to prepare for the changes resulting from the 1992 initiative. GM Europe, for example, underwent a major cost-cutting effort in order to be competitive with Japanese auto manufacturers, which are coming to Europe in force.[1] Other firms, such as IBM, are busy establishing alliances with European firms such as Bull and Siemens.[2]

However, Europe after 1992 is only one part, albeit a major part, of the global business story. The potential for East-West economic integration, the reunification of Germany, the resurgence of capitalism in China, and the emergence of Latin American countries, especially Mexico, as major economic entities are but a few of the trends and events moving management onto a global plane. This process has been under way for many years. The Japanese have for years successfully penetrated U.S. markets in automobiles, electronics, steel, and other manufactured goods. Each day thousands of Americans purchase shoes from Reebok, a British company that manufactures in Korea. Each year the British purchase thousands of automobiles made by an American company, Ford, that have been assembled in England with parts manufactured in thirteen European countries.[3] In addition, many U.S. firms have moved some of their manufacturing facilities to Mexico. In sum, the globalization of business is having a significant impact on the practice of management.

This chapter addresses key issues in the globalization of business and examines how management will have to change in response. However, bear in mind that these changes will not occur quickly or easily. One of the major challenges facing management in the 1990s is the need to adapt management practices to other countries. A global management process is emerging as managers in many countries learn from one another, but this is only the core of a process that must still be adapted to accommodate cultural variations.

The reunification of Germany was a major event that helped move management onto a global plane. By the year 2000, a united Germany will be one of the world's dominant economies.

The Globalization of Business

A "brave new world" is emerging in which trade will occur almost without regard to national borders. Hybrid products are emerging that are attractive to consumers in more than one nation. Joint ventures, mergers, acquisitions, and other kinds of alliances will characterize the business world in the future. Ford Motor Company's new compact car, the Probe, was designed in Detroit, engineered in Hiroshima by the company's equity partner, Mazda, and assembled in Michigan. Similarly, Mitsubishi and Chrysler jointly produced two versions of two almost identical cars, the Mitsubishi Eclipse and the Plymouth Laser, which were engineered and manufactured in the United States, as well as the Dodge Stealth and the Mitsubishi 3000XD, which were designed in the United States and manufactured in Japan. Hewlett-Packard and Canada's Northern Telecom pooled their know-how to tap the enormous new market for corporate information systems. A leather-processing subsidiary of Tata, the Indian conglomerate, is teaming up with France-based TFR to compete with Italian firms in marketing upscale leather goods. Caterpillar and Mitsubishi are teaming up to make giant earth movers.[4]

Business forecasters have identified the move toward global business as one of ten key changes that are occurring now and will occur in the near future.[5] In describing the American CEO of the next century, *The Wall Street Journal* makes it clear that he or she will be experienced abroad and may very well be from abroad.[6] Major U.S. corporations are already actively engaged in global management training for their younger managers.[7]

Among the most significant changes taking place are those involving the nature of business. Firms are moving from simply accepting the possibility of international opportunities and threats to recognizing that global considerations must be part of their overall game plan. Another key change is that non-U.S.-based firms are gaining more power in the global marketplace. For example, eight of the world's ten largest banks are Japanese, compared to only one in 1980.[8] (See Table 3.1.) Whether measured by the size of deposits or assets, only one U.S. bank—Citicorp—made it into the top twenty-five in 1991, and it lost ground from its 1988 rank of twentieth in asset size. As shown in Table 3.2, in 1991, ten of the world's twenty-five largest industrial companies were American. Ten were European, four Japanese, and one Korean. In 1980, none of the twenty-five largest industrial companies in the world was headquartered in Japan or Korea.

The United States ran a foreign-trade deficit of $100 billion a year or more for five consecutive years, from 1984 to 1988 ($155 billion in 1987).[9] Much of this deficit occurred in trade with Japan and other Pacific Rim countries. As the Japanese sold vast quantities of products overseas and amassed huge assets, Japanese banks became large and powerful. The trade deficit is also one of the reasons for the enormous impact of Japanese banks on the U.S. capital market. The United States went from being the world's largest lending nation in 1980, with a surplus of $106 billion, to being the world's largest debtor nation in 1987, with a debt of $368 billion.[10] Because they hold much of that debt, Japanese banks and firms have a major influence on the availability of capital for investment in American businesses.[11]

In 1992, EEC firms created a home market of 340 million people (including 17 million former East Germans). U.S. firms have a home market of 243 million people, and Japanese firms have a home market of 120 million people. Thus, for the first time in history, European firms have a consumer base large enough to make them true global competitors.

TABLE 3.1 World's Largest Banks, 1991 (ranked by assets)

Rank 1991		Headquarters	Assets ($ Million)	Deposits ($ Million)
1	Dai-Ichi Kangyo Bank	Japan	475,831.4	374,631.7
2	Sumitomo Bank	Japan	464,113.7	367,266.7
3	Fuji Bank	Japan	455,357.6	352,896.8
4	Sakura Bank	Japan	448,291.0	360,389.1
5	Sanwa Bank	Japan	445,027.2	357,150.9
6	Mitsubishi Bank	Japan	432,092.9	349,294.6
7	Industrial Bank of Japan	Japan	333,321.5	254,553.6
8	Norinchukin Bank	Japan	311,033.9	261,530.4
9	Crédit Agricole	France	306,316.4	211,639.0
10	Crédit Lyonnais	France	305,450.4	125,088.4
11	Deutsche Bank	Germany	295,446.8	265,328.0
12	Banque Nationale de Paris	France	275,079.7	132,682.6
13	Tokai Bank	Japan	270,974.7	211,663.6
14	Mitsubishi Trust & Banking	Japan	261,561.5	221,252.2
15	Barclays Bank	Britain	257,709.5	210,188.1
16	Long-Term Credit Bank of Japan	Japan	255,663.4	209,476.6
17	Bank of Tokyo	Japan	247,187.9	149,707.3
18	ABN Amro Holding	Netherlands	242,374.2	188,964.7
19	Sumitomo Trust & Banking	Japan	234,917.1	214,111.5
20	Société Générale	France	234,070.5	177,321.3
21	National Westminster Bank	Britain	231,510.9	200,583.8
22	Bank of China	China	229,385.3	147,372.9
23	Kyowa Saitama Bank	Japan	227,270.7	184,936.1
24	Mitsui Trust & Banking	Japan	226,658.4	201,675.0
25	Citicorp	U.S.	216,922.0	146,475.0

SOURCE: Adapted from "The World's Largest Commercial Banking Companies," *Fortune* (August 24, 1992), p. 213. © 1992 Time Inc. All rights reserved.

Another factor affecting global business is the massive debt of the developing nations. Fortunately, economic reforms in Latin America have helped reduce the intensity of this problem.[12]

It is also becoming clear that the United States' leadership role in the world, especially in the world of business, is being challenged.[13] In the near term, the United States is likely to retain its global leadership on the basis of its strengths, principally its consumer base and its military power. However, with the world changing so fast and the role of military power diminishing in many nations, it is difficult to predict the global distribution of economic power a few years from now.[14]

As firms have entered the global marketplace, they have become increasingly larger, often eclipsing whole countries in terms of their economic impact. Table 3.3 provides some striking comparisons between the revenues of global

TABLE 3.2 World's 25 Biggest Industrial Corporations, 1991

Rank 1991	1990	Company	Headquarters	Sales ($ Millions)	Percent change from 1990	Profits ($ Millions)	Rank	Percent change from 1990	Assets ($ Millions)	Rank
1	1	General Motors	U.S.	123,780.1	(1.1)	(4,452.8)	490	—	184,325.5	1
2	2	Royal Dutch/Shell Group	Britain/Neth.	103,834.8	(3.1)	4,249.3	2	(34.0)	105,307.7	4
3	3	Exxon	U.S.	103,242.0	(2.5)	5,600.0	1	11.8	87,560.0	6
4	4	Ford Motor	U.S.	88,962.8	(9.5)	(2,258.0)	488	(362.5)	174,429.4	2
5	6	Toyota Motor	Japan	78,061.3	21.0	3,143.2	3	5.0	65,178.7	8
6	5	Intl. Business Machines	U.S.	65,394.0	(5.3)	(2,827.0)	489	(147.0)	92,473.0	5
7	7	IRI	Italy	64,095.5	4.3	(254.1)	459	(127.4)	N.A.	
8	10	General Electric	U.S.	60,236.0	3.1	2,636.0	5	(38.7)	168,259.0	3
9	8	British Petroleum	Britain	58,355.0	(2.0)	802.8	55	(70.9)	59,323.9	11
10	11	Daimler-Benz	Germany	57,321.3	5.6	1,129.4	30	8.4	49,811.8	13
11	9	Mobil	U.S.	56,910.0	(3.2)	1,920.0	8	(0.5)	42,187.0	22
12	12	Hitachi	Japan	56,053.3	10.6	1,629.2	16	10.3	60,641.0	10
13	17	Matsushita Electric Industrial	Japan	48,595.0	11.7	1,832.5	10	11.1	62,312.5	9
14	15	Philip Morris	U.S.	48,109.0	8.5	3,006.0	4	(15.1)	47,384.0	14
15	13	Fiat	Italy	46,812.0	(2.0)	898.7	46	(33.3)	69,736.4	7
16	16	Volkswagen	Germany	46,042.2	5.3	665.5	65	2.1	46,111.8	16
17	24	Siemens	Germany	44,859.2	14.4	1,135.2	29	24.3	41,785.0	23
18	14	Samsung Group	South Korea	43,701.9	4.4	347.3	126	4.1	43,290.3	19
19	20	Nissan Motor	Japan	42,905.7	6.7	340.9	128	(57.8)	45,916.4	17
20	21	Unilever	Britain/Netherlands	41,262.3	3.2	1,842.6	9	29.2	25,340.3	43
21	18	EMI	Italy	41,047.3	(1.7)	872.0	48	(48.6)	N.A.	
22	22	E.I. Du Pont de Nemours	U.S.	38,031.0	(4.5)	1,403.0	22	(39.3)	36,117.0	26
23	19	Texaco	U.S.	37,551.0	(8.9)	1,294.0	26	(10.8)	26,182.0	41
24	23	Chevron	U.S.	36,795.0	(6.3)	1,293.0	27	(40.1)	34,636.0	27
25	26	Elf Aquitaine	France	36,315.8	10.3	1,737.1	12	(11.0)	46,539.7	15

SOURCE: "The World's Biggest Industrial Corporations," *Fortune* (July 27, 1992), p. 179. © 1992 Time Inc. All rights reserved.

corporations and the gross domestic products (GDPs) of several countries. According to Secretary of Labor Robert B. Reich, global corporations are increasingly wielding tremendous power and, in fact, are becoming stateless in nature. Their top managers feel less allegiance to the countries in which these firms are headquartered and more allegiance to the corporation itself. Decisions about where to manufacture, for example, are made less on the basis of national allegiance than on the basis of the firm's ability to compete globally.[15]

The Triad of Key Markets

Triad of key global markets: North America, Europe (EEC), and Japan.

Kenichi Ohmae, senior partner in the consulting firm of McKinsey & Company in Tokyo, has identified a **triad of key global markets:** Japan, Europe, and North America.[16] Any corporate player desiring a global presence must be able to

TABLE 3.3 How Revenues of the Top Ten Global 500 Compare with Some National Economies

Firm	Sales	Country	1991 GDP
1. General Motors	$123,780	Finland	$126,630
2. Royal Dutch Shell Group	$103,835	Norway	$106,320
3. Exxon	$103,242	Turkey	$103,800
4. Ford Motor	$88,963	Thailand	$92,010
5. Toyota Motor	$78,061	Hong Kong	$82,680
6. IBM	$65,394	Greece	$70,130
7. IRI (Italian Holding Company)	$64,095	Portugal	$68,980
8. General Electric	$60,236	Israel	$57,880
9. British Petroleum	$58,355	Venezuela	$52,660
10. Daimler Benz	$57,321	Malaysia	$47,940

SOURCE: Alison Rogers, "*Fortune* Plays Benchmarker," *Fortune* (July 27, 1992), p. 16. © 1992 Time Inc. All rights reserved. (Source of data: WEFA.)

compete in each of those markets. In this section we will examine each of the major players in the triad.

Japan

The Japanese economy has, like a phoenix, risen from the ashes of World War II to unparalleled heights. In the following paragraphs, we discuss what makes the Japanese so successful; we then review some of the changes affecting their potential for continued success.

SOURCES OF SUCCESS

The official view of the Keidanren, the powerful federation of Japanese businesses, is that Japanese success results from a complex interaction of macro and micro variables involving government, capital, labor, and technology, as shown in Table 3.4. Items 3 and 4 in the table—macro and micro labor factors—are essentially those that William G. Ouchi identified in his research on the relationship of Japanese management practices to Japanese success.[17] In addition, such factors as a highly educated work force, favorable government policy, and a high savings rate are important. A survey of Japanese business executives indicated that a majority of them believe cultural factors to be the predominant cause of Japanese business success.[18] U.S. experts attribute part of Japan's success to restrictive trade barriers against the products and services of firms based in other countries. Those experts also point to cartels, old-boy networks, and corruption as factors in the success of Japanese firms.[19]

At the level of the firm, individual Japanese corporations attempt to establish a "winner's competitive cycle."[20] The cycle begins with growth: Japanese companies believe that they must grow faster than their competitors; they must increase their market share so that their volume of business will increase at a greater rate than their competitors'. This, in turn, depends on a higher rate of investment, which can take many forms, including price cutting, expansion of capacity, advertising, and development of new products. Failure to take these steps will ultimately lead to the failure of the firm in the Japanese system of competition.

CHANGES IN THE JAPANESE SUCCESS FORMULA

While it seems clear that by the year 2000 Japan will probably be second only to the United States in overall economic power (although a unified Germany may give it a run for its money), it is uncertain how it intends to reach that level of economic performance. Japan suffered through a recession in 1992 and a three-year, 60 percent decline in the Nikkei stock market average from 1990 to 1992.[21] Moreover, tensions have developed over Japan's trade practices, which the United States and European countries consider unfair. Those tensions may result in import quotas. In addition, Japan's development as one of the world's financial capitals is threatened by its government's stringent regulation of business.

A number of cultural as well as economic and historical factors also seem to be creating problems for Japan.[22] Many observers believe that the Japanese educational system is too rigid for the twenty-first century. More innovation will be needed if firms are to remain competitive, but the Japanese educational system stifles creativity.

Another difficulty faced by Japanese firms is that the work ethic appears to be eroding, especially among younger workers. That generation is becoming restless, more Westernized, and less willing to work long, hard hours. These

---

TABLE 3.4 Factors Contributing to the Success of the Japanese Economy

1. Macro Capital Factors:
   - high savings rate
   - effective industrial financing through the banking system
   - industrial grouping, such as the large trading companies
   - government industrial policy

2. Micro Capital Factors:
   - modern management: ownership and management are separated
   - middle and long-term gains, emphasizing the long-term view
   - capital investment by individual corporations
   - fund raising made easy through excellent access to sources

3. Macro Labor Factors:
   - high educational levels of the workforce
   - flexible manpower supply moving from declining to growth industries
   - good labor-management cooperation; only 32% unionized
   - wages are kept within productivity

4. Micro Labor Factors:
   - an employment system characterized by three elements: (1) life-time employment, (2) promotion system based on seniority, to which wages are tied, and (3) incentives for training employees
   - deciding by consensus, popularly called "bottom-up management"
   - labor transfers within the company: given employment security, employees are most willing to move

5. Macro Technology Factors:
   - Japan has aggressively imported overseas technology, and integrated and improved that technology
   - development of production technology
   - effective research and development that, while low, is helped by the government's implementation of policy

6. Micro Technology Factors:
   - TQC—total quality control system
   - workers' suggestions
   - parts availability through small business
   - highly competitive technologically; i.e., keeping abreast of and using new technology

SOURCE: Adapted from Masaya Miyoshi, managing director, Kendron, Tokyo, as published in Norman Coates, "Determinants of Japan's Business Success: Some Japanese Executive's Views," *Academy of Management Executives* (January 1988), p. 70.

shinjinrui, as Japanese young people are known, are indeed "new human beings" (the term's literal meaning) who prefer playing to working. Employee loyalty is waning as employees switch firms in search of better work and higher pay.[23] The role of women in Japan is also changing, slowly but surely, with the result that women are entering the work force in larger numbers.[24]

The Japanese have paid a high price for their economic success in terms of family life and personal sacrifice. Rates of alcoholism, emotional breakdown, and suicide are increasing, and wives are growing more resentful of their executive spouses' devotion to work.[25] In addition, Japan's population is aging.[26] This means that an increasing proportion of the population will consist of social security recipients and occupants of nursing homes, placing an additional economic burden on younger workers.

Despite these problems and challenges, the Japanese are still the dominant financial power in the world and could eventually replace the United States as the number 1 economic power.[27] Japan has been a great imitator and is becoming a good inventor. It is building a new economic power base throughout Asia and the Pacific. It is moving rapidly ahead in Thailand, the Phillippines, Indonesia, Malaysia, and China and is beginning to develop ties with Taiwan, Korea, Singapore, and Hong Kong. It seems certain that Japan will replace the United States as the most powerful economic influence in Asia.[28] It has invaded the European market, positioning itself to take advantage of the 1992 initiative.[29] Moreover, it is likely that Japan's financial strength will continue to grow.

Japanese firms are already beginning to dominate key science technologies—superconductivity, biotechnology, and microelectronics—and are taking great pains to improve their research capability.[30] They also are restructuring to accommodate slower growth.[31] One company that has taken to heart the need to restructure its own economic situation is Toshiba. Badly battered by the 1991–1992 recession, Toshiba symbolizes the leaner Japanese firm of the future, as this chapter's Global Management Challenge shows.

ASIA'S "FOUR TIGERS"

In addition to Japan, four Pacific Rim nations—South Korea, Taiwan, Hong Kong, and Singapore—have been rewarded with increasing prosperity for their hard work, competitive spirit, and free-enterprise economies. These so-called Four Tigers account for more than 11 percent of the United States' 1991 trade deficit. Despite considerable pressure to do so, they have done little to remove barriers to trade. Taiwan, however, has a "buy American" policy in which U.S. companies are favored for major purchases and projects. (For example, Japanese companies are not permitted to bid on Taipei's new subway, but U.S. firms are.)

A number of economic and political factors affect trade between the Four Tigers and the West. Hong Kong and Singapore have pegged their currencies to the U.S. dollar, with the result that U.S. trade deficits with those countries will continue. South Korea has balked at opening its borders to U.S. firms and is not offering much hope for compromise.[32] In 1997, Hong Kong will revert to Chinese rule, and this will undoubtedly affect its trade relations with the West. Finally, China is beginning to exert its economic strength and may soon be a fifth "tiger."

Europe After 1992

Europe, the second member of the triad, is potentially the most economically significant. Europe's economic future depends on the outcome of the 1992 unification effort and the East-West economic integration that began in 1989. A unified Germany has increased the potential for European economic growth.

AT APPLE: Apple has learned how to compete in Japan, partly relying on an insider's knowledge of the market. It has taken the fight to its competitors' home markets. This is an important part of being a true global competitor.

AT APPLE: The globalization of business caused Apple to reassess its European strategy. Apple wanted to be in a position to take advantage of new opportunities and meet the challenge of its global competitors.

Toshiba: Leaner and Meaner

It could be a variation on the old favorite: Where does a 500-pound gorilla sit during a recession? In the case of Toshiba Corporation, one of the largest makers of computer chips, home appliances, and heavy machinery, the answer is "*Almost anywhere it likes.*"

This is not to say that the recession is having little impact on the manufacturing giant. Its profits fell by 58 percent in 1991, to $827 million. Stock prices have plunged, and Toshiba's famous laptop computers are not jumping off the shelves. In 1992, Toshiba fared little better because of the high value of the yen and the recession at home.

In response, the company's executives are enacting a bevy of changes: investment and export strategies, product cycles, and ventures with outsiders are all under review. However, when the going gets rough, it helps to start from the winner's circle, and Toshiba's world-class engineers and factories constitute a big plus: The company is likely to emerge stronger once the recession is over.

While it's retrenching, Toshiba is doing what doesn't come naturally. Capital spending was trimmed by an estimated 25 percent in 1992, to $1.4 billion. More troubling, Toshiba could be forced to reconsider its breakneck pursuit of product development—something its rivals have already done.

Also in response to flagging demand, Toshiba finds itself cutting more and more deals with rivals like Motorola Inc., IBM, General Electric Co., Siemens, and Time Warner Inc. Such deals guarantee partners, but they also involve massive transfers of Toshiba's expertise.

Still, the engineering powerhouse does not have to worry too much. Although computer chips and consumer electronics have been hit hard by the recession, sales of heavy electrical equipment and energy systems have been robust, yielding $7 billion in revenues in 1991. While its frenzied investments in the 1980s left Toshiba with substantial bills, they also produced a network of factories and new products poised to take off when people start spending again.

Meanwhile, Toshiba continues to plow money into high-definition TV,

THE 1992 INITIATIVE

Europe 1992 initiative: The movement to form an integrated market for the twelve countries of the EEC.

The **Europe 1992 initiative**—the concept of an integrated market for firms in the EEC—extends to much of the rest of Europe as well. For example, Austria, Sweden, and Finland have applied to join the EEC, as will most of the rest of Western Europe, and many Eastern European countries are leaning in that direction. The new EEC could easily swell to twenty-five members, with a total population of 450 million, by the year 2000.[33] (EEC countries as of 1993 are shown in Figure 3.1.) This integration of markets will give European firms the ability to compete on a global basis for the first time. Their home market will be large enough to test a product that can then be marketed globally. It will help to eliminate, although not totally, the need to create specialized products for various countries or regions of Europe, which have different cultural preferences. It will make commerce and trade much easier because the main barrier to a true common market has been the existence of local regulations.

In response to increased competition and the impact of the 1991–1992 recession in Japan, Toshiba was forced to enact a number of changes, including trimming capital spending and making deals with business rivals.

liquid-crystal displays, next-generation batteries, and high-risk fields such as warm-temperature superconductors. The immediate future may present some difficulties, but there is little danger that Toshiba will lose its way. Corporate planners promise to maintain a "long-term perspective."

SOURCES: John W. Verity, "The Japanese Juggernaut That Isn't," *Business Week* (August 31, 1992), pp. 64–66; and Neil Gross, "Toshiba: Rethinking the Way It Does Business," *Business Week* (April 27, 1992), p. 55.

These regulations affect virtually every facet of business, but they are especially problematic when they prevent the standardization of products across national borders. For example, before the 1992 initiative there were no common standards for auto emissions, radio wavelengths, mobile telephones, or capitalization rules for banks. Insurance companies were even prohibited from selling insurance in more than one country. All this changed as a result of the 1992 initiative. Among the areas affected are national borders (no passports after January 1, 1993), air travel (any European carrier can fly between EEC countries), taxes (a 15 percent minimum value-added tax), and standards (a rule approved in one country applies to all). There have been modest changes in rules governing airlines, telecommunications, autos, and finance.[34] In sum, as Cor van der Klugt, president of Philips, Europe's largest consumer electronics company, has observed, "What Europe is doing is gigantic. The drive for economic unity is the most important thing that will happen for the next fifty years."[35]

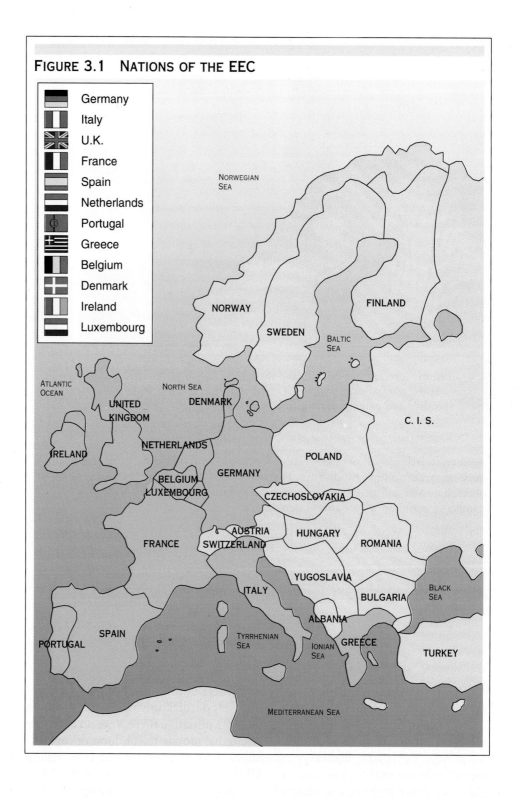

FIGURE 3.1 NATIONS OF THE EEC

Germany
Italy
U.K.
France
Spain
Netherlands
Portugal
Greece
Belgium
Denmark
Ireland
Luxembourg

    Not everyone is certain that a complete integration will occur, however. As of early 1993, not all of the EEC countries have ratified the treaty, and a two-tiered system of poorer countries (e.g., Italy) and richer ones (e.g., Germany) may emerge.[36] Nevertheless, the requirements for success in this new environment are quite different from those of the past. There have been obvious changes in the strategies of European firms as a result. Marketing has become very important, and firms that are skilled in marketing have been able to seize the opportunities created by the 1992 initiative in advance of their competitors.

Many firms are changing their cost structures—for example, by automating production processes—and attempting to cut costs. Huge restructurings have occurred. Philips, for example, has eliminated 20 percent of its work force— 47,000 employees—but can still barely turn a profit.[37] Firms have also sought to employ differentiation strategies. In some countries, such as Spain and southern Italy, firms have gained advantages as a result of such factors as lower wage rates.

Responses to the 1992 initiative have varied from one country to another. Germany, for example, has focused on reunification, sometimes at the expense of the 1992 initiative. Denmark, France, and Great Britain have not offered much support for the initiative, but other nations, such as Spain, have moved ahead in preparing for economic integration. The cultural problems associated with European integration will be complex, and not all of the region's economic problems will be eliminated. It is likely that a single currency will evolve, although it is not clear when. There has already been a period of bank consolidation, creating a significant shift of power among European banks.[38]

A TYPICAL STRATEGY FOR AN EEC-BASED FIRM

Avery International, a U.S.-based office supply firm with one-third of its sales coming from its European subsidiary, has substantially altered its European strategy to respond to the 1992 initiative. G. J. van den Akker, head of Avery Europe, outlined the strategies the firm has followed:

1. Moving to a service-oriented strategy that will provide the product to any customer in Europe within twenty-four hours
2. Cutting the number of distribution warehouses from one for each country to five regional warehouses
3. Reducing inventories
4. Reducing transportation and administrative costs
5. Moving to an integrated data network
6. Increasing emphasis on quality
7. Eliminating non-value-adding work
8. Tracking common product lines to ascertain the characteristics of products needed in 1992
9. Reexamining price and quality competitiveness in the firm[39]

This chapter's Quality Management Challenge highlights GM Europe's strategies for coping with the environment in Europe after 1992. Note that the company's managers are aware that they cannot afford to rest on their laurels but must take action if the firm is to remain competitive.

A TYPICAL STRATEGY FOR A NON-EEC-BASED FIRM

Non-EEC-based firms have attempted to establish a presence in Europe through acquisitions, mergers, and other entry strategies. GE, for example, has merged with GE of Britain and made several acquisitions on the Continent, including some in Eastern Europe, in order to prevent being locked out of Europe after 1992.

By the middle of 1992, 285 directives covering economic and legal issues related to the establishment of the Common Market had been proposed. Though several major issues remain, it now seems apparent that most directives will pass.[40] These will affect the strategies of foreign firms.

AT APPLE: Apple, which already had a substantial market share in Europe, took the actions that were necessary for a non-EEC-based company to survive and prosper after 1992.

GM Europe's Strategy of Continuous Improvement

In the business world of the 1990s, no one ever promised anyone a rose garden. A case in point is GM Europe, which ought to feel safe and secure these days. It has enjoyed huge successes and hefty profits for more than five years and has run rings around its major competitor, Ford of Europe. It has done so well that its former chief, John F. Smith, Jr., was brought back to Detroit early in 1992 to head the parent company. So why is GM Europe running scared?

The answer is that Japanese auto makers are poised to become a major factor in Europe. Although their combined market share constituted only 12 percent in 1992, representing only about one-third of their share of U.S. sales, Nissan, Toyota, and Honda will all be opening their own plants in England soon, and the new competition will put pressure on prices.

So GM Europe, the maker of Opels in Germany and Vauxhalls in England, plans to cut costs—completely overhauling the way it develops and manufactures cars. "Lean" production methods will slash inventory, factory space, equipment, and employees.

In the vanguard of the new production system is an assembly plant recently acquired by GM in Eisenach, in the former East Germany. Having cast off communism, east German workers are more malleable and more open to change than workers in GM's existing factories. "If we can take a work force in a former Communist country and make it the most efficient in Europe," says Louis R. Hughes, GM Europe's president, "it will send an incredibly strong signal to our organization."

GM Europe has a history of aggressively launching products and cutting costs.

- It pioneered running auto plants around the clock, maximizing the use of costly machinery. So far, no other auto maker has done this.
- It moved its headquarters to a small suburban building in Zurich, thereby avoiding bureaucracy and a German old-boy network at Opel's headquarters in Frankfurt.
- It reduced its parts bill by terminating relationships with existing suppliers and acquiring parts outside GM and outside Germany.
- It cultivated a "green" image, introducing catalytic converters on a full range of models.
- It created a "strategy board," a group of fifteen top executives with authority to act promptly on virtually any important issue. The idea has now been imported into GM's U.S. operations as well.

THE POTENTIAL FOR EAST-WEST ECONOMIC INTEGRATION

In 1989, a series of changes in political and economic structure began in Eastern Europe. It is not immediately clear what the impact of those changes will be, but their economic significance could surpass that of the 1992 initiative. Poland, Czechoslovakia, Hungary, and the former East Germany have already benefited

In keeping with its history of aggressively launching products and cutting costs, in 1992 GM opened its first dealership in Russia.

Boosting efficiency is now GM Europe's top priority. Its leaner plants are projected to produce about 75 percent more cars per worker than its old-style, mass-production plants, where conveyor belts and storage bins for parts represent the wave of the past. Although assembly-line inventories have been cut in some places, such as the Opel factory at Bochum in the Ruhr Valley, further cuts are required. Cuts in the work force of around 20 percent in the next five years are expected.

The leaner, Japanese-style plants will be filled with details that create huge efficiencies in the aggregate. For example, delivery trucks will unload parts a few meters from the assembly line. They will drive in one door and out another; they won't back up. The assembly line won't *push* cars at workers; cars will move only when workers signal that they're ready.

The result? Higher production, less inventory, fewer errors. The means? Worker training. "When you get into this system and live with it for a while," says Tom LaSorda, director of the Eisenbach plant, "you become a disciple. Then you can't go back."

SOURCE: Paul Ingrassia and Timothy Aeppel, "Worried by Japanese, Thriving GM Europe Vows to Get Leaner," *Wall Street Journal* (July 27, 1992), pp. A1, A6.

from the easing of economic and political constraints. However, eventually all nations in Eastern Europe and the former Soviet Union will probably benefit from these changes. The reunification of Germany has somewhat slowed progress toward comprehensive economic integration. Germany will probably be one of the world's three greatest economies by the year 2000, overshadowing the rest of Europe and much of the rest of the world.

North America

The principal economic powers in North America are the United States and Canada. These two nations signed a trade pact that took effect on January 1, 1989, calling for the abolishment of all tariffs over the next ten years. The pact has had a significant impact on some firms, but the potential impact of the North American Free Trade Agreement is much greater. That agreement would create a free-trade zone between the United States, Canada, and Mexico. Designed to take effect in late 1993 or early 1994, the agreement will give North American firms access to new markets and an inexpensive work force in Mexico; Mexico will benefit from increased investment and new jobs.[41] On the negative side, the U.S. and Canadian economies will lose high-paying jobs to Mexico.

DECLINING COMPETITIVENESS

Perhaps the most significant feature of U.S. and Canadian firms in recent years has been their declining global competitiveness. North American firms have found themselves at a competitive disadvantage on a global basis in both manufacturing and service industries, for a number of reasons: the transition from a manufacturing to a service economy, declining investment in heavy manufacturing, disadvantageous wage rates and benefit structures, technology transfer from the United States to foreign competitors, and a short-term perspective with regard to the returns expected from an organization.[42] Other factors in the reduced competitiveness of North American firms include diversification strategies, the subsequent adoption of decentralized organizational structures, and evolutionary changes in the nature of the capital market.[43]

The principal effect of these factors has been reduced investment in long-term product/market development. Innovation has been shortchanged both by the short-term perspective and by the absence of funds for investment in organizations that take a long-term perspective. In fact, it has been argued very strongly that U.S. competitiveness has declined principally because of a decline in innovation.[44] The firms that have survived, and that remain competitive internationally, have had to change how they think. A perfect example is Caterpillar, which totally revised its strategy, its management style, its organizational structure, and its marketing in order to beat global competitors.[45] Most firms in the United States and Canada are now becoming more competitive in the global marketplace.

Effects of Other Global Changes

The former Soviet Union—now the Commonwealth of Independent States (CIS)—first under Mikhail Gorbachev and more recently under Boris Yeltsin, has, through the policies of *perestroika* and *glasnost*, attempted to improve the well-being of its populace. The possibility exists that economic changes even greater than those occurring in Europe may occur in the CIS and China, despite China's political setback in the 1989 Tiananmen Square incident. Both the CIS and China are moving toward capitalism. Thus, two of the world's largest markets are opening up for European, Japanese, and American competitors alike.[46] In addition, South America—especially Brazil and Argentina—has become a major economic force.[47]

Management and the Global Environment

Global management is the performance of management activities on a truly global basis. It embodies the concept of a product sold in numerous countries, even though it may have to be tailored somewhat to the needs of customers in those countries. It requires a degree of coordination among activities that is not experienced in multidomestic/international operations.[48] **Multidomestic firms** are organizations that operate across national boundaries but treat each country as a separate market, developing products solely for that market.[49] Firms like AT&T and Federal Express are multidomestic; they do not design a product for a global market but take a product that worked in the United States and sell it in another country. They operate without a highly coordinated international manufacturing/service operation, in conjunction with marketing, finance, and human resources. In contrast, firms like Ford Motor Company, GM, Unilever, Mazda, Matsushita Electric Company, Sony, and GE are global companies. They produce products for global markets. However, even within these large corporations, especially GE and GM, there may be major divisions that operate in a multidomestic fashion. Both global and multidomestic companies are multinational corporations. A **multinational corporation** (MNC) is simply a firm that has significant operations in more than one country. MNCs may also be multinational enterprises—a group of corporations with businesses in several different countries but with a single headquarters.[50]

Most organizations don't become multinational or global overnight. Typically, they start as domestic organizations and move through a series of stages, gradually reaching multidomestic, and in some cases global, stages of multinationalization. Neil H. Jacoby and Christopher M. Korth have each identified a series of stages through which organizations pass on their way to becoming multinational.[51] Korth's model of these stages is depicted in Table 3.5; Jacoby's findings are integrated into this model. A fifth stage has been added to reflect the concept of global competition. In examining the table, bear in mind that not all organizations reach either the fourth or the fifth stage, and some may reach them and subsequently withdraw. For example, when Renault sold American Motors Corporation to Chrysler in 1987, it retreated from a global to a multidomestic strategy.

One of the major changes in moving from stage 1 to stage 5 is that products designed for the domestic market are first sold overseas. In later stages, manufacturing and financing may occur in foreign countries; in the fifth stage, the organization becomes totally global, designing products for more than one national market and using coordinated manufacturing, financing, human resources, and information management to manage the global competitive situation. This five-stage evolutionary process has been shown to be typical of U.S. firms.[52]

In the following paragraphs, we will examine management in multinational environments, analyzing how the four environmental forces are different and how they affect the organization's economic and management functions.

Environmental Factors

Four types of environmental forces affect organizations and their management: economic/competitive, political/legal, sociocultural, and technological. Each of them is significantly influenced by the change from domestic to multinational operations. In this section, we will take a close look at each category.

Global management: The performance of management activities on a truly global basis; embodies the concept of a product sold in numerous countries, requiring a degree of coordination among activities that is not experienced in multidomestic/international operations.

Multidomestic firm: An organization that operates across national boundaries but treats each country as a separate market, developing products solely for that market.

Multinational corporation: A firm that has significant operations in more than one country.

TABLE 3.5 Five Degrees of Internationalization

	Stage 1 First-Degree International- ization	Stage 2 Second-Degree International- ization	Stage 3 Third-Degree International- ization	Stage 4 Fourth-Degree International- ization	Stage 5 Fifth-Degree International- ization
Nature of contact with foreign markets	Indirect, passive	Direct, active	Direct, active	Direct, active	Direct, active
Focus of international operations	Domestic	Domestic	Domestic and international	Domestic and international	International
Orientation of company	Domestic	Domestic	Primarily domestic	Multinational (domestic operations viewed as part of the whole)	Global (with domestic modifications)
Type of international activity	Foreign trade of goods and services	Foreign trade of goods and services	Foreign trade, foreign assistance contracts, foreign direct investment	Foreign trade, foreign assistance contracts, foreign direct investment	Foreign trade, foreign assistance contracts, foreign direct investment
Organizational structure	Traditional domestic	International department	International division	Global structure	Global structure

SOURCES: Adapted from Christopher M. Korth, *International Business, Environment of Management*, 2nd ed. (Englewood Cliffs, N.J.: Prentice-Hall, 1985), p. 7 and Neil H. Jacoby, "The Multinational Corporation," *The Center Magazine* (May 1970), pp. 37–55.

ECONOMIC/COMPETITIVE FACTORS

Organizations that operate multinationally will be confronted with a myriad of economic and competitive environmental factors. They will face different monetary systems; they will be operating in countries that are going through varying stages of economic development; they may even be confronted with different economic systems, such as a moderate form of socialism in Great Britain, new capitalistic socialism in Hungary, a modified form of communism that allows some capitalism in China, a capitalist/socialistic approach in France, or a blend of capitalism and socialism in Canada. There will be fierce global competitors, powerful or weak customers and suppliers, new entrants into the market, and an increased number of substitute products or services.

POLITICAL/LEGAL FACTORS

Multinational corporations also face widely varying political/legal systems. In much of Europe, government takes an active role in business, frequently changing monetary and fiscal policy and taxation programs, as well as offering incentives for plant location or industrial development. Similarly, in Japan the government has close ties to its multinationals. It provides R&D funds and steers firms toward selected industries. In Europe prior to 1992, organizations were faced with at least twelve different sets of laws, controls, and policies—a situation that has continued, to some extent, since then but will soon no longer be the case. Throughout the world, property rights and laws governing the operation of business differ. Very few "free trade" countries exist, and controls on imports and exports are common.

R. Hall Mason notes that host countries—that is, countries allowing MNCs to operate within their borders—often impose restrictive policies on their actions. These restrictions include required shared ownership with the host country or its citizens, reservation of certain management and technical jobs for local hires, profit and fee ceilings, contract renegotiations, external debt capital, development of the host country's personnel and export market, and a preference for technology-based industries over extractive industries (which take raw materials out of a country).[53]

SOCIOCULTURAL FACTORS

Multinational corporations must learn to operate in a widely varying cultural context. Educational systems, for example, vary widely from one country to another. Stefan Robock and Kenneth Simmonds have identified several distinct cultural differences: assumptions and attitudes; personal beliefs, aspirations, and motivations; interpersonal relations; and social structure.[54] With respect to assumptions and attitudes, U.S. and Canadian management systems have been greatly influenced by their societies' belief in self-determination. In many other countries, however, the culture is much more fatalistic—a dominant belief is that human beings really cannot control their own future. Problems may arise in other areas as well—for example, with respect to time. Being "on time" is very important in most Western societies but is of little importance in China. In fact, being late is more common there than being on time.

With respect to personal beliefs, aspirations, and motivations, the need to achieve is much less significant in non-Western/capitalist/Protestant countries (for example, India and Peru) than it is in Western societies. Underlying beliefs about authority also affect how management functions. In Japan, teamwork is more readily accepted than in the United States or in Europe, although the latter are moving toward more teamwork in managing. The status of women in the workplace varies throughout the world. In the Middle East, women are almost always second-class citizens. In Europe, there are varying degrees of acceptance of women in organizations. Scandinavian countries accept them wholeheartedly,

Organizations that operate multinationally will be confronted with myriad economic and competitive environmental factors, including the growth of capitalism in China. Shown here are workers in the Concord Camera Factory in Shenzhen.

while Spain is more resistant to allowing women to hold managerial or professional positions. In the United States, women are a major part of the work force at all levels. In Japan, they play almost no part in the organization other than as front-line workers. With the passage of an equal employment opportunity act in 1987, however, Japanese women are slowly beginning to be accepted in managerial and professional positions.

With respect to social structure, social status and interclass mobility play important roles in many cultures. Britain has a very strong class structure, whereas Canada and the United States do not. The Japanese focus much of their energy on a group-oriented, patriarchical organizational structure. In sum, sociocultural factors can have a very significant impact on management. Managers must learn to operate within the cultural context of each individual country. Also significant are differences in verbal and nonverbal communication. Language, body language, symbols, and other aspects of communication vary, and these must be learned if management is to be effective. For example, the "OK" hand sign is an obscene gesture in southern Europe and much of South America.

These variances in sociocultural factors have led wise corporations to train their employees in the cultures of the countries to which they will be sent. This chapter's Diversity Management Challenge describes the efforts of several companies to deal with issues of cultural diversity. What experiences, if any, have you had with issues related to cultural diversity?

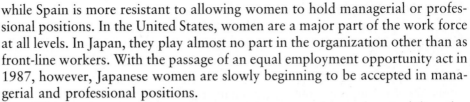

DIVERSITY MANAGEMENT CHALLENGE

How Companies Train Employees in Other Countries

Of all the major U.S. companies that send managers abroad, only about half give them any training in what to expect when they get there.

More surprising still, that represents an *increase* from a decade ago, when only about 10 percent bothered to orient overseas-bound executives and their families.

The orientation, called cross-cultural training, is usually a crash course in the political history, business practices, social customs, and nonverbal gestures in the new country. The training prepares expatriates to handle some of the common problems of culture shock, such as self-pity. Equally important, it helps them recognize and cope with the cultural differences they will encounter.

Suppose that a family has been posted to Kenya. Cross-cultural training might alert them to avoid these mistakes:

- Don't signal "just a minute" by raising an index finger. The finger itself will offend.
- Don't hold business dinners at restaurants. Married women in Kenya associate dining in restaurants with loose morals.

TECHNOLOGICAL FACTORS

Within the triad nations, technology is easily transported and is waning as a source of competitive advantage. Organizations must be prepared to reformulate products and services quickly, improving on existing technologies in order to maintain a competitive advantage. In the future, the Japanese and Europeans are likely to be at the forefront of technological change. In developing countries, multinationals will find different levels of technological development and will have to function within those various levels or bring in their own advanced technology.

Impacts on Management Functions

Managers everywhere must adapt to the effects of these four environmental factors. The five principal functions of management will be carried out differently in different multinational situations. Managers must learn not only how to adapt to different situations in their own country, but also how to transfer good management practices from one culture to another and adapt them to the environmental factors operating in that situation. However, sometimes management practices that are effective in one country are simply not transferable to others. In the following paragraphs, we will explore some of the impacts of environmental forces on management functions in international settings.

> *AT APPLE:* U.S. managers working for Apple in Europe and Japan, as well as European and Japanese managers working for Apple in the United States, will have to adapt to new situations.

- When entertaining at home, don't be surprised if guests arrive an hour early or an hour late, or announce their departure four times.

Cross-cultural training is on the rise among American businesses because corporations that move their executives overseas want to curb the substantial costs of unsuccessful transplants. The orientation can cost a company about $6,000 for three days. Global-minded businesses lose an estimated $2 billion to $2.5 billion a year as a result of failed assignments. Reynolds Metals Company's high rate of expatriate burnout fell "to almost zero," the company claims, after cross-cultural training was initiated in the late 1970s.

Despite massive cost cutting lately, General Motors still spends nearly $500,000 a year on training for about 150 Americans and their families heading abroad. The company believes that the training contributes significantly to its less than 1 percent rate of premature returns—compared with 25 percent at firms that do not properly select and coach expatriates.

In a survey of corporate clients, Berlitz International found that corporations wanted cultural orientation even more than its trademark foreign-language training. Berlitz quickly set up a cross-cultural division.

The best training may occur only after families have arrived overseas. At Procter and Gamble Company, for example, orientation doesn't even begin until expatriates have reached their posts. Deep-rooted, subtle concepts are more effectively tackled this way, trainers believe. However, they hasten to add that training anywhere is more helpful than none at all.

SOURCE: Joann S. Lublin, "Companies Use Cross-Cultural Training to Help Their Employees Adjust Abroad," *Wall Street Journal* (August 4, 1992), pp. B1, B7.

PROBLEM SOLVING

Although the basic stages of problem solving must be followed in any country, the way decisions are made may differ—for example, in the degree of creativity applied. Firms in several European countries, such as Philips in the Netherlands, are much more innovation oriented than most firms in the United States; yet U.S. firms are, on average, more innovative than European firms. The level of creativity in product development is generally higher in U.S. firms than in Japanese firms, but Japanese firms are more creative in innovating new processes (for example, in cutting manufacturing costs).[55] By contrast, on average, Japanese firms engage in participative decision making much more than most American firms, which in turn surpass most European firms in this respect. The ability to use analytical processes in decision making often depends on the availability of computers, and in this respect American and Japanese managers are far ahead of managers in the rest of the world.

Finally, there is the issue of who controls decision making. In most organizations in most countries, strategic decisions are still made at the top of the organization, although there may be varying degrees of participation in relevant decisions at lower levels.

PLANNING

Planning is more acceptable in some societies than in others. For example, the Chinese are much less interested in strategic planning than the Japanese.[56] However, in most of the developed nations planning and strategic planning are acceptable. Strategic planning is the aspect of planning that is of most concern to multinationals. Strategic plans for multinationals focus on such issues as how and to what extent a company should enter into or expand within a country or countries; whether to be a multidomestic or global competitor; and how to proceed through the various stages of growth toward global competition (see Table 3.5).

Donald A. Ball and Wendell H. McCulloch, Jr., suggest that the various reasons for "going global" are either aggressive or defensive:

Aggressive Reasons

1. Seek new markets
2. Yield higher profits/cut costs
3. Obtain additional products for other markets
4. Satisfy top management's desire to expand

Defensive Reasons

1. Protect home markets
2. Protect other markets
3. Guarantee raw-material supply
4. Acquire technology
5. Diversify geographically
6. Obtain bases for new operations[57]

Table 3.5 presents the various stages through which an organization may pass in developing a global strategy. When to take such actions, on what basis to take them, and what countries to enter are among the most important strategic decisions.

The Decision: Domestic, Multidomestic, or Global?

Not all products or services can be readily transferred to other nations; however, in an increasingly homogeneous international environment more and more

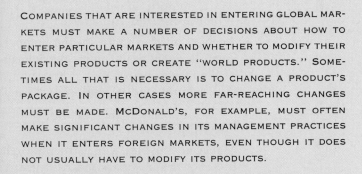

COMPANIES THAT ARE INTERESTED IN ENTERING GLOBAL MAR-
KETS MUST MAKE A NUMBER OF DECISIONS ABOUT HOW TO
ENTER PARTICULAR MARKETS AND WHETHER TO MODIFY THEIR
EXISTING PRODUCTS OR CREATE "WORLD PRODUCTS." SOME-
TIMES ALL THAT IS NECESSARY IS TO CHANGE A PRODUCT'S
PACKAGE. IN OTHER CASES MORE FAR-REACHING CHANGES
MUST BE MADE. MCDONALD'S, FOR EXAMPLE, MUST OFTEN
MAKE SIGNIFICANT CHANGES IN ITS MANAGEMENT PRACTICES
WHEN IT ENTERS FOREIGN MARKETS, EVEN THOUGH IT DOES
NOT USUALLY HAVE TO MODIFY ITS PRODUCTS.

AT APPLE: *Apple has already made the decision to be a global company. It has chosen direct investment as its primary means of entering foreign markets, but it also has some joint ventures.*

products are being accepted in different countries. Organizations typically move to overseas locations for the reasons outlined by Ball and McCulloch. The decision whether to be multidomestic or global depends on a large number of variables, but principally on the size of the firm and the nature of the industry in which it competes. Most authorities believe, for example, that companies in the automobile industry must be able to compete globally.[58] This perception, for example, caused Ford to revise its strategy and build a platform (underbody) for a "world car," a car that could be sold anywhere in the world with a few style changes.[59] In other industries, such as fast food, it may be possible to take the existing domestic product and sell it globally without altering it or creating a world product. This has certainly been the case with McDonald's hamburger chain. Although it may obtain raw materials, and in a sense "manufacture" the product in various countries, McDonald's generally has not had to tailor its product to other countries.[60]

How to Enter a Country?

Most firms enter a country first on a marketing or manufacturing basis. From a marketing perspective, the firm may choose to import or export, to license, to invest directly, or to enter joint ventures. Joint ventures are becoming increasingly important to global competitiveness. Kenichi Ohmae, Howard V. Perlmutter, and David A. Heenan argue that global alliances are vital to competing globally. Global companies must defray immense fixed costs to compete globally; partners can help them in this respect.[61]

Which Countries to Enter?

Analysts must examine all the major factors to determine which countries to enter. In recent years, political risk has been studied especially closely.[62] All four of the major environmental forces must be assessed: economic, political/legal, sociocultural, and technological. (See Table 3.6.)

ORGANIZING

Managers must learn the structural relationships that prevail in various countries. For the most part, macro structures are similar, but the amount of authority delegated varies significantly from country to country, and even from region to region within the same country. As is true in the United States, authority relationships vary considerably from one company to another and even from one department to another within a company. Micro structures such as work group and supervisor/subordinate relationships vary significantly. Some countries do not use team approaches, for example, while others do.

LEADING

Appropriate leadership behaviors for managers vary greatly in different countries. For example, firms in some countries, such as Japan, do not set specific performance objectives for subordinates, while firms in other countries, including the United States, do. Rewards for performance are stressed in very few countries; they receive more emphasis in the United States, for example, than in heavily unionized countries such as France. Manager/subordinate relationships are important in some countries, such as Finland, but much less so in others, such as Germany. Participation is highly developed in Japan, but not in Spain. Concern for attitudes while performing the leadership behaviors just discussed varies greatly around the globe.

CONTROLLING

While many countries have similar information and control systems, exactly what is controlled may vary significantly. Firms in Great Britain, for example, tend to be very concerned about managing assets and liabilities, while firms in the United States are more concerned about controlling income and expenses. In Japan, group performance is controlled, as opposed to individual performance in Canada.

Impacts on Economic Functions

Managing in the multinational or global arena has major implications for each of the organization's economic functions: marketing, finance, operations, human resources, and information. For example, products and advertising must be formulated to match local consumer preferences. Financing arrangements, terms, and the like vary from one country to another. Firms may choose to place operations in different countries in order to take advantage of lower wage rates or specialized skills. Human resources practices also vary widely from country to country. Sophisticated information systems may be available in one country and nonexistent in another.

TABLE 3.6 Political Risk of Investment in Foreign Countries

Sources of Political Risk	Groups Through Which Political Risk Can Be Generated	Political Risk Effects: Types of Influences on International Business Operations
Competing political philosophies (nationalism, socialism, communism)	Government in power and its operating agencies	Confiscation: Loss of assets without compensation
Social unrest and disorder	Nonparliamentary opposition groups (e.g., anarchist or guerrilla movement working from within or outside of country)	Expropriation with compensation: Loss of freedom to operate
Vested interests of local business groups	Nonorganized common interest groups: students, workers, peasants, minorities	Operational restrictions: Market shares, product characteristics, employment policies, locally shared ownership
Recent and impending political independence	Foreign governments or intergovernmental agencies, such as the EEC	Loss of transfer freedom: Financial (dividends, interest payments), goods, personnel, or ownership rights
Armed conflicts and internal rebellions for political power	Foreign governments willing to enter into armed conflict or to support internal rebellion	Breaches or unilateral revisions in contracts and agreements
New international alliances		Discrimination (taxes, compulsory subcontracting)
		Damage to property or personnel from riots, insurrections, revolutions, and wars

SOURCE: Stefan H. Robock and Kenneth Simmonds, *International Business and Multinational Enterprise,* 3rd ed. (Richard D. Irwin, 1983), p. 342, reprinted by permission.

Global Competitiveness

Michael Porter, a strategic consultant, author, and researcher, has thoroughly analyzed the nature of global competition. He suggests that whether or not a firm will be competitive globally depends on the four key factors identified in Figure 3.2: factor conditions; demand conditions; related and supporting industries; and company strategy, structure, and rivalry.

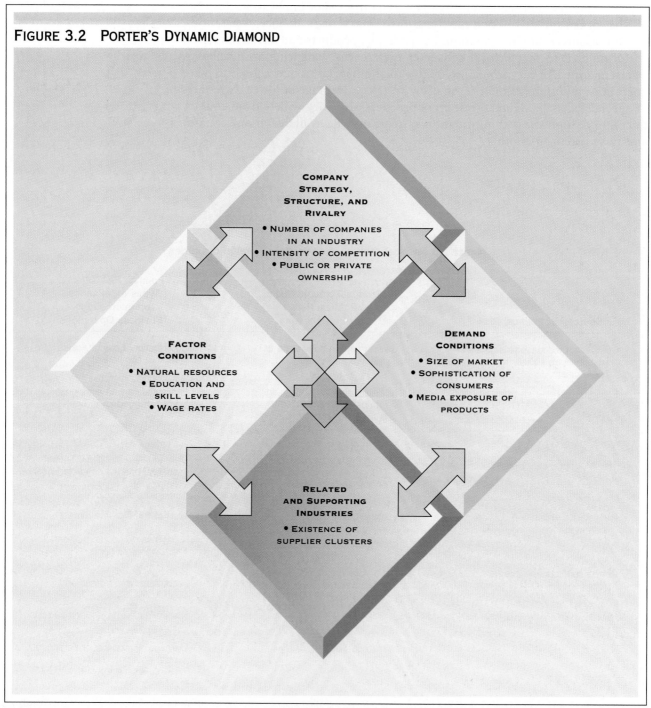

FIGURE 3.2 PORTER'S DYNAMIC DIAMOND

COMPANY STRATEGY, STRUCTURE, AND RIVALRY
• NUMBER OF COMPANIES IN AN INDUSTRY
• INTENSITY OF COMPETITION
• PUBLIC OR PRIVATE OWNERSHIP

FACTOR CONDITIONS
• NATURAL RESOURCES
• EDUCATION AND SKILL LEVELS
• WAGE RATES

DEMAND CONDITIONS
• SIZE OF MARKET
• SOPHISTICATION OF CONSUMERS
• MEDIA EXPOSURE OF PRODUCTS

RELATED AND SUPPORTING INDUSTRIES
• EXISTENCE OF SUPPLIER CLUSTERS

SOURCE: MICHAEL PORTER, THE COMPETITIVE ADVANTAGE OF NATIONS, (NEW YORK: FREE PRESS, 1990). REPRINTED WITH PERMISSION OF THE FREE PRESS, A DIVISION OF MACMILLAN, INC. COPYRIGHT © 1990 BY MICHAEL E. PORTER.

Factor conditions are a nation's abilities to turn basic factors—natural resources, education, and infrastructure—into a specialized advantage. **Demand conditions** are the number and sophistication of domestic customers for the industry's product or service. **Related and supporting industries** (the company a company keeps) include both suppliers and competitors. Finally, **company strategy, structure, and rivalry** (the conditions governing a nation's businesses, especially competition) completes the "dynamic diamond" envisioned by Porter.[63]

To determine its global competitiveness, a firm would compare its domestic industry to the same industry in other countries in terms of the factors in the diamond. The more points of the diamond are positive for the firm's domestic industry, the more likely it is that the firm will have a sustainable competitive advantage. Porter proposes, for example, that Japanese firms are more likely to have a sustainable competitive advantage than U.S. firms because they have intense domestic competition and U.S. firms do not; the Japanese educational system is superior (although it does not promote creativity and innovation); Japanese firms have strong supportive industries; and there is strong domestic demand for many Japanese products. Porter also identifies chance and government as two factors that influence a firm's success. Chance is outside a firm's influence, but government is not. As noted earlier, Japanese firms have closer ties to government than U.S. firms do.

Factor conditions: Conditions that enable a nation to turn basic factors—natural resources, education, and infrastructure—into a specialized advantage.

Demand conditions: The number and sophistication of domestic customers for an industry's product or service.

Related and supporting industries: The infrastructure of firms that support firms in a particular industry.

Company strategy, structure, and rivalry: The conditions governing business in a nation, especially competition.

Applying Management Practices Abroad

The management practices of one country usually have at least some, and often considerable, applicability in other countries. Generally, however, they have not been shown to be universally applicable.[64] Geert Hofstede, a scholar and international consultant, has shown that the values of various societies differ substantially on four basic dimensions: power distance, uncertainty avoidance, individualism and collectivism, and masculinity.[65] These differences help explain why management practices are not universally applicable.

Power distance refers to the degree to which the culture accepts variances in power in organizational relationships, specifically superior/subordinate relationships. Low power-distance countries, such as Austria, Israel, and New Zealand, have small power variances, which means that there is very little difference between the power of managers and subordinates. In high power-distance countries, such as the Philippines, Mexico, and India, there are tremendous differences in authority between individuals at different levels of the organizational hierarchy.

The **uncertainty avoidance** dimension is the degree to which a culture dislikes uncertainty or risk and therefore tries to reduce or avoid it. Weak avoidance countries generally accept and tolerate uncertainty, whereas strong avoidance countries are unwilling or unable to tolerate it. Countries whose cultures are weak in avoidance of uncertainty include Singapore, Denmark, Great Britain, and the United States. Those that are strong in avoidance of uncertainty include Greece, Japan, and France.

The **individualism versus collectivism** dimension indicates the degree to which a culture is either individualistic or group oriented (collectivist). Individualistic countries include the United States, Canada, and the Netherlands. Collectivist countries include Venezuela, Pakistan, and Taiwan.

The fourth dimension, **masculinity,** is concerned with characteristics that most cultures would attribute to men: acquisition of money and possessions,

Power distance: The degree to which the culture accepts any variance in power in organizational relationships, specifically those between superiors and subordinates.

Uncertainty avoidance: The degree to which a culture dislikes uncertainty or risk and therefore tries to reduce or avoid it.

Individualism versus collectivism: The degree to which a culture is oriented toward the individual or the group.

Masculinity: A set of characteristics that many cultures would attribute to men, including acquisition of money and possessions, pursuit of advancement, and assertiveness.

pursuit of advancement, and assertiveness. Among the more "masculine" countries are Japan, Austria, and Italy. Among the more "feminine" countries—those that show a preference for relationships, caring for the weak, modesty, and emphasis on quality of life—are Sweden, Norway, and Switzerland. The United States ranked thirty-sixth of the fifty nations studied, toward the "masculine" end of the scale.

The consequences of these differences are significant. Moreover, there are important differences in these dimensions *within* some countries. Managers can therefore expect to have some difficulty transferring their management styles to foreign countries or to other regions within a country. Conversely, though, as cultures become more similar it is likely that the variances in these dimensions will diminish. However, this will require many years of cultural diffusion and assimilation. Japanese management styles appear to be generally applicable to other cultures. Indeed, as we saw in Chapter 2, many of the characteristics of Japanese management have been transferred to American organizations. Japanese management styles have been transferred to European firms, as well. For example, Jaguar and Ford of Europe have copied many Japanese management systems, especially those related to consensual decision making, long-term employment, and less specialization in careers.[66] Many U.S. management styles and actions have also been adopted globally.

Unique Problems for Multinational Corporations

Organizations doing business overseas face several unique problems. Among these are political instability, terrorism, conflicts with host governments, monetary transactions, and human rights issues. In this section, we will take a brief look at each of these types of problems.

Political Instability

Political instability can be a major problem in developing nations. Governments may rise and fall quickly in these nations because of economic instability and outside political forces. Organizations doing business in countries with high levels of political risk prefer to enter into licensing, joint venture, or export arrangements, rather than make direct investments. However, in many cases the desirability of investment is so high that political risk must be taken. Table 3.6 indicates several sources of political risk and their effects on international business operations.

Terrorism

For personnel of MNCs operating overseas—especially in developing countries but also in Europe—terrorism, kidnapping, and extortion are major problems. In addition, the physical plants of many companies are often targets for terrorists. For example, in the early 1990s the IRA repeatedly bombed areas of London. Because of incidents like these, many firms invest heavily in security fencing and guards. Bodyguards are often employed by managers working in high-risk areas.

Conflicts with a Host Country's Government

The government of a host country often places restrictions on multinational corporations operating within its geographic territory. The restrictions may create conflicts between MNCs and the host country's government. Regardless of the country involved, an organization can take steps to reduce the potential for conflict.

Currency Fluctuations

The value of currencies relative to those of other countries fluctuates tremendously. In the early 1980s, U.S. currency was very strong relative to foreign currencies; U.S. firms, which were actually making money in overseas operations in other countries' currencies, were losing money when they exchanged those currencies for American dollars. By contrast, in the early 1990s, the devaluation of the dollar enabled American firms to reap substantial benefits because they had overseas income that translated into more dollars when exchanges were made. As a result of such fluctuations, it is almost impossible to factor in the appropriate figures for currency exchange in long-term strategic planning.

Human Rights

In developing countries, and even in some "developed" countries, human rights are often neglected. In recent years, for example, South Africa has been a major human rights offender from the standpoint of the United States and many other nations. American companies doing business in South America have been caught in an ethical dilemma. Many employ black South Africans who would lose their jobs if the company were to leave, or perhaps would be treated less well by new owners. Yet by staying, the company appears to support the South African government's racially discriminatory *apartheid* policies. To withdraw would, for all practical purposes, mean that the company could not return to South Africa, a sizable market, and hence would experience a major loss on its capital investments. Nevertheless, American companies have been under pressure to pull out of South Africa. Pressure has been applied by stockholders of investment funds and universities, as well as by the federal government and antiapartheid groups.

This bottling plant in Johannesburg was divested by Coca-Cola in 1986 in response to protests against South Africa's apartheid policies.

Many firms have chosen to withdraw or to reduce their presence in South Africa in order to lessen the negative publicity associated with remaining there.[67]

South Africa is not the only country in which human rights are violated. Significant violations of human rights have occurred in Tibet, in South and Central America, in many Eastern European countries, and in some Pacific Rim nations. Businesses typically have tried not to get involved in such internal issues, but in many cases, as in South Africa, they have been forced to respond in some way. Firms must develop strategies for coping with such complex situations. Some guiding principles have been proposed, but in many cases organizations are on their own in determining an ethical course of action that balances many variables.

Summary

(Before reading this summary, look again at the objectives listed at the beginning of the chapter.)

1. Globalization of business means that the organization creates a single product for markets in a number of different countries, sometimes tailoring the product to particular markets. It also means that firms are entering numerous markets throughout the world.

2. The triad of key markets consists of North America, Europe (the EEC), and Japan. Europe has 340 million people, the United States 240 million, and Japan 120 million.

3. Japanese firms seek to grow faster than their competitors by increasing their market share so that their volume of business will increase at a greater rate. Increased volume means decreased costs, and decreased costs mean more profitability and financial strength.

4. The Four Tigers' principal strengths are their relatively low labor costs and their ability to adapt foreign technology to their own purposes.

5. In 1992, the EEC became a true common market with essentially no barriers to free trade. So far, North American firms have not been frozen out of that market. Many were already operating in Europe, and most of them took action to strengthen their positions. Others entered the market quickly by arranging for mergers, alliances, acquisitions, and joint ventures.

6. The potential for East-West integration offers even greater opportunities than the Europe 1992 initiative. The reunification of Germany is especially significant.

7. It is clear that managers must change the way they work when they operate in different countries, although as business becomes more global, countries will become more similar. Both economic and management functions are modified by differing economic, political/legal, sociocultural, and technological forces.

8. It is often difficult to apply the management techniques used in one country when operating in another country. Research has shown that underlying cultural dimensions in different countries vary significantly.

9. Companies entering foreign markets may export or license, become multidomestic firms, or develop into fully global enterprises.

10. Global organizations have essentially the same organizational structures as others, but functional or client-based structures are uncommon. Typically, global organizations begin with multiproduct structures and eventually have a divisional structure, either by country or by major region.

11. Leadership varies in different countries. Leadership styles that function well in Japan, for example, may not function well in Argentina or the Middle East. Most of

the countries in the triad of key markets are moving toward more teamwork—that is, toward greater sharing of decision-making authority. Even within similar markets, however, leadership styles may need to differ significantly.

12. Control in a global situation depends very much on the ability to develop strategic information systems.

13. Some of the unique problems faced by firms operating in foreign countries include political instability, human rights violations, terrorism, conflicts with the host country's government, and currency fluctuations.

General Questions

1. Describe how management, while becoming more complex, is also becoming more interesting because of the globalization of business.

2. Describe the major changes occurring in the globalization of business since 1991. Indicate their impact on the functions of management.

3. In terms of Porter's dynamic diamond, what must U.S. firms do to become more globally competitive? How has the 1992 initiative helped European multinationals become better competitors?

4. Enumerate the reasons that Japanese firms have been so successful as global competitors.

5. Describe the actions taken by EEC-based firms and non-EEC-based firms to respond to the Europe 1992 initiative.

6. What problems does Japan face that may cause it to become less competitive in global markets?

7. Why are joint ventures and acquisitions so popular for firms operating in foreign markets, especially in Europe?

Questions on the Management Challenge Features

GLOBAL MANAGEMENT CHALLENGE

1. What makes Toshiba successful?

2. What actions is Toshiba taking to prepare for the management challenges of the future?

QUALITY MANAGEMENT CHALLENGE

1. What actions is GM taking to prepare for the entry of Japanese auto firms into European markets after 1992?

2. How do continuous improvement and quality enter into GM's strategy?

DIVERSITY MANAGEMENT CHALLENGE

1. Describe the training programs of the companies mentioned in this feature.

2. Why are such actions necessary?

Apple Computer: Global Competitor par Excellence

Apple is diversifying its product line as a way of beating global competition, primarily because other firms now have the capability to emulate the Macintosh's capabilities. To do so, it has used alliances. In addition, it is moving rapidly into new product markets. It is becoming a consumer electronics company. For example, its Newton, a personal digital assistant, will have advanced capabilities beyond those of the Macintosh. It will be smaller and able to recognize handwriting and store it digitally. It will not be a free-form personal computer like Macintosh but instead will do a few things well. Apple has also moved into the information systems market, realigning its sales force so that it can offer total system solutions. The company is also working on voice recognition systems designed to make computers more user friendly.

Its project for the last part of the twentieth century or the first year or so of the twenty-first century, the Knowledge Navigator, will combine video phone, voice recognition, networking with mainframes, database management, and huge memory and calculating capabilities in a PC the size of a notebook.

Apple is diversifying its product line as a way of beating global competition, primarily because other firms are now able to emulate the Macintosh's capabilities. Shown here is Newton, a personal digital assistant that can recognize handwriting and store it digitally.

DISCUSSION QUESTIONS

1. Describe Apple's overall plan for achieving global success.
2. How has the Europe 1992 initiative played an important part in that plan?
3. Discuss how global alliances with cutting-edge firms lead to the development of products like Newton and the Knowledge Navigator.

To Invest or Not to Invest?

Phillip Knight was the CEO of a $200-million-a-year paper manufacturing subsidiary of a U.S. conglomerate with headquarters in New York City. Knight had recently completed a five-year turnaround of the firm, moving it from losses of more than $30 million in 1985 to profits of $26 million in 1989. He was then asked to lead a task force to study business investment in the paper and related industries in Europe, principally in Eastern Europe.

As part of that endeavor, Knight and two company analysts made a fifteen-day trip to Europe with stopovers in Italy, Hungary, Poland, and Turkey. In each country, the trio toured existing plants and facilities with the aim of determining which of four companies the parent company would purchase. Knight ruled out the Turkish company immediately, on the basis of the age of its plant and equipment and cultural problems related to productivity. The Hungarian-owned plant posed a different set of problems, although the owners and the state were more than willing to negotiate. This, too, he rejected.

Knight and the analysts believed that both the Italian and Polish companies could be turned into highly profitable operations within a few years. Because both were similar in function, design, and age, and because the company would be saddled with excess capacity if both were acquired, it was necessary to choose between them. The financing was similar, so the decision had to be based on other factors. But negotiations with both companies encountered unexpected obstacles. Suddenly the Hungarian plant looked more promising.

Knight and the analysts considered such factors as national infrastructure, existing and potential management styles, employee motivation, cultural differences, and political risk. Much of what they knew was subjective. They had to do a considerable amount of political, social, cultural, and economic forecasting. Other factors had to be considered as well, such as the desire on the part of top corporate management to be positioned in both EEC countries as well as in Eastern Europe.

DISCUSSION QUESTIONS

1. Examine the factors Knight had to consider and discuss how they might manifest themselves in the two countries. Recognizing that facts may not be readily available, try simply to isolate the *types* of differences that might exist.

2. What other factors might Knight need to consider?

3. What are the potential problems associated with *not* investing in each of the three countries?

Note: On January 1, 1993, Phillip Knight signed a contract to purchase the Hungarian firm on behalf of the U.S.-based conglomerate.

Factors to Consider

MANAGE
YOURSELF

The instructor will ask the class to break up into groups to discuss the following situation. You have received a job offer with your current U.S.-based firm for a management position at a subsidiary in Paris. You jump at the opportunity. Your employer wants you to go to Paris to talk with personnel there before you formally accept the job. You speak only a minimal amount of French and would have to become conversationally skilled in the language as well as able to read it. For you that poses no problem. However, because you will be in management, and because you will have to adjust to a new culture, you realize that you need to consider factors other than language. What are those factors, and how might you adapt to each?

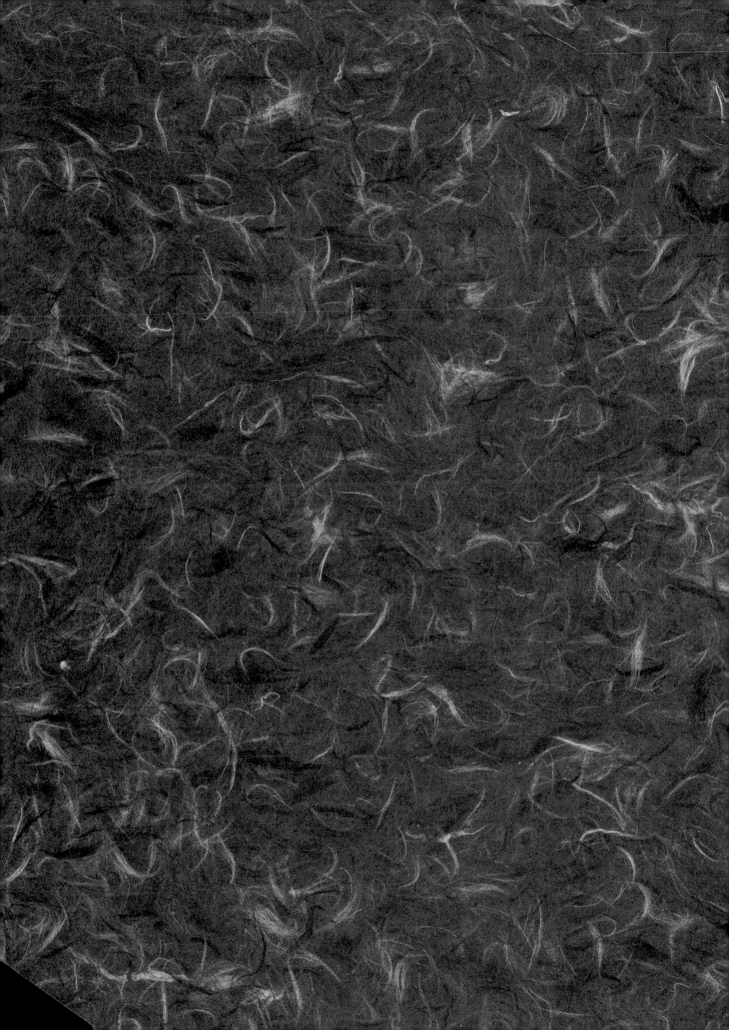

PART TWO

Creative Problem Solving

At the core of management is the creative problem-solving process. Creative problem solving is involved in planning, organizing, leading, and controlling, as well as in the minor functions of management. In recent years, managers have increasingly shared their creative problem-solving role with subordinates in a process known as self-management. This trend will continue into the future. Part of the reason for this sharing is that the organization's external environment is much more complex and dynamic than it was a few years ago. Those closest to the environment—often the firm's operative employees—are believed to be able to make better decisions than those who are farther removed. Regardless of who makes them, all decisions should be made in an ethical and socially responsible manner.

Chapter 4 examines creative problem solving, what it involves, and how to go about it. The chapter reviews the types of problem solving, the conditions under which it occurs, and other aspects, including the pros and cons of group and individual problem solving. Chapter 5 studies the dynamic nature of the environments in which managers operate, both the internal and external environments. The topics of ethics and social responsibility are discussed. Ethical behavior is viewed as a necessity for a socially responsible firm.

"All decision is compromise."

—Herbert Simon,
Nobel laureate
in economics

"The key to success for Sony and to everything in business, science, and technology, for that matter, is never to follow the others."

—Masaru Ibuka,
co-founder,
Sony Corporation

The Manager as a Decision Maker and Creative Problem Solver

Man_ANAGEMENT CHALLENGES DISCUSSED IN THIS CHAPTER:

Accelerating rates of change.

Transition from an industrial to a knowledge-based economy.

Complexity of the managerial environment.

Federal Express: Sorting Out a Mess

In the spring of 1992, Federal Express faced a major problem. As many as 4,300 packages a month were still missing their flights, even though additional employees had been assigned to the "minisort"—the frenzied last effort to get packages on their assigned flights each night. Because the company "absolutely, positively" guarantees overnight delivery, the packages that missed their flights had to be put on commercial flights at a cost of $16.60 per package. The company was spending $875,000 a year just to ship packages that had missed their flights. A team of twelve minisort workers was chosen to solve this problem.

A manager, Melvin Washington, headed the team, but he served primarily as a facilitator. The team met mostly on its own time, usually over breakfast, after spending long hours sorting packages on the night shift. The team interviewed many fellow employees, managers of other divisions, and staff personnel and discussed numerous possible problem areas. They used a four-step creative problem-solving technique that Federal Express had taught them in conjunction with a total quality management program.

After many hours of hard work, the team determined that several factors were contributing to the problem. First, there were too many people working on the minisort, which only added to the confusion. Second, many of those workers didn't know what they were supposed to do. The team recommended that the number of minisort workers be reduced from 150 to 80 and that steps be taken to improve workers' understanding of their tasks. For example, sorting codes had been relatively easy to memorize in the beginning, but as the firm had grown, more and more codes had been added, making memorization impossible. The team recommended that codes be posted so that workers could see them. They also worked with other sorting departments to increase their quality control efforts, thereby reducing the number of packages sent to the nightly minisort. Finally, a "traffic cop" was appointed to direct the tractors carrying sorted packages to the right planes.

The results were impressive. The time spent on minisort dropped from more than an hour a night to 38 minutes. In one year, the number of packages missing their flights fell to about 1,800 a month. The firm saved $938,000 in eighteen months. "It seems so simple," Washington observes, "but it wasn't. The hardest part was selling it to everyone." The team members were pleased with their solutions, even though what they proposed ended up costing each of them about $50 a week in lost wages because their work hours were reduced.

SOURCE: Martha T. Moore, "Sorting Out a Mess," *USA Today* (April 10, 1992), p. 5B.

The manager's primary function is to solve problems creatively, but in the changing managerial environment, this function is also changing. The manager's role as a facilitator of the problem-solving efforts of subordinates and others is expanding. This trend will continue as organizations attempt to become more productive and individuals seek more control over the decisions that affect their jobs and their lives. The creative problem-solving team at Federal Express is typical of such teams in many organizations, in which subordinates solve problems and managers facilitate the process. Managers must not only excel at creative problem solving, but also be able to help others solve their problems creatively. They must lead the way in the development of a learning organization.

Today, managers and other problem solvers are finding it necessary to be more creative in their problem-solving efforts than they were in the past. For example, the members of the Federal Express team sought creative, not just standard, solutions to their problems. They kept trying until they found solutions that would work. Their success resulted from many hours of searching for new ways to solve their problem.

In this chapter we will explore the stages of creative problem solving; the conditions under which decisions are made; structured versus unstructured decisions; individual versus group problem solving; the behavioral aspects of decision making; problem solvers' styles and preferences; intuitive and rational thinking; and deciding when a participative approach is appropriate. These key concerns are shown in Figure 4.1.

When Federal Express established a problem-solving team to help solve the "minisort" problem, the outcome was impressive. As a result of the changes recommended by the team, the firm saved more than $930,000 in eighteen months.

FIGURE 4.1 KEY ISSUES IN THE CREATIVE PROBLEM-SOLVING PROCESS (CPS)

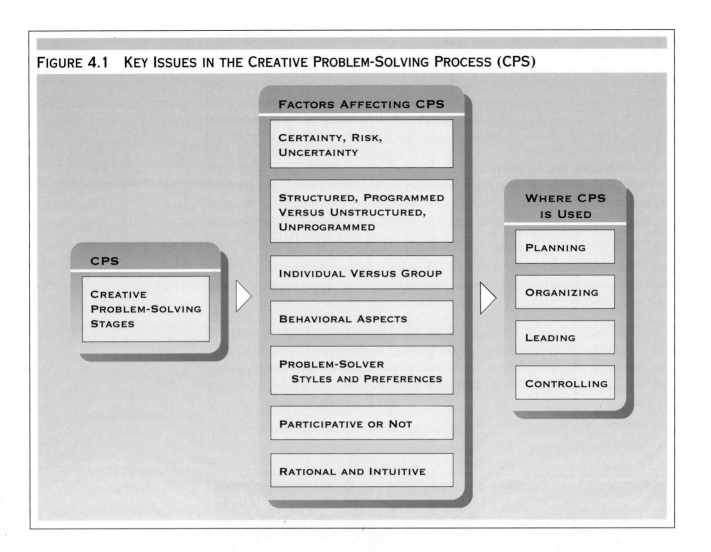

Problem Solving: The Core Management Function

The single action that makes or breaks an organization is creative problem solving. As noted in Chapter 1, creative problem solving is management's core function. It is, for example, fundamental to total quality management.[1] As Figure 4.1 shows, whether they are planning, organizing, leading, or controlling, managers must seek out and solve problems. They must be aware that a problem exists; they must be certain they know what the real problem is; they must make assumptions about the problem situation; they must develop alternative solutions to the problem; they must choose among those alternatives; they must implement their choices; and they must check to see that they have solved the problem.

Situations calling for problem-solving skills can be either problems or opportunities. A problem exists when a level of performance is less than the established objectives. This can result from an organization's internal weakness or from an external threat. An opportunity exists when there is potential for exceeding the established objectives. Opportunities result from an organization's internal strengths or a favorable external environment. Typical problems and opportunities that may arise in each of the management functions are listed in Table 4.1. Note, too, that the weaknesses of one organization may create an opportunity for another: Toshiba Corporation began to dominate the U.S. laptop computer market in the late 1980s because other computer manufacturers did not have a highly competitive product in that market segment. Later Toshiba's market share dropped drastically as the value of the yen rose, enabling competitors to undercut Toshiba's prices.

Not too many years ago, problem solving was defined largely as a rational effort. As scientists and management researchers tried to improve the process, they focused on analysis and quantitative factors. In recent years, however, they have come to realize that a strictly rational approach misses the whole point of problem solving. Creativity is vital to successful problem solving. It is especially important in generating alternatives, but it can be employed in the other stages as well. Thus, the problem-solving process is now widely referred to as **creative problem solving (CPS).**[2] Firms that understand the importance of CPS give their

Creative problem solving (CPS): An eight-stage process for solving problems creatively.

TABLE 4.1 Typical Creative Problem-Solving Decisions Faced by Managers

Planning

What is the mission of the organization?
What are our objectives?
What are the objectives of our work unit?
What are our strengths, weaknesses, opportunities, and threats?
What actions are our competitors taking and how should we react to them?
What are the relevant needs of our customers that we aren't meeting?
What should our strategies be?
How can we carry out our strategies?

Organizing

What specific tasks are needed?
How should we combine jobs into departments?
How much authority should be delegated?
What staffing needs are there within the organization?
How can we best train people to perform their jobs?

Leading

How do we achieve productivity?
How do I influence my subordinates to make them more effective and efficient?
What are the needs of my subordinates?
What are the key group dynamics of my subordinates' work group?
What other factors affect my leadership choices?

Controlling

What are our standards?
What is the level of performance compared to those standards?
How often should we measure level of performance?
What control systems are needed?
If we haven't achieved our objectives, why not?
How can we increase performance in the future?

Problem Solving

How can I improve my problem solving?
Are there new, creative ways to make decisions?

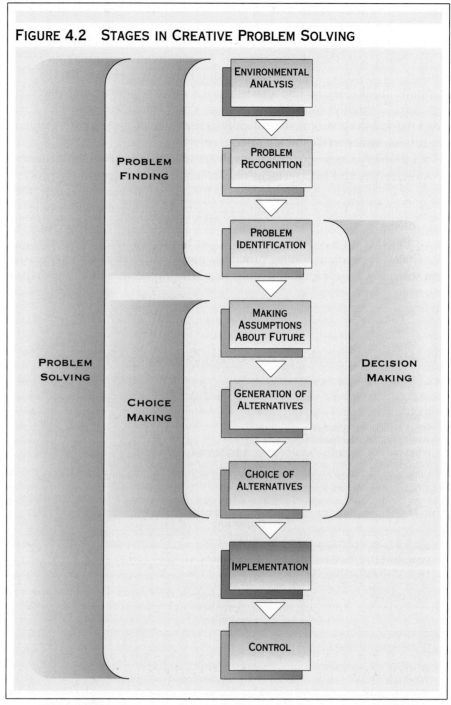

FIGURE 4.2   STAGES IN CREATIVE PROBLEM SOLVING

PROBLEM FINDING

ENVIRONMENTAL ANALYSIS

PROBLEM RECOGNITION

PROBLEM IDENTIFICATION

PROBLEM SOLVING

CHOICE MAKING

MAKING ASSUMPTIONS ABOUT FUTURE

GENERATION OF ALTERNATIVES

CHOICE OF ALTERNATIVES

DECISION MAKING

IMPLEMENTATION

CONTROL

SOURCE: ADAPTED FROM GEORGE T. HUBER, MANAGERIAL DECISION MAKING.
SCOTT, FORESMAN AND COMPANY, 1980, P.8

managers special CPS training. Frito-Lay reports that in just five years CPS training resulted in $500 million in identifiable savings and/or increased revenues.[3] As shown in Figure 4.2, creative problem solving includes eight key stages:

1. Constantly analyzing the environment.
2. Recognizing the problem.
3. Identifying the problem.
4. Making assumptions about the future.
5. Generating alternatives.
6. Choosing among the alternatives.
7. Implementing the chosen alternative.
8. Controlling to ensure that objectives are achieved.

A **decision** is a choice among alternatives. Technically, therefore, it encompasses only items 3 through 6 on the preceding list.[4] In solving a problem, as opposed to making a decision, you would carry out the other steps—that is, in addition to identifying the problem and finding a solution, you would scan the environment in search of problems; once you had reached a decision, you would implement your choice and monitor the results to determine whether your decision was a good one. Although it is important to recognize that there is a difference between solving a problem and making a decision, in this book we will use these terms interchangeably, using the definition of problem solving given earlier.

Decision: A choice among alternatives.

The Creative Problem-Solving Process

The creative problem-solving process consists of the eight stages identified in Figures 4.2 and 4.3. In Figure 4.3, three substages have been added: determining criteria for a successful solution, determining the primary factors in the situation, and determining the outcomes of various alternatives to aid in the choice process. In this section we will examine each of these stages and substages in detail.

Constant Environmental Analysis

Problem solvers must constantly scan their environments—external and internal—for signs of problems. They must also keep environmental factors in mind during the other steps of the decision process. Some firms, such as Anheuser-Busch, have sophisticated environmental-analysis systems to assist their managers. Such systems contain information on customers, competitors, the economy, and other important factors. They are computer based and often use computer simulations. Rapidly changing and increasingly complex environments make this process absolutely critical.

While analysis of the environment tends to be a rational process, interpreting the meaning of the information obtained often requires the use of intuition. As you will see later in the chapter, managers have personal preferences for how they gather and evaluate information, which can greatly affect the kinds of decisions they make.

AT FEDERAL EXPRESS: Federal Express monitors package location at all times. It carefully monitors customer satisfaction, and it constantly scans its environment.

FIGURE 4.3   PROBLEM SOLVING/DECISION MAKING

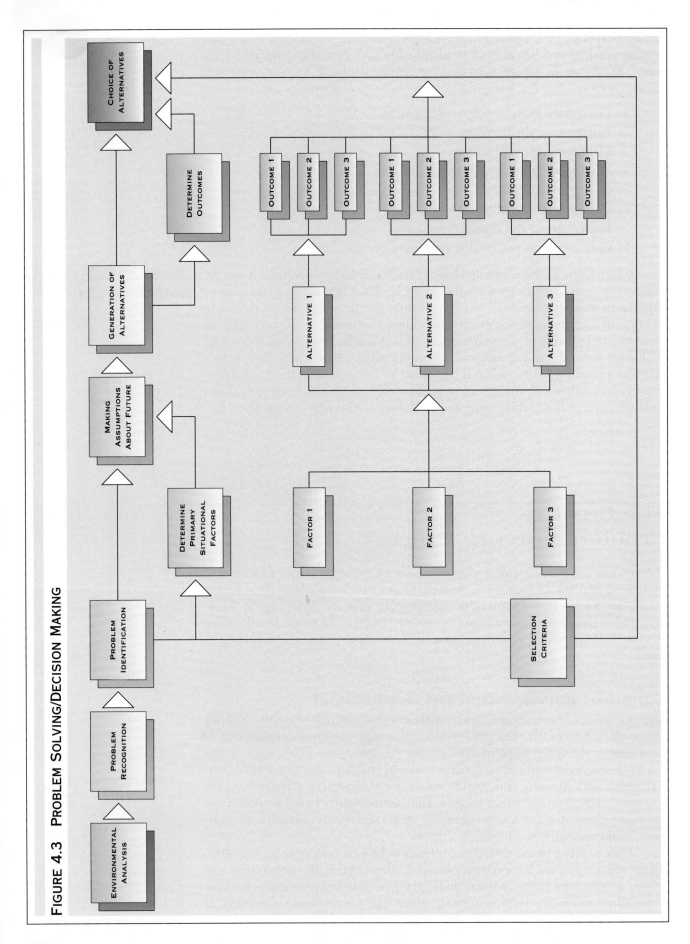

Recognition of Problems or Opportunities

A problem solver is concerned with either problems or opportunities.[5] In the recognition stage, problem solvers depend on formal and informal information systems—and often on their intuition as well—to alert them to a possible problem. In the recognition stage, problems are not precisely defined. Rather, the problem solver often has a vague feeling that something is amiss or that a tremendous opportunity exists.

Research by W. F. Pounds has shown that most managers simply do not ask themselves often enough, "How do we know that we have a problem?" Problem recognition tends to be informal and intuitive. Pounds indicates that managers might be able to find problems in four ways:

1. Comparing a current with a past experience.
2. Comparing a current experience with current objectives or plans.
3. Comparing performance with models of desirable outcomes.
4. Comparing performance with that of other organizations or subunits.[6]

The most preferred of these methods would be the second—because managers should always be striving to achieve current objectives. However, Pounds found that the first method is most often used, whereas the third and fourth are seldom used. Pounds' studies reveal that business managers do not usually compare current performance against current objectives; rather, they rely on other benchmarks, such as last year's performance, as a basis for comparison. He suggests that "consequently they may be defining the wrong problem or may not recognize one when it exists."[7]

Later research by Marjorie A. Lyles and Ian I. Mitroff confirmed that problem recognition is typically informal and intuitive. They collected case histories from top managers in major organizations. Eighty percent of the managers reported that they had recognized the existence of a problem before being told about it by subordinates or supervisors or before it appeared in some type of formal information system, such as a financial statement. When asked how they knew about those problems, they replied, "informal communication and intuition."[8]

Too often, managers fail to recognize problems at all.[9] More attention must be given to problem recognition and identification if CPS is to be successful.[10] For example, at Wang Computers, successive CEOs failed to recognize the problem of not having a personal computer as part of the company's product line, a failure that eventually led to bankruptcy. If they had been more alert, and had recognized this problem, Wang might have prospered.[11]

Finding problems or opportunities depends on constant environmental scanning and analysis. Successful managers are continually alert, always monitoring, always watching. They actively pursue problems and opportunities. For example, in service industries they might perform customer satisfaction surveys to determine potential problems. They might also use customer complaint records, focus groups, and employee input.[12]

Alert managers recognize weak signals as well as strong ones. In *Innovation and Entrepreneurship,* Peter Drucker observes that many managers fail to recognize opportunities and, hence, fail to take advantage of them.[13] Apparently, very few managers actively seek opportunities.[14] However, the entrepreneurial manager—that is, one who acts like an independent businessperson—is constantly aware of opportunities and takes advantage of them. Some companies encourage entrepreneurship among their managers; most do not. However, more top-level managers are beginning to do just that. In high-technology areas, sophisticated techniques, such as market-opportunity analysis, have been developed to help identify opportunities for developing and applying new technologies.[15]

Problem Identification

The creative problem solver seeks to determine the *real* problem.[16] During the recognition stage, the manager knows that a problem exists but is not sure exactly what it is. In the identification stage, the manager attempts to get at the roots, or cause, of the problem. In most organizations there is a complex series of problems; frequently, however, one or a few of them seem to cause most of the others. For example, lower profits may have resulted from lower sales, which may have resulted from reduced advertising as part of a cost-cutting program. Inadequate worker performance may be the result of poor leadership, inadequate training and knowledge, a change in the quality of materials, improper procedures, boredom, excessive workloads, pay scales that seem unfair,

lack of penalties for poor performance, and lack of rewards for excellent performance, to name a few possible causes.[17]

The manager must determine which problem or problems are the causal ones. Errors are highly likely at this stage because of differences in managers' perceptions and self-images.[18] Managers solve problems according to their perceptions of them. If they misperceive a problem, their efforts to solve it will be misdirected. A manager's self-image often affects his or her perceptions. For example, a manager with a weak self-image might perceive a threat in a situation where none exists in reality.

Two management consultants, Charles Kepner and Benjamin Tregoe, suggest that asking a few questions often helps to identify the problem. Table 4.2 lists their questions.

IKEA Furniture, the giant Swedish furniture chain, saw an opportunity based on cost. It has seized that opportunity and become the store that customers hate to love, as this chapter's Global Management Challenge reveals. As you read this feature, think about how the firm could improve its services and yet keep costs low.

Analysts all agree that IKEA has found—or formed—a substantial niche. In an industry split between two types of stores—trendy, big-ticket department stores such as Nordstrom and Bloomingdale's and price cutters such as Kmart, Home Depot, and Staples—IKEA attracts the denizens of both camps.

Its strategy has several components:

- a large selection of stylish, sturdy, functional furniture

- low prices

- a $10-millon advertising budget

- highly visible sites that are easily accessible from major highways

The tradeoff? Service. Customers shouldn't be surprised by long lines, little sales help, and furniture that's frequently out of stock (and that can't be ordered).

Shoppers seem willing to accept these disadvantages, however. Sales for the year ending August 1991 were $284 million, compared with $169 million for the previous fiscal year.

IKEA reports that the 1991 figure represents no profit for that year because it spent so much on expansion. It also invests heavily on advertising when it opens a store, which it has been doing at the rate of one or two a year.

IKEA's greatest strength may be its iconoclasm: Like its typical customers, it is willing to try something new. It designs its own furniture, for example, instead of buying it at the North Carolina furniture markets. This helps keep costs down and assures quality standards. IKEA is so price conscious that it can use components from four different manufacturers to make a single chair. It uses more than 15,000 suppliers in more than 45 countries.

So the next time you want a sofa bed, coffee table, armchair, wall unit, and small table for under $1,500, you might roll up to IKEA in a rented truck. Just be prepared to wait in line. Several lines.

SOURCE: Jeffrey A. Trachtenberg, "IKEA Furniture Chain Pleases with Its Prices, Not with Its Service," *Wall Street Journal*, September 17, 1991, pp. A1, A6.

TABLE 4.2 The Kepner-Tregoe Problem Definition Worksheet

Problem Symptoms

Describe, as specifically as possible, the nature of the symptoms.

Describe where the symptoms occurred.

Describe when the symptoms occurred.

Describe the extent of the symptoms.

Describe any changes that occurred.

Do the changes explain the symptoms?

If not, examine other changes.

SOURCE: Adapted from Charles H. Kepner and Benjamin B. Tregoe, *The Rational Manager.* Copyright © 1965, McGraw-Hill Company. Reprinted with permission of McGraw-Hill, Inc.

CRITERIA FOR A SUCCESSFUL SOLUTION

As part of the problem-identification stage, problem solvers must establish criteria for a successful solution. They must determine and specify, preferably both quantitatively and qualitatively, what constitutes a "good" decision. In other words, before they choose a solution they must decide what it must accomplish. They also need to identify desirable, but not necessarily critical, criteria. In the choice stage, they will compare each alternative to these criteria in order to make their choice. (See Figure 4.3.)

A. M. Castle, one of the nation's largest suppliers of metal products, has based virtually all of its strategic decisions on one critical criterion: Does it improve customer service? As a consequence, the firm has developed numerous innovative programs to assist customers, including designing specific products for them, helping them assess their needs, and showing them how they can improve their profitability. A. M. Castle's market share and profits have increased dramatically as a result.[19]

DETERMINING KEY SITUATIONAL FACTORS

Before making assumptions and generating alternatives, it is necessary to identify the key situational variables. These are the factors that are prominent parts of the problem, that will influence your ability to solve the problem, and that will be included in the solution. In making leadership choices (how to influence others' motivation), for example, the key factors are usually a manager, a subordinate, the work group, the task, the organization's structure and culture, and other critical variables.[20]

Making Assumptions About the Future

After analyzing the environment and recognizing and identifying the problem or problems, decision makers must make assumptions about the conditions of various elements in the decision situation. In planning, for example, it is necessary to make an assumption about whether competitors will continue to compete in the same way. In organizing, an assumption might be required about the probable effectiveness of giving someone more work to do. In leading, it might be necessary to make an assumption about how someone would react to a particular type of managerial style. On the basis of these assumptions, problem solvers generate and evaluate alternatives and make choices.

AT FEDERAL EXPRESS: It took a lot of guts to decide that the solution was fewer, not more, people at Federal Express. The team had to get to the real problem. They were not fooled by the surface problems to which others had reacted.

AT FEDERAL EXPRESS: The team assumed that management would support its recommendations. It assumed that the other employees would, also.

A KEY STEP IN THE PROBLEM-SOLVING PROCESS IS GENERATING A NUMBER OF POSSIBLE SOLUTIONS TO THE PROBLEM. IT IS IMPORTANT TO CONSIDER SEVERAL ALTERNATIVES RATHER THAN SIMPLY ATTEMPTING TO IMPLEMENT THE FIRST SOLUTION THAT COMES TO MIND. A VARIETY OF CREATIVE IN-DIVIDUAL AND GROUP TECHNIQUES CAN BE USED TO GENERATE ALTERNATIVES. SHOWN HERE ARE THREE GROUP TECHNIQUES: VISUALIZATION, THE INNOVATION GAME, AND ROLE PLAYING, A PRAC-TICE EXERCISE DESIGNED TO IMPROVE INNOVATION AND GROUP INTERACTION.

Generating Alternatives

Once a manager has recognized a problem, identified the underlying cause or causes, and made assumptions, he or she must generate alternatives to solve it and related problems. Realistically, unless the problem is extremely simple, alternative solutions need to be generated for a model of the situation—that is, for a simplification of the real situation. The search for alternatives can be time consuming and complicated. Herman Miller, probably the nation's most innovative furniture design company, encourages its employees to generate numerous alternatives, even wild and crazy ones, in the hope of uncovering something special. It has even designed its office areas to provide plenty of informal gathering spaces to encourage the interchange of ideas.[21]

AT FEDERAL EXPRESS: The team finally arrived at three key solutions after many weeks of discussion: Reduce the number of people in minisort, provide workers with a clearer understanding of their jobs, and work to reduce the number of packages sent to minisort by other departments.

Evaluating and Choosing Among the Alternatives

After generating a set of alternative solutions, the manager must choose one or more alternatives that will meet the criteria for a successful solution. Determining the likely outcomes of these various alternatives allows for a better comparison with the criteria and improves the likelihood that the choice eventually made will be an appropriate one. Choosing an alternative seems like a rational process, but in fact it is often intuitive, involving social and political relationships. Even a rational decision-making process may involve many complex variables, sometimes making the situation controversial and almost untenable. For example, the decision to launch a new product involves many complex variables. Top managers may disagree on the right action to take. Many times, therefore, the CEO makes a choice based on intuition.

Risk propensity: Willingness to undertake risk for possible gain.

One factor that greatly affects the choice of alternatives is the problem solver's **risk propensity,** or willingness to undertake risk for possible gain. Some individuals are willing to take high risks; others are not. Research by Danny Miller reveals that top managers with a high risk propensity often make choices that leave their organizations in dire straits.[22] Are you willing to take risks? Take the Manage Yourself test at the end of the chapter to find out.

Implementing the Choice

Implementation: Actions taken to carry out a selected problem solution.

Implementation is the action that is taken to carry out a decision. Once managers have made a choice, they must implement it. Managers should consider the difficulty of implementation when they choose among alternatives. Many choices may seem appropriate, but if they are difficult to implement they are not good ones. Factors such as lack of resources and a negative political situation in the organization could influence a manager to choose one alternative over another. Whatever choice is made, implementation requires mustering resources, gaining support for the project, and then taking the series of actions necessary to carry out that choice.

AT FEDERAL EXPRESS: The team found it necessary to "sell" its solutions to the other employees before the solutions could be implemented.

Control

Once the solution has been implemented, its success must be evaluated. During the control stage, decision makers find out whether they have solved the problem, have a continuing problem, or have a problem they hadn't discovered.

FIGURE 4.4 CONDITIONS UNDER WHICH DECISIONS ARE MADE

DECISION MAKING UNDER CERTAINTY

PROBLEM	ALTERNATIVE 1	100%	OUTCOME 1	ALTERNATIVES ARE KNOWN, CONDITIONS SURROUNDING EACH ARE KNOWN. OUTCOMES ARE CERTAIN.
	ALTERNATIVE 2	100%	OUTCOME 2	
	ALTERNATIVE 3	100%	OUTCOME 3	

DECISION MAKING UNDER RISK

PROBLEM	ALTERNATIVE 1	70%	OUTCOME 1	ALTERNATIVES AND RELATED CONDITIONS ARE NOT KNOWN, BUT PROBABILITIES ARE ESTIMABLE. OUTCOMES ARE UNKNOWN.
	ALTERNATIVE 2	20%	OUTCOME 2	
	ALTERNATIVE 3	10%	OUTCOME 3	
		100%		

DECISION MAKING UNDER UNCERTAINTY

PROBLEM	ALTERNATIVE 1	UNKNOWN	OUTCOME 1	ALTERNATIVES, NUMBER OF ALTERNATIVES, RELATED CONDITIONS, AND PROBABILITIES ARE UNKNOWN.
	ALTERNATIVE 2	UNKNOWN	OUTCOME 2	
	ALTERNATIVE 3	UNKNOWN	OUTCOME 3	
	ALTERNATIVE N	UNKNOWN	OUTCOME N	

Conditions Under Which Decisions Are Made

The conditions under which managers make decisions have a tremendous impact on the choices they make. Figure 4.4 shows three possible degrees of certainty about the outcomes of decisions. The less routine, the less anticipated, and the more complex the problem, the more uncertain the decision-making environment usually is.

Problem Solving Under Conditions of Certainty

Certainty exists in a problem-solving environment when the decision maker can predict the results of implementing each of the alternatives 100 percent of the time. For example, when a city's treasurer leaves the city's money in a bank overnight, he or she knows exactly how much interest that account will gener-

Certainty: A condition in which a decision maker can predict the results of implementing each alternative 100 percent of the time.

ate. The treasurer also knows with certainty the results of other alternatives, such as not leaving the money in the overnight account. Managers seldom know with 100 percent certainty the results their decisions will have. Many times, however, they act as if they did.

Problem Solving Under Conditions of Risk

Risk: A condition in which problem solvers lack complete certainty about the outcomes of their actions.

Under conditions of **risk,** problem solvers do not have complete certainty about the outcomes of their actions, but neither are they completely uncertain about what might result. Rather, they can assign a probability to the outcome of each alternative, if it were to be implemented. Probabilities are usually expressed as a percentage—for example, a 10 percent chance of occurrence.

Risk is probably the most frequent situation confronting a manager. When a manager believes there is a one-in-ten chance that a new pay procedure will fail, but a nine-in-ten chance that it will succeed, he or she is making a decision under conditions of risk.

Problem Solving in Uncertain Environments

Uncertainty: A condition in which managers cannot assign even a probability to the outcomes of the various alternatives that the problem-solving process generates.

Uncertainty exists when managers cannot assign even a probability to the outcomes of the various alternatives generated by the problem-solving process. Managers may not even know about all the alternatives. Uncertainty forces managers to rely on hunches, intuition, creativity, or "gut feel." It is not that the numbers are not analyzed; they usually are. However, the manager must also rely on nonrational decision processes. Unstructured, complex, unanticipated situations almost always occur in uncertain environments. For example, when Sony released Data DiscMan®, it had no idea how successful the product would be. Sony's managers were working in an uncertain environment. They were unsure about the probabilities of various demand levels.

Types of Problems and Decisions

Structured Versus Unstructured Problems

Structured problems: Routinely occurring problems that have readily identifiable attributes—the factors involved and their interrelationships. They have standard, almost automatic solutions, often referred to as programmed decisions.

Structured problems are those that occur routinely and have readily identifiable attributes (the factors involved and their interrelationships). They have standard, almost automatic solutions, often referred to as *programmed decisions*. When a student's grade-point average falls below a certain level, the student is sent an official warning. When a computer signals a malfunction, a maintenance person is dispatched to fix it. Both of these cases illustrate recurring, routine events that trigger a structured response.

Unstructured problems: Nonroutine, complex problems with difficult-to-identify attributes. They normally have not been faced before and lead to unprogrammed decisions.

Unstructured problems are nonroutine, complex problems with difficult-to-identify attributes. They lead to *unprogrammed decisions*. Normally, unstructured problems are being faced for the first time. One of the most complex unstructured problems ever analyzed is how to rid Los Angeles of smog. Biology, earth sciences, chemistry, and physics are all involved. Industry, automobiles, and even drive-through hamburger stands are major issues. A 500,000-equation computer simulation has been developed to help solve the problem, but its developer admits that the model is only as good as the assumptions it is based on—many of which are the result of complex, often intuitive thought processes.[23] Because structured responses cannot be employed, nonroutine problems demand that the manager engage in creative problem solving. Solving these types of problems requires intuition, creativity, and heuristics (rules of thumb).

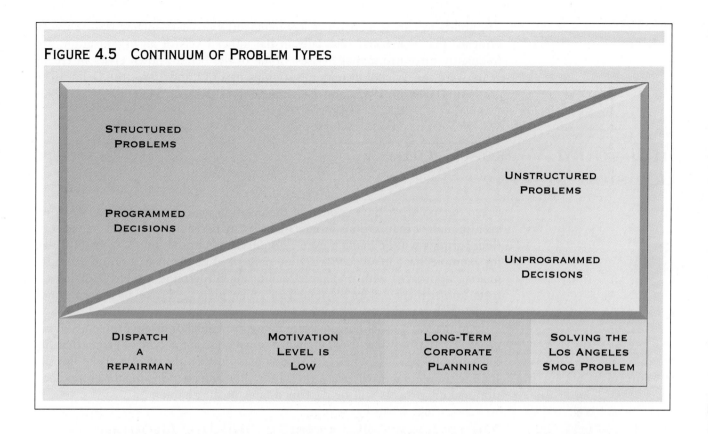

FIGURE 4.5 CONTINUUM OF PROBLEM TYPES

STRUCTURED
PROBLEMS

UNSTRUCTURED
PROBLEMS

PROGRAMMED
DECISIONS

UNPROGRAMMED
DECISIONS

| DISPATCH A REPAIRMAN | MOTIVATION LEVEL IS LOW | LONG-TERM CORPORATE PLANNING | SOLVING THE LOS ANGELES SMOG PROBLEM |

Figure 4.5 shows how problems can be placed on a continuum of structuredness. Some problems are clearly structured, some clearly are not. Most problems, however, vary in the degree to which the factors involved are readily identifiable and can be related to each other. For example, a problem of low employee motivation is more structured than the problem of long-term planning for a company, which tends to be more unstructured.

Anticipated Problems Versus Surprises

Another way of looking at managerial problems is to consider whether they were anticipated or were surprises. Good managers anticipate the problems that may occur as a result of most, if not all, of their actions and decisions. They should anticipate the potential problems of any situation in which they find themselves, regardless of whose decisions brought them to it. Such monitoring prepares them to anticipate a diverse range of problems having to do with productivity, motivation, concerns about pay, concerns about not being promoted, the failure of an advertising campaign, or failing to gain a certain market share.

Some problems are surprises. Equipment breakdowns, power failures, a competitor's strategy, or a sudden loss of market share may take a manager by surprise. The less complex of these surprises may be handled by routine solutions. Good managers recognize that, over time, certain events may occur. These surprises can be anticipated to some extent. Absenteeism, tardiness, and similar personnel problems, for example, may be handled through specific policies and rules. While the exact timing of this type of event is unknown, its occurrence is almost assured.

On the other hand, any manager may face a crisis, the most extreme form of unanticipated problem. It often requires quick problem-solving actions under highly stressful conditions, as well as the expenditure of considerable resources.

AT FEDERAL EXPRESS:
When the Federal Express minisort team began to deal with the problem of missed flights, it faced a complex problem that it had not faced before. There were no ready-made solutions. They had to be invented.

The ability to handle a crisis is a key managerial problem-solving skill. There is evidence that managers, especially in the upper levels of an organization, are frequently forced to manage crises. Some of the better-known crises in recent years were the Tylenol cyanide poisonings in 1982 and 1986, the Delta 1011 crash in Dallas in 1985, and General Motors' loss of $4.5 billion in 1991.

Individual Versus Group Decision Making

Up to this point we have spoken of the decision maker as an individual. However, in many organizations groups make many decisions. If current trends continue, groups will be making even more decisions in the future. General Mills, for example, has already converted 60 percent of its plants to a group decision-making approach, with managers facilitating the groups' problem-solving efforts. Future plans call for all of General Mills' plants to be run by these autonomous work teams.[24]

Managers must choose whether to use individual or group problem-solving processes. If groups are used, managers must choose the type of group that fits the situation best. They must be able to pick not just the type of group but the specific techniques it will use. Criteria for choosing an individual or group decision-making process will be described later in the chapter.

Major Types of Decision-Making Groups

Interacting group: A group whose members meet face-to-face with open interchange.

Group processes can raise the level of creativity in problem solving because more people will generate more ideas and people can build on the ideas of others. There are three major types of problem-solving groups: the interacting group, the nominal group, and the Delphi group. These groups are similar, yet distinct. Most groups are interactive. Nominal and Delphi groups are designed to overcome some of the problems interactive groups encounter, such as domination by a member with a strong personality. Generally speaking, there are many types of interactive group techniques, but only one major nominal group technique and one Delphi technique.

INTERACTING GROUPS

Interacting groups meet face-to-face and have an open interchange of ideas. They are usually unstructured, although many have an agenda and objectives. In creative problem-solving situations, interactive group meetings usually begin with the group leader stating the problem. An open, unstructured discussion follows. Problem recognition and identification, the generation of alternatives, and choice processes are focal points. A simple majority usually controls the eventual result. Three highly productive, interactive, creative group processes are brainstorming, storyboarding, and the lotus blossom technique.

Brainstorming

Brainstorming: A group creative problem-solving process in which no negative feedback is allowed on any suggested alternative until all alternatives have been generated.

Brainstorming is a group creative problem-solving process that focuses on the following procedures:

1. No negative feedback is allowed on any suggested alternative until all alternatives have been generated.
2. Piggybacking on other people's ideas is encouraged.
3. Quantity of ideas, not quality, is the key. Evaluation comes later.
4. Free thinking is pursued. Let the "wild and crazy" ideas flow.

Brainstorming sessions have a leader and a recorder; the recorder writes the ideas, usually on a board, where all participants can see them. Sessions last about thirty minutes. There are usually six to ten participants. Ideas are evaluated after the brainstorming process has been completed. Brainstorming is especially useful for generating alternative solutions. It is often used in advertising but can be used to solve any well-defined problem. Brainstorming is the most widely used group idea generation technique. A version of brainstorming was used by Honda's engineering team to develop the highly fuel efficient engine for the 1992 Honda Civic.[25]

Storyboarding

Storyboarding is a structured but flexible brainstorming process designed to identify major issues and then brainstorm each of them.[26] In this technique participants put together a complete picture ("story") of the problem, one piece at a time. The "story" is then transcribed for all to see, usually on some type of wallboard. Storyboards involve two thinking sessions—one creative, the other critical. Basic brainstorming rules are followed in the creative thinking session. In the critical session, ideas are evaluated and the list of ideas is reduced to a manageable number. Storyboarding is good for analyzing a problem as well as generating alternatives. Implementation may also be an issue for a storyboard. A leader and recorder are used in a group that ranges from six to ten participants. Each thinking session lasts about thirty minutes. Storyboarding is used to solve complex, less well-defined problems—for example, determining what to do about low levels of worker motivation, a problem in almost all industries. PepsiCo, Disney Companies, and Sun-Trust Banks are just a few of the hundreds of major firms that use this technique.

Storyboarding: A structured but flexible brainstorming process that focuses on identifying major issues and then brainstorming each of them.

Lotus Blossom

Lotus blossom is a creativity technique developed by the Japanese that uses a core thought as the basis for the expansion of ideas into an ever-widening series of surrounding windows (or "petals"). The core idea is surrounded by eight windows, each of which becomes the core thought for another set of eight windows. The process begins by using the core thought to trigger other thoughts, which are then placed in the eight surrounding windows. Each of these new core thoughts is then brainstormed for related thoughts. As with the other two techniques, the emphasis in lotus blossom is on generating quantity; the resulting ideas may be evaluated subsequently.[27]

Lotus blossom: A creative problem-solving technique that uses a core thought as the basis for the expansion of ideas into an ever-widening series of surrounding windows (or "petals").

The creative technique known as storyboarding can be used to identify major issues and analyze them. It is best suited to complex problems.

Lotus blossom is especially useful for developing future scenarios. Each scenario, in turn, might become the core of another round of brainstorming until all key issues have been identified. For example, if the core thought is future trends in education, the eight surrounding thoughts might be computer usage, videos, the instructor's role, types of students, textbooks, facilities, funding, and classroom pedagogy. Each of these would then be the subject of a brainstorming session. The eight ideas surrounding computer usage might be presentations, laptops, required features, additional features, integration into classes, data base/image, testing, and ethics.

NOMINAL GROUPS

Nominal group: A decision-making technique in which much of an interacting group's interpersonal exchange is eliminated in order to preclude the influence of a dominant personality.

André L. Delbecq and Andrew H. Van de Ven originated the **nominal group** technique in 1968, partly as an outgrowth of their dissatisfaction with interactive group processes. A nominal group is more structured than an interactive one. It intentionally eliminates much of the interpersonal exchange of the interacting group. The primary purpose of this process is to eliminate dominance of the choice process by one or a few people.[28] It follows four steps:

1. Group members independently write down their ideas about the group's problem.
2. Each group member then presents each of his or her ideas to the other members, one at a time. Each idea is summarized on a chalkboard (or some other device) so that all the members can see it. No ideas are discussed until all of them have been presented and recorded.
3. An open discussion of ideas follows, but only to clarify ideas that some members do not understand. No attack or defense of ideas is allowed.
4. Next, a secret ballot is held. Group members list their top ideas in order of priority. The ballots are tallied, and then a second round of voting usually occurs. The nominal group's eventual decision is a pooled outcome of this vote.

DELPHI GROUPS

Delphi group: A decision-making technique utilizing a series of questionnaires administered by a central individual to experts who never meet face-to-face.

The **Delphi group** technique was developed by Norman Dalkey and his associates at the RAND Corporation. It utilizes a series of questionnaires that are administered by a central individual to experts who never meet face to face. As the respondents reply, their responses are summarized. A new questionnaire based on their responses is then developed and sent to them. This process is repeated until a group consensus has been reached. Normally, only two repetitions of the process are necessary.

The Delphi technique has four principal uses:

1. Generating alternative futures (forecasts)
2. Examining a situation for underlying assumptions or to gain additional information
3. Discovering information that might lead to a consensus among the participants
4. Combining expert opinions from different disciplines

AT FEDERAL EXPRESS: The Federal Express minisort team accomplished objectives that none of its members could have accomplished individually. More ideas, more resources, and more efforts were brought to bear on the problems the company faced.

The Delphi technique has been used by the Singapore tourism industry to predict its environment in the year 2000, by the Taiwan information industry to determine its government's apparent priorities in information technology, and by the Arthur Andersen Consulting Group to examine the degree of uncertainty in the European insurance industry as a result of the 1992 initiative.[29]

Advantages and Disadvantages of Group Decision Making

Groups offer six advantages over individual decision making:

1. The group can provide a superior solution. Groups collectively have more knowledge than an individual. Interactive groups not only combine this knowledge, but create a knowledge base that is greater than the sum of its parts as individuals build on each other's inputs.
2. There is a greater likelihood that the final decision will be accepted when those who will be affected by it or must implement it have a say in making it.
3. Group participation leads to a better understanding of the decision.
4. Groups help ensure a broader search effort.
5. Risk propensity is balanced. Individuals with a high risk propensity often fail. Groups moderate this propensity. Groups also encourage the risk avoider to take more risks.
6. A collective judgment is usually better.[30]

On the other hand, group decision making has certain liabilities. Among them are the following:

1. In interactive groups there is pressure to conform. Sometimes these groups become guilty of what is known as *group think,* in which people begin to think alike and new ideas or ideas that are contrary to the group's ideas are not tolerated.
2. One individual may dominate the interactive group, with the result that his or her opinions, not the group's, are accepted. Nominal groups are designed to overcome this problem. Delphi groups usually do not have this problem because the participants never meet face to face.
3. Groups typically require more time to come to decisions than individuals do.
4. Groups usually make better decisions than the average individual, but they seldom make better ones than the superior individual. In fact, a superior performance by a group may result from the efforts of one superior individual.
5. The total time spent by a group to solve a problem may negate the advantages of the decision it reaches.
6. Groups often make riskier decisions than they should. The propensity of groups to endorse a riskier position is known as the *risky shift.*[31,32]

Behavioral Aspects of the Decision Process

Decision making in an organization seems to follow one of two behavioral models: economic and administrative. The economic model revolves around the rational, systematic perspective discussed earlier; the administrative model focuses on the psychological, interpersonal aspects of decision making. For many years, the economic model was believed to be the way decisions were actually made.

Classical, or economic, model: A model of decision making that describes how decisions are made from a conceptual, analytical viewpoint.

We now know that the administrative approach is the more realistic of the two. People simply do not make decisions in a strictly rational manner. Rather, various psychological and interpersonal factors affect the process.

The Economic Model of Decision Making

The eight-stage model of decision making provided earlier—analyzing the environment, recognizing a problem, identifying the problem, making assumptions, generating alternatives, making a choice, implementing the choice, and controlling—follows the economic perspective. It describes how decisions are made from a conceptual, analytical viewpoint. The assumptions underlying this **classical,** or **economic, model** follow:

1. Objectives are known and agreed upon.
2. The existence of the problem is recognized and its nature has been determined.
3. The consequences of implementing each alternative are certain, or a probability may be assigned to each.
4. Criteria for the best decision are known and agreed upon. Decision makers will seek to maximize their situation by choosing the "best alternative" indicated by these criteria.
5. Managers are rational. They can assign values, order preferences, and make the best possible decision.
6. Managers have complete knowledge of the situation.

The Administrative Model of Decision Making

Research by Nobel laureate Herbert A. Simon, management researcher James G. March, and others reveals that decision making is often dominated by nonrational social and political processes.[33] Moreover, these researchers have found that the assumptions of the economic model do not conform to reality. Their combined efforts have led to the construction of the **administrative model** of decision making. This model is based on a concept identified by Simon and known as *bounded rationality.*[34] It suggests that decision makers are restricted in the decision process and must settle for something less than an ideal solution. The administrative model is based on the following assumptions:

Administrative model: A model of decision making that suggests that decision makers experience "bounded rationality" and must settle for something less than an ideal solution.

1. Objectives of the decision are often vague, conflicting, and not agreed upon.[35]
2. Often managers do not recognize that a problem exists.[36]
3. Managers often do not go through the identification process and do not have a clear idea of the nature of the problem (this has been called "making an error of the third kind").[37]
4. Decision makers and problem solvers solve models of their world. These models never encompass all the variables, facts, or relationships involved in the actual problem. Therefore, if and when rationality is applied, it is applied only to a part of the total problem. Research reveals several biases in the construction of such models: poor modeling of the problem, the nature of evidence itself, and anchoring on a piece of information associating a solution with a past success. For example, managers make decisions based on the most readily available evidence, which may not be the best evidence. They also often select alternatives that involve overcoming financial hurdles even if "better" alternatives exist.[38]

5. Only a few of the possible alternatives are considered because the decision maker's knowledge of the situation is usually limited.

6. Few managers search for the best possible alternative. Most will settle for the first alternative that minimally satisfies minimally considered objectives—what Simon calls "satisficing" criteria.[39] Managers often do not seek the best decision, only the decision that improves, or satisfies, their situation and that time constraints allow them to make.

7. Managers base decisions on rules of thumb and frequently will not even evaluate alternatives according to specified criteria. Past experience is often the basis for making decisions.

8. The decision-making process, especially in the higher levels of an organization, is greatly affected by social relationships. Coalitions of decision makers vie for power. Problem solvers must gain the support of powerful individuals and coalitions to ensure that their solutions are chosen and implemented.

9. Decisions often occur in a series of small steps. There are few "great leaps," especially in large organizations.

In sum, while the economic model is widely accepted as the basis for decision making in organizations, the process is often anything but rational. It is also political, social, and "satisficing." What makes for the "best" decision is not always apparent. All decision makers must be aware of their own limitations and the constraints of the situation. They must also anticipate the political and social realities not only of the decision process, but of the implementation and control processes as well. This often requires participation, or "selling" the decision to others. Managers must recognize these constraints and work within them. They should also seek to reduce the limitations on the decision process.

> *AT FEDERAL EXPRESS: Management had to determine whether it could succeed in solving the minisort problem by itself or would have to involve numerous other members of the organization. Full participation by a strong team was the obvious solution.*

Problem-Solving Styles and Tendencies

Historically, managers have tended to deal with problems in three ways: by avoiding them, solving them, or seeking them out.[40] Some managers avoid problems by refusing to recognize that a problem or opportunity exists. For example, some believe that the Bush administration avoided the problem of the federal budget deficit rather than face it head on. Other managers solve problems as they arise. IBM's PCjr was completely redesigned after it failed to penetrate the market. Although it was ultimately scrapped because it tried to meet the demands of a market that did not exist, IBM personnel met the problem head on.[41]

Problem-seeking managers actively search for potential problems or opportunities, attempting to anticipate them. Royal Dutch Shell, for example, is well known for its strategic-planning simulation systems, which actively monitor all the signals from its internal and external environments. The company has developed the ability to recognize even weak signals of potentially dangerous situations.[42] Its rapidly changing environment caused it to do so.

Problem-Solving Styles

According to researchers James L. McKenney and Peter G. W. Keen, managers develop preferences for one of two basic problem-solving styles: systematic or intuitive.[43] These individual preferences probably stem from, or are at least

Systematic thinkers: People
who approach a problem in
a logical and rational
manner.

partly related to, differing preferences for gathering and processing information.[44] **Systematic thinkers** approach a problem in a logical and rational manner. They divide the problem into smaller parts, analyze each of them, reassemble the problem, and apply various complex analytical techniques to reach a decision. They tend to "look for a method, make a plan for problem solving, be very conscious of their approach, defend the quality of the solution largely in terms of the method, define specific constraints of the problem early in the process, discard alternatives quickly, move through a process of increasing refinement of analysis, conduct an orderly search for additional information, and complete any discrete analysis that they begin."[45] **Intuitive thinkers** are especially good at keeping track of many variables that may defy ordinary analytical techniques. The term *intuitive* implies that positions are reached without rational and analytical thought. The solution or the observation simply "comes to" the individual via insight. Intuitive thinkers tend to "keep the overall problem continuously in mind, redefine the problem frequently as they proceed, rely on verbalized guesses, even hunches, to find a solution, consider a number of alternatives and options simultaneously, jump from one step of analysis to research and back again, and explore and abandon alternatives quickly."[46] Intuitive thinkers can handle extremely complex problems spontaneously. They seem to be able to view the entire situation better than someone who is strictly rational and analyti-

Intuitive thinkers: People
who approach a problem
more intuitively than
logically.

ETHICAL MANAGEMENT CHALLENGE

Levi-Strauss: A Values-Driven Company

Ever since Robert Haas became CEO at Levi-Strauss in 1984, following in the footsteps of his uncle, father, and grandfather, everyone at Levi has agreed on one thing: Henceforth, it's OK to disagree.

The freedom to be honest and express one's point of view is a value that Levi supports throughout the company. In fact, it's an Aspiration.

Levi-Strauss codified its values into an Aspirations Statement in 1987. Many firms pay lip service to the idea of "values," but Haas has gone to unusual lengths to have such commitments actually drive day-to-day business.

In the old days, a real difference existed, Haas says, between the "soft stuff," such as commitment to the work force, and the "hard stuff" that *really* mattered: getting pants out the door. Now they're increasingly intertwined: What the company stands for and what its people believe in actually govern the company's day-to-day operations.

The old boundaries and expectations have broken down, Haas maintains, because of the dislocations of the 1980s: increased competition, corporate restructurings, the globalization of enterprises, and a new generation of workers. As a result, the old distinctions between suppliers and customers—or workers and managers—no longer "go without saying," and a traditional, hierarchical, command-and-control organization is no longer desirable. If a company is to be able to react quickly to market changes, it must put more accountability, authority, and information into the hands of those closest to its products and customers.

In other words, in a more volatile marketplace, a business is propelled by its *ideas,* not by a manager with authority.

Levi's ideas are summarized in a short, two-part Aspirations Statement. The first part describes the kind of company Levi aspires to be. (Sample: "We all want a

cal. Thus, against the advice of his attorney, Ray Kroc purchased a small hamburger chain because he had a feeling that the chain had tremendous potential. He was right—with that decision, McDonald's as we know it was born.

Problem Solving and Ethics

So far, we have discussed creative problem solving primarily from a technical viewpoint. But managers and others applying CPS often have wide latitude in making decisions, and significant pressures are often brought to bear on them to make the "right" decision. The values of the decision makers therefore greatly affect the outcome of the decision-making process. This chapter's Ethical Management Challenge examines how values drive problem solving at Levi-Strauss. Much of the next chapter deals with the ethics of decision making.

How Much Participation, and When?

Managers need some way to determine when members of their work groups, individually or collectively, should participate in managerial decisions and when they should not—and how much they should participate if they do. These are not easy decisions to make. We gave some guidelines in the previous section, when we focused on individual versus group decision making, but the factors involved affect more than just the superiority of the decision.

company that our people are proud of and committed to, where all employees have an opportunity to contribute, learn, grow, and advance based on merit, not politics or background.") The second part describes the type of leadership required to realize these goals. (Sample: "New Behaviors: Leadership that exemplifies directness, openness to influence, commitment to the success of others, willingness to acknowledge our own contributions to problems, personal accountability, teamwork, and trust.")

How do the Aspirations pan out in the real world? Haas says they make it possible to say things that didn't get said easily before—especially by workers. (Sample: "It doesn't seem aspirational to be working with that contractor because, from what we've seen, that company really mistreats its workers." Or "that company has been a supplier for a long time, and it's struggling right now. Wouldn't it be better in terms of the partnership we're trying to create with our suppliers to pay our bills on time?")

Haas says that even he has sometimes had trouble adjusting to the new empowered company. "It has been difficult for me to accept the fact that I don't have to be the smartest guy on the block—reading every memo and signing off on every decision." However, he's reconciled to having his cake and eating it too: "In reality, the more you establish parameters and encourage people to take initiatives within these boundaries, the more you multiply your own effectiveness by the effectiveness of other people."

Haas cites the success of the Dockers line, introduced in 1986 and one of the fastest-growing new products in the history of the apparel industry, as an example of the potential of the new, collaborative style of management. "We didn't have a business plan for Dockers. We had managers who saw the opportunity. They created a product and went out and made commitments for production that were greater than the orders they had in hand because they believed in the product and its momentum. And five years later it's a staple in the American wardrobe."

SOURCE: Robert Howard, "Values Make the Company: An Interview with Robert Haas," *Harvard Business Review* (September–October 1990), pp. 133–144.

Managers must determine when members of their work groups, such as these employees at a Nissan plant in Tennessee, participate in managerial decisions.

Victor Vroom and P. W. Yetton have constructed a model that uses a decision tree to help answer the questions of when and how to allow participation in decision making. They suggest that by following their decision tree, which includes the factors that are critical to each decision point, a manager will be able to make an appropriate decision with respect to whether and how much participation should occur. Five management decision styles are described in Table 4.3—AI, AII, CI, CII, and GII. These are offered as possible solutions to the fourteen possible problem types shown. Those problem types result from decisions related to seven primary decision variables, A, B, D, E, F, G, and H, characterized in Figure 4.6. For several problems, more than one participative style may be appropriate, as is indicated in Table 4.3.

TABLE 4.3 Decision Methods for Group Problems

AI. You solve the problem or make the decision yourself, using information available to you at the time.

AII. You obtain the necessary information from your subordinates, then decide the solution to the problem yourself. You may or may not tell your subordinates what the problem is in getting the information from them. The role played by your subordinates in making the decision is clearly one of providing the necessary information to you, rather than generating or evaluating alternative solutions.

CI. You share the problem with the relevant subordinates individually, getting their ideas and suggestions without bringing them together as a group. Then *you* make the decision, which may or may not reflect your subordinates' influence.

CII. You share the problem with your subordinates as a group, obtaining their collective ideas and suggestions. Then you make the decision, which may or may not reflect your subordinates' influence.

GII. You share the problem with your subordinates as a group. Together you generate and evaluate alternatives and attempt to reach agreement (consensus) on a solution. Your role is much like that of chairman. You do not try to influence the group to adopt "your" solution, and you are willing to accept and implement any solution which has the support of the entire group.

SOURCE: Reprinted from Victor Vroom and P. W. Yetton, *Leadership and Decision Making* by permission of the University of Pittsburgh Press. © 1973 by the University of Pittsburgh Press.

FIGURE 4.6   DECISION-PROCESS FLOW CHART

A. IS THERE A QUALITY REQUIREMENT SUCH THAT ONE SOLUTION IS LIKELY TO BE MORE RATIONAL THAN ANOTHER?

B. DO I HAVE SUFFICIENT INFO TO MAKE A HIGH QUALITY DECISION?

D. IS THE PROBLEM STRUCTURED?

E. IS ACCEPTANCE OF DECISION BY SUBORDINATES CRITICAL TO EFFECTIVE IMPLEMENTATION?

F. IF I WERE TO MAKE THE DECISION BY MYSELF, IS IT REASONABLY CERTAIN THAT IT WOULD BE ACCEPTED BY MY SUBORDINATES?

G. DO SUBORDINATES SHARE THE ORGANIZATIONAL GOALS TO BE ATTAINED IN SOLVING THIS PROBLEM?

H. IS CONFLICT AMONG SUBORDINATES LIKELY IN PREFERRED SOLUTIONS?

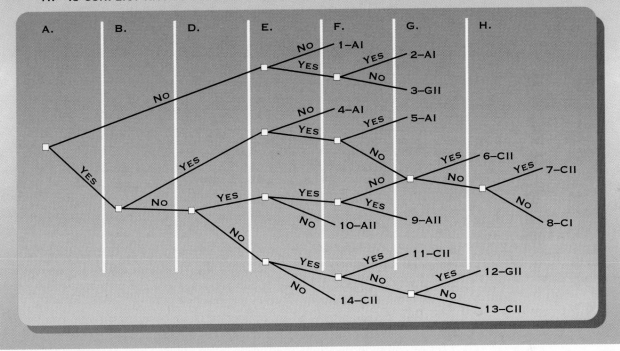

SOURCE: REPRINTED FROM VICTOR VROOM AND P.W. YETTON, <u>LEADERSHIP AND DECISION MAKING</u> BY PERMISSION OF THE UNIVERSITY OF PITTSBURGH PRESS ©1973 BY THE UNIVERSITY OF PITTSBURGH PRESS.

These styles range from authoritarian, in which subordinates have no input in decisions, to highly participative, in which subordinates essentially make the decisions. The A types of decisions are authoritarian; AI decisions are more authoritarian than AII. The C types are consultative, with CII more consultative than CI. In consultative decision making, subordinates serve as advisors to the manager. The G type of decision is group oriented. In it, subordinates make the decision in conjunction with the manager. The Vroom-Yetton model gives managers a practical means of determining which of these styles they should choose.[47]

To use the model, managers state the problem and then answer questions A, B, D, E, F, G, and H sequentially. Each question can be answered with a yes or a no; hence, managers follow one branch or another of the decision tree as a

TABLE 4.4 Problem Types and the Feasible Set of Decision Methods

Problem Type	Acceptable Methods
1	AI, AII, CI, CII, GII
2	AI, AII, CI, CII, GII
3	GII
4	AI, AII, CI, CII, GII*
5	AI, AII, CI, CII, GII*
6	GII
7	CII
8	CI, CII
9	AII, CI, CII, GII*
10	AII, CI, CII, GII*
11	CII, GII*
12	GII
13	CII
14	CII, GII*

*Within the feasible set only when the answer to question G is yes.

SOURCE: Reprinted from Victor Vroom and P. W. Yetton, *Leadership and Decision Making* by permission of the University of Pittsburgh Press, © 1973 by the University of Pittsburgh Press.

consequence of their answer, proceeding to the next relevant question. Managers work through the decision tree until they reach an optimal decision point. Figure 4.6 and Table 4.4 indicate the preferred and the possible decision styles for each decision point.

This decision tree is an important step forward in the management problem-solving process because it identifies the major contingency variables for a set of common decisions used in problem solving and prescribes what to do about them.

Using the Model

Suppose that you are the professor in a typical Introduction to Management course. Your problem is to choose a book for the course. Think through each of the following questions from a professor's perspective.

> *Question A:* Is one book likely to be of better quality than another? The answer is yes. This places the professor at B.
> *Question B:* Does the professor have sufficient information to choose the best book? The answer is yes. If you are following Figure 4.6, this places the professor at E.
> *Question E:* Is the students' acceptance of the book critical to using it successfully? The answer is yes. This places the professor at F.
> *Question F:* If the professor chooses a book, will the students use it? The answer is yes. This yields 5AI as a solution under G. An AI decision means that the manager solves the problem and makes the decision using the available information.

Suppose, on the other hand, that you are the sales manager for a software manufacturer and are faced with developing a new sales promotion technique. Let's go through the questions again.

> *Question A:* Is one technique likely to be better than another? Yes. This places you at B.
> *Question B:* Do you, as sales manager, have sufficient information to make a high-quality decision? The answer could be yes or no. If you suppose it to be no—because you are not familiar enough with the requirements of the territory to decide by yourself—you move to D.
> *Question D:* Is the problem structured? The answer is no. This problem is seldom faced, and there are no obvious or easy answers. You then move to E.
> *Question E:* Is acceptance of the solution by subordinates critical? The answer is yes. You move to F.
> *Question F:* If you make the decision alone, is it likely to be accepted by your subordinates? The answer could be yes or no. Suppose, however, that because of your subordinates' past independence the answer is no. You must move to G.
> *Question G:* Do subordinates share the organizational goals to be attained in solving this problem? The answer is yes. The solution is 12GII, which is a highly participative solution to this problem. You made some assumptions that could just as easily have been different, so your solution could have been different.

The Vroom-Yago Model

In 1988, Vroom and Arthur G. Yago proposed that an additional factor needed to be considered in the basic model itself: whether the subordinate has sufficient information to make the decision. They also suggested that two versions of the model exist: one based on whether time is an overriding factor—that is, the amount of time available to make decisions—and the other on whether the manager is driven to develop subordinates' decision-making skills. Vroom and Yago have computerized the decision-process flowchart for each of these two models. They have also refined, in considerable detail, when and when not to use the various decision methods. They do so for groups and for individuals. Time and space do not permit us to review these here in detail. However, it is important to grasp the underlying concepts of how to make choices using the basic model. You must also be aware that insufficient time may override the choices that would normally be made, as might the desire to improve the decision-making skills of the subordinates.[48]

The Manager as a Creative Problem Solver

The increased complexity of the managerial environment, the personalities and expectations of decision makers and other members of the organization, as well as the other management challenges noted in Chapter 1, are changing the way problems must be solved. Managers are not only moving toward more participatory decision making, but also responding to the need for the decision maker to be more creative and innovative.

Innovation: An outcome of the creative process that has a significant impact on an organization, a society, or an industry; it can be a product, a process, or an approach to marketing or management.

Creativity results in something new that has value. **Innovation** results in something new that has significant value in an organization, industry, or society. Innovation is how firms make money from creativity. There are four types of innovation: product, process, marketing, and management.[49] Many experts believe that innovation in the management process is essential if U.S. firms are to compete successfully in the 1990s and beyond.[50] Many firms are actively seeking new ways of planning, organizing, leading, and controlling in order to become more competitive.[51]

As society changes—technologically, socially, economically, and politically—and as customers and competitors change, the need for creative solutions increases. As firms become more competitive, as product life cycles are shortened, as more and more new entrants supply products and services in all market areas, more creativity and innovation are needed.

3M—Masters of Innovation

Like most U.S. firms, 3M found itself facing stiff competition in the mid-1980s. To improve its situation, the company turned to what it knew best: innovation—not just innovation in product development, where it had always been strong, but also in process innovation, in cutting costs. In 1985, Chairman and CEO Allen (Jake) Jacobson initiated his J-35 program (J for Jake, 35 for 35 percent cuts in labor and manufacturing costs by 1990). It worked.

Spencer Silver, the innovator of 3M's Post-it note pads, displays some items in the Post-it product line.

There are two other reasons for becoming more creative and innovative in problem solving: First, today the computer does the number crunching. Problem solvers no longer have to spend so much time on the mechanics of the process. They need to learn how to use information more creatively to make better decisions. Second, an intuitive individual who also uses rational and analytical approaches has an advantage over someone who is simply rational and analytical.[52] Especially in complex problem-solving situations, the intuitive person generates better decisions than those produced by the single-mindedly rational individual.

Creativity is extremely important at all stages of problem solving and decision making. Although we tend to think of creativity as being principally concerned with generating alternatives, it also takes creativity to analyze the environment, search out problems and separate them from symptoms, choose good

3M's penchant for innovation propelled the firm to a $1.15 billion profit in 1991. How does 3M do it? It has paid close attention to cultivating a culture that incorporates the ingredients of both creativity and innovation. Specifically, 3M's management

1. tolerates creative people and their ideas.
2. believes in the long-term potential of creativity.
3. encourages entrepreneurial spirit and activity.
4. allows people to make mistakes, looking for a good batting average rather than a home run every time at bat.
5. ties salaries and promotions to innovation.
6. allows innovators of good products to run their own businesses.
7. lets nothing, especially politics, get in the way of innovation.
8. keeps divisions small, usually under $200 million in sales.
9. encourages information-sharing meetings among employees.
10. has specific financial hurdles to be overcome by new products.
11. forms new-product teams.
12. uses a 25 percent rule: 25 percent of a division's profits must come from products that didn't exist five years before.
13. uses a 15 percent rule: 15 percent of an employee's time may be spent on anything, as long as it leads to new-product development.
14. uses objectives to elicit process innovations.
15. encourages front-line employees to contribute.
16. develops close relationships with customers.
17. provides seed money to develop a product.
18. formally spreads technology to all divisions.
19. keeps corporate rules to a minimum.
20. allows virtually unfettered creative thinking.

Has this culture fostered innovation? Absolutely. 3M has more than sixty thousand products, including such notables as Scotch tape, Scotchgard®, and Post-it-Notes®.

SOURCE: "Masters of Innovation—How 3M Keeps Its New Products Coming," *Business Week* (April 11, 1989), pp. 58–63; 3M, Annual Report, 1991.

solutions and implement them in an effective way, and develop effective control systems.

Achieving creativity in problem solving depends on the "four P's" of creativity: product, processes, possibilities, and personal creativity.

- *The product:* Creative services, products, or ideas result when the other three "P's" are present.
- *Processes:* Individuals or groups may use some one hundred processes to improve creativity, including three that we discussed earlier: brainstorming, storyboarding, and lotus blossom.[53]
- *Possibilities:* Creativity also requires a certain type of organizational culture. Rewards must be provided, creativity must be encouraged, and open communication and trust should dominate. Innovative companies such as 3M, Hewlett-Packard, and Merck possess such organizational cultures.[54] Milliken even has an "Innovator's Hall of Fame."[55] The 3M Company, widely regarded as the most innovative large company in the United States, is discussed in this chapter's Innovation Management Challenge.
- *Personal creativity:* Creativity can be increased in two ways. First, most people have been socialized against being creative. Overly burdensome rules, regulations and procedures, and attitudes opposed to new ideas dominate most organizations. Therefore, employees need to be *resocialized* to overcome negative attitudes and noncreative habits.[56] Second, several techniques can be used to develop intuition and improve creativity.[57] Research by Weston H. Agor reveals that many top executives emphasize the importance of intuition in successful problem solving. They also emphasize, however, that intuition is only one way of approaching a problem and that rational analysis must come first.[58]

Visitors to Milliken Company's Hall of Fame view the awards the company's employees have received for ideas that have led to innovations in products, processes, marketing, or management. The Hall of Fame helps instill in employees the belief that innovation is important.

Increasing Problem-Solving Effectiveness

The title of this chapter, "The Manager as a Decision Maker and Creative Problem Solver," is intended to convey the importance of using creativity in problem solving. Unfortunately, most educational processes develop only systematic thinking skills. Although some decisions lend themselves readily to systematic thinking, others do not. The more complex, unstructured, and infrequent the decision, the more likely it is that intuition and creativity will be necessary. It has been shown, for example, that CEOs need to employ intuition in strategic planning because some complex problems almost defy rational approaches.[59] (Chapter 23 discusses creativity and innovation in detail.)

In addition to using greater creativity and intuition, however, managers can increase their problem-solving effectiveness by working on the rational stages—for example, improving environmental analysis and problem identification. Problem solving can also be improved by recognizing the conditions under which the problem is to be solved, the structure of the problem, the relevance of group decision making, and the behavioral factors involved. Finally, as group problem solving becomes more common, managers must learn facilitative skills like those discussed in Chapter 15.

Summary

(Before reading this summary, look again at the objectives listed at the beginning of the chapter.)

1. Creative problem solving is the core function of management. Problem solving consists of eight stages: environmental analysis, problem recognition, problem identification, making assumptions, generating alternatives, evaluation and choice, implementation, and control.

2. Decisions are made under three principal conditions. Under conditions of certainty, alternatives, conditions, and probabilities are known and outcomes are certain. Under conditions of risk, alternatives and conditions are known and probabilities can be estimated; outcomes are unknown. Under conditions of uncertainty, alternatives, the number of alternatives, conditions, probabilities, and outcomes are all unknown.

3. Problems can be placed on a continuum from highly structured, or programmed, to highly unstructured, or unprogrammed. Structured problems are routine and simple and lead to routine decisions. Unstructured problems are unique and complex and require one-of-a-kind solutions. Top managers tend to face more unstructured problems, whereas lower-level managers tend to face more structured problems.

4. The advantages of group problem solving include potentially superior solutions, greater acceptance of decisions, improved understanding, a broader information base, balanced risk propensities, and better collective judgment. The disadvantages of group problem solving include conformity, dominance by one person, the amount of time it takes to make a decision, and the phenomenon of risky shift.

5. Theoretical explanations of decision making generally follow the economic model. However, the administrative model, which takes into account the behavioral aspects of decision making, portrays the process more accurately. Individual psychological, social, and political forces often enter into the decision-making process.

6. Managers' problem-solving styles can be classified as either intuitive or systematic.

7. The Vroom-Yetton model provides guidelines about when and how much participation in decision making a manager should allow.

8. Most organizations and many people, especially managers, will have to become more creative in the near future. Being creative requires learning creative problem-solving techniques.

9. Innovation is needed to solve contemporary management challenges and problems. Creativity leads to innovation in the right kind of organizational culture.

General Questions

1. Why is creative problem solving the primary responsibility of managers?

2. Describe a decision you have witnessed or participated in as a member of an organization. Indicate which stages of the creative problem-solving process were followed.

3. Review the major decisions you have made in the last month. Which of these were structured and which were unstructured? Were they made under conditions of risk, uncertainty, or certainty?

4. Think of an organization to which you have belonged. Describe its typical problem-solving process in terms of the classical and administrative models of decision making.

5. Describe the politics of decision making in organizations. Use personal examples.

6. Do you use rules of thumb in decision making? If so, describe them.

7. Review the pros and cons of individual and group problem solving.

8. What is your problem-solving style?

9. Describe each of the three major types of problem-solving groups and how each might be used.

10. Why do managers need more creativity in solving problems, especially in complex situations? Why do they need more innovation?

Questions on the Management Challenge Features

GLOBAL MANAGEMENT CHALLENGE

1. What makes Ikea so successful? Why are people willing to wait in long lines for its products?

2. What could you do to make Ikea more successful without ruining its basic strategy?

ETHICAL MANAGEMENT CHALLENGE

1. Describe the relationship among values, cultural diversity, and ethics at Levi-Strauss.

2. How does Robert Haas influence the company's values?

INNOVATION MANAGEMENT CHALLENGE

1. Describe the characteristics that make 3M an innovative corporation.

2. Describe another company with which you are familiar in terms of these characteristics.

Federal Express: Sorting Out a Mess

The twelve workers on the minisort team were mostly part-time, hourly workers. They were challenged to get rid of a headache, the problem of packages missing flights. Working on minisort was often viewed as a sort of punishment. Many workers believed that if their manager was mad at them, he or she would send them to minisort. Other departments viewed the minisort as a solution to their own quality problems—"If we can't sort it right, minisort will always be there to take care of it." Therefore, they didn't do the best job they could to correct their own quality problems.

The members of the minisort team were willing to take a cut in pay, partly because the company listened to them. "For management to listen to me, that's important," commented team member Dawn Mason. Also important was realizing that the four-step CPS quality improvement technique they had been taught really worked. Team member Jeff Acree declared, "When people started smiling down there [in the minisort room], that's when quality started meaning something to me."

DISCUSSION QUESTIONS

1. In what ways can this situation serve as a model for other firms to follow?
2. What role did CPS play in this group's decision-making efforts?
3. How is quality related to CPS?
4. What kind of manager does group decision making require?

Excellence in Teaching

The five faculty members carefully examined the documents in front of them. As members of Roger Warren's tenure committee, they had to determine whether he met the school's standards for tenure. Determining whether a colleague should be awarded tenure is a serious responsibility, not one to be taken lightly. Tenure would normally be granted if the committee determined that the candidate had successfully achieved the levels of performance embodied in the school's tenure criteria. The approval of the dean, the university president, and the board of trustees was also necessary but was usually given if the committee recommended it. These were the five criteria for tenure:

1. Teaching excellence
2. Publications
3. University service
4. Community service
5. Professional development

There was no question that Warren had satisfied the last four criteria. He had written a sufficient number of articles in the proper journals, and one book. He was on a major committee at the university. He provided community seminars and had attended several professional meetings. But teaching excellence was another matter.

The business school, of which Warren was a member, had recently defined teaching excellence as "consistently at or above the mean score for all school faculty on student evaluations." Unfortunately for Warren, the faculty average for the business school was 7.5 on a 9.0-point scale for virtually all of the twenty-six items rated. This was the highest in the university, and it made it difficult for Warren, or for anyone else, to achieve the desired standard on this criterion. Obviously, unless everyone achieved the same score, someone had to be below average for an average to exist.

Warren taught three undergraduate courses. His student evaluation averages were 6.2 for two of his classes and 7.4 for the third. The lower averages were in difficult, required accounting classes. The higher-average course was an elective accounting course for accounting majors. During the last two years for which they were available, the averages for the two introductory courses had changed substantially each fall. Warren's ratings seemed to go up slightly in the spring.

The committee had discussed the definition of the standard of teaching excellence, the impact of the change in the content of those courses on evaluations, the impact of the nature of the courses on evaluations, and the previously determined policy of using supplementary materials in addition to the student evaluations to show teaching effectiveness. However, after an hour of calm but emphatic discussion, the issue still was not settled. The committee largely favored granting tenure, but felt that it needed additional information, perhaps provided by the candidate, to substantiate its position. The committee chair agreed to obtain such information before the following Friday, when the committee would meet again.

The committee members returned to their offices to be alone with their thoughts. One member, Carlos Alvarez, a tenured full professor of finance, was particularly bothered by what had just taken place. He felt that Warren had made a solid contribution to the school. Yet Warren's approach to teaching was very boring, in what many consider to be a very boring discipline. While Alvarez had heard many students complain about the way Warren taught, he knew there were other students who liked him. Alvarez thought back to one committee member's argument that because the total faculty averages were so close to Warren's it could not be said that Warren was not at the average. He also recalled a recent presentation on student evaluations and performance appraisals by Kate Stanford of the management department. She indicated that student evaluations often measure their perceptions of teaching style—especially liveliness, humor, and wit—as well as enthusiasm and rigor. Those evaluations do not measure actual performance in terms of changing student behaviors. Ultimately, performance would be determined by what students did after they left the college. Alvarez wondered how that could be measured. Finally, his thoughts turned to Warren's other contributions, which he felt were certainly worthwhile. He was not sure Warren was an excellent teacher, but some decision had to be made.

DISCUSSION QUESTIONS

1. Show how Alvarez and the other committee members are attempting to use the rational approach to decision making. What role should intuition play here?

2. Indicate how the committee may be applying an administrative approach to decision making.

3. Describe the tenure problem in terms of the stages of the problem-solving process.

4. What would your decision be if you were Alvarez and the additional data provided by Warren substantiated what you already knew? Why?

5. Put yourself in Warren's place. What kinds of comments could you make to indicate that you should be considered an excellent teacher?

The Farley Test for Risk Takers

Answer yes or no to each item as it applies to you (check your answer).

1. I would take the risk of starting my own business rather than work for someone else.   YES NO

2. I would never take a job that requires lots of traveling.   YES NO

3. If I were to gamble, I would never make small bets.   YES NO

4. I like to improve on ideas.   YES NO

5. I would never give up my job before I was certain I had another one.   YES NO

6. I would never invest in highly speculative stocks.   YES NO

7. To broaden my horizons, I would be willing to take risks.   YES NO

8. Thinking of investing in stocks does not excite me.   YES NO

9. I would consider working strictly on a commission basis.   YES NO

10. Knowing that any particular new business can fail, I would avoid investing in one even if the potential payoff was high.   YES NO

11. I would like to experience as much of life as possible.   YES NO

12. I don't feel that I have a strong need for excitement.   YES NO

13. I am high in energy.   YES NO

14. I can easily generate lots of money-making ideas.   YES NO

15. I would never bet more money than I had at the time.   YES NO

16. I enjoy proposing new ideas or concepts when the reactions of others—my boss, for example—are unknown or uncertain.   YES NO

17. I have never written checks without having sufficient funds in the bank to cover them.   YES NO

18. Business deals that are relatively certain are the only ones I would engage in.   YES NO

19. A less secure job with a large income is more to my liking than a more secure job with an average income.   YES NO

20. I am not very independent-minded.   YES NO

If you answered yes to questions 1, 3, 4, 7, 9, 11, 13, 14, 16, 19, give yourself 1 point for each answer. If you answered no to items 2, 5, 6, 8, 10, 12, 15, 17, 18, 20, give yourself 1 point for each answer. If your total score is 17 or 18 or higher, this might suggest financial-risk-taking potential and type-T tendencies. However, this questionnaire is not definitive. Scores may vary from person to person and from time to time.

source: Test used with permission of Frank Farley.

"Change is the order of the day, either choose it or chase it. Adapt or die."

—Theodore Levitt,
Editor,
Harvard Business Review

"We have become far too careless, self-indulgent, and cruel in the pain we inflict on these creatures (laboratory test animals) for the most frivolous, unworthy purposes."

—Meg Greenfield,
Editorialist,
Newsweek

Ethics, Social Responsibility, and the Managerial Environment

CHAPTER OBJECTIVES

When you have read this chapter you should be able to:

1. Describe the major components of a firm's internal, competitive, and general environments.
2. Define the concept of a stakeholder.
3. Describe the organization in terms of the complexity of the environment in which it operates and show how that environment is changing.
4. Identify the four principal components of social responsibility for a business.
5. Describe the major issues of social responsibility.
6. List and discuss the possible philosophies of response.
7. Define and discuss business ethics.
8. Identify the factors to be considered in making decisions in an ethical manner.

Mᴀɴᴀɢᴇᴍᴇɴᴛ CHALLENGES DISCUSSED IN THIS CHAPTER:

 Accelerating rates of change.

 Increasing demands by constituents.

 Unstable market and economic conditions.

 Complexity of the managerial environment.

CHAPTER OUTLINE

The Exxon Valdez Oil Spill

Not every management decision is a sound one. Far from it. One of the worst series of management decisions imaginable accompanied the worst oil disaster to occur in North American waters. In March 1989, 240,000 barrels (10 million gallons) of oil leaked from the tanker *Exxon Valdez* into Alaska's Prince William Sound. The spill covered more than 900 square miles, taking a catastrophic toll on animals—sea otters, birds, whales, walruses, herring, and salmon. (More salmon spawn in the waters around the town of Valdez than anywhere else on earth.) Several of the fisheries were protected, but many fishermen saw their livelihoods and way of life destroyed by the spill. One consequence of the spill was that at least four lawsuits were filed against Exxon and Alyeska, the pipeline company formed by the seven firms that share the oil field.

On Friday, March 24, 1989, at 12:04 A.M., Third Mate Gregory T. Cousins, who was illegally in command of the tanker while Captain Joseph Hazelwood reportedly was asleep in his cabin, ordered the *Exxon Valdez* to execute a strange series of right turns in an attempt to dodge floating ice. The ship ran aground and the oil spilled. At 12:30 A.M., Alyeska Pipeline dispatched an observation team to the scene, but it did not have containment equipment. Meanwhile, Alyeska was attempting to put together a containment operation, but its people were in total disarray. By 3:23 A.M., the Coast Guard was aboard the *Exxon Valdez* and found that it had already lost 138,000 barrels of oil. According to the government-approved containment plan, Alyeska should have arrived with the containment equipment by then, but it had not. When the containment barge was finally loaded, it was loaded with the wrong equipment. It had to be reloaded, further delaying the response to the catastrophe.

Ironically, the Alyeska containment operation was understaffed. There should have been fifteen crew members on hand, but there were only eleven. Until 1981, Alyeska had had a containment team standing by around the clock, but state officials had allowed the company to cut this expense from its budget.

At 6:00 A.M., Exxon officials flew over the spill for the first time.

At 9:00 A.M., the Coast Guard tested Captain Hazelwood for alcohol consumption. It had been reported that he had had alcohol on his breath at the time of the spill. Apparently, the *Exxon Valdez*'s captain had a history of alcoholism but had been retained nonetheless. At 2:30 P.M., the Alyeska crew finally arrived with the containment equipment. At 11:00 A.M., the *Exxon Valdez* was finally encircled by an Alyeska containment boom, but the oil spill already covered 12 miles. The spill was out of control.

It is estimated that it may take as many as ten years for Prince William Sound to recover fully. Early in the pipeline project, Alyeska officials had promised that state-of-the-art spill-prevention equipment would be used by any tanker passing through the sound. A few of the ships in the Exxon fleet employed such equipment, but the *Exxon Valdez* did not.

Lee Raymond, president of Exxon Corporation, made excuses for the company, claiming that it was in a situation beyond its control. He blamed "ultimately the Coast Guard" for prohibiting it from moving as quickly as it could. But the evidence clearly indicated otherwise.

SOURCES: Kim Wells and Charles McCoy, "Out of Control: How Unpreparedness Turned the Alaska Spill into an Ecological Debacle," *Wall Street Journal* (April 3, 1989), pp. A1, A4; Ken Wells and Marilyn Chase, "Paradise Lost: Heartbreaking Scenes of Beauty Disfigured Follow Alaska Oil Spill," *Wall Street Journal* (March 31, 1989), pp. A1, A4; "Smothering the Water," *Newsweek* (April 10, 1989), pp. 54–57; "Environmental Politics," *Newsweek* (April 17, 1989), pp. 18–19; and Meg Greenfield, "In Defense of the Animals," *Newsweek* (April 17, 1989), p. 78.

The Exxon Valdez oil spill represents the worst in management decision making, negligence, and unpreparedness. The results were devastating. Unfortunately, such decisions are not isolated incidents. Thousands of similar events occur every day in all types of businesses and governments. Most of these decisions lack the impact of the one just described, but collectively they could create problems even more devastating than those witnessed at Valdez.[1] Concern about such events led to the Earth Summit, which was held in Rio de Janeiro in June 1992. On that occasion, most of the world's national leaders convened to continue an ongoing dialogue on how to protect the natural environment. There was much to discuss.[2]

The 1980s and early 1990s, for example, brought widespread recognition that the "greenhouse effect" is a fact. The earth is getting warmer, as is evidenced by record temperatures, drought, and forest fires caused by dryness.[3] Many believe that this warming will alter weather patterns and cause the flooding of low-lying lands.[4] The earth's ozone layer is being depleted, and the incidence of skin cancer and other cancers is bound to increase as a consequence.[5] Acid rain is deforesting much of the United States, Canada, and Europe and destroying fish in lakes and rivers.[6] The world's oceans are dying as a consequence of industrial pollution dumped into rivers or directly into the oceans. Developers are using up the nation's shorelines, which prevent the natural cleansing of the sea and fish breeding.[7]

That is not all. Overfishing is threatening numerous species.[8] The world's water supply is becoming polluted.[9] Plastic waste is choking oceans and rivers, killing millions of animals, destroying beaches, and disintegrating into lethal chemicals.[10] About 40,000 square miles of tropical forests are destroyed every year, mostly by burning, which adds to the carbon dioxide already in the atmosphere and, more important, decreases the amount taken out of the atmosphere by trees.[11] The former Soviet Union, now the Commonwealth of Independent States, is a toxic wasteland, the product of a policy of encouraging economic growth at any price.[12]

These examples relate to just one of numerous points at which the concerns of society and the organization overlap: the natural environment. A business

At the Rio de Janeiro Earth Summit, most of the world's leaders convened to discuss a wide range of global environmental problems.

must also be concerned about customers, competitors, and suppliers changes in technology, and threats to its domain from government, special-interest groups, and the larger society. Additional issues may arise in such areas as equal employment opportunity; consumerism; energy use; labor relations; corporate philanthropy; and employee health, education, and welfare. These issues, which all have to do with social responsibility, are identified in more detail in Table 5.1. To varying degrees, these issues and others may also arise in other countries.

TABLE 5.1 Categories of Social Responsibility

Product Line

Internal standards for products
Average product life
Product performance
Packaging impacts

Marketing Practices

Sales practices
Credit practices against legal standards
Accuracy of advertising claims—specific government complaints
Consumer complaints about marketing practices
Provision of adequate consumer information
Fair pricing
Packaging

Employee Education and Training

Policy on leaves of absence
Dollars spent on training
Special training program results (systematic evaluations)
Plans for future programs
Career training and counseling
Failure rates
Personnel understanding

Corporate Philanthropy

Contribution performance
Selection criteria for contributions
Procedures for performance tracking of recipient institutions or groups
Programs to permit and encourage employee involvement in social projects
Extent of employee involvement in philanthropy decision making

Environmental Control

Measurable pollution
Violations of government (federal, state, local) standards
Cost estimates to correct current deficiencies
Extent to which various plants exceed current legal standards (e.g., particulate matter discharged)
Resources devoted to pollution control
Competitive company performance (e.g., capital expenditures)
Effort to monitor new standards as proposed
Programs to keep employees alert to spills and other pollution-related accidents
Procedures for evaluating environmental impact of new packaging of products

External Relations

Community development
Support of minority and community enterprises
Investment practices
Government relations
Specific input to public policy through research and analysis
Participation and development of business/government programs

Ethics is also of major importance to business management. In the 1980s, accepted standards of business ethics were violated by numerous firms. The roll call of firms and/or individuals involved in unethical practices reads like a Who's Who of American business: Anheuser-Busch for improper payments and kickbacks;[13] Northrop Corporation for substantial improper charges made to the U.S. Air Force on contracts;[14] Raytheon for its kickback scheme;[15] E. F. Hutton for a check-floating scheme aimed at defrauding banks of interest payments;[16]

External Relations

Political contributions
Disclosure of information (communications)
Extent of public disclosure of performance by activity category
Measure of employee understanding of programs (relations/communications with stockholders, fund managers, major customers, etc.)
International relations
Comparisons of policy and performance with those of other countries and against local standards

Employee Relations, Benefits, and Satisfaction with Work

Comparison of wage and other policies with competition and/or national averages
Comparison of operating units on promotions, terminations, hires
Performance review system and procedures for communication with employees whose performance is below average
Promotion policy—equitable and understood
Transfer policy
Termination policy (e.g., how early is notice given?)
General work environment and conditions
Fringe benefits as percentage of salary at various salary levels
Evaluation of employee benefit preferences (questions can be posed as choices)
Evaluation of employee understanding of current fringe benefits
Union/industrial relations
Confidentiality and security of personnel data

Employment and Advancement of Minorities and Women

Current hiring policies in relation to requirements of affirmative action programs
Company versus local, industry, and national performance
Percent minorities and women employed in major facilities in relation to minority labor force available locally
Number of minorities and women in positions of high responsibility
Promotion performance of minorities and women
Specific hiring and job upgrading goals established for minorities and women
Programs to ease integration of minorities and women into company operations (e.g., awareness efforts)
Specialized career counseling for minorities and women
Special recruiting efforts for minorities and women
Opportunities for the physically handicapped

Employee Safety and Health

Work environment measures
Safety performance
Services provided (and cost of programs and human resources) for safety equipment, instruction, special safety programs
Comparisons of health and safety performance with competition and industry in general
Developments/innovations in health and safety
Employee health measures (e.g., sick days, examinations)
Food facilities
AIDS policies

SOURCE: Adapted from *Business and Society Review*, Summer 1973, Copyright © 1973, Business and Society Review. Reprinted with permission.

GE and General Dynamics for overcharging the U.S. government on defense contracts;[17] much of the construction industry in New York City for its apparent ties to organized crime and its use of extortion and bribery in securing contracts;[18] the U.S. Postal Service and other major U.S. government agencies for bribery and kickback schemes involving the purchase of computers;[19] Shearson and Lehman Brothers for laundering gambling funds;[20] and Ivan Boesky for insider trading on Wall Street—to just name a few. The 1990s brought the Bank of Credit and Commerce International (BCCI) scandal and the Dow-Corning silicon-gel implant impropriety, among others. BCCI, a global bank, was involved in numerous illegal activities in many countries, including the United States and much of Europe.[21] Dow-Corning apparently continued to sell breast implants even though it was aware that they could cause serious problems.[22]

As we have noted in earlier chapters, the environment of business is rapidly becoming more complex, with a large number of groups demanding action to satisfy their needs. Moreover, that environment is subject to much more change than it was a few years ago. Theodore Levitt, editor of the *Harvard Business Review,* suggests that "Change is the order of the day, either choose it or chase it. 'Adapt or die' is the tag mark that covers almost every business and organization."[23] Only businesses that adapt to the many new problems and opportunities they face will be successful.

Cooperation between nations will be necessary to solve many of the problems confronting businesses. The 1992 Earth Summit was aimed at furthering global solutions to environmental problems, but it was just the beginning of a long and difficult process.[24]

This chapter explores the nature of the business environment, examining the internal and external environments. The two main external environments are the competitive environment and the general environment. The general environment has four main components: economic/competitive, political/legal, social/cultural, and technological. The chapter then discusses the social responsibilities of business, defining the issues and noting the range of responses possible in light of society's needs. Issues of ethics, a vital topic in today's society, are also discussed. Subsequent chapters will focus on other aspects of these environments.

The Nature of the Business Environment

External environment: All elements outside the boundaries of the organization that have the potential to affect the organization.

Competitive environment: All the elements that affect the organization's competitive situation.

As discussed in Chapter 2, most organizations are open systems. They interface in various ways with other elements of society. A closed system, on the other hand, does not interact with other elements. Managers who act as if their organizations are closed systems, except for interactions with customers and suppliers, will suffer severely and cause severe suffering, as the case of the *Exxon Valdez* oil spill revealed.

Figure 5.1 shows that the organization has two principal environments: an external environment and an internal environment. The organization's **external environment** consists of all elements outside the boundaries of the organization that have the potential to affect the organization.[25] The external environment has two principal parts: the competitive environment and the general environment.[26] The **competitive environment** comprises all the elements that affect the organization's competitive situation. Its major components include customers,

FIGURE 5.1 THE ORGANIZATIONAL ENVIRONMENT—DOMESTIC AND INTERNATIONAL

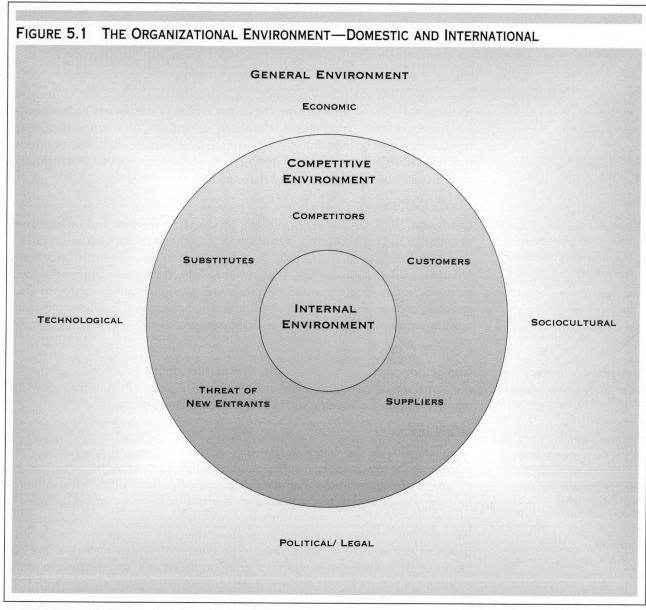

SOURCES: ADAPTED FROM L. J. BOURGEOIS, "STRATEGY AND THE ENVIRONMENT: A CONCEPTUAL INTEGRATION," ACADEMY OF MANAGEMENT REVIEW (JANUARY 1980), PP. 25–39. MICHAEL PORTER'S COMPETITIVE FACTORS ARE SUBSTITUTED FOR THOSE IN BOURGEOIS'S TASK ENVIRONMENT: AND REPRINTED WITH THE PERMISSION OF THE FREE PRESS, A DIVISION OF MACMILLAN, INC. FROM COMPETITIVE STRATEGY: TECHNIQUES FOR ANALYZING INDUSTRIES AND COMPETITORS BY MICHAEL E. PORTER. COPYRIGHT © 1980 BY THE FREE PRESS.

competitors, suppliers, substitutes, and new entrants.[27] The **general environment** includes elements—such as society, technology, the economy, and legal/political factors—that have less contact with the organization but occasionally influence it or are significantly influenced by it. The increasing use of personal computers and the changing value of the dollar are just two such factors out of thousands. The **internal environment** includes all the elements contained within the organization's boundaries—corporate culture, current employees, stockholders, management, leadership style, and organizational structure, for example.

An organization may operate both within and across national boundaries, making its competitive environment and its general environment global as well as local. If the organization is a global firm, it may operate within local environ-

General environment: Elements—such as society, technology, the economy, and political/legal factors— that occasionally influence the organization or can be significantly influenced by it.

Internal environment: All the elements that are contained within the organization's boundaries.

ments in many different countries. For example, the strategy Mazda uses to sell cars in England may differ significantly from its strategy in Germany because it is adapting to different local markets.

The Competitive Environment

The competitive environment consists of elements that have a direct, ongoing relationship with, or an effect on, the organization as it transacts its business. It includes customers, competitors, suppliers, substitutes, and potential new entrants.[28] It is part of the economic situation that firms face, but it is so important that it is viewed as a separate environment. In this section we will look briefly at each element of the competitive environment.

CUSTOMERS

Customers: Individuals and organizations that consume an organization's products or services.

Customers consume the organization's products or services and include both individuals and organizations. Thanks to management critics such as Thomas J. Peters and Robert H. Waterman, Jr., organizations have begun to pay more attention to their customers.[29] The customer is becoming a focal point of competitive efforts. Physicians and hospitals are providing better service to their patients; colleges are more concerned about their students' welfare; and many airlines are taking better care of their passengers.

COMPETITORS

Competitors: Organizations that market similar products or services to the same set of customers.

Competitors are other organizations that market similar products or services to the same set of customers. For example, in the personal-computer industry, Apple Computer competes with IBM, Compaq, and others.

SUPPLIERS

Suppliers: Organizations and individuals that provide the materials an organization uses to produce outputs (including raw materials, subassemblies, labor, computer programs, energy, and others).

Suppliers provide the materials that the organization uses to produce outputs. These may be raw materials, subassemblies, labor, computer programs, energy, or a host of others. In the manufacturing process, relationships with suppliers have become critical in recent years as organizations have attempted to improve product quality. One of the major suppliers is labor. Every organization has to have the right people with the right skills at the right time to perform the jobs necessary to achieve organizational objectives. Numerous factors affect the labor supply—unions, demographics, competitors, wages, and the growth of the economy.

Competitors are organizations that market similar products or services to the same set of customers. In the personal-computer industry, Apple Computer and IBM are direct competitors.

SUBSTITUTES

Substitutes include products or services that have a similar function to those produced by the organization. Automobile rentals are substitutes for air travel, for example. Firms are concerned about substitutes because they can reduce sales of their products.

NEW ENTRANTS

A firm must be concerned about the threat of **new entrants** into its industry because these affect its ability to compete successfully. For example, when Lexus and Infiniti entered the luxury-car market, they took market share from Mercedes, BMW, and Jaguar.

The General Environment

The **general environment** is not a direct competitive factor, although technology greatly affects a firm's ability to compete. Organizations must constantly scan this environment for threats and opportunities. Companies that operate in more than one country are confronted with many, usually different, general environments. Even within the same country there may be different environments as a result of history, racial composition, ethnic origin, or geographic isolation. Thus, in Spain the Basques and Catalonians create different environments from those found in other regions; in the United States, there are Hispanic populations in California and Asian Americans in cities like New York and San Francisco. The dimensions of the general environment include technology, society and culture, the economy, and law and politics.

TECHNOLOGY

Technology includes existing technology as well as technological advances. One of the principal means by which organizations compete is by differentiating their products or services from those of other firms. This means somehow improving current products or creating new ones. One of the main ways in which this occurs is through new technology. Radial tires replaced standard-ply tires. The digital watch replaced the pin-lever watch. Photocopying machines replaced carbon copies. The laser is replacing the high-speed drill in dentistry. According to two studies, once a major technological advance has been introduced in an industry, the formerly dominant firms find it almost impossible to recover.[30] Thus, it behooves an organization not only to stay current with technology, but to be on the technological edge. Also important is the firm's ability to bring a product to market very rapidly, using its own technology or that of others.[31] Japanese firms have been quick to see the possible applications of technologies developed by firms in other countries.

SOCIETY AND CULTURE

The **societal/cultural** element of the general environment includes the social, cultural, and demographic characteristics of the society or societies in which the organization operates. If, for example, a society becomes more concerned about environmental pollution, organizations will be forced to respond to new values in that area. These will often be expressed in laws. Such events occurred in the early 1990s as part of a new wave of social activism. Americans, along with citizens of many other nations, began a new war on pollution.[32] In Europe, environmental laws associated with the 1992 initiative placed tighter controls on firms operating in those countries. The firms responded with "greening" programs—for example, increased emphasis on recycling. In Germany, firms can expect to take back and recycle every product they make, not just cans and bottles but perhaps eventually whole automobiles.[33]

Other values that might affect business include the perceived importance of education, equal employment opportunity, and health care. Demographic trends that will influence a firm's actions include an aging population, the baby boomers, a substantial growth in the Hispanic population, and population shifts from north to south in both the United States and Europe. U.S. firms, for example, will be hiring more older workers in an effort to capitalize on their skills. They will also be learning how to manage a more diverse work force as the composition of the labor force changes.[34]

Sometimes businesspeople try to improve their environment. One example is Martin Koldyke, the subject of this chapter's Quality Management Challenge. Why did Koldyke do what he did? How did he do it? What did he accomplish?

THE ECONOMY

Economy: The general economic condition of a country (or countries) or region (or regions) in which an organization operates, represented by inflation rates, interest rates, currency values, and numerous other factors.

The **economy** includes the general economic condition of the country (or countries) and region (or regions) in which the organization operates. Inflation rates, interest rates, currency values, consumer purchasing power, employment levels, budget deficits, trade deficits, and numerous other factors must be analyzed for their impact on the organization. In the early 1990s, for example, the continuing decline of the value of the dollar made many U.S. firms more competitive globally, resulting in additional exports, which helped offset record imports. Similarly, as interest rates rise, the housing market invariably declines, affecting not only builders and resellers, but also building supply companies, real estate agents, and the overall economy. The converse is not always true, however. In 1991 and 1992, lowering interest rates did little to stimulate the housing market.

One of the major changes occurring in the U.S. and other domestic economies is their increasing interdependence. What happens in the United States often greatly affects the economies of many other countries, and vice versa. International cooperation to solve joint economic problems has thus become imperative.[35]

THE LEGAL/POLITICAL ELEMENT

Legal/political element: Laws and regulations at the local, state, national, and international levels, as well as individuals and organizations that attempt to influence the legal environment, such as lobbyists and protest groups.

The **legal/political** element includes laws and regulations at the local, state, national, and international levels, as well as individuals and organizations that attempt to influence the legal environment, such as lobbyists and protest groups. The national and state governments have issued numerous laws related to the treatment of unionized workers, occupational safety and health, equal employment opportunity, protection of the natural environment, consumer protection, and honesty in business practices.

Numerous groups attempt to influence government at various levels in their efforts to regulate business and other organizations. The National Association for the Advancement of Colored People (NAACP), for example, lobbies heavily for civil rights legislation and the enforcement of equal opportunity laws. The Sierra Club pressures for increased protection for the natural environment. Organizations such as MADD (Mothers Against Drunk Drivers) have initiated legislation directed at companies that sell alcoholic beverages. At the same time, business organizations themselves may attempt to influence laws that affect their political situations through lobbyists and political action committees. Most of this activity means more responsibilities for businesses.[36]

The general environment and all of its components are subject to constant change. These changes are occurring throughout the world, as this chapter's Management Challenge indicates. In what ways has Oxford's general environment changed?

Martin Koldyke

It may not be news to you that all schools are not created equal, but the extent of the disparities certainly surprised Chicago venture capitalist Martin Koldyke, chairman of Frontenac Company.

Koldyke's life-style in the Chicago suburb of Kenilworth has always been consonant with his position: good schools for his four children; two country clubs; three vacation homes; and plenty of equally affluent friends.

Then came the Academy Awards.

Koldyke got his start as a suburban "do-gooder"—his phrase—while watching the awards one night in the mid-1980s. "Why can't there be such awards for teachers?" he asked his wife. (He taught school briefly in his twenties.)

Responding to his own question, he founded the Golden Apple Foundation. Initially the foundation distributed one-semester college scholarships, $2,500, and a computer to extraordinary Chicago-area teachers. Eventually the mission expanded to helping to pay for college for students who were willing to commit themselves to teaching in the Chicago public schools. More than seventy-nine would-be teachers have been sponsored so far.

Then Koldyke found out what the inner-city schools were really like. He visited Crane High School, one of the city's roughest. "I realized that the people who were sending their kids to Crane were powerless," he says. "It was clearly a place that didn't work." Lockers without locks, graffiti everywhere, teachers who appeared shell shocked. "My good neighbors in Kenilworth wouldn't put up with that for more than five minutes."

Most disturbing were the standards. Few graduates had adequate verbal or math skills. Koldyke began pounding the table at meetings of educators—his frustration with incompetence at all levels in the schools has become well known, as has his disenchantment with "governmental indifference to the bottom third of society." He is no supporter of simple volunteerism as a solution to the problems of the poor. Still, his own volunteer efforts have received increasing attention—and support.

Koldyke continually addresses business groups and exhorts them to get involved with the schools. At one of his talks, a futures trader pledged $250,000 to Golden Apple—on the spot.

"I'm better off working with the establishment," Koldyke says. "I want my friends who really do have power to trust me, to think that the things we're doing are all right."

In addition to Golden Apple, where his wife now works full time and his daughter sits on the board, Koldyke has started Teachers for Chicago, which enables people to become teachers in mid-career, without having to take time off to go to school. He also works at getting city agencies, neighborhood groups, and schools—potential foes—to work together.

Koldyke no longer thinks of retiring to Florida. He talks of leaving the suburbs and moving to the city. He plans to devote his retirement to working with the poor. He's still haunted by a 1990 encounter with a fourth-grader at one of the city's most troubled public-housing complexes. She approached him as he was about to leave and said, "You'll be back, won't you?"

"I told her I'd be back."

SOURCE: Alex Kotlowitz, "A Businessman Turns His Skills to Aiding Inner-City Schools," *Wall Street Journal* (February 25, 1992), pp. A1, A13.

Cracks in the Ivory Tower

Oxford University, famed for its Gothic architecture, is the beneficiary of eight centuries of benevolent patronage from a host of notables, including Henry VIII, Cardinal Wolsey, and Cecil Rhodes. In the 1980s the university faced major budget cuts by Prime Minister Margaret Thatcher. Thatcher was determined to make England's universities more self-sufficient and businesslike in their operations. The government was cutting Oxford's $185 million operating budget by 11 percent over a four-year period. Government funds, which at one time paid two-thirds of Oxford's operating budget, paid only 45 percent in 1988. A hundred academic posts were vacant in 1988 because of lack of funds. An estimated two thousand positions were vacant in various British universities.

In 1988, Oxford University launched a $400 million American-style fund-raising campaign to improve its library, laboratories, and staff. Among the targets of the endowment campaign were Oxford's eight thousand American graduates as well as American corporations and charitable foundations.

One of the major consequences of the budget cuts was a change in the time-honored tradition of the tutorial, the one-on-one instruction of undergraduates. In the future, tutorials are expected to include at least two students. Another area in which Oxford has felt the pinch is in its library. Many of its books are held together by ribbons. It will take ten years to computerize the card catalog. Purchases of books and periodicals have been cut back. The library's hours have been shortened, and funding for research has all but dried up.

Faced with such dire straits, Oxford's staid management decided to take up the ungentlemanly art of fund raising. In 1988, it launched a $400 million American-style fund-raising campaign to improve Oxford's library, laboratories, and staff. It hired Henry Drucker, an American political scientist, as its first fund-raising director, recognizing that magnificent buildings and art collections don't pay professors' salaries. A major target of the endowment campaign was Oxford's eight thousand American graduates and American corporations and charitable foundations. Oxford hoped to raise 30 percent of the total needed from these sources. It even set up a three-person fund-raising office in Japan because its reputation there is legendary.

SOURCE: Peter Schmeisser and Wendy Anderson, "Cracks in the Ivory Tower," *U.S. News and World Report* (December 5, 1988), pp. 65–66.

External Environments: Stability and Complexity

British researchers Tom Burns and G. M. Stalker first called attention to two types of external environments: stable and unstable. **Stable** environments change very little; **unstable** environments change constantly. Burns and Stalker also identified two types of responses to these external environments: mechanistic and organic.[37] A **mechanistic organization** focuses on hierarchical relationships and tends to be rigid in the worst sense of the word *bureaucratic*. An **organic organization** is characterized by openness, responsiveness, and a lack of hierarchy.[38]

Burns and Stalker's study indicated that firms operating in stable environments tend to use mechanistic designs, whereas firms operating in unstable environments tend to use organic designs. The necessity for employing these particular designs in those types of situations has been demonstrated over and over again. As mechanistic firms encounter changing environments, they find the transition difficult, if not impossible. Organizations that are able to make the transition to an organic structure will survive; those that are not able to do so will fail. Contrast, for example, Eastern Airlines and American Airlines. American Airlines was able to adapt to changes in its environment and even to change its environment. It became more organic: Authority was decentralized and innovation encouraged. Programs such as Frequent Flyer (an industry first) were introduced. Eastern Airlines remained mechanistic and bureaucratic and eventually declared bankruptcy; it was unable to adapt to its environment.[39] Burns and Stalker were quick to recognize that no organization is purely mechanistic or organic. Nor do they indicate that either design is superior. Rather, each design best fits a particular environmental situation. However, as organizations face more unstable environments, the organic structure is the preferred design.

Robert B. Duncan, an academician, later conceptualized the external environment as involving not just stability but also complexity.[40] Simple environments are characterized by few products, few competitors, few locations, and simple technology. Complex environments usually have a large number of products, a large number of geographic locations, a change in the nature of consumers, and, often, complex technology. Figure 5.2 suggests the possible combinations of these factors—environmental complexity and environmental change—indicating the resulting degree of uncertainty in each situation. Environments with high levels of instability and complexity exist now and are forecasted for most organizations in the future. As a result, CEOs need broader-based experience and must spend more time analyzing the external environment than ever before.[41]

Stable environments: Environments that change very little.

Unstable environments: Environments that change constantly.

Mechanistic organization: An organization that focuses on hierarchical relationships and tends to be bureaucratic.

Organic organization: An organization characterized by openness, responsiveness, and a lack of hierarchy.

AT EXXON: *Exxon's competitive environment is stable, but also complex. Exxon appears to be treating it as if it were simple. Its response to an environmental catastrophe was slow, as it might have been in response to a competitor's action.*

The Organization/Environment Interface

Organizations can interface with their environments in either of two ways: They can adapt to them or change them. Organizations adapt to their environments primarily through the strategic planning process, in which they assess the situation, establish major objectives, and establish strategic plans accordingly. To be adaptive, an organization needs a structure that is flexible and responsive—in other words, organic. Normally, this means allowing for decision making by the managers directly involved in a situation, as opposed to having all major deci-

FIGURE 5.2   FRAMEWORK FOR ASSESSING ENVIRONMENTAL UNCERTAINTY

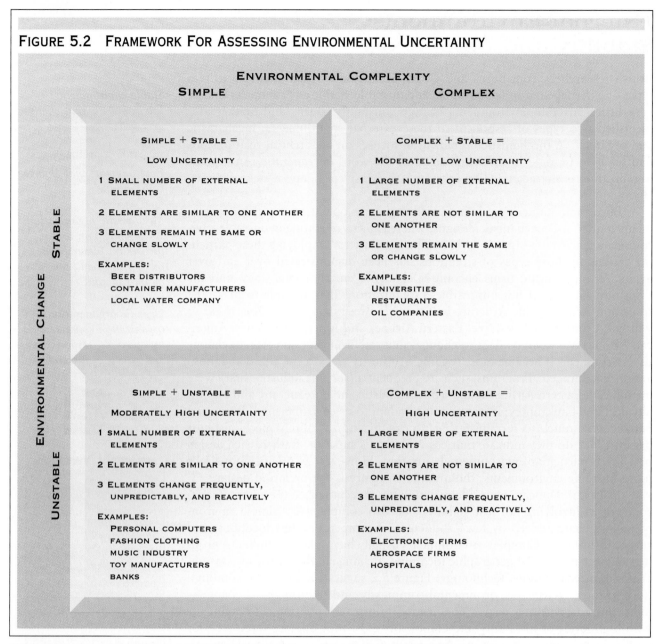

ENVIRONMENTAL COMPLEXITY

SIMPLE — COMPLEX

ENVIRONMENTAL CHANGE

STABLE

SIMPLE + STABLE =

LOW UNCERTAINTY

1 SMALL NUMBER OF EXTERNAL ELEMENTS

2 ELEMENTS ARE SIMILAR TO ONE ANOTHER

3 ELEMENTS REMAIN THE SAME OR CHANGE SLOWLY

EXAMPLES:
BEER DISTRIBUTORS
CONTAINER MANUFACTURERS
LOCAL WATER COMPANY

COMPLEX + STABLE =

MODERATELY LOW UNCERTAINTY

1 LARGE NUMBER OF EXTERNAL ELEMENTS

2 ELEMENTS ARE NOT SIMILAR TO ONE ANOTHER

3 ELEMENTS REMAIN THE SAME OR CHANGE SLOWLY

EXAMPLES:
UNIVERSITIES
RESTAURANTS
OIL COMPANIES

UNSTABLE

SIMPLE + UNSTABLE =

MODERATELY HIGH UNCERTAINTY

1 SMALL NUMBER OF EXTERNAL ELEMENTS

2 ELEMENTS ARE SIMILAR TO ONE ANOTHER

3 ELEMENTS CHANGE FREQUENTLY, UNPREDICTABLY, AND REACTIVELY

EXAMPLES:
PERSONAL COMPUTERS
FASHION CLOTHING
MUSIC INDUSTRY
TOY MANUFACTURERS
BANKS

COMPLEX + UNSTABLE =

HIGH UNCERTAINTY

1 LARGE NUMBER OF EXTERNAL ELEMENTS

2 ELEMENTS ARE NOT SIMILAR TO ONE ANOTHER

3 ELEMENTS CHANGE FREQUENTLY, UNPREDICTABLY, AND REACTIVELY

EXAMPLES:
ELECTRONICS FIRMS
AEROSPACE FIRMS
HOSPITALS

SOURCE: ADAPTED AND REPRINTED FROM "CHARACTERISTICS OF PERCEIVED ENVIRONMENTS AND PERCEIVED ENVIRONMENTAL UNCERTAINTY" BY ROBERT B. DUNCAN, PUBLISHED IN ADMINISTRATIVE SCIENCE QUARTERLY 17(3) (1972): 313-327 BY PERMISSION OF THE ADMINISTRATIVE SCIENCE QUARTERLY COPYRIGHT © 1972 BY CORNELL UNIVERSITY. THE ABOVE EXAMPLES WERE EDITED FOR THE 1990 ENVIRONMENT.

sions made by top management. Companies have several strategic and tactical options for changing their environments. Among them are public relations, politics, trade associations, and illegal activities.

Public Relations

Through the media, and often through advertising, firms may influence various conditions in their environments. Advertising is most often used to stimulate demand, but it can also be used to influence public opinion for other reasons. In the late 1980s and early 1990s, firms in the chemical industry attempted to show increased concern for the natural environment. Dupont, for instance, advertised that it would stop making chlorofluorocarbons by the end of the 1990s in order to help protect the earth's ozone layer.[42]

Politics

Corporations often attempt to influence state, federal, and local governments. Their principal weapons are personal contacts, lobbyists, and **political action committees (PACs)**—committees organized by companies to support political candidates who favor particular policies. Large businesses and trade associations have been using lobbyists for years as a way of influencing government; however, small businesses have recently turned to this means as well—for example, to lobby for special tax breaks or exemptions from the full requirements of workers' compensation laws.[43]

Political action committees (PACs): Committees organized by companies to support political candidates who favor particular policies.

Trade Associations

Trade associations have long been a favorite organizational tool for influencing customers, suppliers, government, and even competitors. Associations often employ lobbyists to represent their members' interests to these various constituencies.

Unfortunately, companies sometimes resort to illegal activities in an effort to change their environments. To some, these actions seem necessary. It is reported, for example, that you cannot be a major player in the New York City construction industry without paying bribes, often to criminal organizations.[44] Firms often simply yield to the pressure and commit such acts in order to gain an advantage over competitors.

Social Power and Social Responsibility

The organization interacts with a large number of constituents in its environment. Each of those constituents may be affected by the organization's actions. The constituents may also take actions that will affect the organization. Because of its considerable **social power**—the power to influence various constituents— business is perceived by many components of society as inheriting a commensurate level of social responsibility.[45,46] **Social responsibility** can be defined as the obligation of an organization to solve problems and take actions that further the best interests of both society and the company.[47] Although this definition seems relatively straightforward, in practice it is often difficult to determine what constitutes social responsibility. For example, if a company dumps pollutants into a river that, while approved for dumping by state and federal law, contaminate a city's water supply, is this act socially responsible? When Japanese firms flood the American market with products, selling them below cost in order to gain market share, is this act socially irresponsible even though consumers may benefit from it? Arguments for and against corporate social responsibility have been identified. They are listed in Table 5.2.

Social power: The power to influence various constituents.

Social responsibility: An organization's obligation to solve problems and take actions that further both its and society's interests.

TABLE 5.2 Major Arguments For and Against Business Social Responsibility

For Social Responsibility

1. It is in the best interest of a business to promote and improve the communities where it does business.
2. Social actions can be profitable.
3. It is the ethical thing to do.
4. It improves the public image of the firm.
5. It increases the viability of the business system. Business exists because it gives society benefits. Society can amend or take away its charter. This is the "iron law of responsibility."
6. It is necessary to avoid government regulation.
7. Sociocultural norms require it.
8. Laws cannot be passed for all circumstances. Thus, business must assume responsibility to maintain an orderly legal society.
9. It is in the stockholders' best interest. It will improve the price of stock in the long run because the stock market will view the company as less risky and open to public attack and therefore award it a higher price-earnings ratio.
10. Society should give business a chance to solve social problems that government has failed to solve.
11. Business, by some groups, is considered to be the institution with the financial and human resources to solve social problems.
12. Prevention of problems is better than cures—so let business solve problems before they become too great.

Against Social Responsibility

1. It might be illegal.
2. Business plus government equals monolith.
3. Social actions cannot be measured.
4. It violates profit maximization.
5. The cost of social responsibility is too great and would increase prices too much.
6. Business lacks the social skills to solve societal problems.
7. It would dilute business's primary purposes.
8. It would weaken the U.S. balance of payments because the price of goods will have to go up to pay for social programs.
9. Business already has too much power. Such involvement would make business too powerful.
10. Business lacks accountability to the public. Thus, the public would have no control over its social environment.
11. Such business involvement lacks broad public support.

SOURCE: R. Joseph Mansen, Jr., "The Social Attitudes of Management," in Joseph W. McGuire, ed., *Contemporary Management* (Englewood Cliffs, N.J.: Prentice-Hall, 1974), p. 616.

Contrasting Views of Social Responsibility

There are varying views on what constitutes social responsibility. Social responsibility is both an issue of obedience to the law and a question of ethics—adherence to the society's norms and values.[48] (What is ethical varies with a particular society's values and norms.)[49] There are at least three important contrasting views of social responsibility: the profit concept, the stakeholder concept, and the social power/social responsibility concept.

THE PROFIT CONCEPT

Nobel Prize-winning economist Milton Friedman is the primary proponent of the profit concept. Friedman takes a narrow view of corporate social responsibility. He believes that an organization's sole social responsibility is to make a profit. The **profit concept** embodies his belief that the single purpose of a business is "to use its resources and energy and activities to increase its profits, so long as it stays within the rules of the game."[50] Friedman has expressed the viewpoint of the traditional economist: The free market system is the best system for regulating the conduct of a business, and it is up to society to establish the rules within which it operates.

Profit concept: The belief that the primary responsibility of business is to make a profit.

THE STAKEHOLDER CONCEPT

Stakeholders include all the individuals and organizations that are directly or indirectly affected by a firm's decisions. The **stakeholder concept** suggests that management must account for its impact on its stakeholders when it makes decisions, and it must take their interests into account.[51] Determining what is socially responsible depends on the values placed on the leading interests of each of the stakeholder groups. Some may be in conflict—for example, stockholders versus suppliers versus consumers versus special-interest groups. The organization must balance all these successfully if it is to be a truly socially responsible corporate citizen. For example, if a firm spends money to reduce pollution outputs beyond what is legally required, it may decrease the returns to stockholders at the same time that it meets the demands of environmental groups.

THE SOCIAL POWER/SOCIAL RESPONSIBILITY CONCEPT

The **social power/social responsibility concept** suggests that business has a certain social responsibility because of the power it wields. If it fails to carry out that responsibility, it will find itself at the mercy of societal constraints on its operations. This is known as the Iron Law of Social Responsibility.[52] It is easy to see how it operates. In the 1960s and 1970s, for example, numerous laws were passed to make businesses adhere to society's interests in the areas of equal employment opportunity, prevention of water and air pollution, occupational safety and health, and consumer protection. Because companies had not adhered to society's norms, society took action and created laws to force them to do so.

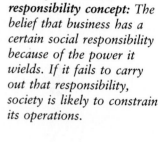

The three contrasting perspectives can be summarized as follows:

1. Organizations should seek a profit but play by the rules. If businesses do not play by the rules, they may be punished.
2. Organizations should minister to the needs of their stakeholders.
3. With social power comes social responsibility.

Archie Carroll, a management researcher and author, has developed a model of social responsibility that incorporates all these differing viewpoints.

Social responsibility involves balancing the interests of different stakeholder groups. For example, if a firm spends money to reduce pollution outputs beyond what is legally required, it may decrease the returns to stockholders at the same time that it meets the demands of environmental groups.

Carroll's model is shown in Figure 5.3. In the rest of this section, we will describe the model in detail.

Levels of Responsibility

Levels of responsibility: A model of social responsibility consisting of four principal components: economic, legal, ethical, and philanthropic responsibility.

Carroll's model of the **levels of responsibility** has four principal components: economic, legal, ethical, and philanthropic responsibility.[53] The four levels encompass the three principal perspectives (profit, stakeholder, and social power) described earlier.

ECONOMIC RESPONSIBILITY

A business is first of all an economic unit. Its economic responsibility is to make a profit. "All other business rules are predicated on this fundamental assumption."[54] If a firm does not make a profit, it cannot stay in business and therefore cannot engage in other socially responsible activities.

LEGAL RESPONSIBILITY

Business must also play by the rules. No one would view a firm as socially responsible if it broke the law to obtain profits. Society has laid out laws, rules, and regulations, thousands of which exist at the international, national, state, and local government levels to regulate all types of businesses. Government can

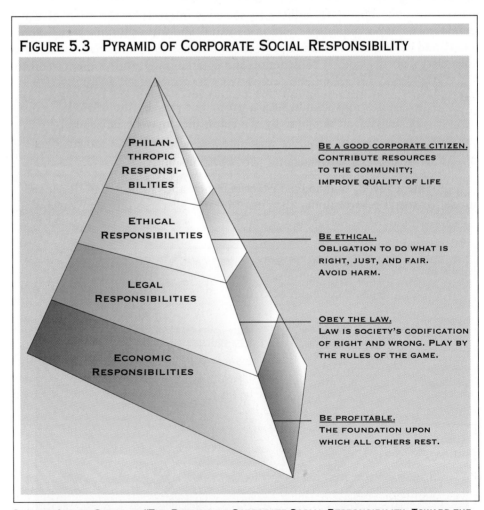

FIGURE 5.3 PYRAMID OF CORPORATE SOCIAL RESPONSIBILITY

PHILAN-THROPIC RESPONSI-BILITIES — BE A GOOD CORPORATE CITIZEN. CONTRIBUTE RESOURCES TO THE COMMUNITY; IMPROVE QUALITY OF LIFE

ETHICAL RESPONSIBILITIES — BE ETHICAL. OBLIGATION TO DO WHAT IS RIGHT, JUST, AND FAIR. AVOID HARM.

LEGAL RESPONSIBILITIES — OBEY THE LAW. LAW IS SOCIETY'S CODIFICATION OF RIGHT AND WRONG. PLAY BY THE RULES OF THE GAME.

ECONOMIC RESPONSIBILITIES — BE PROFITABLE. THE FOUNDATION UPON WHICH ALL OTHERS REST.

SOURCE: ARCHIE CARROLL, "THE PYRAMID OF CORPORATE SOCIAL RESPONSIBILITY: TOWARD THE MORAL MANAGEMENT OF ORGANIZATIONAL STOCKHOLDERS." REPRINTED FROM BUSINESS HORIZONS (JULY–AUGUST 1991), P. 42. COPYRIGHT © 1991 BY THE FOUNDATION FOR THE SCHOOL OF BUSINESS AT INDIANA UNIVERSITY. USED WITH PERMISSION.

affect business through legislation, judicial actions, agency administration (bureaucracy), or executive actions (see Figure 5.4). Some legitimate businesses break laws or rules, as the Pentagate scandal of the late 1980s (in which defense contractors defrauded the Pentagon) revealed. However, such behavior is not condoned by society. Thus, firms have not only an economic responsibility but also a legal one.

ETHICAL RESPONSIBILITY

Ethics is a broad term referring to written and unwritten rules about right and wrong, as defined by a particular society, industry, profession, group, or individual.[55] **Ethical behavior** is behavior a society, an organization, a profession, a group, or an individual considers acceptable and appropriate; **unethical behavior** is outside the norms of these reference groups.[56] When we speak of **ethical responsibility,** we are referring to the responsibility to act within the norms of these reference groups, whether or not the norms have been transformed into laws or rules.

Every manager functions within a society. *Societal ethics* defines which behaviors are acceptable and ethical within that society. The manager also functions within an organization. *Organizational ethics* defines the behaviors that are considered ethical within the organization. Managers also often function within a profession, and many believe that management itself is a profession. *Professional ethics* refers to behaviors that are prescribed by professional associations as appropriate to members of that profession. *Group ethics* refers to behaviors prescribed by a particular group, such as the work group. Finally, managers are individuals. *Personal ethics* consists of the behaviors that an individual considers appropriate. The elements of an individual's ethical system are derived from a variety of sources: societal, organizational, and professional ethics as well as the norms of religious institutions, the family, and peer groups.

A crisis may reveal, and sometimes alter, the ethical values of an individual or an organization. This chapter's Ethical Management Challenge describes the impact of the AIDS crisis on management at Pacific Bell.

The difficulty of maintaining a high standard of ethical responsibility becomes clear when one examines a company like W. R. Grace. Grace is nationally known for its efforts to reduce the federal deficit by running provocative ads on television, showing the potential consequences of continued deficits. Yet, at the same time, it has settled out of court on charges of water contamination by one of its chemical companies and, in a different case, was found guilty of fraudulently obtaining an oil and gas loan from Continental Illinois National Bank & Trust Company, for which it was fined $100 million.[57]

Finally, it should be noted that what is perceived to be ethical in one society may not be ethical in another. This often poses a problem for businesses operating across national boundaries. Multinational corporations find, for example, that in most less developed countries, bribery is an accepted way of doing business. However, it is illegal in the United States, and it is illegal for U.S. businesses to commit bribery even in countries where it is legal.[58] Despite the apparent need to do so, some companies have refused to pay bribes in order to do business in foreign countries.[59]

PHILANTHROPIC RESPONSIBILITIES

Philanthropic responsibilities are those for which there are no societal laws, rules, or ethical statements, but for which expectations may exist nonetheless. These are matters of personal or organizational choice. Philanthropic responsibilities are the highest form of social responsibility because they are voluntary. This is not just charitable giving, although that is an important responsibility.

Ethical behavior: Behavior that is considered acceptable and appropriate by a society, organization, profession, group, or individual.

Unethical behavior: Behavior that is outside the norms of a particular reference group.

Ethical responsibility: The responsibility to act within the norms of a particular reference group, whether or not those norms have been transformed into laws or rules.

Philanthropic responsibilities: Responsibilities for which there are no societal laws, rules, or ethical statements, but for which expectations may exist nonetheless.

FIGURE 5.4 TYPICAL BUSINESS–GOVERNMENT RELATIONSHIPS IN THE UNITED STATES

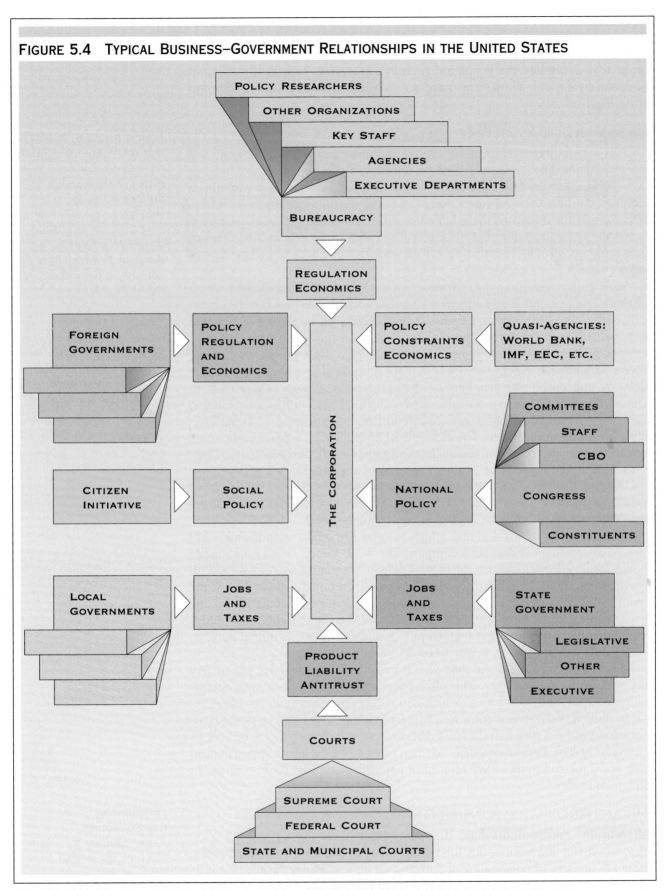

SOURCE: R. EDWARD FREEMAN, STRATEGIC MANAGEMENT: A STAKEHOLDER APPROACH (BOSTON: PITMAN, 1984), P. 15.
COPYRIGHT © 1984 BY R. EDWARD FREEMAN.

Dayton-Hudson, a department store chain, has given 5 percent of its taxable income to charitable institutions since 1945 and urges other corporations to do so as well.[60] A major area of philanthropic responsibility is environmental protection. Environmentally concerned firms are described as "green." Green firms do more than the law requires of them. Thus, when Pacific Gas and Electric determined that energy conservation was preferable to building nuclear power plants, it was partly a rational economic decision and partly an exercise in philanthropic responsibility.[61]

Identifying the Issues

Societies generally spell out the issues they want business to address in the form of laws, rules, and regulations. However, when a new issue emerges, such as how to prevent the destruction of the earth's protective ozone shield, a period of debate often ensues before a response to the issue becomes mandated by law. Thus, businesses must scan their environments not just for competitive factors but for social responsibility issues as well.

The Philosophy of Responsiveness

When confronted with societal demands, an organization may respond in ways that range from very uncooperative to extremely cooperative. There are four basic response modes: reactive, defensive, accommodative, and proactive.[62] These are highlighted in Figure 5.5. In this section we will take a closer look at each of them.

REACTIVE ORGANIZATIONS

A **reactive organization** "fights all the way" against taking responsibility for its actions.[63] Typically, it denies involvement, discounts the evidence, and attempts to obstruct individuals or groups that could show that it has acted irresponsibly. The company might accept its economic responsibility but deny its legal and ethical responsibilities. Tobacco companies, for example, have for years denied the evidence that smoking leads to cancer and other diseases.

DEFENSIVE RESPONSE

A **defensive response** occurs when the company admits that it has made a mistake but defends itself as having been caught up in circumstances beyond its control; it may even take minor actions to offset its error. When General Dy-

AT EXXON: In the case of the oil spill at Valdez, Exxon followed a reactive strategy to some degree. Lee Raymond, Exxon's president, told ABC News that he blamed "ultimately the Coast Guard" for delaying the use of dispersants. His position was contradicted by the evidence.

Reactive organization: A response to societal demands in which the organization "fights all the way" against taking responsibility for its actions.

Defensive response: A response to societal demands in which the organization admits its mistakes but claims that they are due to circumstances beyond its control.

FIGURE 5.5   POSSIBLE SOCIAL RESPONSIBILITY RESPONSES

REACTION	DEFENSE	ACCOMMODATION	PROACTION

DO NOTHING ←——————————————————→ DO MUCH

SOURCE: ARCHIE CARROLL, "A THREE-DIMENSIONAL CONCEPTUAL MODEL OF CORPORATE PERFORMANCE," ACADEMY OF MANAGEMENT REVIEW (1979), P. 502.

with AIDS as it would anyone with a life-threatening illness. It held a series of seminars to educate workers. It was also the first company to produce a video about AIDS, a hard-hitting program that pulled no punches but helped reduce fears and calm emotions.

Jim Henderson, the company's director of human resources policy and services, noted bluntly, "People with AIDS are sick; we don't fire sick people." As it turned out, this policy was not only humane but affordable. The company reexamined its health care benefits for long-term terminal patients. It found that when hospices and other home-care programs were used, patients got better-quality care than they would receive in a hospital. In addition, it saved the company millions of dollars. The average AIDS patient cost no more to treat than patients with other terminal illnesses. At Eriksen's urging, the company also published information about AIDS in its corporate newspaper "Update." The first article appeared on July 22, 1985, the day actor Rock Hudson revealed that he had AIDS.

Pacific Bell has historically been a conservative company. Steve Poulter, Pacific's director of consumer affairs, had to use a great deal of persuasion to reduce top management's skepticism. He was able to convince them that the company's competitive situation could be improved if the company adopted an AIDS policy and education program—especially because the company had a negative image in San Francisco's gay community, which had a disproportionate number of AIDS cases. The company had an opportunity to do good and at the same time do good for itself.

One of Pacific Bell's managers, Chuck Woodman, was transformed by the AIDS crisis. Woodman had very negative views toward AIDS patients. But when one of his repairmen, Dave Goodenough, contracted AIDS, his attitude changed. Working with Goodenough and keeping him employed was the toughest managerial challenge Woodman had faced in four years at Pacific. "When I look at where I was and where I am now," he commented, "AIDS has had a bigger impact on my thinking about people than anything I have come up against." Woodman educated himself about AIDS and became an advocate for AIDS patients. With 25 of his 750 employees diagnosed with AIDS, he juggles his schedule so that they can all work when they are physically able to.

SOURCE: David Kirp, "Uncommon Decency: Pacific Bell Responds to AIDS," *Harvard Business Review* (May–June 1989), pp. 140–151.

tal laws in Louisiana. Bethlehem Steel Corporation is helping to clean up the Chesapeake Bay. These corporate actions were not voluntary. They were the consequence of "citizens' suits," a popular weapon in the fight against industrial polluters.

Today, companies are being sued more frequently than ever before by citizens seeking redress for damage to society. As such social activism becomes more frequent, companies are more likely to take action voluntarily, or at least to settle out of court and agree to take action in order to avoid stiffer penalties.[65] Thus, McDonald's, facing constant pressure from environmental groups, has become a crusader for recycling and is trying to become a major force in educating the populace on environmental issues. These actions have been taken principally because the firm recognized that it must be socially responsible. McDonald's and other companies are taking voluntary action on issues of social responsibility because they recognize that if they do not, citizen pressure groups may force them into even more stringent actions.[66]

PROACTIVE FIRMS

A **proactive firm** goes beyond what is legally and ethically required. It leads its industry, seeking ways to improve its community. Typical of this approach is that taken by the American Express Company. "At American Express, we measure performance by profitability and return on investment. There is, however, another significant measure: how we fulfill our responsibility to the communities from which our profits are derived. Public responsibility is a fundamental corporate value at American Express."[67] The company has long been a leader in many areas of social responsibility: equal employment, employing and marketing to the disabled, protecting consumer interests, assisting worthy causes, practicing corporate ethics, and serving customers in times of crisis. It recently increased its goals for hiring minorities, including seeking minority candidates for four top management positions, and doubled its corporate contributions to the United Way for the period from 1988 through 1991.[68]

Some other companies have been less proactive about carrying out their social responsibilities, as this chapter's Global Management Challenge reveals. These firms have polluted Mexico's environment in an effort to cut costs and compete globally. Because Mexico has few pollution control laws, they followed standards that were less rigid than those they would have faced in the United States. Can these companies be considered socially responsible?

GLOBAL MANAGEMENT CHALLENGE

Poisoning the Border

Maquiladoras, commonly called *maquilas*, are American firms, large and small, that move to areas of Mexico near the U.S. border in order to enjoy cheap labor and generous tax breaks from both nations—and the freedom to pollute the environment.

The migration has been under way for the last twenty-five years, and it has transformed once-quiet border towns into sprawling urban centers. Close to 2,000 plants employing half a million workers now dot the 2,000 miles of border. In 1990, the *maquiladora* program generated $3.5 billion in foreign exchange for the Mexican economy—second only to $9 billion from oil exports. However, it also generated a bleak legacy of health problems and environmental degradation.

Some U.S. companies admit that they have moved south to avoid expensive U.S. environmental requirements. They then create more pollution than they would in the United States. Mexico has scant resources to enforce its 1988 cleanup laws. Although the United States spent $24.40 per capita on environmental protection in 1992, Mexico could afford only 48 cents—a major increase from the 8 cents it spent in 1989.

The American Medical Association has called the border area "a virtual cesspool and breeding ground for infectious disease" for the following reasons:

- Indiscriminate dumping and long-term storage of industrial garbage and hazardous wastes poison the water and soil.
- Chemically laced industrial waste water pumped into canals and rivers causes widespread gastrointestinal illness, hepatitis, and other long-term health problems.
- Massive discharges of toxic fumes occur in chemical plants and other factories.

Improving Social Responsiveness

Corporate social responsiveness can be improved in two ways: by institutionalizing social responsibility through a social policy process (planning) and through a process known as the social audit (control). The organization must also be concerned with its potential legal liabilities, which it can identify by means of a litigation audit.

The Corporate Social Policy Process

In the corporate social policy process, the organization institutionalizes society's needs and wants within the organization's policy framework.[69,70] As reflected in Figure 5.6, the corporate social policy process is an all-encompassing way of institutionalizing business ethics, corporate social responsibility, and corporate social responsiveness. Without the institutionalization envisioned by this model, it is unlikely that the type of performance sought will be forthcoming. Kathleen Black, publisher of *USA Today*, offers an important insight into this process. She comments that the CEO must "make it happen." Al Neuharth, former CEO of *USA Today*'s partner company, Gannett Company, Inc., made it happen with regard to equal employment opportunity. Neuharth tied bonuses and promo-

- Female employees, who start work as young as thirteen, are exposed to toxic substances and other hazards that can cause severe birth defects in their infants.

The *maquilas* have grown explosively in the last five years—by 15 to 20 percent. As a result, tens of thousands of workers are packed into shantytown *colonias*, living in shacks improvised from cinder blocks, tin sheets, scrap lumber, plastic, and cardboard but without benefit of electricity, sewers, or drinking water. Wages start at $27 for a 49-hour week, $47 is average, but in the border economies, food and other necessities are often as expensive as they are in the United States.

Health problems are endemic, particularly in the electronics-assembly industry. Some plants supply protective gloves, but few women wear them because they hamper dexterity—and therefore threaten the fast-paced production schedule. Workers in the American-owned plants have been found to be three times as likely to give birth to low-birthweight infants as other local women. Half of the underweight babies are born prematurely.

Water samples at some of the *maquila* sites can contain pH levels so severe that they cause acidic or caustic burns to the skin. Solid-waste dumps can contain acre after acre of industrial detritus—plastic, metal, rubber, resins, paint sludge. The health threats from solid waste generally remain confined to the local area, but the polluted industrial effluents and untreated sewage are migrating into the United States and creating serious water-borne health problems north of the border.

Meanwhile, industries that generate large amounts of toxic garbage—furniture manufacturing, metal polishing, chemicals, fiberglass, and electronics—continue to migrate south.

SOURCE: Michael Satchell, "Poisoning the Border," *U.S. News & World Report* (May 6, 1991), pp. 32–41.

FIGURE 5.6 CONTRIBUTIONS OF BUSINESS ETHICS, CORPORATE SOCIAL RESPONSIBILITY, AND CORPORATE SOCIAL RESPONSIVENESS TO THE CORPORATE SOCIAL POLICY PROCESS

BUSINESS ETHICS

VALUE-BASED REFLECTION AND CHOICE CONCERNING THE MORAL SIGNIFICANCE OF INDIVIDUAL AND ORGANIZATIONAL ACTION BY BUSINESS DECISION MAKERS. THIS REFLECTION AND CHOICE EMANATES FROM AND PERTAINS TO CRITICAL ISSUES AND PROBLEMS CONFRONTING THE ORGANIZATION AND ITS LEADERS.

CORPORATE SOCIAL POLICY PROCESS

INSTITUTIONALIZATION WITHIN THE CORPORATION OF PROCESSES FACILITATING VALUE-BASED INDIVIDUAL AND ORGANIZATIONAL REFLECTION AND CHOICE REGARDING THE MORAL SIGNIFICANCE OF PERSONAL AND CORPORATE ACTION. INDIVIDUAL AND COLLECTIVE EXAMINATION OF THE LIKELY OVERALL CONSEQUENCES OF SUCH ACTIONS, THEREBY ENABLING THE FIRM'S LEADERS BOTH INDIVIDUALLY AND COLLECTIVELY WITHIN THE ORGANIZATIONAL SETTING TO ANTICIPATE, RESPOND TO AND MANAGE DYNAMICALLY EVOLVING CLAIMS AND EXPECTATIONS OF INTERNAL AND EXTERNAL STAKEHOLDERS CONCERNING THE PRODUCTS (SPECIFIC ISSUES OR PROBLEM-RELATED CONSEQUENCES) OF ORGANIZATIONAL POLICIES AND BEHAVIOR.

=

+

CORPORATE SOCIAL RESPONSIBILITY

DISCERNMENT OF SPECIFIC ISSUES, PROBLEMS, EXPECTATIONS AND CLAIMS UPON BUSINESS ORGANIZATIONS AND THEIR LEADERS REGARDING THE CONSEQUENCES OF ORGANIZATIONAL POLICIES AND BEHAVIOR ON BOTH INTERNAL AND EXTERNAL STAKEHOLDERS. THE FOCUS IS UPON THE PRODUCTS OF CORPORATE ACTION.

+

CORPORATE SOCIAL RESPONSIVENESS

DEVELOPMENT OF INDIVIDUAL AND ORGANIZATIONAL PROCESSES FOR DETERMINING, IMPLEMENTING, AND EVALUATING THE FIRM'S CAPACITY TO ANTICIPATE, RESPOND AND MANAGE THE ISSUES AND PROBLEMS ARISING FROM THE DIVERSE CLAIMS AND EXPECTATIONS OF INTERNAL AND EXTERNAL STAKEHOLDERS.

SOURCE: EDWIN M. EPSTEIN, "THE CORPORATE SOCIAL POLICY PROCESS: BEYOND BUSINESS ETHICS, CORPORATE SOCIAL RESPONSIBILITY, AND CORPORATE SOCIAL RESPONSIVENESS." CALIFORNIA MANAGEMENT REVIEW (SPRING 1987), P. 107. COPYRIGHT 1987 BY THE REGENTS OF THE UNIVERSITY OF CALIFORNIA. REPRINTED FROM THE CALIFORNIA MANAGEMENT REVIEW, VOL. 29, NO. 3. BY PERMISSION OF THE REGENTS.

tions to EEO goals. Gannett and *USA Today* have excellent records for hiring and promoting women and minorities. For example, in 1989, middle management at *USA Today* was 34 percent female and 11 percent minority. Black believes that Neuharth's policies are responsible.[71]

The Social Audit

The second principal way in which organizations can improve their social responsiveness is through management control. Even though the corporate social policy process attempts to use planning—goals, objectives, strategies, policies, rules, and procedures—to achieve social responsiveness, it is also necessary to measure an organization's performance to ascertain whether it has actually

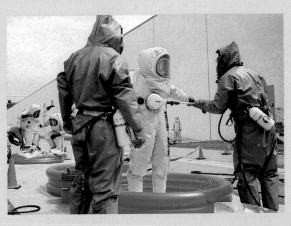

ORGANIZATIONS RESPOND IN A VARIETY OF WAYS TO THE DE-
MANDS PLACED ON THEM BY SOCIETY. *REACTIVE* ORGANIZA-
TIONS DENY RESPONSIBILITY FOR EVENTS OR CONDITIONS
THAT ARE HARMFUL TO SOCIETY. THIS CAN BE SEEN IN THE
CASE OF ACID RAIN (ABOVE), WHICH IS BELIEVED TO BE
CAUSED BY POLLUTANTS EMITTED BY MANUFACTURING PLANTS
AND HAS DESTROYED THOUSANDS OF ACRES OF FORESTS. A
DEFENSIVE ORGANIZATION ADMITS THAT IT HAS CAUSED AN
EVENT SUCH AS AN OIL SPILL, BUT CLAIMS THAT THE EVENT
WAS BEYOND ITS CONTROL; THE SPILL BY THE TANKER *BRAER*
IN QUENDALE BAY, SCOTLAND (TOP LEFT), IS AN EXAMPLE OF
SUCH A SITUATION. AN ORGANIZATION MAY MAKE AN *ACCOMMO-
DATIVE* RESPONSE, SUCH AS HELPING TO CLEAN UP POLLUTED
AREAS (RIGHT), IN ORDER TO FORESTALL CRITICISM BY GROUPS
SEEKING REDRESS FOR DAMAGE TO SOCIETY. FINALLY, A *PRO-
ACTIVE* ORGANIZATION GOES BEYOND WHAT IS LEGALLY AND
ETHICALLY REQUIRED, FOR EXAMPLE, IN PROTECTING ITS EM-
PLOYEES AGAINST POTENTIAL HAZARDS (TOP RIGHT).

achieved this goal. The idea of a **social audit**—an audit of an organization's social performance—dates back at least to 1940.[72] Since that time, the concept of a social audit has remained essentially unchanged, but the particulars of what is audited and what organizations ought to be accomplishing in terms of social goals have evolved considerably.[73] Companies now perform social audits focusing on several issues, such as environmental pollution and equal employment opportunity.[74] In the 1980s, interest in the social audit seems to have waned, but renewed interest is likely in the 1990s as social activism regains momentum. Table 5.3 provides an example of how a company might "keep score" with its various stakeholders. In Europe, where environmental issues are a major concern, firms are making increasing use of this technique.[75]

The Litigation Audit

Attorney David Silverstein suggests that companies should periodically perform a **litigation audit** to determine potential corporate exposure to litigation. This audit requires, first, that management recognize an evolving legal issue; second, that it forecast the direction in which that issue will move; and third, that it decide how best to respond. Many companies suffering from legal problems failed to follow this process and suffered financial loss as a result. An example is

TABLE 5.3 A Sample Scorecard for "Keeping Score with Stakeholders"

Stakeholder Category	Possible Near-Term Measures	Possible Long-Term Measures
Customers	Sales ($ and volume) New customers Number of new customer needs met ("tries")	Growth in sales Turnover of customer base Ability to control price

Suppliers	Cost of raw material
	Delivery time
	Inventory
	Availability of raw material
		Growth rates of
		  Raw material costs
		  Delivery time
		  Inventory
		New ideas from suppliers

Financial Community	EPS (Earnings per share) Stock price Number of "buy" lists ROE (Return on equity)	Ability to convince Wall Street of strategy Growth in ROE
Employees	Number of suggestions Productivity Number of grievances	Number of internal promotions Turnover
Congress	Number of new pieces of legislation that affect the firm Access to key members and staff	Number of new regulations that affect industry Ratio of "cooperative" vs. "competitive" encounters
Consumer Advocate (CA)	Number of meetings Number of "hostile" encounters Number of times coalitions formed Number of legal actions	Number of changes in policy due to CA Number of CA initiated "calls for help"
Environmentalists	Number of meetings Number of hostile encounters Number of times coalitions formed Number of EPA complaints (Environmental Protection Agency) Number of legal actions	Number of changes in policy due to environmentalists Number of environmentalist "calls for help"

SOURCE: R. E. Freeman, *Strategic Management* (Boston: Pitman Publishing, Inc., 1984), p. 179. Copyright © 1984 by R. E. Freeman. Reprinted by permission.

Johns Manville, which knowingly exposed workers and customers to the hazards of asbestos.[76] A litigation audit at least keeps the firm moving toward meeting society's requirements.

Corporate Social Responsibility and Profitability

Management theorists have divergent views regarding the relationship between a company's social responsibility and its financial performance. The three major perspectives follow:

1. A firm incurs costs by being socially responsible; these put it at an economic disadvantage relative to other firms.
2. Firms actually invest very little in corporate social responsibility and benefit from socially responsible actions because they increase productivity or morale.
3. The costs of social responsibility can be significant, but they may be offset by a reduction in some of the firm's other costs.[77]

A number of research studies have attempted to analyze relationships between social responsibility and financial performance (in terms of stock market values and financial accounting measures). Those studies have had mixed results—only in some was there a correlation between social responsibility and future performance.[78] A study by Jean B. McGuire, Alison Sundgren, and Thomas Schneeweis revealed that past performance is more closely correlated with social responsibility than future performance. These authors surmise that one possible explanation might be that firms with high levels of financial success may act in more socially responsible ways than firms that are not financially successful. They also found that socially responsible firms tend to take less risky actions than firms that are not socially responsible.[79]

External Social Controls

Managers must contend with three levels of external social controls: (1) those that focus on the individual firm or industry (e.g., breaking up AT&T); (2) those that focus on specific practices or business functions (e.g., regulations on accounting for taxes); and (3) those that are systematic and apply to all firms in an industry or society (e.g., regulation of the airline industry).[80]

There is more than one model or philosophy of control, and all of them can be used at each of the levels just noted. For example, the government may attempt to let the market have more control over the company, perhaps by bringing antitrust suits against companies that have a near-monopoly of their industry. The government may also initiate regulations, such as those concerned with equal employment opportunity. Pressure groups may call for social audits, and stockholders may bring lawsuits against a company. Managers must formulate strategies for coping with these and other forms of external social control.

Business Ethics

It is debatable whether anyone can really teach you ethics at this point in your life. What someone else can do is teach you how to think through an **ethical dilemma,** a situation in which there is a conflict between the firm's economic performance and its social performance. For most ethical dilemmas, the ethical answer is obvious; however, for many there are multiple alternatives, whose

Ethical dilemma: A situation in which there is a conflict between the firm's economic goals and its social responsibility.

consequences are uncertain and extend beyond the immediate decision. There can be personal implications for the manager involved, and the available choices may be subject to mixed outcomes (positive and negative).[81] Your instructor can give you some guidance in identifying your own values and society's. Then, if you are faced with an ethical dilemma in an organization, you will know what to look for and how to think about it.[82]

The disconcerting reality about ethics is that the "ethical signposts do not always point in the same direction."[83] There may be information indicating that opposite courses of action are equally appropriate. For example, when Goodyear Tire and Rubber Company had to decide whether to remain in South Africa, it was faced with a choice between staying (thereby preserving the jobs of its 1,500 black employees and meeting the needs of stockholders) or leaving (thereby satisfying the demands of constituent groups attempting to place economic pressure on South Africa). Both choices had positive and negative aspects.

Often, managers must not only resolve their personal ethical dilemmas but also make decisions for others, weighing numerous variables. This is not an academic debate; business ethics is "applied ethics." Managers have to come up with real answers, as Table 5.4 suggests.

A corporate culture establishes its own values. There is tremendous pres-

---

TABLE 5.4 Dimensions and Boundaries of Ethical Conduct

1. Business ethics is "applied" ethics. It has to come up with an answer, not just a debate. It relates to specific patterns of conduct, not eliminating but going beyond such generalized attributes as honesty or fairness.
2. Business ethics deals with relationships. It must be accepted as well as asserted; its validity depends upon mutual acceptance.
3. Business ethics can often be institutionalized, with systematic procedures and rules for administering and implementing them.
4. Business ethics is designed to provide a common denominator of understanding and communication between parties to a transaction or relationship, vastly simplifying the negotiation process by providing predictability and dependability in the conduct of affairs.
5. A business ethic (or pattern of conduct) is valid only for the area of common acceptance by the parties affected by the transaction involved.

SOURCE: Henry B. Arthur, "Making Business Ethics Useful," *Strategic Management Journal* (October–December 1984), pp. 319–332. Reprinted by permission of John Wiley & Sons, Ltd.

sure to perform, and this often compromises personal principles. People tend to lose sight of their personal values because of the demands the organization places on them.[84] The need to perform to avoid being fired may cause them to lie or cheat in order to give the appearance of achieving mandated performance levels.

How the Individual Manager Should Decide

Managers often face complex decisions with many variables. There are few guidelines for making such decisions in an ethical manner, but academician Laura L. Nash has provided a list of twelve questions managers should ask themselves:

1. Have you defined the problem correctly?
2. How would you define the problem if you stood on the other side of the fence?
3. How did this situation occur in the first place?
4. To whom and to what do you give your loyalty as a person and as an employee?
5. What is your intention in making this decision?
6. How does this intention compare with the probable result?
7. Whom could your decision or action injure?
8. Can you discuss the problem with the affected parties before you make your decision?
9. Are you confident your decision will be as valid over a long period of time as it seems now?
10. Could you disclose without qualm your decision or action to your supervisor, your CEO, your board of directors, your family, and society as a whole?
11. What is the symbolic potential of your action if understood? If misunderstood?
12. Under what conditions would you allow exceptions to your stand?[85]

Management theorist Arthur Bedeian suggests that the toughest question the manager must answer is, "How willing are you to discuss your decision on national television with Mike Wallace on '60 Minutes' next Sunday evening?" He suggests that if the decision will really enhance the corporation's image when it gets exposure on national television, it is probably an ethical decision.[86]

Business ethics vary in different countries. Managers must understand the ethics of the countries in which they operate and attempt to strike a balance between them and those of their own country. For example, Japanese computer chip manufacturing firms have historically been much less responsive than their U.S. counterparts to the need to reduce toxic wastes. One result was a very high level of mercury poisoning in Japan for many years.

How Companies Can Improve
Their Ethical Performance

Companies can use a variety of techniques to improve their ethical performance. Among these are codes of ethics, whistleblowing, ombudsmen, corporate ethics committees, task forces, and training programs. It is also important to control for compliance.[87]

CODES OF ETHICS

In an effort to improve their managers' ethical conduct, more and more corporations are installing codes of ethics. Although some observers have caustically referred to the idea of business ethics as an oxymoron, in reality business leaders take ethics very seriously. A recent survey by the Conference Board Inc. reveals that companies are tightening their codes of ethics, requiring compliance by managers and employees at lower levels of the organization and instituting procedures to assure continuing concern for ethics in the firm.[88] Most firms hold seminars to inform employees of what they expect.[89] Companies such as Chemical Bank, Xerox, General Mills, and Johnson & Johnson have fired people for violating their ethics codes.

How valuable are such codes? Certainly they help, but they are not a guarantee of ethical behavior by all members of the organization.[90] Part of the problem with codes of ethics is that managers' personal values may differ from those embodied in the code. For example, in 1988 Hertz Car Rental Company admitted to overcharging motorists and insurance companies $13 million for repairs. Hertz had a code of ethics and required its employees to sign a compliance statement, but neither of these policies made a difference. Most of the problem resulted from charging retail prices for repairs for which Hertz actually paid much less (it received a volume discount because of its size). Allen Blicker, the company's national accident control manager, was viewed as the "architect" of this and other fraudulent practices that eventually led to a grand jury probe. Blicker and eighteen other managers were fired; the company refunded more than $3 million to customers and insurers, but the damage had been done—despite a code of ethics and signed compliance statements.[91]

WHISTLEBLOWING

Whistleblowing: Disclosure of an illegal, immoral, or unethical action by members of the organization performing the action.

Another way to improve corporate social responsibility is not only to allow whistleblowing, but to actively encourage it.[92] **Whistleblowing** occurs when an employee discloses an illegal, immoral, or unethical action committed by a member of the organization.[93] Unfortunately, the available evidence suggests that most firms not only discourage, but actually punish whistleblowing. For example, after Morton Thiokol, Inc., engineers Allen J. McDonald and Roger Boisjoly graphically demonstrated the problems with the "O-ring" on the shuttle booster rocket and testified in Congress about their objections to the launch of the *Challenger* space shuttle, they were stripped of their responsibilities and transferred to lower-level jobs. Eventually, they regained their original positions, but only after pressure was placed on the company by the media and public opinion.[94]

OMBUDSMEN, CORPORATE COMMITTEES, AND TASK FORCES

Other techniques employed by organizations to improve their social responsibility performance include ombudsmen, committees, and task forces. These individuals or groups oversee programs for encouraging ethical behavior, reviewing violations of codes of ethics, and taking action on whistleblowers' observations of illegal, immoral, or unethical actions.

TRAINING PROGRAMS

Organizations must provide training for managers, professionals, and other employees at all levels, especially for those in sensitive positions, such as purchasing, waste disposal, personnel, R&D, sales, and manufacturing, where social responsibility issues could be involved. Examples of such issues include equal employment opportunity, treatment of animals in R&D, bribery in purchasing, and pollution resulting from manufacturing. This training must be aimed at improving the social performance of the individuals involved by helping them understand ethical dilemmas, possible consequences, and company policies on such issues.

CONTROLLING COMPLIANCE—THE ETHICS AUDIT

Periodically, an organization should perform ethics audits—audits that examine the ethical performance of the organization's members. It is not enough just to have a code of ethics. Ninety percent of Fortune 500 companies have them, yet many have seen their employees violate the codes. Dow-Corning, for example, has been a leader in the corporate ethics movement, yet it recently was involved in serious ethical lapses.[95] Thus, the firm must actively investigate its members for compliance with its code of ethics.[96]

Social Responsibility, Ethics, and Problem Solving

Social responsibility issues are problems. They can be solved by applying the problem-solving model discussed in Chapter 3. When ethical dilemmas are encountered, they, too, should be viewed as problems and should be solved by applying the standard problem-solving model. Ethical and social responsibility perspectives also enter into the solution of other problems: The problems encountered by managers can be solved in ethical and/or socially responsible ways. In such cases, ethical and social responsibility would be integral parts of the problem, but not the problem itself.

Summary

(Before reading this summary, look again at the objectives listed at the beginning of the chapter.)

1. An organization's environment has two principal components: internal and external. The external environment consists of the competitive environment and the general environment, which affect the organization at both the domestic and international levels. Organizations may face many variations of these environments if they function in different countries.

2. The stakeholder concept requires that firms take into account the impact of their decisions on their various stakeholders.

3. Organizations face much more complex and unstable environments today than they did in the past. They must learn to adapt to or change their environments in order to survive.

4. Social responsibility—corporate social performance—has been shown to have four principal components: economic, legal, ethical, and discretionary.

5. Key issues of social responsibility include environmental pollution, equal employment opportunity, employee health and safety, consumer protection, the quality of the work life, product safety, and business ethics.

6. An organization may respond to social responsibility issues in several ways. Those responses can be described as reactive, defensive, accommodative, or proactive.

7. Ethics refers to the norms and values defining conduct. Ethical systems can be societal, organizational, professional, group, or personal.

8. In determining whether a decision is ethical, managers should ask themselves whether it would stand up under the scrutiny of higher management, the board of directors, and society as a whole.

General Questions

1. What is an ethical dilemma, and why is it so difficult to make decisions in such a situation?

2. Why does Milton Friedman say that the only responsibility of a business is to make a profit? How would you argue against this decision, or would you?

3. Name a company that illustrates each of these descriptions of levels of social responsibility: economic, legal, ethical, and discretionary.

4. Describe the social responsibility performance of various companies in such areas as air pollution, water pollution, equal employment opportunity, consumer protection, employee safety and health, and product safety. Try to find companies that illustrate the philosophical positions of reaction, defense, accommodation, and proaction.

5. If you were to construct a social audit of equal employment opportunity for your college, what questions would you ask to determine whether the college is socially responsible in this area?

6. Air and water pollution are two of the major problems facing the world in the next twenty years. If you were a major chemical producer, what kinds of actions could you expect to have to take in the next fifteen years in order to avert increased legal activity by citizens or federal law enforcement agencies?

7. To what factors would you attribute the ethics "crisis" that seems to have peaked in the late 1980s?

8. Devise strategies for coping with two or three types of external social control over business—for example, federal legislation or consumer pressure groups.

9. Discuss what should be done to prevent another major oil spill anywhere in the world.

Questions on the Management Challenge Features

QUALITY MANAGEMENT CHALLENGE

1. Why would Martin Koldyke undertake such a challenge?

2. How could schools reach the level of productivity of those described in this feature?

3. What impact do cultural differences have on these schools' productivity?

MANAGEMENT CHALLENGE

1. How has Oxford's world changed?

2. Besides raising more funds, what else could be done to improve educational processes and facilities at Oxford?

ETHICAL MANAGEMENT CHALLENGE

1. Into what category of social responsibility do Pacific Bell's actions fit?

2. What, specifically, was ethical about Pacific Bell's actions?

GLOBAL MANAGEMENT CHALLENGE

1. Describe the level of social responsibility being displayed by these firms.

2. What can citizens of Mexico and the United States do to improve their social responsibility performance?

E   P   I   L   O   G   U   E

The Exxon Valdez Oil Spill

Exxon was forced to return to Prince William Sound to do additional cleaning up in the summers of 1990 and 1991. The enormity of the spill and the subsequent cleanup effort, as well as the spill's catastrophic consequences, point to the financial problems that can be involved in transporting oil through U.S. waters and to the need for better management of operations with the potential for environmental damage. Oil companies are discussing the possibility of unloading oil outside U.S. waters in order to avoid spillage problems. This, of course, will not improve the situation in Alaska, but it could reduce potential liabilities for spillage inside U.S. waters. Federal legislation passed in 1990 gave states the right to sue for an unlimited amount of liability for oil spills.

DISCUSSION QUESTIONS

1. How could companies like Exxon and Alyeska be so haphazard in their actions?

2. What role did the state government play in this catastrophe? The federal government?

3. Describe the strategy used by Exxon to extricate itself from this problem.

4. What can be done to prevent such catastrophes in the future?

CHAPTER 5   ETHICS, SOCIAL RESPONSIBILITY, AND THE MANAGERIAL ENVIRONMENT   185

A Question of Ethics

Sue Barnes was an administrator of special projects in a large health care organization located in a major city in the southern United States. She supervised the work of specialty project teams, as well as a staff of six professionals and two secretaries. Previously, she had managed the work of from eight to ten supervisors, each of whom had eight to ten subordinates.

Both Barnes and her boss, Mike Murray, were enrolled in MBA programs. She was attending an evening program at a local college; he was enrolled in a correspondence program with a "Big Ten" university. One day Murray asked Barnes to let him look at one of her papers. She said sure, thinking he was interested in her work. A few weeks later, he showed her a paper he had mailed to his faculty advisor in his MBA program. Seventy-five percent of it was verbatim plagiarism of her paper. She couldn't believe it. She vowed to herself not to let him have any more of her papers. She was starting to tell him what she thought when he interrupted her and said, "Have you had the statistics course in your school yet? I need another paper for my course."

She spoke bluntly, "You can't do that. It's unethical."

"As a manager, I can get my subordinates to do my work here, so why not for school?" he replied flippantly.

"Well, for one reason, because that's not how it works in school. You're supposed to do your own work," she retorted.

"Well, if you're going to be uncooperative with your boss, that could cause you serious problems," he threatened.

"If you want to dance, we will," she said angrily, implying that he could not threaten her.

The conversation continued in the same vein for several minutes. Barnes left knowing that Murray knew that she thought he was a cheater and that she would not help him cheat. If it caused her "serious problems," she would be forced to go straight to the president of the company.

DISCUSSION QUESTIONS

1. Is this situation an ethical dilemma for Barnes? Why or why not?
2. If you were Barnes, what would you have said to Murray in addition to what she said?
3. What would you say to Murray's boss if such a conversation became necessary?

MANAGE
YOURSELF

Grappling with
Controversial Issues

The instructor will ask the students to form small groups to discuss the following questions. Each group is to arrive at a consensus and report its findings to the class. Further discussion may take place at that point.

1. Contrast "situational ethics" with the belief in absolute rules of right and wrong. Which view is correct? Why?
2. Discuss the issue of paying bribes in order to do business in underdeveloped countries, even though this is against the law in the United States. For example, one U.S. corporate official reports that in Mexico a tax agent would not accept a U.S. firm's tax payment without a bribe. If he was not bribed, he would report the payment as late and fine the company. What should a manager do in such a case?

Strategic Problem Solving at Intel

By mid-1992, Intel Corporation's CEO, Andrew Grove, had clearly established a set of strategies for dealing with a number of problems confronting the firm. These major plans of action to achieve corporate objectives typified the results of the creative problem-solving process in this firm, the world's leading PC chip maker. Intel's grip on the PC chip market resulted in a fourfold increase in revenues from 1986 to 1992; during the same period, its profits doubled. However, increased competition, a huge R&D and capital expenditure commitment, and a changing culture all posed serious problems for the firm. As you read the following paragraphs, examine how Grove and Intel's other top managers have solved each of the problems identified, and note how the solutions form a cohesive strategy for coping with the external environment.

INCREASING COMPETITION

Intel faced numerous new competitive situations, first from cloners of its highly successful 386 chip, the key ingredient in most new PCs, and more recently from cloners of its new 486 chip, which will be the key ingredient in new PCs in 1993 and 1994. It was also threatened by firms with competitive technologies, such as the RISC (reduced instruction-set computing) processors that are the primary component of workstations, which can compete in many ways with PCs.

Grove's primary solution is a simple one: "Ultimately, speed is the only weapon we have." Intel will strive to get its products to market faster and faster. By doing so, it will cut down on the advantages of clones—cheaper prices and, often, better features. Cloners take a firm's chips (or other product) apart and re-create them. Since they don't have to spend the money on R&D to develop the chip, they can manufacture it more cheaply. By introducing new products faster, the firm can reduce the cloner's advantage. Speed also provides an advantage by introducing new technologies that are superior to existing ones. Intel's Pentium (586) chip essentially eliminates any advantage of RISC technology.

But getting to market faster is not easy, especially when each new chip is at least twice as powerful and two to five times faster than its predecessor. Intel's solution was twofold. First, the firm would always be developing two chips at the same time in an overlapping fashion. Thus, once the 486 was completed, the 486 development team immediately went to work on the 686 chip. The 586 team began work on the 786 chip once the 586 was completed. The development teams share members and resources. The 586 team shared information and members with the 686 team so that what was learned on one chip could be used on another. Projects overlap for about a year.

Second, the firm is spending whatever money is necessary to achieve these goals. It spent $800 million on R&D and $1.2 billion on capital expenditures in 1992. It has purchased special software to help in the design and testing processes. These purchases have helped reduce the product development time. Since no other firm in the industry has the cash flow that Intel does, Grove believes no other firm can keep up. (But if profit margins slip with increased competition, Intel may not be able to maintain this pace either.)

Speed has some disadvantages, however. A significant one is the lead time for writing software for a new chip. If hardware isn't designed in a coordinated way, there won't be much user demand for chips. And if software for the new hardware isn't readily available, people will not demand the new PCs based on the new chip.

Intel's solution was to become customer oriented. If the firm simply announces a new chip upon completion and begins taking orders, as Intel used to do, working on two chips at once does not give it a significant advantage. By sharing information with hardware and software developers before completion, the firm is able to provide advance notice of the chip's capabilities and applications, thereby increasing demand. And by listening to customers (another reversal of past engineering practices), the firm is able to incorporate customers' requirements into a new chip; again, demand is higher as a result. For example, when the team began designing the 586 chip, it visited every major hardware customer and key software house to find out what they wanted. The result was a list of 147 features, many ranked quite differently than expected.

Another solution to the problem of cloners is to take them to court for patent violations. Still another is to cut prices drastically once they move into Intel's markets. This reduces Intel's margins but makes it very difficult for the cloners to make money.

Intel has also begun to diversify away from just making chips for PCs. It now has interests in several other businesses—making PCs for firms like DEC, which will sell them under its own label; producing chips for uses other than in PCs; and developing enhancement products, supercomputers, and flash memory (units that retain memory when the power is off). Grove doesn't view these other businesses as simple hedges against a downward spiral in PC chips. Rather, he sees them as an integrated set of businesses that provide synergy and enhance the firm's overall effort to stay on the cutting edge.

R&D AND CAPITAL BUDGET EXPENDITURES

As noted earlier, in 1992 Intel spent $2 billion for R&D and capital expenditures. It now faces the problem of maintaining the cash flow to support these expenditures. In this case, the problem is the solution. There is no problem as long as the firm can maintain the pace of new-chip introductions, and that pace can be maintained only as long as the firm invests in R&D and capital assets.

CHANGING THE ORGANIZATIONAL CULTURE

Changing Intel's culture was not easy, but it has happened. The former arrogance has been replaced by concern for the customer. A number of actions contributed to the change. Grove himself led the effort. Craig R. Barrett was promoted to executive vice-president in charge of daily operations and assigned the task of revamping the product development process. Other important elements of the effort to change Intel's culture focused on employee behavior: setting objectives for activities that lead to customer satisfaction, rewarding those who excelled at the new activities, and changing the way employees talked about customers. Now no one at Intel wants to be called a *chiphead,* the firm's new term for someone who acts like an engineer who is unconcerned about the customer.

DISCUSSION QUESTIONS

1. Identify the problems faced by Intel and the solutions that evolved.
2. Describe how these decisions fit together to form a cohesive approach to increasing the firm's competitiveness.

SOURCE: Robert D. Hof, "Inside Intel," *Business Week* (June 1, 1992), pp. 86–94.

PART THREE

Planning

Planning is the first mission function of management and the first stage in the management process. When a successful product, such as the Hewlett-Packard palm top computer, is launched, it all begins with planning. When Mazda introduced its Miata, planning led to the creation and introduction of the new model. When Airborne Express launched its services as a low-price competitor to Federal Express, it engaged in extensive planning to determine prices and service levels.

Chapter 6 reviews the basics of the planning process. Important topics include the basic components of the planning process; key issues in planning, such as SWOT analysis (strengths, weaknesses, opportunities, and threats); organizational purpose; and managing by objectives, results, and rewards systems. Chapter 7 discusses strategy formulation and implementation. Important considerations include defining strategic management; strategizing in turbulent environments; key issues in strategy formulation, such as strategic intent; strategies at the corporate and business levels; types of strategists; strategy formulation in a global environment; and implementation of strategy. Chapter 8 reviews quantitative methods as used in problem solving and planning. Included in this chapter are discussions of basic quantitative methods such as statistics, quantitative methods used in problem solving, forecasting as a key quantitative technique for planning, additional quantitative planning techniques, and the use of computers in decision making and planning.

> "**M**anagement's job is to see the company not as it is . . . but as it can become."
>
> —John W. Teets,
> Chairman,
> The Greyhound Corporation

> "**I**f you don't know where you're going, you'll probably end up somewhere else."
>
> —David P. Campbell

CHAPTER 6

The Planning Process and Organizational Purpose

CHAPTER OBJECTIVES

When you have read this chapter, you should be able to:

1. Describe the planning process and its two principal parts: its purpose (what is to be accomplished) and the plan (how, where, when, and by whom it is to be accomplished).

2. Indicate why planning can be reviewed as "problem solving for the future."

3. Identify the relationships between planning and the other functions of management.

4. Identify differences in the planning problems that confront different levels of management.

5. Discuss the key issues in the scope and characteristics of planning.

6. Enumerate the limitations of planning and why people often fail at it.

7. Describe the relationships between vision, mission, goals, and objectives.

8. List the characteristics of sound objectives.

9. Describe the MBO and MBORR processes and the differences between them.

CHAPTER OUTLINE

Plans and Planning
 THE IMPORTANCE OF PLANNING
 LEVELS OF PLANNING
 STANDING VERSUS SINGLE-USE PLANS
 CRITERIA FOR PLANS
 PLANNING AND CONTROL
 SWOT ANALYSIS
 THE LIMITATIONS OF PLANNING
 WHY PLANNING FAILS
 ESTABLISHING AN ENVIRONMENT CONDUCIVE TO PLANNING

Organizational Purpose
 VISION AND MISSION
 GOALS AND OBJECTIVES

Managing by Objectives
 MANAGEMENT BY OBJECTIVES, RESULTS, AND REWARDS (MBORR)
 ALTERNATIVES TO OBJECTIVE-BASED SYSTEMS
 SETTING PERSONAL OBJECTIVES

Planning as a Problem-Solving Process

MANAGEMENT CHALLENGES DISCUSSED IN THIS CHAPTER:

 Accelerating rates of change

 Increasing globalization of business

 Increasing levels of competition

 Complexity of the managerial environment

General Accident Revises Its Mission

In 1988 and 1989, General Accident Insurance Company (GA), a global insurance firm headquartered in Perth, Scotland, experienced its highest profits. In 1990, it experienced its greatest loss ever, losing over $100 million. Top management, led by Walter Farnham, determined that the losses were caused not by a one-time event but by fundamental changes in the insurance industry and the firm's lack of an appropriate strategy for coping with them. Although the firm had been monitoring these changes, it had not been significantly affected by them until the global recession began in 1990. In addition to the recession, the primary factors affecting most insurance firms around the world, including GA, were increased competition, high levels of insurance losses, the consumer movement to lower insurance rates, encroachment by banks on insurers' markets, the U.S. junk bond debacle, increased regulatory controls, and an increasingly hostile legal environment.

Top management undertook an examination of the firm's fundamental purposes and its strategies, structure, systems, and organizational culture. Since customer service had become so critical to the industry, much of the investigation focused on how each of these areas was affected by the demand for better service. In-depth interviews with employees quickly revealed that few of them knew the firm's vision and mission and that the importance of customer service had not become part of the organizational culture. Many employees did not know what the term *strategy* meant, much less that the company's strategy was to differentiate itself from competitors by providing superior performance. The organization's performance measurement and reward systems were not directed toward improving customer service. Finally, the organization's structure was extremely rigid in terms of coordinating rules and policies. Thus, while the structure was flat, it nonetheless hindered independent initiatives to make customers happy.

A program of change was initiated by mid-1991; it focused on changing the company's culture—that is, its shared values. At the center of this program was a change in the firm's mission and strategies and an effort to educate employees about this change. Systems and structure were changed to accommodate new goals, strategies, and systems and incorporate them into the organization's culture.

SOURCE: Stephen E. Bailey, Robert C. Capobianco, and Karen H. Sparkman, "General Accident—A Case Analysis," unpublished working paper, Roy E. Crummer Graduate School of Business, Rollins College, December 2, 1991. Also see "British Insurers: Another Disaster," *The Economist* (September 7, 1991), pp. 83, 86.

General Accident Insurance Company of Scotland is typical of a company in a highly competitive, changing environment. To cope with these challenges, it has found it necessary to change its vision and mission. It is aligning its objectives and plans with its new mission of providing improved customer service.

Planning is problem solving for the future in a changing environment.[1] As more and more changes take place in the external business environment, planning becomes more important and more difficult. The planning process is divided into two parts. The first is determining **purpose**—what is to be accomplished. Purpose is first defined in terms of a directional and motivational *vision,* then as a general *mission,* and then more definitively in terms of *goals.* Goals are then stated in terms of specific *objectives.* These guide the organization's subunits and each individual in it.

The second part of the planning process is determining how, where, when, and by whom the purpose is to be accomplished. The result is a **plan:** a set of actions designed to achieve an objective, goal, mission, or vision. The major plans of action to achieve the organization's purpose are called strategies. Strategies are the concern of top management. Intermediate (tactical) plans and operational plans, which are aimed at achieving less encompassing objectives, are the concerns of middle and lower levels of management. Other kinds of plans include budgets, policies, procedures, and rules.

Planning is an organization's best means of determining its purpose, gaining support for that purpose, and assuring individuals that they have a stake in what the organization seeks to accomplish. The planning process is an opportunity for individuals to see beyond their own department, share a common vision, and solve their own problems. High levels of rational and creative endeavor are required in planning the future of an organization, department, group, or individual. Planning is also the organization's best way of coping with strategic changes. Changes are going to happen, and the organization should plan for them.[2]

This chapter first examines the basic planning process: plans and planning; the importance of planning; the scope of planning in an organization; the char-

Planning: Problem solving for the future in a changing environment.

Purpose: The first step in planning—deciding what is to be accomplished.

Plan: A set of actions designed to achieve an objective, goal, mission, or vision.

Planning is an organization's best means of determining its purpose, gaining support for that purpose, and assuring individuals that they have a stake in what the organization seeks to accomplish. With so much depending on the planning process, considerable time, effort, and creativity are required if it is to succeed.

acteristics of plans and planning; the limitations of planning; and why people fail at planning. The second section examines the purposes of planning—vision, mission, goals, and objectives—and how they are determined. Finally, planning and objective setting are discussed from the standpoint of their effectiveness as problem-solving processes. This theme is continued in the next two chapters: Chapter 7 reviews the strategic planning process, and Chapter 8 describes the major quantitative techniques that can be used to improve decision making of all types, with special attention to planning.

Plans and Planning

Planning is concerned not with future decisions but with the future impact of decisions made today.[3] Planning involves assessing the future and preparing for it, or creating it. Planning is *the* fundamental function of management. Everything the organization attempts to accomplish, everything any manager attempts to achieve, and everything any individual employee attempts to bring about depends on setting objectives and formulating plans to reach those objectives. Whether a manager is at the strategic, intermediate, or operational level, whether he or she is the CEO or a front-line supervisor, planning is the starting point for everything else the manager does.

As Figure 6.1 shows, all management activity stems from planning. Organizing and leading are done in order to carry out plans and achieve objectives. Controlling is done to determine whether the objectives have been achieved and the plans carried out. However, planning also depends on what happens in the

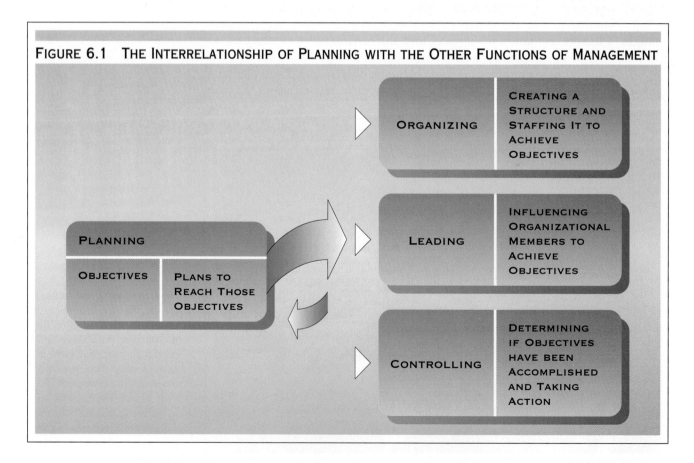

FIGURE 6.1   THE INTERRELATIONSHIP OF PLANNING WITH THE OTHER FUNCTIONS OF MANAGEMENT

Downsizing at AT&T

An upper-level manager in the AT&T Information System Division had to determine how to combine two data centers and eliminate fifty jobs. He knew what his objectives were; they had been given to him by top management. But he had to establish a plan of action to achieve them. The complexities of that decision were immense. The entire company had been forced to downsize as a result of deregulation. He did not want to hurt anyone's future, but he knew that, somewhere along the line, many people would no longer be employed in the Bell systems. He had to take the best course of action within six months to help meet company objectives, help the affected employees find other jobs, satisfy his own values, and solve the problem ethically.

The manager decided to invite the fifty people who would be affected to participate in the problem-solving process—that is, to help him find ways to achieve his multiple, conflicting objectives. This was a unique solution in a company that was noted for less than careful attention to human concerns. To the manager's satisfaction, the employees understood the problem, appreciated his willingness to share a difficult situation with them, and with few exceptions recognized and accepted the fact that certain actions had to be taken. They were able to formulate a plan that would, through a combination of attrition (employees voluntarily leaving or retiring) and outplacement, satisfy most of the job needs of most of the people involved. The two data centers were combined, and the manager felt that he had retained the best people for the new center.

---

other functions; this is suggested by the smaller arrow pointing to planning in Figure 6.1.

Throughout the planning process, the manager is making decisions and solving problems, focusing on current decisions that will lead to future results. The process is often difficult, not only in terms of solving the problems but from an emotional and ethical perspective as well, as this chapter's Ethical Management Challenge illustrates.

The Importance of Planning

Planning is fundamental to the success of the organization for several reasons. It helps the organization, as well as the individuals and groups within it, think about and prepare for the future, and especially for future change. As the rate of change increases, planning becomes more important and more difficult. It results in the establishment of performance objectives that can be used to measure progress, and it provides motivation. Planning is the primary basis for the other management functions: organizing, leading, and controlling. It initiates systematic, proactive problem solving, as opposed to reactive decision making, and provides for the integration of organizational, group, and individual efforts.

Levels of Planning

Planning occurs at the organization's three major levels: top, middle, and lower. As shown in Figure 6.2, at the top level the manager is concerned with strategic planning—the planning that has a significant impact on the organization as a

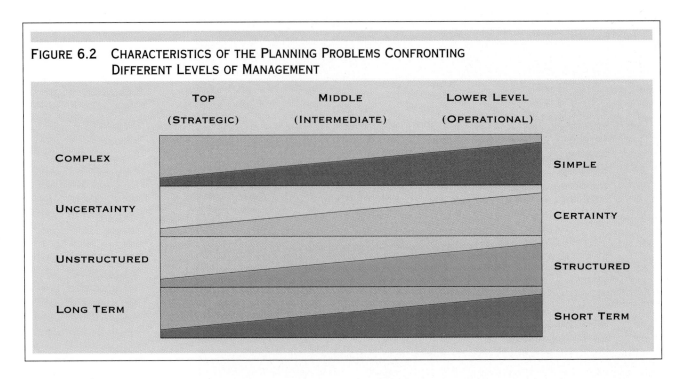

FIGURE 6.2   CHARACTERISTICS OF THE PLANNING PROBLEMS CONFRONTING
DIFFERENT LEVELS OF MANAGEMENT

whole and usually involves a major commitment of resources. Middle- and lower-level managers are concerned primarily with implementing these strategic plans. Their goal is to achieve the most effective and efficient use of an organization's resources in carrying out its strategic plans.

Figure 6.2 shows that the planning problems confronting top management are more complex, have a higher degree of uncertainty, are more unique and unstructured, and cover longer periods than those confronting middle- and front-line managers. This is not to say that such problems occur only at top management levels. They may occur at other levels as well. Nor is it to say that top managers do not face some simple, certain, routine, structured, and short-term problems. They do. Normally, however, the characteristics of the planning problems confronting the various levels of management are as shown in Figure 6.2.

Top managers usually face a myriad of interdepartmental environmental variables, such as how to allocate resources within the organization. They usually are uncertain about the likelihood of various events taking place and almost always face situations that are not likely to recur and for which no simple rule will work. Top managers usually plan one to three years in advance. They may also engage in very general, visionary "strategic thinking"—simply thinking about the environment and making plans for coping with it over the next few years.[4] Middle managers typically plan a few months to two years in advance. Lower-level managers normally plan a few weeks to a year in advance. It should come as no surprise that top managers also spend much more time planning than managers at other levels.

Middle- and lower-level managers work within the policies and strategies created by top management. Managers at these two levels are concerned with implementing those policies and strategies; they are often required to achieve specific objectives but are usually allowed to develop their own plans (although sometimes they are given the plans). Their principal concerns are not *what* must be done but *who* should do it, *where* and *when* it should be accomplished, and *how* it should be achieved. Lower- and middle-level managers make significant

TABLE 6.1 Selected Plans Created by Each Level of Management

Top-Level Management

Chief Executive Officer (CEO)

5-year strategic vision

3-year strategy for acquiring other businesses

3-year strategy for developing an advantage over competition

Chief Operating Officer

3-year capital budget for purchasing major items such as plant and equipment

2-year operating budget—revenues and expenses

1-year plan for acquiring other businesses

Marketing Executive

3-year marketing plan

Production Executive

3-year plan for how many plants and how much equipment will be needed to sustain operations

Human Resource Management Executive

3-year staffing plan

Chief Financial Officer

3-year plan describing how much cash will be needed by the company

1-year operating budget

Middle-Level Management

Sales Manager

1-year sales plan

Financial Manager

1-year plan for providing cash to build facilities

Human Resource Management Manager

1-year recruitment plan

Lower-Level Management

Regional Sales Manager

1-year sales plan for Midwest region

Financial Investments Officer

1-year plan to achieve 20% return on investments

Human Resource Management Manager of Training and Development

1-year plan to train 220 managers in organizational culture management

inputs into the information system used by top managers to develop strategic plans. Lower-level managers make similar inputs into the information system used by middle-level managers to make intermediate-level plans. Table 6.1 provides a list of plans that might typically be generated by selected managers at each level of an organization with only one major business.

Standing Versus Single-Use Plans

Plans are classified as either standing plans or single-use plans. Both types are used to pursue organizational goals and objectives, but in very different ways, as Figure 6.3 suggests.

STANDING PLANS

Standing plans guide activities that recur over time. There are three principal types of standing plans: policies, procedures, and rules and regulations.

Policies are plans that provide general guidance. They vary from one organization to another, both in which subjects are covered by policies and in how the issues relating to a subject will be treated. For instance, many companies have policies permitting managers to give subordinates time off to go to college, but how much time they can take and how frequently are among the issues that are likely to be treated differently by each business.

Policies: Plans that provide general guidance.

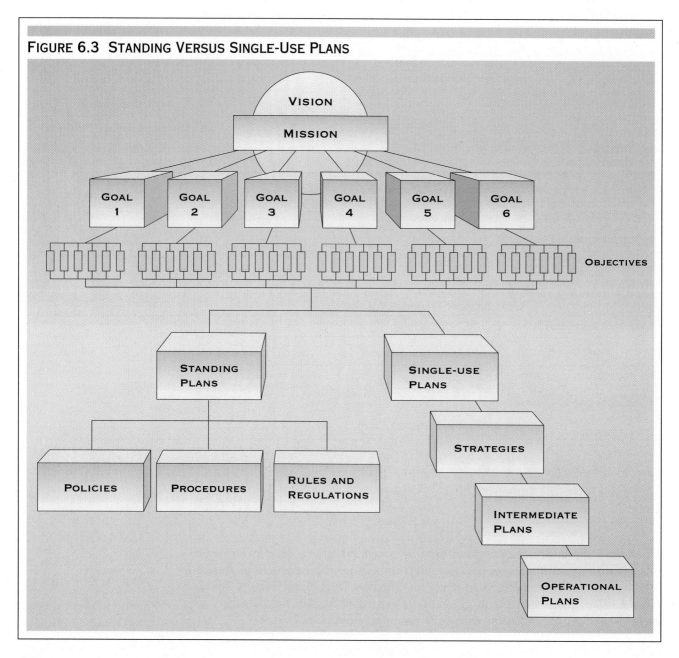

FIGURE 6.3 STANDING VERSUS SINGLE-USE PLANS

Procedures are plans that describe the exact series of actions to be taken in a given situation. For example, many companies have a policy of at least partially reimbursing employees for educational expenses. When this occurs, the employee must follow a set procedure in order to be reimbursed. He or she may have to fill out company Form 1063, attach a copy of his or her grades, take both documents to the personnel office for processing, and wait for the check to arrive in the mail. Companies may have hundreds, if not thousands, of procedures.

Rules and regulations are plans that describe exactly how one particular situation is to be handled. "No smoking" is a rule. Whereas policies guide decision making, procedures and rules make the decision for you. Procedures and rules differ primarily in what they apply to. Procedures describe a series of steps to accomplish a particular objective, whereas rules state an action to be taken (or not taken) in response to a certain situation.

SINGLE-USE PLANS

Single-use plans are used once and then discarded. In some cases, it may take ten years to carry out such a plan. In other situations, this type of plan could be carried out in a single day. There are three types of single-use plans: strategies, intermediate plans, and operational or operating plans. (See Figure 6.3.)

STRATEGIES

Strategies are major plans that commit large amounts of the oganization's resources to proposed actions designed to achieve its major goals and objectives. Managers are often concerned with three levels of strategy:[5]

1. A **corporate strategy** is a strategic plan that identifies the business or businesses in which an organization will engage and how it will conduct that business. When Compaq Computers determined that it needed to develop and diversify its products, it was establishing a corporate strategy.[6]

2. A **business strategy** is a strategic plan that indicates how an organization competes in a particular business. If an organization has more than one business, each is referred to as a **strategic**

Procedures: Plans that describe the exact series of actions to be taken in a given situation.

Rules and regulations: Plans that describe exactly how a particular situation is to be handled.

Single-use plans: Plans that are used once and discarded.

Strategies: Major plans that commit large amounts of the organization's resources to proposed actions designed to achieve its major goals and objectives.

Corporate strategy: A strategic plan that identifies the business (or businesses) an organization will engage in and how it will fundamentally conduct that business.

Business strategy: A strategic plan that indicates how an organization competes in a particular business.

When Compaq Computers—whose chairman, Ben Rosen, is shown here—determined that it needed to develop and diversify its products, it was establishing a corporate strategy.

Strategic business unit (SBU): A business within a multibusiness organization that serves a particular set of customers with a group of products or services that are distinct from those offered by other SBUs in the same organization.

Functional strategy: A strategic plan that states how an organization can use its resources most effectively and efficiently to carry out corporate and business strategies.

Intermediate plans: Plans that help translate strategy into operations.

Program: An intermediate plan that covers a broad set of activities.

Project: Usually a subset of a program; the term is sometimes used as a substitute for program.

Product plans: Plans that cover the activities related to a project for a set period, often a year.

Divisional plans: Plans for an organization's major divisions—for example, the marketing plan for the year.

Operating plans: Plans that deal with day-to-day operations, typically for a period of less than one year.

Annual operating plan: The one-year plan of action that states how a strategy will be implemented.

business unit (SBU). Each SBU serves a particular set of customers with a group of products or services distinct from those offered by other SBUs in the same organization. However, most companies compete in only one business. Having determined that it wanted to expand its paper business, Georgia-Pacific moved rapidly to add many new products and market them in a more sophisticated way. This was a business strategy.[7]

3. A **functional strategy** is a strategic plan that addresses how an organization can use its resources most effectively and efficiently to carry out corporate and business strategies. Typical areas addressed by functional strategies are marketing, finance, operations, human resources, information management, R&D, and management. Wal-Mart, for example, emphasizes low prices, cost cutting, and service—functional strategies aimed at keeping it the number 1 retailer in the United States.[8]

INTERMEDIATE PLANS

Intermediate plans, sometimes called *tactics,* help translate strategy into operations. These plans normally commit far fewer resources than strategies do. Again, there are several types of intermediate plans. The main types follow:

1. A **program** covers a large set of activities.[9] An example is Intel's development of the 486 computer chip.
2. A **project** is usually a subset of a program; the term is sometimes used as a substitute for *program.* When British Airways undertook a program to recapture business by providing superior service, one of the projects was to establish a business class lounge—which has been a huge success.[10]
3. **Product plans** cover the activities related to a product for a set period, often a year. As part of its product plan, Caesar's World spent $150 million to modernize its Las Vegas casino to make it more competitive with newer casinos.[11]
4. **Divisional plans** are plans for an organization's major divisions— for example, the marketing plan for the year, or the plan for one of the product divisions for the year. Thus, each year Red Lobster, a major division of General Mills, must develop a plan to guide its operations.

OPERATING PLANS

Operating plans deal with day-to-day operations, typically for a time frame of less than one year. They commit far fewer resources than strategies or intermediate plans. There are several types of operating plans:

1. The **annual operating plan** is the one-year plan of action that states how strategy will be implemented. It applies to the whole organization but commits resources for only one year. At Mrs. Fields' Cookies, for example, the annual operating plan is input into a computer. Progress is checked against the plan each day.[12]
2. The **budget** is the annual operating plan, together with the revenues and expenses anticipated for each of the actions necessary to carry out the plan. For example, Parker-Hannifin, an important manufacturer of fluid power systems and components, emphasizes strategic cost accounting—and, hence, budgets—in making operating decisions.[13]

3. A **departmental plan** is typically, but not necessarily, a department's annual operating plan. Departmental plans may include longer- or shorter-term plans that apply to the entire department. In a large law firm, for example, the litigation department will have an annual operating plan detailing expected billings and expenses.

4. A **group plan** is developed for a work group. Typically, but not necessarily, it consists of the group's intended actions for carrying out its part of the annual operating plan. For example, new-venture teams at General Foods plants develop plans to speed product development.[14]

5. An **individual plan** is developed by an individual to contribute to the accomplishment of the organization's objectives. For example, at Cypress Semiconductor, individual employees develop plans for achieving weekly objectives, all aimed at achieving longer-term corporate objectives.[15]

Criteria for Plans

Regardless of the type or level of planning, the manager must test the plan against a variety of criteria. It is important to ensure that the complexity and comprehensiveness of the plan are appropriate. The plan's likely impact must be kept in mind, as well as the need for both quantitative and qualitative content. The manager must also be aware of whether strategic or operational perspectives are involved and whether the plan can be revealed publicly or should remain confidential. Other factors that should be considered are what parts of the plan are written and unwritten and whether it is formal or informal. The manager should also evaluate the plan in terms of ease of implementation, balance of rationality and creativity, and flexibility. Finally, it is important to be aware of the cost of carrying out the plan.

In the rest of this section we will take a closer look at each of these criteria.

COMPLEXITY VERSUS SIMPLICITY

GM's strategic decision to spend $40 billion (it eventually spent $77 billion) to upgrade technology to make the company more competitive was a complex plan. It led to thousands of additional strategic, intermediate, and operational plans. It required a tremendous amount of coordination, and its implementation consumed hundreds of millions of hours.[16] In contrast, an example of a simple plan might be the daily schedule of one of the work groups seeking to achieve a small part of that complex plan.

COMPREHENSIVE VERSUS NARROW COVERAGE

Comprehensive plans have broader coverage than narrow ones; they affect a larger portion of the organization, and they tend to be concerned with corporate, business, or functional strategies, as opposed to departmental, group, or individual plans. An example of a comprehensive plan is Coors Beer's strategy of entering several diverse businesses.[17] (Coors later decided to sell those businesses.)[18] A narrower plan would be one in which a division of an insurance company chose to employ a lower price and intensive personal selling over a two-month period in order to increase sales by 20 percent.

MAJOR VERSUS MINOR IMPORTANCE

Strategic plans are very significant; operational plans are less so. North Carolina National Bank's acquisition of C&S/Sovran was a major plan. The result was a huge new bank, Nation's Bank, which is now the United States' fourth largest.[19]

Budget: The annual operating plan, together with the revenues and expenses anticipated for each of the actions necessary to carry out a plan.

Departmental plan: Typically, a department's annual operating plan; it may include longer- or shorter-term plans that apply to the whole department.

Group plan: A plan developed for a particular group—typically, but not necessarily, the actions it will pursue in carrying out its part of the annual operating plan.

Individual plan: A plan developed by an individual to contribute to accomplishing the organization's objectives.

GM's strategic decision to spend $40 billion (it eventually spent $77 billion) to upgrade technology and make the company more competitive was a complex plan. One product of the upgrade plan is the control room of General Motors' highly automated Saginaw Vanguard plant.

Decisions about how to change office procedures when the acquisition was complete were part of a minor plan for managers at C&S/Sovran.

QUALITATIVE VERSUS QUANTITATIVE PLANS

Most business plans are not entirely quantitative. Many involve complex qualitative judgments as well. For example, when Microsoft decided to take its stock public, its manager established a range of values for the stock that would be acceptable. The plan included the goal of achieving a stock offering price within that range—a value based not only on a quantitative examination of the organization's financial condition, but also on qualitative forecasts of the organization's future.[20]

STRATEGIC VERSUS OPERATIONAL PLANS

Strategic plans involve significant commitments of resources. Operational plans employ considerably fewer resources. Thus, when the Federal Aviation Agency (FAA) awarded Harris Corporation a $1.66 billion contract to help revamp air traffic control systems, the award was part of the FAA's strategic plan for overhauling the $15 billion system. Securing the contract was part of Harris's strategic plan to diversify away from the defense industry. Harris also had a carefully thought out operational plan that enabled it to win the contract in the final year of a long bidding war with AT&T.[21]

CONFIDENTIAL VERSUS PUBLIC PLANS

Confidential plans are proprietary. Most major companies make their strategic plans available to the public, at least in a general way. Almost all announce their strategic goals, often in their annual reports. IBM, for example, has consistently listed its four cornerstone goals as growth, product leadership, efficiency, and profitability.[22] These goals are so vague and broad that competitors cannot use their knowledge of them to gain an advantage. However, the specifics of an organization's plan would be useful to competitors and therefore are kept confidential. IBM is extremely concerned about industrial espionage and has established high levels of security at many of its facilities in order to protect its confidential plans.[23]

IBM is extremely secretive about its plans. It has established high levels of security to protect its confidential plans about new products like the liquid crystal display shown here.

WRITTEN VERSUS UNWRITTEN PLANS

Many plans, especially those made at lower levels of the organization, are unwritten. Aspects of a plan are often unwritten but assumed. For example, a supervisor for Bell Labs may read the strategic plan, the related policies, and the intermediate plans he or she is given and from them determine a work schedule for the upcoming year. From time to time, the manager may make verbal changes in that schedule.

FORMAL VERSUS INFORMAL PLANS

Most smaller organizations, such as your local print shop, manufacturing company, or record store, have informal plans. The plans of entrepreneurial organizations are usually carried in their owner's head. Many times, these are not really plans but simply reactions to events. Most larger organizations—IBM, Hewlett-Packard, American Airlines, the U.S. Department of Agriculture, the Teamsters Union, and others—have formal written plans that were drawn up as a consequence of an established series of procedures.

EASE VERSUS DIFFICULTY OF IMPLEMENTATION

Some plans are very easy to implement; others are not. The manager is responsible for ensuring that a plan can be implemented and that ease of implementation has been considered as part of the planning process. Japanese firms spend significantly more time on planning for implementation of a plan than American firms do.[24]

RATIONAL VERSUS CREATIVE PLANNING

The planning process must be both rational and creative. As we saw in Chapter 4, creativity is part of any problem-solving process, but the changing nature of the organizational environment makes creativity even more important than it once was. The increased rate of change, the increasing level of competition, the nature of decision making in the computer age, and the edge that intuitive managers have in making decisions combine to put a premium on creativity. This is why companies like Apple Computer make an effort to instill creativity in all members of its organization. Even Apple's names for its conference rooms—Lust, Envy, Greed—are designed to promote motivation and creativity.[25]

FLEXIBLE VERSUS INFLEXIBLE PLANS

In the changing management environment, managers must create more flexible plans. It must be possible to adjust a plan smoothly and quickly to the requirements of changing conditions.[26] For example, Boeing knows that for years it has made a considerable portion of its profits (70 percent) from the 747 aircraft. Management realized that it had to be flexible to remain competitive in the aircraft market. However, it had difficulty being flexible enough to meet the challenge posed by Europe's Airbus, which is heavily subsidized by its owner governments.[27] The importance of flexibility cannot be overstated. The executives in charge of strategic planning at General Electric, for example, suggest that attempting to forecast beyond three years is folly. Even over a three-year period, situations change so rapidly that strategic planning provides direction, not hard-and-fast plans.[28] With such short time horizons, flexibility is crucial.

COST

One of the key factors involved in implementing plans is their cost. Appropriate cost estimates must be attached to plans so that their cost can be held to a reasonable level.

Planning and Control

Planning and control are inseparably linked. The standards established in planning are used to determine whether the desired results were achieved.[29] A plan is not likely to be implemented successfully without some mechanism of control. In most organizations, the budget is the device most frequently used to control performance. A well-thought-out budget integrates an organization's strategy, structure, management, and resources, and the tasks it must accomplish.[30] Across all economic functions of the organization—marketing, finance, operations, and human resources—the objectives established in planning provide the basis for control. The control process is often improved if those who must implement the plan participate in the planning process.

SWOT Analysis

Before making a decision, the decision maker performs a situational analysis. The contents of that analysis depend on the level of management involved—top, middle, or lower. In virtually any planning situation the manager is looking for problems to solve, and in many cases the problems are opportunities. An **opportunity** is a chance to improve the organization's situation significantly—for example, a change in customer demographics that might lead to more sales. The problems encountered may also be threats or weaknesses. A **threat** is an external environmental situation, such as a new competitor, that may keep an organization from achieving its objectives. **Weaknesses** are internal situations—such as poorly trained employees—that might keep the firm from achieving its objectives. To achieve its objectives, the organization must rely on its **strengths**—internal situations, such as high cash reserves—to overcome threats, overcome weaknesses, and take advantage of opportunities. Examining these four factors—strengths, weaknesses, opportunities, and threats, or SWOT—produces a situational analysis.[31]

At the upper levels of the organization, the manager's focus is largely external. In a single-business organization the manager is concerned primarily with competing in the marketplace. In organizations composed of several business units, upper-level managers are concerned with managing the company's "portfolio" of businesses. The top-level manager of each business unit is concerned with competing in his or her business. Farther down in the organizational hierar-

AT GA: At General Accident, the culture now fosters planning. It also fosters creativity. This combination creates an internal environment in which the company can meet the challenges of an ever-changing external environment.

AT GA: At General Accident, authority is decentralized. Regional and branch managers are allowed to develop their own plans of action to achieve objectives. However, the company controls performance very closely.

Opportunity: A chance to improve the organization's situation significantly.

Threat: An external environmental situation that may keep an organization from achieving its objectives.

Weaknesses: Internal situations that might keep the firm from achieving its objectives.

Strengths: Internal situations that will help an organization achieve its objectives, overcome threats, overcome weaknesses, and take advantage of opportunities.

chy, managers are more concerned with specific organizational functions. Their plans usually have a more internal focus (unless they are in such areas as sales or purchasing). Goals and objectives, strategies, policies, procedures, and rules are already defined for middle- and operational-level managers. Their planning must occur within these constraints and guidelines; upper-level managers, on the other hand, look to vision, mission, and goals and some policies in formulating the strategies and key results expected of others.

In planning at all levels, the manager is searching for the key set of factors that will help identify the real problem. An important factor for a middle- or operational-level manager is the upper-level manager to whom he or she reports; it is this individual who defines the conditions under which the manager must operate. Similarly, at upper levels, a board of directors, a chairman of the board, or a CEO may be a key factor in the situation. SWOT analysis is discussed further in Chapter 7.

The Limitations of Planning

There are several limitations on the planning process. Managers must be aware of them and take action to overcome them.[32] Among the most important barriers to planning is the fact that external environmental events cannot always be controlled. In addition, there may be internal resistance to planning. Other problems that may have to be overcome include the fact that planning is difficult and expensive; the tendency to focus on current crises; and the failure to understand the weaknesses of the premises on which a plan is based. We will now take a closer look at each of these limitations.

EXTERNAL ENVIRONMENTS

In the early 1990s, the number of people taking the Graduate Management Aptitude Test (GMAT) declined, and so did the number of applicants to graduate programs in business. Business executives were complaining about the high salaries of people with MBAs and the increasing difficulty of placing such people in sufficiently challenging jobs. Numerous articles reported that there was an oversupply of MBAs, and demographic studies suggested that fewer students would seek higher education in the future. Many MBA program executives lowered their expectations for future enrollments and did not increase their schools' faculties or expand their facilities. As a result, if the demand for MBAs does increase in the mid-1990s, many programs will be unprepared to take advantage of the opportunity. Demand is often an uncontrollable external environmental factor.

INTERNAL RESISTANCE

Without the proper levels of participation and careful planning for implementation, proposed plans and objectives will invariably be resisted by some members of the organization. For example, in the information system division of a major entertainment company, a new, systematic approach to planning for the division was resisted by employees, primarily out of fear. People were uncertain about the many changes occurring within the division. Some of the changes involved critical skills, causing many employees to wonder whether their jobs would exist in a few weeks. They were not trying to sabotage the program, but they were concerned enough so that they did not support the program as fully as top management would have liked.[33]

COST

Effective planning requires a lot of time and energy. The more committed to planning an organization is, the more time and energy it devotes to it. Moreover, in today's managerial environment, plans have to be updated constantly to take advantage of, or react to, rapidly changing situations. The cost of planning will rise as a result, but the cost of being unprepared will be still higher.

CURRENT CRISES

Managers in many American firms seem constantly to be dealing with current crises. Many such crises occur because of poor or no planning. Many others occur because of uncontrollable environmental circumstances, such as government policy actions, technological changes, or a competitor's marketing strategy. Managers need to develop new ways of planning so that they can react effectively to such events.

WEAK PREMISES

Premises: Assumptions about a situation and the future condition of factors in that situation that must be made as part of the planning process but should not be made without thorough consideration.

Premises, or assumptions about a situation and the future condition of factors in that situation, must be made as part of the planning process, but they should not be made without thorough consideration. Premises also need to be continually reevaluated to make sure they are still relevant. This chapter's Management Challenge reveals how Komatsu Ltd. assumed that it could compete in global markets on the basis of quality and price. It did not expect U.S.-based Caterpillar Inc. to match it, but Caterpillar did. Now Komatsu seeks to diversify, having reconsidered its assumptions.

THE DIFFICULTY OF PLANNING

As noted earlier, planning requires a tremendous amount of creativity, as well as a rational and analytical capability. Many variables must be considered, and plans are often based on uncertain assumptions. Moreover, planning is often very time consuming. Two hundred pages of documentation may be necessary for important purchases or programs, and hundreds or even thousands of em-

almost since its formation. Komatsu Dresser's unit market share dropped from 20.3 to 18 percent between 1990 and 1991. Caterpillar's U.S. market share rose from 34.5 to 36.4 percent in the same period.

"The proverbial synergy that was supposed to develop [between Komatsu and Dresser] never materialized," says one industry analyst.

Komatsu Dresser's chief operating officer, Masahiro Sakane, says that the U.S. venture is "on track" to be profitable when the recession ends, but he acknowledges that "both parent companies are not pleased we are losing money." The venture's 1991 operating loss widened to $74 million from $14 million in 1990, as sales fell by 25 percent, to $1.01 billion from $1.35 billion.

In response, Dresser plans to bail out, spinning off to shareholders its half-share in the venture. Dresser expects to concentrate on oil and gas services.

Komatsu realizes that its planned diversification could divide its resources but maintains that the company must accept that risk if it wants to grow. The determination to diversify is so strong that executives ordered the removal of the bulldozer that once sat on top of the company's downtown headquarters. Explains the official in charge of international operations, "Komatsu isn't only for a bulldozer anymore."

SOURCES: Thomas N. Cochran, "Cat Fancier," *Barron's* (July 9, 1990), p. 30; Ronald Henkoff, "This Cat Is Acting Like a Tiger," *Fortune* (December 19, 1988), pp. 70–76; and Robert L. Rose and Masayoshi Kanabayashi, "Komatsu Throttles Back on Construction Equipment," *Wall Street Journal*, May 13, 1992, p. B–4.

ployee hours may be required to create them. Meanwhile, the managerial environment is changing. Planning is especially difficult for European firms that are trying to adjust to the 1992 initiative (see Chapter 3) and the globalization of business. Volkswagen's efforts to make this adjustment are described in this chapter's Global Management Challenge.

Komatsu Ltd. did not expect U.S.-based Caterpillar Inc. to match its prices and quality in the global market, but Caterpillar succeeded in doing so. To achieve these goals, Caterpillar had to greatly increase its productivity, especially by cutting costs.

Volkswagen's Plans for Global Competition

According to the *Harvard Business Review*, Volkswagen AG could be the most daring company in Europe today. This claim is based on the breathtaking program of expansion the firm has undertaken since the early 1980s. The automaker is building or refitting plants from East Germany to China and from Mexico to Spain.

The appetite for keener global competition seems no less breathtaking in light of its price: $35 billion—$7 billion a year on average, which is $3 billion more than the company's reported annual cash flow.

The expansion represents the strategic vision of Carl H. Hahn, chairman of the board of management since 1982. Under his leadership, in addition to Volkswagen and Audi, the company acquired the Spanish carmaker Seat in 1986 and Czechoslovakia's Skoda in 1990.

Hahn believes that Europe is a microcosm of the world in the 1990s, and that by concentrating on the European market—where it already boasts the largest market share of any automaker, 15 percent—Volkswagen will be situating itself on an unparalleled platform for global competition.

The watchword of Hahn's faith is *federalism.* He plans to turn Volkswagen into a federated European company—a true multinational. The firm will offer a wider variety of cars and build them in comparatively low-wage regions.

"Profits nowadays come mostly by satisfying narrower and narrower groups of customers," he says. "We want to be able to customize closer to where European drivers acquire and express their tastes. Norway is not Spain. We want integrated factories and design centers to offer consumers the touches they really want."

Hahn believes that the other half of the plan—reducing costs—can be accomplished because Europe is varied: It now comprises higher- and lower-cost

Why Planning Fails

Planning can fail for a number of reasons. Managers must be prepared to overcome or anticipate a variety of problems. Among these are lack of commitment to planning, failure to implement plans properly, failure to see planning as both a rational and a creative process, absence of proper controls, poor leadership, and resistance to change. Also contributing to failure in some cases is the lack of a planning approach for use in complex, changing environments.

Establishing an Environment Conducive to Planning

The planning process itself must be planned, organized, led, and controlled if it is to succeed. There must be a planning system, and it must be adhered to. The organization should establish a culture that is receptive to planning—that not only encourages it but demands it, facilitates it, and rewards it. Such a culture encourages top managers to review the plans of their subordinates, who in turn review the plans of those working under them. Individuals should be recognized and rewarded when they reach planned goals and encouraged, through delegated authority and an emphasis on risk taking, to participate in the process.

regions, more and less developed countries. Volkwagen pays its German workers upward of $25 to $28 an hour. By contrast, the Skoda factory provides a "particularly wonderful opportunity," Hahn says. Engineering skills are high, but costs and wages aren't.

Compared with most European auto companies, which are nationally oriented, Volkswagen has always had to think beyond Germany and even Europe, Hahn notes. It has never had a protected market at home and has always had to develop markets abroad. In retrospect, he observes, "this imperative to globalize has been advantageous to us."

Americans may be unaware of Volkswagen's strength because the company did not do well here in the late 1980s—it commands only 1.5 percent of the market—but, "We are number 1 in Europe," Hahn says. "We have more than held our own in Canada. We are number 1 by far in Mexico, as well as Brazil. By investing in several ventures in China, where we have also become the number 1 car manufacturer, we have established an important starting position in Asia. . . . We are also . . . the number one importer [in Japan], though this still amounts to about 50,000 cars a year."

Another component of the plan is an ever-increasing commitment to traditional German automation. At the company's headquarters in Wolfsburg, where about 60 percent of the Volkswagen Group's 3 million cars were made in 1990, 1,200 company-made robots complete about 80 percent of each car's assembly. Automation has resulted in a significant improvement in quality, as machines check machines. It also humanizes the workplace, as workers supervise overall quality and concentrate on customization and trim. Automation also increases manufacturing flexibility: Because robots can be programmed to perform a variety of tasks, during one run a production line can make a variety of models with different features.

SOURCE: Bernard Avishai, "A European Platform for Global Competition: An Interview with VW's Carl Hahn," *Harvard Business Review* (July–Agust 1991), pp. 103–113.

Organizational Purpose

There are several types of organizational purposes, which are shown in Figure 6.4. The organization's most general purpose, with the broadest scope, is its vision. Its mission, goals, and objectives are more specific and narrower in scope.

Vision and Mission

Managers today are increasingly recognizing the need to have a "vision" of what the organization is to become.[34] **Vision** is nonspecific directional and motivational guidance for the entire organization; it is normally provided by an organization's CEO. It describes where the company is going in the most general terms, but it must also provide emotional direction.[35] Most visions are aimed at improving the organization's competitive standing.[36] To be effective, visions must be inspiring; they must also be clear and challenging. "To make a contribution to the world by making tools for the mind that advance mankind" was Steven Jobs's vision for Apple Computer. This was a compelling statement of direction.

Based on the opinions of corporate CEOs, James C. Collins and Jerry F.

Vision: Nonspecific directional and motivational guidance for the entire organization.

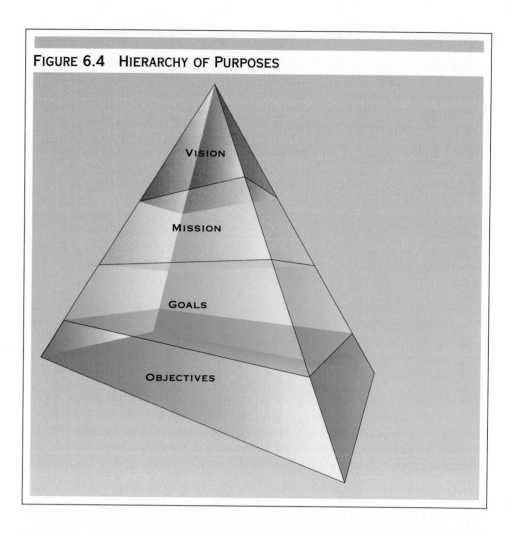

FIGURE 6.4 HIERARCHY OF PURPOSES

VISION

MISSION

GOALS

OBJECTIVES

Porras expand the definition of vision to include a guiding philosophy.[37] This is consistent with the increasing importance being given to organizational values.

A company's vision often changes when its CEO changes, other organizations are acquired or merged, the environment changes, or management challenges are encountered. While it may seem easy to conceive of a vision, this is not the case. The CEO must spend sufficient time to make the vision clear and compelling.[38]

Mission: A broad statement of business scope and operations that distinguishes an organization from other, similar organizations.

An organization's **mission** is its reason for being. Mission adds specificity to vision. It is easy to say that an organization's mission is to make money or to serve society, but these are not true mission statements. Rather, as Philip Kotler and John A. Pearce, II, suggest, an organization's mission is its widely stated definition of its basic business scope and operations, a definition that distinguishes it from other similar organizations.[39] The primary thrust of an organization's mission statement is external: It focuses on customers, markets, and fields of endeavor. Every objective, every plan, and every action of every individual and group in the organization should be developed and carried out with the organizational mission in mind.

The exact nature of a mission statement varies from one organization to another. Some mission statements include descriptions of basic corporate concerns, such as product quality, location of a facility, and perceived strategic advantage. Many mission statements reveal not simply purpose but philosophy as well. Research by Pearce and Fred David suggests that the more comprehensive the mission statement, the more likely the firm is to make a profit.[40] Andrew

Lexmark International Inc.'s CEO, Marvin Mann, is shown here meeting with a team of employees at the company's Lexington, Kentucky, facility, where it manufactures laser printers, typewriters, and keyboards. Every objective, plan, and action of every individual and group in an organization like Lexmark International should be developed and carried out with the organization's mission in mind.

Campbell and Sally Yeung of the Ashridge Strategic Management Center in England have concluded that a mission statement should contain four elements: "Purpose—why the company exists; strategy—the competitive position and distinctive competence of the organization; behavior standards—the policies and behavior patterns that underpin the distinctive competence and the value system; and values—what the company believes in."[41] Table 6.2 presents representative portions of organization mission statements.

Periodically, organizations redefine their mission or purpose. In the last twenty years, probably no organization has had to change its mission more dramatically than AT&T. When the government's policy of deregulation became effective in 1984, the company's goals, objectives, strategies, plans, and culture—its whole way of life—were changed. All of those changes were embodied in its planning process: the process of establishing vision, mission, goals, and objectives and the plans for achieving them. As this chapter's Ethical Management Challenge reveals, the changes had a profound impact.

Although the process of establishing a mission statement might seem to be a simple one, it is not. As Pearce notes, "The critical role of the company mission as the basis of orchestrating managerial actions is repeatedly demonstrated by failing firms whose short-run actions are ultimately found to be counterproductive to the long-run purpose."[42] Because employees look to the corporate mission for guidance, the mission statement can significantly affect the organization's future. Recognizing the importance of the mission statement, Compaq Computer's CEO, Eckhard Pfeiffer, recently changed the company's mission to include a focus on customer satisfaction; he felt that the change was necessary to reverse a decline in sales.[43]

Goals and Objectives

An organization's **goals** are refinements of its mission. Goals are more specific than mission and address key issues within the organization, such as market standing, innovation, productivity, physical and financial resources, profitability, management performance and development, worker performance and attitude, public responsibility,[44] treatment of employees, growth, efficiency, treatment of customers, and returns to owners.[45] However, goals are not as specific

Goals: Refinements of an organization's mission that address key issues within the organization.

TABLE 6.2 Mission Statement Components

1. Customer Market	We believe our first responsibility is to the doctors, nurses, and patients, to mothers and all others who use our products and services. (Johnson & Johnson)
2. Product/Service	AMAX's principal products are molybdenum, coal, iron ore, copper, lead, zinc, petroleum and natural gas, potash, phosphates, nickel, tungsten, silver, gold, and magnesium. (AMAX)
3. Geographic Domain	We are dedicated to the total success of Corning Glass Works as a worldwide competitor. (Corning Glass)
4. Technology	Control Data is in the business of applying microelectronics and computer technology in two general areas: computer-related hardware and computing-enhancing services, which include computation, information, education, and finance. (Control Data)
5. Concern for Survival	In this respect, the company will conduct its operations prudently and will provide the profits and growth which will assure Hoover's ultimate success. (Hoover Universal)
6. Philosophy	We believe human development to be the worthiest of the goals of civilization and independence to be the superior condition for nurturing growth in the capabilities of people. (Sun Company)
7. Self-concept	Hoover Universal is a diversified, multi-industry corporation with strong manufacturing capabilities, entrepreneurial policies, and individual business unit autonomy. (Hoover Universal)
8. Concern for Public Image	Also, we must be responsive to the broader concerns of the public, including especially the general desire for improvement in the quality of life, equal opportunity for all, and the constructive use of natural resources. (Sun Company)

SOURCE: J. A. Pearce, II, and F. R. David, "Corporate Mission Statements: The Bottom Line," *Academy of Management Executive* (May 1987), vol. 1, no. 2, pp. 109–116.

as objectives. They are open-ended statements of purpose to be used when managers do not want to become entangled in specifics.[46] Goals help describe an organization's philosophy. **Objectives** are specific statements of anticipated results that further define the organization's goals. Typically, each goal is subdivided into a set of very specific objectives. Thus, if the goal is to increase sales, the specific objective might be a 5 percent increase in the first year.

Objectives: Specific statements of anticipated results that further define the organization's goals.

THE IMPORTANCE OF GOALS AND OBJECTIVES

Goals are important because they allow the organization to explain its mission in philosophical terms. Some of Hewlett-Packard's goals are presented in Table 6.3.

Objectives are important to the organization for eight reasons:[47]

1. They provide specific direction.
2. They provide for the integration of employee actions.
3. They provide mechanisms for control. Objectives are typically broken down into standards of performance. Workers are held accountable for meeting those standards.[48]
4. They motivate those who are assigned the task of accomplishing them.
5. They help relieve boredom by providing a way of keeping score.
6. Feedback on the attainment of objectives can help provide recognition.
7. Achieving objectives helps raise self-esteem.
8. Achieving objectives, when combined with feedback, can lead to

TABLE 6.3 Hewlett-Packard's 1992 Goals

1. Profit Objective: To achieve sufficient profit to finance company growth and to provide the resources we need to achieve our other corporate objectives.

2. Customer Objective: To provide products and services of the highest quality and the greatest possible value to our customers, thereby gaining and holding their respect and loyalty.

3. Fields of Interest Objective: To participate in those fields of interest that build upon our technology and customer base, that offer opportunities for continuing growth, and that enable us to make a needed and profitable contribution.

4. Growth Objective: To let growth be limited only by our profits and our ability to develop and produce innovative products that satisfy real customer needs.

5. Our People Objective: To help Hewlett-Packard people share in the company's success, which they make possible; to provide employment security based on their performance; to ensure them a safe and pleasant work environment; to recognize individual achievements; and to help them gain a sense of satisfaction and accomplishment from their work.

6. Management Objective: To foster initiative and creativity by allowing the individual great freedom of action in attaining well-defined objectives.

7. Citizenship Objective: To honor our obligations to society by being an economic, intellectual, and social asset to each nation and each community in which we operate.

SOURCE: Hewlett-Packard Company, Inc., Corporate Objectives, 1989, confirmed by company officials in 1992.

increased liking for the task and increased satisfaction with performance.

CHARACTERISTICS OF SOUND OBJECTIVES

Effective objectives possess four common characteristics: (1) the goal area or attribute sought, (2) an index for measuring progress toward the attribute, (3) a target to be achieved or a hurdle to be overcome, and (4) a time frame within which the target is to be achieved.[49] A sample of each of these characteristics is given in Table 6.4. These characteristics are relevant whether the objectives are set by top managers or by a front-line manager. They are also relevant for objectives that anyone might establish for personal planning purposes.

AT GA: General Accident develops very general goals, such as service, growth, and profit. Several specific objectives are then derived from each of those goals.

Goals are important because they allow the organization to explain its mission in philosophical terms. Objectives are typically broken down into standards of performance, and workers are held accountable for meeting those standards. These Hewlett-Packard employees operate almost totally autonomously.

TABLE 6.4 Characteristics of Effective Objectives

Possible Attributes	Possible Indices	Targets and Time Frame		
		Year 1	Year 2	Year 3
Growth	Dollar sales Unit sales	$100 million 1.00 × units	$120 million 1.10 × units	$140 million 1.20 × units
Efficiency	Dollar profits Profits/sales	$10 million 0.10	$12 million 0.10	$15 million 0.11
Utilization of resources	ROI ROE	0.15 0.25	0.15 0.26	0.16 0.27
Contributions to owners	Dividends per share Earnings per share	$1 $2	$1.10 $2.40	$1.30 $2.80
Contributions to customers	Price Quality Reliability	Equal to or better than competition	Equal to or better than competition	Equal to or better than competition
Contributions to employees	Wage rate Employment stability	$3.50/hour <5% turnover	$3.75/hour <4% turnover	$4.00/hour <4% turnover
Contributions to society	Taxes paid Scholarships awarded, etc.	$10 million $100,000	$12 million $120,000	$16 million $120,000

SOURCE: C. W. Hofer, "A Conceptual Scheme for Formulating a Total Business Strategy," no. BP-0040 (Dover, Mass.: Case Teacher's Association, 1976), p. 2. Copyright 1976 by C. W. Hofer. Reproduced by permission.

Managing by Objectives

Management by objectives (MBO): *A process in which objectives are determined and distributed to succeeding levels of management; managers at each level participate in the formulation of action plans; and the plans are implemented.*

Managing by objectives was first employed by General Motors in a system known as Managing for Results.[50] In the 1960s, it was popularized by management consultant and author George Odiorne as **management by objectives (MBO)**.[51] At one time, about half of the Fortune 500 industrial firms employed some form of MBO.[52] More recently, Heinz Weihrich has examined MBO systems as a way of instilling managerial excellence. One of his major contentions is that MBO must be integrated thoroughly into all the other organizational systems—strategic management, organizational development, and human resource development—to be effective.[53]

The MBO process is a relatively simple one, consisting of just a few steps at each level of management:

1. Objectives are determined and distributed to the next-lower level of management.
2. Action plans are formulated.
3. Some degree of participation occurs in setting objectives and formulating plans.
4. Implementation occurs.

In the remainder of this section we will take a closer look at each of these steps.

DETERMINING OBJECTIVES

As noted earlier, an organization's mission is defined in terms of goals. Goals, in turn, are further defined in terms of more specific objectives. Related subobjectives are established for each major function or division of the organization. Objectives are then distributed down the management hierarchy. This process occurs until each manager in the organization, as well as every other person in

PLANNING TAKES PLACE AT EVERY LEVEL OF THE ORGANIZATION AND IN A WIDE VARIETY OF ENVIRONMENTS. IT MAY INVOLVE FORMAL GROUP PROBLEM-SOLVING TECHNIQUES OR AN INFORMAL BULL SESSION OVER COFFEE. COMPUTERS PLAY AN IMPORTANT ROLE IN PLANNING TODAY, WHETHER IN THE OFFICE OR ON THE WAY TO A CONVENTION OR A MEETING WITH A CLIENT.

the organization who has control of the content of his or her job, has a particular share of each of the objectives established by top management.

Researchers Gary P. Latham and Gary Yukl have examined numerous studies of MBO and have reached the following conclusions:

1. The more specific the objective, the more likely it is that the level of performance will increase.
2. Difficult objectives, if they are accepted by the subordinate, stimulate higher levels of performance.
3. Setting objectives works well at both management and operative levels.
4. Whether objectives are assigned or established mutually by the manager and the subordinate, they serve to improve performance.[54]

An MBO system is most effective if there are between six and twelve objectives. If there are more than twelve, it is difficult to give each of them full consideration. Objectives should be challenging, but they should not be so demanding as to frighten, discourage, or create fear of failure. Research suggests that stating specific objectives—such as "Improve service levels by 5 percent" or "Cut customer complaints by 10 percent"—is more effective than simply saying "Do the best you can."[55]

DEVELOPING ACTION PLANS

Once objectives have been set for each level of the organization, plans must be formulated to accomplish them. Normally, managers formulate their own action plans, which are then approved by higher-level managers.

PARTICIPATION

One of the major issues in any MBO system is the degree to which the subordinate is involved in establishing objectives and plans. Although there is usually some room for negotiation, in most organizations top management suggests objectives to the next-lower level of management; those managers in turn suggest objectives to the level below them, and so on until all the managers and other employees involved in the system have received their objectives. On the other hand, in most organizations, the individual manager determines how to achieve the objectives. There is often a high level of participation in the total planning process. Managers who attempt to develop their subordinates' skills are more likely to allow them to participate in setting objectives.[56] In addition, managers are more likely to encourage participation by subordinates when it is necessary to respond quickly and frequently to changes in the environment.

IMPLEMENTATION OF ACTION PLANS

Implementing action plans is a very complex process at all levels of the organization. It involves leadership, communication, motivation, staffing, human resource management, culture management, systems management, and information management.

ADVANTAGES AND DISADVANTAGES OF MBO

MBO systems have both positive and negative aspects.[57] On the positive side, they often lead to increases in both the quantity and quality of performance. A study of seventy MBO programs found that productivity had increased in sixty-eight of them.[58] MBO can also improve communication and understanding, increase job satisfaction, and enhance individual growth. The clarification of role prescriptions that occurs as a result of MBO is a highly beneficial effect because people have a better understanding of what is expected of them. Finally, as noted earlier, objectives provide motivation.

The disadvantages of MBO include various problems with the objectives themselves: Objectives may be set too high or too low, may be inflexible, and are sometimes rejected. It also is difficult to set objectives in nonquantifiable areas, such as employee morale. Another disadvantage is that managers become more critical when using MBO and often use objectives as whips. In many MBO systems, rewards are not tied to performance or may be lacking altogether. Moreover, MBO is very time consuming and usually does not take group dynamics into consideration.

MBO has certain disadvantages for the individual as well as the organization. Each individual has physical and mental limitations that may not be taken into consideration when objectives are being established. On the other hand, objectives often place an upper limit on performance, even if that level could be exceeded.

Still another limitation of MBO is that it has historically worked best in a slowly changing environment. However, as we have seen at several points in the preceding chapters, the managerial environment is changing increasingly quickly. Under these conditions, MBO systems are likely to be less effective.

Although the disadvantages of MBO outnumber the advantages, the importance of the positive aspects should not be overlooked. Virtually all studies of MBO have found that the most common reasons for the failure of MBO programs are that the results are not evaluated; rewards are not tied to performance; and the program has not been implemented properly—for example, there has been too little or too much participation by lower-level managers or employees.[59]

Additional research by Robert Rogers and John E. Hunter suggests that the commitment of top management is essential to the success of an MBO program. When top management was highly committed, productivity increased by 56 percent. When top management was barely committed, productivity increased by only 6 percent.[60]

The benefits and liabilities of MBO are illustrated in this chapter's Innovation Management Challenge. Could you work in such an environment, under such a program?

Management by Objectives, Results, and Rewards (MBORR)

As already indicated, available evidence suggests that MBO does not always produce the desired results, unless actual results are measured and considered in performance appraisals and rewards are given for the successful attainment of objectives. Using MBO in combination with checking for results and rewarding performance is known as **management by objectives, results, and rewards (MBORR)**[61] An outstanding example of a successful MBORR program is the one used by Cypress Semiconductor, discussed in this chapter's Innovation Management Challenge. It is not just an MBO system; it also checks for results and provides appropriate rewards.

Management by objectives, results, and rewards (MBORR): Broadening MBO to include checking for results and rewarding performance.

SETTING PRIORITIES

Every manager faces a conflict when it comes to assigning priorities to the objectives he or she has established. At the strategic level, for example, what does the chief executive sacrifice in efficiency in order to achieve a higher market share? At the supervisory level, a front-line manager may have personal-development objectives for each subordinate, but to achieve those objectives he or she may temporarily have to sacrifice productivity by sending an employee to a course or seminar. At every level of the organization, there are almost always conflicts between long- and short-term objectives. In addition, an individual's personal

Competing in Silicon Valley

How do you make money in a business in which everyone else is losing money? One way is by using Turbo MBO. T. J. Rodgers, president of Cypress Semiconductor Company of San Jose, California, swears by his MBO system. Every day, by reading a computer printout, he knows what his 1,400 employees are doing, how close they are to achieving their objectives, or whether they are failing to achieve

T. J. Rodgers, president of Cypress Semiconductor Company, knows what his 1,400 employees are doing, how close they are to achieving their objectives, or whether they are failing to achieve those objectives just by reading a computer printout.

objectives may be in conflict with organizational priorities. Finally, functional objectives are often in conflict. The problem is made more complex because objectives are often interdependent. For example, the organization's financial managers may wish to keep finished-goods inventories at low levels to reduce holding costs, while its operations managers wish to keep them higher in order to be able to satisfy customer needs.

How, then, does the manager assign priorities? Only a few systems exist for setting priorities.[62] Most managers therefore develop a system for themselves. As in any problem-solving situation, the manager must consider the alternatives—in this case, alternative objectives—and evaluate them according to specific criteria. Thus, the key step is to develop criteria for prioritizing the needs of customers, bosses, or subordinates and for balancing resources, time frames, and impact on the company. All of these factors and others may be used to determine priorities.

Alternatives to Objective-Based Systems

Fundamental to any objective-based system is the belief that an individual's job can be clearly separated from those of other members of the organization. It is easy to see how MBORR-type systems would work in sales and in manufacturing, where each person clearly affects the company's performance. It is even possible to identify the contributions of many jobs in service industries or service

those objectives. Every Wednesday at noon Rodgers assembles his top managers for a status report on goal achievement by each of the company's departments. There is no escape; the computer knows all. The large screen containing computer-generated graphics and performance charts details the status of each executive's weekly objectives.

Rodgers likes to call his system Turbo MBO. Every Monday morning, project leaders meet with their staffs and assign the jobs that need attention that week. Everyone's new objectives are input into a minicomputer, which is linked to all of the company's executives and managers via personal computers. A spreadsheet program is used to display the objectives. On Tuesday, priorities are given to individual objectives. On Wednesday, any manager who is "delinquent" in achieving 35 percent of his or her objectives must give the reason. The computer alerts the president when an executive is delinquent on 20 percent of his or her objectives.

Turbo MBO has its critics. One engineer who left the firm said that he is a self-motivating professional and does not need to have someone looking over his shoulder all the time. Julian Philips, a San Francisco principal at McKinsey & Company, believes that MBO systems like the one at Cypress Semiconductor cannot keep up with a changing environment. Rodgers disagrees. He feels that the Turbo MBO system allows managers to adjust quickly to changes. The important thing, he says, is to have frequent meetings about the status of objectives, rather than wait six months to find out whether they have been achieved. This is why he has weekly and daily performance reviews on the computer. His competitors may surprise him, but he wants no surprises from his organization.

SOURCES: T. J. Rodgers, "No Excuses Management," *Harvard Business Review* (July–August 1990), pp. 84–98; and Steve Kaufman, "Going for the Goals," *Success* (January–February 1988), pp. 38–41.

functions in manufacturing or sales. Accounts payable clerks, for example, can be required to process a certain number of invoices in a certain period; a hospital nurse can be required to receive positive evaluations from 98 percent of his or her patients. However, many jobs are difficult to describe in terms of the specific objectives to be achieved. For example, what does a trainer in a personnel department accomplish? Can the trainer's objectives be defined in terms of the number of people trained or how they are trained, or is there some productivity measure that can be seen to increase as a result of the training given? Take the case of the company's financial manager: What factors are under this individual's control? What can he or she accomplish? Can the president of the company actually increase profits? If so, to what identifiable degree?

It is sometimes necessary to provide a behavioral description of what is expected, rather than objective measurements, and to hold people accountable for applying that description. A technique known as the **behaviorally anchored rating scale (BARS)** does just that. It lists a series of behavioral activities that should be undertaken in a particular job, accompanied by verbal descriptions of several levels of performance for each activity. BARS are expensive to create and time consuming to use as a method of planning and control, but they are very useful in situations like the ones just described.[63] Managers and human resource management experts are still attempting to objectify what it is that people are supposed to accomplish in many jobs. BARS are very useful in situations in which this has not been established.

Behaviorally anchored rating scale (BARS): A series of behavioral activities that should be undertaken in a particular job, accompanied by verbal descriptions of several levels of performance for each activity.

FIGURE 6.5 PLANNING AS PROBLEM SOLVING

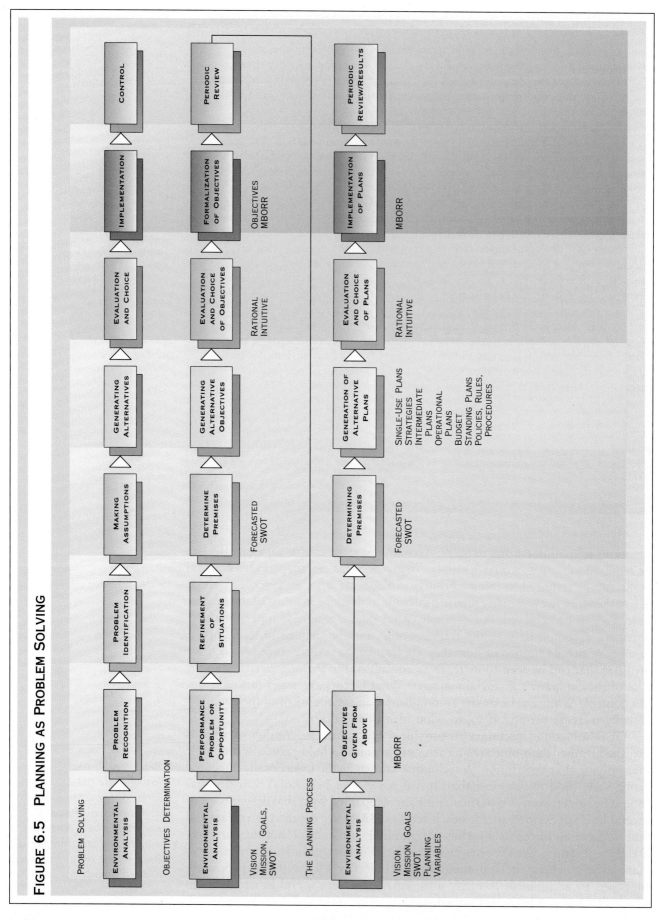

PROBLEM SOLVING

ENVIRONMENTAL ANALYSIS → PROBLEM RECOGNITION → PROBLEM IDENTIFICATION → MAKING ASSUMPTIONS → GENERATING ALTERNATIVES → EVALUATION AND CHOICE → IMPLEMENTATION → CONTROL

OBJECTIVES DETERMINATION

ENVIRONMENTAL ANALYSIS → PERFORMANCE PROBLEM OR OPPORTUNITY → REFINEMENT OF SITUATIONS → DETERMINE PREMISES → GENERATING ALTERNATIVE OBJECTIVES → EVALUATION AND CHOICE OF OBJECTIVES → FORMALIZATION OF OBJECTIVES → PERIODIC REVIEW

VISION
MISSION, GOALS,
SWOT

FORECASTED
SWOT

RATIONAL
INTUITIVE

OBJECTIVES
MBORR

THE PLANNING PROCESS

ENVIRONMENTAL ANALYSIS → OBJECTIVES GIVEN FROM ABOVE → DETERMINING PREMISES → GENERATION OF ALTERNATIVE PLANS → EVALUATION AND CHOICE OF PLANS → IMPLEMENTATION OF PLANS → PERIODIC REVIEW/RESULTS

VISION
MISSION, GOALS
SWOT
PLANNING
VARIABLES

MBORR

FORECASTED
SWOT

SINGLE-USE PLANS
STRATEGIES
INTERMEDIATE
  PLANS
OPERATIONAL
  PLANS
BUDGET
STANDING PLANS
POLICIES, RULES,
  PROCEDURES

RATIONAL
INTUITIVE

MBORR

Another problem facing organizations today is the increasing complexity of their external environments. To meet these challenges, MBORR systems must be made more flexible. It may be necessary to state objectives in the form of target zones rather than specific standards. More flexible objectives and more frequent performance reviews are also desirable. Ten years ago, for example, banks readily fit the mold of companies that could use an MBORR system effectively. Today, while banks may need an objective/performance-driven system more than ever, their environments are changing quite rapidly. They need to be able to respond quickly to those changes while being able to describe performance in objective terms. Two approaches to this problem are emerging. On the one hand, rather broad statements of objectives with acceptable ranges of performance are being established. On the other, frequent reviews of very specific, but very flexible, objectives are being used in many companies; these systems are often computerized.

Another alternative to objective-based systems is total quality management. W. Edwards Deming, the leading proponent of this approach, declares that MBO systems defeat their own purposes. Workers, he believes, should set their own objectives. Processes, rather than objectives, should be managed, both by managers and by those they manage.[64] Both perspectives are probably correct. MBO has been shown to work, and so have the approaches suggested by Deming, which are usually based on work groups acting as autonomous teams. If you recall the description of GE at the beginning of Chapter 1, you will remember that GE has discovered that it needs to use both approaches. Managing objectives alone often results in processes getting out of hand.

Setting Personal Objectives

Part of a manager's responsibility is to set personal objectives—not just those related to the organization, but those he or she must achieve to become a more productive member of the organization (and of society).[65] Although most of a manager's objectives should be tied directly to the organization's mission, goals, and objectives, the manager should, and probably will, be alert to the need to develop and grow beyond the objectives of a particular job. Personal objectives may include physical, psychological, social responsibility, interpersonal, and family objectives, among others. Many of these stem directly from organizational objectives, but some may be in conflict with them. For example, working overtime can conflict with family objectives.

Planning as a Problem-Solving Process

Throughout this chapter we have seen that planning is a problem-solving process. In fact, the only major difference between problem solving and general planning is the time horizon. Even though most problems are solved for the immediate future, most planning is expected to bring results over an extended period. The key in planning, perhaps more than in any other type of problem solving, is to search the environment for important pieces of information. In organizing, leading, and controlling, much more of the information necessary to make the choice to solve the problem is usually readily available. Problem solving in planning often deals much more with unknown factors. The manager must search for this information in a more organized way.

The manager goes through the problem-solving process at least twice for each plan developed: the first time to determine objectives and the second time to formulate the plans to achieve those objectives. Figure 6.5 expands these two processes by showing how the key terms and concepts introduced in this chapter fit into them.

Often, the manager is assigned specific objectives. Going through the problem-solving process for each objective is simply a matter of making certain that other factors do not warrant a change in that objective. For example, the manager may have been given the objective of reducing the scheduled work hours of employees in a program or service area by 10 percent. However, if the manager is aware that sales are expected to increase beyond what top management could have known when determining this objective, this manager must indicate the inappropriateness of the objective. In addition, as seen in the figure, certain assumptions, or premises, exist at any level of the planning process. The manager must always be as certain as possible about the validity of those premises.

Summary

(Before reading this summary, look again at the objectives listed at the beginning of the chapter.)

1. The planning process consists of two parts: determining a purpose (vision, mission, goals, or objectives) and formulating plans to achieve it.

2. Planning is problem solving for the future in a changing environment; it involves making decisions today that will determine the organization's actions tomorrow.

3. Planning leads to the other three functions of management. It provides the objectives and plans of action that the organization's structure is designed to achieve. Leadership is used to influence individuals in that structure to accomplish those objectives and goals. Control determines whether the objectives of planning have been achieved.

4. Planning is more complex, more uncertain, more unique, less structured, and longer-term in nature at higher levels of management than at middle or lower levels. At lower levels few factors are involved, there is more certainty, many of the decisions are routine or structured, and planning typically is for the short term.

5. Plans must be tested against a variety of criteria. Characteristics that may be appropriate for some plans will not be for others. Before making a decision, the decision maker performs a situational analysis. This entails examining strengths, weaknesses, opportunites, and threats and, hence, is often called SWOT analysis.

6. Among the limitations on the planning process are external events, internal resistance, cost, current crises, weak premises, and the difficulty of planning. The reasons that planning may fail include lack of commitment to planning, failure to implement plans properly, failure to see planning as both rational and creative, absence of proper controls, poor leadership, resistance to change, and the lack of a planning approach for use in complex, changing environments.

7. Vision is a broad general direction for the organization; it has emotional content. Mission describes an organization's line of business and how it intends to proceed in that business. Goals are broad statements that further define an organization's mission. Objectives provide specific definitions of goals.

8. Effective objectives have the following characteristics: the goal area or attribute sought, an index for measuring progress toward the attribute, a target to be achieved, and a time frame in which the target is to be achieved.

9. Management by objectives (MBO) consists of the determination and distribution of objectives, the formulation of action plans, some degree of participation by subordinates, and implementation. MBORR adds requirements for measuring results and providing related rewards.

General Questions

1. Describe the planning process in an organization with which you are familiar.

2. Discuss planning in a not-for-profit organization like the United Way or the American Heart Association and indicate how it might differ from planning in a for-profit organization.

3. What is the relationship between standing plans and single-use plans?

4. Given what you know about management and the changing external environment of most companies, how useful do you think intermediate planning will be in the future? How might planning be improved in changing environments?

5. Discuss each of the basic characteristics of plans for an organization with which you are familiar.

6. Will planning increase or decrease in importance in the future? Why?

7. With respect to your own personal planning, do you plan for the short or the long term, or do you plan at all? Write down five success-oriented goals for yourself for the next year and for the next three to five years.

8. Are there any conflicts in the objectives you developed in answering the preceding question? How would you determine priorities for those objectives?

9. How would you integrate the objectives and plans of different business units for a multibusiness firm like GE?

10. The chapter lists several reasons why the planning process can fail. How would you try to overcome each of them?

Questions on the Management Challenge Features

ETHICAL MANAGEMENT CHALLENGE

1. Why was this an ethical issue?
2. How else might this problem have been solved?

MANAGEMENT CHALLENGE

1. What assumptions did Komatsu have to rethink in its battles with Caterpillar?
2. What changes in strategy resulted?

GLOBAL MANAGEMENT CHALLENGE

1. What is Carl Hahn's vision for Volkswagen?
2. How has he developed plans to meet the challenges of Volkswagen's different environments around the world?

INNOVATION MANAGEMENT CHALLENGE

1. Describe Turbo MBO as a management innovation, a valuable new way of managing.
2. What are the pros and cons of such a system?

General Accident Revises Its Mission

General Accident and other major British insurance companies suffered major losses in 1991. General Accident's losses totaled £105.2 million. These losses were credited to a recessionary economy; however, it should be noted that a substantial increase in premiums (20–25 percent) cost General Accident a severe loss in market share, as 20 percent of its policyholders left the firm. General Accident did post a profit of about £10 million for the second quarter of 1992.

DISCUSSION QUESTIONS

1. Do you think GA's change in mission caused some of its losses? If so, how?
2. What other factors contributed to the losses?
3. Evaluate the decision to raise premiums.

An Information Services Division

Lou Follett, head of the East Coast department of the information systems division of a major global company, pondered the situation he faced. His boss, Bob Morris, had instituted a management by objectives (MBO) program for the division as part of a management shift in which increased authority was given to various divisions, making them more autonomous. Consequently, the information division, which had been a cost center providing service to internal users (captive customers), would function as a profit center and would compete against outside companies for customers. Follett decided that the department's human resource manager needed to be involved and could give him some guidance. He called a meeting with Karen Stone, the personnel manager, and her assistant, Marian Matthew, to solicit ideas. As a result of the meeting, he asked Stone to draw up a plan of action. She was to use the forms and limited information on MBO provided by the West Coast human resource department. She would also arrange for Morris to talk about MBO with all the East Coast managers. Beyond that, she was on her own and could move forward as she saw fit, with Follett reserving the right to approve of any plans she and Matthew might make.

DISCUSSION QUESTIONS

1. If you were the personnel manager, what actions would you propose to Follett?
2. How might an MBO system best be used in this situation—for planning, for control, and for employee development?

Learning About MBORR

MANAGE
YOURSELF

How well do you understand the MBORR system? Let's find out. Your instructor has established objectives for you for the semester; surely you have done so, too. It is time to formalize those objectives. At this point your MBORR system is only partly participatory. You have been assigned objectives, but you are also establishing some for yourself. You have the ability to choose a plan of action to achieve your objectives. In the space below, indicate your instructor's objectives for you, your own objectives, and how you plan to achieve both sets. When the course is over, write the results and the rewards you received.

Your Instructor's Objectives for You in This Course

Your Objectives for Yourself in This Course

Your Plans for Reaching Those Objectives

1. Instructor's Objectives
2. Your Objectives

Results

Rewards

"Of all the contrasts between the successful and the unsuccessful business, or between the corporate leader and its followers, the single, most important differentiating factor is strategy."

—Thomas Cannon

"We are not managing this company for the next quarter. We are building it for the next generation."

—Sam Johnson,
Chairman and CEO,
S. C. Johnson & Son, Inc.

CHAPTER 7

Strategy Formulation and Implementation

CHAPTER OBJECTIVES

When you have read this chapter you should be able to:

1. Describe the strategic management process in organizations.
2. Identify the major levels of strategy and describe each briefly.
3. Describe the major steps in the strategic planning process.
4. List and describe the major types of corporate strategies.
5. State the three questions that strategic planning answers.
6. Describe the roles of the following in strategic management: core competencies, capabilities, resource bases, and organizational learning.
7. Identify the principal types of strategists in an organization.
8. Describe the role of human behavior in the strategic management process.
9. Discuss strategic planning in different types of organizations.
10. Discuss the implementation of strategies.

M ANAGEMENT CHALLENGES DISCUSSED IN THIS CHAPTER:

 Increasing globalization of business.

 Increasing levels of competition.

 Unstable market and economic conditions.

 Complexity of the managerial environment.

CHAPTER OUTLINE

Baldor's Success Depends on Functional Strategies

In the mid-1980s Baldor, a manufacturer of industrial motors located in Fort Smith, Arkansas, was confronted with declining profits. It had to determine whether to move its manufacturing operations to other countries, as other motor manufacturers such as GE, Reliance Electric, and Emerson Electric had, or to stay at home. Roland Boreham, Jr., Baldor's chairman and CEO, believed that any price advantage of moving abroad would be lost if, as was likely, the value of the dollar relative to foreign currencies began to fall. He also feared that product quality might suffer. Quality was Baldor's competitive advantage in a market in which more than 50 percent of its products were customized, and he didn't want the company to lose this advantage. The decision to remain a domestic manufacturer was often criticized, but Baldor stayed the course.

Baldor had invested substantially in new plant and equipment from 1977 to 1982. To overcome the decline in sales and profits that it experienced from 1982 to 1985, the company invested heavily in its personnel. It sent all ninety-six middle managers to the three-day seminar at Phil Crosby's Quality College and more than 80 percent of its 2,500 employees to in-house training programs. Manufacturing functional strategies were altered as well. Speed of delivery was emphasized; Baldor can now design, produce, and deliver a high-quality motor in six weeks. Using a home-grown version of just-in-time manufacturing called flexible flow, in which inventories were reduced to the amount needed for that production run, Baldor cut its batch-order manufacturing process from four weeks to five days.

New products were developed, and innovation was stressed in both design and manufacturing. In flexible flow, for example, progressive assembly was eliminated. Each worker now assembles an entire motor by following directions on a computer printout. A worker can assemble as many as twenty different motors in a day. This helps reduce boredom and increase autonomy and pride. More than three hundred new motors were listed in Baldor's last catalog, and it has developed some unique new products, such as a motor that can work well in the very damp environment necessary for growing mushrooms.

In addition, several motivational programs have been instituted; for example, employees are encouraged to sign their work. Baldor has not laid off an employee in Fort Smith since 1962, a policy that increases employee loyalty. The company's success has also been buoyed by its decision to train workers in new technologies. Workers have had to learn many new skills to do all that Baldor requires to be competitive.

Baldor's decision not to move its manufacturing operations abroad turned out to be the right one, although it initially met with heavy criticism. The company's sales jumped 40 percent between 1985 and 1988 and reached $286 million in 1991, despite increased foreign competition. Baldor even managed to penetrate the Japanese market with one of its motors. As CEO Boreham observes, "Pride takes you one direction, short-term profit another. Pride usually wins out, if you're a confident person."

SOURCES: Baldor: Motors and Drives: 1991 Annual Report (Fort Smith, Ark.: Baldor, 1992); Stephen J. Mraz, "Teaching Workers the Three Rs Is Good for the Bottom Line," *Machine Design* (January 24, 1991), pp. 25–27; and Alan Farnham, "Baldor's Success: Made in the U.S.A.," *Fortune* (July 17, 1989), pp. 101–106.

A mong the most important actions of top managers are those associated with formulating and implementating strategies.[1] Strategy formulation and implementation occur at an organization's corporate, business, and functional levels, as shown in Figure 7.1.[2]

Corporate strategy defines the business or businesses the firm should be in, the criteria for entering those businesses, and the basic actions the firm will follow in conducting business. At Baldor, for example, the firm chose to be an innovative manufacturer of high-quality custom electric motors.

Most organizations operate in only one business area, although they may have many products; examples include Wendy's, Kroger's Food Stores, and Mrs. Fields' Cookies. Some firms, such as Walt Disney Companies, have more than one business. Each business an organization engages in must function competitively in its own marketplace. To do so, it formulates a business strategy. Baldor's business strategy is to differentiate its products from those of competitors on the basis of quality and to speed customized products to market.

Functional strategies must support the business's corporate and business strategies. Within any business there are two types of functional strategies: economic functional strategies such as marketing, operations, finance, and human resources management, and management functional strategies such as planning, organizing, leading, controlling, and problem solving. To achieve its strategy of differentiation, Baldor must have a manufacturing strategy that leads to high quality, a human-resource strategy that stimulates both quality and innovation,

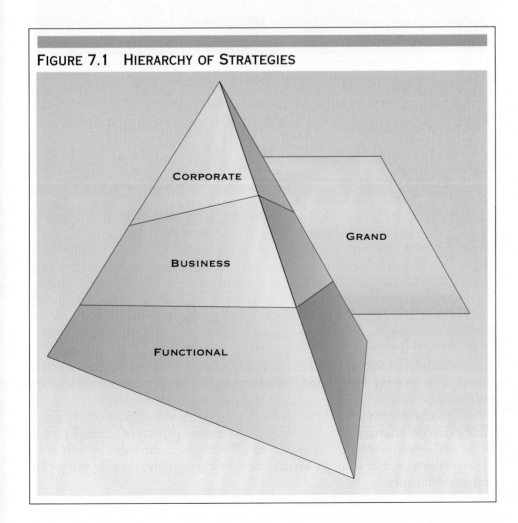

FIGURE 7.1 HIERARCHY OF STRATEGIES

Each business an organization engages in must function competitively in its own marketplace. Baldor's business strategy is to differentiate its products from those of competitors on the basis of quality and to speed customized products to market.

Grand strategy: The fundamental strategy from which all of the organization's other strategies and plans are derived.

and a research and development strategy that enables the firm to bring new products to market quickly.

Finally, every business has a **grand strategy,** the strategy from which virtually all other strategies and plans are derived. This is the organization's driving force. The grand strategy may be growth, diversification, or any of a number of others.[3] Grand strategies are usually corporate or business strategies, but they can also be functional. At Baldor, the grand strategy is customized quality.

The purpose of a strategy is to achieve the strategic objectives established earlier in the strategic management process. Strategy formulation is a complex problem-solving process. Not only does it involve different types of strategies for each of the three distinct levels of strategy, but it also involves a number of additional interrelated strategic factors. Each set of strategic objectives established, each strategy formulated, follows the planning/problem-solving model portrayed in Figure 4.2.[4]

This chapter explores the three levels of strategy and various other factors involved in the strategic decision process.[5] Numerous aspects of strategy formulation and implementation are discussed. The chapter concludes by exploring the evolving nature of strategic management in increasingly complex and turbulent environments.

Strategic Planning, Strategic Management, and Strategic Thinking

In the preceding chapter we discussed the process of setting objectives. Here we turn to the formulation of strategies. **Strategic planning** is the problem-solving process of establishing strategic objectives and formulating plans to accomplish those objectives. Any strategic plan is based on the answers to three questions:

1. Where are we now?
2. Where do we want to be?
3. How do we get there?

Strategic planning can be applied to any major area in an organization; most often it focuses on the marketplace. It is concerned primarily with long-term actions to achieve objectives, but it could also be concerned with significant short-term actions.

The Strategic Management Perspective

Strategic management is the process of managing the pursuit of an organization's mission while managing its relationship to its environment.[6] Strategic management is broader than strategic planning. It includes implementation and control as well as planning, and involves a much broader environmental analysis than that associated with strategic planning. As environments continue to change, strategic management becomes both more important and more difficult.

The strategic management process follows a series of five steps (see Figure 7.2):

1. Environmental analysis (discussed in Chapters 5 and 6)
2. Determination of vision, mission, goals, and strategic objectives (see Chapter 6)
3. Formulation of strategies (discussed in this chapter)
4. Implementation of strategies (discussed in this chapter)
5. Evaluation and control of strategies (discussed in Chapters 18 and 19)

Each of these steps is a problem-solving exercise in and of itself.

Organizational and managerial concern with strategy has evolved through a series of stages.[7] Historically, strategy in business organizations was directed mainly toward trying to beat the competition in the marketplace. In the 1970s,

> *Strategic planning: The process of establishing strategic objectives and formulating plans to accomplish those objectives.*

> AT BALDOR: *Baldor faces a changing environment. Competition is fierce. Focusing on one business seemed more reasonable to Baldor than being a multibusiness firm.*

> *Strategic management: The process of managing the pursuit of an organization's mission while managing its relationship to its environment.*

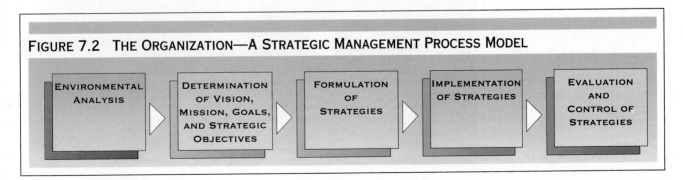

FIGURE 7.2   THE ORGANIZATION—A STRATEGIC MANAGEMENT PROCESS MODEL

| ENVIRONMENTAL ANALYSIS | DETERMINATION OF VISION, MISSION, GOALS, AND STRATEGIC OBJECTIVES | FORMULATION OF STRATEGIES | IMPLEMENTATION OF STRATEGIES | EVALUATION AND CONTROL OF STRATEGIES |

however, strategic planners also became concerned with many nontraditional aspects of the organization's environment. Managers began to recognize that strategy is not simply a competitive process but involves virtually every major aspect of running an organization. Of special concern during this period were stakeholders, groups with a stake in an organization's strategic decisions that normally would not have been considered when those decisions were being made. Among those groups were environmental groups, minorities, and consumer groups. During the same period, efforts were also made to develop a way of strategizing for multiple-business organizations. Strategies for the management functions, such as planning, organizing, leading, and controlling, also became more formal.

Although strategic management has received considerable attention, even the largest organizations have only recently attempted to take an integrated approach to strategic management. Michael E. Naylor, then executive in charge of corporate strategic planning for GM, reports that it was not until the late 1970s that GM began to take an integrated strategic management approach to its corporate strategy. It, too, had focused narrowly on the marketing and financial perspectives of individual businesses, not formulating a total corporate strategy or fully considering the various stakeholders affected by its strategies.[8] Walt Disney Companies did not begin corporatewide strategic planning until 1984.[9] It is only recently that management researchers have begun to recognize fully the various aspects and impacts of strategic management.[10]

Strategizing in Complex, Turbulent Environments

In recent years, firms have realized that their environments are becoming more dynamic and often more complex. As a result, they have begun to engage in **strategic thinking**.[11] This means that strategists "think through" the strategy, recognizing that they are doing so principally to provide direction and that at any moment their objectives and strategies may have to change. Because circumstances change, organizations develop **scenarios** of events that might occur, as

Although strategic management has received considerable attention, even the largest organizations, such as General Motors, have only recently attempted to take an integrated approach to strategic management. Shown here is the control room of GM's Orion, Michigan, assembly plant.

discussed in Chapter 6.[12] They also formulate **contingency plans**—here contingency strategies—alternative plans that can be put into effect if the chosen plan becomes inappropriate. Firms often generate multiple scenarios so that they can have contingency plans ready to be implemented when circumstances change. For example, Norwegian Oil and Gas Company developed scenarios of the oil supply situation in Europe for varying degrees of success of the 1992 EEC initiative. It then developed contingency strategies depending on those scenarios.[13] When one of the scenarios begins to materialize, they will be better prepared to take the appropriate strategic action.

Even though firms prepare scenarios of possible futures, they often do not formalize their contingency plans—rather, they determine approximately what they should do. Having thought through the scenarios and the necessary plans, they can implement the latter quickly when deemed necessary.

An increasingly important strategic concept in such environments is **organizational learning**—the process through which organizations learn.[14] Both the content and the speed of learning are critical. In fast-changing environments the ability to learn, to lead the market, and to adapt to it becomes increasingly important. In fact, Ray Stata, CEO of Analog Devices, suggests that "the ability to learn faster than your competitors may be the only sustainable competitive advantage."[15]

Strategic thinking: Thinking through a strategy in order to provide direction.

Scenario: A predicted or imagined sequence of events.

Contingency plan: An alternative plan that may be put into effect if the chosen plan becomes inappropriate.

Organizational learning: The process through which organizations learn.

Strategy Formulation

Strategy formulation, whether corporate, business, or functional, consists of the following steps (see Figure 7.3):

1. It commences with an internal and external environmental analysis.
2. Strategists review the organization's vision, mission, and goals.
3. The analyses are used to determine strengths, weaknesses, opportunities, and threats. This SWOT analysis helps answer the strategic question, "Where are we now?" A forecasted SWOT (for example, for five years from now) is then prepared. This helps answer the question, "Where do we want to be?"
4. Planning premises must be developed. Premises are the assumptions on which strategic objectives and related strategies will be based. Forecasts of the future states of both internal and external environments are involved in formulating premises.
5. Strategic objectives are determined. These define "where we want to be."
6. Alternative strategies are developed.
7. Choices must be made among those alternatives. These answer the question, "How do we get there?"

Strategy formulation: The process by which a corporation, business unit, or functional department determines its overall strategy.

AT BALDOR: *The formulation of business strategy at Baldor involved redefining the purpose of many of the organization's components. Quality became critical. Most aspects of the organization were changed—including manufacturing, marketing, human resources, and R&D.*

SWOT Analysis

Determining alternative solutions depends greatly on both internal and external environmental analyses. The purpose of these analyses is to determine the organization's strengths, weaknesses, opportunities, and threats relative to each other.[16] This process becomes more complex as the environment becomes more turbulent.

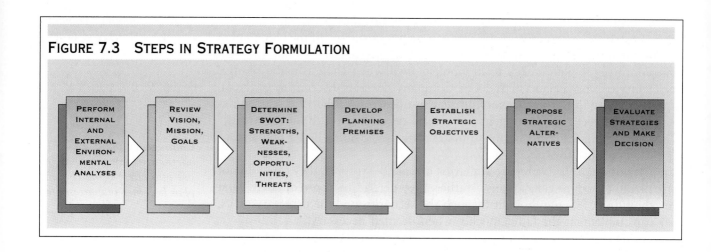

FIGURE 7.3 STEPS IN STRATEGY FORMULATION

| PERFORM INTERNAL AND EXTERNAL ENVIRON- MENTAL ANALYSES | REVIEW VISION, MISSION, GOALS | DETERMINE SWOT: STRENGTHS, WEAK- NESSES, OPPORTU- NITIES, THREATS | DEVELOP PLANNING PREMISES | ESTABLISH STRATEGIC OBJECTIVES | PROPOSE STRATEGIC ALTER- NATIVES | EVALUATE STRATEGIES AND MAKE DECISION |

EXTERNAL ENVIRONMENTAL ANALYSIS

As discussed in Chapters 1, 5, and 6, the manager is confronted with four principal sets of external factors: technological, economic/competitive, political/legal, and social. These in turn include numerous subfactors. The competitive environment is so important that it is analyzed separately. Each of the organization's **stakeholders**—individuals and groups with a vested interest in the actions of an organization's management—anticipates and often demands certain actions by management. Top management must consider these elements in formulating a strategy.

INTERNAL ENVIRONMENTAL ANALYSIS

Within the organization the strategic manager, depending on his or her function and level, is confronted with a host of internal environmental factors. These include the organization's other functions; the general management; the owners—usually stockholders; others who direct the organization (for example, the trustees of a nonprofit organization); members of management throughout the organization; various management systems; a host of nonorganized employees; the organization's culture; the organization's rules, policies, and procedures; and the organization's strategy and structure. In formulating strategy, the manager must be able to balance the needs and requirements of all of these factors against each other, as well as against the demands of the external environment.

Core Competencies, Capabilities, and Resource Bases

In the early 1990s, three approaches to analyzing and building internal strengths became prominent. Two noted researchers and consultants, C. K. Prahalad and Gary Hamel, proposed that an organization's key strengths are its **core competencies**—the organization's collective learning, especially as related to the technology and manufacturing processes that make the firm competitive. For example, Honda knew how to make engines better than anyone else. This allowed it to make automobiles as well as motorcycles and gain a dominant position in both.[17] McKinsey & Company consultants George Stalk, Philip Evans, and Lawrence E. Shulman have developed a broader concept than core competencies. Their term **capabilities** refers to collective, cross-functional, value-adding organizational processes that create competitive advantages. Capabilities require investment in support activities beyond what might seem necessary on the surface. Wal-Mart, for example, developed a superior logistics system that en-

Stakeholders: Individuals and groups with a vested interest in an organization's actions.

Core competencies: The organization's collective learning, especially as related to the technology and manufacturing processes that make it competitive.

Capabilities: Collective, cross-functional, value-adding organizational processes that create competitive advantages.

Sam Walton was a shrewd strategist. First he found a niche. As his firm gained strength, he mounted a direct campaign against Kmart. Wal-Mart's superior logistics system enabled it to beat Kmart's prices.

abled it to beat Kmart's prices.[18] Broader still is the concept of competing through **resource bases.** A number of management experts have suggested the need to build substantial resource bases, including those consisting of intangible assets such as employee skills and organizational knowledge. These resource bases then serve as a basis for competition; hence, the term **resource-based strategy.** They allow firms to seize opportunities and ward off threats.[19] GE actively practices the resource-based approach, stockpiling assets (resource bases), both tangible and intangible, in order to be in a position to seize opportunities and ward off threats. Many experts consider this approach critical to strategizing in complex, changeful environments.

Resource bases: Collections of resources, including intangible assets such as employee skills and organizational knowledge, that serve as a basis for competition.

Resource-based strategy: Strategy based on the accumulation of resource bases.

Planning Premises

Once the current SWOT analysis has been completed, a forecasted SWOT must be prepared. The same SWOT or an updated SWOT used to determine objectives will be used in establishing premises and strategic alternatives. The strategist seeks to use current and predicted strengths, core competencies, capabilities, and resource bases to overcome weaknesses and threats and take advantage of opportunities to achieve strategic objectives.

In order to determine the organization's future SWOT, strategists must make *premises*—certain assumptions about the future condition of these and other environmental conditions.[20] For example, what will the prime interest rate be three years from now? What will competitors' product strategies look like two years from now? What major technological advances will be made in the next three years? What major social and demographic changes will occur in the next five years? Will the new management system we want to install make us better able to meet the demands of the marketplace? What will be the terms of the union contract to be negotiated next year? These and hundreds of other assumptions (of which a few will be critical) must be made in the course of strategic planning.

No matter how carefully a strategy is developed, the results are not always what is sought. Porsche, the subject of this chapter's Global Management Challenge, assumed it could offer only high-priced models in the United States and still be profitable. Those assumptions proved false. Read the feature on Porsche and determine what the company should have done. What should its strategy be now?

Strategic Intent: Strategic Fit versus Leveraging Resources

Hamel and Prahalad have provided another important concept: **strategic intent**, meaning ambition out of proportion to resources and capabilities, an obsession with winning. Strategic intent is more than blind ambition. It is an active management process that includes focusing the organization's attention on winning, motivating people by communicating the value of the target, leaving room for individual and team contributions, sustaining enthusiasm by providing new operational definitions as circumstances change, and using intent consistently to guide the allocation of resources.

Hamel and Prahalad argue that most U.S. corporate strategists are caught up in the practice of **strategic fit**, trimming ambitions and matching strategy according to the corporation's current SWOT analysis. They argue that firms ought to **leverage resources**—focus on strategic intent and the actions needed to achieve that intent. Strategy should be matched to opportunities. Future strengths, or core competencies, should be created and current weaknesses and threats overcome. Japanese firms, they claim, practice leveraging resources rather than strategic fit; they innovate and achieve.

According to Hamel and Prahalad, innovation results from having a strategic intent but few resources.[21] For example, if Toyota's strategists had practiced SWOT analysis and strategy formulation the way U.S. strategists do, they might have gotten out of the automobile business in 1960. Toyota's leaders, however, established the firm's strategic intent as someday being the number 1 automobile firm in the world. Toyota is now the number 3 firm and is likely to pass Ford as number 2 by 1995.

Establishing strategic intent and leveraging resources to achieve it are two of the most important actions a firm can take. As firms encounter the management challenges, especially global competition, changing technology, and a complex marketing and economic environment, they must stretch themselves to reach their objectives.[22]

Strategic intent: Ambition out of proportion to resources and capabilities; an obsession with winning.

Strategic fit: Trimming ambitions and matching strategy according to the corporation's current SWOT analysis.

Leveraging resources: Focusing on strategic intent and the future actions needed to achieve that intent.

Toyota's strategic intent is to become the world's leading automobile firm. Toyota is now the number 3 firm and is likely to become number 2 very soon.

238

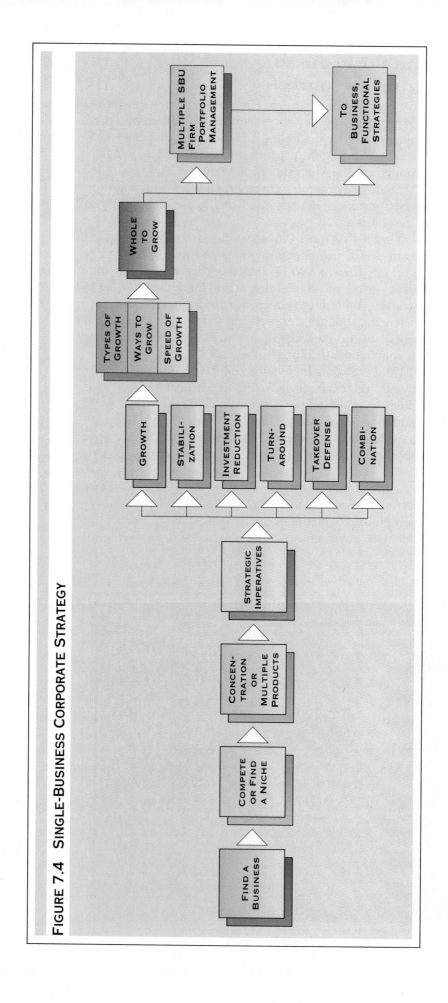

FIGURE 7.4   SINGLE-BUSINESS CORPORATE STRATEGY

Strategy Formulation at the Corporate Level

The conceptual steps the manager follows in strategic management are essentially the same at the corporate level as they are at the business and functional levels. They involve three major stages: strategy formulation, implementation, and control.

However, the specifics of the strategic planning process at the corporate level differ from those of the planning process at the business or functional level. The focus of **corporate strategy** is on determining what business(es) the company is in or should be in and how that business is to be operated. The focus of **business strategy** is on determining how the firm will obtain a strategic advantage and how it should use that advantage to beat the competition. The focus of a **functional strategy** is on determining how best to use the company's resources to support the competitive efforts included in the business strategy.

Single-Business Corporate Strategy

The underlying question in formulating any corporate strategy is, "What business(es) are we in or should we be in?" At the level of the single strategic business unit (SBU), as shown in Figure 7.4, the firm begins by asking itself the following questions:

1. Is there some business in which the organization has a natural strategic advantage or an innate interest? If it is already in that business, does that advantage or interest still exist?

2. Does the company want to compete directly or find a niche in which there is no head-on competition?

3. Does the company want or need to concentrate on one product line or many (or multiple businesses)?

4. Has the company followed the strategic imperatives for the 1990s of innovation, quality, continuous improvement, flexibility, and speed (of getting products to market)?

COMPETE OR FIND A NICHE

An organization always competes with others in a general sense. The question is whether it competes directly with others or finds a niche in which there is no real head-on competition. For example, in the past Wal-Mart has tended to "niche" in small cities, avoiding head-on competition with Kmart. Now, however, it seldom looks for niche market situations but competes directly with Kmart.

CONCENTRATE ON ONE PRODUCT OR MANY

Organizations may concentrate on a single product or product line. Random House, for example, publishes books and does nothing else. Conversely, an organization can market numerous products or product lines. Thus, Procter & Gamble has hundreds of products in numerous segments of many markets.

STRATEGIC IMPERATIVES

Five *strategic imperatives* have been identified for firms seeking to meet the challenges of the 1990s:[23]

1. *Innovation:* Both product innovation (new products or services) and process innovation (especially marketing and management innovation) must occur.

Corporate strategy: Strategy that focuses on what business(es) the company is in or should be in and how that business is to be conducted.

Business strategy: Strategy that focuses on how the firm will obtain a strategic advantage and how it should use that advantage to beat the competition.

Functional strategy: Strategy that focuses on how best to use the company's resources to support its competitive efforts.

AT BALDOR: Baldor followed the strategic imperatives of innovation, quality, flexibility, and speed. It also sought continuous improvement.

2. *Quality:* Firms must produce high-quality goods and services.[24]
3. *Continuous improvement:* Products and processes must be continuously improved upon to keep pace with or stay ahead of competitors.
4. *Flexibility:* Firms must be able to react quickly and change their actions quickly in anticipation of future events.
5. *Speed:* New products and services must be brought to market quickly.[25]

BASIC ACTION STRATEGIES

Basic action strategies: The fundamental strategies open to a single-business organization.

When a single-business organization has completed the analysis just described, it can choose among a number of **basic action strategies.** It may grow, stabilize, reduce its investments, defend itself against a takeover or seek one, turn its fortunes around, or some combination of these options. Let us take a closer look at each of these basic strategies.

GROWTH

Organizations can choose to grow or not to grow. They may increase their sales or profits by employing any number of strategies. They may grow in other ways as well. For example, a firm may seek new markets for existing products (as McDonald's did when it entered Europe and Japan) or develop new products for old markets (as McDonald's did when it added salads to its menu) or choose to diversify in order to avoid having all its eggs in one basket.

STABILIZATION

Firms may choose to stabilize, perhaps to consolidate, until further growth is advisable. For example, when Burroughs acquired Sperry Corporation to form Unisys, then CEO Michael Blumenthal chose to consolidate the firms and stabilize their strategies and operations before pursuing growth.

REDUCING INVESTMENTS

Organizations may choose to cut costs, sell off assets, or both. Multiple-SBU organizations may divest whole firms. Organizations may even choose to liquidate, sell, or extract profits from a cash-generating operation without investing any more funds.

DEFENDING AGAINST A TAKEOVER OR SEEKING ONE

Some organizations, because of their particular financial condition or because of the inabilities of management, or both, are particularly attractive targets for takeover by other firms. A firm must prepare a defense against a possible takeover or it may find itself in a crisis situation. If it is unprepared, its top managers may do dangerous and stupid things to prevent a takeover. Conversely, some organizations benefit greatly by seeking out organizations that can be acquired.

TURNAROUND

Organizations that find themselves in dire straits must seek a way to turn the situation around. Thus, when Sir Colin Marshall became chairman of British Airways in 1987, the company's situation was bleak. Through adroit management of labor relations, the organization's culture, employee motivation, and corporate image, Marshall transformed British Airways from "bloody awful" into "bloody awesome."[26]

An organization can choose among a number of basic action strategies. If it chooses to grow, it can do so in a variety of ways. It may seek new markets for existing products, as McDonald's did when it opened stores in Moscow and Tokyo. It may also diversify, as Walt Disney Companies did when it developed a line of toys based on its familiar cartoon characters and began producing motion pictures like *Beauty and the Beast* that are designed to appeal to older viewers as well as to young children.

COMBINATION

Often, organizations engage in some combination of the strategies just described. For example, between 1984 and 1986, Apple Computer first employed a turnaround strategy to overcome its degenerating market situation. It used cost-cutting measures to shore up profits while new products were created. After the financial situation was stabilized, new products were introduced to enable the firm to grow successfully.

Multiple-Business Corporate Strategy

Organizations that function in more than one business formulate corporate strategy in much the same way as a single-business organization. They review vision, mission, and goals; examine the internal and external environments; determine SWOT, core competencies, capabilities, and resource bases; develop planning premises; establish strategic objectives; propose strategic alternatives; and, finally, evaluate the alternatives and make a decision. However, the objectives and strategies are very different from those found at the business level. Strategic management of a series of businesses is concerned primarily with portfolio management—that is, management of a group (portfolio) of SBUs.[27]

Portfolio strategies have several objectives: to balance the shape, size, and risk of cash flows; to keep new products coming into the marketplace; to ensure the long-term viability of the organization; to provide synergistic marketing, production, financial, human resource, or R&D effects; to increase returns on investment; and to increase profits.[28] Sometimes the analysis of what is best for a multiple-business organization, in terms of what businesses to retain, can have some ironic outcomes. For example, Singer no longer makes sewing machines, and Greyhound no longer runs a bus company.[29]

To achieve their objectives, multiple-business firms acquire and divest other firms, and they invest to varying degrees in the firms currently in their portfolios. Three basic strategies emerge from these actions: Invest and grow (includes acquisition); use very selective investment and watch earnings; or harvest (cash flows and profits) and divest.

A number of techniques are employed in making these strategic choices. One of the more popular ones is the **portfolio matrix.** Characteristics of the market and the industry are plotted against the characteristics of the firm to form a matrix. Various locations on the matrix call for one of the three basic strategies.[30]

THE BCG MATRIX

An example of such a matrix is shown in Figure 7.5. The **BCG matrix,** developed by the Boston Consulting Group (BCG), is used by strategists to plot each business's relative competitive position (horizontal axis), as expressed by relative market share, against the business's growth rate (vertical axis). Each business is represented by a circle on the matrix; the size of the circle represents the size of the business (usually total sales). The matrix is divided into four cells representing the relative desirability of various combinations of competitive position and growth. These four cells are symbolized by a star, a question mark, a cash cow, and a dog. "Stars" represent the greatest profit potential, "dogs" the least. Stars are invested in; dogs are usually divested (sold off). "Question marks" have poor cash flows and must be monitored. Some will continue to be invested in, others sold. "Cash cows" have the best cash flows, as they require little or no investment and yield high levels of profit and cash.

Once a business has been positioned in the matrix, the appropriate portfolio strategy can be identified. The main assumption underlying the matrix—and,

Portfolio matrix: A technique in which characteristics of the market and industry are plotted against the characteristics of the firm, forming a matrix.

BCG matrix: A technique developed by the Boston Consulting Group in which each business's relative competitive position, as expressed by relative market share, is plotted against its growth rate.

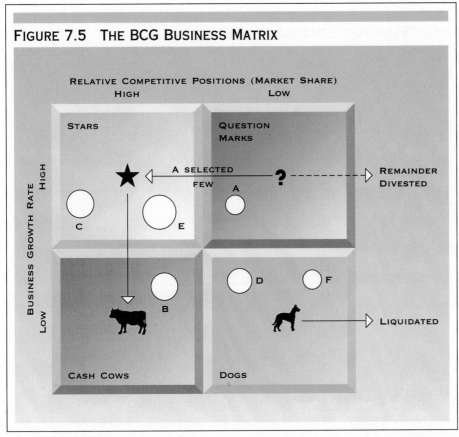

FIGURE 7.5   THE BCG BUSINESS MATRIX

RELATIVE COMPETITIVE POSITIONS (MARKET SHARE)

HIGH   LOW

BUSINESS GROWTH RATE — HIGH / LOW

STARS

QUESTION MARKS

A SELECTED FEW

REMAINDER DIVESTED

C   E   A

B   D   F

CASH COWS

DOGS

LIQUIDATED

SOURCE: REPRINTED FROM LONG RANGE PLANNING, BARRY HEDLEY, "STRATEGY AND THE BUSINESS PORTFOLIO," (FEBRUARY 1977), P. 10. COPYRIGHT 1977, WITH KIND PERMISSION FROM PERGAMON PRESS, LTD., HEADINGTON HILL HALL, OXFORD OX3 0BW, UK.

thus, the strategies to be used—is that higher market share in fast-growing markets leads to profitability, whereas in slowly growing markets obtaining a high market share requires too much cash.[31] Thus, when Avery Dennison, which produces labels and pressure-sensitive materials, was formed by a merger between Avery International and Dennison Manufacturing, the Boston Consulting Group used the BCG matrix and other analyses to determine that $135 million of Dennison's businesses should be divested and another $45 million shut down.[32]

The BCG matrix has been criticized as being overly simple. For example, depending on how the terms are defined, 60 to 70 percent of firms could be classified as dogs when they really do not warrant that description.[33]

THE GE STOPLIGHT PORTFOLIO MATRIX

Another matrix, the **GE portfolio matrix,** is shown in Figure 7.6. General Electric Co. pioneered the development of this matrix to enable top management to determine which SBUs or major products it wished to retain in its portfolio, which it wished to divest, and how it wanted to treat those it retained. With minor adjustments in the criteria employed, this matrix can also be used to evaluate potential acquisitions, mergers, or new products.

The GE Strategic Business Planning Grid, or "stoplight strategy" as it is often called, employs different-colored cells in a nine-cell matrix to indicate which strategies should be followed for various businesses. SBUs or products are located on the grid on the basis of an evaluation of the attractiveness and

GE portfolio matrix: A technique developed by General Electric Co. to enable top management to determine which SBUs to retain in its portfolio, which to divest, and how to treat those it retains.

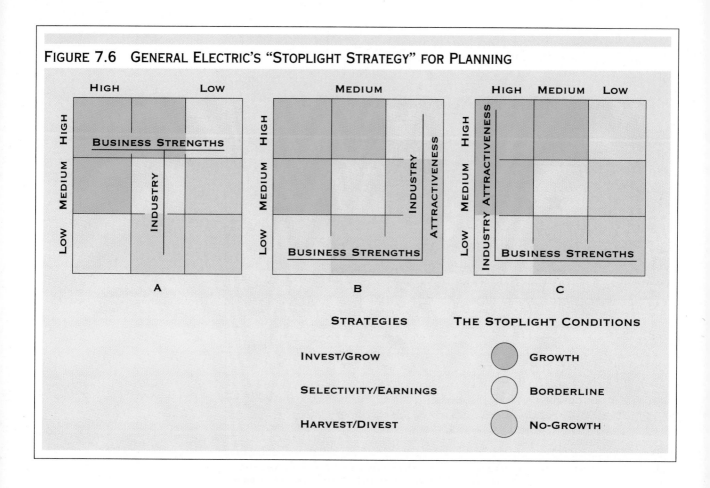

FIGURE 7.6   GENERAL ELECTRIC'S "STOPLIGHT STRATEGY" FOR PLANNING

STRATEGIES

INVEST/GROW

SELECTIVITY/EARNINGS

HARVEST/DIVEST

THE STOPLIGHT CONDITIONS

GROWTH

BORDERLINE

NO-GROWTH

strengths of the industry in which they are found. Both industry attractiveness and business strength are rated as high, medium, or low.

The term *stoplight strategy* is applied to this matrix because of the green, yellow, and red color coding employed to identify various classifications of businesses or products according to their desirability. SBUs that turn up in the green cells will be invested in and will employ growth strategies. Those that turn up in the red cells will no longer be invested in and may become cash cows or be divested. Those that end up in the yellow cells will be monitored for change in either industry attractiveness or business strengths. Large SBUs may have products that fall into each of these three categories.

In Figure 7.6, stoplight grid A indicates that the organization has medium business strengths but high industry attractiveness. Because the evaluations intersect in a green cell, the appropriate strategy would be "invest and grow." Stoplight grid B portrays a case in which business strength and industry attractiveness are low. As a result, the business is in a red zone and will be harvested and ultimately divested; investment will be reduced or terminated and cash will be extracted where possible before divestment. Stoplight grid C represents a firm with low business strengths but high industry attractiveness. Consequently, the firm lands in a yellow cell of the matrix and, hence, will be monitored for progress.

The GE matrix is backed by a significant amount of analysis and can be helpful in developing appropriate strategies. Firms that prove worthwhile from the standpoint of potential earnings will be selected for invest-and-grow strategies. Those that do not will be divested. Note, however, that the matrix is used only as a guide; it is not an ironclad procedure.

OTHER MULTIPLE-SBU STRATEGIES

Portfolio management is the primary multiple-SBU strategy. The noted researcher and consultant Michael E. Porter has identified three others: sharing activities such as distribution, transferring skills, and restructuring.[34] The first two would seem to lead to the creation of core competencies and capabilities.

Besides the strategies described so far, creating alliances and managing organizational culture have recently become major corporate strategies for multiple-SBU firms.[35] Strategic alliances can help firms enter new markets, such as Europe and Japan. They can also help reduce costs because costs are shared. Managing organizational culture is a way of sharing knowledge and increasing worker productivity.

Strategy and the Industry Life Cycle

Product and industry life cycles are important to strategy formulation at the multiple-business level. These cycles have four major stages: introduction, growth, maturity, and decline. Firms attempt to have several businesses in each life cycle stage; this is known as a balanced growth portfolio. There must always be new products or businesses to replace older, less profitable ones. For example, GE has in its portfolio firms with mature products, such as lightbulbs; firms with products in the growth stages, such as certain types of electronic components; and firms with new products, such as brain scanners. As product life cycles have been compressed by global competition, consulting firms such as P. E. Handley-Walker Company, Inc., have carved out a niche for themselves by teaching firms how to get new products to market faster through innovation, continuous improvement, and close relations with customers.[36]

Strategy Formulation at the Business Level

Corporate strategy focuses on choosing a business (or businesses) and deciding how to conduct that business. It prepares the firm for engaging in competition. Business strategy states how the firm will compete in the marketplace. The major issues are how to use generic strategies to create a competitive advantage (a strength that allows a firm to compete successfully) and the role of strategy throughout the product life cycle.

Generic Strategies—The Porter Competitive Strategies

Some experts believe that organizations should follow very specific strategies at the business level in order to be successful. Michael E. Porter argues that there are three strategies among which organizations should choose in order to compete successfully.[37] These **generic competitive strategies** are

1. *Cost leadership:* Producing a product at the lowest possible cost. Hyundai, the Korean automobile manufacturer, followed this strategy in 1986, when it introduced the Hyundai XL for $4,999. This low-price strategy was based on the ability to produce the car at a very low cost. If a firm can sell a low-cost product at a high price, it garners very high profit margins. For several years Apple Computer enjoyed such margins with its Macintosh PC.

Generic competitive strategies: According to Michael E. Porter, the three strategies among which organizations should choose in order to compete successfully are cost leadership, differentiation, and focus on a particular market or product.

2. *Differentiation:* Somehow distinguishing the product or service from similar products or services offered by other firms.[38] Budweiser follows a differentiation strategy in its "Why Ask Why, Try Bud Dry" advertising. Providing more service to customers than competitors was a major differentiation strategy in the 1980s. Another differentiation strategy being employed by many firms today is speed—providing customers with new products or services quickly. Hewlett-Packard and Brunswick, for example, have developed special teams to get products to customers faster.[39] Many times it takes real creativity to differentiate an organization's products or services from those of other firms, as this chapter's Innovation Management Challenge reveals.

3. *Focus:* Serving a particular target market extremely well. The underlying assumption is that by so doing the firm can serve the market better than the competition. As they say at Kentucky Fried Chicken, "We do chicken right." In reality, low cost and differentiation are applied either broadly or narrowly. Thus, it is most accurate to speak of either a cost or a differentiation focus.[40]

Table 7.1 indicates some of the requirements for these generic competitive strategies. Although there is only limited research evidence to support the appropriateness of these strategies, they have an intuitive appeal.[41] Growth is the basic action strategy underlying each of these strategies.

Industry analysis: Analysis of the five factors that form an industry's structure: the strength and nature of the existing competition; potential entrants; the threat of substitutes; the bargaining power of suppliers; and the bargaining power of buyers.

The choice of which of Porter's strategies to use is based on the condition of the five factors shown in Figure 7.7: the strength and nature of the existing competition; potential entrants; the threat of substitutes; the bargaining power of suppliers; and the bargaining power of buyers. Together these five factors form an industry's structure. The analysis of these five factors is known as **industry analysis.** The specific concerns related to each factor are also shown in the figure. When considering the existing competition, for example, the strategist might be concerned with industry growth, industry capacity, loss of capital, and the strength of each competitor.

TABLE 7.1 Requirements for Generic Competitive Strategies

Generic Strategy	Commonly Required Skills and Resources	Common Organizational Requirements
Overall cost leadership	Sustained capital investment and access to capital Process-engineering skills Intense supervision of labor Products designed for ease in manufacture Low-cost distribution system	Tight cost control Frequent, detailed control reports Structured organization and responsibilities Incentives based on meeting strict quantitative targets
Differentiation	Strong marketing abilities Product engineering Creative flair Strong capability in basic research Corporate reputation for quality or technological leadership Long tradition in the industry or unique combination of skills drawn from other businesses Strong cooperation from channels	Strong coordination among functions in R&D product development and marketing Subjective measurement and incentives instead of quantitative measures Amenities to attract highly skilled labor, scientists, or creative people

SOURCE: M. E. Porter, *Competitive Strategy* (New York: Free Press, 1980), pp. 40, 41. Reprinted with permission of The Free Press, a Division of Macmillan, Inc. Copyright © 1980 by The Free Press.

The goal of a focus strategy is to serve a particular target market extremely well, thereby meeting its needs better than the competition. As they say at Kentucky Fried Chicken, "We do chicken right."

Some experts believe that organizations should follow very specific strategies at the business level in order to be successful. Budweiser follows a differentiation strategy in its "Why Ask Why, Try Bud Dry" advertising campaign.

Hall's Competitiveness Model

In a study of the relationship between strategic planning and competitive success at a number of firms, William K. Hall concluded that there are really two primary generic strategies—high differentiation relative to competitors and low cost relative to competitors. Hall's **competitiveness model** is portrayed in Figure 7.8. Firms that have relatively low costs or a very high degree of relative differentiation possess "power alleys" in the marketplace. Hyundai and Mercedes are examples of each (although Mercedes's differentiation has been successfully challenged by Lexus and Infiniti). The firm that has both is in the Garden of Eden; the firm with neither is in Death Valley. Mazda's Miata is an example of a product in the Garden of Eden; in the 1970s, most of the firms in the U.S. steel industry were in Death Valley. Combinations of these two strategies yield varying degrees of ability to compete.[42] Unlike Porter, Hall does not see differentiation and low cost as mutually exclusive.[43] Several research studies support Hall's view.[44]

Competitiveness model: A model developed by William K. Hall that an organization can use to determine the optimal combination of two strategies—high differentiation relative to competitors and low cost relative to competitors.

Other Generic Strategies

There are a host of other generic strategies. For example, Raymond E. Miles and Charles C. Snow propose that organizations should act in one of four basic ways: as defenders, prospectors, analyzers, or reactors.[45] Defenders seek stability. Prospectors look for new opportunities. Analyzers are somewhere between defenders and prospectors. Reactors react; they do not really have a strategy and therefore usually fail. Various portions of a firm may use different strategies, thus creating the problem of how to integrate them. For example, managers of existing product lines at Procter & Gamble might be defenders, but managers of new products would be prospectors. Integrating them under the same corporate umbrella would require different motivational programs, budget perspectives, and objectives (e.g., profit versus market penetration).

Additional research reveals that firms seeking a high market share emphasize product or service quality, spend considerable amounts of money on marketing, and invest heavily, strategies that usually—eventually—give them a high return on investment.[46] Other researchers have identified strategies that best suit firms seeking intensive growth, as well as strategies for companies with a low market share, for those competing in stagnant industries, for dominant firms, for firms in declining industries, for regulated firms, and others.[47]

FIGURE 7.7 FORCES DRIVING INDUSTRY COMPETITION

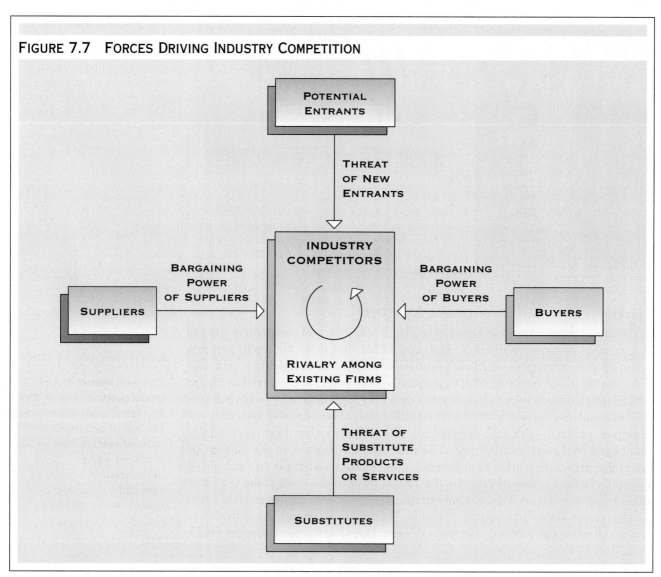

Although numerous types of generic strategies have been suggested by various authors, none has proven to be a panacea. Strategic managers must be very much aware of the various prescribed alternatives available to them, but they must also recognize their limitations. They must recognize that many of the prescriptive or generic strategies—for example, the Porter strategies—may or may not be valid in their firm's situation. Even though there is much anecdotal evidence of their validity, research has not provided clear evidence that any of them works in other than very narrow circumstances. These strategies therefore should be viewed as general guidelines rather than as specific prescriptions.

Creating a Competitive Advantage

Although the distinction between competitive strategy and competitive advantage may seem subtle, it is anything but. Competitive strategy focuses on *what* the firm wants to do in the marketplace and the basic options available to it.

FIGURE 7.8 HALL'S COMPETITIVENESS MODEL

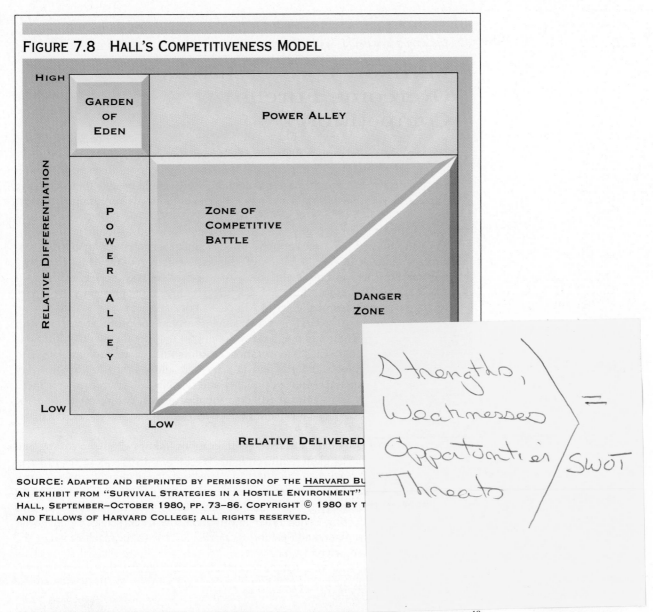

SOURCE: ADAPTED AND REPRINTED BY PERMISSION OF THE HARVARD BU...
AN EXHIBIT FROM "SURVIVAL STRATEGIES IN A HOSTILE ENVIRONMENT"
HALL, SEPTEMBER–OCTOBER 1980, PP. 73–86. COPYRIGHT © 1980 BY T...
AND FELLOWS OF HARVARD COLLEGE; ALL RIGHTS RESERVED.

Competitive advantage addresses the issue of *how* it carries out those options.[48] Successful competitive strategy in the long term is impossible without a sustainable competitive advantage—whatever it is that enables the firm to outdo its competitors in the marketplace.[49] Competitiveness has become a critical issue for most companies, especially in terms of competing effectively with foreign firms.[50] Thus, finding a competitive advantage is even more critical to success than ever before. U.S. firms competing in Latin America, for example, have found that proprietary technology, good will based on brand name, and economies of scale in production have served them well in those markets.[51]

A major part of obtaining a competitive advantage is being close to the customer—knowing customer needs, involving customers in the development of new products and services, leading customers to new ideas, and establishing close relationships with customers. Another vital part is **competitor analysis**—performing a SWOT analysis of competitors in order to understand their strategies and determine where they are vulnerable. After studying its competitors' weaknesses, Chrysler stressed its comparative strengths in the advertising campaign for its LH series of cars, which were introduced in 1992 and 1993.

Competitive advantage:
Any factor that enables a firm to outdo its competitors in the marketplace.

Competitor analysis: A SWOT analysis of competitors for the purpose of understanding their strategies and determining where they are vulnerable.

Milliken Uses Creativity to Overcome Foreign Competition

The textile manufacturer Milliken and Company, Inc., with sales of more than $2 billion, found itself facing extremely stiff foreign competition. Recognizing that it was physically closer to the customer and therefore should be able to get closer in a market sense as well, Milliken initiated a series of innovative programs to do just that.

Milliken's first step was to establish more than 1,000 customer action teams (CATs) to unearth new market opportunities in partnership with an existing customer. To launch a CAT, the customer joins representatives of the Milliken factory and sales, finance, and marketing staffs to seek creative ways to serve current or new markets. Well over a hundred such projects may be implemented in a year, adding many millions of dollars to Milliken's bottom line.

An example of a CAT is a year-long "partners-for-profit" program with apparel maker Levi-Strauss that has revolutionized the way the two organizations do business together. Close cooperation enables Milliken to produce fabric to Levi's exacting color standards and in sizes that allow Levi's to exploit every square inch of material. Milliken's quality and reliable delivery record convinced Levi's to omit its inspection of Milliken-supplied goods. Milliken can ship the goods directly to Levi's factory, and Levi's does not have to warehouse the material.

State-of-the-art data and telecommunications linkups eliminate sorting and storing steps at Levi's plant. Milliken loads fabrics into its trucks in the order in which Levi's will need them; in effect, the trucks are meticulously stocked warehouses on wheels. The fabrics are unloaded in the exact order in which they will be needed at Levi's factory, as determined by computers interacting between the two firms. With exact, time-coded order information, the truck brings exactly what Levi's needs to the plant, and the fabric is carried directly to the machine where the garment is cut and sewn.

Levi's makes tags at a remote location for each bolt of fabric manufactured. Via another electronic hookup, the appropriate tags arrive at Levi's finishing plant

Concern with Product and Industry Life Cycles

Many strategic options, including which competitive advantage to seek, are dictated at least to some extent by the life-cycle stage of a particular product line or perhaps a whole business.[52] Strategic managers must be aware of desirable strategies for each stage of their product's life cycle. Strategies for all of the economic functions for each stage of the life cycle have been suggested.[53]

The classic example of how product life cycle affects strategy is the pricing strategy IBM followed for its personal-computer line. In 1982, 1983, and early 1984, when it had a unique position in the business market (its only major competitor was Apple), IBM was able to charge an extremely high price for its products. As that segment of the computer industry grew, however, competitors entered the market with IBM PC clones at lower prices. IBM was forced to lower

This Levi-Strauss factory has become much more efficient because of the creative "partners for profit" program developed by Milliken. For example, Strauss can now concentrate on finished products rather than on the management of raw-materials inventories.

just as the Milliken truck pulls up; they are attached as the truck is unloaded. The result is a monumental savings of cost and delivery time for Levi-Strauss, plus previously unheard-of flexibility in responding to today's lightning-fast fashion trends. Milliken shares the financial benefit. More important, it keeps an order that might otherwise be lost to a foreign competitor.

Milliken involves its customers in solving quality problem as well. By using groups made up of company representatives and customers, Milliken has improved its already high level of customer satisfaction. These and other efforts by Milliken helped it win the Malcolm Baldrige National Quality Award in 1989.

SOURCES: Bruce Whitehall, "How Milliken's Action Teams Involve Clients in Quality," *Business Marketing Digest* (First Quarter 1992), pp. 11–16; and Tom Peters, "The Home Team Advantage," *U.S. News & World Report* (March 31, 1986), p. 49.

the price of its original computers, although it did not have to match the prices of the clones because its name and reputation allowed it to charge a higher price. As the PC reached the maturity stage of the product life cycle, IBM was forced to charge even lower prices. However, it continued to introduce new versions of the product—first the IBM AT and then the IBM XT. These more powerful PCs initially had few competitors, so IBM was able to charge higher prices. Again its prices came down as clones and competitors entered the marketplace. In fact, IBM not only lowered its prices to meet those of competitors, but lowered them far enough to force competitors out of the market. It could produce PCs at a lower cost than many of its competitors could.[54] IBM followed the same cycle with its PS/2 series, introduced in 1990. As close competitors entered the market, it again matched their low prices. In this situation, however, IBM's profit margins were eroded to such an extent that the company suffered financially, especially in 1992.

Strategy Formulation at the Functional Level

The principal concern of functional strategies is efficient use of the organization's resources. Functional strategies support corporate- and business-level strategies. They include strategies related to the organization's economic functions: marketing, finance, operations, human resources, R&D, and logistics. They also include strategies related to the management functions: planning, organizing, leading, controlling, and creative problem solving. A typical financial strategy might be to sell and lease back crucial real estate or plants and equipment. The pricing of the various IBM PCs, discussed earlier, is an example of a marketing strategy. The prominent concerns of the economic functional strategies are shown in Table 7.2.

Types of Strategists

There are four principal types of strategists in any organization: the entrepreneurial leader who makes most or all of the strategic decisions; the informal coalition of top managers; the professional planner; and the division manager.

TABLE 7.2 Economic Functional Strategies

Economic Functions	Major Concerns
Marketing	Marketing mix—the combination of the following four factors: Product mix—the types and number of products or services Pricing Promotional efforts—image Distribution channels—how, where, and when the products are distributed to customers Identification of target market
Finance	Debt Dividends, returns Capitalization structure—how the firm is financed Asset management—especially cash Liability management
Operations	Production technology Layout and design of physical plant Productivity Quality Location
Human Resources and Human Resource Practices	Organizational design and development Management of culture Productivity Government regulations Management of change
R&D and Product Development	Speed Innovation New products and services

Lee Iacocca of Chrysler Corporation epitomizes the entrepreneurial type of manager. Such individuals are usually found in small firms but occasionally are found in larger ones. They make all or almost all of the organization's strategic decisions.

In larger organizations, strategic planning decisions are often made by an informal group of upper-level managers known as a *coalition*.[55] In most large organizations there are several coalitions vying for power. In an organization dominated by a coalition the decision process is often an incremental one, involving a series of small steps as the decision moves from group to group up and down the hierarchy.

In a very limited number of organizations, a professional strategic planner has a profound impact on strategic actions. The professional planner is an advisor whose recommendations may become, in effect, strategic decisions because he or she is most familiar with the strategic situation. In recent years, the role of professional planners has been reduced in many organizations as they restructured and reduced the level of staff support. This has forced strategic decision making farther down in the hierarchy, placing it in the hands of division managers.

As organizations have decentralized, they have sought to have division managers become entrepreneurs within the organization—hence the term *intrapreneurs*. This decentralization has occurred because the evidence suggests that the managers who are closest to the market can make certain decisions better than the very top managers. Moreover, it is thought that having a financial interest, such as a significant profit-sharing incentive, will stimulate managers to do much more successful strategic planning.[56]

Strategic Planning in Global Businesses

As with all management functions, strategic planning varies greatly in the international arena. There are at least four major reasons:

1. The international marketplace is highly competitive. For example, U.S. firms in such industries as autos and PCs face strong competition from firms in Hong Kong, Germany, Brazil, Singapore, Japan, Korea, Taiwan, and Great Britain.

2. Operations are conducted in widely varying economic, legal, political, social, and cultural environments; as a result, people's needs, wants, desires, and capabilities differ.

3. The values of currencies fluctuate, and currency translations can turn a profit into a loss.

4. Host country governments can make life extremely difficult for foreign companies.[57]

AT BALDOR: Imagine the human variables involved in significant changes such as those Baldor underwent. For example, the managers who had formulated previous strategies would have very mixed emotions about seeing them altered. Many would have a vested interest in retaining the old strategies, if only for ego's sake.

From a strategic-management perspective, the strategies of U.S.-based global or multinational firms are often influenced more by the governments of other countries than by the U.S. government. In much of Europe, for example, union representatives are required to sit on large companies' boards of directors. Information gathering is often much more difficult, and the information needed is often quite different, as are the markets. How the people in other cultures view time, their aspirations, their perspectives on authority, how rank and social status are determined, the roles of women, and the meaning of nonverbal communication must all be considered. These and other factors influence an organization's ability to plan strategically, especially when doing business in the global marketplace.

Implementation of Strategy

Once a strategy has been formulated, it must be implemented.[58] In fact, implementation should be considered as one of the SWOT factors when strategy is being formulated. There are four key ingredients in successful implementation: proper organizational structure, suitable management systems, appropriate leadership style, and astute management of organizational culture.[59]

Organizational Structure

"Strategy follows structure."[60] Matching organizational structure to strategy is an extremely important aspect of implementation. Without the proper structure—jobs, departmentalization of jobs, and distribution of authority—an organization cannot carry out its chosen strategies successfully. Managers have six or seven important ways in which to structure the whole organization. These are discussed in Chapter 9.

Various factors affect the choice of a structure. An organization's structure and strategies should match the company's growth stage. In the early stages, an organization typically has a different structure than it will have later. And firms in certain industries, such as aerospace, often have different structures than firms in other industries because of the magnitude of the projects involved and because those projects change frequently.

Structures are not static. They are dynamic. One of the outstanding structural changes that occurred in many firms in the 1980s was the elimination of many staff and middle-management positions. These changes were part of an effort to cut costs and distribute authority farther down the chain of command so that line managers could make more decisions. This increased decision-making authority allows managers to respond to local conditions and situations better than upper-level managers probably would. One of the major strategic structural choices being made today concerns how much authority to delegate. In addition, organizations are beginning to be designed around processes such as information flow, as opposed to functions such as marketing or production.

Management Systems

Operational planning systems; integrated planning and control systems; organizational leadership, motivation, and communication systems; and managing human resources from a system perspective are all critical to successful implementation. It is not enough simply to have strategic objectives and strategic plans; there must be operational and sometimes intermediate planning programs to carry them out. There must be budgets—annual or eighteen-month to two-year financial operating plans. There must be programs to provide leadership and develop a certain style of managing throughout the company. There must be compensation systems and other reward systems to encourage proper implementation. There must be communication systems, such as meetings, attitude surveys, policies, rules, procedures, and bulletin boards, so that people know what to do and how, when, where, and why to do it. There must be human resource management systems. To ensure proper utilization of human resources, the human resources department must actively engage in personnel planning, recruiting and attracting, selecting, training and developing, orienting, providing

STAGES IN
TEAM DEVELOPMENT

FORMING
(Establishing Trust)

STORMING
(...rifying Leadership And
...Other Roles)

...ORMING
(... The Rules For
... As A Team)

...RMING
(... At Maximum
...nd Efficiency)

Structures are not static, but dynamic. An important structural change occurring in many organizations today is the formation of autonomous work groups and teams. The Ford Motor Co. managers shown here are participating in a team development program.

compensation, assuring employee health and safety, facilitating group relationships, evaluating employees, controlling the performance of individuals, managing change, observing equal employment opportunity requirements, and improving communication within the organization. Finally, management must develop systems of control and numerous other management systems to ensure the successful implementation of strategy.

Leadership Style

Successful implementation of a strategic plan requires that managers at all levels of an organization be cognizant of, and be skilled in, communication and leadership. Each manager must be aware of how individuals are motivated and be able to influence that motivation. He or she must develop a satisfactory leadership style, a pattern of leading subordinates. A manager must be skilled in interpersonal relationships and able to "sell" the strategy to those who will implement it, to those who must approve it, and to other key parties.[61]

Organizational Culture

As shown in Figure 7.9, organizational culture—the organization's shared values—is at the center of strategic management.[62] McKinsey & Company developed the framework shown in the figure, called the Seven Elements of Strategic Fit, or the Seven S's. The Seven S's are defined briefly in Table 7.3.

The basic concept underlying the Seven S's is that the organization's efforts in each area must be coordinated—aimed at the same objectives and moved in

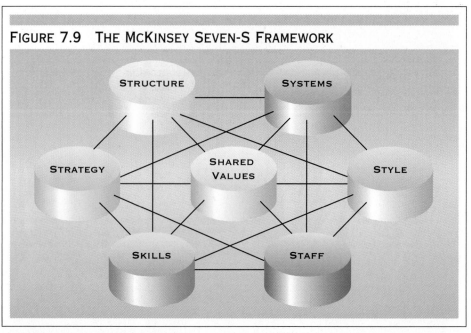

FIGURE 7.9 THE McKINSEY SEVEN-S FRAMEWORK

STRUCTURE

SYSTEMS

STRATEGY

SHARED VALUES

STYLE

SKILLS

STAFF

the same direction—to produce synergy. "The whole is greater than the sum of its parts" is the conceptual basis of the Seven-S framework.

The Seven-S framework embodies the major concepts of implementation introduced earlier: strategy, structure, systems, managerial/leadership style, and culture, or shared values. "Staff" is a demographic consideration, and "skills" is the synergistic competitive edge the organization obtains if the other six S's work in concert. These skills are similar to the strategic capabilities discussed earlier in the chapter.

John Hancock Companies provides an example of the achievement of synergy through the seven S's. When John Hancock made the strategic decision to become a multiple-SBU, highly competitive player in the financial services industry, it had to change the other six S's in its mutual life insurance SBU. It previously had been a bureaucratic organization with many employees. To become more competitive, it had to give employees the authority to make decisions. Some staffing changes were necessary, along with changes in motivational systems, leadership style, and organizational culture. This chapter's Diversity Management Challenge examines a firm in which culture is critical to strategy implementation.

Strategic Management in Complex and Turbulent Environments

The environments confronting strategic planners today are increasingly complex and turbulent.[63] Internal and external environments, as well as the competitive environment, are posing significant challenges to top management. Conse-

TABLE 7.3 Summary of the Seven S's

1. *Strategy:* A coherent set of actions aimed at gaining a sustainable advantage over competition, improving position vis-à-vis customers, or allocating resources.

2. *Structure:* The organization chart and accompanying baggage that show who reports to whom and how tasks are both divided up and integrated.

3. *Systems:* The processes and flows that show how an organization gets things done from day to day (information systems, capital budgeting systems, manufacturing processes, quality-control systems, performance measurement systems).

4. *Style:* Tangible evidence of what management considers important by the way it collectively spends time and attention and uses symbolic behavior. What managers say is less important than the way they behave.

5. *Staff:* The people in the organization. Here it is very useful to think not about individual personalities but about corporate demographics.

6. *Shared values (or superordinate goals):* The values that go beyond, but might well include, simple goal statements in determining corporate destiny. To fit the concept, these values must be shared by most people in an organization.

7. *Skills:* A derivative of the rest. Skills are those capabilities that are possessed by an organization as a whole, as opposed to the people in it. (The concept of corporate skill as something different from the skills of the people in it seems difficult for many people to grasp; yet some organizations that hire only the best and the brightest cannot get seemingly simple things done, while others perform extraordinary feats with ordinary people.)

SOURCE: Robert H. Waterman, Jr., "The Seven Elements of Strategic Fit," *Journal of Business Strategy,* Faulkner & Gray Publishers, New York, NY. Reprinted with permission.

quently, firms are undertaking a series of actions to improve their strategy formulation. Among those actions are strategic thinking; flexible strategic plans; resource-based strategies (improving resources to cope with potential environments); scenario forecasting; improving information systems; better scanning of the environment; increasing capacity for change; speed strategies (getting products to market faster); frequent reviews of plans; contingency plans; alliances; and simulations. At a time when strategic planning is most needed, it unfortunately has become more difficult. Innovative strategic planning is becoming increasingly necessary. These rapid changes, this turbulence, is what makes organizational learning so critical to success.

Strategic Management as a Problem-Solving Process

It is important to keep in mind that strategic management in any environment is a creative problem-solving process. It involves planning—that is, making decisions about the future. As Figure 7.10 suggests, it is a problem-solving activity. It stems from a situation that must be resolved and results in a choice among alternatives. The figure shows that many of the concepts covered in this chapter are themselves problem-solving processes: strategic planning, strategic thinking, strategic management, strategy formulation for all types of strategies, and strategy implementation. Strategists could engage in all parts of the process, and the McKinsey Seven-S model relates to all of them as well.

FIGURE 7.10 STRATEGIC MANAGEMENT AS PROBLEM SOLVING

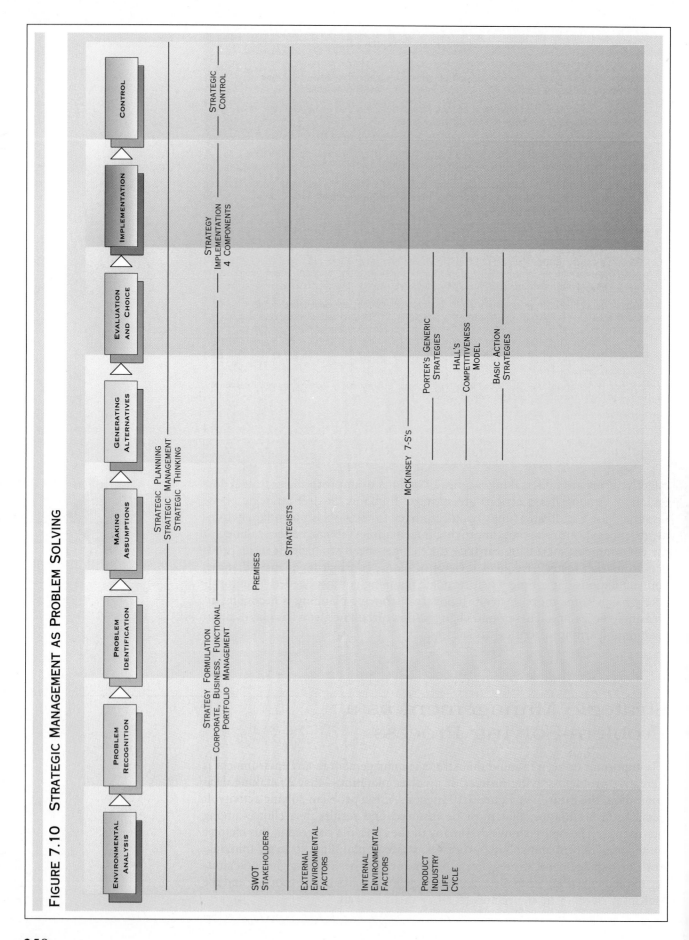

Hitachi: Diversity in a Land of Sameness

All Japanese companies are alike. Right? Wrong! Giant Hitachi, with sales of $62 billion (which accounts for 2 percent of Japan's gross domestic product), is egalitarian and individualistic in a country where other firms are hierarchical and demand conformity. The company's structure is so amorphous and so decentralized that it's sometimes hard to figure out who is in charge. The spirit of individualism that results sometimes leads to spectacular rebelliousness. For example, in the 1980s a former Hitachi CEO decided that hydroelectric power was passé and ordered the research team in that sector disbanded. The team disobeyed and went underground. Taking advantage of generous unallocated research time, the team continued its work, surfacing a few years later with a significant new system that power companies found desirable because of its positive impact on the environment.

Decentralization is the rule throughout the company. Most of its twenty-eight plants operate as separate companies, spending freely on research and development as they deem necessary. The company began as a loose federation of fiercely independent engineers, and this may help explain its amorphous structure. The firm diversified and expanded without a dominant leader like Sony's Akio Morita.

Heading Hitachi is Tsutomu Kanai, a converted Christian and avowed nonconformist. A nuclear engineer, he maintains R&D efforts even in tough times. But he isn't afraid to make hard decisions. Recently he cut top management's pay, including his own, by 15 percent. "Our ordinary workers have been hit hard. Managers must experience the same kind of pain," he explained. Not many Japanese CEOs would take such action; even fewer U.S. CEOs would.

Kanai and a team of ten managing directors steer the firm's strategy. They are in constant contact with division and plant managers. Hitachi's strategy is based on expanding product frontiers in the company's four major business groups: chips, computers, and telephones; power plants, steel mills, trains, and robots; electric wire, special steels, and ceramics; and TVs and VCRs.

Hitachi's 1,200 scientists and engineers are the company's real heroes and are allowed to pursue their projects to the fullest extent. For example, Yasutsugu Takeda, managing director of R&D, helped develop semiconductor lasers. When he couldn't get any Hitachi factory interested in making them for sale, he lined up numerous sales with customers such as IBM, Xerox, and Canon. He presented these orders to one of the chip-making factories and thus began Hitachi's very successful optoelectronics business.

SOURCE: Neil Gross, "Inside Hitachi," *Business Week* (September 1992), pp. 92–100.

Summary

(Before reading this summary, look again at the objectives listed at the beginning of the chapter.)

1. Strategic management is concerned with accomplishing the organization's mission while managing its external relationships. It encompasses strategy formulation, implementation, and control. It is much more comprehensive than strategic planning.

2. There are three levels of strategy: corporate, business, and functional. Corporate strategy is concerned with which business or businesses an organization should be in. Business strategy is concerned with how to compete in a particular business. Functional strategy is concerned with effective and efficient use of resources in carrying out corporate and business strategies. Organizations may choose among several basic action strategies: competing or finding a niche, concentrating on multiple products, growing, stabilizing, reducing investments, defending against a takeover or seeking one, turning around the company's fortunes, or some combination of these.

3. Strategy formulation consists of the following steps: reviewing vision, mission, and goals; performing an environmental analysis; determining strengths, weaknesses, opportunities, and threats (SWOT); developing planning premises; establishing strategic objectives; proposing strategic alternatives; evaluating strategies; and making a decision. Strategists must consider both internal and external environments when establishing objectives and formulating strategy. Planning premises are based on forecasted SWOT. The product life cycle plays a very important role in the formulation of business strategy.

4. Corporate strategy for multiple-business organizations is essentially a portfolio management exercise using such tools as the BCG matrix and the GE matrix.

5. Strategic planning answers three questions: where are we now, where do we want to be, and how do we get there?

6. Core competencies, capabilities, and resource bases are types of strengths on which strategy can be based. Fast organizational learning is a skill and can offer a competitive advantage.

7. There are four types of strategists: the entrepreneurial manager, the coalition, the professional planner, and the division manager.

8. Strategic planning is greatly affected by human behavior—for example, the strategist's needs and values and social relationships. It is and should be much more intuitive than is often thought.

9. Strategic planning varies widely in different types of organizations: large versus small, international versus domestic, not-for-profit versus for-profit, and regulated versus unregulated.

10. Implementation of strategy is most concerned with organizational structure, systems, management style, and shared values.

THINKING
ABOUT
MANAGEMENT

General Questions

1. Why are organizations so concerned about strategic management today?

2. Describe how strategic management in a Du Pont chemical division would differ from strategic planning in the same division.

3. Choose a company with which you are familiar, or a well-known company such as Coca-Cola, and indicate how it would accomplish each of the stages in the strategy formulation process.

4. Describe the major concerns for AT&T at the corporate level, at the business level, and at the functional level.

5. Select a company and describe its basic action strategies.

6. Select a nonprofit organization and describe its possible strategies using Porter's generic strategies.

7. Describe an organization that uses each of the Miles and Snow typologies.

8. Why do multiple-business organizations seek to have businesses in each of the three areas of the GE business screen and in each stage of the product, market, and industry life cycles?

9. Describe what the major concerns of strategies for the management functions might be.

10. Describe how the processes of strategy formulation and implementation might differ for each of the following: large businesses, small businesses, international businesses, not-for-profits, regulated businesses.

11. Relate both a successful and an unsuccessful example of implementation using the Seven-S model.

12. Describe how organizational learning might take place.

Questions on the Management Challenge Features

GLOBAL MANAGEMENT CHALLENGE

1. What error in strategic premises (decision assumptions) did Porsche make?

2. How should it correct its situation?

INNOVATION MANAGEMENT CHALLENGE

1. How does innovation help Milliken succeed?

2. How could Milliken's approach be applied in other firms?

DIVERSITY MANAGEMENT CHALLENGE

1. How does Hitachi's culture differ from those of other Japanese firms?

2. Why has its culture developed as it has?

E P I L O G U E

Baldor's Success Depends on Functional Strategies

Baldor has moved forward with its ambitious program to be a world class competitor. It has adopted a major program of employee empowerment, giving front-line workers the authority to make work-related decisions that formerly were made only by managers. It has entered into extensive employee training programs to give them the skills to compete as a global work force. In many cases, this means bringing workers up to twelfth-grade reading and math capability. A major emphasis has been placed on teaching workers the skills necessary to perform statistical quality control. Baldor has also broadened and diversified its markets to include food handling and fitness, thereby reducing its dependence on its major customers in the oil and agricultural industries.

DISCUSSION QUESTIONS

1. What is Baldor's key strategy?

2. What had to change, in addition to strategy, in order for this strategy to be successful? (Try the Seven S's.)

RP Finds Quality Through Innovation

In 1991, Tom Kirkman, director of strategy for RP, a large European oil firm, was directed by the firm's CEO to prepare a strategy for improving quality. Kirkman hired a group of consultants to help develop the program. Massive training and development programs were undertaken to educate first top management, then the rest of management, and finally all the staff and operative employees in total quality management, and to help change the corporate culture to place greater emphasis on quality. The results were dramatic in terms of reduced costs and increased customer satisfaction.

In 1993, the CEO asked Kirkman to turn his attention to innovation as a key component of the corporate strategy. Innovation was one of five key values included in the firm's statement of values; quality was another. The CEO specifically stated that he did not want to dilute the firm's efforts to improve quality and that he wanted to ensure that employees did not see innovation as a gimmick. Kirkman hired a consultant who specialized in innovation management to provide a series of seminars on innovation management, first to top management and later to the rest of the firm's managers. The consultant suggested that a theme of quality through innovation would help achieve the ends sought by the CEO. Kirkman agreed.

DISCUSSION QUESTIONS

1. How do quality and innovation fit together as strategies for increasing customer satisfaction?

2. Think about how innovation could be integrated into a quality problem-solving program. More specifically, quality is a problem-solving process that often involves measuring performance against quality standards, redesigning work to eliminate steps so that fewer mistakes will be made, and automating (in manufacturing) in order to achieve higher levels of efficiency. How might innovation be applied in such situations?

Strategy Formulation

Select a well-known national company and list its current strengths, weaknesses, opportunities, and threats. Then try to identify its probable opportunities and threats five years from now.

Company
Current Strengths
Current Weaknesses
Current Opportunities
Current Threats
Future Opportunities
Future Threats

Now formulate a corporate strategy for the entire organization and a grand strategy for at least one of its businesses.

Corporate Strategy
Business Strategy
Functional Strategy
Grand Strategy

"Imagination is more important than knowledge."

—Albert Einstein

"There are three kinds of lies: lies, damned lies, and statistics."

—Benjamin Disraeli

When you have read this chapter, you should be able to:

1. Describe how quantitative 'methods and management science techniques can be used in problem solving.

2. Indicate the advantages and disadvantages of quantitative methods.

3. Discuss the quantitative and qualitative aspects of decision making.

4. Discuss the importance of various decision science techniques.

5. Define statistical analysis and decision theory techniques and describe how you would use them.

6. Define sales forecasts and describe how you would use them.

7. Define time series and causal techniques and describe how you would use them.

8. Define the qualitative methods of forecasting and describe how you would use them.

9. List the five basic steps in the forecasting process.

10. Define break-even analysis, linear programming, networking models (PERT and CPM), and project management and describe their use.

11. Indicate the uses of computers in decision making.

12. Describe the use and importance of simulation in problem solving.

13. Describe how quantitative methods aid in the problem-solving process.

MANAGEMENT CHALLENGES
DISCUSSED IN THIS CHAPTER:

 Accelerating rates of change.

 Increasing levels of competition.

 A more diverse work force.

Quantitative Methods for Problem Solving and Planning

American Airlines Embraces Quantitative Methods

American Airlines has long been known as an innovative company. It was the first firm in the airlines industry to use an advanced computer-based reservation system, a frequent-flyer program, and two-tier wage systems (in which two people performing the same job may receive significantly different wages). American is concerned with doing whatever is necessary to succeed, and it uses whatever management approaches will work. So it's no wonder that American has embraced management science.

American uses management science in several areas. Among these are crew pairing and maintenance scheduling. These are important functions for quantitative analysis. A 1 percent saving in crew pairing costs amounts to $13 million. Every month an optimization program known as TRIP (trip re-evaluation and improvement program) grinds away for 500 hours on an IBM mainframe, pairing some 8,300 pilots and 16,200 flight attendants on 510 aircraft operating within Federal Aviation Administration constraints, customer demands, and union contract requirements, always arriving at the lowest-cost solution. Recent changes in the optimization program have resulted in $20 million in annual savings for American.

Overbooking is the practice of selling more reservations for a flight than there are actual seats on the airplane. Airlines use overbooking to offset cancellations and no-shows. Without overbooking, approximately 15 percent of all seats would fly empty. Discount allocation involves determining the number of discount fares to offer on a flight. On more popular flights these are held to a minimum, but on less popular flights airlines offer numerous discount fares. Traffic management involves providing the optimal revenue mix of flights that connect at various hubs. This involves matching multiple-flight passengers and single-flight passengers and the number of flights coming and going from each hub. Clearly proper yield management is absolutely essential to profitable airline operations in the 1990s.

American has also developed a system called DINAMO (dynamic inventory maintenance and optimizer) as a way of preventing spoilage of inventory (failure to sell seats). DINAMO is an automated decision-making system that balances the three requirements of yield management. An optimization model, DINAMO incorporates several different, complex interactive mathematical models, several of which are being used for the first time in any firm. The DINAMO system became operational in 1988, and in the subsequent three years it saved the firm $1.4 billion in potentially lost revenue. The rate of spoilage was held to 3 percent. It is estimated that the program will continue to save $500 million a year.

SOURCES: Barry C. Smith, John F. Leimkuhler, and Ross M. Darrow, "Yield Management at American Airlines," *Interfaces* (January–February 1992), pp. 8–31; Ranga Anbil, Eric Gelman, Bruce Patty, and Rajan Tanga, "Recent Advances in Crew-Pairing Optimization at American Airlines," *Interfaces* (January–February 1991), pp. 62–74.

Because of the critical importance of increasing productivity in order to become more competitive, managers are seeking to make decision making more rational and to reduce the levels of uncertainty in the alternatives they choose. To do so, they have increasingly turned to management science, the use of quantitative methods and other techniques to improve the decision-making process. At American Airlines, management science has helped make the company more competitive and more profitable. American has become more analytical in its approach to problem solving, and the use of management science techniques has spread throughout the company.

Although quantitative techniques can be employed in any of the stages of problem solving, their principal applications are in two stages of the process:

1. They help managers analyze situations in a more rational manner in order to recognize and identify problems better.
2. They help problem solvers improve the actual choices they make.

The two systems discussed in the opening case perform both of these functions for American's managers.

Management science as we know it today evolved from operations research (OR) conducted during World War II in an effort to improve production capabilities and the utilization of scarce resources in the military and supporting industries. However, even before the war, people like Frederick W. Taylor, Frank and Lillian Gilbreth, and Henry L. Gantt attempted to base the problem-solving process more on fact than on gut reaction or rules of thumb (see Chapter 2). Management science techniques did not change significantly between the early 1950s and the late 1970s, but their usage increased greatly. In recent years, with the advent of the personal computer (PC) and minicomputers with substantial mainframe capability, their usage has increased even more. Spreadsheet analysis and computer simulations are available for use by almost anyone. Numerous PC programs have been developed to aid managers in making more rational decisions. Quantitative programs and decision support systems have been developed to enable managers to make more scientific decisions.

For virtually every technique that will be discussed in this chapter, numerous software packages are available to perform the quantitative analysis. Some even help with the actual decision process. Not many of the techniques are new; existing techniques have been computerized, making them easier to use. This chapter reviews the major quantitative techniques available to aid in the decision process, focusing on those that are used most consistently. The chapter begins

An analyst at Merck & Company compares a computer-generated control report with a Gantt chart of expected performance.

with a brief discussion of the foundations of quantitative methods and their advantages and disadvantages. Quantitative problem-solving techniques are then reviewed, followed by a section on quantitative planning techniques, including forecasting. The chapter closes with a review of the use of computers in problem solving. Included are discussions of spreadsheets, simulations, and other uses of decision software in management.

Foundations of Quantitative Methods

Management science: A broad term that encompasses virtually all rational approaches to managerial problem solving that are based on scientific methods.

Management science is an extremely broad term, encompassing virtually all the rational approaches to managerial problem solving that are based on scientific methods. This chapter deals primarily with quantitative methods that assist in problem solving and decision making. A managerial problem may have either qualitative or quantitative aspects. The aspects that lend themselves to qualitative analysis include such variables as competitors' intentions and worker motivation. The aspects that can be analyzed from a quantitative perspective include such factors as the costs of raw materials, market share, and the history of customer purchase decisions.

Quantitative methods: A group of techniques that can improve problem solving by making it a more rational, analytical process.

The primary focus of **quantitative methods** is improving the problem-solving process by making it more rational and analytical. Most quantitative methods are based on economic decision criteria. You will recall from the discussion of decision making in Chapter 4 that there are two models of the decision process: the economic model and the administrative model. Quantitative methods attempt to improve the manager's ability to make decisions according to the economic model.[1] These methods rely on mathematical models, and in recent years they have come to rely on the use of computers to perform the calculations in the models.

When using management science and quantitative methods within the standard problem-solving model, a manager proceeds as follows. In formulating the problem, the manager identifies key elements as usual, but identifies the relationships among the key elements in mathematical terms. As part of the process, he or she must determine the variables involved, which will be either controllable or uncontrollable. Decision criteria must also be identified. The result of this analysis will be a mathematical model based on formulas describing the relationships among objectives and variables. The model is then manipulated to determine possible alternative solutions, given various values of the variables and constraints.

The implementation of quantitative methods often requires special effort, as managers may fail to understand their importance. Some managers resist the use of quantitative methods—often because they do not understand them or their relevance.[2] In some situations, however, quantitative methods are essential. Imagine designing and manufacturing a space shuttle vehicle with hundreds of thousands of parts without some type of computer assistance. The task would be impossible.

While most quantitative techniques have been applied to operations management, financial management, and R&D—and, to some extent, to market research—even the seemingly simple act of approaching a boss or a subordinate about a problem can be examined quantitatively. Moreover, more complex interpersonal tasks can be assisted by using quantitative methods, as this chapter's Global Management Challenge suggests.

Advantages and Disadvantages of Quantitative Methods

The future appears to belong to those who can master the computer to enhance their problem solving.[3] However, despite the obvious need to use computer-based quantitative methods, those methods have both advantages and disadvantages.

Advantages

Quantitative methods can assist the problem solver in a number of very useful ways.[4] Among these are the following:

1. They enhance rationality. For many years, managers have relied on intuition to make decisions. Although we have suggested that intuition is a critical component of problem solving, and one that was neglected until recently, intuition is best used after the manager has "crunched the numbers." The numbers to be crunched, as well as the actual crunching, are provided by quantitative methods. Typically, managers have relied on rules of thumb, general knowledge, or organizational policies and rules to guide them. Now they can also rely on powerful quantitative tools, often PC based, to aid in the problem-solving process.

2. They can simplify complex problems and help managers organize them more effectively. By breaking complex problems into parts, managers can understand them more readily and devise better solutions.

3. They provide a means for evaluating risk. Many of the models ask for some estimate of risk. This requirement helps the manager choose among alternatives.

4. The costs of information, computers, and software have dropped significantly. Many managers now have a portable desktop computer that costs less than $2,000 and enables them to perform calculations that twenty years ago were possible only with a large mainframe that cost several hundred thousand dollars and filled a large room. Managers could not afford to ask "what if" questions then; the cost was prohibitive. Today, virtually anyone using a spreadsheet program or a relatively inexpensive simulation can ask such questions. The level of uncertainty in recognizing and identifying problems and in making choices among alternatives has been greatly reduced as a result.

5. Improved software allows managers with limited computer skills to employ quantitative methods. The "user friendliness" of software has improved substantially in recent years, and PCs have become increasingly powerful. Two million bytes of information storage capacity is now the industry standard, with twenty million easily added. Hence, more and more of the machine's memory can be used to provide user-friendly features such as easy-to-understand instructions; and with such large memories, the machine can perform more and more complicated tasks. The evidence suggests strongly that in the future much more software that can readily be used by the average manager will be available.

AT AMERICAN AIRLINES: American's experience shows that using quantitative methods can increase profits. Without scientific management, American would have been significantly less profitable.

The Finnish Parliament Applies Quantitative Methods to Energy Policy

In the 1980s, the Finnish Parliament was confronted with a complex issue: how to provide sufficient power to meet the nation's future needs. Forecasts had shown varying levels of need, but it was clear that additional power would be needed. A number of extremely complex and interdependent variables was involved. The legislators asked for expert assistance.

With a grant from the Academy of Finland, Raimo P. Hamalainen of the Helsinki University of Technology devised a quantitatively based model to assist them. The model focused on the issue of whether an additional nuclear power plant should be constructed. If the answer was yes, construction needed to begin right away, as eight to ten years are required to construct a nuclear power plant. A 1983 poll had shown that less than 50 percent of the Finnish population favored the use of nuclear power. Interviews by the Finnish Parliament revealed that one-third were in favor, one-third against, and one-third uncertain. All sides in the debate had vested interests. For example, Finnish power companies feared that a no vote would eliminate nuclear power as an option for many years. Those opposed to nuclear power feared problems such as atomic and nuclear accidents.

Hamalainen chose a PC-based model of the analytical hierarchy process (AHP) to incorporate the values of all the constituencies involved. Society's overall benefit, an elusive goal indeed, was the criterion used as the basis for decision making in the model. As revealed in Figure 8.1, numerous key variables were involved. The AHP weights preferences for alternative solutions according to the vote of each constituency. All the alternatives are paired against all other possible choices.

Interviews with members of Parliament were used to determine the values (preferences) associated with each of the major variables; numerical statistics were based on those values. This technique revealed that the decision was one of nuclear power versus coal-fired plants. As the debate continued, however, the Chernobyl nuclear accident occurred (1987) and the power companies withdrew their application for a nuclear power plant license.

SOURCE: Raimo P. Hamalainen, "Computer Assisted Policy Analysis in the Parliament of Finland," *Interfaces* (July–August 1988), pp. 12–23.

6. It is generally believed that using management science techniques leads to greater profitability. This was certainly true at American Airlines and has been shown to be true of other firms in a study of Fortune 500 companies.[5]

Disadvantages

Unfortunately, certain problems are inherent in the use of quantitative methods:

1. Quantitative methods typically employ models of reality— simplified versions of actual situations. In many software programs increased user friendliness is achieved by formulating an even simpler model. Some of the more complex simulations enable managers to model an entire system, but few can afford this type

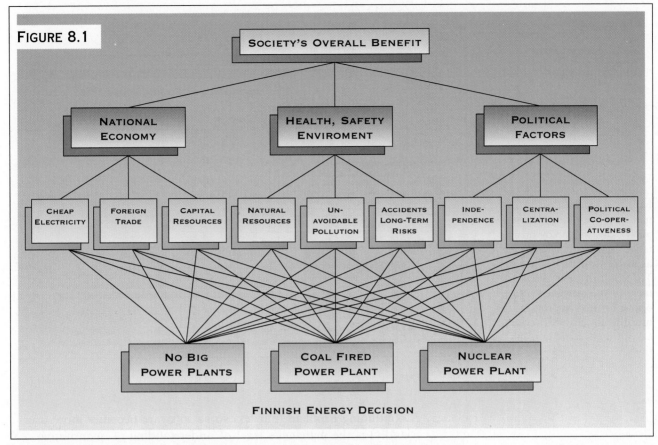

FIGURE 8.1

SOCIETY'S OVERALL BENEFIT

NATIONAL ECONOMY

HEALTH, SAFETY ENVIROMENT

POLITICAL FACTORS

CHEAP ELECTRICITY

FOREIGN TRADE

CAPITAL RESOURCES

NATURAL RESOURCES

UN-AVOIDABLE POLLUTION

ACCIDENTS LONG-TERM RISKS

INDE-PENDENCE

CENTRA-LIZATION

POLITICAL CO-OPER-ATIVENESS

NO BIG POWER PLANTS

COAL FIRED POWER PLANT

NUCLEAR POWER PLANT

FINNISH ENERGY DECISION

SOURCE: RAIMO P. HAMALEINER, "COMPUTER ASSISTED POLICY ANALYSIS IN THE PARLIAMENT OF FINLAND," INTERFACES (JULY–AUGUST 1988), P. 17.

of model. It is therefore critical to make certain that key variables are not left out of the model. In any case, there is a trade-off between simplification, providing for ease of solution, and the possibility of omitting one or more important factors from the model.

2. All-encompassing simulations may be too expensive. A model of the U.S. economy costs hundreds of thousands, if not millions, of dollars to build. Few organizations can afford to construct their own model. Fortunately, at least three are willing to sell their models of the U.S. economy to others, but that is not an option for most complex situations.[6]

3. Quantitative methods usually meet with resistance when they are first introduced. There may be resistance again later, when new techniques are introduced. Many people have not overcome their fear of computers, and many organizations fail to introduce their personnel to the programs in a way that reduces resistance to change.

4. Not every problem can be modeled satisfactorily using quantitative methods. In many cases, the decision is almost totally qualitative. Moreover, quantitative methods do not account for many of the social-psychological variables involved in problem solving. Interpersonal problems, for example, are difficult to quantify; nor have many models yet been designed to aid in the creative aspects of problem solving.

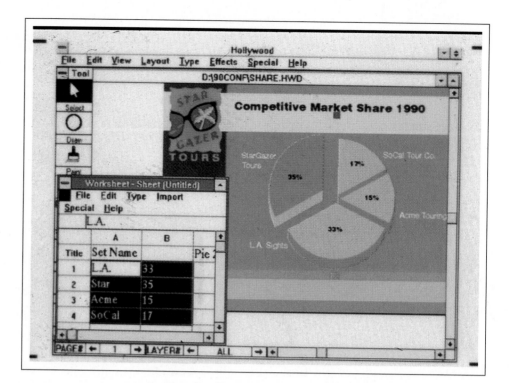

Improved software enables managers with limited computer skills to employ quantitative methods that were not available to them in the past. The new programs allow more of the machine's memory to be used to provide user-friendly features such as easy-to-understand instructions.

5. A continuing problem (but less so as software becomes more user friendly) is the manager's level of understanding of quantitative methods. With user-friendly software, the manager becomes semiexpert in using a quantitative method. Yet he or she often is not fully conversant with the theory behind the technique. Managers must understand the meanings of the numbers the software gives them, not just how to obtain those numbers.

6. Insufficient time to solve extremely complex problems limits the use or applicability of many quantitative methods. There may not be enough time to construct models or analyze the problem scientifically. If a decision must be made immediately, intuition often must suffice. On the other hand, quite complex problems can be modeled in a page or two; thus, many complex problems can be modeled even when time is short. Available evidence indicates, however, that many strategic problems almost defy scientific analysis because of their complex interdependent relationships. In these cases, intuition must be used.[7] Moreover, while rigorous rational analysis of problems is necessary, creativity can often add to the number and quality of potential solutions.[8]

The advantages and disadvantages of quantitative methods are summarized in Table 8.1.

Basic Quantitative Decision-Making Techniques

There are a variety of basic quantitative decision-making techniques. We will introduce some of them briefly here and discuss them more fully later in the chapter.[9]

TABLE 8.1 Advantages and Disadvantages of Quantitative Methods for Problem Solving and Planning

Advantages

1. The rationality of the problem solver is enhanced.

2. Problems are simplified and managers helped to organize a problem better.

3. A means of risk evaluation is provided for various alternatives.

4. Nonprohibitive cost of computer usage for quantitative methods makes computation and analysis relatively inexpensive.

5. User-friendly software makes it possible for almost any manager to use quantitative methods.

Disadvantages

1. Models are simplified versions of reality.

2. All-encompassing simulations may be prohibitively costly.

3. Resistance to change, to computers, and to quantitative methods occurs initially in every situation.

4. Not every problem can be modeled satisfactorily.

5. A person can use a method without fully understanding it.

6. The short amount of time available to spend on very complex problems may limit the use or applicability of many quantitative methods.

Inventory models: Used to determine how much inventory to order and when.

Queueing theory: Applied to determine the number of service units that will minimize both customer waiting time and cost of service.

Network models: Build on the GANTT chart to break large, complex projects into smaller segments that can be managed independently.

Forecasting: Includes a number of techniques for making predictions, largely on the basis of past experience.

Regression analysis: Indicates relationships among two or more variables. Once a relationship has been defined, it can be projected into the future.

Simulation: Produces a model of a problem; a computer is then used to solve the problem in different ways, altering variables to determine their effects.

Linear programming: Determines how to allocate resources among potentially competing uses.

Sampling theory: Applied to determine appropriate samples of populations for marketing research and other purposes.

Statistical decision theory: Used to determine characteristics in models on the basis of probabilities.

Quantitative techniques like those just listed are applied in numerous areas. In 1979, G. Thomas and J. DaCosta surveyed large corporations to determine which areas of application used management science techniques most frequently.[10] Their results are summarized in Table 8.2.

A survey by Norman Gaither, also conducted in 1979, isolated three principal areas of manufacturing in which quantitative techniques are employed: production planning and control, project planning and control, and inventory

TABLE 8.2 Quantitative Methods Used by Corporations

Method	Percent Using
Statistical Analysis	93
Simulation	84
Linear Programming	79
PERT/CPM	70
Inventory Theory	57
Queueing Theory	45
Nonlinear Programming	36
Heuristic Programming	34

SOURCE: Adapted from G. Thomas and J. DaCosta, "A Sample Survey of Corporate Operational Research," *Interfaces* (1979), no. 4, pp. 102–111.

analysis.[11] A survey by W. Ledbetter and J. Cox, shown in Table 8.3, revealed that several techniques are used quite often by business managers in arriving at decisions.[12] A recent survey of the chief financial officers of Fortune 500 firms by James S. Moore and Alan K. Reichert reports that such techniques are being used selectively, but significantly, as shown in Table 8.4. (Note the differences in responses in Tables 8.4 and 8.2, which are due to differences in the respondents to the two questionnaires.)

Literally hundreds of quantitative methods are employed in organizations today. In this section we will focus on the commonly used techniques—statistical analysis, decision theory, and decision trees—and then review the

TABLE 8.3 Areas in Which Management Science Studies Are Applied

Area of Application	Percentage of Companies Reporting Applications in that Area
Forecasting	88
Production Scheduling	70
Inventory Control	70
Capital Budgeting	56
Transportation	51
Plant Location	42
Quality Control	40
Advertising and Sales Research	35
Equipment Replacement	33
Maintenance and Repair	28
Accounting Procedures	27
Packaging	09

SOURCE: W. Ledbetter and J. Cox, "Are OR Techniques Being Used?" Reprinted from *Industrial Engineering* magazine, February 1977. Copyright 1977, Institute of Industrial Engineers, 25 Technology Park/Atlanta, Norcross, Georgia 30092.

TABLE 8.4 Areas in Which OR Techniques Are Being Used

Technique	Percentage of Firms Indicating Frequent/ Regular Use
Sales Forecasting Models	76
Project/Product Models	61
Inventory Management Models	60
Break-Even Analysis	47
Simulation	29
Linear Programming	24

SOURCE: Adapted from James S. Moore, "A Multivariate Study of Firm Performance and the Use of Modern Analytical Tools and Financial Techniques," *Interfaces* (May–June 1987), p. 81.

vital planning aids of forecasting, linear programming, PERT/CPM, decision-support software, and simulations. Techniques that are widely used in production and operations management are discussed in Chapter 21.

Statistical Analysis

Studies of the use of quantitative methods in business find that statistical analysis is the most frequently cited technique. **Statistics** are data that have been assembled and clarified in some meaningful way. They are divided into two principal types: descriptive and inferential (predictive). **Descriptive statistics** describe a situation as it currently exists. **Inferential,** or **predictive, statistics** are used to predict what will happen in a given situation in the future. The two types are closely related. Most often, statistics about current situations are used to predict future situations. (Note: This approach can be misleading. A better technique is to use scenarios to generate future-based statistics to make predictions.) For example, marketing researchers often analyze samples of selected market populations in order to determine their characteristics. These descriptive statistics are then used to suggest whether new products might be successful in that marketplace and what the characteristics of a successful product might be (inferential statistics). Marriott used this approach in designing the features of its Courtyard Motels. It analyzed the interactive effects of numerous factors on the various design possibilities—for example, lobby and restaurant size and location versus ease of customer parking. These efforts were successful; the Courtyard chain has prospered.[13] Production personnel, especially those in quality control, often examine a sample of products to determine how many contain errors. This descriptive statistic is used to predict the rate of errors in the larger "population" of products. (Most Japanese firms seek 100 percent product perfection and therefore have "zero defects" programs. Many U.S. firms are moving in this direction as well.)

For the average manager, descriptive statistics are more important than predictive ones. Managers use statistics in the preparation of charts, graphs, tables, indexes, and the like, designed to help them understand trends and perhaps even make some inferences about the future. Managers making presentations to upper-level managers or to their subordinates or fellow managers are likely to employ descriptive statistics. They may, for example, combine information from software packages, such as spreadsheet analysis of production costs, with a professional presentation package. It is important for managers to have a

Statistics: Data that have been assembled and clarified in some meaningful way.

Descriptive statistics: Statistics that describe a situation as it currently exists.

Inferential, or predictive, statistics: Statistics used to predict what will happen in a given situation in the future.

Japanese firms like this automobile manufacturer are attempting to achieve zero defects. Many U.S. firms are moving in this direction as well.

clear understanding of the data they are using. This entails more than a concern with how statistics can be used to predict future situations. For example, in coming years, human resource managers will increasingly be called upon to use statistics to support their personnel decisions, as this chapter's Diversity Management Challenge suggests.

Although the typical manager generally uses descriptive statistics, there are times when inferential statistics are useful. For example, managers may use regression or correlation to describe certain situations. Assuming that the situation described will not change, the resulting statistics can be used to make predictions about the future. Trained statisticians almost never use them in that way. They are more concerned about the existing relationships between variables than their future relationships. However, a manager can determine whether a relationship that existed historically will have any meaning in the future. He or she can then make decisions based on how useful that relationship is in predicting the future.

In such situations, good judgment is vital. If it were demonstrated, for example, that a strong correlation exists between the birthrate in New York City and the number of storks nesting in Canada, would you see them as related? A manager in Gerber's baby food division might say that an increase in stork nesting in Canada would mean that the company should produce more baby food. It is not likely, however, that a production manager would make such a decision because it seems clear that, while a rise in the birthrate might be accompanied by a rise in the number of nesting storks, there is probably not a cause-and-effect relationship between them. In short, managers must make such determinations carefully.

Decision Theory: Decision Trees and Expected Value

Techniques such as decision trees and concepts such as expected value can be used in determining optimal choices when confronted with several alternatives under conditions of uncertainty or risk.

DECISION TREES

Employees in the Fabrication Division of Boeing's Commercial Airplanes Group use statistical process control to improve product quality, reduce costs, and provide continuous product improvement. They use decision trees to help determine what data to collect and what control charts to use.[14] A decision tree describes the interrelationships among complex problems involving a series of sequential choices.[15]

It is a visual representation of the alternatives available to the decision maker, their interconnectedness in the environment, and their consequences. Figure 8.2 illustrates a typical decision tree. The organization portrayed in this figure is attempting to determine whether to sell its consulting services in Atlanta or in Boston. In either city, services may have a high level of demand or a low level of demand. In Boston there is a 70 percent chance of high demand. The conditional payoff from choosing the condition (i.e., Boston) would be $2 million. The probability of low demand is 30 percent. The conditional payoff is $.5 million. The expected value is the sum of the conditional payoffs times the conditional probabilities: ($2,000,000 × .7) + ($500,000 × .3) = $1,400,000 + $150,000, for a total of $1,550,000. Consulting services in Atlanta have a high-demand probability of .9. The conditional payoff is $1.5 million. The low-demand probability is .10. The conditional payoff is $.4 million. The expected value is ($1,500,000 × .9) + ($.4 million × .1) = $1,350,000 + $40,000, for a total of $1,390,000. The expected value of establishing consulting services in

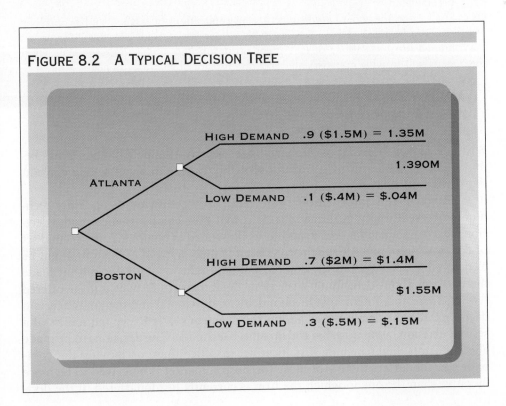

FIGURE 8.2   A TYPICAL DECISION TREE

HIGH DEMAND   .9 ($1.5M) = 1.35M

1.390M

ATLANTA

LOW DEMAND   .1 ($.4M) = $.04M

HIGH DEMAND   .7 ($2M) = $1.4M

$1.55M

BOSTON

LOW DEMAND   .3 ($.5M) = $.15M

Using Statistics to Assure Legal Compliance

Do you like paperwork? Do statistics turn you on? If so, consider a career as a human resource manager. As a result of the 1991 Civil Rights Act, companies need to *prove* that their personnel decisions are not discriminatory—even unintentionally discriminatory. Human resource managers must keep increasingly detailed records, which constitute the proof.

Without such statistical data, companies can face expensive lawsuits.

According to the 1991 act, the employer's motive is not an issue in determining the legality or illegality of hiring and promotion processes. Instead, courts will look at two criteria. First they will examine the impact of the qualifications used. Each "qualification" will be examined to determine whether it statistically screens out more minorities or women than whites or males. In situations in which employers evaluate a number of qualifications, if statistics show that fewer minority individuals or women make it through the process, the legality of the entire process will be in doubt.

Second, courts will compare the candidate pool (race, sex, and national origin) with the work force selected.

To be prepared in the event of an allegation of unintentional discrimination, a human resource manager can take several steps to maintain data that would be useful in a statistical battle. Here are some suggestions:

Collect and maintain data on applicant flow. Record who actually applied for each position, who was chosen, and why. On a separate form, unavailable to those making the hiring decisions, record information about the applicants' age, sex, race, and national origin. If a challenge ensues, such information will help in determining the actual makeup of the applicant pool for that position. In the absence of such specifics, assumptions about the work force can be easily made and manipulated.

Limit the pool of applicants. Accept applications only when a job is open and ready to be filled. Advise applicants that their applications are "live" for only a limited time, say thirty days. Accept no unsolicited applications by mail. These steps will provide a statistically accurate history of the real applicant pool.

Boston is higher than that of establishing services in Atlanta. All other things being equal, the decision maker would probably choose to begin selling consulting services in Boston.

Although this information could have been portrayed using other techniques, the real utility of decision trees is that they can be used to model decisions that are sequential. For example, as illustrated in Figure 8.2, the second set of decision alternatives for the path chosen (a high demand in Boston) might be to determine what actions the company should take, or not take, until it made the decision about consulting services in Boston. It could wait until it offered services there and until a high level of demand developed and then make certain decisions. But the decision tree allows the problem solver to see the results of a second decision, assuming that the first has been made. The decisions to be made about Boston might include just locating an office there or moving the company's headquarters there—because the Boston market is perceived to be more lucrative than the one in which the firm is currently headquartered. If the deci-

A human resource manager must collect and maintain data on all applicants for positions in the organization, including information about each applicant's age, race, sex, and national origin. This information is kept separate from test scores and is not made available to those making the hiring decisions.

Use written job descriptions. Because the 1991 act focuses on which qualifications adversely affect minorities and whether those qualifications are related to a particular job, job descriptions should outline all duties and qualifications, as well as any relevant standards for quantity or quality of production.

Use job posting. To substantially reduce the number of candidates for a promotion, post openings and include specific criteria and application deadlines.

Use objective criteria (thereby eliminating many unqualified candidates).

Maintain records on all employment decisions. The 1991 Civil Rights Act shifts the burden of proof to the employer. Human resource managers need to retain records to show that statistical disparities are a result of innocent causes.

SOURCE: John C. Cook, "Preparing for Statistical Battles Under the Civil Rights Act," *HR Focus* (May 1992), pp. 12–13.

sion makers choose just to open an office, key questions are where in Boston to open it—a central-city location versus a perimeter highway location—and how much to spend. An additional alternative might be to go ahead and begin to do some consulting in Atlanta because the difference in the expected values of the two original alternatives is not very large. One of the real advantages of using decision trees is their flexibility, as Figure 8.3 suggests. They can be adjusted to suit different needs.

Decision analysis is being used in more organizations as its utility is recognized. A division of Eaton Corporation, for example, used the decision tree technique to determine whether to acquire the rights to a night safety device. Honeywell uses expected values to aid in growth planning in its defense industry segment.[16] The U.S. Forest Service uses decision tree analysis to guide its decisions to control-burn certain areas in order to prevent forest fires from covering much larger areas.[17] Decision tree analysis has been used to help people choose which mortgage is best for them and to determine where to drill for oil.[18] The

A decision tree describes the interrelationships among complex problems involving a series of sequential choices. Software to guide decision makers through the process is becoming more available.

use of decision trees will probably increase as software to guide decision makers through the process becomes more available. In fact, many software programs use the decision tree as a graphic presentation device.

When substantial amounts of money are involved, decision makers can make effective use of these decision-analysis tools. However, they must be especially careful to apply judgment and intuition to the statistics obtained in this way.

FIGURE 8.3 SEQUENTIAL DECISIONS SHOWN ON A DECISION TREE

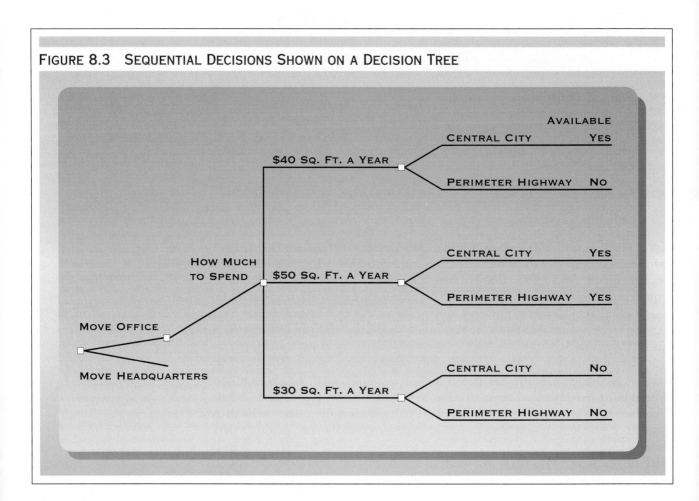

Quantitative Techniques for Problem Solving

In addition to statistics and decision trees, several other quantitative methods are available to facilitate problem solving. Among them are inventory models, queueing models, and distribution models.

Inventory Models

Inventory models provide guidance in managing inventory, most often in determining how much inventory to maintain at a particular point in time. Inventory modeling is limited to managers in operations situations. Inventory models can be used with raw-material, work-in-process, and finished-goods inventories. There are costs associated with having too little or too much of each of these. Too little inventory of raw materials or work-in-process goods may halt the production process while additional inventory is being acquired. Too little inventory of finished goods may upset customers when they cannot purchase a good because of a stockout. Too much of all three types of inventory means excessive carrying charges (the costs of maintaining high inventory levels), as well as money tied up in goods that have not yet been sold. In addition, there are costs associated with ordering raw materials and supplies. Inventory holding costs must be balanced against the costs of continually changing production runs. Normally, the longer the production run, the cheaper the per unit cost because start-up costs can be averaged over a larger number of products.

One of the more recent innovations in inventory management is just-in-time inventory, in which only enough inventory for one day's manufacturing is kept in work-in-process and raw-material inventories. Suppliers have to meet production requirements or lose the contract. Thus, as we saw in Chapter 7, Milliken supplies Levi-Strauss with exactly one day's materials requirement for its manufacturing facilities.[19] The advantages of just-in-time inventory are that holding costs are kept to virtually zero, production runs are at maximum for the plant's capacity for the day, and finished goods can be shipped to the customer as they are completed. However, there are two disadvantages: problems in maintaining control of the quality of the inputs and in making sure that needed materials are there in time. Inventory models have recently begun to incorporate the impact of pricing and advertising on inventory levels.[20] Because inventory models are so critical to the production situation, they are discussed in more detail in Chapter 21.

Inventory models: Models that provide guidance in managing inventory, most often in determining how much inventory to maintain at a particular point in time.

AT AMERICAN AIRLINES: American used inventory modeling to help fill its planes to capacity. Seats were the finished-goods inventory in this situation.

Queueing Models

Queueing models assist in making choices about waiting-line problems. We have all had the experience of waiting in line at banks, grocery stores, and airline ticket counters.[21] The number of tellers or clerks available to serve us has probably been determined on the basis of some waiting-line model. As in the case of an inventory model, there are both costs and benefits to various levels of "inventory"—in this case the number of people waiting. Customers do not like to wait, so an organization may lose customers in the long or even the short term if they have to wait very long. On the other hand, if a company has enough personnel to make sure a customer does not have to wait, its personnel costs are likely to be very high. The organization thus must balance the two factors. Personnel costs are known, but the effect of waiting on revenues must be estimated. This is done by means of queueing models.

Queueing models: Models that help a manager make choices about waiting-line problems.

A queueing model describes the system's operating characteristics—the percentage of time the service facilities are not being used; the anticipated number of people waiting in line at any point in time; and the average time that the organization would like each person to spend in line, among others. Such models are quite versatile. New York City, for example, used a queueing model to determine whether to change the location of service areas for its police patrol cars. The travel time of the cars to their patrol areas was used as the "waiting-line time."[22] L. L. Bean Inc., the noted mail order firm, developed a queueing model for handling customers' calls that resulted in $10 million in annual savings in the allocation of resources for its telemarketing program.[23]

Distribution Models

Distribution models:
Models that help a manager determine where products are to go and how they are to be shipped.

Logistics and marketing managers are particularly concerned with the effective and efficient distribution of an organization's products. To understand their distribution systems better, they employ distribution models, sometimes referred to as transportation models. **Distribution models** help a manager determine where products are to go and how they are to be shipped. Shipping costs differ for each type of transportation. The manager must determine the optimum means of transportation and the optimum route. Most firms attempt to have vehicles full when they return as well as when they leave—whether the vehicles are the company's or are leased. For example, Hughes Supply Company, a $300-million wholesale/retail commercial construction supply firm, has translated the goal "No truck returns empty" into an objective of at least 60 percent full.[24]

Most distribution models are developed using linear programming, a technique that will be described shortly. However, more extensive computer simulation models may also be employed. For example, Marshall's, an off-price retail clothing chain, had been experiencing rapid growth at a compound annual rate of 30 percent. This growth was coming primarily from the addition of new outlets. The pattern of clothing inventory flows from warehouses to stores was changing constantly, straining existing corporate logistics models. Marshall's put together a team of consultants augmented by specialists in logistics software. They chose to use an IBM AT as their hardware. The model they developed actually consisted of three submodels analyzing inflows, inventories, and outflows. There are as many as twenty thousand links in the system. The model helped Marshall's solve its distribution management problem by enabling distribution managers to satisfy store managers' inventory requirements better than before. Through the model, distribution managers can see how all of the stores and warehouses are interrelated.[25]

Forecasting—A Key Quantitative Technique for Planning

Several quantitative approaches can be used to improve the planning process. To begin with, most plans are based on premises, which in turn are based on forecasts. In this section we will discuss a variety of forecasting techniques. In the next section we will examine other quantitative techniques available for planning: linear programming, break-even analysis, network analyses, and simulations.

 Forecasts are predictions of the future. In business they are often expressed in financial terms.[26] Forecasting becomes more difficult as the managerial environment changes more rapidly.

NUMEROUS QUANTITATIVE METHODS CAN BE EM-
PLOYED TO FACILITATE PROBLEM SOLVING. INVEN-
TORY MODELS ASSIST IN DETERMINING THE QUAN-
TITIES OF FINISHED GOODS THAT SHOULD BE KEPT
IN STOCK AND WHEN ADDITIONAL QUANTITIES
SHOULD BE ORDERED. QUEUEING MODELS HELP
SOLVE PROBLEMS INVOLVING WAITING LINES,
SUCH AS HOW TO HANDLE PASSENGERS AT AIRLINE
CHECK-IN COUNTERS. DISTRIBUTION MODELS USE
LINEAR PROGRAMMING AND COMPUTER SIMULA-
TIONS TO DETERMINE WHERE PRODUCTS ARE TO GO
AND HOW THEY ARE TO BE SHIPPED.

The principal strategic planning forecast that organizations must make is the sales forecast. Forecasts may also be necessary for utilizing material resources and cash. Several techniques can be employed in forecasting. Among them are the quantitative techniques of time series analyses and causal analyses—including regression and correlation—and the qualitative techniques of executive opinion, sales force opinion, expert opinion, and consumer surveys.

Sales Forecasting

Sales forecasting: The process of predicting future sales.

Sales forecasting is the process of predicting future sales. All organizations depend on inflowing financial resources for current and future operations, so predicting their level is an important task. For nonprofit organizations, revenue forecasting, tax forecasting, and other processes are equally relevant and are similar in nature. Your local school authority, for example, must make a forecast of tax funds to determine whether it can give its teachers a 2.5 percent raise this year.

The organization's four principal economic functions—marketing, finance, operations, and human resources—depend on the sales forecast to some degree for the completion of their jobs. (See Figure 8.4.) Because so much depends on the sales forecast, it is usually one of the very first steps in strategic planning. Sales forecasts typically cover a range of possibilities—for example, a growth rate of 8 to 15 percent. Managers must be prepared to operate within that range. Different actions will be possible with a growth rate of 15 percent than with a rate of 8 percent.

Virtually all of an organization's expenses are based on some assumption about the amount of sales that will be made during the forthcoming year or years. The marketing department's promotion, pricing, and distribution efforts are carried out in response to the sales forecast. The R&D department must determine the need for new products. The finance department must determine how to finance related expenses such as compensation, which must be calculated and planned for on the basis of the estimated availability of funds (also based on the sales forecast). Operations managers work in conjunction with marketing managers to determine how much of the product or service to create—also on

A key quantitative technique for planning is sales forecasting, which provides information needed by all the other functional departments of the organization.

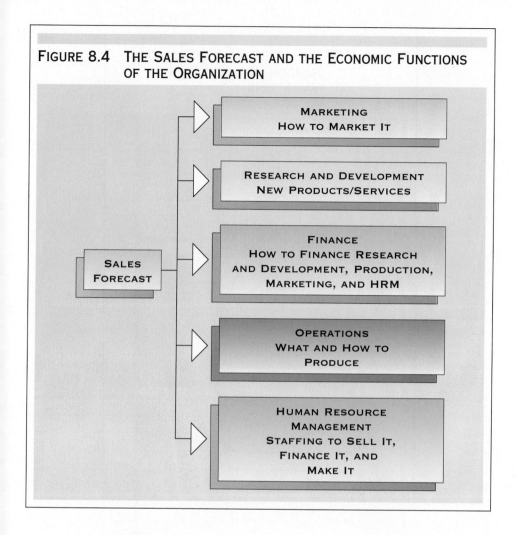

FIGURE 8.4   THE SALES FORECAST AND THE ECONOMIC FUNCTIONS OF THE ORGANIZATION

SALES FORECAST

MARKETING
HOW TO MARKET IT

RESEARCH AND DEVELOPMENT
NEW PRODUCTS/SERVICES

FINANCE
HOW TO FINANCE RESEARCH AND DEVELOPMENT, PRODUCTION, MARKETING, AND HRM

OPERATIONS
WHAT AND HOW TO PRODUCE

HUMAN RESOURCE MANAGEMENT
STAFFING TO SELL IT, FINANCE IT, AND MAKE IT

the basis of the sales forecast. The human resources department uses this information to decide how to staff operations.

Staffing levels, supply budgets, and travel budgets all depend on the sales forecast. For example, an MBA program in a small college might concern itself with the accuracy of sales forecasts (number of incoming students) made by the dean of admissions. Just a few students more or less can cause a 10 percent variance in the program's full-time operating budget. No one wants to be "under budget." A thorough understanding of the forecasts is vital to using them correctly.[27]

Forecasting Techniques

Forecasting techniques are either quantitative or qualitative. Quantitative techniques can be further subdivided into time series or causal techniques.

TIME SERIES TECHNIQUES

One of the key assumptions of forecasting is that the past is a good predictor of the future. This is often true of sales. Time series analyses therefore are very common in sales forecasting. Data that occur over a long period, such as sales, can be analyzed using **time series analyses** in which the variable under study is plotted against time, as shown in Figure 8.5.

Underlying time series analyses is the assumption that time series data will take one of four forms: trend, cyclical, seasonal, and irregular or random. Most

Time series analysis: A technique in which the variable under analysis is plotted against time.

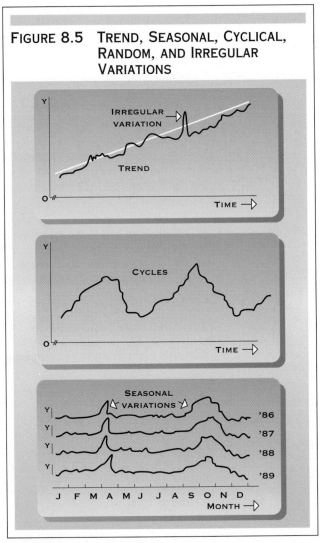

time series data exhibit some sort of trend over a long period. In Figure 8.4 a hand-estimated best "fit" line is used to indicate a trend. More precise computations can be used to determine that trend. Once a trend has been determined, the line can be extended past the current database to predict future points on that line—in this case, future sales.

It is extremely important to adjust time series data for seasonal and cyclical effects. Economic cycles, for example, have a major impact on forecasts of housing starts. It is not too difficult to adjust seasonal effects because a four-quarter or twelve-month analysis will usually reveal the seasonal impact. The Walt Disney World theme parks, which include the Magic Kingdom and Epcot Center, report that attendance is lowest in May, September, and January and extremely high in June, July, August, December, February, March, and April. Knowing this allows them to staff the parks at appropriate levels to keep "waiting lines" to a minimum.[28] Cyclical effects are more difficult to predict because economic cycles, industrial cycles, and product-technology cycles vary significantly, with often unpredictable effects on the economy, industry, or technology.

AT AMERICAN AIRLINES: American used quantitative methods, including expert systems, to forecast demand and schedule seat availability.

CAUSAL TECHNIQUES

The other principal type of quantitative forecasting technique is the causal technique. **Causal techniques** suggest causes of the behavior of dependent variables and often use them to predict events. The two principal types of causal models are regression analysis and the econometric model.

Regression analysis is a statistical technique that determines the relationships between two or more variables—a dependent variable and one or more independent variables. By their very nature, regression techniques are descriptive. However—again assuming that relationships among the variables will be the same in the future as in the past—the manager will often extend the regression line to some future date.

A typical regression equation follows:

$$Y = AX_1 + BX_2 + C$$

where

Y = the dependent variable (sales of hamburgers)

X_1, X_2 = independent variables (businesses having more than 50 employees; number of high school students in the area)

A, B = weights for the independent variables calculated according to an analysis of past data

C = a constant derived from the same data

In this case, hamburger sales are highly dependent on business and student populations in the area. The formula could be used to estimate sales for a new store or to predict the amount of increased sales resulting from increased business or student populations in the area. The manager could substitute various values for X_1 and X_2 in the equation and determine the potential increase in sales.

New York City used regression analysis to help it determine the most efficient way to clean the streets. This chapter's Management Challenge feature shows how the city went about doing so.

Econometric models use a complex series of interdependent regression equations, combining both theory and applied research, to predict the performance of some dependent variable, often the national economy. Because econometric forecasts are costly to create, corporate strategists usually buy forecasts to use in their strategic planning rather than develop them themselves. Such forecasts are available not just for the total economy but for various industries as well. They are provided by a number of services, such as Data Resources, Wharton Econometric Forecasting Associates, and the Evans Group. Forecasts from different sources will offer different predictions, even though they are presumably derived from the same basic information: Each organization's chief forecaster has different beliefs, values, perceptions, and assumptions.[29]

Qualitative Methods

Qualitative forecasting methods are judgments and opinions used in forecasting. Many times, when a forecast must be prepared quickly, there simply is not enough time to gather and analyze quantitative data. At other times, when perceived environmental variables are changing rapidly, the past may not be a good predictor of the future.[30] Moreover, when managers seek to determine the potential impact of new events or wish to determine how to launch new products, it may be advisable to rely on judgment or opinion.

Several techniques are commonly used in such situations. They include executive opinion, sales force composites, expert opinion (including the Delphi technique), and consumer surveys. Another important technique is the techno-

Causal techniques: Techniques that can be used to suggest causes of the behavior of dependent variables and to predict events.

Regression analysis: A statistical technique that determines the relationships between two or more variables, a dependent variable and one or more independent variables.

Econometric models: Models that use a complex series of interdependent regression equations, combining both theory and applied research, to predict the performance of some dependent variable, often the national economy.

Qualitative forecasting: An approach to forecasting that involves the use of judgments and opinions.

Polishing the Big Apple

In a city the size of New York, street cleaning is an ongoing necessity. There are twelve thousand employees in the sanitation department, which spends about half a billion dollars per year on street cleaning. How do you determine optimal manpower levels, and how do you determine the relationship between the number of street cleaners required and factors such as illegally parked cars?

In 1980, the sanitation department was faced with several major problems, including dirtier streets, 1,500 fewer employees than it had in 1965, and low morale among workers. Moreover, it had no knowledge base to use in making decisions, little or no coordination with other city agencies, weak support from top management, and no support from the city council.

A regression analysis helped the New York City Sanitation Department save about $12 million a year in reduced salary and benefits costs.

To answer its questions and solve its problems, the department conducted a regression analysis aimed at improving the conditions of the streets and the efficiency of the work force. A project team built a database, which was then regressed to determine the relationship between employee levels and their effectiveness (as measured by a cleanliness score from the city). Different models were used for analyzing the effects of other factors. The program achieved both of its major goals. After the analysis was conducted, the department achieved five consecutive years of improved cleanliness ratings. Its 1986 rating was 68.7 percent, compared to a low of 53 percent, using seven hundred fewer people. There was a savings of about $12 million a year in reduced salary and benefit costs.

SOURCE: Lucius C. Riccio, Joseph Miller, and Ann Litke, "Polishing the Big Apple: How Management Science Has Helped Make New York Streets Cleaner," *Interfaces* (January–February 1986), pp. 83–88.

logical forecast, which is used primarily to keep the organization abreast of changes in technology. L'Eggs Products' forecasting department, for example, has found it very desirable to include the marketing brand group's qualitative observations in its forecasting efforts. The head of the forecasting department also meets with the head of marketing to review forecasts.[31]

The Limits of Forecasting

There are a wide variety of forecasting techniques; however, several limitations are common to all.[32] Among these limitations are the following:

1. Forecasting techniques generally assume that factors that existed in the past will continue to exist in the future. This is not necessarily the case. Accelerating rates of change pose a special problem.
2. Forecasts are rarely perfect; actual results usually differ from those that were predicted.
3. Forecasts for groups of items such as products or services tend to be more accurate than forecasts for individual items because forecasting errors among items in a group tend to cancel each other out.
4. Forecasts are more accurate for the short term than for the long term. Accelerating rates of change make long-term forecasts more difficult.

Forecasts: A Summary

There are five basic steps in the forecasting process:

1. Determine the purpose of the forecast and when it will be needed.
2. Establish a time horizon that the forecast must cover.
3. Select a forecasting technique.
4. Gather and analyze the appropriate data and then prepare the forecast. Identify any assumptions that are made in conjunction with preparing and using the forecast.
5. Monitor the forecast to see if its predictions are accurate.[33]

A final step is "selling" the forecast to management. Forecasters must be prepared to be persistent in selling their forecasts. At pharmaceutical giant Parke-Davis, for example, the sales forecasting department slowly but surely won management's confidence. One of the means it used was to place confidence levels on each forecast.[34]

Knowing which forecasting technique to use is often a troublesome decision in itself. Numerous issues are involved: the length of time the forecast covers, the availability of computer software, the changefulness of the external environment, and the need for accuracy. These various factors must be weighed and balanced in choosing a technique. David M. Georgeoff and Robert G. Murdick have created an easy-to-use and readily available guide that can be used to reduce the complexity of the process of choosing a forecasting model.[35]

Additional Quantitative Planning Techniques

In addition to forecasting techniques, a number of other quantitative techniques are available for use in planning. Four of the most widely used techniques are break-even analysis, linear programming, network models (PERT/CPM), and simulations. In this section we will examine each of these techniques in detail.

Break-Even Analysis

Whenever new products or services are launched, whenever new projects are undertaken, or whenever managers consider enacting an annual operating plan, there will be a point at which the revenue generated from the product, service, or project is going to equal the cost of generating that revenue. This is known as the **break-even point.** Managers perform a **break-even analysis** to determine the point at which revenues equal costs, along with other relevant information. The principal reason for determining this point is to make certain the organization does not carry out a plan that will not result in a profit. A break-even analysis compares the forecasted demand for the product and the resulting income from the project against the costs of the project. If demand is less than the break-even point, the project should not be undertaken. Managers may also use break-even analysis to examine the effects of different prices or output levels, or to compare alternative allocations of production capacity.

Break-even analysis also points out the need to cut costs. For example, Japanese firms have found that their corporate break-even points have slipped upward in recent years, in many cases reaching 90 percent of revenue, as competition has increased. As a consequence, they have been reducing investment, cutting production costs, leasing, and reducing staff. Nissan decided to bring out new models only every five years instead of every four. Fujitsu has halved its capital spending. Japan Air Lines has started leasing airplanes instead of buying them. Large Japanese firms are hiring fewer college graduates.[36]

As shown in Figure 8.6, all projects or products incur certain levels of **fixed costs**—costs that tend to remain constant regardless of the volume of output. These include factors such as depreciation of plant and equipment, overhead items such as managerial salaries, and insurance costs. **Variable costs** are costs that vary with the volume of output. Normally these include direct labor and materials costs. Variable costs per unit typically remain the same regardless of the volume of output, whereas fixed costs per unit decrease as volume increases. The total cost of any product or service is equal to the fixed cost plus the variable cost per unit times the number of units. These relationships are shown graphically in Figure 8.6.

Also shown in Figure 8.6 is how revenue varies with volume. Like variable costs, revenue varies per unit. Hence, total revenue has a linear relationship with output—that is, a change of a certain magnitude in the independent variable (output) causes a change in the dependent variable (revenue) of a directly related magnitude, regardless of the value of the independent variable.[37] At some point, total revenue will equal total cost. This is the break-even point. Figure 8.6 calculates this point. It can also be calculated algebraically. For example, assuming a fixed cost of $3 million, variable costs of $400 per unit, and revenues of $700 per unit, the volume necessary to break even turns out to be 10,000 units.

Let:

$$TFC = \text{total fixed costs}$$
$$VC = \text{variable cost per unit}$$
$$P = \text{price per unit}$$
$$BEP = \text{break-even point}$$

The formula for calculating the break-even point is

$$BEP = \frac{TFC}{P - VC}.$$

FIGURE 8.6 GRAPHICAL REPRESENTATION OF BREAK-EVEN ANALYSIS

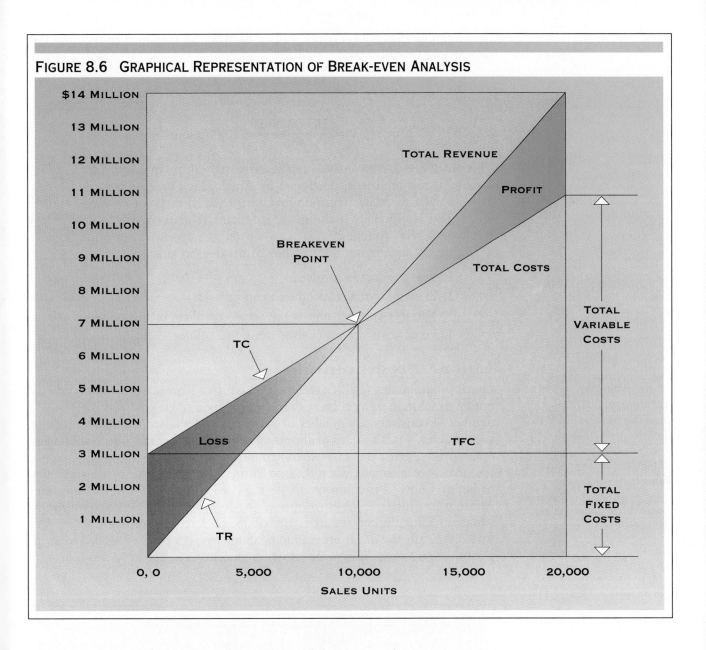

In the preceding example, the formula would be calculated as follows:

$$BEP = \frac{\$3 \text{ million}}{700 - 400} = \frac{\$3 \text{ million}}{300} = 10,000 \text{ units.}$$

Break-even analysis is very good for determining the answers to "what if" questions: What if we wanted a profit of so much, what if we raised prices by so much, what if we could cut costs by so much . . . what would the results be?

In order to determine the required volume (V) to generate a desired profit (DP), the formula would be

$$V = \frac{DP + TFC}{P - VC},$$

where V is actually just a higher break-even point.

Suppose that the company wanted to make $3 million. The required volume would be calculated as follows:

$$V = \frac{\$3,000,000 + \$3,000,000}{700 - 400}$$

$$V = \frac{\$6,000,000}{300} = 20,000 \text{ units.}$$

This use of break-even analysis can be extremely critical in profit planning. One version of this approach, developed by Armco, Inc., uses an expanded break-even analysis to relate return-on-investment (ROI) targets to various volume levels. This is especially useful in capital-intensive markets, where ROI is very sensitive to sales volume.[38]

The key underlying assumptions of break-even analysis follow:

1. One product is involved.
2. Everything that is produced can be sold.
3. Variable cost per unit is the same regardless of the volume.
4. Fixed costs do not change when the volume changes.[39]

Linear Programming

Linear programming: A technique in which a sequence of steps leads to the optimum solution of a problem characterized by a single goal and objective, a number of constraints, a number of variables, and a linear relationship among the variables.

Linear programming (LP) is a technique in which a sequence of steps leads to the optimum solution of a problem characterized by a single goal and objectives, a number of constraints, a number of variables, and a linear relationship among the variables.[40] It is a means of allocating resources or facilities on a project in an optimal way, given the selected constraints—perhaps price and availability of resources. For example, when Ralston Purina makes Dog Chow, Fit and Trim, or Puppy Chow, it is confronted with the need to combine a variety of grains whose prices differ. It seeks to offer a dog food that uses the cheapest grains while providing the content advertised on the package. To solve this problem, it would typically use linear programming. Similarly, if a country needed to airlift personnel and cargo to a wide variety of locations in a short period, using a

Linear programming is a technique in which a sequence of steps leads to the optimum solution of a problem characterized by a single goal and objectives, a number of constraints, a number of variables, and a linear relationship among the variables. Ralston Purina uses this technique to determine how to combine a variety of grains whose prices differ.

Joy Love Peace Happiness Happiness Joy Love Peace Happiness

Be with you
at this season
and
throughout
the year

Blessings
Sister Pamela

and the

Weekend College Staff

College of Notre Dame of Maryland

limited number of aircraft, LP would be used to determine how best to allocate available resources.[41]

Most LP problems are solved on a computer because the equations involved require a large number of calculations. LP problems are solved in a series of steps. The model literally "closes in" on the optimal combination of variables. (You can solve a very basic problem in linear programming, one involving only one possible product and two variables, by graphing it; however, most LP problems are more complex than that.)

LP is an extremely valuable tool. It can be used in a number of situations but is probably most frequently used as a production scheduling device or in cost determination. United Airlines, for example, uses it to schedule four thousand workers.[42] LP can also be used in such diverse areas as allocating sales representatives to territories or selecting an optimal portfolio of investments.[43] One of the advantages of LP is that it allows the manager to perform sensitivity analysis, examining the effects of changes in variables; this is similar to exploring "what if" questions in break-even analysis. One version of LP is capable of handling extremely complex problems with numerous variables and solution possibilities.[44]

Network Models

The **program evaluation and review technique (PERT)** and **the critical path method (CPM)** are network models used to plan and coordinate large-scale projects.[45] PERT and CPM graphically display a project's activities, provide estimates of how long the project and its component activities will take, indicate which activities are the most critical at the time of project completion, and suggest how long an activity within the project can be delayed without delaying the entire project.[46] Although PERT and CPM were developed separately, and there originally were many differences between the two, over time these project planning techniques have become almost identical.[47] PERT was developed through the joint efforts of Lockheed Aircraft, the U.S. Navy Special Projects Office, and the consulting firm of Booz, Allen & Hamilton in an effort to speed up the Polaris missile submarine project. CPM was developed by J. A. Kelley of the Rand Corporation for use by the Du Pont Corporation in planning and coordinating maintenance projects in chemical plants.[48] We will use PERT as an example, although most of what we say could also apply to CPM: Both PERT and CPM use network models to portray major project components—activities and the sequential relationships among them.[49]

A Gantt chart for the activities of a bank opening a new branch is shown in Figure 2.1 (p. 47). Figure 8.7 portrays the same activities in terms of a single-project network diagram. As the figure shows, the PERT network basically consists of circles or squares indicating the beginning or ending of an activity, and arrows indicating the activities themselves. The activities are arranged sequentially from left to right. This network diagram is superior to the Gantt chart in portraying a sequence of activities. Simultaneous activities are represented by dual or multiple paths. Notice that certain activities need to be performed either simultaneously or before others, and that some can be carried out independently.

One of the manager's principal concerns is to determine the **critical path** through the network. The critical path is the sequence of activities that takes the longest amount of time to get from the starting circle to the finishing circle. The manager is interested in determining the longest path through the network because it determines how long it will take to complete the project. The activities on the critical path are the critical activities. Activities on paths that are shorter

Program evaluation and review technique (PERT) and critical path method (CPM): Network models used to plan and coordinate large-scale projects.

Critical path: In a large-scale project, the sequence of activities that requires the most time for completion.

PERT enables Navy contractors to complete highly complex projects, such as this nuclear submarine, on time and at a lower cost than if other project management systems were used.

than the critical path can experience delays and still not affect the completion date of the project. Delays in activities on the critical path will affect the time it takes to complete the project.[50] In Figure 8.7, the critical path takes twenty weeks—from the beginning point, locating facilities (eight weeks), through remodeling (eleven weeks) and moving in.

ADVANTAGES AND DISADVANTAGES OF PERT

Like many of the techniques we have discussed, PERT has both advantages and disadvantages. The advantages follow:

1. The manager is forced to organize and quantify plans and obtain information that is not readily available.
2. PERT provides a visual display of the project and its major activities. Visual displays usually aid in the planning process.
3. PERT identifies the critical activities that might delay the project and should be closely monitored. It also indicates activities that can be delayed without delaying the project.
4. Resources can be reallocated, if by doing so the length of time required to complete the entire project would be shortened.

The disadvantages of using PERT include the following:

1. An important activity may be overlooked in the network.
2. Sequential relationships may not be correct as shown.
3. Time estimates are just that—estimates—and therefore are subject to the problems associated with basing activities on estimates.
4. A computer is necessary to use PERT for large projects.[51]

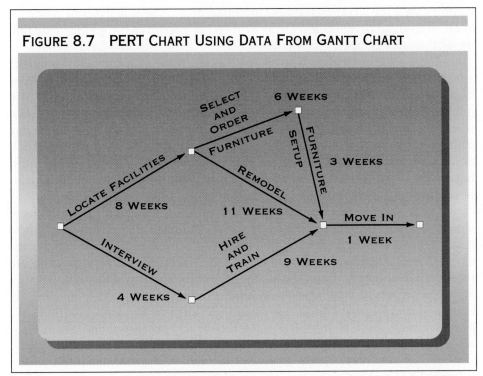

FIGURE 8.7 PERT CHART USING DATA FROM GANTT CHART

SOURCE: ADAPTED FROM WILLIAM J. STEVENSON, PRODUCTION-OPERATIONS MANAGEMENT, 3RD ED. (HOMEWOOD, ILL.: IRWIN, 1986), P. 701.

Some three thousand contractors and subcontractors were involved in various segments of the Polaris project for which PERT was developed. Coordination of those contractors' activities might have been impossible without PERT. At the very least, the Navy estimates that it completed the project two years earlier than it would have without PERT. Today, PERT is used in almost all major construction projects. For example, Blount Brothers Construction Company employed PERT when it constructed the Superdome in New Orleans.[52] In 1993, after the below-ground levels of the World Trade Center in New York City were seriously damaged by a car bomb, CPM was used to plan and coordinate the process of repairing or rebuilding the support structures, electrical wiring, heating and cooling systems, and many other complex, interconnected systems that must be back in operation before the huge office towers could be reopened. In sum, even though there are some problems with PERT and CPM, these techniques are used in virtually every major project management situation.[53]

The Use of Computers in Decision Making and Planning

The use of computers in problem solving is increasing rapidly. Mainframes, minicomputers, and PCs have more power, are available at a lower cost, and have more widespread applications than ever before. Perhaps most important, with the advent of powerful PCs, most of the techniques discussed in this chapter are available in relatively inexpensive computer software packages, well within the price range of most small businesses. **Decision support systems** (DSS), software packages that improve the decision-making process, are becoming widely available. Most businesses can certainly afford them; there are more

Decision support systems: Software packages that improve the decision-making process.

complex ones for larger businesses. Increased quantitative analyses of problems at all levels of an organization are anticipated as a result of the greater availability of these programs.

There are even programs, such as Idea Generator, that can help a manager structure any decision.[54] PERT and CPM, financial planning, LP, spreadsheets, break-even analysis, inventory planning and control, and numerous other programs are readily available for PCs. DSS software will become even more useful when applied in conjunction with artificial intelligence (in which computers emulate the human decision process) and expert systems (which provide additional information to aid managers in making decisions).[55] Perhaps the most important use of the computer, with respect to planning and problem solving, is in conducting simulations.

The use of databases, large computer-stored deposits of information from which needed information can be extracted, is another area of vital concern to managers today. New York City, for example, placed all of its personnel records on a database management system. Known as PRISE—Personnel Reporting and Information System for Employers—the system significantly improved the city's ability to service its two hundred thousand employees, expedite personnel actions, and control personnel decision making. The program also allowed the city to decentralize more of its personnel decisions and thereby reduce its bureaucracy.[56]

Simulations

Simulation: A model of a real-world situation that can be altered to show how changes in its various components would affect other parts of the model.

A **simulation** is a model of a real-world situation that can be altered to show how changes in its various components would affect other parts of the model. Typically, managers simulate company operations or external environments to learn how changes in input levels, production processes, sales, or other factors might affect the total operation or some specific part thereof.

Computers have long been touted as one means of meeting the challenge of an increasingly competitive environment. Until recently, there seemed to be little

A simulation is a model of a real-world situation that can be altered to show how changes in its various components would affect other parts of the model. Redstone uses a LAN-based portfolio management system called PORTIA. The system has a "what-if" capability: When analysts enter the proposed trades, it tells them what the portfolio will look like.

hard evidence to support this belief. Office automation did not prove advantageous at first, and the effectiveness of robotics was being reevaluated. (For example, GM's inability to reap full benefits from its robotized, highly computerized plants revealed flaws in the basic concept.)[57] However, there is growing evidence from a number of sources that computer simulations of production situations such as inventory modeling and plant layouts are increasing productivity. One of the keys to this change is managers' receptivity to the use of simulations. Animation has aided this receptivity. Graphic displays take the mathematician's simulation rationale and put it into readily understandable pictorial language that the average manager can understand.[58] Another key factor in managerial receptivity is the growing number of programs for PCs that bring simulation within the capabilities of many small manufacturers, most of which will benefit substantially from using the programs.

Engineers at Northern Research and Engineering Corporation, a subsidiary of Ingersoll Rand, saved the Torrington Company $750,000 when they simulated the production line facility that Northern was designing for Torrington. Originally, seventy-seven machines were considered necessary, but the simulation indicated that the facility could operate with only seventy-three. Numerous smaller firms are finding that simulations allow them to improve their just-in-time inventory scheduling, a service required of many of these firms by the larger manufacturers they supply.

Polaroid Corporation uses simulation to study production lines. It still employs inventories between segments of its production lines as "buffers"—that is, to keep the lines from being shut down because of lack of parts. Simulation of these inventory buffers indicated that 25 percent of the inventories could be eliminated. This saved the company thousands of dollars as well as substantial floor space. Polaroid also uses simulations to study its capital investment decisions and staffing policies.[59]

Simulations can be used very effectively in a number of situations, such as training. They are often used in pilot training, for example. Weyerhaeuser has developed a simulation that assists in improving the use of raw materials. It trains its log cutters to make better decisions, thereby increasing the yield of usable lumber from each tree.[60] Another use of simulations is described in this chapter's Innovation Management Challenge.

Simulations are extremely useful for examining complex situations. Historically, simulations have been expensive and have been employed only by very large organizations with significant financial resources. More recently, relatively inexpensive simulation software for PCs and minicomputers has become available. Moreover, minicomputers now do the work that was done by much more expensive mainframes just a few years ago; this has helped bring down the cost of simulation. Users of PC simulation software must sacrifice complexity for ease of operation, but even with their limitations, such simulations can be valuable to small organizations.

Readily available spreadsheet programs allow a company to model its financial situation and change various inputs, such as projected sales, to determine their effects on total income, expenses, assets, liabilities, and equity. The break-even point, for example, can be determined using a spreadsheet program. It can be viewed as a series of "what if" questions. The computer can also be asked to indicate what the volume must be for profit to be zero. Some spreadsheet programs have a "goal-seek" feature that automatically calculates the break-even point.

A major feature of recent spreadsheet programs is optimization analysis, an extension of what-if questions. Decision variables are changed until the objective—profit—is maximized without violating any constraints. Only a few

Football (Soccer) Match Simulations

Simulation is particularly valuable in training situations in which the appropriate decisions are context-dependent. An example is police crowd control: Reactions must be swift but not excessive, and decisions must be made amid noise and distraction that can hamper clear thinking, at the very least.

In England, the London police use simulations to reproduce some of the trickiest situations they are required to manage: the volatile conditions among fans at soccer matches (they call it *football*). British football matches are frequently the scene of violence among spectators.

The complex simulations reproduce the stimuli that accost officers at a match. They then present the consequences of the trainees' decisions.

The system consists of a network of computers connected to 12-inch laser disk video players. The video can show someone informing an officer of an incident or can reproduce scenes typical of the stadium during the officer's patrol. Each laser disk video player represents a single vantage point: Participants can see the scene only from their own viewpoint.

The simulation begins as a senior officer triggers an incident that evolves as the scenario progresses. Images can be combined, and video, text, graphics, or audio information can be fed in, as in these examples:

- An officer sees a video clip of an incident of ticket touting. The illegal sale is accompanied by the ticking of a decision countdown clock in a corner of the screen. Further cues for action increase the pressure.

spreadsheet programs have this feature, but many are adding it. The Southern California Gas Company uses optimization software to schedule its meter readers.[61]

Bethlehem Steel Corporation uses a microcomputer for production planning and cost analysis. It has an optimization model of steel flows through the plant, based on the Lotus 1-2-3™ spreadsheet program and run on an IBM PC. It assesses the impact of changes in demand on facilities, capacities, and costs. It allows the user to ask what-if questions. For example, how many eight-hour shifts will the plate mill require if this year's demand for steel plate products is 500,000 tons? Or, how much will the cost of products be raised if the price of natural gas goes up 20 percent? All five of Bethlehem's plants use the model.[62]

Like the decision-making techniques discussed in the early part of this chapter, the planning techniques just described tend to be employed only in certain areas of an organization. However, computer software packages can and should be used wherever possible. It would be worthwhile for any manager to purchase one of the general problem-solving packages to improve his or her decision-making techniques. Quantitative methods, especially simulations and related techniques, are important tools of organizational learning. In the future, organizational learning—an organization's ability to learn from its environment and from its own actions—may separate successful organizations from unsuccessful ones.[63]

- Another trainee confronts two fans claiming the same seat.

- Shortly before the final whistle, an officer receives a report that one of the main gates cannot be opened. The stock response would be to block off the exit with a row of officers and divert the fans with loudspeakers. The simulation accommodates less conventional responses, too, ever since the testing phase, when one experienced controller asked for a Range Rover and a chain to pull the gates off in time to let the spectators through.

At football matches, though roving groups of officers are generally equipped with radios, the radios are often useless because of crowd noise. "Unless you sat at the back of a stand, you could have no conception of the working environment," one officer says. As a result, the simulation blasts the roars and chants of the crowd through powerful speakers. To make working with the radio even more lifelike, trainees can use their radios only when the channels are clear. If one trainee hogs the airwaves, another could be blocked at a critical time. Throughout, the aim is to reproduce the stress under which people must make their decisions.

Jonathan Crego, technology training advisor to London's Metropolitan Police Force, hopes to heighten the realism of the simulations still further by injecting riot footage into the video bank. At present, the simulation stops and debriefing begins before the results of bad management can be seen. Crego feels that some onscreen crowd carnage might enliven the trainees' experience.

SOURCE: Phil Hilton, "A Match for the Crowd," *Personnel Management* (June 1992), pp. 57–58.

Management Science as Decision Support for Problem Solving

Management science was designed to enhance problem solving. Its very purpose is to improve the rationality of the process. Increased use of computers and user-friendly software have greatly enhanced management science in recent years. Managers now find it much easier to employ the techniques described in this chapter and other quantitative techniques as well. To implement management science effectively, managers must learn to rely on these techniques and consider their use part of the normal decision-making process.[64] But they must use them as decision support, not as a substitute for making a decision. Judgment must be applied to the results derived from quantitative methods. As mentioned in Chapter 4, some managers are more rational than others, tend to use a more scientific approach, and tend to think rather then intuit. Others tend to avoid the use of rational and analytical approaches. However, both are vital, especially in more complex decisions.

Figure 8.8 provides additional insight into how various key terms and concepts discussed in this chapter might be used in problem solving. Note that while only a few are identified as important in more than one stage of the process, many can be used in some way in more than one stage.

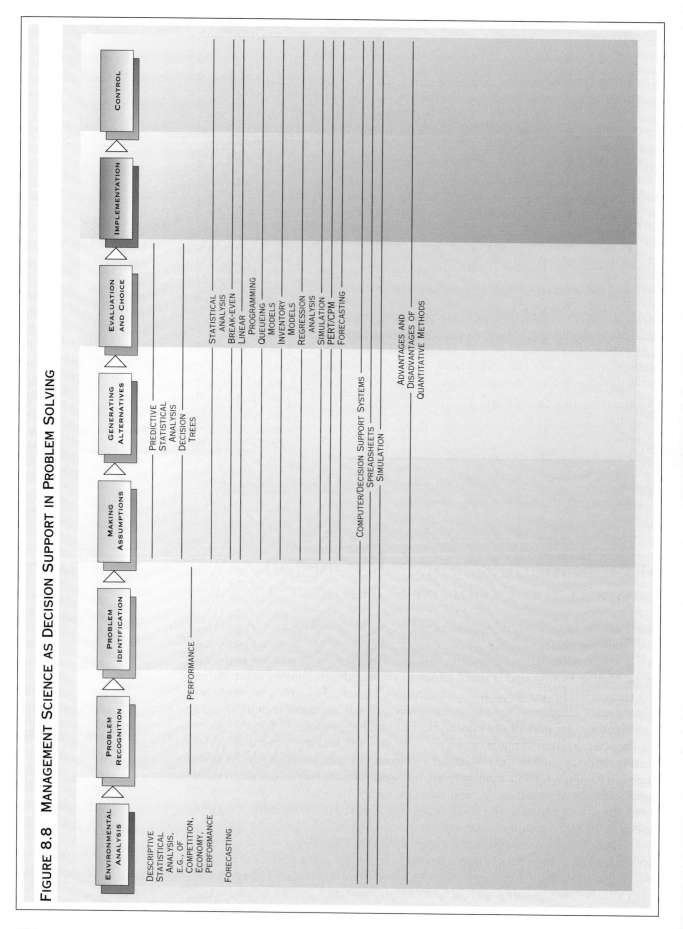

FIGURE 8.8   MANAGEMENT SCIENCE AS DECISION SUPPORT IN PROBLEM SOLVING

Summary

(Before reading this summary, look again at the objectives listed at the beginning of the chapter.)

1. Management science aims to improve problem solving by making it more rational and analytical. It formulates a problem as a mathematical model, which aids in all phases of decision making, especially problem recognition, problem identification, and choice among alternative solutions.

2. There are several advantages to using quantitative methods. Such methods enhance rationality, simplify problems, provide means for evaluating risk, and utilize user-friendly software, which makes it possible for almost anyone to use them. These methods are much less costly today than they were in the past.

3. There are certain disadvantages to using quantitative methods: Models are simplified versions of reality, substantive simulations may be too expensive, and people often resist change. Moreover, not all problems can be modeled satisfactorily; some require human judgment. Managers may not understand the theory behind the techniques they use, and for complex problems there may not be enough time to build the models and run them.

4. Methods such as forecasting, production scheduling, inventory control, capital budgeting, transportation, plant location, quality control, statistical analysis, simulation, LP, and PERT/CPM are frequently utilized in organizations.

5. Statistical analyses are used either to describe or to predict. They are most often used to describe current situations. They may also be used to predict and to forecast. Decision theory assists greatly in understanding a problem. Decision trees may be used for any problem in which sequential decisions occur. The concept of expected value allows managers to choose between alternatives in risk situations.

6. Forecasting is critical to an organization, especially in strategic planning. Sales forecasting is the basis for an organization's budget and all of its economic functions. Marketing, finance, operations, and human resources all depend on forecasts of future revenues.

7. Forecasting techniques may be either quantitative or qualitative. Quantitative techniques include time-series and causal techniques. Time-series techniques help identify the effects of trend, seasonal, cyclical, and random variations from a set of data. Causal techniques describe the relationships between independent and dependent variables. The formulas derived through the use of these techniques are often extrapolated to predict future events.

8. Qualitative methods include executive opinions, sales force composites, expert opinion, and consumer surveys. Technological forecasts help an organization remain competitive. Without proper understanding of their environment, organizations usually fail to respond successfully to competitors' actions.

9. The five basic steps of the forecasting process are (a) determining the purpose of the forecast and when it will be needed, (b) establishing the time horizons that the forecast must cover, (c) selecting a forecasting technique, (d) gathering and analyzing the appropriate data and then preparing the forecast, and (e) monitoring the forecast to see if it is performing satisfactorily.

10. Break-even analysis is used to determine the point at which revenues equal costs. It is especially important to use break-even analysis to determine if the projected project, product, or service will make a profit at the desired level. It can also be used for asking what-if questions. Linear programming is especially useful in situations with known goals, multiple variables, and multiple constraints. Network models (PERT and CPM) are especially useful for showing the relationships among activities within large-scale projects and for the scheduling of those activities.

11. Computers are increasingly being used in problem solving. Decision support software is readily available.

12. Simulation is coming into more widespread use in problem solving to show the impact of choosing various alternatives.

13. Computer programs, including simulation, assist in decision making by making it more rational.

General Questions

1. What is the purpose of using quantitative methods in management?

2. Why should managers be familiar with management science techniques?

3. What are the key differences between the standard approach to problem solving and problem solving using quantitative methods?

4. Describe ways in which you might be able to use some of the quantitative methods described in this chapter.

5. Describe how quantitative methods can help managers in various management situations.

6. Describe the likely scenario relative to increased use of computers and more widespread use of management science.

7. As the environment changes more rapidly, how do you think you might go about improving forecasting?

8. Give examples of quantitative and qualitative forecasting.

9. How could you improve the implementation of management science techniques?

10. Do intuition and qualitative decision making have any relevance to management science? If so, where do they fit in?

Questions on the Management Challenge Features

GLOBAL MANAGEMENT CHALLENGE

1. Can you think of other quantitative techniques that might be used in such situations?

2. How could the analytic hierarchy process be used in business situations?

DIVERSITY MANAGEMENT CHALLENGE

1. Why are statistics so critical in complying with government regulations?

2. Why are statistics crucial in this compliance situation?

MANAGEMENT CHALLENGE

1. Describe how New York City used quantitative methods to help solve its street cleaning problems.

2. What other typical problems of city management might lend themselves to quantitative techniques?

INNOVATION MANAGEMENT CHALLENGE

1. How is simulation used by the London police?

2. Why does the use of computers result in superior simulations?

American Airlines Embraces Quantitative Methods

American Airlines considers quantitative methods so important to achieving its mission that it has established a four hundred-person subsidiary, Decision Technologies, to provide it with quantitative support. Decision Technologies is the largest supplier of decision support to the transportation industry. As with Sabre, its computer-based reservation system, American is willing to supply other airlines with the services of its decision-support division in return for a hefty consulting fee. In addition to yield management, the division supplies support in the areas of capacity management, management of airport resources, management of maintenance and engineering facilities and operations, air-space simulations, pricing, and tariff analysis. The division combines industrial engineering with operations research approaches, using high-speed mainframe computers and workstations.

DISCUSSION QUESTIONS

1. In addition to those mentioned, what areas might a supplier like Decision Technologies become involved in?

2. Are you surprised at the number of possible applications of quantitative methods in just one firm?

Forecasting at Perfumery on Park

David Currie, co-owner with his wife, Anna, of Perfumery on Park (Avenue), pondered the best way to forecast the next year's sales. Since its opening in 1985, the perfumery had experienced steady growth in sales at a rate of about 10 percent each year. In 1992, however, sales during November and December, the two biggest sales months, had increased by 30 percent, causing sales for the year to increase by 22 percent.

David wondered whether to assume that sales would continue to increase at a 10 percent rate, at the recently experienced 22 percent rate, or at a rate somewhere in between. The consequences of the forecast were important. David and Anna had been considering hiring a full-time clerk so that Anna could pursue the company's new mail-order business. Moreover, inventories had to be ordered, and the problems resulting from not having a customer's perfume in stock could have an impact on future sales. The year 1992 had not been a strong one for the U.S. economy, but neither had it been a down year. David wasn't quite so sure what had caused the increase in sales. He wondered how to forecast for 1993.

DISCUSSION QUESTIONS

1. How does a small business forecast? Is forecasting by a small business really any different from forecasting by a larger firm?

2. How could break-even analysis be used to factor in the salary of the full-time clerk?

3. How would you go about forecasting Perfumery on Park's sales for 1993?

Using PERT/CPM to Build a Custom Sports Car

Use this table to find out how well you understand the PERT/CPM methodology.

The Maser is a new custom-designed sports car. An analysis of the task of building the Maser reveals the following list of relevant activities, their immediate predecessors, and their duration.

Job Letter	Description	Immediate Predecessors	Normal Time (Days)
A	Start		0
B	Design	A	8
C	Order special accessories	B	0.1
D	Build frame	B	1
E	Build doors	B	1
F	Attach axles, wheels, gas tank	D	1
G	Build body shell	B	2
H	Build transmission and drive train	B	3
I	Fit doors to body shell	G, E	1
J	Build engine	B	4
K	Bench-test engine	J	2
L	Assemble chassis	F, H, K	1
M	Road-test chassis	L	0.5
N	Paint body	I	2
O	Install wiring	N	1
P	Install interior	N	1.5
Q	Accept delivery of special accessories	C	5
R	Mount body and accessories on chassis	M, O, P, Q	1
S	Road-test car	R	0.5
T	Attach exterior trim	S	1
U	Finish	T	0

SOURCE: The author is indebted to Peter L. Pfister for the material on which this case is based.

1. Draw an arrow diagram of the project "Building the Maser."
2. Mark the critical path and state its length.
3. If the Maser had to be completed two days early, would it help to
   a. buy preassembled transmissions and drive trains?
   b. install robots to halve engine-building time?
   c. speed delivery of special accessories by three days?
4. How might resources be borrowed from activities on the subcritical paths to speed activities on the critical path?

SOURCE: James A. F. Stoner and Charles Wankel, *Management,* 3rd ed. (Englewood Cliffs., N.J.: Prentice-Hall, 1986), p. 195.

Toyota: An Aggressive Strategy
Despite a Problematic Environment

Toyota Motor Corporation had sales of $81.3 billion for the fiscal year ended June 30, 1992, ranking it third in global auto sales behind Ford and General Motors. It held 9.1 percent of the U.S. auto market, placing it fourth—behind GM, Ford, and Honda and just ahead of Chrysler. At a time when other automakers are closing plants in Japan, the United States, and Europe, Toyota is building or expanding six assembly plants around the world, five in key export markets outside Japan: Britain (to be used as a launching pad for gaining market share in Europe), Pakistan, Thailand, Turkey, and the United States.

But not everything is as rosy as Toyota might like. Its profits fell in 1992, and it is expecting another 20 percent drop in profits for 1993. These lowered profits resulted from declining sales in Japan owing to the recession there, and from decreasing margins in the United States. (Although U.S. market share increased slightly in 1992, profits were hurt because of the high value of the yen relative to the dollar, which meant that the firm had to reduce prices to remain competitive.) Moreover, a huge capital expansion program has put a strain on profits, which have suffered from the combined effects of increased interest payments on the debt used to finance the expansion, decreased interest earnings from spending $10 billion in cash on the capital improvements, and the depreciation taken on the plant and equipment.

As if these problems weren't enough, Toyota has been so successful in executing its strategy that it has created enemies both at home and abroad. Competitors are demanding that their governments act to reduce Toyota's power. Japanese firms, for example, have pressured their government to increase Toyota's model cycle time (the number of years a model stays on the market) from four years to five. This would save them huge amounts in research and development investment. U.S. and European auto manufacturers have lobbied their governments to increase tariffs and impose quotas in the hope of slowing the penetration of their markets by Japanese auto firms.

The Japanese government has put pressure on Toyota to reduce its employees' workload to 1900 hours a year by the end of 1993. This would make Toyota comparable to U.S. auto firms, whose employees work 1920 hours a year. The reduction in hours is part of the Japanese government's efforts to improve the quality of work life and overall quality of life for its citizens, who are known for working excessively long hours. Finally, there is a shortage of labor in Japan. The auto industry is especially hard hit because most young Japanese men would rather go into banking or other prestigious service industries.

TOYOTA'S STRATEGY

As could be expected of this highly effective and efficient firm, Toyota rapidly developed a series of strategies for dealing with these problems. Recognizing that profits were being pinched both at home and abroad, it undertook an unprecedented cost reduction program with several key facets. First and foremost, manufacturing costs were to be reduced through work redesign and by replacing human labor with robots (but only when it made good business sense). Overtime work by white-collar employees was eliminated and desirable but unnecessary business expenses were trimmed heavily (for example, travel expense budgets were cut in half). Two thousand part-time workers were let go.

Automation of manufacturing had been a long-standing practice at Toyota, and recent capital investment programs had stepped up the pace. But like GM before it, Toyota discovered that automating everything isn't necessarily the way to go. Only when it is cheaper to do so should jobs be automated. Mikio Kitano, a member of the board of directors, oversees a special program aimed at improving productivity. He believes very strongly in replacing human labor with machines only when necessary. "The key to productivity is simplicity. Men control machines, not the other way around," he declares. He insisted on less automation at the new plant in Kyushu and was able to justify his position on a cost basis. Millions of dollars were saved in the first few months of this program alone. However, automation was increased not just to save money, but because of the labor shortage. Toyota also determined that it would build new plants on the outer islands, rather than at the traditional location in Toyota City near Tokyo. This way, it could recruit workers who had less chance of finding jobs in more fashionable industries.

Finally, Toyota has reexamined the concept of lean manufacturing. It has even created buffer inventories in part of its assembly process, something it has never done since it instituted just-in-time inventories in the early 1950s. To reduce political pressures at home and abroad, it suggested that it would lengthen its model cycle time to five years and reduce its imports, but a year later it had not made either change.

It also moved some of its focus for expansion to the Pacific Rim and Eastern Europe, where it would not face complaints by competitors about its appetite for market share.

DISCUSSION QUESTIONS

1. Identify the problems Toyota faced and how it solved each of them.
2. Discuss the probable impact of Toyota's strategies on those of its competitors.

SOURCES: Karen Lowry Miller, "The Factory Guru Tinkering with Toyota," *Business Week* (May 17, 1993), pp. 95, 97; Alex Taylor III, "How Toyota Copes with Hard Times," *Fortune* (January 25, 1993), pp. 78–81; and Joseph B. White and Clay Chandler, "Peace Overture: Pressed by All Sides, Hard Driving Toyota Trims Back Its Goals," *Wall Street Journal* (May 19, 1992), pp. A1, A10.

Organizing

Organizing is concerned mostly with organizational structure: the jobs of the organization's members, how they are grouped together into departments, the authority granted to subordinates to perform their jobs, how many subordinates a manager has, and how all this is coordinated. At the strategic level, organization focuses on macro structure—how the firm as a whole is organized. At the tactical and operational levels, organizing focuses on the micro structure—jobs, groups of jobs, and departments. In addition to structural concerns, organizing is concerned with allocating resources and making other preparations for the implementation of plans. Certain aspects of organizing, such as scheduling worker assignments, overlap with planning and are covered in Part III. However, organizing is also concerned with how human resources are allocated. Of special concern is the increased cultural diversity found in organizations today. Recently, organizing has also begun to focus on the organization's culture and how it is managed, and on how the organization manages change.

Chapter 9 reviews basic concepts that are relevant to organizing. The types of macro structures are discussed, and selected micro-level issues are noted. Chapter 10 is concerned with organizational design—that is, with how the firm is structured at the macro level. Chapter 11 focuses on important micro-level issues such as job design and team management. Chapter 12 discusses staffing and human resource management, and Chapter 13 reviews the management of organizational culture, cultural diversity, and change.

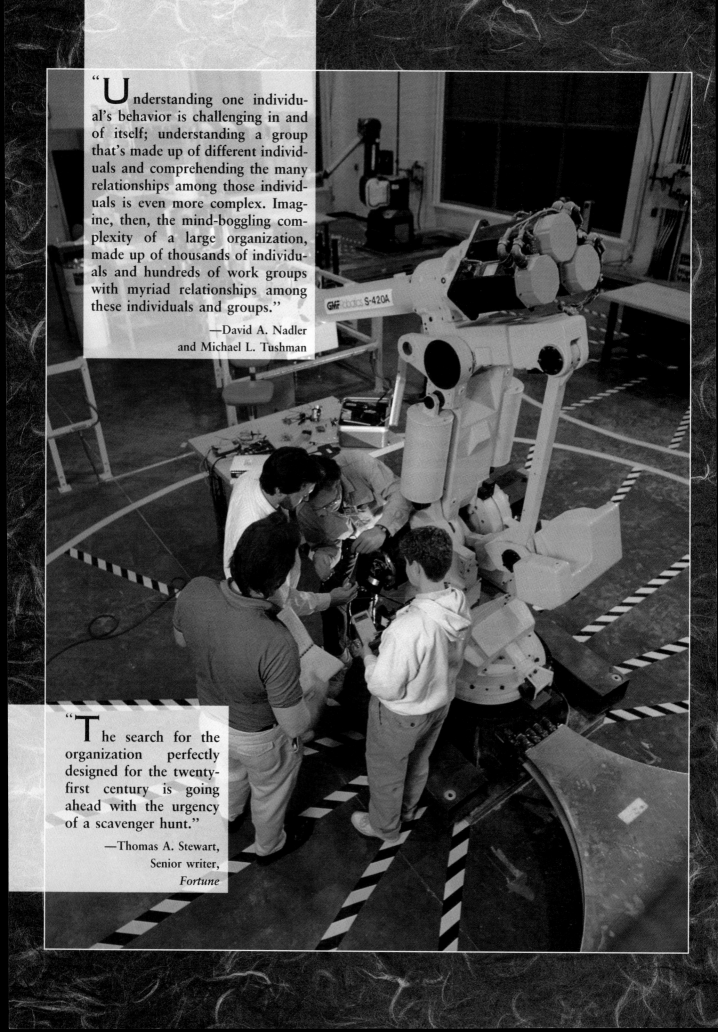

"Understanding one individual's behavior is challenging in and of itself; understanding a group that's made up of different individuals and comprehending the many relationships among those individuals is even more complex. Imagine, then, the mind-boggling complexity of a large organization, made up of thousands of individuals and hundreds of work groups with myriad relationships among these individuals and groups."

—David A. Nadler
and Michael L. Tushman

"The search for the organization perfectly designed for the twenty-first century is going ahead with the urgency of a scavenger hunt."

—Thomas A. Stewart,
Senior writer,
Fortune

When you have read this chapter you should be able to:

1. Define the organizing process and indicate its relationship to planning.
2. Describe the choices managers must make in structuring an organization.
3. Define an organization.
4. Indicate the differences between formal and informal organizations.
5. Discuss how the combinations of jobs and the authority to perform those jobs—together with departmentation, span of control, and coordination—result in organizational structure.
6. Interpret an organization chart.
7. Indicate how resources other than human resources are organized.

MANAGEMENT CHALLENGES
DISCUSSED IN THIS CHAPTER:

 Accelerating rates of change.

 Increasing globalization of business.

 Increasing levels of competition.

 Changing technology.

CHAPTER 9

The Organizing Process

C H A P T E R   O U T L I N E

Organizing

Division of Labor—The Job
DIVISION/SPECIALIZATION OF LABOR
DIFFERENTIATION
THE ORGANIZATION CHART

Delegation of Authority
AUTHORITY
DELEGATING AUTHORITY
THE SCALAR CHAIN OF COMMAND
THE ACCEPTANCE THEORY OF AUTHORITY
THE PARITY PRINCIPLE
CENTRALIZATION VERSUS DECENTRALIZATION
LINE AND STAFF AUTHORITY
FUNCTIONAL AUTHORITY

Departmentation
THE COMPLEXITIES OF PYRAMIDAL STRUCTURES
THE MANAGERIAL SPAN OF CONTROL
"FLAT" VERSUS "TALL" ORGANIZATIONS

Coordination
FORMALIZATION
COMPLEXITY
INTEGRATION AND DIFFERENTIATION
THE MANAGER AS A LINKING PIN
ADDITIONAL COORDINATION DEVICES

Additional Types of Structures
PROJECT STRUCTURE
THE TEAM
THE MATRIX STRUCTURE
JOINT VENTURES AND STRATEGIC ALLIANCES
NETWORK ORGANIZATIONS
INFORMAL STRUCTURE

Organizing as a Problem-Solving Process

Simply Better

When a merger of two companies occurs, it is usually heavily one-sided—one of the two is larger or stronger and imprints its style on the merged corporation. When Philadelphia's SmithKline Beckman and London's Beecham, Ltd., merged in 1989, however, it was a match of equals. The pharmaceutical companies were similar in size, both were multinational, and both were takeover targets. Their CEOs felt that industry forces would foster consolidation among their competitors, and that they needed to grow to survive. In each other, they found a good match with complementary products and facilities. From the beginning, the merger was planned to create a new company that maintained the strengths of each of the principals.

Robert Bauman, former chairman of Beecham and CEO of SmithKline Beecham, the merged company, believed that there are five requirements for a successful merger: It must be based on sound business reasoning; it must be accomplished quickly; members of the merged organization must be involved in the reorganization; the organization must begin planning for the future; and the implementation of merger plans must be monitored.

Each of these points has been carefully attended to, some quickly and easily, others requiring more effort. In particular, reorganization involved the formation of more than three hundred project teams consisting of more than two thousand employees of the merged company to analyze existing structures and practices and create new ones. They found redundancies, closed sites, and eliminated layers of management, centralizing some activities and decentralizing others. Some of the teams even eliminated their own jobs. All of this planning was geared to where the company wanted to be in ten years. Over the six-month period of the teams' work, SmithKline Beecham's employees saw how the others performed, and when positions were finally assigned, no one doubted that they had been assigned on merit. Nobody cared any longer who had come from which premerger company.

Top management established five values for the new company designed to give it a long-term competitive advantage. They also developed nine leadership practices that would foster those values, and distributed the values and practices throughout the company. The interpretation and implementation of the practices were left to the individual employee. Thus, all employees were given the broad outline of the organizational culture the company wanted, helpful guidelines for creating it, and the freedom to create it themselves.

Clearly, the merger had been one of that rare breed, a real merger, rather than a takeover. The outcome, SmithKline Beecham, is greater than the sum of its parts.

SOURCES: Robert P. Bauman, "Creating a Global Health Care Company," *Journal of Business Strategy* (March–April 1992); and W. Warner Burke and Peter Jackson, "Making the SmithKline Beecham Merger Work," *Human Resource Management* (Spring 1991), pp. 69–87.

hat happened at SmithKline Beecham is happening in thousands of companies across the United States, including Eastman Kodak, AT&T, TRW, Eastern Airlines, Xerox, Du Pont, GE, and GM. It is also happening in Europe to firms like Philips and Mercedes Benz, and in the Pacific Rim nations to firms like Nissan and Matsushita. Organizations are restructuring and reorganizing. They are changing the content of jobs, combining some and eliminating others. In addition, they are changing how jobs are grouped; the size of work groups; the amount of authority delegated to individuals and groups to accomplish their jobs; and the manner in which the whole organization is coordinated.[1] At SmithKline Beecham, restructuring occurred because of a merger necessitated by a changing managerial environment. As discussed in Chapters 1 and 5, managers face increased levels of competition, a need for faster new-product development, a quest for lower costs, demands for higher quality, and the potential for lower profit margins in virtually all industries. Consequently, the need to reorganize has become pervasive. Never before in the history of American industry has the organizing function been so critical. More than ever, appropriate organizing is viewed as a prerequisite for success.[2]

Organizing

Organizing is the process of determining how resources are allocated and prepared to accomplish an organization's mission. The organizing process results in an **organizational structure** that defines the following aspects of the organization:

1. The relationships between tasks and authority for individuals, groups, and departments.
2. Formal reporting relationships—for example, the number of levels in the organization's hierarchy and the span of control; as well as the reporting relationships among groups in different departments involved in accomplishing the same corporate objectives.
3. The grouping of individuals into work groups, groups into departments, and departments into organizations.
4. The systems for coordinating effort in both vertical (authority and functions) and horizontal (tasks and processes) directions.[3]

Organizing: The process of determining how resources are allocated and prepared in order to accomplish an organization's mission.

Organizational structure: The result of the organizing process; consists of relationships among tasks and authority, reporting relationships, groupings of jobs, and systems of coordination.

Organizing is the process of determining how resources are allocated and prepared to accomplish an organization's mission. One result of this process is the grouping of individuals into work groups like the one shown here.

There are two types of structures in an organization: formal and informal. They differ in terms of legitimacy. **Formal structure** is sanctioned by the organization and designed to achieve organizational objectives. **Informal structure** refers to whatever structure exists that has not been prescribed by the formal organization. For example, two of an organization's employees may meet while at work for reasons unrelated to accomplishing the organization's mission.

An **organization** is a group of people working together to achieve a common purpose.[4] While it has always been understood that structure had to be matched to strategy for the strategy to succeed, there is increasing research evidence for this belief.[5] The manager's principal concerns with regard to structuring an organization follow:

Formal structure: An organizational structure sanctioned by the organization and designed to achieve its objectives.

Informal structure: Any structure within an organization that has not been formally prescribed by it.

Organization: A group of people working together to achieve a common purpose.

1. *Division of labor:* Determining the scope of work and how it is combined in a job, or how it is combined in a set of jobs assigned to a work group.
2. *Delegation of authority:* Determining how much authority should be granted to individuals and groups to do their jobs.
3. *Departmentation:* Grouping jobs into work units, teams, or departments on some rational basis.
4. *Span of control:* Determining how many subordinates each manager should have.
5. *Coordination:* Of individuals, groups, and departments as they perform their jobs.[6]

In the remainder of this chapter we will examine each of these concerns in detail. Chapters 10 and 11 offer more specific guidance for structuring at the total organization (macro) and individual job or group (micro) levels.

Division of Labor—The Job

Job: A collection of tasks assigned to one individual.

A **job** is a collection of tasks assigned to one individual; it is designed to achieve specific objectives and carry out related plans. A job is designed on the basis of the division of labor, the principle of specialization, and the need to divide the organization into subunits in response to external factors.

Division/Specialization of Labor

Division of labor: The subdivision of objectives and plans into smaller and smaller units until they reach the task level.

Specialization of labor: The division of a task into smaller and smaller subunits until it can be repeated easily and successfully by an individual or group.

Division of labor is the subdivision of objectives and plans into smaller and smaller units until they reach the task level. This is often referred to as the **specialization of labor.** Historically, division of labor has focused on the jobs of individuals. More recently, it has become apparent that the work group may be the basic functional unit in organizations. Thus, group objectives and group tasks may soon be the focus of the division of labor.[7] For example, GE's Bayamón plant in Puerto Rico has been restructured to focus on the group's work rather than on the individual's. Teams of workers are given task assignments. Members of teams work together to accomplish their interconnected tasks, rather than their own independently designed tasks. These teams cross functions, and each worker is expected to make the entire process successful, not just his or her part.[8]

As we saw in Chapter 2, specialization of labor is one of Fayol's fourteen principles. It was introduced into management and made a prominent component of organization structure design, especially job design, by Adam Smith. Specialization allows an individual to work on one part of a larger project. No individual could build a space shuttle, but specialization allows many individuals to construct specific parts that are then assembled to create a space shuttle. Specialization causes an individual's work to be highly repetitive and, hence, less prone to errors. However, there is a negative side to repeating a job numerous consecutive times without error: The worker will become bored. The analytical part of the brain falls asleep and the worker begins to daydream and to make errors.

Specialization of labor is a fundamental element in almost all organizations. For example, McDonald's, Wendy's, Burger King, and other hamburger chains are noted for their ability to routinize the handling of customers' requests, filling customers' orders in a way that gives credence to the term *fast food*. They could not do this without specialization. They have continually studied and examined the number of specialized tasks necessary to perform their hamburger "manufacturing" jobs.

Sometimes, however, specialization creates too many jobs, including some that are unnecessary. This is a major reason for restructuring. Also, as computers begin to control more of the labor process, work is sometimes being recombined into new processes that can be managed in less specialized groupings.[9]

Differentiation

Each organization, and each department within an organization, adapts its subcomponents—including structure, processes, and member behaviors—to meet the constraints of its specific environment. This process of adaptation to the environment is known as **differentiation**.[10] A marketing research department, for example, would be expected to have a more freewheeling structure—a more autonomous structure in which more authority is delegated—than would be found on a highly routinized manufacturing assembly line. Similarly, the spans of control in a March of Dimes campaign, where volunteer fund collectors are largely self-supervising, would be expected to be larger than those found in a complex computer-programming environment where projects are closely supervised by project leaders. In both cases, each of the fundamental elements of structure described—jobs, delegation of authority, departmentation, span of control, and coordination—is differentiated in response to environmental circumstances.

Differentiation: The process through which each organization, and each department within an organization, adapts its subcomponents, including structure, processes, and members' behaviors, to meet the constraints of its specific environment.

These McDonald's employees have highly specialized jobs. Their physical movements have been carefully calculated to provide the fastest, most economical service possible.

The Organization Chart

Organization chart: A pictorial representation of an organization's formal structure.

The relationships between tasks and the authority to do those tasks are best represented in an **organization chart,** a pictorial representation of an organization's formal structure. Such a chart is presented in Figure 9.1. By examining it, we can determine the following relationships:

1. *The division/specialization of labor:* Each box on a typical organization chart represents a job position that combines a certain number of tasks. Typically, the chart also indicates the type of work that is being performed by individuals in the various positions. (Note how this will change to show the grouping of jobs as work teams become more common.)

2. *Relative authority:* Normally, a position higher up on the chart has more authority than positions below it. This is not always true, as some charts are designed with greater complexity; usually, however, positions on the same level have the same amount of authority, and they have more authority than those below them.

3. *Departmentation:* Organization charts normally depict groupings of positions in what are known as departments.

4. *Span of control:* Visual scanning of the chart readily indicates the number of subordinates a manager has.

5. *The levels of management:* A quick look down an organization chart reveals the number of levels of management in the organization.

6. *Coordination centers:* By observing an organization chart, you can see who would most likely be expected to coordinate the activities of various subunits. The president, for example, would be expected to coordinate the activities of the vice-presidents; the vice-presidents would coordinate the actions of their reporting divisions; and the division chiefs would coordinate the actions of managers of reporting subunits.

7. *Communication channels:* Communication channels through which coordination would occur are clearly indicated on the organization chart. However, communication may occur diagonally or horizontally between positions, not just vertically. Day-to-day operational communication involves complex interactions that are not shown on the chart.

8. *Decision responsibility:* By observing the preceding factors, it usually is possible to determine who will be responsible for making a decision on a particular matter. However, exactly how much authority is delegated to each position is not apparent on an organization chart, so decision authority may vary somewhat from what the chart seems to indicate. In the case of autonomous work teams, determining authority and responsibility within the group will be very difficult because ordinarily group members are equal in status.

Organization charts are typically presented on paper and read from top to bottom. Most such charts depict organizational structures as pyramids. The top of the pyramid represents top management; the bottom, the operational employees. Various levels of management and staff are shown in between. Chapter 13 includes an organization chart that has been intentionally inverted in order to emphasize the importance of serving the customer.

FIGURE 9.1   A TYPICAL MULTIDIVISIONAL ORGANIZATION

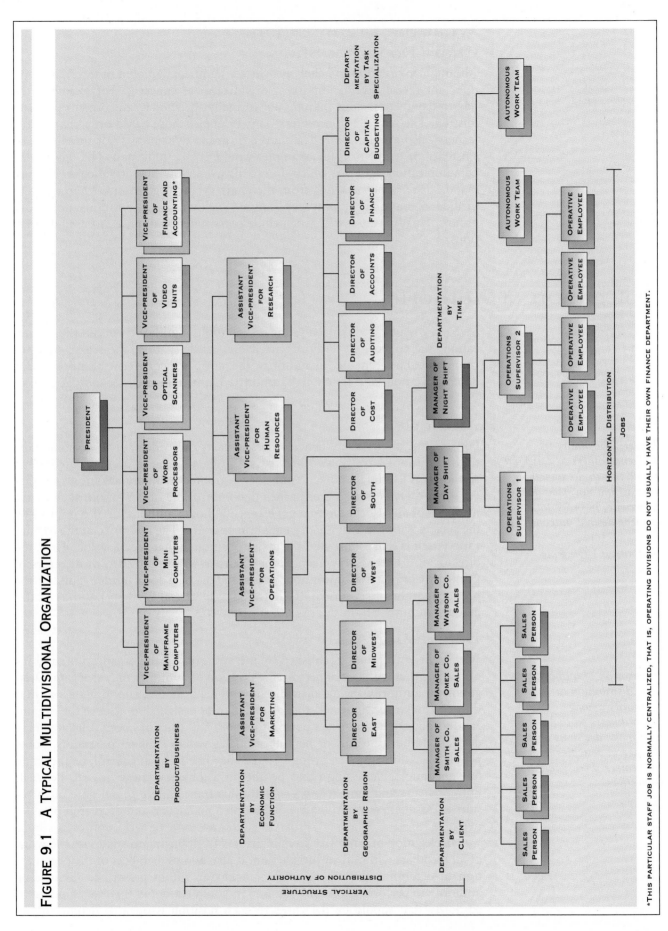

*THIS PARTICULAR STAFF JOB IS NORMALLY CENTRALIZED, THAT IS, OPERATING DIVISIONS DO NOT USUALLY HAVE THEIR OWN FINANCE DEPARTMENT.

What the Organization Chart Does Not Show

Although an organization chart provides a significant amount of information, it does not reveal several important organizational concerns. For example, the day-to-day relationships that are not formally specified by the organization are missing. The real decision centers—for example, those based on a charismatic leader—also are not clear. The nature of group dynamics is not revealed. The existence of teamwork, for example, would not be indicated. The day-to-day communication patterns, which do not always follow the formal chain of command, also are not obvious from the chart. Many organization charts do not include operational employee positions—neither single positions nor work groups. Finally, very few charts include cross-functional, process-based interactions.[11]

Delegation of Authority

Seven key issues are involved in the distribution of authority within the organization: the concept of authority itself and its delegation, the scalar chain of command, the acceptance of authority, the parity principle, centralization versus decentralization, and functional authority. Let us take a closer look at each of these issues.

Authority

Power: The ability to influence others to carry out orders, or to do something they would not have done otherwise, in order to achieve desired outcomes.

Power is the ability to influence others to carry out orders, or to do something they would not have done otherwise, in order to achieve desired outcomes.[12] **Authority** is legitimate power. Authority is granted to an organization's managers by its owners or by other parties that control the organization, such as the members of an association or a governmental body; authority is also granted by the society within which the organization operates. The authority of the organization itself is said to rest with the major position in that organization. Thus, the director of a United Way agency, the chairperson of the board of directors of Compaq Computer Corporation, the president of a local bridge club, or the president of the International Brotherhood of Electrical Workers has the greatest amount of authority in the organization.

Authority: Legitimate power.

Delegating Authority

Delegation of authority: The distribution of authority among subordinates so that they can make decisions and engage in activities designed to achieve the organization's objectives.

Within the constraints established by the authority of the organization and his or her position within it, a person in a position of authority may delegate. **Delegation of authority** means distributing authority among subordinates so that they can make decisions and engage in activities designed to achieve the organization's objectives. In turn, a person to whom authority has been delegated may delegate authority to his or her subordinates within similar constraints. Some people have difficulty delegating because they like to be in control, or they may feel uncomfortable letting other people do a job they know how to do well. Entrepreneurs and most managers share this trait. Failure to delegate often results in dissatisfied subordinates, overworked managers, and decreased productivity.

Delegation of authority frees managers from having to supervise the work of all members within their jurisdiction. It also allows members of the organization to determine the nature of their behavior within prescribed limits. The authority to perform a job is essential to its completion, but the exact amount of authority that should be delegated to each position is open to debate. Many

Authority is granted to an organization's managers by its owners or by other parties that control the organization. The authority of the organization itself is said to rest with the major position in that organization, for example, the chair of the board of directors.

individuals can gain power in addition to the authority delegated to them, for example, by becoming expert in a field, so that others come to them for help, or by becoming leaders of informal groups. Others fail to use their authority fully and lose power as a result. For example, a manager who fails to control subordinates' performance will no longer be seen by those subordinates as having power.

It is important to note that delegation of authority does not mean that the manager is not responsible. He or she is still held accountable for the actions and decisions of subordinates.

The Scalar Chain of Command

The **scalar chain of command** is the formal distribution of organizational authority in a hierarchical fashion. The scalar chain simply defines the relationships of authority among different levels of the organization. In the scalar chain, individuals higher up on the chain have more authority than those below them. This is true of all succeeding levels of management, from first-line employees to top management. The scalar chain helps define authority and responsibility and, thus, accountability. Figures 9.1 and 9.3–9.7 include examples of the scalar chain as portrayed in organization charts.

Scalar chain of command: The formal distribution of organizational authority in a hierarchical fashion; defines authority relationships among individuals at different levels of the organization.

The Acceptance Theory of Authority

As noted in Chapter 2, Chester Barnard's **acceptance theory of authority** states that a manager has true authority only if subordinates choose to accept his or her formal authority as real.[13] Otherwise, authority does not truly exist. In the 1970s, for example, the workers at GM's Lordstown assembly plant refused to produce more than 65 cars per hour, even though the ultramodern plant was capable of producing 100 cars per hour.[14] They did not accept management's authority to determine the rate of production. Unions are often able to influence their members not to accept management's authority. Millions of employees in

Acceptance theory of authority: A manager has true authority only if subordinates choose to accept his or her formal authority as real.

all types of organizations do not always perform at peak levels because they do not accept the authority of their managers. Often they do not directly disobey; they just do not cooperate fully.

The Parity Principle

Parity principle: Anyone who is assigned the responsibility for achieving an objective should also be given the authority to achieve it.

The **parity principle** states that when someone is assigned the responsibility for achieving an objective, he or she should also be given the authority to achieve it. This seems obvious, but the rule is often violated. Problems typically arise when a manager is assigned a task outside the normal chain of command. The manager may be required to lead several people to whom his or her authority has not been made clear or who feel that the "outsider" has no authority over them. When heading a committee or a task team, managers often need to supervise and get cooperation from employees over whom they have no formal authority. For example, a project team leader on the space shuttle booster rocket program works with people from many technical disciplines, yet that leader has only limited formal authority over any of them. It is easy for team members to disregard the manager's authority and instructions, especially in deference to the orders of their normal functional manager, who in most cases will still complete the team member's performance appraisal.

Centralization Versus Decentralization

Centralized organization: An organization in which authority is not widely delegated and virtually all important decisions are made by top management.

In a **centralized organization,** authority is not widely delegated. Hence, virtually all important decisions—in some cases, virtually all decisions—are made by top management. Such a structure is often dysfunctional. Consider the case of a U.S. Air Force missile wing commander, a colonel, who simply would not delegate. With an annual operating budget of almost $100 million, the colonel demanded that he personally approve all purchase orders over $50.00. He eventually came under the scrutiny of his boss, a three-star general, for his failure to achieve objectives because of lack of delegation.[15] Numerous similar examples of inability to delegate can be found in business organizations. For example, Kenneth Olsen, Digital Equipment Corporation's founder and until recently its CEO and chairman, directed the firm almost single-handedly, leading it up, and down, through several business cycles. His insistence on pursuing what critics felt was the wrong strategy (neglecting major products such as laptop computers) led to his replacement.[16] Had he delegated, new-product development in the right product areas would have occurred sooner.

Decentralized organization: An organization in which authority is widely delegated to subordinates.

In a **decentralized organization,** authority is widely delegated to subordinates. There is a broad range in the amount of authority that can be delegated, as Figure 9.2 reveals. A decentralized organization can be characterized as delegating authority to managers to enable them to make decisions that are relevant to their departments, divisions, or businesses within organizational guidelines. A substantively decentralized organization carries the delegation process one step further and delegates to subordinates the authority to make decisions their bosses would usually make.[17] Today this would be called an empowered organization. **Empowerment** means giving subordinates substantial authority.[18] It is believed to be critical to the successful implementation of team-based organizational structures and will be discussed further in Chapters 10, 11, and 16.

Empowerment: Giving subordinates substantial authority.

Somewhere between the decentralized organization and the empowered one is Johnson & Johnson. Numerous other firms, awed by Johnson & Johnson's success, have tried to emulate its decentralized approach. This chapter's Innovation Management Challenge reviews the approach that has enabled Johnson & Johnson to be one of the world's most innovative companies for more than sixty years. Identify the structural characteristics that make Johnson & Johnson innovative.

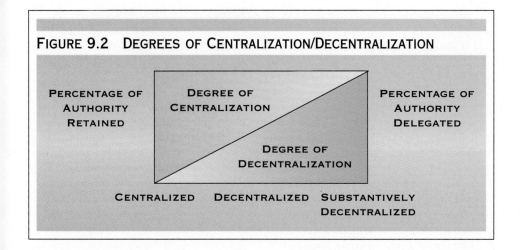

FIGURE 9.2 DEGREES OF CENTRALIZATION/DECENTRALIZATION

PERCENTAGE OF
AUTHORITY
RETAINED

DEGREE OF
CENTRALIZATION

PERCENTAGE OF
AUTHORITY
DELEGATED

DEGREE OF
DECENTRALIZATION

CENTRALIZED   DECENTRALIZED   SUBSTANTIVELY
DECENTRALIZED

Managers must decide how much decentralization is appropriate for their organization or subunit. This is a complex question. Research studies have shown that a decentralized organization is better able to adapt to the demands of a changing environment.[19] Yet as information systems provide top management with more information about the external environment, these findings could change because managers will be able to respond faster. Moreover, subunits will vary in degree of decentralization. It is possible to have a centralized organization with some decentralized subunits, and vice versa.

In recent years, there has been renewed interest in decentralization. Much of the momentum for this trend is a result of Japanese firms' positive experiences with worker participation in decision making. A decentralized organization is not always more productive, but it is more productive in most situations, when all factors are considered. Business firms operating in stable external environments, for example, can prosper using centralized organizational structures. However, firms operating in dynamic external environments (as most firms will in the future) need decentralized structures in order for various departments to respond more readily to environmental demands.

Virtually all personal-computer firms, for example, attempt to decentralize decision making in order to respond to the unpredictability of the marketplace. The pace of change is so rapid in the personal-computer industry that without decentralization a firm could not survive. Decentralization allows the members of the organization with the most knowledge about the problem at hand to make the decisions necessary to solve that problem. There are disadvantages to uncontrolled decentralization, however. For years Hewlett-Packard was characterized as the epitome of the decentralized organization, and for years it responded superbly to the marketplace. In the mid-1980s, however, it found itself in a computer hardware market calling for machines that could communicate—that is, interface with each other. Its products could not communicate because they had all been designed by separate, decentralized units.[20] So Hewlett-Packard initiated another decentralized approach to product development, one that used committees, so that all departments and divisions affected were involved. At first, this approach was considered innovative, but eventually it led to "death by committee." It gave rise to a CYA (cover your answers) mentality that led nowhere. No one wanted to take responsibility for a decision. Only when CEO John Young, in desperation, decided to create "czars" to head new-product development groups did the firm finally turn around. It quickly launched a series of new products, all of which were successful. There may be several morals to this story, but perhaps the most poignant one is that in times of

AT SMITHKLINE BEECHAM: While many changes were made in specific areas, the overall balance between centralized power and decentralized empowerment was more or less retained after the merger.

Johnson & Johnson

Johnson & Johnson's raison d'être is innovation. Roughly 25 percent of current sales—$12 billion in 1991—was from products introduced during the previous five years. The key to successful innovation at J&J is the company's long-standing policy of decentralization.

J&J consists of over 160 separately chartered companies, such as Johnson & Johnson Baby Products, McNeil Consumer Products (Tylenol), and Ortho Pharmaceuticals. Each company has its own president, and the presidents act independently. They choose their staff and decide what they will produce and to whom they will sell. They prepare their own budget and marketing plans. Many oversee their own R&D. Some see their bosses at headquarters as rarely as four times a year.

Long before "empowerment" became a buzzword elsewhere in America, it prevailed at J&J. Longtime chairman Robert Wood Johnson encouraged decentralization as early as the 1930s. More than fifty years later, J&J is a model of how to make it work.

One way it *doesn't* work is by remaining the same. Management has constantly needed to fine tune the decentralized operation at J&J; the current chief executive, Ralph S. Larsen, is in the middle of one such tune-up. He hopes to make J&J more efficient by encouraging the units to share more services, such as payroll processing, computer services, purchasing, distribution, accounts payable, and benefits. He also hopes to eliminate redundancies and to facilitate relationships with J&J's biggest customers.

When a promising new device or product is acquired at J&J, a division is often set up within a larger company to incubate the idea. A management team is then appointed, and the unit is eventually broken out into a freestanding company. In this way, the product gets the best of both worlds—the financial backing of a corporate colossus and the undivided attention of a dedicated and undistracted management.

Of course, decentralization can have its downside: Company presidents have no one to blame if they make bad decisions. They are solely responsible.

Free of headquarters bureaucracy, J&J's operating units are among the most aggressive marketers in the United States. Since 1980, yearly profits have averaged more than 19 percent, and annual sales have risen by more than 10 percent in five of those years. "We're always folding some company and creating others," Larsen says. But even though the emphasis on innovation fosters an appearance of controlled chaos, the commitment to decentralization will not be altered any time soon.

SOURCE: Joseph Weber, "A Big Company That Works," *Business Week* (May 4, 1992), pp. 124–132.

Line and staff concept: An approach to organization based on the distinction between line and staff officers, in which line officers make decisions directly related to the organization's objectives and staff officers provide advice and support.

rapid change a centralized approach, with inputs from the front line, may in fact be superior to a decentralized approach.[21] The advantages and disadvantages of decentralization are indicated in Table 9.1.

Line and Staff Authority

Most organizations have historically employed what is known as the **line and staff concept** in their organizational structures. This concept evolved from the military distinction between line and staff officers. Line officers made battle-

This Hewlett-Packard team is working on various stages of a software package. The history of Hewlett-Packard's performance shows that in times of rapid change a centralized approach, with inputs from the front line, may in fact be superior to a decentralized approach.

related decisions. Staff officers provided advice but could not make the decisions. **Line authority** is authority within a given unit's chain of command. **Staff authority** is advisory and comes from outside that unit's chain of command. The line has, over time, come to be defined in a macro sense as all functions the organization cannot do without.[22] Marketing, operations (production or service operations), and finance have traditionally been considered the three major functions without which an organization could not survive. The basic idea is that, regardless of the service or product, it must be possible to sell it, make it, and finance the selling and making of it before an organization can exist.

All functions that are not **line** functions are designated as **staff**. Staff functions generally involve providing advice or assistance to the line functions. Thus,

Line authority: Authority within a given unit's chain of command.

Staff authority: Advisory authority that comes from outside a given unit's chain of command.

Line: All functions that the organization cannot do without.

Staff: All functions that are not designated as line functions; they generally involve providing advice or assistance to the line functions.

TABLE 9.1 Advantages and Disadvantages of Decentralization

Advantages	Disadvantages
1. **Efficiency:** Decentralization spreads the management load and reduces red tape and bottlenecks. If management at lower levels can make on-the-spot decisions, less time is lost in getting approvals up the line.	1. **Control:** When managers have great latitude in making decisions, coordinating overall activities is more difficult.
2. **Flexibility:** Managers who can make decisions have the ability to cope with changing conditions and adjust for unexpected circumstances.	2. **Duplication:** If all department managers are autonomous, there is a greater danger of duplicating efforts. Several offices might be keeping identical records on customers, shipments, inventory, and so on.
3. **Initiative:** It is very challenging and motivating for managers to make decisions regarding problems and solutions in their own departments.	3. **Centralized Expertise:** Managers with a lot of decision-making latitude may tend to overlook home-office expertise.
4. **Development:** The best training for management development is to encourage managers at lower levels to run their own departments.	4. **Competency:** Additional decision making by lower-level managers strains the organization to produce competent managers at all levels.

SOURCE: Gerald H. Graham, *Understanding Human Relations: The Individual, Organization, and Management* (Chicago, Ill.: Science Research Associates, 1982), p. 137. Copyright 1982 by Science Research Associates Inc.; reprinted by permission of the publisher.

human resource management (personnel), logistics, research, corporate planning, and similar functions have usually been considered staff functions. Today, line authority is often defined as the relationship between a manager and a subordinate. This is a commonly accepted definition, but the older perspective survives as well.

Traditionally, only line managers have had authority over line operations. More recently, line authority has meant that only managers have authority over their subordinates. Staff personnel advise but do not normally have authority over line activities. Thus, members of the personnel department can advise the production department that it needs to improve its hiring procedures or face increased absenteeism, but the personnel department cannot make the production department follow this advice if the organization uses a line-authority approach. Although the line and staff concept still governs the delegation of authority in most organizations, the distinction between the two is diminishing.

Concurrent authority: A system in which all decisions by the line must be concurred with by the staff.

Under the concept of **concurrent authority,** the organization may require that staff concur in all decisions. This initialing, or signing off, by staff members on line members' proposals gives staff considerably more power. For example, in most organizations, the strategic-planning department (staff) must concur with divisional plans (functional or business strategies) before top corporate management will agree to them. In addition to concurrent authority, staff positions are occasionally granted functional authority over certain matters.

Functional Authority

Functional authority: A system in which a person, work group, or department is given line authority over decisions in other departments related to their area of expertise.

Functional authority gives a person, work group, or department line authority over decisions in other departments that are related to their areas of expertise. This allows them to intervene in line chains of command. In the case just noted, the personnel department could order the production department to make changes in its hiring practices if it possessed functional authority. Today, many organizations operate under a functional-authority concept, in which functional managers make all decisions related to their areas of expertise regardless of where the problem is.

Organizations may encounter problems when using this approach because many decisions overlap. Line and staff are often in conflict. The accounting department, for example, may say that costs can be reduced by cutting inventory, but the marketing department may say that sales will be hurt by such a practice. A joint decision must be arrived at. Giving either department functional authority to determine inventory levels could prove disastrous. Because staff is advisory and line has command authority, the two often disagree on what actions the line should take.

Departmentation

Departmentation: The grouping of jobs under the authority of (usually) a single manager, according to some rational basis, for the purposes of planning, coordination, and control.

Organizations divide up work in order to benefit from specialization. The tasks that comprise a job are identified. Jobs are then grouped into departments. **Departmentation** is the grouping of jobs under the authority of (usually) a single manager, according to some rational basis, for the purposes of planning, coordination, and control. The work group is the basic unit of departmentation. Work groups are grouped into larger departments, the largest of which are known as divisions.

There are eight bases for departmentation: economic function, process, product, strategic business unit, geography, task specialization, time, and client or customer. Figure 9.1 provides an example of each of these. The first five—

functional, process, product, SBU, and geography—often comprise the first level of the organization's structure below the CEO. The other three—task specialty, time, and client—are usually subdivisions of the others.

Departmentation by Economic Function

Departmentation by economic function is the most common basis for an organization's overall or macro structure. The reason for this is that most organizations are small and not complex, sell only one or a few products, and therefore are best organized on a functional basis. In this form of departmentation, the managers of major economic functions report directly to the company president or other senior executive. Typically, the marketing, operations, finance, and human resource managers report to the CEO. Figure 9.3 shows one example of functional departmentation, modified to meet the needs of a particular company. Table 9.2 indicates the possible advantages and disadvantages of functional departmentation.

Functional departmentation often occurs as a subpart of a more complex organizational environment with multiple products or businesses. For example, First National Bank is one of several businesses owned by Ford Motor Company. Its internal structure is functional, but it fits within a Ford macrostructure based on lines of business—that is, SBUs.

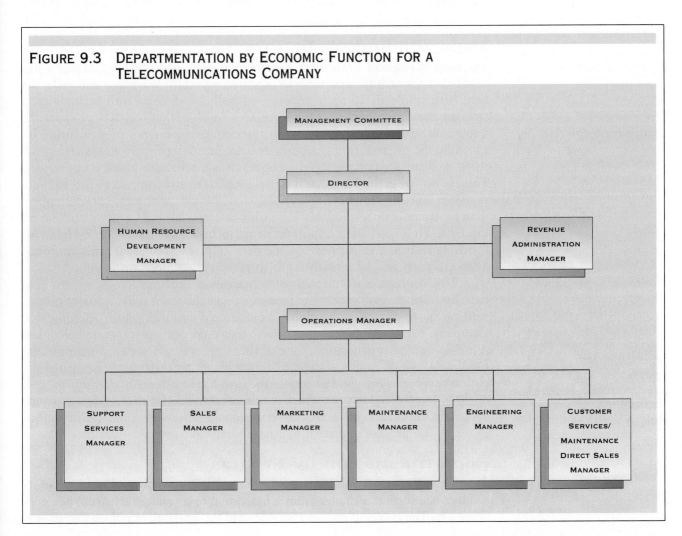

FIGURE 9.3   DEPARTMENTATION BY ECONOMIC FUNCTION FOR A TELECOMMUNICATIONS COMPANY

TABLE 9.2 Advantages and Disadvantages of Departmentation by Economic Function

Advantages

Suited to smaller, less complex organizations, with few products or services.

Allows coordination from a holistic perspective.

Staffing consistent with technical training.

Allows for total organizational reaction to market situations, if coordinated properly.

Reduces demands on the supervisor for technical knowledge.

Fosters development of specialization in areas of expertise.

Fosters more expert-based problem solving.

Disadvantages

Often results in a "functional orientation," with divisions competing rather than cooperating.

Overspecialized management and other employees (they can't see the forest for the trees).

Slowed response times to market situations in larger organizations, especially those with many products.

Problems referred up the hierarchy when they should be solved at lower levels.

General managers not developed.

Can lead to problems of functional coordination.

Departmentation by Process

The need to respond to the management challenges identified in Chapter 1 has resulted in a search for new ways to organize, especially ways that will make the firm better able to compete, operate globally, and cope with technological changes and a more diverse work force. One result of that search is an approach known as **structuring by process.** In this approach, instead of structuring by function, the organization examines its basic customer-related needs and structures itself to satisfy those needs. The result is a structure based on processes. You are probably thinking that it is more logical to structure according to functions—marketing, finance, operations, and human resources, for example— than to structure on a seemingly less profit-oriented basis. The jury is still out on this issue. However, a few important firms, including Xerox, GE, and Hallmark Cards, have begun to organize on the basis of processes because this approach helps cut costs and apparently leads to greater customer satisfaction.[23]

Structuring by process: An approach to organizational design in which the organization examines its basic customer-related needs and structures itself to satisfy those needs.

This concept, also referred to as **horizontal organization,** is so new that most authorities on management have not yet evaluated it fully. A major proponent of this approach is the global management consulting firm McKinsey & Company. McKinsey consultants believe that there are a certain number of key processes in any organization. One of those processes is order generation and fulfillment, which begins when a customer places an order and ends when the customer receives the good or service the firm has to offer. Another key process might be integrated logistics, which would concern itself with the flow of materials within the firm. A series of cross-functional teams would manage these processes.[24] The process approach is discussed and illustrated in Chapter 10.

Horizontal organization: An approach to organizational design based on the belief that there are a certain number of key processes in any organization and that its structure should be based on those processes rather than on functions.

Departmentation by Product

At some point, an organization will have a sufficient number of products in its product line so that a change from a functional to a product structure becomes necessary. The choice is not an easy one, and the criteria are not easy to define.

ALTHOUGH DEPARTMENTATION BY ECONOMIC FUNCTION IS THE MOST COMMON BASIS FOR AN ORGANIZATION'S OVERALL OR MACRO STRUCTURE, SEVERAL OTHER APPROACHES ARE POSSIBLE AS WELL. ONE APPROACH, KNOWN AS STRUCTURING BY PROCESS, INVOLVES EXAMINING THE ORGANIZATION'S CUSTOMER-RELATED NEEDS AND DEVELOPING A STRUCTURE TO MEET THOSE NEEDS. THIS RELATIVELY NEW APPROACH RESULTS IN A HORIZONTAL ORGANIZATION. A MORE FAMILIAR APPROACH, USED BY MULTIBUSINESS ORGANIZATIONS LIKE WALT DISNEY COMPANIES, IS TO BASE THE ORGANIZATION'S STRUCTURE ON STRATEGIC BUSINESS UNITS (SBUS). DEPARTMENTATION BY TASK SPECIALTY OCCURS WHEN A DEPARTMENT BECOMES SO LARGE AND COMPLEX THAT IT IS NECESSARY TO FORM SUBDEPARTMENTS AND SMALLER GROUPS TO PERFORM PARTICULAR FUNCTIONS.

The advantages and disadvantages of both structures must be weighed. How big should a company be to adopt a product structure? Should the decision be based on the number of products or on the amount of revenue from each product? When should the firm change to a global structure? How can it cut costs, other than by closing plants and laying off workers? For Apple Computer, the answers to all of these questions were related. When John Sculley became CEO in 1983, he soon merged the Lisa and Macintosh product lines, giving the company two product divisions instead of three. In 1985, he merged the Apple II and Macintosh divisions, essentially returning the company to a functional structure. This move revealed that Sculley did not think Apple was big enough for a product structure. The company cut costs by eliminating duplicate staffs, and it streamlined its marketing efforts. Apple did not abandon the personal-computer market, where cheap products abound, but it did focus on the office market. Then, in 1988, Sculley reorganized the company again, changing from a functional structure to a geographically based SBU structure with functional support. Three geographic SBUs—North America, Europe and Africa, and Asia—along with an R&D division, report directly to Sculley. This structure was chosen because of increased revenues in Europe and potential revenues in Asia.[25]

A typical product structure (in this case, services) is shown in Figure 9.4. Perhaps the best-known product structure is that of Procter & Gamble, with more than seven hundred product departments. Table 9.3 identifies the advantages and disadvantages of this structure.

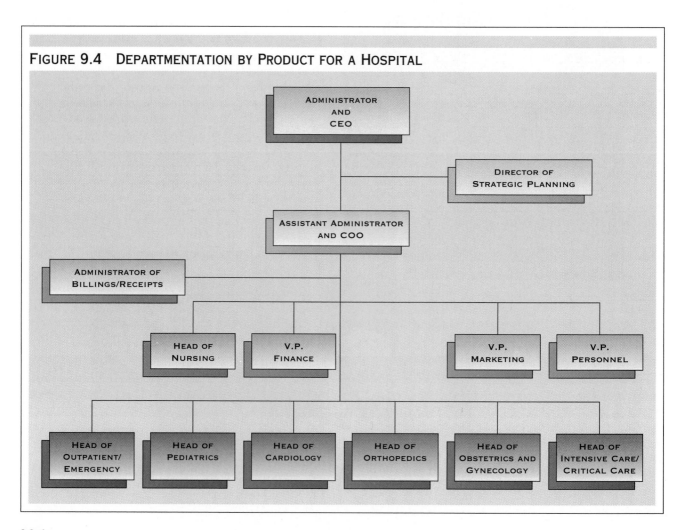

FIGURE 9.4   DEPARTMENTATION BY PRODUCT FOR A HOSPITAL

TABLE 9.3 Advantages and Disadvantages of Product Structure

Advantages

Responsiveness to market.

Facilitates interfunctional coordination.

Enhances product visibility, product development.

Develops general managers.

Possible synergies among products, distribution, and so on.

Disadvantages

Specialization and related expertise may wane.

Competition between product managers is fostered—a different but similar type of problem to that experienced in functional structure between functional managers.

Holistic perspective is limited.

Functions are still critical, but often have little power.

Functional efficiencies may decline.

Functional efforts may be duplicated.

Costs are duplicated.

AT SMITHKLINE BEECHAM: There are five sectors, of which four are equivalent to SBUs. The predominant one is Pharmaceuticals, with Consumer Brands smaller, followed by Animal Health and Clinical Laboratories. The overall corporate management is considered the fifth sector.

Departmentation by Strategic Business Unit

The primary macrostructure for between 500 and 1,000 U.S. businesses and 100 or so sizable U.S. not-for-profit organizations is based on the **strategic business unit (SBU).** An SBU is a major division within a multibusiness organization that operates much like an independent company and offers a set of distinct products to a distinct market. For example, in 1993, Walt Disney Companies' theme parks—Disneyland and Walt Disney World—were included in one of Disney's seven SBUs; among the others were movies, consumer products, cable television, and real estate development.

When a company has a large number of SBUs, it creates group divisions to reduce spans of control and increase coordination. The advantages and disadvantages of the SBU structure, also known as the multibusiness, multidivisional, or "M-form" structure, are listed in Table 9.4. (Figure 9.1 is an example of this structure.)

Strategic business unit (SBU): A major division within a multibusiness organization that operates much like an independent company and offers a set of distinct products to a distinct market.

Departmentation by Geography

For many organizations it is desirable to be located near customers, especially for marketing and direct sales. Sales forces, if they are not divided into client or customer departments, are typically divided into geographic territories, such as the St. Louis and Chicago offices, or the Midwest or Northeast sales territory. Geographic departmentation is based on the assumption that by being physically close to customers, the organization can serve them better. Figure 9.5 presents an organization chart for the Sales Department of Macmillan Publishing Company's College Division. It is based on geographic departmentation. Table 9.5 enumerates the advantages and disadvantages of departmentation on a geographic basis.

Sometimes operations divisions are structured geographically in order to provide ready support to the company's marketing efforts. Large companies like

TABLE 9.4 Advantages and Disadvantages of SBU Structure

Advantages

Only structure that satisfactorily suits a multibusiness organization.

Enhances flexibility of response to marketplace.

Retains business orientation to market.

Retention of advantages of functional (or other) structures for each business.

Permits more even revenue flows and risks among businesses.

Disadvantages

The complex structure is often subject to overstaffing at corporate levels.

Intense coordination is required.

Each business unit possesses certain disadvantages of the functional (or other) structures.

There is mixed evidence that the multiple business structure offers any profit advantages over SBUs—that is, why not operate as separate companies rather than as SBUs of the same company?[a]

This structure may reduce innovation. It clearly causes a short-term focus, as opposed to a long-term focus.[b] Profits are viewed as the critical measure of SBU performance. Top management turns over frequently, and their compensation is almost always based on short-term profit, thus causing them to reduce long-term investment, for example, for R&D.

[a]For a brief review of the evidence, see James M. Higgins and Julian W. Vincze, *Strategic Management: Text and Cases,* 5th ed. (Hinsdale, Ill.: Dryden, 1993), pp. 221–224.
[b]Charles W. Hill, Michael A. Hitt, and Robert E. Horkison, "Declining U.S. Competitiveness: Reflections on a Crisis," *Academy of Management Executive* (February 1988), pp. 51–60.

IBM have numerous manufacturing facilities distributed throughout the United States, Europe, and other foreign countries in order to reduce transportation time and costs. As the U.S. economy becomes more globally competitive, increasing geographic departmentation will be required for companies doing business in and among various countries. Moreover, there is a growing belief that as companies enter into more global alliances, a new form of geographic departmentation is occurring. A new form of organization—a global network with geographic nodes structured around a central corporate core—appears to be emerging. The nodes are often acquired companies or alliances.[26]

Departmentation by Task Specialty

Departmentation by task specialty typically occurs in extremely large organizations. For example, at one time Lockheed Georgia employed more than three hundred accountants. They were all housed in the same large, open area but were departmentalized by task specialty. There were departments for cost accounting, budgetary accounting, capital asset accounting, and project accounts (such as C130, C141, C5-A, and Jet Star, all major types of airplanes). Even within some of these task specialties there were subdepartments based on task specializations. Cost accounting, for example, was divided into journal ledger and contract departments. Employees in the journal ledger department were responsible for entering costs into the ledger by making various voucher entries; those in the contract area helped work up cost information on airplane contract proposals.[27] Figure 9.1 portrays task specialization in a typical accounting department.

An interesting phenomenon occurring in several U.S. manufacturing industries is a move toward departmentation on a micro basis according to task

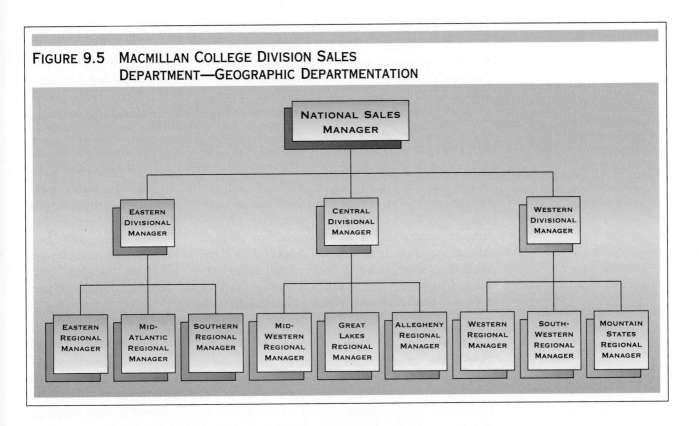

specialization. This is being done to cut costs and improve quality, in order to compete better with Japanese firms. Outboard Marine, for example, no longer has sprawling plants with thousands of workers on an assembly line producing outboard motors. Such plants are simply too large for a single manager to plan, organize, and control. The company therefore automated its plants and reduced the number of workers to five hundred in each of five plants, each of which was assigned a specific set of specialized tasks. This form of organization eliminates

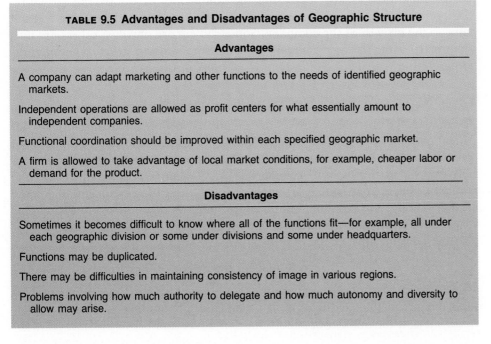

TABLE 9.5 Advantages and Disadvantages of Geographic Structure

Advantages

A company can adapt marketing and other functions to the needs of identified geographic markets.

Independent operations are allowed as profit centers for what essentially amount to independent companies.

Functional coordination should be improved within each specified geographic market.

A firm is allowed to take advantage of local market conditions, for example, cheaper labor or demand for the product.

Disadvantages

Sometimes it becomes difficult to know where all of the functions fit—for example, all under each geographic division or some under divisions and some under headquarters.

Functions may be duplicated.

There may be difficulties in maintaining consistency of image in various regions.

Problems involving how much authority to delegate and how much autonomy and diversity to allow may arise.

errors, raises quality, and cuts costs. Engine blocks are cast at the Spruce Pine, North Carolina, plant using a rare "lost-form" technique that produces smaller but more powerful engines at less cost. The blocks are trucked to Burmanth, North Carolina, for pistons, fuel systems, and other equipment and then on to either Rutherfordton, North Carolina, or Calhoun, Georgia, for transmissions.[28] Note how this counters the trend toward process-based organizations.

Departmentation Based on Time

A frequently employed form of departmentation is based on time and usually consists of a day shift, a night shift, and a swing shift. In hospitals, for example, the day shift usually runs from 7:00 AM to 3:00 PM, the swing shift from 3:00 PM to 11:00 PM, and the night shift from 11:00 PM to 7:00 AM. More complex time arrangements are also possible. For example, in the Air Force, crews on a Minuteman missile launch site might be on duty for twenty-four hours two or three days a week. Some bomber and fighter crews might be "on alert" for a week, living in an alert shack and waiting for possible scrambles of the airplanes. Figure 9.1 portrays this type of departmentation.

Departmentation by Client or Customer

One of the main reasons organizations departmentalize is to ensure that decisions are made by the individuals who are most familiar with the situation. A client or customer orientation significantly increases an organization's chances of success.[29] Departments based on clients are usually found in sales divisions. Figure 9.1 shows this type of departmentation for a sales division.

The Complexities of Pyramidal Structures

Pyramidal structures are even more complex than the preceding discussion suggests because various combinations are possible. Ian C. MacMillan and Patricia E. Jones suggest that numerous major combinations exist for functional, product, geographic, and customer departmentations; they cite several strengths and weaknesses for each configuration.[30] Such combinations could also involve process departmentation. In addition, an SBU structure could be overlaid on each of the combinations, greatly increasing the complexity of the overall structure. Managers must decide which forms of departmentation are necessary at each point in the growth of the company. Some choices are obvious; others are not. Chapter 10 contains some general guidelines for choosing structural configurations.

The Managerial Span of Control

Managerial span of control: The number of people a manager directs.

The **managerial span of control** is the number of people a manager directs. Of critical concern to managers is determining the appropriate size of the span of control—that is, how many subordinates a manager can effectively direct. In studying the span-of-control concept, V. A. Graicunas postulated that as the number of subordinates increases arithmetically, there is an exponential increase in the number of possible relationships among them. This is known as **Graicunas's theory**. He devised the following formula to calculate the number of possible relationships:

Graicunas's theory: The theory that as the number of subordinates increases arithmetically there is an exponential increase in the number of possible relationships among them.

$$R = n(2^{n-1} + n - 1)$$

where R = number of relationships managers might have with subordinates and subordinates might have with each other, and n = number of persons supervised. Thus, if the number of subordinates is 3, the number of possible relation-

For most jobs, the span of control should not exceed a certain number of subordinates. That number varies with factors such as the manager's leadership style and the subordinates' abilities.

ships is $R = 3(2^2 + 3 - 1) = 18$; as n increases, the number of relationships increases rapidly. Suppose that $n = 5$; then $R = 5(2^4 + 5 - 1)$; and $R = 100$. The more people there are, the more relationships there are to be managed.

For most jobs, the span of control should not exceed a certain number of subordinates. That number, however, varies with other factors. Among these are the nature of the job itself (is the work stable and routine or dynamic and changing?); the manager's leadership style; the time available for managing; the manager's abilities; the subordinates' abilities—such as training and skill; the organization's culture; the nature of the organization's management systems; the availability of rules and procedures; whether subordinates are concentrated in one location or not; and the organization's performance objectives. In one large manufacturing organization, the maintenance engineering manager had seventy-five people reporting directly to him; he was able to manage them effectively because their jobs were largely self-contained.[31]

Assembly-line managers typically have large spans of control, whereas managers of professional groups typically have much smaller ones—at least partly because of the more frequent need to seek advice and confer with other managers. Most top managers have few direct subordinates because of the complexity and changing nature of their tasks and the limited time they have to supervise others directly. There is no absolute span of control that applies to all jobs, but a good rule of thumb is five to nine people.[32]

The size of a manager's span of control affects the management style that will be appropriate. A management style that emphasizes relationships is more difficult to utilize when the span of control is large. Large spans of control also imply that each employee will work in a particular job with little supervision. There is usually a high degree of delegation of authority. A large span of control also may result in managers spending less time rewarding and controlling subordinates' performance than they otherwise would. Conversely, smaller spans of control imply closer relationships between manager and subordinates, less delegation of authority, more controlling, and more time spent rewarding subordinates' behavior.

Spans of control may be adjusted to encourage particular management styles. Some firms may want subordinates to make decisions; they will develop a structure with larger spans of control. The span of control in amusement parks, where managers may supervise as many as forty people, reflects both the desire to cut costs and the fact that the jobs are easy to learn and are essentially self-directed.[33] Naturally, larger spans of control lead to the emergence of informal groups within the formal groups. Typically, managers of such groups must depend heavily on their cooperation.[34]

In addition to management philosophy and other factors noted earlier, the factors that influence the span of control include the similarity of functions supervised and their complexity and geographic contiguity; the direction and control needed by subordinates; the amount of coordination necessary; the planning required of the manager; and how much assistance the manager receives from the organization.[35] Spans of control are expected to increase in the 1990s as firms flatten their structures.[36]

"Flat" Versus "Tall" Organizations

The way an organization structures itself will cause it to become either "tall"—reflecting small spans of control, more levels in the chain of command, and centralization—or "flat"—reflecting large spans of control, fewer levels in the chain of command, and decentralization. GM provides important lessons on some of the consequences of such choices. GM saw its U.S. market share plummet from 48 percent in 1979 to 36 percent in 1987. An evaluation of its strategic situation revealed a number of problems, including the company's structure. GM realized that with eleven to fourteen layers of management (depending on the division), compared to Toyota's five, and a more centralized structure than Toyota's, it had become less responsive to the marketplace than its competitors. Customer needs were blurred, and it took far too long to make decisions. For example, GM might take seven years to launch a new product from conception to showroom, whereas Toyota would take only four years. These additional layers in the scalar chain also meant that GM's management costs were higher than Toyota's. Figure 9.6 characterizes the situation: The more centralized organization is taller than the decentralized organization.

In an effort to become more competitive, GM made a series of severe cuts in its managerial and professional staff. It still has more layers of management than Toyota, but it has substantially reduced the number of layers from the 1987 level.[37]

Coordination

Coordination: *The process of integrating the efforts of individuals and departments to achieve the organization's purpose.*

Coordination is expected to be an increasingly important part of organizational structure as structures become ever more complex. **Coordination** is the process of integrating the efforts of individuals and departments to achieve the organization's purpose.[38] It involves several structural issues: formalization, complexity, integration and differentiation, and the linking-pin concept. In this section we will examine each of these issues in some detail.

Formalization

Formalization: *The extent to which written documentation occurs within an organization.*

Formalization is the extent to which written documentation occurs within an organization. It focuses on objectives and related job descriptions but may also include policies, strategies, procedures, and systems manuals. A highly formalized organizational structure would have policies and strategies; detailed job descriptions, objectives, and procedures; and detailed sets of rules—all in writing. Normally, smaller, more cohesive, family-type organizations are not very formalized. However, as an organization grows, it eventually becomes necessary to formalize its structure in order to avoid confusion, clarify roles, and eliminate ambiguity. A typical example is Philip Crosby and Associates, Inc., one of the

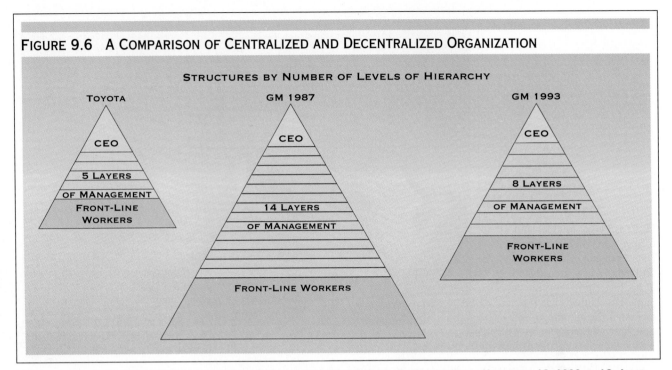

FIGURE 9.6 A COMPARISON OF CENTRALIZED AND DECENTRALIZED ORGANIZATION

STRUCTURES BY NUMBER OF LEVELS OF HIERARCHY

SOURCES: JOSEPH B. WHITE, "GM AIMS TO BREAK EVEN BY NEXT YEAR," *WALL STREET JOURNAL*, NOVEMBER 13, 1992, P. A3; JOLIE SOLOMEN, "CAN GM FIX ITSELF?" *NEWSWEEK* (NOVEMBER 9, 1992) PP. 54–59 (REPRINTED FROM MARCH 16, 1987 ISSUE OF *BUSINESS WEEK* BY SPECIAL PERMISSION, COPYRIGHT © 1987 BY McGRAW-HILL, INC.); WILLIAM J. HAMPTON AND JAMES R. NORMAN, "GENERAL MOTORS: WHAT WENT WRONG?" *BUSINESS WEEK* (MARCH 16, 1987), PP. 102–110; AND JACK A. SEAMONDS AND KENNETH R. SHEETS, "GM'S NOVEMBER MASSACRE," *U.S. NEWS AND WORLD REPORT* (NOVEMBER 17, 1986), P. 56.

nation's leading quality consultants. When the firm had 105 employees, it was still as informal as it had been when it was founded three years earlier. However, its rapid growth caused employees to become uncertain of their job responsibilities and the firm's expectations. A massive formalization effort led to an easing of this problem and a recognition of overlapping job responsibilities.[39]

There is evidence that even if formalization occurs, employees may not feel that the detailed objectives and job descriptions have much relevance to them. Thus, it is necessary not only to formalize the structure as the organization grows, but also to make certain that the resultant written statements are accepted as valid and necessary by employees.

Some organizations strive to be "informal." Electronic Data Systems' founder and former CEO, H. Ross Perot, prided himself on having no written memos in his huge time-sharing company. The reality, though, was that a lot of his company's rules, regulations, policies, procedures, and job descriptions were highly formalized in what has been described as a "militaristic"—centralized and rule bound—culture.[40]

AT SMITHKLINE BEECHAM: By offering guidelines in its Leadership Principles and leaving implementation to lower-level management, top management at SmithKline Beecham had the best of both worlds—a formal overall policy statement with informal lower-level policy details.

Complexity

The **complexity** of an organization refers to the number of different jobs and departments it encompasses and their interrelationships. An organization's structure is said to be complex if it includes a large number of different jobs and departments and/or if there are a number of loosely structured arrangements among them—for example, autonomous teams in a horizontal arrangement or internal or external networks (for example, between work units or with customers and suppliers). Normally, the more complex an organization's structure, the more numerous and difficult the problems encountered in managing it. Complex organizations such as GM tend to have slower communications and to make

Complexity: The number of different jobs and departments in an organization and the interrelationships among them.

H. Ross Perot, founder and former CEO of Electronic Data Systems, prided himself on having no written memos in his huge time-sharing company. He claimed that this increased the amount of free time he could enjoy.

decisions more slowly (unless they are highly decentralized) than less complex organizations.

Complex organizations often tend to be too tightly controlled. Members of such organizations frequently feel that they are tied up with "red tape." Organizations like the U.S. Department of Agriculture are so complex and formalized that decisions on many issues can take virtually forever. In addition to formalization, one of the reasons that complex organizations are slow in making decisions is that so many of their internal units must have a role in the decision process. Overcoming the negative consequences of complexity may require changes in certain organizational behaviors. It may be necessary, for example, to increase the level of participation by subordinates in decision making. Computerized information systems offer a means of dealing with complexity that was not available until recently.[41] Organizations that become mired in bureaucracy may also require major restructuring. Some organizations are reluctant to take the necessary actions, as this chapter's Global Management Challenge reveals.

Integration and Differentiation

As noted earlier, organizations and their subunits differentiate their structures, processes, and members' behaviors according to the requirements of their environments. For example, an accounting department is structured differently than a sales department because they operate in different environments. Differentiation has numerous other structural ramifications as well, such as those related to client and product departmentation, described earlier in the chapter. For example, a firm may choose a client-based structure—major accounts, in a sales department—in order to serve its customers better. Spans of control may grow smaller in response to a highly unstable external environment.

Paul R. Lawrence and Jay W. Lorsch suggest (as did Henri Fayol) that differentiated subunits tend to view the organization's purpose from a "differentiated," or biased, perspective.[42] That is, because subunits differ from other units within the organization, they have a tendency to be parochial in their views and to lose sight of the organization's purpose. To counteract this tendency, organizations must be integrated. **Integration** is the direction of differentiated

Integration: The direction of differentiated subunits' efforts toward the fulfillment of an organization's central purpose or mission.

Rousing a Sleepy Giant

From April 27 to June 29, 1990, the stock price of N. V. Philips, the Dutch electronics giant, plunged from 40 Netherlands guilders per share to 31 guilders per share on the Amsterdam Stock Exchange. The company's performance had been lackluster throughout the 1980s. It had suffered heavy losses in computers and semiconductors in 1989 and in the first quarter of 1990. Despite efforts by CEO Cornelis van der Klugt to trim excess layers of management and to deal with the impacts of European market unification in 1992, Philips still plodded along. On July 1, 1990, van der Klugt stepped down and was succeeded by Jan Timmer, the head of the firm's consumer products division.

Analysts cited the need for major cuts in the firm's bloated employment levels and the need to sell its computer and semiconductor businesses in order to improve profitability significantly. Timmer declined to sell the unprofitable businesses and said that he would eliminate only 10,000 of the firm's 293,000 employees, not 50,000 as some analysts recommended. He did, however, promise major cost cutting in the computer division and signaled a retreat from the minicomputer market. Timmer soon found, however, that he had no choice but to make even more significant cuts in the company's work force. By late 1992, 47,000 people—20 percent of the work force—had been let go. Morale is low, and the thought of more reorganizations is likely to drive it even lower. Yet Timmer must take such actions if he is to turn the company around.

SOURCES: Stewart Toy, "Europe's Shakeout," *Business Week* (September 14, 1992), p. 44; and Bob Hagerty, "Philips' Timmer Faces Challenge Rousing Sleepy Electronics Giant," *Wall Street Journal* (June 29, 1990), p. A10.

subunits' efforts toward the fulfillment of an organization's central purpose or mission. Typically, objective setting and planning systems are a major source of integration because they direct the whole organization toward the same purposes.

Research findings suggest that the most successful organizations are those that are both highly differentiated and highly integrated.[43] The implication is that the organization must plan to accomplish both differentiation and integration—that the organization's structure must be altered to meet the environment of each subunit and then coordinated to achieve its mission. Differentiation and integration, including related research, will be discussed in more detail from another perspective in the next chapter.

The Manager as a Linking Pin

Organizations are formed around groups of people—work groups, teams, departments. The manager of each work unit is a **linking pin** among at least three groups: the group he or she leads and manages (A), the group of peer managers (managers at the same level in the same work group) of which he or she is a member (B), and the group of managers higher in the organizational hierarchy (C), of which the manager's boss is a member, as shown in Figure 9.7.[44] In addition to linking basic work groups, a manager may also serve as a link between autonomous, or self-managed, work teams and units outside the organization. The manager, thus, is the vital connecting point for many of the elements

Linking pin: The idea that the manager of each work unit serves as a linking pin among at least three groups: the group that he or she leads and manages, the group of managers at the same level of which he or she is a member, and the group of managers higher in the organizational hierarchy, of which the manager's boss is a member.

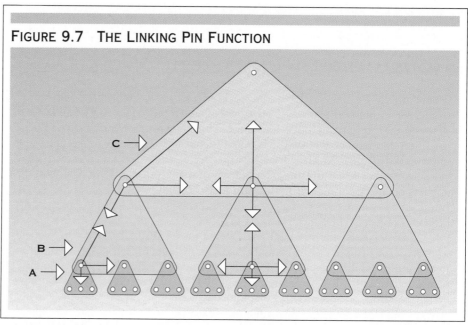

FIGURE 9.7 THE LINKING PIN FUNCTION

SOURCE: RENSIS LIKERT, NEW PATTERNS OF MANAGEMENT, NEW YORK: MCGRAW-HILL, P. 165. REPRODUCED WITH PERMISSION.

of structure discussed previously: span of control, departmentation, delegation, decentralization, formalization, acceptance of authority, and parity.

As a linking pin, the manager is primarily responsible for implementation. This requires coordination of the organizational objectives that come from higher levels of the hierarchy with the individual objectives that come from lower levels. Influencing motivation is also an essential task. Coordination with peer managers facilitates these processes. Because of the increasing emphasis on team approaches and the increased use of networks, managers need to develop the skills that will enable them to perform the linking function more effectively.[45]

The manager of each work unit is a linking pin among at least three groups. Because of the increasing emphasis on team approaches and the increased use of networks, managers need to develop the skills that will enable them to perform the linking function more effectively.

Additional Coordination Devices

Richard L. Daft has identified several devices in addition to objectives and planning that organizations can use to improve coordination. These additional coordination devices include the following:

1. *Add levels of positions to the hierarchy.* If the manager is overworked, adding positions may improve coordination. (This solution has not been shown to be effective in the 1990s.)

2. *Use information systems better.* Providing managers with better information in periodic reports—for example, information from computer database summaries—may improve their ability to coordinate. Electronic mail can be especially useful.

3. *Exchange paperwork.* Managers can improve coordination by exchanging information with other managers.

4. *Increase personal contact.* Have more direct contact with subordinates and other managers.

5. *Emphasize liaison.* Liaison roles can be created to improve the coordination of individuals, groups, and departments. It may be necessary to appoint a full-time integrator.

6. *Employ task forces.* A person in a liaison role can usually coordinate two or more departments. When more departments need to be coordinated, temporary task forces can be established, made up of representatives from each department affected by a problem. They join to solve the problem, or at least to coordinate efforts to solve it.

7. *Teams can be created* to achieve coordination.[46] In addition, networks, groupware (software for group decision making), and horizontal structures can be used to improve coordination.

Additional Types of Structures

Up to this point, the traditional pyramidal form of structure and variations of it have been this chapter's principal concern. However, six other forms should also be noted. They are the project, the team, the matrix, the joint venture, other strategic alliances, and the network.

Project Structure

A **project structure** is a temporary, function-based structure designed to carry out a specific project. It is disassembled in parts as each stage of the project is completed. (For example, the R&D portion of the structure would be dissolved once the project was articulated.) The project structure is used principally in the construction industry, but until the 1970s it was used in the aerospace industry as well. One difficulty with the project structure is that employees are retained only as long as their part of the project continues. In the construction business this is not a significant problem, as there is usually an available pool of labor that moves from project to project in any given city. In the aerospace industry, in contrast, engineers in a given city typically do not have many projects to choose from; hence, they tend to resist termination of a project. The project structure closely resembles the product structure, except that groups of products are usually produced over long periods, whereas projects endure for only a few months or years.

Project structure: A temporary function-based structure that is designed to carry out a specific project and is disassembled as each stage of the project is completed.

The Team

Team: An egalitarian, highly cooperative, close-knit work group striving to achieve a set of mutually desirable objectives.

AT SMITHKLINE BEECHAM: *Teams were created during the initial transition period to study and implement the merger at an organizational level. The team approach generated closer ties between members of the two premerger companies and helped spread the idea that everyone was "in this together."*

A **team** is an egalitarian, highly cooperative, close-knit work group striving to achieve a set of mutually desirable objectives. Just as a pyramid best represents the distribution of authority in a classical organizational structure, a circle best represents the distribution of authority in team management situations. Conceptually, each member of a team is equal in authority. In true teams, managers participate as members. They do not impose their decisions on others but, in most cases, facilitate the group's efforts. Teams generally have no more than ten members.

In a broader sense, team management means building cohesive work groups. Authority may be shared up to a certain level, but in many teams the manager retains ultimate authority. Team management involves helping the team perform more effectively and at the same time helping team members satisfy their needs. It has been used extensively in businesses and in the federal government to increase productivity and encourage collaborative problem solving.[47]

Quality circles are formal groups of employees that meet periodically during work hours to solve company problems. They are an example of the team concept in its purest form. The manager facilitates, coaches, counsels, and provides resources but does not intervene in the group's problem-solving process.

Team management is usually found at the micro level of organizational structure. Teams may be found in the pyramid as well as the other types of structures. In industrial situations, team management has been applied throughout organizations with up to about two hundred people. For example, a milk-processing plant organized its employees into twenty teams with ten members each, representing various levels of the organization. The teams were successful in raising productivity above the levels achieved under a hierarchical management system.[48]

Thousands of U.S.-based companies, including many of the Fortune 500 firms, have successfully implemented team management. The same can be said of thousands of companies in Europe and Japan and other Pacific Rim countries. Even companies in countries with emerging economies have turned to teams as a

A team is an egalitarian, cooperative, close-knit work group striving to achieve a set of mutually desirable objectives. This Saturn team is working on a highly innovative robotic training project.

way of becoming more competitive.[49] Cross-functional teams, in which representatives from different departments—marketing, finance, and operations, for example—meet to solve a problem, are especially useful in improving customer satisfaction. They also help overcome divided loyalties and speed project development. Chapter 15 discusses groups and team management in more detail.

The Matrix Structure

The **matrix structure** is characterized by the simultaneous authority of project and functional managers over line and/or staff. As a pyramid represents hierarchical authority and a circle represents the equal authority of the team, a rectangle represents the distribution of authority in a matrix organization. An example of the matrix form of management is displayed in Figure 9.8. The matrix form of management is found principally in aerospace and banking.

The matrix organization was designed principally as a way to avoid the shortcomings of project management. When a project was completed, employees were terminated. New projects were begun, often without phasing in and out of other projects in order to retain employees. Each project was managed as a

Matrix structure: A structure characterized by the simultaneous authority of project and functional managers over line and/or staff.

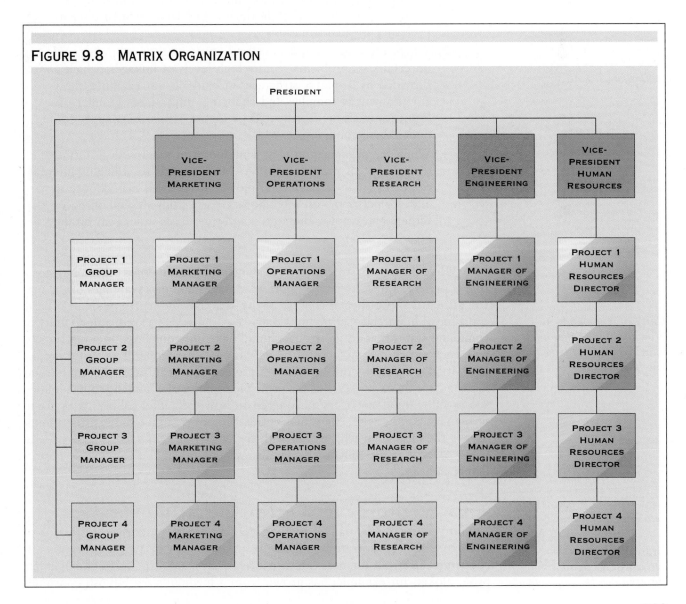

FIGURE 9.8 MATRIX ORGANIZATION

separate entity. A major difficulty with this approach was that companies that used the project structure found it difficult to rehire employees. The matrix structure was designed to keep employees in a central pool and to allocate them to various projects according to the length of time they were needed. If a firm had a large number of projects, it could retain a permanent labor force and simply move employees from project to project. The key was in timing a project's life cycle. The matrix organization is seldom found in pure form. All sorts of variations exist. Normally the matrix is part of a much larger pyramid, although it can comprise 80 or 90 percent of the pyramid. The horizontal organization, discussed previously, looks somewhat like a matrix in terms of its organization chart, but the functional chain of command is much less important than in the true matrix.[50]

Stanley M. Davis and Paul R. Lawrence have identified three conditions that should lead to the use of the matrix structure:

1. There are two critical requirements related to outputs—demands for technical quality and for frequent new products. These demands are a central feature of the aerospace industry. Such requirements mean that power must be shared within the organization. The dual authority of the matrix structure seems necessary in such situations.

2. Where the organization's external environment is complex and uncertain, its problems require high levels of linkages, which are provided by a matrix structure. In banking, for example, the environment is complex and changing, and a large number of branches must be coordinated. A matrix structure is appropriate under these conditions.

3. When the organization is at a midpoint in its growth in terms of the number of products it offers, and it needs to utilize its internal resources (such as engineers) more efficiently, it may choose to allocate personnel on a temporary basis from a common pool rather than employ them on a full-time basis in a given product area.

While the matrix structure solves some problems, it poses others. No structure is perfect. Table 9.6 portrays the advantages and disadvantages of the matrix structure.[51] Of special concern is the fact that the matrix violates a basic principle of hierarchical structures: unity of command. The principle of **unity of command** states that an individual should have only one boss. In a matrix system, each person has two bosses by definition: a functional boss and a project boss. If an individual works on enough projects in a year, he or she can have as many as five or six bosses. For the principle of unity of command to be violated successfully, these managers must agree on how their joint subordinates are to be managed. Otherwise, chaos may ensue. Moreover, although the project manager is the individual who works with the employee on a day-to-day basis, in many cases it is the functional manager who fills out the employee's performance appraisal.[52]

Unity of command: A principle stating that an individual should have only one boss.

Joint Ventures and Strategic Alliances

A **joint venture** is essentially a partnership between corporations; it is a type of strategic alliance. A **strategic alliance** is an agreement by two corporations to cooperate. Strategic alliances can turn a relatively small firm into a global enterprise. Nokia, for example, has grown from a medium-sized Finnish consumer

Joint venture: A partnership between corporations.

Strategic alliance: An agreement by two corporations to cooperate.

TABLE 9.6 Advantages and Disadvantages of Matrix Organizational Structure

Advantages
Provides coordination necessary to satisfy dual environmental demands.
Flexible use of human resources.
Suited to complex and changeful environments.
Leads to functional and integration skill development.

Disadvantages
Members of the organization experience dual authority, which leads to role ambiguity, frustration, and confusion.
Managers and other participants need sound interpersonal skills.
Extensive training is required.
It is time consuming to resolve conflicts and to reach agreement on objectives and actions.
Without cooperation the matrix will not work.

SOURCE: Adapted from Robert Duncan, "What Is the Right Organizational Structure: Decision Tree Analysis Provides the Answer." Reprinted by permission of publisher, from *Organizational Dynamics*, Winter 1979, p. 429. © 1979, American Management Association, New York. All rights reserved.

goods conglomerate to a world-class communications and electronics company. It has operations in thirty-three countries and production in sixteen, largely through strategic alliances. Nokia has alliances with Tandy and AT&T in mobile phones; with Philips, Thomson, and Bosch in the European high-definition television project; and with Technophone Ltd. in the cellular market in the United Kingdom.[53]

Even Sears and IBM have joined in a venture, Prodigy, that is aimed at providing videotech services for shopping, banking, electronic-mail information, and education. These services would provide home subscribers with video/computer capabilities to transact business in each of these areas. Through late 1987, the two companies had jointly invested $250 million in the venture. Their belief is that if every home has a computer, it can be linked to multiple information services by telephone. As of early 1992, Prodigy had 1.4 million subscribers.[54]

Network Organizations

One consequence of the challenges to management in today's environment is the emergence of the **network organization** structure. This consists of clusters of firms or specialized subunits that are coordinated by market mechanisms rather than by traditional chains of command.[55] The network is better able to anticipate and respond to its environment than other structures because it is smaller, has fewer layers of management, and is closer to its markets. In other ways, too, this form of organization can mitigate threats and take advantage of opportunities; for example, it helps build close relationships among individuals and groups both inside and outside the organization. The latter extend beyond the normal "let's do business" relationships. They involve making customers and suppliers part of the company and encouraging collaboration by interdependent functional units. Network organizations employ numerous communication devices to improve these relationships. Such organizations are often global firms, but domestic firms may also use this type of structure.[56]

Network organization: A cluster of firms or specialized subunits coordinated by market mechanisms rather than by traditional chains of command.

FIGURE 9.9   ORGANIZING AS PROBLEM SOLVING

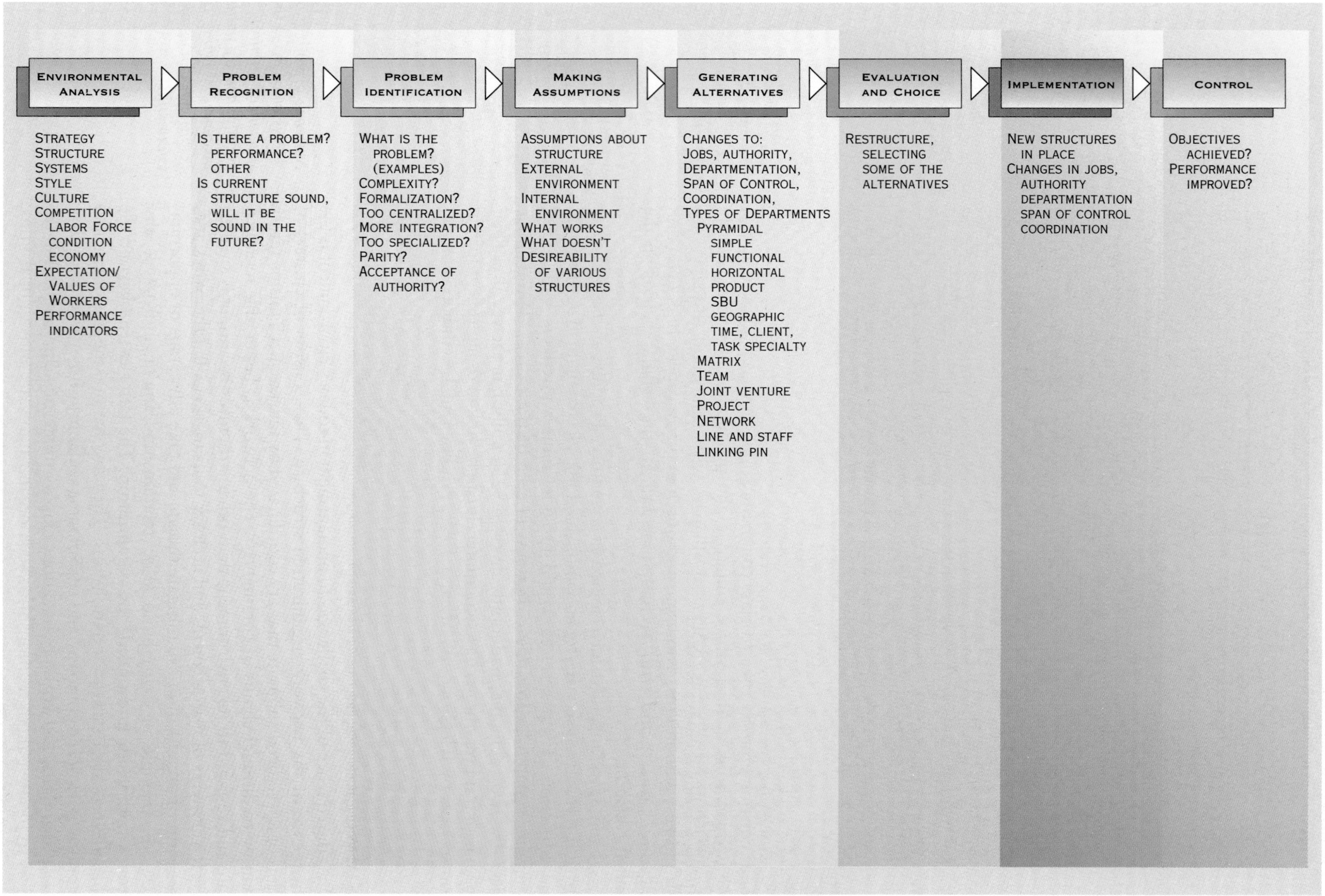

ENVIRONMENTAL ANALYSIS	PROBLEM RECOGNITION	PROBLEM IDENTIFICATION	MAKING ASSUMPTIONS	GENERATING ALTERNATIVES	EVALUATION AND CHOICE	IMPLEMENTATION	CONTROL
STRATEGY STRUCTURE SYSTEMS STYLE CULTURE COMPETITION LABOR FORCE CONDITION ECONOMY EXPECTATION/VALUES OF WORKERS PERFORMANCE INDICATORS	IS THERE A PROBLEM? PERFORMANCE? OTHER IS CURRENT STRUCTURE SOUND, WILL IT BE SOUND IN THE FUTURE?	WHAT IS THE PROBLEM? (EXAMPLES) COMPLEXITY? FORMALIZATION? TOO CENTRALIZED? MORE INTEGRATION? TOO SPECIALIZED? PARITY? ACCEPTANCE OF AUTHORITY?	ASSUMPTIONS ABOUT STRUCTURE EXTERNAL ENVIRONMENT INTERNAL ENVIRONMENT WHAT WORKS WHAT DOESN'T DESIREABILITY OF VARIOUS STRUCTURES	CHANGES TO: JOBS, AUTHORITY, DEPARTMENTATION, SPAN OF CONTROL, COORDINATION, TYPES OF DEPARTMENTS PYRAMIDAL SIMPLE FUNCTIONAL HORIZONTAL PRODUCT SBU GEOGRAPHIC TIME, CLIENT, TASK SPECIALTY MATRIX TEAM JOINT VENTURE PROJECT NETWORK LINE AND STAFF LINKING PIN	RESTRUCTURE, SELECTING SOME OF THE ALTERNATIVES	NEW STRUCTURES IN PLACE CHANGES IN JOBS, AUTHORITY DEPARTMENTATION SPAN OF CONTROL COORDINATION	OBJECTIVES ACHIEVED? PERFORMANCE IMPROVED?

Informal Structure

Informal relationships develop among members of an organization while they are working and when they get together away from work. Such relationships are based on friendship or common interests.[57] They are not typically sanctioned by the formal organization, although it is usually aware of them. There are times when such relationships are encouraged in order to maintain the cohesiveness of the work group.

An organization's informal structure can affect power relations within the organization. When, for example, a secretary wields informal power because he has access to the boss, he may develop a group of followers who attempt to gain access to the boss through him. When an administrative assistant knows more than anyone else about how to use a spreadsheet program, she may have considerable influence on other members of the organization, even though she has been granted no formal authority. Remember that even though individuals may report to a manager, they may not recognize his or her authority and may go to someone else for needed opinions or technical information.

The informal structure can also have positive effects. Informal groups often are responsible for maintaining cohesiveness—that is, a sense that it is desirable to remain in and participate actively in the group. Cohesiveness assists the manager in keeping a group working toward its objectives. The informal group can provide important, quite accurate information to people in the organization's informal communication network. Informal structure also helps satisfy the social needs of individuals and can provide a sense of satisfaction of higher-level needs, such as esteem. On the other hand, informal groups that are extremely cohesive but are not aligned with the organization's objectives can hinder the accomplishment of those objectives. They may provide inaccurate information, circulate rumors, or resist change. The manager must therefore learn how to manage informal groups. Chapter 15 provides more insight into how this may be accomplished.

Organizing as a Problem-Solving Process

This chapter has introduced various organizational structures and their advantages and disadvantages. Chapters 10 and 11 will provide more information about the factors that influence the choice of a structure. Figure 9.9 examines structure from a problem-solving perspective.[58]

In approaching organizing as a problem-solving process, a manager would continually analyze environmental information for signals of a need to change the organization's structure. The factors shown in the figure are the major ones, but they are only a few of those that need to be considered. Top management would be concerned mainly with overall macro structure—divisions and departments; lower-level managers would be concerned with micro structures—small departments, work groups, and individual jobs.

At lower levels, managers recognize and identify structural problems, often in response to the dictates of upper-level managers. Thus, as discussed earlier in the chapter, when Hewlett-Packard restructured in the early 1990s, lower-level managers followed upper management's guidelines in restructuring their work groups and the jobs of subordinates. In essence, the problem was already recognized and identified for them. Conversely, top management was responding to market conditions. Wanting to be more responsive to customers and develop products faster, CEO John Young changed the company's structure in order to eliminate innovation-stifling committees. He created product "czars" to take control and move products to market faster.[59] To do so, he had to change the corporation's overall structure, which allowed each of the company's separate businesses to operate independently but in a coordinated way. In the problem-identification stage, Young determined that those businesses needed to be better integrated.

Young assumed that the competitive environment of the future would dictate this change in strategy and, hence, structure. He also assumed that Hewlett-Packard's basic structure was satisfactory and needed to be modified, not totally changed. He therefore developed a number of alternatives related to redefining the jobs and authority of division chiefs and product development leaders and improving coordination among them. Lower-level managers had to make as-

---

ETHICAL MANAGEMENT CHALLENGE

Is Downsizing Ethical in Japan?

The 1991–1993 recession hit hard in Japan. Sales in basic industries slumped in the face of increasing competition. Manufacturing firms were shown to be less efficient than many believed. During the 1980s they had become less lean and mean. Nissan, Japan's second-largest car maker, was a case in point, having lost money in 1992 because of several factors, including a flexible manufacturing strategy gone awry, the lowest car sales in Japan in twenty years, and the global recession. Drastic changes were badly needed.

Yoshifumi Tsuji, Nissan's new president, set the tone when he declared, "A bloodless change isn't going to do us any good. Reform and pain go together." Soon thereafter, the firm announced that it was closing its Zama plant, just outside Tokyo, the first major closing of a manufacturing facility in Japan since the end of World War II and the first ever of an auto plant. Zama's workers were guaranteed work at another plant (in an undesirable location), but many indicated that they would not move. The lifetime employment guarantee common in Japanese firms was in jeopardy at Nissan. Further threatening that guarantee was the announcement that the work force would be cut by 10 percent (5,000 out of 48,000) in the next three years through attrition. Realistically, given the slow attrition rate, such a turnover is unlikely. And if the recession continues, the firm may be forced to find alternatives to attrition. Thus, the lifetime employment guarantee may all go by the wayside at Nissan.

Other Japanese firms find themselves in similar straits. Nippon Telephone & Telegraph, for example, has announced a 10 percent cut in its work force, amounting to a reduction of 30,000 people. Some wonder if this can be done without layoffs. Many Japanese firms have already made the easy cuts, eliminating temporary workers (almost all of whom are women) and offering early-retirement programs. Layoffs appear to be just around the corner as it is estimated that Japanese firms are employing at least 1 million redundant workers.

In Japan, layoffs raise a major ethical question. How do you eliminate workers who have been guaranteed a job for life? Hiroyuki Mizuno, a Matsushita executive, suggests that the Japanese are moving toward the tougher American style of management that they have long disdained. "We are coming to the U.S. way. Our

sumptions about such issues as what aspects of the structure should remain in place, how to reward employees who were willing to make changes, and how to use people effectively in the new structure. They would then develop alternatives based on their perceived situation.

Both top management and lower-level management would choose the approach to restructuring that best fit their circumstances. Hewlett-Packard's top management chose to stick with an SBU structure and to increase coordination; they also chose, in several situations, to change significantly the degree of autonomy granted to division and product-development chiefs. Management at all levels then took the necessary actions to implement these structural changes, including removing an entire division. Management also analyzed changes in performance to determine whether the structural changes had been effective. Finally, management had to determine whether these decisions were ethical,

The lifetime employment guarantee common in Japanese firms was in jeopardy at Nissan when it lost money in 1992. Further threatening that guarantee was the announcement that the work force would be cut by 10 percent in the next three years through attrition.

management has to be changed," he says. As an example of this shift, several Japanese firms have rescinded contract offers to university graduates, a practice unheard of in a protocol-conscious society.

SOURCES: Karen Lowry Miller, "Stress and Uncertainty: The Price of Restructuring," *Business Week* (March 29, 1993), p. 74; Clay Chandler and Michael Williams, "Strategic Shift: A Slump in Car Sales Forces Nissan to Start Cutting Swollen Costs," *Wall Street Journal* (March 3, 1993), pp. A1, A6; John Bussey, Clay Chandler, and Michael Williams, "The Other Shoe: Japanese Recession Prompts Corporations to Take Radical Steps," *Wall Street Journal* (February 24, 1993), pp. A1, A5.

Hewlett-Packard relies heavily on automation, such as the production line automation shown here. When the company restructured in the early 1990s, lower-level managers followed upper management's guidelines in restructuring work groups and the jobs of subordinates.

given Hewlett-Packard's corporate culture and society's general perception of such actions. As shown in this chapter's Ethical Management Challenge, Nissan now faces the same issue. What unique ethical problems are raised by downsizing in Japan?

Summary

(Before reading this summary, look again at the objectives listed at the beginning of the chapter.)

1. Organizing is the process of determining how resources are allocated and prepared for accomplishing an organization's mission. Structure is designed to carry out the organization's strategy and other plans.

2. In structuring an organization, managers must be concerned with (a) the division of labor (determining a scope of work and how it is combined in a job), (b) delegation of authority (determining how much authority should be granted to individuals and groups to do their jobs), (c) departmentation (grouping jobs into work units and departments on some rational basis), (d) spans of control (determining how many subordinates each manager should have), and (e) coordination of individuals, groups, and departments.

3. An organization is a group of people working together to achieve a common purpose.

4. Formal organization consists of the structure that is sanctioned by the organization. Informal structure consists of all other relationships that develop within the organization.

5. By examining an organization chart, we can determine the following relationships: division and specialization of labor, relative authority, departmentation, span of control, levels of management, coordination centers, communication channels, and decision responsibility.

6. Organizational structure results from the interaction among the content of individual jobs based on specialization of labor; the amount of authority delegated; the groupings of individuals, groups, and departments; the sizes of spans of control; the types of departmentation used—task specialization, time, customer, geography, product, process, economic function, or strategic business unit; and the amount of complexity, formalization, integration, and coordination.

7. Resources other than human resources are organized through planning and scheduling.

General Questions

1. Describe an organization you know in terms of each of the five fundamental elements and their components. For example, is departmentation based on product, economic function, or SBU? Do you see evidence of departmentation based on task specialization? What are the spans of control?

2. Draw a simple organization chart for the organization you described in the preceding question.

3. How do you think the structures of for-profit and not-for-profit organizations might differ?

4. Describe the difference between formal and informal structure within organizations and describe how the informal structure actually alters the authority of the formal structure.

5. Discuss the advantages and disadvantages of structures based on economic function, product, SBU, and matrix.

6. Why is organizing important?

7. Describe the relationship of authority to job performance.

8. Why is there no ideal span of control?

9. Is your college centralized or decentralized, in terms of the degree of authority delegated to instructors?

10. How would you go about delegating authority in an organization?

Questions on the Management Challenge Features

INNOVATION MANAGEMENT CHALLENGE

1. Describe how decentralization stimulates innovation at Johnson & Johnson.

2. What else accounts for Johnson & Johnson's high rates of innovation?

GLOBAL MANAGEMENT CHALLENGE

1. Why did Philips have to restructure so drastically?

2. What has to be done to make the remaining employees more productive?

ETHICAL MANAGEMENT CHALLENGE

1. Why would Nissan consider it ethical to lay off employees now even though it was never done so before and has guaranteed lifetime employment?

2. What are the pros and cons of this decision?

Simply Better

The new management at SmithKline Beecham recognized the value of symbols and language in instilling a new corporate culture in employees. On the first day following the merger, both U.S. and UK corporate headquarters had new signs with the new company name prominently installed. And each employee in the company was greeted by signs in six languages proclaiming "Now We Are One." Playing on the initials of the merged company, the slogan "Simply Better" was adopted. It is used as a guide for interpreting the new corporate culture at all levels within the company. The company's internal magazine for management, "Communiqué," centers on cultural issues.

"Simply Better" also designates the ongoing effort involving change that is guiding the company toward its ten-year goals. It emphasizes that the analysis and thought that went into the reorganization cannot be just a one-time effort.

DISCUSSION QUESTIONS

1. Why did Bauman bother to change the organization of SmithKline Beecham? Would it have been easier to retain Beecham's structure and integrate SmithKline Beckman's employees into it? Why or why not?

2. Discuss Bauman's five requirements for a successful merger in relation to the SmithKline Beckman–Beecham merger.

Coping with Overgrowth

Rita Sanchez was the new president of a small service company with 345 employees. Concerned about cost and an overly large labor force, she began examining various departments throughout the organization. In the last ten years the company's sales, adjusted for inflation, had not increased. Yet the number of employees had grown from 285 to 345. She wondered why.

A few years ago the personnel department consisted of only three people—an administrator and two secretaries. Now it included six people, and if you counted the affirmative-action director there were seven. Sanchez discovered that a new director, appointed three years ago, had added the additional staff. The affirmative-action director had been appointed by the recently retired president in an effort to improve the company's record in hiring and promoting women and minorities.

Sanchez wondered how many people the personnel department, as well as other departments in the organization, really needed.

DISCUSSION QUESTIONS

1. What could account for the growth in the number of employees throughout the company?

2. What might account for the growth in the number of employees in the personnel department?

3. Recognizing that the company suffered a 15 percent attrition each year in salaried positions (about half of the work force) but only a 5 percent attrition in the hourly work force, what kinds of actions could Sanchez take to reduce staffing to previous levels within two years?

Designing a New Organizational Structure

Tom Andrews has been promoted to the job of administrator of Cobb General Hospital, a 600-bed hospital located in a suburb of New Orleans. He is excited about the promotion but has some doubts as well.

Andrews was the associate administrator for three years, but he was really more of a "gofer" for the former administrator, Bill Collins. Because of his enthusiasm and his M.A. in Hospital Administration, he was offered the administrator's job after the board of directors asked for Collins's resignation.

Andrews is looking at the organization chart for the hospital, which Collins had pieced together over the years. In reality, each time a new unit had been added or a new function started, Collins merely had the new person report directly to him. Andrews is worried about his ability to handle all the people who are currently reporting to him in his new position. If you were Andrews, how would you redraw the organization chart?

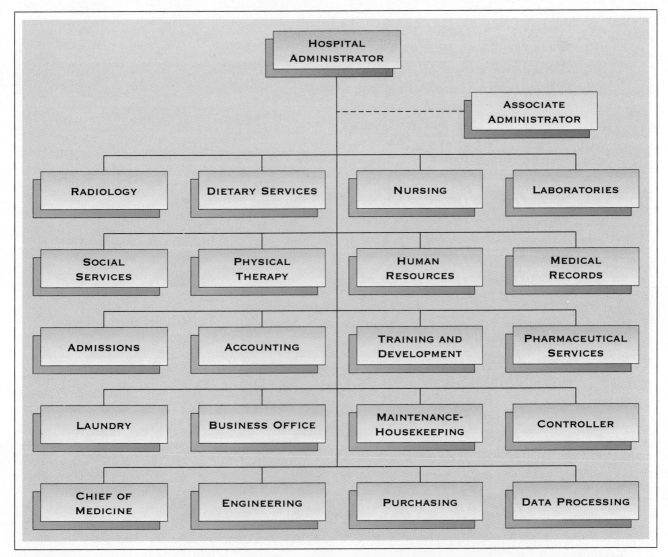

SOURCE: LESLIE W. RUE, LLOYD L. BYARS, MANAGEMENT: THEORY AND APPLICATION, 4TH ED. (HOMEWOOD, ILL.: IRWIN, 1986), P. 257.

"The challenge is not to design organizational structures that are perfect, but to design structures that are better than those of your competitors."

—Ian C. MacMillan and Patricia E. Jones

"The traditional organizational map describes a world that no longer exists."

—Larry Hirschborn and Thomas Gilmore, Principal and vice-president, respectively, Wharton Center for Applied Research

When you have read this chapter, you should be able to:

1. Describe the organizational design process.

2. Describe how each of the following affects organizational design: strategy, management philosophy, environment, geographic dispersion, technology, and size.

3. Distinguish between mechanistic and organic organizations.

4. Indicate the importance of the Woodward studies of technology to organizational design.

5. Describe the "shape of things to come."

MANAGEMENT CHALLENGES
DISCUSSED IN THIS CHAPTER:

  Accelerating rates of change.

  Increasing globalization of business.

  Increasing levels of competition.

  Changing technology.

  Complexity of the managerial environment.

CHAPTER 10

Organizational Design

Making the Elephant Dance

Eastman Kodak Co., like many of the older giants of American business, has faced higher costs, declining profits, and increased competition in the last decade. In particular, Kodak lost part of its film market to Fuji Photofilm Company because Fuji was more innovative in product design and was underpricing Kodak on existing products.

In 1982, Walter A. Fallon, then chairman of Kodak, observed, "It's time to make this elephant dance." Between 1982 and 1989, Kodak reorganized four times. It had been highly centralized, with the chairman becoming involved in far too many decisions. The first restructuring involved decentralizing control, adding businesses, making the company more entrepreneurial, and delegating decision making to front-line supervisors, a slow transition because the supervisors had to gain new skills. Subsequent restructurings by then CEO Colby Chandler reduced the work force by 11 percent, cut marginal products, and modified the corporate culture to make it more market driven, again a difficult task because of the long history behind the corporate values that needed changing.

Kodak's three major divisions are photo products, drugs and chemicals, and copiers and printers. More than one third of its sales and the majority of its profits come from the photo products group. Drugs and chemicals are slightly profitable, but the copier and printer group is losing money. A number of products originally seen as having opportunities for high growth fizzled out. Seeing the potential in the electronic picture business, Kodak introduced an 8mm camcorder, only to withdraw it after losing out to the VHS format. The Disk Camera had to be withdrawn because it made fuzzy pictures. Although the copier and printer line has not

been withdrawn, many models in that line suffer from problems of reliability. In addition to Fuji's inroads, store brand film (much of it 3M's ScotchColor 100) has taken a healthy bite out of Kodak's greatest strength, film sales, because of its low price (roughly 35 percent lower than Kodak's). Kodak is shifting some of its product advertising budget over to promotional incentives to try to regain some of its lost market.

It is obvious that trying to find a single breakthrough product is no longer the best strategy for ensuring the company's health. Kodak's latest effort, the Photo CD, lets customers transfer their photos to CD format and display the images on their TV screen. Unlike Kodak's other electronic imaging devices, Photo CD is expected to turn a profit by 1994. And if Photo CD really catches on, it could help boost sales in the photo products line as well.

There are, however, two large problems that Kodak must solve in the near future if it is to remain profitable in the next decade. The first is the erosion of its film market. The second is what to do about the unprofitable copier and printer line. One possibility is to sell it; this would probably bring $1 billion to $1.5 billion. However, a successful copier and printer line would enhance Kodak's position in the electronic imaging market.

Because of the problems it faces, Kodak is likely to restructure again. The number of jobs that will disappear is uncertain, but it is clear that cuts will be made.

SOURCES: Peter Pae, "Kodak to Again Restructure Operations," *Wall Street Journal* 18 August, 1989, p. B-2; Clare Ansberry, "Uphill Battle: Eastman Kodak Company Has Arduous Struggle to Regain Lost Edge," *Wall Street Journal* 2 April, 1987, pp. 1, 20; and Judith H. Dobrzynski, "Getting the Picture: Kodak Finally Heeds the Shareholders," *Business Week* (February 1, 1993), p. 25.

When Fallon analyzed Kodak's situation, he found that the company needed dramatic changes in both strategy and structure. To make these changes, he added to Kodak's basic mix of businesses, reduced the work force to save costs, decentralized and delegated substantial power to existing product groups, began to rely more on front-line managers for decisions, and added entrepreneurial units. Similarly, when Chandler restructured the company he changed the organization's design to make it more competitive. Kodak is typical of many U.S. companies that have found it necessary to undergo **restructuring,** a redesign of the organization that almost always results in *downsizing,* or reductions in employee levels.[1]

While top managers perform most of the activities involved in organizational design, lower-level managers must implement their decisions. Therefore, lower-level managers must be able to understand the purpose of a new design and how their efforts can help make the design work. Moreover, they must be able to explain the changes to subordinates. They must also understand how the changes affect the design of their own jobs and those of their subordinates. All employees must understand these issues if changes in organizational design are to succeed.

Top managers have three basic organizational design structures to choose from, whether they manage a large department, a division, or the entire organization. Those structures are the hierarchical pyramid, the matrix, and the team. (The team and the pyramid are the primary options of lower-level managers.) In most cases, managers will choose the pyramid, which can take any of the eight forms described in Chapter 9. They may choose to incorporate the matrix and team approaches within the pyramid; however, virtually all organizations are pyramidal in nature. Thus, the key problem-solving issue in organizational design is how to structure the pyramid. Managers must decide on the best variations and combinations of division of labor, delegation of authority, departmentation, span of control, and coordination in order to accomplish the organization's objectives.

Restructuring: Redesigning the organization, often downsizing in an effort to make it more competitive.

AT KODAK: *The structure has been changed as times require. For a very long time, Kodak dominated the photo products market, and its highly centralized structure reflected that position. With increasing competition from Fuji and 3M (through store brands), a more organic structure has evolved.*

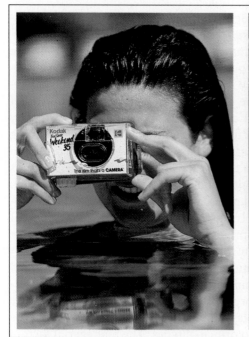

Kodak is typical of many U.S. companies that have found it necessary to undergo *restructuring,* a redesign of the organization that almost always results in downsizing, or reductions in employee levels. Kodak has suffered severe setbacks in its photo products division, despite the introduction of new products such as disposable cameras.

Earlier chapters have emphasized that the external environment affects virtually all decisions in an organization to some degree; that strategy (planning) leads to structure (organizing); and that the existing structure (along with other factors) affects the choice of future structures. This chapter will show how several specific factors affect the macro structure of the organization and how the nature of these factors in a particular situation can affect top management's choice of structural design. It will also show that because flexibility is so critical to competing successfully, organizations often choose to have several different structures.[2]

As Alfred D. Chandler, Jr., discovered after studying Sears, GM, Du Pont, and Standard Oil of New Jersey, macro structure should follow strategy.[3] For example, when Ford Motor Company decided to compete on the basis of quality, it had to decentralize so that front-line workers could make decisions that would improve quality. Chandler's findings have been supported by additional research.[4] However, structure is also a function of five other key variables: the size of the organization, the technology employed, the external environment, management philosophy, and the geographic dispersion of subunits, as revealed in Figure 10.1.[5] Other influential variables might include management systems, management style, organizational culture,[6] the characteristics of employees,[7] and the informal organization.

This chapter explores how each of the six factors identified in Figure 10.1 affects organizational design. Where possible, the related changes in specific structural elements are noted. A discussion of the changing nature of structure follows. The chapter concludes with a discussion of organizational design as a problem-solving process. It is important to recognize that no macro structure is ever perfect, and that constant fine tuning and occasional major restructurings are to be expected in most organizations. Restructuring, to some degree, is occurring almost all the time.

Organizational Design

Organizational design: The process of determining the best overall, macro structure for the organization and its major components, as well as the characteristics of structural elements such as spans of control and departmentation.

Organizational design is the process of determining the best overall macro structure for the organization and its major subcomponents, as well as the characteristics of structural elements such as spans of control and departmentation. The concept of organizational design has evolved over time. It began with the classical approach to structure, drawn largely from models used in the military, government, and the Catholic church. The classical approach reflected the belief that job design leads to organizational design. This approach resulted mostly from the belief that jobs were designed to carry out strategy and that grouping jobs in some logical fashion resulted in a macro organizational structure. Research supports this view but also notes that other situational variables, such as those shown in Figure 10.1, affect the optimal design of an organization as well. With the advent of increasingly complex situations, a situationally based approach to organizational design is evolving. A recent survey of 390 CEOs of major corporations suggests that appropriate organizational design is one of the four key criteria for business success in the twenty-first century.[8]

Job design: Determining the content of individual jobs (and more recently groups of jobs) in such a way as to implement strategy.

It appears that **job design**—determining the content of individual jobs (and more recently teams of jobs) so as to implement strategy—while still an important factor, no longer dominates the organizational design process. The other factors identified in Figure 10.1 also play important roles in the process.[9] The factors identified in the figure are of two principal types. The managerial factors are strategy and management philosophy. The contextual variables are the ex-

FIGURE 10.1   MACRO STRUCTURE—MANAGERIAL AND CONTEXTUAL FACTORS

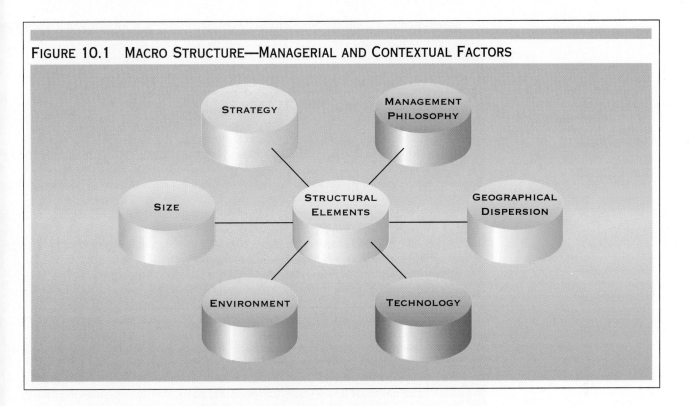

ternal environment, the technology employed, the organization's size, and the geographic dispersion of the organization's subunits. Strategy is closely linked to one of the contextual factors—environment. Usually, some element of the external environment leads to a change in strategy, which then leads to a change in structure. Therefore, these two factors will be discussed together here.

Strategy, the Environment, and Organizational Design

The purpose of organizing is to prepare resources to carry out plans. It follows that the purpose of structure is to carry out strategy. Strategy, as determined by top management, would naturally be expected to have a powerful impact on structure. If the structure is inappropriate, the strategy often fails.

However, researchers David J. Hall and Maurice A. Saias have substantiated that structure does not always follow strategy; sometimes, strategy follows structure.[10] Typical of companies whose strategy was dictated to some extent by their structure is General Motors. It has been unable to regain its former level of competitiveness at least partly because of its unwieldy structure, which is extremely bureaucratic and inflexible. When GM had to change its strategy in response to changes in the external environment, notably the emergence of strong competition, it was not able to respond as quickly as it would have liked, largely because of a structure designed for a different set of environmental circumstances.

Strategies and Structures

An organization's structure is usually related to its basic strategies. For example, an organization that focuses on innovation as a way of differentiating itself from its competitors would normally choose a structure that is highly decentralized

Reorganizing Makes ABB More Competitive

The electrical equipment giant ABB (Asea Brown Boveri) is global—but stateless. Its creator, Percy Barnevik, himself a Swede, merged a venerable Swedish engineering group, Asea, with a flagship Swiss competitor, Brown Boveri. Barnevik added seventy more companies in Europe and the United States to create a giant multinational company. With a nominal address in Zurich, the firm's thirteen top managers meet frequently in a variety of countries. They share no common language and speak only English—a second language for twelve of them.

ABB is a world leader in high-speed trains, robotics, and environmental control. It is larger than Westinghouse and competes with GE. Yet in his five years at the helm, Barnevik has launched a personal war on excess capacity. He has cut jobs by more than 20 percent, closed dozens of factories, eliminated staff at numerous headquarters offices in Europe and the United States, and shunted whole businesses from one country to another. A corps of 250 global managers now leads 210,000 employees.

Observers believe that the layoffs, plant closings, and product exchanges will characterize many other European industries in the future, including autos, steel, and telecommunications.

The model of competitive enterprise that Barnevik is pioneering—he calls it a multidomestic organization—combines global-scale and world-class technology with roots in local markets. It fleshes out the "think globally, act locally" idea.

The organization, or matrix, is based on two axes. One is a distributed global network. National borders are irrelevant as managers around the world make decisions on product strategy and performance. "Global managers have exception-

and encourages innovation.[11] Similarly, a diversified conglomerate typically would be highly decentralized, allowing each SBU to manage in its own right. TransAmerica, a financial services company serving the financial and insurance industries, has fewer than one hundred people on its corporate staff to manage

These laboratory researchers operate almost independently of supervision. In the organization of the future, many workers, knowledge workers especially, will operate autonomously. More and more jobs can be expected to become knowledge-based jobs, and organizational structures will change accordingly.

ally open minds," Barnevik says. "They respect how different countries do things, and they have the imagination to appreciate why." But they also push the limits. "Global managers don't passively accept it when someone says, 'You can't do that in Italy or Spain because of the unions,' or 'You can't do that in Japan because of the Ministry of Finance.' They sort through the debris of cultural excuses and find opportunities to innovate."

The other axis of the matrix consists of the traditionally organized national companies that make up ABB, each optimally serving its home market. Barnevik cites a recent order—ABB considers it the "order of the century"—to build freight-hauling locomotives for the Alps. "If we expect to win those orders, we had *better* be a Swiss company. We had better understand the depth of the Swiss concern for the environment, which explains the willingness to invest so heavily to get freight moving on trains through the mountains to Italy or Germany and off polluting trucks. We had better understand the Alpine terrain and what it takes to build engines powerful enough to haul heavy loads. We had better understand the effects of drastic temperature changes on sensitive electronics and build locomotives robust enough to keep working when they go from the frigid, dry outdoors to the extreme heat and humidity inside the tunnels."

If ABB can resolve its internal contradictions—if it can be global and local, big and small, decentralized with centralized reporting—its matrix will be widely emulated. Some believe that the matrix is too rigid or simplistic. Barnevik says, "But what choice do you have? To say you don't like a matrix is like saying you don't like factories or you don't like breathing. It's a fact of life. If you deny the formal matrix, you wind up with an informal one—and that's much harder to reckon with."

SOURCES: Carla Rapoport, "A Tough Swede Invades the U.S.," *Fortune* (June 29, 1992), pp. 76–79; and William Taylor, "The Logic of Global Business: An Interview with ABB's Percy Barnevik," *Harvard Business Review* (March–April 1991), pp. 91–105.

the numerous diversified businesses in its portfolio.[12] Each of those businesses functions independently. Conversely, organizations that have chosen Michael E. Porter's cost leadership strategy have historically been extremely centralized in order to retain tight control over all the organization's functions.[13] In such cases, it can be clearly demonstrated that strategy leads to structure.

Sometimes it is difficult to tell where the impacts of the environment on strategy and of strategy on structure leave off. Henry A. Mintzberg defines strategy as "the long-term adaptation of the organization to its environment."[14] In that context, strategy is a direct function of the environment, and structure is a direct function of strategy. It is therefore true that structure is most often an indirect function of the environment. This chapter's Diversity Management Challenge reveals just how important the appropriate organizational design can be to ensuring the successful implementation of strategy.

The next few pages discuss several key issues related to strategy, the environment, and organizational design: mechanistic versus organic organizations, vertical versus horizontal organizations, hollow corporations, virtual corporations, and the insights gained from the Lawrence and Lorsch study.

Mechanistic Versus Organic Structures

As discussed in Chapter 5, Tom Burns and G. M. Stalker first called attention to two types of organizational-design responses to external environments: mechanistic and organic.[15] The **mechanistic** model focuses on hierarchical relation-

Mechanistic: A term used to refer to organizations characterized by rigidity, bureaucracy, and a strict hierarchy.

Organic: A term used to refer to organizations characterized by openness, responsiveness, and lack of hierarchy.

ships and tends to be rigid in the worst sense of "bureaucratic." **Organic** organizations are characterized by openness, responsiveness, and lack of hierarchy.[16] Table 10.1 indicates the differences between these two structures.

Burns and Stalker described environments as either stable or unstable, basing the distinction on the amount of change in the environment. Their study indicated that firms operating in stable environments tend to use mechanistic organizational designs, whereas firms operating in dynamic, unstable environments tend to use organic designs. The necessity for employing these types of design in these situations has been demonstrated over and over again. As mechanistic firms encounter changeful environments, they find the transition difficult, if not impossible. Organizations that are able to make the transition to an organic structure will survive; those that are not will fail.

Contrast, for example, Eastern Airlines and American Airlines. American Airlines was able to adapt to changes in its environment. It became more organic. It adapted a two-tier wage system in which new employees received much lower wages than senior employees. This enabled American to compete in a very cost-conscious market. Similarly, American created the first "frequent-flyer" program, which gave it a competitive edge for a while. Eastern Airlines remained

TABLE 10.1 Mechanistic Versus Organic Organizational Design

Mechanistic	Organic
1. Tasks are highly fractionated and specialized; little regard is paid to clarifying the relationship between tasks and organizational objectives.	1. Tasks are more interdependent; there is an emphasis on the relevance of tasks and organizational objectives.
2. Tasks tend to remain rigidly defined, unless altered formally by top management.	2. Tasks are continually adjusted and redefined through the interaction of the organization's members.
3. Specific role definition (rights, obligations, and technical methods) is prescribed for each member.	3. Role definition is generalized (members accept general responsibility for task accomplishment beyond individual role definition).
4. Hierarchic structure of control, authority, and communication exists. Sanctions derive from an employment contract between employee and organization.	4. There is a network structure of control, authority, and communication. Sanctions derive more from community of interest than from contractual relationship.
5. Information relevant to the situation and the organization's operations is formally assumed to rest with the chief executive.	5. The leader is not assumed to be omniscient; knowledge centers are identified where they are located throughout the organization.
6. Communication is primarily vertical, between superior and subordinate.	6. Communication is both vertical and horizontal, depending upon where information resides.
7. Communications primarily take the form of instructions and decisions issued by superiors. Information and requests for decisions are supplied by inferiors.	7. Communications primarily take the form of information and advice.
8. Loyalty to organization and obedience to superiors are insisted on.	8. Commitment to the organization's tasks and goals is more highly valued than loyalty or obedience.
9. Importance and prestige are attached to identification with the organization and its members.	9. Importance and prestige are attached to affiliations and expertise in the external environment.

SOURCES: Richard M. Steers, *Organizational Effectiveness: A Behavioral View* (Santa Monica, Calif.: Goodyear, 1977), p. 90. Adapted from Tom Burns and George M. Stalker, *The Management of Innovation* (London: Tavistock, 1961), pp. 119–122. Used by permission of Tavistock Publications Ltd.

more mechanistic and bureaucratic, failed to adapt, and was unable to gain wage concessions from the machinists' union. It became less competitive on a cost basis with other airlines and went bankrupt as a result.[17]

Burns and Stalker were quick to recognize that no organization is purely mechanistic or organic. Both designs will continue to exist. Nor did they claim that either design is superior. Rather, each design is best suited to a particular environmental situation. However, because situations to which mechanistic organizations are best suited are rapidly declining in number, and those to which organic organizations are best suited are increasing in number, organic organizations should dominate future organizational designs.

Robert B. Duncan later conceptualized the environment as not just an issue of stability but also one of complexity.[18] Simple environments have few products, few competitors, few locations, and simple technology. Complex environments have a large number of products, a large number of geographic locations, and many different consumers, and they may employ complex technologies. Figure 10.2 suggests the possible combinations of these factors (environmental complexity and rate of change), indicating the resulting degree of uncertainty in each situation.

Henry A. Mintzberg has suggested the conditions under which structure should be centralized or decentralized, mechanistic or organic, on the basis of degree of environmental complexity and rate of change, as shown in Figure 10.2. Turin's (Italy) Gruppo GFT, the world's largest manufacturer of designer apparel, with sales in more than seventy countries, is an example of an organization that shifted to a decentralized organic structure in order to compete globally. Its objective is to become an insider in each of its markets. To do so, it has created highly autonomous manufacturing and sales units, which are coordinated by the corporate staff. It has a multifaceted organizational structure.[19]

Sometimes, however, organizations can become too organic, as this chapter's Global Management Challenge suggests. Honda, which had hitherto been a perfect example of a flexible organization, took on certain structural characteristics modeled on those of American firms because it was becoming less competitive. After you read this feature, you should be able to identify those characteristics and explain why Honda chose to become less loosely structured.

Vertical Versus Horizontal Organizations

As discussed in Chapter 9, organizations have historically been designed on the basis of economic functions—marketing, finance, operations, human resources, information management. Even when firms have moved to product, SBU, and geographic structures at their top levels, the next level has almost always been functionally based. However, the need to respond to complex, rapidly changing, highly competitive global environments has caused organizations to seek new ways of structuring. In the early 1990s, a number of consultants and academics, especially the global consulting firm McKinsey & Company, began to favor the **horizontal organization,** a design based largely on processes rather than on functions, as the organizational design mechanism that firms should follow in the future.[20] Figure 10.3 portrays such an organization. As the figure shows, a horizontal organization is made up of autonomous, cross-functional work teams designed around critical processes. A firm that wished to organize in this way would first identify its key processes, which must be related to customer satisfaction. There may be six to eight such processes in any organization. Then the firm should flatten the hierarchy, using these processes as its primary structure. Because autonomous, cross-functional work teams are the primary components of this design—rather than individual jobs, as in vertical, functionally based orga-

Horizontal organization: A design based largely on processes rather than on functions.

Honda Tries to Strike a Balance

When the new president of Honda, Nobuhiko Kawamoto, took over in 1990 and reorganized Japan's third-largest automaker, he visited Honda's legendary founder, Soichiro Honda, to explain the changes he envisioned. "Not many people criticize Mr. Honda," Kowamoto says. "But I told him, 'I'm sorry to say it, but not everything you said is correct now.'"

What is no longer correct—especially for the American-based part of the operation—is the Japanese style of consensus management. It is being replaced with American-style organization charts: specific hierarchies and spheres of responsibility.

Under Soichiro Honda, *organization* was almost a dirty word. "First there are people, then there is work, and a minimum necessary organization follows so the people and work are efficiently managed," he would say. "An organization exists to serve its members or people, not the other way around."

Kawamoto, on the other hand, sees great challenges ahead for Honda and all automakers in the 1990s, and he wants the faster decision making and tighter control that a strong new structure will afford.

Formerly, Honda was run from the legendary tenth floor of its Tokyo head-quarters, where its thirty-two top executives shared an office and an unusually collegial atmosphere. When decisions were required, board members would talk things over until they reached a consensus. No formal reporting relationships existed among the executives.

Even more surprising, only twelve of the thirty-two executives had specific responsibilities. The arrangement worked well when Honda was an upstart. Now that it is no longer small, however, the tenth floor has come to be seen as an unwieldy impediment to timely decision making.

Kawamoto's reorganization assigns a specific responsibility to each executive. When a decision must be made in a particular area, the single executive responsible makes it.

Now that the tenth floor has been broken up, executives can get out of the office more and supervise operations. They can be on hand when production decisions are made, and they can stay in better touch with dealers, suppliers, and customers.

Honda is a giant company, with 87,000 employees in 38 countries. Half its

---

AT KODAK: In the 1980s and again in 1993, Kodak eliminated a significant number of jobs. One of its current options is to sell its copier and printer division. Both actions will result in downsizing.

nizations—continuous improvement of work flows that are cross-functional in nature is possible. The hierarchy can also be flattened because these teams take on the work of management and because constant coordination, often using computers, eliminates the need for some management positions. Table 10.2 presents McKinsey & Company's ten-part guidelines to creating horizontal structures based on processes.

Among the firms that have successfully instituted process-based design are Hallmark Cards, which has completely redesigned its new-card development cycle around a process design; Kodak, which achieved huge cost savings and productivity improvements after it redesigned its black-and-white film manufacturing operations around processes; General Electric, which is experimenting with process design in many operations and whose Bayamón, Puerto Rico, plant reported significant productivity improvement after conversion to process de-

The new president of Honda, Nobuhiko Kawamoto, sees great challenges ahead for Honda and all automakers in the 1990s. He wants the faster decision making and tighter control that a strong new structure will afford.

sales are in North America, and the president of its North American operations, Koichi Amemiya, says its organizational restructuring has improved communication and speeded decision making. "There's a much shorter distance between American Honda and the head office than before. If something is wrong, now I can call Kawamoto directly."

SOURCE: Alex Taylor, III, "A U.S.-Style Shakeup at Honda," *Fortune* (December 30, 1991), pp. 115–120.

sign; Xerox, which is performing a massive overhaul of the entire company based on this approach; and the San Diego Zoo, which increased customer satisfaction levels and productivity significantly after switching to a process-based design.[21]

Another horizontal form of organization, not necessarily based on processes, is the network. Internally, a **network organization** is coordinated horizontally; externally, it is coordinated with other organizations at the value-adding or process level. Thus, for example, the purchasing manager would create a network with related internal logistics functions to ensure proper handling of purchasing logistics, and with external suppliers to ensure high-quality, low-cost material and/or service inputs.[22] The network is viewed as critical in highly changing environments as a means of "capturing" customers, suppliers, and other external constituents by giving them a vested interest in the company. This

Network organization: A form of organization, not necessarily based on processes, in which coordination occurs horizontally rather than vertically.

FIGURE 10.2 ORGANIZATIONAL DESIGNS IN FOUR TYPES OF ENVIRONMENTS

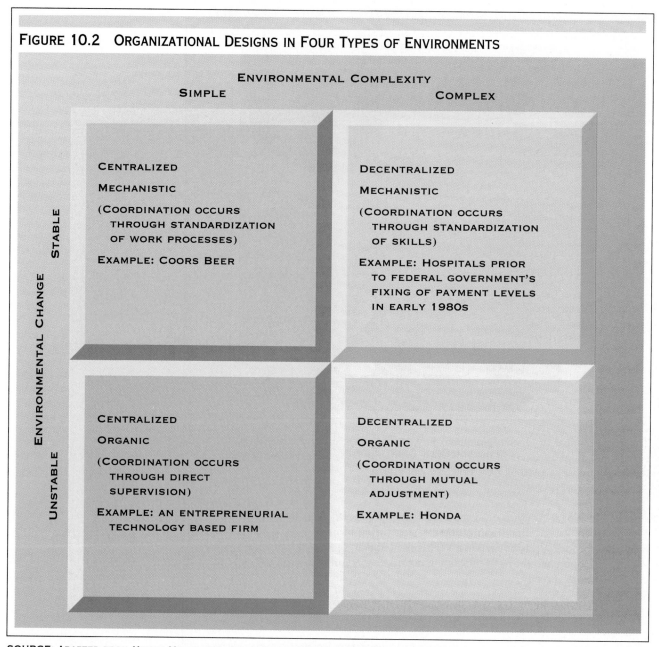

SOURCE: ADAPTED FROM HENRY MINTZBERG, <u>STRUCTURE IN FIVES: DESIGNING EFFECTIVE</u>
<u>ORGANIZATIONS</u> (ENGLEWOOD CLIFFS, NJ: PRENTICE-HALL, 1983), P.144.

makes it an especially important organizational structure for global businesses.[23] Networks provide flexibility as well as locking constituents into the firm.[24] They readily accommodate alliances and acquisitions.[25]

The Hollow Corporation

Another type of organization has been suggested: the hollow corporation, in which a few top corporate officials run a corporation that outsources all of its functions to other firms (that is, hires other firms to perform its basic economic functions).[26] Partial hollow corporations already exist; they outsource a variety of functions, including manufacturing, human resources, management, and in-

FIGURE 10.3 COMPARING VERTICAL AND HORIZONTAL ORGANIZATIONS

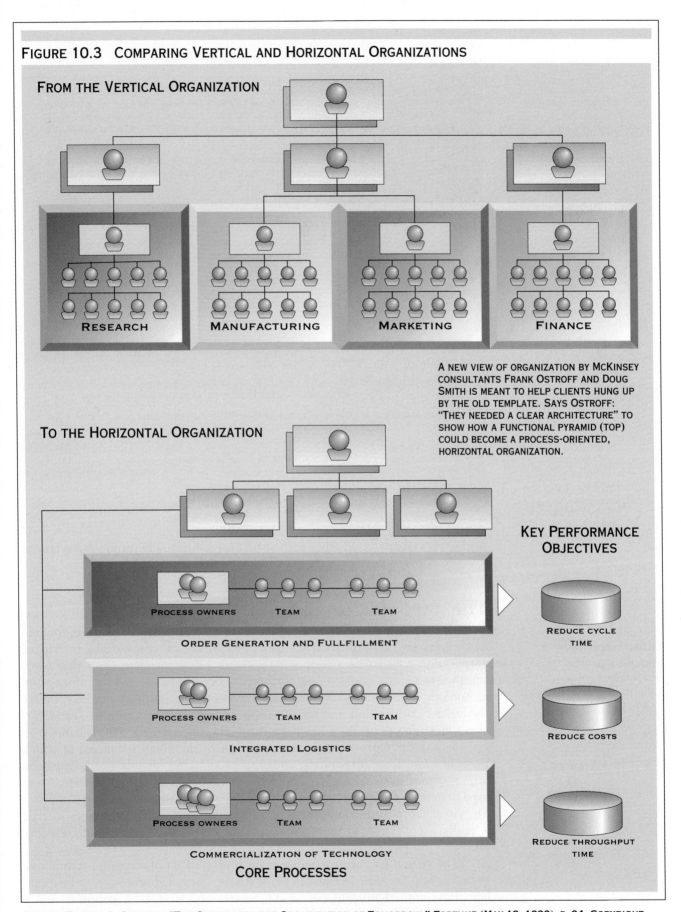

FROM THE VERTICAL ORGANIZATION

RESEARCH   MANUFACTURING   MARKETING   FINANCE

A NEW VIEW OF ORGANIZATION BY McKINSEY CONSULTANTS FRANK OSTROFF AND DOUG SMITH IS MEANT TO HELP CLIENTS HUNG UP BY THE OLD TEMPLATE. SAYS OSTROFF: "THEY NEEDED A CLEAR ARCHITECTURE" TO SHOW HOW A FUNCTIONAL PYRAMID (TOP) COULD BECOME A PROCESS-ORIENTED, HORIZONTAL ORGANIZATION.

TO THE HORIZONTAL ORGANIZATION

KEY PERFORMANCE OBJECTIVES

PROCESS OWNERS   TEAM   TEAM
ORDER GENERATION AND FULLFILLMENT

REDUCE CYCLE TIME

PROCESS OWNERS   TEAM   TEAM
INTEGRATED LOGISTICS

REDUCE COSTS

PROCESS OWNERS   TEAM   TEAM
COMMERCIALIZATION OF TECHNOLOGY

REDUCE THROUGHPUT TIME

CORE PROCESSES

SOURCE: THOMAS A. STEWART, "THE SEARCH FOR THE ORGANIZATION OF TOMORROW," FORTUNE (MAY 18, 1992), P. 94. COPYRIGHT © 1992 TIME INC. ALL RIGHTS RESERVED. (TONY MIKOLAJCZYK FOR FORTUNE. SOURCE OF DATA: McKINSEY & CO.)

formation systems.[27] Whether such structures will actually proliferate is not yet known, but it is possible that many such firms will exist.

The Virtual Corporation

Virtual corporation: A temporary network of independent companies that unite to exploit a specific opportunity.

Some management experts believe that in the future the virtual corporation will be an important type of structure. Similar to the hollow corporation, the **virtual corporation** consists of a temporary network of independent firms that come together to exploit a specific opportunity. They are connected by information technology. They share skills, costs, and access to one another's markets. Unlike the hollow corporation, the virtual corporation has no central office or hierarchy. Once the opportunity has been exploited, the network will disband.

The virtual corporation is an extension of the alliance concept at which firms like Corning Corporation and Apple Computer already excel. The term *virtual* comes from the early days of computing, when "virtual memory" was used to make a computer act as if it had more storage capacity than it really did. The virtual corporation appears to be a single firm with vast capabilities when it is really a collection of many smaller firms collaborating to achieve specific needs.

The virtual corporation depends on sophisticated information technology to make the process of working together easier. The collaborators must be excellent firms with significant core competencies and strategic capabilities and a shared sense of opportunism.[28]

ORGANIZATIONS HAVE HISTORICALLY BEEN STRUCTURED ACCORDING TO THEIR ECONOMIC FUNCTIONS: MARKETING, OPERATIONS, AND SO ON. HOWEVER, IN THE EARLY 1990S CONSULTANTS AND ACADEMICS BEGAN RECOMMENDING A PROCESS-BASED OR HORIZONTAL STRUCTURE. AMONG THE ORGANIZATIONS THAT HAVE SUCCESSFULLY INSTITUTED A PROCESS-BASED DESIGN IS HALLMARK CARDS; THE ARTIST SHOWN HERE IS PARTICIPATING IN THE DEVELOPMENT OF A NEW LINE OF CARDS. THE SAN DIEGO ZOO HAS ALSO SWITCHED TO A PROCESS-BASED DESIGN AND REPORTS HIGHER LEVELS OF CUSTOMER SATISFACTION AS A RESULT. ALSO SHOWN HERE ARE KODAK "ZEBRAS"—PERSONNEL IN THE COMPANY'S NEWLY REDESIGNED BLACK-AND-WHITE FILM MANUFACTURING OPERATION.

The virtual corporation is an extension of the alliance concept at which firms like Corning Corporation excel. The virtual corporation appears to be a single firm with vast capabilities, but it is really a collection of many smaller firms collaborating to achieve specific needs.

The Lawrence and Lorsch Study

Chapter 9 discussed coordinating (integrating) the objectives and efforts of an organization's differentiated subunits. This chapter examines the reasons behind the differentiation process. Paul R. Lawrence and J. W. Lorsch examined firms in the plastics, food, and container industries and discovered that the degree to which firms adapt to the environment, or differentiate, and the extent to which differentiated subunits are integrated, have much to do with those firms' success.[29] Differentiation was seen as occurring to enable the firm to adapt to the particular environment encountered by each subunit of the organization.[30]

In their study, Lawrence and Lorsch defined **differentiation** as the tendency of organizational subunits to become structurally different from each other because their structures result from the process of adapting to different environments.[31] Although this definition may make differentiation sound like another term for specialization of labor, the concept of differentiation also includes departmentation and organizational behavior. Lawrence and Lorsch placed subunits of the organizations they studied on a continuum from mechanistic to organic. They also examined integration, the "process of achieving unity of effort among various subsystems and the accomplishment of the organization's task."[32]

Lawrence and Lorsch were concerned with the degree to which the external environment affects differentiation and also integration, especially for firms in rapidly changing environments. In their view, the environment is divided into three key subunits: the market subenvironment, made up of customers, competitors, distribution systems, and advertising agencies; the technical/economic subenvironment, comprising labor, raw materials, and equipment; and the science subenvironment, made up of rapidly changing developments in products and technologies, research centers, professional associations, and the study of science. These three subenvironments correspond to the marketing, production, and R&D functions within a typical organization. Lawrence and Lorsch found that each subunit will differentiate differently and that mechanisms for integrating subsystems vary from one organization to another. Their study's most important finding was that organizations must both differentiate and integrate in

Differentiation: The tendency of organizational subunits to become structurally different as a result of the need to adapt to different environments.

According to Lawrence and Lorsch, the environment is divided into three subunits: the market subenvironment, the technical/economic subenvironment and the science subenvironment. The science subenvironment is characterized by rapid change in products and technologies, research centers, professional associations, and the study of science.

order to be highly successful. Another important finding was that the higher the level of uncertainty, the more differentiation occurs and, hence, the more integration is required.

In the broadest sense, an organization adapts to environmental factors through strategy. The strategist must carefully review the environment when determining whether the structure should be mechanistic or organic, centralized or decentralized, vertical or horizontal. The Lawrence and Lorsch study clearly indicates that the manager must be concerned about both differentiation and integration in relation to the environment. The manager must realize that there is no one best structure but, rather, there is a structure that is best suited to a particular set of environmental circumstances. Moreover, the manager must recognize that no structure is perfect and that all structures are compromises. Finally, as environments continue to move toward less stable conditions, and as they become increasingly complex, the manager must be able to modify the structure to fit the environment. Flexible organizations are the wave of the future in most industries.[33] Further structural differentiation will occur as a result, and the need for coordination will increase. In sum, as competition, especially global competition, increases, environments become more complex, and the rate of change accelerates, organizations will seek structures that enable them to function better in those environments. They will seek to learn faster than their competitors.[34] This requires a flexible, organic organization, normally decentralized but occasionally centralized. It requires high levels of both differentiation and integration, and it is clearly leading to the development of networks and process-based organizations.

Size, Age, Growth, and Organizational Design

Growth Theories of the Firm

Growth theories of the firm explain how an organization's size, age, and growth influence its structure. Organizations pass through a series of stages as they grow and become older.[35] Most business organizations begin as entrepreneurial endeavors, with a simple structure consisting of owner and employees. At some point, the firm becomes large enough to enter a second stage of development: It departmentalizes on the basis of economic function or, more recently, on the basis of processes. In either case, the first set of divisions beneath the chief executive on the organization chart will be marketing, finance, operations, human resources, and information management.

In the third stage, the firm moves from a functional, or process, structure to a product structure. The divisions reporting to the chief executive are product divisions. Each division will usually have departments based on economic functions, or processes, reporting to it. The fourth stage of development involves a shift from the product structure to the SBU structure, with the SBU being the first level of departmentation beneath the chief executive on the organization chart. The next level may be based on products, functions, or processes.[36] These structures are indicated in Figure 10.4.

Project and matrix structures are characteristic of late stages of growth in certain industries. Geographic, client, and task specialization departmentations may occur under any of these structures, although normally geographic and client departmentations occur only after functional structure has been achieved. Because the process-based horizontal structure is so new, it has not yet been incorporated into the growth theories. However, because it is viewed as an

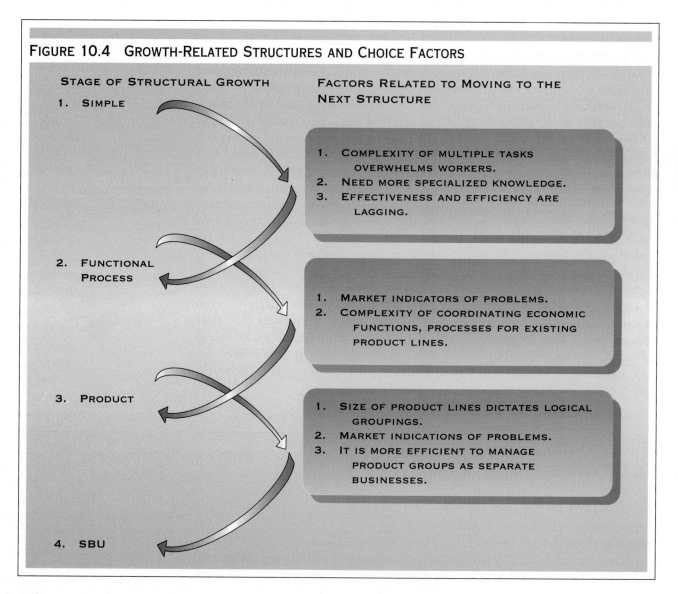

FIGURE 10.4 GROWTH-RELATED STRUCTURES AND CHOICE FACTORS

STAGE OF STRUCTURAL GROWTH

1. SIMPLE

2. FUNCTIONAL PROCESS

3. PRODUCT

4. SBU

FACTORS RELATED TO MOVING TO THE NEXT STRUCTURE

1. COMPLEXITY OF MULTIPLE TASKS OVERWHELMS WORKERS.
2. NEED MORE SPECIALIZED KNOWLEDGE.
3. EFFECTIVENESS AND EFFICIENCY ARE LAGGING.

1. MARKET INDICATORS OF PROBLEMS.
2. COMPLEXITY OF COORDINATING ECONOMIC FUNCTIONS, PROCESSES FOR EXISTING PRODUCT LINES.

1. SIZE OF PRODUCT LINES DICTATES LOGICAL GROUPINGS.
2. MARKET INDICATIONS OF PROBLEMS.
3. IT IS MORE EFFICIENT TO MANAGE PRODUCT GROUPS AS SEPARATE BUSINESSES.

alternative to functional departmentation, it is included in Figure 10.4 in parentheses.

The major issue in this sequence of transitions is determining the points at which the organization should change structures from simple to functional (process), from functional (process) to product, and from product to SBU. The other departmentations—geographic, client, and task specialization—though important, typically do not significantly affect the organization's macro structure (although geography obviously affects the structure of a global firm). These choices are essentially based on the organization's ability to meet the demands of its customer groups and other constituents. As the organization grows, the need to perform numerous different economic functions becomes too great for individual members of the organization. Specializing by function (or process) becomes a necessity for achieving both effectiveness and efficiency.

As a function- or process-based organization grows, it begins to acquire a large number of product offerings. At some point, its ability to satisfy customer needs is taxed. Although this is a critical point in the organization's growth, it is difficult to determine exactly when it is reached. Eventually it will become obvious: As the organization moves through the product-based stage, it loses momentum again. Managers should again be monitoring the environment for signs of problems.

The move from a product-based structure to an SBU structure occurs as the organization's managers recognize the need to group products according to categories or markets. It becomes more efficient to run these groups of products as separate businesses. Today, the effects of size on structure are being moderated as organizations become smaller yet more productive. Within this decade, therefore, new growth theories and their relationships to structure will emerge.

Another critical issue is that organizations proceed through a complete series of stages known as a firm's life cycle. Firms are born and eventually die, unless the organization is renewed in some way.[37] (Renewal of firms is discussed in Chapter 13.) The manager must be keenly aware not only of environmental and strategic concerns, but also of the impact of size and growth on organizational structure. The manager must balance the impacts of these factors, keeping in mind that organizations must be responsive to their environments while managing their size and growth.

In the late 1980s, it became fashionable to suggest that effective organizations do not allow subunits to grow beyond certain size limits—for example, five hundred people per location. Most consultants suggest that these units should be given significant autonomy and, where possible, be run as profit centers.[38] The general belief is that it is easier to identify the contributions of individual employees and that employees are more satisfied, and more manageable, under such circumstances. For example, Hewlett-Packard, which employs 76,000 people, has only one unit with more than 1,000 people. There are many reasons for this. In addition to the ability to identify individual contributions, overhead costs are lower and the organization is less bureaucratic. One study of the relationships among size, bureaucracy, and performance suggests that smaller, less bureaucratic organizations outperform smaller, more bureaucratic organizations, but that more bureaucratic large organizations outperform less bureaucratic ones.[39]

AT KODAK: While Kodak is primarily a mass-production manufacturer, all its manufacturing is highly technical. In addition, the film and paper production operations are virtually continuous processes. You would therefore expect to find Kodak's functional departments, especially its R&D operations, to be different from those in other manufacturing firms.

Management Philosophy

Management may, at any time and at any level of the organization, determine that it wants a particular type of structure in order to achieve some chosen end or express its management philosophy. If, for example, one of the company's

Whatever the intent, it is clear that management philosophy does affect structure. Lee Iacocca, former CEO of Chrysler Corporation, Linda J. Wachner, CEO of Warnaco, and John Sculley of Apple Computer each put their personal stamp on their organizations. The resulting structures reflected their individual needs, expectations, and personalities.

strategies is to cut costs, this could be done by reducing the number of managerial positions not directly involved with customers. Whatever the intent, it is clear that management philosophy does affect structure. Henry Ford of Ford Motor Company, Lee Iacocca, former CEO of Chrysler Corporation, John Sculley of Apple Computer, and Linda J. Wachner, CEO of Warnaco (the only female head of a Fortune 500 industrial company), each put their personal stamp on their organizations.[40] The resulting structures reflected their individual needs, expectations, and personalities. Indeed, the history of many organizations reflects the personalities and philosophies of their top managers.

Downsizing Versus Rightsizing

Downsizing: A restructuring process through which the organization becomes smaller; it may involve eliminating individual positions, groups, departments, and even whole business units.

Downsizing is a restructuring process through which the organization becomes smaller. Individual positions, groups, departments, and even whole business units may be eliminated. Downsizing can be accomplished by any number of tactics, including layoffs, voluntary-retirement incentives, the selling off of poorly performing business units, plant closings, and various subsequent reorganizations. In theory, downsizing reduces costs. If employees, a major cost in most organizations, are let go, it is expected that those who remain will figure out a way to get the work done. They will cut out unnecessary tasks and redesign work appropriately. In practice, the evidence suggests that, at best, only about half of the firms that downsize come close to meeting their cost-cutting objectives, and fewer than one-third improve profitability to their satisfaction—and those moderate gains are made at the expense of employee morale.[41] Firms often find that they need to rehire many of the same employees within a short period.[42] Thus, the problem with traditional downsizing efforts is that they focus on superficial changes rather than on the fundamental inefficiencies that caused the firm to need to be restructured in the first place.[43]

Rightsizing: Taking a long-term strategic perspective when examining the organization's human resource requirements. The focus is on creating not merely a lean organization, but one that provides high value to the customer.

Problems like those just described have spurred interest in **rightsizing**—taking a long-term strategic perspective when examining the organization's human resource requirements. The focus is on creating not merely a lean organization but one that provides high value to the customer.[44] It is this kind of thinking that has led some firms to switch to horizontal forms of organization, especially structures based on processes. Massive layoffs simply do not bring the anticipated returns: The basic flaw in organizational design remains after the people are gone. Yet, as this chapter's Innovation Management Challenge suggests, some firms seem to have no choice. The results of downsizing at Rank Xerox (UK) have been nothing short of spectacular. New products and sizable

Rank Xerox Restructures

During the 1960s and 1970s, Rank Xerox (UK) was synonymous with *copies*. Xerox introduced the plain paper copier—which *Fortune* magazine called "the most successful business product ever introduced"—in 1959. The next fifteen years represented a golden age for the company. Xerox had created not only a product but an industry, and it felt that it owned it. Patent protection meant that competition was virtually nonexistent.

In 1976, the Japanese entered the low end of the market, and profits plummeted.

"We had to do something," says Rob Walker, a Rank Xerox director. "That 'something' was to begin a total change in the culture of the company!"

Step one was competitive benchmarking: a commonsense comparison of how you do things with how they are done by companies considered to be "best in class" inside or outside the industry. The idea, of course, is to close the gap and ultimately surpass your models.

Xerox benchmarked with the competition for product development, manufacturing cost, distribution, marketing and sales, billing, product support, internal organization, and internal technical support. "The results were shocking," Walker says. "Our costs were too high—not by a little, but a lot. One study found that Xerox's unit manufacturing cost was equal to the Japanese selling price—and they were making a profit. It took us twice as long as the Japanese to bring a new product to market. We used five times the number of engineers, had four times the number of design changes and three times the design costs."

Benchmarking outside the industry for billing, inventory control, and distribution revealed comparable problems.

In response, Xerox established its "Leadership Through Quality" program in 1983. The program revolutionized both management philosophy and organizational structure at Xerox. It constitutes a total commitment to meeting customer requirements. Here are two of its key features:

- *Management philosophy.* The classical "command-and-control" organization was scuttled. In its place is a cross-functional and participative organization. Team orientation and self-managed work groups emerged. The role of manager changed from "director and inspector of results" to "coach, facilitator, and inspector of the process."

- *Organizational structure.* Discrete functions, such as sales, marketing, service, manufacturing, personnel, and finance, are recognized as breeding grounds of conflict and bureaucracy. In their place, Xerox has developed a more holistic view of "how to achieve our common goals, with greater realization between functions of how they had to integrate to deliver to our customers."

With customer satisfaction the number 1 priority under the new program, managers behave differently with both customers and employees. They are now outward facing, Walker says, rather than internally focused, and their aim is to support front-line employees in understanding and delivering customer requirements.

Accompanying the change is an empowerment strategy, in which responsibility and accountability devolve to the employees closest to the customer. Problems can be fixed speedily without requiring authorization through a chain of command.

SOURCE: Rob Walker, "Rank Xerox—Management Revolution," *Long Range Planning* (February 1992), pp. 9–21.

profits have resulted. Ask yourself why this firm was able to downsize successfully when so many others have been far less successful.

Technology

Technology: The equipment, knowledge, materials, and experience employed in performing tasks within an organization.

Technology, in its broadest sense, refers to the equipment, knowledge, materials, and experience employed in performing tasks within an organization.[45,46] Technology affects any type of organization and any type of job, be it a college professor teaching English, a worker on a robotized assembly line, a person selling computers, or a nurse assisting patients in a hospital.

Technology affects macro organizational design through its impact on the design of jobs, departmentation, spans of control, delegation of authority, and coordination. While environment and size tend to dictate the overall macro structure, technology has a greater effect on departments and individual jobs.[47] It is easy, for example, to see how the design of each brewery at Anheuser-Busch would be greatly affected by technology, while the corporation's overall size would probably determine its macro structure. Many types of technologies affect the whole organization and/or specific departments; information technologies such as PCs are an example.[48] PCs and related information systems help shape corporate structures because they improve coordination in an era of extreme complexity.[49]

The Woodward Studies

Much of the most influential research on the relationship between technology and organizational structure was carried out in the 1950s by Joan Woodward, a British industrial sociologist, and her colleagues.[50] They collected data from one hundred manufacturing firms in Essex County in southern England. Information regarding the firms' histories, objectives, manufacturing processes, structural elements, and performance was gathered. The researchers used a narrower definition of technology than the one presented at the beginning of this section. They were concerned with equipment and related production processes—"the methods and processes of manufacture"—as opposed to the broader definition, which focuses on knowledge and experience.[51]

Unit (small batch) production: The manufacture of a product or small number of products according to specific and unique customer requirements.

Woodward's group described three types of technology in manufacturing situations: unit or small batch production; mass production; and process production. **Unit,** or **small batch, production** refers to the manufacture of a product or small number of products according to specific and unique customer requirements. The volume is low and the skill level of employees is usually high. Stamos yachts and Gulfstream corporate jet planes are examples of unit production. **Mass production** is production in large quantities on assembly lines, with standardized parts and high specialization of labor. Sharp Electronics uses mass production technology to manufacture amplifiers, CD players, speakers, and other electronic components. **Process production** refers to the production of materials or goods in a continuous flow. Petroleum production is a process production technology, as is the brewing and bottling of beer. Woodward's classification of the firms her group studied is shown in Figure 10.5.

Mass production: Production in large quantities on assembly lines, with standardized parts and high specialization of labor.

Process production: The production of materials or goods in a continuous flow.

Woodward and her associates discovered that technology, organizational design, and performance are closely related. Successful small batch and process production organizations were simpler, less formalized, and more decentralized than their less successful counterparts. They were "organic" organizations. The successful mass production organizations were more complex, more formalized,

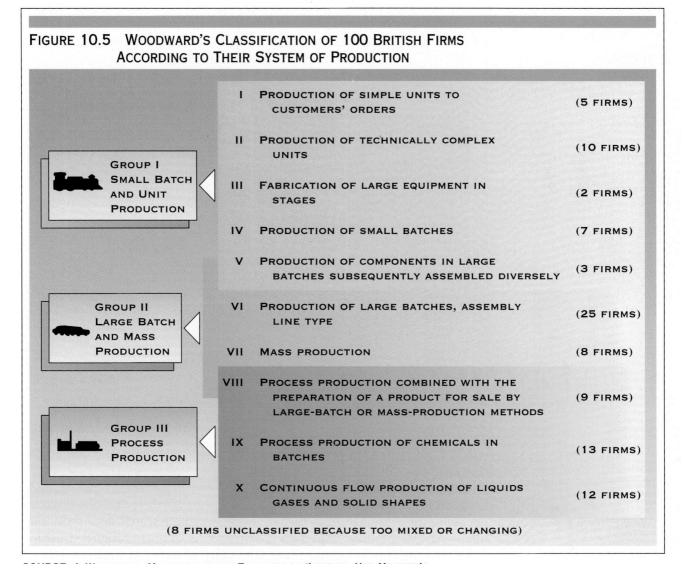

FIGURE 10.5   WOODWARD'S CLASSIFICATION OF 100 BRITISH FIRMS ACCORDING TO THEIR SYSTEM OF PRODUCTION

GROUP I SMALL BATCH AND UNIT PRODUCTION	I PRODUCTION OF SIMPLE UNITS TO CUSTOMERS' ORDERS	(5 FIRMS)
	II PRODUCTION OF TECHNICALLY COMPLEX UNITS	(10 FIRMS)
	III FABRICATION OF LARGE EQUIPMENT IN STAGES	(2 FIRMS)
	IV PRODUCTION OF SMALL BATCHES	(7 FIRMS)
GROUP II LARGE BATCH AND MASS PRODUCTION	V PRODUCTION OF COMPONENTS IN LARGE BATCHES SUBSEQUENTLY ASSEMBLED DIVERSELY	(3 FIRMS)
	VI PRODUCTION OF LARGE BATCHES, ASSEMBLY LINE TYPE	(25 FIRMS)
	VII MASS PRODUCTION	(8 FIRMS)
GROUP III PROCESS PRODUCTION	VIII PROCESS PRODUCTION COMBINED WITH THE PREPARATION OF A PRODUCT FOR SALE BY LARGE-BATCH OR MASS-PRODUCTION METHODS	(9 FIRMS)
	IX PROCESS PRODUCTION OF CHEMICALS IN BATCHES	(13 FIRMS)
	X CONTINUOUS FLOW PRODUCTION OF LIQUIDS GASES AND SOLID SHAPES	(12 FIRMS)

(8 FIRMS UNCLASSIFIED BECAUSE TOO MIXED OR CHANGING)

SOURCE: J. WOODWARD, MANAGEMENT AND TECHNOLOGY (LONDON: HER MAJESTY'S STATIONERY OFFICE, 1958), P.11. DIAGRAM IS REPRODUCED WITH THE PERMISSION OF THE CONTROLLER OF HER BRITANNIC MAJESTY'S STATIONERY OFFICE.

and more centralized than less successful organizations of this type. They were "mechanistic" organizations.

Some of Woodward's research findings appear in Figure 10.6. The findings tell us that each type of technology is characterized by different structural arrangements for successful firms using that type of technology. For example, in successful mass production organizations, a supervisor would have a very large span of control. The span of control would be smaller in a successful firm using unit or small batch production technologies, and smaller still in successful firms using process technology. The sizes of these spans of control reflect the need to differentiate structure according to the technology involved.

Mass production technologies create job designs with low range (variety of tasks) and low depth (amount of decision authority). These types of jobs are best organized in the classical way. Conversely, unit and process technologies create job designs with high range and high depth, which lead to a "lean," highly decentralized structure. With unit and process technologies, employees need

AT KODAK:
Empowerment at lower levels, a reduction of major levels of management from seven to five, and administrative layoffs have all served to make Kodak's structure more organic.

FIGURE 10.6 THE RELATIONSHIPS BETWEEN CERTAIN ORGANIZATIONAL CHARACTERISTICS AND TECHNOLOGY

	UNIT OR SMALL BATCH	MASS PRODUCTION	PROCESS MANUFACTURING
MEDIAN LEVELS OF MANAGEMENT	3	4	6
MEDIAN EXECUTIVE SPAN OF CONTROL	4	7	10
MEDIAN SUPERVISORY GAIN OF CONTROL	23	48	15
MEDIAN DIRECT TO INDIRECT LABOR RATIO	9:1	4:1	1:1
MEDIAN INDUSTRIAL TO STAFF WORKER RATIO	8:1	5.5:1	2:1

SOURCE: JOAN WOODWARD, INDUSTRIAL ORGANIZATION: THEORY AND PRACTICE (LONDON: OXFORD UNIVERSITY PRESS, 1965), PP. 52–62.

considerable latitude in performing their jobs, whereas with mass production they need very little.

Additional research on the relationship between technology and structure has generally supported Woodward's findings, although there are some limits on the ability to generalize from them.[52] However, the research does show that technology has a distinct impact on certain features of organizational structure. A series of studies performed at the University of Aston in England, and by others following their methodology, revealed a complex, interdependent relationship among strategy, environment, size, and technology.[53]

Technology has the greatest impact on small units in an organization. It does not have a significant effect on macro organizational structure, but it has a major effect on departmental structures.[54] Within their own departments, managers must recognize the impacts of technology on structure and the need to adapt structure to technology. This is easy to say and hard to do. For example, when introducing different types of software to support the professional staff of a university, it might be advantageous to adopt a participative structure because the cooperation of the users is necessary to make the change effective. As firms shift to advanced manufacturing technologies and flexible manufacturing, the structure of the units involved will change dramatically.[55] And as firms face increasingly complex environments, Woodward's findings may not hold up.

Geographic Dispersion

As global competition emerges as a dominant force in the 1990s and beyond, structures for coping with global operations must be established. Even operations that are not global, but within which subunits are widely dispersed, will

IBM's Risc System 6000 technology. Within their own departments, managers must recognize the impacts of technology on structure and the need to adapt structure to technology.

need to modify their structures. Eventually, firms will find it advisable, if not necessary, to organize geographically in order to adapt to local environments. In general, the farther apart individuals, groups, departments, and major divisions are in geographic terms—and, more important, the farther they are from headquarters or from their managers—the more likely it is that the organization will be decentralized and that authority will be delegated.

The old saying "out of sight, out of mind" applies here as well, although this is changing somewhat as computers provide management with the information needed to control performance from a distance. However, top management does not want to become overburdened. Even if more information is available than before, managers still may not have the time or the expertise to make all the necessary decisions. Therefore, as noted previously, the network organization is becoming the preferred structure in globally competitive firms.

Choosing the Appropriate Structure

An organization's structure must match its strategy, management philosophy, environment, size, technology, and geographic dispersion. Other factors also must be considered: organizational culture, management systems, management style, characteristics of employees, and the informal organization. In addition, noted consultant and author Peter Drucker suggests that structural options should be evaluated in light of the following criteria:

- Clarity, as opposed to simplicity. The Gothic cathedral is not a simple design, but your position inside it is clear; you know where to stand and where to go. A modern office building is exceedingly simple in design, but it is very easy to get lost in one; it is not clear.
- Economy of effort to maintain control and minimize friction.
- Direction of vision toward the product rather than the process, the result rather than the effort.

FIGURE 10.7 ORGANIZATION DESIGN AS A PROBLEM-SOLVING PROCESS

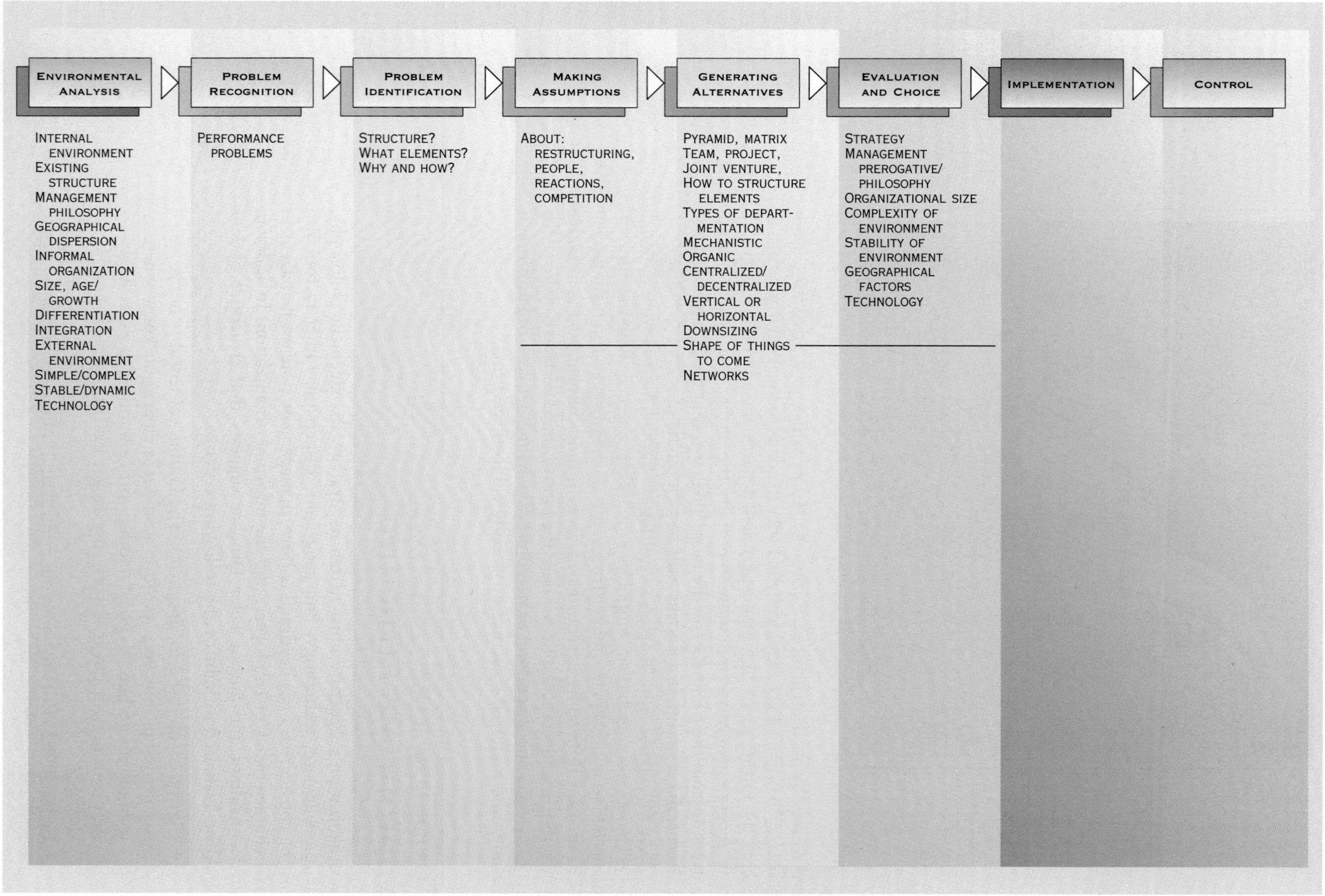

ENVIRONMENTAL ANALYSIS	PROBLEM RECOGNITION	PROBLEM IDENTIFICATION	MAKING ASSUMPTIONS	GENERATING ALTERNATIVES	EVALUATION AND CHOICE	IMPLEMENTATION	CONTROL
INTERNAL ENVIRONMENT EXISTING STRUCTURE MANAGEMENT PHILOSOPHY GEOGRAPHICAL DISPERSION INFORMAL ORGANIZATION SIZE, AGE/ GROWTH DIFFERENTIATION INTEGRATION EXTERNAL ENVIRONMENT SIMPLE/COMPLEX STABLE/DYNAMIC TECHNOLOGY	PERFORMANCE PROBLEMS	STRUCTURE? WHAT ELEMENTS? WHY AND HOW?	ABOUT: RESTRUCTURING, PEOPLE, REACTIONS, COMPETITION	PYRAMID, MATRIX TEAM, PROJECT, JOINT VENTURE, HOW TO STRUCTURE ELEMENTS TYPES OF DEPART- MENTATION MECHANISTIC ORGANIC CENTRALIZED/ DECENTRALIZED VERTICAL OR HORIZONTAL DOWNSIZING SHAPE OF THINGS TO COME NETWORKS	STRATEGY MANAGEMENT PREROGATIVE/ PHILOSOPHY ORGANIZATIONAL SIZE COMPLEXITY OF ENVIRONMENT STABILITY OF ENVIRONMENT GEOGRAPHICAL FACTORS TECHNOLOGY		

- Understanding by each individual of his or her own task, as well as that of the organization as a whole.
- Decision making that focuses on the right issues, is action oriented, and is carried out at the lowest possible level of management.
- Stability, as opposed to rigidity, to survive turmoil, and adaptability to learn from it.
- Perpetuation and self-renewal, which require that an organization be able to produce tomorrow's leaders from within, helping each person develop continuously; the structure must also be open to new ideas.[56]

In designing the organization's macro structure, work groups, and individual tasks at lower levels, it is important to realize that results are often slow in coming. For example, it took ten years for Westinghouse's redesign effort to show a significant financial return.[57]

The Shape of Things to Come

We are in a time of structural change. Organizations are seeking ways to manage their resources better. Environments are changing. The structures that will dominate organizations in the future are uncertain. They may not even exist yet, but some trends can be identified.

As organizations face increasingly dynamic and complex environments, with increased levels of competition, they must create structures that are more responsive to the marketplace. At the same time, they must be able to cut costs. Restructuring is one way of accomplishing both objectives.[58] Decentralization is also likely to occur. This reduces the need for middle management and, in many cases, for support staff. Decentralization makes a firm more responsive to its environment; reducing middle management and support staff makes it more cost effective. Decentralization also helps satisfy workers' expectations of greater decision-making authority. The implications of this trend for the U.S. work force are discussed in more detail in Chapter 12.

The organizations of the future will become more horizontal, based on processes and networks. On the other hand, a recurring theme is the SBU type of organization: a small corporate staff and small, independent businesses, usually structured on the basis of functions. In another view of the future, Peter Drucker suggests that the symphony orchestra may be a useful model: It consists of a conductor and everybody else. He allows for "first-chair" positions to achieve coordination, but the point is that organizations will become much flatter and have far fewer managers.[59]

A final, very important factor is that the organization must develop a structure for its anticipated future environment and in anticipation of its future strategy. It should not wait until the strategy is in place to think about structure. It should be changing its structure to meet the requirements of the new strategy.[60]

Organizational Design as a Problem-Solving Process

As should be clear from the preceding discussion, organizational design is a complex problem-solving process involving a large number of interdependent variables.[61] Examining Figure 9.9 in conjunction with Figure 10.7 will help you

There used to be six people performing the work that these four now perform at Chevron. One consequence of Chevron's slimming down exercise was that work had to be prioritized, and some work was simply not done. As is often the case, Chevron discovered that a lot of unnecessary work was being done and could be dispensed with.

understand the issues involved and the complexity of the process. Most of the key terms and concepts examined in this chapter could be placed under more than one stage of problem solving in Figure 10.7. They have been placed under the stage(s) where they are significant factors.

A manager would work through Figure 10.7 as follows. Suppose that a problem has been detected in the performance of the organization as a whole. Competitors are making decisions faster, responding to customer needs more quickly, and producing products at lower cost. In analyzing the environment, top management concludes that the existing structure worked well in a simple and stable environment, but that the environment has become complex and dynamic. In further identifying the problem, top management determines that there are too many layers of management; the same amount of productive work could be done with fewer managers being involved; decisions could be made faster with fewer levels of management; customers could be responded to faster; and costs would be lowered by reducing overhead.

The next step is to consider several alternative ways of cutting middle management. Also involved are issues related to information systems, how the work will continue to be done, and what tasks must be reassigned. Several decisions result. The organization is to become more organic and more decentralized—flatter, in terms of the pyramid. During implementation, an improved information system is installed to assist the flow of information, because there are fewer managers to summarize and process it. A significant number of managers (20 percent of all managers) are either given early retirement or terminated with three months' pay. A process-based work-redesign program is begun on a trial basis. Top management monitors costs, customer reaction time, and decision times to determine whether the changes in the organization's macro design were appropriate.

Summary

(Before reading this summary, look again at the objectives listed at the beginning of the chapter.)

1. The organizational design process consists of determining the effects of each of the following major factors: strategy, environment, size, management philosophy, technology, and geographic dispersion. The impacts of each of these factors must be balanced. The manager must determine which of the principal forms of departmentation to use and how the structural elements should be characterized.

2. Organizational design is affected by the major factors just listed in the following ways:

a. Strategy leads to structure, but sometimes structure leads to strategy. It is clear that certain strategies must be carried out within particular structures in order to be successful.

b. Environment affects structure through its impact on strategy. In addition, subunits of the organization must differentiate on the basis of environmental influences. Environments may be simple or complex, stable or dynamic. Each of the resulting four types of environments calls for a specific form of organization relative to combinations of mechanistic or organic, centralized or decentralized structures.

c. As organizations grow, they typically pass through a series of stages; the type of structure shifts from simple to functional to process to product to SBU.

d. Managers can choose to structure an organization at any time according to their beliefs about how a particular structure will affect their ability to manage.

e. Technology has its primary effects on small units of an organization but can influence any part of the organization and any position within it.

f. As organizations become more global or more geographically dispersed, organizational structures tend to become decentralized. Networks are common in global firms.

3. Mechanistic organizations are highly specialized, task oriented, rigidly defined, hierarchical, highly controlled, and usually centralized. Communication is from the top down. Organic organizations are collaborative and knowledge based. They are continually defining tasks, and communications flow both from the top down and from the bottom up.

4. The Woodward studies provided the first scientific evidence that technology affects the design of structure and that matching structure to technology would result in higher levels of performance.

5. The shape of things to come is uncertain but seems to be moving in the direction of a return to smaller organizations with simpler structures, large organizations with relatively few middle managers, process-based organizations, and networks.

General Questions

1. Think of an organization with which you are familiar. Describe that organization in terms of its structural design and the factors that probably led to the selection of this structure.

2. Describe the potential for horizontal structuring in the organization you selected in response to the preceding question.

3. Describe the type of technology used and its impact on organizational structure.

4. Describe the characteristics of the organization's environment and their effects on strategy and structure.

5. Discuss how managerial and contextual factors interact to determine organizational structure at GM.

Questions on the Management Challenge Features

DIVERSITY MANAGEMENT CHALLENGE

1. What are some of the cultural diversity problems ABB faces as a global corporation?

2. How does the company solve these problems?

GLOBAL MANAGEMENT CHALLENGE
1. Why did Honda reorganize along the lines of an American corporation?
2. How might the company's culture be improved or harmed by these actions?

INNOVATION MANAGEMENT CHALLENGE
1. Describe the structural changes made by Rank Xerox.
2. What were the benefits of those changes?

E P I L O G U E

Making the Elephant Dance

Kodak executives must solve two large problems in the near future if the company is going to remain profitable in the next decade. The first problem, erosion of the film market, was discussed earlier. The second problem is what to do about the unprofitable copier and printer line. One possibility is to sell, which would probably bring $1 million to $1.5 billion. However, a successful copier and printer line would enhance Kodak's place in the electronic imaging market.

More generally, Kodak confessed to its stockholders that 1992 was another bad year, and that it is time to pay more attention to earnings and stock price. Management announced lowered aspi-rations for the growth of the photo products group—3 percent instead of 6 percent; two thousand layoffs, mostly in administration and R&D; and reduced aspirations in electronic imaging. Also, certain managers' salaries have been tied to company profits, and top managers are required to hold from one to five years' salary in company stock to develop a closer relationship between performance and compensation.

All of these changes have been praised by the business community, but while Kodak's stock price and net profit are up, it is likely that additional changes will be made in the near future.

DISCUSSION QUESTIONS

1. How should Kodak structure its R&D efforts to help solve its major problems?
2. How would a change in the marketing of photo products to compete on the basis of price affect the structure of Kodak?

SOURCE: *Business Week* (February 1, 1993), p. 25.

Someone Has to Be Let Go

Ken Mulligan was a senior vice-president of one of the nation's leading quality consulting firms. In four years, the company's personnel had expanded from 8 (the founder, a secretary, two full-time trainers, and four part-time trainers) to 125 full-time employees. Fifteen of these were full-time "account executives," trainers with limited sales and customer-service responsibility. About 70 percent of the company's revenues came from training courses on quality management. Revenues and profits had grown by leaps and bounds. But in the summer of the fourth year, revenues dropped drastically as the economy hit a mild recession and expected revenues from the company's biggest client, IBM, failed to materialize.

Mulligan was assigned the task of determining what changes to make in the company's structure. A loss was projected for the current quarter, and the president and chairman of the board—the founder—had decreed that all members of the work force who were not productive had to be let go. A target of twenty-five people had been set. Mulligan had been placed in charge of a three-person task force and given one week to develop a plan, including the names of those to be released and the timing of their releases. All releases had to be completed within three weeks.

The company had grown so rapidly that it had not had time to complete any job descriptions. It was common knowledge that a lot of people, including some account executives, had little to do. There had never been any evaluations of employees other than the training staff.

At the end of the briefing session in which Mulligan was assigned this task, the president commented: "Good luck, you're going to need it."

DISCUSSION QUESTIONS

1. If you were Mulligan, where would you start? How would you proceed?
2. What is the obvious course of action? Should Mulligan take that action?
3. How can you rationally make the choices Mulligan must make?

Understanding Factors Related to Structure

MANAGE YOURSELF

Either individually or in small groups, review or discuss an organization you are familiar with—perhaps one you work for, have worked for, or have belonged to—in terms of how its structure is or was affected by each of the following factors:

STRATEGY   GEOGRAPHIC DISPERSION
MANAGEMENT PHILOSOPHY   TECHNOLOGY
ENVIRONMENT   SIZE

Was the organization's structure affected by

THE INFORMAL GROUP?

When the review or discussion is complete, each person or group's observations should be shared with the rest of the class.

"Without work, all life goes rotten. But when work is soulless, life stifles and dies."

—Albert Camus

"We cannot achieve breakthroughs in performance by cutting fat or automating existing processes. Rather, we must challenge old assumptions and shed the old rules that make the business underperform in the first place."

—Michael Hammer,
Consultant,
Harvard Business Review

Job Design

CHAPTER OBJECTIVES

When you have read this chapter, you should be able to:

1. Describe the situational model of job design and its components.

2. List and define each of the five core dimensions and the three contextual dimensions that help define a job.

3. Describe each of the following job design options: work simplification, job rotation, job enlargement, job enrichment, autonomous work teams, and quality circles.

4. Describe a typical job enrichment program in terms of the core job dimensions, including critical psychological states, related implementation concepts, and personal and work outcomes.

5. Indicate how the need for growth acts as a moderating factor in job enrichment.

6. Indicate how technology, especially robotics and personal computers, affects job design.

7. Indicate how the changing nature of the work force and workers' expectations and values affect job design.

8. Describe job design as a problem-solving process.

MANAGEMENT CHALLENGES
DISCUSSED IN THIS CHAPTER:

 Increasing levels of competition.

 Changing technology.

 A more diverse work force.

Job Redesign at Volvo

In the late 1960s and early 1970s, Volvo, a major Swedish automobile company, faced a series of complex personnel problems. Sweden has a small, homogeneous population and a very stable government with many state-supported services. Swedes tend to be well educated and have high expectations regarding their personal well-being. Consequently, most of the firm's facilities experienced worker turnover at rates of 50 percent or more annually, with absenteeism approaching 20 percent. Because very few students graduating from Swedish high schools wanted to take factory jobs, 58 percent of the firm's work force came from foreign countries. In an effort to address these problems, Volvo engaged in a job redesign program. Efforts were made both to increase the number of tasks each worker would perform (job enlargement) and to allow each worker—as an individual or as a member of a group—to make more decisions (job enrichment). These efforts met with mixed results—one project was successful, another largely unsuccessful.

Despite the mixed results, Volvo committed itself to a major organizational design and job redesign effort. Its new automobile plant at Kalmar was designed to incorporate job enlargement, job enrichment, job rotation, and autonomous work teams. The Kalmar plant is noted for its unique physical facilities, including large exterior windows. It is also known for its use of the team approach and its emphasis on the use of computers to help teams manage. Jobs at the plant are designed to give each worker a large number of tasks and the authority to perform them.

It cost 10 to 30 percent more to produce an automobile at the Kalmar plant than at a conventional plant; the Kalmar plant's production capacities were extremely limited, compared to those of U.S. plants, because of the reduced levels of specialized labor and the increase in decision making by employees. However, Volvo executives were satisfied with the results: higher product quality, improved worker attitudes, lower rates of absenteeism and turnover, and reduced numbers of supervisory personnel. Fifteen years after its inception, the Kalmar plant was performing well beyond expectations.

In the mid-1980s, confronted with similar problems—the absenteeism rate at one plant was 24 percent—Volvo went even further with its Uddevalla plant. In fact, this plant has dispensed entirely with the assembly line. Work teams of eight to ten people assemble a car in one location. Each car is attached to a "tilt," which lifts and rotates the car body as workers assemble it. Parts appear as if by magic in this industrial Disneyland, arriving on carts guided by magnetic strips in the floor.

The Uddevalla plant is essentially run by the workers. Weekly production goals are set by assembly teams in consultation with management. Membership in the teams is 57 percent male and 43 percent female. Ten thousand units a year were assembled in this 85,000-square-foot facility in the late 1980s. Although Volvo officials predicted that 40,000 units would be produced annually by 1991, only about 23,000 units were produced. Some of the assembly teams report having difficulty coping with their new management responsibilities, and friction has occasionally developed between top management and the work teams and within the work teams themselves. Still, few of Volvo's workers wish to return to the old ways, with management making all the decisions.

SOURCES: Robert R. Rehder, "Sayonara, Uddevalla?" *Business Horizons* (November/December 1992), pp. 8–18; Robert R. Rehder, "Building Cars as if People Mattered: The Japanese Lean System vs. Volvo's Uddevalla," *Columbia Journal of World Business* (Summer 1992), pp. 56–70; Berth Jonsson and Alden G. Lank, "Volvo: A Report on the Workshop on Production Technology and Quality of Working Life," *Human Resource Management* (Winter 1985), pp. 455–465; "Kalmar, Ten Years Later," *Via Volvo* (Spring–Summer 1984), pp. 14–19; and "Auto Plant in Sweden Scores Some Success with Worker Teams," *Wall Street Journal* (March 1, 1977), p. 1.

When Volvo's managers revised the content of the jobs at the Kalmar and Uddevalla plants, they were performing job design. **Job design** is the process that determines the content of a job or group of jobs, including the degree of authority associated with the job. Volvo's job design efforts were part of a larger organizational design process. Two of the most important tasks in which any manager can engage are job and organizational design. Although few managers will have an opportunity to design an entire organization, most have an ongoing opportunity to redesign the work of those who report to them. Managers most frequently redefine individual jobs and the relationships among them.

Job design: The process of determining the content of a job or group of jobs, including the degree of authority associated with the job.

As portrayed in Figure 1.1, planning leads to organizing. The strategy developed in the strategic planning process and the operational plans formulated by a line or staff manager or by a group of managers must be put into place. Job and organizational design are important because they define how the organization will achieve the goals set forth in its strategic and operational plans. Job and organizational design must work in concert.

One of the primary management challenges of the 1990s is to make organizations more competitive. It is increasingly apparent that organizational and job design are important ways of improving competitiveness by increasing productivity. As a result, there is growing interest in **reengineering** the firm—that is, totally redesigning work to eliminate inefficiencies.[1] Organizations are shifting to horizontal structures and autonomous work teams. Japanese business organizations have successfully redesigned work to make it more productive, and a growing number of North American firms have done so also. Organizations throughout the world will be forced to redesign work if they wish to be competitive. Many European firms, for example, are undergoing major restructurings in order to become more competitive.[2]

Reengineering: Completely redesigning work to eliminate inefficiences.

Also contributing to the movement toward work redesign is the demand by U.S. employees for more participation in decision making. To successfully delegate authority, it is necessary to redesign the job. Thus, in the next few years,

The majority of engines for Volvo cars and commercial vehicles are manufactured at the Volvo Components Corporation's facilities in Skövde, Sweden. About 4,000 people work at the Skövde plant.

most managers will become very familiar with job design whether they want to or not. This chapter focuses on actions that companies and managers can take to redesign work to meet the management challenges of the 1990s.

Job design takes place in the context of a specific situation. Environmental factors, organizational factors, and individual characteristics affect the content of any job—its primary dimensions—as well as the performance and other requirements associated with that job, as shown in Figure 11.1. The first section of this chapter presents this situational model of job design. The components of the job and its primary dimensions are defined, and the contextual factors of the job—the environment, the organization, and the individual—are discussed. Aspects of job redesign such as job enlargement, job enrichment, and job rotation are then reviewed. The impact of technology on job design is discussed, with emphasis on the impacts of computers and robotics. The quality of work life (QWL) and related issues are explained. The impact of Total Quality Management on job design is discussed. Finally, job design is portrayed as a problem-solving process.

AT VOLVO: Volvo redesigned jobs at the Kalmar and Uddevalla plants according to the basic contextual factors: the environment, the organization, and the individual.

A Situational Model of Job Design

During your working life you will spend more time at your job than you will at any other activity, including sleeping. As noted in Chapter 10, a *job* is a collection of tasks designed to achieve an organization's objectives. It can be exciting, glamorous, and rewarding, or dull, monotonous, and unsatisfying. A job can satisfy basic needs by supplying money to provide food, clothing, shelter, and security. It can satisfy social needs by providing friends and a chance for interpersonal relationships. It can provide esteem, and it may even provide opportunities for self-fulfillment, achievement, and the attainment of power.[3] But a job may also do none of these. Some people's jobs do not even provide enough

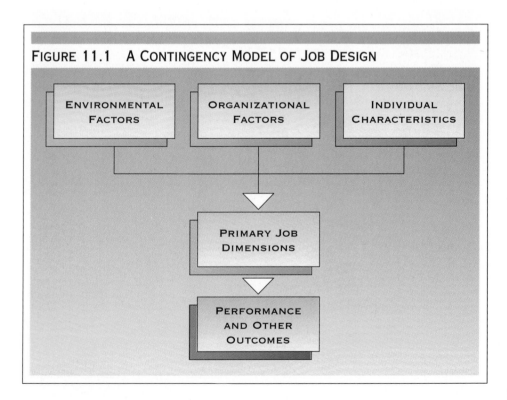

FIGURE 11.1   A CONTINGENCY MODEL OF JOB DESIGN

ENVIRONMENTAL FACTORS

ORGANIZATIONAL FACTORS

INDIVIDUAL CHARACTERISTICS

PRIMARY JOB DIMENSIONS

PERFORMANCE AND OTHER OUTCOMES

money to cover the basic necessities of life, much less satisfy other needs. Moreover, jobs that seem glamorous or satisfying to some people are not glamorous or satisfying to others. Managers and management researchers are learning that certain kinds of jobs lead to more productivity and satisfaction than others. Managers must design jobs with the appropriate content if they are to meet the management challenges of the 1990s.[4]

The outcomes of any given job, such as performance and satisfaction, are a function of four major sets of factors:

1. *Environmental factors:* The economy, the marketplace, society, government, employees and potential employees, unions, and technology are key environmental factors.

2. *Organizational factors:* Mission, goals, objectives, strategy, operational plans, macro structure, management systems, leadership style, organizational culture, and group dynamics all affect the design of individual jobs.

3. *Individual characteristics of the job holder:* Personality, needs, self-image, attitudes and values, modes of perception and learning, motivation, and aspirations cause job holders to behave in certain ways. (If a group of jobs was being examined for design purposes, this factor would include the dynamics of the work group.)

4. *The primary job dimensions:* The elements that constitute a job naturally affect its outcomes.[5] There are five core job dimensions and three contextual dimensions. (These are defined in the next section.)

Job design is the process of allocating work-related tasks and authority to individual and work group positions. When designing or redesigning a job, the manager must take into account not only the five elements that constitute a job but also the other three sets of factors that will affect its design and how an individual performs it. Figure 11.1 presents a situational model of job design.

Structural Elements at the Micro Level

A single job is composed of tasks (the horizontal component) and the authority to accomplish those tasks (the vertical component). Each job has varying amounts of these components, known respectively as range and depth (analogous concepts work at the group level as well). **Range** indicates the variety and number of tasks in a job. **Depth** indicates the amount of decision-making authority available to the job holder. Figure 11.2 reveals how a cross section of jobs would contain varying amounts of range and depth. For example, an anesthesiologist has a limited number of tasks to perform but has a high level of authority; a surgical nurse also has a limited number of tasks but has a low level of authority.

Horizontal and vertical structure can be further analyzed in terms of various dimensions. The **core job dimensions,** as identified by management researchers J. Richard Hackman and Greg R. Oldham, follow:

1. *Skill variety:* The degree to which a job requires employees to perform a wide range of operations or to use a variety of procedures in their work.

2. *Task identity:* The extent to which employees do a complete piece of work and can clearly identify the results of their efforts.

3. *Task significance:* The extent to which employees perceive a significant impact on others as a result of their efforts.

Range: The variety and number of tasks in a job.

Depth: The amount of decision-making authority available to the job holder.

Core job dimensions: The key dimensions identified by Hackman and Oldham: skill variety, task identity, task significance, autonomy, and feedback.

FIGURE 11.2   TYPICAL RANGES AND DEPTHS OF SELECTED JOBS

		RANGE				
		LOW				HIGH
DEPTH — HIGH		ASSEMBLY LINE WORKER AT A FORD MOTOR CO. PLANT	ANESTHESIOLOGIST	COLLEGE PROFESSOR	ASSEMBLY LINE WORKER AT KALMAR	DOCTOR	COMPANY PRESIDENT
DEPTH — LOW		TYPICAL ASSEMBLY LINE WORKER	SURGICAL NURSE	GRADUATE ASSISTANT	ASSEMBLY LINE WORKER WITH "ENLARGED" JOB	NURSE IN A HOSPITAL WARD	MANAGER OF ACCOUNTS PAYABLE
TYPE OF ORGANIZATION		BUSINESS	NON-PROFIT	NON-PROFIT	BUSINESS	NON-PROFIT	BUSINESS

SOURCE: ADAPTED FROM JAMES L. GIBSON, JOHN M. IVANCEVICH, AND JAMES H. DONNELLY, JR., ORGANIZATIONS: BEHAVIOR, STRUCTURE, PROCESSES, 6TH ED. (PLANO, TEX.: BPI, 1988), FIGURE 13.2, P. 466.

4. *Autonomy:* The extent to which employees have substantial freedom and independence and a major say in scheduling their work, selecting the equipment they will use, and deciding on procedures to be followed.

5. *Feedback:* The degree to which employees receive, in the course of their work, information that reveals how well they are performing the job.[6]

The **contextual dimensions** that help define a job include the following:

1. *Interpersonal relationships:* The extent to which the individual engages in meaningful human interactions on the job with peers, subordinates, and superiors.

2. *Authority and responsibility for goal setting:* The degree of authority and responsibility delegated to and inherent in a position—particularly the amount of latitude an individual has in setting objectives.

3. *Communication patterns:* Formal and informal communications associated with a job.[7]

Contextual dimensions: *Dimensions that help define a job; they include interpersonal relations, authority and responsibility for goal setting, and communication patterns.*

The dimension of skill variety deals primarily with range, whereas the dimensions of autonomy, feedback, and authority and responsibility for goal setting deal primarily with depth. Task identity and task significance relate to the degree to which an individual's need for self-esteem might be satisfied. Interpersonal relationships and communication patterns relate to the satisfaction of social needs on the job. Although much attention has been given to the five core job dimensions, the three contextual dimensions—interpersonal relations, authority and responsibility, and communication patterns—should not be overlooked.

The eight dimensions just listed affect both the design of the job and the outcomes of the job holder's efforts—the consequences of work for the individual, the organization, and the society. North American business organizations have become extremely interested in how all these dimensions fit together in the

Interpersonal relationships are an important contextual dimension of a job. Meaningful human interactions on the job are highly valued by employees like these steelworkers at the Ford Engine Plant in Cleveland, Ohio.

design of a job. Many have begun to redesign work in an attempt to compete better with Japanese and other Pacific Rim firms, which have a cost advantage because of lower labor rates, as well as advantages resulting from better utilization of human resources and technology. General Electric has adopted a worker-paced assembly line in its Louisville, Kentucky, dishwasher plant. GE needed the increased product quality, the resulting lower cost of warranty repairs, the associated reduced level of customer complaints, and overall lower cost—all of which have enabled the company to compete better. Traditionally, GE and other appliance manufacturers have employed continuous assembly lines without worker control. This GE line, however, moves faster than a continuous line, yet workers do not object and quality is higher. Units with problems are set aside to be repaired later.[8]

These eight factors constitute a job. When a manager, the job holder, a personnel specialist, or a consultant attempts to design or redesign a job, these factors are the building blocks they use. When a job is designed for a salesperson, secretary, company president, director of purchasing, carpenter, or airline pilot, it will consist of varying elements from each of these eight dimensions. A job can have more or less task variety, identity, significance, autonomy, feedback, interpersonal relationships, goal setting, or communication. It is the job designer's responsibility to ensure that the appropriate level of each factor is designed into the job.

When these dimensions are combined appropriately, they can provide job satisfaction for the individual job holder. Job satisfaction is important inasmuch as it is often related to productivity—although not necessarily on a one-for-one basis. Normally, however, individuals who are satisfied in their work tend to perform at higher levels than those who are not.[9]

When designing a job, the manager must also take into account how old ways of designing jobs restrict visions of how jobs and groups of jobs can be designed. Managers must look for entirely new ways of designing work, looking at systems, flows, and processes rather than viewing jobs in isolation. They must pay special attention to how information technology can improve job design.[10]

Job Design and the Quality of Work Life

Believing that job satisfaction leads to higher levels of performance and that providing a satisfying workplace is an important goal, many organizations have become concerned with the **quality of work life** (QWL).[11] This term has been

Quality of work life (QWL): *The extent to which individuals' needs in the workplace are satisfied.*

defined in several ways, but it essentially means improving the satisfaction of individuals' needs in the workplace. Richard E. Kopelman suggests that QWL is generally viewed as "a philosophy of management that enhances the dignity of all workers; introduces changes in an organization's culture; and improves the physical and emotional well-being of employees."[12] Richard E. Walton suggests that an assessment of an organization's QWL should review the following eight criteria:

1. Adequate and fair compensation
2. Safe and healthy working conditions
3. Immediate opportunity to use and develop human capacities
4. Future opportunity for continued growth and security
5. Social integration in the work force
6. Employee rights to privacy, speech, equity, and due process
7. The balance between the job holder's role as work related and the rest of his or her life
8. A socially responsible work organization[13]

Items 2, 3, 4, 5, and 7 on the preceding list are directly concerned with job design. This is not surprising because QWL has to do with work and, hence, is concerned largely with the job itself. The content of the job must eventually be matched with the needs, personality, and other characteristics of the job holder. Many companies—GM, Westinghouse, GE, and Volvo among them—have taken action to improve QWL by focusing on matching individuals to their jobs. Because QWL is a major underlying component of total quality management (TQM) programs, we can expect to see QWL improve as more firms move to TQM.[14]

The quality of work life has been defined in several ways, but it essentially means improving the satisfaction of individuals' needs in the workplace. Shown here are workers at the assembly line of Toyota and GM's "NUMMI" joint venture.

Job Design at the Individual Level

Managers who wish to redesign jobs to enhance the quality of work life may choose among several options. The primary options follow:

1. *Job enlargement:* Increasing the range of a job
2. *Job enrichment:* Increasing the depth of a job
3. *Job rotation:* Rotating workers from job to job
4. *Work simplification:* Reducing the range and usually the depth of a job
5. *Quality circles:* Increasing the range and depth of a group of jobs
6. *Autonomous work teams:* Significantly increasing the range and depth of a group of jobs, forming the group into a team
7. *Process redesign:* Designing jobs around processes rather than functions

Historically, most redesign programs have focused primarily on job enlargement and job enrichment. Today, however, there is a trend toward autonomous work teams, which are discussed in more detail in Chapter 15, and process redesign, discussed in Chapters 9 and 10.

Job Enlargement and Job Enrichment[15]

During the 1960s, it became evident that several factors—including increased employee expectations about work, especially in highly specialized jobs—were leading to unacceptable levels of absenteeism, inferior performance, and even sabotage.[16] It was clear that specialization was yielding diminishing returns. Management researcher Chris Argyris spoke early (in 1957) and often of the incongruity between the needs of human beings and the needs of the organization. According to Argyris, an individual's drive toward maturity is frustrated by

Employees at Coca-Cola attend a job enrichment seminar. Job enrichment is a means of changing the depth of jobs and improving employee motivation.

organizational rules, procedures, hierarchy, and specialized division of labor. This results in boredom, daydreaming, absenteeism, apathy, negativism, and lowered productivity.[17] Douglas McGregor, another management theorist, addressed the same issue, but from the perspective of how managers' leadership style may thwart the needs of their subordinates. McGregor observed that managers who assumed that employees were lazy, unmotivated, and controllable (referred to as Theory X assumptions) treated them that way, and the results were as predicted. Similarly, managers who assumed that subordinates were mature, self-motivated, and self-controlled (Theory Y assumptions) treated them that way, and again the results were as predicted. Management style, then, leads to self-fulfilling prophecies about the performance of subordinates.[18]

In 1971, Frederick W. Herzberg became one of the first advocates of increasing the range of jobs—**job enlargement**—and/or the depth of jobs—**job enrichment**—as a means of changing these conditions and improving employee motivation. By "motivation" Herzberg meant influencing employees to do more on the job or to do a better job than they had been doing, in contrast with the more traditional view in which it is acceptable for an employee simply to do the job as assigned. (Chapter 14 reviews Herzberg's views of motivation in more detail.) Herzberg does not see job enlargement primarily as a way of improving motivation. Rather, he views it as a way of counteracting the problems associated with specialization of labor. He views motivation as resulting from the provision of satisfiers that are intrinsic to the job itself, such as autonomy, feedback, and authority and responsibility for goal setting.

Herzberg believes that motivated individuals have a sense of achievement, that they receive recognition, that their efforts produce opportunities for advancement, and that they grow as individuals. He thinks that factors that are extrinsic to the job—"hygiene factors" such as salary, relationships with others, company rules, and policies and procedures—do not "motivate." In his words, "If I kick my dog . . . , he will move. And when I want him to move again what must I do? I must kick him again. . . . It is only when [a person] has his own generator that we can talk about motivation. He then needs no outside stimulation. He wants to do it."[19] Among the many companies that have used job enrichment as suggested by Herzberg are Texas Instruments, IBM, and General Foods.[20]

Work Simplification

In **work simplification** the job is reduced to a very narrow set of tasks involving standardized procedures with little or no opportunity for decision making. This is the classic result of specialization of labor. Work simplification goes against the current trend in job design. It might be attempted in situations in which the job could be done better if it were simplified, where workers are willing to tolerate highly specialized jobs, or in firms that hire mentally handicapped workers, in order to provide them with an appropriate amount of challenge. It could also be used in programs that allow employees to redesign their own jobs to eliminate unnecessary steps. Such actions can also lead to improved product or service quality. Such was the case at Granville-Philips, an instrument and gauge manufacturer based in Boulder, Colorado. This small company taught its seventy-four employees work design techniques. The employees, in turn, simplified their jobs, improving efficiency and quality.[21]

This chapter's Global Management Challenge describes how Nissan workers are simplifying their jobs to help their firm cut costs.

Job enlargement: An approach to job design that focuses on task variety, a meaningful work module, performance feedback, ability utilization, and worker-paced control.

Job enrichment: An approach to job design that encompasses employee participation, goal internalization, autonomy, and group management.

AT VOLVO: *Volvo recognized that its workers were not as productive as they could be. It also recognized that its workers' QWL was not as high as might be desirable. Both job enlargement and job enrichment were carried out.*

Work simplification: An approach to job design in which the job is reduced to a very narrow set of tasks involving standardized procedures with little or no latitude for making decisions.

Nissan Redesigns to Survive

The 1991–1993 recession hit hard in Japan. Nissan, Japan's second-largest car maker, was not immune to its effects. By combining flexible manufacturing with high quality and unique styling, Nissan had hoped to capture more market share by satisfying the whims of customers. But the hoped-for sales failed to materialize, even though Nissan had developed several stylistic winners with the newly designed 300ZX, Maxima, and Pulsar. The market did not seem to be aware of the new styles. And while the firm thought it was giving customers what they wanted by creating more styles with more options in more colors, as it turned out it was merely giving itself a lot of headaches.

After studying the situation, Nissan took drastic actions, including the first-ever closing of a Japanese automobile plant. The goal of Nissan's "reformation" is to cut annual production costs by 200 billion yen (about $1.68 billion) and to increase productivity by about 30 percent. Much of the savings will come from using fewer and cheaper parts and materials. As customer options are eliminated, fewer parts will be needed and there will be fewer steps in the production process. This, in turn, will lead to the simplification of many jobs.

Tadashi Arai, a screw designer at Nissan's R&D center southwest of Tokyo, is designing himself out of a job. His team's assignment is to cut the number of fasteners in each car in half, from an average of 6,000 to an average of 3,000 or less. "I used to derive happiness from designing different types of things," says the 54-year-old engineer. But over his desk sits a sign of the times—"Behold! This is our bulky state."

SOURCES: John Bussey, Clay Chandler, and Michael Williams, "The Other Shoe: Japanese Recession Prompts Corporations to Take Radical Steps," *Wall Street Journal* (February 24, 1993), pp. A1, A5; and Clay Chandler and Michael Williams, "Strategic Shift: A Slump in Car Sales Forces Nissan to Start Cutting Swollen Costs," *Wall Street Journal* (March 3, 1993), pp. A1, A6.

Job Rotation

In **job rotation** an employee moves from one job to another. This is a very effective way to train workers. Bank management training programs typically employ job rotation. Such programs, often lasting as long as two years, give trainees an opportunity to learn how all major functions contribute to the accomplishment of the bank's mission. Hospitals are beginning to use this technique as well, rotating their management trainees through a series of positions over a one- or two-year period. An individual who completes a job rotation program is presumed to be prepared to manage one part of the system while understanding the entire system.

Job rotation can help reduce boredom and lessen the impact of career plateaus—situations in which people are unlikely to advance farther up the corporate hierarchy.[22] It can be an effective means of improving job design and can help improve the quality of work life. Swissair has found that the rotation of managers increases their interest in their jobs. Managers are moved from one department to another several times during their careers, often to areas that are completely unfamiliar to them. Top management feels that the firm benefits because managers have a strategic view, rather than a narrow one; are loyal because they appreciate the growth opportunities available to them; and learn to

Job rotation: A system in which an employee moves from one job to another.

At Thomson Consumer Electronics, job rotation is used to reduce rates of employee accidents and disorders caused by repetitive motions and lifting of heavy objects.

work more closely with managers in other departments.[23] Some rotation programs, however, prove frustrating because the employee has a series of dull, boring jobs instead of just one.

Not all job rotation programs are undertaken in order to improve QWL. For example, job rotation can be used to reduce rates of employee accidents and disorders caused by repetitive motions and lifting of heavy objects. Thomson Consumer Electronics in Bloomington, Indiana, reduced such disorders by 46 percent through the use of job rotation.[24]

Job Design at the Group Level

Three important job design options at the group level are quality circles, autonomous work teams, and process redesign. Although work simplification, job rotation, job enlargement, and job enrichment are usually applied to individuals, the principles involved can also be applied to groups. Work reengineering efforts are also likely to focus on groups.

Quality Circles

Quality circle: A group-based job design program in which a formal group of employees meets periodically during working hours to solve problems.

Quality circles are an important group-based job design program.[25] Lori Fitzgerald and Joseph Murphy describe **quality circles** as groups that "consist of three to twelve employees who perform the same work or share the work area. They . . . meet on a regular basis, normally one hour per week on company time, in order to apply specific techniques and tools, learned in extensive training, to problems affecting their work and work area. Subsequently, they present solutions and recommendations to their management for the authorization of these solutions."[26] To a much lesser degree than autonomous work teams, quality circles provide job enrichment. Their principal concern is solving problems related to their work; in so doing, they provide task variety, identity, significance,

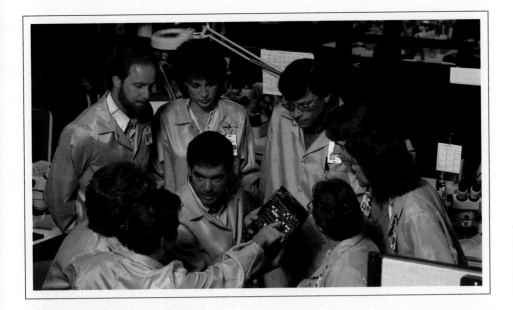

This quality circle at Westinghouse is examining an electronic device to determine how to improve the process for manufacturing it.

autonomy, and feedback, even if only to a limited degree. They also result in increased levels of interpersonal behavior and communication. Hence, they satisfy all eight job dimensions to some degree.

Most Fortune 500 firms have at least investigated quality circles, and many have tried them. Quality circles are usually introduced in manufacturing and in highly competitive clerical areas such as claim processing in insurance companies. Although they are not usually thought of as a job design technique, quality circles effectively produce some of the same results: high levels of internal motivation, high-quality performance, and increased levels of job satisfaction.[27] Quality circles are a type of continuous improvement process and therefore are an important factor in competitiveness.[28] Autonomous teams and quality circles are discussed in more detail in Chapter 15.

Autonomous Work Teams

Applying job enrichment to groups creates **autonomous work teams,** self-managed work teams that have the authority to accomplish work group objectives, usually in relation to projects, products, or processes. Because much work is performed in groups, the group is a natural unit around which to design jobs. Jobs are designed interdependently rather than separately. Autonomous work groups may establish the pace of work, the distribution of tasks among members, the group's membership, the training and development of members, and perhaps even their own compensation.[29]

Many, if not most, QWL efforts are based on the use of work teams and improving teamwork within work groups. M&M Mars has a plant in Waco, Texas, that is run by self-managing work teams. Similarly, the Skippy Peanut Butter plant in Little Rock, Arkansas, has no fixed jobs, no fixed job descriptions, no inspectors, and no supervisors. A general manager, a human resource manager, and a quality manager act as advisors to the one hundred or so employees, who arrive at decisions through a process of consensus building.[30] Teams develop new cars and manufacturing processes at Chrysler and solve problems at Federal Express.[31]

This chapter's Diversity Management Challenge discusses the efforts of British Petroleum to create multicultural teams. When you have read this feature you should be able to discuss the problems and solutions associated with such teams.

Autonomous work team: A self-managed work team that has the authority to accomplish work group objectives, usually on projects, products, or processes.

AT VOLVO: Volvo's Kalmar and Uddevalla plants were designed to function around autonomous work teams. Work teams at Volvo select team members, control their own performance, and determine job rotation, job scheduling, and the pace of the work.

BP's Multicultural Teams

When BP decided to establish a European Centre in Brussels, the team leader and manager of the new operation, Rob Ruijter, chose his staff from among European and United Kingdom associates as well as other BP finance centers around the world. What he wanted, Ruijter says, is what anyone would want in such circumstances: the highest possible level of professional skill.

What he got was forty people from thirteen nations, all moving to a new environment.

Ruijter wanted the trust and commitment of each member of his staff, and he wanted them to become a close-knit team as quickly as possible. It was soon clear that to achieve these objectives his multicultural team would need support in several respects.

If people come from different cultures, they do not necessarily share any underlying assumptions about what a team is. Their views, in fact, can be radically different. A French executive often assumes that the authority to make decisions is a right of office and a privilege of rank. In the Netherlands, Scandinavia, and the United Kingdom, managers expect their decisions to be challenged—and probably made in a more collaborative manner in the first place.

Coalescing people who hold such divergent views into an efficient, high-performing team can clearly present some challenges. The main concern is whether their attention can be deflected from their differences so that they can focus on their work.

A two-day event was organized to bring the team together to discuss how they would carry out their roles: "how to communicate with each other and with outsiders, make decisions, delegate, lead, conduct meetings, appraise performance and, most importantly, deal with conflict," according to the conference organizers.

The event included group discussions, simulated and real cross-cultural conversations, and guided negotiations. It helped the new co-workers realize that they

Process Redesign

Numerous other programs are being experimented with. This is especially true in organizations that have chosen a macro design based on core processes. Process designs depend heavily on cross-functional work teams to achieve their objectives.[32]

As mentioned in earlier chapters, one of the major structural changes occurring in organizations today is a shift toward organizing by process. Process redesign suggests that each process be examined to eliminate unnecessary steps. Process redesign is an important means of reducing costs. Normally it results in the simplification of jobs, but in some cases it leads to job enrichment.

The Job Design Process

In any job design effort, the designer works with range and depth. As shown in Figure 11.3, most simplified jobs involve no depth and little range. Job rotation and enlargement mean increased range, but little if any increase in depth. Quality circles result in more range and more depth. Job enrichment and autonomous work teams result in substantially more depth.

share the same challenge—to work together as a multicultural team. Many participants were surprised at what others perceived as challenges. The Dutch wanted assurance that they would be able to express opinions openly. The Germans, that proper procedures would be implemented as soon as possible.

There were lighter notes as well. The Americans were astonished that the French shake hands with everyone in their work group every morning: The custom is a sign of friendliness in France but a formal token of politeness in the United States.

After the two-day event, a small cultural-awareness team was organized to create informal get-togethers, seminars, and induction training for subsequent arrivals. It also provided a support network for members who might be having difficulty with cross-cultural issues.

After a year, a follow-up workshop was held to assess progress. The team had performed well, but not as well as had been hoped at the outset. This was attributed partly to its cultural mix.

Training advisers Rosemary Neale and Richard Mindel note that when multicultural teams perform well they usually perform exceptionally well, but it almost always takes them longer to reach that point than monocultural teams. The BP team felt that its training had not completely eliminated misunderstandings, but that when misunderstandings occurred, individuals had learned to listen to each other, to be more tolerant, to avoid irritation, to take broader perspectives, and to see differences in perception as creative challenges.

In hindsight, the trainers recognize that family members would have profited from such an orientation as well, either at the two-day event or at one organized separately for them, "as it is always the family which bears the brunt of adjusting to a new environment."

SOURCE: Rosemary Neale and Richard Mindel, "Rigging Up Multicultural Teamworking," *Personnel Management* (January 1992), pp. 36–39.

A Closer Look at Job Enrichment and Job Enlargement

Kae H. Chung and Monica F. Ross reviewed the literature on job enlargement and job enrichment in order to identify the key characteristics of these concepts. Their research provides us with a better understanding of the differences between the two concepts as well as their similarities. In their view, job enlargement "involves reversing the work simplification or specialization process somewhat."[33] It embodies one or more of the following features:

1. *Task variety:* More and different tasks are performed.
2. *A meaningful work module:* By working on the complete unit of work, the employee gains an appreciation of his or her contribution to the entire product or project.
3. *Performance feedback:* Performance feedback is increased when a larger number of tasks involved in producing a more complete work unit are performed.
4. *Ability utilization:* Satisfaction (and hence motivation, according to Herzberg) is increased when the work unit is enlarged to permit the use of a wider variety of skills and abilities.

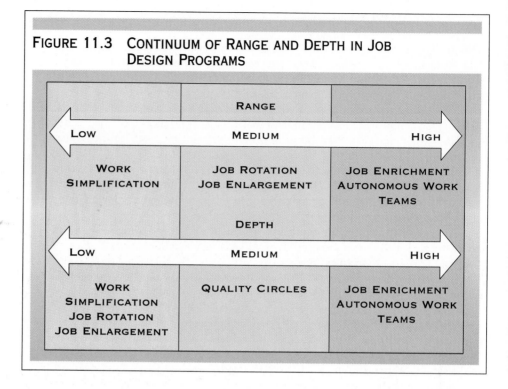

FIGURE 11.3   CONTINUUM OF RANGE AND DEPTH IN JOB DESIGN PROGRAMS

RANGE		
LOW	MEDIUM	HIGH
WORK SIMPLIFICATION	JOB ROTATION JOB ENLARGEMENT	JOB ENRICHMENT AUTONOMOUS WORK TEAMS

DEPTH		
LOW	MEDIUM	HIGH
WORK SIMPLIFICATION JOB ROTATION JOB ENLARGEMENT	QUALITY CIRCLES	JOB ENRICHMENT AUTONOMOUS WORK TEAMS

5. *Worker-paced control:* When work activity is no longer paced by a machine, the employee's desire to control some part of his or her environment is satisfied; again, motivation results.[34]

Chung and Ross define job enrichment as enabling nonmanagerial employees to perform functions that were previously restricted to managerial and supervisory personnel (in essence, increased depth). They view job enrichment as encompassing four characteristics:

1. *Employee participation:* Employees participate in the decision process (but only at the level of the job, not at the management level, as with worker councils, junior boards, and so on); thus, they feel personally responsible for carrying out their tasks.
2. *Goal internalization:* Workers set goals for their own jobs.
3. *Autonomy:* Workers need a high degree of control over the means they will use to achieve the objectives they have set; thus, they evaluate their own performance, take risks, and learn from their mistakes.
4. *Group management:* Because most employees whose jobs are appropriate for enrichment work in groups, assignments and job redesign are often subject to team consensus.[35]

Most authorities on the subject would probably agree that job enlargement is concerned with range and is less motivating than job enrichment, which is concerned with depth. However, most would also agree that job enlargement reduces boredom and thus encourages employees to perform at minimally satisfactory levels. Organizations often pursue both paths. For example, Sometown, Inc., a fairly large, privately held manufacturing firm, redesigned its accounting department so that its junior accountants became product accountants. These employees had previously been little more than bookkeepers, but after their jobs

JOB ENLARGEMENT AND JOB ENRICHMENT MAY INCORPORATE ANY OR ALL OF SEVERAL FEATURES. A KEY FEATURE OF JOB ENLARGEMENT IS INCREASING THE VARIETY OF TASKS, ESPECIALLY FOR ASSEMBLY LINE WORKERS LIKE THIS WOMAN CHECKING JARS IN A SKIPPY PEANUT BUTTER PLANT (ABOVE RIGHT). JOB ENLARGEMENT MAY ALSO TAKE THE FORM OF TRAINING TO IMPROVE WORKERS' SKILLS AND ABILITIES. WORKERS AT GM'S SATURN PLANT ARE GIVEN TRAINING IN COMPUTERIZED PRODUCTION METHODS (ABOVE LEFT). KEY FEATURES OF JOB ENRICHMENT INCLUDE EMPLOYEE PARTICIPATION IN DECISION MAKING, ILLUSTRATED IN THE EMPLOYEE CONFERENCE (RIGHT), AND GOAL INTERNALIZATION, ILLUSTRATED IN THE SHOP FLOOR SLOGAN (BELOW).

were redesigned they became an integral part of the information management team. They were "motivated" to assume responsibility for managing at least two clerical subordinates. Both the range and the depth of their jobs were increased, as were task identity and feedback. To a limited extent, autonomy was increased as well.[36]

Reflections on Job Enrichment

Job enrichment requires a change in management philosophy for most organizations. It requires delegation of authority and participative, rather than authoritarian, behavior. The management profession tends to attract people with a high need for power, a desire to control others. (This characteristic of managers will be discussed in more detail in Chapter 14.)[37] Job enrichment is not very compatible with this type of personality. Moreover, in the United States and Canada, unions have generally opposed job enrichment/enlargement programs, or at best have failed to support them. This situation is changing, however.[38] European unions, in contrast, have supported enrichment and participation programs.

Employees who find themselves doing increased amounts of work with no corresponding increase in extrinsic rewards are not likely to be satisfied and, hence, will not be motivated. Thus, managers who initiate enrichment programs must be prepared to reward increased levels of performance. One front-line supervisor recounts how he merged "typists" and "word processing personnel" into the same "word processing pool." Several of the typists quit, partly because they were fearful of the more complicated work; however, we can surmise that they were also unhappy because they had enriched jobs but were not receiving any additional pay. After the firm increased their compensation, the remaining typists adjusted satisfactorily to their enriched jobs.

Although the vast majority of workers readily accept job enrichment, this approach is not appropriate for everyone.[39] Employees who do not want responsibility, do not share the belief that work should be fulfilling, and want to do just enough to get by will not adapt well to job enrichment or enlargement. Management cannot embrace a single job design technique and expect it to work for everyone. People are different. Nevertheless, job enrichment works for many people. It is important, though, to keep Herzberg's "hygiene" factors at acceptable levels. For example, if pay is perceived as too low or supervision is perceived as too authoritarian, employees will not be satisfied by their "enriched" jobs.

Not every job can be enriched. Trade-offs are involved in virtually every situation. Costs must be weighed against benefits. Absenteeism and turnover may be reduced by job enlargement or enrichment, but productivity may decline when jobs become less specialized. Workers may be dissatisfied for any number of reasons. The problem may not be the job at all. Managers must attempt to uncover other possible problems. Bernard J. White analyzed the responses of fifteen hundred workers who were asked to rank various factors, both internal and external to the job, according to their importance. He concluded that managers could ignore neither hygiene factors nor motivators.[40]

Matching Job Design to Individual Growth Needs

J. Richard Hackman, Greg R. Oldham, Robert Janson, and Kenneth Purdy have developed the models shown in Figures 11.4 and 11.5, which relate growth needs to core job characteristics and to the core dimensions discussed previously: skill variety, task identity, task significance, task autonomy, and feedback. They have also identified the critical psychological states that result from

AT VOLVO: Despite Volvo's success with job enrichment, there were problems. At Uddevalla, for example, workers had trouble coping with the additional responsibility. There was friction between the work teams and management, and the costs were higher than at plants using more traditional approaches.

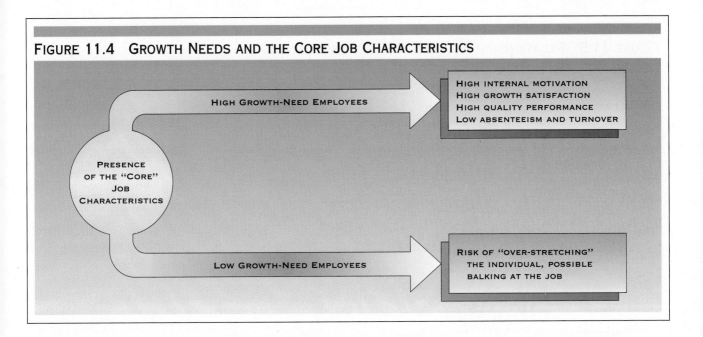

FIGURE 11.4   GROWTH NEEDS AND THE CORE JOB CHARACTERISTICS

PRESENCE OF THE "CORE" JOB CHARACTERISTICS

HIGH GROWTH-NEED EMPLOYEES

HIGH INTERNAL MOTIVATION
HIGH GROWTH SATISFACTION
HIGH QUALITY PERFORMANCE
LOW ABSENTEEISM AND TURNOVER

LOW GROWTH-NEED EMPLOYEES

RISK OF "OVER-STRETCHING" THE INDIVIDUAL, POSSIBLE BALKING AT THE JOB

various job characteristics. For example, task variety, identity, and significance help make work more meaningful. Task autonomy leads to a feeling of responsibility for the outcomes of the work. Feedback will lead to knowledge of the actual results of work activities.

Hackman and his colleagues indicate that these three critical psychological states must be realized in order for employees to develop the intrinsic work motivation Herzberg believes necessary. Their model is extremely important because it suggests that individuals will not all respond to the five core job characteristics in the same way. Some will reach the critical psychological states and some will not. The moderating variable is the strength of the employee's need for growth. Employees who have a high need for growth, who want to develop as human beings, will respond favorably to intrinsic job satisfaction. Those who have a lower need for growth will respond negatively, or at least in a neutral manner, to attempts to incorporate the core job characteristics in a job's design. The relationship between need for growth and the core job characteristics is portrayed in Figure 11.4. As you can see, the combination of the core job characteristics and high growth needs results in high levels of motivation, satisfaction, and performance; the combination of the core job characteristics and low growth needs results in reduced motivation, satisfaction, and performance.

Figure 11.5 presents five implementation concepts that can be used to include the core dimensions in a job's design: combining tasks, forming natural work units, establishing client relationships, vertical loading, and opening feedback channels. With the exception of opening feedback channels, each of these concepts affects more than one core job dimension. The implementation concepts are defined here:

1. *Combining tasks:* The implementation tactic of combining tasks reverses the trend toward high task specialization resulting from the scientific management approach. A variety of tasks are combined into the job, affecting both task variety and task identity.

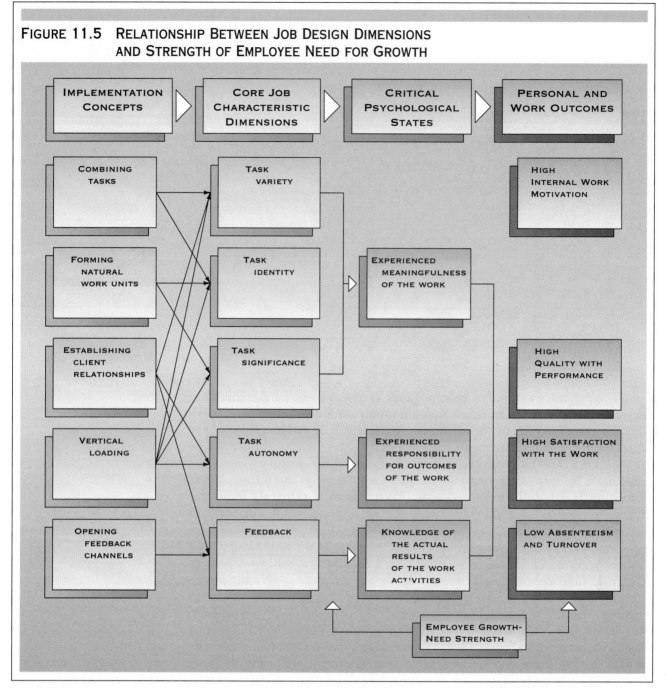

FIGURE 11.5   RELATIONSHIP BETWEEN JOB DESIGN DIMENSIONS AND STRENGTH OF EMPLOYEE NEED FOR GROWTH

SOURCE: J. RICHARD HACKMAN, GREG OLDHAM, ROBERT JANSON, AND KENNETH PURDY, "A NEW STRATEGY FOR JOB ENRICHMENT." COPYRIGHT 1975 BY THE REGENTS OF THE UNIVERSITY OF CALIFORNIA. REPRINTED FROM THE CALIFORNIA MANAGEMENT REVIEW, VOL. 17, NO. 4. BY PERMISSION OF THE REGENTS.

2. *Forming natural work units:* The feeling of ownership of the job is increased when an employee is given responsibility for an identifiable unit of work. For example, employees might assemble an entire motor, as opposed to simply attaching the piston to the crankshaft. Forming natural work units affects both task identity and task significance.

3. *Establishing client relationships:* Allowing workers to become familiar with clients by developing ongoing relationships with them

enables them to gain a new perspective on their work. Establishing client relationships affects task variety, task autonomy, and feedback.

4. *Vertical loading:* Vertical loading aims to give the employee responsibility for the outcome of the work. It includes such decisions as setting schedules, choosing work methods, quality control, the development of other workers, establishing the pace of work, and problem solving. It affects four of the five core job dimensions: task variety, task identity, task significance, and task autonomy.

5. *Opening feedback channels:* Giving employees feedback is extremely important to the satisfaction of their needs and to their understanding of their level of job performance. Feedback channels may be either external or built in as part of the job.

Volvo's experience at the Kalmar and Uddevalla plants exemplifies the implementation concepts shown in Figure 11.5. Tasks are combined; individuals perform more than one task and can exchange jobs as often as they wish. Natural work units have been formed in which a team of workers handles a general area, such as upholstery fitting, door assembly, or electric wiring. Although distinct relationships with clients have not been formed, the emphasis is on providing quality for the client.

Vertical loading can be seen in the fact that workers are allowed to vary the pace of their work as long as they keep up the general flow of production. Workers are allowed to solve problems and are in charge of quality control. Finally, feedback channels take the form of an internal computerized report for each team, indicating progress, problems, and quality issues.

The Kalmar and Uddevalla plants incorporate all the job enrichment implementation concepts that affect the core job dimensions. The critical psychological states have been attained. Workers experience their work as meaningful, take responsibility for outcomes, and are aware of the actual results of their work. Consequently, they have increased levels of internal work motivation, produce a high-quality product with reasonably high levels of performance, and are highly satisfied with the work; rates of absenteeism and employee turnover have been reduced.

The experience at the Kalmar plant, combined with that of GM's joint venture with Toyota in Fremont, California, reveals that it is not necessary to design a plant with a small workshop orientation to obtain the desired results.[41] Work can be redesigned using job enrichment, autonomous work teams, and quality circles (and probably process redesign). Such actions reduce the high overhead cost of a specially designed assembly line but yield the benefits of work redesign.

Effects of Job Redesign on Other Jobs

Pragmatically speaking, there are only so many tasks and so much authority to go around. If a job is redesigned, an increase in tasks or authority must come from another job or jobs. Similarly, if tasks or authority are eliminated from a job, they must be transferred elsewhere. Tasks may be taken from or given to any of the following:

1. Prejobs—jobs that occur before the job in question.
2. Postjobs—jobs that occur after the job in question. For example, in order to give an assembler of small motors an additional task, it might be necessary to remove the task of putting the housing on

AT VOLVO: *The danger of overly "humanizing" the workplace, as was done at Uddevalla, is that such plants are not cost competitive with plants in Japan, Korea, or even the United States.*

the motor from the next stage in the manufacturing process and give it to the assembler of motors.

3. Other jobs.

Authority may be taken from or given to other employees, either to peers or to others who are higher or lower in the hierarchy.[42]

The same type of analysis can be made for work groups, but in this case it is the manager's job that is most affected because he or she gives up tasks and authority to the group. The manager becomes more of a facilitator and less of a decision maker. In process redesign, managerial jobs are often eliminated.

Technology and Job Design

Technology: The organization of knowledge to achieve practical purposes.

Just as technology affects the macro structure of the organization, as discussed in Chapter 10, it has a major impact on the structure of individual jobs and groups of jobs. Until recently, no other factor has had as dramatic an effect on job design as specialization. Today the trend toward specialization is being reversed, partly as a result of the use of computers to perform some functions automatically.

Technology, in one form or another, affects everyone's job, whether one is a manager, a manufacturing employee, a clerk, or an accountant. Many people think of **technology** as machinery and equipment,[43] but it can also be defined more broadly as "tools in a general sense," to include intellectual tools such as computer languages and analytical and mathematical techniques. In its broadest interpretation, technology is the organization of knowledge to achieve practical purposes.[44] Most research, especially at the macro level, has been done using the narrower definition. However, we will consider tools of any kind used in any job. Of special interest is the sociotechnical interface: the point at which people work with technology.

As the use of technology grows by leaps and bounds, its impact on human beings increases in significance. Two technological developments are reshaping job design. First, robotics has been introduced into manufacturing facilities at a significant rate. Second, office automation, especially the personal computer, has the potential to reshape nearly everyone's job.

Robotics

One future scenario is almost a certainty: More and more manufacturing jobs will be automated and robotized. Most of the push to increase the use of robots comes from concern about the ability of U.S. firms to compete with foreign firms, especially firms in Pacific Rim countries. David Packard, former chairman of Hewlett-Packard, observes, "We have no choice but to automate because foreign competitors are doing so."[45] Robots have enabled many manufacturing firms to achieve extremely high levels of effectiveness and efficiency. Many jobs that were formerly held by human beings in steel and automobile plants and in virtually any major manufacturing facility are now performed by robots. In some contexts, robots have replaced human beings altogether. For example, in the Mazak Corporation's plant in northern Kentucky, from midnight to 8:00 A.M. the totally automated third shift is busy making parts for the Ford Motor Company and for appliances manufactured by GE. If a problem occurs, the machines will shut down and will be repaired the next day. Normally, the plant operates all night long without anyone there.[46]

The GMFanuc Robotics Corporation is an example of the increased use of automation and robots in manufacturing jobs in response to concern about the ability of U.S. firms to compete effectively with foreign firms.

Another scenario is also a certainty: The future will not see as much robotization as was once predicted. One reason is that experience has taught managers that total robotization is usually less productive than a combination of well-managed individuals and automated machinery working together. The GM joint venture with Toyota to manufacture Chevy Novas has shown quite clearly that this strategy works. GM's Fremont plant, which was once notorious for its inefficient and unproductive work force, became the most efficient and most productive plant in the GM system in a matter of months. The "new" operation uses automation with some robotization but stresses management of the work force as a key factor. Japanese management style, featuring participative management, proved to be a key factor in the operation's success.[47]

Millions of unionized workers are horrified at the thought of robotization. Thousands of unionized jobs disappear every year, and while the major setbacks in the automobile industry seem to be over, there is evidence that technological changes, especially robotization, may be reshaping the U.S. economy. There is great fear that the economy may become segmented into a large number of low-paying service jobs and a few high-paying high-technology jobs. Some observers fear that the middle class may disappear as a result.[48]

Robotization does not seem compatible with demands by workers for increased participation. Most jobs in highly automated situations, as well as the jobs left after robotization, are rather mundane and routine, often monotonous. Another concern is that highly automated, robotized work often reduces opportunities for self-management. Not only is the number of available jobs reduced, but those that are left are often reduced in both range and depth. It also becomes more difficult for workers to pace their own work—although computer software can alleviate this problem.

One of the major challenges for managers in the future will be to reconcile the increased expectations of individuals for participation and for more exciting jobs with the apparently decreasing number of opportunities caused by increasing levels of robotization and automation of all types.[49] Even when managers subscribe to a philosophy of encouraging personal growth in their employees, their ability to provide opportunities for growth may be limited in such cases. In addition, some people are fearful of change and have difficulty working in an environment where there are few people. On the other hand, Apple Computer's experience with robotization has been very favorable. Apple's Macintosh manufacturing facility in Fremont, California, produces 80,000 computers per month, one every twenty-three seconds, using fewer than 300 people, most of whom are not involved directly in manufacturing but engage in quality control and distribution. These jobs tend to be more enriched than they would have been without robotization. The mundane work has been automated, thereby freeing workers for decision making. Management realizes that more automation and robotization will be required for the plant to remain competitive. Peter Baron, the plant manager, comments, "We have to be the lowest-cost producer in the world by the time the Japanese figure out how to make a good computer."[50]

Office Automation and Electronic Communication

The power of the personal computer is only beginning to be realized, with the increased availability of user-friendly software often allowing groups to function as a team.[51] It seems inevitable that every manager, every professional, and perhaps even every staff member and operational employee will be using a PC, workstation, laptop, palm top, or personal digital assistant before the year 2000. Many firms, such as Federal Express, have already computerized their operations.[52] The PC is a form of technology that affects the design of almost everyone's job.[53] PCs allow their users not only to make more and faster decisions but to make better decisions. Because the PC handles number crunching, the individual (or group) problem solver has the time to be more creative.

A computer can be used in every phase of the problem-solving process. It can monitor the environment and analyze environmental factors to indicate potential problem areas or opportunities. It therefore helps the manager recognize and identify problems. The computer can also help generate solutions through what-if scenarios and can be used in evaluating alternatives, in implementation and control, and in monitoring the progress of action plans.

One consequence of the increased use of computers and related information systems is the flattening of the traditional pyramid. As more and more computers are networked, there is less need for middle-level managers and staff to process information up and down the hierarchy. Hercules, Inc., a diversified company engaged in construction, chemicals, aerospace, and defense, was able to reduce its levels of management from twelve to six, trimming about eighteen hundred jobs (about 7 percent of its work force), as a result of the introduction of a high-speed information network system.[54] Job reengineering depends heavily on the use of networked PCs for electronic mail, voice mail, and other electronic communication systems, which enable work to be redesigned around processes, teams, and networks.[55]

By the year 2000 it is likely that every manager, professional, and staff member will be using a computer of some kind, perhaps a laptop or notebook like the one shown here. Computers can be used in every phase of the problem-solving process.

Work at Home

One of the implications of PCs is that many people can perform their jobs at home. Individuals whose jobs consist largely of data analysis or data processing, such as insurance claim processors, can perform much of their work at home, receiving and transmitting data over telephone lines. A little more than 11.7 million Americans are self-employed at home, 9.4 million "moonlight" (perform a second job) from their home, and 13.7 million keep an office at home.[56] The desirability of working at home has been mentioned for many years, especially for people who have low-paying jobs or need to care for young children. It would not be possible for typical assembly-line work to be done at home, nor is this arrangement desirable for people who have to interact with others in order to perform their functions. There are other kinds of problems as well. People tend to overeat when they work at home, and there is no particular evidence that their productivity is increased.[57] However, some benefits accrue to individuals who work at home. For example, they spend less money on gas, lunch, and child care. Some benefits also accrue to the firm, such as reduced absenteeism; and to society, such as less pollution.[58] It is estimated that by the year 2000 one-third of the work force will work at home on a full- or part-time basis.[59]

Worker Expectations

Another important factor affecting job design is the expectations of the average employee with respect to his or her job. It is evident that the expectations of workers in Canada and the United States have risen in the last fifty years. Basic physiological and security needs are satisfied by most jobs; if they are not satisfied on the job, they will usually be satisfied by government support programs. Hence, workers tend to have higher-level social, esteem, or self-fulfillment needs.[60] They therefore want to participate more in the organization's decision-making processes.[61]

Also important from the standpoint of job design is the increasing diversity of the work force. Between 1990 and 2000, only 15 percent of the net new workers added to the labor force will be native-born white males. The remainder will be women and male minority-group members.[62] These changes in the composition of the work force are generating different worker expectations. There is greater concern for the quality of work life, which most often translates into a need for job enrichment. Fortunately, many of these expectations are compatible with the need for companies to become more competitive. Table 11.1 reveals how important various job experiences have been to workers. These expectations need to be considered in designing jobs.

The reality remains that workers in virtually all situations today have higher expectations than their predecessors did. They want more from their jobs.[63] To accomplish this and other ends, more and more firms have experimented with job enrichment, especially autonomous work teams. Job enrichment is being attempted in service as well as manufacturing firms. Citibank, for example, attempted to provide job enrichment for very pragmatic reasons, as this chapter's Quality Management Challenge reveals.

Another factor in workers' changing expectations is the dual wage earner family, sometimes called DINKS—"double income, no kids"—although many double-income families do have children. People in this group expect more from their work than other workers do. Still another factor is the aging of the work force: In 1970 the median age in the United States was twenty-eight, in 1980 it was thirty, and by 2000 it should be about thirty-five.[64] Much of this has to do with the aging of the baby boom generation as it moves through the total population, together with the fact that over the past few years birthrates have decreased and then stabilized. Daniel L. Yankelovich, a well-known surveyor of

---

TABLE 11.1 The Importance of Various Job Experiences

Rank Order of Importance

1. Chance to do something that makes you feel good about yourself.
2. Chances to accomplish something worthwhile.
3. Chances to learn new things.
4. Opportunity to develop your skills and abilities.
5. The amount of freedom you have on your job.
6. Chances you have to do things you do best.
7. Resources that you have to do your job.
8. Respect you receive from people you work with.
9. The amount of information you get about your job performance.
10. Your chances for taking part and making decisions.
11. The amount of job security you have.
12. The amount of pay you get.
13. The way you are treated by the people you work with.
14. The friendliness of people you work with.
15. The amount of praise you get for a job well done.
16. The amount of fringe benefits you get.
17. Chances for getting a promotion.
18. Physical surroundings of your job.

SOURCE: Patricia Winwick, "What You Really Want from Your Job," *Psychology Today* (May 1978). Reprinted with permission from *Psychology Today* Magazine, copyright © 1978 (PT Partners, L.P.).

Citibank's Job Enrichment Program

Citibank sought to achieve greater market penetration. To do so, it needed superb front-line employee/customer relations. But when it surveyed its customers it learned that its employees were not very customer oriented, at least not as perceived by the customer. Citibank recognized that it faced a serious management challenge.

According to bank vice-president George E. Segers, when management examined the causes of this problem, it concluded that employees were not customer oriented because they "didn't feel like somebody." The employees were very dissatisfied with their mundane jobs, and they therefore reacted to customers in an unenthusiastic manner. Keeping in mind that everyone wants to "feel like somebody," management redesigned many of the front-line and other positions in the bank. Among the changes were the following:

1. Delegating more authority so that one individual handles an entire transaction from the time it comes into the bank until it is completed.
2. Allowing employees to have more contact with customers and to use computers more extensively in performing their jobs.
3. Encouraging communication between departments.
4. Polling employees to find out what was dull and routine about their jobs before the bank automated those positions.
5. Engaging in substantial training and development for the entire work force.

Considerable training was required because new attitudes had to be formed by both managers and workers, and the actual skills involved had to be developed in those who would use them. Citibank has found its program to be quite successful.

SOURCE: Roy W. Walters, "Citibank Project: Improving Productivity Through Work Design," in Donald L. Kirkpatrick, ed., *How to Manage Change Effectively* (San Francisco: Jossey-Bass, 1985), pp. 195–208.

societal values, has observed the new values of the work force. He sees three key values increasing in importance: the need for leisure, the symbolic significance of having a paid job, and the insistence that jobs must become less depersonalized.[65] Yankelovich asserts that "throughout history, and certainly during the last century, American individualism stopped at the workplace door. Now it is knocking that door down, demanding entrance."[66]

Time Factors in Job Design

Jobs vary not only in content, but also in when they are performed. In an effort to solve a variety of problems, including absenteeism, tardiness, turnover, and the cost of benefits—as well as to satisfy employees' desire to spend more time with their families and to have more personal time—employers have made some changes in hours of work. Among the approaches used are flexi-time, part-time work, the compressed work week, and job sharing.[67]

Flexi-time

Many jobs now incorporate **flexi-time,** a system in which a worker is allowed to set his or her own hours within common ranges, as long as the total is forty hours a week. For example, an individual may choose to come in at 10:00 A.M. and leave at 6:00 P.M., as opposed to coming in at 9:00 and leaving at 5:00. In a truly flexible time system, the worker could come in and leave at different times each day or work for different segments of the day during the week.

Part-Time Workers

An increasing number of jobs that were formerly full time are now being performed by part-time employees. One of the key reasons is that this helps reduce the costs of employees to the organization. Benefits are typically much less extensive for part-time employees, and basic pay rates are usually lower as well.[68] Firms also employ workers part time in order to keep valued employees who do not want to work full time.[69] When employees who choose to work part-time are included, fully 25 percent of the work force, or 25 million people, are part-time workers.[70]

The Compressed Work Week

Another approach to work scheduling is the **compressed work week,** in which forty hours of work are scheduled to be completed in fewer than the traditional five days—usually in four days.[71] Organizations that have adopted this program include Atlantic Richfield, R. J. Reynolds, John Hancock, and General Dynamics. It is generally believed that the compressed work week offers employees the advantage of an extra day off and offers employers a means of reducing absenteeism and tardiness. However, the level of worker fatigue usually increases, especially with a three-day work week.

One clothing manufacturing plant has used the compressed work week successfully.[72] The plant improved its productivity in an industry in which a large number of job holders are single parents who need the additional time for family responsibilities. No lowered productivity at the end of the day was in evidence. The workers were, however, paid a piece rate, which may help explain the continuing high levels of productivity. Other companies have had less success and have terminated their compressed work week programs.

Job Sharing

Job sharing is another alternative approach to work scheduling. Typically, two individuals split the work day, although the sharing could be done on alternating days as well. Job sharing appeals to people who have children and cannot spend the whole day at work, who are retired or semiretired, or who simply do not want to work a full day. The employer gains the expertise of two people on the job, and if one worker is sick, only a half day of work is lost.[73] Because job sharing is a new technique, it is too soon to determine how effective it will be.

TQM and Job Design

Total quality management programs depend on and may also influence job design. For example, TQM programs change the nature of jobs by increasing employee decision-making power through job enrichment, autonomous work teams, and quality circles. They change the content of jobs through changes in inventorying procedures such as JIT (just-in-time) inventory systems. Continuous improvement is often incorporated into the worker's job as part of TQM. Concern for quality and taking the actions necessary to achieve quality are always part of employees' jobs in TQM. TQM also often uses advanced manufacturing technology, which also affects job design.[74]

Job Design as a Problem-Solving Process

As can be seen in Figure 11.6, a considerable amount is known about job design as a problem-solving process. This chapter has indicated the factors to be analyzed in the external environment and the organization, along with the relevant employee characteristics. The key issues identified were technology, computers, and the changing nature of work force demographics, values, and expectations. To recognize and identify problems, these and other factors must be considered, as must the job's existing design. Generating alternatives for changing a job's design focuses on changing the job's eight key dimensions. Some of the typical alternatives include work simplification, job rotation, job enlargement, job enrichment, autonomous work teams, quality circles, and other participative programs.

A manager might approach a job design problem in the following way: Suppose that a control report indicates a performance problem and the manager suspects that an employee might lack motivation. The manager might attribute the problem to the design of the employee's job. Or higher-level management might direct the manager to change the job's design as part of the company's strategy to become more competitive by reducing costs. The manager would analyze the situation—in this case, the unmotivated employee's characteristics and the organization's objectives. In that way he or she could determine what to do with the eight key job dimensions to make the job in question more motivating or more efficient. The manager would have to make certain assumptions about the nature of the individual in the job to be redesigned. The manager would then choose among the job design options described earlier in the chapter. The solution—say, job enrichment—would be implemented, perhaps by forming more natural work units or vertical loading. The manager might allow the employee to participate in redesigning his or her job. After a specified period, the manager would evaluate the effectiveness of the redesign.

FIGURE 11.6 JOB DESIGN AS A PROBLEM-SOLVING PROCESS

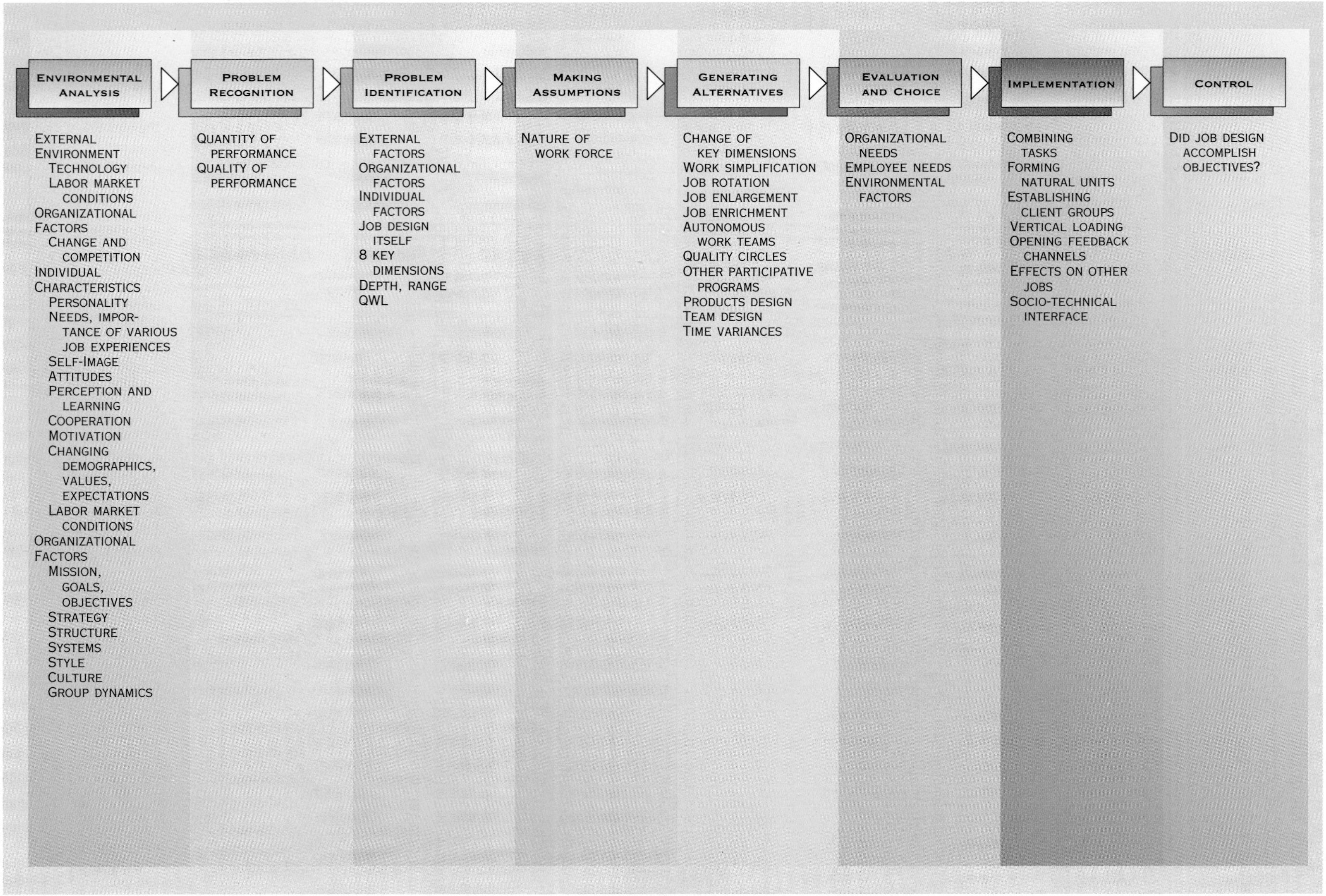

ENVIRONMENTAL ANALYSIS

EXTERNAL ENVIRONMENT
TECHNOLOGY
LABOR MARKET CONDITIONS
ORGANIZATIONAL FACTORS
CHANGE AND COMPETITION
INDIVIDUAL CHARACTERISTICS
PERSONALITY
NEEDS, IMPORTANCE OF VARIOUS JOB EXPERIENCES
SELF-IMAGE
ATTITUDES
PERCEPTION AND LEARNING
COOPERATION
MOTIVATION
CHANGING DEMOGRAPHICS, VALUES, EXPECTATIONS
LABOR MARKET CONDITIONS
ORGANIZATIONAL FACTORS
MISSION, GOALS, OBJECTIVES
STRATEGY
STRUCTURE
SYSTEMS
STYLE
CULTURE
GROUP DYNAMICS

PROBLEM RECOGNITION

QUANTITY OF PERFORMANCE
QUALITY OF PERFORMANCE

PROBLEM IDENTIFICATION

EXTERNAL FACTORS
ORGANIZATIONAL FACTORS
INDIVIDUAL FACTORS
JOB DESIGN ITSELF
8 KEY DIMENSIONS
DEPTH, RANGE
QWL

MAKING ASSUMPTIONS

NATURE OF WORK FORCE

GENERATING ALTERNATIVES

CHANGE OF KEY DIMENSIONS
WORK SIMPLIFICATION
JOB ROTATION
JOB ENLARGEMENT
JOB ENRICHMENT
AUTONOMOUS WORK TEAMS
QUALITY CIRCLES
OTHER PARTICIPATIVE PROGRAMS
PRODUCTS DESIGN
TEAM DESIGN
TIME VARIANCES

EVALUATION AND CHOICE

ORGANIZATIONAL NEEDS
EMPLOYEE NEEDS
ENVIRONMENTAL FACTORS

IMPLEMENTATION

COMBINING TASKS
FORMING NATURAL UNITS
ESTABLISHING CLIENT GROUPS
VERTICAL LOADING
OPENING FEEDBACK CHANNELS
EFFECTS ON OTHER JOBS
SOCIO-TECHNICAL INTERFACE

CONTROL

DID JOB DESIGN ACCOMPLISH OBJECTIVES?

Summary

(Before reading this summary, look again at the objectives listed at the beginning of the chapter.)

1. The situational model of job design has three components: recognition of the impact of environmental and organizational factors, the individual characteristics of the job holder, and the primary job dimensions. The interaction of these components produces performance and job satisfaction.

2. The core job dimensions are task variety, task identity, task significance, autonomy, and feedback. The three contextual dimensions that help define a job are interpersonal relations, authority and responsibility for goal setting, and communication patterns.

3. The major job design options are work simplification, job rotation, job enlargement, job enrichment, autonomous work teams, and quality circles. Work simplification involves reducing the job to as narrow a set of tasks as possible. Job rotation means moving a person from one job to another. Job enlargement means increasing the number of tasks in an individual's job (range). Job enrichment means increasing the individual's decision-making authority (depth). At the group level, autonomous work teams and quality circles increase decision making by team members.

4. Each of the five implementation actions will affect one or more of the core job characteristics. Employees will attain one or more of three critical psychological states—experiencing the work as meaningful, taking responsibility for outcomes, and being aware of the results of work activities—depending on the strength of the employee's need for growth. If these states are reached, the desired personal and work outcomes will occur.

5. An individual who has a high need for growth will respond more favorably to the core job characteristics than will one with a low need for growth.

6. Technology affects job design by changing the tasks necessary to perform a job. Robotics often eliminates jobs and drains enrichment from those that remain. Computers aid managers in every stage of problem solving and free them to be more creative.

7. Workers today expect more from their jobs in terms of satisfaction of higher-level needs.

8. Job design can be viewed as a problem-solving process in which the manager identifies a problem related to the characteristics of a particular job and solves it by redesigning that job.

General Questions

THINKING ABOUT MANAGEMENT

1. Why are so many employers concerned about the quality of work life?

2. Which would you consider to be a "superior" form of job redesign, one that improves range or one that improves depth? Explain your answer.

3. Think of several jobs with which you are familiar. Do these jobs need to be enlarged? Enriched? Could they be performed better by autonomous work teams or quality circles? Can you think of jobs that could not be enriched, at least not on a cost-benefit basis?

4. Why do you think so many union leaders typically oppose job enrichment and job enlargement?

5. Indicate how technology affects the design of a job you have held.

6. How has the personal computer changed the design of the job of college student?

7. Select a typical job and describe how you would use the core job dimensions to enrich it.

Questions on the Management Challenge Features

DIVERSITY MANAGEMENT CHALLENGE

1. What are some of the problems of having staff members from thirteen different countries working together in teams?

2. How did BP solve those problems?

QUALITY MANAGEMENT CHALLENGE

1. Why did Citicorp embark on a job enrichment program?

2. What were the results?

GLOBAL MANAGEMENT CHALLENGE

1. Why was Nissan forced to redesign jobs?

2. The most likely effect of job redesign is work simplification. How do you think Japanese workers will react? What are the implications for productivity?

Job Redesign at Volvo

In late 1992 Volvo announced that it would close its Udevalla and Kalmar plants. In the end, declining sales and the need to become more cost competitive had spelled doom for these two plants.

DISCUSSION QUESTIONS

1. Is there any way to make enriched jobs more productive?
2. How do you think these plants were affected by the European 1992 initiative and the success of Japanese firms in European markets?

Shifting the Focus from Operations to Customers

One of the first actions David O'Neal took when he became director of the Orange County Convention Center was to give his subordinates an interaction survey. The survey asked respondents to indicate the importance of their interpersonal activities on the job. Such a survey is used to determine the need to locate certain people's offices near each other, to determine whether the existing patterns of communication are appropriate, and to determine who or what activity is the focal point of the organization. The results were surprising. The operations manager turned out to be at the hub of the organization. (See the organization chart.) Interviews with subordinates revealed that because of this situation there were communication roadblocks and that more attention was given to staging the shows and physically supporting them (the operations function) than to satisfying customers' needs. Moreover, there was no one in charge of bookings, and there were only two evening coordinators, whose function was principally to serve as a liaison with the client groups (exhibitors at conventions held in the facility). The coordinators were not spending much time on customer service. O'Neal wondered how to redesign certain jobs and whether to create new ones.

DISCUSSION QUESTIONS

1. What job(s) would you create if you were O'Neal?
2. How would you restructure existing jobs?

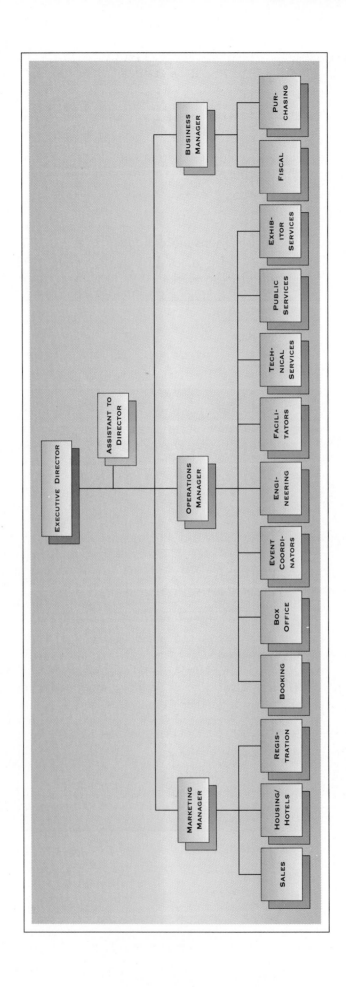

416

The Eight Primary Job Dimensions

Think about the jobs you have had or the job you would like to have when you graduate. How important have the various primary job dimensions been to you? How important are they to you now? How important will they be in future jobs? What are you looking for in the job you will get upon completion of this course? In the space provided, rank the eight dimensions in accordance with their importance to you, from 1 (most important) to 8 (least important).

Primary Job Dimensions	Rank in Current or Last Job, or Job upon Graduation	Rank in Next Job After That
Task Variety	_____	_____
Task Identity	_____	_____
Task Significance	_____	_____
Autonomy	_____	_____
Feedback	_____	_____
Interpersonal Relationships	_____	_____
Authority and Responsibility for Goal Setting	_____	_____
Communication	_____	_____

Why did you rank these items as you did? What will be different in your future job than in your current job? What do the rankings tell you about your needs previously, now, and in the future?

"Only 15 percent of the net growth in the work force—those entering minus those leaving—will be comprised of white males by the year 2000."

—Hudson Institute's "Work Force 2000" report

"Traditional ways of managing a work force don't work anymore."

—Donna Taylor, Manager, Valuing Differences Program, Digital Equipment Company

Staffing and Human Resource Management

419

Toyota, an Exacting Employer

When you invest $800 million in a plant in Georgetown, Kentucky, as a spearhead for your sales operation in the United States, you want to be doubly sure that you hire the right three thousand people to run it. And when you compete on the basis of quality, manage by teamwork, seek flexibility in your work force, and also want loyal employees, you want to be quadruply sure you hire the right people. How do you ensure that the right workers will be hired?

If you are Toyota, you run them through twenty-five hours of tests, including a grueling final interview. You probe not just for educational levels and technical skills, but for personality factors as well. You test people with paper-and-pencil tests and with job simulations. Applicants are even put through job simulations for positions they are not applying for. Their interpersonal skills are noted. There are mock production lines where they must actually assemble something. The company is looking for people who can maintain a fast pace and endure tedious work, yet remain alert.

Only one applicant in twenty makes it to the interview, which is conducted by a team made up of representatives of various Toyota departments. Some say that this "fussiness" is aimed at keeping out pro-union workers. Others say the reason is that Japanese firms fear that American workers lack good work habits. Some government officials fear that Toyota's system can be traced to racial discrimination. At Toyota, the proportion of minority group members in management positions is lower than the proportion of applicants from minority groups, and the same is true for women. Regardless of the reasons, Toyota is taking great pains to select the proper people. There is no shortage of applicants for the 2,700 production jobs and the 300 office jobs, either. A labor pool of more than 60,000 people applied for the production jobs, so Toyota can afford to be choosy.

SOURCES: Chuck Cosentino, John Allen, and Richard Wellins, "Choosing the Right People," *HR Magazine* (March 1990), pp. 66–70; and Richard Koenig, "Exacting Employer: Toyota Takes Pains, and Time Filling Jobs at Its Kentucky Plant," *Wall Street Journal* (December 1, 1987), pp. 1, 31.

Never before has an organization's strategic success depended so heavily on its human resources, and never before has managing human resources been so difficult.[1] From the standpoint of global competitiveness, the changing nature of the work force poses a very great management challenge to U.S. firms.[2] Firms like Toyota carefully select their employees in order to eliminate the problems associated with the U.S. work force: lack of education, lack of skills, questionable motivation, increasing cultural diversity (which makes management more complex), and in some cases lack of the simple coping skills required in a work environment. Most other firms do not have the luxury of being able to pick and choose among applicants. As a result, they often must educate their employees—teaching them basic skills—and they must learn how to manage cultural diversity.

This chapter discusses the topics of human resource management and staffing. **Human resource management** (HRM) is the process of first placing employees in jobs and then managing those employees. HRM thus can be described as the process of putting the right people with the right skills in the right place at the right time with the right motivation in order to achieve the organization's strategy.[3] **Staffing** relates to the individual manager's role in the HRM process. Toyota is representative of a number of companies that are taking a new approach to staffing and HRM, an approach that differs in several ways from the one used by most firms:

- It is more strategic in nature.[4]
- Human resources are now considered more critical to accomplishing the organization's mission.
- There is greater concern with overall governance of the work force, as opposed to simple labor relations.
- Emphasis is placed on managing the organization's culture.
- There is a renewed interest in teamwork.
- There is more concern with outcomes.
- There is increased recognition of the importance of human resources to total quality management (TQM) as well as to the other strategic imperatives—innovation, continuous improvement, flexibility, and speed.
- There is a movement from training in specific skills to broader development of the employee on a long-term basis.
- There is greater recognition of the need to manage cultural diversity.[5]

At Toyota, for example, there is an emphasis on team management. The employee is viewed from a strategic perspective, and programs have been developed to improve the utilization of human resources in the organization. The emphasis is on long-term employee development and overall management of human resources, as opposed to simply dealing with traditional personnel issues. Results are important.

In most organizations with one hundred or more employees, there is a human resource management or personnel department. As an organization grows, and as its commitment to HRM increases, the size, strength, power, and importance of the HRM department also increase. The role of the individual manager in the staffing process also changes; normally it decreases.

HRM is managed like any other function of the organization and any other management problem. Planning, organizing, leading, and controlling are integral parts of HRM. As with any other management function, staffing and HRM are problem-solving processes.

Human resource management (HRM): *The process of first placing employees in jobs and then managing those employees; putting the right people with the right skills in the right place at the right time with the right motivation in order to accomplish the organization's strategy.*

Staffing: The individual manager's role in the HRM process.

At Toyota, the employee is viewed from a strategic perspective; programs have been developed to improve the utilization of human resources in the organization. These prospective employees are taking tests that they must pass if they are to become Toyota employees.

Human Resource Management Practices

HRM practices, whether they are part of the individual manager's staffing activities or performed by the HRM department, are of two principal types: those concerned with placing the employee in the job, and those concerned with the relationship between the job holder and the organization. (See Figure 12.1.) The first series of practices occurs sequentially, whereas the second occurs in the same period on an ongoing basis. In the remainder of this chapter, these practices are described in more detail: first from the perspective of the HRM department, then in terms of the manager's role, and finally from the standpoint of equal employment opportunity (EEO). These three-part descriptions are designed to help you understand the setting within which the individual manager operates and what is expected of him or her.

Equal Employment Opportunity (EEO)

Equal employment opportunity (EEO): *A set of regulations barring employers from basing HRM decisions on race, sex, color, religion, national origin, physical or mental handicap (disability), pregnancy, age, or veteran status.*

As can be seen in Figure 12.1, **equal employment opportunity** (EEO) is an externally imposed requirement that affects HRM practices in virtually all organizations (those with fifteen or more employees, in most cases). EEO laws bar organizations from making human resource decisions on the basis of race, color, sex, religion, national origin, physical and mental handicap (disabilities), pregnancy, age, or veteran status. EEO law is enforced principally by the Equal Employment Opportunity Commission (EEOC) of the federal government. It is also enforced by various state EEO agencies. A number of laws (shown in Table 12.1) define the standards to which employers must adhere. These laws are defined in great detail in guidelines issued by various federal EEO enforcement agencies, principally the EEOC. Often the courts further define which personnel practices are or are not acceptable. Major EEO issues often end up in the United States Supreme Court.[6]

Employers must also adhere to state EEO laws and guidelines. These vary from one state to another and in some cases are more stringent than federal laws and guidelines.

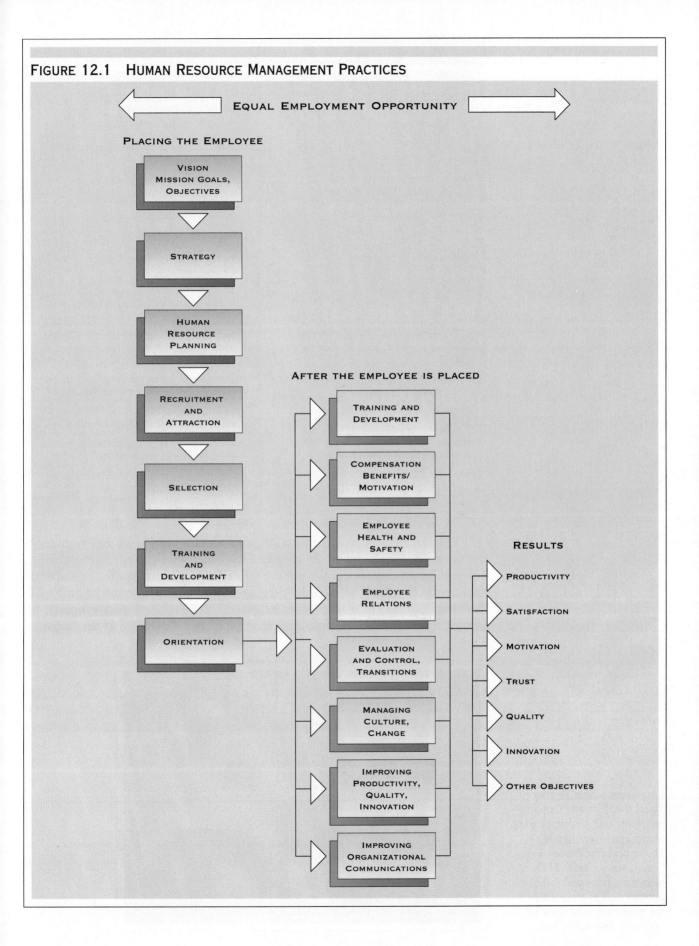

FIGURE 12.1   HUMAN RESOURCE MANAGEMENT PRACTICES

EQUAL EMPLOYMENT OPPORTUNITY

PLACING THE EMPLOYEE

VISION
MISSION GOALS,
OBJECTIVES

STRATEGY

HUMAN
RESOURCE
PLANNING

RECRUITMENT
AND
ATTRACTION

SELECTION

TRAINING
AND
DEVELOPMENT

ORIENTATION

AFTER THE EMPLOYEE IS PLACED

TRAINING AND
DEVELOPMENT

COMPENSATION
BENEFITS/
MOTIVATION

EMPLOYEE
HEALTH AND
SAFETY

EMPLOYEE
RELATIONS

EVALUATION
AND CONTROL,
TRANSITIONS

MANAGING
CULTURE,
CHANGE

IMPROVING
PRODUCTIVITY,
QUALITY,
INNOVATION

IMPROVING
ORGANIZATIONAL
COMMUNICATIONS

RESULTS

PRODUCTIVITY

SATISFACTION

MOTIVATION

TRUST

QUALITY

INNOVATION

OTHER OBJECTIVES

TABLE 12.1 Principal Federal EEO Laws and Related HRM Requirements

Federal Law	Requirements
Title VII, Civil Rights Act of 1964, as amended in 1972, and by the Equal Employment Opportunity Act of 1978	Prohibits discrimination in employment decisions based on race, color, sex, religion, and national origin, for employers of 15 or more employees in both public and private sectors.
Executive Orders 11141, 11246, and 11375, of 1964, 1965, and 1967	Prohibit discrimination in employment decisions based on age, race, color, sex, religion, and national origin, for federal government contractors and subcontractors.
Pregnancy Discrimination Act of 1978 (amendment to Title VII)	Requires pregnancy/maternity to be treated as any other significant disability would be treated.
Equal Pay Act of 1963	Prohibits wage discrimination on the basis of sex. Mandates equal pay for equal work.
Age Discrimination in Employment Act of 1967 as amended in 1978, 1986, and 1988	Prohibits employment discrimination on the basis of age. Specifically protects individuals age 40 or older.
Rehabilitation Act of 1973 as amended in 1986	Prohibits employment discrimination on the basis of physical and mental handicaps.
Vietnam-Era Veteran's Readjustment Act of 1974	Provides for affirmative action for Vietnam-era veterans and for disabled veterans.
Americans with Disabilities Act of 1990 (became effective July 26, 1992)	Protects 43 million Americans from discrimination in employment.
Civil Rights Act of 1991	Makes it easier for employees to bring suit claiming job discrimination.

Historically, the major thrust of equal employment laws and regulations was access to employment. As greater access has been gained, more attention has been given to how employees are treated. Daily management of the work force has been greatly affected by these laws, and managers must be attuned to their implications. Managers must be careful to treat employees properly, according to the law. A significant implication of these laws is that the organiza-

Employers adhere to state Equal Employment Opportunity laws and guidelines when hiring employees like telephone operator Nancy Thibeault, shown here. EEO laws vary from one state to another and in some cases are more stringent than federal laws and guidelines.

tion and its managers must carefully document HRM actions in the event that a person complains to the EEOC or another enforcement agency or files a suit claiming discrimination.

In the 1990s, the major EEO-related issues confronting business include complying with the Americans with Disabilities Act; eliminating "glass ceilings" that limit the upward mobility of women and members of minority groups; accommodating employees with AIDS; accommodating employees with children or other dependents; preventing sexual harassment; and helping employees overcome problems related to alcohol and drug abuse.

Companies and nonprofit organizations respond to these laws and issues in varying ways. Some comply unwillingly and minimally. Others respond positively, even wholeheartedly, as this chapter's Diversity Management Challenge reveals. When you have read this feature, you should be able to describe the U.S. West program.

Placing the Employee

Placing employees in jobs involves all the practices that occur up to the point at which the employee is able to carry out assigned tasks on the job. Thus, human resource planning, recruitment, selection, orientation, and training and development are components of placement. In the following sections we will discuss each of these practices in detail.

Human Resource Planning

Historically, the HRM department has been responsible for human resource planning. **Human resource planning,** often referred to as personnel planning, is the process of determining the staffing requirements necessary to carry out an organization's strategy. It is part of the organizing and systems components of strategy implementation, as shown in Figure 12.2. There was very little human resource planning in most business organizations until recently, when the strategic importance of human resources came to be recognized more fully.

The human resource planning function involves refining the specifics of the macro organizational structure discussed in Chapters 9 and 10. The job design

Human resource planning: The process of determining the staffing requirements necessary to carry out an organization's strategy, also referred to as personnel planning.

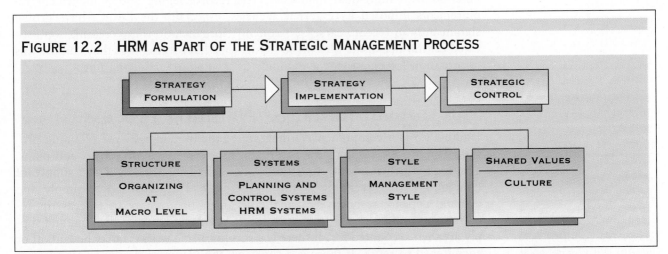

FIGURE 12.2   HRM AS PART OF THE STRATEGIC MANAGEMENT PROCESS

SOURCE: ADAPTED FROM FIGURE 8.2, STRATEGIC MANAGEMENT, TEXT AND CASES, 5TH ED., BY J. HIGGINS AND J. VINCZE, COPYRIGHT © 1993 BY THE DRYDEN PRESS, INC., A DIVISION OF HOLT, RINEHART AND WINSTON, INC., REPRINTED BY PERMISSION OF THE PUBLISHER.

A Woman-Friendly Company

Companies can benefit and encourage women employees in a variety of ways. Some attempt to decrease the travel time, relocation requirements, and long hours that could discourage women with family responsibilities. Others offer extended leaves, flexi-time, and elder care assistance. Those that are serious about retaining and promoting women pursue policies aimed at preventing discrimination and sexual harassment.

But for those who wish to be genuinely woman-friendly, such policies don't tackle the real barriers, which are more subtle and more complex. To create an environment in which everyone actually has an opportunity to contribute, participate, *and advance,* some traditional corporate practices must be challenged. This appproach can involve goals for promoting women as well as for increasing men's awareness of unfair practices. It includes recognizing that the top echelon of business has historically been reserved for men, and that women still need to work harder than men to enter it and remain in it. "When they excel," notes *Business Week,* "it's generally without the support, gossip, glad-handing, and socializing that ease the way for men. Add to that the outright bias many male executives still harbor, and you've got one lumpy playing field."

One company that is seeking to level the field is U.S. West Communications. At the top 1 percent salary level ($68,000 and up), women hold 21 percent of the jobs at U.S. West. Management intends to increase this number, already higher than at most American firms, to 35 percent within ten years. U.S. West—like a few other exceptional companies in industries as varied as chemicals, computers, and banking—is attempting to smooth the way to the top for the women in its ranks.

The attempt to encourage women at U.S. West has been a sustained one.

---

activity discussed in Chapter 11 is also usually considered part of human resource planning and is normally carried out by the HRM department in conjunction with individual managers. The recordkeeping and management requirements imposed by external agencies, especially the EEOC, have grown significantly in recent years. Consequently, organizations are creating sophisticated central personnel files. In so doing, they have found that they can use this information for employment planning as well as for reporting purposes.

The Human Resource Planning Process

AT TOYOTA: Toyota focuses on matching employees to strategic tasks. The company therefore is extremely careful about the people it hires, what they can do, and how its strategy can best be carried out.

Figure 12.3 is a comprehensive diagram of the human resource planning process. The process begins with an organization's strategic objectives and plans. The requirements for meeting these are then compared with the supply of human resources available in the marketplace. Human resource supply and demand depend, respectively, on the organization's ability to forecast its requirements and on its existing work force. Variances between demand and supply are then accounted for. If there is a surplus, some workers may be laid off or encouraged to retire. If there is a shortage, the firm may decide to recruit new employees or pay existing employees to work overtime, among other options.

Sensitivity training on gender issues has been provided for fifteen years. Women's groups have been active within the company and have helped to change its culture and expand opportunities.

Top management views pluralism as a business strategy. In 1987, the company began an accelerated development program for women of color after a study revealed the following numbers: One out of every 21 white males reached middle-management positions or higher, but only one out of 138 white women and one out of 289 nonwhite women did so. Women were leaving the company primarily because they did not see opportunities to advance, according to the program's director.

The program sought to identify the women of color with the greatest leadership potential, including good communication skills, strategic planning ability, ability to handle adversity, and diversity of experience. It included a week-long workshop in which participants played games to show, among other things, that women "are taught to be helpless." Other workshops assessed their potential to be corporate officers with exercises on mergers and acquisitions, marketing strategies, and public-relations crises. Within two years, half the women who had participated had been promoted, some twice. None had left the company. And the number of nonwhite women reaching middle management had increased to one in 189.

U.S. West attacked another side of the problem by developing a Pluralism Performance Menu. The menu evaluates the top 125 corporate officers on how well they meet particular criteria, the overall profile of their organization, and whether their work force reflects the composition of the labor force in their geographic area. If the population base is diverse and managers hire and promote only white males, their salaries may be reduced or their annual bonuses forfeited.

SOURCES: Walecia Konrad, "Welcome to the Woman-Friendly Company," *Business Week* (August 6, 1990), pp. 48–55; and Cathy Trost, "Firms Heed Women Employees' Needs," *Wall Street Journal* (November 22, 1989), p. B1.

The Impact of Cultural Diversity

Figure 12.4 details several changes in the demographics of the American work force and U.S. society in general. Each of these changes will require modifications in HRM practices in the next few years. One of the major consequences of these changes is increased emphasis on managing **cultural diversity,** a situation in which several cultures coexist within the same organization or the same society. Broadly interpreted, this includes the emergence of women and older workers as well as ethnic minorities as major components of the work force.[7] In an even broader context, it can mean people from several countries working together. Cultural diversity is discussed in more depth in Chapter 13.

Other factors that will influence HRM practices in the future include the lack of skills among many workers in these population groups, which means that employers must train them in these skills. The changing expectations of workers will lead employers to revise their motivation systems. Also significant is the existence of two age waves in the population—the baby-boomers followed by the baby-busters—which cause periodic shortages and surpluses of labor. These age waves, in turn, result in various efforts to adjust the size of the work force by, for example, hiring part-time workers.[8]

Today, part-time or contingent workers account for about 25 percent of the labor force. The benefits of such workers to the corporation are obvious.

Cultural diversity: The existence of different cultures within an organization or society; includes the emergence of women, older workers, and ethnic minorities as major components of the work force, as well as people from different countries working together.

FIGURE 12.3 THE HUMAN RESOURCE PLANNING PROCESS

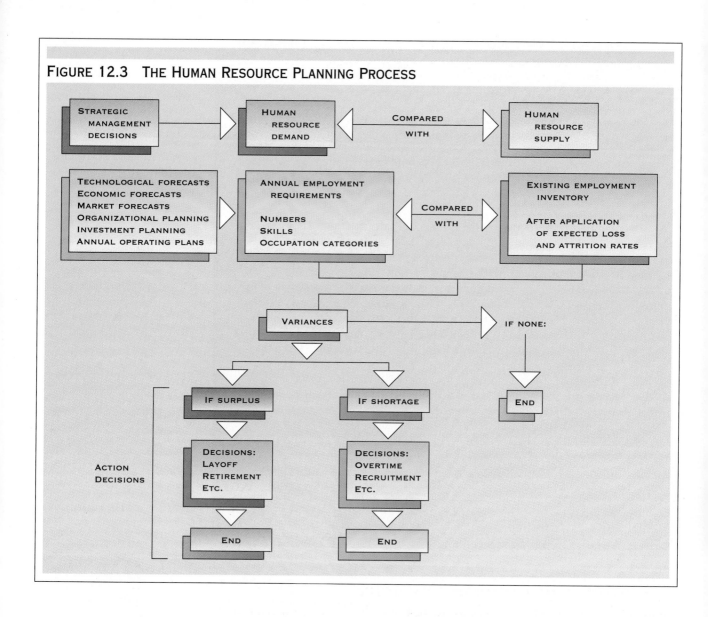

STRATEGIC MANAGEMENT DECISIONS → HUMAN RESOURCE DEMAND ← COMPARED WITH → HUMAN RESOURCE SUPPLY

TECHNOLOGICAL FORECASTS
ECONOMIC FORECASTS
MARKET FORECASTS
ORGANIZATIONAL PLANNING
INVESTMENT PLANNING
ANNUAL OPERATING PLANS

ANNUAL EMPLOYMENT REQUIREMENTS

NUMBERS
SKILLS
OCCUPATION CATEGORIES

COMPARED WITH

EXISTING EMPLOYMENT INVENTORY

AFTER APPLICATION OF EXPECTED LOSS AND ATTRITION RATES

VARIANCES → IF NONE:

IF SURPLUS   IF SHORTAGE   END

ACTION DECISIONS

DECISIONS:
LAYOFF
RETIREMENT
ETC.

DECISIONS:
OVERTIME
RECRUITMENT
ETC.

END   END

Publix is one of the many employers that have found that hiring retired workers for part-time jobs pays off. With a shortage of available teenage labor due to changing demographics, older workers are an excellent source of labor for service industries.

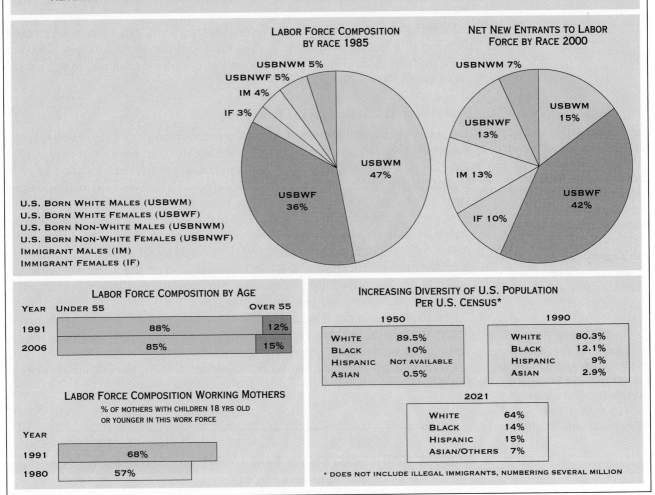

FIGURE 12.4 CHANGES IN THE AMERICAN WORK FORCE

THE SHEER SIZE OF THE BABY-BOOM GENERATION, THE LARGE NUMBERS OF WOMEN ENTERING THE WORK FORCE, AND SUCH OTHER FACTORS AS HISPANIC IMMIGRATION HAVE DRAMATICALLY ALTERED THE PROFILE OF THE "TYPICAL" AMERICAN WORKER.

LABOR FORCE COMPOSITION BY RACE 1985

USBNWM 5%
USBNWF 5%
IM 4%
IF 3%
USBWM 47%
USBWF 36%

NET NEW ENTRANTS TO LABOR FORCE BY RACE 2000

USBNWM 7%
USBWM 15%
USBNWF 13%
IM 13%
USBWF 42%
IF 10%

U.S. BORN WHITE MALES (USBWM)
U.S. BORN WHITE FEMALES (USBWF)
U.S. BORN NON-WHITE MALES (USBNWM)
U.S. BORN NON-WHITE FEMALES (USBNWF)
IMMIGRANT MALES (IM)
IMMIGRANT FEMALES (IF)

LABOR FORCE COMPOSITION BY AGE

Year	Under 55	Over 55
1991	88%	12%
2006	85%	15%

LABOR FORCE COMPOSITION WORKING MOTHERS

% OF MOTHERS WITH CHILDREN 18 YRS OLD OR YOUNGER IN THIS WORK FORCE

Year	
1991	68%
1980	57%

INCREASING DIVERSITY OF U.S. POPULATION PER U.S. CENSUS*

1950		1990	
WHITE	89.5%	WHITE	80.3%
BLACK	10%	BLACK	12.1%
HISPANIC	NOT AVAILABLE	HISPANIC	9%
ASIAN	0.5%	ASIAN	2.9%

2021	
WHITE	64%
BLACK	14%
HISPANIC	15%
ASIAN/OTHERS	7%

* DOES NOT INCLUDE ILLEGAL IMMIGRANTS, NUMBERING SEVERAL MILLION

SOURCES: KATE BALLEN, "HOW AMERICA WILL CHANGE OVER THE NEXT 30 YEARS," FORTUNE (1992), P. 12; "A PORTRAIT OF AMERICA: HOW THE COUNTRY IS CHANGING," BUSINESS WEEK (SPECIAL ISSUE, "REINVENTING AMERICA," 1992), PP. 51–58; "NEEDED: HUMAN CAPITAL," BUSINESS WEEK (SEPTEMBER 19, 1988), PP. 102–103.

When employees work only part-time or for short periods, their wages are usually lower, they are entitled to fewer benefits, and the cost of the worker to the employer is significantly reduced. An individual might prefer to keep a job at a reduced total compensation rate rather than lose it.[9]

Another trend in employment planning is a consequence of the shortage of unskilled labor. Because of changes in the age makeup of the population, there are fewer people in the eighteen- to twenty-five-year-old age group than formerly. Therefore, many employers are hiring more older workers. Employers like McDonald's are finding that older people are excellent employees when placed in the right job. Also, they often require fewer benefits, especially if they work part-time and are already receiving social security benefits.

The individual manager works within the HRM policies established by the organization, whether those are made by an HRM department or by the president of a small company. The manager may help design job descriptions and specifications but often is involved in only a minor way in human resource planning. Most managers are not involved in the strategic planning aspects of employment planning. Instead, their role is to determine certain aspects of individual job designs and job descriptions. Often it is the manager who must hire or terminate people according to the strategic HRM plan. Managers tend to be reactive rather than proactive in staffing. The manager's role is portrayed in Figure 12.5.

Firms today, especially large firms, and their managers must begin to think in terms of a global work force.[10] They must look for applicants in other countries, not just in the United States. Scientific talent, for example, may be much more readily available overseas.[11]

Job Analysis and Design

Job analysis: The process in which existing and potential jobs are analyzed or reanalyzed, designed or redesigned, to ensure that they help fulfill the company's mission.

Job description: A description of the responsibilities and duties of a job.

Job specification: A description of the kind of person needed to perform a job, in terms of skills, knowledge, and abilities; used as the basis of recruitment and selection.

Job analysis is a major part of human resource planning. This process, which ultimately leads to job design, helps create the demand portion of Figure 12.3. Existing and potential jobs must be analyzed or reanalyzed, designed or redesigned, to ensure that they help fulfill the company's mission. Job analysis begins with an examination of the job and its place in the organization. It continues with an in-depth analysis of the activity and concludes by producing a **job description**—the responsibilities and duties included in the job—and a **job specification**—the skills, knowledge, and abilities needed by the person performing the job. The job specification is the basis for recruitment and selection. Most job analyses are performed by professional job analysts, but supervisors, the job holder, or both may also perform the analysis.

Job analysis is performed through observation; interviews with job incumbents, supervisors, or others; questionnaires; or the use of a diary or log to describe an individual's job performance.

There is no standard format for a job description, but it usually includes the following:

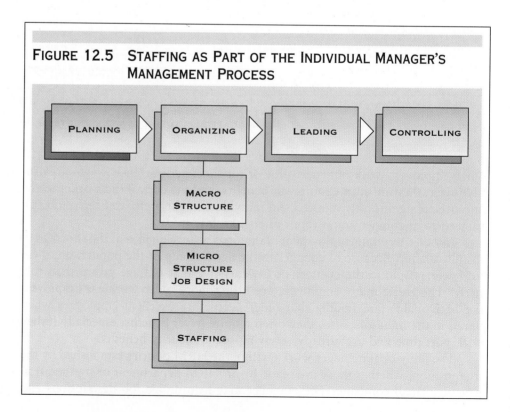

FIGURE 12.5   STAFFING AS PART OF THE INDIVIDUAL MANAGER'S MANAGEMENT PROCESS

There is no standard format for a job description, but it usually includes relevant working conditions and the physical environment: lighting, noise levels, heat, hazardous conditions, and the like. Many workers would not be comfortable in hectic environments like the Foreign Exchange trading floor at the Deutsche Bank, shown here.

1. *The job title.* (More than twenty thousand titles are available in the *Dictionary of Occupational Titles.*[12])
2. *A job summary:* A brief statement of the content of the job.
3. *A description of job activities:* Descriptions of the tasks performed and materials used and the extent of supervision given or received.
4. *Relevant working conditions and physical environment:* Lighting, noise levels, heat, hazardous conditions, and the like.
5. *The job's social environment:* Information about the work group and interpersonal relationships required to perform the job.
6. *Compensation and benefits:*[13]

Job design can be accomplished through the rational approach or the behavioral approach. The *rational approach* emphasizes the scientific study of a series of tasks and the design of jobs so that each job includes as few tasks as possible and therefore can be performed efficiently by any worker. The *behavioral approach* examines a job's core dimensions—those that lead to meaningful work, responsibility for outcomes, or knowledge of results—and builds the job around them.[14]

Often a manager supervises individuals in jobs designed by others, principally job analysts and personnel specialists or engineers. Nevertheless, the manager should look for opportunities to improve the design of those jobs, not only scientifically but also in terms of the core job dimensions. Managers must be able to help identify candidates who match the specifications that result from job analysis. Managers should also ensure that job descriptions are accurate and timely. In the future, many jobs will be designed around teams of workers. The members of those teams will share the contents of jobs that were formerly independent.

Forecasting the Need for Human Resources

The organization must predict its future needs and compare them with its current supply of job holders. Future human resource requirements depend heavily on the existing and potential demand for the organization's products or services.

Managers must forecast the anticipated demand for labor and staff accordingly.[15] Because the labor force will undergo dramatic demographic changes during the 1990s, careful human resources planning is more critical now than ever.[16]

An important consideration is the mix of current employees. A human resource audit—a systematic inventory of personnel—can be used to provide this information. Such an audit produces a human resource inventory database. In many organizations, obtaining this database is an ongoing process; the data are updated periodically. The database provides information about employees who could be promoted, the need for training and development, and whether certain workers should be replaced. The necessary data can be extracted from the overall human resource information system.

The need for such a database should be obvious. In fact, however, relatively few organizations maintain one, although more are recognizing the need to do so.[17] Organizations like IBM, Disney, and the U.S. Civil Service Commission have databases that allow them to plan for their employees' careers and to match individuals to the jobs for which they are best suited.[18]

Job Specifications and EEO

Job specifications must not include requirements beyond those that are truly necessary to perform in the job. (This subject is discussed in more detail later in the chapter.) Unnecessary requirements, such as arbitrary education levels, would eliminate certain applicants from consideration and, hence, might be used to discriminate. Such discrimination is prohibited under EEO guidelines.

Recruitment

Recruitment: A series of activities intended to attract a qualified pool of job applicants.

Recruitment consists of a series of activities intended to attract a qualified pool of job applicants. It involves the HRM actions taken from job design through the filing of an application form by a prospective employee. Once that first contact has been made, the selection process begins. Individuals who are recruited have abilities that match the job specifications determined in the human resource planning process. Once a pool of qualified applicants has been obtained, the selection process will determine which applicant will be hired to perform the job.

Recruitment can occur either internally or externally. Current employees have a legal right under EEO laws to apply for other jobs in the company. Similarly, the company must notify current employees of available positions. This normally takes place through the "posting" of job openings on bulletin boards or through memos. Most firms try to promote from within as well as hire from outside. If positions are filled only through promotion, the company will not benefit from ideas brought in by new employees. If it does not promote at least some of its current employees, morale suffers. As firms attempt to achieve greater cultural diversity in management, it is likely that more jobs will be filled by promoting from within.

Recruitment can also be conducted either actively or passively. *Active recruitment* involves placing advertisements in various media—newspapers, radio, television, trade journals, and the like; visiting high schools, colleges, and other places where applicants may be found; and making contacts with people who will seek applicants for the organization—employment agencies and union hiring agents, for example. *Passive recruitment* means that the organization simply waits for applicants to walk in and apply for the available jobs. Passive recruitment is quite common in many industries. Banking, for example, attracts numerous suitable applicants because of its positive image (though not because of high salaries). Banks seldom have to recruit applicants for any positions except low-paying front-line jobs, such as tellers, and certain highly specialized or top-management positions.

Most organizations must actively recruit employees. Location, specialization, low pay, the condition of the economy, competition for employees, and poor working conditions are among the reasons that active recruitment may be necessary. For example, the shortage of skilled employees expected in the 1990s means that employers will have to recruit actively and work hard to retain their current employees.[19] EEO is another reason for active recruitment. For example, as Hispanics account for an increasing percentage of the labor force, firms will need to hire representative numbers from this population group and may have to actively recruit them.[20]

Factors Affecting Recruitment

Government, unions, labor market conditions, the composition of the work force, the location of the organization, the preferences of job applicants, and available resources affect an organization's ability to recruit satisfactory applicants. Because the labor force is changing both demographically and in terms of worker expectations, recruitment practices will change as well. Moreover, firms may have to hire employees whom they might not otherwise accept and may have to train many of them in basic skills. This chapter's Innovation Management Challenge portrays the efforts of one firm to bring recruits up to par through basic skills training.

Matching the Recruit with the Organization

Once job descriptions and specifications have been determined, the organization advertises the job and contacts applicants. A preliminary screening process will usually disqualify some of the applicants because they fail to meet some of the job specifications. Once the initial pool of applicants has been determined, line managers become involved and the selection process begins. Typically, the personnel department sends applicants to a line manager for consideration. Often, the line manager makes the final decision. The evidence strongly indicates that when an employer makes a conscious effort to match applicants to jobs, both the employer and the employees will be more satisfied.[21]

AT TOYOTA: A team of interviewers helps make the final selection of new employees.

Who Recruits?

Most recruitment is carried out by members of the organization, but some recruitment is done by individuals and agencies outside the firm. In very large organizations, the human resources department normally does the recruiting. In the largest organizations, there may be a staff of professional interviewers and recruiters. In such organizations, managers need to be familiar with the established recruitment process but are not directly involved in recruiting. In smaller organizations, the manager or a personnel or staff specialist may do the recruiting and needs to know the entire process.

The initial treatment of potential applicants is extremely important, regardless of who is doing the recruiting. Applicants will form a negative impression of the organization if they feel that they are being treated casually.[22] The recruiter is usually the first person the applicant meets. It is important that he or she give a positive impression of the company as well as a realistic one.

External recruiters can include employment agencies, unions, or "headhunters" (employment agencies that place professional or managerial candi-

Aetna's Institute for Corporate Education

Aetna Life & Casualty Company in Hartford, Connecticut, found itself with a shortage of qualified workers in entry-level positions. Workers in the available pool were often woefully lacking in basic reading and writing skills. Aetna needed innovative solutions to the problem. One solution had the company's Institute for Corporate Education begin working with local organizations to teach nineteen- to twenty-four-year-olds basic reading and writing. The institute works with them until they can read the kind of material they would have to read at Aetna. Then Aetna will employ them. Aetna has hired more than one thousand people in this way. Badi Foster, head of the institute, indicates that the company is "looking for a payoff from five to eight years" later. Many of the people being taught are members of minority groups.

In a related action, Aetna has also developed an education program on managing cultural diversity. At first, some managers resisted the program because they saw it as "fuzzy-headed, soft-hearted" thinking, recounts Foster. But, he notes, "If you don't get the managers to see this as a business problem, no matter what you do for the entry level, it won't be enough."

SOURCES: Amanda Bennett, "Company School: As Pool of Skilled Help Tightens, Firms Move to Broaden Their Role," *Wall Street Journal* (May 8, 1989), pp. A1, A4; and Art Duritz, "A Critical Role for Corporate Education," *Personnel* (August 1991), p. 5.

dates). These organizations serve a vital function for employers: They help internal recruiters in areas with which they are unfamiliar (such as conducting a national search for an engineer) or in which they have no jurisdiction (such as hiring union members).

Sources of Job Applicants

Internal means of attracting job applicants include posting jobs (advertising job openings in company media, usually bulletin boards), recruiting friends of current employees, and searching human resource databases for people with the needed skills. External sources include employment agencies, educational institutions, advertisements, unions (through their hiring halls), and candidates who simply come in looking for work.

Resourceful Recruiting

Special approaches to recruiting may be necessary under certain circumstances— for example, when the job market is tight, as it will be in the 1990s; in recruiting engineers and scientists; and in recruiting female or minority managers. A number of techniques that go beyond traditional help-wanted advertising may be used in such cases. Among them are:

- telerecruiting
- talent scout cards

Aetna Life & Casualty in Hartford, Connecticut, found itself with a shortage of qualified workers in entry-level positions. The company's Institute for Corporate Education began working with local organizations to teach nineteen- to twenty-four-year-olds basic reading and writing skills.

- point-of-sale messages
- hiring from other companies' layoffs or closings
- posters and door hangers
- direct-mail campaigns
- radio ads
- new recuitment agencies
- employment hot line
- newspaper ads (other than help-wanted)
- public relations and marketing
- recruiting via databases
- government-funded programs
- information seminars
- welcome wagons and realtors
- referral incentives
- sign-on bonuses[23]

When Dime Savings Bank of New York faced a scarcity of qualified candidates, it ran a series of ads piggybacked to its customer service system. When customers called in about their accounts, a voicemail system provided descriptions of job opportunities. Interested parties could leave a voicemail message, and applicants with appropriate qualifications were called by an interviewer. In a little over a year, twenty-four employees were hired at a savings of $1,529 each, compared to normal recruitment methods.[24]

The Application Form

The cornerstone of both recruitment and selection is the job application itself. The application form may be given to all applicants, or it may be given only to those who pass a preliminary screening process. Because of federal and state EEO laws, many employers have increased their levels of preliminary screening, asking every person who inquires about a job to fill out an application form.

EEO Considerations

Recruitment has been greatly affected by EEO laws. The recruitment process, especially if it includes application forms, may be investigated for discriminatory content or impact. Moreover, EEO laws require employers to give careful attention to matching applicants' qualifications with job descriptions and specifications. Although technically this may be part of the selection process, initial screening often occurs during the recruitment phase. Screening has become increasingly important as a way of saving money by weeding out unsatisfactory candidates early in the process.

EEO guidelines prohibit employers from asking applicants questions about their race, color, age, sex, national origin, veteran status, religion, and mental or physical handicaps, unless a bona fide occupational qualification (BFOQ) is allowed for a particular job. That is extremely rare but does occur. A church-affiliated college, for example, might be allowed to hire employees for certain positions on the basis of religion and could therefore inquire about an individual's religious preference. Information about race, color, sex, and so on can be requested once an individual has been hired so that the organization can provide employee insurance. Such information may not be used to discriminate in any way.

As a consequence of EEO laws, employers that fail to show appropriate percentages of minorities or women in various job classifications must make a special effort to recruit them. This may mean recruiting at minority or women's colleges, in minority housing areas, or in minority newspapers or women's magazines. Such recruitment would be part of an **affirmative-action program,** a set of actions undertaken by the organization to fulfill its EEO obligations in a

Affirmative-action program: A set of actions undertaken by an organization to fulfill its EEO obligations in a systematic way.

EEO guidelines prohibit employers from asking applicants questions about their race, color, age, sex, national origin, veteran status, religion, and mental or physical handicaps, unless a bona fide occupational qualification is allowed for a particular job.

systematic way. The requirements for such programs are spelled out in federal (and some state) regulations.

Selection

When a pool of applicants has been chosen, the organization must decide which applicant best matches the job specifications—that is, who is most qualified to fill the position. This process is known as **selection** and consists of the following steps:

1. Completion of the application form or a biographical data form
2. One or more employment interviews
3. Testing
4. Reference checks and recommendations
5. A physical examination
6. Selection

Selection: A process occurring before employment in which the organization determines the candidate best qualified to fill a particular position.

Some companies are extremely rigorous in their selection process. Major Japanese firms are particularly stringent, as can be seen in the description of Toyota's hiring practices at the beginning of the chapter. In the future, firms will need to pay even more attention to selection because of the changing skill levels in the labor force.

The Application Form

The application form is used in both recruitment and selection. Once the organization begins to make choices among candidates, the application form becomes part of the selection process. Application forms have been subjected to close scrutiny for compliance with EEO legislation.

AT TOYOTA: Toyota was concerned about technical and interpersonal skills. It assessed applicants in both areas.

Interviews

The interview is perhaps the weakest link in the selection process, but it is often the most critical. Vital information can be exchanged in the interview, but research has shown that the interview is susceptible to a number of problems. Unless each candidate is asked the same questions, for example, the same information will not be gathered for each. When managers evaluate candidates on the basis of the information obtained from an interview, they may be comparing apples and oranges. An interview is also subject to bias created by such factors

The interview is perhaps the weakest link in the selection process, but it is often the most critical. A major reason for the use of interviews is the belief that face-to-face interaction provides information about the candidate's personality and sociability that cannot be obtained using other techniques.

as the candidate's appearance.[25] Nevertheless, interviews are widely used. A major reason for their use is the belief that face-to-face interaction provides information about the candidate's personality and sociability that cannot be obtained using other techniques. Structured interviews based on job requirements, related activities, and related performance dimensions (such as relevant knowledge) can alleviate the problems commonly associated with interviews. A manager conducting an interview should carry out the following steps:

1. Plan for the interview; review the job description and specification. Prepare questions related to requirements, activities, and performance dimensions.
2. Create a good climate for conducting the interview.
3. Allow sufficient time for an uninterrupted interview.
4. Screen questions beforehand to avoid those that might be construed as discriminatory. The wording of questions is critical. To ask whether a person has children is illegal, but to ask whether he or she can work overtime is not.
5. Press for answers to all questions and check them for inconsistencies.
6. Write notes about the interview immediately upon its completion.[26]

If you are a candidate for a job, the following guidelines can help you make a positive impression in an interview:

1. Be prepared: Find out all you can about the potential employer.
2. First impressions are critical: It is absolutely vital that you create a positive image. Be neatly and appropriately dressed and well groomed.
3. Prepare answers for typical interview questions such as questions about your personal ambitions and life experiences.
4. Probe for information about the company during the interview.

The manager often interviews candidates and therefore must know what he or she can legally ask. The manager must also be able to structure interviews, use probing questions effectively, and learn to avoid the pitfalls of the interviewing process. To the extent that the manager helps devise tests and application forms, he or she should be aware of the legalities involved. Finally, in making choices, the manager must be able to balance criteria for hiring. For example, employees will have differing levels of skills related to various job specification criteria. The manager must be able to determine which employee has the right balance of skills for the job.

Employment Testing

Some companies use tests to help them make employment decisions. Most tests are administered before hiring.[27] Typical tests include tests of job skills, such as typing, and psychological tests, which are administered to applicants in certain occupations, such as sales and management. When employees are being considered for promotion, testing may also include performance appraisals. Drug testing is also common both before and after hiring. To be used legally, a test (or any other selection device) must have **validity**—it must actually be able to distinguish between candidates who will be successful in a job and those who will not.[28] It must also have **reliability**—it must produce the same results when taken by the same person more than once or when various forms of the same test are taken by the same person.[29]

AT TOYOTA: *An important part of Toyota's selection process consists of interviews. They help ensure that specific criteria will be satisfied.*

Validity: *The requirement that a test must be able to distinguish between candidates who will be successful in a job and those who will not.*

Reliability: *The requirement that a test must produce the same results when taken by the same person more than once or when various forms of the same test are taken by the same person.*

EEO CONSIDERATIONS

Historically, the EEOC has required a demonstration of validity before permitting an organization to use a test or other selection device. (Interviews and performance appraisals are both viewed as tests by the EEOC.) Moreover, a test cannot be used if it may have an adverse impact on a group protected by EEO laws—that is, if it disqualifies a significantly larger percentage of applicants in that group than in other groups.

Many organizations have used tests as part of their selection process. However, because of the difficulty and cost of proving that a test actually predicts future job performance, many employers have abandoned formal testing except for the most critical jobs. They have settled instead for a first-come, first-hired, "hear thunder, see lightning" approach. However, as the skills required of front-line employees—and, hence, their cost to the organization—have increased, many firms have resumed testing.

PERSONALITY TESTS

With employees needing more interpersonal skills than ever before, and with front-line employees costing more than ever before, how can organizations ensure that their selection process produces the "right" person? One increasingly popular way is to use tests that reveal personality factors.[30] Robert Goehing, manager of human resources development for Kimberly Clark Corporation, a manufacturer of disposable personal and health care products and paper and specialty products, comments: "Ten years ago we didn't expect as much from people. Now we have participative organizations that foster a high degree of responsibility even at the operator level." At Kimberly Clark's newest plant, applicants for nonunion machine operator jobs must participate in "leadership simulation" exercises. In a typical exercise, the applicant might play the part of a supervisor who has to direct a seasoned employee to switch to a more demanding job. An actual supervisor would play the worker's role. Goehing adds, "We are looking for people who can assume work-group leadership even if they wouldn't have that responsibility initially."[31]

AT TOYOTA: Toyota employees are chosen according to job-related criteria, both technical and interpersonal.

Criticisms of such tests abound. Some critics claim that the most sought-after personality traits are not necessary for all employees and therefore may violate EEO laws. Others, such as union leaders, are concerned that companies are using personality inventories to weed out pro-union applicants. Critics also charge that simulations are only as good as the people judging them. Research suggests, however, that personality tests, especially those based on job content, have high validity when predicting job success.[32] More and more companies are employing such tests as a means of predicting which applicants will be successful on the job.

One of the most popular personality tests is the Myers-Briggs Type Indicator, or MBTI as it is commonly known. Responses to more than one hundred questions are used to indicate why an individual would be classified toward one or the other end of four dimensions:

1. Social interaction: introvert or extravert
2. Preference for gathering data: intuitive or sensor
3. Preference for decision making: feeling or thinking
4. Style of making decisions: perceptive or judgmental (organized, planned out)

Combinations of these preferences result in the sixteen personality types shown in Figure 12.6. Users of the MBTI believe that it is important to identify these types because they affect the way people interact and solve problems. Knowl-

FIGURE 12.6   THE SIXTEEN PERSONALITY TYPES IDENTIFIED BY THE MBTI

		SENSING TYPES S		INTUITIVE TYPES N	
		THINKING T	FEELING F	FEELING F	THINKING T
INTROVERTS I	JUDGING J	ISTJ SERIOUS, QUIET, EARN SUCCESS BY CONCENTRATION AND THOROUGHNESS. PRACTICAL, ORDERLY, MATTER-OF-FACT, LOGICAL, REALISTIC, AND DEPENDABLE. TAKE RESPONSIBILITY.	ISFJ QUIET, FRIENDLY, RESPONSIBLE, AND CONSCIENTIOUS. WORK DEVOTEDLY TO MEET THEIR OBLIGATIONS. THOROUGH, PAINSTAKING, ACCURATE. LOYAL, CONSIDERATE.	INFJ SUCCEED BY PERSEVERANCE, ORIGINALITY, AND DESIRE TO DO WHATEVER IS NEEDED OR WANTED. QUIETLY FORCEFUL, CONSCIENTIOUS, CONCERNED FOR OTHERS. RESPECTED FOR THEIR FIRM PRINCIPLES.	INTJ USUALLY HAVE ORIGINAL MINDS AND GREAT DRIVE FOR THEIR OWN IDEAS AND PURPOSES. SKEPTICAL, CRITICAL, INDEPENDENT, DETERMINED, OFTEN STUBBORN.
	PERCEIVING P	ISTP COOL ONLOOKERS—QUIET, RESERVED, AND ANALYTICAL. USUALLY INTERESTED IN IMPERSONAL PRINCIPLES, HOW AND WHY MECHANICAL THINGS WORK. FLASHES OF ORIGINAL HUMOR.	ISFP RETIRING, QUIETLY FRIENDLY, SENSITIVE, KIND, MODEST ABOUT THEIR ABILITIES. SHUN DISAGREEMENTS. LOYAL FOLLOWERS. OFTEN RELAXED ABOUT GETTING THINGS DONE.	INFP CARE ABOUT LEARNING, IDEAS, LANGUAGE, AND INDEPENDENT PROJECTS OF THEIR OWN. TEND TO UNDERTAKE TOO MUCH, THEN SOMEHOW GET IT DONE. FRIENDLY, BUT OFTEN TOO ABSORBED.	INTP QUIET, RESERVED, IMPERSONAL. ENJOY THEORETICAL OR SCIENTIFIC SUBJECTS. USUALLY INTERESTED MAINLY IN IDEAS, LITTLE LIKING FOR PARTIES OR SMALL TALK. SHARPLY DEFINED INTERESTS.
EXTROVERTS E	PERCEIVING P	ESTP MATTER-OF-FACT, DO NOT WORRY OR HURRY, ENJOY WHATEVER COMES ALONG. MAY BE A BIT BLUNT OR INSENSITIVE. BEST WITH REAL THINGS THAT CAN BE TAKEN APART OR PUT TOGETHER.	ESFP OUTGOING, EASYGOING, ACCEPTING, FRIENDLY, MAKE THINGS MORE FUN FOR OTHERS BY THEIR ENJOYMENT. LIKE SPORTS AND MAKING THINGS. FIND REMEMBERING FACTS EASIER THAN MASTERING THEORIES.	ENFP WARMLY ENTHUSIASTIC, HIGH-SPIRITED, INGENIOUS, IMAGINATIVE. ABLE TO DO ALMOST ANYTHING THAT INTERESTS THEM. QUICK WITH A SOLUTION AND TO HELP WITH A PROBLEM.	ENTP QUICK, INGENIOUS, GOOD AT MANY THINGS. MAY ARGUE EITHER SIDE OF A QUESTION FOR FUN. RESOURCEFUL IN SOLVING CHALLENGING PROBLEMS, BUT MAY NEGLECT ROUTINE ASSIGNMENTS.
	JUDGING J	ESTJ PRACTICAL, REALISTIC, MATTER-OF-FACT, WITH A NATURAL HEAD FOR BUSINESS OR MECHANICS. NOT INTERESTED IN SUBJECTS THEY SEE NO USE FOR. LIKE TO ORGANIZE AND RUN ACTIVITIES.	ESFJ WARM-HEARTED, TALKATIVE, POPULAR, CONSCIENTIOUS, BORN COOPERATORS. NEED HARMONY. WORK BEST WITH ENCOURAGEMENT. LITTLE INTEREST IN ABSTRACT THINKING OR TECHNICAL SUBJECTS.	ENFJ RESPONSIVE AND RESPONSIBLE. GENERALLY FEEL REAL CONCERN FOR WHAT OTHERS THINK OR WANT. SOCIABLE, POPULAR. SENSITIVE TO PRAISE AND CRITICISM.	ENTJ HEARTY, FRANK, DECISIVE, LEADERS. USUALLY GOOD IN ANYTHING THAT REQUIRES REASONING AND INTELLIGENT TALK. MAY SOMETIMES BE MORE POSITIVE THAN THEIR EXPERIENCE IN AN AREA WARRANTS.

SOURCE: INTRODUCTION TO TYPE BY ISABEL BRIGGS MYERS (PALO ALTO; CONSULTING PSYCHOLOGISTS PRESS INC. 1980), PP. 7, 8.

edge of personality types, if identified and acted upon, can allow managers, subordinates, and peers to interact and solve problems more meaningfully. If your boss is a sensor and you are an intuitor, for example, you will gather information in different ways. A sensor prefers facts, an intuitor gut reactions. To work well with your boss, you will need to emphasize the facts in a situation and keep your gut reactions to yourself.

Users of MBTI also believe that different types of people perform better in different jobs. Thus, to get the most from the selection process, the organization should try to match the personality type of the applicant with the characteristics of the job.

EMPLOYERS MAY CONDUCT SEVERAL KINDS OF TESTS TO DETER-
MINE WHETHER PROSPECTIVE EMPLOYEES ARE QUALIFIED FOR THE
JOBS THEY SEEK. SOME EMPLOYERS USE PERSONALITY TESTS TO
ASSESS THE INTERPERSONAL SKILLS AND PERSONALITY TRAITS OF
CANDIDATES; THESE TESTS OFTEN TAKE THE FORM OF LENGTHY
QUESTIONNAIRES. DRUG TESTING IS COMMON BOTH BEFORE AND
AFTER HIRING. EMPLOYERS WITH A VIEW TO THE FUTURE MAY RE-
QUIRE NEWLY HIRED EMPLOYEES TO IMPROVE THEIR WRITING AND
OTHER SKILLS IN FORMAL TRAINING PROGRAMS.

Reference Checks

One of the best ways to verify the desirability of an individual for a particular job is to check his or her references. Lately, however, this has proven difficult to do. Former employers are afraid to talk about ex-workers, even in a positive way, for fear of potential lawsuits.[33] An employee might, for example, bring suit against a former employer that provided an unfavorable job reference for him or her. Some firms will not say anything about former employees without their written consent.[34]

Physical Examinations

Until recently, many organizations asked job applicants to undergo a physical examination. This makes sense when the ability to perform certain physical actions is required to do the job. However, under the Americans with Disabilities Act (ADA), which took effect in 1992, this is an ill-advised policy because it may be illegal.[35] In a related matter, testing for drug use is becoming more common, both before and after hiring.

EEO CONSIDERATIONS

The ADA bars employers from discriminating against people with disabilities unless the disability would directly interfere with the performance of a particular job. Broadly interpreted, such disabilities might include drug use and AIDS, but this is not yet clear.[36] Employees with disabilities must be accommodated within reason. Before the passage of the ADA, employers often screened out individuals with various kinds of disabilities. For example, they might avoid hiring individuals with a high risk of heart attack in order to keep their insurance rates low, even though the condition might have nothing to do with the ability to perform in the job.[37] As a consequence of potential difficulties with EEO law, most employers that require a physical examination do so only after the offer to hire has been made. Many have abandoned it altogether.

Employment Decisions

In most organizations, the final hiring decision rests with the line manager who will supervise the new employee. In some organizations, the personnel department may make the decision with respect to lower-level jobs, but this practice is becoming less common. There is also a trend toward allowing work groups and teams to make decisions on the hiring of their new members.

Harvey MacKay, president of MacKay Envelope Corporation, suggests that there is one acid-test question about a potential employee: "How would you feel if he (or she) worked for your competition?"[38] If you would not want a competitor to benefit from the applicant's skills and knowledge, hire him or her yourself.

It is important to remember that the employment decision is a two-way street. The prospective employee must be sufficiently convinced of the merits of joining the organization. In addition to pay, he or she must also consider issues such as centralization versus decentralization, job autonomy, amount of travel, and opportunities for promotion.

Assessment Centers

Assessment center: A two- or three-day program consisting of simulation exercises, tests, interviews, and problem-solving assignments used to measure an individual's potential for promotion or assignment to a specific job.

One of the most successful techniques for selecting managers is the assessment center. An **assessment center** is a two- or three-day program consisting of simulation exercises, tests, interviews, and problem-solving assignments that are used to measure an individual's potential for promotion or assignment to a specific job. Assessment centers provide very valid predictions of future success in management. Several measures are used to evaluate a candidate, and the actual components of the job are used as part of the testing process. Their primary drawback is their expense because, in most cases, a few candidates are supervised by a large number of administrators.

Realistic Job Previews

In the recruitment process, both the employer and the potential employee should seek to make their presentations to each other as realistic as possible. The potential employee wants to get the job but does not want to exaggerate his or her abilities. Similarly, the firm needs to present a realistic job preview, clearly indicating expectations, requirements, culture, and leadership style, among other factors. Studies reveal that such previews help reduce turnover and increase employee satisfaction.[39]

Orientation

Orientation introduces the employee to the organization—to the requirements of the job, to the social situation in which he or she will be working, and to its norms and culture. Most organizations use some type of checklist to orient the employee to a job. Orientations usually include an overview of the company, policies and procedures, compensation, benefits, safety and accident prevention, employee and union relations, physical facilities, and economic factors. Department functions; job duties and responsibilities; policies, rules, procedures, and regulations; the autonomy of the department; and an introduction to the work group may also be included. A sound orientation process is vital.[40]

Managers are directly involved in orienting new employees to the specific job situation. In effect, the new employee is undergoing a socialization process. It is important that managers recognize this and conduct the orientation in a professional manner.

Orientation: The introduction of a new employee to the organization—the requirements of the job, the social situation in which he or she will be working, and the organization's culture.

Training and Development

Training helps the employee gain the specific job-related skills that will ensure effective performance. **Development** is the process of helping the employee grow, principally in his or her career but perhaps also as a human being. It is a long-term investment.[41] Selection for training and development is part of the career planning process.

Training and development to increase skills is widely viewed as a means of achieving global competitiveness. United Airlines, for example, transformed itself from a largely domestic company into a full-fledged global competitor in five years by using an extensive training program called Best Airline—The Global Challenge.[42] Despite widespread acceptance of the importance of training and development, U.S. firms trail their foreign counterparts in financial commitment to such programs. For example, Fortune 500 employees spend about 2 percent of their time in training programs, whereas comparable Japanese and German workers spend 10 percent of their time in training. U.S. firms spend about half as much money per worker on employee training as German firms.[43]

Training and development can occur on or off the job. On-the-job training occurs while the individual is actually performing in the work setting. Off-the-job training and development typically occur in classrooms or similar training situations such as hotel conference centers. Training and development may be

Training: Programs designed to help employees gain specific job-related skills that will ensure effective performance.

Development: The process of helping an employee grow, principally in his or her career but perhaps also as a human being.

More and more training and development will be necessary in the future to acquaint old and new employees with new job responsibilities. This IBM seminar is just one of perhaps a hundred that a career employee might be expected to attend.

carried out in the workplace by either the manager, the human resources department, or consultants and seminar leaders. Employees may also be sent to seminars at sites away from the workplace.

Classroom instructional techniques include lectures and discussion, case studies, simulations, and role playing. Lectures and discussion tend to be knowledge oriented, whereas case studies, simulations, and role playing are skill oriented. In a lecture and discussion situation, the employee is largely passive; with the latter three techniques, the employee is a participant.

One of the most important trends in employee training and development is the increasing amount of basic education by business. Faced with a smaller labor pool than in the past, organizations are having difficulty finding workers with the degree of education they require. This means that they must train many employees in basic skills.[44] (This chapter's Innovation Management Challenge described one firm's efforts in this area.) Another consequence of the shortage of skilled workers is that firms are hiring more learning-disabled workers than in the past.[45]

Business is also investing more in employee development in order to become more competitive. Workers' skills, for example, can become outdated as a result of rapid technological change.[46] More and more firms are using computers and interactive video programs to train employees.[47] As organizational learning becomes a more dominant philosophy, the emphasis on employee development is likely to increase.[48]

Human resource management does not end with the placement of an employee on a job. The HRM function includes a number of ongoing tasks and programs, among which are continuing employee development and training, compensation and benefits, employee health and safety, employee relations, employee evaluation and control, employee transitions, managing culture and change, improving productivity and quality, and improving organizational communications. In the remainder of the chapter we will take a closer look at each of these.

Continuing Employee Development

The manager's principal training and development function is to make certain that the individual first receives adequate training to do the job and later is encouraged to grow beyond the job. The manager must ascertain whether an employee needs more training and development and should ensure that the employee is promotable in the long run. From time to time, an employee will have to be trained for a specific new job. The manager should manage his or her own training and development as well as that of subordinates.

Employee development is a long-term process; it is not as directly job related as training.[49] It tends to provide general skills and knowledge that are useful both in the current job and later in an individual's career. Development is a critical element in the strategic management of human resources. It is based on the recognition that employees should be integrated into the organization and developed as a resource for future strategic actions.[50] Development tends to take place after the individual has been on the job for a while. A number of companies, including IBM, AT&T, GTE, Wang, Motorola, and Xerox, operate their own internal "universities," teaching employees a wide variety of technical and managerial subjects.[51]

The term **intellectual capital** is often used to describe a firm's intellectual assets. It is tied to organizational learning and viewed as a major competitive weapon.[52] Developing intellectual capital is therefore a major function of continuing employee training and development.

Intellectual capital: A term often used to decribe the firm's intellectual assets.

Compensation and Benefits

The HRM department plays a critical role in employee motivation through the design of compensation and benefit programs. Such programs define the limits within which individual managers can use compensation or benefits as motivators. The classic method of influencing employee motivation is through financial compensation. Direct compensation is generally based on time worked, performance, or some combination of the two. To be effective, compensation programs should be designed to reward performance while taking other factors, such as seniority, into account.

There are numerous forms of compensation, including hourly wages, salaries, overtime pay, merit pay, bonuses, incentive plans, stock options, profit sharing, piece rates, commissions, and group incentives. Benefits are part of total compensation and constitute approximately 37 percent of the average employee's salary.[53] If current trends continue, that proportion could reach 40 to 45 percent.[54] Typical benefits are life and health insurance, unemployment compensation, retirement benefits (including social security), paid vacations, paid holidays, and sick leave. It is difficult to use benefits as a way of influencing motivation because they are provided regardless of an employee's performance.

Because of the rapid increase in health care costs, employers' health insurance costs have risen dramatically.[55] This problem was further compounded in 1989 with the passage of the Technical and Miscellaneous Revenue Act of 1989 (TAMRA), which requires that virtually all employees be provided with benefits equivalent to those of "highly compensated employees." In most cases, employers have faced increased costs and paperwork as a result.[56,57]

Most organizations perform job evaluations in order to establish the wages to be paid for various jobs. **Job evaluation** is the systematic determination of the

Job evaluation: The systematic determination of the relative worth of a job in an organization.

relative worth of a job in an organization. It allows the organization to rank jobs hierarchically. A successful job evaluation depends on up-to-date job descriptions and specifications.

Factors affecting compensation and benefits and related decisions include the worth of the job and the employee; market compensation and benefit conditions; collective bargaining; the organization's ability to pay; perceptions of employee equity in terms of wages; and EEO laws and guidelines.

The wages actually paid are often influenced by the results of wage, salary, and benefit surveys in the community in which the organization is located. Most local personnel associations perform such surveys annually, so that member employers' compensation and benefit packages will be "in the same ballpark." Sometimes organizations simply cannot hire people at the wages they wish to pay and, hence, are forced to increase their compensation and benefit levels.

EEO CONSIDERATIONS

Comparable worth: Compensation on the basis of the job's worth to the organization regardless of the sex of the job holder.

The Equal Pay Act of 1963 prohibits the payment of different wages for equal work on the basis of sex. Title VII of the Civil Rights Act of 1964 prohibits discrimination on the basis of sex (and other factors noted earlier) in any employment practice. More recently, the issue of **comparable worth**—the idea that employees should be compensated on the basis of the job's worth to the organization, regardless of the sex of the job holder—has received significant attention. A number of lawsuits have been filed claiming that organizations in both the public and private sectors were paying women less than men holding jobs of comparable worth.[58] As a result of such suits, the evaluation systems used to determine the worth of a job are being revised. At Bank of America, for example, physical labor has been redefined to include tasks that can cause eye strain, allowing many female-dominated clerical jobs to be evaluated at a higher level of pay.[59]

Employee Health and Safety

Employee health and safety are primary concerns of most employers. Medical insurance is part of most benefit packages. However, much of management's concern is focused on the work environment—air, water, and noise pollution; other health hazards; and the safety of equipment. Federal requirements regarding safety in the work area, as well as certain hazards to health, are defined in considerable detail in the Occupational Safety and Health Act (OSHA) of 1970. OSHA requires employers to make their work areas safe and eliminate environmental hazards.

Accident prevention programs are a critical part of employee health and safety programs. Extensive feedback from management about safety issues and positive reinforcement of safe behavior have been shown to produce favorable results for bakers, bus drivers, paper mill employees, and employees of farm machinery manufacturers.[60] Unfortunately, as employers push for increased productivity, accident levels increase significantly.[61] Sonoco Products Company found that one of the best ways to increase safety was to involve employees in designing safety policies and practices.[62]

In addition to preventing accidents, employers need to eliminate the illness and disease caused by hazards in the workplace. Among those hazards is stress. In a number of legal cases, employers have been found guilty of creating too stressful an environment.[63] Consequently, many organizations are developing wellness programs. For example, Metropolitan Life Insurance Company has such a program for its 9,500 headquarters employees. The program includes

The Union Pacific Corporation's worker safety truck is part of the company's accident prevention program. Extensive feedback from management about safety issues and positive reinforcement of safe behavior have been shown to produce favorable results.

blood pressure control, cholesterol reduction, weight training, stress management, and smoking prevention. Numerous other companies have developed physical-fitness programs in an attempt to make employees healthier and reduce health care costs.[64]

An issue related to employee health is drug use. The use of drugs, including alcohol, is widespread in many industries. More and more employers are making drug testing part of the hiring process. For example, Denver-based Coors, the nation's fourth-largest brewer of beer, has dropped lie detector tests in favor of drug testing.[65] There is considerable controversy over whether such testing is legal, but the answer appears to be yes.[66]

Managers are responsible for the day-to-day occupational safety and health of their subordinates. The manager typically must enforce rules, regulations, and procedures. Stretching the law is unethical as well as dangerous. Managers in certain occupations, such as construction, often face moral dilemmas because employers ask or even demand that they bend safety rules.

AIDS (acquired immune deficiency syndrome) is a potential managerial problem in all organizations. Many employers have special policies and programs for employees with AIDS. Most of these deal with such matters as shifting work schedules to accommodate periods of illness. Basing employment decisions on whether a person has AIDS probably violates the Americans with Disabilities Act of 1990. With the exception of a few health care organizations, employers are not testing for AIDS when screening potential employees. Managers must use their best interpersonal skills not only to assist employees afflicted with AIDS, but to increase the understanding of subordinates working alongside AIDS victims.[67]

Employee Relations

Employee (labor) relations is concerned with managing a unionized work force. An organization's relationships with organized labor are vital to its success. Traditionally, a major part of the human resources department's efforts in

Employee (labor) relations: The concerns of managing a unionized work force.

unionized firms has been to manage labor relations; in nonunionized firms, the main thrust has been to prevent unions from organizing the work force. In many large unionized firms, the human resource function is performed by two departments, one to handle employee relations and one to handle all other personnel functions.

The employee relations department is responsible for managing and administrating the union contract, grievances, compensation, work rules, and other issues that arise from time to time. A principal concern of employee relations is negotiation of the union contract. Today, most unions, in addition to seeking higher wages, are attempting to protect existing jobs for current members. They face difficult times; competition, especially from foreign firms, has forced many givebacks by unions and has caused management to take tougher negotiating positions. Unions seek to gain new members, especially in service industries, to counter the effects of the loss of jobs in traditionally unionized industries such as autos and steel.[68]

A manager in a unionized situation must supervise within the requirements established by the union contract as well as by company policies, rules, and procedures. Such a manager's decision environment is highly defined, and his or her latitude for decision making is extremely limited. Normally, work rules, compensation, grievance procedures, and disciplinary choices are spelled out in very specific terms either by the contract or by company policy. As with EEO issues, the manager must maintain precise records. It must be possible to prove that the requirements of the contract have been met; otherwise, disciplinary actions may fail or be disallowed by an arbitrator.

Employee Evaluation and Control

The HRM department must establish procedures for employee evaluation and control. These include performance appraisals, disciplinary systems, and grievance procedures. A number of actions may hinge on these procedures, such as promotion, bonuses, disciplinary actions, and employee transitions.

Performance Appraisal

There are several types of performance appraisals. Those used most frequently are:

1. *Graphic rating scales:* Employees are rated on a scale, usually from 1 to 10, on traits and/or behavior such as intelligence, neatness, and quantity of work accomplished.

2. *Management by objectives, results, and rewards:* Objectives are established, plans determined, performance reviewed, and rewards given, as described in Chapter 6.

3. *Forced choice:* The evaluator is required to choose among a set of descriptions of employee behavior, which are then scored according to a key.

4. *Simple ranking:* Raters simply rank subordinates from best to worst on the basis of perceived performance.

5. *Critical incidents:* Raters identify positive and negative aspects of employee performance.

6. *Essay:* Raters describe employee performance in an essay format.

Each of these approaches is better for certain situations than for others. None is appropriate for all situations.

A number of people may do the evaluating: the employee, the immediate supervisor, a second-level supervisor, an external consultant, subordinates, peers, or a combination of these. Currently, the most frequently recommended system is one in which the employee and the supervisor perform independent evaluations. They exchange their evaluations and then discuss any significant differences between them.

Performance appraisals were originally instituted for the purpose of controlling performance, but they also greatly influence motivation and set and communicate goals as part of the planning process. There are some problems with performance appraisals, however. For example, raters may have a tendency to rate too leniently or too strictly.[69]

EEO CONSIDERATIONS

The EEOC views the performance appraisal as a test. Therefore, it must meet validity requirements if it is used to determine promotion—it must be objective and job related.[70] It can also be used as a standard for disciplining or terminating employees. Managers and the HRM department must carefully document the reasons and justifications for the evaluations given. A disgruntled employee might claim discrimination or unfairness, or that there was insufficient justification for the actions taken. For example, a number of lawsuits have been brought against Japanese firms such as Sumitomo, Honda, and C. Itoh & Company claiming that their promotion practices discriminate against non-Japanese employees.[71]

Disciplinary Programs

Many organizations have disciplinary programs that consist of a series of five steps:

1. *Verbal warnings:* The manager talks with the subordinate about the problem. The focus is on the problem, not on blaming the employee.
2. *Written warning:* The manager presents a written warning notice to the employee, detailing the undesirable behavior. In many situations, especially in unionized organizations, it has become necessary to have the employee sign this notice or to have a witness present.
3. *One-day suspension:* If the undesirable behavior is repeated after the written warning, a one-day suspension without pay is usually prescribed.
4. *Three-day suspension:* If the undesirable behavior continues, the employee is suspended for three days without pay.
5. *Termination:* If the employee's behavior still has not improved, the employee is terminated.

Normally it is the manager's job to carry out these steps. However, often a manager will ask a team to straighten out its own problems.

Grievance Procedures

Organizations may provide a system that enables employees to air their grievances. A **grievance system** provides policies, rules, and procedures for use in appraising performance, disciplining, and handling grievances. Such a system is almost always included in a union contract. Normally, a grievance system follows the chain of command; however, special grievance committees, or a

Grievance system: Policies, rules, and procedures for use in appraising performance, disciplining, and handling grievances.

Personnel Management in Spain

If you're a personnel manager, Spain may not be the best place to practice your trade.

When the graduate business school at the University of Navarra, Barcelona, known as IESE, surveyed the personnel function in Spain, its researchers found that conditions were less than optimal in some respects.

The challenges that managers face in Spain in the 1990s are familiar to executives in all countries preparing to enter the single European market: greater employee mobility, more demanding professional qualifications, and new career opportunities for staff. In Spain, other factors affecting the picture include demographic change, with fewer young workers and more women in the labor force; greater demands for training, produced by new technology and structural changes in the economy; higher training standards; and union demands beyond economic issues.

To assess the state of the personnel function, IESE sent questionnaires to a sample of 700 companies with more than 500 employees. Responses from 70 of the companies were included in the final study. Among the findings were the following:

The personnel function itself: About 95 percent of the companies had a personnel unit; in 75 percent, the head of personnel enjoyed the same status as the heads of other key functions.

Employee professional development: About 85 percent of employers run training, 66 percent organize human resource development, 63 percent conduct appraisals of potential, and 56 percent conduct performance appraisals.

Job descriptions: While 87 percent of the companies had updated organizational charts, only 15 percent had planning succession charts reflecting possi-

grievance-handling staff, are not uncommon. The HRM department establishes the system, and the manager must function within it.

Employee Transitions

Various kinds of employee transitions must be managed; employees may quit, receive promotions and demotions, be laid off or transferred, retire, die, or be terminated. The HRM department designs procedures for managing these transitions, and the manager carries them out in relation to his or her subordinates. Many companies are attempting to ease the pain of some transitions, such as layoffs. Hughes Aircraft Company, for example, went to great lengths to provide generous severance packages ($17,000 per employee) and job placement assistance when it laid off twelve thousand workers in 1992.[72] Companies are also trying to learn how to handle these transitions more appropriately, in part to avoid being sued.

ble changes three to five years away. More than 30 percent of the companies lacked formal job descriptions. Even those that had them tended to have them for supervisors and technicians (65 percent) but not for manual workers (45 percent).

Recruitment: More than half of the companies lacked a formal recruitment strategy. Interviews and experience, not recruitment tests, counted most in evaluating candidates. Orientation and socialization procedures were "not highly developed."

Training: Although economists have emphasized the importance of training, one-third of the companies had no training plans at all. Training support systems were "poorly developed."

Appraisal: More than 40 percent of the companies had no performance appraisal. Within occupational areas, 63 percent of department heads underwent such appraisal, but only 25 percent of manual workers did so.

Compensation: "Although compensation management is one of the oldest personnel activities," writes José Rodriguez, head of the department of organizational behavior at IESE, "it is surprisingly underdeveloped in Spain." Fixed compensation is a constant, but 60 percent of the companies use financial incentives.

Employee relations: About 62 percent of the companies have a collective-bargaining agreement. Pay and benefits are the main reasons for strikes. For 80 percent of the companies, absenteeism is no higher than 6 percent. More than 60 percent of the companies use flexible hours, but new forms of organization—job enrichment, job enlargement, and autonomous work groups— "have only developed modestly."

Rodriguez looks forward to a wider vision of the human resources mission and increased professionalism within personnel's four main areas of responsibility: employee influence, human resources flow, reward systems, and work systems.

SOURCE: José Rodriguez, "Spanish Customs," *Personnel Management* (April 1991), pp. 23–24.

HRM and Organizational Strategy

The purpose of all the HRM practices described in this chapter is to help the organization carry out its corporate, business, and functional strategies.[73] Each organization faces its own unique set of environmental and organizational circumstances. Hence, HRM practices are conducted on a contingency basis. For example, in high-technology industries there has been an increase in incentive-type compensation programs because firms in those industries are simultaneously faced with a very competitive marketplace and a shortage of qualified workers. Other firms are located in areas experiencing labor shortages. For example, Walt Disney World took only one in ten applicants in 1985, but in the early 1990s, as the labor pool in the central Florida area shrank and the demand for labor increased, Disney began hiring one in 2.5 applicants.[74] Such firms often must make special efforts to recruit new workers using the techniques listed earlier.

FIGURE 12.7 HUMAN RESOURCE MANAGEMENT AND STAFFING AS PROBLEM SOLVING

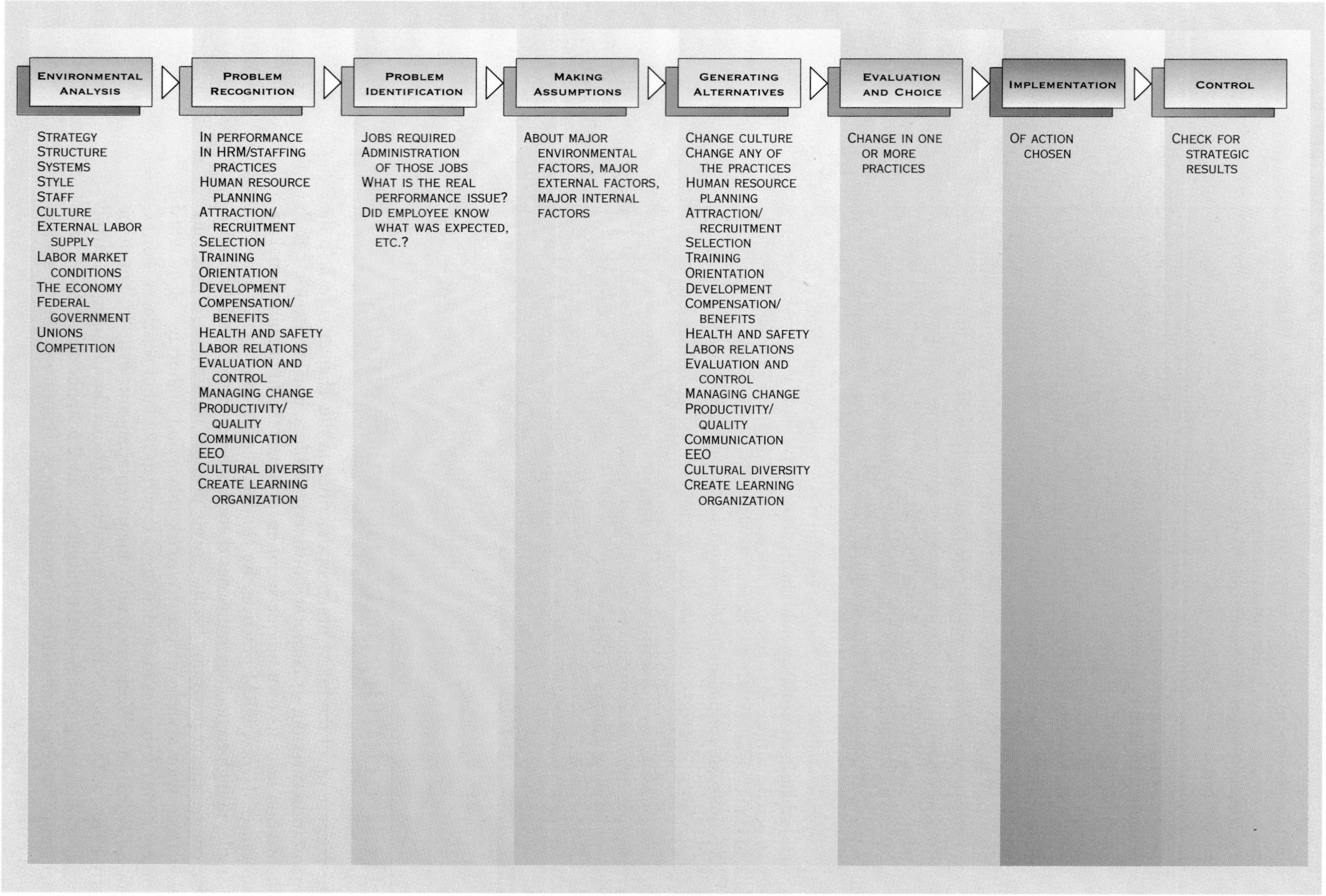

ENVIRONMENTAL ANALYSIS	PROBLEM RECOGNITION	PROBLEM IDENTIFICATION	MAKING ASSUMPTIONS	GENERATING ALTERNATIVES	EVALUATION AND CHOICE	IMPLEMENTATION	CONTROL
STRATEGY	IN PERFORMANCE	JOBS REQUIRED	ABOUT MAJOR	CHANGE CULTURE	CHANGE IN ONE	OF ACTION	CHECK FOR
STRUCTURE	IN HRM/STAFFING	ADMINISTRATION	ENVIRONMENTAL	CHANGE ANY OF	OR MORE	CHOSEN	STRATEGIC
SYSTEMS	PRACTICES	OF THOSE JOBS	FACTORS, MAJOR	THE PRACTICES	PRACTICES		RESULTS
STYLE	HUMAN RESOURCE	WHAT IS THE REAL	EXTERNAL FACTORS,	HUMAN RESOURCE			
STAFF	PLANNING	PERFORMANCE ISSUE?	MAJOR INTERNAL	PLANNING			
CULTURE	ATTRACTION/	DID EMPLOYEE KNOW	FACTORS	ATTRACTION/			
EXTERNAL LABOR	RECRUITMENT	WHAT WAS EXPECTED,		RECRUITMENT			
SUPPLY	SELECTION	ETC.?		SELECTION			
LABOR MARKET	TRAINING			TRAINING			
CONDITIONS	ORIENTATION			ORIENTATION			
THE ECONOMY	DEVELOPMENT			DEVELOPMENT			
FEDERAL	COMPENSATION/			COMPENSATION/			
GOVERNMENT	BENEFITS			BENEFITS			
UNIONS	HEALTH AND SAFETY			HEALTH AND SAFETY			
COMPETITION	LABOR RELATIONS			LABOR RELATIONS			
	EVALUATION AND			EVALUATION AND			
	CONTROL			CONTROL			
	MANAGING CHANGE			MANAGING CHANGE			
	PRODUCTIVITY/			PRODUCTIVITY/			
	QUALITY			QUALITY			
	COMMUNICATION			COMMUNICATION			
	EEO			EEO			
	CULTURAL DIVERSITY			CULTURAL DIVERSITY			
	CREATE LEARNING			CREATE LEARNING			
	ORGANIZATION			ORGANIZATION			

Managing Organizational Culture

Of special concern to the HRM department is the management of organizational culture. The HRM department typically creates cultural indoctrination programs for use during orientation; such programs are designed to mold recruits into employees who can function within the organization's culture.[75] Most cultural management programs are part of **organizational development,** "a long-range (planned) effort to improve an organization's problem-solving and renewal processes, particularly through a more effective and collaborative management of organizational culture, with special emphasis on the culture of formal work teams, with the assistance of a change agent or a catalyst, and the use of theory and technology of applied behavior science, including research."[76]

Organizational development normally begins with a survey or other diagnostic effort, such as a series of interviews, to determine what needs to be done. Next, a plan is formulated to prepare for change, to make the changes, and to reinforce the changes. Anheuser-Busch is an example of a company that has undertaken extensive organizational development in an effort to move toward a more participative and team-oriented culture in many of its plants.[77] The management of culture, change, and cultural diversity will be discussed in more detail in Chapter 13.

Organizational development: A long-range (planned) effort to improve an organization's problem-solving and renewal processes, particularly through more effective and collaborative management of organizational culture.

Improving Productivity and Quality

Productivity and quality are the cornerstones of competitiveness in the 1990s. The HRM department helps establish programs designed to increase employee productivity. It also designs related programs aimed at continuous improvement and innovation that are implemented by individual managers. Quality and innovation are discussed in depth in Chapter 23.

Global Perspectives

As firms increasingly operate on a global basis, their HRM practices will have to be tailored to the requirements of each country in which they operate while adhering to overall corporate policies. Firms can also learn from the HRM practices of foreign firms—for example, the recruitment practices of Japanese firms. Organizations that operate globally must also understand the HRM practices of the firms against which they are competing. This chapter's Global Management Challenge provides information on the HRM practices of Spanish firms. Note the difference between these practices and those of U.S. firms.

HRM and Staffing as Problem-Solving Processes

The environment within which HRM and staffing occur is changing rapidly. HRM and staffing practices must change accordingly. Figure 12.7 shows in broad terms how HRM and staffing can be approached as problem-solving processes.

This model can be applied to each aspect of HRM and staffing. For example, the human resources department might encounter a labor shortage. After careful analysis of the environment, and assuming that the shortage will continue, it might decide to hire more retired workers, realizing that they would be employed for only a few years. Implementation of this plan would probably involve special recruiting efforts. Similarly, in response to the personnel department's actions, the individual manager might have to change his or her selection process in hiring older workers. That, in turn, might require a change in leadership style.

Summary

(Before reading this summary, look again at the objectives listed at the beginning of the chapter.)

1. Human resource management (HRM) is more strategically oriented today than it was in the past. HRM has also become more concerned with overall governance of the work force, as opposed to simple labor relations; and more emphasis is being placed on managing organizational culture and cultural diversity.

2. There are two main categories of HRM practices: those concerned with placing the employee in the job and those concerned with the relationship between the job holder and the organization. The former include human resources planning, recruitment, selection, orientation, and training; the latter include employee development, compensation and benefits, employee relations, employee health and safety, and employee evaluation and control.

   a. The principal concern of human resources planning is to make certain that the human resources necessary to carry out an organization's strategy have been identified and planned for.

   b. Recruitment aims to provide the proper number of employees with the right skills at the right place and the right time to carry out the organization's strategy.

   c. Selection consists of a series of steps that may include preliminary screening, interviewing, testing, reference checks, and a physical examination. The final decision is aimed at selecting the best applicants from the pool created by the recruitment effort.

   d. Orientation is designed to socialize the individual into the organization, acquainting him or her not only with the job, but with general rules and procedures and the social aspects of the work situation.

   e. Training provides new employees with the skills needed to do a specific job.

   f. Development provides employees with additional skills, abilities, and knowledge as they make various transitions within the organization.

   g. Compensation and benefit systems not only enable the organization to recruit employees but also influence individual and group motivation.

   h. In companies with unions, major HRM concerns include negotiation and administration of the contract.

   i. Evaluation and control are necessary to achieve satisfactory performance levels and develop personnel. Employee transitions such as promotions, transfers, retirements, and terminations must be managed carefully.

   j. A major concern of the HRM department is managing organizational culture. Programs for increasing productivity, quality, and innovation are also spearheaded by the HRM department.

3. Equal employment opportunity (EEO) law affects every employment practice, especially human resources planning, selection, benefits and compensation, evaluation, and control.

THINKING
ABOUT
MANAGEMENT

General Questions

1. Describe briefly how HRM has changed in the last few years. Why has it changed?

2. How have EEO and affirmative action affected employment practices?

3. How are human resources planning and strategy related?

4. How will the changing characteristics of the work force affect employment practices?

5. Why should a test have validity, regardless of EEO requirements?

6. Why are firms having to invest more in educating new employees?

7. What is the role of HRM in implementing strategy?

Questions on the Management Challenge Features

DIVERSITY MANAGEMENT CHALLENGE

1. Why is the U.S. West program so successful? Why don't other firms emulate it?

2. What role do values play in the formulation of such programs?

INNOVATION MANAGEMENT CHALLENGE

1. What was innovative about Aetna's approach?

2. What else may be required in the future?

GLOBAL MANAGEMENT CHALLENGE

1. Identify the differences between these practices and those you would expect to find in U.S. firms.

2. How can you find out what U.S. firms really do?

E P I L O G U E

Toyota, an Exacting Employer

In 1992, Toyota opened an assembly plant in the United Kingdom. This move was part of its strategy of entering Europe in preparation for the lowering of import quotas throughout Europe, which will occur in 1999.

DISCUSSION QUESTIONS

1. How might Toyota have to adjust its employment processes for the UK labor market?

2. Find out some characteristics of this market and refine your answer to question 1.

Managing the Work Force of the 1990s

Linda Sampieri, director of employee relations for Red Lobster Restaurants, had been challenged by her boss, the vice-president for human resources, to develop appropriate HRM programs for the restaurant's first-line employees and their managers. Her boss believed that because the work force would change dramatically in the next few years, new programs would be necessary. In Chapter 1's "Managers at Work" you were asked to suggest a new motivational program for Sampieri to use with the new work force. Here, she—and you—must contemplate what other HRM issues need to be addressed and how to deal with them.

The firm has the standard set of personnel practices—employee benefits, grievance procedures, and compensation programs—that a major food service company would be expected to have for full-time employees. Sampieri needs to determine what else must be done, or what could be done instead of what is being done now. Costs are critical, as the restaurant industry will experience little or no real growth in the 1990s and competition is expected to increase.

DISCUSSION QUESTIONS

1. What changes in work force composition and diversity would you expect to occur in the restaurant industry?

2. What changes in HRM practices might be necessary as a consequence of those changes?

Lawful or Unlawful?

MANAGE YOURSELF

The following questions and requests frequently appear on job application forms and in interviews. With an eye toward possible discrimination, test yourself on the legality of these items, circling *L* for lawful and *U* for unlawful.

1. What is your maiden name?	L	U
2. What was your previous married name?	L	U
3. Have you ever worked under another name?	L	U
4. What is your title—Mr., Miss, Mrs., or Ms.?	L	U
5. What is your marital status?	L	U
6. What is your birthplace?	L	U
7. What is the birthplace of your parents, spouse, or other relatives?	L	U
8. Submit proof of age (birth certificate or baptismal record).	L	U
9. What is your religious denomination or affiliation? (or church, parish, pastor, or religious holidays observed)	L	U
10. Are you available for Saturday or Sunday work?	L	U
11. Are you a citizen of the United States of America?	L	U
12. Are you a naturalized citizen?	L	U
13. On what date were you granted citizenship?	L	U

14. Submit naturalization papers or first papers.   L   U
15. List past work experience.   L   U
16. List organizations, clubs, societies, and lodges to which you belong.   L   U
17. What is your wife's maiden name?   L   U
18. Submit names of persons willing to provide professional and/or character references.   L   U
19. Supply names of three relatives other than father, husband or wife, or minor-age dependent children.   L   U
20. What relative can we notify in case of accident or emergency (name and address)?   L   U
21. What foreign languages can you read, write, or speak?   L   U
22. How did you acquire the ability to read, write, or speak a foreign language?   L   U
23. Have you ever been arrested for any crime? If so, stipulate when and where.   L   U
24. List names of dependent children under the age of eighteen.   L   U
25. What arrangements have you made for the care of minor children?   L   U
26. What is the lowest salary you would accept?   L   U
27. What is your height and weight?   L   U
28. Have you ever had your wages garnisheed?   L   U
29. Have you ever been refused a fidelity bond?   L   U
30. Do you own a home? a car? have charge accounts?   L   U
31. What kind of work does your spouse do?   L   U
32. Attach a photograph to the application form.   L   U
33. Please submit a photograph (optional).   L   U

SOURCE: Reproduced from Suzanne H. Cook, "The 1.5 Million Dollar Interview," *Management World* (December 1977), with permission from the Academy of Administrative Management, Chicago, IL 60661.
ANSWERS: Except for questions 11, 15, 18, and 21, the questions could reasonably be construed to be discriminatory, unless the employer has a very good and statistically valid reason for asking them.

Managing Organizational Culture, Cultural Diversity, and Change

CHAPTER OBJECTIVES

When you have read this chapter you should be able to:

1. Define organizational culture and indicate why managing culture is essential to increasing the level of organizational performance.

2. Discuss how to manage culture in an organization.

3. Indicate the relationships between the McKinsey Seven S's and organizational culture.

4. Describe how organizations instill their culture in their members.

5. Define and describe organizational climate and its impact on culture.

6. Describe how best to manage cultural diversity.

7. Describe the Likert system of climate types.

8. Describe the process of change management.

9. Define organizational development and describe its purposes.

10. Discuss resistance to change and various strategies for coping with it.

M ANAGEMENT CHALLENGES DISCUSSED IN THIS CHAPTER:

 Accelerating rates of change.

 Increasing globalization of business.

 Increasing levels of competition.

 A more diverse work force.

British Airways: From Bloody Awful to Bloody Awesome

When Sir Colin Marshall became CEO of British Airways at the beginning of 1983, the airline was £1.2 billion in debt and had suffered a £500 million loss in 1982. Morale was terrible; there was no coordinated marketing program; and little attention was given to customers. Passengers rated BA the airline they would least like to fly. The firm suffered from problems associated with government ownership. Marshall's challenge was to take the airline private and make it profitable. This meant changing the corporate culture.

One of Marshall's greatest concerns was getting the company to focus on customers. He began a profit-sharing program for employees and established a two-day seminar, "Putting People First," that all employees were required to attend. These changes were based on the belief that employees would not treat customers better until they themselves were treated better. The focus of the seminar was on relationships—all relationships employees might have, be they with other employees, managers, customers, or family members. The program contributed significantly to improved morale and better customer relations.

Another step toward changing BA's culture was its development program, "Managing People First." This five-day residential seminar was eventually attended by all BA managers. Marshall addressed each session personally—about a hundred seminars in all—for an hour or more. He felt that it was necessary to demonstrate top management's commitment in order to elicit employee commitment.

Among Marshall's other actions were creating a whole new look for the firm—new uniforms, new exterior paint on the planes, new interiors for the planes, new passenger lounges, and an expensive advertising campaign to sell the "new" BA. A four-person creative marketing team was formed. TV cameras were installed in passenger disembarking areas, enabling passengers to register complaints immediately upon landing. All complaints are analyzed in a timely manner and the passenger is informed of what actions have been taken.

In 1992, BA initiated two one-day seminars based on the theme of "Winning for Customers." One seminar, "Winners," is for employees; the other, "Managing Winners," is for managers.

SOURCES: Sir Colin Marshall, "From Bloody Awful to Bloody Awesome," speech delivered to the Strategic Management Society, London, October 15, 1992, and Patricia Sellers, "How to Handle Customers' Gripes," *Fortune* (October 24, 1988), pp. 88–97.

B ritish Airways' changes in management and culture were bound to have a major impact on the working lives of employees. The radical change in social environment was accompanied by a similar change in attitudes. Colin Marshall's personal involvement contributed to the success of the changes. Like British Airways, many companies are undergoing severe changes because of economic stress or changes in leadership. How to manage such changes in a positive way is a difficult challenge.

In both global and domestic firms, managing cultural diversity is also a critical challenge. Managers in firms like General Electric, Xerox, Nissan, Johnson & Johnson, Philips, and American Airlines have had to manage not only a changing culture but a more diverse work force as well. This chapter explores the management of organizational culture, cultural diversity, change, and resistance to change.

The Management of Organizational Culture

Strategic management and social responsibility were the major concerns of top management in the 1970s, but during the 1980s the focus shifted to managing organizational culture and restructuring. Change, quality, organizational learning, and innovation are the primary issues for top management in the 1990s. Managing organizational culture is the key to effective management in all of these areas.

Recall the McKinsey Seven S's framework presented in Figure 7.9. Culture (shared values) is at the core of that framework. It influences and is influenced by strategy, structure, systems, staff, style, and skills. **Organizational culture** is the pattern of shared values and norms that distinguishes an organization from

Organizational culture: The pattern of shared values and norms that distinguishes an organization from all others.

The radical change in the social environment at British Airways was accompanied by a similar change in attitudes among employees. Playing tiddlywinks helps junior managers work as a team rather than as individuals.

all others.[1] These values and norms define "what is important around here." They provide direction, meaning, and energy for members of the organization. Managing culture involves defining the organization's values, instilling those values in new and veteran employees, integrating culture into the organization through the use of cultural artifacts such as myths and symbols, controlling organizational climate, and changing culture as necessary. Culture and the rest of the Seven S's are highly interdependent. For example, if strategy is changed, culture must be changed also. As organizational learning becomes a major strategic weapon, firms must modify their cultures to include organizational learning as a highly valued activity.

The success of most Japanese firms, as well as many American firms, in managing their organizational cultures so as to increase productivity and become more competitive has provoked interest in the management of culture.[2] Not all such efforts have been successful, however, especially when they have involved transferring organizational cultures from one society to another. European firms have found that the assimilation of different cultures must occur on a country-by-country basis.[3] For example, because French managers tend to be elitist and authoritarian, it would not be easy to use Japanese participative management techniques in France. Many English firms, in contrast, have incorporated these techniques into their more egalitarian structure.

Culture as Revealed in Artifacts

An organization's culture is revealed in four kinds of artifacts: myths and sagas; language systems and metaphors; symbols, ceremonies, and rituals; and identifiable value systems and behavioral norms.[4] In this section, we will take a closer look at each of these.

CORPORATE MYTHS AND SAGAS

Corporate myths and sagas reveal important historical facts about an organization—its early pioneers and products, its past triumphs and failures, and the visionaries who have transformed the company. Myths and sagas identify the organization's shared values and norms and reinforce them. Such stories help shape the attitudes and behavior of new as well as veteran employees.

Mary Kay Ash, founder of Mary Kay Cosmetics, believes strongly in the right of women to succeed, and she has a clear understanding of the women she is trying to motivate. She motivates them principally with money and symbols of success—mink coats, diamonds, and pink Cadillacs. She also provides recognition and opportunities for success. She often tells how, in her early career as a salesperson, she found few opportunities for women. In order to provide such opportunities, she started her own company with a $5,000 investment. Today, Mary Kay Cosmetics is a multimillion-dollar international company, and Ash's success story has become a corporate saga.

Ash's concern for people has also found its way into the corporate culture. Her employees are fond of telling the story of how she bakes cookies for each class of new recruits and serves them herself in her own home.[5] Such stories serve to promote the values and norms she seeks for her company: A place where women can succeed and gain self-esteem, motivation is high, performance is rewarded, and management cares about employees.

When top management changes, the organization's culture often changes as well. For example, for years GE's culture stressed innovation. The company's slogan was "Progress is our most important product." In time, GE became a multinational conglomerate, with hundreds of businesses grouped into several major divisions. Eventually, however, the company became stagnant. Some of its businesses, such as the television division, seemed incapable of innovation.

AT BA: Upon joining BA, Marshall was faced with numerous problems, many of which involved BA's culture. His efforts changed the culture from lethargic and adversarial to disciplined, competitive, and committed. Without this managed change of culture, it is likely that BA would be either bankrupt or a minor player in its industry.

Along came John F. Welch, Jr., in 1981. Within five years he eliminated one hundred thousand employees, more than one-fourth of the work force; sold off the ailing businesses; and acquired others, including RCA. Welch claims that he transformed the company into a "lean and mean fighting machine." Others disagree. They see Welch as a cost cutter who does not understand strategy. They refer to him as "Neutron Jack" and claim that, like a neutron bomb, he gets rid of people while the buildings remain. Nevertheless, it is clear that Welch's actions changed the company's culture.[6] GE's myths and sagas, rituals, and values and norms now focus on low cost, high productivity, and innovation.

Welch is again attempting to change GE's culture (see the opening case in Chapter 1). This time he is focusing on generating innovation through participation in order to make the firm more competitive.[7] Welch recognizes that to be competitive, the firm must be productive; to be productive, it must be innovative; and for innovation to occur, employees at all levels must be involved.

LANGUAGE SYSTEMS AND METAPHORS

The language systems and metaphors used in organizations often indicate their shared values. Some companies focus on the competition—they must "do battle" or "capture" market share. Their leaders talk about ambushes and shoot-outs with competitors.[8] Others focus on the technologies or processes they use. Professors often speak of pedagogical devices, course content, and presentation techniques; a high-tech firm might be concerned with nuclear accelerators or photon lasers or working on "the project." Bureaucrats in Washington, D.C., often use acronyms: PUD—Planned Urban Development; DEA—Drug Enforcement Administration; DOD—Department of Defense. When people who work for the Walt Disney Companies talk about the Magic Kingdom, imaginary characters like Mickey Mouse and Donald Duck come to mind. Everyone at Disney is a "member of the cast," not an employee. Everyone is constantly "on stage," a reference to the company's original business—movies.

SYMBOLS, CEREMONIES, AND RITUALS

Symbols, ceremonies, and rituals also reveal what is important in a particular organization.[9] A company's logo, flag, and slogan convey the importance it places on certain ideas or events. So do its ceremonies. Celebrations of successful sales campaigns, for example, are often flamboyant. Versitek, a Xerox subsidiary that manufactures computer printers, celebrated a very successful year in a unique way. In the words of Robert Murray, director of corporate communication, "We hired an elephant and the Stanford University marching band. It is quite a job to get eight hundred employees into a building without letting them know what was going on. We got them inside and the VPs announced this year's highlights. . . . 'We can't say how big the numbers are,' one said, 'so let's see how big they really are.' Then we slid open the door and in marched the band, and they all thought it was fairly impressive."[10]

Mottos also say a lot about organizations. A good motto meets the following criteria:

1. It conveys and promotes the organization's core philosophy.
2. It has an emotional rather than a rational or intellectual appeal.
3. It is not a direct exhortation for loyalty, productivity, quality, or any other organizational objective.
4. It is mysterious to the public but not to members of the organization.[11]

Semper Fidelis ("Always Faithful"), the U.S. Marine Corps motto, meets all of these criteria; so does *Je me souviens*, French for "I Remember," the motto of the Canadian province of Quebec.[12] Ford Motor Company's "Quality is Job 1" is a motto that has helped transform the company into a manufacturer of high-quality automobiles.

IDENTIFIABLE VALUE SYSTEMS AND BEHAVIORAL NORMS

Identifiable value systems and behavioral norms are reflected in an organization's strategy, structure, systems, style, staffing, and skills, and in its policies, rules, and procedures. They can also be seen in what is rewarded and what is not. Values and norms are passed on in informal communications. How an organization is structured—for example, the size of its corporate staff or the extent to which it allows individuals to participate in decision making—is a critical component of its value system. The recent concern for quality among automobile firms and other American manufacturers shows a trend toward placing a higher value on competitiveness.[13]

The Westin Kauai (Kauai, Hawaii) is an 850-room megaresort. About a year after the hotel opened, it became obvious to General Manager Jim Treadway that the "share the fantasy" theme (a Disney-like theme park concept) did not fit the resort. He initiated a management-by-values program that involved employees in determining a more appropriate theme. The fantasy theme was dropped in favor of one derived from the local Hawaiian culture. Corporate uniforms were replaced by flowing Hawaiian garb, and nearby Mt. Haupu was chosen as the hotel's symbol. Significant improvement in service and guest satisfaction resulted, at least partly because employees felt more comfortable with a theme that reflected their life-style.[14]

Eaton Corporation provides another example. Two decades ago Eaton began the long, difficult process of transforming its HRM techniques through an experiment with an all-salaried plant. That experiment, and the results of similar approaches at other facilities, convinced the company to pursue a participative management approach at all of its facilities. Called the Eaton Philosophy, its goal is to place a high value on the individual and thereby create an atmosphere in which employees can and will work to their full potential.[15]

It is becoming increasingly evident that organizations with an identifiable and properly managed culture have a source of sustainable competitive advantage. Conversely, those whose cultures are not clearly identified or well-managed are usually less successful.[16] Ralph H. Kilmann found that *norms*, or informal standards of behavior, play an important part in establishing an organization's culture.[17] Typical norms are "Don't express your feelings," "Tell the boss what he or she wants to hear," "Don't be late," "Don't be associated with a failure," "Don't upstage the boss," and "Keep plenty of records to protect yourself." Kilmann also found that about 90 percent of organizational norms have negative connotations. This finding suggests that, at least in the organizations he studied, culture, as expressed in norms, could have a negative effect on performance.

Culture and Strategy

Corporate and business strategies are major influences on corporate culture. Conversely, organizational culture affects strategy and must support that strategy if it is to succeed. In this section, we will explore the relationship between strategy and culture and describe four common types of corporate culture.

An organization's culture is revealed through four kinds of cultural artifacts: myths and sagas; language systems and metaphors; symbols, ceremonies, and rituals; and value systems and behavioral norms. Each of these types is represented here. Mary Kay Ash (above, standing at left) has carefully fostered myths and sagas about herself and her company. At Walt Disney Companies, key metaphors are the notion that employees are "members of the cast" who are constantly "on stage." The use of symbols can be seen in Ford Motor Company's "Quality is Job 1" motto. Value systems and norms are represented by Hewlett-Packard's norm stating that people should not only be healthy but have fun, too.

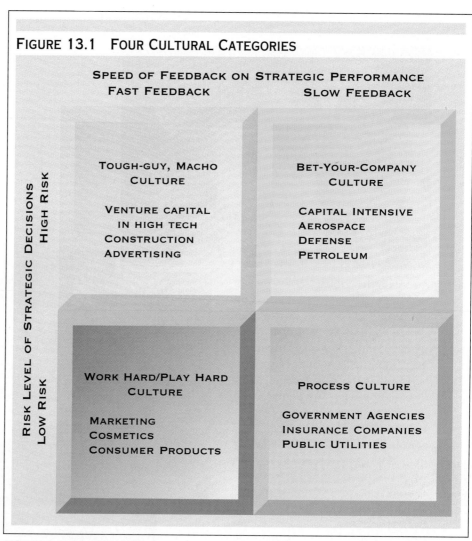

FIGURE 13.1   FOUR CULTURAL CATEGORIES

SPEED OF FEEDBACK ON STRATEGIC PERFORMANCE
FAST FEEDBACK   SLOW FEEDBACK

RISK LEVEL OF STRATEGIC DECISIONS
HIGH RISK

TOUGH-GUY, MACHO CULTURE

VENTURE CAPITAL
IN HIGH TECH
CONSTRUCTION
ADVERTISING

BET-YOUR-COMPANY CULTURE

CAPITAL INTENSIVE
AEROSPACE
DEFENSE
PETROLEUM

LOW RISK

WORK HARD/PLAY HARD CULTURE

MARKETING
COSMETICS
CONSUMER PRODUCTS

PROCESS CULTURE

GOVERNMENT AGENCIES
INSURANCE COMPANIES
PUBLIC UTILITIES

SOURCE: TERRENCE E. DEAL AND ALLAN A. KENNEDY, <u>CORPORATE CULTURES</u>, © 1982 BY ADDISON-WESLEY PUBLISHING COMPANY, INC. REPRINTED WITH PERMISSION OF THE PUBLISHER.

Culture as a Strategic Weapon

An organization's culture can be used as a strategic weapon. This occurs when management creates and reinforces values that support the company's purposes and strategies. In terms of the McKinsey Seven S's model discussed in Chapter 7, the better aligned the Seven S's, the greater the commitment of employees and the greater the likelihood of success. Culture can also be used as a strategic weapon when values are shared by the company, its customers, and its suppliers.

Terrence E. Deal and Allan A. Kennedy suggest that the relationship between strategy and culture is very pronounced and results in the four readily identifiable cultural categories shown in Figure 13.1: tough-guy, macho culture; bet-your-company culture; work hard/play hard culture; and process culture.[18] These categories are based on combinations of the speed of the feedback given following strategic performance and the degree of risk taken in making strategic decisions. Cultures may change from one type to another over time, sometimes intentionally, sometimes as a consequence of changing circumstances.

TOUGH-GUY/MACHO CULTURE

When strategic problem solvers commit large sums of money in highly competitive situations, the organization is characterized by a **tough-guy/macho** culture.

Managers operating in such a culture quickly learn the consequences of their high-risk strategic decisions. Tough-guy cultures are typical of high-tech manufacturers of products with short life cycles, such as computer work stations or PCs; large construction projects like the $650 million International Trade Building in Washington, D.C.; and advertising companies competing for new clients. Leaders in this culture tend to be the heroes, the ones who pull off the big deals. The stories told involve past risks that resulted in success. Slogans are battle cries, and ceremonies focus on problem solving.

Tough-guy/macho culture: An organizational culture that develops when strategic problem solvers commit large sums of money in highly competitive situations.

BET-YOUR-COMPANY CULTURE

The **bet-your-company** culture results from decisions for which feedback is slow but risks are high. Large financial investments are made in highly competitive environments where payoffs take a while to develop. This culture is common in capital-intensive industries (those requiring major investments in plants, equipment, or R&D), such as aerospace, defense, and petroleum. Boeing Aircraft, for example, has spent billions of dollars to develop its 777 airplane, but it will not know for several years whether this investment will pay off.[19] Genentech, the leading biotechnology company in the 1980s, invested hundreds of millions of dollars in R&D and hired a marketing staff before it had any products. It literally bet the company and its investors' money on its ability to develop products that did not exist when the company was founded.[20]

The heroes in this culture are sage and experienced. They have survived over the long haul and know what is involved in betting the company. The culture's ceremonies typically call for formal meetings to reduce uncertainty.

Bet-your-company culture: An organizational culture that develops where feedback on decisions is slow but the risks are high.

WORK HARD/PLAY HARD CULTURE

The **work hard/play hard** culture emerges in situations characterized by fast feedback and low risk. It is a fast-paced culture in which fun is important and there is plenty of action for everyone. This culture encourages creativity in problem solving.

The work hard/play hard culture often occurs in marketing-oriented firms. Certain types of retail stores, consulting firms, and large computer manufacturers often have this type of culture. Managers make many decisions, but most of

Work hard/play hard culture: An organizational culture that emerges in situations characterized by fast feedback and low risk.

The tough-guy/macho culture is illustrated by Donald Trump, who often undertakes high-risk construction projects. A work hard/play hard culture may be found at Procter and Gamble. Here P&G laundresses test detergents in washing machines from various countries.

them involve little risk. The new product either sells or does not sell; the effect of its sales on total company sales is minimal, although for the product manager it may be significant. For example, at Procter & Gamble, a company with more than seven hundred products, a product manager's efforts will have little effect on the company as a whole, but failure could lead to the manager's being fired. The heroes in such a culture are super salespeople, yet they are often team players. Sales conventions, meetings, contests, and parties all reinforce the values of hard work and hard play. Mary Kay Cosmetics, for example, is well known for its extravagant annual convention.

PROCESS CULTURE

Process culture: An organizational culture that evolves from situations in which feedback on decisions is slow and risk is low.

The **process culture** evolves from situations in which feedback is slow and risk is low. Organizations with such a culture typically include government agencies, insurance companies, and public utilities. Note, however, that cultures in some of these organizations—for example, insurance companies—are beginning to change because the environments they face involve higher risk than was once true. (In some cases there is also faster feedback.) The term *process* refers to how problems are solved and decisions made. Because it is often difficult to tell what the results of decisions are, and because there is no particular risk, the key value is the way in which decisions are made—that is, the process. Such organizational environments are activity oriented rather than result oriented. Organizations with a process culture are described as mechanistic. The U.S. Department of Health and Human Services is a classic example of a process culture.

AT BA: The process culture best characterizes the situation at BA before Sir Colin Marshall took over. After Marshall's arrival, the firm shifted toward a bet-your-company culture, but it also had elements of a tough guy/macho culture.

Heroes in this culture devise new processes and perform maintenance roles for the organization; they act to keep the company going, perhaps by providing recognition or passing on information. Ceremonies reward performance in carrying out processes. A thirty-year pin is a symbol of success in such an organization.

Culture and Shared Values

Since 1924, IBM has charted its course with three key values articulated by its founder, Thomas J. Watson, Sr.:

1. *Respect for the individual:* Caring about the basic rights of each person in the organization and not just when it is convenient or expedient to do so.
2. *Customer service:* Giving the best customer service of any company in the world, not some of the time but all of the time.
3. *Excellence:* Believing that all job holders and products should perform in a superior way.[21]

This credo appears everywhere at IBM—on the walls, in manuals, in discussions among employees. If you ask any IBM employee, he or she will tell you that the customer comes first, that IBM cares about the individual, and that all of IBM's products and services must have a high level of quality. In recent years, as tough competition has forced it to downsize, IBM has reaffirmed these values—focusing again on customer service and excellence and still showing respect for the individual by not laying off personnel until all other alternatives had been exhausted. Even then, the number let go was small compared to the numbers receiving early retirement or contract layoffs.

More and more organizations are beginning to recognize the importance of publishing statements of their core values.[22]

If you want to know what an organization's culture is like, ask its members what is important. Have them describe their strategy, structure, systems, style, staff, skills, shared values, norms, rules or policies, and procedures. Have them describe their heroes, their ceremonies, their symbols, their stories, their slogans. If they say the customer is important, ask them what they do for customers. AM International, a worldwide sales and service firm serving the graphic arts industry, inverted its organization chart, putting the customer at the top. The "players," or front-line employees, are at the next level, followed by the "coaches" and "scorekeepers."[23] This unique organization chart is shown in Figure 13.2. In such a situation, management's role changes from order giver to facilitator, counselor, and supporter.

What about the culture of innovative organizations? This chapter's Innovation Management Challenge provides some insight into the question. In reading about Herman Miller, try to discover a few of the values that are important to an innovative company.

Fitting Employees into the Corporate Culture

Corporate culture is an expression of an organization's shared values, but the values of individuals vary. This implies that the values of individual employees must be changed to match those of the group and the organization or that, at the very least, the employee must adopt new values. For example, if a blue suit, white shirt or blouse, and dark tie or scarf constitute the company "uniform," the individual must dress that way regardless of his or her personal preferences.

On the basis of a study of numerous corporate cultures, Richard T. Pascale proposed that organizations with strong cultures fit employees into the company

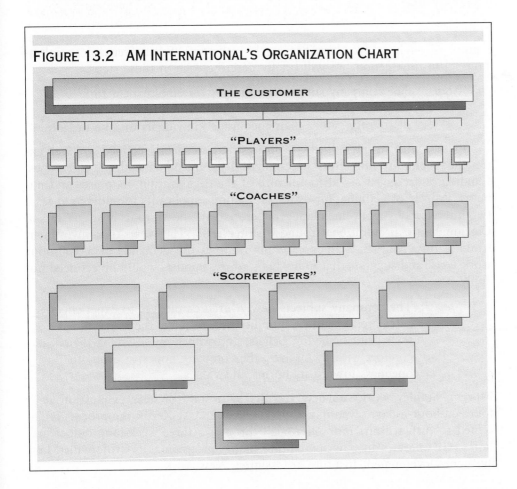

FIGURE 13.2 AM INTERNATIONAL'S ORGANIZATION CHART

THE CUSTOMER

"PLAYERS"

"COACHES"

"SCOREKEEPERS"

The Creative Organizational Culture

What are some of the characteristics of a creative organizational culture? An organization with such a culture tolerates extremely creative people, rewards creative ideas, trains people to be creative, celebrates creative successes, and tends to be democratic. Herman Miller, Inc., an office furniture design company, believes that the key to creativity lies in eliminating the stresses and inconveniences of the daily work routine. It has provided informal meeting areas throughout its offices. These give people a place to sit and chat whenever ideas occur. The company lets employees design their own offices, believing that different people need different types of work spaces. It has located its research department far from the main office, giving researchers real as well as symbolic freedom. Herman Miller also believes in participative management and in sharing profits with employees. Open communication and a trusting environment also characterize this firm. These values help make Herman Miller the most innovative office furniture company in the United States.

SOURCES: James M. Higgins, *Profile of the Innovative Organization: A Seven S's Perspective* (forthcoming); Joani Nelson-Horchler, "The Magic of Herman Miller," *Industry Week* (February 18, 1991), pp. 11–17; Charles O'Reilly, "Corporations, Culture, and Commitment: Motivation and Social Control in Organizations," *California Management Review* (Summer 1989), pp. 9–25; and "Eureka! New Ideas on Boosting Creativity," *Success* (December 1985), p. 27.

AT BA: Enculturation begins with a very rigorous selection process, but BA also needed to indoctrinate the employees it already had. Once that was done, BA could follow the seven steps of socialization for new employees.

culture through a seven-step process he calls the "Seven Steps of Socialization."[24] In this section, we will briefly describe each of those steps.

> *Step 1:* The company subjects candidates for employment to a selection process so rigorous that it often seems designed to discourage rather than encourage individuals to take the job.

Companies with strong cultures—cultures that are clearly defined and well entrenched—employ numerous selection devices, including multiple interviews. Candidates are given a realistic picture of the organization, its pluses and minuses. Procter & Gamble, for example, requires applicants to undergo at least two interviews by front-line managers before being flown to its headquarters in Cincinnati for an additional round of interviews. The New York investment banking firm Morgan Stanley carefully outlines the demands of a 100-hour work week and suggests that individuals whose families would object need not apply.

> *Step 2:* The company subjects newly hired employees to experiences calculated to induce humility and to make them question their prior behavior, beliefs, and values. By lessening their comfort with themselves, the company hopes to promote openness toward its norms and values.

Morgan Stanley works its new recruits to a state of near exhaustion with fourteen-hour-a-day, seven-day-a-week schedules. At Xerox the process is designed to turn recruits into "Xeroids" through a three-week-long indoctrination.[25] GE operates an extensive culture change program at its Crotonville Management Development Institute in Ossining, New York.

GE operates an extensive culture change program at its Management Development Institute in Crotonville, New York.

The Crotonville Institute does much more than teach traditional business courses like accounting and finance. It also spreads Chairman John Welch's vision of the company. It helps indocrinate GE's culture into its employees. Its success has caused several companies to emulate it, including Hitashi, Limited, which built a virtual replica of Crotonville in Japan. The focus is on teamwork and learning from others. For example, river raft races help build camaraderie as well as leadership. Crotonville's mission reads "to make GE managers more action-oriented, more risk-oriented, more people-oriented." Welch observes, "It's supposed to develop leaders, not just managers. Yesterday's idea of the boss, who became the boss because he or she knew one more fact than the person working for them, is yesterday's manager. Tomorrow's person needs to envision a shared set of values, a shared objective."[26]

Step 3: The companies send the newly humbled recruits into the trenches, pushing them to master one of the disciplines at the core of the company's business. The newcomers' promotions are tied to how they do in that discipline.

At Delta Airlines, Morgan Stanley, McKinsey & Company, IBM, and a host of other major companies, new recruits must work their way up through the organization. It takes six years to become an IBM marketing representative. Advancement is slow and is based on performance.

Step 4: At every stage of the new manager's career, the company measures the results he or she has achieved and grants rewards accordingly.

IBM makes certain that its managers adhere to the company's three credos. Especially important is courteous and fair treatment of others. IBM has been known to punish managers who failed to treat subordinates properly; they have been reassigned to less desirable jobs. At Procter & Gamble, the performance of new professionals is evaluated against three core criteria: building volume, building profits, and conducting changes.

Step 5: All along the way the company promotes adherence to its transcendent values, those overarching purposes that go far beyond the quest for profits.

At Delta Airlines, new recruits learn about "the family." All employees are members of the family, and the family works together through thick and thin. Members take pay cuts so that other members of the family will not be laid off. Senior pilots may work for reduced hours to avoid cutbacks. Sacrifices are necessary, but the family survives.

Step 6: Great emphasis is placed on watershed events in the organization's history that reaffirm its culture. The organization's folklore reinforces a code of conduct—how we do things around here.

A story that is frequently told at Procter & Gamble reveals its emphasis on honesty: A top brand manager was fired because he had overstated a product's features. At AT&T, stories focus on keeping the telephone system working in emergency situations. These stories not only carry a moral, but encourage similar behavior by the recruit.

Step 7: The company supplies promising individuals with role models. These models are consistent—each exemplary manager displays the same traits.

IBM, 3M, and AT&T all provide role models for employees to imitate. They may be peers or supervisors. The protégé watches the role model make presentations, write memos, handle conflicts, and manage, and attempts to duplicate those efforts. In many firms, relationships between role models and protégés develop more or less by accident, but effective organizations make a point of providing models for employees.[27]

Managing Culture

The effective manager must identify the organization's existing culture and its impact on effectiveness and efficiency. He or she must then determine whether that culture is appropriate and, if not, change it.

Culture must be understood at two levels: the mythical level, which includes the organization's myths, stories, heroes, symbols, slogans, and ceremonies; and the normative level—"the way we do things around here."[28] The normative level of culture is indicated in strategy, structure, systems, style, staffing, and skills, as well as in rules, procedures, and policies. The manager, whether a department manager or CEO, must learn to manage both levels of organizational culture.

MULTIPLE CULTURES

The management of culture is further complicated by the variations in culture within the organization, which often reflect variations within the society in which it operates. There is usually a widely shared, or mainstream, culture and a set of subcultures. In addition, there are often varying degrees of acceptance or rejection of the key values of each culture.[29] Numerous factors—a particular manager or group of managers, a particular set of environmental circumstances or corporate pressures, disagreement with company policies and procedures, differing interpretations of values—can lead to different behaviors within an organization.

Multiple cultures exist in an organization for several reasons, the most obvious of which is that organizations are made up of people of different races, ethnicities, nationalities, gender, and ages. This condition, known as cultural diversity, will be discussed in more depth shortly. Multiple cultures may also exist as the result of a merger of two companies, a change in top management, multinational operations or alliances, and different functional, product, or SBU-based cultures.

Multiple cultures naturally exist within an organization immediately after a merger.[30] For example, when General Motors acquired Electronic Data Systems, the cultures of the two organizations clashed severely. H. Ross Perot, founder and CEO of EDS, ran a militaristic organization whose management ranks were much thinner than GM's. Perot's entrepreneurial values were quite different from those of GM's CEO, Roger Smith. Only when GM purchased all of Perot's shares in the company was GM able to begin to resolve the clash of cultures.[31] As it turned out, Perot was right. GM became more like EDS as it downsized significantly, closed numerous plants, and eventually eliminated about half of its white-collar work force.

A change in top management often leads to the presence of multiple cultures within the organization. Again using the example of GM, when Robert Stempel took over from Roger Smith, he attempted to change the organization's culture. When Jack Smith took over from Stempel, he too sought cultural change.[32] In both cases, many employees who had lived through eleven years of a culture led by Roger Smith still adhered to the norms of that culture, while others were more willing to accept the new culture.[33] The old culture was bureaucratic, inefficient, and indecisive, and pay (including bonuses) was unrelated to performance. The new culture honors hard work, pay for performance (for white-collar workers), efficiency, and competitiveness.

Multinational firms must deal not only with the cultural diversity of their employees but also with the varying cultures of the countries in which they operate. Such firms sometimes hire a *cultural integrator,* someone familiar with several cultures, who coordinates the activities of groups operating in different cultures.[34] A firm doing business in all the countries of the European Economic Community, for example, must deal with a minimum of twelve cultures. Employees who work overseas must become familiar with the cultures of the countries in which they do business. This chapter's Diversity Management Challenge examines how Korea's Samsung Corporation trains its personnel for overseas assignments. How do you think its practices differ from those of U.S. firms?

Managing Cultural Diversity

As discussed in Chapter 12, cultural diversity refers to the existence of more than one culture within an organization or a society. While the focus is on ethnic minorities, in a broader context the term includes women and older workers, as well as people from different countries working together in a multinational firm. Historically, the U.S. labor force has consisted primarily of white males. In recent decades, however, the composition of the labor force has changed, and it continues to change. From 1989 to 2000, only 15 percent of the new members added to the labor force will be native-born white men, compared to 48 percent in 1988. The remainder will be nonwhite and immigrant men and women and native-born white women (42 percent).[35] Moreover, the number of married women working outside the home will continue to increase. There will also be more divorced people and single parents in the labor force. The proportions of black and Hispanic workers will increase at a higher rate than that of white workers. As a result, the labor force will be more racially and ethnically diverse,

Samsung Prepares Employees for Other Cultures

Samsung is Korea's largest company, with assests of nearly $16 billion and operations in fifty-five countries. Like many Korean companies, it has been export-driven for the past twenty years. And now it is ready to *think international*.

The idea of internationalization—or *kukjewha*—is new in Korea. Companies used to believe that they could sell whatever they built. However, the international environment has changed. Korean firms are losing market share, sandwiched between low-paid workers in China and Malaysia on the one hand and high technology from the United States and Japan on the other.

Giant Korean firms like Samsung believe that they need to anticipate consumer desires and respond to competition. To do that, Samsung has launched an internationalization campaign.

with fewer male head-of-household wage earners.[36] Finally, the proportion of older workers will be higher than in the past. In addition, as noted earlier, two major age groups, the baby-boomers and the baby-busters, are moving through the work force.

Many companies have initiated programs to help their members work within such an environment. Digital Equipment Corporation is an example. DEC's cultural diversity program—"Valuing Diversity"—cuts across all levels of the organization. Barbara Walker, its founder, labels it "good business," not just doing good.[37] Similarly, Corning Corporation believes that managing a multicultural work force in the best way possible makes good business sense.[38]

Managing cultural diversity is a complex and difficult task, both from the perspective of the organization and from that of the individual manager. Train-

As a result, Korean giants like Samsung feel that they need to anticipate consumer desires and respond to competition. To do that, they have to learn more about foreign countries.

"We are ignorant of foreign culture," explains the manager of Samsung's personnel department. A case in point is the 1991 wall calendar that was sent to overseas customers and partners. For each month, a female model is depicted holding a Samsung product. For July, the model wears a see-through blouse. When they learned that some Americans were offended, Samsung executives quickly recalled the calendar.

In the future, Samsung hopes not just to avoid blunders but to be more culturally sensitive. To achieve this objective, it has launched an internationalization campaign. Executives are encouraged to learn English or Japanese. Managers bound for overseas assignments attend a kind of boot camp with a curriculum that includes table manners, dancing, and avoiding sexual harassment. And about four hundred of the most promising young employees are being sent abroad for a year to "develop international tastes."

The costs of the overseas postings are substantial—around $80,000 per employee—and they take key people out of circulation. But Samsung is confident that the cultural immersion will create savvier managers for its international operations.

Samsung employees working abroad have experienced many of the dismaying features of life in their host countries. In New York City, one manager had all his belongings stolen from a rental car—and was afraid to tell the police. In Moscow, another had his car stolen. In South Africa, an employee with a black belt in tae kwon do was attacked in a Soweto pub, knocked unconscious, and relieved of both his money and his car. He thought his Karate skills would protect him, but he was mistaken.

Samsung does not send women employees abroad. "Samsung corporate culture is that women are not involved in corporate operations," explains the general manager of the group's personnel department. "Taking into account Korea's cultural climate, we will delay that."

Meanwhile, back at the boot camp for managers heading abroad, considerable attention is given to dealing with women. Employees are warned not to ask female job applicants whether they are married, when they intend to marry, their age, or their religion.

SOURCE: "Korea's Biggest Firm Teaches Junior Execs Strange Foreign Ways," Wall Street Journal (December 30, 1992), pp. A1, A4.

ing and development programs aimed at increasing awareness of cultural diversity and promoting positive attitudes toward cultural differences are critical to successfully managing cultural diversity. Such programs should begin with top management and involve all levels of the organizational hierarchy. It is important to instill a positive attitude toward diversity.[39] Part of the management of diversity is convincing people that diverse cultures create a richer and more innovative experience, more open to change and better at problem solving than homogenous groups.[40] Various other programs must be modified or initiated to accommodate a more diverse work force. For example, compensation programs should be modified to meet the needs of various groups; job sharing may be needed to accommodate parents of young children; on-site day care or elder care may be necessary; and so on.

One of the principles of DEC's cultural diversity program is that diversity is something that should be celebrated. Another is that diversity can be managed in ways that benefit both the company and its employees.

R. Roosevelt Thomas, director of the American Institute for Managing Diversity at Morehouse College in Atlanta, suggests the following ten steps for managing cultural diversity successfully—that is, so that no member of a diverse work force experiences an unnatural advantage or disadvantage:

1. *Clarify your motivation:* The goal is to cope effectively with a change in the managerial environment.
2. *Clarify your vision:* Help people understand that a properly managed, culturally diverse work force unleashes everyone's greatest potential.
3. *Expand your focus:* Managing cultural diversity goes beyond integrating minorities and women into the work force. Its goal is to create a heterogeneous culture in which people differ in many ways, including age, education, background, function, and personality.
4. *Audit your corporate culture:* To create the culture you want, you need information about the existing culture.
5. *Modify your assumptions:* The organizational culture's real values must be found and changed to meet the requirements of the new culture. Destructive assumptions about members of other cultural groups must be rooted out.
6. *Modify your systems:* Modifying assumptions makes it possible to change systems, such as those related to promotions, mentoring, and performance appraisal.
7. *Modify your models:* A second reason for modifying assumptions is that models of appropriate managerial and employee behavior will change.
8. *Help people pioneer:* Managing diversity involves managing change. This may require helping some members of the organization overcome obstacles and recover from failures.
9. *Apply the special consideration test:* A cultural diversity program should focus on more than one group; otherwise it is not truly managing diversity.
10. *Initiate affirmative action:* Cultural diversity begins with an affirmative action program.[41]

It quickly becomes obvious that managing diversity is a complex process. However, there are many success stories to emulate, and commitment will lead

Managing cultural diversity goes beyond integrating minorities and women into the work force. Its goal is to create a heterogeneous culture in which people differ in many ways, including age, education, background, function, and personality. This principle is illustrated in a painting by Mark Hess that appeared on the cover of *Fortune* magazine.

to future successes. Moreover, cultural diversity programs are not limited to the ten factors just listed. Companies can adjust their programs to meet their specific needs. Avon created ethnic networks for blacks, Hispanics, and Asians as part of implementing Thomas's ten-point program.[42] Other firms may choose other tactics. UPS, for example, has had a culturally diverse work force for many years. To help facilitate managers' understanding of differing perspectives, it created its Community Internship Program in 1968. Upper and middle managers are taken off the job for one month to work as community interns. During that time they may serve meals to the homeless, help urban neighborhoods fight drug abuse, build temporary housing for migrant workers, or help teachers manage disadvantaged children. About forty managers a year serve as community interns.[43] Throughout this book there are examples of situations involving issues of diversity in multinational firms.

Organizational Climate

Organizational climate refers to the desirability of the work and social environment within an organization. It can be seen in how people communicate, make decisions, establish objectives, lead, and control. Climate is a function of many variables, including managers' actions, employees' behavior, work-group behav-

Organizational climate:
The desirability of the work and social environment within an organization.

ior, and other factors both internal and external to the organization.[44] Climate is a critical component of organizational culture.[45]

Every organization should periodically assess its climate. Systems for measuring organizational climate have been developed by several management experts, including Rensis Likert, Keith Davis, George Litwin and Robert Stringer, Garlie Forehand and B. Von Haller Gilmer, and Andrew W. Halpin and D. B. Crofts.[46] The best known and most widely used of these is the Likert system. (See Figure 13.3.) Likert identified four basic types of organizational climate: exploitive authoritative, benevolent authoritative, consultative, and participative. These are referred to as Systems 1, 2, 3, and 4, respectively. Each system is part of a continuum based on degree of participation. In an exploitive authoritative climate, the manager makes decisions regardless of employee needs. In a benevolent authoritative climate, the manager makes decisions in a quasi-parental way, having considered employee needs. In a consultative authoritative climate, the manager makes decisions but asks subordinates for input. In a group participative climate, the group makes the decisions. According to Likert, System 4 is the most appropriate style of management in most situations.

Likert and his associates at the Center for Social Research at the University of Michigan developed an employee questionnaire for use in assessing organizational climate. Four responses are provided for each question; each response is a behavior representing one of the four systems. The questions are subdivided into six issue areas: leadership, motivation, communication, decisions, objectives, and control. Figure 13.3 presents a shortened version of the questionnaire. Why not complete it as directed, basing your responses on a current or past work situation? Read the question on the left, and circle the answer to the right that best describes your experience. You can use either your immediate supervisor and work group or the total organization as a point of reference.

After you have answered the questions, score one point for each System 1 answer; two for each System 2 answer; three for each System 3 answer; and four for each System 4 answer. Add up the points you scored and divide the total by 19. The average score should be between 1 and 4. Comparing it with the descriptive titles of Systems 1, 2, 3, and 4 will give you a rough idea of your organization's climate. A score of 2.4, for example, would be about halfway between Systems 2 and 3—that is, halfway between benevolently authoritative and communicative.

According to Likert and his associates, the higher the score, the better the management style. Allowance must be made for contingencies, of course; no

In a consultative climate like that of the typical advertising firm, shown here, the manager makes decisions but asks subordinates for input. In a group participative climate, the group makes the decisions.

FIGURE 13.3 LIKERT'S FOUR STYLES OF MANAGEMENT

	SYSTEM 1 EXPLOITIVE AUTHORITATIVE	SYSTEM 2 BENEVOLENT AUTHORITATIVE	SYSTEM 3 CONSULTATIVE	SYSTEM 4 PARTICIPATIVE GROUP
HOW MUCH CONFIDENCE IS SHOWN IN SUBORDINATES?	NONE	CONDESCENDING	SUBSTANTIAL	COMPLETE
HOW FREE DO THEY FEEL TO TALK TO SUPERIORS ABOUT JOB?	NOT AT ALL	NOT VERY	RATHER FREE	FULLY FREE
ARE SUBORDINATES' IDEAS SOUGHT AND USED, IF WORTHY?	SELDOM	SOMETIMES	USUALLY	ALWAYS
IS PREDOMINANT USE MADE OF 1 FEAR, 2 THREATS, 3 PUNISHMENT, 4 REWARDS, 5 INVOLVEMENT?	1, 2, 3, OCCASIONALLY 4	4, SOME 3	4, SOME 3 AND 5	5, 4 BASED ON GROUP SET GOALS
WHERE IS RESPONSIBILITY FELT FOR ACHIEVING ORGANIZATION'S GOALS?	MOSTLY AT TOP	TOP AND MIDDLE	FAIRLY GENERAL	AT ALL LEVELS
HOW MUCH COMMUNICATION IS AIMED AT ACHIEVING ORGANIZATION'S OBJECTIVES?	VERY LITTLE	LITTLE	QUITE A BIT	A GREAT DEAL
WHAT IS THE DIRECTION OF INFORMATION FLOW?	DOWNWARD	MOSTLY DOWNWARD	DOWN AND UP	DOWN, UP AND SIDEWAYS
HOW IS DOWNWARD COMMUNICATION ACCEPTED?	WITH SUSPICION	POSSIBLY WITH SUSPICION	WITH CAUTION	WITH AN OPEN MIND
HOW ACCURATE IS UPWARD COMMUNICATION?	OFTEN WRONG	CENSORED FOR THE BOSS	LIMITED ACCURACY	ACCURATE
HOW WELL DO SUPERIORS KNOW PROBLEMS FACED BY SUBORDINATES?	KNOW LITTLE	SOME KNOWLEDGE	QUITE WELL	VERY WELL
AT WHAT LEVEL ARE DECISIONS FORMALLY MADE?	MOSTLY AT TOP	POLICY AT TOP, SOME DELEGATION	BROAD POLICY AT TOP, MORE DELEGATION	THROUGHOUT BUT WELL INTEGRATED
WHAT IS THE ORIGIN OF TECHNICAL AND PROFESSIONAL KNOWLEDGE USED IN DECISION MAKING?	TOP MANAGEMENT	UPPER AND MIDDLE	TO A CERTAIN EXTENT, THROUGHOUT	TO A GREAT EXTENT THROUGHOUT
ARE SUBORDINATES INVOLVED IN DECISIONS RELATED TO THEIR WORK?	NOT AT ALL	OCCASIONALLY CONSULTED	GENERALLY CONSULTED	FULLY INVOLVED
WHAT DOES DECISION-MAKING PROCESS CONTRIBUTE TO MOTIVATION?	NOTHING: OFTEN WEAKENS IT	RELATIVELY LITTLE	SOME CONTRIBUTION	SUBSTANTIAL CONTRIBUTION
HOW ARE ORGANIZATIONAL GOALS ESTABLISHED?	ORDERS ISSUED	ORDERS, SOME COMMENT INVITED	AFTER DISCUSSION, BY ORDERS	BY GROUP ACTION (EXCEPT IN CRISIS)
HOW MUCH COVERT RESISTANCE TO GOALS IS PRESENT?	STRONG RESISTANCE	MODERATE RESISTANCE	SOME RESISTANCE AT TIMES	LITTLE OR MORE
HOW CONCENTRATED ARE REVIEW AND CONTROL FUNCTIONS?	HIGHLY AT TOP	RELATIVELY HIGHLY AT TOP	MODERATE DELEGATION TO LOWER LEVELS	QUITE WIDELY SHARED
IS THERE AN INFORMAL ORGANIZATION RESISTING THE FORMAL ONE?	YES	USUALLY	SOMETIMES	NO—SAME GOAL AS FORMAL
WHAT ARE COST, PRODUCTIVITY, AND OTHER CONTROL DATA USED FOR?	POLICING, PUNISHMENT	REWARD AND PUNISHMENT	REWARD, SOME SELF-GUIDANCE	SELF-GUIDANCE, PROBLEM SOLVING

SOURCE: R. LIKERT, NEW PATTERNS OF MANAGEMENT, © 1961, MCGRAW-HILL INC. REPRINTED WITH PERMISSION OF MCGRAW-HILL.

management prescription works for all situations. The national average on the Likert scale is about 2.4, but scores vary between organizations and within the same organization at any point in time as well as over time. Firms with scores below 2 have cause for concern. Such organizations are less desirable places to work and probably are less productive.

Beginning in 1969, Likert demonstrated the correlation between Likert scale scores and organizational performance, using two GM plants in the same city. The plant that scored lower on the scale had low morale and low productivity. The plant that scored higher had high morale and high productivity. Moreover, when the low-scoring plant adopted the other's management practices, its morale, productivity, and climate scores all improved dramatically.[47]

Likert's System 4 is highly group oriented. Some individuals would not benefit from this type of climate. For example, highly creative or achievement-oriented individuals may not want to work in teams or groups. Participation may not be effective when subordinates are not sufficiently mature. In some situations, such as military organizations, authoritarian management styles are necessary. Given recent changes in employee expectations and educational levels, it would seem that System 4 is probably more desirable than in the past. Each system, however, may be appropriate in some situations.

Managing Change

Managing change: A process in which the individual and the organization develop plans to influence change, implement it, and control its effects, as opposed to simply letting change happen.

The effective management of change is a necessity for all businesses today. **Managing change** means that the individual and the organization develop plans to influence change, implement it, and control its effects, as opposed to simply letting change happen. In this section, we discuss the issues of accelerating change and changes in the business environment. We then review organizational development—that is, the planning and implementation of a program for managing change. Finally, resistance to change and how to overcome it are discussed.

Accelerating Rates of Change

In 1970, Alvin Toffler's book *Future Shock* sounded an alarm, claiming that the future would be dominated by changes that would increase at an accelerating rate, as revealed in Figure 13.4.[48] Toffler's predictions have come true. Changes are occurring at accelerating rates in science and technology, industrial competition, organizational structure, social relationships, law, social structure, and global events. As such changes come faster and faster, both individuals and organizations find it more difficult to cope with them. The result is "future shock."

In 1982, John Naisbitt identified the ten "megatrends" that appear in Table 13.1. Like Toffler's, Naisbitt's predictions have come true to a large extent. It is clear, for example, that we live in an information-based society, that firms are operating in an increasingly global economy, that organizations are decentralizing, that the level of participation in organizations is increasing, that networked structures are becoming more common, that there is a movement of power to the southern United States, and that people have many choices regarding how to live their lives.

In early 1990, Naisbitt and his wife, Patricia Auberdene, identified ten new megatrends for the year 2000: a global economic boom, a renaissance in the arts, the emergence of free-market socialism (in Europe, Eastern Europe, and the Soviet Union, but perhaps in Asia as well), global life-styles and cultural nation-

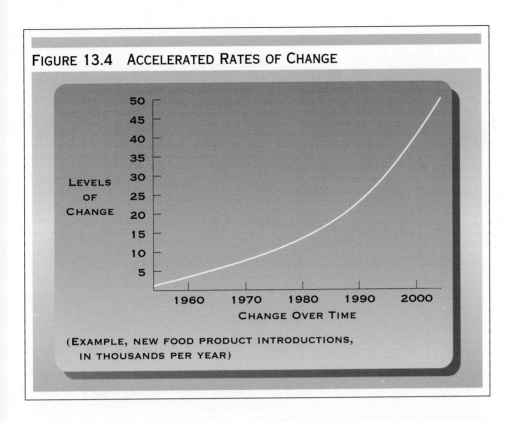

FIGURE 13.4   ACCELERATED RATES OF CHANGE

LEVELS OF CHANGE

50
45
40
35
30
25
20
15
10
5

1960   1970   1980   1990   2000

CHANGE OVER TIME

(EXAMPLE, NEW FOOD PRODUCT INTRODUCTIONS, IN THOUSANDS PER YEAR)

alism, the privatization of the welfare state, increasing prosperity in Pacific Rim nations, an increase in the number of women in leadership positions, major advances in biology, religious revival, and the triumph of the individual.[49] Some of these trends, such as free-market socialism, are already in evidence.

TABLE 13.1 Megatrends

Changing from	Changing to
1. Industrial society	Information society
2. Forced technology	High tech/High touch: In a high-technology society, high levels of interpersonal relations are necessary to counterbalance the impersonalness of this technology.
3. National economy	World economy
4. Short-term perspective	Long-term perspective
5. Centralization (of organization and society)	Decentralization (of organization and society)
6. Institutional help	Self-help
7. Representative democracy (in society and organization)	Participation (of organization and society)
8. Hierarchies in structures of organizations	Networking
9. North (geographic migration in the United States)	South (geographic migration in the United States)
10. Either/or (personal choices)	Multiple options (personal choices)

SOURCE: John Naisbitt, *Megatrends* (New York: Warner Books, 1982).

FIGURE 13.5 A WORLD TURNED UPSIDE DOWN

	WAS/IS	MUST BECOME
1. MARKETING	MASS MARKETS, MASS ADVERTISING, VIOLENT BATTLES TO SHIFT A SHARE POINT (MARKET SHARE), FUNCTIONAL INTEGRITY OF MARKETING PROS	MARKET CREATION, NICHE FOCUS, INNOVATION FROM BEING CLOSER TO MARKETS, THRIVING ON MARKET FRAGMENTATION, CEASELESS DIFFERENTIATION OF ANY PRODUCT (NO MATTER HOW MATURE)
2. INTERNATIONAL	"GLOBAL" BRANDS WHICH ARE MANAGED FROM THE U.S., INTERNATIONAL AS AN ADJUNCT ACTIVITY, FOR BIG FIRMS ONLY	FOCUS ON NEW MARKET CREATION, DEVELOPMENT DONE OFFSHORE FROM THE START, ESSENTIAL STRATEGY FOR FIRMS OF ALL SIZES.
3. MANUFACTURING	EMPHASIS ON VOLUME, COST, HARDWARE, FUNCTIONAL INTEGRITY	PRIMARY MARKETING TOOL (SOURCE OF QUALITY, RESPONSIVENESS, INNOVATION), PART OF PRODUCT DESIGN TEAM FROM THE START, SHORT RUNS, FLEXIBILITY, PEOPLE SUPPORTED BY AUTOMATION
4. SALES AND SERVICE	SECOND-CLASS CITIZENS, "MOVE THE PRODUCT" PREDOMINATES	HEROES, RELATIONSHIP MANAGERS (WITH EVERY CUSTOMER, EVEN IN RETAIL), MAJOR SOURCE OF VALUE ADDED, PRIME SOURCE OF NEW PRODUCT IDEAS
5. INNOVATION	DRIVEN BY CENTRAL R&D, BIG PROJECTS THE NORM, SCIENCE- RATHER THAN CUSTOMER-DRIVEN, CLEVERNESS OF DESIGN MORE IMPORTANT THAN FITS AND FINISHES, LIMITED TO NEW PRODUCTS	SMALL STARTS IN AUTONOMOUS AND DECENTRALIZED UNITS THE KEY, EVERYONE'S BUSINESS, DRIVEN BY DESIRE TO MAKE SMALL AND CUSTOMER-NOTICEABLE IMPROVEMENTS
6. PEOPLE	NEED TIGHT CONTROL, TRY TO SPECIALIZE AND DIMINISH ROLE	PEOPLE AS PRIME SOURCE OF VALUE ADDED, CAN NEVER TRAIN OR INVOLVE TOO MUCH, BIG FINANCIAL STAKE IN THE OUTCOME
7. STRUCTURE	HIERARCHICAL, FUNCTIONAL INTEGRITY MAINTAINED	FLAT, FUNCTIONAL BARRIERS BROKEN, FIRST-LINE SUPERVISORS GIVE WAY TO SELF-MANAGED TEAMS, MIDDLE MANAGERS AS FACILITATORS RATHER THAN TURF GUARDIANS
8. LEADERSHIP	DETACHED, ANALYTIC, CENTRALIZED STRATEGY PLANNING, DRIVEN BY CORPORATE STAFFS	LEADER AS LOVER OF CHANGE AND PREACHER OF VISION AND SHARED VALUES, STRATEGY DEVELOPMENT RADICALLY BOTTOM-UP, ALL STAFF FUNCTIONS SUPPORT THE LINE RATHER THAN VICE VERSA
9. MANAGEMENT INFORMATION SYSTEMS (MIS)	CENTRALIZED FOR THE SAKE OF CONSISTENCY, INTERNALLY AIMED	INFORMATION USE AND DIRECT CUSTOMER/SUPPLIER LINKUPS AS A STRATEGIC WEAPON MANAGED BY THE LINE, DECENTRALIZATION OF MIS A MUST
10. FINANCIAL MANAGEMENT AND CONTROL	CENTRALIZED, FINANCE STAFF AS COP	DECENTRALIZED, MOST FINANCE PEOPLE TO THE FIELD AS "BUSINESS TEAM MEMBERS," HIGH SPENDING AUTHORITY DOWN THE LINE

SOURCE: ADAPTED FROM THOMAS J. PETERS, THRIVING ON CHAOS: HANDBOOK FOR A MANAGEMENT REVOLUTION, PP. 42–43. COPYRIGHT © 1987 BY EXCEL, A CALIFORNIA LIMITED PARTNERSHIP. REPRINTED BY PERMISSION OF ALFRED A. KNOPF, INC.

Echoing the alarm sounded by Toffler and Naisbitt, Thomas J. Peters warned that managers are going to have to learn to manage in a world of increasing change—indeed, they are going to have to learn to thrive on chaos.[50] Peters recognized that accelerated rates of change, megatrends, and similar events have a direct impact on organizational life and, hence, on management. Ten areas in which change is accelerating are identified in Figure 13.5.

Chapter 1 described ten management challenges. Most of those challenges are a consequence of change. Numerous other areas of rapid change have been suggested by several authors.[51]

Organizational Development

Two ways to manage change in the organization are strategy and organizational development. Strategy was discussed in Chapter 7. In this section, we focus on organizational development. In its broadest sense, **organizational development** (OD) is any planned program for managing change. This definition would include strategies of all types.[52] More commonly, however, organizational development is construed as the management of change in organizational cultures. Wendell French and Cecil Bell have provided a widely accepted definition of OD: "a long-range effort to improve an organization's problem-solving and renewal processes, particularly through a more effective and collaborative management of organizational culture, with special emphasis on the culture of formal work teams, with the assistance of a change agent or catalyst, and the use of the theory and technology of applied behavioral science, including action research."[53] Let us take a closer look at each element of this definition.

Organizational development (OD): *In its broadest sense, any planned program for managing change; it is usually construed as the management of change in organizational cultures.*

LONG-RANGE EFFORT

Most OD programs require from two to five years to complete the cycle of diagnosis, planning, implementation, stabilization, and evaluation that characterizes the process. An example of a company that uses OD is Anheuser-Busch, which applies it to solve specific problems at its various facilities. At one brewery, management styles were changed from authoritative to participative, and productivity increased substantially as a result. Management expects each OD program to take at least several months and possibly several years, depending on the circumstances.[54] The reason OD interventions require so much time is that the behavioral changes sought require fundamental changes in attitudes and values. The diagnostic process leading to a decision about what actions to undertake also requires a significant amount of time. Typically, surveys, interviews, and performance analyses are employed in the diagnosis stage.

IMPROVING THE PROBLEM-SOLVING AND RENEWAL PROCESSES

The purpose of OD is to improve the way problems are solved in an organization and to make the organization self-renewing. The central focus of most such efforts is increased participation in decision making—giving those involved in a situation a chance to make decisions about how to improve it. The second goal of OD, renewal, stems from the tendency of organizations to stagnate as they age.[55]

COLLABORATIVE MANAGEMENT OF ORGANIZATIONAL CULTURE

At the core of OD is the management of shared values (values having to do with strategy, structure, systems, style, staff, skills, and other key factors in the organization) and norms (the informal "do's and don'ts" of organizational life).

SPECIAL EMPHASIS ON THE CULTURE
OF FORMAL WORK TEAMS

The emphasis in OD is almost always on improving the effectiveness and efficiency of work groups. Team-building exercises are typically employed. The manager's role changes from one of "boss" to one of counselor, coach, and facilitator. Quality circles, creativity circles, and autonomous work teams can all be part of an OD effort.

ASSISTANCE OF A CHANGE AGENT OR CATALYST

A **change agent** is a consultant, sometimes internal but usually external to the organization, who helps initiate and then guides the OD program. OD is unique in the management consulting field because the consultant remains with the organization to help implement the plans he or she recommends rather than simply writing a report and then leaving for another assignment. A **catalyst** is any event, such as a decline in productivity or profits, that triggers recognition of the need for an OD program. For example, Harley-Davidson experienced a decline in market share that became the catalyst for an OD effort to regain its dominance in the United States.

USING APPLIED BEHAVIORAL SCIENCE
AND ACTION RESEARCH

OD relies both on theory and on the results of relevant research. The OD consultant diagnoses the situation and makes recommendations about the actions necessary. This is known as **action research.** If a particular practice has been shown to be effective in one situation, it is usually transferred to another.

Changing Views of
Organizational Development

Until recently, OD has had a somewhat negative connotation among managers, partly because it did not seem sufficiently performance oriented, tended to ignore the realities of organizational politics, included terminology (and tech-

The emphasis in organizational design is almost always on improving the effectiveness and efficiency of work groups. The manager's role changes from one of "boss" to one of counselor, coach, and facilitator.

niques) that "turned off" many managers, and had produced poor evaluations when it came to measuring results.[56] As the underlying premises of OD have become more acceptable to U.S. managers, largely because of the success of foreign competitors using team-based OD efforts, and as OD has become more performance oriented (for example, through the incorporation of TQM programs), more companies have been willing to consider it.[57] In the future, the management of culture is likely to focus on creating learning organizations, encouraging innovation, and stimulating continuous improvement.[58]

Resistance to Change

FORCE-FIELD ANALYSIS

OD is one of several ways of managing organizational change. Regardless of which approach is used to manage change, the manager will invariably be faced with resistance. To better manage change, the problem solver needs to understand **force-field analysis**. This concept—developed by Kurt Lewin, a pioneer in the study of change—suggests that change results from the relative strengths of driving and restraining forces.[59] The driving forces push the organization toward change; the restraining forces push against change. The actual change that results is a consequence of the interaction of the two sets of forces. According to Lewin, the driving forces activate the restraining forces. If you want change, you

Force-field analysis: A view of change as resulting from the relative strength of driving and restraining forces.

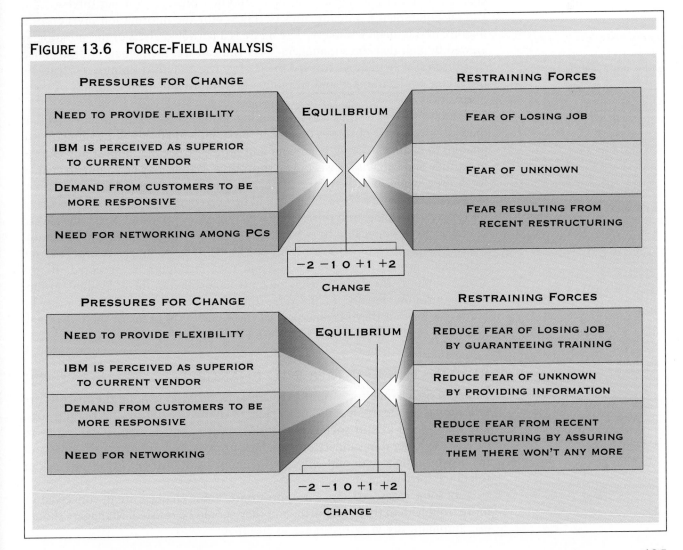

FIGURE 13.6 FORCE-FIELD ANALYSIS

FIGURE 13.7 THE CHANGE PROCESS

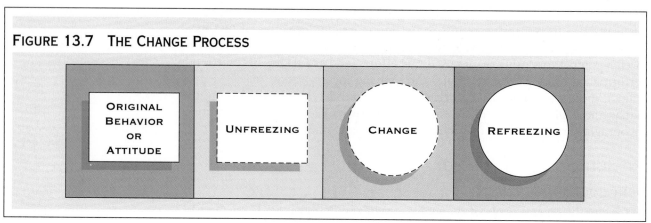

SOURCE: ADAPTED FROM JAMES A. F. STONER AND CHARLES WANKEL, MANAGEMENT, 3RD ED. (ENGLEWOOD CLIFFS, NJ: PRENTICE-HALL, 1986), P. 35.

should push. However, the natural tendency of those you are pushing is to push back. Lewin suggests that decreasing the restraining forces is a more effective way of encouraging change than increasing the driving forces.

Figure 13.6 portrays the use of force-field analysis to reduce resistance to a change from using a single computer vendor, UNISYS, to using three—IBM, Digital Equipment Company, and UNISYS—for the information division of a major entertainment company. The figure is a partial analysis of the situation as viewed by that division's managers.[60] As you can see, the managers determined that the best way to move toward the change was to reduce employees' fears by providing job guarantees and training—and to provide open channels of communication.

Lewin sought to find ways of making change effective. He discovered that there are two major obstacles to change. First, individuals are not willing (or are unable) to change existing behaviors and attitudes. Second, almost any change in attitude and behaviors lasts only a short time. People may be willing to change for a little while, but then they often revert to their original behavior. Lewin suggested that these two problems could be overcome by a three-step process of unfreezing, changing, and refreezing (see Figure 13.7). He and others developed a model that is applicable to individuals, groups, or organizations.[61] In the unfreezing stage, present behavior must be shown to be no longer desirable to the individual, group, or organization—and that fact must be accepted. In the changing phase, the desired behavior must be instilled in the individual, group, or organization. Finally, in the refreezing stage, behavioral changes must be reinforced so that they become part of the behavior patterns of the individual, group, or organization in the long term.

REASONS FOR RESISTANCE TO CHANGE

People resist change for a number of reasons. Primary among the reasons are self-interest and fear—fear of failure, fear of change itself, fear of economic loss, and fear of the loss of social relationships. Also contributing to resistance to change are general misunderstanding, lack of trust, and different perceptions of the organization's goals and objectives. Finally, resistance can stem from lack of tolerance for change.[62]

In some cases, resistance is appropriate. Some changes are ill conceived or more trouble than they are worth, and they should be resisted. Managers should not automatically view resistance as negative.

OVERCOMING RESISTANCE TO CHANGE

Managers cannot allow their efforts to achieve their objectives to be thwarted. They must develop satisfactory strategies for overcoming resistance to change. Each of the following strategies is commonly used in certain situations and has distinctive advantages and disadvantages, as summarized in Table 13.2.

Education and Communication

Many times, employees simply need more information about a planned change. Absence of information often leads to fear. By providing logical and rational reasons for a change, managers can smooth the way for acceptance and weaken the forces working against change.

Participation and Involvement

Lester Coch and John French found that a useful approach to reducing resistance to change is to encourage participation by those involved in determining how they will be affected by the change.[63] Participation is a prominent characteristic of successful Japanese management systems. People who participate "buy into the project" and do not have to be convinced to do so later.

Facilitation and Support

Managers who offer support to their subordinates, perhaps through retraining or through emotional support, are likely to see resistance fade. Managers may

TABLE 13.2 Approaches to Reducing Resistance to Change

Approach	Commonly Used When . . .	Advantages	Disadvantages
1. Education + communication	There is a lack of information or inaccurate information and analysis.	Once persuaded, people will often help implement the change.	Can be very time-consuming if many people are involved.
2. Participation + involvement	The initiators do not have all the information they need to design the change, and others have considerable power to resist.	People who participate will be committed to implementing change, and any relevant information they have will be integrated into the change plan.	Can be very time-consuming if participants design an inappropriate change.
3. Facilitation + support	People are resisting because of adjustment problems.	No other approach works as well with adjustment problems.	Can be time-consuming, expensive, and still fail.
4. Negotiation + agreement	Some person or group with considerable power to resist will clearly lose out in a change.	Sometimes it is a relatively easy way to avoid major resistance.	Can be too expensive if it alerts others to negotiate for compliance.
5. Manipulation + co-optation	Other tactics will not work, or are too expensive.	It can be a relatively quick and inexpensive solution to resistance problems.	Can lead to future problems if people feel manipulated.
6. Explicit + implicit coercion	Speed is essential, and the change initiators possess considerable power.	It is speedy and can overcome any kind of resistance.	Can be risky if it leaves people angry with the initiators.

SOURCE: Reprinted by permission of the *Harvard Business Review*. An exhibit from "Choosing Strategies for Change" by John P. Kotter and Leonard A. Schlesinger (March–April 1979). Copyright © 1979 by the President and Fellows of Harvard College. All rights reserved.

also help reduce resistance by bringing in outside facilitators or acting as facilitators themselves.

Negotiation and Agreement

Sometimes there is a need for negotiation between those who seek change and those who resist it. For example, companies often negotiate with unions to obtain changes in work rules. It may be necessary to negotiate with a variety of powerful individuals or groups in order to achieve change.

Manipulation and Co-Optation

Although they are not recommended, manipulation and co-optation are possible means of reducing resistance to change. In co-optation, managers may assign the most resistant subordinates to key roles in the change process in order to elicit their support covertly. This approach can be used either with individual subordinates or with the leader of a work group.

GLOBAL MANAGEMENT CHALLENGE

Air France Must Change

Air France needs to do something new these days—make a profit.

Until recently, the state-owned carrier enjoyed the security of a protected environment; the French government owns 99 percent of the airline. In the past three years, however, airlines have reported large losses. At Air France, losses for 1990 and 1991 totaled 1.4 billion francs, and 1992 figures were not expected to be much better.

"They need to make a big profit; it's as simple as that," says an airline consultant. "The problem is, the way to do that goes against decades of tradition." Critics say that Air France betrays the mentality of a public utility.

But no more. Profitability is now the top priority, according to Chairman Bernard Attali, who was recently reappointed by the French government. For his new three-year term, his goal will be "to come back to profitability—quickly."

Attali and his fellow executives are trying to reach the goal in a variety of ways, including changes in the airline's fleet and route structure, performance reviews for managers, and a corporate reorganization. They hope to be able to decrease expenses by about 1.5 billion francs ($293 million) per year, or about 4 percent of costs. They are even ready to look at cuts in staffing levels—something once considered impossible for a French carrier.

Still, to achieve such a decrease in expenses is a monumental task, even with a government backer. Air France's route structure reflects its mission as a government-owned airline. Its flights often accommodate low-traffic routes at the expense of more profitable combinations. "We are used to being a public service, and now we have to change that," says Christian Boireau, a recently appointed sales and marketing executive. "You cannot do it in a few weeks."

Boireau has been charged with improving productivity and employee attitudes toward the importance of making a profit. Recently he supervised the introduction of a series of training and refresher courses whose goal is to teach more than two thousand employees the importance of meeting customer demands. Performance reviews for workers constitute another innovation.

SOURCE: Brian Coleman, "Air France Chairman Makes Profitability a Top Priority," *Wall Street Journal* (July 3, 1992), p. B3.

Explicit and Implicit Coercion

Not infrequently, managers threaten to punish resisters or reduce their rewards as a means of gaining support for change. This strategy potentially increases resistance, especially in the long term. Once used, coercion may make future changes even more difficult.

This chapter's Global Management Challenge provides an insight into managing change and resistance to change. Having seen what worked for British Airways, what suggestions do you have for overcoming resistance to change at Air France? How might national culture affect the appropriateness of the techniques used by the two companies?

The Management of Culture as a Problem-Solving Process

Managing organizational culture, cultural diversity, and change is a problem-solving process, and managers need to enhance their skills in managing all three areas. Figure 13.8 provides insight into how each area can be approached as a problem-solving situation.

As an example, suppose that top managers examine the organization's internal environment and identify several performance problems. In studying the external environment, they observe stronger competition in their markets. Further examination uncovers low morale among employees and a general belief that the company is mired in such a tough competitive situation that it is doomed to failure. The organization's culture must be changed drastically. Top management embarks on a major campaign, involving managers at all levels of the hierarchy in changing the company's vision, mission, goals, and objectives. Those who are successful in implementing the new strategy are cast as heroes, and efforts are made to create opportunities for people to succeed and to reward success. Teams of managers and workers are formed at all levels to devise ways to make the new strategy work.

Summary

(Before reading this summary, look again at the objectives listed at the beginning of the chapter.)

1. An organization's culture is the set of shared values and norms that distinguishes it from other organizations. It has two levels—a mythical level and a normative level. The available research and anecdotal evidence suggest that a strong organizational culture can be a long-term competitive advantage.

2. The management of culture involves establishing values, instilling those values in new and current employees, integrating culture through the use of cultural artifacts, controlling climate, and changing culture as necessary.

3. McKinsey's Seven S's are strategy, structure, systems, style, staff, skills, and shared values. They are interdependent, even though all are based on strategy. Organizational culture plays a major role in each of these areas. Terrence E. Deal and Allan A. Kennedy have identified four principal types of culture: tough guy, bet-your-company, work hard/play hard, and process.

FIGURE 13.8 MANAGEMENT OF CULTURE AND RESISTANCE TO CHANGE AS PROBLEM SOLVING

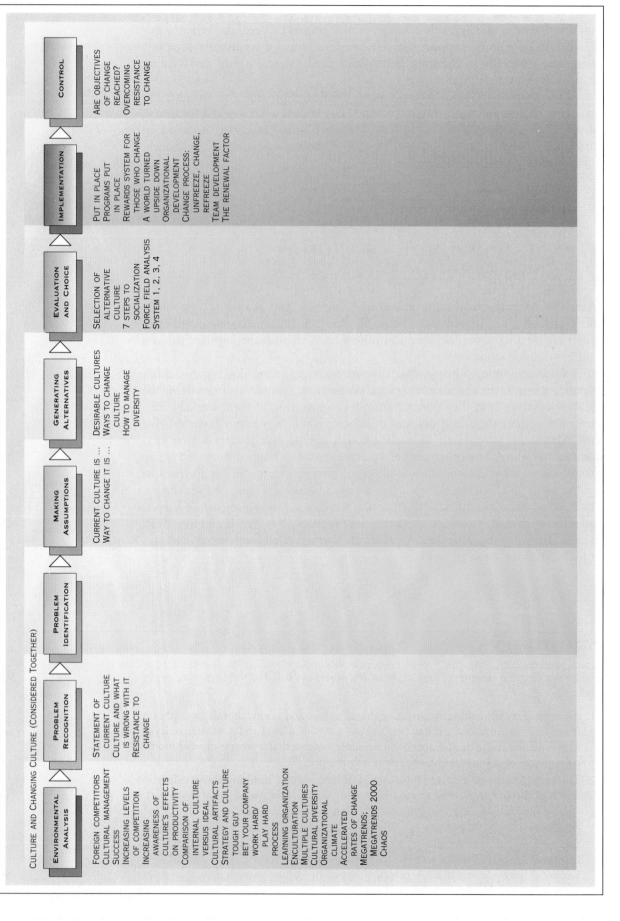

CULTURE AND CHANGING CULTURE (CONSIDERED TOGETHER)

ENVIRONMENTAL ANALYSIS	PROBLEM RECOGNITION	PROBLEM IDENTIFICATION	MAKING ASSUMPTIONS	GENERATING ALTERNATIVES	EVALUATION AND CHOICE	IMPLEMENTATION	CONTROL
FOREIGN COMPETITORS CULTURAL MANAGEMENT SUCCESS INCREASING LEVELS OF COMPETITION INCREASING AWARENESS OF CULTURE'S EFFECTS ON PRODUCTIVITY COMPARISON OF INTERNAL CULTURE VERSUS IDEAL CULTURAL ARTIFACTS STRATEGY AND CULTURE TOUGH GUY BET YOUR COMPANY WORK HARD/ PLAY HARD PROCESS LEARNING ORGANIZATION ENCULTURATION MULTIPLE CULTURES CULTURAL DIVERSITY ORGANIZATIONAL CLIMATE ACCELERATED RATES OF CHANGE MEGATRENDS; MEGATRENDS 2000 CHAOS	STATEMENT OF CURRENT CULTURE CULTURE AND WHAT IS WRONG WITH IT RESISTANCE TO CHANGE		CURRENT CULTURE IS ... WAY TO CHANGE IT IS ...	DESIRABLE CULTURES WAYS TO CHANGE CULTURE HOW TO MANAGE DIVERSITY	SELECTION OF ALTERNATIVE CULTURE 7 STEPS TO SOCIALIZATION FORCE FIELD ANALYSIS SYSTEM 1, 2, 3, 4	PUT IN PLACE PROGRAMS PUT IN PLACE REWARDS SYSTEM FOR THOSE WHO CHANGE A WORLD TURNED UPSIDE DOWN ORGANIZATIONAL DEVELOPMENT CHANGE PROCESS: UNFREEZE, CHANGE, REFREEZE TEAM DEVELOPMENT THE RENEWAL FACTOR	ARE OBJECTIVES OF CHANGE REACHED? OVERCOMING RESISTANCE TO CHANGE

4. Organizations instill culture in their members through a seven-step process outlined by Richard T. Pascale and referred to as the Seven Steps of Socialization.

5. Organizational climate refers to the desirability of the organization's work and social environments. Climate is a major determinant of culture because it reflects the organization's values relative to how people are managed, especially how much participation in problem solving is encouraged.

6. R. Roosevelt Thomas has suggested ten steps for properly managing cultural diversity: clarify your motivation, clarify your vision, expand your focus, audit your corporate culture, modify your assumptions, modify your systems, modify your models, help people pioneer, apply the special consideration test, and initiate affirmative action.

7. The Likert system describes four types of management style relative to problem-solving authority: exploitive authoritative, benevolent authoritative, consultative, and group participative. These can be placed on a continuum from very authoritative to highly participative.

8. Managing change requires objectives and strategy. Managing cultural change usually requires organizational development (OD).

9. OD is a long-range effort to improve an organization's problem-solving processes through more effective management of organizational culture. There is special emphasis on the culture of formal work teams, with the assistance of a change agent or catalyst, using the theory and technology of applied behavioral science, including action research. The stages of OD are diagnosis, planning, implementation, and stabilization/control.

10. Any forces for change seem automatically to evoke forces acting against, or resisting, change. Resistance to change occurs for a variety of reasons and may be overcome by one or a combination of six strategies: education and communication, participation and involvement, facilitation and support, negotiation and agreement, manipulation and co-optation, and explicit and implicit coercion.

General Questions

THINKING ABOUT MANAGEMENT

1. Describe the culture of an organization with which you are familiar.

2. Discuss the interrelationships among the McKinsey Seven S's at that organization.

3. Discuss myths and sagas; language systems and metaphors; symbolism, ceremonies, and rituals; and the identifiable value systems and behavioral norms of that organization.

4. Of the four types of culture identified by Deal and Kennedy, which one best describes the culture of your organization?

5. How does your organization socialize new recruits into its culture?

6. Why do you suppose that, according to Ralph H. Kilmann's research, most behavioral norms have negative connotations?

7. Where do you think the faculty of the school at which you are taking this course would rank their situation on the Likert scale?

8. How would you change a poorly managed culturally diverse organization into a well-managed one?

9. Describe a typical organizational development program.

10. Indicate the relationships among OD, culture, and planned change for an organization with which you are familiar.

11. What are the major changes taking place in American society? In the management of U.S. firms?

12. Why do people resist change?

13. How can resistance to change be overcome?

Questions on the Management Challenge Features

INNOVATION MANAGEMENT CHALLENGE

1. What are the values at Herman Miller that make it an innovative company?

2. What other values might be appropriate? (See Chapter 23.)

DIVERSITY MANAGEMENT CHALLENGE

1. Describe the successes and failures of the Samsung program.

2. Just as Samsung must prepare its employees for the cultural diversity of the U.S. work environment, U.S. firms must prepare employees who will work in Korea to manage a male-dominated work force. Discuss the implications for U.S. firms.

GLOBAL MANAGEMENT CHALLENGE

1. What changes will Air France's CEO need to make in the organization's culture?

2. Which of British Airways' CEO's actions would be appropriate for Air France?

E P I L O G U E

British Airways: From Bloody Awful to Bloody Awesome

In March 1993, the Clinton administration approved British Airways' $300 million investment in USAir, which gave BA a 24.6 percent share of USAir's total equity and 19.9 percent ownership of its voting stock. This move continued BA's drive to become a global, rather than just a European, airline. The firm intends to invest another $450 million in USAir if the administration approves the plan; approval is linked to the further opening of Heathrow and other UK airports to U.S. airlines.

As part of the pact, BA and USAir agreed to a reservation code-sharing arrangement linking USAir's domestic routes to BA's international flights. The program would provide USAir customers from thirty-eight states with "seamless" service to transatlantic destinations, including one-time check-in and automatic luggage transfer. Simpler and cheaper airfares are expected to result. USAir will also lease planes and crews to BA for two transatlantic routes.

DISCUSSION QUESTIONS

1. While USAir has focused on customer service, its service is not rated as high as BA's. What changes in USAir's culture might be necessary to make it more like BA's culture? How might those changes be carried out?

2. How do you go about merging two organizational cultures?

Hughes Supply Company

Stewart Hall, executive vice-president of Hughes Supply Company, is wondering how to continue the process of cultural change at Hughes Supply. The firm sells construction and building supplies through 121 branches in nine southeastern states, mostly to contractors and professional builders. It also has some retail outlets. Inventory accounts vary with the size of the store, which in turn depends on the size of the market in which it competes. Sales for the year ending December 31, 1991, were $481 million.

Competition has been increasing significantly in almost all of Hughes Supply's markets. In the past most of the competition came from smaller independent firms. Now large discount retailers like Home Depot are cutting into Hughes Supply's markets, as are more traditional building supply companies such as Lowes.

Each branch manager in essence runs his or her own business, but most are ill-prepared to manage in an increasingly complex and dynamic environment. All of the branch managers worked their way up from sales positions in the stores.

Top management has initiated several programs aimed at improving customer service, and these have been well received. Ongoing training has been provided to branch managers to help them cope with their situation, and the training has been judged to be effective. Yet the competition is relentless. Hall and other members of the management team want to continue the improvement in customer relations. They are looking for some innovative ideas.

DISCUSSION QUESTIONS

1. What actions would you pursue if you were Hall?
2. Several different cultures are represented in Hughes Supply's management, which is largely white but includes some blacks and a small number of Hispanics. What issues does this raise for Hall's program of cultural change?

What Kind of Manager Are You?

MANAGE YOURSELF

If you have not already done so, take the self-test shown in Figure 13.3, "Likert's Four Styles of Management," score it, and discuss the results in class.

Reinventing the Chrysler Corporation

In 1989, Chrysler Corporation was faced with a series of problems, including an aging line of cars, a bulging cost structure, and declining profits. Top management, spearheaded by Lee Iacocca, recognized the need for a completely new strategy if the company was to be competitive. Chrysler had to develop new platforms (basic car bodies around which models are built), achieve superior advanced designs, reach the highest levels of quality to entice the typical U.S. buyer of Japanese cars, and cut unnecessary costs—and it had to do all this as quickly as possible. The phrase "reinventing the Chrysler Corporation" became synonymous with the effort to achieve a competitive advantage. It quickly became evident, however, that to make the new strategies effective, the firm also had to drastically change its structure, leadership style, management systems, and organizational culture.

CHIMNEYS AND PLATFORM TEAMS

Among the first problems tackled was that of getting new products to market faster with higher quality and higher levels of customer satisfaction. At Chrysler, as at most U.S. corporations, design had historically been isolated from other functional units. The product went from design to engineering to procurement and supply to manufacturing, and finally to marketing and sales. Each of these functional units had its own bureaucracy that did not communicate with the others unless they balked at proposed plans; then top management had to settle the matter. This structure led to constant bickering. Each functional unit was like a chimney, billowing its own smoke upward to top management. Designs that were created and manufactured in isolation were forced on customers by the sales force, whose job was to sell the product whether customers liked it or not. Meanwhile, the finance department was trying to forecast costs and revenues in isolation from the normal flow of information.

Chrysler decided to adopt cross-functional development teams, called *platform teams*. Four teams were created: large car, small car, minivan, and jeep/truck. Representatives from each of the functional departments, plus customers, were integrated into the product development, manufacturing, and marketing process. Finance was included in the information loop, but the teams were charged with bringing products to market within precise cost levels. The teams were given a high degree of autonomy to achieve their objectives, eliminating the need for management to continually settle disputes.

To facilitate product development, the work of the teams, and the cross-functional nature of their operations, Chrysler officially opened its $1 billion Chrysler Technology Center (CTC) in the fall of 1991. Each platform team has its own floor in the CTC. Team members use shared databases and communication systems to keep in constant contact with each other. Suppliers are involved at early stages of design and throughout the process. Through focus groups, questionnaires, and interviews, customers are also involved throughout the process. The CTC includes a manufacturing facility where prototype manufacturing processes can be developed at the same time that a new car is being developed in order to speed manufacturing and improve quality. The platform team works in conjunction with assembly line workers to create the most efficient manufacturing process.

CHANGES IN MACRO STRUCTURE, LEADERSHIP STYLE, MANAGEMENT SYSTEMS, AND CULTURE

One of the major changes in structure that occurred during this period was the empowerment of employees to make decisions relevant to their jobs. In the past, the supervisor typically made all the decisions. But management recognized that this approach was not entirely effective. In the new structure, the supervisor would become a coach and facilitator. Part of the effort to cut up to $4 billion in costs depended on employees making suggestions for reengineering work to cut out unnecessary tasks.

The changes in Chrysler's structure, style, and culture are reflected in the New Castle, Indiana, plant. Once targeted for closing, the plant went from losing $5 million a year in 1988 to saving the firm a net $1.5 million in 1991. This impressive turnaround was accomplished by empowering employees, making sure they knew that change was necessary, and creating a learning environment. Information systems were updated to provide employees with the information they needed in order to make the right decisions.

RESULTS

The results of those changes have been impressive. Chrysler posted significant profits in 1992 and the first quarter of 1993. Profit estimates for 1993 have been continually revised upward. Chrysler's stock price soared from a low of $10.50 per share in late 1991 to $47 in July 1993. The profits and stock price reflect Chrysler's tremendous success with the Dodge Viper, an exciting and pricey new sports car; the latest Jeep Cherokee; and the LH series of cars, which entered the medium-price market against European and Japanese competitors and proved extremely successful. Trendy, with many popular features, the cars have proven so successful that Chrysler's only problem is manufacturing them fast enough. Additional new models anticipated for 1994 and 1995 are also receiving positive reviews.

DISCUSSION QUESTIONS

1. Describe how changes in strategy led to changes in structure, systems, leadership style, and organizational culture.
2. How is Chrysler typical of the firm of the future?

SOURCES: Brian S. Moskal, "Chrysler Polishes the Creative Wheel," *Industry Week* (March 16, 1992), pp. 40–42; Peter M. Tobias and Shari Johnson, "Chrysler Harnesses Brainpower," *Industry Week* (September 21, 1992), pp. 16–20; Gary S. Vasilash, "Chrysler Gets Serious About Success," *Production* (January 1992), pp. 58–60; and Gary S. Vasilash, "Teams are Working Hard at Chrysler," *Production* (October 1991), pp. 50–52.

Leading

The essence of the new management may very well be leadership. As we move from an administratively oriented, boss-centered approach to management to an approach geared toward collaborative activity for mutual benefit, leadership becomes ever more critical. To lead, the manager must understand motivation and its relationship to performance. Also important are communication, the dynamics of the groups in which much of an organization's work will be accomplished, and the activity of leadership itself.

Chapter 14 discusses the basics of human motivation and how they are related to performance. The actions that managers and the organization can take to influence motivation are reviewed. Chapter 15 reviews group dynamics and discusses some of the major types of groups used to improve organizational performance. Chapter 16 examines the leadership process. Especially important to this discussion are factors that managers use in choosing among possible actions, and the actions themselves. Finally, Chapter 17 is a commentary on the communication process, with observations on what the manager and the organization can do to utilize communication to achieve the organization's purposes.

"Successful companies address the human needs and give them priority."

—Thomas J. Peters
and Robert H. Waterman, Jr.

"The results of a twenty-year study are in. The answer to the question 'What really motivates people?' is 'Go ask your people.' "

—Vincent S. Flowers
and Charles L. Hughes

When you have read this chapter, you should be able to:

1. Discuss the various types of needs and need theories and the Herzberg theory of need satisfaction.

2. Be able to describe the expectancy-instrumentality, equity, reinforcement, and attribution theories and their implications for motivation.

3. Describe the difference between motivation and performance, and discuss the factors that turn motivation into performance.

4. Determine whether or not a person can continue to be motivated in the same way again once he or she has completed the motivation-performance cycle.

5. Describe management's role in each of the stages of the MPC.

6. Describe how you would use the motivation/performance cycle to motivate a subordinate.

M──ANAGEMENT CHALLENGES
DISCUSSED IN THIS CHAPTER:

 Accelerating rates of change.

 A more diverse work force.

 Complexity of the managerial environment.

CHAPTER 14

Motivation and Performance

CHAPTER OUTLINE

Nucor

The American steel industry has taken a beating since the early 1980s, when overseas competition exposed its weaknesses: oversized, outmoded production facilities and ingrown, stodgy management. Modern mini-mills have recaptured part of the business lost, but the steel industry has not been associated with the words *growth* and *profit* for quite a while now. That is, except for Nucor Corp.

In 1965, a near-bankrupt company, named Nuclear Corporation of America at the time, reorganized and made current CEO Ken Iverson president. Since then, the steel joist manufacturer and mini-mill operator has grown to the seventh-largest steel company in the United States. The then-young (39) Iverson worked with the division vice-presidents to create a highly decentralized structure with only four levels of management. Each plant is its own division, with a vice-president as manager, and is run with little interference from corporate headquarters. There is, however, a great deal of monitoring of performance of all divisions by headquarters, and frequent exchange of information among the managers. Because few other companies have either the productivity or growth of Nucor, the divisions compete (on paper, because the actual markets are divided geographically) with each other for a few points increase in efficiency.

How do you get workers in a retrenching field to be so productive? First of all, the company as a whole is designed to be competitive, making it possible for workers to feel pride in their employment. All facilities are modern and efficient. However, the autonomy of each division means that the facilities and the operations can be changed when the workers using them see a need for such change. This structural aspect, the local empowerment of the managers, means each division feels it can control its performance, an essential ingredient to actually exercising that control.

Compensation is tied directly to production. Bonuses are paid above a certain base for each extra ton of production, with a bonus sometimes almost doubling a production worker's paycheck. Similar incentives exist for all workers in the company. Thus financial reward is tied to continued productivity, and this is true for all employees—there are no luxurious "perks" for executives. The no-nonsense approach to corporate management is exemplified by Iverson's using the New York subways when he visits Wall Street. If the top management isn't wasting money, the lower management and staff are less likely to.

While the company has no retirement plan per se, there is a profit-sharing plan with a deferred trust for each employee. Half of the shared profit, if earned, is given in a yearly bonus and the other half put into the trust. While there is often a high initial turnover when a new plant opens because many workers don't fit into the company's "hard-work" profile, after a while the turnover drops to a very low level, and at the same time productivity rises.

SOURCE: F. C. Barnes, "A Nucor Commitment," in James M. Higgins and Julian W. Vincze, *Strategic Management: Text and Cases*, 5th ed. (Ft. Worth, TX: Dryden Press, 1993).

Motivation is an internal drive to satisfy an unsatisfied need. While motivation itself is internal to the individual, its strength and direction may be influenced by outside forces. One of the manager's most important jobs is to influence subordinates so that they are motivated to achieve the organization's objectives in an effective and efficient manner.[1] The manager must utilize his or her knowledge of motivation to channel efforts to transform individual and group needs into actions that will enhance performance.

Motivation: An internal drive to satisfy an unsatisfied need.

Nucor Corp. motivates its employees on several levels. Compensation is tied directly to production at all levels, and employees have the power to affect their level of productivity.

This chapter explores the motivation cycle an individual goes through in an attempt to satisfy his or her needs. The cycle begins when a person becomes consciously or subconsciously aware of personal needs. The person then proceeds through a series of steps aimed at satisfying those needs until the cycle begins again. After learning about each stage in the individual motivation process, you will learn about the principles that allow managers and organizations to influence an individual's motivation cycle. The two issues, individual motivation and how it is influenced, are integrated into a ten-stage model. This model is used to show the interdependencies among various theories of motivation, along the lines suggested by academicians Lyman W. Porter and Edward E. Lawler, III.[2] The model also provides a vehicle for understanding how motivation theories can be applied. Specific actions that managers can take in each of these stages to influence the strength and direction of motivation are reviewed.

It is important to realize that the model is just that, a simplification of a very complex set of processes. Moreover, no set of actions will always, or even usually, influence another individual's motivation. Finally, each theory that has been integrated into this model can be applied independently as well. The model is used primarily so that the interdependencies among them will be accounted for and so that all parts of this complex puzzle will be considered.

One of the manager's most important jobs is to influence subordinates so that they are motivated to achieve the organization's objectives in an effective and efficient manner. Employees at the Citibank Trading Center in New York City have the power to affect their own productivity. Compensation is tied directly to production.

The Motivation Cycle

Motivation cycle: A sequence of events that begins with unsatisfied needs and ends after the individual has assessed the consequences of attempting to satisfy those needs or when the process is interrupted for some reason.

The **motivation cycle** begins with unsatisfied needs. It ends after the individual has assessed the consequences of attempting to satisfy those needs or when the process is interrupted for some reason. Motivation is a cyclical process consisting of six stages:

1. An individual has an unsatisfied need.
2. Because the individual is driven to attempt to satisfy this need, he or she searches for alternatives that might satisfy it.
3. The individual chooses the "best" way to satisfy the need.
4. The individual is motivated to take action to obtain the need satisfier.
5. The individual reexamines the situation, contemplating what has taken place.
6. Depending on the outcomes of these efforts, the individual may or may not be motivated again by the same type of need and need satisfier.[3]

The stages in this motivation cycle are presented in Figure 14.1. One of the manager's major functions—perhaps the primary function—is to influence this motivation cycle in order to achieve the organization's objectives.

As shown in Figure 14.2, at each stage of the motivation cycle the manager must take certain actions. Notice that several related stages involving actions designed to influence motivation have been added to the original motivation cycle. These are the actions that managers (and the organization) should take in attempting to influence the strength and direction of motivation. These stages relate the individual's motivation cycle to its enactment in an organizational context.

Performance: Achievement of objectives in an effective and efficient way.

Motivation/performance cycle (MPC): A ten-stage model showing how managers can influence the motivation of subordinates.

The manager's principal concern is to motivate the individual to achieve the organization's objectives in an effective and efficient way. This is **performance**. Performance is critical to the discussion of motivation in an organizational context. Figure 14.2 presents the **motivation/performance cycle** (MPC). The following paragraphs examine the relationship between motivation and performance revealed in Figure 14.2. This chapter's Global Management Challenge illustrates how understanding the MPC can improve workers' motivation and performance. Note the various programs used in addition to job design.

Content theories: Theories concerned with the internal factors that motivate people—needs and how they can be satisfied.

Content and Process Theories

Two types of theories are included in the MPC model: content and process. **Content theories** are concerned with the internal factors that motivate people—needs and how they can be satisfied. **Process theories** are concerned with how people are motivated—specifically, with how they choose need satisfiers and how external factors affect that process. Content theories are examined in stages 1 and 3 in Figure 14.2. Process theories are examined in stages 2, 4, 6, 8, 9, and 10. Stages 5 and 7 deal with results.

Process theories: Theories concerned with how people are motivated—specifically, with how they choose need satisfiers and how external factors affect that process.

Stage 1 of the MPC: Needs

Need: Something we must have or want to have.

A **need** is something we must have or want to have. Unsatisfied needs motivate us. Managers are responsible for determining the need satisfiers that will lead us to attempt to achieve the organization's objectives while satisfying our needs. A

502

FIGURE 14.1 THE INDIVIDUAL MOTIVATION PROCESS

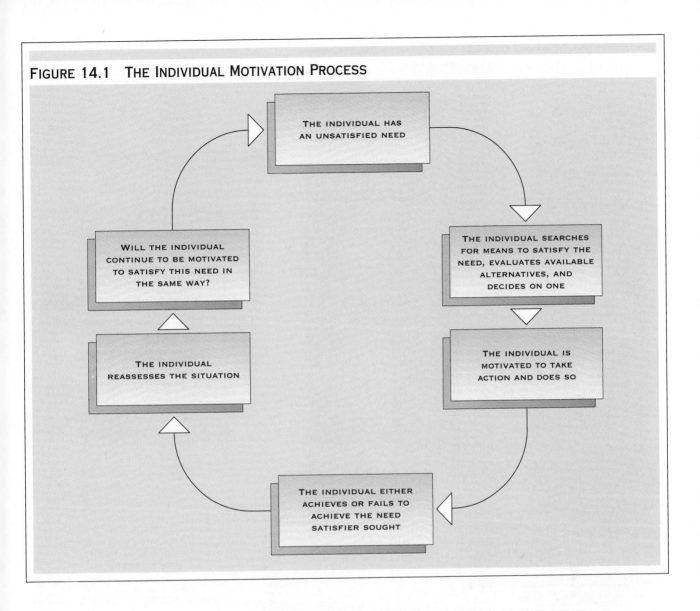

THE INDIVIDUAL HAS AN UNSATISFIED NEED

THE INDIVIDUAL SEARCHES FOR MEANS TO SATISFY THE NEED, EVALUATES AVAILABLE ALTERNATIVES, AND DECIDES ON ONE

WILL THE INDIVIDUAL CONTINUE TO BE MOTIVATED TO SATISFY THIS NEED IN THE SAME WAY?

THE INDIVIDUAL IS MOTIVATED TO TAKE ACTION AND DOES SO

THE INDIVIDUAL REASSESSES THE SITUATION

THE INDIVIDUAL EITHER ACHIEVES OR FAILS TO ACHIEVE THE NEED SATISFIER SOUGHT

few general need satisfiers, such as pay and recognition, are often used, but these do not work for all of us all the time. To the extent possible, the manager attempts to help satisfy employee needs within the framework of the organization's motivation system.

The Hierarchy of Needs

Most experts believe that needs are ordered in a hierarchy based on their importance to the individual. Two well-known hierarchy theories were formulated by Abraham Maslow and C. P. Alderfer. Both theories suggest that human needs are ordered in a hierarchical fashion, but each has a different number of levels in the hierarchy and a different set of rules for how the hierarchy functions.

Maslow's Hierarchy

On the basis of extensive research on the problems of his patients, clinical psychologist Abraham Maslow concluded that people's needs are ordered in a hierarchy of prepotency.[4] As shown in Figure 14.3, **Maslow's hierarchy** suggests that when a lower-level need in the hierarchy has been satisfied, it is no longer the individual's primary motivator. Instead, the next need in the hierarchy be-

AT NUCOR: A comprehensive set of satisfiers was developed for the various needs of employees. The structuring of those satisfiers helped align the needs of the employees with those of the company.

Maslow's hierarchy: Human needs are ordered in a hierarchy such that lower-level needs must be satisfied before a higher-level need can be a primary motivator.

FIGURE 14.2   THE MOTIVATION/PERFORMANCE CYCLE (MPC)

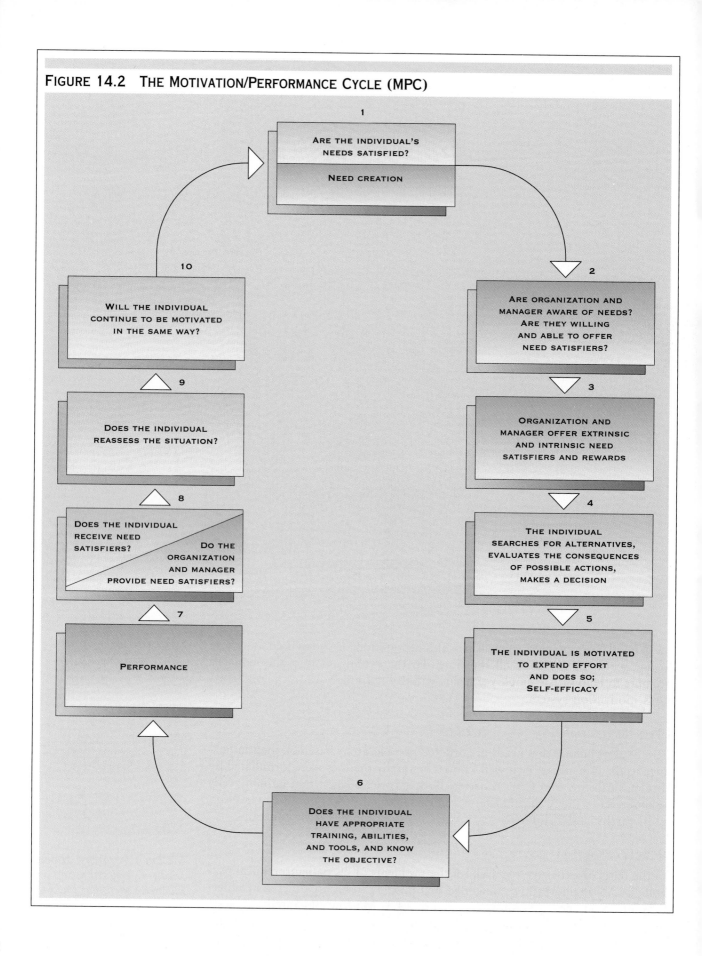

FIGURE 14.3 MASLOW'S HIERARCHY OF NEEDS

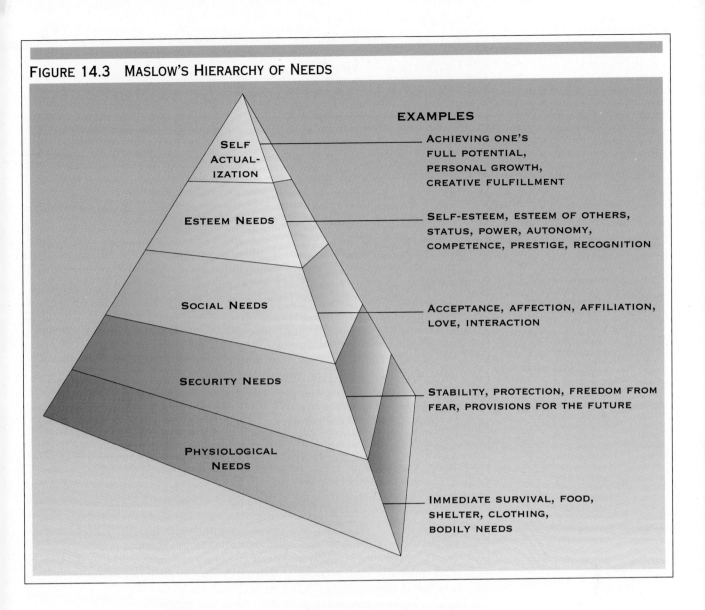

comes the strongest motivator. Thus, as physiological needs are satisfied, security needs become important; as those needs are satisfied, social needs become more important; and so on. Maslow hypothesized that the journey up the hierarchy would take most of a lifetime. In fact, some people might never reach the highest levels. Moreover, if a formerly satisfied need were no longer satisfied, the individual would drop back to a lower level of the hierarchy. If an individual who was motivated predominantly by social needs lost his or her job, for example, security might become the most important need. If he or she were unemployed long enough, physiological needs might become dominant.

Maslow also noted that some people might ignore lower-level needs because they are fixated on a higher-level need. Martyrs, for example, seem to ignore the need for security altogether. Teachers, nurses, and other people in low-paying but socially beneficial occupations are often satisfying higher-level needs at the expense of lower-level ones.

A number of research studies have focused on Maslow's hierarchy. These strongly suggest that there are actually fewer than five levels of needs. In addition, Maslow's findings are somewhat suspect because he used his patients as the basis for the theory; his hierarchy is bound by both cultural and economic factors.[5] Thus, it may not be possible to generalize the hierarchy to all people; it

Worker Motivation at Volvo

In Chapter 11, we looked at how Volvo manages job design. Perhaps even more challenging is how such a quality-oriented company manages the job of motivating its workers.

There is general agreement on why a good level of motivation is essential in an economy with high labor costs, such as Sweden's. Obviously, high motivation enhances competitiveness—of particular importance now that Japan and the Far East are seen as major threats to Sweden's traditional markets. In addition, Sweden's industrial policy deliberately sets out to produce goods with sound technology for the high end of the market, and Volvo understands that quality goods are more likely to be produced by a well-motivated work force that takes pride in its work.

Swedish companies have moved in several ways to reorganize the work environment. They secure commitment throughout a company through such means as structural decentralization, small autonomous work groups, incentive bonuses, and development agreements.

Structural decentralization: Most plans to increase motivation involve decentralization. Decentralization aims to provide shorter lines of communication so that production can respond quickly to market changes. It also aims to ensure a shared understanding of the need for profits. Because decentralized units are relatively small and personal initiative is encouraged within them, they increase motivation. So, too, does the widespread use of feedback on performance. At Volvo, decentralization has been characterized by the division of the company into autonomous profit centers.

Small autonomous work groups: Work groups increase job satisfaction by expanding the content of an individual's job. The underlying idea is that the operator is not an extension of the machine and should be able to vary the pace of work throughout the day. When changes in the production process at Volvo enabled people to work in small teams, job satisfaction was enhanced.

Incentive bonuses: Pay incentives are short-term motivators that yield immediate results. In some sections of Volvo's Olofstrom plant, for example, workers now get an extra percentage in their wages for each one percent increase in shop output. Bonuses have had remarkable effects on productivity at Olofstrom, which

probably differs from one country to another and from one economic group to another in the same country. Edwin C. Nevis, for example, has found that in China belonging is the first level of needs, followed by physiological needs, safety, and self-actualization in the service of society. The latter differs from our view of individual self-actualization: Serving the community is a very important need in China.[6]

It is not clear whether a hard-and-fast hierarchy of needs exists. What is clear is that there are major types of needs and that some are more important than others to a given individual at a given time. If we view the hierarchy as a lifelong process, as Maslow did, it is a reasonable conceptualization of how people's needs are ordered in North American society.

ALDERFER'S THEORY

After examining Maslow's approach and related research, Clayton P. Alderfer proposed that the hierarchy of needs can be more accurately conceptualized as having only three levels, as indicated in Figure 14.4: existence needs, relatedness

In some sections of Volvo's Olofstrom plant, workers now get an extra percentage in their wages for each one percent increase in shop output.

was already achieving good standards of performance as a result of work groups and mechanization.

Development agreements: In countries like Sweden, there has been an increase in collaborations among employers, blue-collar unions, and white-collar unions. At Volvo, managers and foremen have daylong educational sessions in groups of twenty; the sessions are designed to increase understanding of Volvo's operating values, particularly its emphasis on customer requirements. The point is to improve knowledge and skills throughout the company in order to stimulate constructive thought and action.

SOURCE: H. G. Jones, "Motivation for Higher Performance at Volvo," *Long Range Planning* (October 1991), pp. 92–104.

needs, and growth needs. There is some research to support this model as a more universally applicable one.[7] Note that Alderfer's hierarchy does not require the satisfaction of lower-level needs before an upper-level need can be activated. His theory does, however, allow for regression to lower-level needs. For example, if someone whose primary need is for personal growth loses his or her job, existence might become the most dominant need, although growth might continue to be important.

The Nature and Strength of Current Needs

Up to this point, we can summarize what we know about needs as follows:

1. Human beings have many needs, which can be classified into several major types. This allows the manager to offer the specific need satisfiers that are likely to satisfy the needs of a particular group of workers. A manager can seldom know exactly which needs are dominant or offer precisely what an employee needs.

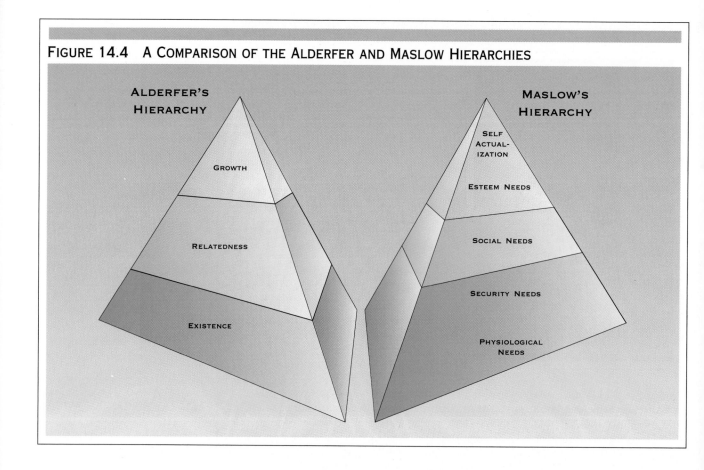

FIGURE 14.4 A COMPARISON OF THE ALDERFER AND MASLOW HIERARCHIES

ALDERFER'S HIERARCHY

GROWTH

RELATEDNESS

EXISTENCE

MASLOW'S HIERARCHY

SELF ACTUAL- IZATION

ESTEEM NEEDS

SOCIAL NEEDS

SECURITY NEEDS

PHYSIOLOGICAL NEEDS

Rather, the manager must depend on general satisfiers such as pay. Moreover, as the cultural diversity of the work force increases, it becomes more difficult to find the right set of need satisfiers. There are many diverse groups to deal with—not just ethnic and gender groups, but also age groups (for example, baby-busters, people over fifty, and baby-boomers); employees at difficult job levels (for example, professional staff and middle managers); and employees with different family circumstances (for example, single parents and dual-income couples with no children). Each group may require special need satisfiers.[8]

2. Needs and the rewards that satisfy them can be either tangible or intangible. They tend to become more intangible as the individual develops—that is, as he or she progresses up the hierarchy.

3. Current needs, regardless of their position in the hierarchy, tend to dominate a person's goals, driving his or her behavior. Needs often change, and an individual may be motivated by more than one need at the same time. People's needs also change as a result of changes in their environment. For example, the increasing use of technology may create a need for more human interaction.

Managerial Implications

The hierarchy theories are interesting in themselves, but their importance to management lies principally in the ability of the manager and others to identify dominant needs in individuals and groups. In order to influence the motivation process, the manager must know or have a good estimate of each person's or group's needs and must attempt to satisfy those needs for the benefit of the individual and the organization. Because of the changes occurring in subordinates' needs—for example, as a result of lower average educational levels and greater cultural diversity—managers will need training in identifying needs.

Another factor contributing to the complexity of work force motivation is a change in attitudes toward work. Young employees, especially those in their teens and early twenties, have significantly lower levels of self-motivation than employees in other age groups. There seems to be almost a disdain for work among many young people. Employers and managers will need to focus on control procedures as well as need satisfiers to ensure satisfactory levels of performance for that group.[9] Improved selection instruments that can identify candidates with a strong work ethic can also help.[10] Yet companies and their managers cannot ignore individuals in this age group who hold more traditional values regarding work. Their needs must be satisfied too.

Finally, as shown in Stage 1 of the motivation/performance cycle, another action the manager can take is to create needs in the individual—or, more appropriately, to strengthen existing needs and make them dominant. At Merrill-Lynch, for example, a catalog of very expensive items is distributed to stockbrokers to strengthen existing needs for luxury items.[11] Finally, as more work is performed by autonomous work teams, team-based incentives are becoming more important.[12]

Achievement Motivation

David C. McClelland also contributed to our understanding of human needs. He found that a small percentage of people have an unusually high **need for achievement** (or nAch, defined primarily in economic terms). Such people tend to possess a consistent set of traits:

1. They prefer to set their own goals and pursue tasks for which the probability of success is moderately high.
2. They prefer to work at tasks that give them quick feedback, which helps them gauge their success levels.
3. They prefer tasks in which their own efforts will have a significant impact on the accomplishment of the task. This gives them a feeling of achievement.
4. They constantly search for ways to improve their performance.[13]

People with a high need for achievement typically choose occupations like business management and sales.

Need for achievement: A motivating drive that causes an individual to seek high levels of achievement, defined primarily in economic terms.

These teenagers are applying for a job at a fast-food restaurant. Employers today may need to utilize improved selection instruments to identify workers with a strong work ethic.

Achievement need theory:
Individuals with a high
need for achievement
(nAch) also usually have a
need for power (nPower)—
control over others—and a
relatively low need for
affiliation (nAff)—social
interaction.

McClelland identified two other needs that complement the achievement need in their **achievement need theory:** the need for power (nPower, or control over others) and the need for affiliation (nAff, or social interaction). A successful business manager typically has a high need for achievement and power but a low need for affiliation. A successful entrepreneur is similarly motivated.[14]

An important principle underlying this theory is that these needs are largely culturally determined. (It is generally believed that the need for achievement can also be developed through training.) The following circumstances contribute to a high need for achievement:

1. When the dominant belief system of a society or culture encourages and allows individuals to be successful, to achieve, and to make money, economic development will occur and high achievers will emerge. Some societies stress achievement in other areas besides economic success. When the prevailing belief system is opposed to economic achievement, as was the case in Western civilization before the Protestant Reformation and in the former Soviet Union prior to *perestroika,* few people will have a high need for achievement.[15]

2. When the stories children hear and the television programs they watch emphasize economic achievement, children tend to learn that achievement is important.

3. The family plays an extremely important part in the development of high achievers. High achievers come from families that stress high levels of performance; give positive recognition for performance and take a problem-solving attitude toward failure; provide continuous feedback; and are characterized by democratic rather than authoritarian decision making.

It is not clear exactly how, or even if, achievement fits into the hierarchy theory. Achievement could be a specific type of self-actualization need, or it might be one of several needs that do not fit neatly into the hierarchy.

In the former Soviet Union, few people had a high need for achievement. Today, as a result of the enormous changes that have occurred since the end of communist rule, need for achievement is a desirable trait among entrepreneurs like those shown here.

In most business organizations there are many people who are motivated by the need to achieve. People with a high need for achievement seem to be invaluable to organizational performance. The manager should create (or seek out) opportunities to satisfy achievement needs.

Charles A. Garfield studied more than 250 managers, salespeople, and entrepreneurs who were carefully selected through a peer review process in which fellow managers, salespeople, and entrepreneurs recommended individuals for the study. He and his associates found that peak performers share the following characteristics:

1. Vision and the ability to plan strategically.
2. The drive to surpass previous levels of performance.
3. High levels of self-confidence and self-esteem.
4. A pronounced need for responsibility and control.
5. Strong communication and salesmanship skills.
6. The habit of mentally rehearsing before critical events.
7. Little need for outside praise or recognition.
8. A willingness to take risks.
9. The ability to accept feedback and make self-corrections.
10. An ownership attitude toward their ideas and products.[16]

People with a high need for achievement tend to gravitate toward positions in sales, management, and other areas in which demonstrated performance is usually rewarded, feedback is frequent, and there are opportunities to set goals and achieve them. Thus, it makes sense for organizations to seek out high achievers to fill positions of importance.

How to manage such individuals is a challenge. The best way seems to be to provide them with jobs that allow them to make decisions, that provide them with feedback, and that reward them. Team-based work also seems to provide motivation for people with a strong drive to achieve.[17]

Because the achievement need is a cultural phenomenon, a culturally diverse organization will be made up of people with differing levels of that need. People from cultures dominated by philosophies or religions that do not place a high value on success are unlikely to be high achievers. Similarly, people from disadvantaged backgrounds normally receive little encouragement to be high achievers.[18] The organization needs to find ways of motivating workers from such backgrounds as well as from more achievement-oriented cultures. This is usually a very difficult task.

Additional Categories of Needs

There are several additional types of needs that do not fit cleanly into the hierarchies. Among them are role motivation; objectives as motivators; the need to contribute to society; and the need for truth, beauty, and justice.

ROLE MOTIVATION

John Miner has formulated a theory of human needs known as **role motivation**.[19] His research indicates that certain individuals enjoy the managerial role and seek it out. There is no reason to believe, though, that only managers feel the need to fulfill their particular roles.

The manager must identify the roles, if any, that people desire and then help them fulfill those roles, provided that doing so influences their motivation to achieve the organization's objectives efficiently. For example, offering an employee a promotion to a higher level of management is a way of helping him

Role motivation: A drive stemming from enjoyment of the managerial role itself.

or her fulfill that role. Managers must also be attuned to their own needs for role fulfillment.

OBJECTIVES AS MOTIVATORS

People strive to achieve goals. Therefore, objectives can be used to influence motivation.[20] Both Maslow's and Alderfer's hierarchies are based on levels of needs that are also goals, in contrast to non-goal-oriented needs such as the need for truth and beauty or for closure.[21] People seek to achieve objectives that enable them to satisfy their needs. Sales quotas, for example, help motivate salespeople. Some individuals are motivated to accomplish objectives regardless of their position in the hierarchy, or perhaps in addition to their interest in satisfying other needs. Managers' expectations regarding subordinates' performance, especially if positive, do seem to be a motivational force.[22] The astute manager provides an environment in which an individual can accomplish objectives.[23]

Chapter 6 described a management system called management by objectives. Organizations and their managers use such systems not only as part of planning and control processes but also as ways of influencing motivation. The setting of objectives, or goals, is discussed in more detail later in the chapter.

ACTIONS THAT CONTRIBUTE TO SOCIETY

Many people feel a **need to contribute to society.** Teachers, nurses, doctors, and others may feel that they are giving themselves to society through their occupations. Environmentalists and advocates of social causes may have a similar need.

A manager in an organization that serves society, such as an adoption agency, should seek out people with this type of need. A manager in a socially responsive organization, such as IBM, should select people with a high need to contribute to society for certain tasks—for example, raising money for the United Way campaign.

THE NEED FOR TRUTH, BEAUTY, AND JUSTICE

Maslow recognized certain needs that do not fit into his hierarchy, such as the needs for truth, beauty, and justice. These are not goal-oriented needs. There are other types of needs outside the hierarchy, such as the need for symmetry and the need for closure.[24]

Determining Employee Needs

Managers must be attuned to employee needs. They must also be alert to the impact of needs on performance. A manager must constantly seek to discover what subordinates' needs are. Most of them can be learned by asking, either in person or through questionnaires, and by observation. The manager must then offer appropriate need satisfiers as described in stages 2 and 3 of the motivation/performance cycle. This challenge is made more difficult by the fact that needs are always changing.

Stage 2 of the MPC: Recognizing Needs and Being Able and Willing to Offer Need Satisfiers

Once the individual becomes aware of certain needs, he or she searches for ways to satisfy them. Managers should take action to identify subordinates' needs, but unfortunately they often fail to recognize them. For example, managers often

AT NUCOR: From the production level, where 4 percent of the base salary is added per ton of steel produced, to the executive level, where the percentage is based on return on assets, every worker at Nucor has a clear objective set with the rewards for achieving it spelled out.

Need to contribute to society: *A motivating drive stemming from the desire to give something to society through one's occupation.*

forget to acknowledge good performance—or worse, they may overlook an employee's need for respect as a human being. Constant interaction with employees should minimize such failures.

The need recognition process is further complicated by the fact that today's employees have different needs than previous generations of employees.[25] Also, an individual may be driven by multiple needs. Salespeople, for example, clearly seek recognition, but they also need autonomy. Too often, the latter is ignored.[26]

One survey of supervisors' perceptions of what employees want from their jobs reveals that managers often badly misjudge their subordinates' needs. For example, supervisors ranked "good wages" as the most important employee need, but employees ranked it fifth in importance. Employees felt that "interesting work" was their most important need; "full appreciation of work well done" was second in importance. Supervisors ranked these as fifth and eighth, respectively, in importance to workers.[27]

The manager must take the necessary actions to determine the needs of subordinates. However, the manager must also assess whether he or she is able or wants to satisfy those needs. Various constraints may prevent the manager from offering the satisfiers that employees need: The funds may not be available; promotion may not be possible; or there may be limited time to spend with each subordinate.

Sometimes the manager may be able, but not willing, to satisfy an individual's needs. An employee with a high need for affiliation often tries to spend time talking to other employees. The manager will not be willing to satisfy that need because it detracts from the employee's performance. Sometimes managers do not offer need satisfiers for less legitimate reasons. For example, they may not reward an employee they dislike, regardless of performance. As more companies recognize the impact of personal needs on performance, they are making a greater effort to satisfy those needs—for example, by providing such services as

At Black and Decker, the CEO makes a point of personally rewarding employees for their contributions to the firm. Such positive reinforcement does much to maintain motivation.

on-site child care centers.[28] Need recognition is more difficult in a culturally diverse organization because employees from different backgrounds have different priorities and needs.

Stage 3 of the MPC: Offering Extrinsic and Intrinsic Need Satisfiers

Hygiene factors: Need satisfiers extrinsic to the job; they are often referred to as dissatisfiers, meaning that if these items are absent, employees will be dissatisfied and may not perform as well as they would if the factors were present.

Motivators: Need satisfiers intrinsic to the job; often referred to as satisfiers.

Frederick A. Herzberg's research on job design, discussed in Chapter 11, is part of an overall theory that also deals with the use of need satisfiers to influence motivation. According to Herzberg, there are two basic types of need satisfiers: hygiene factors and motivators. The **hygiene factors** are extrinsic to the job and include pay and supervision. They are often referred to as dissatisfiers, meaning that if they are absent, employees will be dissatisfied and may not perform as well as they would if such factors were present. **Motivators** are intrinsic to the job and include achievement and recognition for performance. Motivators are often referred to as satisfiers. Herzberg suggests that an organization and its managers should attempt to provide opportunities for intrinsic satisfaction and not be concerned only with extrinsic satisfaction.[29]

Herzberg believes that hygiene factors do not increase an individual's motivation level, but that motivators do. Remember that by *motivation,* Herzberg means motivation to do a better job, not just an adequate job, and that he is concerned with motivation in the long term. This refinement may help explain some of the differences between his results and those found by other researchers. Herzberg's concern is with raising motivational levels, whereas managers are often concerned with maintaining them—which can usually be done by supplying hygiene factors. If an individual is intrinsically satisfied, he or she will be motivated to perform at a higher level. Herzberg is careful to point out that decreased levels of motivation are caused by the lack of extrinsic factors; however, supplying those factors will not increase levels of motivation. Only intrinsic satisfiers will lead to higher levels of motivation, according to his theory.

Herzberg's theory has been severely criticized for several reasons: It was formulated using a limited sample of accountants and engineers—two groups of workers whose lower-level needs are satisfied. The research methodology used provided for individual storytelling in response to questions and is subject to personal attribution biases (in which people attribute their motivation to factors that might not have been the actual cause). He also overlooked certain responses that did not agree with his theory—for example, items that are satisfiers for some people may be dissatisfiers for others. Some research has revealed opposite results, notably that hygiene factors may act as satisfiers rather than dissatisfiers.[30] Finally, Herzberg's belief that money does not lead to increased levels of motivation disagrees with the findings of about 95 percent of all other studies of this issue.[31]

This chapter's Quality Management Challenge demonstrates that incentives play a critical role in motivation. Whirlpool raised productivity dramatically through gain sharing—a program in which profits resulting from improved productivity are distributed to employees. What else besides employee efforts contributed to increased productivity at Whirlpool?

Herzberg's observations are useful because they point managers toward types or groups of satisfiers that can be offered to meet different kinds of employee needs. For example, it might be necessary to provide hygiene factors for workers dominated by lower-level needs in order to influence their motivational

Improving Quality at Whirlpool

The Whirlpool factory at Benton Harbor, Michigan, isn't any prettier than it used to be—the air still smells oily, the floor is grimy, and the equipment is mostly old and very noisy. But workers are a lot happier. The reason is a gain-sharing plan that has linked productivity to pay—and put an extra $2,700 in each worker's pay packet in 1991.

Whirlpool's gain-sharing plan could serve as a model for many U.S. businesses seeking to improve quality and productivity. Whirlpool has been "in the forefront" of the appliance industry's productivity drive, according to one industry analyst.

The Benton Harbor factory transforms metal rods into washer and dryer parts. Since 1988, productivity there has surged more than 19 percent, to 110.6 parts per worker-hour from 92.8. Quality also has improved: The number of parts rejected has sunk to a minuscule 10 per million from 837 per million. As a result, the average factory worker's pay has risen nearly 12 percent *despite a labor contract offering no regular wage or cost-of-living increases during that time.*

How did Whirlpool do it? Instead of building a state-of-the-art plant, it overhauled its manufacturing process and taught workers to improve quality. According to one veteran, workers used to feel that "if a machine broke, you just sat down" until someone came to fix it—sooner or later. But in the late 1980s, many factories on the southeastern shore of Lake Michigan closed. They included a larger Whirlpool operation at Benton Harbor; the smaller tooling and plating facility saw the writing on the wall. The company offered the workers one hope: Increase productivity. The gain-sharing agreement was hammered out in 1988.

Gain sharing is straightforward. The bigger the gain in output, the bigger the kitty that workers share with the company. The exact percentage of the workers' share depends on the quality of their output—that is, on how few parts are rejected. Workers receive equal shares of their pool; the company's shares are divided between shareholders and consumers (i.e., balancing profits and prices).

It's like getting a raise—but workers accept all the initial risk; they get more only if they produce more. Interestingly, they're producing more even though the foremen are telling them to emphasize quality over quantity. Efforts to improve quality create a win-win situation: With less time wasted on making bad parts, productivity increases automatically. The cost of scrapping bad parts decreases, and less inventory needs to be stored.

Managers have "talked quality for nearly thirty years," says Lloyd Spoonholtz, the local union chief. "Now they're finally living it."

SOURCE: Rick Wartzman, "A Whirlpool Factory Raises Productivity—and Pay of Workers," *Wall Street Journal* (May 4, 1992), pp. A1, A4.

---

levels, or at least to maintain them at satisfactory levels. On the other hand, employees dominated by upper-level needs would probably require motivators rather than hygiene factors to increase their motivational levels. As people move upward in the Maslow or Alderfer hierarchy, they have higher expectations about their jobs. Work force expectations are clearly headed in this direction. They are among the challenges that are changing the nature of management, as discussed in Chapter 1. Job designs must often be changed as a result. On the other hand, while money will motivate many, if not most, workers in the short run, compensation programs may need to be redesigned to make them more effective. Figure 14.5 shows how the various types of needs suggested by Maslow might be matched by need satisfiers according to Herzberg. Note how empowerment, a major tactic for improving productivity, satisfies the higher-level needs that characterize many of today's employees. Autonomous work teams, which usually provide high levels of satisfaction, also help satisfy high-level needs.

Stage 4 of the MPC: Choosing Among Alternatives and Evaluating Possible Consequences

Having become aware of a need, the individual searches for alternative ways to satisfy it. When faced with more than one alternative, he or she must evaluate them and make a choice. Two theories of motivation—the expectancy and equity theories—greatly aid our understanding of this stage.

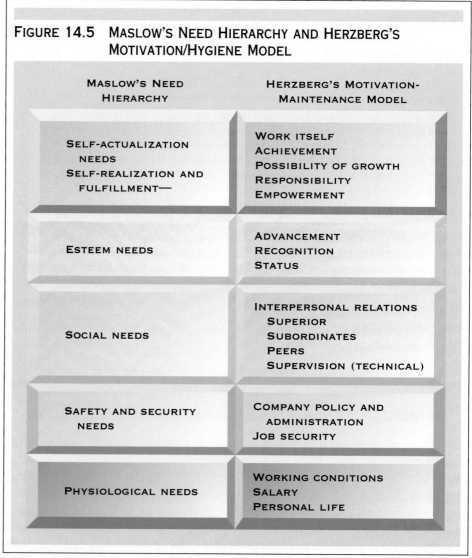

FIGURE 14.5   MASLOW'S NEED HIERARCHY AND HERZBERG'S MOTIVATION/HYGIENE MODEL

MASLOW'S NEED HIERARCHY	HERZBERG'S MOTIVATION-MAINTENANCE MODEL
SELF-ACTUALIZATION NEEDS SELF-REALIZATION AND FULFILLMENT—	WORK ITSELF ACHIEVEMENT POSSIBILITY OF GROWTH RESPONSIBILITY EMPOWERMENT
ESTEEM NEEDS	ADVANCEMENT RECOGNITION STATUS
SOCIAL NEEDS	INTERPERSONAL RELATIONS SUPERIOR SUBORDINATES PEERS SUPERVISION (TECHNICAL)
SAFETY AND SECURITY NEEDS	COMPANY POLICY AND ADMINISTRATION JOB SECURITY
PHYSIOLOGICAL NEEDS	WORKING CONDITIONS SALARY PERSONAL LIFE

SOURCE: JAMES HIGGINS, HUMAN RELATIONS: BEHAVIOR AT WORK, 2ND ED., P. 69, © 1987, MCGRAW-HILL, INC. REPRODUCED WITH PERMISSION OF MCGRAW-HILL.

Expectancy-Instrumentality Theory

Victor Vroom and others have proposed a theory, known as **expectancy-instrumentality theory**, that describes how an individual chooses among alternative need satisfiers. According to this theory, the individual contemplates the consequences of his or her actions in choosing alternatives to satisfy personal needs.[32] Vroom's theory assumes a rationally determined decision, but other possibilities exist. Much of the time individuals react habitually, emotionally, or instinctively when choosing among alternative need satisfiers. However, when they do contemplate the consequences of their actions, their motivation to expend effort depends on the answers to the following questions:

1. Can I perform the task? (Can I do the job?)
2. If I perform the task, what is the probability that I will receive the expected outcome? (If I do the job, will I get the reward?)
3. What is the outcome worth to me? (What is the reward worth to me?)

Expectancy-instrumentality theory: Individuals contemplate the consequences of their actions in choosing alternatives to satisfy their needs.

In the organizational context, this translates into the individual's perception of the situation.

More formally, expectancy theory is based on the following assumptions:

1. A combination of forces within the individual and in his or her environment determine behavior.
2. People make decisions about their own behavior and that of organizations.
3. People have different types of needs, goals, and desires.
4. People make choices among alternative behaviors on the basis of the extent to which they think a certain behavior will lead to a desired outcome.[33]

Figure 14.6 summarizes the expectancy model of employee motivation.[34] An **expectancy** is the probability that an action will result in a certain consequence. In this model motivation is believed to lead to effort, which leads to performance. Performance leads to various outcomes, each of which has an associated value known as a **valence**. Such values are unique to each individual. Most immediate outcomes, such as compensation, are associated with secondary outcomes, such as being able to make a car payment. Additional important considerations shown in the figure include

Expectancy: The expected probability that an action will result in a certain consequence.

Valence: The value attached to a particular outcome by a particular individual.

1. an effort-to-performance expectancy.
2. a performance-to-outcome expectancy.
3. degrees of relationship between outcomes and values.

THE EFFORT-TO-PERFORMANCE EXPECTANCY

"Can I perform the task?" An individual's perception of the probability that effort will lead to high performance is defined as having a value somewhere between 0 and 1. If the expectancy is high, the value is 1; if it is low, the value is near 0. When an individual believes that he or she can perform a particular task, the expectancy will be 1. When an individual believes that he or she cannot perform the task, or that a low level of performance will result regardless of the effort expended, the expectancy is weak and close to 0. IBM sets its sales goals so that 80 percent of its salespeople can reach their goals. As a result, expectancy is high, and so is performance.[35]

FIGURE 14.6 THE EXPECTANCY MODEL OF EMPLOYEE MOTIVATION

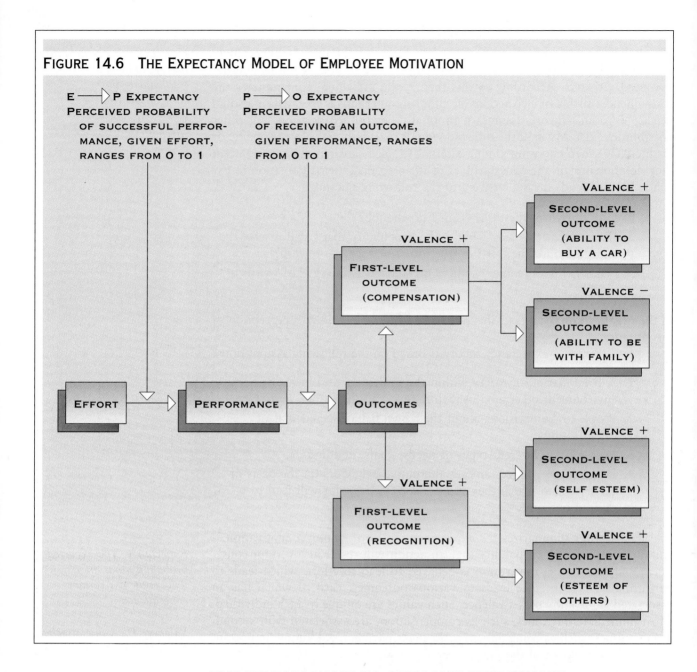

THE PERFORMANCE-TO-OUTCOME EXPECTANCY

"If I perform, what is the probability that I will receive the expected outcome?" If the individual thinks the answer is yes, or nearly yes, the expectancy approaches 1. If he or she feels that high performance may not have a bearing on the outcome, then a lower expectancy, somewhere between 1 and 0, would result. If he or she thinks there may be no relationship between performance and outcome, the expectancy is 0. IBM salespeople who meet their goals are automatically members of the 100 Percent Club. This is an expectancy of 1, as is the probability of financial reward for meeting quotas.[36]

THE RELATIONSHIP BETWEEN OUTCOMES AND VALENCES

"If I receive the expected outcome, what is it worth to me?" When an individual asks this question, he or she is attempting to estimate the value, or valence, of the outcome. A high performer may receive pay raises, fast promotions, substan-

THE EXPECTANCY MODEL OF EMPLOYEE MOTIVATION IS BASED ON THE THEORY THAT MOTIVATION LEADS TO EFFORT, WHICH IN TURN LEADS TO PERFORMANCE. PERFORMANCE CAN HAVE VARIOUS OUTCOMES, EACH OF WHICH IS VALUED DIFFERENTLY BY DIFFERENT INDIVIDUALS. IN THIS MODEL, THEREFORE, THE EMPLOYEE ASKS THREE QUESTIONS: (1) "CAN I PERFORM THE TASK?" (FOR EXAMPLE, CAN I DO THE WORK OF A QUALITY CONTROL INSPECTOR?) (2) "IF I PERFORM, WHAT IS THE PROBABILITY THAT I WILL RECEIVE THE EXPECTED OUTCOME?" (IF I DO A GOOD JOB REPAIRING TELEPHONE LINES, WILL I GET THE RECOGNITION I DESERVE?) (3) "IF I RECEIVE THE EXPECTED OUTCOME, WHAT IS IT WORTH TO ME?" (ARE REWARDS SUCH AS RECEIVING AN AWARD IMPORTANT TO ME?) IF THE EMPLOYEE IS ABLE TO PERFORM THE TASK AND VALUES THE EXPECTED OUTCOMES, MOTIVATION WILL OCCUR.

tial praise, and critical assignments but would also be subject to fatigue, stress, jealousy, and political manipulations. Such a person may find, for example, that money, a first-level outcome, is not a motivating reward because it does not have much comparative value if it takes him or her away from family, a second-level outcome. Each outcome (reward) is being compared to the rewards that result from other behaviors.

For motivated behavior to occur, three conditions must be met:

1. The individual must have a reasonably high expectancy that effort will lead to performance.
2. The individual must have a reasonably high expectancy that performance will lead to the desired outcome.
3. The desired outcomes, both first- and second-level, must have reasonably high valences. Technically, as long as the expectancies are greater than 0 and the valences are stronger than those of other alternatives, some motivated behavior should result.[37] However, if organizations and managers want to influence behavior, they should increase the valence of the perceived consequence of success.[38]

Equity Theory

In addition to expectancies and the valences of outcomes, the individual assesses the degree to which the potential rewards will be distributed equitably. J. Stacy Adams's **equity theory** contends that people will seek rewards only if they perceive that the rewards will be distributed equitably.[39] The term *equity* implies that a person is being treated equally or fairly compared to others who behave in a similar way.

As shown in Figure 14.7, employees compare their inputs and outcomes (rewards) with those of other employees, especially those who are performing the same basic job. When they find evidence of inequity, they must adjust their behavior to make the situation more acceptable. If they feel that they are in an inequitable situation, they can reduce their inputs—amount of effort, for example—or they can increase their outputs by trying to build psychological benefits for themselves ("I do better work than Jane"). They can also attempt to secure greater rewards, or they can leave the job. Conversely, if they feel that they are benefiting unduly from a situation, they can increase their inputs or (an unlikely scenario) seek to have their outcomes reduced.

A worker in a unionized organization, for example, may produce a higher-quality product, be more diligent, and pay more attention to details than a peer while receiving the same amount of pay. Such a worker may perceive the situation as inequitable and feel that something should be done to correct it. The worker may make this adjustment by decreasing inputs or increasing rewards. If inputs are adjusted, the worker will put in less effort. If rewards are increased, they will have to be nonfinancial rewards, because wages are fixed by the union contract. The worker might, for example, seek praise for his or her efforts or talk about how enjoyable the work is. If the employee still considers the situation inequitable, he or she may quit. In some instances, workers steal from their employers to compensate for perceived inequities.[40]

It has been proposed that people have varying degrees of sensitivity to the equity of a situation.[41] This sensitivity varies along a continuum based on the preferred ratio of inputs to outcomes relative to those of co-workers.[42] Generally, the manager should attempt to create a situation that subordinates perceive as equitable. This can be accomplished both by providing actual equity and by

Equity theory: People will seek rewards only if they perceive that the rewards will be distributed equitably.

AT NUCOR: *Perceived equity is exceptionally high. Not only are specific bonuses spelled out in detail for all, but the more nebulous "perks" of executive privilege have been eliminated.*

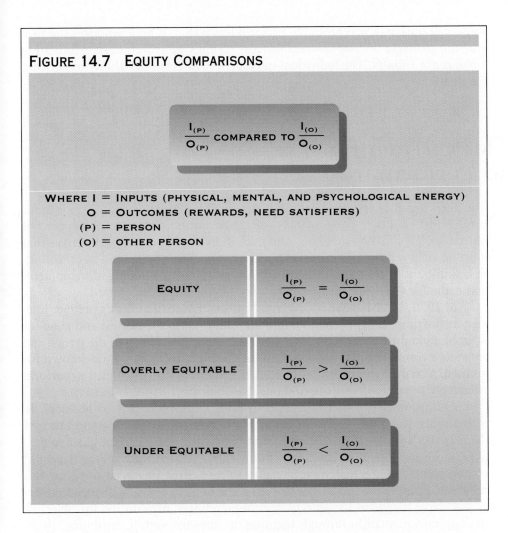

FIGURE 14.7   EQUITY COMPARISONS

$$\frac{I_{(P)}}{O_{(P)}} \text{ COMPARED TO } \frac{I_{(O)}}{O_{(O)}}$$

WHERE I = INPUTS (PHYSICAL, MENTAL, AND PSYCHOLOGICAL ENERGY)
O = OUTCOMES (REWARDS, NEED SATISFIERS)
(P) = PERSON
(O) = OTHER PERSON

| EQUITY | $\dfrac{I_{(P)}}{O_{(P)}} = \dfrac{I_{(O)}}{O_{(O)}}$ |

| OVERLY EQUITABLE | $\dfrac{I_{(P)}}{O_{(P)}} > \dfrac{I_{(O)}}{O_{(O)}}$ |

| UNDER EQUITABLE | $\dfrac{I_{(P)}}{O_{(P)}} < \dfrac{I_{(O)}}{O_{(O)}}$ |

maintaining good communication regarding nonequitable outcome distributions.

Have you ever perceived inequities on the job? What did you do about them? How did you make your inputs/outcomes ratio equal to those of others? Have you ever felt that your ratio was higher than someone else's? What did you do then?

Stage 5 of the MPC: Motivation to Expend Effort

If an individual has completed the preceding stages of the MPC satisfactorily, he or she will be motivated to expend effort to accomplish the organization's objectives. The degree to which a person is willing to take action, and the strength of that motivation, depends on the answers to the questions asked earlier. Only if the answers are sufficiently positive will the individual be motivated to take the actions desired by management.

There is considerable evidence that **self-efficacy**—a person's estimate of his or her capacity to affect performance on a specific task—influences how well a person performs. A person who thinks he or she can perform well on a task probably will perform well. A person who believes that he or she cannot per-

Self-efficacy: An individual's estimate of his or her capacity to affect performance on a specific task.

form well on a task will probably perform less well.[43] It thus behooves the firm and the manager to improve employees' feelings of self-efficacy. Motivation alone is not enough. The individual must believe in his or her ability to perform the task.

Stage 6 of the MPC: Turning Motivation into Performance

Managers are not concerned only with motivation. They must ensure that motivated effort results in performance—effective and efficient accomplishment of objectives. This involves making sure each individual knows the objectives that must be achieved; knows the tasks necessary to achieve them; and has the abilities, skills, and tools to accomplish the necessary tasks. Training, development, and capital investment are obviously very important in this regard.

In 1970, Jim Marshall, one of the National Football League's premier linemen at the time, caught a fumble in midair and ran to the nearest end zone for what he thought was a touchdown. Unfortunately, he had run to the wrong end zone; as a result, the play was a safety for the other team, not a touchdown for his own. Marshall was highly motivated, but in this instance he failed to perform effectively because of confusion about the objective.

Confusion over which direction to take arises frequently in business. In recent years, therefore, there has been greater recognition of the importance of the manager's goal-setting actions to motivation. As noted earlier, goals (objectives) motivate. Edwin A. Locke (in 1968) was the first to focus on this aspect of management.[44] Since that time, considerable research has been done on this subject.[45] From the manager's perspective, the objective-setting process consists of five steps: diagnosis for objective-setting readiness, preparation for objective setting, implementation through focusing on objective-setting attributes, an intermediate review to adjust objectives, and final review.[46]

These steps are largely self-explanatory, except for the implementation of step 3. This requires that the manager set objectives in light of desirable attributes. Objectives should be specific—that is, quantifiable and clear. Because the level of difficulty affects performance, the manager must carefully weigh the difficulty of each objective. In addition, the manager must treat objective setting in a way that demonstrates commitment to the outcomes.

Research on objective setting reveals the following:

1. More specific objectives, such as a 10 percent increase in annual sales, lead to higher levels of performance than general statements like "Do as much as you can."

2. The more difficult the objective, the higher the level of performance, assuming that the individual is committed to achieving the objectives.

3. The actual process of setting objectives may encounter a variety of problems, as discussed in Chapter 6.[47]

The importance of objectives as an influence on motivation helps explain the results of the management-by-objective programs discussed in Chapter 6. These programs focus on the goal-setting process and thus take advantage of its impact on motivation. From the subordinate's perspective, commitment to an objective leads to performance. If an employee is not committed to an objective, he or she is less likely to reach it. The manager can have a significant influence on subordinates' commitment.[48] Designing programs to increase commitment may be essential in the future.

Stage 7 of the MPC: Performance

If an individual is highly motivated and the appropriate conditions are present, high levels of performance—effective and efficient accomplishment of objectives—will result. How performance is defined varies from one organization to another and from one situation to another. In some organizations performance is not clearly defined in advance, although it should be. In most organizations, especially large ones, an individual's performance results from numerous factors, including competition, organizational support, and cooperation among departments. As competition increases, greater emphasis is placed on performance. Sometimes, in fact, organizations push their employees too hard. They expect and demand too much, as this chapter's Ethical Management Challenge reveals. Have you ever worked in an organization where performance was more important than the well-being of the individual? What are the implications of such treatment for the organization and the individual?

Stage 8 of the MPC: Obtaining or Not Obtaining Need Satisfiers

Need satisfiers are essential to any attempt to influence motivation. As we have seen, an individual is originally motivated by unsatisfied needs. He or she is motivated to take action in the expectation that effort will lead to performance, that performance will lead to an outcome with value, and that the need satisfiers will be distributed equitably. If these conditions are not met by stage 8 of the cycle, the individual, having assessed the situation (stage 9), is unlikely to continue to be motivated in the same way (stage 10).

Reinforcement of Effort

Much of our understanding of Stage 8 of the MPC results from reinforcement theories of motivation. **Reinforcement theories** suggest that behavior that produces rewarding consequences is likely to be repeated, whereas behavior that produces no rewards or has punishing consequences is less likely to be repeated. Note that these are tendencies, not absolutes.

Much of the original research in this area was done by the psychologist E. L. Thorndike, who, in 1898, formulated the **law of effect**: "Of several responses to the same situation, those that are accompanied or closely followed by satisfaction . . . will be more likely to recur; those which are accompanied or closely followed by discomfort . . . will be less likely to occur."[49] Since the late 1930s another psychologist, B. F. Skinner, has been a major force in demonstrating how reinforcement works.[50] Figure 14.8 uses the language of reinforcement theory to explain human motivation.[51] This phenomenon is widely known in its applied form as **organizational behavior modification** (OBM).[52]

Reinforcement theory is almost the converse of expectancy theory. In expectancy theory, the individual focuses on expectations of success and associated values before performing a particular behavior or response. This is shown

Reinforcement theories: Behavior that produces rewarding consequences is likely to be repeated, whereas behavior that produces no rewards or has punishing consequences is less likely to be repeated.

Law of effect: Of several responses to the same situation, those that are accompanied or closely followed by satisfaction will be more likely to recur; those that are accompanied or closely followed by discomfort will be less likely to occur.

Organizational behavior modification (OBM): Application of the law of effect to motivate members of an organization to behave in specific ways.

Do Some Firms Push Too Hard?

In the effort to downsize, get fit, and become lean and mean, some corporations are being just plain mean to their employees.

In a survey of employees at 171 big corporations over the last eighteen years, the number of managers who have felt overworked rose from 34 percent to 46 percent in the last five years. Among nonmanagers, 39 percent now feel that they have too much to do, up from 30 percent. A survey of 201 large and small corporations shows that one in four employees experiences anxiety or stress-related disorders. Sixteen work days are lost per employee per year owing to emotional exhaustion or depression. Research suggests that these conditions and the substance abuse they frequently engender cost $183 billion annually in lost productivity, faulty workmanship, and medical bills.

Employees are typically pushed too hard in two kinds of situations: labor-intensive industries such as supermarket chains, where profits are created by human output, and large companies that are downsizing—reducing the work force but not the workload.

Often, when companies are downsizing, the soon-to-be ex-workers are given severance payments as well as the services of outplacement firms, but the survivors are left with profound insecurities and only one certainty: more work.

One firm that tried to handle its restructuring more humanely was Sea-Land. After giving severance payments to 440 employees, the company made work elimination a priority. Job descriptions for all the remaining positions were rewritten, many reduced from five pages to one. A new rule of thumb: If another department needs a task done more than yours, let the people in that department do it. Often they will find that they do not really need the task done either.

At Pizza Hut, a typically labor-intensive operation, management took some of the pressure off employees by asking them to suggest ways to redesign their work. Store managers were also asked to help decide what paperwork the parent company could forgo. The manager overseeing the eighty-one stores in St. Louis even opted to set up an administration independent of the parent company and launched his own payroll system—with more generous bonuses for managers. According to the president of Pizza Hut, this semiautonomous experiment, which has fewer layers of management than the parent company, boasted 40 percent sales growth in eighteen months. The next experiment: Hourly workers are being invited to help decide on questions such as scheduling their hours and selecting their uniforms. "We're doing focus groups with employees that we normally do with customers," says the president.

SOURCE: Thomas A. Stewart, "Do You Push Your People Too Hard?" *Fortune* (October 22, 1990), pp. 121–128.

in Figure 14.8 as a path from stimulus to response. In reinforcement theory, there is more emphasis on what happens after a given behavior. After performing the behavior (response), the individual experiences certain consequences. When the individual faces the same choices again, the response will depend on whether the consequences of previous responses were pleasant or not. If the consequences were pleasant, the individual is likely to make the same response (Path 4). If the consequences were unpleasant, the individual is likely to seek a new response (Path 5).

FIGURE 14.8 THE REINFORCEMENT THEORY OF MOTIVATION

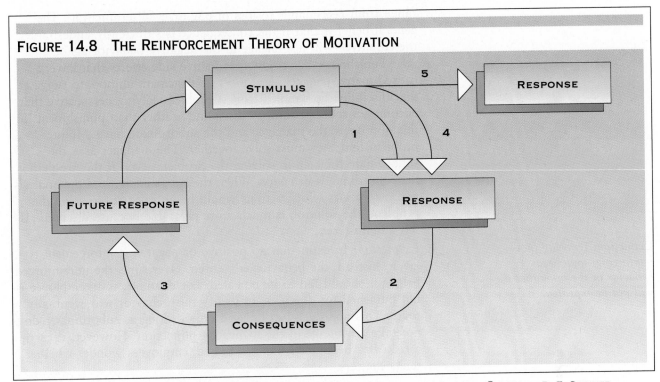

SOURCE: B. F. SKINNER, BEYOND FREEDOM AND DIGNITY (NEW YORK: KNOPF, 1971). COPYRIGHT © 1971 BY B. F. SKINNER. REPRINTED BY PERMISSION OF ALFRED A. KNOPF, INC.

Types of Reinforcement

Reinforcement theory suggests that there are four types of reinforcement: positive and negative reinforcement, punishment, and extinction. Positive and negative reinforcement strengthen or maintain a particular behavior. Punishment and extinction weaken or decrease a particular behavior. Let us take a look at each of these types.

1. *Positive reinforcement:* In **positive reinforcement** something positive is given after the behavior occurs. An easy way to provide positive reinforcement in an organization is to give the person a raise. Another is to send a timely, personal, short memo outlining the person's performance successes.[53] Similarly, when a manager responds in a positive way to friendly interpersonal actions, subordinates are encouraged to be friendly and sociable toward others.

   Positive reinforcement: Giving a reward after the desired behavior occurs.

2. *Negative reinforcement:* In **negative reinforcement** something negative is removed or does not occur when the desired behavior is performed. An employee may, for example, be motivated to perform at high levels in order to avoid being reprimanded by a manager. New recruits in a military training camp seek to perform at extremely high levels in order to avoid the reprimands of the drill sergeant.

   Negative reinforcement: The removal or lack of occurrence of a negative condition when the desired behavior occurs.

3. *Punishment:* Managers often use **punishment** to discourage undesirable behaviors. According to reinforcement theory, if the consequence of a behavior is unpleasant, that behavior will not be repeated. One of the manager's most unpleasant chores is to discipline employees—for coming in late, for being absent, for poor-quality work, or for a low quantity of work. The punishments used

   Punishment: Reinforcement in which an undesired behavior is followed by an unpleasant consequence.

range from reprimands to loss of pay or even termination. The general belief is that if the consequence is sufficiently undesirable, the employee will not engage in the negative behavior again.

Punishment has counterproductive side effects that have caused many managers and most management authors to suggest that discipline be handled from a problem-solving perspective that encourages self-determined "discipline" rather than punishment. In this approach, the manager and the subordinate have a joint problem that they must solve together. The manager asks the subordinate for help in solving the problem, even if the problem is the subordinate's behavior. When the subordinate does the analysis and determines which actions would be appropriate to solve the problem, the solution is much more palatable because discipline is self-administered.

4. *Extinction:* In **extinction** no positive or negative reinforcement is given. Instead, the behavior is ignored. Over time, the unreinforced behavior should fail to be repeated. For example, if an employee is not punished for absences, in theory this behavior will eventually cease. This approach can be used only as long as subordinates do not take advantage of the manager's nonaction. However, it carries a risk: If a behavior is not reinforced, employees wonder whether it really matters.

Extinction: *Ignoring (not reinforcing) undesired behavior in the hope that it will not be repeated.*

Schedules of Reinforcement

The schedule of reinforcement—when and how often rewards are tied to performance—is critical. There are two basic types of reinforcement schedules: continuous and intermittent. In **continuous reinforcement schedules,** a reinforcement

Continuous reinforcement schedules: *Reinforcement follows every occurrence of the desired behavior.*

TABLE 14.1 Reinforcement Schedules and Their Effects on Behavior

Schedule	Description	When Applied to Individual	When Removed by Manager	Organizational Example
Continuous	Reinforcer follows every response	Fastest method for establishing new behavior	Fastest method to cause extinction of new behavior	Praise after every response, immediate recognition of every response
Fixed interval	Response after specific time period is reinforced	Some inconsistency in response frequencies	Faster extinction of motivated behavior than variable schedules	Weekly, bimonthly, monthly paycheck
Variable interval	Response after varying period of time (an average) is reinforced	Produces high rate of steady responses	Slower extinction of motivated behavior than fixed schedules	Transfers, promotions, recognition
Fixed ratio	A fixed number of responses must occur before reinforcement	Some inconsistency in response frequencies	Faster extinction of motivated behavior than variable schedules	Piece rate, commission on units sold
Variable ratio	A varying number (average) of responses must occur before reinforcement	Can produce high rate of response that is steady and resists extinction	Slower extinction of motivated behavior than fixed schedules	Bonus, award, time off

SOURCE: Adapted from O. Behling, C. Schriesheim, and J. Tolliver, "Present Theories and New Directions in Theories of Work Effort," *Journal of Supplement Abstract Service of the American Psychological Association* (1974), p. 57.

follows every occurrence of the behavior. In **intermittent reinforcement schedules,** a reinforcement follows some occurrences of the behavior but not others. There are four types of intermittent reinforcement schedules: fixed interval, variable interval, fixed ratio, and variable ratio. Each has different impacts (see Table 14.1):

Intermittent reinforcement schedules: Reinforcement follows some occurrences of the desired behavior but not others.

1. *Continuous schedule:* Reinforcement follows every behavioral response. If a manager praises a subordinate every time he or she succeeds at a task, continuous reinforcement is being used. Emery Air Freight used continuous reinforcement (feedback on container usage) to improve employee performance in using containers of appropriate sizes from 45 to 95 percent, saving the company $650,000 in one year.[54]

2. *Fixed-interval schedule:* A reward is given at regular intervals. The best example of such a schedule is the regular paycheck. There is little, if any, correlation between reward and performance. Thus, in Stage 9, when the individual asks the question, "Is the outcome related to performance?" the answer is often no and there is little incentive to do good work.

3. *Variable-interval schedule:* Time is the basis for reinforcement, but the interval between reinforcements varies. Sometimes this reinforcement schedule provides little incentive to perform because reinforcement occurs regardless of behavior.

4. *Fixed-ratio schedule:* Reinforcement is given after a fixed number of behaviors, regardless of the amount of time that has passed. This typically results in a higher level of effort. For example, if a person working in a telephone "boiler room" (a high-pressure sales activity) receives a bonus of $25 for every ten subscriptions he or she obtains, motivation will be high because there is a definite relationship between performance and outcomes.

Motivation is high for employees of the Home Shopping Network because there is a definite relationship between performance and outcomes.

5. *Variable-ratio schedule:* Reinforcement occurs after a varying number of behaviors and a varying length of time. Research has shown that this is the most powerful reinforcement schedule for maintaining desired behavior. Exactly why this is true is not clear. A manager who praises an employee lavishly after two or three successful performances and again after the eighth or the tenth successful performance is using a variable-ratio schedule. Such an approach would be very difficult to use for formal rewards such as pay.

The Effectiveness of Organizational Behavior Modification

A review of the applications of organizational behavior modification (OBM) indicates that it almost always has positive results. It has been used successfully to increase performance, reduce absenteeism, improve customer service, increase sales, reduce cash shortages, set better goals, improve feedback, reduce errors, increase efficiency, and reduce workplace hazards.[55] Despite these successes— and others in areas ranging from the increasing use of seatbelts and earplugs to increasing the fuel efficiency of truck drivers—OBM is not widely used. Perhaps one reason is that OBM is often perceived as manipulative. However, pay-for-performance systems are coming into greater use as a means of improving productivity. Of special interest are pay-for-group-performance programs.[56]

Reinforcement research clearly indicates that if desired performance is to be maintained, the consequences of the individual's actions must be pleasant.[57] This means that management must give the reward promised as an incentive on either a fixed- or a variable-ratio schedule. However, providing rewards for performance, though conceptually appealing, is often difficult outside of sales and manufacturing, where the direct contributions of individuals are readily identifiable. Even in these areas there may be problems caused by jealousy or bias. Poorly trained managers may not recognize performance, and some man-

IBM has recently tightened its performance evaluation system in order to identify high performers and employees who should be let go.

agers use inappropriate criteria. Moreover, performance appraisals often suffer from "grade inflation" and hence fail to differentiate accurately between good and mediocre performance. (IBM has recently tightened its performance evaluation system in order to identify high performers and employees who should be let go.[58]) Finally, in some situations, performance—as measured by service calls handled per hour, for example—may be in conflict with customer satisfaction, another measure of performance.[59]

Stage 9 of the MPC: Reassessing the Situation

At this point in the motivation/performance cycle, the individual may reassess the situation in a rational manner. Some people simply continue to behave on the basis of past experience or in a reactive, habitual, or emotional way. However, when an individual reexamines the situation, he or she asks the same questions as in Stage 4, except that "Can I perform the task?" is replaced by "Was the outcome related to performance?" The other questions asked include "Was I rewarded?" "What is the valence (value) of the reward?" and "Were the rewards distributed equitably?" Depending on the answers, the individual may or may not be motivated in the same way again.

The implications of this process can be enormous, and more and more companies are realizing its significance. Quaker Oats Company, for example, has developed a plan for its Lawrence, Kansas, plant that ties hourly employees' annual pay adjustments to the plant's performance.[60] Burlington Northern Railroad caps the pay of its three thousand workers while making them eligible for bonuses tied to the company's overall success.[61]

Stage 10 of the MPC: Continued Motivation

The answer to the question of whether an individual will continue to be motivated in the same way depends on the factors discussed earlier. From a very broad perspective, continued motivation depends on the individual's satisfaction with the MPC process and its results.[62] This level of satisfaction is influenced by the work environment and the individual's personality.

Continued motivation may also depend on the individual's self-image and the impact of the MPC process on that image. For example, a number of studies indicate that if the process strengthens an individual's self-image, he or she is likely to be motivated in the same way again.[63] If the impact on self-image is negative, the individual may not continue to be motivated in the same way. The results of research on this subject clearly show that people with high self-esteem are likely to be more motivated, have higher job satisfaction, and be more productive than those with low self-esteem.[64] It therefore behooves managers to attempt to improve or maintain high levels of self-esteem in their employees. Low levels of self-esteem can also affect the workings of expectancy theory. People with high self-esteem may see expectancies and values realistically, whereas those with low self-esteem may underestimate the probability of success.[65]

Attribution Theory

One of the most critical factors in determining future motivation is attribution: the individual's attribution of success or failure and the manager's attribution of subordinates' successes or failures. Psychologist Albert Bandura has formulated a theory, known as **attribution theory**, that states that individuals tend to attribute success to themselves and failure to outside variables. This theory appears to explain attributions by individual employees. However, managers tend to attribute the failures of subordinates to the subordinates themselves and to attribute their successes to outside factors.[66] Recent research suggests that managers are more likely to attribute a subordinate's failures to external factors when the employee has a good work history than when he or she has a poor one.[67] The length and nature of superior–subordinate relationships also affects attribution.[68] For example, a negative relationship might lead to the attribution of employee failure to internal factors, despite the presence of external causes. The manager should clarify the situation and make certain that the individual understands the process and the results. If the subordinate's needs cannot be satisfied, it is necessary to explain why. If there is a misperception of attribution, this also must be clarified.

Attribution theory:
Individuals tend to attribute success to themselves and failure to outside variables.

MANAGEMENT CHALLENGE

Working in a Japanese Company

John E. Rehfeld, president and chief operating officer of Japan-based Seiko Instruments USA, has worked for Japanese companies since 1981. He believes that Japanese management techniques are effective and that they change behavior—including his. Many of those techniques, he insists, could be equally effective in the United States. These are among his top ten:

Budget for six months: Initially, a six-month cycle felt like twice as much work, Rehfeld says, but he soon welcomed the opportunity to adjust the budget at Toshiba, another Japanese firm, because the computer world changed so much in six months. And having two deadlines each year means less time for procrastination. If you find that you are missing your targets after the first quarter, you have only three months—not nine—to catch up, and you work harder to do so. Moreover, the six-month budget is good for motivation: Each new budget is a clean slate, and managers can adjust goals that no longer seem achievable.

Fix the problem, not the blame: When Toshiba's PC sales never really got off the ground, Rehfeld expected trouble. "Everyone was under stress. I was prepared for a knock-down-drag-out fight over who was to blame for our lousy performance." It never happened. "The discussions were always calm, and the focus was always on solving the problems. No one seemed the least bit interested in laying blame." As a result, Rehfeld felt that he was part of the team and worked even harder. "I realized others in the company had a lot of trust in me, and I wanted to live up to it." He contrasts what might have happened in a typical U.S. company: "The instinct is to find a scapegoat. I probably would have

Motivation is highly sensitive to culture. This chapter's Management Challenge details how one manager learned to work in a new culture and use what it had to offer relative to motivation.

Motivating as a Problem-Solving Process

Influencing the motivation of subordinates can be viewed as a form of creative problem solving. Figure 14.9 indicates how the key terms and concepts discussed in this chapter enter into the problem-solving process. The manager must first recognize that there is a problem having to do with motivation and/or performance. He or she must then identify the needs that are dominant and require action. Next, the manager must determine which satisfiers are available to be used to influence the subordinate in the desired direction. The manager must determine which alternative will be most effective and the best way to offer it. Then the manager must implement his or her decision by providing the satisfi-

been fired and replaced. And the problems would still be there for the new person to deal with."

Don't rest on your laurels: When Rehfeld and his managers finally made their budget in the third year and continued to do so thereafter, he felt pleased. Great, in fact. But "I never got a thank-you." His staff felt discouraged, too, and complained, "Do the Japanese think we're their slaves?" Eventually, Rehfeld realized that the deemphasis on thanking employees is part of the process of *kaizen,* or "continuous improvement." The Japanese *plan* something, *do* it, and then stop and *see* the results to determine how they could be improved. "The Japanese are not interested only in the results; they are equally interested in the process and in how you can do it better next time." In other words, they do not rest on their laurels before pursuing their next goal.

Get people to buy into the decision: When you go through the painstaking process of talking to distributors, dealers, and users, gathering data, and *then* deciding what is needed (even though you already know), the process may seem to be a waste of time, but in reality it isn't. When the other groups buy into the decision, they do so with a vengeance, and the value of their commitment more than outweighs the liability of a slow start. For an American version of the Japanese consensus approach, Rehfeld suggests that *collaborative* decision making works virtually as well: It requires only 20 percent effort to achieve 80 percent buy-in. "In the United States, the majority rules, so no one seems to expect 100 percent agreement anyway."

SOURCE: John E. Rehfeld, "What Working for a Japanese Company Taught Me," *Harvard Business Review* (November–December 1990), pp. 167–176.

FIGURE 14-9 INFLUENCING MOTIVATION AS PROBLEM SOLVING

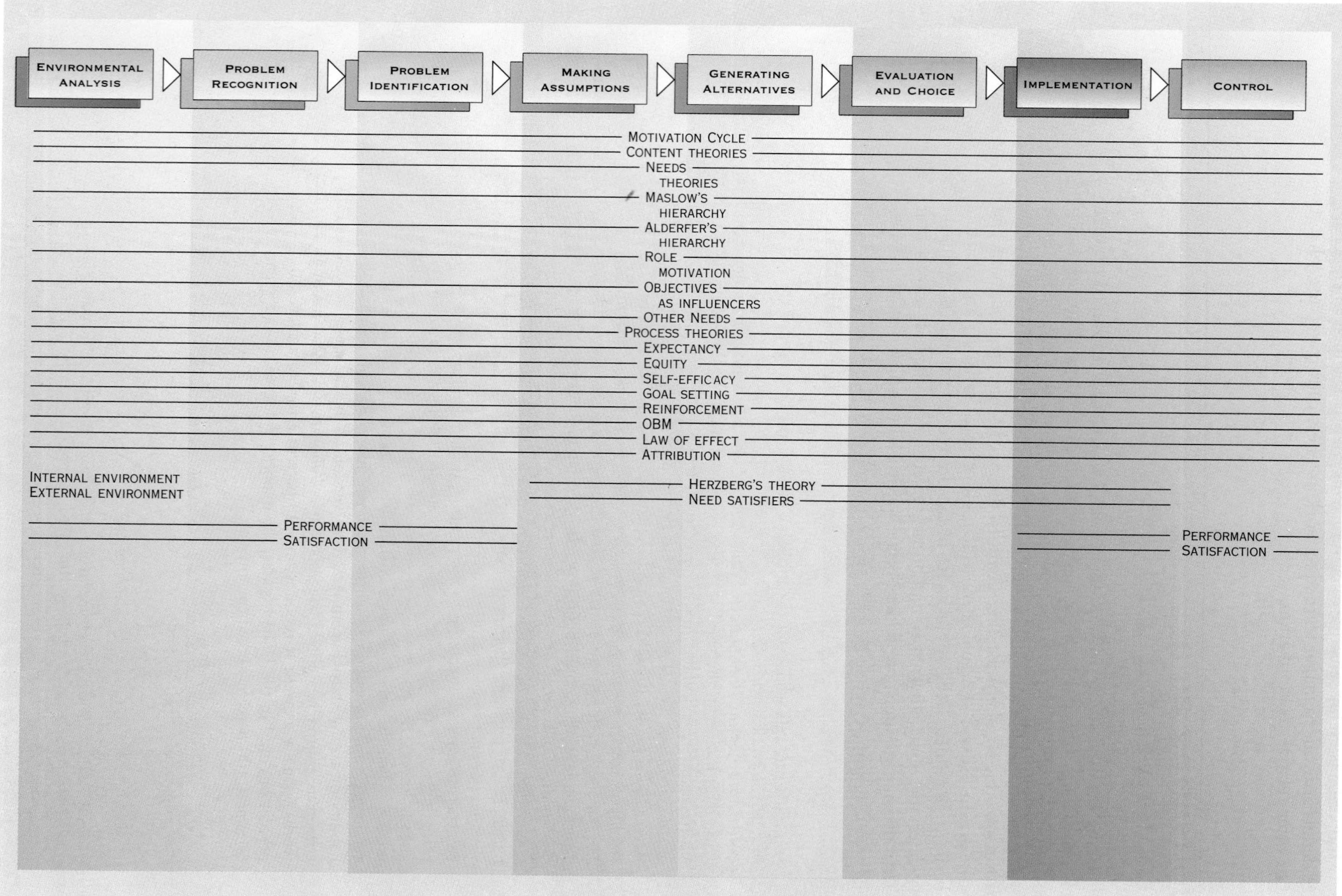

ers in an appropriate manner. Finally, the manager must ascertain whether the problem has been solved. Many of the firms and managers discussed in this chapter have been creative problem solvers.

Guidelines for Using the Motivation/Performance Cycle

The questions presented here can serve as guidelines for using the motivation/performance cycle. These questions can be used not just by managers but by anyone who wishes to influence motivation, including self-motivation. They correspond to the stages of the cycle presented in Figure 14.2.

1. What are the individual's dominant needs?

2. Are there any other important needs? How do I know? Am I able to satisfy these needs? Am I willing to satisfy them? Will satisfying these needs help overcome performance problems? What are the implications of my answers to these questions?

3. What need satisfiers are available, both extrinsic and intrinsic? What satisfiers are there outside the normal reward system? Will offering these satisfiers help overcome performance problems?

4. How is this person likely to react to the satisfiers offered: rationally, emotionally, habitually? Are these satisfiers contingent on performance? Are they likely to induce effort? Can the individual perform sufficiently well to receive these satisfiers? What is the probability of reward? Are these rewards worth the effort I'm asking? Are they going to be distributed equally? How are these rewards likely to be perceived by the individual? What should I do as a result of the answers to these questions?

5. Has this person been motivated to expend mental or physical effort? Is this effort adequate? If not, why not? Does the person think he or she can do the job?

6. Does the individual have sufficient ability and training to perform? Does he or she know the series of tasks necessary to accomplish the objectives? Does he or she know the specific objectives? Have I worked diligently enough at setting goals? Have I made the proper tools and technology available so that this person can perform well? Is the job designed to provide the right types of intrinsic satisfiers for this person?

7. Is performance at a satisfactory level? If not, why not?

8. Have I provided the need satisfier I promised? If not, why not? If not, have I explained why?

9. Does the individual perceive the rewards as contingent on performance, of sufficient value, and equitably distributed? How do I know? What do the answers mean?

10. Will this individual continue to be motivated in the same way in the future, or will I have to offer him or her different need satisfiers? What are the impacts of attribution, esteem, and rewards on my answer? What should I do now?

Summary

(Before reading this summary, look again at the objectives listed at the beginning of the chapter.)

1. According to Maslow's hierarchy of needs, there are five levels of needs: physiological, security, social, esteem, and self-actualization. According to Alderfer, there are three levels: existence, relatedness, and growth. In addition to these needs, there are needs for achievement, power, and affiliation, and the needs to achieve objectives, perform roles, and contribute to society. Herzberg suggests that need satisfiers are of two types: hygiene factors and motivators.

2. Expectancy-instrumentality theory suggests that people examine their situation in the light of potential need satisfiers, asking "Can I do the job?" "If I do the job, will I get the reward?" and "What is the reward worth to me?" Equity theory holds that workers compare ratios of inputs to outcomes for themselves and others doing similar work; when they perceive imbalances, they adjust their inputs. Reinforcement theories suggest that rewarded behavior is likely to be repeated and unrewarded or punished behavior is not. Attribution theories propose that people tend to attribute success to themselves and failure to outside forces; managers, however, tend to attribute subordinates' success to outside forces and their failures to characteristics of the subordinates themselves.

3. The difference between motivation and performance is the difference between effort and results. The manager can turn motivation into performance by providing objectives, coaching, training, tools, technology, and equipment.

4. Whether or not a person can be motivated in the same way in the future as in the past depends on the results of his or her previous experiences with the MPC. The central issues are whether or not the individual has been satisfied and the effect of the MPC on his or her self-esteem.

5. The manager should create needs (stage 1); make an effort to recognize needs and be able and willing to satisfy them (stage 2); offer need satisfiers (stage 3); clarify the situation as necessary (stage 4); provide objectives, coaching, training, tools, technology, and equipment (stage 6); measure and reward performance, giving the satisfiers offered (stage 8); and clarify the process (stages 9 and 10).

6. In using the MPC, a manager must be alert to the individual's dominant needs, the available need satisfiers, the individual's likely reaction to the satisfiers, whether the person has been motivated to expend effort, whether the person has sufficient ability and training, whether performance is at a satisfactory level, whether the promised need satisfier has been provided, whether the individual perceives the reward as contingent on performance, and whether the individual will continue to be motivated in the same way in the future.

THINKING ABOUT MANAGEMENT

General Questions

1. Define motivation and performance.
2. Describe each of the major motivational theories presented in this chapter and indicate how each is integrated into the MPC.
3. Give examples of actions that would occur in each of the ten stages of the MPC.
4. What motivates you to perform really well?
5. Critique the following theories: Maslow's hierarchy of needs, Herzberg's motivators and hygiene factors, achievement needs, goal setting, expectancy, equity, reinforcement, and attribution.

6. Describe creative reward systems that you have observed, or design some yourself.

7. Why do most organizations reward (pay) people on fixed-interval rather than variable-ratio schedules, even though the latter seem to be more effective?

8. Evaluate the grading system used in your course in terms of the MPC.

Questions on the Management Challenge Features

GLOBAL MANAGEMENT CHALLENGE

1. Describe the four broad concepts of motivation used by Volvo.

2. Discuss how these can be used to make a firm more competitive.

QUALITY MANAGEMENT CHALLENGE

1. How did Whirlpool use incentives to improve quality?

2. What else contributed to the improvement in productivity?

ETHICAL MANAGEMENT CHALLENGE

1. Describe how companies push too hard, what happens as a result, and some possible alternative solutions.

2. Discuss the ethical implications of pushing too hard.

MANAGEMENT CHALLENGE

1. Describe motivation as a cross-cultural phenomenon.

2. What can we learn about motivation from other cultures?

E P I L O G U E

Nucor

There are some criticisms of Nucor's incentive system. Absence or tardiness results in loss of the bonus, and a worker might be encouraged by the system to work when ill. However, each of these leads to a real loss of productivity for that worker and for the production team as a whole, and the system should still work in the long run. Production workers aren't alone—if a whole division isn't as productive, everyone in the division loses. In fact, after his 1981 earnings of $300,000, in 1982 Iverson himself received only his base salary of $110,000 because corporate return on assets was too low for the executives to get any bonus.

However overbearing Nucor may seem to outsiders, its employees don't see it that way. Attempts to unionize the company have failed, probably because of the high salaries taken home—in North Carolina, Nucor's workers average more than twice the state average for hourly wage earners. But money alone isn't the whole picture. The unified philosophy of the company, which addresses numerous needs on both sides and provides assurances over the long run, is the real success.

Morale and company loyalty are high. As one worker told an NBC interviewer, "I enjoy working for Nucor because Nucor is the best, the most productive, and the most profitable company that I know of."

1. Describe the stages of the MPC as it is applied at Nucor.
2. Why don't more companies adopt motivation systems like Nucor's?

Motivating the Difficult Employee

Lynn Atkinson had been supervising eight programmers for just three weeks, and already she was running into problems. Previously, she had been a programmer herself. She knew when she accepted the job that she would face a difficult task. She knew the personalities of her subordinates all too well. Two of them were extremely difficult to work with. Both believed that they were all-knowing and infallible when it came to programming. Arnold Baxter was really good; Mary Roberts was not as good as she believed herself to be.

On Atkinson's first day on the job, a change order had been received for one of the existing programs. Baxter and Roberts had been assigned to the task of making the changes. Both resented being taken off their current assignments, but Atkinson had assured them that they were needed, so they had agreed to do it. Two weeks into the project, Roberts complained that she could not work with Baxter any more because he was too immersed in his part of the project to cooperate with her as he should. Baxter retorted that she simply did not understand what was going on. Atkinson asked her boss for advice. He told her that her job was to manage the situation and that he would stand behind her 100 percent, no matter what course of action she chose.

Atkinson thought about the problem. Both Baxter and Roberts earned very high salaries and could get jobs anywhere they wanted at a moment's notice. They were both good at their work. Roberts tended to whine; Baxter liked to tell people how good he was, but he was intolerant of other people's inadequacies. Atkinson herself had had a few run-ins with him when she had been a programmer. The previous manager had let Baxter and Roberts have their own way most of the time. However, Atkinson was determined to get them to fit into the work group better.

DISCUSSION QUESTIONS

1. What seems to be driving Baxter and Roberts?
2. What options does Atkinson have for getting them to cooperate?

How Important Are Various Needs on the Job?

If you are currently employed, circle the number on the scale (1 = very unimportant, 7 = very important) that reflects the importance of each item to your job. If you are not employed, think of a job you would like to obtain or a job you have held in the past.

1. The feeling of self-esteem a person gets from being in my job.
   1 2 3 4 5 6 7

2. The opportunity for personal growth and development in my job.
   1 2 3 4 5 6 7

3. The prestige of my job inside the company (that is, the regard received from others in the company).   1 2 3 4 5 6 7

4. The opportunity for independent thought and action in my job.
   1 2 3 4 5 6 7

5. The feeling of security in my job.   1 2 3 4 5 6 7

6. The feeling of self-fulfillment a person gets from being in my job (that is, the feeling of being able to use one's unique capabilities, realizing one's potential).   1 2 3 4 5 6 7

7. The prestige of my job outside the company (that is, the regard received from others not in the company).   1 2 3 4 5 6 7

8. The feeling of worthwhile accomplishment in my job.
   1 2 3 4 5 6 7

9. The opportunity in my job to give help to other people.
   1 2 3 4 5 6 7

10. The opportunity in my job for participation in the setting of goals.
    1 2 3 4 5 6 7

11. The opportunity in my job for participation in the determination of methods and procedures.   1 2 3 4 5 6 7

12. The authority connected with my job.   1 2 3 4 5 6 7

13. The opportunity to develop close friendships in my job.
    1 2 3 4 5 6 7

Need	*Score*	
Security:	List score for Question 5.	_____
Social:	Add scores for Questions 9 and 13 and divide by 2.	_____
Esteem:	Add scores for Questions 1, 3, and 7 and divide by 3.	_____
Autonomy:	Add scores for Questions 4, 10, 11, and 12 and divide by 4.	_____
Self-actualization:	Add scores for Questions 2, 6, and 8 and divide by 3.	_____

Your instructor will provide some typical scores for purposes of comparison.

SOURCE: Adapted from Lyman W. Porter, *Organizational Patterns of Managerial Job Attitudes* (New York: American Foundation for Management Research, 1964), pp. 17, 19.

"Groups and individual factors are merely different aspects of the same phenomena in constant interaction with each other."

—Kurt Lewin

"I feel much more comfortable knowing that I have 420 people worried about my business than just 10 or 15 people worried about my business. Empowering employees—giving them responsibility for business—is the key."

—Debra Boggan,
Plant Manager,
Northern Telecom

Group Dynamics

CHAPTER OBJECTIVES

When you have read this chapter, you should be able to:

1. Discuss, from a manager's perspective, why groups form, types of groups, and the role of groups in formal and informal organizations.

2. Understand how managers work with and through groups to achieve the organization's objectives.

3. Describe the stages of group development, how groups function, and some of the more important characteristics of groups.

4. Discuss four special types of groups.

5. Describe the essence of conflict management.

MANAGEMENT CHALLENGES DISCUSSED IN THIS CHAPTER:

 Increasing globalization of business.

 Increasing levels of competition.

 A more diverse work force.

Improving Productivity Through Work Teams

Aid Association for Lutherans (AAL), a ninety-year-old fraternal benefit society that operates a huge insurance business, recognized the need to increase productivity in an industry in which profits were being squeezed by higher levels of competition. In August 1987, the company reorganized its five hundred-person insurance staff into largely self-managing cross-functional work teams. Prior to the reorganization, claims had been sent to each of the functionally based departments—health insurance, life insurance, and support services. Any one of the 1,900 field agents might have to contact personnel in each of those departments (each of which had two major divisions) at various times. In situations involving multiple, complex claims, the insured party or the agent might be shuffled from department to department. An inquiry could take thirty days. Now, each team of twenty to thirty employees can handle all of the 167 procedures that were formerly split among the three functional departments.

The results of the reorganization have been dramatic. Employment has been cut by 12 percent, yet the productivity of the remaining employees has risen by 40 percent. Forty supervisory positions and four levels of management have been eliminated because the teams have assumed most management tasks. Customers and agents receive responses within a few days, and the agents are able to develop ongoing relationships with specific teams, resulting in improved customer service. Employees are rewarded for their new responsibilities and no one was laid off when the teams were formed. Those whose positions were eliminated were offered other jobs in the organization if they wanted them. The implications of AAL's success for other insurers, banks, and other service firms are staggering.

SOURCES: Robert Janson and Richard L. Gunderson, "The Team Approach to Companywide Change," *National Productivity Review* (Winter 1990–1991), pp. 35–44; "Work Teams Can Rev Up Paper-Pushers, Too," *Business Week* (November 28, 1988), pp. 64–72; and telephone interviews with AAL personnel, March 1993.

One of the major changes in management in recent years is the increasing use of work groups to improve productivity and quality. Organizations have always been structured around work groups, each led by a manager, but only recently have managers begun to learn how to work truly effectively with groups. AAL's self-managing cross-functional work teams are but one of myriad examples of the use of teamwork in organizations. For example, TQM and productivity enhancement programs often depend on autonomous work teams. New-product development teams, joint venture teams, and problem-solving task forces are other important examples of this approach.

Why are groups so important to organizations and individuals? Why are some groups more effective than others? Why are so many organizations concentrating on better management of the group as a means of becoming more productive and raising quality, and why have they not done so before?

This chapter explores these questions. First it examines the types of groups that exist—both formal and informal—and why they are formed. Then it explores the organizational context of groups, how groups function, and the positive results of groups. (See Figure 15.1.) The latter portion of the chapter focuses on what managers can do to work well with four specific types of groups: the autonomous work team, the task force, the quality circle, and the creativity circle. The chapter concludes with a discussion of conflict management.

Why Examine Groups?

Much of the work of organizations is accomplished through group activity. Work is usually organized around groups, and the organization is a system of overlapping groups. Tasks are usually assigned to groups before being assigned to individuals. The work group can often function more productively as a team than its members can as individuals. Groups dominate life away from work as well. The family is a group; friends meet in groups; a fraternity is a group; athletic teams are groups. Groups naturally form to satisfy individuals' needs.

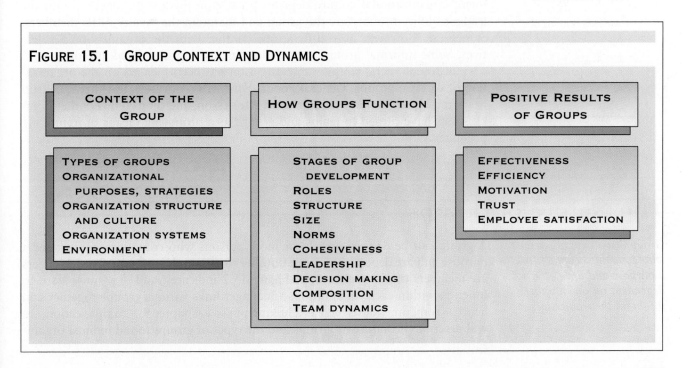

FIGURE 15.1   GROUP CONTEXT AND DYNAMICS

CONTEXT OF THE GROUP	HOW GROUPS FUNCTION	POSITIVE RESULTS OF GROUPS
TYPES OF GROUPS ORGANIZATIONAL purposes, strategies ORGANIZATION STRUCTURE AND CULTURE ORGANIZATION SYSTEMS ENVIRONMENT	STAGES OF GROUP DEVELOPMENT ROLES STRUCTURE SIZE NORMS COHESIVENESS LEADERSHIP DECISION MAKING COMPOSITION TEAM DYNAMICS	EFFECTIVENESS EFFICIENCY MOTIVATION TRUST EMPLOYEE SATISFACTION

Aid Association for Lutherans' self-managing cross-functional work teams are but one example of the use of teamwork in organizations. Here, members of a self-managed work team at AAL discuss a project at their national headquarters in Appleton, Wisconsin.

AT AAL: *Cross-functional work teams were used to improve productivity. Decision making was improved and the level of innovation increased.*

Within the organization, groups often make decisions. Groups are believed to make better decisions than their members would normally make individually. Yet a group probably does not arrive at better decisions than a superior individual would make independently. On the other hand, groups tend to take more risks than individuals, and this spurs creativity and innovation. When the sharing of information is important and division of labor is useful, groups tend to make better decisions than individuals.[1]

Groups also establish norms and influence their members to adhere to them. Organizational culture depends greatly on the group, together with the leader's ability to motivate the group and maintain the loyalty of its members. Sometimes, however, a group's norms conflict with the organization's objectives. Some informal groups may undermine or oppose formal authority.

In recent years, considerable attention has been focused on the organization of work in groups. General Foods, Ford, GM, Chrysler, Lockheed, Martin Marietta, Hyatt, Honeywell, Foremost-McKesson, and thousands of other organizations have turned to teams and groups as a promising means of improving productivity.

The Nature of Groups

Group: Two or more people who come into contact for a purpose and are dependent on one another to obtain their objectives.

A **group** can be defined as two or more persons who come into contact for a purpose and are dependent on one another to obtain their objectives.[2] Managers are members of many groups, as Figure 15.2 indicates, and they must learn to function within each. In addition, a manager links various groups together and hence is sometimes described as a linking pin (see Chapter 9).[3] In this section, we will describe the nature of groups and the types of groups found in most organizations.

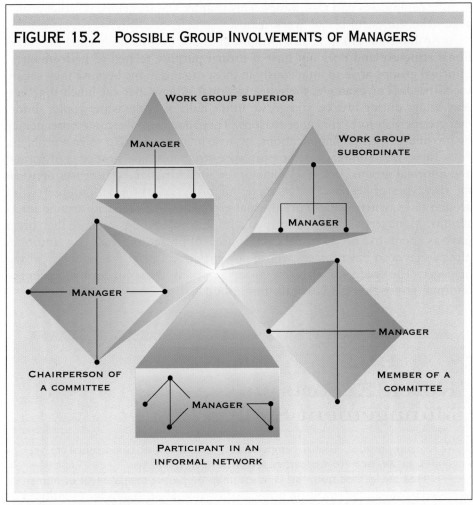

FIGURE 15.2   POSSIBLE GROUP INVOLVEMENTS OF MANAGERS

WORK GROUP SUPERIOR

MANAGER

WORK GROUP
SUBORDINATE

MANAGER

MANAGER

MANAGER

CHAIRPERSON OF
A COMMITTEE

MANAGER

MEMBER OF A
COMMITTEE

PARTICIPANT IN AN
INFORMAL NETWORK

SOURCE: JOHN R. SCHERMERHORN, JR., JAMES G. HUNT, AND RICHARD N. OSBORN, MANAGING ORGANIZATIONAL BEHAVIOR, 3RD ED. (NEW YORK: WILEY, 1988), P. 201. REPRINTED BY PERMISSION OF JOHN WILEY & SONS, LTD.

Formal and Informal Groups

There are two basic types of groups—formal and informal. Each is formed for various reasons, but both operate within an organizational context.[4] Each operates within an organization that has purposes and strategies, structure, a culture (shared values), and systems. Each also functions within an external environment—that is, external to the organization within which the group exists.

A **formal group** is created by the organization and has specific tasks aimed toward achieving the organization's objectives. It is part of the organization's structure.[5] The members of a formal group work together, either on a series of group tasks (the **task group**) or simply because of the lines of authority within the organization (the **command group**).[6] The task group, or **work group,** is extremely important because it is charged with transforming materials and other resources into products or services.[7] Examples of such groups are the teams that assemble various portions of Martin Marietta's Patriot missile in Orlando, Florida. An example of a command group is the faculty of the business school at a university. Very little, if any, of their primary function—teaching—is performed in a group, yet faculty members are placed together in the organization's hierarchy of authority. Work groups may be either permanent or temporary. Permanent work groups include departments or divisions. Temporary work groups

Formal group: A group created by the organization; its specific tasks are aimed at achieving the organization's objectives.

Task group: A group that comes together to solve a specific problem or type of problem.

Command group: The structure of a formal group along the lines of authority within the organization.

Work group: A group charged with transforming materials and other resources into products or services.

Informal group: *Any group that is not part of the formal organizational structure and does not have a formal purpose related to performance.*

include committees and task forces. This chapter's Management Challenge discusses the successful use of work teams.

An **informal group** is any group that is not part of the formal organizational structure and does not have a formal purpose related to performance.[8] Informal groups arise spontaneously in most organizations because they satisfy social needs. For example, there are informal groups that eat lunch together, play bridge during breaks, and gossip in the halls or at the water cooler. Informal groups also form for other reasons. They may help overcome bureaucracy by providing faster communications, or arise in a crisis to help solve a problem.

Table 15.1 summarizes the purposes, structures, and processes of formal and informal groups. It reveals some of the similarities and differences between the two types of groups. For example, the processes of formal groups revolve around tasks, whereas those of informal groups revolve primarily around interactions. Managers are very concerned with informal groups because they often serve as alternative need satisfiers and sources of power for employees. Informal groups may also have leaders whose power detracts from the authority of the manager. The leader of a formal group normally does not lead the primary informal group that exists within that group.

MANAGEMENT CHALLENGE

Korea Exports Its Management Style

We're being invaded. Global competition is rampant. Our competitors are very good. Can we, or have we learned from them? Yes, and yes.

First we learned from the Japanese that the proper management of human resources could substantially improve productivity. Their lessons for us included the increased use of group decision making, viewing the employee as a human being, and building commitment. Now the Koreans are beginning to teach American managers additional lessons.

Hai Min Lee, president of Samsung USA Inc., eats lunch in the employee cafeteria, wears a blue Samsung uniform like that of a line worker, and works out of a spartan office. He practices an egalitarian management style more pronounced even than that of the Japanese—who are often said to have invented the practice. The Koreans are apparently more flexible than the Japanese and more willing to listen to other people's views. They too emphasize worker participation in decision making: "The person who knows the factory process best should not be left out," observes Lee. Much of this participation occurs in work teams.

Americans seem to like the Korean style. Myrtel Sanders, a Samsung employee, comments, "I used to work at an RCA plant, and they took the employees for granted. You can voice your opinion here. I once spoke up to a manager. I would have been fired anywhere else, but it was O.K. There's no union here, but we get all the benefits we need."

Employee benefits are numerous. "If a worker is buying a house or getting a divorce, we get the company lawyer," Lee commented. The Koreans openly celebrate events that are important to employees, such as birthdays. Employees are kept informed and are often actively involved in creative problem solving. Views are openly exchanged.

SOURCE: Laurie Baum, "Korea's Newest Export: Management Style," *Business Week* (January 19, 1987).

TABLE 15.1 The Purposes, Structures, and Processes of Formally and Informally Organized Groups

	Purpose	Structure	Process
Formal organization	Adequate financial return for effort, investment, and risk	Jobs, positions, organizational units; formal roles, relations, and rules; designated authority and accountability	Tasks, procedures, work-flow sequences, formal organizational policies
Informal organization	Satisfaction of personal, social, and psychological needs	Personal influence or power based on interpersonal and group skills, friendships, cliques, likes and dislikes, and ability to use job processes to advantage	Interpersonal processes, group processes, intergroup processes
Possible consequences of serious mismatch	Low productivity, low profitability, may fail	Management and supervision have authority but lack power to make things happen the way they should and lack respect of workers. Low productivity, low profitability, may fail.	Formal processes misused to satisfy personal needs. Production wasteful, inefficient; everything bogged down in red tape. Buck passing, finger pointing, game playing. Low productivity, may fail.

SOURCE: From *Organizational Team Building* by Earl J. Ends and Curtis W. Page. Copyright © 1977. Reprinted by permission of Winthrop Publishers, Inc., Cambridge, Massachusetts.

Why Groups Form

All groups form for the purpose of satisfying needs. Formal groups are formed to satisfy organizational needs. Informal groups are formed to satisfy needs that are not satisfied in other ways. Simple proximity also contributes to the development of groups; that is, people who work together are likely to become members of an informal group.

Formal groups are formed for the purpose of accomplishing the organization's mission or objectives. A formal group's objective may be winning a football championship (the Dallas Cowboys), putting together the most efficient hamburger products operation (Wendy's), or having the most productive sewing line in the shirt industry (Polo). All of an organization's objectives are assigned to formal groups or to individuals to be accomplished. The logical grouping of

At Herman Miller, formal groups are formed for the purpose of accomplishing the organization's mission or objectives. The logical grouping of tasks and the distribution of authority to accomplish them are the bases of organizational structure.

these tasks and the distribution of authority to accomplish them are the bases of organizational structure.

Informal groups form for one primary reason: to satisfy needs that the organization or manager does not satisfy. The organization (and its managers) should satisfy as many employee needs as is practical. Any needs they do not satisfy may be satisfied elsewhere. Obviously, no organization can satisfy all needs of all employees, nor should it; however, whatever needs it is capable of satisfying should be satisfied efficiently, as long as both the organization and the individual benefit. Otherwise, informal groups may form with objectives that are opposed to the aims of the organization and its managers.

Not all informal groups are negative from the standpoint of the organization. **Friendship groups,** which arise to satisfy social needs, result naturally from interactions among people working near each other. **Interest groups** are formed on the basis of common interests, such as playing cards during lunch hour or organizing a clothing drive. As the diversity of the work force increases and as businesses become more global, more informal groups are likely to form within organizations. Table 15.2 examines how informal groups provide need satisfiers.

From the standpoint of the manager and the organization, the important issues raised by informal groups are why certain needs are not being satisfied by the organization and what can be done about the situation. If the organization is not satisfying needs it is capable of satisfying, the potential for trouble exists. For example, groups may form to seek ways to satisfy grievances. Sometimes such groups become formal groups—that is, unions.

Managers must recognize that their power may be opposed or undermined by informal groups. They need to know how to work with these groups and their leaders. These and related issues are addressed later in the chapter.[9]

Friendship groups: Groups that arise to satisfy social needs; the natural result of interactions among people working near each other.

Interest groups: Groups formed on the basis of common interests.

AT AAL: *The organization made a conscious effort to build work group teams. It established a culture within which those teams could function well. Recognition was given to team successes.*

TABLE 15.2 How Informal Groups Satisfy Needs

Need	Example of How This Need Is Satisfied by Informal Groups
Physiological	Groups may be able to negotiate for more compensation and other benefits.
Safety or Security	There is safety in numbers. Groups may counteract bad management.
Social Needs	Groups provide the opportunity to fulfill social needs through interaction.
Esteem Needs	Informal leadership positions or simple membership in a group may raise self-esteem.
Self-actualization	Leadership and group accomplishment are important contributors.
Role Fulfillment	People contribute through the roles offered by the group, perhaps to lead or to follow, or to do what the group was formed to do.
Power	There is strength in numbers. Leadership allows for control over others. Groups control various situations.
Achieving Objectives	Informal groups come together for some purpose, whether it's to play poker, bowl, or counteract the company.
Truth, Beauty, and Justice	Some groups form to go to museums, to go hiking or fishing, to read, and so on.

Influences on Group Structure and Tasks

The organization's purposes—its vision, mission, goals, and objectives—lead to strategies that, in turn, result in the tasks groups are expected to perform and the way those tasks are distributed. The organization's structure and culture largely determine the size and composition of groups and how they are structured. The organization's systems, especially its reward systems, directly affect how group members will be influenced to perform. Other systems affecting behavior include objective-setting and control systems, each of which should be linked to reward systems. The environment of the organization also affects its strategies and, hence, work group objectives and tasks. It also aids or detracts from performance under certain conditions. For example, in a growth environment, with plenty of available resources, a group would act much differently than it would in a recessionary economy or in an organization that is attempting to cut costs.

How Groups Function

The way groups function can greatly affect the results they obtain. A group's effectiveness is influenced by its stages of development; the roles people play within the group; its structure, size, norms, cohesiveness, and leadership; the decision process; and its composition.

Stages of Group Development

Every group passes through a series of stages of development.[10] Different studies have labeled those stages differently, but the sequence is similar in all cases.[11] From a decision-making perspective, the stages identified by J. Steven Heinen and Eugene Jackson are most appropriate: *forming, storming, initial integration,* and *total integration.* A final stage, *dissolution,* will also eventually occur.

FORMING

In the *forming* stage, the members of the group become acquainted. They learn about each other and about the objectives and tasks they are to accomplish. Members examine these issues in view of their own needs and the personal need satisfaction that may result from being in the group. During this stage, members learn to accept one another. Sometimes this process can be difficult if some members have had negative experiences with others in the group.

STORMING

The *storming* stage is a period of high emotion. Cliques and coalitions of subgroups may form, and these are often accompanied by tension. Members learn more about their expected objectives and roles and how their needs may be satisfied. Conflict may occur as each member seeks to have his or her agenda adopted by the group. The amount of storming varies considerably from one group to another. In some cases, it may be almost nonexistent; in others it may be highly charged. Some decision making may occur at this stage, but more often the focus is on group dynamics, as opposed to accomplishing tasks.

INITIAL INTEGRATION

In the initial stage of integration, the group begins to function cooperatively. This stage is sometimes referred to as the norming stage because members are establishing the rules of acceptable conduct, or norms, for the group. Most individual needs become less important than the needs of the group as a whole,

AT AAL: It took several months for the cross-functional teams to become fully functioning. They had to come together and go through each of the stages of group development.

and most hostility ceases. Decision making occurs relative to the task, but maintenance of the group may be more important at this stage than task accomplishment. A sense of closeness and group purpose emerges.

TOTAL INTEGRATION

At the stage of total integration, the group becomes fully functional. Productive decisions are made. Members are well organized, concerned about the group and its results, and able to deal with task requirements and conflict in rational and creative ways. The group's primary concerns at this stage are continuing to achieve results and adapting to changing conditions. A mature, totally integrated group will score high on the criteria for such groups, as shown in Figure 15.3.

DISSOLUTION

All groups eventually dissolve. Temporary groups do so when their task has been accomplished. Permanent groups do so when work is restructured or the work of the group is no longer necessary for some other reason.

In an ongoing group, the preceding stages may be repeated when new members are admitted. The new members must be accepted by and must accept the older members (forming stage); they have to learn to work out their needs and interpersonal relations (storming stage). The reconstituted group eventually begins to function in an integrated way (initial integration stage) and finally becomes fully functioning once more (total integration stage).

Knowing these stages, managers can take actions to ensure that groups progress toward total integration. For example, managers may be especially nurturing toward groups in the storming stages, when group members feel uncertain about their need satisfaction. Similarly, they may find it necessary to practice conflict resolution in these stages and to help the group focus on objectives. Later, they may delegate more power to group members or use other techniques to help the group continue to adapt and perform.

Both formal and informal groups go through these stages when they first come into existence and when their membership is changed.[12] This chapter's Global Management Challenge describes the formation of teams in the Rover auto plant at Lonebridge, England.

Group Roles

Both formal and informal groups have two primary membership roles: task roles and building and maintenance roles. In addition, certain individual roles are enacted in both types of groups.

TASK ROLES

Task roles: Roles related to the task that has been assigned to a formal group or that an informal group has determined to undertake, such as offering new ideas, gathering information, and giving opinions.

Task roles are roles related to the task that has been assigned to a formal group or that an informal group has determined to undertake. These are problem-solving, decision-making, or solution-seeking roles. Kenneth Benne and Paul Sheats have identified twelve largely self-defining task roles, including those concerned with offering new ideas, gathering information, giving opinions, coordinating group actions, refining problems and solutions, energizing the group, and record keeping.[13] In a typical pyramidal organization, it is assumed that these roles are performed by the manager; often, however, especially in a democratic/participative management situation, any group member may assume

FIGURE 15.3 CRITERIA OF GROUP MATURITY

1. **ADEQUATE MECHANISMS FOR GETTING FEEDBACK:**

| POOR FEEDBACK MECHANISMS | 1 | 2 | 3 | 4 | 5 | EXCELLENT FEEDBACK MECHANISMS |

2. **ADEQUATE DECISION-MAKING PROCEDURE:**

| POOR DECISION-MAKING PROCEDURE | 1 | 2 | 3 | 4 | 5 | ADEQUATE DECISION-MAKING |

3. **OPTIMAL COHESION:**

| LOW COHESION | 1 | 2 | 3 | 4 | 5 | OPTIMAL COHESION |

4. **FLEXIBLE ORGANIZATION AND PROCEDURES:**

| VERY INFLEXIBLE | 1 | 2 | 3 | 4 | 5 | VERY FLEXIBLE |

5. **MAXIMUM USE OF MEMBER RESOURCES:**

| POOR USE OF RESOURCES | 1 | 2 | 3 | 4 | 5 | EXCELLENT USE OF RESOURCES |

6. **CLEAR COMMUNICATIONS:**

| POOR COMMUNICATION | 1 | 2 | 3 | 4 | 5 | EXCELLENT COMMUNICATION |

7. **CLEAR GOALS ACCEPTED BY MEMBERS:**

| UNCLEAR GOALS—NOT ACCEPTED | 1 | 2 | 3 | 4 | 5 | VERY CLEAR GOALS—ACCEPTED |

8. **FEELINGS OF INTERDEPENDENCE WITH AUTHORITY PERSONS:**

| NO INTERDEPENDENCE | 1 | 2 | 3 | 4 | 5 | HIGH INTERDEPENDENCE |

9. **SHARED PARTICIPATION IN LEADERSHIP FUNCTIONS:**

| NO SHARED PARTICIPATION | 1 | 2 | 3 | 4 | 5 | HIGH SHARED PARTICIPATION |

10. **ACCEPTANCE OF MINORITY VIEWS AND PERSONS:**

| NO ACCEPTANCE | 1 | 2 | 3 | 4 | 5 | HIGH ACCEPTANCE |

SOURCE: ADAPTED FROM EDGAR H. SCHEIN, PROCESS CONSULTATION, 2ND ED., COPYRIGHT © 1988, ADDISON-WESLEY PUBLISHING COMPANY INC. "A MATURE GROUP PROCESS," REPRINTED WITH PERMISSION.

Rover's Teams Improve Quality

When the Rover Group began developing its first volume car engine in thirty years, the K series engine, the launch was not only financially significant, with an overall investment of 150 million British pounds and acquisition of the latest production technology; it also kicked off a new approach to employee relations at the UK automaker—an opportunity to experiment with new ways of working.

One of the earliest innovations in employee relations was the introduction of *cross-functional teamwork,* a project-based management style that crosses functional boundaries. (The company realized that it was important to change the attitudes of managers first.) After courses intended to alter participants' attitudes toward change and training in cross-functional teamwork, cross-functional project groups were established to confront quality issues and other common problems.

Inspired by the success of team-based product development and manufacturing with the K series and the Land Rover Discovery four-wheel drive, Rover announced a new initiative to shape its structure to accommodate the new approach. Known as *teamwork in engineering,* the simultaneous-engineering approach involves the division of both Rover cars and Land Rover into six business units, each reponsible for the engineering, development, and production of specific product lines. The focus is on projects, not components, and it allows individuals to build commitment by identifying with the outcome of their work. Hierarchical layers are reduced and cross-functional contacts are encouraged.

These improvements in communication are enhanced by Rover's practice of *conformance engineering,* whereby employees performing process, quality, and industrial engineering functions work together as a resource team. They report to the conformance manager, who reports to the manufacturing manager.

Functional flexibility is crucial to effective teamwork. Operators' responsibilities are broader. They include assisting the highest-loaded operator in the team, altering the next level of maintenance, rotating jobs within the team's assignment, establishing priorities for improvement, collecting and examining data, finding solutions and presenting them to management, informing and involving other team members, and confirming that the solutions work.

A more stable industrial relations atmosphere has prevailed at Rover in recent years, and management has moved away from unilateral decision making to a more sophisticated, consultative style of employee relations. According to one production manager and senior steward, Rover has "not seen anything like it, in terms of cooperation and openness, for the last twenty years."

SOURCE: Frank Muller, "A New Engine of Change in Employee Relations," *Personnel Management* (July 1991), pp. 30–33.

them. For example, in the GM Saturn Project, work teams perform these roles, operating without foremen.[14] In an informal group, these roles are often performed by members as well as by leaders.

Earlier we noted the importance of the manager as a linking pin between groups. Much of the manager's success in this function depends on his or her ability to perform task roles successfully. As Chapter 4 emphasized, leaders

At GM's Saturn plant, work teams in the Robotic Training Project perform tasks without being supervised by foremen.

should facilitate problem solving and task completion. They establish the "right climate." They help members satisfy their individual needs, within reason. They represent the group, its values, and its objectives when the group interacts with other groups or other members of management. Most important, they are responsible for moving the organization forward—that is, for achieving its objectives. The same comments apply to informal leaders. They, too, facilitate, represent, establish climates, and help their groups achieve their objectives.

BUILDING AND MAINTENANCE ROLES

Members of groups must also perform actions that tend to maintain the group. According to Benne and Sheats, there are seven major **building and maintenance roles**: roles devoted to encouraging members, mediating differences, compromising, communicating, setting standards, observing, and following passively.[15] These roles mean exactly what their names suggest.

Some of these roles are performed by the manager, but many are not. Obviously no one can be all things to everyone. Thus, group leaders need to draw others into performing some of these roles, but they must also be aware of how these roles affect their leadership actions. Leaders must be prepared to recognize which group members perform these roles naturally, making use of their inherent abilities.

Building and maintenance roles: Roles devoted to building and maintaining the group, such as encouraging members, mediating differences, compromising, communicating, and setting standards.

INDIVIDUAL ROLES

Most groups have some members who play **individual roles** in the group setting in an effort to satisfy their own needs rather than those of the group. Benne and Sheats identify the following as typical individual roles: aggressor/attacker, blocker/resister, recognition seeker, dominator, and special-interest pleader.[16] The manager must make certain that group roles are carried out and that individual roles are minimized because they contribute nothing to the group's purposes. In certain cases, however, some individual roles can be useful. For example, the blockers/resisters may prevent self-destructive change. The manager

Individual roles: Roles played by some group members to satisfy their own needs rather than the group's.

must learn to recognize when individuals are contributing to the group's efforts and when they are merely trying to satisfy their own needs.

If you take a few minutes to reflect on groups to which you have belonged, you can identify people who fill several roles in each of the three major categories just described.

Group Structure

In the 1940s J. L. Moreno, a sociologist, developed an approach to the structure of groups known as **sociometry.**[17] Using his scheme, Figure 15.4 identifies group structure as consisting of a leader, a primary group, a fringe group, and an out-group.

The primary group (also known as the in-group) consists of the highest-status members of the group—active members and others who are accorded all the rights and responsibilities of group members. In Figure 15.4, *A, B, C, D, E,* and *F* are members of the primary group. They share information, help each other, and establish rules of behavior.

The fringe, or secondary, group consists of people who have lesser status and fewer group privileges but still have greater acceptance than people whom the group does not recognize as members at all. *G, H, I,* and *J* are members of the fringe group. They might be "let in" on some group activities or knowledge, such as knowledge about how to do a job better.

The out-group consists of people who have no membership, no privileges, and no interest in the group under discussion. These people may belong to many other groups, but not to this one.

Communication tends to be highest among members of the primary group. They are on friendly, but more distant, terms with members of the fringe group.

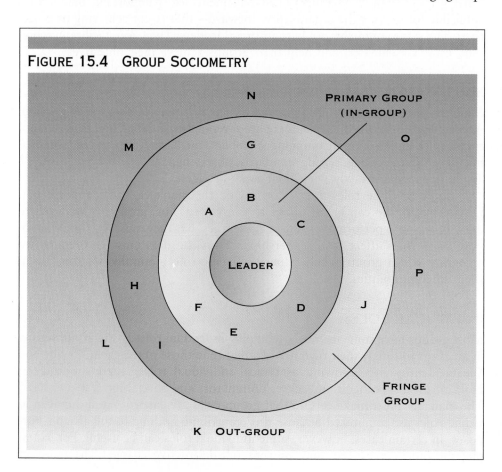

FIGURE 15.4   GROUP SOCIOMETRY

They do not communicate at all with the out-group. In the work environment, the manager must ensure that communication occurs among all group members and must take steps to forestall, or at least minimize, the exclusion of an out-group.

OVERLAPPING GROUP STRUCTURES AND THE GRAPEVINE

Secondary members of one group may be primary members of another group, and vice versa. When members of these overlapping groups talk among themselves, they create a phenomenon called the grapevine—so named because its tendrils seem to reach everywhere. Much has been said and written about the grapevine. Just what is it? The **grapevine** is the path of communication within the organization that exists outside its formal communication channels. It is generally accurate and often faster than the formal channels. Some experts believe that such communication should be kept to a minimum. Others say that managers should use the grapevine to their advantage. Figure 15.5 depicts how the grapevine might function in a typical organization.

Keith Davis, a human relations expert, has examined the grapevine phenomenon for more than thirty years.[18] "With the rapidity of a burning powder train," he asserts, "information flows out of the woodwork, past the manager's

Grapevine: The path of communication within an organization that exists outside the organization's formal communication channels.

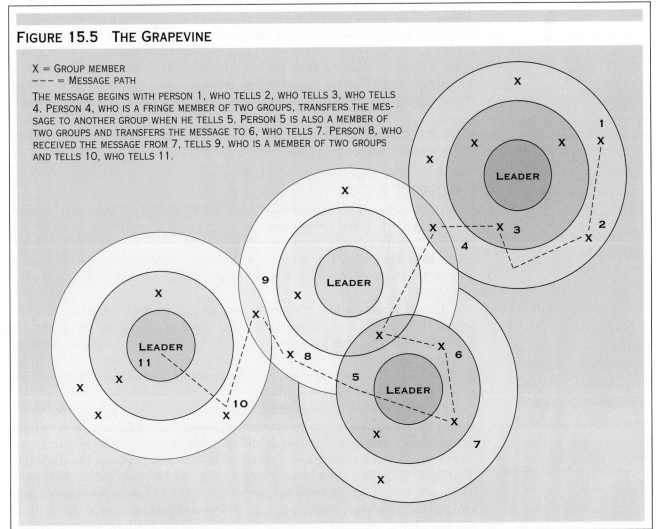

FIGURE 15.5 THE GRAPEVINE

X = GROUP MEMBER
– – – = MESSAGE PATH

THE MESSAGE BEGINS WITH PERSON 1, WHO TELLS 2, WHO TELLS 3, WHO TELLS 4. PERSON 4, WHO IS A FRINGE MEMBER OF TWO GROUPS, TRANSFERS THE MESSAGE TO ANOTHER GROUP WHEN HE TELLS 5. PERSON 5 IS ALSO A MEMBER OF TWO GROUPS AND TRANSFERS THE MESSAGE TO 6, WHO TELLS 7. PERSON 8, WHO RECEIVED THE MESSAGE FROM 7, TELLS 9, WHO IS A MEMBER OF TWO GROUPS AND TELLS 10, WHO TELLS 11.

SOURCE: JAMES M. HIGGINS, <u>HUMAN RELATIONS: BEHAVIOR AT WORK</u>, 2ND ED., P. 176, © 1987, MCGRAW-HILL, INC. REPRODUCED WITH PERMISSION OF MCGRAW-HILL.

door and the janitor's mop closet, through steel walls or construction-glass partitions." The messages communicated via the grapevine are often "symbolic expressions of feelings."[19] For example, if rumor says that the boss may quit even if this is not the case, it may be that the employees wish it were true. Among Davis's findings are the following:

1. Grapevines are accurate 75 to 95 percent of the time, although they are sometimes extremely inaccurate.
2. A few sources supply the entire network.
3. The grapevine is a psychological reflection of employee interest in the organization or its members.
4. Levels of activity in the informal communication network parallel those in the formal network.
5. Troublemakers sometimes use the grapevine.
6. All untrue rumors, whether started by troublemakers or not, are best countered by truth, told directly to employees by management early in the situation.

Davis concludes that wise managers "feed, water, cultivate the grapevine" because it "cannot be abolished, rubbed out, hidden under a basket, chopped down, tied up, or stopped. It is as hard to kill as the mythical glass snake which, when struck, broke into fragments and grew a new snake out of each piece."[20] A manager can nurture the grapevine by developing friendships with key members of the network and giving them useful information from time to time. The manager should not abuse the grapevine but listen to it and keep it informed. More recent surveys show that employees view the grapevine as the most reliable source of information within the organization.[21] To reduce the negative impacts of the grapevine, firms and their managers must provide open and honest communications.[22]

Group Size

Groups of various sizes can function adequately, but the optimum size appears to be between five and seven members when problem solving is involved and frequent communication must occur.[23] Various studies show that different group sizes are optimal in different situations.[24] GM's Saturn Project work groups, for example, have from six to fifteen members, depending on the job performed.[25]

Larger groups allow for more interaction, more decision inputs, and greater division of labor. At the same time, however, the larger the group, the less chance each member has to contribute to the discussion and the less time the manager can devote to each member. Subgroups may emerge within large groups. Each of these subgroups may be attempting to achieve its own goals rather than those of the main group.

Communication becomes more difficult as the size of a group increases, and openness among members appears to diminish. In addition, in very large groups—say, sixty members—it is difficult for every member to participate fully.[26] It is difficult even to know everyone in such a large group, but the leader must make that effort. Moreover, a larger group may actually reduce productivity in carrying out certain tasks because of the difficulties of coordination. Large groups tend to be more difficult to lead and to maintain because of the complex number of interrelationships among their members—which multiply geometrically with increases in group size, thereby reducing the quality of communication, or at least making it more difficult.[27]

Members of the Digital Equipment Company's marketing team make decisions together and work closely together to achieve organizational objectives. Communication is not difficult in a group of this size.

The optimal size of a group is just large enough to serve the group's function. That size is determined by examining the major variables in the situation—for example, the group's purpose. As groups grow, they tend to become less intimate and less homogeneous, to offer fewer opportunites for individual participation, and to be less concerned with their central interest or task. Thus, tasks such as selection of personnel and solving emotionally charged problems are not performed as effectively in large groups as in small ones. Realistically, a group with more than twelve members becomes difficult to manage, but there are certain trade-offs to be considered. Smaller groups necessitate paying the salaries of the extra managers needed to manage them, unless the groups are self-managing.

Group Norms

Norms are the standards of performance or other behavior established by a group. They are the behavior that group members "ought" to engage in. J. R. Hackman has identified five characteristics of norms:

1. They represent the structural characteristics of the group. They are its "personality."
2. They apply strictly to behavior and not to private thoughts and feelings.
3. They are developed only for behavior judged to be important by the majority of group members.
4. Although they usually develop slowly, norms can be developed rapidly if the need arises—for example, in a crisis.
5. Not all norms apply to all members. For example, productivity norms will be established for each job, and thus will differ according to the member's job.[28]

Some typical norms are shown in Table 15.3.

The members of a group adhere to its norms in varying degrees, but important norms are usually adhered to very strictly by most, if not all, members. Members who deviate from these norms may be subjected to disciplinary action and sanctions.[29] In some groups such disciplinary actions might be limited to verbal chastisement, whereas in others physical punishment is possible. Union

Norms: Standards of performance or other behavior established by a group.

AT AAL: *The team's norms were in agreement with the company's objectives. The teams therefore performed well.*

TABLE 15.3 Typical Norms

There are hundreds of norms in every organization, and maybe just as many in each work group. Norms can be positive or negative, productive or unproductive, healthy or unhealthy. Examine the following norms of one large company as perceived by more than 100 of its top managers. As you review them, put a check mark beside those you feel are productive and should be enforced. Put a minus mark beside those that are unproductive.

Do	Don't
—Dress conservatively	—Turn down promotions
—Be punctual	—Associate with lower-level employees
—Be frugal	—Discuss salaries
—Stress accepted values or be quiet	—Ask embarrassing questions
—Operate through a chain of command	—Admit weakness
—Eat with a work-defined group	—Use profanity
—Consider an invitation a command	—Cross departmental lines to handle a problem
—Be a self-starter	—Work late in the office
—Answer your own phone	—Disagree with immediate supervisor
—Be prompt in answering mail	—Go over boss's head
—Be available	—Grow a beard
—Be cooperative and diplomatic with other departments	—Socialize with your boss
—Be conservative with expenses	—Eat lunch with clerical employees
—Be accurate	—Leave the lunch table until the boss does, even if he or she arrives late
—Stay at your desk and look busy	—Leave early
—Be discreet about goofing off	—Spread rumors
—Decorate your office conservatively	—Moonlight
—Defer to superiors	—Lose your self-control
—Respond instantly to vice-presidents	—Close your office door
	—Call in sick on a long weekend

SOURCE: Adapted from Robert W. Goddard, "Everything Swings Off #1," *Manage* (January 1984), p. 8.

members might physically abuse another member who crossed a picket line, for example. Group members may also be punished for "positive" deviance. High achievers who go beyond the group's productivity norms or the formal organization's standards in the workplace may be accused of "rate busting" and be punished by other members of the group.

Group norms are more likely to be enforced strongly if they ensure the success or survival of the group and reflect the preferences of powerful group members—for example, supervisors or informal leaders. Norms that simplify, or make predictable, the behavior expected of group members, reinforce members' roles, and help the group avoid embarrassing interpersonal problems are also likely to be enforced.[30]

Group Think: The Problem of Conformity

Because of their need to belong to groups and because of the control groups have over their members, people often conform to rather rigid and sometimes irrational group requirements. When self-esteem becomes extremely dependent on the group and individualism is not highly regarded, the behavior of group members will become quite similar. For example, the informal group may establish productivity norms that are lower than, or even occasionally higher than, company standards. To feel that they belong, members of the group usually conform to those norms.

In some groups, conformity may be so high that group think results. **Group think** is a condition that exists when "concurrence seeking becomes so dumb that in a cohesive 'in' group it tends to override realistic appraisal and alternative courses of action."[31] There is a definite tendency in extremely cohesive groups to attempt to achieve complete unity of opinion. This phenomenon can be detrimental to decision making for both the group and its leader. The eight symptoms of group think identified by Irving Janis (who coined the term) follow:

Group think: A condition that exists when the tendency of members of a cohesive group to seek concurrence becomes so strong that it overrides realistic appraisal and alternative courses of action.

1. *Illusions of invulnerability:* Members become overconfident and willing to assume great risk.
2. *Collective rationalization:* Problems with the beliefs or actions of group members are "rationalized" away.
3. *Unquestioned belief in group morality:* Decisions of the group come to be viewed as morally correct.
4. *Stereotyping the enemy:* The targets of group decisions are stereotyped as evil, weak, or stupid.
5. *Direct pressure to conform:* For example, at Cleveland-based Lincoln Electric, the world's leading manufacturer of welding equipment, less productive employees are pressured by peers to increase their level of performance.
6. *Self-censorship of deviant behavior:* Members convince themselves that it is inappropriate to voice opinions contrary to the group's.
7. *An illusion of unanimity:* Members believe that every decision made by the group is supported by every other group member.
8. *Self-appointed "mind guards":* Some members feel that it is necessary to protect the group from adverse information.[32]

Group think can lead to unethical behavior.[33] As this chapter's Ethical Management Challenge reveals, when a leader is surrounded by "yes men" it is easy to understand how unethical decisions might emerge for reasons of fear, greed, or belongingness. How could more ethical decisions have been made at Dow-Corning?

The dangers of group think can be reduced or avoided. Team building, organizational development, management development, education of leaders and group members, and an organizational culture that honors and rewards original thinking can all serve to reduce group think. Managers can also take specific actions to curb the ills of group think, such as encouraging dissent, rewarding critical thinking, dividing employees into groups to critique ideas, and testing ideas before implementation.[34]

If an organization is to be effective, it must work through, not against, group norms. Managers must make certain that the organization's objectives are congruent with group norms. Ideally, work groups should embrace organizational objectives as their goals. An outstanding example of this approach is the U.S. Marine Corps. The welfare of the corps is far more important than the welfare of any individual marine. By applying group norms in support of the corps, the corps capitalizes on the group process rather than resisting it.

The Dow-Corning Cover-Up—A Group-Think Phenomenon?

If you're a marketing manager, there is about a 70 percent chance that you will face a serious ethical dilemma in the course of your career. The consequences of the decision you make will not be merely personal; your choice could affect your organization and society as a whole.

Take the case of Dow-Corning Corporation. Although neither Dow Chemical Company nor Corning Inc. made silicone breast implants, they were equal partners in their joint venture, Dow-Corning. While Dow-Corning was the largest supplier of silicone implants, sale of the implants accounted for only 1 percent of its revenues. However, the implants were sold for thirty years. Then, in the late 1980s, an increase in complaints of hard, painful fibrous tissue around the implants was documented. The implants also leaked silicone, and expert testimony linked silicone to autoimmune diseases such as rheumatoid arthritis. The devices were also found to impede mammograms.

Although breast implants were the third most popular form of cosmetic surgery, after nose and liposuction operations, before 1988 the Food and Drug Administration (FDA) did not require data from manufacturers to determine whether they were safe. In April 1991, the FDA began requiring implant manufacturers to prove that their products were safe. But investigations revealed that for at least a decade the industry had been aware of animal studies linking the implants to cancer and other illnesses. Women were not told about these risks until years later.

Dow-Corning's actions appear to have been clouded by its corporate goals, and its reactions to the revelations about implants have generally been characterized as "too little, too late." Ironically, Dow-Corning was among the first firms to establish an ethics program—and that program was considered the most elaborate in corporate America. Launched in 1976, it began with a series of audits to monitor ethical compliance and communicate with employees about ethics. The audits were conducted by a committee of company executives. Some ethicists believe it failed to uncover the implant problems because few managers will speak candidly on moral issues in large groups of employees—especially in groups that include the boss.

Although neither Dow Chemical Company nor Corning Inc. made silicone breast implants, they were equal partners in their joint venture, Dow-Corning.

SOURCES: John A. Byrne, "The Best-Laid Ethics Program . . . ," *Business Week* (March 9, 1992), pp. 67–69; Michele Galen, "Debacle at Dow-Corning: How Bad Will it Get?" *Business Week* (March 2, 1992), pp. 36, 38; and Tim Smart, "Breast Implants: What Did the Industry Know, and When?" *Business Week* (June 10, 1991), pp. 94–98 (Industrial/Technology Edition).

RESEARCH HAS SHOWN THAT MOST GROUPS DEVELOP BOTH A FORMAL LEADER AND AN INFORMAL LEADER. THE FORMAL LEADER IS CONCERNED WITH ACHIEVING THE GROUP'S OBJECTIVES AND IS LIKELY TO FOCUS ON TASK-ORIENTED ACTIONS. THE INFORMAL LEADER IS MORE CONCERNED WITH THE NATURE OF THE INTERACTIONS AMONG GROUP MEMBERS. THE COCA-COLA COMPANY'S GROUP DECISION-MAKING TRAINING PROGRAM ATTEMPTS TO BUILD TRUST BETWEEN GROUP MEMBERS THROUGH GAMES LIKE THE ONE SHOWN HERE.

Marine Corps recruits at boot camp on Parris Island learn that the Corps is more important than any individual member. The group process is used to build teams of men who are willing to fight and die for the Corps.

Group Cohesiveness

Cohesiveness: The tendency of group members to want to belong to the group, as opposed to wanting to leave it.

Cohesiveness is the tendency of group members to want to belong to the group, as opposed to wanting to leave it.[35] Cohesiveness, productivity, and member satisfaction are most positively correlated when the group's members agree with its formal objectives. Thus, if cohesiveness can be created within the group, productivity and member satisfaction will usually increase. However, because cohesiveness is related to productivity in complex ways, it is not always easy to utilize it effectively.[36]

Conditions that foster cohesiveness in a group include a friendly atmosphere, similarity among members, interdependence among members, high status, a threatening external environment, attractive objectives, and small size. Forces that diminish group cohesiveness include low public image, disagreement over group activities, membership in other groups, and unpleasant demands.[37] Sometimes the cohesiveness of a group is based on opposition to the organization or to a particular manager. In such cases the organization's objectives are seldom achieved, at least not efficiently.

Research indicates that there is a strong correlation between group norms and productivity. Where norms strongly favor productivity, the group will have high levels of output. Where the norms are strong but are opposed to productivity, there will be low levels of output.

Leadership in Groups

Within any group there are usually two leaders, the formal leader and the informal leader. The formal leader can employ a wide range of actions to influence employee motivation. These can be classified into four categories: performing task-oriented actions (those aimed at achieving group objectives); performing relationship-oriented actions (those designed to build relationships and increase cohesiveness); offering intrinsic and extrinsic rewards; and encouraging subordinates to participate in decision making. The informal leader can use similar actions, but his or her power is likely to be based on something other than formal authority. The formal leader must be aware of, and take into account, the informal leader's power.

Of increasing importance is the shift in leadership skills necessary to manage an autonomous work group, as opposed to a more typical hierarchical work group. The focus is on coaching, advising, and facilitating, as opposed to controlling and directing. In such teams, the terms *manager* and *employee* begin to lose their traditional meanings. Workers become self-managed.[35] The leadership role is explained in more detail in Chapter 16.

Decision Making

Groups go through distinct processes as they attempt to make decisions. In the **group decision process,** each member makes a large number of inputs and other members build on them. Groups' decisions are often superior to those of individuals in both quantity and quality. Typically, the bases for groups' success are their closeness to the problem, the larger number of ideas generated because more people are working on them, and the group's ability to build on a solution recommended by others. All of these factors contribute to the desirability of group decision making.[39] Yet, as noted in Chapter 4, there is little evidence to suggest that group decisions are necessarily better than those made by individuals, especially superior individuals.[40]

Group decision process: A decision-making procedure in which each member of a group makes a large number of inputs on which other members build.

The Composition of Groups

Group members display a range of personalities, work styles and motivations, backgrounds, and racial and religious characteristics, among other differences. The composition of a group can greatly affect its productivity. One of the manager's greatest challenges is managing culturally diverse groups. As business becomes more global, this will include managing multicultural work teams. In addition, the percentage of handicapped workers in the work force is expected to increase. Managers need to learn new skills for selecting and managing such teams.[41]

The Results of Group Activity

Only if the manager functions properly, so that the group functions properly, are the organization's objectives likely to be achieved. The main results of proper group functioning are effectiveness (achieving objectives) and efficiency (achieving them with the least amount of resources), which together lead to productivity, motivation, trust, and employee satisfaction. Motivation occurs if groups are led and rewarded properly. Trust develops when the leader's and members' behaviors are appropriate. The final positive result, employee satisfaction, does not necessarily contribute to the other five, but it usually does.[42]

An effective work group is one that achieves high levels of performance and also maintains good interpersonal relations.[43] Barry M. Staw has provided the following guidelines for utilizing groups to enhance both performance and member satisfaction:

1. Organize work around intact groups, as opposed to starting new ones.
2. Have groups select, train, and reward members.
3. Have groups enforce strong norms, with groups involved in on- and off-the-job activities.
4. Distribute resources on a group, rather than an individual, basis.
5. Allow, even promote, intergroup rivalry in order to build within-group solidarity.[44]

AT AAL: Teams were formed expressly to achieve higher levels of performance. The company stressed clear, concise, agreed-upon goals and objectives; well-defined roles; appropriate leadership; an open and trusting environment; rewards; and recognition.

Other factors that play an important part in the effectiveness of groups include task interdependence—how closely group members work together; outcome interdependence—whether, and how, group performance is rewarded; and potency—members' belief that the group can be effective.[45] Highly effective work groups possess the characteristics shown in Table 15.4. It is not yet known whether these characteristics will carry over to autonomous work teams.

A Comprehensive Look at Groups

As Figure 15.1 indicates, groups form for various reasons, but all of those reasons are related to needs.[46] All groups develop through essentially the same stages and function in approximately the same ways. The results of group activities are related to the reasons for the group's formation, though not always directly. The formal and informal reasons are not always the same, and the objectives for which a group was formed are not always achieved.

The precise effects of cultural diversity on group dynamics are not yet known.[47] It seems obvious that there could be a significant impact, especially with ethnically diverse groups. Some experts believe that using the group to enculturate diverse members would be appropriate.[48] We know, for example, that multicultural international teams can function well together after the team-building process has been completed.[49] A recent review of the available research suggests that in problem solving, while multiple perspectives are perceived to be beneficial, in reality they create obstacles to achieving consensus.[50]

Managers' knowledge of groups can be misused. In one instance, a manager at a newspaper attempted to use the group to make himself look better. He knew that a survey of organizational climate would be given to all employees in a few weeks and sensed that he might not be evaluated positively. He also knew that top management would be interested in subordinates' ratings of their managers. He therefore took steps to ensure that his ratings would be high. He began bringing in donuts for the members of his group each morning and "buddying up" to them. But he was overzealous, and his goals were obvious. The group became cohesive, but in opposition to him rather than in support of him. As a result, his ratings were very negative. He then punished the group, which responded (via the grapevine) by exerting enough influence to get him transferred to a nonmanagerial position within a few months.

Groupware: Software for the Team

"Groupware"—software that enables work groups and teams to tackle problems together through networked personal computers—has become widely available. Groupware is especially effective for task forces and autonomous teams. Previously, workers used PCs independently and then met to discuss the results. Groupware allows problem solvers to share results simultaneously.[51]

WordPerfect's "Office" and Lotus 1-2-3's "Notes" allow employees to schedule meetings jointly, share messages, access databases, and track project statuses. Arthur Andersen & Company, a major management consulting firm, purchased twenty thousand copies of "Notes" in order to improve group problem solving.[52] Action Technologies' "Coordinator" bases its functioning on "categories" of conversations. The user composes a message, assigns it to a category, and then transmits it to other users over phone lines. Coordinator reminds users of pending commitments, tracks conversations, and keeps a record of a project's status. Coordinator is used at General Motors' Dayton offices and at GTEL, a California retailer of telephone equipment. Still another program, Broderbund's "For Comment," allows up to sixteen users to work jointly on a document such as a business plan. Wilson Learning Corporation and Xerox have developed networked software to allow simultaneous brainstorming;[53] and Microsoft's group-oriented "Windows" program appeared in 1992.[54] Groupware programs work best when a group is already cooperative and collaborative.[55]

Groupware: Software that enables work groups and teams to tackle problems together through networked PCs.

Special Types of Groups

Managers work with groups, especially groups of subordinates, every day. Sometimes a manager encounters other types of groups or works with his or her subordinate group in special ways. In this section, we review four special types of groups: the team, the task force, the quality circle, and the creativity circle.

Autonomous Work Teams

An important type of group in many organizations today is the autonomous work team. A **team** is a group of people, normally within the same department, who work together to identify and solve work-related problems. Teams may also be cross-functional. An **autonomous work team** is a relatively small, highly

Team: A group of people with shared authority, normally within the same department, who work together to identify and solve work-related problems.

Autonomous work team: *A relatively small, highly trained, autonomous work group that takes responsibility for a product, project, service, or process.*

trained, autonomous work group that takes responsibility for a product, project, service, or process.[56] Special training is usually necessary to increase cohesiveness among team members and improve their ability to find, analyze, and solve problems. Teams typically are ongoing work units.

The dynamics of teams resemble those of mature groups. However, the leader's role in facilitating group activity is much more important in teams. In addition, much of the decision making is shifted to the group, so members' problem-solving skills become more critical. In most cases, training in those skills is required.[57] The jobs of team members are often redesigned, usually resulting in greater cohesiveness, and autonomous teams often select their own members and occasionally critique their performance as well. In teams it is especially important to make roles, responsibilities, and priorities clear; to ensure open communication; to resolve conflicts appropriately; and to help members cooperate.[58]

Task Forces

Task force: *A special type of group that comes together to solve a specific problem or series of problems.*

A **task force** is a special type of group that comes together to solve a specific problem or series of problems. It is normally interdepartmental or, at the very least, composed of numerous specialists.[59] Task forces are very useful when a problem is multidisciplinary—for example, in product design. Team-type training is often provided for members of task forces, and in many organizations *team* and *task force* are synonymous.

Teams and task forces are often used in concert. For example, when managers at United Hospitals, Inc., in Philadelphia are confronted with interdepartmental problems, they turn to task forces for solutions. When they want to solve problems, they often rely on competition between work teams. Task forces have been used to solve numerous problems, including interdepartmental scheduling, coordination of tests for patients undergoing surgery, and reduction of patient-care "downtime"—times when a professional arrives to treat a patient but the patient is not there. Similarly, the hospital has used a team competition program to reduce costs, enhance morale, and improve patient satisfaction.[60]

Thomas J. Peters believes that self-managed work groups may be the most effective tool for increasing productivity.[61] Systematic research on such groups indicates that they produce very positive results over time.[62] This chapter's Quality Management Challenge details how a team significantly improved quality in a functional area of a hospital.

Team building: *A planned series of steps that begins with an examination of a group's functioning and ends with the implementation of changes to improve effectiveness.*

The effectiveness of a team can be enhanced by **team building**, a planned series of steps that begins with an examination of the functioning of a group and ends with the implementation of changes to improve effectiveness.[63] Team building often involves redesigning jobs and attempting to open up communication among team members and between team members and the rest of the organization. This can pose problems in a unionized organization. Unions usually resist changes that reduce the number of workers needed, as autonomous work teams often do. Labor strife, such as the United Auto Workers' lengthy strike against Caterpillar in 1992, can undermine or destroy agreements to work together for the good of the company.[64]

Quality Circles

Quality circles: *Specially formed groups consisting of three to twelve employees who meet on a regular basis to apply specific techniques and tools to problems affecting their work and work area; they subsequently present solutions and recommendations to their management for authorization.*

Specially formed groups known as **quality circles** "consist of three to twelve employees who perform the same work or share the same work area and function and meet on a regular basis, normally one hour per week on company time, in order to apply specific techniques and tools learned in extensive training to problems affecting their work and work area; subsequently they present solu-

A Team Cuts X-ray Processing Time

One of the most valuable weapons in the physician's arsenal is the X-ray; in many instances it takes the guesswork out of diagnosis. But three days is a rather long time to wait for one—or so they thought at Sentara Norfolk (Virginia) General Hospital, where the average time elapsing between an X-ray order and the delivery of a written report to the doctor ordering it was 72.5 hours.

"We were all embarrassed by that turnaround," admits the hospital's chief radiologist. To solve the problem, Sentara formed a quality-improvement team. The team consisted of nine employees and managers. Its investigations revealed subtle bottlenecks, wasted motion, and the need to upgrade technology.

Pat Curtis, head of cardiac nursing and *not* part of the radiology department, served as the quality-improvement team's facilitator. "As an outsider, I wasn't threatening," she explains.

Although the team met only eleven times, members had heavy information-gathering assignments and often conferred informally. Changes were enacted as soon as the need for them became apparent. Some were simple, "like eliminating hand-stamped physicians' signatures or adding the word *permanent* to printouts so they aren't thrown out." Others were more complex, such as persuading management to replace its dictation system with a digital one, eliminating rewind and mechanical searches. In the end, the team reshaped the entire X-ray processing system, eliminating fourteen of its forty steps.

The result: The waiting time of 72.5 hours was reduced to an average of 13.8 hours—an astonishing 81 percent improvement that amazed even those with great expectations for the project. The success in the X-ray department has inspired the creation of more than 250 quality teams in the Sentara system—and numerous inquiries from local companies. As one vice-president and team member put it, "This can work anywhere."

SOURCE: Kevin Anderson, "Dramatic Turnaround," *USA Today* (April 12, 1992), p. 5B.

tions and recommendations to their management for the authorization of these solutions."[65] Quality circles have been used in the United States to help companies compete more effectively, especially with firms in Pacific Rim countries. To be successful, quality circles should have several basic characteristics: First, there must be a sincere desire on the part of management to assist each employee's growth to the maximum of his or her potential. Second, employees must participate voluntarily. Third, there must be a structured process for problem solving in which individuals are trained in problem-solving techniques. Fourth, it is especially important that all levels of management be committed to the concept. Management must support the program by creating the necessary time and space and considering the results. Finally, union and employee commitment are vital.[66]

It is not known how many quality circles exist in the United States or how many firms have adopted this practice. However, it is safe to say that most of the Fortune 500 manufacturing firms have considered quality circles and the majority have tried them, usually successfully. Quality circles are frequently introduced only in selected areas and typically are not found throughout the organi-

Employees at GE's assembly plants are grouped into specialized quality circles. They apply scientific techniques and tools learned in extensive training to problems affecting their work.

zation. Experience has shown that they work extremely well in manufacturing situations but are less effective in service situations. Most quality circles have more than paid for themselves, with payback rates as high as five to one.[67]

The American quality circle is not exactly like its Japanese counterpart. For example, in Japan the foreman runs the quality circle; in the United States, an external facilitator often manages the circle for several months. After that time, the foreman or an elected leader may lead it. The role of the facilitator is to promote and help implement the program; train members; guide initial meetings; solve any problems that may arise; and serve as liaison between the quality circle and staff personnel controlling the resources needed by the group.[68]

In Japan, quality circles meet on their own time, whereas in the United States they are paid for the time they devote to the program. In addition, in the United States, an infrastructure is created within the administrative system to provide support for the program because it may meet with internal resistance. For example, several specialists may manage quality-circle programs even in a small company. The *Los Angeles Times* has three such specialists, even though it has only forty quality circles among its three hundred employees.[69]

Quality circles can help improve the job satisfaction of those involved. They are a form of job enrichment—that is, they give their members more decision-making power. Members are taught new problem-solving skills and various decision-making tools. Quality circles involve teamwork and thus, to some extent, help satisfy the individual's need to belong to a group. They also provide a mechanism for communication. Last, but perhaps most important, they provide a way of improving self-esteem. American workers tend to believe that they are underutilized. Quality circles allow workers to show that they can perform at higher levels than are expected in a typical manufacturing job.

Quality circles sometimes fail because they are introduced in the wrong context, training is inadequate, or there are flaws in the techniques employed. Often managers expect too much in the short term, and those expectations may not be realized. There may also be resistance on the part of managers (who fear that they are losing authority) as well as employees and possibly unions. Quality circles may also fail in situations in which workers are dissatisfied by aspects of their jobs that cannot be improved by joining the quality circle.[70] Teams may become disheartened when their proposed solutions fail despite their best efforts. Quality circles need stability to function properly,[71] and it is essential that top management support the program wholeheartedly.[72]

Quality circles have been treated as a fad by some firms. If they did not turn out to be a panacea for all kinds of problems, they were quickly dropped. To be effective, quality circles must be part of a total quality philosophy.

Some organizational cultures—highly authoritative ones, for example—will not support quality circles. It is also possible that some of the success of the program is a result of the Hawthorne effect (see Chapter 2) and will not necessarily continue. Finally, any technique, if not renewed, will tend to lose its effectiveness over time.[73] For example, in the late 1970s, Toyota Auto Body found that its quality circles were losing momentum and failing to provide the kinds of results they had provided in the past. Toyota therefore renewed its program by making quality circles responsible for new areas, such as customer complaints.[74]

Employees benefit from participation in quality circles in several ways. First, supervisors of quality circles seem to become more self-assured, knowledgeable, and poised.[75] Front-line employees benefit for the following reasons:

1. *Communication improves:* Trust is increased, people learn how to handle conflict, and interpersonal relations among group members improve.
2. *Individual skills develop:* Circle leaders are trained in valuable interpersonal skills and teach them to other circle members. Creativity is fostered. Decision-making ability is developed.[76]
3. *Self-esteem rises:* Participating and seeing the effects of their decisions raises members' self-esteem.[77]
4. *Employees become agents of change:* Resistance to change is reduced or eliminated because employees choose the changes that will be made.

In the future, successful quality circles will probably be part of total quality management. Using quality circles without the other components of TQM can dilute their effectiveness. Moreover, TQM is becoming more common and is likely to be the dominant quality program in the 1990s.

Creativity Circles

Although they have not yet been widely adopted in the United States, creativity circles have had a major impact in Japan and are increasingly being used in Europe.[78] **Creativity circles** are groups of employees who meet to solve problems facing the work group. They are a natural extension of quality circles. The primary difference is that quality circles focus on problems of quality and the use of statistics in solving them, whereas creativity circles focus on a wide range of problems, and their members are taught a variety of creative problem-solving techniques. Creativity circles are likely to become increasingly important in the United States as firms turn to innovation as a way of coping with the management challenges.

Creativity circles: Groups of employees who meet to use creative techniques to solve problems facing the work group.

Leading Groups as a
Problem-Solving Process

Whatever type of group is employed, the manager must determine how best to lead the group. He or she can chose among a number of leadership techniques (discussed in Chapter 16), basing the choice partly on the condition of the factors shown in Figure 14.1.

Leadership of a group can be viewed as a problem-solving process. For example, suppose that there are problems with a product's quality. The manager would use contextual factors to determine whether to use a group to solve the problem and, if so, what type of group would be appropriate—task or command, permanent or temporary. Other choices the manager would have to make include the size of the group, its composition, and how to deal with an informal group. Similarly, the manager might examine a group's cohesiveness, the strength of informal leadership, group norms and roles, and the like before making changes in the job assignments of members of a permanent work group. A good manager is constantly attuned to the work group's contextual factors, how the group is functioning, and the results it is achieving.

Conflict Management

Conflict has historically been viewed as undesirable, something to be avoided. The contemporary view is that conflict cannot always be avoided, but it can be managed.[79] Conflict is inevitable in any organization. All of the individuals and groups in the organization have their own objectives and needs. No two of them can ever agree completely because they will not perceive the same situation in precisely the same way. For example, engineers and production managers clash over the best way to construct an engine. Top management often clashes with personnel administrators over compensation programs. Supervisors clash with upper managers over operational procedures. In short, conflict is pervasive in modern organizations.

Conflicts can arise between individuals, between individuals and groups, between groups, between the organization and the individual, between the organization and the group, and between organizations. Several sources of conflict have been identified. Among them are aggressive or conflict-prone personalities; ambiguous or conflicting roles; differences in objectives, values, or perceptions; inadequate authority; oppressive management; inadequate resources; and unsatisfactory communication.

Consequences of Conflict

Although many people would like to eliminate all conflict, it seems more realistic to try to keep it within bounds and to make use of it. Conflict can have positive as well as negative consequences.

POSITIVE CONSEQUENCES

Much change depends on conflict. Competition tends to enhance the general welfare, provided that the level of conflict is not too high. The offensive and defensive units of a football team may compete to see which does its job better, and in so doing win the game. Branch A and Branch B may compete, and in so doing cause the bank to grow at a much faster rate than it would otherwise. Conflict in the form of competition ordinarily increases a group's cohesiveness, which in turn usually increases its productivity. Loyalty normally increases when people unite against a common foe. If problems are recognized, solutions may be forthcoming. Change results, and the organization survives and prospers. Researcher and consultant Richard Pascale suggests that conflict is vital to organizational success because it helps push the firm forward in time of rapid change and prevents it from stagnating.[80]

NEGATIVE CONSEQUENCES

When conflicts are not resolved, people stop talking to each other. Activities, not results, become important. Biased perceptions of "the other guys" are reinforced and unbiased communication is blocked. Strong leaders are sought—and such leaders often become autocratic in conflict situations. The organization's overall objectives are forgotten. The conflict may become a test of wills, of who can outlast the other person, group, or organization. Sometimes individuals, rather than problems, are attacked. At the very least, inappropriate types or levels of conflict are counterproductive.

Resolving Conflict

The manager's role is to choose appropriate **conflict management** techniques and keep conflict at a reasonable level. Many of the sources of conflict identified earlier give rise to difficulties that can be avoided if appropriate steps are taken in time.

The commonly attempted technique of asserting dominance over the opponent will not suffice as a long-term method of conflict resolution. The conflict situation should be viewed as a problem that can be solved in a rational manner, like any other problem.

Conflict management: The choice of appropriate techniques for keeping conflict at a reasonable level.

MANAGING CONFLICT

Because not all conflict can be eliminated and some is even desirable, managers must learn to manage conflict. Several conflict management methods have been proposed. Kenneth W. Thomas suggests that these approaches can be explained in terms of the degree of cooperativeness and assertiveness of one of the contending parties with respect to intentions concerning the conflict.[81] Figure 15.6 modifies his approach to include aggression.

Thomas's approach can be used as a vehicle for discussing major conflict resolution techniques:

1. *Avoidance:* No assertiveness, no cooperation. Most unpleasant realities can be avoided in this way. The problem is not solved, only postponed. In the short run, this technique may work. It is not uncommon, for example, for people who do not have the strength to oppose their bosses to avoid them, perhaps in the hope of delaying a decision until they gain strength.

2. *Accommodation:* No assertiveness, cooperation. Some people simply give in to others. Sometimes it is necessary to accommodate other people. For example, for many years U.S. auto manufacturers accommodated most union demands in the interest of labor harmony. However, as foreign competition cut into profits, unions became more willing to accommodate management.

3. *Smoothing:* Low assertion, low cooperation. Smoothing is a mild attempt at problem solving. It focuses on similarities rather than on differences, and seeks resolution. The intent is to move the parties toward a common goal. Political parties often use this approach after a primary election campaign.

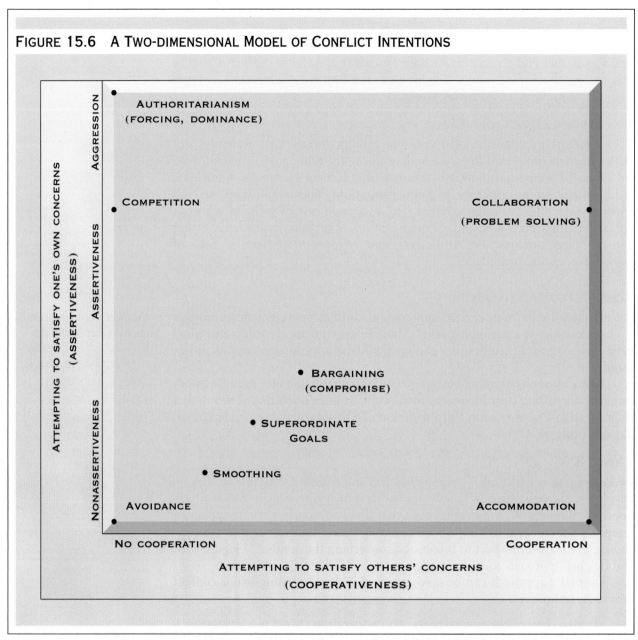

FIGURE 15.6   A TWO-DIMENSIONAL MODEL OF CONFLICT INTENTIONS

SOURCE: ADAPTED FROM KENNETH W. THOMAS, "INTRODUCTION" (TO A SERIES ON CONFLICT MANAGEMENT ENTITLED, "CONFLICT AND THE COLLABORATIVE ETHIC"), <u>CALIFORNIA MANAGEMENT REVIEW</u>, WINTER 1978, VOL. XXI, NO. 2, P. 57. © 1978 BY THE REGENTS OF THE UNIVERSITY OF CALIFORNIA. BY PERMISSION OF THE REGENTS.

4. *Competition:* Assertiveness, no cooperation. This is a win–lose approach, but the competitors must adhere to certain rules. The assertive person does not seek to harm the other's self-image. Change and success in a free-market economy are based on competition.

5. *Bargaining (compromise):* Moderate assertiveness, moderate cooperation. This is a give-and-take approach. Negotiations between labor and management usually follow this pattern. Both parties satisfy some of their needs but not all of them.

6. *Superordinate goals:* Increasing assertiveness, increasing cooperation. The parties attempt to find a common set of

objectives that will cause them to forget their differences. Superordinate goals may be imposed from above. Such goals do not solve the underlying problem but do provide a focus. Thus, members of a football team may fight among themselves during the week, but on game days their differences are forgotten because they have a superordinate goal.

7. *Authoritarianism (forcing, dominance):* Aggression, no cooperation. A party that believes it must win at any cost is using aggression. The unfriendly business takeover in which all of a company's managers are terminated by the new management is an example of this approach.

8. *Collaboration:* Assertiveness, cooperation. This approach is characterized by a genuine attempt to find solutions that satisfy all the needs of both parties. The difference between collaboration and compromise lies in the participants' attitudes: While trying to achieve their own objectives (assertiveness), they become increasingly cooperative.

CHOOSING A CONFLICT RESOLUTION TECHNIQUE

A great deal has been written about the need to collaborate, as if it were the preferred mechanism for resolving all conflicts. The truth is that each of the conflict resolution techniques just described is appropriate in certain circumstances. The manager's task is to base a decision on the critical factors in each situation, beginning with the cooperativeness and assertiveness of both parties. Sometimes the conflict will be between equals; at other times, one party will be dominant and the other subordinate. The same factors that should be considered in leadership decisions apply here: the personality of the decision maker, the personalities of those involved in the conflict, the nature of the groups involved, the organizational climate, the task, and other factors.[82]

Summary

(Before reading this summary, look again at the objectives listed at the beginning of the chapter.)

1. Groups form to satisfy needs. Formal groups form to satisfy an organization's needs. Informal groups form to satisfy needs of their members that are not satisfied by the formal group.

2. The organization's structure results from the grouping of jobs and the distribution of authority in order to achieve organizational objectives. Managers serve as linking pins in this structure, linking various authority levels and work groups. A major function of managers is leading groups.

3. All groups, whether formal or informal, go through similar stages of development: *forming, storming, initial integration,* and *total integration.* All groups include task roles, building and maintenance roles, and the individual roles that members choose to play. Groups establish norms that define acceptable conduct for their members. Successful groups are characterized by effectiveness, efficiency, and the satisfaction of their members' needs.

4. Four special types of groups are autonomous work teams, task forces, quality circles, and creativity circles.

5. Conflict management requires that the manager choose a conflict resolution technique that is appropriate to the situation, depending on the degree of cooperativeness and assertiveness of those involved.

General Questions

1. Think of groups to which you belong or have belonged. Trace those groups through the model presented in Figure 15.1.

2. What sanctions might the group impose against rate busters in various work situations, such as construction (carpenters, electricians, bricklayers); manufacturing (sewing-machine operators, tool and die makers, welders); clerical (accounts payable clerks, secretaries); and professionals (accountants, lawyers, college teachers)?

3. Think of a committee meeting you attended recently. Critique the leader's performance. Then critique the effectiveness of various members in performing task and maintenance roles. What were the results of the meeting? How good were those results?

4. On the basis of what you know about groups, explain how the leader of an informal group might be an aid or an obstacle to the leader/manager of a formal group. What can the formal group leader do to ensure the informal group leader's assistance?

5. If you were the leader of a formal work group and the informal group seemed to be undermining your authority, what strategies could you follow to change the situation?

6. Demonstrate your knowledge of group processes by showing how Figure 15.1 applies to quality circles.

Questions on the Management Challenge Features

MANAGEMENT CHALLENGE

1. Japanese and Korean managers are portrayed as having similar managerial styles. It is unlikely that their styles are identical. Why? See if you can find information about research comparing the two styles.

2. If worker participation in decision making is so successful, why don't more U.S. firms use it?

GLOBAL MANAGEMENT CHALLENGE

1. Why did Rover adopt group-based programs?

2. Describe these programs and their results.

ETHICAL MANAGEMENT CHALLENGE

1. How did group think contribute to this debacle?

2. Why were codes of ethics and ethics training unable to prevent the problem?

QUALITY MANAGEMENT CHALLENGE

1. Describe what the team accomplished and how.

2. Why was this team so effective?

Improving Productivity Through Work Teams

The AAL has moved forward with its team program in three areas: performance appraisal, employee selection, and employee compensation. A few teams conducted performance evaluations of their members, but it was determined that this was not an appropriate activity for teams because of the high skill levels required. However, teams are permitted to provide input to managers when they complete the evaluation forms.

Teams have been allowed to interview candidates and even select team members without the involvement of their managers. With respect to compensation, some teams were allowed to determine their members' compensation on a test basis. This process caused some turbulence in group relations, and eventually it was determined that each team member would receive an equal amount of incentive compensation.

AAL is currently conducting research on some complex issues: employee satisfaction and the quality of work life; productivity; and customer satisfaction. It is also investigating the interrelationships among these issues. Managers and staff have discovered that factors underlying these three areas sometimes come into conflict. For example, the factors that lead to customer satisfaction may not necessarily contribute to higher productivity or job satisfaciton. Yet the firm would like to achieve all three of these goals simultaneously.

DISCUSSION QUESTIONS

1. Why do you believe performance evaluation and decisions regarding compensation were not handled effectively by the teams?

2. Can you think of additional examples of conflict between factors leading to customer satisfaction, productivity, and employee satisfaction? How could the firm resolve such conflicts so that all three goals are achieved?

Groups May Be the Answer

Martin Marietta's plant in Orlando, Florida, had landed major defense contracts through expert salesmanship. But as the plant began to build the products, it discovered that it was not manufacturing as efficiently as it would have liked. The plant's operations managers, led by Charles Hardin and Bob Jones, set out to find ways to improve productivity.

Hardin had been exposed to the quality circle concept while obtaining his MBA. He knew the value of such groups, but the culture at Martin Marietta was too authoritarian to allow for participative quality circles. Moreover, the company wanted a solution that worked primarily to make production more efficient. Hardin, Jones, and the other operations managers set out to examine all alternatives, with the goal of somehow using groups to improve productivity. Some fifteen hundred operations employees would be involved in any solution they proposed.

DISCUSSION QUESTIONS

1. Suggest a solution involving groups that would fit Martin Marietta's needs.
2. What types of implementation problems would you foresee, given the authoritarian culture described?

Team-Building Checklist

The following exercise is designed to reveal the types of questions that might be asked of actual managers and team members to determine whether a team-building program is necessary. After you have completed the form and scored it, your instructor will discuss the questionnaire with you.

Problem identification: To what extent is there evidence of the following problems in your work unit? (If you are not now employed, use a previous work group or any other group to which you have belonged.)

	Low Evidence	Some Evidence	High Evidence
1. Loss of production or work-unit output.	1 2	3	4 5
2. Grievances or complaints within the work unit.	1 2	3	4 5
3. Conflicts or hostility between unit members.	1 2	3	4 5
4. Confusion about assignments or unclear relationships between people.	1 2	3	4 5
5. Lack of clear goals, or low commitment to goals.	1 2	3	4 5
6. Apathy or general lack of interest or involvement of unit members.	1 2	3	4 5
7. Lack of innovation, risk taking, imagination, or taking initiative.	1 2	3	4 5
8. Ineffective staff meetings.	1 2	3	4 5
9. Problems in working with the boss.	1 2	3	4 5
10. Poor communications: People are afraid to speak up, are not listening to each other, or are not talking together.	1 2	3	4 5
11. Lack of trust between boss and member or between members.	1 2	3	4 5
12. Decisions made that people do not understand or agree with.	1 2	3	4 5
13. People feel that good work is not recognized or rewarded.	1 2	3	4 5
14. People are not encouraged to work together in a better team effort.	1 2	3	4 5

Scoring: Add up the score for the fourteen items. If your score is between 14 and 28, there is little evidence that your unit needs team building. If your score is between 29 and 41, there is some evidence, but no immediate pressure unless two or three items are very high. If your score is between 43 and 56, you should think seriously about planning a team-building program. If your score is over 56, team building should be a top priority for your work unit.

SOURCE: William Dyer, *Team Building: Issues and Alternatives*, 1977, Addison-Wesley Publishing Company, Inc., Chapter 4, pp. 36–37. Reprinted with permission.

"A business short on capital can borrow money, and one with a poor location can move. But a business short on leadership has little chance of survival."

—Warren Bennis and Burt Nanus
Leaders

"Transformational leadership is about change, innovation, and entrepreneurship. It is a leadership process that is systematic, consisting of purposeful and organized search for changes, systematic analysis, and the capacity to move resources from areas of losses to greater productivity. It is a behavior process capable of being learned and managed."

—Noel M. Tichy
and Mary Anne Devanna
The Transformational Leader

M ANAGEMENT CHALLENGES DISCUSSED IN THIS CHAPTER:

 Accelerating rates of change.

 Increasing globalization of business.

 A more diverse work force.

 Transition from an industrial to a knowledge-based economy.

CHAPTER 16

Leadership

CHAPTER OUTLINE

Morehouse College Trains
Middle-Class Blacks to Lead

For years Morehouse College administrators have asked themselves how best to train college students to become leaders. Each year they reaffirm a simple credo: "Whatever you do in this hostile world, be the best." Little known among white Americans, Morehouse College, a men's college located in Atlanta, has played a prominent role in shaping the black middle class, producing doctors, lawyers, teachers, and perhaps most notably, civil rights activist Martin Luther King, Jr.

Morehouse's impact on the black community and elsewhere far exceeds its limited number of graduates. Much of its success is attributed to its creation of the "Morehouse man." This phrase was first coined by Benjamin Mays, who became president of the college in 1940 and dominated the institution for decades. The Morehouse man is expected to possess the qualities of self-discipline, self-confidence, and above all, strength. Although this mission was conceived in a segregationist world, it is still considered relevant for today's environment, one that many believe continues to be plagued by prejudice and discrimination.

How is the Morehouse man created? The process is complex and demanding. It begins with an indoctrination period similar to boot camp that takes place when the student arrives on campus. The academic process itself is rigorous. On the average, only half of the students in any given class graduate. Lectures on subjects ranging from black history to etiquette (twice a week the first year, once a week thereafter) and an uncompromising attitude toward performance in the classroom also help form the Morehouse man. Active student participation in clubs, athletics, and other extracurricular activities provides many opportunities to lead. The high level of performance demanded of students results in leaders with high expectations and performance capabilities. Finally, Morehouse men are challenged to accept the responsibility to make a difference.

SOURCES: Jack Gordon, "Rethinking Diversity," *Training* (January 1992), pp. 23–30; and Linda Williams, "Molding Men: At Morehouse College, Middle Class Blacks Are Taught to Lead," *Wall Street Journal* (May 5, 1987), pp. 1, 25.

Everyone agrees that leadership is essential to an organization's success, but precisely what is meant by leadership is uncertain. There are almost as many definitions as there are people using the term.[1] Most would agree, however, that leadership involves influencing others, and all would agree that a leader is a person who has followers. Most would also agree that leaders have followers because they take certain actions and behave in certain ways. **Leadership,** then, is the process of making choices about how to treat people in order to influence them, and then translating those choices into actions.[2] Martin Luther King, Jr., a Morehouse College graduate, was a powerful leader with many followers.

Managers are not necessarily leaders; indeed, all too often they are not good leaders.[3] Some organizations spend millions of dollars training their managers in leadership skills.[4] Moreover, as employees increasingly manage themselves, the role of the manager requires additional leadership, rather than administrative, skills.[5]

Most successful managers are leaders with sound human relations skills and thus are able to influence others to carry out the work of the organization. If managers cannot become leaders, they may find themselves with nothing to manage. A manager without followers soon finds that work is not getting done. Some managers, of course, try to do all the work themselves. But that is not managing, let alone leading.

This chapter discusses the basic issues of organizational leadership: how it is defined, the factors that affect its success, the major leadership theories, and practical approaches to improving leadership ability. Research on leadership ranges from the study of traits shared by successful leaders to studies of the behaviors of successful leaders in specific situations. The section on approaches to leadership includes a model of leadership that suggests the factors on which leadership choices should be based in any given situation. The chapter concludes with discussions of five important issues in management: leadership skills in autonomous work teams; empowerment; the need for managerial leaders who can meet the demands of highly competitive and changeful environments; leadership training and development; and the multicultural aspects of leadership.

Leadership: The process of making choices about how to treat people in order to influence them and then translating those choices into actions.

Management and Leadership

There are some inherent differences between managers and leaders.[6] Generally, managers are rational problem solvers; leaders are more intuitive. Leaders are concerned primarily with results; managers must also be concerned with the efficiency of results. Managers perform several administrative functions in addition to leadership, such as planning, organizing, controlling, decision making, and communicating. Managers are concerned primarily with achieving the organization's objectives, whereas leaders must also represent their followers' objectives. Leaders obtain their power from below; managers obtain theirs from above.

Some experts believe managers and leaders are so different that managers cannot be made into leaders, but this is a narrow view.[7] As organizational environments change, it is becoming increasingly clear that it is necessary to improve managers' leadership skills. Managers who seek to be leaders must use these skills to balance the needs of the organization and those of their followers. Noel M. Tichy and Mary Anne Devanna, authors of *The Transformational Leader,* believe that the development of these skills will be critical to organizational success in the future.[8]

James M. Korzes and Barry Z. Posner, authors of *The Leadership Challenge*, studied five hundred managers who were also leaders and concluded that effective leaders rely on five principles of action:

1. Leaders challenge the process. They are pioneers and innovators. They encourage those with ideas.
2. Leaders inspire a shared vision. They are enthusiastic.
3. Leaders enable others to act. They are team players.
4. Leaders model the way. They show others how to behave as leaders.
5. Leaders "encourage the heart." They openly and often celebrate achievements.[9]

Leadership, Power, and Influence

Power: The ability to control others by influencing the strength and direction of their motivation.

The ability to influence others is the most important quality of leadership. Although there are many ways to influence others, all forms of influence are based on some type of **power**—the ability to control others by influencing the strength and direction of their motivation. Managers have power because of their position in an organization. Thus, they normally have more sources of power than leaders outside of formal organizations. However, the manager's power still must be accepted by followers if he or she is to be effective.

Chester Barnard recognized that unless followers accept a manager's power, the manager will have no influence.[10] For example, it is not uncommon for athletes to break training and go into town for a few beers or a late-night date. On such occasions they refuse to recognize the authority of their coaches. Workers sometimes go on strike rather than recognize the authority of their bosses. Students sometimes question the authority of their professors and refuse to complete homework assignments they consider unreasonable. When subordinates do not accept the authority of someone in a superior position, that person lacks influence, at least temporarily.

It has been suggested that the only successful leadership is that which is dictated by the followers.[11] Thus, if a leader fulfills certain expectations of subordinates, the subordinates will reciprocate with high levels of performance and esteem for the leader.[12] In this view, the followers become the leaders, in contrast to the conventional view in which leaders lead and followers follow. There is an element of truth in both views, and a successful leader realizes this. The leader must take responsibility for his or her power and influence and recognize followers as human beings with needs that must be satisfied.

People possess power for various reasons. Social psychologists John R. P. French and Bertram Raven have identified five key sources of power: legitimate, reward, coercion, expertise, and reference.[13] The first three of these are a consequence of the leader's position and are often referred to as *position* power. The latter two result from personal characteristics and are termed *personal* power.

1. *Legitimate power,* or authority, results from a person's position in the organization. A leader who depends exclusively on this type of power may suffer in the long run. Ordinarily, followers will follow a leader only as long as their needs are reasonably well satisfied.[14]
2. *Reward power* depends on the leader's ability to control the rewards given to other people. A good leader is able to provide desired rewards.

Referent power depends on personal appeal, magnetism, and charisma. John F. Kennedy and Martin Luther King, Jr., had this kind of power.

3. *Coercive power* depends on the ability to punish others. Fear of punishment is a motivator, but it does not motivate many people very highly for long. Nevertheless, some managers attempt to motivate through fear.[15]

4. *Expert power* depends on special skill or knowledge. Think of someone who is very good at what he or she does. Does that person have followers? In most circumstances, the answer will be yes. In many college business administration programs, student computer experts have many followers because people who are less skilled at using computers need their help.[16]

5. *Referent power* depends on personal appeal, magnetism, and charisma. John F. Kennedy and Martin Luther King, Jr., had this kind of power. Can you think of ways in which both of these men also used the other types of power at their disposal?

Managers need to remember, first, that they have choices as to the way they treat subordinates, and second, that the way they carry out those choices determines their success or failure and that of the organization. Managers can select the appropriate way to treat subordinates only after they have considered all of the major factors in a situation. Unfortunately, leadership behavior is often based either on learned authoritarian or emotional responses or on bad examples. Because much leadership behavior is learned from inappropriate role models, leadership development and training become even more vital to an organization's success. Most major U.S. firms, including General Electric, Ford, Xerox, and Hewlett-Packard, spend significant resources on developing their managers' leadership skills.

Approaches to Leadership

From the dawn of history through the early twentieth century, most leaders used authoritarian methods. Early leadership was often charismatic and/or coercive. The influence of learned reactions and emotions on leadership style was great.

During this time there was very little use of the more effective rational, ethical, and assertive approaches to leadership. There was little emphasis on objectives, little delegation of authority, little maintenance or building of subordinates' egos, little participation in management by subordinates, and very little knowledge of how to manage properly.

The large organizations that existed throughout most of this period were primarily governmental (military) or religious—or state governments run by churchmen. Almost all of them had extremely authoritarian structures and climates. In the United States and Canada and in some European nations, governments, and to some extent businesses, were more democratic than elsewhere, and some more effective leadership practices were followed. However, it was only as the business organization began to grow in size and influence that more modern and successful leadership styles began to flourish and the role of the manager as leader developed and became important.

There are many theories about what makes for successful leadership. There are approaches based on the traits, abilities, or characteristics of successful managers; behavioral approaches, which suggest that successful leaders act in certain ways; and contingency, or situational, approaches, which propose that leadership choices should be based on the major variables in a situation. These approaches are discussed in detail in the following sections. Each contributes in some way to an integrated model of leadership known as the Leadership TRRAP, which is described in more detail at the end of the chapter.

Trait Approaches

Trait theories: *Leadership theories that attempt to identify the common traits possessed by successful leaders.*

AT MOREHOUSE: *The college seeks graduates who possess most of the traits and skills listed in Table 16.1.*

AT MOREHOUSE: *In some ways, the Morehouse approach to leadership is a trait approach. Morehouse expects its students to acquire certain traits, such as persistence.*

Management was not studied scientifically until the late nineteenth and early twentieth centuries, when Henri Fayol, Frederick Taylor, Frank and Lillian Gilbreth, and others began their research. Leadership was not examined in depth until the 1940s. At that time, leadership was approached from the perspective of traits. In **trait theories,** successful leaders are considered to possess common traits. What are the traits of successful leaders? How tall are they? What color are their eyes? How intelligent are they?

Much early trait research focused on inherited physical and mental traits, but researchers eventually examined intellectual, personal, emotional, social, and other traits. The researchers studied not only managers, but political and religious leaders as well. The trait approach came into existence partly because of the continuing dominance of powerful families like the Hapsburgs, who ruled much of Europe for several centuries, and the Roosevelts, who dominated American politics and government for fifty years. People noted common traits in members of these families and assumed that all leaders possessed them. When the traits of different families were examined and compared, however, few common characteristics emerged. Early trait research failed to produce either a list of traits common to successful leaders or a theory that would predict what leaders would actually do in a given situation.

Early efforts to formulate a trait theory were confusing and fraught with methodological problems. Most authorities agreed then that the trait approach was, at best, weak.[17] Later studies, using improved definitions and methodologies, proved more fruitful. Table 16.1 contains lists of the traits and skills that appear most frequently in successful leaders. More recently, Shelley A. Kirkpatrick and Edwin A. Locke concluded that research findings indicate that leaders have six fundamental traits: drive (achievement, ambition, energy, tenacity, initiative), leadership motivation (the desire to lead), honesty and integrity, self-confidence, cognitive ability, and knowledge of the business.[18]

The trait approach came into existence partly because of the continuing dominance of powerful families like the Roosevelts, who dominated American politics and government for fifty years.

Even these traits are not universally accepted as characteristic of all successful leaders, and they are not effective in all leadership situations. While they are identifiable traits of successful leaders, it is clear that they are not necessarily inborn, but can be developed. It is also clear that while individuals may possess certain traits that enhance their ability to lead, the situation also plays an important role. "Certain traits increase the likelihood that a leader will be effective,

TABLE 16.1 Traits and Skills Most Frequently Found to Be Characteristic of Successful Leaders

Traits	Skills
Adaptable to situations	Clever (intelligent)
Alert to social environment	Conceptually skilled
Ambitious and achievement oriented	Creative
Assertive	Diplomatic and tactful
Cooperative	Fluent in speaking
Decisive	Knowledgeable about the group task
Dependable	Organized (administrative ability)
Dominant (desire to influence others)	Persuasive
Energetic (high activity level)	Socially skilled
Persistent	
Self-confident	
Tolerant of stress	
Willing to assume responsibility	

SOURCE: Gary Yukl, *Leadership in Organizations* (Englewood Cliffs, N.J.: Prentice-Hall, 1981, p. 70.

but they do not guarantee effectiveness, and the relative importance of different traits is dependent on the nature of the leadership situation."[19]

Despite its limitations, the trait approach contributes to our understanding of leadership by pointing out the need to consider the relationship between individual characteristics and leadership choices. These characteristics are related to personality and needs, which, in turn, affect the leader's response to a given situation.[20]

Theory X and Theory Y

One of the major components of personality is the individual's assumptions about other people. In his classic book *The Human Side of Enterprise,* Douglas T. McGregor (1906–1964) postulated that managers tend to make two different assumptions about human nature. He called these views Theory X and Theory Y.[21] (See Table 16.2.) Theory X tends to lead to authoritative, perhaps even aggressive, managerial behavior, and Theory Y to a more participative style. McGregor insisted that Theory Y managers are just as concerned about productivity as Theory X managers but are more "adult" and less "parental" about achieving results.

McGregor believed that the assumptions managers make about their employees influence how they treat them. Theory X managers tell people what to do, are very directive, are very control oriented, and show little confidence in their subordinates. They foster dependent, passive behavior. Theory Y managers, on the other hand, allow for more participation in making decisions, delegate more authority, and offer people more interesting jobs.

McGregor's approach is heavily influenced by Maslow's hierarchy of needs (see Chapter 14). McGregor recognized that social, esteem, and self-actualization needs had become more dominant in the postwar period. A management

TABLE 16.2 Theory X and Theory Y Assumptions

Theory X

1. The average human being has an inherent dislike of work and will avoid it if he or she can.

2. Because of this human characteristic, most people must be coerced, controlled, directed, and threatened with punishment to get them to put forth adequate effort toward the achievement of organizational objectives.

3. The average human being prefers to be directed, wishes to avoid responsibility, has relatively little ambition, and wants security above all.

Theory Y

1. The expenditure of physical and mental effort in work is as natural as play or rest.

2. External control and the threat of punishment are not the only means for bringing about effort toward organizational objectives. People will exercise self-direction and self-control in the service of objectives to which they are committed.

3. Commitment to objectives is a function of the rewards associated with their achievement.

4. The average human being learns, under proper conditions, not only to accept responsibility but to seek it.

5. The capacity to exercise a relatively high degree of imagination, ingenuity, and creativity in the solution of organizational problems is widely, not narrowly, distributed in the population.

6. Under the conditions of modern industrial life, the intellectual potentialities of the average human being are only partially utilized.

style based on Theory X therefore was no longer appropriate. McGregor urged managers to base their behavior on the assumptions of Theory Y. Not all people fit those assumptions, but most probably do.

McGregor made a pioneering contribution to leadership theory. His approach links assumptions to action. However, he proposed his theories during the 1960s. More recent approaches to leadership focus more on actual behavior and the situation in which it occurs.

Behavioral Approaches

After the trait approach failed to discover a set of traits that could be used to predict leadership success, a number of studies were carried out in an attempt to identify successful leadership behaviors. In other words, attention shifted from what leaders are like to what they do. Noteworthy studies were performed at Ohio State University and the University of Michigan. Additional behavioral theories were proposed by Gary M. Yukl and by Robert Blake and Jane Mouton.

The Ohio State and Michigan Studies

A series of studies at Ohio State University indicated that two behavioral dimensions play a significant role in successful leadership. Those dimensions are **consideration** (behavior that indicates friendship, mutual trust, respect, and warmth) and **initiating structure** (behavior that organizes and defines relationships or roles and establishes well-defined patterns of organization, channels of communication, and ways of getting jobs done). Studies conducted at the University of Michigan revealed two similar aspects of leadership style that are correlated with effectiveness: **employee orientation**—the human-relations aspect, in which employees are viewed as human beings with individual, personal needs—and **production orientation,** or stress on production and the technical aspects of the job, with employees viewed as the means of getting the work done.[22]

As you can see, these conceptualizations are quite similar. As noted in Chapter 15, they have come to be known as relationship and task orientations. Successful leaders, defined in terms of productivity and employee satisfaction, engage not in one behavior or the other but in both to varying degrees. Thus, to be successful most of the time, the leader must behave in a manner consistent with task orientation (initiating structure and concern for productivity) and also in a manner consistent with relationship orientation (consideration and concern for people). It is important to understand that in both the Ohio State and Michigan studies, numerous behaviors were statistically collapsed into the two general categories discussed here.

The Yukl Studies

Gary M. Yukl, author of *Leadership in Organizations,* felt that there was a void in existing descriptions of leader behavior.[23] Although those descriptions were easily comprehended and relevant to many kinds of leaders, they did not provide specific guidelines for behavior in varying situations. Yukl and his colleagues spent several years conducting research on this question. They isolated eleven leadership behaviors, which fall into the four broad categories shown in Table 16.3. Note, however, that although the choices of behaviors are well defined, the factors that would cause a manager to stress one behavior more than another have not been identified.

Consideration: Behavior that indicates friendship, mutual trust, respect, and warmth.

Initiating structure: Behavior that organizes and defines relationships or roles and establishes well-defined patterns of organization, channels of communication, and ways of getting jobs done.

Employee orientation: A leadership style in which employees are viewed as human beings with individual, personal needs.

Production orientation: A leadership style that stresses production and the technical aspects of the job, with employees viewed as the means of getting the work done.

AT MOREHOUSE: The Morehouse approach to leadership can be seen as a behavioral approach. For example, Morehouse teaches that a high level of performance is always necessary.

As the nature of subordinates' needs and expectations changes, some of these behaviors become more necessary. For example, number 2, "supporting," and number 8, "consulting and delegating," will become more important as companies make increasing use of autonomous work teams.

In this chapter's Global Management Challenge, Kim Woo-Choong, founder of Daewoo, describes the behaviors he believes are characteristic of good leaders. Do they match those on Yukl's list? Why or why not?

Kim Woo-Choong

According to Kim Woo-Choong, whose South Korea-based Daewoo Group posted sales of $25 billion in 1991, a good leader is just what the word suggests: one who provides a model for his or her followers. He is critical of the "If you've got it, flaunt it" style of leadership common among American executives. He recalls a party at the New Jersey home of the late Malcolm Forbes. Corporate executives from all over the country arrived by limousine and helicopter. "Everyone wore black tie—except me. I came in a business suit. . . . I wondered how top executives could spend so much time and money to attend a party. I was proud to come in a business suit."

Kim is proud of some other aspects of his leadership as well. "I have never played golf. I have never gone to the theater or to concerts. . . . My hobby is work." Do not feel sorry for Daewoo's founder and chairman. The feeling that he ought to have some fun at times "could come only from people who have never experienced the true joy of work, the utter joy that comes with accomplishment. No one who has poured him- or herself into work has ever failed."

According to Kim Woo-Choong, whose South Korea-based Daewoo Group posted sales of $25 billion in 1991, a good leader is just what the word suggests: one who provides a model for his or her followers.

Another secret of successful leadership, according to Kim, is respect for—and respectful use of—time. "We actually work double the time of other companies. Instead of working the conventional 9 A.M. to 5 P.M., we work from 5 A.M. until 9 P.M.," he says. "Life is too precious to waste. Do not take even a moment for granted, for things are built upon the accumulation of moments."

A corollary of Kim's view of time: "We have a tradition at Daewoo of not having meetings during working hours. We hold meetings either before or after work."

Successful leadership also depends on attitude. "People who come up with 'It may not work' or 'What are we going to do if it fails?' do not have the credentials to be businessmen. If there is only a 1 percent chance of success, a good businessman sees that 1 percent as the spark to light a fire. The business world is not a world where you put one and one together to get two. It is a world where you see one turning into ten and ten turning into fifty."

SOURCE: Kim Woo-Choong, "Every Street Is Paved with Gold," *Success* (October 1992), pp. 62–63.

The Leadership Grid

Leadership Grid: A model of leadership consisting of a 9-x-9 grid that shows how a manager's concerns for people (relationships) and production (tasks) can be combined.

The fourth behavioral theory, the **Leadership Grid,**® was developed by Robert Blake and Jane Mouton. Like most leadership models, it focuses on the production/relationship orientations uncovered in the Ohio State and Michigan studies. Blake and Mouton went further, however; they created a grid based on leaders' concern for people (relationships) and production (tasks).[24] Figure 16.1 shows how these concerns interact in various management styles.

Like other behavioral theories, the Leadership Grid® proposes that there is a best way to manage people. It is the way used by the "9,9 manager," who has 9 units of concern for productivity and 9 for people. Six other major styles are indicated: 1,1, 9,1, 1,9, 5,5, paternalist, and opportunist. Typical characteristics of these styles are presented in Table 16.4.

The grid is often used in organizational development programs. Before training, leadership style is measured by means of a self-assessment instrument. Leaders determine their grid style—that is, they assign themselves to a position on the grid, such as 3,6. After training, in which the leaders receive feedback and

FIGURE 16.1 THE LEADERSHIP GRID®

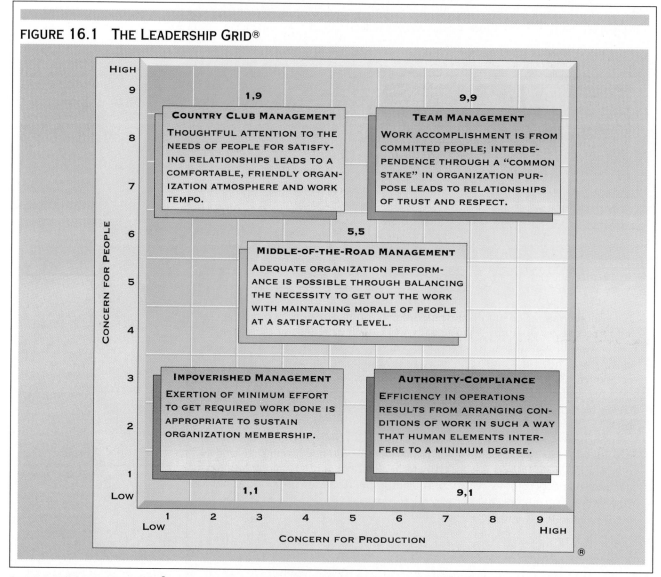

SOURCE: THE LEADERSHIP GRID® FIGURE FROM LEADERSHIP DILEMMAS—GRID SOLUTIONS, BY ROBERT R. BLAKE AND ANNE ADAMS MCCANSE (FORMERLY THE MANAGERIAL GRID FIGURE BY ROBERT R. BLAKE AND JANE S. MOUTON). HOUSTON: GULF PUBLISHING COMPANY, P. 29. COPYRIGHT© 1991 BY SCIENTIFIC METHODS, INC. REPRODUCED BY PERMISSION OF THE OWNERS.

TABLE 16.4 The Major Leadership Grid® Styles

1,1	**Impoverished management,** often referred to as laissez-faire leadership. Leaders in this position have little concern for people or productivity, avoid taking sides, and stay out of conflicts. They do just enough to get by.
1,9	**Country Club management.** Managers in this position have great concern for people and little concern for production. They try to avoid conflicts and concentrate on being well liked. To them the task is less important than good interpersonal relations. Their goal is to keep people happy. (This is a soft Theory X approach and not a sound human relations approach.)
9,1	**Authority-Obedience.** Managers in this position have great concern for production and little concern for people. They desire tight control in order to get tasks done efficiently. They consider creativity and human relations to be unnecessary.
5,5	**Organization Man management,** often termed middle-of-the-road leadership. Leaders in this position have medium concern for people and production. They attempt to balance their concern for both people and production, but are not committed to either.
9 + 9	**Paternalistic "father knows best" management,** a style in which reward is promised for compliance and punishment threatened for non-compliance.
Opp	**Opportunistic "what's in it for me" management,** in which the style utilized depends on which style the leader feels will return him or her the greatest self-benefit.
9,9	**Team management.** This style of leadership is considered to be ideal. Such managers have great concern for both people and production. They work to motivate employees to reach their highest levels of accomplishment. They are flexible and responsive to change, and they understand the need to change.

SOURCE: Robert R. Blake and Jane S. Mouton. *The Managerial Grid III* (Houston: Gulf Publishing Company, copyright © 1985), chaps. 1–7 as modified here. Reproduced by permission of the owners.

critique from colleagues, they reevaluate their grid position and determine what changes may be necessary to strengthen their contributions to the organization. The desired objective is to be a 9,9 leader.

According to this theory, 9,9 is always best, and managers should strive to come as close to it as they can. If they develop high levels of concern for both production and people, their concerns will be translated into sound leadership behavior.[25] The importance of this concern for both people and productivity has intuitive appeal and substantial research support.[26]

Contingency Approaches

The behavioral approaches contributed significantly to our understanding of leadership by identifying what it is that successful leaders do—what actions they take. However, they did not identify *when* certain actions should be taken. The contingency approaches described here attempt to do that.

Contingency theories propose that for any given situation there is a best way to manage. Contingency theories go beyond **situational approaches,** which observe that all factors must be considered when leadership decisions are to be made. Contingency theories attempt to isolate the key factors that must be considered and to indicate how to manage when those key factors are present. Six such theories will be reviewed here.

The Continuum of Leadership Behavior

The first of the six contingency models was Robert Tannenbaum and Warren H. Schmidt's continuum of leadership behavior.[27] Their model, shown in Figure 16.2, was the first to frame leadership in terms of the choices managers may

Contingency theories:
Leadership theories suggesting that for any given situation there is a best way to manage.

Situational approaches:
Leadership theories suggesting that all factors must be considered when leadership decisions are to be made.

FIGURE 16.2 CONTINUUM OF LEADERSHIP BEHAVIOR

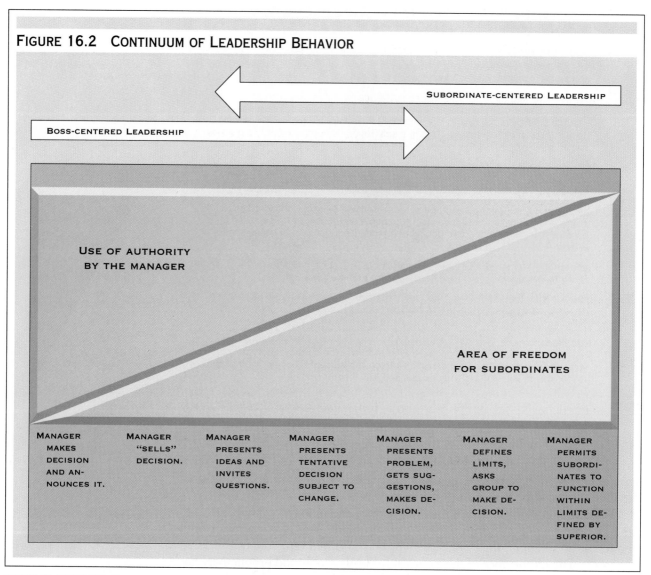

SUBORDINATE-CENTERED LEADERSHIP

BOSS-CENTERED LEADERSHIP

USE OF AUTHORITY
BY THE MANAGER

AREA OF FREEDOM
FOR SUBORDINATES

| MANAGER MAKES DECISION AND ANNOUNCES IT. | MANAGER "SELLS" DECISION. | MANAGER PRESENTS IDEAS AND INVITES QUESTIONS. | MANAGER PRESENTS TENTATIVE DECISION SUBJECT TO CHANGE. | MANAGER PRESENTS PROBLEM, GETS SUGGESTIONS, MAKES DECISION. | MANAGER DEFINES LIMITS, ASKS GROUP TO MAKE DECISION. | MANAGER PERMITS SUBORDINATES TO FUNCTION WITHIN LIMITS DEFINED BY SUPERIOR. |

make regarding subordinates' participation in decision making. The actions shown at the left side of the continuum are relatively authoritarian; those at the right side are relatively participative. The manager's choices depend on three factors:

1. *Forces in the manager:* The manager's value system, confidence in subordinates, leadership inclinations, and feelings of security in an uncertain situation.

2. *Forces in the subordinate:* Expectations, need for independence, readiness to assume decision-making responsibility, tolerance for ambiguity in task definition, interest in the problem, ability to understand and identify with the goals of the organization, and knowledge and experience to deal with the problem.

3. *Forces in the situation:* Type of organization, effectiveness of the group, the problem itself (the task), and time pressure.

In 1975, research by Jerome Franklin indicated that organizational structure and climate are more important than Tannenbaum and Schmidt's model indicates. Leaders must function in accordance with the "rules of the game" established by the organization.[28]

Fiedler's Contingency Model

In Fred E. Fiedler's contingency model, leadership is effective when the leader's style is appropriate to the situation, as determined by three principal factors: the relationship between leader and followers, the structure of the task, and the power inherent in the leader's position. These factors are defined here:

1. *Leader-member relations:* The nature of the interpersonal relationship between leader and follower, expressed in terms of good through poor, with qualifying modifiers attached as necessary. It is obvious that the leader's personality and the personalities of subordinates play important roles in this variable.

2. *Task structure:* The nature of the subordinate's task, described as structured or unstructured, associated with the amount of creative freedom allowed the subordinate to accomplish the task, and how the task is defined.

3. *Position power:* The degree to which the position itself enables the leader to get the group members to comply with and accept his or her direction and leadership.[29]

These factors enable the manager to influence (motivate) subordinates. After analyzing these factors by means of questionnaires developed by Fiedler, the manager would choose between task and relationship leadership styles.

Fiedler and his associates have shown how the two leadership styles and combinations of the three factors are related to productivity. As Figure 16.3 shows, a leader who has good relations with group members, a structured task, and strong position power should use a directive (task oriented) management style because that style is associated with high productivity under those conditions. Other combinations of favorable and unfavorable conditions call for the management styles indicated in the rest of the figure. One of Fiedler's conclusions is that the manager should attempt to change the situation to match his or her style. (Note that this suggestion would create major staffing problems if all managers attempted to carry it out.)

Fiedler's theory identifies specific situational factors and the behaviors that are appropriate when those factors occur in certain combinations. However, management researcher Robert Vecchio has pointed out that this research does not address all the variables in most managerial situations. Moreover, Fiedler's methodology is weak in some respects. The sample for his original study was drawn from a wide variety of groups. Replications of his study have had mixed results, and even Fiedler has difficulty explaining the results of his research.[30]

Path-Goal Theory

Robert J. House and Terrence R. Mitchell have proposed that leaders can be effective—that is, affect the satisfaction, motivation, and performance of group members—in two primary ways.[31] The first is by making rewards contingent on the accomplishment of objectives. Second, the leader can aid group members in attaining rewards by clarifying the paths to goals and removing obstacles to performance. This view of leadership, **path-goal theory**, depends heavily on the expectancy theory discussed in Chapter 14, in which the person to be influenced asks three questions: (1) Can I perform the task? (2) If I perform the task, what

Path-goal theory: A leadership theory that focuses on the need for leaders to make rewards contingent on the accomplishment of objectives and to aid group members in attaining rewards by clarifying the paths to goals and removing obstacles to performance.

FIGURE 16.3 HOW EFFECTIVE LEADERSHIP STYLE VARIES WITH THE SITUATION

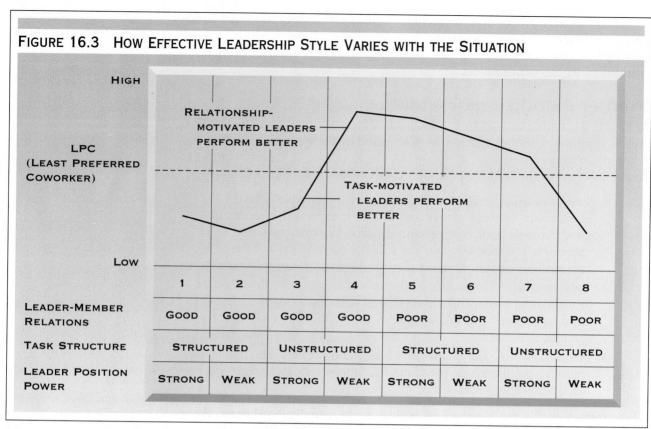

SOURCE: FRED E. FIEDLER AND MARTIN M. CHEMERS, LEADERSHIP AND EFFECTIVE MANAGEMENT (GLENVIEW, ILL.: SCOTT, FORESMAN, 1974), P. 80. REPRINTED BY PERMISSION OF FRED E. FIEDLER.

is the probability that I will get the reward? and (3) What is the reward worth to me? The leader's activity is designed to show subordinates that a given action will produce a valued reward and that they can be successful in carrying out that action.

According to path-goal theory, there are four primary styles of leadership, as shown in Figure 16.4:

1. *Directive leadership:* The leader explains the performance goal and provides specific rules and regulations to guide subordinates toward achieving it.

2. *Supportive leadership:* The leader displays personal concern for subordinates. This includes being friendly to subordinates and sensitive to their needs.

3. *Achievement-oriented leadership:* The leader emphasizes the achievement of difficult tasks and the importance of excellent performance and simultaneously displays confidence that subordinates will perform well.

4. *Participative leadership:* The leader consults with subordinates about work, task goals, and paths to resource goals. This leadership style involves sharing information as well as consulting with subordinates before making decisions.[32]

SITUATIONAL DIFFERENCES

The leader attempts to match his or her style to the situation (see Figure 16.4). According to path-goal theory, there are two major differences in leadership situations. The first is related to the nature of subordinates. Is their ability and

FIGURE 16.4 THE PATH-GOAL MODEL OF LEADERSHIP

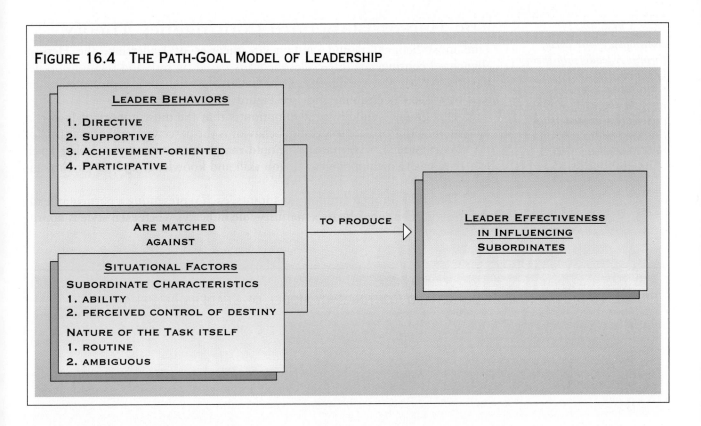

knowledge adequate to the task or do they need additional training? What are their feelings relative to control of their destiny—do they feel that they are in control or that they are at the mercy of an outside force? The second factor deals with the nature of the job itself. The task may be routine, and subordinates may have dealt with it many times and feel comfortable doing it; or the task may be ambiguous (not clearly defined or understood) or somewhat new, and subordinates may require help, or may need to be inventive, to master it.

A manager may face many different kinds of situations. The following examples indicate the logic that might be used to determine the appropriate leadership style for a given situation:

- Directive leadership would be used when subordinates have low levels of training and the work they are doing is partly routine and partly ambiguous.
- Supportive leadership would be used when subordinates are doing highly routine work and have been doing it for some time.
- Achievement-oriented leadership would be used when subordinates are doing highly innovative and ambiguous work and already have a high level of knowledge and skill.
- Participative leadership would be used when the work is moderately ambiguous and subordinates have medium levels of experience doing it.

Path-goal theory reveals that certain **substitutes for leadership** exist. These are systems that help define behavior and preclude the need for direct managerial actions. For example, if the leader's role is to clarify the path to the goal and make it easier to pursue, clear and precise rules and plans would be substitutes for leadership, as would good incentive systems. Routine tasks, or tasks providing intrinsic satisfaction, would also be substitutes.[33]

Substitutes for leadership: Systems that help define behavior and preclude the need for direct managerial actions.

The Hersey-Blanchard Contingency Theory

Like most behavioral and contingency theories of leadership, the **Hersey-Blanchard contingency (life-cycle) theory** is based on task and relationship behaviors.[34] Each of these dimensions of leadership behavior is represented on an axis of a two-dimensional grid (see Figure 16.5).

This model's underlying assumption is that the most important factor in determining appropriate leadership behavior is the perceived level of maturity of the subordinate(s). The manager should match his or her style to that level. Maturity has two components: (1) job skill and knowledge and (2) psychological maturity.

The grid is broken into four quadrants, each representing a particular leadership style. The subordinate's maturity line indicates when each style is appro-

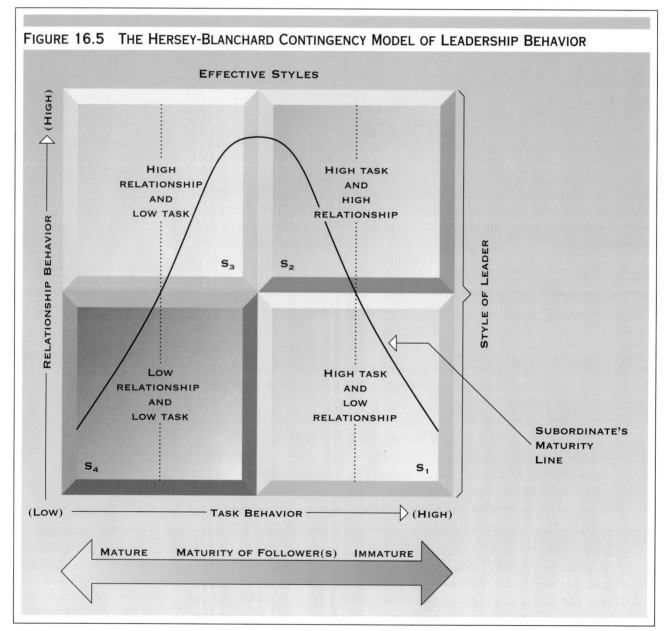

FIGURE 16.5 THE HERSEY-BLANCHARD CONTINGENCY MODEL OF LEADERSHIP BEHAVIOR

EFFECTIVE STYLES

RELATIONSHIP BEHAVIOR (HIGH)

HIGH RELATIONSHIP AND LOW TASK — S₃

HIGH TASK AND HIGH RELATIONSHIP — S₂

LOW RELATIONSHIP AND LOW TASK — S₄

HIGH TASK AND LOW RELATIONSHIP — S₁

STYLE OF LEADER

SUBORDINATE'S MATURITY LINE

(LOW) — TASK BEHAVIOR → (HIGH)

MATURE — MATURITY OF FOLLOWER(S) — IMMATURE

priate. The maturity line does not represent the actual maturity of a subordinate but, rather, the amounts of task and relationship behaviors that are appropriate, given the manager's perception of the subordinate's maturity.

As an illustration, assume that a single subordinate begins with a low level of maturity. As the subordinate's maturity increases (or if it begins at a relatively high level), the emphasis shifts from a high-task, low-relationship orientation to a high-task, high-relationship one. As the subordinate matures further, the style shifts to a low-task, high-relationship one. Finally, when the subordinate reaches full maturity, a low-relationship, low-task style becomes preferable. At this point, the subordinate should be able to manage him- or herself. The intuitive appeal of this approach is great. (The model would function in the same way for a work group as for a single subordinate.)

There are numerous combinations of task and relationship orientations within each style. Ordinarily, the changes in task or relationship orientation occur incrementally. Few managers make sudden sweeping changes in their leadership styles.

A questionnaire, the Leader Effectiveness and Adaptability Description (LEAD), can be used to ascertain a leader's most commonly used style and the range of this style—that is the leader's adaptability to the situation. (Will the leader shift to the appropriate style or continue to use the style he or she is accustomed to using?) The LEAD reveals the leader's ability to change styles according to the maturity levels of subordinates.

There is little empirical evidence for the validity of the Hersey-Blanchard theory, but its intuitive appeal is great. Moreover, virtually all theories of motivation and leadership can be explained at least partially by this model. To apply this approach, the leader needs considerable skill in diagnosing subordinates' maturity levels. However, this is true of most leadership models. The value of this model lies in its recognition of the importance of adaptation to the subordinate's personality. Just about everyone needs some recognition (relationship behavior), and managers should take this need into account whether they use the model or not. Most employees will not be productive without some recognition.

This approach identifies an important variable in successful leadership: the match between the characteristics of the manager/leader and those of the subordinate. Many organizations, including Holiday (Inns) Corporation and Xerox Corporation, have adopted this approach. However, the available research offers mixed evidence on whether it can accurately predict successful leadership behavior.[35] This is probably because it leaves out several important variables that need to be considered, such as position power, work group dynamics, and the nature of the task.

The Vroom-Yetton-Yago Model

In Chapter 4, the Vroom-Yetton-Yago decision tree model for determining degrees of participative leadership was discussed. The focus was on participation as an aspect of problem solving. Here the issue is participation from the leader's viewpoint.[36] The Vroom-Yetton-Yago model enables the leader to determine when to allow subordinates to participate in decision making.

The Muczyk-Reimann Model

Jan P. Muczyk and Bernard C. Reimann suggest that "participation" behavior is concerned with the degree to which subordinates are allowed to be involved in decision making. They separate this from "direction," which they view as the degree of supervision exercised in the execution of the tasks associated with carrying out the decision. They conclude that managers should always emphasize tasks, relationships, and rewards.[37] Thus, the major issue in adapting leadership style to the situation is related to delegation, as applied in both participation and direction.

In the Muczyk-Reimann model, the combination of high and low levels of participation and direction leads to four leadership styles related to the delegation of decision making and the execution of decisions:

1. The *directive autocrat* makes decisions unilaterally and closely supervises the activities of subordinates.
2. The *permissive autocrat* makes decisions unilaterally but allows subordinates a great deal of latitude in executing them.
3. The *directive democrat* wants full participation but closely supervises subordinates' activities.
4. The *permissive democrat* allows high participation in both decision making and execution.

Muczyk and Reimann describe the types of situations in which each of these styles might be used. For example, the directive autocrat would function well in situations in which time is at a premium and subordinates are less mature in terms of job skills or psychological development. Conversely, for the permissive democrat to function well, there must be plenty of time to make decisions, and subordinates must be very mature.

Leaders as Communicators

Leaders need to use certain communication styles to carry out specific leadership styles.[38] For example, a leader may choose to be supportive but have a very aggressive communication style. In that case, the behavior may not be perceived as supportive. Similarly, a leader may choose to be very directive but have a passive communication style that makes the directive style ineffective. Studies of communication styles and their effect on leadership success suggest that an assertive approach to communication may be appropriate to all leadership styles, although an aggressive style may be desirable for a person with a more task-oriented leadership style.[39] Chapter 17 examines the manager/leader's role as a communicator in more detail.

Leadership as a Problem-Solving Process

Figure 16.6 shows that a manager's personality, needs, and characteristics would affect all stages of problem solving. For example, a manager with a need to control others might view his or her environment in terms of power struggles. Such a manager might perceive a problem if a subordinate attempted to make a decision alone rather than ask for help. The manager's choice of leadership actions would clearly be affected by his or her need for power. Similarly, the various management behaviors would affect all stages of the problem-solving process, especially generating alternatives and selecting and implementing a solution.

In examining all of the various studies mentioned in this chapter, several important factors emerge that must be taken into account in choosing leadership behaviors. Those factors include the subordinate's personality and needs, the

CONTINGENCY THEORIES PROPOSE THAT FOR ANY GIVEN SITUATION THERE IS A BEST WAY TO MANAGE. THERE ARE SEVERAL SUCH THEORIES. IN PATH-GOAL THEORY, A LEADER MUST CONSIDER THE ABILITY AND KNOWLEDGE OF SUBORDINATES AND THEIR FEELINGS, AS WELL AS THE NATURE OF THE JOB ITSELF. THE HERSEY-BLANCHARD MODEL ASSUMES THAT THE MOST IMPORTANT FACTOR IN DETERMINING APPROPRIATE LEADERSHIP BEHAVIOR IS SUBORDINATES' PERCEIVED LEVEL OF MATURITY. JAMES SEELEY BROWN, VICE-PRESIDENT OF ADVANCED RESEARCH, AND FRANK SQUIRES, VICE-PRESIDENT OF RESEARCH OPERATIONS (BELOW, LEFT), ARE TYPICAL OF THE THOUSANDS OF XEROX MANAGERS WHO HAVE BEEN TRAINED USING THE HERSEY-BLANCHARD MODEL. ANOTHER APPROACH, THE MUCZYK-REIMANN MODEL, IS BASED ON DIFFERENT COMBINATIONS OF MANAGERIAL DIRECTION AND SUBORDINATE PARTICIPATION. AT THE MARKETING FIRM SHOWN HERE (BELOW, RIGHT), THERE IS A HIGH LEVEL OF SUBORDINATE PARTICIPATION IN THE CREATION OF AN ADVERTISING CAMPAIGN.

FIGURE 16.6 LEADERSHIP AS PROBLEM SOLVING

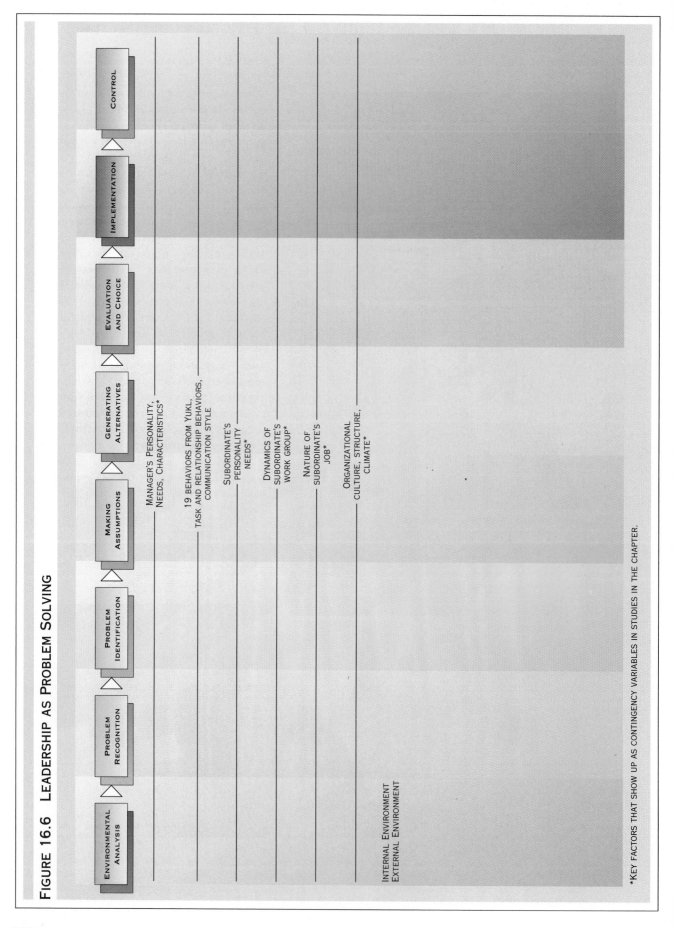

ENVIRONMENTAL ANALYSIS

PROBLEM RECOGNITION

PROBLEM IDENTIFICATION

MAKING ASSUMPTIONS

GENERATING ALTERNATIVES

EVALUATION AND CHOICE

IMPLEMENTATION

CONTROL

MANAGER'S PERSONALITY, NEEDS, CHARACTERISTICS*

19 BEHAVIORS FROM YUKL, TASK AND RELATIONSHIP BEHAVIORS, COMMUNICATION STYLE

SUBORDINATE'S PERSONALITY NEEDS*

DYNAMICS OF SUBORDINATE'S WORK GROUP*

NATURE OF SUBORDINATE'S JOB*

ORGANIZATIONAL CULTURE, STRUCTURE, CLIMATE*

INTERNAL ENVIRONMENT
EXTERNAL ENVIRONMENT

*KEY FACTORS THAT SHOW UP AS CONTINGENCY VARIABLES IN STUDIES IN THE CHAPTER.

dynamics of the subordinate's work group, the nature of the subordinate's job, and the overall organizational culture, climate, and structure. For example, a manager faced with a subordinate who is difficult to motivate should determine that person's needs and personality and choose an appropriate leadership style. The manager should also analyze the job to see whether it is detracting from the subordinate's motivation. Finally, he or she should consider the culture and structure of the organization. Taking all of these factors into account, the manager would choose one or more of the available leadership behaviors to influence the employee's motivation.

The major leadership issues discussed in this chapter and elsewhere in the book can be integrated into a situational model of leadership. The basic premise underlying the model is that the leader makes choices and takes action on the basis of the following variables:

1. Characteristics of the leader (personality, needs, perception of the situation)
2. Characteristics of the situation
3. Available leadership behaviors
4. Expected results

Figure 16.7 shows how these four variables can be combined to create a general model of leadership. The Leadership-TRRAP model (Figure 16.8) is a specific version of this model.

Figure 16.8 shows that leaders are faced with five major sets of choices. These have to do with how much and/or what kind of task, relationship, reward, attitude, and participation behaviors to employ or emphasize.[40] (Hence the acronym *TRRAP*.) The attitude component refers to the leader's attitude while engaging in the other four types of behaviors. It is critical because "how you say it" is just as important, if not more so, than "what you say."[41] Yukl's eleven behaviors or any other list of leadership behaviors could easily be substituted for the behaviors shown in the figure.

These choices occupy various positions on a continuum, as Figure 16.9 suggests. The consistent combination of task orientation, relationship orientation, reward orientation, participation orientation, and attitude determines a person's style of leadership. Table 16.5 provides examples of each of these behaviors.

The choice of a leadership behavior should be made only after the major factors affecting the situation have been considered. According to the TRRAP model, the manager must function within the context created by the situation. The manager's choices must be adapted to the environment created by the personalities of the people involved; the dynamics of the work group; the nature of the task or job; the culture, structure, and climate of the organization; and any other factors that affect the situation. Knowing just how much emphasis to place on task, relationship, reward, and participation behaviors and what attitude to

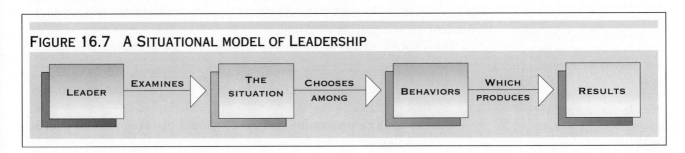

FIGURE 16.7   A SITUATIONAL MODEL OF LEADERSHIP

LEADER → EXAMINES → THE SITUATION → CHOOSES AMONG → BEHAVIORS → WHICH PRODUCES → RESULTS

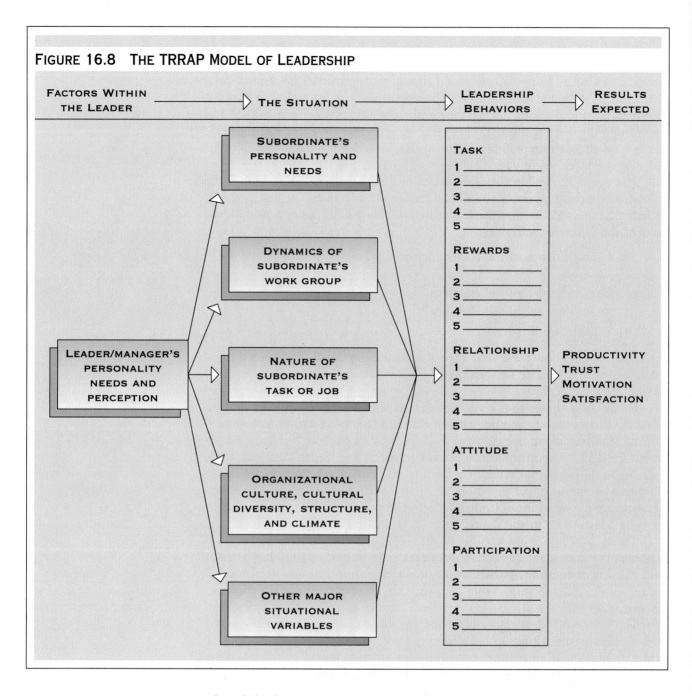

FIGURE 16.8   THE TRRAP MODEL OF LEADERSHIP

FACTORS WITHIN THE LEADER	THE SITUATION	LEADERSHIP BEHAVIORS	RESULTS EXPECTED

SUBORDINATE'S PERSONALITY AND NEEDS

DYNAMICS OF SUBORDINATE'S WORK GROUP

LEADER/MANAGER'S PERSONALITY NEEDS AND PERCEPTION

NATURE OF SUBORDINATE'S TASK OR JOB

ORGANIZATIONAL CULTURE, CULTURAL DIVERSITY, STRUCTURE, AND CLIMATE

OTHER MAJOR SITUATIONAL VARIABLES

TASK
1 _____
2 _____
3 _____
4 _____
5 _____

REWARDS
1 _____
2 _____
3 _____
4 _____
5 _____

RELATIONSHIP
1 _____
2 _____
3 _____
4 _____
5 _____

ATTITUDE
1 _____
2 _____
3 _____
4 _____
5 _____

PARTICIPATION
1 _____
2 _____
3 _____
4 _____
5 _____

PRODUCTIVITY
TRUST
MOTIVATION
SATISFACTION

TRRAP model of leadership: A model of leadership showing that leaders face five major sets of choices having to do with how much and/or what kind of task, relationship, reward, attitude, and participative behaviors to employ or emphasize.

take while doing so is critical. This model suggests that the manager should strongly emphasize task, rewards, and relationships, along with a positive attitude, most of the time. That is, subordinates know that the manager expects high levels of performance and will clarify roles and facilitate their efforts, will reward performance, is concerned about them and works to build relationships, and has a positive attitude. The degree of participation chosen is more highly dependent on the specific situation.

The **TRRAP model of leadership** is based on the following concepts:

1. Managers can choose among a variety of leadership behaviors.
2. Certain behaviors have been shown to be appropriate most of the time.
3. The leader's personality and needs should be taken into account in choosing leadership behaviors.

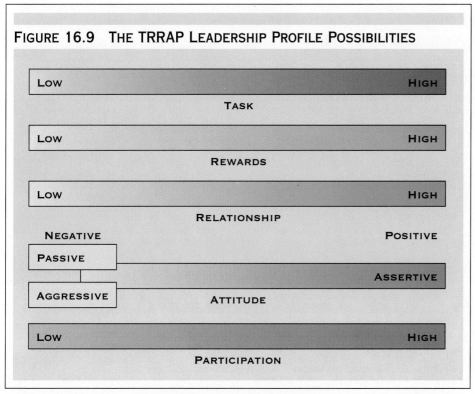

FIGURE 16.9   THE TRRAP LEADERSHIP PROFILE POSSIBILITIES

LOW	HIGH

TASK

LOW	HIGH

REWARDS

LOW	HIGH

RELATIONSHIP

NEGATIVE   POSITIVE

PASSIVE

                                      ASSERTIVE

AGGRESSIVE   ATTITUDE

LOW	HIGH

PARTICIPATION

SOURCE: JAMES HIGGINS, <u>HUMAN RELATIONS: BEHAVIOR AT WORK</u>, 2ND ED., P. 208, © 1987, MCGRAW-HILL, INC. REPRODUCED WITH PERMISSION OF MCGRAW-HILL.

4. Probably the single most important factor to be considered in making these choices is the subordinate's personality and needs.

5. The dynamics of the work group should also be considered.

6. The task to be performed by the subordinate is important to the leader's choice of behavior; some tasks require closer supervision than others.

7. Organizational culture, structure, and climate influence the choice of a leadership behavior. All such choices must be made within the context of the organization's rules, procedures, and policies.

8. Other variables, such as time, may enter into the process.

9. In the long run, managers should choose leadership behaviors that increase or maintain subordinates' self-image. Negative leadership behaviors may be effective in the short run, but the long-term consequences of continuing such behavior can be disastrous.

10. When the appropriate behaviors are chosen, higher levels of motivation, productivity, satisfaction, and trust result.

11. Trust is an important ingredient in this process and is highly correlated with continued performance.[42]

12. Managers' leadership choices combine varying degrees of emphasis on task, reward, relationship, attitude, and participation (TRRAP).

This discussion has assumed that productivity and employee satisfaction are the criteria by which leadership is to be judged. This is not always the case. When organizations seek leaders who meet other criteria—such as people who can be counted on not to rock the boat—much of what has been said here becomes less meaningful.

TABLE 16.5 Behaviors Associated with the Elements of the TRRAP Model

Task	Reward	Relationship	Attitude	Participation
Assigning objectives	Giving raises	Communicating openly	(−)Acting passively	Deciding jointly
Making certain subordinates know how to do their jobs	Providing recognition	Being friendly	(−)Being submissive	Delegating responsibility
Periodically reviewing and discussing others' performances	Giving praise	Supporting subordinates with top management when they're right	(−)Not saying what you think	Implementing quality control
Emphasizing objectives	Patting people on the back	Attending to others' personal needs (family, illness, birthdays, etc.)	(−)Not making waves	Using job enrichment
Planning	Being equitable	Building trust	(+)Acting assertively	Asking for others' opinions
Organizing resources	Giving promotions	Working well with groups	(−)Showing impatience	Using others' inputs in making choices
Creating structure	Providing incentives	Listening to others	(+)Respecting others	Letting others make decisions
Providing direction to achieve goals	Publicly reporting successes	Providing ego support	(+)Acting honestly	
Knowing how to do subordinates' jobs well enough to correct performance	Tying rewards to performance	Representing values of group	(+)Confronting others	
Developing subordinates' job skills	Tying rewards to objectives	Working with informal group leader	(−)Acting aggressively	
			(−)Showing contempt	
			(−)Showing indifference	
			(−)Being deceitful	

(−) means a negative managerial attitude.
(+) means a positive managerial attitude.

Today a successful manager must be a complete leader/manager. Such a manager practices not just one or two of the relevant leadership skills but all of them. In addition, he or she realizes that there are no formulas that can be applied to all situations. Instead, the manager analyzes the factors just listed in the context of each situation and selects the appropriate behavior.

Emerging Issues in Leadership

Transformational Leadership

Transactional leadership: A type of leadership in which the leader exchanges something he or she values for something valued by followers.

Over the years, the study of leadership has focused on leadership in small groups, which is applicable throughout the organization. More recently it has focused on transformational leadership, which is applicable primarily at the upper levels of an organization.[43] James McGregor Burns has identified two types of political leadership: transactional and transformational.[44] **Transactional leadership** occurs when one individual approaches others for the purpose of exchanging something that is valued. That is, the leader will exchange something he or she values for something valued by followers. **Transformational leadership** involves changing the beliefs, needs, and values of followers. It involves more than simply asking for their compliance. According to Burns, it "is the result of mutual stimulation elevation that converts followers into leaders and may convert leaders into morale agents."[45]

Leadership researcher Bernard Bass has applied Burns's ideas to organizational management.[46] He notes that transactional leaders "look to consider how to marginally improve and maintain the quantity and quality of performance, how to substitute one goal for another, how to reduce resistance of particular actions, and how to implement decisions."[47] This is typical of the type of small-group leadership discussed in this chapter. However, Bass goes on to note that transformational leaders, in contrast, "attempt and succeed in raising colleagues, subordinates, followers, clients, or constituencies to a greater awareness about the issues of consequence. This heightening of awareness requires a leader with vision, self-confidence, and inner strength to argue successfully for what he [or she] sees as right or good, not for what is popular or acceptable according to established norms."[48]

Bass notes that charisma is an important part of transformational leadership. He identifies Lee Iacocca, former CEO of Chrysler Corporation, as the premier example of a transformational leader with vision and charisma. He also argues that such leadership does not occur only at the top but may occur throughout the organization. He cites the case of a sergeant who transforms troops into extremely loyal followers.[49]

As organizations face more change and increased levels of competition, it appears that transformational leadership will be vital to their success. For example, Compaq Computers faced a dramatically altered PC industry. Its "quality at a high price" strategy was failing. In one year a new CEO, Eckhard Pfeiffer, transformed the company by changing its marketing, product, and manufacturing strategies and its organizational culture.[50]

Noel M. Tichy and David O. Ulrich have identified three key sets of activities associated with transformational leadership: creation of a vision, mobilization of commitment to that vision, and institutionalization of change throughout the organization. Transformational leaders engage in these activities in order to transform their organizations and their subordinates into willing agents of

Transformational leadership: A type of leadership that involves changing the beliefs, needs, and values of followers.

AT MOREHOUSE: The Morehouse approach is transformational: It teaches young black men how to make a difference.

Leadership researcher Bernard Bass identifies Lee Iacocca, former CEO of Chrysler Corporation, as the premier example of a transformational leader with vision and charisma.

change.[51] Tichy and Mary Anne Devanna examined the case histories of numerous transformational leaders and concluded that organizations must train their leaders to be transformational and must promote managers with the potential to transform the organization.[52] This chapter's Innovation Management Challenge describes a transformational leader, CEO Linda Wachner of Warnaco.

Leadership Skills for Autonomous Teams

Autonomous work teams vary in degree of empowerment. Consequently, the leadership skills necessary to manage such teams also vary. In general, a manager would be expected to play different roles at various stages of the team's development. In the early stages, the manager would be involved in planning the team and determining its composition (if it is not a natural work group). In the next stage, the manager would be involved in training team members and facilitating group behavior. In the maturity stages, the manager would focus on administration, coaching, and providing resources and information. Facilitating skills would have to be mastered. Performance measurement must also occur, but it can be carried out by the team as well as by the manager.[53] To some degree, the manager must be able to help team members become more self-motivated.

INNOVATION MANAGEMENT CHALLENGE

Linda Wachner
Transforms Warnaco

In 1992, Linda Wachner was the only female CEO of a Fortune 500 industrial company and, according to *Fortune,* was America's most successful businesswoman. She has infused the lingerie and apparel maker Warnaco with cachet, purpose, and financial stability. Since she took over in 1986, she has cut the company's debt by 40 percent and increased its operating cash flow from $50 million to $92 million. She also brought the company public. The price of its shares has risen 75 percent since the initial offering.

Wachner achieved her success in a period that has been brutal for American retailers. Like other managers who have learned to prosper in difficult times, Wachner has developed a fervent devotion to three principles: Stay close to the customer; keep on top of the business; and watch the till.

Wachner's drive to strengthen Warnaco has been unrelenting, and it has been accompanied by a forcefulness that has drawn some criticism. Her first move was to reduce the Warnaco portfolio from fifteen businesses to two. Retained were the intimate-apparel labels, such as Warner's and Olga, and the menswear lines, such as Christian Dior and Hathaway. Among the discards were several women's apparel lines, including White Stag, Geoffrey Beene sportswear, and Pringle of Scotland sweaters, which faced stiff competition and provided meager returns.

In addition to its mid-priced Warner's and Olga brands, Warnaco now has licensing agreements with fashion designers such as Ungaro and Scaasi to produce higher-priced garments under their names. It makes private-label goods for Victoria's Secret. And it will manufacture lower-priced bras under the Fruit of the Loom label, to be sold in Wal-Mart and KMart.

Wachner follows retail sales reports closely and roams shops that buy her brands. Says one buyer, "[Her] strength is that she is constantly in touch with customers in the stores and her retailers." She spends long hours chatting with salespeople, gleaning information about what people are buying and why.

For teams with a relatively low level of empowerment, in which tasks are assigned but the team determines how they will be carried out, the leadership skills just mentioned are sufficient. When teams are totally self-managed, including setting their own goals, choosing their own members, evaluating their performance, establishing compensation for their members, and so on, the terms *manager* and *subordinate* no longer describe the relationships found in many organizations.[54] In some firms, the traditional hierarchical leader may cease to exist. Leadership is distributed among the members of the team.[55] Where teams retain a formal leader, that individual needs to be able to instill self-motivation in team members and help them develop self-management skills. Facilitation becomes critical. Such managers often facilitate more than one team at a time.

Leadership Training and Development

Leadership is becoming an increasingly important factor in organizational success. While some people may argue that leadership is a quality of character, most management authorities believe that it is a set of skills that can be taught.[56] A recent survey by the American Society for Training and Development found that 60 percent of the nation's largest employers offer leadership training as an ele-

In 1992, Linda Wachner was the only female CEO of a Fortune 500 industrial company and, according to *Fortune,* was America's most successful businesswoman.

To put the information she gathers to work, Wachner has devised two strategies. One is a letter faxed to her every Friday night by the head of each of Warnaco's seven divisions, describing any potential problems in shipping or delivery; the problems can be attacked promptly on Monday. The other is a spiral notebook carried by each top executive, Wachner included. Entitled *DO IT NOW,* the notebook contains notes about meetings and conversations, business projections, and anything else needing prompt attention. "If you want to do something with all your heart," says Wachner, "then it deserves your immediate attention."

SOURCE: Susan Caminiti, "America's Most Successful Businesswoman," *Fortune* (June 15, 1992), pp. 102–108.

ment of management development.[57] Firms like GE require that managers participate in leadership training at each stage of their careers. Managers work on solving real problems as part of their training.[58] In the 1990s, leadership training is emphasizing the development of global managers. Coca-Cola, for example, rotates more than three hundred professionals and managers from one country to another each year to help them develop a global perspective.[59]

Empowerment

Empowerment: The process of giving employees the maximum amount of power necessary to do their jobs as they see fit.

Empowerment is the process of giving employees the maximum amount of power necessary to do their jobs as they see fit. Empowerment is substantive delegation. It has also been described as a set of actions that strengthen subordinates' belief in their effectiveness.[60] In this sense, leadership becomes "the art of empowering others."[61]

With the exception of the focus on increasing people's perceptions of their capabilities, empowerment is essentially participative management. As with autonomous work teams, however, empowerment seems to have a range of meanings, depending on the amount of delegation involved. When organizations and managers speak of empowering their employees, therefore, they are not all referring to the same degree of delegation of authority. When Pacific Gas & Electric "empowered" its employees, it did so by instituting a strong suggestion program and allowing individuals to decide how to do their jobs.[62] But when Federal Express "empowered" its employees, it developed a corporate philosophy that fostered respect for the individual, encouraged employee input, provided job security to encourage risk taking, developed pay-for-performance programs, gave awards and recognition for individual and team performance, and redesigned jobs to include more decision authority.[63] Federal Express also taught its employees problem-solving skills, including the skills required for working in groups.

However it is defined, empowerment involves major changes in the attitude of most managers and in the philosophy of most corporations about the roles of employees in the problem-solving process. It often involves the use of autonomous work teams. Whatever set of actions gives employees a greater sense of power can be termed empowerment.

Multicultural Aspects of Leadership

Little research has been done on how leadership styles are affected by gender, race, ethnicity, age, and other differences in the social and cultural backgrounds of leaders. A review of possible differences in leadership style between male and female leaders concluded that there are no major differences. Male and female leaders exhibited the same degrees of people and task orientation, and no significant differences were found in their needs or values.[64] A recent study suggests, however, that women have begun to manage differently than men. They are not imitating the styles men have found successful but, rather, are managing in ways that seem more natural to them. Whereas the men studied tended to manage transactionally, the women behaved more transformationally. Part of this difference is the result of differences in how men and women communicate. Women tend to be less demanding than men, for example.[65] Still, the preponderance of evidence suggests that there is little difference in leadership styles between men and women.

Leadership styles often differ from one company to another, and these must be reconciled when companies merge. For example, when SmithKline Beckman Corporation merged with Beecham PLC to form SmithKline Beecham, top management recognized the need for a common leadership style. It laid out

Recent studies suggest that women managers like Patricia Cole, president of Cole Financial Services, manage more transformationally than men.

nine key leadership guidelines for all of its managers to follow.[66] The guidelines include finding opportunities to challenge and improve one's personal performance and working with subordinates individually and as a team to set targets and develop programs to achieve higher standards of performance.

It is also clear that leadership practices acceptable in one country are not necessarily acceptable in another. Most of these differences can be traced to differences in national cultures, as discussed in Chapter 3. Even in countries with seemingly similar cultures, differences in management styles can be readily identified. For example, in Asia, three broad styles have been identified: East Asian, South Asian, and Southeast Asian.[67] Over time, we would expect leadership practices in different nations to become more similar as managers in one culture learn from managers in other cultures. This chapter's Diversity Management Challenge profiles the development of French managers and identifies some of their unique attitudes toward leadership and management.

Leading the Learning Organization

The importance of organizational learning has been noted at several points in earlier chapters. For an organization to become a learning organization, leadership styles must be modified.[68] Peter M. Senge, who has written extensively on organizational learning, suggests that the role of the leader is drastically different in a learning organization than in a traditional bureaucracy, where controlling (which can stifle learning) is the major concern. "Leaders are designers, teachers, and stewards. These roles require new skills: the ability to build shared vision, to bring to the surface and challenge prevailing mental models, and to foster more systemic patterns of thinking. In short, leaders in learning organizations are responsible for building organizations in which people are continually expanding their capabilities—that is, leaders are responsible for learning."[69]

Ikujiro Nonaka, a professor at Hitotsubashi University in Tokyo, suggests that the role of a manager in a knowledge-creating company (similar to a learning organization) is to orient employees' knowledge creation in a purposeful direction. Managers do this by creating a conceptual framework that helps employees make sense of their experiences.[70] Part of a manager's job in the learning organization is increasing the organization's intellectual assets and treating knowledge and the people who have it as assets; this requires investing in those assets. Leaders then need to use the resulting knowledge to its fullest extent.[71]

Finally, leaders must learn themselves as well as help subordinates learn. They must be open to new ideas; they must be systematic in their thinking—able to see connections between issues, events, and data; they must be creative; they must have a strong sense of personal efficacy; and they must be empathetic.[72]

Summary

(Before reading this summary, look again at the objectives listed at the beginning of the chapter.)

1. Leadership involves making choices and carrying out those choices in order to influence people's motivation.

2. A manager is not necessarily a leader but should be. Leaders are concerned with effectiveness, managers with both effectiveness and efficiency. Leaders receive their power from their followers; managers receive theirs from the authority of the organization.

3. There are five bases of power: legitimate, reward, coercive, expert, and referent.

4. Existing contingency models are useful, but none can predict appropriate managerial leadership behavior in all situations.

5. Certain behaviors seem to lead to successful leadership most of the time: a high task, relationship, and reward orientation; a positive and assertive attitude; and allowing medium to high levels of participation by subordinates.

6. Transformational leadership is becoming increasingly critical to successful management in a rapidly changing world.

General Questions

THINKING ABOUT MANAGEMENT

1. Indicate the major differences between leadership and management.
2. Describe leadership as a process of influencing others.
3. Describe leadership as a process of making choices.
4. Why did the trait theory of leadership not hold up? Why does a skills approach seem to have some merit?
5. Are you a Theory X or a Theory Y person?
6. Which of Yukl's eleven behaviors are more likely to be important in the future? Why?
7. Which of the leadership grid styles is best? Why?
8. How is the Hersey-Blanchard model used to select an appropriate leadership style?
9. What does path-goal theory contribute to leadership style?
10. Explain the Muczyk-Reimann model.
11. Describe a leadership situation you have witnessed and indicate how the leader should have handled it, using the TRRAP model.
12. Discuss current issues in leadership.

Questions on the Management Challenge Features

GLOBAL MANAGEMENT CHALLENGE
1. What are the behaviors that Kim Woo-Choong suggests make good leaders?
2. How do these compare to the behaviors in Yukl's list?

INNOVATION MANAGEMENT CHALLENGE
1. How did Linda Wachner transform Warnaco?
2. Why did the company become more innovative as a result?

DIVERSITY MANAGEMENT CHALLENGE
1. Describe the leadership characteristics of French managers.
2. How do these differ from what you would expect of a typical U.S. manager?

Morehouse College Trains Middle-Class Blacks to Lead

Morehouse College is at the forefront of an organized approach to changing how companies manage cultural diversity. It has established the American Institute for Managing Diversity, which is headed by R. Roosevelt Thomas, Jr.

According to Thomas, the problem of diversity is not limited to questions of race, gender, ethnicity, and disabilities. Rather, it is an issue of mismanagement if the members of an organization are not all allowed to contribute the full extent of their ability. For example, if women and minority employees are clustered at the bottom of the organizational hierarchy because they are not given opportunities to rise, human resources are being mismanaged. The issue, in short, is one of management rather than a legal, social, or moral issue. Thomas notes that research has shown that well-managed heterogeneous groups are more productive than homogeneous groups. He believes that managing diversity is a means of improving corporate performance.

DISCUSSION QUESTIONS

1. How does Morehouse College create the Morehouse man?
2. How does managing cultural diversity fit into this leadership perspective?

Transforming a Law Firm

William C. Martin, managing partner and chairman of the board of Akerman, Senterfitt & Eidson, a law firm with 30 partners and 180 employees, pondered his firm's future. Like all law firms, his faced increasing levels of competition. New firms often used low-price strategies to acquire business. Thus, the firm was vulnerable to losing some of its business when it could not demonstrate a clear advantage to justify higher fees.

The firm hired students who had graduated in the top 15 to 20 percent of their class at law schools, so it had a talented work force. But attorneys' needs were changing. Most of the associates were not willing to work as long hours as the partners. Increasing the number of billable hours worked was a major concern of the firm, and top management needed to find ways of motivating associates to work longer hours.

The firm had been seeking a way to differentiate itself from others. It had settled on a full-service, high-quality approach, but Martin was not convinced that it would work. Most other large firms would be attempting a similar strategy, and he was not sure his firm could clearly differentiate itself from them.

The firm believed in participation and in providing a high quality of work life for its members. Yet it needed a vision that probably only the managing partner could provide. Martin was a studious, articulate, and rather quiet leader, not given to flamboyance. He was surrounded by many people with large egos and knew that he had to balance many needs and wants in shaping a vision for the firm.

DISCUSSION QUESTIONS

1. How does transformation occur? What would it mean in the case of this law firm?
2. How might Martin go about being "the leader" in a participatory firm?

Assessing Your Managerial Style

Respond to the following items according to how you would probably behave (A = always, F = frequently, O = occasionally, S = seldom, N = never).

If I were a work group manager, . . .

1.	I would act as group spokesperson.	A F O S N
2.	I would allow group members complete freedom in their work.	A F O S N
3.	I would encourage the use of uniform procedures.	A F O S N
4.	I would permit group members to use their own judgment in solving problems.	A F O S N
5.	I would needle group members for greater effort.	A F O S N
6.	I would let group members perform their jobs the way they think best.	A F O S N
7.	I would keep the work moving at a rapid pace.	A F O S N
8.	I would settle conflicts when they occur in the group.	A F O S N
9.	I would decide what should be done and how it should be done.	A F O S N
10.	I would turn group members loose on a job and let them go to it.	A F O S N
11.	I would be reluctant to allow group members any freedom of action.	A F O S N
12.	I would assign group members to particular jobs.	A F O S N
13.	I would push for increased production.	A F O S N
14.	I would be willing to make changes.	A F O S N
15.	I would schedule the work to be done.	A F O S N
16.	I would persuade others that my ideas are to their advantage.	A F O S N
17.	I would refuse to explain my actions.	A F O S N
18.	I would permit the group to set its own pace.	A F O S N

Scoring

1. Underscore the item numbers for activities 1, 3, 5, 7, 9, 11, 13, 15, and 17 and write a "1" next to the underscored items to which you responded A (always) or F (frequently).

2. Write a "1" next to the items not underscored to which you responded A (always) or F (frequently).

3. Circle the "1's" you have written next to items 2, 4, 6, 8, 10, 12, 14, 16, and 18. Count the circled "1's." This is your concern for people score.

4. Count the uncircled "1s." This is your concern for production score.

SOURCE: Adapted from Thomas J. Sergiovanni, Richard Metzcus, and Larry Burden, "Toward a Particularistic Approach to Leadership Style: Some Findings," *American Educational Research Journal* (January 1969), 62–79. © 1969, American Educational Research Association, Washington, D.C.

"We rule men with words."
—Napoleon Bonaparte

"Perfect understand-ing between human be-ings is impossible. Grasp that concept."
—James W. Newman

CHAPTER OBJECTIVES

When you have read this chapter, you should be able to:

1. Describe the functions of communication in an organization.

2. List the seven steps in communication.

3. Indicate the importance of communication.

4. Discuss the various forms of verbal and nonverbal communication.

5. Identify the barriers to effective communication.

6. Explain how listening skills can be developed.

7. Discuss the use of organizational communication approaches.

8. Improve managerial communications.

9. Identify how electronics is changing communications.

Managing Communication

CHAPTER OUTLINE

MANAGEMENT CHALLENGES DISCUSSED IN THIS CHAPTER:

Accelerating rates of change.

Increasing globalization of business.

Changing technology.

A more diverse work force.

Philips' Global Communication Day

Netherlands-based Philips, Europe's largest electronics firm, with about 300,000 employees at locations throughout the world, faced serious threats as Europe 1992 unfolded and U.S. and Japanese firms moved to increase their stakes in the European market. Philips recognized that it had to become a global, rather than merely European, competitor. The company made substantial layoffs to reduce costs, and invested heavily in R&D to create new products, but it did not significantly improve its competitive position. In fact, it was barely breaking even.

CEO Jan Timmers believed that strong action had to be taken to plant the seeds of change in the minds of employees. He wanted to involve all of Philips' employees in helping to solve the company's problems. At the suggestion of several top managers, he considered the possibility of a global communication day. On that day as many of the company's offices as possible would be linked to headquarters by satellite for a problem-solving session on a global scale.

At first, three of the firm's top managers refused to go along with the program, believing that it displayed improper managerial style and did not reflect the corporation's traditional values. Eventually, after much discussion and considerable risk taking by the program's primary supporters, they agreed to participate.

The logistics involved were staggering. Division managers and plant managers had to be "sold" on the program so that their subordinates would participate actively. Satellite linkages had to be established with as many plants as possible. At each location, broadcast screens and monitors had to be arranged. Group leaders had to be trained to lead the problem-solving sessions. The right issues had to be addressed and materials for analyzing those issues had to be developed. A plan for the day had to be written and distributed.

With thousands of hours of preparation and the commitment of millions of dollars, the Global Communication Day became a reality in the summer of 1992.

SOURCE: Jan Post, presentation to the Strategic Management Society, London, October 15, 1992.

Corporate communications is undergoing a major revolution as electronics— fax machines, television, cellular phones, computers, and local area networks—makes instantaneous communication across vast distances a reality.[1] In many cases, the more personal aspect of communication is missing. For example, only words appear in faxes or on a computer screen. As a result, communication skills related to writing well, in addition to speaking well, become necessary. As the managerial environment changes, the manager's communication function and skills also are changing.

Communication is the transfer of information from one communicator to another through the use of symbols. For communication to be complete, both parties must understand what has been transferred. Every management function involves communication.[2] In fact, the activity all managers share in addition to problem solving is communication.[3] The understanding and proper use of communication therefore are essential to successful management. Indeed, some experts believe communication is a manager's most important activity.[4]

Most managers are less effective at communicating than they would like to admit. Few actively practice the skill. Most seem to take for granted that they know how to communicate. All too often, however, they do not. CEO Jan Timmers recognizes the importance of letting people know what is going on in his company. He also recognizes the scale of the revolution occurring in communication and uses it to his advantage. That is why he has turned to television to get his message across.

The average manager spends 50 to 70 percent of his or her time communicating in some way.[5] Professionals, staff, and first-line employees often communicate as much or more than managers. The coordination required to achieve organizational objectives depends on effective communication. Yet subordinates as well as managers often do not know how to communicate effectively.

Sam Walton, founder and long-time CEO of Wal-Mart, was so convinced of the importance of communication that he visited the managers of each of the company's stores (750 at the time) at least once a year. Eventually this task became impossible as the firm grew and added more stores. At the company's annual meeting, he would call every manager by name and recall details of each store's operations. His concern for communication reflected his concern for peo-

Communication: The transfer of information from one communicator to another through the use of symbols.

The late Sam Walton was famous for his ability to communicate with his employees. He knew them and joined them in many activities. An open communication style was one reason for his immense success.

ple.[6] Numerous other CEOs are turning to improved communication as a means of improving corporate performance.[7]

This chapter first briefly examines the functions of communication and then describes the basic communication process, using a two-communicator model. The various verbal and nonverbal forms of communication are then explored. You may be surprised to discover just how many ways of communicating exist and how they complement or detract from one another. It is just as important to know the meanings conveyed by pointing a finger as it is to understand the words that may accompany the gesture. The common problems associated with communication are noted, and some solutions are suggested. Systems to improve communication are reviewed. Finally, there is a brief discussion of the electronic revolution in communication. Chapter 20 covers these issues in more detail.

The Functions of Communication

William G. Scott and Terrence R. Mitchell have identified four major functions of communication within the organization: the emotive, motivation, information, and control functions.[8] A communication normally involves at least one of these functions and often more than one.

The Emotive Function

It is people who communicate, even when one of the communicators is a group or organization. People have emotions, which they express to others through communication. The emotive function of communication is oriented toward feelings. Within the organizational framework, emotive communication is aimed at increasing acceptance of the organization's goals and actions. For example, Occidental Chemical Corporation is so concerned with the emotional side of its safety program that it began holding safety congresses to encourage its employees to initiate and develop their own safety programs. Employee representatives from various company facilities attend these congresses, work on safety issues, and return to their plants with ideas for improvement.[9] This is an example of emotive communication at work.

The Occidental Chemical Corporation employees shown here are processing a safety checklist at the Lake Charles petrochemical facility. Occidental is so concerned with the emotional side of its safety program that it began holding safety congresses to encourage its employees to initiate and develop their own safety programs.

Citibank's Ethics Game

If you're playing games on the job, you usually have to conceal the fact. At Citibank, you're just getting with the program.

The program is *The Work Ethic,* a board game developed by Citibank to reinforce the company's ethical standards. The game exposes employees to genuine ethical dilemmas and issues of professional integrity. None of the scenarios used is simple or can easily be labeled right or wrong. Instead, employees are challenged to think and question and are sensitized to complex—and realistic—issues.

Employees can play the game at one of four levels: entry level, supervisor, manager, and senior manager. More points are won or lost at the higher levels, where the consequences of decisions have greater implications and the individual's behavior sets an example for larger numbers of junior managers and employees. The game cards present dilemmas dealing with such issues as insider trading, customer confidentiality, conflicts of interest, and sexual harassment. Four possible solutions are provided for each dilemma, none of them perfect or obvious.

An example: You are a corporate recruiter and a colleague tells you that you must move a poorly performing manager out of his unit within three months. What do you do? (A) Insist that the manager be counseled on his performance before any transfer is made. (B) Present him to your fellow recruiters with no mention of the performance problem. (C) Refuse to be involved in the transfer. (D) Present the candidate to recruiters but reveal the performance issues. Note that the most comfortable solution—taking the problem to a supervisor—is not available.

The higher-scoring alternatives in this case are A and D, which net 20 points and 10 points, respectively. C (refusing involvement) scores zero; and B (silent dissimulation) yields a score of −10.

To encourage dialogue, an appeals process is built into the game. A trained facilitator and several senior managers sit in on each session. Players who disagree with one of the printed answers can challenge it, and the appeals board can override it with a unanimous vote.

Initially tested in 1987, the game has since been translated into Spanish, Portuguese, French, German, Flemish, and Japanese. It has been played in 54 countries by more than 30,000 staffers.

SOURCE: Karin Ireland, "The Ethics Game," *Personnel Journal* (March 1991), pp. 72–75.

The Motivation Function

Communication concerned with motivation (that is, influencing others) is designed to elicit commitment to the organization's objectives. Virtually all the approaches to motivation detailed in Chapter 14, plus the leadership approaches described in Chapter 16, require this type of communication. Most of the major activities of leaders, especially those involved in the implementation of plans, require communication. Instructing, rewarding, disciplining, informing subordinates about objectives, and defining roles all require communication.

AT PHILIPS: Timmers used his global TV day not only to inform but also to motivate. He wanted employees to buy into his changes.

The Information Function

The objective of the information function is to provide the information necessary for decision making. The information involved is often technical. Financial information, for example, is part of the technical information necessary to make major purchase decisions. Much of the communication involved in the information function takes place through the organization's formal management information systems. Whenever a manager is ready to make a decision, he or she needs information—which meeting to go to, what to do when the plane arrives, where the lecture is to be given, whether performance is measuring up to standards, and the like. A manager obtains that information through communication. For example, strategists at the world's largest women's apparel firm, Liz Claiborne, use a computerized customer survey feedback program to make marketing and product development decisions. The firm also employs 150 specialists to solicit feedback from customers in stores throughout the United States.[10]

The Control Function

Reports, policies, and plans function to control the behavior of an organization's members. They define roles; clarify duties, authority, and responsibilities; and reinforce organizational structure (defined as jobs and the authority to do them). By providing a means of checking for the achievement of objectives, these types of communication further the organization's mission. For example, communicating control information is especially important in total quality management programs. If standards are not communicated, employees do not know how quality is defined.[11]

Sometimes a company will go to extraordinary lengths to communicate with its employees. This chapter's Ethical Management Challenge describes Citibank's unusual effort to highlight corporate ethics for its ninety thousand employees.

The Communication Process

Encoding: The process of transforming ideas into symbols that others will understand.

Decoding: The process of interpreting a message.

The communication process, shown in Figure 17.1, begins when the sender (which may be a person, a group, or an organization) wishes to share a thought, feeling, idea, or concept with another entity, the receiver.[12] This message must be **encoded,** or converted into symbols, in a form that the receiver can easily recognize. The message may be transmitted either verbally or nonverbally. Communications can be transmitted in person, in print, in memos, on television, or through any other communications medium. The message is received through the senses and by intuition.

Once the message has been transmitted, it must be **decoded,** or interpreted, by the receiver. The receiver transforms the message into thought and (ideally) understands or finds its meaning. Are you understanding this message? If not, is it you or I—the receiver or the sender—who is at fault? Is the message being interfered with by some external factor (noise) or by some internal factor pertaining to the sender, the receiver, or both? Such factors as personality, role, status, perception, and self-image influence the communication process. They affect the sender's ideation, encoding, and transmission of the message, and they have an equal impact on the way the receiver receives, decodes, understands, and acts on that message. Finally, if communication is to be effective, the sender must receive feedback from the receiver during or after the communication process.

Ideation

Ideation: The conception of an idea or thought; the first step in the communication process.

The conception of an idea or a thought is known as **ideation;** it is the first step in the communication process. Ideation encompasses everything that occurs before the idea is encoded—that is, before it is expressed in an understandable language for transmission. Consider an individual who has developed a new prod-

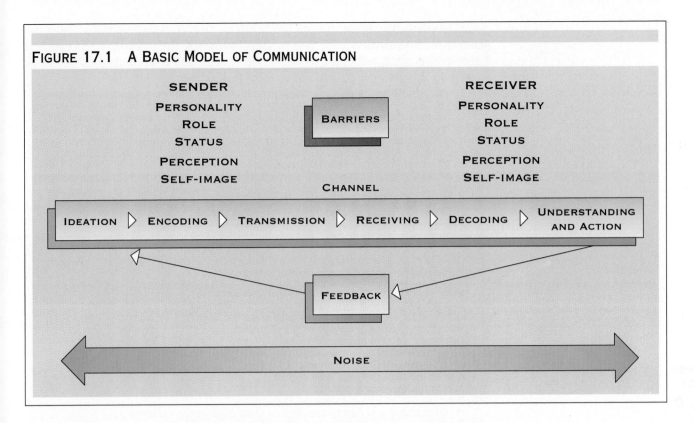

FIGURE 17.1 A BASIC MODEL OF COMMUNICATION

SENDER	BARRIERS	RECEIVER
PERSONALITY		PERSONALITY
ROLE		ROLE
STATUS		STATUS
PERCEPTION		PERCEPTION
SELF-IMAGE		SELF-IMAGE

CHANNEL

IDEATION ▷ ENCODING ▷ TRANSMISSION ▷ RECEIVING ▷ DECODING ▷ UNDERSTANDING AND ACTION

FEEDBACK

NOISE

uct, a social group that has established norms of acceptable behavior, or an organization that has established rules and procedures for achieving its objectives. The conception of the product, norms, or rules occurs as part of the ideation process. Before the product developer, the group, or the organization can convey a message, it must formulate an idea.

Encoding

The person, group, or organization that wishes to communicate must express the message in some transmittable language, either verbal or nonverbal. The essence of encoding is to transform ideas into symbols that others will understand. Verbal languages include not only oral encodings, but written language and silence as well. Nonverbal languages can be as simple as body movements or as complex as a work of art that conveys many messages in a language all its own. The individual's personality, the personality of group members, and the personalities of those who are given the task of encoding messages affect the encoding process and the content of the message. Each person has his or her perception of what a message should accomplish and how it should be symbolized. Encoding requires careful selection of the appropriate verbal or nonverbal symbols to convey the exact idea that was originally conceived. This process is complicated by the fact that symbols can only represent and approximate the idea.[13]

If you have ever had to write rules, directives, policies, or procedures for others to follow, you recognize the difficulty of the encoding process. We often need to write and rewrite, practice and repractice our communications until the message is exactly as we would like it to be. Even then we sometimes fail to communicate. The difficulty of the encoding process can be seen in instructions for assembling bicycles, lawnmowers, barbecue grills, and fertilizer spreaders. Manufacturers' encodings often leave a lot to be desired. Table 17.1 presents some examples of incorrect encodings.

TABLE 17.1 Say What You Mean

It is said that back in the 1940s, the following message was prominently displayed at the front of the main chemistry lecture hall at a major university.

"The English language is your most versatile scientific instrument. Learn to use it with precision."

In the intervening years, the teaching of proper grammar in the public elementary and high schools fell into disfavor. The inevitable result is that the manuscripts submitted to us are often full of grammatical errors, which their authors probably do not recognize (and often would not care about if they did).

We regard this state of affairs as deplorable, and we want to do something about it. For many years we have tried to correct the grammar of papers that we publish. This is toilsome at best, and sometimes entails rather substantial rephrasing. It would obviously be preferable to have authors use correct grammar in the first place. The problem is how to get them to do it.

One fairly effective way is to provide examples of what not to do; it is particularly helpful if the examples are humorous. We have recently seen several grammatical examples of this type. A few weeks ago we found, taped to a colleague's office door, the most complete one we have seen. (He tells us it was passed out in a class at Dartmouth—not in an English class—at the time a term paper was assigned.) We reproduce it here in the hope that it will have some effect. (Each sentence contains the error it describes.)

1. Make sure each pronoun agrees with their antecedent.
2. Just between you and I, the case of pronouns is important.
3. Watch out for irregular verbs which have crope into English.
4. Verbs have to agree in number with their subject.
5. Don't use no double negatives.
6. Being bad grammar, a writer should not use dangling modifiers.
7. Join clauses like a conjunction should.
8. A writer must not shift your point of view.
9. About sentence fragments.
10. Don't use run-on sentences you got to punctuate.
11. In letters essays and reports use commas to separate items in a series.
12. Don't use commas, which are not necessary.
13. Parenthetical words however should be enclosed in commas.
14. Its important to use apostrophes right in everybodys writing.
15. Don't abbrev.
16. Check and see if you any words out.
17. In the case of a report, check to see that jargon wise, it's A-OK.
18. As far as incomplete constructions, they are wrong.
19. About repetition, the repetition of a word might be real effective repetition—take, for instance the repetition of Abraham Lincoln.
20. In my opinion, I think that an author when he is writing should definitely not get into the habit of making use of too many un-necessary words that he does not really need in order to put in his message.
21. Use parallel construction not only to be concise but also to clarify.
22. It behooves us all to avoid archaic expressions.
23. Mixed metaphors are a pain in the neck and ought to be weeded out.
24. Consult the dictionary to avoid misspellings.
25. To ignorantly split an infinitive is a practice to religiously avoid.
26. Last but not least, lay off cliches.

SOURCE: "Grammar," *Physical Review Letters* (March 19, 1979), pp. 747–748. Reprinted by permission of George L. Trigg.

Transmission

Once the sender has determined the content of the message, it is transmitted across one or more of the available methods of transmission, or channels. Communication channels include spoken words, body movements, written words, television, radio, an artist's paint and canvas, a photographer's film, electronic mail, and any other medium through which a message can be transmitted. Each type of channel has certain advantages over others; some may be used in certain situations but not in others. For example, organizations that communicate information to employees via television have found this medium to be superior in many ways to company newspapers. The speed of message delivery, cost effectiveness, and availability are important considerations when choosing a channel and a medium. Fax machines, which make it possible to send pictures and other

AT PHILIPS: The channel chosen—television—enabled Timmer to deliver his message visually to all the intended receivers at once. He could not have done this by any other means.

Both verbal and nonverbal communication play an important part in information transfer. CEO Lawrence Bossidy utilizes both methods in this meeting with employees.

visual messages over telephone lines, are becoming so important to doing business that not having a fax machine can hinder small businesses. Mark Eisen, director of marketing for Retail Planning Associates of Columbus, Ohio, goes so far as to say that he wonders about firms without fax machines: "What's wrong—a gap in management sophistication?"[14]

Oral communication most often flows between individuals. A leader who talks to a group of followers may be speaking as an individual; but if the leader is speaking on behalf of an organization, it is the organization that is communicating with the group. Once the transmission is under way, the message is no longer under the sender's control. It is then up to the receiver to receive the message, decode it, and extract meaning from it. Feedback from receiver to

Electronic mail is a popular channel through which messages are transmitted. Speed of message delivery, cost effectiveness, and availability are important considerations when choosing a channel.

sender may cause the sender to restate the message in order to improve the receiver's understanding.

Communication Channels

Managers can choose among a variety of channels for communicating with subordinates, managers, and other members of the organization. Memos, telephone calls, and face-to-face conversation are among the commonly available channels. The number of possible channels has expanded greatly in recent years and now includes video and audio tapes, electronic bulletin boards, fax machines, voice mail, computer conferencing, and teleconferencing.[15]

Richard L. Daft and Robert H. Lengel have studied how managers choose among communication channels in order to enhance communication effectiveness.[16] They have found that channels differ in their capacity for communicating information. This capacity is influenced by three characteristics:

1. Ability to handle multiple cues simultaneously—for example, eye, face, hand, and body language indicators.
2. Ability to facilitate rapid feedback.
3. Ability to establish a personal focus for the communication.

Channel richness: The degree to which a communication channel can handle multiple cues simultaneously, facilitate rapid feedback, and establish a personal focus for communication.

The degree to which these three criteria can be satisfied is termed **channel richness.** It is the amount of information that can be transmitted during a communication episode. The hierarchy of channel richness is illustrated in Figure 17.2. As you can see, face-to-face conversation involving physical presence is the richest channel and is best used for nonroutine, ambiguous, and difficult messages. At the other end of the hierarchy are impersonal static channels—those that do not allow for feedback—such as fliers, bulletins, and general reports; these are sufficient for routine, clear, and simple messages. In choosing a channel, managers must make sure that it has the right level of richness for the message. If it does not, the message may not be understood and acted on.[17]

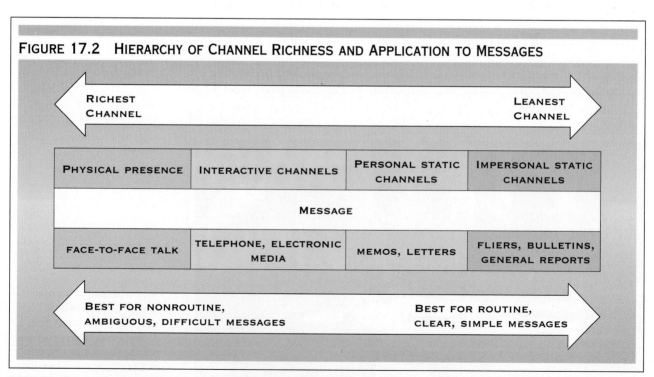

FIGURE 17.2   HIERARCHY OF CHANNEL RICHNESS AND APPLICATION TO MESSAGES

RICHEST CHANNEL			LEANEST CHANNEL
PHYSICAL PRESENCE	INTERACTIVE CHANNELS	PERSONAL STATIC CHANNELS	IMPERSONAL STATIC CHANNELS
MESSAGE			
FACE-TO-FACE TALK	TELEPHONE, ELECTRONIC MEDIA	MEMOS, LETTERS	FLIERS, BULLETINS, GENERAL REPORTS

BEST FOR NONROUTINE, AMBIGUOUS, DIFFICULT MESSAGES   BEST FOR ROUTINE, CLEAR, SIMPLE MESSAGES

SOURCE: RICHARD L. DAFT, MANAGEMENT (HINSDALE, ILL.: DRYDEN PRESS, 1988), P. 436.

Walter St. John, director of educational services and management development at National Food Associates, recommends the following guidelines for channel selection:

1. Important messages should be shared both orally and in writing.
2. Face-to-face communication is usually best; do not rely too heavily on written communication.
3. Provide for feedback.
4. Use a variety of media.
5. Customize the medium—for example, create a television program (channel) just for the organization.
6. Be sure you understand the message and follow up on it.
7. Be cautious about using cost criteria in choosing channels.[18]

Choosing the best channel is a complex process, and there is not always a "best" channel. Key issues are clarity and feedback. Memos, graphs, and reports provide clarity. Telephones, interactive videos, and face-to-face conversations allow for feedback.[19]

Receiving

The process of **receiving** a message is more complex than might be assumed. The various senses must work in combination to detect the message and report it to the brain. There, the *perceptual set*, the person's remembered experiences, will be consulted and meaning will be given to the perceived message. Ideally, understanding and action will result.

Numerous factors affect the receiving process. They include the degree to which the senses and brain are already engaged in other activities, sensory and extrasensory capabilities (such as intuition), and physical and mental capacities. External "noise" (interference of any type) also affects the receiving process.

Receiving: The process in which various senses work in combination to detect a message and report it to the brain.

Decoding

The sensory information that arrives from the sender must be decoded—that is, interpreted by the receiver. Messages that are received are interpreted in light of the factors that affect the perceptual process, especially the receiver's self-image, needs, and personality. If the sender is sending two contradictory messages at once, the task of decoding is made more difficult. The interpretation of sensory inputs depends greatly on individual perceptions, which can alter meanings significantly.

Understanding and Action

If all has gone well up to this point, the receiver understands the message. But all does not always go well. In fact, perfect understanding is impossible because no two communicators will perceive the same event identically. Most people therefore settle for a satisfactory level of understanding most of the time. A message must be understood if it is to be acted on. The receiver must be motivated to take action, even if the action consists of storing the information for later retrieval.

Communication is subject to noise at any stage of the process. **Noise** is any factor that interferes with communication. During ideation, noise may take the form of unclear conceptualization. During encoding, the use of slang to communicate with someone who does not understand it will result in noise. If the message is garbled during transmission, as when a television signal breaks up, the result is noise. If a word, symbol, or event has a different meaning for the receiver than for the sender, their differing perceptions will cause noise during

Noise: Any factor that interferes with communication.

the decoding process. If the receiver does not link the parts of the message together as the sender intended, the resulting noise will interfere with understanding. Many of these problems have to do with word meanings and individual personalities. Common problems or barriers to communication are discussed in more detail later in the chapter.

Feedback

Feedback: *A message sent by the receiver to the sender during a communication.*

The receiver must not only listen but also provide feedback.[20] **Feedback** is a message sent by the receiver to the sender during a communication. For example, a frown on the receiver's face as the sender is talking may be interpreted as disagreement or incomprehension and cause the sender to alter the message. Feedback facilitates understanding and increases the potential for appropriate action. When the sender and receiver do not use the same encoding and decoding processes, miscommunication may result.[21]

AT PHILIPS: *Unlike most television shows, the one used by Philips to communicate with employees provided for feedback.*

Feedback is being viewed as increasingly critical to successful communication. For example, in autonomous work groups open feedback is necessary if conflict is to be resolved.[22]

The Role of Perception in Communication

Perception: *The process of organizing and interpreting incoming sensory information in order to define ourselves and our surroundings.*

Perception is the process of organizing and interpreting incoming sensory information in order to define ourselves and our surroundings.[23] It is our window on the world. Every decision, every action hinges on our ability to perceive.

It is important to realize that our senses do not give meaning to objects and events in our environment; they merely extract raw data for processing by the brain. The brain gives meaning to those data. Through **selectivity**, the brain sorts out what it believes to be the key stimuli from the thousands being received.

Selectivity: *A process in which the brain sorts out what it believes to be the key stimuli from the thousands being received.*

Once key stimuli have been selected, they are evaluated with reference to an individual's **perceptual set,** or existing information base. When we encounter new stimuli and compare them with similar ones stored in our perceptual set, we are **interpreting** them. "Reality" consists of the meanings we give to those stimuli. Once meanings have been assigned to stimuli, we can act on them, even if our action is to dismiss them as unimportant.

Perceptual set: *An individual's existing information base.*

Note that every individual's perceptual set includes a self-image component. Our interpretations of stimuli therefore are colored by our self-image. An insecure employee, for example, might not admit to poor performance and might interpret a supervisor's corrective comments as overly critical.

Interpreting: *The process of comparing new stimuli with similar ones stored in our perceptual set.*

Significant insights into the content of the perceptual set have been provided by neurological research. One of the major early contributors to this field was surgeon Wilder Penfield, whose research findings led him to conclude that every event we have ever consciously experienced is probably stored in our brain. Most such events are eventually forgotten, but they apparently can still be remembered under certain conditions. When their brains were stimulated electrically, Penfield's patients remembered not only long-forgotten events, but also the emotions those events had aroused—no matter how unimportant the event and no matter how long ago it had occurred.[24] Thus, the perceptual set influences emotional as well as factual interpretations. This knowledge helps us understand why a seemingly unimportant event can trigger a highly emotional reaction: The mind associates it with a similar, remembered piece of information that is charged with emotion.

As noted earlier, our perceptual sets include factors related to our self-image, status, personality, and background—for example, to our cultural background. Managers must be attuned to the impact of these factors on the communication process. For example, a timid employee might not communicate to a manager, even if the manager encouraged him or her to do so. Similarly, a manager must be attuned to cultural differences when communicating with foreign-born employees or with members of a culturally diverse work force.[25] For example, French workers are more formal than Americans. They would never address a person they had just met by his or her first name.[26] More and more organizations are beginning to recognize the need for training in communication skills, especially for managers.[27] One such training program is described in this chapter's Management Challenge.

Forms of Communication

There are two major forms of communication: verbal and nonverbal. **Verbal communication** consists of either speech (oral communication) or writing. **Nonverbal communication** consists of body language and the use of time, space, touch, clothing, appearance, and aesthetic elements to convey a message. In this section we will discuss each of these in detail.

Verbal Communication

Verbal communications are transmitted by means of two primary channels: hearing (in oral communication) and sight (in written communication). Oral communication frequently involves other channels as well. For example, we see another communicator's body movements, facial expressions, eye contact, and gestures. However, written communication usually depends solely on what is committed to paper. No other clues, such as tone of voice, can be given or received to help us encode or decode the message. Feeling, smell, hearing, and touch normally do not come into play.

ORAL COMMUNICATION

We probably spend more time in **oral communication**—speaking and listening—than in any other activity except sleeping. Speech involves ideation, encoding, and transmitting messages through language and **paralanguage**—tone of voice, inflection, speed, volume, and silence. Variation of any of these elements can give the message an entirely different meaning.

Language is communication that is carried out through the manipulation of recognizable symbols. It varies by country, culture, social class, age, sex, and other factors.[28] Even when two people have all these factors in common, they may not agree on the meanings of all words. Slang and colloquial definitions also affect meaning. In much of Georgia, for example, people say "fixin' to get ready," meaning preparing rather than repairing, which is a more common definition of the word *fixing*. No two people have exactly the same perception of a word's meaning because no two people have identical life experiences on which to base their definitions. If we are to be effective speakers, we must be alert to the subtle differences in meanings and sentence construction that could have significance to different listeners.

Tone is the quality of voice that gives some indication of the speaker's attitude. Voice tones can be assertive, bashful, aggressive, angry, passive, and much more. *Inflection* is a change in tone that increases our knowledge of the speaker's attitudes. Tone and inflection are vital elements of effective communi-

Verbal communication: Communication consisting of either speech (oral communication) or writing.

Nonverbal communication: Body language and the use of time, space, touch, appearance, and aesthetic elements to convey a message.

Oral communication: Speaking and listening.

Paralanguage: Tone of voice, inflection, speed, volume, and silence.

Language: The manipulation of recognizable symbols.

Improving Managers' Communication Skills

The manager of personnel services at Questar Corporation in Salt Lake City observed a number of supervisors experiencing problems because of poor communication skills. Productivity suffered when new supervisors could not communicate properly; many of the experienced supervisors also lacked good communication skills. With the help of a communications consultant, the manager designed a new program for teaching communication skills.

Before launching the program, the personnel services department evaluated the situation. The evaluation revealed that new supervisors received a "new supervisor's first-aid kit" that contained a list of resource people and guidelines on various personnel matters—compensation, performance appraisal, benefits, and policies. New supervisors also received a supervisor's guide and attended an orientation program. This was followed by some practical courses; for example, supervisors learned how to administer performance appraisals and to work within EEO guidelines. Each of these programs assumed that managers already had a certain level of communication skills. This assumption proved to be unfounded.

The new training program, called Communication Skills Training for Selected Supervisors, emphasized assertiveness as the fundamental communication skill for supervisory personnel. Role playing, self-awareness, active listening, self-talk, and other key techniques were discussed. The assertiveness training involved asking individuals to role-play situations. These sessions were videotaped and the participants' communication practices were critiqued and evaluated. The company has been very satisfied with the improvement in the attendees' communication skills.

This instructor is leading a skill-building exercise during a seminar in the Questar "Communication Skills Training for Selected Supervisors" program.

SOURCE: N. Patricia Freston and Judy E. Lease, "Communication Skills Training for Selected Supervisors," *Training and Development Journal* (July 1987), pp. 67–70.

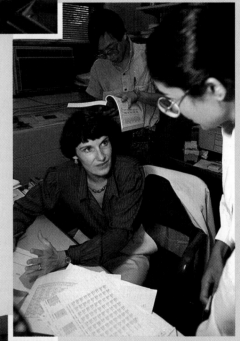

WE PROBABLY SPEND MORE TIME IN ORAL COMMUNICATION—
SPEAKING AND LISTENING—THAN IN ANY OTHER ACTIVITY
EXCEPT SLEEPING. A NUMBER OF FACTORS CONTRIBUTE TO
THE EFFECTIVENESS OF COMMUNICATION, INCLUDING PER-
CEPTIONS OF MEANING, INFLECTION AND TONE OF VOICE,
AND THE SPEED AND VOLUME OF SPEECH. THE LAYOUT OF AN
OFFICE CAN AFFECT THE EASE OF ORAL COMMUNICATION BY
INCREASING OR DECREASING THE AMOUNT OF NOISE AND
OTHER DISTRACTIONS IN THE ENVIRONMENT. ALSO SIGNIFI-
CANT ARE CULTURAL DIFFERENCES, WHICH CAN AFFECT THE
WAY LISTENERS PERCEIVE THE MEANINGS OF WORDS. NON-
VERBAL COMMUNICATION—FACIAL EXPRESSIONS, GES-
TURES, USE OR AVOIDANCE OF EYE CONTACT—CAN ALSO IN-
FLUENCE THE EFFECTIVENESS OF ORAL COMMUNICATION.

cation, especially for managers. A manager who must reprimand a disruptive employee will not be effective if the message is delivered in a tentative tone.

Rapid communication is appropriate for some messages but not for others. Important points normally should be made slowly. Less important points can be covered more quickly. Speed also indicates attitude. Nervous people usually talk more rapidly than people who are confident. Thus, varying the speed of your speech and paying attention to the speed of others' speech can enhance your communication efforts.

Volume can be employed to stress certain points. Sometimes high volume indicates the subject's importance. Sometimes, however, a manager can capture a listener's attention most effectively by almost whispering the most important points. Unvarying volume or speed becomes monotonous; it is better to vary both of these factors throughout a conversation or presentation.

SILENCE

Silence—pauses, lack of response, blank stares—communicates. If someone pauses before making a point, the pause tends to attract the listener's attention. If a speaker pauses before speaking, the pause seems to lend importance to what he or she is about to say. Not responding to a statement can communicate disagreement or lack of respect.

LISTENING

Research findings suggest that we spend as much as 80 percent of our time communicating and that 45 percent of that time is spent listening. As a student, you probably spend 60 to 70 percent of your class time listening. Unfortunately, most people are inefficient listeners. Studies have revealed that most people cannot recall more than half of what they have heard within a few minutes of having heard it.[29] The cost of poor listening to an organization is staggering.

Listening is much more than just hearing. Effective listening involves interpretation, understanding, and action. It requires hard work and self-discipline. Becoming a good listener takes patience, practice, and persistence, but it can be done.

If you want to listen effectively, you must be motivated to listen. Why might a manager want to listen? Among other reasons, to solve a problem, receive a raise or a promotion, make a friend of a subordinate, or find that other people will listen. Professional sports agent Mark McCormack feels strongly about the importance of listening. He claims that if he devotes the first few minutes spent with a new acquaintance to listening, he can learn enough about that person's personality to formulate a strategy for working and negotiating with him or her.[30]

Top managers at the Sperry Corporation (now part of UNISYS) became concerned about communication among its members and with various constituents. They believed customers' needs were not being heard and that insufficient listening was lowering productivity and might be having a negative effect on the company's climate and culture. They decided to solve the problem by starting a listening program. The Manage Yourself exercise at the end of the chapter presents Sperry's quiz on listening. Test yourself and find out how good a listener you are.

Now that you have tested yourself on your listening skills, you are probably wondering what you can do to improve them. The keys to effective listening found in Table 17.2, which are part of the Sperry listening program, provide some insights into what it takes to be an effective listener.[31]

TABLE 17.2 Ten Keys to Effective Listening

Keys to Effective Listening	The Bad Listener	The Good Listener
1. Find areas of interest	Tunes out dry subjects	Opportunitizes: asks "What's in it for me?"
2. Judge content, not delivery	Tunes out if delivery is poor	Judges content, skips over delivery errors
3. Hold your fire	Tends to enter into argument	Doesn't judge until comprehension is complete
4. Listen for ideas	Listens for facts	Listens for central themes
5. Be flexible	Takes intensive notes, using only one system	Takes fewer notes. Uses 4–5 different systems, depending on speaker
6. Work at listening	Shows no energy output. Fakes attention.	Works hard, exhibits active body state
7. Resist distractions	Is easily distracted	Fights or avoids distractions, tolerates bad habits, knows how to concentrate
8. Exercise your mind	Resists difficult expository material; seeks light, recreational material	Uses heavier material as exercise for the mind
9. Keep your mind open	Reacts to emotional words	Interprets color words; does not get hung up on them
10. Capitalize on the fact that *thought* is faster than *speech*	Tends to daydream with slow speakers	Challenges, anticipates, mentally summarizes, weighs the evidence, listens between the lines to tone of voice

SOURCE: "Your Personal Listening Profile," Sperry Corporation, 1980. p. 9. Reprinted by permission. Courtesy of Sperry Corporation.

WRITTEN COMMUNICATION

Because of the absence of tone, inflection, speed, volume, and silence, the effectiveness of **written communication** is almost totally a function of the words chosen and the structuring of sentences and paragraphs. Managers must frequently communicate in writing. No matter how simple an idea may seem to you, it may not be so simple to the people to whom you are writing. One way to test the effectiveness of a written communication is to ask yourself: If I knew nothing about what I have just written, would I understand it?

The widespread use of electronic mail has made writing skills more important than in the past. Yet many organizations are facing a variety of problems related to written communication. The ability of the average employee to use language effectively and write understandably has declined. At the same time, people who are trained in such specialties as engineering and accounting often have difficulty communicating in any language other than mathematics. These problems have led many organizations to establish special programs to teach their members writing and communication skills.

Written communication: The transmission of symbols in writing.

Nonverbal Communication

Oral communications are accompanied by nonverbal forms of communication such as body language. We need to be aware of these forms of communication because they account for so much of face-to-face communication; in fact, up to 90 percent of a message may be communicated by these means.[32]

Entering Japanese Markets

Most U.S. firms find it extremely difficult to gain entrance into Japanese markets because of the many barriers in their path. But a few firms have managed not only to enter the Japanese market, but also to succeed there. Among them are the Coca-Cola Company and IBM. One of the reasons these firms succeed is that they are willing to work hard to understand the Japanese culture, including its language. They are therefore able to communicate the important features of their products and services to Japanese consumers.

Communicating with the Japanese is a matter of learning how they communicate. For example, although the Japanese avoid giving criticism, many Westerners still perceive them as hostile. Moreover, they do not like to give definitive yes or no answers, a trait that sometimes causes Westerners to believe that negotiations are going well when they actually are not.

One reason firms like IBM have succeeded in the Japanese market is that they are willing to work hard to understand the Japanese culture, including its language.

SOURCES: Farid Elashmawi, "Japanese Culture Clash in Multicultural Management," *Tokyo Business Today* (February 1990), pp. 36–39; and Carla Rapaport, "Understanding How Japan Works," *Fortune* (Pacific Rim Special Issue, 1990), pp. 14–18.

We all learn to read the subtleties in other people's body language, but few of us are as aware of this nonverbal form of communication as we should be. In addition to body language (primarily facial expressions, eye contact, hand gestures, and body postures), the physical distance between people (proxemics) and their attitudes toward time (chronemics) are important types of nonverbal communication. Status symbols, touching, appearance, and aesthetic elements also communicate messages.

BODY LANGUAGE

Body language: *A form of nonverbal communication that has four major components: facial expressions, eye contact, gestures, and body postures.*

If you know people fairly well, you should be able to detect the meanings of their **body language**—their facial expressions, postures, and gestures and their use or avoidance of eye contact. Body language can take many forms and have many meanings. It is important to interpret those meanings even though there are no definitions that apply to all types of body language in all situations.[33] Holiday

Inns, Inc., teaches its employees to read body language in order to improve customer satisfaction.[34]

The meanings of body language are very much affected by culture. Some gestures have commonly accepted meanings within most cultures, but others vary in meaning from one culture to another. For example, the gesture we commonly use to indicate "come here"—hand upright, palm facing the body, fingers curled, waving one onward—means goodbye in many Latin American countries. In fact, most forms of body language have different meanings in other cultures. Hence, when we communicate with members of other cultures, or even of subcultures within our own country, confusion may result. Table 17.3 lists some forms of body language and their meanings in the United States.

Body language is more readily interpreted when its four primary components—facial expression, eye contact, gestures, and body posture—occur in combination. For example, when someone stands with arms crossed, lips pursed, and eyes narrowed, maintains steady eye contact, and leans forward toward another person, what message is being conveyed? Body language is also best interpreted within the context of the situation: Who is involved? What has happened? What is about to happen?

If you want to see just how important body language can be, tune in to your favorite television show, turn off the sound, and see whether you can determine the plot of the story. It will be less difficult to do so than you might think because verbal and nonverbal messages usually reinforce each other.

Body language provides clues to the real meaning of a speaker's words. As communication expert Norman Sigband has noted, when nonverbal messages conflict with verbal messages, most of the time you should probably believe the nonverbal ones.[35]

TABLE 17.3 Commonly Accepted Interpretations of Various Forms of Body Language in the United States

Body Language	Interpretation
Facial expressions	
Frown	Displeasure, unhappiness
Smile	Friendliness, happiness
Raised eyebrows	Disbelief, amazement
Narrowed eyes, pursed lips	Anger
Eye contact	
Glancing	Interest
Steady	Active listening, interest, seduction
Gestures	
Pointing finger	Authority, displeasure, lecturing
Folded arms	Not open to change, preparing to speak
Arms at side	Open to suggestions, relaxed
Hands uplifted outward	Disbelief, puzzlement, uncertainty
Body postures	
Fidgeting, doodling	Boredom
Hands on hips	Anger, defensiveness
Shrugging shoulders	Indifference
Squared stance or shoulders	Problem solving, concerned, listening
Fidgeting, biting lip, shifting, jingling money	Nervousness
Sitting on edge of chair	Listening, great interest
Slouching in chair	Boredom, lack of interest

USE OF SPACE

AT PHILIPS: *One of the advantages of television is that it allows several forms of verbal and nonverbal communication to occur simultaneously.*

Proxemics: *The study of interpersonal space.*

Think of conversations you have observed. How close did the speakers stand to each other? Why did one person stand closer to some people than to others? Who sits at the head of the table at important meetings? Why does someone stand up when he or she wants a person who is already standing to view him or her as an equal?

The study of the use of interpersonal space is termed **proxemics.** An important finding of this research is that we allow some people to be closer to us than others. The amount of space between two people reveals quite accurately the degree of intimacy of their conversation, their status, and the respect they accord each other. The intimacy involved decreases as the space between them increases. Edward T. Hall has distinguished among four zones of interpersonal space: intimate distance from physical contact, eighteen inches; personal distance, from eighteen inches to four feet; social consultive distance, from four to eight feet; and public distance, from eight to twelve feet or more.[36]

These zones of interpersonal space vary among cultures. For example, a distance that indicates intimacy to us would not necessarily indicate intimacy to an Arab, who is likely to seek much closer contact with other people than most Westerners prefer. Knowledge of such variations will become more important as business becomes increasingly global in scope.

Violations of these unwritten rules about personal space can be used to manipulate others. One manager in a steel plant constantly violated other people's personal space and intimidated them by doing so. He always stood right next to someone when he spoke. He usually got his way, partly because of his use of personal space.

Companies communicate their respect and concern for their employees by their use of space. Large, nicely appointed offices, and offices on upper floors, usually go to top managers. During the 1970s, many companies adopted the open-office concept, with partitions and no doors. Such offices were designed to save costs and promote "an open atmosphere for communication." Westinghouse's Turbine Generator Division adopted this concept expressly to encourage

The amount of space between two people reveals quite accurately the degree of intimacy of their conversation, their status, and the respect they accord each other.

openness.[37] Today, however, with productivity declining, many companies consider "open" to mean "noisy." Xerox, for one, has reversed its position because of the problems created by noise and lack of privacy.[38] In a recent Steelcase Office Environment Index survey, 65 percent of the office workers surveyed indicated that they preferred private offices to open areas, 23 percent favored partitioned areas, and 11 percent favored bull-pen arrangements.[39]

As a student you, too, should be interested in space—not only because it can be used to communicate, but because it is related to grades. Abner M. Eisenberg has shown that the classroom space students choose is directly correlated with participation in discussions. The students who sit in the middle of the row at the front of the room participate more than those in other seating positions.[40] If you were taking a course such as business policy, which requires a high degree of participation, you might raise your grade by sitting in one of those seats—and, of course, participating.

USE OF TIME

When was the last time you were late for an appointment with your boss or your professor? What happened? Have you been late to a meeting recently? You probably noticed some raised eyebrows. Maybe you have missed a plane because you were late. Such experiences reveal the importance of the use of time.

The study of the use of time is known as **chronemics.** This research has provided information that can be useful to managers. It has shown, among other things, that people communicate disrespect, lack of concern, and lack of interest when they are late. It has also revealed significant cultural variations in the use of time.

Chronemics: The study of the use of time.

In the United States, Canada, and parts of Western Europe, "time is money." The more efficiently you use time, the more money you can presumably make. In other parts of the world, however, other uses of time are more important. Sigband notes, for example, that in Ethiopia, low-level bureaucrats take a disproportionately long time to make simple decisions in order to enhance their apparent importance in the eyes of the people who are waiting for those decisions.[41]

Other cultural variations can be seen in the allocation of time to negotiations. An Alabama manufacturing firm found that Japanese negotiators like to have documents signed when they are ready to leave, even if the negotiations are not complete. Although the American negotiators expected to meet again, the Japanese had allocated only a certain amount of time to the process. Either the deal was made or it was not, but no more time could be spent on it.[42]

STATUS SYMBOLS

Many employers use **status symbols** as reward systems. Status symbols can become extremely important to some people, probably because they enhance their self-image and the esteem in which others hold them. Common status symbols used by organizations include the size, location, and furnishings of offices; first-class versus coach air travel; job titles; reserved parking spaces; executive lunchrooms and bathrooms; country club memberships; and chauffeurs.

Status symbols: Rewards used by an organization to enhance members' self-esteem and the esteem in which others hold them.

TOUCHING

Touching and the avoidance of touching play important roles in communication. A handshake, a slap on the back, a tender touch on the arm or body, holding hands, an embrace—all convey messages. In some organizations, touching is strictly forbidden; in others it is not.

PERSONAL APPEARANCE

"Clothes make the man," goes an old saying—and the woman, too. What impact does clothing have? Several books stress the importance of clothing and other aspects of personal appearance as a means of communication.[43] They are believed to have a great impact on success in the business world. For years men in many firms could wear suits of any color—as long as it was gray or black. Now navy blue appears to be the color associated with power and prestige. Look at what you are wearing. What messages are you conveying? If you want a white-collar job, do not go to the interview dressed in jeans and a tee shirt. What message does such an appearance convey? Clothing is only part of your appearance; your hair, teeth, and physical fitness also communicate a message. What about the appearance of your desk and study area—what messages does it convey?

Communicating in Organizations

Formal Communication

*Formal communication:
Communication that occurs
through official channels
and is sanctioned by the
organization.*

Formal communication occurs through official channels and is sanctioned by the organization. Memos, policies, procedures, and reports of committee meetings are examples of formal communication. Formal communication can occur in three directions: downward, upward, and horizontally. (See Figure 17.3.) Managers must learn to communicate in each of these directions.

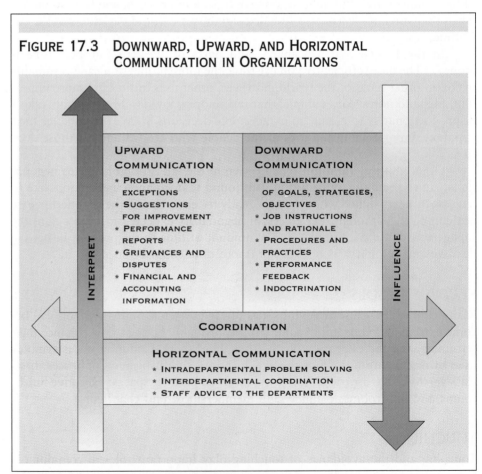

FIGURE 17.3   DOWNWARD, UPWARD, AND HORIZONTAL COMMUNICATION IN ORGANIZATIONS

UPWARD COMMUNICATION
* PROBLEMS AND EXCEPTIONS
* SUGGESTIONS FOR IMPROVEMENT
* PERFORMANCE REPORTS
* GRIEVANCES AND DISPUTES
* FINANCIAL AND ACCOUNTING INFORMATION

DOWNWARD COMMUNICATION
* IMPLEMENTATION OF GOALS, STRATEGIES, OBJECTIVES
* JOB INSTRUCTIONS AND RATIONALE
* PROCEDURES AND PRACTICES
* PERFORMANCE FEEDBACK
* INDOCTRINATION

INTERPRET

INFLUENCE

COORDINATION

HORIZONTAL COMMUNICATION
* INTRADEPARTMENTAL PROBLEM SOLVING
* INTERDEPARTMENTAL COORDINATION
* STAFF ADVICE TO THE DEPARTMENTS

SOURCE: FROM <u>ORGANIZATIONS: A MICRO/MACRO APPROACH</u> BY RICHARD L. DAFT AND RICHARD M. STEERS, P. 538. COPYRIGHT © 1986 BY SCOTT, FORESMAN AND COMPANY. REPRINTED BY PERMISSION OF HARPERCOLLINS PUBLISHERS.

A survey of 250 firms by The Hay Group showed that 54 to 67 percent of employees see top-down communication as positive, but only 30 to 42 percent see bottom-up listening programs as positive.[44] This implies that companies are better at telling things to their employees than they are at listening to them. Similarly, a survey of forty-eight thousand employees by the Opinion Research Corporation, a division of the consulting firm Arthur D. Little, determined that "downward communication, measured by employees rating their company on letting them know what is going on, is rated favorably by fewer than half the employees in all groups."[45] This implies that companies may not even be very good at telling things to their employees.

British Petroleum Exploration, an oil exploration firm based in the United Kingdom, works hard at communication. Recently it initiated a program of "upward feedback" in which employees evaluate their managers on the way they manage subordinates. Managers are given a *Tactics Guide* to help turn the feedback information into positive behavior.[46]

Informal Communication

Informal communication occurs outside formal channels. It occurs continuously and includes impromptu discussions and conversations among friends. The manager must be attuned to the nature of informal communication, the amount of information flowing, and the accuracy of the information. Often the manager can learn important pieces of information from the grapevine—such as the potential for employee relations problems. Informal communication is usually accurate but tends to become inaccurate when emotional issues are involved.[47] The best way to counter negative rumors is to provide the facts.

Informal communication: Communication that occurs outside formal channels.

Common Barriers to Communication

Many problems can interfere with the smooth transmission of thought from one communicator to another. Those problems stem from the characteristics of the sender or the receiver.[48] Some stem from the nature of the organization and others from aspects of culture. In the culturally diverse work world of the 1990s, barriers to communication are likely to become more numerous and more difficult to overcome.

The most common barrier to communication is language. The symbols chosen are abstractions of thoughts, feelings, and concepts. It is impossible to communicate every single sensed aspect of life, or even all of the most important ones. Rather, language enables us to communicate the aspects we perceive to be most important. Because the words we use are abstractions, other people may not interpret them the way we do.

Poor speaking and listening habits pose another barrier to communication. Few of us know how to speak properly in every situation, and most of us are not good listeners. Speaking too quickly or too slowly, failing to use the appropriate tone of voice, and failing to make eye contact lead to ineffective communication. Similarly, a person who does not listen well reduces the likelihood that a message will be transmitted effectively.

Physical and social differences can also create barriers to effective communication. For example, barriers may exist between managerial and first-line employees, between men and women, between blacks and whites, between employees in the plant and those in the home office 500 miles away. Messages can

Effective communication is a skill that must be developed and requires hard work.

be misinterpreted when such factors cause noise. Even if interpretation is accurate, these problems may interfere with understanding.

Still another common barrier to communication is poor timing. Managerial communications such as instructions to change product lines, set up new operations, or delay payments must be issued when the need arises.

Wordiness in written as well as oral messages can be a significant barrier to communication. The receiver can grasp the meaning of a message much more quickly and accurately if the sender keeps the message simple. (This principle is embodied in the well-known acronym KISS: "Keep It Simple, Stupid.") Companies can do much to improve communication by reducing wordiness. Loew's, Inc., a conglomerate with interests in tobacco, hotels, financial services, broadcasting, and watches, has gone so far as to eliminate written memos.[49]

Characteristics of the Sender and Receiver

Personality plays an important role in communication. It helps give meaning to reality through the perceptual process. Although people with similar experiences develop similar perceptual sets, enough differences remain to require us to be attuned to others' perceptions.

Two other characteristics that greatly influence the communication process are role and status. A parent may communicate in a certain way, sending authoritative messages to children in certain instances but listening attentively in others. The roles of doctor, lawyer, dentist, accountant, carpenter, engineer, manager, subordinate, friend, professor, and student affect the nature of individuals' messages. Differences in status can create barriers to communication. When the sender and receiver do not have the same status, their perceptions differ.

A good part of communication involves protecting our self-image. As a result, not only may we hear only what we want to hear and see only what we want to see, but our own messages may be distorted. This is one reason that maintaining or improving a subordinate's self-image is a vital managerial activity. In addition, as noted in Chapter 14, the manager's efforts to influence a subordinate's motivation must have a positive effect on the subordinate's self-image if the motivation/performance cycle is to continue. If the impact on self-image is negative, motivation will decline.

Unintentional perceptual problems can also lead to problems in interpretation. When we speak with someone whose native language is different from ours, and when we realize that some of the words we use have as many as fifteen or twenty different definitions, the difficulty of accurate interpretation becomes obvious.

Information Overload

Information overload, or too much information, boggles the mind. Today's managers are frequently swamped by information, the result of excessive communication.[50] They must constantly guard against a tendency to create too many memos, reports, and other documents. They also need to avoid calling too many meetings or including too many people in any given meeting. The objective of any information system should be to provide only what is needed and usable.

Information overload: An excess of information, resulting from excessive communication.

Coping with Barriers to Communication

Human beings have a well-established tendency to do things the way they have always done them. The first step in improving communication is to decide what we want to do. This may sound like the old joke in which the patient says, "Doctor, it hurts when I do this," and the doctor replies, "So don't do it." However, there is some truth in such jokes. If anything you have been doing interferes with your communication, you should stop doing it.

Role playing can help managers learn how to handle various types of communication situations. Because we cannot rehearse every possible situation, learning general guidelines on how to determine appropriate behavior is crucial. It is also important to recognize that emotions may hamper rational problem solving; as a result, not every situation will be resolved satisfactorily.

When sending a communication, be as open with the other person as possible. Be direct and honest. Maintain eye contact and provide a positive communication environment. Select words carefully and keep the language simple. Use repetition and as many channels, or media, as necessary to get your message across. Be aware of your receivers' situation and avoid putting them on the defensive. Have empathy for them. State your position on issues, including your feelings.

The receiver needs to listen actively, to hear what is said and what is not said. The receiver must be attentive and maintain eye contact, try to understand the other person's position, provide feedback, and learn to filter out noise. The receiver should avoid being defensive and try not to evaluate what is said until the other person has finished speaking.

To be effective communicators, managers should learn specific communication skills such as active listening and assertiveness. **Active listening** is a program designed to teach individuals to listen to the content and emotional aspects of what is being said, to provide feedback to the speaker, or both.[51] Active listening is a valuable tool for helping someone work through a problem. You listen to what the person has to say, summarize the content, and tell him or her what you heard. Perhaps more important, you describe the feelings you heard expressed, feelings that the speaker may not be aware of. You do not, however, offer solutions.

Active listening: A program designed to teach individuals to listen not only to the content of what is being said but also to its emotional aspects, to provide feedback to the other person, or both.

Assertiveness training is a program designed to teach people to communicate in a way that satisfies their needs while respecting the rights of others. A passive individual allows others to satisfy their needs at his or her expense. An aggressive individual satisfies his or her needs at the expense of others. An assertive individual manages the communication so that the needs of both parties are satisfied. As communicators, managers need to be assertive, not passive or aggressive.[52]

Assertiveness training: A program designed to teach individuals to communicate in a way that satisfies their needs while respecting the rights of others.

Organizational Communication

To achieve productive, positive communication with employees, customers, and others, an organization must create the proper communication climate. Such a climate exists when management recognizes that employees have certain rights relative to communication. When the organization keeps employees informed of actions that affect their jobs, treats them with respect, provides feedback on their performance, and communicates relevant objectives; and when the organization recognizes employees' rights to fair and equitable treatment and a reasonable amount of participation in decision making, as well as their right to question policy, an appropriate communication climate exists.

Organizations can improve communication (and, hence, productivity) by means of either structural or informational approaches. Structural approaches attempt to change the organization's structure in order to improve communication; informational approaches attempt to improve organizational communication primarily by disseminating information.

Structural Approaches

Structural approaches attempt to improve communication by changing job content, creating new or different jobs, changing the way jobs are grouped, or altering the distribution of authority within the organization. Improved communication systems usually call for increased delegation of authority, equalization of power, and participation by subordinates in decision-making processes. Much of the structural approach is implemented through personnel practices. In this section, we will briefly review several types of programs that have been instituted in an effort to improve organizational communication.[53]

EMPLOYEE ASSISTANCE PROGRAMS, ACTION LINES, AND COUNSELING

Some firms call them employee action lines; others call them counseling programs: They are programs designed to help employees solve personal problems, including those that are not job related.[54] Many firms employ full- or part-time psychologists to counsel employees. General American's action line focuses primarily on job-related problems; Monsanto's employee assistance program focuses on personal problems.

Sometimes employers must be creative to get employees to make good use of such programs. The Golden Nugget Casino is a good example. Located in Atlantic City, New Jersey, the casino employs thirty-five hundred people, most of them in high-pressure jobs. They must deal with customers, provide excellent service, and handle large amounts of cash. Consequently, many of the casino's workers have problems with alcohol, drugs, and unstable marriages. Through the research of an employee relations firm, the casino's managers discovered that employees were reluctant to use the firm's counseling service because they were afraid they would be fired if their personal problems were revealed. As a consequence, the casino developed a 24-hour, toll-free hot line. Employees and their families can call and discuss their problems without fear. If the problem is serious, employees are referred to one of eighteen counselors in the area. Most calls are related to stress on the job, but some deal with very serious problems, including thoughts of suicide. The company spends $125,000 a year on the program but feels that it is worth the expense because it has helped so many employees lead better lives. It has also contributed to the development of a high level of loyalty among employees.[55] (Such programs are not always beneficial to the corporation. Employees at some other companies have claimed that treatment received under such programs has caused them psychological harm and have even sued the company for damages.[56])

GRIEVANCE PROCEDURES

Grievance procedures are formalized ways for employees to present grievances against the organization and its managers. Not all organizations have such procedures, nor are all such programs perceived as being fair or effective in solving employees' complaints. If they are not effective, employees are likely to decrease their productivity through absenteeism, shoddy work, tardiness, balking at orders, and the like. From the viewpoint of the organization, therefore, effective grievance procedures are vital.

Grievance procedures:
Formal ways for employees to present grievances against the organization and its managers.

ATTITUDE SURVEYS

Surveys, questionnaires, and interviews with employees have grown in popularity as a way of keeping tabs on employees' needs, their perceptions of the organization, and potential problem areas. Frederick A. Starke and Thomas W. Ferratt propose that organizations develop a "behavioral information system" based partly on surveys. The system would enable management to remain aware, at least periodically, of employees' perceptions of major factors within the organization.[57] IBM has added a procedure in which employees complete attitude surveys via computers. Each survey is instantaneously added to an on-line database of responses. Employees prefer this type of survey to a written questionnaire. Each screen contains a small number of questions that are color coded to make them more user friendly.[58] The first companywide attitude survey often turns up some bad news. The key is to respond and let employees know what actions have been taken to solve problems.[59]

OMBUDSMEN

Many organizations have created a position or department to handle employee questions, complaints, and problems. Usually the person in this position, often called an ombudsman, reports directly to the head of the organization, keeping communications with employees confidential. The **ombudsman** must have the capability to motivate line managers to take action on employee problems; otherwise this function will become a dead end and employees will cease to use it. Frederick W. Smith, chairman of Federal Express, believes employee complaints are so important that he spends every Tuesday addressing them. His efforts are just part of an overall grievance system that costs the company more than $2 million a year. However, the program results in many benefits, including improved morale and fewer legal problems.[60]

Ombudsman: A position or department created to handle employee questions, complaints, and problems.

OPEN-DOOR POLICIES

Managers who keep "open doors" indicate to their subordinates that they are available to listen to problems and complaints at any time. The open door indicates a climate of trust and willingness to communicate. Some managers have an official open-door policy but do not make the commitment this practice requires. Many subordinates are reluctant to take advantage of the open door because they hesitate to bypass other managers in the chain of command. Only if the organization's climate is one of trust can such inhibitions be overcome.

SUGGESTION PROGRAMS

Suggestion programs can make significant contributions to an organization. They provide a channel through which employees can contribute their ideas. Suggestion programs do have some drawbacks, though. After a while, when all the practical suggestions seem to have been offered and further suggestions are

Home Depot Stresses Quality Service

Different jobs make different demands. If you work for the fast-growing Home Depot chain of discount hardware stores, be prepared to get up early on Sunday morning to watch TV.

Home Depot uses its own broadcast system to communicate with its employees. An example is "Breakfast with Bernie," a 6:30 A.M. talk-show-style session with Chief Executive Bernard Marcus and President Arthur M. Blank. "Breakfast with Bernie" takes place in one store and is broadcast to dozens of others in the area. At a typical show, sales figures for the year are announced and greeted with enthusiasm. Then a video shows some of the company's employees helping a foster mother build an addition to her already well-utilized house. Spirits soar along with the sales figures.

Home Depot makes sure that its employees are unusually knowledgeable. Its worker training is intense. Its staff can offer immediate how-to information on such subjects as electrical installation and laying tile. Staff are instructed to ask

not accepted, employees may become resentful. Overall, though, such programs can be effective.

Sometimes an extra push is needed. American Airlines' IdeAAs in Action suggestion program uses IdeAAdvocates, volunteers who help promote the program, to increase employee participation, improve the quality of suggestions, and provide immediate feedback to employees who make suggestions.[61] Similarly, Pacific Gas & Electric found it necessary to decentralize approvals in order to speed up the process. After the change, for suggestions that would lead to a saving of less than $50,000 the award could be bestowed by the originating unit without the need for higher-level approval.[62]

Informational Approaches

As noted earlier, information approaches focus primarily on disseminating information. Occasionally new jobs are created in this process, but usually established positions simply expand their information functions. Several means of disseminating information in addition to those ordinarily included in a firm's information distribution system are available. They include periodic meetings with employees, television broadcasts, in-house publications (including newsletters, bulletin boards, and magazines), athletic programs, company manuals, and periodic performance reviews.

PERIODIC MEETINGS WITH EMPLOYEES

Periodic meetings with employees, whether held daily, weekly, or at longer intervals, are extremely important. Such meetings give employees a chance to learn what the organization is all about, what it is accomplishing, and what it hopes to accomplish. Employees, especially lower-level managers, often feel that they are the "last to know." Managers who keep employees informed about the organization's situation can expect them to be more interested, dedicated, concerned, and loyal.[63]

Pitney-Bowes, an international manufacturer of office equipment, stresses

shoppers "What project are you working on?" so that they can go through customers' lists with them. New hires, often experienced electricians or carpenters, begin by attending five days of classes on subjects ranging from the history of the firm to how to greet customers. Once on the staff, they regularly attend seminars on topics such as painting and tiling, so they can answer customers' questions accurately.

Service is a high priority. "Never just point to another aisle," cautions an assistant store manager. "Walk the customer over, and find someone to help." Even though the stores are often crowded, customers generally feel that the service and selection are good.

One key to the good rapport between customers and salespeople at Home Depot is that the latter do not work on commission. Customers buy what they need, not what salespeople need to sell. Another factor that produces high-quality customer service is the autonomy enjoyed by managers. They are free to take initiatives, such as organizing free weekend classes on topics of interest to customers.

"Bernie" Marcus insists that his high standards won't slip no matter how big Home Depot grows. "We've been able to preserve our culture from 5,000 employees to 30,000 employees, so I see no reason why we can't go to 100,000," he says.

SOURCE: Walecia Konrad, "Cheerleading, and Clerks Who Know Awls from Augers," *Business Week* (August 3, 1992), p. 51.

informative, open communication with its employees. Its management believes that "informed employees are the best employees." Each month, all employees meet with their supervisors to discuss problems and policies. The process of discussion moves upward through the hierarchy, conveyed by elected representatives, until problems have been resolved.[64]

TELEVISION BROADCASTS

One of the problems associated with relaying information to employees is that they may not all receive the same message at the same time. The same is true when newspapers and newsletters are distributed. Moreover, not all employees may read the same meanings into the messages received. One way to alleviate such problems (but not to eliminate them) is to broadcast information to employees on television.

Television can also be used to reduce the costs and fatigue of travel. Ford Motor Company, for example, has eliminated the need for its salespeople to gather in one place for its national sales meeting. It has installed television broadcasting and reception equipment at thirty sites around the country. Atlantic Richfield and TRW, a major diversified manufacturing firm, are among hundreds of other firms that now conduct conferences by television.[65] Domino's Pizza, Federal Express, and Empire Savings Bank of America are just a few of the firms that use television to get their company's messages across to employees.[66] To improve the quality of service, Home Depot relies heavily on video, as this chapter's Quality Management Challenge reveals.

PUBLICATIONS AND BULLETIN BOARDS

Management can make employees feel that they are important simply by printing their names in company newsletters and newspapers. This form of recognition is relatively inexpensive but has proved to be effective for many firms. In large organizations, the key seems to be to personalize the medium used. Employees want to know about the company as a whole, but they especially want to know about their plant, their office, their friends and acquaintances, and

Domino's pizza uses television broadcasting to relay information. These Domino's employees are listening to Don Vleck, distribution vice-president, as he discusses ways to improve customer service.

most important, themselves. Video bulletin boards using television monitors are becoming popular as a means of communicating such information.[67]

ATHLETIC PROGRAMS

Company athletic programs communicate positive messages to employees. Such programs say, "We are a team. We need to stick together. The organization cares about your health and your friendships. The company that plays together stays together." An example of such a program is the New Publishers League, in which softball teams representing various New York City publishing companies compete for a trophy.

MEMOS AND HANDBOOKS

Communications that are written in "bureaucratese" that the average employee cannot understand, or that communicate lack of concern, will not be well received by employees. One soft-drink bottler's retirement program was so complex that even the company lawyer had difficulty understanding it. Most employees could not comprehend it and wondered whether the company was trying to deceive them. Finally, after realizing the effect on morale, the firm ordered a simple interpretation of the program to be written. After much diffi-

Company athletic programs communicate positive messages to employees and instill the idea that the organization cares about their health and fitness.

culty, a communication that could be understood by virtually all employees was completed, distributed, and explained.

John Mackay, founder and CEO of Austin-based Whole Foods Market, uses a handbook to tell employees what the company is all about. It does not contain the typical dos and don'ts but rather discusses history, philosophy, and purpose. Mackay keeps his employees informed about strategy and other important issues through this handbook.[68]

The Impact of Technology

Technology is changing the way managers communicate. Fax machines, laptop computers, video phones, video conferencing, cellular phones, electronic mail, and voice mail are causing managers—as well as salespeople, clerks, and other employees—to change the way they communicate. More and more workers are working at home. Fax machines instantly transmit visual material between two locations at a very reasonable cost, and electronic mail enables managers to distribute information to a large number of employees with minimal effort.[69]

At Westinghouse Electric Corporation, for example, electronic mail has proven invaluable. Faced with the need to improve its information flow, improve customer relations, increase productivity, and cut costs, Westinghouse adopted electronic mail, commonly known as E-mail. Some 6,000 personal computers connect 10,700 of the company's managers and employees along with about 1,000 customers. E-mail links the company's U.S. operations with offices in thirty-seven foreign countries. Telephone tag no longer occurs because electronic-mail and voice-mail systems allow respondents to reply without talking directly to the other person. The company feels that the ability to transfer information so quickly has given it a competitive edge.[70]

Communication as a Problem-Solving Process

This chapter does not include a chart describing communication as a problem-solving process because the topic is too broad to be contained in a single illustration. However, it should be apparent that many aspects of communication involve decision making in all its phases. To give just a few examples, decision making is involved in choosing how to code messages; which channels to use—whether downward or upward—and how to use them; which particular skills to use; whether to train employees in communication skills; and how to interpret nonverbal communication.

Summary

(Before reading this summary, look again at the objectives listed at the beginning of the chapter.)

1. Communication has four major functions: to express emotions, to activate motivation, to inform, and to control.

2. The seven steps in the communication process are ideation, encoding, transmission, receiving, decoding, understanding and action, and feedback.

3. Communication takes place in every interaction between managers and other members of the organization. Effective communication is therefore fundamental to sound management.

4. Communication may be verbal or nonverbal. Verbal communication consists of oral and written words. Nonverbal communication, or paralanguage, consists of body language, the use of space and time, status symbols, touching, and personal appearance.

5. Among the barriers to communication are language limitations, poor speaking and listening habits, physical and social differences, problems of timing, and wordiness.

6. Listening is critical to successful oral communication. The best way to develop listening skills is to practice.

7. Organizations may use both structural and informational approaches to improve communication. Structural approaches include employee action programs, grievance procedures, attitude surveys, ombudsmen, suggestion programs, and similar techniques. Information approaches include periodic meetings with employees, publications and bulletin boards, athletic programs, written communications, and the like.

8. Managers can learn specific skills—such as listening, active listening, assertiveness, and transactional analysis—to improve their communication efforts.

9. Technological advances such as fax machines and cellular phones are having a major impact on communication in organizations.

THINKING
ABOUT
MANAGEMENT

General Questions

1. What are the four major functions of communication? Give examples of each.

2. Think of a recent communication between you and another person. Follow the communication process through each of its steps.

3. Give examples of various types of verbal and nonverbal communication.

4. How many different meanings can you give to the statement "You should not have done that" by varying your tone, inflection, speed, and volume and using silence?

5. Describe how perception affects communication.

6. Discuss the electronic revolution in communication.

7. Discuss how barriers to communication can be overcome.

Questions on the Management Challenge Features

ETHICAL MANAGEMENT CHALLENGE

1. Describe the Citicorp ethics game.
2. Why is this a good way of communicating ethical principles?

MANAGEMENT CHALLENGE

1. Why is communication a critical management skill?
2. How did Questar Corp. improve its managers' communication skills?

GLOBAL MANAGEMENT CHALLENGE

1. Why is communication between North American and Japanese individuals often difficult?
2. What impact can this have on a business arrangement?

QUALITY MANAGEMENT CHALLENGE

1. How does Home Depot improve the quality of its employees' customer service?
2. What role does video play in that effort?

E P I L O G U E

Philips' Global Communication Day

Philips' Global Communication Day went well. The morning began with an address by Timmers to personnel linked by satellite at more than one hundred locations. (Those who were not linked by satellite participated by telephone.) Throughout the day, teams at numerous plants were interviewed over the TV hookup so that their experiences could be shared by teams at other locations. At the end of the day Timmers presented a summary of what had been accomplished and where the firm would go from there.

It is too early to tell what impact the Global Communication Day will have on the firm. Organizational development and other major changes like those Timmers was initiating may not bear fruit for months or even years.

DISCUSSION QUESTIONS

1. What risks were Timmers and other supporters of the Global Communication Day taking?
2. What positive results might the event have?
3. What else must be done for this effort to succeed?

Deciphering Communication

Mike Mancuso had worked at Weldon Manufacturing Company for six years. He and his coworkers had a close relationship. Several of them bowled together in the same league, and they often got together for parties. Everyone was elated when Mancuso was promoted to be supervisor of the unit. Things went smoothly for several weeks, but then Mancuso began to detect a change in the attitudes of his old friends—they were no longer eager to talk to him. He had dropped out of the bowling league, feeling that a manager should not be so close to subordinates.

Mancuso sensed that something was wrong, but he was not sure what. He reflected on his management style. He made sure all his subordinates knew what their jobs and objectives were. He checked their work periodically. He tried to be friendly but did not always have a chance to pat everyone on the back, as he would like to. He thought about a recent incident with David Jenkins, who had been a close friend before Mancuso was promoted. Mancuso was approaching him from the side, and Jenkins caught a glimpse of him from the corner of his eye. Mancuso knew that Jenkins had turned away to keep from having to talk to him, but he began a conversation anyway. He had to, because Jenkins was not doing his job right and Mancuso felt that he had to set him straight. Jenkins had not been receptive, and Mancuso had sensed some anger in his voice.

Then there was the incident with Julie Metzger. Metzger had always been a good employee, but her work had fallen off lately. Mancuso had counseled her on her performance, but she had not responded favorably. She had used the new assembly process as an excuse, but Mancuso knew better. Something was bothering her. She seemed nervous. A couple of other incidents came to mind. Many managers might have assumed that these problems stemmed from subordinates' inability to cope with a friend becoming their manager. But Mancuso was perceptive enough to realize that he might be part of the problem, maybe a major part. He wondered what steps to take next. He contemplated asking the personnel director for advice, and he considered having a meeting with his subordinates to allow them to express their feelings.

DISCUSSION QUESTIONS

1. One of the most difficult problems all managers face is determining what is on an employee's mind. It may take a while for a manager to realize that something is wrong. Some managers are so inner-directed that they never realize something is amiss. What clues did Mancuso have, as noted here? What other types of clues might he have had?

2. How does nonverbal communication provide clues to such problem situations? Are men or women, on the average, better at reading nonverbal behavior?

3. Should Mancuso go to the personnel director or directly to his subordinates? Why?

Listening

MANAGE
YOURSELF

LISTENING HABIT	FREQUENCY					SCORE
	ALMOST ALWAYS	USUALLY	SOME-TIMES	SELDOM	ALMOST NEVER	
1. CALLING THE SUBJECT UNINTERESTING						
2. CRITICIZING THE SPEAKER'S DELIVERY OR MANNERISMS						
3. GETTING <u>OVER</u>-STIMULATED BY SOMETHING THE SPEAKER SAYS						
4. LISTENING PRIMARILY FOR FACTS						
5. TRYING TO OUTLINE EVERYTHING						
6. FAKING ATTENTION TO THE SPEAKER						
7. ALLOWING INTERFERING DISTRACTIONS						
8. AVOIDING DIFFICULT MATERIAL						
9. LETTING EMOTION-LADEN WORDS AROUSE PERSONAL ANTAGONISM						
10. WASTING THE ADVANTAGE OF THOUGHT SPEED (DAYDREAMING)						

TOTAL SCORE

KEY:
FOR EVERY "ALMOST ALWAYS" CHECKED, GIVE YOURSELF A SCORE OF 2
FOR EVERY "USUALLY" CHECKED, GIVE YOURSELF A SCORE OF 4
FOR EVERY "SOMETIMES" CHECKED, GIVE YOURSELF A SCORE OF 6
FOR EVERY "SELDOM" CHECKED, GIVE YOURSELF A SCORE OF 8
FOR EVERY "ALMOST NEVER" CHECKED, GIVE YOURSELF A SCORE OF 10

THE AVERAGE SCORE IS 62. OF COURSE THE BEST WAY TO FIND OUT JUST HOW GOOD A LISTENER YOU ARE IS TO HAVE SOMEONE WHO KNOWS YOU WELL RATE YOU ON THESE ITEMS.

SOURCE: "YOUR PERSONAL LISTENING PROFILE," SPERRY CORPORATION, 1980, P. 7. REPRINTED WITH PERMISSION.

Women Managers Give Their Views on Leadership

Do women manage differently than men? Yes and no. The evidence suggests that women attempted to manage like men when they first began entering management in large numbers. They tried to be stern, discipline oriented, perhaps even macho. More recently, however, women have begun to realize that a more instinctive or intuitive approach may have some advantages.

While most women lack the leadership skills that many men develop in the team sports in which they participate as boys and young adults, most women possess interpersonal skills that many men lack. And since interpersonal skills are becoming much more important, these skills and the orientation toward people that most women possess offer them the opportunity to manage in ways that suit their natural perspectives better than simply emulating men.

When *Inc.* magazine interviewed numerous female entrepreneurs, it discovered many similarities in management style, as well as many differences, just as it would have among a sample of male executives. But each woman interviewed clearly believed that women have something different to bring to the situation than men would typically bring. They respected the male perspective, but they also wanted to emphasize that they can offer certain unique skills.

Inc. singled out five women entrepreneurs to provide their perspectives on how women manage. Ernesta Procope is the CEO of a New York City insurance agency with thirty-six employees. Sharlyne Powell owns a franchise-granting firm, Women at Large, that specializes in fitness programs for heavier women based in Yakima, Washington. Georgena Terry owns a small, but very successful, company in Rochester, New York, that manufactures bicycles especially for women. Cynthia Hudson owns Waterfront Corporation, a Philadelphia-based corporation that repairs bridges and other structures in the Philadelphia area. Rosemary Voss owns the fifth-largest Century 21 real estate firm in the United States.

The following paragraphs summarize the views of these female entrepreneurs.

- Women manage differently than men, and they should. Women are generally more concerned about people than men. This helps them deal with the majority of problems in a business, which are people problems. The women interviewed by *Inc.* found that being concerned about people is a very positive behavior for a CEO. So are listening, caring, and helping others.

- Women tend to be more cooperative than competitive. They are also horizontally rather than vertically oriented. That is, they rely less on power than on a peer, group, or shared authority perspective, in contrast to men, who depend more on the power of the organizational hierarchy to support their decisions. The women indicated that they tended to let things slide rather than confronting a person who was posing a problem, but that they had learned that this is the wrong approach.

Each of the women felt that managers shouldn't worry about what others think of their decisions (women tend to be more concerned about this than men); just do it. Otherwise, people will question their ability to make decisions, and ultimately the business will fail. The bottom line seemed to be that you can't please everyone, so you have to please yourself.

These women entrepreneurs believe that women find it difficult to delegate. So do most male entrepreneurs. However, women who are striving to prove their value are even less likely to delegate than men because they have so much to prove. They also sometimes have difficulty recruiting because many men are unwilling to work for a female boss.

DISCUSSION QUESTIONS

1. In what ways would the female management style be more or less effective than the traditional male style?

2. It has been noted that in the future women will probably make better managers than men. Is this true? Why or why not?

SOURCE: "Women in Business," *Inc.* magazine video tape (Boston, 1987).

PART SIX

Controlling

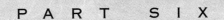

Controlling is the final step in the management process. Managers must determine whether objectives have been achieved and if not, what actions to take. Control is a process that can be applied at any level of the organization: strategic, tactical, or operational. Today the control process is changing as management itself changes. It is becoming much more prominent, and managers are trying to anticipate events rather than determine the results several days, weeks, or months after they have occurred.

Chapter 18 introduces the control process, reviewing the fundamental steps and major issues involved in properly managing control. Chapter 19 examines management control systems, both financially based systems and more broadly based systems focusing on issues such as employee performance, quality, and innovation. Chapter 20 reviews the relationship between information systems and control. One major concern of this chapter is the learning organization and the role of information in such an organization.

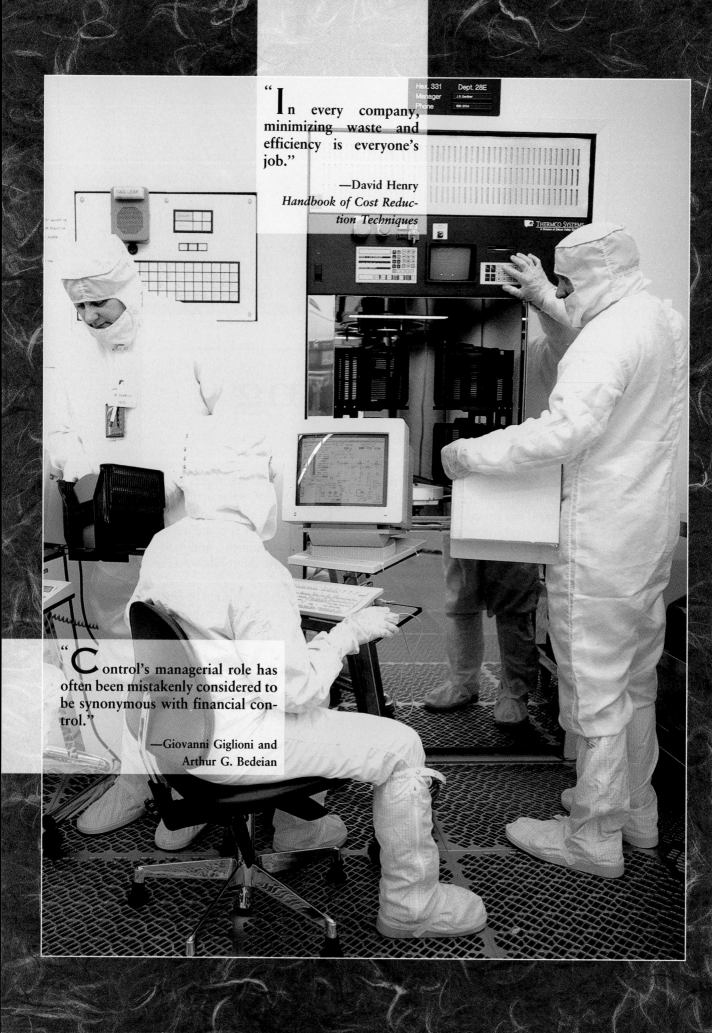

"In every company, minimizing waste and efficiency is everyone's job."

—David Henry
Handbook of Cost Reduction Techniques

"Control's managerial role has often been mistakenly considered to be synonymous with financial control."

—Giovanni Giglioni and
Arthur G. Bedeian

When you have read this chapter you should be able to:

1. Define the control process and enumerate its steps.

2. Indicate why controlling is important.

3. Discuss the relationship of planning to control.

4. Indicate the relationships between control and management style.

5. Describe the characteristics of effective control systems.

6. List the dysfunctional aspects of control.

7. Identify the major types of controls.

8. Discuss current trends in control management.

MANAGEMENT CHALLENGES
DISCUSSED IN THIS CHAPTER:

 Accelerating rates of change.

 Increasing levels of competition.

 Quality and innovation as managerial imperatives.

 Complexity of the managerial environment.

Controlling Performance: Strategic, Tactical, and Operational Control

CHAPTER OUTLINE

The Challenger Tragedy

Seventy-three seconds after launch on January 28, 1986, the space shuttle *Challenger* was destroyed along with its seven occupants—six astronauts and one civilian passenger, a teacher, Christa McAuliffe. In the months that followed, the presidential commission formed to investigate the tragedy, headed by former Secretary of State William Rogers, uncovered evidence of mismanagement throughout the National Aeronautics and Space Administration (NASA), not just at the Kennedy Space Center. The decision to launch the *Challenger* was not merely a bad decision, but a bad decision that was inevitable in a system gone awry. Several aspects of control were involved.

First, NASA's top managers had become isolated. Information from control systems often failed to reach them. The agency's leaders had become preoccupied with raising money. They spent far too much time in Washington and far too little managing the agency and the Marshall, Kennedy, and Johnson space centers.

Second, there were clear indications of violation of safety procedures. On the evening of January 27, Allan McDonald, the senior engineer representing Morton Thiokol, the manufacturer of the booster rocket, refused to sign off on the launch, even after a lengthy argument with Lawrence Mulloy, rocket-booster manager at Huntsville, Alabama, who was also at the cape for the launch. Mulloy went over his head and received permission from Joe Kilminster, a Morton Thiokol vice-president, to sign the launch authorization. He did so shortly before midnight.

Third, there were several communication problems. For example, physical inspection of the vehicle before the launch turned up extremely cold spots on the skin of the right booster rocket, but for some reason this information was not fed back to Launch Control.

The Rogers commission discovered that information was not shared within or among the three space centers on a day-to-day basis. Even when information was made available, it was often lost in a sea of paperwork. This paperwork was intended to establish control over a decentralized organization. However, it tended to cover up problems rather than identify them.

Fourth, the defect in the booster rocket's O-ring that caused the explosion had been documented in NASA's written information systems since 1978. Budget cuts and demands to meet impossible flight schedules had pushed the issue aside.

Fifth, it became evident during the investigation that the decision to launch was a political as well as an economic one. Millions of schoolchildren were waiting to watch a teacher conduct class from space. The delayed launch would indicate failure, and politicians do not like failures, especially nationally televised ones.

Finally, the commission found that safety standards had been sacrificed in not just one, but numerous areas of the launch program in order to meet deadlines. As one key official commented to his subordinates, "Safety is like caviar, a little bit is good but too much of it makes you sick."

SOURCES: "After the Challenger—How NASA Struggled to Put Itself Back Together," *Newsweek* (October 10, 1988), pp. 28–38; David Bailey, "NASA's Ace Space Boss," *Florida Trend* (January 1988), pp. 47–52; Michael Brody, "NASA's Challenge: Ending Isolation at the Top," *Fortune* (May 12, 1986), pp. 26–32; Ed Magnuson, "Fixing NASA," *Time* (June 9, 1986), pp. 14–27; "Questions Get Tougher," *Time* (March 3, 1986), pp. 14–16; and Tim Smart, "Rogers: NASA Came Close to a Cover-Up," *Orlando Sentinel* (May 11, 1986), pp. A1, A18.

The Challenger disaster was inevitable, given the circumstances, but it could have been prevented if the appropriate control systems and mechanisms had been established and if approved control procedures had been followed. Probably no event in recent history more vividly illustrates the need for appropriate levels, types, and degrees of control. As millions of people around the world watched, a series of control failures erupted into a national disaster. Ultimately, it was found that political and economic factors had led to an expedient choice in a decentralized system over which top management had failed to exercise proper control.

Every day, newspaper articles present other examples of failure to exercise proper control: General Motors' cost inefficiencies, the U.S. federal budget deficit, the Defense Department bribery scandals, Digital Equipment Corporation's failure to get new products to market on time, the embezzlement of millions of dollars by Phar-Mor Inc.'s founder, Michael I. Manus, the failures of the numerous corporations that file for bankruptcy, and the financial statements of firms that failed to control their cost and competitive strategies.[1] In all these cases, managers failed to exercise proper control.

In this age of accelerating change, increasing competition, increasingly global business, changing technology, a more diverse work force, and other management challenges, control becomes more difficult, yet ever more important. A revolution is occurring in control as new methods and technologies are being used to cope with these challenges.[2] Many of these emulate Japanese approaches, such as strategic cost systems and continuous improvement.[3] Others, such as interactive control systems, benchmarking, and expert systems, are home-grown approaches to improving control in the organization.[4] Even new types of performance appraisal systems are being developed to cope with such factors as the need to be sensitive to differences in management styles in different countries.[5] Finally, all control systems are expected to function more quickly, as time is of the essence in management today.

This chapter begins by defining control and indicating its importance. Then it examines the stages of the control process. The general characteristics of

AT NASA: *Had NASA exercised appropriate control, seven people would not have died and NASA would not have experienced a two-and-a-half-year delay in shuttle launches.*

The seven members of the crew of the space shuttle *Challenger,* who lost their lives when the shuttle was destroyed shortly after launch.

the process are noted, the interrelationships of planning and control discussed, and the types of management control strategies and styles described. Next, the types of control and the characteristics of effective control systems are reviewed. The problems of controlling in a changing environment are noted. Finally, control as a problem-solving process is discussed.

The Importance of Control

Control: The systematic process by which managers ensure that the organization is achieving its objectives and carrying out the associated plans effectively and efficiently.

Control is the systematic process by which managers ensure that the organization is achieving its objectives and carrying out the associated plans effectively and efficiently.[6] Robert J. Mockler describes this process as follows: "Management control is a systematic effort to set performance standards for planning objectives, to design information feedback systems, to compare actual performance with today's predetermined standards, to determine whether there are any deviations and to measure their significance, and to take any action required to assure that all corporate resources are being used in the most effective and efficient manner possible in achieving corporate objectives."[7]

Control is the fourth major function of management. It is the concluding phase in the management cycle of planning, organizing, leading, and controlling. Appropriate control leads to the attainment of objectives and the fullfillment of plans. Planning and control are closely interdependent.

The term *control* as used here can be traced to Frederick W. Taylor's *Scientific Management*. In fact, control was the "central idea" of scientific management.[8] Even as late as the early 1970s, it was generally agreed that control was neglected and not well understood.[9] Only recently have control and types of control mechanisms been seen as being of major importance.[10] Control remains a major problem in many organizations. As can be seen in the *Challenger* example, controlling a large organization is often a complex process involving not just simple control systems but organizational structures, leadership styles, and the objectives and plans that are the driving force of organizations. Not only must planning, organizing, and leading be controlled, but so must control itself. Finally, throughout all of these functions the decision-making process must be controlled.[11]

The repercussions of failure to exercise control can be horrendous. In medicine, for example, software "bugs" can literally kill patients, radiation machines may give lethal doses, pacemakers may stop unexpectedly, and computer-produced medicines may be hazardous to health.[12] In business organizations, especially manufacturing firms, failure to control can lead not only to loss of profits but ultimately to bankruptcy. Japanese and other Pacific Rim firms have put many U.S. firms out of business through their ability to provide superior product quality. Quality control has therefore become a crucial element of U.S. firms' efforts to become more competitive.[13]

Control is important because it helps organizations cope with uncertainty, complex environments, and limitations in people's ability to carry out plans. Control helps in coping with uncertainty and complexity because managers and their subordinates must continually check to determine what progress is being made. This often means changing plans that no longer fit the circumstances. Control helps overcome the problems of human limitations, especially through the delegation of authority, because it involves continually checking to ascertain how objectives are being reached and how plans are being carried out.

AT NASA: Control designed to address the problem of human limitations was noticeably absent at NASA.

Steps in the Control Process

There are four steps in the control process:

1. Establishing performance objectives and standards
2. Measuring actual performance
3. Comparing actual performance to objectives and standards
4. Taking necessary action based on the results of the comparison[14]

The relationships among these steps are shown in Figure 18.1. In this section, each step will be described in detail.

Establishing Performance Objectives and Standards

The first step in control involves establishing performance standards. Those standards state the objectives of the organization and its subunits, providing targets for individuals and groups to achieve; actual performance can be compared with those targets. When those whose performance is to be measured are involved in developing standards, they are likely to have more positive attitudes toward meeting those standards. A highly refined management by objectives, results, and rewards program includes standards for every job, from maintenance engineer to company president. Sometimes standards are difficult to establish properly or are not changed to fit new circumstances. For example, radar on board the British frigate *Sheffield* was designed to detect Soviet missiles. When dispatched to the Falkland Islands, the frigate was attacked by Argentinian Exocet missiles supplied by French arms makers. Because the frigate was unable to detect this type of in-bound missile, it was sunk.[15]

Methods for measuring performance must be designed for each standard established. Whether the standard is number of patients per hour, sales per month, rejects per day, calls per hour, or productivity per year, a means of measuring performance against that standard must be determined. Sometimes it is difficult to establish standards for service jobs, in which specific objectives may not be readily identifiable. For example, what are the objectives of a grocery store checkout clerk? To put through X units of sales per hour? To keep customers happy? Similarly, for a psychologist, should the objective be to see a certain number of patients per day or to cure a certain number of patients per year? Despite the difficulties involved, to the extent possible, specific standards

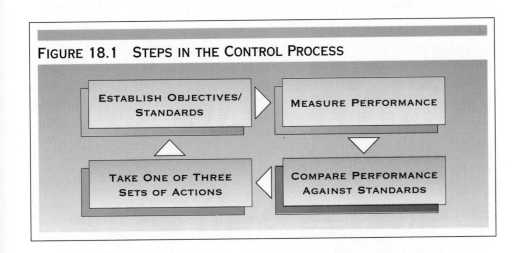

FIGURE 18.1   STEPS IN THE CONTROL PROCESS

ESTABLISH OBJECTIVES/ STANDARDS → MEASURE PERFORMANCE → COMPARE PERFORMANCE AGAINST STANDARDS → TAKE ONE OF THREE SETS OF ACTIONS

These Genentech researchers are shown celebrating the development of a new heart drug. Unfortunately, however, the actual performance of the new drug, as measured by sales, was well below the level that had been forecasted.

of performance must be identified for every job, and ways of measuring performance against those standards must be determined. Moreover, those standards must be accepted and utilized by all involved. Today, many organizations are using benchmarking and best-practices studies of competitors to set standards.[16]

Measuring Actual Performance

AT NASA: The standard of performance tolerance for the O-ring was continually ignored by the individuals involved in the launch decision process. Thus, although standards were defined, they were not applied.

Once systems for measuring performance against standards have been designed, actual performance by an individual, group, or department must be calculated. It is necessary to achieve a balance between too much information and too little. For example, the typical cost information provided in manufacturing and service operations, which is principally used for controlling the use of labor and machinery, has not been sufficient for making strategic decisions such as whether to delete product lines. Thus, while the organization may be performing efficiently from one perspective, its performance from another perspective—such as meeting the needs of the market—may not be measured appropriately.[17] As a result, many companies are revising their management cost accounting systems.[18]

Comparing Actual Performance to Objectives and Standards

Comparing actual performance against the standards established previously can help determine whether objectives have been achieved. A football coach, for example, continually compares a player's performance against a set of expectations for blocking, tackling, running, passing, and scoring. The coach, in turn, is evaluated by the number of games won by the team during a season.

Taking Necessary Action

Once actual performance has been compared to performance standards, the manager must choose among three possible actions:

1. If performance is below the standards, the manager must take corrective action. He or she must first determine whether performance is the problem. If so, efforts to improve performance

must be made. Another possibility is that the standards were too high to begin with. For example, GM's sales forecasts were consistently overly optimistic and its costs consistently too high. This eventually resulted in the replacement of the chief financial officer and the president of the corporation in April 1992.[19] Later that year most members of the top management team, including the CEO, were replaced as GM found itself losing billions of dollars.[20]

2. If performance (or anticipated performance) is below the standard, the manager must take preventive action to ensure that the problem will not recur. This goes beyond merely taking corrective action. As management author William T. Greenwood has observed, it is insufficient simply to correct problems. Rather, the manager must take action to make sure the problems will not recur.[21]

3. If performance is greater than or equal to standards, the manager may choose to reinforce the behaviors that led to achievement of the standard.

Corrective actions are relatively easy to carry out in most cases, but complex situations often defy rational solution. Political, economic, and social relationships must be adjusted, often to no one's satisfaction, as this chapter's Ethical Management Challenge reveals. What factors led to the problems at this Swiss bank?

Characteristics of the Control Process

As can be seen in Figure 18.1, the control process is cyclical. Standards are established; performance is measured against the standards; deviations from the standards lead to action; and the cycle begins again. Control tends to be viewed as a negative endeavor, but the process results in an extremely positive contribu-

Preliminary and continuing analysis can help prevent deviations from the norm. Such analysis is particularly important to Bethlehem Steel. Molten metal must be constantly monitored so that it will not get too hot or too cool for too long.

Rothschild Bank AG

For more than two hundred years the Rothschilds have been a dynasty of fabulously wealthy financiers discreetly bankrolling royalty, governments, and the merely rich. Their near-legendary status has been swathed in secrecy, discretion, and the customary silence in which Swiss banking is traditionally conducted. But two centuries of privileged privacy came to a sudden and startling end late in 1992, when a senior executive and credit manager of the private Rothschild Bank AG in Zurich did something most extraordinary for a Swiss banker: talk about the bank's affairs.

The credit manager is Juerg Heer, who has worked for the bank since 1972. In 1992, he was arrested for making improper loans to companies that have since failed. The bank says he deceived its directors, broke its rules, and got kickbacks for providing the loans. It estimates the resulting damage to its business at around $155 million, and it is suing Heer, who is under criminal investigation.

Heer admits to receiving around $20 million in commissions for the loans but says that other bank officers knew of and approved his actions. Moreover, he is so incensed at his treatment by the bank that he is publicizing all that he knows about the secretive institution—and that's plenty.

The picture he paints is devastating for the Rothschild institution. It includes the assertion that the bank has been carelessly managed, has operated for years on the fringes of legality, and has been entangled in some of the largest recent financial scandals. Among other things, he claims that the Rothschilds' Zurich bank was involved with Banco Ambrosiano, whose former chairman, Roberto Calvi, was found hanging under Blackfriars bridge in London in 1982. Heer says he personally handed over a suitcase stuffed with $5 million for Calvi's killers. The bank was also involved in lucrative schemes to help rich Italian families evade capital controls and taxes. Heer claims that he helped Baron Elie de Rothschild, the now-retired chairman of the Zurich bank, create a series of front companies to hide the actual ownership of Italian assets behind the bank's name.

Heer's most substantial allegations concern the front companies designed to hide the ownership of assets. Swiss banks have adopted "due diligence" guidelines that prohibit them from assisting in the flight of capital, and they are supposed to be vigilant about the possibility of tax fraud as well. Yet Heer says that the baron himself acted as a trustee for some of the bank's best clients, using a Panama-based company as a cover and earning $2 million to $3 million a year in commissions. The bank confirms that units located outside the country held "certain assets for certain clients," but adds that such practices are normal and legal.

SOURCE: Peter Gumbel, "A Swiss Bank Squirms as Officer It's Suing Tells of Sleazy Deals," *Wall Street Journal* (December 11, 1992), pp. A1, A6.

tion to organizational success. The trend toward self-control, as opposed to control imposed by others, should help satisfy the increasing needs of individuals for autonomy and lead to a more positive perspective on the control process.

The typical control process described here is retrospective, but control can and should be anticipatory as well.[22] Preliminary and continuing analysis can help prevent deviations from the standards. This is especially important in some industries, such as steel. Molten metal must be constantly monitored so that it will not get too hot or cool for too long. Otherwise, the whole batch could be lost. Much of the change occurring in U.S. control methods involves such **feed-forward control,** in which changes are anticipated. In fast-paced, complex global environments, businesses must anticipate surprises and be prepared to deal with turbulence in advance of its occurrence.[23]

Feedforward control: Control systems that anticipate changes rather than merely react to them.

Finally, control must occur throughout the organization. Although many organizations tend to rely on financial controls because they offer a common denominator by which to measure success, true control cannot be achieved unless all the factors leading to those numbers—such as quality, inventory levels, service, and theft—are controlled as well. Control must occur at all the critical points at which performance can be matched against plans.[24]

No set of control points or standards is suitable for every manager because of the differences among organizations and departments, the variety of products and services to be controlled, the types of behaviors involved, and the various types of plans to be evaluated.[25] However, standards tend to fall into one of eight categories, as Table 18.1 reveals.

Although these categories may suffice for examining the total organization, each subunit, department, and individual within it must determine relevant control points for its assigned task. As discussed in Chapter 2, an organization is an input-transformation-output system. This is true of each subunit of the organization as well. Thus, there must be control points for inputs, for various phases of transformation, and for outputs. Whether the process being controlled results in a physical product, a service, or an idea, standards must be established, performance measured and then compared to standards, and action taken where necessary for each of the control points established. McDonald's establishes control points for its franchises in such areas as housekeeping, quality, timeliness, and employee appearance. When it inspects franchise facilities, the control cycle is followed for each of these areas.

TABLE 18.1 Eight Types of Standards

1. Physical Standards: Nonmonetary measurements are common at the operating level—for example, units of production per machine hour.

2. Cost Standards: Monetary measurements are also common at the operating level—for example, costs per plane reservation.

3. Capital Standards: The application of monetary measurements is made to physical items. These are concerned with the capital invested in the company and its utilization—for example, the desired ratio of return on investment.

4. Revenue Standards: Monetary standards are relative to sales—for example, sales per capita.

5. Program Standards: The successful implementation of plans involved in a program may be used as a standard of performance—for example, the successful development of a new product.

6. Intangible Standards: Where job performance is difficult to describe, intangible standards are often employed—for example, customer loyalty.

7. Objectives Standards: Many companies are now moving to specific objectives for virtually every job—for example, salespeople trained per year for a personnel training specialist.

8. Strategic Plans: Control points are used for strategic control—for example, checking at each stage of action to see if a strategy is successful.

SOURCE: Harold Koontz and Heinz Weihrich, *Management*, 9th ed. (New York: McGraw-Hill, 1988), pp. 493–494. Reproduced with permission of McGraw-Hill.

The Interrelationships of Planning and Control

As can be seen in Figure 18.2, planning and control are intimately related. The management cycle begins with planning and ends with control. Control is concerned with whether objectives have been achieved and plans carried out. Typically, different members of the organization are involved in planning and control. Communication between them is critical.

As plans become increasingly flexible, control processes and standards must also become more flexible. A major part of strategic planning is an "early warning system," a control system that "alerts management to potential opportunities and problems before they affect the financial statements."[26] For example, executive information systems (EISs) such as Commander EIS continuously track the progress a firm is making toward accomplishing its objectives. At San Diego's Home Federal Savings and Loan, Commander helps provide early warning of potential problems.[27]

Strategic plans should serve as a means of establishing control. As discussed in Chapter 7, for example, Michael E. Porter identifies taking a low-cost position relative to competitors as one of the three key strategies.[28] High levels of quality, achieved through rigorous control efforts, have been identified as a key way of providing differentiation in the marketplace. If consumers perceive the quality of a firm's products or services as higher than that of competitors' products or services, it has successfully differentiated them.[29]

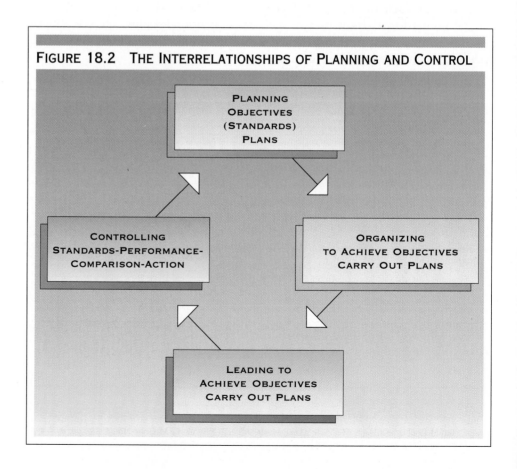

FIGURE 18.2   THE INTERRELATIONSHIPS OF PLANNING AND CONTROL

PLANNING
OBJECTIVES
(STANDARDS)
PLANS

CONTROLLING
STANDARDS-PERFORMANCE-
COMPARISON-ACTION

ORGANIZING
TO ACHIEVE OBJECTIVES
CARRY OUT PLANS

LEADING TO
ACHIEVE OBJECTIVES
CARRY OUT PLANS

Management Control Styles

William G. Ouchi, who introduced many U.S. managers to Japanese management practices, has identified three principal control strategies, or styles, that managers may choose to employ when designing and managing control systems: market control, bureaucratic control, and clan control.[30] These three styles can be used simultaneously because each serves a different purpose. They are based on the belief that cooperation between a firm's subunits is a function of the exchanges taking place between those subunits and between individuals in the organization. For example, individuals exchange their labor and time for money, security, and job satisfaction. Organizations exchange materials, outputs, services, and products to achieve some objective or purpose. All such exchanges have a cost associated with them that Ouchi calls a transaction cost and defines as "any activity which is engaged in to satisfy each party to an exchange that the value given and received is in accord with his or her expectations."[31] The components of these three control styles are identified in Figure 18.3.

Market Control

A **market control** strategy allows market mechanisms such as competition to establish the standards of the control system. This strategy assumes that market mechanisms are most efficient in setting the prices or costs identified with certain transactions. This style of control relies on external forces to control behavior within the firm. It is a quantitatively oriented strategy. There must be an identifiable product or service whose contributions to the organization can be

Market control: A control strategy in which market mechanisms are allowed to establish the standards of the control system.

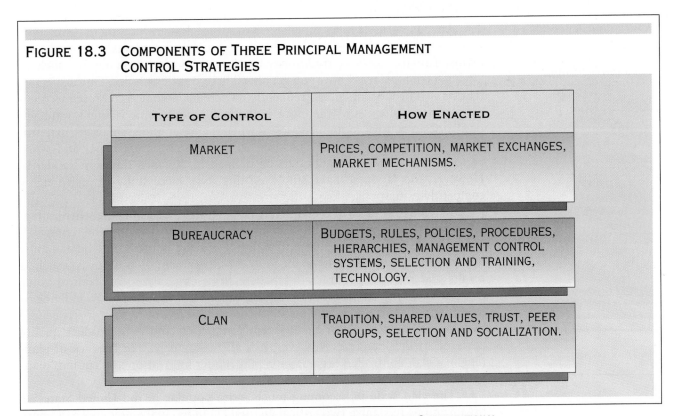

FIGURE 18.3 COMPONENTS OF THREE PRINCIPAL MANAGEMENT CONTROL STRATEGIES

TYPE OF CONTROL	HOW ENACTED
MARKET	PRICES, COMPETITION, MARKET EXCHANGES, MARKET MECHANISMS.
BUREAUCRACY	BUDGETS, RULES, POLICIES, PROCEDURES, HIERARCHIES, MANAGEMENT CONTROL SYSTEMS, SELECTION AND TRAINING, TECHNOLOGY.
CLAN	TRADITION, SHARED VALUES, TRUST, PEER GROUPS, SELECTION AND SOCIALIZATION.

SOURCES: WILLIAM G. OUCHI, "A CONCEPTUAL FRAMEWORK FOR THE DESIGN OF ORGANIZATIONAL CONTROL MECHANISMS," MANAGEMENT SCIENCE (1979), PP. 833–838; "MARKETS, BUREAUCRACIES, AND CLANS," ADMINISTRATIVE SCIENCE QUARTERLY (1980), NO. 1, P. 130.

measured. Typically, divisions of the company become *profit centers*—their contributions to the company are measured by the profits they generate.[32] For example, the Walt Disney Companies have seven major divisions, each run virtually as a separate business: theme parks, movies, consumer products, cable television, Disney Development (real estate), hotels, and imagineering (creative designs).

Bureaucratic Control

Bureaucratic control: A control strategy based on authority and carried out through rules, regulations, and policies.

Sometimes market control is inadequate, especially when there is little or no competition or one subunit is very powerful. In such cases, bureaucratic control is a reasonable approach. **Bureaucratic control** is based on authority and is carried out through rules, regulations, and policies. It depends on compliance rather than commitment and requires well-defined job descriptions and standards. Standardization of activities is at the core of this system. Any well-managed assembly line, for example, depends on repetition of activity according to highly refined specifications for its success. Hierarchy, formalized control systems, computerized reporting systems, and similar methods of control are utilized.

In bureaucratically controlled organizations, decision making is depersonalized. The rules determine what is to be done, and statements like "You can't go against the rules" or "That's company policy" are commonly heard. Large American organizations, such as Xerox and American Airlines, often use both market and bureaucratic control systems.

Clan Control

Clan control: A control strategy that relies on social needs and is established largely through cultural artifacts.

The **clan control** style relies on people's social needs—their desire to belong to a group. Control is established largely through cultural artifacts like rituals and myths. Rituals, such as traditional Christmas bonuses, and myths, such as "Being a team player is how you get ahead here," are examples. Ouchi suggests that clan control occurs most frequently "where teamwork is common, technologies change often, and therefore individual performance is highly ambiguous."[33] Clan control is often employed when the other two systems are inappropriate—when competition is lacking or powerful subunits exist, and when performance is too ambiguous to be defined in advance through standards. However, the Japanese have employed this style successfully in many highly competitive situations.

Bureaucratic control is characteristic of American businesses, whereas Japanese firms are more likely to be characterized by clan, or cultural, control.[34] Whereas most U.S. firms attempt to apply market control and bureaucratic methods in conjunction with some type of management by objectives—such as results and rewards programs—Japanese firms emphasize clan control while also partly relying on the other two styles. Japanese firms often allow individuals to set their own objectives and pursue a cooperative effort. Many experts believe that this is one reason for the efficient production and high product quality achieved by the Japanese. However, it is also recognized that the lack of planning in a clan-controlled organization may hinder innovation and cut into management's ability to handle radical changes.[35]

The clan style is becoming much more popular in the United States as organizations recognize two critical factors: (1) Individual employees seek more self-control, and (2) proper management of organizational culture can lead to more efficient and effective organizations. Many organizations are switching from market and bureaucratic control to a mixture of bureaucratic, market, and

A MARKET CONTROL STRATEGY ALLOWS MARKET MECHANISMS TO ESTABLISH THE STANDARDS OF THE CONTROL SYSTEM. DISNEYLAND USES SUCH AN APPROACH. BUREAUCRATIC CONTROL, IN CONTRAST, IS BASED ON AUTHORITY AND CARRIED OUT THROUGH RULES AND POLICIES. THIS APPROACH IS BEST SUITED TO SITUATIONS IN WHICH ACTIVITIES ARE STANDARDIZED, SUCH AS AN AUTOMOBILE ASSEMBLY LINE. THE THIRD STYLE, CLAN CONTROL, RELIES ON PEOPLE'S DESIRE TO BELONG

TO A GROUP. MANY JAPANESE FIRMS USE THIS APPROACH. SHOWN HERE IS THE TOSHIBA BASEBALL TEAM BEING TREATED TO A PARTY IN THE FACTORY.

FIGURE 18.4   CHOOSING A CONTROL STYLE

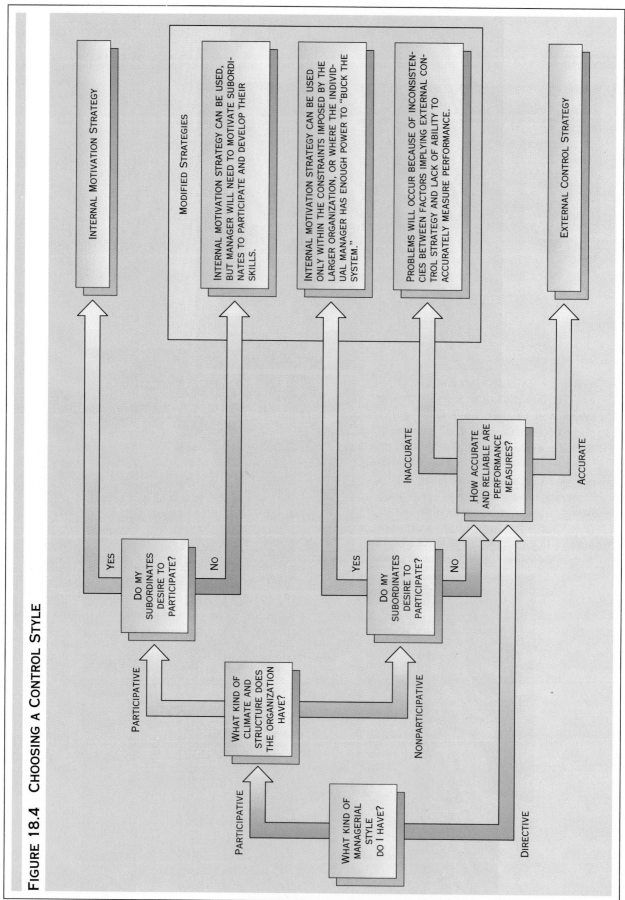

SOURCE: PERMISSION OF THE HARVARD BUSINESS REVIEW FROM "FIT CONTROL SYSTEMS TO YOUR MANAGERIAL STYLE" BY CORTLANDT CAMMANN AND DAVID A. NADLER (JANUARY–FEBRUARY 1976), P. 71. COPYRIGHT © 1976 BY THE PRESIDENT AND FELLOWS OF HARVARD COLLEGE. ALL RIGHTS RESERVED.

clan control. (See the prologue to Chapter 1, which discusses the efforts of General Electric to incorporate clan control by becoming more team oriented.)

Adhocracy Control

Frank Petrock has suggested that there is a fourth type of control style, adhocracy control.[36] There are four types of organizational culture in his model. They can be represented by the four cells of a matrix, using internal versus external focus and stability versus flexibility as the two axes. Clan culture is internally oriented and emphasizes friendliness and loyalty; adhocracy culture emphasizes external focus with a high degree of flexibility and individuality; market culture emphasizes external orientation and stability; and hierarchy culture emphasizes internal orientation and stability. Control styles naturally follow these cultures; consequently, the **adhocracy control** style relies on individual self-control, empowerment, and flexibility. The manager's role is that of facilitator, providing direction but relying on the individual to control his or her own efforts. Clearly, as the managerial environment becomes more complex, clan and adhocracy control styles will become more necessary.

Adhocracy control: A control strategy that relies on individual self-control, empowerment, and flexibility.

Choosing a Management Control Style

Each of the four control styles just described uses a different approach to control. Each can be effective in particular situations. When neither a market nor a bureaucratic control style will suffice, clan control is recommended.[37] At the operating level, the basic choice is between mechanistic (bureaucratic) and organic (clan and adhocracy) types of control. Market control is a more strategic form of control that is imposed on lower-level managers from above.

Cortlandt Cammann and David A. Nadler suggest that most managers essentially must choose between two types of management control styles: an internal motivation style, in which employees control themselves (similar to the clan and adhocracy styles), and an external control strategy, in which rules, regulations, procedures, and external authority are used to control the employee (similar to bureaucratic control, with some elements of the market control strategy).[38,39] Certain situations may call for a mixture of the two strategies.

In choosing a control style, managers should ask themselves the following questions:

1. In general, what kind of managerial style do I have—participative or directive?
2. In general, what kind of culture, structure, and reward systems does my organization have—participative or nonparticipative?
3. How accurate and reliable are the measures of key areas of subordinate performance?
4. Do my subordinates desire to participate in and do they respond well to opportunities to take responsibility for decision making and performance?[40]

In answering these questions, managers should be guided by the chart presented in Figure 18.4. In general, when the manager is participative, the culture is participative, and the subordinates' desire to participate is high, the internal motivation (clan/adhocracy) style should be employed. When the manager is directive, the culture is nonparticipative, and the subordinates do not desire to participate, the external control (bureaucratic) style should be employed.

Problems of Control at Chernobyl

For a country known for bureaucratic, often harsh control, the revelations about the nuclear accident at Chernobyl in Russia provide important lessons about the role of the human element in the control process. The Soviet government was surprisingly candid, blaming "gross" human error for the world's most serious

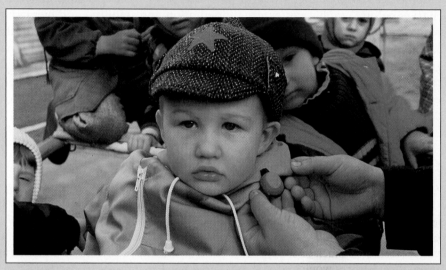

The Chernobyl disaster was a harsh lesson in the role of the human element in the control process. Soviet citizens in the Chernobyl area had to wear radiation detectors like the one shown here being placed on a child.

Designing Effective Control Systems

Management experts have identified the following characteristics of effective control systems:[41]

1. *Strategy, tactics, and operations:* There should be control measures at each level of the planning process—strategic control, management control (i.e., control of tactics), and operational control. It is important to link control to strategy. Control systems should measure performance against where the organization is headed, rather than against behavior that was accepted in the past. In the future, for example, innovation will be much more critical in most firms. Control systems will need to emphasize innovation as well as efficiency.

2. *Acceptability to those who will enforce decisions:* If those who must implement management's decisions are not in agreement with them, there will be dysfunctional consequences. This is an extension of Barnard's acceptance theory of authority, discussed in Chapter 9. Different methods of control have varying degrees of

nuclear accident. In an official report to the International Atomic Energy Agency, it detailed six violations of operating procedures that led to the catastrophe. The blunders occurred as the plant's operators began reducing the Chernobyl reactor's power level so that they could perform a turbine test. Each action was a violation of a rule, and if any one of the violations had not occurred, the accident would have been prevented. Against all odds, however, all six took place. The violations were as follows:

1. The emergency cooling system was turned off to conduct the test.
2. The reactor power output was inadvertently lowered too far, making it more difficult to control.
3. All water circulation pumps were turned on, exceeding recommended flow rates.
4. The automatic signal, which shuts down the reactors if the turbines stop, was blocked.
5. The safety devices that shut down the reactor if steam pressure or water levels become abnormal were turned off.
6. Almost all control rods were pulled from the core.

Nuclear reactors in the former Soviet Union are generally considered to be of an older, unsafe type that is not approved in the United States or Europe. Soviet authorities defended their technology, citing only human error as responsible for the accident. Their response to the catastrophe was immediate, as the site had to be cleaned up and the reactor encased in concrete. For the long term, however, they felt a need not so much to change control policies and procedures as to ensure that such human errors would not recur.

SOURCE: "Anatomy of a Catastrophe," *Time* (September 1, 1986), pp. 26–29.

acceptance.[42] Clan control, for example, depends on trust, cooperation, and commitment for its success, whereas bureaucratic control relies on the acceptance of authority. Sometimes people simply choose to ignore controls, as this chapter's Global Management Challenge reveals. What are some of the results?

3. *Flexibility:* The environment of organizations is changing at an accelerating rate. Consequently, their goals, objectives, and strategies are also changing. The control systems and methods employed must be flexible enough to adapt to changing circumstances.

4. *Accuracy:* Any information system must provide accurate and timely information. Control is no different. Proper decisions cannot be made unless the information on which they are based is accurate. In any business, inaccurate information can have disastrous results. For example, in the health care industry inaccurate information regarding PAP smears has led patients to believe that they had cancer when they did not—or the reverse, which is far worse.[43]

5. *Timeliness:* A decision made too late will be ineffective. Information must be provided in time for managers to make an

appropriate decision. A study of air conditioner manufacturers in Japan found that Japanese managers receive control information twice as fast as their American counterparts; they also respond more quickly than their American counterparts.[44]

6. *Cost effectiveness:* The cost of maintaining control should be no greater than, and at least equal to, the benefits derived. Most added controls increase costs.

7. *Understandability:* If the employee who is charged with the control effort or is being controlled cannot understand the control system, adverse effects are likely.

8. *Objectivity and subjectivity:* Effective control systems balance the requirements for factual and objective information against the occasional need for subjective information. A bureaucratic control strategy would typically require more objective information than a clan control strategy, which would require more subjective information.

9. *Other factors:* Effective control systems are coordinated with planning and other elements of management and the organization. They are realistic, related to the work flow, and justifiable.

Dysfunctional Consequences of Control

If control systems do not possess the characteristics just described—and even if they do—certain dysfunctional consequences may occur. Among those consequences are game playing, resistance to control, inaccurate information, and rigid bureaucratic behavior.

Some people will always view control systems as a challenge, as something to be beaten or a game to be won.[45] Some, for example, might figure out how to pad their budget so as not to be controlled by it. Others might figure out ways of stealing from materials inventories in order to "beat" the rules designed to control those inventories.

People resist control for many reasons. Perhaps the most common reason is excessive control. People tend to resist when an organization is overly controlling.

Inaccurate information can result from a variety of control-related problems. There are clear indications that managers will pass inaccurate information upward in the chain of command in order to make themselves look better.[46] For example, when top management at Boy Scouts of America put pressure on local and regional managers to bring in new members, the managers reported significantly larger numbers of new members than actually existed.[47] More recently, *The Wall Street Journal* revealed that the reporting of false inventories to improve corporate income statements in order to raise stock prices was estimated to be four times as common in 1992 as in 1987.[48] Among the offenders was the Alabama-based electronics maker Comptronix, whose CEO and other executives conspired to raise stock prices by manipulating inventories and other accounts. The CEO was fired, and the firm's stock price quickly dropped from $23.00 a share to $7.50 in response to the information.[49]

A final consequence of ineffective control is rigid bureaucratic behavior. This occurs when people obey a rule beyond a reasonable level. An example is the waiter who refuses a customer's request for additional bread because it is against the rules of the restaurant to provide bread at no extra charge. This behavior is not only excessively bureaucratic, but detrimental to the organization because it could result in the loss of a customer.

Types of Control

There are four major types of control: (1) those defined according to the timing of the control process relative to the transformation process (preaction, concurrent, or postaction control); (2) those defined according to the planning level involved (strategic, management, or operational control); (3) those defined according to the economic function involved (marketing, finance, operations, human resource management, or information management); and (4) those defined according to the management function involved (problem solving, planning, organizing, leading, or controlling). In this section, we will examine each type in detail.

Control Defined by Stage of the Transformation Process

As shown in Figure 18.5, there are three principal types of control defined according to the stages of the input-transformation-output process. They are preaction, concurrent, and postaction controls.[50]

PREACTION CONTROLS

Preaction controls are used to ensure that the necessary human, material, and financial resources are in place before the transformation process begins. Preaction controls—sometimes referred to as preventive controls, precontrols, or feedforward controls—ensure not only that enough resources are available, but also that their quality is sufficiently high to prevent problems once the transformation process is under way. Preaction controls recognize and identify potential problems before they occur.

Preaction controls have received considerable attention in manufacturing firms in recent years. Historically, such firms relied on statistical sampling to ensure that an "acceptable" rate of defects resulted from the manufacturing process. Today, however, they are attempting to make every product perfect. Every input must therefore also be perfect. U.S. firms have traditionally accepted

Preaction controls: Control systems used to ensure that the necessary human, material, and financial resources are in place before the transformation process begins.

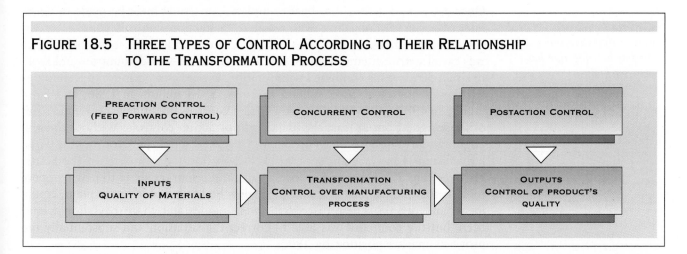

FIGURE 18.5 THREE TYPES OF CONTROL ACCORDING TO THEIR RELATIONSHIP TO THE TRANSFORMATION PROCESS

a certain number of imperfect inputs from their suppliers, but under high-quality management performance standards they are no longer able to do so.[51]

Close attention is also paid to human resource inputs. The human resource department often devotes large amounts of human and financial resources to selecting the best candidates to fill jobs. One of the most exhaustive selection processes in the United States occurs at Toyota's auto assembly plant in Kentucky. Personnel managers sifted through hundreds of applications before each of the 3,000 jobs in the plant was filled.[52] Ironically, in most parts of the country such efforts must be honed in an environment in which the demand for skilled labor is greater than the available supply.[53]

Preaction/feedforward controls become critical in rapidly changing, turbulent environments like those faced by businesses today. Such controls increase the likelihood of spotting potential problems in advance of their occurrence. They require continuous scanning of the environment, the development of alternative scenarios (as discussed in Chapter 7), and an intuitive sense of change.[54]

CONCURRENT CONTROLS

Concurrent controls:
Control systems designed to
detect variances from
standards and undertake
corrective action before a
series of actions has been
completed.

Concurrent controls assess ongoing activities. They are designed to detect variances from standards and undertake corrective action before a series of actions has been completed.[55] Concurrent controls are often referred to as steering controls. This term is derived from the analogy of steering an automobile. The driver will turn the steering wheel many times, even if only slightly, before reaching his or her destination.

An example of concurrent controls can be seen in a power generating plant, where engineers constantly monitor gauges to ensure that all is going well and to avoid power shortages. Similarly, in a brewery, the brewmaster periodically checks the composition of each batch of beer to ensure that it meets standards; a dentist performing a root canal operation checks his or her progress at each stage of the procedure.

Yes/no control: A control
system that consists of a
specific action or series of
actions that must be
accomplished before the
overall process can
continue.

One type of concurrent control is the **yes/no control,** which is used on a specific action or series of actions that must be accomplished before the overall process can continue. Airplane pilots, for example, go down a checklist of items as they prepare for takeoff and landing. Neither process can continue until each item has been checked off.

The ability to control ongoing activities is critical to financial success, as this chapter's Management Challenge indicates. How does S-K-I's concurrent control system work?

POSTACTION CONTROLS

Postaction controls: Control
systems that determine
whether an objective has
been reached.

Once a series of actions has been completed, an effort must be made to determine whether the objective was reached. **Postaction controls** control for the results of completed actions. For example, in the mid-1980s, Bank of America was faced with a financial crisis. Bad loans to third-world countries and high-risk real estate loans combined with inferior services and poor use of technology left it with losses of $337 million in 1985, $518 million in 1986, and $985 million in 1987.[56] Preaction and concurrent controls might have prevented some of those losses, but at least the bank had postaction controls. Without them, it might not have discovered its problems for several more weeks or months. Similarly, Winn-Dixie, a giant supermarket chain located primarily in the South, discovered in 1987 that it was losing substantial market share to new competitors. Its top managers also realized that they had failed to invest in plant, equipment, and people. These discoveries were made later than they should have been, but the company was able to correct the situation and substantially improve its market position by 1992.[57]

Concurrent Control at S-K-I

S-K-I Limited, which owns the two biggest ski resorts in New England—Killington and Mount Snow—takes a technological approach to concurrent control. Ski resorts are a seasonal business. Many operators do not know whether they are making a profit until the season is over, but S-K-I knows where it stands at the end of every day. Founder Preston Smith did not want to wait until the end of the season to find out where the company stood; he knew that computers could track progress on a daily basis. S-K-I uses 370 computer terminals to track the number of tickets sold, restaurant sales, ski lift use, hotel bookings, and other key variables. S-K-I budgets for every day of the season for each major part of the business—restaurants, ski school, snow making, and ski lifts. The results have been impressive. Since 1981, profits have grown at an annual rate of 21 percent, while revenues have climbed by 19 percent each year.

Concurrent control measures allow S-K-I to know where it stands at the end of each ski day, thereby enabling the company to better serve both its customers and its owners.

SOURCE: Sara Smith, "Companies to Watch: SKI Limited," *Fortune* (March 28, 1988), p. 79.

Many organizations use multiple types of control systems. More preaction and concurrent controls will be used in the future, as the managerial environment becomes more complex. Both Bank of America and Winn-Dixie now use multiple types of control systems.

Control Defined by Level of Plan

There are three types of controls defined according to the level of plan involved: strategic, management, and operational (see Figure 18.6).[58]

STRATEGIC CONTROL

Strategic control is concerned with the evaluation of strategy once it has been formulated or implemented. Prior to implementation, strategic control involves asking a series of questions about strategy and its consistency with other factors:

Strategic control: Control concerned with the evaluation of strategy once it has been formulated or implemented.

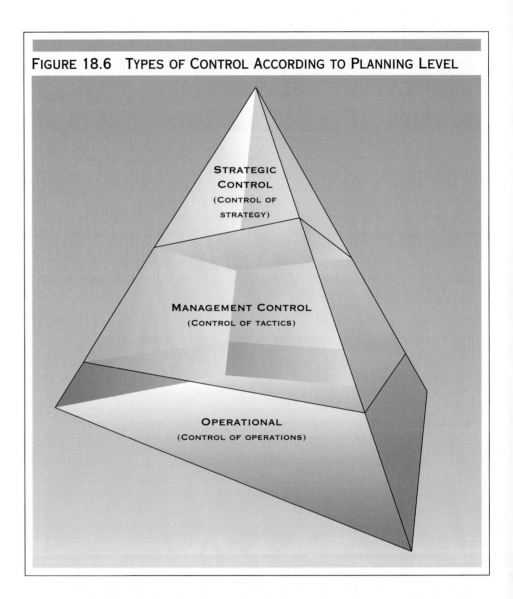

FIGURE 18.6   TYPES OF CONTROL ACCORDING TO PLANNING LEVEL

STRATEGIC
CONTROL
(CONTROL OF
STRATEGY)

MANAGEMENT CONTROL
(CONTROL OF TACTICS)

OPERATIONAL
(CONTROL OF OPERATIONS)

Management, or tactical, control: *Control that focuses on carrying out the subplans included in a given strategy.*

Is the strategy consistent with internal strengths and weaknesses? Does it exploit external opportunities and mitigate threats? Is it timely? Additional external factors to be considered include constituent demand, suppliers, customers, and level of risk. Ease or difficulty of implementation must also be considered.[59] After implementation, results are the focus of control.

MANAGEMENT CONTROL

Management, or **tactical, control** focuses on carrying out the subplans included in a given strategy. As noted in Chapter 7, from the viewpoint of a firm with numerous strategic business units, such as Martin Marietta, the sales and profitability levels of each of its SBUs would be used for tactical control. However, from the perspective of each of the SBUs, that information would be used for strategic control.

OPERATIONAL CONTROL

Operational control: *Control designed to ensure that operational actions are consistent with plans and objectives.*

Operational control is designed to ensure that operational actions are consistent with plans and objectives. It is concerned with individual or group performance appraisals and sometimes with project performance appraisals. These appraisals typically incorporate specific standards for an individual's or a group's job performance, such as quantity and quality levels. Most operational controls are concerned with daily, weekly, monthly, quarterly, or yearly activities. Companies are placing greater emphasis on operational control, as this chapter's Quality Management Challenge suggests, but sometimes this could be too much of a good thing. Why is this so?

Control of Economic Functions

MARKETING CONTROLS

Most efforts to control marketing focus on sales and service. While sales volume is the major concern, there is increasing concern for service as well. Marketing controls may also be concerned with providing information about competitors' efforts, various factors in the marketplace (such as customer preferences), margins, profits, and returns, among other areas.

Marketing controls function at every level of planning—strategic, tactical, and operational. Much of the information about sales volume and service is dependent on the performance of the sales staff. It is usually summarized for groups or departments in tactical and strategic terms. For example, a strategic objective calling for a sales increase of 5 percent in a given year might result in increases of 8 percent in a growing region and 3 percent in a less dynamic region. Individual sales goals might range from a 1 to 2 percent increase to a 10 to 12 percent increase. Performance would then be compared to these goals and necessary steps taken on the basis of the comparison.

FINANCIAL CONTROL

Many people believe that control is almost totally financial in nature. This is not true, but in most organizations financial controls are emphasized more than any other type of control. Top management is certainly interested in "the numbers." Bottom-line results are what most investors, analysts, and managers use to determine whether objectives have been achieved. Marketing, operations, human resources, and information management decisions must all be translated into financial results. Much of the next chapter discusses financial-control reports such as profits, balance sheets, income statements, and ratio analyses.

OPERATIONS CONTROLS

Firms like Apple Computer consider operations controls essential to differentiation and cost strategies. In recent years, operations controls have focused on efficiency and quality. Purchasing, scheduling, and materials controls have also been emphasized, and just-in-time inventory programs have been viewed as increasingly important as a means of competing effectively with foreign firms. Operational control occurs in both service and manufacturing operations. The inputs, transformation process, and outputs differ, but in each situation control points must be determined, performance measured and compared against the standard, and corrective actions taken. **Continuous improvement** in products and/or services has become an especially critical aspect of operations control in recent years. Chapter 20 discusses operations control in more detail.[60]

Continuous improvement: Programs designed to produce continuous improvement in products and/or services.

HUMAN RESOURCES MANAGEMENT (HRM)

Control of human resources occurs throughout the organization. The HRM department focuses on issues such as recruitment, selection, training and development, compensation and benefits, safety and health, equal employment opportunity, labor relations, and employee evaluation and control. Front-line supervisors are primarily responsible for administering policies, rules, and procedures. All managers are involved to some degree, however. The key concerns include productivity levels, quality, innovation, service to the customer, absenteeism, turnovers, and tardiness.

Is There Such a Thing as Too Much Quality?

Quality has been one of the main competitive advantages of Japanese firms for many years. Now, however, it has become the focus of a growing debate among Japanese managers. Japanese CEOs and other top managers are asking if there is such a thing as too much quality. Is it possible to spend too much time and too much money producing too many good products?

"Obviously there's no such thing as overquality," asserts a high-ranking Sony executive. "Quality is good, period," he continues. Yet in an interview in a major Japanese magazine, Sony chairman Akio Morita helped initiate a campaign to slow the pace at which new, high-quality products were being introduced. He did so for several reasons. First, the objective of rapid introduction of high-quality products is increased market share. As Japanese firms gain market share, they alienate foreign competitors and many foreign governments. Second, much of what Japanese firms have accomplished in the areas of quality and rapid new-product development has been achieved at the expense of the employee, who seldom sees his family and often suffers extreme stress and illness. Moreover, customers do not always seek such high levels of quality. Many Tokyo shoppers, for example, would be willing to dispense with the elaborate gift wrapping that most major department stores include in the price of a good; they would prefer lower prices. Finally, many customers are mystified by the vast array of products available. They would appreciate something simpler than a Star Trek remote control for a VCR or TV.

The real question for the Japanese is how to redefine what quality means. And the answer has to begin with the customer. If the customer doesn't want gift wrapping or complex, unnecessary features in a VCR or a washing machine, these do not constitute quality.

Japanese consumers say that they would appreciate simpler products rather than high-tech products with obscure functions. Sony chairman Akio Morita helped initiate a campaign to slow the pace at which new products are introduced by Japanese firms.

SOURCE: Bill Powell, "Japan's Quality Quandary," *Newsweek* (June 15, 1992), p. 48.

INFORMATION MANAGEMENT CONTROLS

Control of information management is largely dependent on the design of control points in the management information system. The primary issues include whether managers are receiving the right information at the right time in order to make effective decisions. Information system audits and control reports are important ways of controlling information management. Many organizations are building decision support systems to aid managers in all areas of the firm. These have built-in information control points and are discussed in more detail in Chapter 20.

Control of Management Functions

At every level of the organization, planning, organizing, leading, controlling, and problem solving must be controlled to ensure that the objectives established for each of these functions are achieved. The control issues related to these functions were discussed in Chapters 1 and 5. Figure 1.6 portrays the management matrix and indicates these interdependent relationships.

Control and the Changing Managerial Environment

The future holds increasing levels of uncertainty and complexity for most organizations. In the past, the control systems and methods described in this chapter have, for the most part, functioned in environments that were reasonably stable and often not very complex. New control models will be necessary for the future. The clan and adhocracy systems, for example, seem to work well in certain types of changeful environments, such as automobiles and electronics, as well as in environments that are more stable and less complex, such as insurance and nursing homes. We can expect to see greater use of these systems, or variations of them. Conversely, some companies, by applying technology (especially computers), have been able to continue to use bureaucratic control systems, although not in isolation. (Cadillac, for example, uses both clan and bureaucratic control.) There is substantial evidence that firms should move toward more individual and group control—that is, to more self-control—in complex situations. Yet there is also evidence that bureaucratic control, with response times speeded up by computerized information systems, may be even more satisfactory.[61]

Control as a Problem-Solving Process

As can be seen in Figure 18.7, controlling is a problem-solving process, paralleling the problem-solving processes discussed in earlier chapters. The primary difference is that the control model makes use of simplified stages of the problem-solving process. All types and methods of control are involved. Managers make control-style choices throughout the process, but the essential consequences tend to be associated mostly with establishing standards, measuring performance, and taking actions that bridge gaps between standards and performance.

A manager operating in a changing environment might make control decisions following the pattern shown in Figure 18.7. He or she would use planning as the basis for action. Failure to reach standards or exceed objectives would

FIGURE 18.7 CONTROL AS PROBLEM SOLVING

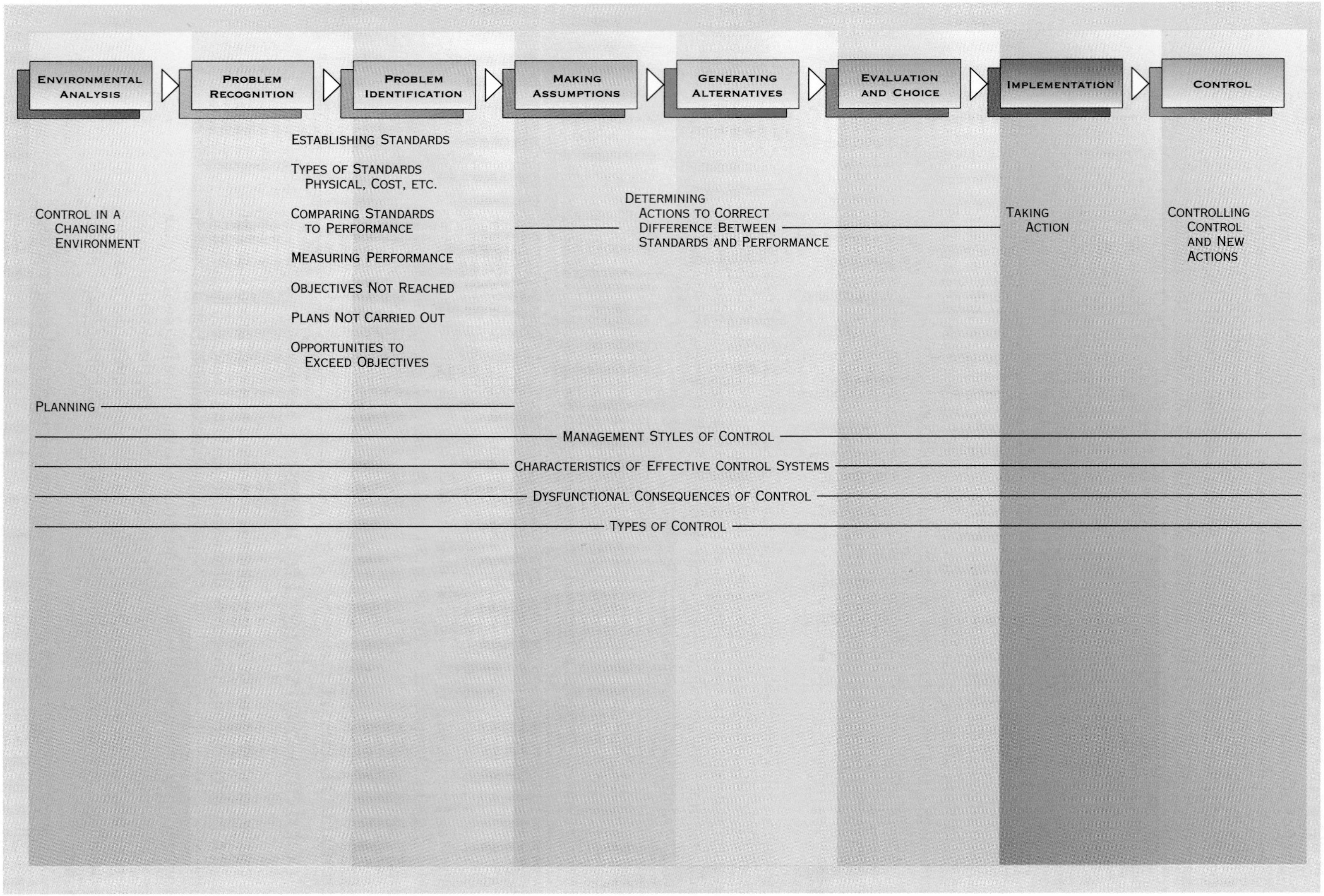

ENVIRONMENTAL ANALYSIS → PROBLEM RECOGNITION → PROBLEM IDENTIFICATION → MAKING ASSUMPTIONS → GENERATING ALTERNATIVES → EVALUATION AND CHOICE → IMPLEMENTATION → CONTROL

CONTROL IN A CHANGING ENVIRONMENT

Establishing Standards

Types of Standards Physical, Cost, etc.

Comparing Standards to Performance

Measuring Performance

Objectives Not Reached

Plans Not Carried Out

Opportunities to Exceed Objectives

Determining Actions to Correct Difference Between Standards and Performance

Taking Action

Controlling Control and New Actions

PLANNING

Management Styles of Control

Characteristics of Effective Control Systems

Dysfunctional Consequences of Control

Types of Control

help in recognizing and then identifying a problem. Following the identification of a problem, the manager would make assumptions and then take the actions necessary to correct the difference between standards and performance. The style of control, the characteristics of the available control systems, and other factors, such as the organization's culture, would affect the manager's problem-solving actions.

Summary

(Before reading this summary, look again at the objectives listed at the beginning of the chapter.)

1. Control is the systematic process by which managers ensure that the organization is reaching its objectives and carrying out plans in an effective and efficient manner. The control process consists of four steps: establishing performance objectives and standards, measuring actual performance, comparing actual performance to objectives and standards, and taking action based on the results of the comparison.

2. Controlling is important because it helps organizations achieve objectives, cope with complex environments, and overcome human limitations.

3. Planning and control are interdependent because controlling depends on the standards that result from the objectives established in planning. Planning, in turn, depends on the results of the control process.

4. There are three main types of management control styles: market control, bureaucratic control, and clan control.

5. Effective control systems measure performance at each level of the planning process. They are accepted by those who will enforce them and are characterized by flexibility, accuracy, and timeliness.

6. The dysfunctional aspects of control include game playing, resistance, inaccurate information, and rigid bureaucratic behavior.

7. Control types are defined by timing relative to the transformation process, by the level of plan involved, or by the economic or management function involved.

8. The primary trends in control are toward self-management and increasing use of clan control. Computers are also affecting the way control is carried out.

General Questions

1. Discuss the importance of control as a management function.

2. Describe the stages in the control process and discuss their use in an organization with which you are familiar.

3. Describe how control is related to the other management functions of planning, organizing, and leading.

4. Discuss how control might differ in marketing, finance, operations, HRM, and information management.

5. How do preaction, concurrent, and postaction controls differ?

6. How would controls differ at the strategic, tactical, and operational levels?

7. Describe the differences among the market, bureaucratic, clan, and adhocracy control styles. When might each style be used?

8. Discuss dysfunctional aspects of control that you have observed in an organization with which you are familiar.

9. Discuss why and how organizational control systems are changing.

Questions on the Management Challenge Features

ETHICAL MANAGEMENT CHALLENGE

1. There are disagreements as to whether Heer's actions were ethical (or legal). What do you think and why?

2. What about the behaviors of others, such as Baron Elie de Rothschild? Were they ethical?

GLOBAL MANAGEMENT CHALLENGE

1. From a control perspective, why did this event occur?

2. What could have been done to prevent it?

MANAGEMENT CHALLENGE

1. How does S-K-I use concurrent control?

2. How could such a system be used in other businesses?

QUALITY MANAGEMENT CHALLENGE

1. Is there such a thing as too much quality? Explain your answer.

2. What actions are Japanese firms taking to solve their problems?

E P I L O G U E

The Challenger Tragedy

As a consequence of the Challenger tragedy, the investigation by the committee, and subsequent layoffs as a result of the two-and-a-half-year delay in shuttle launches, morale at the Kennedy Space Center was terrible. At least fifty major problems in rocket design had been uncovered in the investigation and had to be solved.

In September 1987, retired Air Force General Forrest McCartney assumed control of the Kennedy Space Center. He was the first military officer to head the center, and many observers feared that he would destroy the open and creative environment necessary to solve the problems and move the space program forward. The skeptics were wrong. McCartney had a folksy, low-key, but very demanding style. He restored morale and confidence by paying close attention to details. He worked with employees and showed them that he cared

about every problem, especially theirs. He practiced management by wandering around and talking to people. This was in striking contrast to his predecessor's hands-off approach.

McCartney's approach differed in other ways as well. He held daily 7:30 A.M. meetings for the whole staff; his predecessor had held such meetings only every two weeks. He supervised the rewriting of one hundred thousand pages of documentation for instructions outlining how to perform shuttle-related work. He demanded accountability. He arranged for all the workers to be retrained and involved in formulating an action program.

Before McCartney took over, safety personnel had followed the normal chain of command. Now they are outside the chain of command, and the safety director reports directly to McCartney.

DISCUSSION QUESTIONS

1. Why was a new control style needed?

2. Why was the new style more effective than the old one?

Controlling Paperwork

Doug Harper was an industrial engineer in a large aerospace manufacturing organization. Because of increased competition, the firm felt that it had to cut costs. Top management recognized that there was an excess amount of paperwork at all levels of the organization. Harper was asked to head a seven-member task force to assess the situation and make recommendations for solving whatever problems were uncovered.

The task force decided to survey each middle and first-line manager. The managers were asked to complete a form indicating the reports they filled out, how long they took to complete them, and to whom they were sent. They were asked to complete another form indicating which reports they received and how useful they were. No such analysis of the firm's reporting systems had ever been undertaken. An elaborate computer program was designed to help tabulate the results for the firm's two thousand managers.

DISCUSSION QUESTIONS

1. What results would you expect from such a survey? Why?
2. The survey discovered that, on average, 30 percent of a manager's time was spent writing reports, of which only 15 percent were ever used. What are the implications for control? For cost cutting? For efficiency?
3. How does a situation like the one described here develop?

What Is Cheating?

MANAGE YOURSELF

Cheating is a problem in many universities and colleges. Many schools have honor codes and codes of ethics for students. Students must sign a pledge on their tests, papers, and other graded materials such as projects. A typical pledge is "I have neither received nor given help in creating the specifics of this paper [or test]. I swear that this is my own work." Usually, a student honor council is designated to handle cases of suspected cheating.

Unfortunately, an honor system often is not enough; some students still cheat. What kinds of controls can be used to solve this problem? Your instructor will divide the class into small groups. Each group will devise a system of control to prevent cheating at your university or college. After a specified period, the groups will be asked to report their findings to the class. (*Note:* Before developing a control system, the group needs to define what exactly is meant by cheating.)

"Nearly $100 billion in deposits are gone, with no one but the public to pay." [The actual cost of the savings and loan bail-out is estimated at close to $500 billion.]

—Jane Bryant Quinn
Editor
U.S. News & World Report

"In today's environment we don't think that the numbers really tell the story."

—Patrick S. Parker
Chairman
Parker-Hannifin Corp.

Management Control Systems

When you have read this chapter you should be able to:

1. Discuss the importance of control systems and techniques.
2. Review the core control systems according to the Daft/Macintosh model.
3. Indicate the differences among strategic, management/tactical, and operational control systems.
4. Describe the types of budgets.
5. Identify the role played by each of the various responsibility centers and discuss how control differs in each.
6. Indicate how the balance sheet, income statement, and funds flow analysis might be used in control.
7. Discuss the use of ratio analysis and return on investment.
8. List the various uses of cost analysis.
9. Describe how financial audits, management audits, and strategic audits might be used in control.
0. Describe how control is changing.
1. Discuss the use of performance appraisals in control.
2. Indicate how MBO, disciplinary systems, quality control, and operations controls are used.

MANAGEMENT CHALLENGES DISCUSSED IN THIS CHAPTER:

 Accelerating rates of change.

 Increasing levels of competition.

 Increasing globalization of business.

 Complexity of the managerial environment.

One of a Kind

It is refreshing in this era of bank failures to find a bank whose share of the market, total assets, and return on assets are all increasing. And it is even more refreshing to find that the same bank values local control and autonomy, personal innovation, and quality customer service.

The bank described here is Banc One Corporation, with headquarters in Columbus, Ohio, and branches in eleven mid- and far-western states. Structured as an affiliation of independently chartered banks, with state holding companies when the number of affiliates in a state warrants one, the $61 billion (in assets) bank has increased its earnings per share every year for the past twenty-four years and has tripled its assets since 1986, mainly through acquisitions. Keeping everyone in step in the hundreds of branches is achieved by the use of "blueprints"—policies and training programs that outline services and credit evaluation procedures.

While the central headquarters develops overall policy, programs, and services and provides a centralized data and information system, the local banks are responsible for formulating their own business plans, controlling personnel and lending, determining pricing, and performing marketing functions based on the local conditions. The entire organization uses the bank's Management Information and Control System (MICS) software to conduct continuous monitoring of the business by headquarters and by other branches and banks within the system. This allows for the distribution of risk and power while pooling expertise for major decisions,

which are often made by consensus. Affiliated banks are alerted to new opportunities and anomalies are identified to a much greater extent than was possible when the banks were completely independent.

Often at the forefront of technology (it installed the first ATM in the United States in 1971), Banc One has worked with Electronic Data Systems of Dallas, Texas, to produce the Strategic Banking System™ (SBS) integrated banking system. SBS is intended to allow member banks, as well as banks outside the United States to which Banc One will sell the system, to maintain internal control of key banking processes instead of farming them out to outsiders. With Andersen Consulting, Banc One has built a state-of-the-art credit-card processing system called TRIUMPH®, which it has made available to a limited number of domestic clients. And, together with three other Ohio-Pennsylvania regional banks, Banc One has formed Electronic Payment Services (EPS) to provide speedy, economical processing of electronic point-of-sale data by linking them to automated teller machines (ATMs).

Banc One's leadership in information control is a double-edged sword: Not only does the bank have superior control of its own operations, but it also has a product it can sell to institutions outside its immediate market area.

SOURCES: 1992 Annual Report, Banc One Corporation, Columbus, Ohio; Katherine Burger, "Profit Through Paradox," *Bank Systems & Technology,* (April 4, 1990), pp. 34–36; and Steve Cocheo, "What's So Good About Banc One?" *ABA Banking Journal* (July 1991), pp. 54–58.

C ontrol systems exist for all four of the control strategies discussed in the preceding chapter: the market, bureaucratic, clan, and adhocracy strategies. This chapter focuses primarily on the formal management control systems found in organizations. It explores the six core bureaucratic control systems involved at each of the several levels of the organization, as shown in Figure 19.1, and reviews associated secondary systems that can be employed at each of these levels. The changing nature of control is also reviewed.

Core Control Systems

Figure 19.1 presents the core control systems used by top- and middle-level management in organizations. At the strategic level, the strategic plan, financial analysis, and long-range financial plan are used by top managers for strategy formulation. The operating budget, statistical reports, performance appraisal systems, and policies and procedures are used by middle managers for departmental control and strategy implementation[1] and may also be used in the transformation process at the operational level.[2] (A study by William G. Ouchi and M. A. Maguire suggests, however, that at the operational level, control is usually accomplished through personal influence and surveillance or through output data and records—a results orientation, as shown in Figure 19.1.)[3] Note that while Figure 19.1 represents the most comprehensive view of control systems developed to date, control practices are changing rapidly as the managerial environment changes.[4]

Brief descriptions of the six core bureaucratic control systems follow:

1. *The strategic plan:* As used here, the **strategic plan** is the business unit's principal competitive strategy—its business strategy as defined in Chapter 7. It contains major objectives and plans for reaching those objectives. The term *strategic plan* is actually somewhat of a misnomer. There can be several strategic objectives and several strategies. From a control perspective, the objectives

Strategic plan: As used here, a business unit's principal competitive or business strategy.

Financial analysis, which produces important information such as return on investment, profit margins, and earnings per share, is a form of control occurring at the strategic level.

FIGURE 19.1 CORE CONTROL SYSTEMS

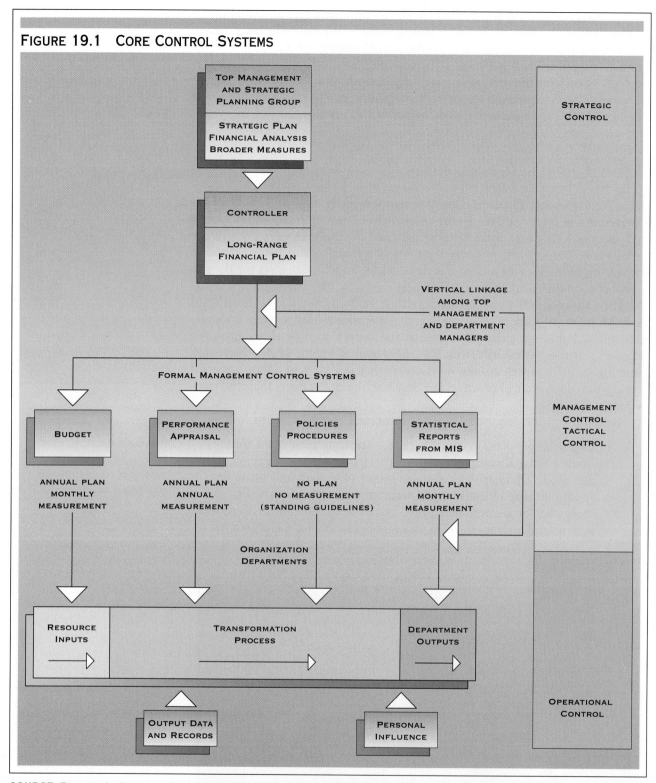

SOURCE: RICHARD L. DAFT AND NORMAN D. MACINTOSH, "THE NATURE AND USE OF FORMAL CONTROL SYSTEMS FOR MANAGEMENT CONTROL AND STRATEGY IMPLEMENTATION," JOURNAL OF MANAGEMENT (1984) NO. 1, P. 60, ADAPTED BY PERMISSION.

toward which these strategies are directed are the principal control mechanisms. As discussed in Chapter 6, objectives might include profits, sales, margins on sales, and growth rates. Financial analysis, which produces important information such as return on investment, profit margins, and earnings per share, may be a dominant form of control at the strategic level. Recently there has been greater use of broader, nonquantitative standards and measurements, such as quality measurements, customer satisfaction indices, and the results of employee satisfaction surveys.[5] As firms move toward new organizational designs, such as cross-functional teams and process-based structures, new measures will be necessary.[6]

2. *The long-range financial plan:* The **long-range financial plan** is essentially a one- to five-year forecast of the organization's anticipated financial performance if the strategy is followed and succeeds to the degree believed necessary.[7] "Pro forma," or forecasted, financial income statements, balance sheets, and cash flows are its principal components. Departmental breakouts may be included. All major companies use both strategies and a financial forecast for strategic control purposes.

Long-range financial plan: A one- to five-year forecast of the organization's anticipated financial performance if the strategy is followed and succeeds to the degree believed necessary.

3. *The operating budget:* The **operating budget** is a financial statement for the forthcoming year, matching revenues and expenses and calculating anticipated profits or losses. Sometimes operating budgets cover a period of eighteen months or two years. In most organizations, the operating budget is composed of a series of sub-budgets. The budget is usually monitored on a monthly, or at least quarterly, basis.

Operating budget: A financial statement for the forthcoming year, matching revenues and expenses and calculating anticipated profits or losses.

4. *Performance appraisals:* **A performance appraisal** is the organization's way of formally evaluating the performance of its employees, including managers. Many companies use some type of management by objectives, results, and rewards system (MBORR) as a basis for performance appraisal. Group evaluations are becoming more common.

Performance appraisal: A formal evaluation of an employee's performance.

5. *Statistical reports:* **Statistical reports** make available information that is used to manage both the transformation process and the interrelationships among units of the organization. Such reports may contain labor efficiency rates, attendance figures, quality control rejects, bookings, accounts payable, accounts receivable, sales reports, the amount of scrap generated, the quality of inputs, and team productivity. This information is found in the organization's management information system (MIS), to be discussed in more detail in Chapter 20.

Statistical reports: Information used to manage both the transformation process and the interrelationships among units of the organization.

6. *Policies and procedures:* **Policies** are general guidelines for taking action. **Procedures** are a set of specific steps to perform a job. Managers use both to ensure that workers perform as well as possible. Normally, procedures are developed for each job. Policies guide managerial actions so that managers do not have to make decisions in recurring situations. The decision to be made is indicated by the policy.

Policies: General guidelines for action.

Procedures: A set of specific steps for performing a job.

Different kinds of information are used for control at the upper levels and at the organization's middle and lower levels. At the upper levels, control information has historically been primarily financial, whereas at the middle and lower levels it has been primarily nonfinancial.[8] This pattern is changing as broader measures are becoming more widely used at the upper levels. At the middle and lower levels, performance appraisals, procedures, and performance-related measures such as quality and efficiency are examined. The budget is used to allocate resources to departments, but the other three tactical control systems are normally based on nonfinancial data. Operational control is also largely nonfinancial, focusing on output measurements and day-to-day interpersonal relationships.

Strategic Control Systems

From a control perspective, the primary concerns at the strategic level are achieving the objectives of the strategic plan(s) and making appropriate use of the financial resources allocated by the long-range financial plan. Most frequently, the results associated with accomplishing objectives are expressed in financial terms and reported in an organization's financial statements: the balance sheet, income statement, and funds flow analysis. The validity of these statements is tested through financial audits. Related analyses of these results focus on ratio analysis or other types of financial analysis.

Cost analysis of operations occasionally plays a major role in strategic control. Cost analysis is especially important when a low-cost strategy is being used.[9] For example, Japanese automobile manufacturers have competed in the United States on the basis of low cost and high quality. In the late 1980s, the

INNOVATION MANAGEMENT CHALLENGE

The Impact of Overcontrol on Creativity

The regimentation characteristic of Japanese firms has been a clear asset in Japan's rush to industrial success. But future success may depend on loosening the reins and allowing more creativity. Basic laboratory research has lagged in Japan compared to the United States. Historically, the Japanese have imitated innovative U.S. products and learned how to make them more cheaply and with higher quality. But they have never been skilled at developing new products.

Yoshihide Tsujimoto, a molecular biologist, left Japan for the freedom of American laboratories. At thirty-four, he supervises five researchers and chooses the research projects he will pursue. He could never have done this in Japan; there he would still be working for a full professor on projects determined by the professor. He complains that the Japanese scientific establishment "idolizes seniority, loathes individualism, and muzzles debate."

Upper-level managers in Japanese organizations, as well as in the government, are beginning to realize that something must change if Japan's industrial growth is to continue. Planners at the Ministry of International Trade and Industry warn that the West will not continue to provide Japan with the fruits of its research. Japanese firms must promote greater creativity. The government is initiating programs to foster creativity and change the centuries-old habits of the scientific establishment. But change will not come easily. Some of the most revered Japanese practices, such as lifetime employment, tend to stifle creativity. There is little opportunity for travel; there are few research grants; and there is little chance of advancement. It is clear that Japan has a long way to go to change its scientific establishment. But unless Japan can change its cultural control systems to allow greater creativity, its economic growth may come to a halt. It has in fact stagnated in the early 1990s.

value of the yen became significantly higher relative to that of the dollar. Consequently, the Japanese engaged in major cost-cutting programs in manufacturing to maintain their cost advantage. However, because reducing costs is used as a motivational device in Japanese firms, those firms use different, more strategically oriented cost systems than do U.S. firms. Many U.S. firms are changing their cost systems so that they can be used more effectively in strategic decision making.[10]

Key results are often expressed in terms of market share, new products developed, and similar measures. A few firms examine themselves from an externally focused, environmentally based strategic perspective. Using social audits or stakeholder audits, for instance, a company might examine its impact on environmental pollution. Broader forms of information, such as quality and customer satisfaction, are also being used.

Strategic control as practiced in the West is largely bureaucratic and formal. By contrast, Japanese firms control strategy through clan or cultural mechanisms, in addition to bureaucratic systems.[11] Sometimes, however, these clan-focused control systems can be as "bureaucratic" as bureaucratic controls, as this chapter's Innovation Management Challenge suggests.

Computer-based strategic control and decision support systems intended for use by executives are becoming more widely available.[12] For example, top

These musicians are typical of the many Japanese who are rebelling against the regimentation of their society. Many observers believe that only through such rebellion, especially against overly bureaucratized research and development programs, can Japan become sufficiently innovative to lead the world in new-product development.

SOURCE: Stephen Kreider Yoder, "Stifled Scholars: Japan's Scientists Find Pure Research Suffers Under Rigid Lifestyle," *Wall Street Journal* (October 31, 1988), pp. A1, A6.

managers at Kraft Inc.'s Grocery Products Group used to face an information nightmare—500 products and 15 separate brands in 33,000 grocery stores. At 3:00 P.M. each day, executives would receive stacks of paper containing the information they needed to determine the previous day's sales performance. Now the same information is available on the computer at 8:30 A.M., sorted by product line and geographic region.[13] (See Chapter 20 for a fuller discussion of the use of information systems in control.)

Financial Analysis

Financial analysis: An examination of the organization's financial statements and the various ratios derived from information on its balance sheet and income statement.

Balance sheet: A financial statement that reveals the condition of the company at a given point in time.

Income statement: A financial statement that shows the condition of the company for a specified period.

Financial analysis consists primarily of examining the organization's financial statements and the various ratios derived from information on its balance sheet and income statement.[14] The **balance sheet** reveals the company's condition at a given point in time. The **income statement** shows its condition for a specified period. The balance sheet looks at assets, liabilities, and equities. The income statement looks at revenues, expenses, and profits or losses. Examples of these statements for the Georgia-Pacific Corporation, a paper products company, are shown in Figures 19.2 and 19.3.

On the balance sheet, the company's total assets are equal to the total of its liabilities and owner's equity. Assets are typically divided into current and long-term or fixed categories, liabilities into short-term and long-term categories. Various types of equities may be listed, but the most frequently found types are common stock and retained earnings.

Income statements typically begin with revenue figures. Revenues, mainly sales, are offset by various types of expenses. Next comes operating income. Taxes are deducted from that amount to yield net income, the so-called bottom line. When managers speak of a bottom-line orientation, this is the number they have in mind. The implication is that all of an organization's actions should be designed to increase net income after taxes, at least in the long term.

FIGURE 19.2   STATEMENTS OF INCOME

GEORGIA-PACIFIC CORPORATION AND SUBSIDIARIES

(MILLIONS. EXCEPT PER SHARE AMOUNTS)	YEAR ENDED DECEMBER 31		
	1991	1990	1989
NET SALES	$11,524	$12,665	$10,171
COSTS AND EXPENSES			
COST OF SALES	9,218	9,738	7,621
SELLING, GENERAL AND ADMINISTRATIVE	1,083	951	689
DEPRECIATION AND DEPLETION	724	699	514
INTEREST	656	606	260
OTHER INCOME	(344)	(48)	—
TOTAL COSTS AND EXPENSES	11,337	11,946	9,084
INCOME BEFORE INCOME TAXES AND ACCOUNTING CHANGES	187	719	1,087
PROVISION FOR INCOME TAXES	266	354	426
INCOME (LOSS) BEFORE ACCOUNTING CHANGES	(79)	365	661
CUMULATIVE EFFECT OF ACCOUNTING CHANGES, NET OF TAXES	(63)	—	—
NET INCOME (LOSS)	$ (142)	$ 365	$ 661
PER SHARE:			
INCOME (LOSS) BEFORE ACCOUNTING CHANGES	$ (.92)	$ 4.28	$ 7.42
CUMULATIVE EFFECT OF ACCOUNTING CHANGES	(.73)	—	—
NET INCOME (LOSS)	$ (1.65)	$ 4.28	$ 7.42
AVERAGE NUMBER OF SHARES OUTSTANDING	85.8	85.3	89.1

FIGURE 19.3 BALANCE SHEETS

GEORGIA-PACIFIC CORPORATION AND SUBSIDIARIES

(MILLIONS, EXCEPT SHARES AND PER SHARE AMOUNTS)	DECEMBER 31 1991	1990
ASSETS		
CURRENT ASSETS		
CASH	$ 48	$ 58
RECEIVABLES, LESS ALLOWANCES OF $36 AND $39	228	409
INVENTORIES		
RAW MATERIALS	329	379
FINISHED GOODS	779	760
SUPPLIES	284	238
LIFO RESERVE	(164)	(168)
TOTAL INVENTORIES	1,228	1,209
OTHER CURRENT ASSETS	58	90
TOTAL CURRENT ASSETS	1,562	1,766
TIMBER AND TIMBERLANDS, NET	1,377	1,630
PROPERTY, PLANT AND EQUIPMENT		
LAND AND IMPROVEMENTS	201	208
BUILDINGS	940	931
MACHINERY AND EQUIPMENT	8,580	8,416
CONSTRUCTION IN PROGRESS	54	493
TOTAL PROPERTY, PLANT AND EQUIPMENT, AT COST	9,775	10,048
ACCUMULATED DEPRECIATION	(4,208)	(3,707)
PROPERTY, PLANT AND EQUIPMENT, NET	5,567	6,341
GOODWILL	1,949	2,042
OTHER ASSETS	167	281
TOTAL ASSETS	$ 10,622	$ 12,060
LIABILITIES AND SHAREHOLDERS' EQUITY		
CURRENT LIABILITIES		
BANK OVERDRAFTS, NET	$ 171	$ 136
COMMERCIAL PAPER AND OTHER SHORT-TERM NOTES	1.210	984
CURRENT PORTION OF LONG-TERM DEBT	346	324
ACCOUNTS PAYABLE	488	550
ACCRUED COMPENSATION	153	160
ACCRUED INTEREST	112	140
OTHER CURRENT LIABILITIES	242	241
TOTAL CURRENT LIABILITIES	2,722	2,535
LONG-TERM DEBT, EXCLUDING CURRENT PORTION	3,743	5,218
OTHER LONG-TERM LIABILITIES	626	404
DEFERRED INCOME TAXES	795	928
SHAREHOLDERS' EQUITY		
COMMON STOCK, PAR VALUE $.80; AUTHORIZED 150,000,000 SHARES; 87,421,000 AND 86,704,000 SHARES ISSUED AND OUTSTANDING	70	69
ADDITIONAL PAID-IN CAPITAL	1,045	995
RETAINED EARNINGS	1,657	1,939
LONG-TERM INCENTIVE PLAN DEFERRED COMPENSATION	(28)	(30)
OTHER	(8)	2
TOTAL SHAREHOLDERS' EQUITY	2,736	2,975
TOTAL LIABILITIES AND SHAREHOLDERS' EQUITY	$10,622	$12,060

A third statement that assists in controlling operations and finances is the **cash flow statement.** It indicates the sources and uses of cash. Typical sources of cash include operating income, depreciation, increased liabilities, and financing activities such as borrowing funds or issuing equity. Typical uses include increases in current assets—inventories and receivables—and purchases of capital assets. Monitoring cash flows is very important to a firm's continued operation. For example, because it is usually necessary to spend large amounts long before the anticipated revenues become available, firms may find themselves short of cash; or they may not generate enough revenues from sales to finance planned expansions, making it necessary to borrow.

Cash flow statement: A statement of the sources and uses of cash, used in controlling operations and finances.

Georgia-Pacific Corporation's success stems in part from its ability to manage large-scale capital equipment successfully.

Financial statement analysis takes on new meaning when applied to firms based in other countries. Accounting standards vary from country to country, and different aspects of financial stability are stressed. For example, U.S. firms focus on income while British firms prefer to build asset bases (e.g., holdings of cash and securities). Japanese firms have less rigid accounting standards than U.S. firms, and financial reports are less consistent from firm to firm.[15]

Ratio Analysis

By examining the ratios between certain figures included on the income statement and the balance sheet, managers may be able to discern the organization's financial condition. There are four principal types of ratios: liquidity, leverage, activity, and profitability. Several other ratios are associated with each of these types. (See Table 19.1.) In the following paragraphs, we discuss the major types of ratios.

LIQUIDITY

Current ratio: A measure of the firm's liquidity—that is, its ability to handle short-term debts and liabilities. It is found by dividing current assets by current liabilities.

Liquidity ratios are concerned with the organization's ability to meet its current debt. A key liquidity ratio is the **current ratio,** which measures the liquidity of the firm—that is, its ability to handle short-term debts and liabilities. It is found by dividing current assets by current liabilities. The result shows how many dollars of current assets exist per dollar of current liabilities. A rule of thumb for manufacturing firms is to maintain a current ratio of at least 2:1 (assets to liabilities), but each firm must compare its position with the industry average. Service firms require a lower current ratio because they have no inventories.[16]

LEVERAGE

Debt-to-total-assets ratio: A leverage ratio that indicates the firm's ability to handle its debts. It is found by dividing total debt by total assets.

Leverage ratios are concerned with a firm's utilization of debt, the relationship of its debt to total assets, and its ability to pay its interest charges. The **debt-to-total-assets ratio** equals total debt (long term) divided by total assets. It is repre-

TABLE 19.1 Selected Financial Ratio Analysis—1992

Ratio	Formula for Calculation	Calculation
Liquidity Current	$\dfrac{\text{Current assets}}{\text{Current liabilities}}$	$\dfrac{\$1,562,000}{\$2,722,000} = .57$ times
Leverage Debt to total assets	$\dfrac{\text{Total debt}}{\text{Total assets}}$	$\dfrac{\$3,743,000}{\$10,622,000} = 35$ percent
Activity Inventory turnover	$\dfrac{\text{Sales}}{\text{Inventory}}$	$\dfrac{\$11,524,000}{\$1,228,000} = 9.4$ times
Profitability Return on total assets	$\dfrac{\text{Net profit after taxes}}{\text{Total assets}}$	$\dfrac{\$(79,000)}{\$10,662,000} = -0.7$ percent

sented as a percentage. Thus, a ratio of 0.50 means that the firm's debt is equal to 50 percent of the value of its assets. Generally, the lower this percentage the better: A high ratio could mean that the firm has little ability to withstand losses. A low ratio indicates that the firm has a buffer of funds available to pay creditors should it become insolvent.

ACTIVITY

The principal concern of activity ratios is to determine how well assets are being utilized. An important activity ratio is the **inventory turnover ratio.** Dividing sales (in dollars) by inventory (in dollars) indicates how many times per year the firm has been able to sell its inventory. The average inventory turnover ratio for U.S. companies is 9, but this figure can vary. More expensive items—such as automobiles, major appliances, and jewelry—normally have lower turnover rates than less expensive items.

Inventory turnover ratio: An activity ratio that shows how well assets are being utilized. It is found by dividing sales by inventory.

PROFITABILITY

The principal concern of profitability ratios is the success of the firm in earning profits, as measured by several tests. An important profitability ratio is **return on total assets** (return on investment), a percentage that is determined by dividing net profit after taxes by total assets. This percentage is compared with the industry average and, when used in conjunction with the firm's profit margin, is an indicator of its earning power. It shows the rate of return the firm is getting per dollar invested in assets.

Return on total assets: A profitability ratio that indicates the success of the firm in earning profits. It is found by dividing net profits after taxes by total assets.

Return on Investment (ROI)

Return on investment (ROI) is a ratio that indicates the organization's income after taxes, relative to its total assets. This provides a *short-term* measure of how well the organization is performing. It shows how well the company has used its assets to produce income. As shown in Figure 19.4, return on investment is itself derived from two ratios, each of which consists of several inputs that can be analyzed in more detail to determine their impacts on ROI. By analyzing each of

Return on investment (ROI): A ratio that indicates the organization's income after taxes relative to its total assets. ROA = ROI

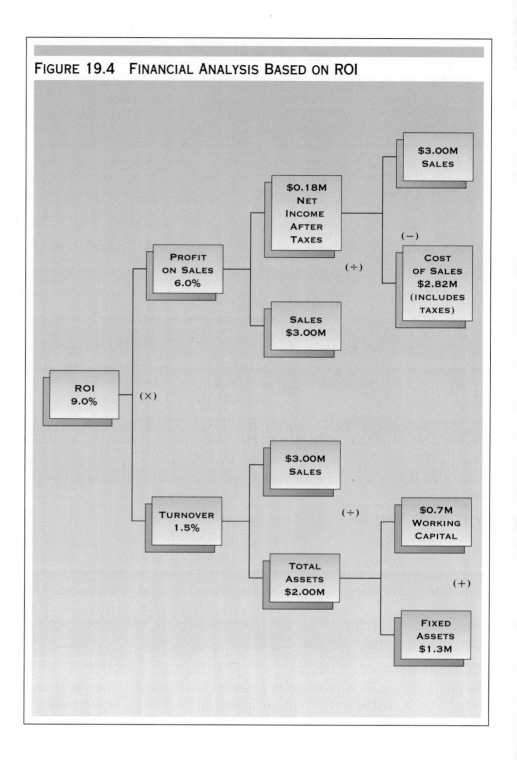

FIGURE 19.4   FINANCIAL ANALYSIS BASED ON ROI

these components of ROI, the organization can determine why a particular operation is effective or ineffective.

Consider an example. In one year, a small manufacturing company showed a substantially reduced ROI. Upon further examination, it became obvious that net income had been reduced—the cost of sales was high as a result of extremely high operating expenses in comparison to previous years. Just before that operating period, the production manager had resigned and had not been replaced. The owner was very sales oriented and had no trouble selling products, but with no one managing production, expenses were running out of control. The owner did not realize how important production management was. His desire to save

$5,000 (by offering a salary below what candidates for the job of production manager were asking) probably cost him $200,000 in profits. Once a new production manager was hired, operating expenses returned to their former lower levels and ROI improved. The decision to hire a manager was prompted by ROI analysis.

A number of strategic problems, as well as operating decisions and policies, affect ROI and its components. For example, the decision to grow rapidly or to cut costs can greatly affect ROI. Managers must be aware of the potential effects of their decisions on ROI.

One drawback of ROI is that it can be manipulated. For example, R&D expenses can be reduced to increase ROI in the short term, but such actions might harm ROI in the long term.[17] Moreover, a focus on ROI causes managers to take a short-term perspective, a common criticism of U.S. strategists. Still, this ratio offers a good, simple measure by which to compare the performance of different firms or the same firm in different periods.

Shareholder Value

Of increasing concern to managers is the concept of **shareholder value,** the belief that a company's performance should be measured in terms of how much shareholders gain from what the business does. The price of the company's stock is often used to reflect this value. Other, more complicated measures are also used. One of the reasons that corporate raiders were prominent in the 1980s was that shareholders were not benefiting significantly from their investments. Raiders often took over a company and improved its performance; stock prices rose dramatically as a consequence.

Historically, most measures of corporate performance, such as ROI, have been accounting oriented. Measures of shareholder value can be designed to cause CEOs and other top managers to look to the future.[18] Francis V. McCrory and Peter G. Gerstberger suggest that firms should use a new formula to account for shareholder value. Net cash flows over the expected life of the business could be discounted by some appropriate rate to give the value of the firm. They believe that comparisons of this value for various investments would yield a truer measure of shareholder value.[19]

Shareholder value: The belief that a company's performance should be measured in terms of how much shareholders gain from what the business does.

Cost Accounting

One of the objectives of any organization is the efficient use of resources. Cost accounting allows organizations to achieve that objective. It is almost impossible to make pertinent decisions on issues such as whether to take on a new product line or project without accurate cost information. Product costing is important for determining efficiency, allocating resources, pricing production, making long-range capacity decisions, making investment decisions, budgeting, and measuring divisional performance. The linkages between planning and cost control are critical. Managers cannot determine whether plans have been implemented successfully without knowing the costs of the operation. Similarly, they cannot plan if they do not know what an operation will cost.

Historically, a major use of cost information was to assign value to inventory for financial and tax statements; however, cost systems designed to assign value to inventory do not give managers the type of information they need to ensure that resources are used efficiently and to measure product costs.[20] Companies have attempted to change their systems to provide additional information, but more and more companies are realizing that they need two, perhaps even three, cost-control systems.[21] A high level of cost control is especially important in today's highly competitive market environment.

To be cost competitive, companies must be able to determine future product costs in order to gauge the long-term advisability of launching a product. Consequently, a few firms have developed whole new cost accounting systems. Traditionally, for example, organizations automated in order to cut costs. Now they can make different investment decisions based on anticipated costs. This type of decision making requires a new approach to cost accounting, including examining variables external to the organization. Investment decisions may be made not just to save on labor costs but to improve quality, reduce inventory levels, add flexibility, cut lead times, and generally provide more customer services.[22] Firms like Parker-Hannifin Corporation, a major manufacturer of motion controls such as hydraulics and pneumatics, have significantly changed their cost accounting systems in order to make better strategic decisions.

Consulting firms, such as Computer-Aided Manufacturing International, Inc., are promoting new accounting systems that some experts believe may revolutionize the way companies figure costs.[23] At the heart of the new systems is **activity-based costing** (ABC). ABC focuses on identifying the real costs of a product by making more accurate allocations of overhead costs, identifying and reducing cost drivers (factors that increase costs), and identifying activities that lead to value for the customer and eliminating those that do not.[24] When used by managers with a future cost perspective, ABC can be extremely beneficial.[25] This chapter's Global Management Challenge demonstrates how important such a perspective can be. It reveals how Japanese firms link product costs to strategic objectives.[26]

Financial Audits

Financial audits examine the organization's financial records and accounting systems.[27] An **internal audit** is performed by members of the organization. Large organizations like the U.S. Air Force, Lockheed Corporation, the Denver Post, John Deere Companies, Boise Cascade, and Boeing typically have a staff of

Activity-based costing (ABC): A focus on identifying the real costs of a product by making more accurate allocations of overhead costs, identifying and reducing cost drivers, and identifying the activities that lead to value for the customer and eliminating those that do not.

Internal audit: An examination of the organization's financial records and accounting systems performed by members of the organization.

Internal audits are performed by members of the organization, such as this auditor at Motorola. Audits focus on major accounts, major areas of decision making, and areas in which there is potential for error or intentional falsification.

Japanese Cost Accounting Practices

What's the best way to reckon how much something should cost? The process of setting a price is approached so differently in Japan that students of the process often feel that their analysis never gets to first base. "We don't keep track of what you're looking for," they are constantly told.

Cost accounting in Japan stands Western practice on its head. In the West, companies typically start by designing a new product. Then they contrive its marketing strategy. *Then* they calculate its cost. If the cost appears prohibitive, they redesign the product—or reconcile themselves to lower profits.

In Japan, the manufacturer begins by deciding on the cost the market is likely to accept. In other words, cost management is market driven. To estimate the cost of a new product, companies don't simply rely on prevailing engineering standards. Instead, they determine target costs by estimating a competitive market price that is usually well below prevailing costs—which are based on standard technologies and processes. Managers then direct designers, engineers, and eventually workers to meet the targets.

As one American analyst explains it, "We tend to build up a model of the product, determine what it's going to cost, and then ask whether we can sell it for that. The Japanese turn it around. They say, 'It's got to sell for X. Let's work backward to make sure we can achieve it.'"

This strategy gives Japanese manufacturers several advantages. Within companies, it allows employees to understand "how their work is translated into the numbers." In other words, the numbers that represent performance are numbers workers can readily grasp and affect: the time it takes to set up a particular manufacturing line, the amount of material wasted through worker error, or the percentage of parts rejected by purchasers.

Another advantage of the Japanese emphasis on target costs is that the people responsible for projecting and measuring those costs are not accountants—who have specialized training but often lack a feel for the product—but *cost engineers*. They often have experience in several departments, such as purchasing, design, and sales. They therefore bring a broad perspective and a unique ability to recognize cost-saving possibilities.

A third advantage of the Japanese system is that the emphasis is not on the individual product but on the portfolio of related products. Decisions are based on the performance of the portfolio as a whole. As one consultant puts it, the attitude is "We're in this business to win. If we believe it makes competitive sense to carry Product X, we will carry it. We will try our damnedest to make it profitable, but whether or not a product is profitable is not the nub of whether we'll be able to win in the overall business."

As an example, take the Sony Corporation's 1989 decision to develop a personal stereo component system even smaller than the so-called Pixy, then ubiquitous in college dorms. Forecasts for the new product, thought to have potential among slightly older customers, were unenthusiastic, but the company decided to take a chance, assuming that it could cover the launch with the higher-margin products in the same group. To Sony's surprise, the smaller version was a big hit with younger customers. Had Sony based its decisions on the product's *standalone* profitability, the new kid on the block would never have been born.

SOURCES: Ford S. Worthy, "Japan's Smart Secret Weapon," *Fortune* (August 12, 1991), pp. 71–75; and Toshiro Hiromoto, "Another Hidden Edge—Japanese Management Accounting," *Harvard Business Review* (July–August 1988), pp. 22–26.

An advantage of the Japanese emphasis on target costs is that the people responsible for projecting and measuring those costs are not accountants but "cost engineers," individuals who have experience in several departments, such as purchasing, design, and sales.

External audit: An audit conducted by individuals or firms outside the organization, typically by certified public accountants (CPAs).

individuals who audit the organization's statements of financial condition. An **external audit** is conducted by individuals or firms outside the organization, typically certified public accountants (CPAs) or CPA firms like Arthur Andersen, Arthur Young, and Kleinveld, Peat, Marwick, and Goerdeler. Only a selected percentage of transactions is examined in detail. Audits focus on major accounts, major areas of decision making, and areas in which there is potential for error or intentional falsification.[28]

Broader Forms of Strategic Control

Recognizing that financial controls alone are insufficient to measure organizational performance, organizations have been searching for additional measures that, when used in concert with financial measures, will more accurately portray the present and the firm's future strategic condition.[29] Professor Robert S. Kaplan and consultant David P. Norton suggest a technique known as the **balanced scorecard** to fulfill this measurement requirement. The scorecard contains four sets of measures: the financial perspective, the internal business perspective, the customer perspective, and the innovation and learning perspective.[30]

Balanced scorecard: A combination of four sets of measures, or perspectives: financial, internal business, customer, and innovation and learning; used to evaluate organizational performance.

The financial perspective indicates how the firm looks to shareholders. Typical concerns are profitability, growth, and shareholder value. The internal business perspective is concerned with what the firm must excel at in order to remain competitive. Key factors include core competencies (see Chapter 7), strategic capabilities, employee skills, and productivity. Because most firms now focus on customers, the customer perspective examines how the firm satisfies their needs. Items to be examined include time, quality, performance, and service. The innovation and learning perspective is concerned with whether the firm can continue to improve. Whereas the customer and internal perspectives tend to look at current situations, the innovation and learning perspective examines the firm's abilities to launch new products, improve processes, and create more value for customers. It also examines the firm's ability to learn.[31] The scorecard makes an important contribution to control of strategy because it measures future capabilities, not just results.

Other broad measures are the management audit and the strategic audit. These are comprehensive examinations of the firm. The **management audit** examines all facets of organizational activity. The **strategic audit** goes a step further and examines in detail the external environment and the organization's interface with it. The latter allows for a complete strengths, weaknesses, opportunities, and threats (SWOT) analysis. As with the scorecard approach, future capabilities are examined. These audits are extremely comprehensive, often involving several hundred different performance measures.[32] They involve the use of benchmarking and best-practices techniques to compare the firm's performance with that of its competitors.[33]

Management audit: An examination of all facets of organizational activity.

Strategic audit: A detailed examination of the external environment and the organization's interface with it.

Management/Tactical Control Systems

Whereas strategic control systems focus largely on total organizational performance, management/tactical control systems focus largely on controlling tactical plans or the budget for the entire organization. There are four principal management/tactical, or middle-management, control systems: budgets and responsibility centers, performance appraisals, statistical reports, and rules and procedures. In this section we will examine budgets and performance appraisals in detail.

Budgets and Responsibility Centers

The resource allocation process is carried out through budgets and responsibility centers. **Budgets** are quantitative statements that allocate resources to various units of the organization, usually for a period of one year or eighteen months. They are normally associated with operating plans, but they may also be drafted for longer-range plans. They help define the boundaries between strategic and tactical plans and between tactical and operational plans.

Budgets generally have three purposes: They help refine organizational objectives, allocate resources in the most effective manner, and promote efficient use of resources. They are stated in monetary terms and cover a specific period. They are usually based on proposals submitted by lower-level managers and reviewed and approved by upper-level managers. Budgets should be modified only under certain extenuating circumstances, such as a dramatic increase or decrease in sales or costs.[34]

The financial resource allocation process ties performance not only to objectives, but also to financial constraints identified by the long-term financial plan or shorter-term operating budget. Many large organizations and some smaller ones establish **responsibility centers** to facilitate long-term financial

Budgets: Quantitative statements that allocate resources to various units of the organization, usually for a period of one year or eighteen months.

Responsibility centers: Subunits of the organization to which resources are allocated for use in attaining specific objectives.

planning, identify responsibility accurately, motivate subordinates, aid in the budgetary process, and provide better control. Responsibility centers are sub-units of the organization to which resources are allocated for use in attaining specific objectives. There are four basic types of responsibility centers: revenue centers; cost or expense centers; profit centers; and investment centers.

REVENUE CENTERS

Revenue centers:
Responsibility centers controlled on the basis of sales of products or services.

Revenue centers are controlled on the basis of sales of products or services and are usually found in sales or marketing departments. No attempt is made to measure the inputs, or expenses, of such centers. Only outputs, or revenues, are measured, and the budget is based on that information. For example, the budget of a hotel's convention sales department will be based on the anticipated revenue generated by the department. Typically, this figure is based on an estimated number of customer contacts.

COST CENTERS

Cost (expense) centers:
Responsibility centers controlled on the basis of costs or expenses generated. Their budget is based on the cost of the inputs utilized in operations.

Cost (expense) centers are controlled on the basis of costs or expenses generated. Their budget is based on the cost of the inputs utilized in operations. A typical cost center for a boat manufacturer might be a manufacturing plant; for a software company, the programming staff might be a cost center.

PROFIT CENTERS

Profit centers:
Responsibility centers controlled on the basis of the difference between revenues and expenses— that is, profit.

Profit centers are controlled on the basis of the difference between revenues and expenses—that is, profit. The principal focus is on the amount of profit contributed to the organization. Large organizations like General Electric may have as many as three hundred profit centers. More and more organizations are attempting to create profit centers to encourage internal entrepreneurship, or intrapreneurship, in the belief that this will enhance competitiveness.[35]

INVESTMENT CENTERS

Investment centers:
Responsibility centers controlled on the basis of profit together with the amount of capital investment made to produce the profit.

Investment centers are controlled on the basis of profit together with the amount of capital investment made to produce the profit. The most commonly used control measure for investment centers is return on investment, obtained by dividing net profits by total assets. SBUs, as defined in Chapter 6, are typical investment centers and would include a company's major businesses, such as Westinghouse's Turbine Generator Division. They might also include less distinct businesses, such as the trust division of First Denver Bank.

Types of Budgets

There are many types of budgets. Most organizations have at least the following types: a master or summary budget for the entire organization, revenue and expense budgets, capital expenditure budgets, cash budgets, and nonmonetary input budgets.

THE MASTER BUDGET

Master budget: A summary statement of the organization's budgets, portraying sales, revenues, expenses, profits, capital employment, ROI, and the relationships among these and other items.

The **master budget** summarizes all of the organization's budgets. It portrays sales, revenues, expenses, profits, capital employment, return on investment, and the relationships among these and other items. The master budget is used to control the entire organization. It integrates the various revenue and expense budgets and capital expenditure budgets. Cash budgets are often derived from the master budget, and resource input budgets are often used in compiling it. Master budgets often cover periods of one year to eighteen months but may be created for a period of a few years.

REVENUE CENTERS ARE CONTROLLED ON THE BASIS OF SALES OF PRODUCTS OR SERVICES. TELEPHONE SALES REPRESENTATIVES WOULD BE PART OF A REVENUE CENTER BECAUSE THEY HELP BRING IN REVENUE FOR THE ORGANIZATION. IN CONTRAST, A COST CENTER IS CONTROLLED ON THE BASIS OF COSTS OR EXPENSES GENERATED. MANUFACTURING PLANTS LIKE THIS STEEL MILL ARE TYPICAL COST CENTERS.

REVENUE AND EXPENSE BUDGETS

Revenue and expense budgets: Statements used by revenue and expense responsibility centers.

Revenue and expense budgets are used by revenue and expense responsibility centers. By far the most common of these are expense budgets; virtually every operating unit is a cost center to some degree and therefore has an expense budget. Only revenue centers, profit centers, and investment centers have revenue budgets.

CAPITAL EXPENDITURE BUDGETS

Capital expenditure budgets: Statements of expenditures for major capital purchases, such as plant and equipment, inventories, and development costs, among others.

Capital expenditure budgets include expenditures for major capital purchases, such as plant and equipment, inventories, and development costs. Normally, some capital expenditures occur each year. A capital expense budget may cover a period of several years, with the current years being integrated into the master budget. Capital budgets are critical because of the relatively large amounts expended over long periods on the basis of decisions made previously.

Controlling the procurement of capital equipment can be especially difficult in large, highly complex organizations like the military. The Pentagon has adopted innovative procurement controls and has shared cost savings with contractors in an effort to cut costs as well as modernize defense contractors' plants.[36]

Mike McGrath, a member of the Pentagon Staff, has helped institute a number of innovative procurement controls and cost-saving activities.

THE CASH BUDGET

The **cash budget** is a forecast of cash receipts and disbursements. This budget is extremely important because it indicates whether the organization is able to meet financial obligations that require payment of cash. It also indicates whether excess cash is available for other purposes.

THE NONMONETARY RESOURCE INPUT BUDGET

The **nonmonetary resource input budget** includes such items as employee hours, units of product, and units of raw material. Eventually these are converted into expense, or revenue, budgets. At some point, the budget must be stated in dollars as well as in units. For example, the manufacturing unit of Eli Lilly Pharmaceuticals would first determine the units of materials needed to manufacture the product quantities scheduled for the year. It would then cost these out—that is, assign dollar amounts to them. The result would constitute part of an expense budget.

The Budgeting Process

The budgeting process begins with a revenue forecast, which is used as a basis for allocating funds to various responsibility centers. Those centers, in turn, develop budgets within the constraints identified by the revenue forecast. In virtually all organizations, however, responsibility centers identify their costs, and in some cases their revenues, long before the revenue forecast is prepared. (The reason for this is that it takes considerable time to prepare the cost estimates.) Cost and revenue budgets are summarized into major types of organizational budgets—cash, expense, and revenue budgets, as shown in Figure 19.5—and matched against the total revenue forecast. When new projects or programs are introduced, they may have their own budgets based on estimated revenue.

Departmental Budgets

At the departmental level, a preliminary budget is developed. It is then sent to upper-level management for review. Upper-level management returns it with recommended changes, and a final budget is prepared.

In preparing departmental budgets, managers typically base their estimates on budget information from previous years. They factor in any major changes that have occurred, and some add a "fudge factor." In virtually all organizations, upper management almost always cuts departmental budgets to some degree. Therefore, many lower-level managers pad their budgets in order to obtain the funds they need.

The budget may be changed from time to time during the budgeted period in response to significant changes in environmental circumstances. A circumstance such as failing to achieve desired sales, or a greatly increased level of sales, would require adjustments in the budget.

Zero-Based Budgeting

Zero-based budgeting was pioneered at the U.S. Department of Agriculture in the 1960s and adopted by Texas Instruments in 1970.[37] It was designed to eliminate some of the problems that occur when present budgets are based on past budgets and the manager concentrates on the differences and on justifying additional funding. Under zero-based budgeting, the budget starts at zero; the manager must justify *all* funding, not just changes. The amounts allocated for the previous year are not automatically available. Numerous firms have switched to zero-based budgeting, including Xerox, Ford, and Playboy Enter-

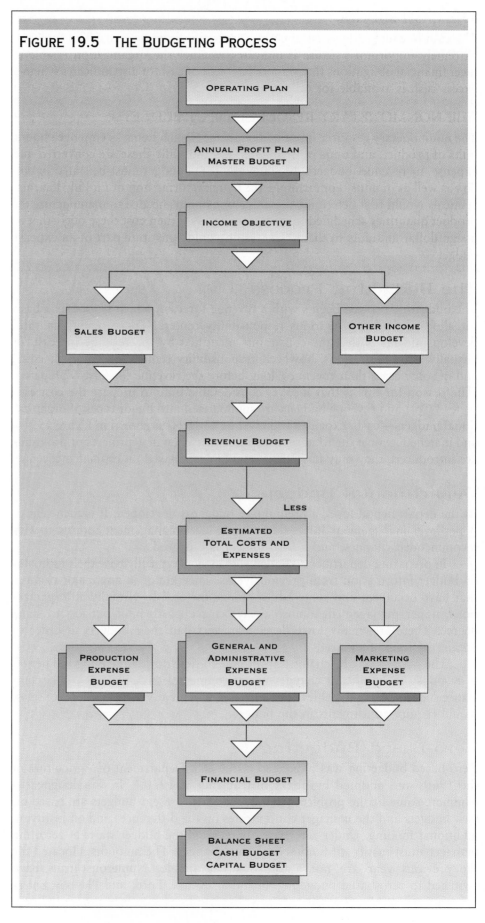

FIGURE 19.5 THE BUDGETING PROCESS

OPERATING PLAN

ANNUAL PROFIT PLAN
MASTER BUDGET

INCOME OBJECTIVE

SALES BUDGET

OTHER INCOME
BUDGET

REVENUE BUDGET

LESS

ESTIMATED
TOTAL COSTS AND
EXPENSES

PRODUCTION
EXPENSE
BUDGET

GENERAL AND
ADMINISTRATIVE
EXPENSE
BUDGET

MARKETING
EXPENSE
BUDGET

FINANCIAL BUDGET

BALANCE SHEET
CASH BUDGET
CAPITAL BUDGET

prises. Numerous federal and state agencies have also adopted the technique. President Jimmy Carter used it as a basis for payroll budgets. Many firms attribute large savings and higher profit levels to their use of zero-based budgeting.[38]

The primary advantage of this approach is that it helps focus the organization on activities that will lead to the accomplishment of its mission. It also helps eliminate waste. The major drawback is that the process is time-consuming and generates a lot of paperwork. Moreover, it does not eliminate the tendency to inflate budget estimates.[39] The future of zero-based budgeting is uncertain. The drive to cut costs in many businesses suggests that the technique might be used more frequently in the future. On the other hand, the time and paperwork it requires are a barrier to increased use of this approach.[40]

Advantages and Disadvantages of Budgets

Budgets are important and have a number of advantages. They are effective control mechanisms, translate objectives into financial terms, coordinate efforts to achieve objectives, provide performance standards, and improve resource allocation. However, a number of weaknesses are associated with them. Budgets are extremely time-consuming. Budget requests are often overstated. They often lead to bad results—for example, when they are used to enhance the power of a particular manager or department—including conflict between departments and the staff that reviews their budgets.[41] Budgets can restrict the organization's flexibility and ability to adapt to change, and they can stifle innovation. Other disadvantages stem from the fact that budgets are oriented toward the short term and focus on financial objectives to the exclusion of others. They discourage initiative by locking management into predetermined courses of action, and they sometimes limit performance by setting expectations at certain levels.[42]

In an ever-changing and more complex managerial environment, the budget as we know it may not survive. Because organizations must change, innovate, and adapt to their environments quickly, many may find budgets too difficult to work with. On the other hand, the use of computers and the ability to change budgets almost instantaneously, or at least to examine them in a "what if" format, may allow budgets to remain an important part of the control process.[43] At the Lord Corporation, a privately held, medium-sized manufacturing and research firm in Erie, Pennsylvania, computerized budgeting enables managers to make major changes in a matter of hours instead of weeks.[44]

Firms can take the following steps to ensure that their budgeting process is successful:

1. Be serious about budgeting; generate commitment to it.
2. Build linkages to connect the firm's long-, medium-, and short-range plans.
3. Adopt detailed and comprehensive procedures for preparing budgets.
4. Analyze budget variances and deviations from standards, and take corrective action.[45]
5. Emulate the Japanese, whose budgets tend to be more flexible and are revised every six months.[46]

Performance Appraisals

Most organizations have some type of formal appraisal system. Performance appraisal is the practice of determining whether an employee is performing his or her job effectively and efficiently. By definition, performance appraisals com-

AT BANC ONE: While each affiliated bank operates on its own and headquarters has no budget control over it, through the information system all banks know what the other affiliates are doing and compete with each other for efficiency.

pare actual performance against the standards for that job. Because of EEO laws, employees must be notified in advance of what constitutes expected performance.[47] Although this requirement seems to call for a management by objectives (MBO) system, a wide variety of appraisal systems exist.

Performance appraisals have several purposes. Among them are control of performance, employee development, motivation, legal compliance, personnel and employment planning, and compensation.[48] The primary purpose of performance appraisal is to make certain that employees are performing up to standards. If they are not, action must be taken to improve their performance. Standards assist in deciding when layoffs or terminations are necessary. They also assist in determining who should receive pay raises and promotions.

Performance appraisals help identify employees who might need more training. They may also be used to indicate the results of training or to encourage supervisors to work more closely with subordinates to improve their performance. This chapter's Ethical Management Challenge provides an interesting view of appraisal.

Knowing that their performance will be measured tends to stimulate employees to perform at higher levels. It develops a sense of responsibility and encourages initiative. When rewards are based on performance, motivation is generally enhanced.[49] In addition, properly designed and administered performance appraisals help justify decisions regarding pay, promotion, transfer, termination, and layoff. To avoid EEO problems, the firm should make sure that the appraisal system is understood by managers and subordinates, instruct managers on its use, require adequate documentation, and make sure subordinates understand their reviews.[50]

Performance appraisals like this one have several purposes. Among them are control of performance, employee development, motivation, legal compliance, personnel and employment planning, and compensation.

Reverse Appraisal at Chrysler

"Reflecting up" means ensuring that one looks good to one's boss. "Often people do a good job of reflecting up," says Debra Dubow, a development specialist at Chrysler. As a result, bosses get a rosy view of the managers who report to them.

But, says Dubow, "the people at the top see managers differently than do the people below." Sometimes bosses have no idea how managers relate to their people. "Thus, any areas of weakness may be blind spots to one's superior, and having just one person give a manager feedback on performance may result in a very narrow, nonobjective view."

The solution being tried at Chrysler is a reverse-appraisal process that allows those who report to a manager to give that manager feedback on his or her performance. The process has three goals: It gives employees a voice in the workplace and input into decisions that affect their work; it improves managers' supervisory skills; and it improves the company's competitive position in the marketplace.

Significantly, most managers at automotive companies like Chrysler have moved up through the ranks on the basis of technical rather than interpersonal skills. Interpersonal relations are a relatively new area of expertise for many managers. Reverse appraisal allows then to try on a new hat—as a coach and facilitator. It also enhances employee spirit and output.

The program wasn't easy to implement. Chrysler has a traditional, hierarchical organization, and reverse appraisal could have met with resistance. It was therefore decided that the results of the process would not be folded into managers' annual performance appraisals.

The rating process began at the higher levels of management in order to engender the feeling that "What's good for the top boss is good for the supervisor." It was hoped that employees who had just evaluated their own bosses would feel less threatened by being evaluated in their turn. Starting at the top also allowed for role modeling. To facilitate accountability, managers were expected to share their appraisal results with their immediate supervisors. They were then encouraged to make an action plan for the coming year, containing goals for improvement and ways to accomplish them.

Here are some sample questions from the six categories evaluated:

- *Teamwork* . . . promotes cooperation and teamwork within our work group.

- *Communication* . . . learns current business information and communicates it to our work group.

- *Quality* . . . demonstrates meaningful commitment to our quality efforts.

- *Leadership* . . . demonstrates consistency through both words and actions.

- *Planning* . . . provides reasonable schedules so that my commitments can be met.

- *Development of the work force* . . . delegates responsibilities and gives me the authority to carry out my job.

SOURCE: Joyce E. Santora, "Rating the Boss at Chrysler," *Personnel Journal* (May 1992), pp. 38–45.

Operational Control

Performance measurements and leadership are the cornerstones of operational control. These mechanisms were discussed in earlier chapters. The systems used in middle management—especially MBORR and performance appraisal, statistical reports, and rules and procedures—also play important roles at the operational level. Virtually every facet of the organization has operational control mechanisms. The disciplinary system discussed in Chapter 12 as an HRM tool is also a key operational control system that cuts across all levels of the organization.

Disciplinary Systems

Most organizations have some kind of system for administering discipline. The purpose of these systems is to control four types of troublesome employee behaviors:

> AT BANC ONE: *The same bank (Banc One, Lafayette, Indiana) received both Banc One's Customer Service Award for 1992 and its Blue One Award for 1992 for outstanding financial performance. Not only is headquarters watching and rewarding desired performance, but its various objectives are compatible with each other.*

1. *Ineffective employees:* Individuals whose performance falls below their capabilities or the expectations of the organization, or who have motivational problems.
2. *Alcoholic or drug-addicted employees:* Employees whose drinking or drug abuse interferes with their performance on the job.
3. *Participants in illegal activites:* Employees who steal from the company or in some other way break the law.
4. *Rule violators:* Individuals who have been counseled but continue to engage in behaviors viewed as undesirable.[51]

Operations Management Control Mechanisms

Chapter 21 reviews a number of mechanisms designed to control performance in operations areas, especially manufacturing. Among these are systems for materials control, quality control, statistical control of manufacturing operations, and charting mechanisms for reviewing performance against planned objectives. These controls work well in isolated environments such as a small factory, but imagine the difficulties faced by the federal government in attempting to control procurement. Think of the costs involved and the potential for bribery. A major investigation begun in the summer of 1988 uncovered the "Pentagate" scandal. Investigators found that information on business competitors could be acquired easily at the Pentagon, and that "classified" documents were passed around like playing cards. The close-knit culture of military procurement helped create these problems.[52]

Control in a Changing Environment

One of the major problems experienced by managers in rapidly changing environments is that the control systems they use may have been designed to function in circumstances that no longer exist, to control factors that no longer need controlling. Worse, they may not be designed to control factors that do need controlling, or to control them quickly enough. A case in point is the financial services industry. Deregulation and consolidation have led to unparalleled changes in many facets of the industry. These changes have had major impacts on budgets, profit center responsibilities, and compensation.[53] Externally, government has failed to control adequately for fraud and bad management, with the result that many financial institutions must be bailed out with federal funds.[54] The securities industry has also suffered from a lack of proper control systems. Insider trading and "junk bonds" have led to major scandals.

To avoid the problems arising from inadequate control, managers must continually assess the situation. Control should be a continuous process. Many firms are taking steps in this direction. Continuous improvement programs are growing in popularity, and control systems are becoming more flexible and future oriented.

Control Systems and the Problem-Solving Process

Control is a problem-solving process, and control systems provide information to be used in all the stages of that process. The environment is analyzed for signs that performance is different from what was expected. Management then must identify the real problem—that is, make certain that performance is not suffering for some reason other than the most obvious ones. Next, assumptions about the key factors in the situation must be made. Among the assumptions made are those related to the probable success of potential solutions once they are generated. Management then chooses among a number of alternative solutions. When the chosen solution is implemented, that effort itself must be controlled. The control systems described in this chapter provide information used in all of the management functions—planning, organizing, and leading as well as controlling.

Summary

(Before reading this summary, look again at the objectives listed at the beginning of the chapter.)

1. Control systems provide managers with the information necessary to determine whether the organization has reached its objectives. Various techniques are used to analyze performance. Without information and analysis, control could not be accomplished effectively.

2. The core control systems are the strategic plan, the long-range financial plan, the operating budget, performance appraisals, statistical reports supplied through the organization's MIS, and policies and procedures.

3. Strategic control systems focus on the performance of the organization as a whole. Tactical control systems focus largely on middle-level management activities and the budget; operational control systems focus on the achievement of front-line organizational objectives.

4. The master budget summarizes all the organization's budgets. Capital expenditure budgets identify major capital costs. The cash budget reviews cash flows for the year. Nonmonetary resource budgets are the source of much budget information.

5. There are four types of responsibility centers. Revenue centers are controlled on the basis of sales of products or services. Cost centers are controlled on the basis of expenses or costs. Profit centers are controlled on the basis of the difference between revenues and expenses (i.e., profit). Investment centers are controlled on the basis of profit, together with the amount of capital investment made to produce that profit.

6. A balance sheet is used to determine the financial condition of an organization at some point in time. An income statement is used to examine the performance of an

organization over a period of time. The funds flow analysis examines the use of funds over a period of time.

7. Ratio analysis enables the analyst to discern a firm's financial condition. ROI gives the manager a single figure that indicates the firm's financial condition for a specific period.

8. Cost systems serve three principal functions: inventory valuation, operational control, and product cost measurement. Increasingly, systems are being designed to enhance strategic marketing decisions.

9. Financial audits help ensure that a firm's financial statements are accurate and that its accounting systems are functioning properly. Management audits take a broader view of the organization, looking at more than the numbers. Strategic audits examine the external environment as well. Both of the latter seek to identify the firm's future capabilities.

10. Control is becoming broader in nature—more future oriented and continuous.

11. Performance appraisals help ensure that members of the organization perform as expected. They also are useful for motivation, for employee development, and for legal compliance; they are used for compensation, in personnel and employment planning, and for administrative purposes.

12. MBO-type systems, disciplinary systems, quality control, and operations control serve, respectively, to provide control over individual performance in pursuit of objectives, behavior relative to rules and procedures, product or service quality, and manufacturing or service operations.

General Questions

1. Discuss the control systems utilized in an organization to which you belong or have belonged.

2. Evaluate the effectiveness of the control systems you discussed in Question 1.

3. Are the control systems used in the organization you discussed in Question 1 market, bureaucratic, or clan systems? Why?

4. Describe the grading process used in this course as a control system, indicating how each step in the control process occurs.

Questions on the Management Challenge Features

INNOVATION MANAGEMENT CHALLENGE

1. What factors lead to the stifling of creativity in Japan?

2. What must Japanese organizations do to overcome these obstacles?

GLOBAL MANAGEMENT CHALLENGE

1. In what ways do Japanese and U.S. firms' approaches to cost accounting differ?

2. Why do these differences give the Japanese a strategic advantage?

ETHICAL MANAGEMENT CHALLENGE

1. Discuss the Chrysler system of subordinate evaluations of bosses.

2. Why is this approach more ethical than a system in which only subordinates are evaluated?

One of a Kind

There is always one participant in a company's operations that is more difficult to control—the customer. Ultimately, the customer calls the shots, and generally the last action in any transaction is payment by the customer. If payment is delayed or defaulted, profit goes out the window. The best customer control for a bank is, of course, to choose customers who will pay—that is, who have a good credit rating and history. Banc One chooses solid commercial customers with good ratings and loans only modest amounts to each customer (the largest customer debt is $90 million, and only seven are more than $50 million). A single default will never amount to more than .2 percent of total assets.

In the credit card business, Banc One also chooses its customers carefully. High-risk groups have been sold off, and the quality of the remaining cards is being emphasized. Lower delinquency rates and losses should offset the lower expected gross yield of credit cards. However, Banc One has also pressed for improvement in the other, less pleasant aspect of customer control—collection of delinquent funds. Banc One uses small, local, quality collection agencies, which do better than large national companies but still recover only a portion of the funds due. However, the bank's innovativeness shows in a successful program to recover funds before the collection stage. When payers are slow, Banc One sends them a video tape to persuade them to pay up. This generally avoids the severed relationship that usually results from collection. While frequently used in marketing, video tapes have not been used before for customer-control functions. Banc One is again at the frontier of technology.

DISCUSSION QUESTIONS

1. As individual banks within Banc One Corporation retain their own charters and are responsible for their own actions, what advantages have they gained by joining the corporation?

2. Banc One's acquisitions are always friendly, and promotion within the company is preferred to hiring outsiders; even state and corporate management is generally recruited from the member banks. How would this serve to facilitate control from the top down?

3. What are the advantages and disadvantages of pursuing the collection of delinquent funds by outside agencies?

Getting a Grip on a New Business

Charles Brandon, part owner and manager of the Winter Park Brewery, a combination restaurant, beer and wine bar, and mini-brewery, was trying to get a grip on the operation. He knew his food costs. He knew the profit margin on each item, but he did not have a complete cost system. Moreover, he had never managed before. He had found that managing low-wage workers was not as easy as it looked. Customers had complained about poor service, and working with the food service managers to whom he had licensed the restaurant portion of the operation had not been easy either.

Brandon had established the Brewery because he wanted to own his own business, had always liked beer and brewing, and saw it as a way to combine a hobby with a business. He began the operation with the vision that the restaurant would be a family restaurant serving only beer and wine; it might even become a sort of neighborhood pub. About halfway through the first year, he realized that the reality was quite different from his vision.

Brandon liked blues and jazz and hoped that offering such music in the restaurant would increase business, which had fallen off. Thursday night became blues night, and bands were scheduled after 9 P.M. on Fridays and Saturdays. The Brewery had no trouble selling all the beer it could make. Capacity had been doubled and aging time cut in half in order to meet demand. But the overall operation was not making money. In this, its tenth month, it had finally reached the break-even point on cash flow, but it had not yet shown a profit.

DISCUSSION QUESTIONS

1. Identify the control problems revealed in this case.
2. Indicate how the control systems discussed in the chapter could be used to help solve these problems.
3. Discuss the strategy and marketing issues raised by this case.

Computing Financial Ratios

Using the information provided in Figures 19.2 and 19.3, compare each of the four financial ratios in Table 19.1 to the industry averages shown here. On the basis of these comparisons, what is your evaluation of Georgia-Pacific's financial condition?

Calculated for Georgia-Pacific	Industry Average*
Liquidity	
Current	1.8 times
Leverage	
Debt to total assets	52.5%
Activity	
Inventory turnover	8 times
Profitability	
Return on total assets	11.7%

Almanac of Business and Industrial Financial Ratios (Englewood Cliffs, N.J.: Prentice-Hall, 1993), p. 73.

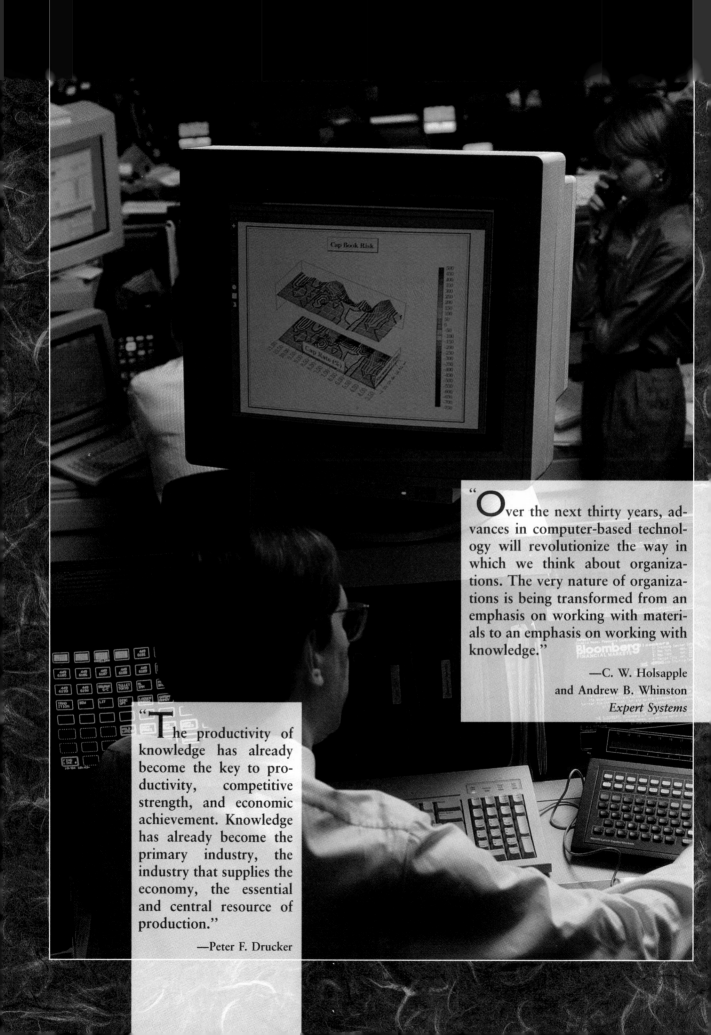

"Over the next thirty years, advances in computer-based technology will revolutionize the way in which we think about organizations. The very nature of organizations is being transformed from an emphasis on working with materials to an emphasis on working with knowledge."

—C. W. Holsapple
and Andrew B. Whinston
Expert Systems

"The productivity of knowledge has already become the key to productivity, competitive strength, and economic achievement. Knowledge has already become the primary industry, the industry that supplies the economy, the essential and central resource of production."

—Peter F. Drucker

Management Information Systems and Knowledge Management

CHAPTER OBJECTIVES

When you have read this chapter you should be able to:

1. Define information and information systems and discuss the role of information as an organizational resource.

2. Describe the purpose of management information systems (MISs).

3. Describe the evolution of MISs.

4. Indicate how MISs are designed.

5. Describe how companies and managers should use an MIS.

6. Describe the functions of a chief information officer (CIO).

7. Identify how microcomputers have affected managers' use of MISs.

8. Describe the impacts of artificial intelligence, decision support systems, networking, and expert systems on management.

9. Indicate how an MIS affects the organization.

10. Describe the knowledge-based organization of the future.

MANAGEMENT CHALLENGES DISCUSSED IN THIS CHAPTER:

 Accelerating rates of change.

 Increasing globalization of business.

 Increasing levels of competition.

 Transition from an industrial to a knowledge-based economy.

 Complexity of the managerial environment.

Levi Strauss & Co. Takes Its Information Systems Seriously

Levi Strauss & Co. makes Levi's jeans, Dockers, and other apparel. It has manufacturing or sales operations in most major countries and competes in a mature market with many major competitors. To accomplish its vision and mission, it has empowered its employees through autonomous teams, training and development, and information systems.

Each of Levi's 2,500 employees has a workstation and access to needed information in the firm's mainframe computer. Bill Eaton, the chief information officer, explains that in order to empower employees, an open systems architecture with complete systems access was necessary. Employees are trained in the skills needed to access various networks to obtain the information they need. Customers and suppliers are linked to the firm through LeviLink, a network electronic data interchange system. Levi's employees are so empowered that they even have access to their personnel files. Through OLIVER (On-Line Interactive Visual Employee Resource), the interactive computer network, they can look at up to 500 screens of personal information. Using OLIVER, employees can examine their total compensation, disability, health care, pension, employee investment plan, survivor benefits, beneficiary, and other information.

All major systems at Levi Strauss, from purchasing to personnel, can communicate with each other. This communication aspect is considered in making all new technology purchases. Levi Strauss has created the position of Director of Quick Response to deal with electronic services to retailers and suppliers. The globalization of its business has caused the firm to install communication networks to keep far-flung operations in touch with each other. Expert systems are also used in several areas, such as inventory management.

SOURCES: David Brousell, "Levi Strauss's CIO On: The Technology of Empowerment," *Datamation* (June 1, 1992), pp. 120–124; Jennifer J. Laabs, "OLIVER: A Twist on Communication," *Personnel Journal* (September 1991), pp. 79–82; and Larry Stevens, "Systems Development vs. the Tower of Babel," *Bobbin* (June 1992), pp. 22, 24.

L evi Strauss's managers know that information is one of the most important ingredients in an organization's success. They know that information enables managers to make better decisions and realize that without information they are shooting in the dark. They also recognize that empowerment of employees requires an information system that enables employees to gain access to their personal files.

The core function of management is problem solving. Current and relevant information about the environment and about the variables in the decision situation are necessary for sound decision making. The decision maker must be able to use this knowledge in following the steps of the decision-making process. In fact, the organization's effectiveness often depends on the information available to its managers.[1]

Information systems have become so sophisticated that decision support systems can assist managers in addressing major issues. More and more frequently, information systems are being designed to do just that. Some information systems can even propose solutions. In short, business is in the midst of an information revolution.

Consider some examples. Insurance giant USAA of San Antonio, Texas, scans every document sent in by customers into an optical disk system. Customer service agents can quickly respond to customer inquiries. Claims are handled more quickly, and customers are happier. USAA's newest information device digitizes customer phone conversations. For example, when someone calls in an accident report, it is digitized into the data bank, and all other information related to this claim is also scanned into optical memory. Later, insurance agents, doctors, and other interested parties can peruse this information on their PCs. USAA will soon have a system whereby even X-rays will be stored on disks. Eventually, conference calls will be carried out via PC over great distances, with all documents and materials available simultaneously to doctors, attorneys, and agents.[2]

American Airlines' Sabre reservation system has 40.2 percent of all U.S. reservation system outlets, giving the company a strategic advantage in reaching agents and booking flights. Sabre accounted for almost all of American Airlines' earnings in 1992 (the airline itself was losing money).[3]

Information systems enable Nissenbaum's auto junkyard in Somerville, Massachusetts, to improve customer service in the "looking for parts" business. Such sales have increased by 75 percent since the company began using a satellite dish–PC system to locate automobile engines and other parts throughout the country. Nissenbaum is connected with six hundred similarly equipped junkyards and parts stores.[4]

McKesson Corporation, a San Francisco wholesaler, is linked by computer to its drugstore customers. Such links cut costs, reduce inventory, increase productivity, and make customers so dependent on McKesson that they rarely switch distributors. For example, McKesson supplies computerized scanners to its customer drugstore managers, allowing them to process inventory needs automatically. It not only ships the materials almost instantaneously, but adds pricing stickers with designated profit margins.[5]

Finally, Merrill Lynch has established a global network linking all of its major offices via a communications satellite. This allows it not only to compete better, but to control its global corporate operations more effectively.[6]

This chapter examines the role of information and information systems in decision making and control. It also discusses management information systems (MISs), common MIS mistakes, and the appropriate use of MIS. The role of the personal computer in managerial decision making and the role of the chief information officer (CIO) are noted. The impact of artificial intelligence, expert sys-

The Sabre reservation system not only gave American Airlines a competitive edge when it was introduced, but now provides substantial revenues for the firm as competitors and travel agencies use its services.

tems, and decision support systems, as well as networking, on the decision process is reviewed. The role of the MIS in the organization—and more important, the role of information in the knowledge-based organization of the future—is discussed.

Management Information Systems (MIS)

Data: Raw, unanalyzed facts.

Information: Data that have been put into a meaningful and useful context and communicated to a recipient who uses it to make decisions.

Data are raw, unanalyzed facts. **Information** "is data that have been put into a meaningful and useful context and communicated to a recipient who uses it to make decisions."[7] Information thus consists of data that have been meaningfully altered for use in decision making.[8] For example, competitors' sales figures are data, but when the organization's sales figures are compared with those of competitors and trends are identified, information is created.

Information is the lifeblood of organizations. Managers need information to recognize and identify problems, make assumptions about solutions, generate alternatives, choose among alternatives, and implement and control the chosen solution. One way to assess a manager's information needs is through a checklist like the one shown in Table 20.1.

Characteristics of Quality Information

Quality information has three attributes: accuracy, timeliness, and relevance. *Accuracy* means that the information is free from mistakes and errors, is clear, and reflects the meaning of the data on which it is based. *Timeliness* means that

TABLE 20.1 Manager's Checklist of Information Needs

1. What types of decisions do you make regularly?

2. What types of information do you need to make those decisions?

3. What types of information do you regularly receive?

4. What types of information would you like to receive that you are not now receiving?

5. What knowledge does this information provide or help provide? (This is important because it is knowledge, not just information, on which the decision will be based.)

decision makers have the information necessary within the relevant time frame. *Relevance* means that the information specifically answers for the recipient the what, why, where, when, who, and how of the issue.[9] To be relevant, information must be complete.

The need for quality information is increasing dramatically. Successfully selling automobiles, providing health care at a profit, or using personal computers or software in the business market requires more information now than at any time in history.[10] In complex, volatile environments, the effectiveness of decisions depends on the decision maker's ability to obtain accurate, timely, and relevant information.

Information Systems and Knowledge

Information and knowledge are essentially synonymous. The purpose of obtaining information is to combine it with other knowledge to arrive at solutions to problems. Knowledge results from learning and experience. People accumulate knowledge about what they do and how they do it.[11] In addition, organizations possess collective knowledge about how to do what they do. To the extent that organizations learn, they can increase their collective knowledge and solve problems better than their competitors. Information systems help organizations learn, accumulate knowledge, and solve problems better and faster. Information systems can help members of the organization share their accumulated knowledge, thereby improving organizational learning and problem-solving capabilities.[12]

Information Needed by Managers

The information needed by managers varies by level—top management, middle management, and operating management—and by economic function (see Figure 20.1).[13] Top management focuses mainly on planning and on broad environmental concerns. Middle management focuses on control, functional areas, and performance. Operating management is concerned primarily with performance, effectiveness, and efficiency. Each of these perspectives requires different information in order to make sound decisions.

The information needed by managers also varies by their function within the organization. Marketing managers need information related to such issues as sales, advertising expenses, sales personnel, sales volume, market penetration, product quality and service, and service cost. Financial managers need information about stock prices, tax rates, interest rates, the state of the economy, the company's performance, and depreciation policies. Operations managers need information related to such issues as efficiency rates, productivity, scrap problems, material utilization rates, labor utilization rates, and union contracts. Personnel managers need information related to the availability of personnel to fill

FIGURE 20.1 THE INFORMATION NEEDED BY LEVEL OF ORGANIZATION

	CHARACTERISTIC	TOP MANAGEMENT	MIDDLE MANAGEMENT	OPERATING MANAGEMENT
1.	FOCUS ON PLANNING	HEAVY	MODERATE	MINIMUM
2.	FOCUS ON CONTROL	MODERATE	HEAVY	HEAVY
3.	TIME FRAME	ONE TO THREE YEARS	UP TO A YEAR	DAY TO DAY
4.	SCOPE OF ACTIVITY	EXTREMELY BROAD	ENTIRE FUNCTIONAL AREA	SINGLE SUBFUNCTION OR SUBTASK
5.	NATURE OF ACTIVITY	RELATIVELY UNSTRUCTURED	MODERATELY STRUCTURED	HIGHLY STRUCTURED
6.	LEVEL OF COMPLEXITY	VERY COMPLEX, MANY VARIABLES	LESS COMPLEX, BETTER DEFINED VARIABLES	STRAIGHTFORWARD
7.	JOB MEASUREMENT	DIFFICULT	LESS DIFFICULT	RELATIVELY EASY
8.	RESULT OF ACTIVITY	VISIONS, GOALS, LONG-TERM OBJECTIVES, AND STRATEGIES	IMPLEMENTATION SCHED-ULES, PERFORMANCE YARDSTICKS	END PRODUCT
9.	TYPE OF INFORMATION UTILIZED	EXTERNAL, INTERNAL, UNCERTAIN ACCURACY	MOSTLY INTERNAL, REASON-ABLE ACCURACY	INTERNAL HISTORICAL, HIGH LEVEL OF ACCURACY
10.*	MENTAL ATTRIBUTES	CREATIVE, INNOVATIVE, AS WELL AS ANALYTICAL	RESPONSIBLE, PERSUASIVE, ADMINISTRATIVE	EFFICIENT, EFFECTIVE
11.	NUMBER OF PEOPLE INVOLVED	FEW	MODERATE NUMBER	MANY
12.	DEPARTMENT/ DIVISIONAL INTERACTION	INTRA-DIVISION	INTRA-DEPARTMENT	INTER-DEPARTMENT

*THIS AREA NEEDS INCREASING INNOVATION AT ALL LEVELS

SOURCE: ADAPTED FROM JEROME KANTER, MANAGEMENT INFORMATION SYSTEMS, 3RD ED. (ENGLEWOOD CLIFFS, NJ: PRENTICE HALL, 1984), P. 6. COPYRIGHT © 1984. ADAPTED BY PERMISSION OF PRENTICE HALL.

jobs, comparative compensation rates, occupational safety and health regulations, and evaluations of employees' performance. MIS managers need information on such issues as utilization of reports, availability of computer time, expert systems being developed or currently available, and rates of information system usage. All managers need information on such issues as quality and innovation.

Defining the MIS

Management information system (MIS): *A formal system for gathering and analyzing information.*

A **management information system** (MIS) is a formal system for gathering and analyzing information. It links three key elements of the organization: management, information, and systems. (See Figure 20.2.) An MIS is created to provide information to managers so that they can make better decisions. It aids management in making decisions by collecting, organizing, and distributing information.[14] The MIS facilitates the problem-solving process in all four of the major functions of management: planning, organizing, leading, and controlling.

Although MISs are usually computerized, they do not have to be. Moreover, in addition to a formal MIS, most organizations also have informal systems for gathering and distributing information. For example, most managers have an informal network of friends within the firm whom they can call when they need information about a particular topic.

The Evolution of the MIS

Organizations have always had some type of MIS, even though it may not have been defined as such. Historically, most information systems have been built around financial—and to some extent marketing—information. Only with the advent of the computer has information about other areas of the organization been extensively collected, analyzed, and distributed. Many people were disappointed with computers and information systems in the 1960s because they failed to meet their expectations.[15] Once computers and the necessary software became more reliable and memory capacities and user-friendliness increased substantially, the computer's tremendous capacity for supplying information was realized and more formal MISs were developed.

The evolution of MISs has occurred in four stages: electronic data processing, management information systems, decision support systems, and expert systems. Each of these stages represents an increase in the sophistication of both hardware and software.

ELECTRONIC DATA PROCESSING (EDP)

In the 1960s and early 1970s, mainframe computers processed information for a limited number of functions, such as accounting, purchasing, and accounts payable. The machines were large and temperamental. For example, they had to be kept at 72 degrees F, plus or minus a degree or two, or they would shut down. Their high cost and complexity made a centralized EDP office mandatory. Data from various departments were processed by the central department. The resulting information was summarized and distributed to managers.

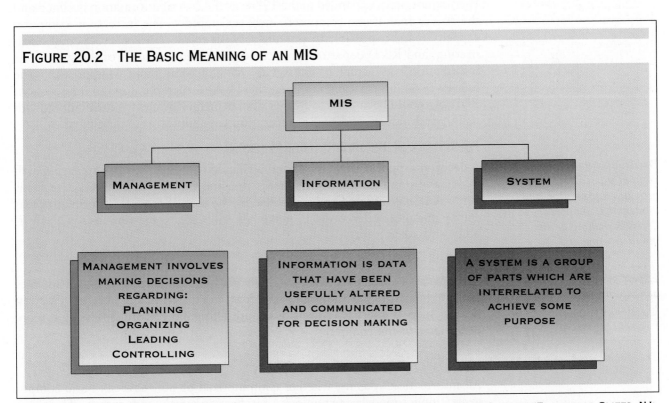

FIGURE 20.2   THE BASIC MEANING OF AN MIS

MIS

MANAGEMENT — INFORMATION — SYSTEM

MANAGEMENT INVOLVES MAKING DECISIONS REGARDING: PLANNING ORGANIZING LEADING CONTROLLING

INFORMATION IS DATA THAT HAVE BEEN USEFULLY ALTERED AND COMMUNICATED FOR DECISION MAKING

A SYSTEM IS A GROUP OF PARTS WHICH ARE INTERRELATED TO ACHIEVE SOME PURPOSE

SOURCE: ROBERT G. MURDICK AND JOEL E. ROSS, INTRODUCTION TO MANAGEMENT INFORMATION SYSTEMS (ENGLEWOOD CLIFFS, NJ: PRENTICE HALL, INC., 1977), P. 8. COPYRIGHT © 1977. ADAPTED BY PERMISSION OF PRENTICE HALL.

Borland International's new dBase IV compiler for DOS features thirty new and enhanced commands and functions in dBase IV, making it easy to create sophisticated business applications for managers.

EDP was designed to process large numbers of transactions. It was based on scheduled computer runs, with integrated files for related jobs. It was not a true MIS.

MISs

EDP departments expanded in the 1970s as the cost of information declined and the size of mainframe computers increased rapidly. The increase in computer capacity made it possible to provide services to more users. Production, engineering, and R&D departments became more frequent users of the system. As information was actually "managed," MISs became more widespread.[16] The focus was on information, not data; there were structured flows of information; EDP jobs could be integrated (rather than being performed for each unit individually); and inquiry and report generation capabilities were developed.

DECISION SUPPORT SYSTEMS (DSSs)

Decision support system: A computer-based MIS that provides information and models that support decision making in an interactive manner.

A **decision support system** is a computer-based MIS that provides managers with information and models that support decision making in an interactive manner.[17] A DSS is initiated and controlled by the user. It provides information that can be manipulated in order to make better decisions; the emphasis is on flexibility and adaptability.

EXPERT SYSTEMS (ESs)

Expert system: An MIS that actually provides guidance to managers.

An **expert system** is an MIS that actually provides guidance to managers. It uses decision heuristics based on the knowledge and experience of experts in a given field to suggest alternative decisions. Both DSSs and ESs are discussed in more detail later in the chapter.

Components of an MIS

All information systems, whether computerized or not, have six basic components: input, models, technology, database, control, and output. These are shown in Figure 20.3.[18] If we think of information as a resource and of the

Managers at Salomon Brothers use decision support systems, computer-based management information systems that provide information and models that support decision making in an interactive manner.

information system as representative of the systems model discussed in Chapter 2, then the inputs, processing (transformation), and outputs model used there applies to information as well. When discussing an information system, processing (transformation) should be broken into four building blocks: models, database, technology, and controls.

INPUTS

Inputs "are all the data, text, voice, and images entering the information system and the methods and media by which they are captured and entered."[19] The most common means of entering transactions for a text are bar-code/laser read-

Inputs: All the data, text, voice, and images entering the information system and the methods and media by which they are captured and entered.

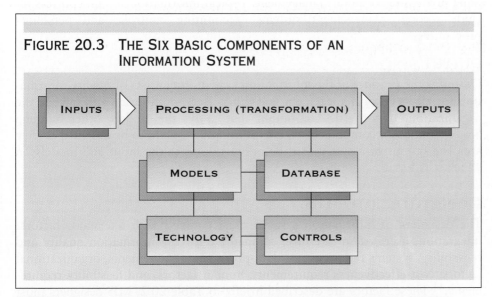

FIGURE 20.3   THE SIX BASIC COMPONENTS OF AN INFORMATION SYSTEM

SOURCE: ADAPTED FROM JOHN G. BURCH AND GARY GRUDNITSKI, INFORMATION SYSTEMS: THEORY AND PRACTICE, 4TH ED. (NEW YORK: WILEY, 1986), P. 36. REPRINTED BY PERMISSION OF JOHN WILEY & SONS, LTD.

ers and the computer keyboard. Voice input is also possible and will become more common during the 1990s.[20] Scanners now provide text input as well.

MODELS

The **models** component of an MIS "consists of a combination of procedural, logical, and mathematical models that manipulate input and store data in a variety of ways, to produce the desired results or output."[21] Models may be very simple, merely updating a file as a consequence of a transaction, or extremely complex, simulating an entire organizational and environmental process—for example, a model of the U.S. economy.

TECHNOLOGY

Technology is the "toolbox" of the information system. "It captures the input, drives the models, stores and accesses data, produces and transmits output, and helps control the total system."[22] Technology has three principal components: technicians, hardware, and software. Technicians are the people who work with the technology, understand it, and make it work. Software programs enable the computer to carry out the processes required by the models. Hardware consists of a variety of computers—large mainframe computers, minicomputers, and PCs. Each of these may be accompanied by various input, central processing, and output devices, as well as storage devices.

DATABASE

The **database** "is where all the data necessary to serve the needs of all users are stored."[23] Data may include text, numbers, voice, and images. Databases may or may not be computerized. The management of databases is becoming ever more significant because various users need different parts of the database. An organization may maintain databases on personnel, parts, services, competitors, inventories, customers, and numerous other kinds of information.

CONTROL

Every computer system should have control systems designed to protect it from natural disasters, such as fire, and from human hazards, such as fraud or sabotage. Most control devices, however, are designed to overcome inadequate operating procedures or poor management. Typical information system controls include records management systems, accounting controls, and personnel procedures.

OUTPUT

Output is the product of the information system. It consists of quality information for all levels of management and other users, both inside and outside the organization. It is the desired output that causes the models, other building blocks, and other components of the information system to be designed as they are. The output of a system can be only as good as the input and models on which it is based.

Designing an MIS

The designers of information systems must contend with ten major factors: integration, user/system interface, competitive forces, information quality and reusability, systems requirements, data-processing requirements, organizational factors, cost-effectiveness requirements, human factors, and feasibility requirements.[24] These factors are described briefly in Table 20.2. MIS designers must assess the relevance of each of these factors.

TABLE 20.2 Ten Primary Design Forces Affecting an MIS

Integration: Information systems must be designed to couple internal organizational units tightly. Manufacturing, marketing, personnel, and finance must be able to network with each other. Furthermore, in the future there will be much more integration with customer systems in order to provide better service.

User/System Interface: The system must be designed to make sure the user has ready access to the system and can use it with as few obstructions as possible.

Competitive Forces: The MIS must be designed to improve the organization's competitiveness and domestic and global market situation in a world of rapid and accelerating change.

Information Quality and Usability: Quality is defined by the user. It is user needs that ultimately determine how a system will be designed. Many times, unfortunately, various users' needs will be in conflict, and many users depending on the same MIS will want different types of information and want to massage it in different ways.

Systems Requirements: The inherent operational requirements of the MIS include reliability, availability, flexibility, installation schedule, life expectancy and growth potential, and ease of maintenance.

Data-Processing Requirements: There are four categories of data-processing requirements that are the detail work of the system: the volume of data involved, the complexity of data-processing information, processing time constraints, and computational demands.

Organizational Factors: There are five key organizational factors that affect the kind of information required. They include the nature of the organization, its primary structure, its size, its management style, and whether it is a functional organization, a divisional organization, or a matrix organization.

Cost-Effectiveness Requirements: Costs and benefits should be identified before a large amount of money is spent to develop an MIS.

Human Factors: Any time technology is introduced into a work situation, human factors become a key element and must be considered in the design of the system. People often fear and resist change.

Feasibility Requirements: Technical, economic, and legal operational and scheduling feasibility must be considered in the design of the system.

SOURCE: Abstracted with permission of John Wiley & Sons, Ltd. from John G. Burch and Gary Grudnitski, *Information Systems: Theory and Practice,* 4th ed. (New York: Wiley, 1986), pp. 41–50.

Figure 20.4 portrays these factors from the standpoint of their impact on the MIS. Sometimes the requirements of one factor will be in conflict with those of another. For example, when competition is very strong, the company must design the system to identify competitors' actions quickly. As a result, it might not pay enough attention to human factors—the needs of the system's users.

USER PARTICIPATION

Just as the participation of subordinates in management decisions leads to greater acceptance of those decisions, the users of an MIS should be involved in its design. Users have a very different perspective on their needs than technicians do.[25] Unless users are involved, they may be overwhelmed by useless information or may not receive the information they need. Moreover, if users do not participate with technicians in designing the system, serious line–staff conflicts may result; even when they do not participate, user satisfaction may not increase.[26] For example, strategists need certain kinds of information about potential product costs to help them make decisions about introducing new products. MIS designers are used to working with historical cost data; if strategists do not participate in the design of the system, their special needs will not be met.

AT LEVI STRAUSS: Considerable thought has been given to the MIS. Information can be communicated globally, not only internally but also to suppliers and customers.

FIGURE 20.4 FORCES IMPACTING ON THE MIS COMPONENTS

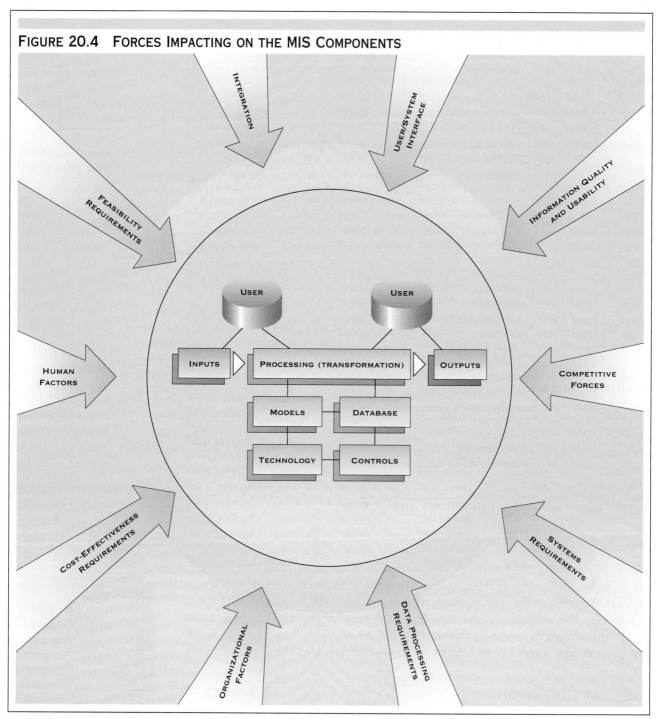

SOURCE: ADAPTED WITH PERMISSION OF JOHN WILEY & SONS, LTD. FROM JOHN G. BURCH AND GARY GRUDNITSKI, INFORMATION SYSTEMS: THEORY AND PRACTICE, 4TH ED. (NEW YORK: WILEY, 1986), P. 42.

Managing an MIS

Once the MIS has been designed and installed, there must be ongoing management of its various components. There must be planning, organizing, leading, controlling, and decision making relative to the information system itself. Much of the responsibility for managing the MIS lies with the MIS director; in larger companies, it lies with the CIO.

Information Requirements in a Changing Environment

Figure 20.5 identifies the types of internal and external environmental information an MIS should provide. As the figure shows, an information system can be both formal and informal and should collect extensive amounts of information so that it can be distributed to users and analyzed.

In Chapter 13 we discussed John Naisbitt's ten megatrends for the 1980s, which are expected to have an ongoing impact throughout the 1990s as well. We also listed his ten megatrends for the year 2000. Most of Naisbitt's predictions have been borne out by the events of the last few years, and the implications for business are tremendous. For example, the migration of the population from the northern United States to the southern and western parts of the country affects distribution systems, manufacturing locations, capital and personnel needs, and the need to train new workers. The trend toward decentralization in organizations directly affects the amount of authority to be distributed. The move from a national to a global economy impels businesses to think and act in global terms. The information requirements of such changes are staggering.[27]

If you combine these megatrends with the areas of major change identified by Tom Peters (listed in Table 13.2) and the ten management challenges identified in Chapter 1, you can see that an organization's environmental information system must change constantly to keep up with rapidly changing internal and external environments. As an example, consider the requirements posed by the increasing globalization of business. Developing information systems for a global business is a complex undertaking; developing a system for a nation-state such as Singapore is even more challenging. This chapter's Global Management Challenge describes how Singapore prepared itself for an information future.

The Strategic Use of Information

Information has become such an important resource that the firm that gathers and processes it most rapidly and utilizes it most effectively gains a strategic advantage over its competitors. Michael E. Porter and Victor E. Miller suggest

Management information systems can collect extensive amounts of diverse information. This control facility is typical of the management information systems being utilized by AT&T around the globe.

FIGURE 20.5 ENVIRONMENTAL INFORMATION PROVIDED BY AN MIS

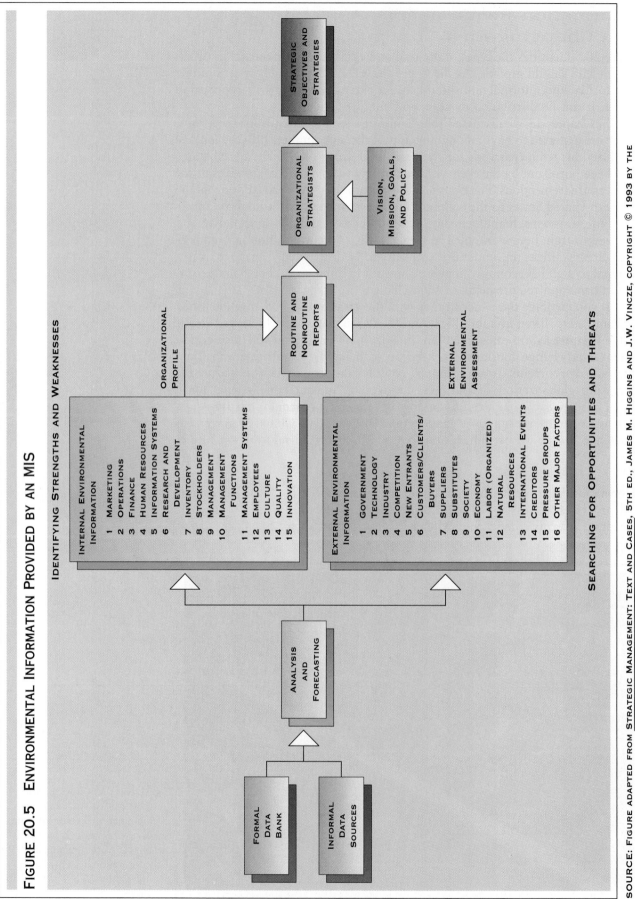

IDENTIFYING STRENGTHS AND WEAKNESSES

SEARCHING FOR OPPORTUNITIES AND THREATS

STRATEGIC OBJECTIVES AND STRATEGIES

ORGANIZATIONAL STRATEGISTS

VISION, MISSION, GOALS, AND POLICY

ROUTINE AND NONROUTINE REPORTS

ORGANIZATIONAL PROFILE

EXTERNAL ENVIRONMENTAL ASSESSMENT

INTERNAL ENVIRONMENTAL INFORMATION
1 MARKETING
2 OPERATIONS
3 FINANCE
4 HUMAN RESOURCES
5 INFORMATION SYSTEMS
6 RESEARCH AND DEVELOPMENT
7 INVENTORY
8 STOCKHOLDERS
9 MANAGEMENT
10 MANAGEMENT FUNCTIONS
11 MANAGEMENT SYSTEMS
12 EMPLOYEES
13 CULTURE
14 QUALITY
15 INNOVATION

EXTERNAL ENVIRONMENTAL INFORMATION
1 GOVERNMENT
2 TECHNOLOGY
3 INDUSTRY
4 COMPETITION
5 NEW ENTRANTS
6 CUSTOMERS/CLIENTS/ BUYERS
7 SUPPLIERS
8 SUBSTITUTES
9 SOCIETY
10 ECONOMY
11 LABOR (ORGANIZED)
12 NATURAL RESOURCES
13 INTERNATIONAL EVENTS
14 CREDITORS
15 PRESSURE GROUPS
16 OTHER MAJOR FACTORS

ANALYSIS AND FORECASTING

FORMAL DATA BANK

INFORMAL DATA SOURCES

SOURCE: FIGURE ADAPTED FROM STRATEGIC MANAGEMENT: TEXT AND CASES, 5TH ED., JAMES M. HIGGINS AND J.W. VINCZE, COPYRIGHT © 1993 BY THE DRYDEN PRESS, INC., A DIVISION OF HOLT, RINEHART AND WINSTON, INC., REPRINTED BY PERMISSION OF THE PUBLISHER.

Singapore Invests in an Information Future

Singapore is perhaps the most technologically advanced environment in the world. Though widely criticized for its repressive policies, its government has diligently invested in technological and human resources, creating an economy in which both individuals and organizations can flourish. Singapore is poised to become the world's first fully networked society, with all homes, schools, businesses, and government agencies interconnected in an electric grid. This small island-city, with almost no natural resources, lying at the tip of the Malay Peninsula is an extraordinarily convenient place to do business.

Singapore's economic strategy is instructive for other small nations, for large nations, and for companies of all sizes. As a result of its recent economic strategy, it has

- capitalized on its only natural advantage—its strategic location—by establishing superb transportation and materials-handling facilities.

- extended that advantage by providing other services, including financial services, to establish a sophisticated infrastructure for communications and information technology.

- constantly upgraded the skills of its work force in order to enable workers to keep pace with the more challenging demands of an information society.

- closely watched developments in global technology and absorbed them as quickly as possible.

The key to Singapore's ability to connect businesses and homes lies in fiber-optics deployment and the availability of ISDN (integrated services digital network). In 1989, Singapore became the first country to achieve 100 percent ISDN availability. (In the United States, the percentage of phone lines that can provide ISDN service ranges from 0.1 percent for Bell Atlantic and Pacific Bell to 1.9 percent for Bell South.) Among the results of Singapore's heavy investment in technology are a variety of networks, including AutoNet (for manufacturing information), RealNet (real estate), LawNet, PortNet, MediNet, BizNet, OrderLink (purchasing departments), InfoLink (databases), $Link (electronic payments), and SchoolLink (connecting all schools with the Ministry of Education).

The efficiency of the networks represents only part of the technological blitz. Public telephones use stored-value telephone cards; coin-operated telephones are obsolete. In 1991, the world's first public videophone booth was introduced by Singapore Telecom. It allows full-color, full-motion video to be sent to ten cities in Japan for about $20 for the first five minutes.

SOURCE: Rajendra S. Sisodia, "Singapore Invests in the Nation-Corporation," *Harvard Business Review* (May–June 1992), pp. 40–50.

ways in which information can be used to give a firm a competitive advantage. Quality strategic information enables a firm to cut costs or differentiate its products better than its competitors. For example, Caesar's Palace, in Las Vegas, was able to cut its budget for complimentary services to "high rollers" by 20 percent by scientifically tracking those customers on its computers. American Express was able to differentiate its travel services from those of other companies by tracking costs and obtaining the lowest fares and rates for its customers via information available on its computer system.

Porter and Miller suggest five steps to be followed in devising an information strategy:

1. Assess intensity of information use.
2. Determine the role of information technology and industry structure.
3. Identify and rank the ways in which information technology might create competitive advantage.
4. Investigate how information technology might spawn new businesses.
5. Develop a plan for taking advantage of information technology.[28]

In a modern organization this means that the manager must have an MIS at his or her disposal—"computers and software that tell managers what is going on in their companies and help them coordinate activities."[29]

Using information as a competitive tool rather than simply to process transactions and keep track of costs has enabled organizations to take the offensive. The ability to react—to make decisions quickly—is in itself a competitive edge. Federal Express provides an example. Its total commitment to the customer allowed it to develop and implement a strategic customer service system called COSMOS. This system is based on an MIS and telecommunications interface. A Federal Express package is tracked at every stage of the delivery process. This system allows the customer to call in to find out the location of any package. Each Federal Express courier is equipped with a hand-held scanner with built-in keyboard, read-out display, and 400K of memory. Packages are logged in and out by the scanner, which plugs into a microcomputer on board each van; the microcomputer, in turn, sends information to a computer at corporate head-

Federal Express used its COSMOS program as a major strategic weapon against other overnight delivery services. Through the use of bar codes transmitted over a telecommunications network, the company can identify the location of a customer's package at any point in the delivery process.

quarters in Memphis, Tennessee. The system was designed "to make it as easy as possible to do business with us." Its purpose is described as "adding value to our products to differentiate them from others."[30]

EISs AND SISs

More and more organizations are striving to develop a strategic MIS system, often referred to as an executive information system (EIS) or a strategic information system (SIS). Such a system supports and/or shapes the business unit's competitive strategy.[31] A strategic MIS offers new competitive opportunities by directly increasing productivity, flexibility, and responsiveness to customers.[32]

An EIS or SIS can be used competitively in many ways. For example, entry by competitors can be blocked by an on-line reservations system that is so convenient that everyone wants to use it. An automated order-entry system can discourage customers from changing suppliers. An EIS can also help the firm choose an optimal pricing strategy,[33] provide the information necessary to spot trends and move ahead of competitors, or provide human resource information for use in more effective implementation of strategies.[34]

One of the major issues in global competitiveness is the ability of Japanese firms to analyze their competitors, to know them almost better than they know themselves. Competitive analysis is a major focus of strategic planning.[35] However, to perform such an analysis, the manager must have an EIS or SIS that provides the necessary information. At present, few U.S. firms have such systems, but more are developing them.[36] This chapter's Ethical Management Challenge discusses the intelligence-gathering practices of some U.S. firms. Do you think these are ethical practices?

The MIS Director and the CIO

The MIS director helps guide management's decisions on hardware, software, system design and development, and system maintenance. He or she leads the professional MIS staff. The director plans, organizes, and controls the management information function.[37]

A **chief information officer** (CIO) is found primarily in larger corporations. The role of the CIO is broader than that of the MIS director. He or she is responsible for managing the use of information and systems from a strategic viewpoint. Take the case of Barnett Bank of Jacksonville, Florida. On the basis of recommendations by its CIO, the bank re-engineered its customer service delivery system, significantly improving customer satisfaction. It was cited by *CIO Magazine* for outstanding achievement in improving quality.[38]

As the need for information increases, CIOs will become more prominent in medium-sized organizations. As more businesses operate globally, many firms will replace CIOs with global information officers (GIOs).[39]

Chief information officer (CIO): *The manager who is responsible for managing the use of information and systems from a strategic viewpoint.*

The Changing Role of the MIS

The role of the MIS is changing in most organizations.[40] Technological changes have greatly increased the power and memory of PCs and enabled managers to manage more information themselves. This has reduced the need for a centralized MIS or data-processing office. PCs can be networked among departments that need to share database information. This also increases the need for large, centralized databases.[41]

An important development is *parallel processing,* in which a problem can be worked on by several computers simultaneously instead of by one computer

The Ethics of Intelligence Gathering

Exactly what constitutes ethical and unethical intelligence gathering is almost always defined in terms of what is legal and what is not. Beyond that, the line between them is rather fuzzy.

Some practices seem clearly ethical. Corning, for example, asks everyone in the firm, from the janitor on up, to provide any information they have about competitors to a central database. The information is analyzed and made available to employees throughout the world. The firm also hires intelligence consultants to provide profiles of competitors.

Nutrasweet's Strategic and Business Information Group recently started creating personality profiles of key decision makers at competing firms. The goal is to better understand and even anticipate competitors' strategic moves. Nutrasweet also monitors those firms' junior executives as they rise through the ranks of management.

Prime Computer's manager of competitor intelligence for the Computervision Division collects sales and product development information about competitors. It also publishes an electronic tipsheet of unfavorable information about competitors that its salespeople can use in appropriate selling situations.

R&D personnel at Merck and Company are expected to research scientific articles to make sure the firm is on the cutting edge of all new drug breakthroughs. If the company finds that a competitor is ahead of it, it tries to license that development. Most drug companies don't stop with this kind of research. They solicit information about their rivals from the federal government's Food & Drug Administration under the Freedom of Information Act. Such information would include data obtained in FDA inspections of competitors' plants.

Questionable ethical practices include the use of private investigators to obtain information about new-product developments. This often means listening to conversations in bars, lounges, and restaurants. It may also mean interviewing competitors' employees for fictitious job openings and prying information from them about critical new developments in their firms.

Some firms even go through competitors' dumpsters, even if the material in them has been shredded. Some managers will accept a competitor's proposal or other materials from valued customers who come into possession of such information.

In short, the lack of a clear definition of ethical behavior seems to have created an "anything goes" environment.

SOURCE: Michele Galen, "These Guys Aren't Spooks, They're 'Competitive Analysts,'" *Business Week* (October 14, 1991), p. 97.

at a time. Kmart uses parallel processing to monitor store-by-store sales in order to spot complex trends.[42] Parallel processing can provide fifty times more power than machines operating independently, making possible unbelievably fast, complex calculations. Such increased power is important to companies like Boeing, which uses parallel processing to simulate aircraft reactions to air flows and to forecast weather accurately 48 hours in advance.[43]

Another significant change is the development of managerial workstations—"systems that serve the manager in the same way that engineering workstations contribute to the productivity of technical personnel."[44] The following functions can be included in a managerial workstation:

1. Spreadsheet processing.
2. Word processing for preparing memos and reports.
3. Database management and a file system for setting up simple personal applications.
4. Presentation graphics for meetings.
5. Electronic mail.
6. Access to external databases.
7. Connection with networks to share data and programs.
8. An increased level of computational power.

Telecommunications and the MIS

Telecommunications consist of a series of technologically based communication techniques and processes that assist in the management decision process. Telecommunications are important accessories to the MIS because they expand its capabilities. Probably the best-known telecommunication technique is electronic mail.

Telecommunications: A series of technologically based communication techniques and processes that assist in the management decision process.

Electronic (E-) Mail

Electronic (E-) mail uses electronic circuitry to transmit written messages instantaneously. One of its best features is that messages can be sent any distance; they can be transmitted around the world via satellite. The message resides in the receiver's computer terminal until the individual turns it on. He or she may then respond in the same manner. This avoids the problem of "telephone tag." E-mail is less expensive than long-distance telephone calls and much faster than a typical letter or even overnight mail. It is extremely useful for communicating with many people simultaneously.

Electronic (E-) mail: The use of electronic circuitry to transmit written messages instantaneously.

As an example of how vital E-mail can be in a competitive situation, consider two TV channels. The Discovery Channel is very similar to the Arts and Entertainment Channel but uses 40 percent fewer employees to acquire, produce, and transmit 200 television programs a month to 4 million homes in the United States. With its 105 staff members constantly traveling, the key to its success is E-mail. Discovery's president, Ruth Otte, receives an average of 100 electronic memos a day in her Landover, Maryland, headquarters—or anywhere she can plug in her laptop PC. She says that she is never out of the office.[45]

AT LEVI STRAUSS: Managers make frequent use of electronic mail. This communication technique saves them hours that might be wasted in "telephone tag."

E-mail has had a significant impact on communications, at least partly because it can be linked with a diverse array of other devices, such as fax machines, PCs, microcomputers, and computer-based managing systems.[46] LTV Aerospace and Defense Company, headquartered in Dallas, uses an E-mail adaptation to give its fourteen thousand employees faster and easier access to corporate information systems and databases. Before this system was installed, few employees took advantage of the information available to them.[47]

Computer conferencing is a multiparty extension of E-mail. Individuals at numerous terminals can communicate with each other simultaneously, sending and receiving messages.

Computer conferencing: A multiparty extension of electronic mail.

The **electronic bulletin board** is a computerized system for distributing memos throughout the organization. Typically these are routine memos on sub-

Electronic bulletin board: A computerized system for distributing memos throughout an organization.

jects like job openings, special events, and policies, rules, regulations, and procedures. The bulletin board can also be used as an electronic library in which all of that information is stored.

The Fax Machine

Fax machine: A machine that uses electronic circuitry and telephone cabling to transmit visual images.

The **fax** machine uses electronic circuitry and telephone cabling to transmit visual images, in much the same way that E-mail transmits written messages. Fax communication has the same benefits as E-mail. It is less expensive than a long-distance telephone call and can be done instantaneously, regardless of the distance between the sender and the receiver. Like E-mail, it is faster than a letter or overnight mail.

The Cellular Phone

Voice mail: A system in which a computer acts as an answering machine, taking messages from callers.

Managers can keep in touch with other members of the organization or with clients while traveling by using a cellular phone. This technology enables executives and nonmanagerial personnel such as salespeople to utilize commuting time between home and office, or between job locations, more efficiently.[48] In the future, pocket-sized phones will be carried everywhere, allowing people to conduct global satellite conversations.[49]

Video conferencing: The use of live television in a conference format.

Voice Mail

In **voice mail** the computer acts as an answering machine, taking messages from callers.[50] Voice-fax mail integration is expected to be a major office product in the 1990s.[51]

Video Conferencing

Video conferencing employs live television in a conference format. Often, but not always, people at numerous sites receiving the video program are able to see each other. The Federal Judicial Center uses video conferencing extensively. Its training clientele numbers more than 17,000, including judges serving in more than 100 federal trial and appellate courts in the United States and its territories. Video conferencing has reduced the difficulty of delivering training quickly and efficiently on time-sensitive issues, such as recent court rulings that might affect cases elsewhere. A number of video conferences have been held using 430 receiving sites, most with audiences of 150 to more than 2,000 people.[52] GE has installed eighty-six video conference centers in more than a dozen countries to help cut travel costs, improve communication, expand markets, and reduce employee fatigue.[53]

Electronic Data Interchange (EDI)

Electronic data interchange (EDI): The exchange of data across organizational boundaries using information technology.

Electronic data interchange (EDI) is the exchange of information across organizational boundaries using information technology.[54] It involves linking database systems among companies, customers, and suppliers. Such systems provide a significant strategic advantage. Many programs link not only their databases but all their electronic telecommunications in order to provide better service. Roger Milliken, head of the textile firm Milliken and Company, claims that this electronic pipeline is "the beginning of a revolution in our industry." It enables his firm and others to compete with their Asian rivals by making it easier for retailers to work with U.S. suppliers.[55] EDI has recently gone global: Citicorp and Motorola jointly developed a global EDI-based trade payments system.[56]

MANAGEMENT INFORMATION SYSTEMS HAVE BEEN TRANSFORMED BY NEW COMMUNICATION TECHNOLOGIES. FOR EXAMPLE, AT MANY RESTAURANTS AND DELIS CUSTOMERS CAN SEND IN THEIR ORDERS BY FAX; THE ORDER WILL BE WAITING FOR THEM WHEN THEY ARRIVE. CELLULAR PHONES ENABLE MANAGERS TO KEEP IN TOUCH WITH OTHER MEMBERS OF THE ORGANIZATION WHILE TRAVELING, AND MANY MANAGERS ARE USING LAPTOP AND NOTEBOOK COMPUTERS IN CONJUNCTION WITH TELECOMMUNICATIONS TO ACCESS DATABASES AND PREPARE REPORTS WHILE AWAY FROM THE OFFICE. FOR LARGER GROUPS, VIDEO CONFERENCING, WHICH EMPLOYS LIVE TELEVISION IN A CONFERENCE FORMAT, MAKES IT POSSIBLE FOR MANAGERS AT SEVERAL LOCATIONS TO HOLD FACE-TO-FACE MEETINGS.

Laptop, Palmtop, and Notebook Computers

Laptop PCs assist an MIS when they can be used in conjunction with telecommunications—for example, to receive voice mail, teleconferencing, database information, or electronic mail. They are used by salespeople to access databases and by anyone wishing to prepare reports while away from the office. Similarly, notebook PCs and palmtops (smaller laptops) can be included in the MIS and be used to access it.

Decision Support Systems (DSSs) and Expert Systems (ESs)

Many organizations are turning to decision support systems (DSSs) to aid their managers in making decisions.[57] DSSs do more than simply provide management information; they actually contribute to the decision-making process.[58] Break-even analysis is an example of a simple DSS. A sophisticated DSS might include an integrated system of spreadsheets, graphics, and databases. All DSSs are MISs, but not all MISs are DSSs. Similarly, all expert systems (ESs) are MISs, but they are not DSSs because they provide solutions. In the following paragraphs, we discuss these three systems and the major differences among them.

DSSs

DSSs are conceived of as supporting, not replacing, managerial judgment.[59] They have been applied in many kinds of organizations to a wide variety of functions. One successful system, which combines traditional MIS functioning and a DSS, helps Air France decide which of its employees should have days off and when, a complicated process in such a large firm.[60] Most authorities in the field believe that the use of DSSs will increase significantly in the future because more user-friendly software will be available.

ESs and Artificial Intelligence (AI)

Artificial intelligence (AI): *Attempts to enable a computer to simulate human reasoning by working with qualitative as well as quantitative information.*

T. H. Winston defines **artificial intelligence** (AI) as "the study of ideas which enable computers to do the things that make people seem intelligent."[61] AI attempts to simulate human reasoning by working with qualitative as well as quantitative information. It often provides rules of thumb that yield good, though not always optimal, solutions. It allows users to deal with "fuzzy" reasoning, in which decisions are not based entirely on rational analysis but involve intuition. Fuzzy logic has caught on in Japan, where firms use it extensively in many kinds of applications.[62] Among the areas in which AI has been applied are robotics, understanding language, and ESs.

Expert systems (ESs) "can be used to preserve and disseminate scarce expertise by encoding the relevant experience of an expert and making this expertise available as a resource to the less experienced person."[63] One of the most important ways in which ESs differ from DSSs and MISs is in their use of heuristic reasoning. DSSs and MISs typically employ algorithms—that is, precise rules that always lead to a correct conclusion. ESs are used for more complex problems for which a "correct" conclusion is not always possible—such as forecasting the weather or diagnosing a disease.[64] In summary, then, ESs differ from MISs and DSSs in the following ways:

AT LEVI STRAUSS:
Expert systems are used in inventory management.

1. They contain facts and additional knowledge that an expert would use to solve a problem.[65]

This technician is analyzing data produced by GTE-Sylvania's Connectionist system, an expert system that tracks variations in heat, pressure, and chemicals used to make fluorescent bulbs and determines the optimum manufacturing conditions.

2. They explain the reasons for the conclusion upon request.
3. They are designed to imitate the human decision-making process.
4. They are normally designed to solve a problem by asking questions, rather than just accepting given input, as DSSs and MISs typically do.[66]
5. They sometimes learn from experience.[67]

It can be quite expensive to develop an ES. For example, the development of INTERNIST, a medical expert system, required the equivalent of a year of work by twenty-six people. However, this comprehensive ES provides doctors with extremely accurate diagnoses of numerous diseases.[68]

Expert systems have the potential to save hundreds of thousands, and perhaps millions, of dollars in certain applications. Arthur Andersen created a driver's license processing system for the state of Pennsylvania in only twenty work days. The system handles 90 percent of all the license processing for the state. This ES replaced a system that took four hundred work days to create but could handle only 25 percent of the processing.[69] A number of ESs have been developed that enable accounting firms to improve productivity significantly. Among these are AUDITOR, TAX ADVISER, TAX MAN, CORP TAX, and PLAN POWER.[70] Increases in productivity ranging from 500 to 1,000 percent are typical when ESs are used.[71]

To some extent, ESs will not only aid decision makers but replace many of them.[72] In fact, much of middle management may disappear as top management makes greater use of ESs. This chapter's Quality Management Challenge describes a successful expert system in some detail.

Executive Information Systems

An **executive information system** includes all information systems tailored to the specific needs of executives. Thus, portions of the MIS, such as the strategic information system, decision support systems, and expert systems, would all be included. Executive information systems are increasingly becoming available in user-friendly formats. Executives have tended to shy away from using PCs, partly because of the time needed to learn how to use software that was not user-friendly, but that is changing. As with other managers, an executive's productivity can be greatly increased by using PCs and related software.

Executive information system: An information system tailored to the specific needs of executives.

United Uses Expert Systems to Reduce Delays at Hubs

United Airlines was confronted by delays at its hubs in Chicago and Denver. Part of the problem was that gate controllers had a huge amount of information to process and made assignments largely on the basis of memory and rules of thumb. To solve this problem, United turned to an expert system called Gate Assignment Display System (GADS). GADS was designed to reduce flight delays related to ground operations. This artificial intelligence program was created by drawing upon the experience and knowledge of United's main controllers and systems analysts through a process known as knowledge engineering transfer.

GADS receives on-line, real-time information from United's central flight information data system, which contains information on current, past, and future United flights. The program incorporates the knowledge and reasoning of the experts who had been making gate assignments. It has eliminated the need for the time-consuming gate boards previously used to process gate assignments. GADS's video graphics presentation provides for overhead displays of aircraft and their gates. The displays indicate such important factors as arrival and departure times and airplane numbers. The system also allows the gate controller to try out different combinations of aircraft and gates before changing gate assignments. GADS automatically adjusts the gate plan as the controller moves a plane from one gate to another. In short, the controller has the ability to play "what if" games with gate assignments.

SOURCE: Carole A. Shifrin, "Gate Assignment Expert System Reduces Delays at United's Hubs," *Aviation Week and Space Technology* (January 25, 1988), pp. 112–113.

Computer Integrated Businesses

Computer integrated business: *A firm whose main functions exchange information constantly and quickly via computers.*

A **computer integrated business** is a firm whose main functions—marketing, operations, finance, distribution, human resources—exchange information constantly and quickly via computers.[73] In essence, the firm's computers talk to each other as often as possible. Networking of computers is vital to such efforts. The main results are improved customer satisfaction and greater productivity. A salesperson, for example, can tell a customer exactly where an order is in the manufacturing process or can place an order and immediately adjust the manufacturing and distribution processes accordingly. Speed is the most compelling reason for integrating computers. Numerous firms, such as Frito-Lay, Saturn Corporation, and Sony, have become computer integrated.[74]

Protecting the Information System

The MIS is subject to a variety of control problems, including controlling the performance of knowledge technicians, controlling the performance capability of the hardware and the software, and controlling the design of the system. Total loss of information may occur as a result of an earthquake or other natural disaster. Disaster protection systems include database duplicates.

One of the most important factors in controlling an MIS is preventing invasion by viruses. A **virus** is a small unit of computer code written by a programmer that can attach itself to other programs, alter them, or destroy data kept on a computer disk.[75] Viruses are capable of reproducing themselves and attaching themselves to other programs stored in the same computer. Typically, a virus is attached to a normal software program, which becomes its "Trojan horse." The virus spreads as the owner of the Trojan horse exchanges software with other computer users, typically through an electronic bulletin board or through the exchange of floppy disks. The more programs are exchanged, the more the virus spreads, but people may not be aware of it for several months because the code may not instruct the virus to take effect until later. Eventually the virus activates itself, usually according to the computer's internal clock. At this point the virus strikes, often wreaking havoc with the computers and programs that have come into contact with it. The process of creation, distribution, infection, and attack is illustrated in Figure 20.6.

To show the pervasiveness and potency of viruses, Richard R. Brandow, publisher of a Montreal computer magazine, and his co-worker, Pierre N. Zovile, created a benign virus. In two months, illegal copying apparently trans-

Virus: A small unit of computer code that can attach itself to other programs, alter them, or destroy data kept on a disk.

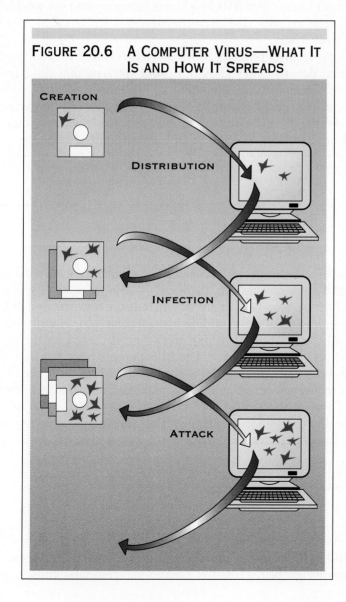

FIGURE 20.6   A COMPUTER VIRUS—WHAT IT IS AND HOW IT SPREADS

CREATION

DISTRIBUTION

INFECTION

ATTACK

One of the most important factors in controlling an MIS is preventing invasion by viruses. Virex is an example of a "vaccine," or antivirus program.

ferred the virus to more than 350,000 Macintoshes around the world. When the virus struck, each machine displayed the message "Universal Message of Peace to All Macintosh Users."[76]

Solving the security problem posed by viruses is tricky. Alert employees are the first line of defense. They should not use software and disks from an unknown source. There are also a number of "vaccines"—that is, software programs that can track down viruses. Security software can be placed on large mainframe computers. Antivirus software is also available, and computer users can use dial-back systems to ensure that incoming phone calls come only from authorized sources.[77] Some companies are spending large sums on protection against viruses.

How an MIS Affects the Organization

Like any type of technology, an MIS arouses a number of somewhat predictable responses from an organization's members. Resistance to change is one. Other key effects of the development of an MIS include the restructuring of the organization; the elimination of many middle-management jobs, as well as certain staff positions; and the creation of *technostress*—stress caused by the introduction and increased use of technology.[78] The MIS changes basic business documents because they have to be tailored to the capacities of the computer.[79] The MIS also changes the way in which individuals make decisions. Because the computer does most of the number crunching, the individual is freed to do more creative thinking. Finally, the MIS may change an organization's culture as it becomes increasingly knowledge based.

The Knowledge-Based Organization

Knowledge-based organizations are the organizations of the future.[80] As C. W. Holsapple and A. B. Whinston observe, "In a most fundamental sense, organizations will increasingly be regarded as joint human-computer knowledge-processing systems. Human participants in these systems, from the most highly skilled to the least skilled positions, can be regarded as knowledge workers. Collectively they will work with many types of knowledge, in a variety of ways, and with various objectives. Their knowledge management efforts will be aided and supported by computers. Not only will these computer co-workers relieve us of the menial, routine, and repetitive, they will also actively recognize needs, stimulate insights, and offer advice. They will highly leverage an organization's uniquely human skills of intuition, creative imagination, value-judgment, the cultivation of effective interpersonal relationships, and so forth."[81]

The organization of the future is dynamically different from the majority of organizations in existence today. However, several organizations, such as Bell Labs and Allen-Bradley Corporation's manufacturing plant in Milwaukee, resemble this description, as do many Japanese firms.[82] There are at least two implications for management. First, the new organization requires changes in management style. New management systems and methodologies will be needed. Managers must learn to manage knowledge (for example, by communicating knowledge throughout the organization). Second, the new organization presents opportunities for increased efficiency and effectiveness.

The **knowledge workers** "are concerned with procuring, storing, organizing, maintaining, reading, analyzing, presenting, distributing, and employing knowledge in order to meet an organization's goals."[83] Some workers will perform all these functions and work with all types of knowledge; others will perform only some. Technological advances in both hardware and software will enable the knowledge worker to employ new kinds of tools in solving problems.

Training the knowledge worker will be critical. A rudimentary level of computer literacy will be necessary but not sufficient for a worker in a truly knowledge-based organization. Workers will have to learn about knowledge itself—how it is organized, the learning process, representation techniques— and they will have to be skilled in using computers to manipulate knowledge. Cooperation and sharing of knowledge among workers will also be extremely important.

Workers of the future—that is, knowledge workers—will be largely self-managed problem solvers; as a result, the nature and scope of management will change. The managerial role will change dramatically, and there will be fewer managers.[84] Instead of resting in the hands of a few members of the organization, management will be performed by everyone. Millions of people will plan, organize, lead, and control themselves as they solve problems at their workstations.

AT LEVI STRAUSS:
Knowledge workers need full access to necessary information. At Levi Struass this includes access to personnel records.

Knowledge workers: Workers concerned with procuring, storing, organizing, maintaining, reading, analyzing, presenting, distributing, and employing knowledge in order to meet an organization's goals.

Managing Information as a Problem-Solving Process

This chapter lacks a summary chart like those found at the ends of earlier chapters. The reason is that the MIS is an important tool at every stage of the problem-solving process. Throughout the process of solving a problem or making a decision, the manager should consider all available information using the MIS (or a DSS or an ES if appropriate).

Summary

(Before reading this summary, look again at the objectives listed at the beginning of the chapter.)

1. Information consists of data that have been put into a meaningful and useful context and communicated to a recipient who uses it to make decisions. Quality information is accurate, timely, and relevant. Information is a vital organizational resource and may even be a strategic advantage when used properly.

2. A management information system (MIS) aids managers in making decisions by collecting, organizing, and distributing information.

3. Information systems have evolved from financial systems to systems dealing with all functional areas of the organization. They have developed from systems based on hand calculations to electronic data processing to formal MISs, DSSs, and ESs.

4. MISs are designed around six components: inputs, models, technology, databases, controls, and outputs. Designers of these systems take into account ten key factors: integration, user/system interface, competitive forces, information quality and reusability, systems requirements, data-processing requirements, organizational factors, cost-effectiveness requirements, human factors, and feasibility requirements.

5. An MIS must be managed on an ongoing basis. It should provide both internal and external environmental information and be able to change as those environments change. This enables management to use it as a competitive tool.

6. The chief information officer (CIO) looks for and develops strategic uses of information.

7. PCs and other microcomputers have enabled managers to use information much more effectively than in the past. This has caused the information management function to be more widely dispersed, with the central MIS department retaining responsibility for databases.

8. Technological advances enable managers to make better, more rational decisions based on greater analysis of information and, more recently, advice on possible solutions.

9. An MIS can result in restructuring, changes in the way decision making occurs, and improved decision making. It can also lead to technostress and resistance to change. The entire organizational culture may change, and people may be freed from routine tasks so that they can engage in more creative work.

10. The knowledge-based organization of the future will feature knowledge workers who use workstations, support centers, communication paths, and knowledge storehouses to make decisions—that is, to solve problems.

THINKING
ABOUT
MANAGEMENT

General Questions

1. Research the MISs used in the college or university at which you are taking this course. Discuss them in terms of type, design, ability to provide the right information, and impact on the organization, and indicate how well they are controlled.

2. Discuss computer viruses and the ways in which organizations can protect themselves against them.

3. Describe the knowledge-based organization of the future.

4. Describe how expert systems will help people manage in the future.

5. Discuss why virtually everyone in business needs to know how to use a computer.

6. Discuss the importance of MISs from the standpoint of the management challenges.

Questions on the Management Challenge Features

GLOBAL MANAGEMENT CHALLENGE

1. Describe how Singapore prepared for an information future.

2. Describe the role of knowledge in this strategy.

ETHICAL MANAGEMENT CHALLENGE

1. Evaluate each company's actions in terms of whether they are ethical or not.

2. What makes an intelligence-gathering practice ethical or unethical?

QUALITY MANAGEMENT CHALLENGE

1. Describe United Airlines' gate program as an expert system.

2. Why is United's program effective?

E P I L O G U E

Levi Strauss & Co. Takes Its Information Systems Seriously

As might be expected in a firm that takes information seriously, the information resources department at Levi Strauss is huge. It has divisions devoted to business communications, engineering, information support, contractor communications, design, finance, graphics, operations services, technical services, user support, and information-processing administration. The department is headed by a chief information officer.

DISCUSSION QUESTIONS

1. What types of information would a firm like Levi Strauss be looking for?

2. Why would a firm want to make its information system available to its employees?

3. Why did Levi Strauss enable its employees to have access to their personal information files?

4. Discuss the complexity of the task of managing information systems in a firm like Levi Strauss.

Gathering Information About Competitors

Bob Jones was an engineering manager for the workstation division of a multinational computer corporation. The workstation division was one of fifteen businesses of the parent company, whose annual sales totaled $10 billion. The parent company had always followed a strategy of building products at a lower cost than competitors, using their technology. But for the first time in its history one of its divisions, the workstation division, had developed proprietary technology that was leading the industry.

The workstation division was headquartered in the Southeast. The firm's major competitor was headquartered in San Diego. A recent story in a computer magazine had indicated that the two firms were neck and neck in technology, and that the other firms in this market had inferior products. The main competitor had more than 25 percent of the market; Jones's firm had 20 percent. With the total market expected to reach $6 billion in five years, Jones's manager wanted to ensure that the firm had a major share.

An important change in the market's structure was expected in the next few months, as new software made the workstation more user friendly and managers, rather than engineers, became its primary users. Jones's boss wanted to know how far along the main competitor was in developing this software and what its overall strategy was for the next five years. He asked Jones to draw up a plan for getting this information.

DISCUSSION QUESTIONS

1. If you were Jones, what types of information would you need to gather?
2. How would you go about gathering that information?
3. How would you design an information system to handle this information?

MANAGE
YOURSELF

Developing an Executive Information System

The instructor will divide the class into small groups. Each group will develop the components of an executive information system for a five hundred-person manufacturing or service firm. Key features should be noted, as well as the major pieces of information needed. After a few minutes, the instructor will ask the groups to report their findings to the class.

AT&T's Universal Card

When AT&T examined its portfolio of businesses and considered alternative ways of investing available funds, it identified many opportunities. One of those was to acquire NCR corporation, which would enable it to enter the workstation and PC markets. Another was to offer a credit card. Many people wondered whether U.S. consumers really needed another credit card. In analyzing the situation, AT&T believed that it had to offer something different in order to be competitive. So it offered a combined calling card and credit card (MasterCard or Visa). Cardholders receive a 10 percent discount on long-distance calls made on AT&T lines, zero-plus dialing, a single itemized bill for charges and long-distance calls, a single customer service number, and no fee for using the card. AT&T Universal Card Services Corporation (UCS) introduced its Universal Card in March 1990, and it quickly became the fastest-growing credit card in history. Within four months UCS had issued 2.6 million accounts. By June 1991, it had issued 10.6 million cards to 6.2 million accounts. It grew so quickly that its resources were strained and it had to cut back on its advertising in order to reduce the number of new accounts to 300,000 per month. By October 1992, UCS was the second largest credit card issuer in the nation. Over 98 percent of customers rate the Universal Card as better than any competing credit card.

From the beginning, the firm wanted high-quality service to be the cornerstone of the new venture. To achieve this goal, it established three imperatives: (1) Delight the customer, (2) delight the employee, and (3) continuously improve service to both.

DELIGHTING THE CUSTOMER

UCS's overall program for quality is known as "Delighting the Customer." More specifically, quality is defined as exceeding customers' expectations in every way. Every employee pays homage to the company slogan, "Customers are the center of our universe." Control plays a special role in delighting the customer. There are three primary means by which the firm listens to the customer and thereby controls

quality: (1) An attribute study is conducted every month to find out what matters to customers. (2) Face-to-face sessions are held with customers in cities throughout the United States. (3) More than 150 measurements of performance by employees and vendors are sampled every day. Eleven monthly surveys track customer satisfaction, and there are eight customer-related databases. The quality pledge has been extended to vendors, and virtually all have agreed to participate in partnership programs to provide high quality. For example, because UCS was concerned that its image might be tarnished by credit applications rejected by credit bureaus, it pushed the three major bureaus to improve customer service by opening service centers that answer calls from individuals who have been denied a Universal Card. The company is also strongly encouraging the bureaus to improve the integrity of the data in their files.

DELIGHTING THE EMPLOYEE

Delighting the employee means that the firm pays careful attention to employee needs because it believes that only if employees are delighted will they delight the customer. For example, the firm has empowered employees to take needed actions on their own to delight the customer. It has provided special reward and recognition programs. And it has paid careful attention to employee benefit programs, which include wellness care, a fitness center, and a day care center. The theme of continuous improvement is reinforced with several measures, including a very successful suggestion program called "Ideas."

CONTINUOUS IMPROVEMENT

Continuously improving service to customers begins with the actions taken to delight the customer. This means reacting to what customers do not like and what they really want. Since its formation, the company has used the Baldridge Award criteria as its quality standards. (UCS won the award in 1992.) Continuously improving service to employees means constant attention to employee needs.

Careful attention has been paid to managing the

organization's culture to ensure that it supports the company's quality and continuous-improvement goals. These include the performance and reward systems and the suggestion program. In addition, cross-functional teams attack problems, offering solutions and developing performance measurement systems to ensure that the solutions were appropriate. For example, the firm has a "Ten Most Wanted List" that depicts the ten most-needed quality improvements. When a problem has been resolved, the item is retired from the list in a brief ceremony.

In addition, there are numerous little recognition programs for employees. One is known as the Power Award. To the sound of a gas-powered noisemaker like those used at football games, a manager marches through the building announcing the bestowing of the Power Award on an employee for outstanding quality service. A little ceremony is held and the employee then displays the award on his or her desk. Employees may also participate in the "Meeting of the Month," attend "Lunch and Learn" sessions with upper management, and join business improvement teams.

INNOVATION

One of the key features of UCS's efforts is innovation in pursuit of quality. Clever, inventive programs and ways of communicating them have bolstered the firm's focus on quality service. And the firm is open to innovation through continuous improvement. Its "Ideas" suggestion program, for example, receives thirty times as many suggestions per employee as the industry average. It elicits so many suggestions because the firm acts on them and reports on its actions or nonactions to those concerned.

DISCUSSION QUESTIONS
1. Describe how control helped AT&T achieve its strategic objectives for its credit card.
2. What role did information systems play in this control process?

SOURCES: "Five Companies Win 1992 Baldridge Quality Award," *Business America* (November 2, 1992), pp. 7–8; "AT&T Universal Card Services," *Business America* (November 2, 1992), pp. 12–13; Linda Punch, "Operational Excellence: AT&T Universal Card—AT&T's Battle for Better Bureaus," *Credit Card Management* (August 1992), p. 24; Kevin T. Keleghan, "Quality of Service: Dancing to the Customer's Tune," *Retail Control* (March 1992), pp. 3–8; James J. Daly, "AT&T's Unfinished Conquest," *Credit Card Management* (August 1991), pp. 52–53; Kate Fitzgerald, "Card Issuers Poised to Fight AT&T," *Advertising Age* (July 2, 1990), p. 12; and Paul C. Kahn, "Not 'Just Another Credit Card,'" *Credit World* (May–June 1990), pp. 38–41.

PART SEVEN

Contemporary Issues in Management

The management process is changing so rapidly that it is impossible to keep track of all the changes or to treat all of them at great length in a text like this one. Throughout this book we have noted the ten management challenges wherever they have been discussed, and most major issues in management have been presented. But three remain that are significant enough to warrant a chapter each.

Chapter 21 examines operations management, a critical component of competition in the 1990s. Because Japanese firms and other competitors have become so proficient at operations management, U.S. managers have been forced to improve their skills in this area, first in manufacturing and more recently in service operations. Chapter 22 discusses the vital topic of entrepreneurship. Many experts believe that the United States' economic success is due to entrepreneurship. But entrepreneurs don't always know how to manage. Among the topics discussed in Chapter 22 are ways in which entrepreneurs could become better managers. Chapter 23 examines two pervasive forces in contemporary management: quality and innovation. These two forces are changing the way people manage and the way people behave in organizations.

"When you aim for perfection, you discover it's a moving target."

—Motorola Corporation
"Power of Belief"

"Being good just isn't good enough any more. We must be better."

—R. E. Heckert
Chairman
E. I. duPont de Nemours and Company

Operations Management

CHAPTER OBJECTIVES

When you have read this chapter you should be able to:

1. Describe the operations management function in manufacturing and service industries.

2. Relate why operations management has become so critical in recent years.

3. Discuss each of the principal strategic, tactical, and operational decisions in operations management.

4. Describe operations as a strategic weapon.

5. Discuss the impact of the globalization of business on the operations function.

6. Indicate why Japanese firms' operations management practices have been so successful.

7. Describe the importance of inventory to manufacturing.

8. Discuss the importance of manufacturing and service quality as it relates to successful business strategy.

9. Describe the factory of the future.

10. Indicate how productivity can be improved.

MANAGEMENT CHALLENGES DISCUSSED IN THIS CHAPTER:

 Increasing globalization of business.

 Increasing levels of competition.

 Changing technology.

 Quality and innovation as managerial imperatives.

CHAPTER OUTLINE

Allen-Bradley's Drive for 21st-Century Manufacturing

Allen-Bradley Corporation (a unit of Rockwell International) specializes in industrial controls. In the mid-1980s, it was faced with increasing levels of competition from Europe and Japan, especially in its electric motor control business. Because contactors and relays are major components in these controls, and European and Japanese models cost less and were smaller, the company decided to protect its core electric motor control business by making European-style contactors and relays; otherwise it would have missed out on a growing market and possibly lost some of its core business.

In an effort to cut costs, the company first explored the possibility of setting up manufacturing operations outside the United States. However, after adjusting for the additional costs of nonautomated factories in order to hire low-cost labor—at $1 an hour in Mexico—it determined that the cost per foreign worker would be an additional $12 per hour, for a total of $13 per hour, $2 short of the $15-per-hour cost of workers in Milwaukee. The company therefore decided to build the most modern computer-integrated manufacturing (CIM) line possible. It invested $15 million in what is now considered the most advanced such factory in the United States and possibly in the world. Recently the CIM factory was expanded at a cost of $9.5 million.

In the new CIM factory a computer analyzes orders and materials requirements and determines the daily production schedule. The totally robotized CIM assembly line is given instructions determining what is to be produced and when and where it is to be shipped, the materials to be employed, and where the materials are to be obtained. All inputs, outputs, and process areas are bar coded, allowing the computer to keep track of the production process. The system is so sophisticated that it can make different products, even a single unit, in a variety of sizes at assembly-line speeds.

Admittedly, manufacturing contactors, relays, and circuit boards is not as complex as manufacturing automobiles or other highly sophisticated and numerous subassembly-type products. However, subassemblies could be manufactured and put together using the same principles. Many other manufacturers have studied Allen-Bradley's plants and are planning to use similar technological applications in their plants.

SOURCES: "Allen-Bradley Invents New CIM Plant Strategy," *Modern Materials Handling* (July 1992), pp. 12–13; Leslie C. Jasany, "How to Regain Competitiveness with a Manufacturing Strategy," *Controls & Systems* (July 1992), pp. 16–17; Joseph F. McKenna, "Not a Facility but a Capability," *Industry Week* (June 15, 1992), pp. 60–61; Gene Bylinski, "Breakthrough in Automating the Assembly Line," *Fortune* (May 26, 1986), pp. 64–66; and John S. DeMott, "American Scene: In Old Milwaukee: Tomorrow's Factory Today," *Time* (June 16, 1986), pp. 66–67.

In recent years, American businesses have accepted the crucial importance of operations management to competing in the global marketplace. Their fiercest competitors, primarily those in the Pacific Rim countries and especially those in Japan and more recently Korea, have become masters of the operations function. They have been able to produce high-quality, low-cost products (and, more recently, services) not only because of lower labor costs, but also because they have made a commitment to their manufacturing processes and have taken the time and effort to perfect them. Allen-Bradley's efforts to improve its manufacturing processes are typical of the efforts of American firms to improve their operations. More and more companies have realized that, to compete in a global marketplace, they must produce high-quality, low-cost products and services.[1,2]

For the first few years after World War II, Japanese products were widely considered inferior to American products. Today, Japanese manufacturers are considered superior to their U.S. counterparts in many industries.[3] In the late 1950s and early 1960s many Japanese firms hired American consultants, who introduced them to the concepts and techniques of quality control. Among the most prominent of those consultants were William Edwards Deming and Joseph M. Juran.[4] A third expert, Phil Crosby, became widely known in the 1980s for his advocacy of "zero defects" as a way of managing.[5]

Through the writings of other management experts, such as Douglas McGregor, the Japanese recognized that traditional authority relationships, symbolized in hierarchical pyramids, were unsuited to achieving the highest levels of productivity.[6] They adopted group-based participative management systems, which fit naturally into their culture.

This combination of a high-quality orientation, continuous improvement, and participative management systems in manufacturing, along with recent technological advances, has propelled the Japanese to world leadership in numerous major products, such as automobiles, electronics, cameras, and steel. Firms in several other Pacific Rim countries have followed those strategies, placing tremendous cost pressures on Japanese firms because they can benefit from much lower wage rates than those prevailing in Japan.[7] Firms in Korea, Taiwan,

To compete in a global marketplace, companies must produce high-quality, low-cost products and services. Allen-Bradley's efforts to improve its manufacturing processes are typical of the efforts of American firms to become more competitive by improving their operations.

Singapore, and Hong Kong have become major competitors with Japanese firms in U.S. markets. They have even made inroads into Japanese markets. Hyundai (automobiles) and Daewoo (electronics and automobiles) are examples.

In this chapter, we will explore how the operations process occurs in both manufacturing and service organizations, how operations can be used to gain a strategic advantage, and the major trends in operations management. Much of the focus of the chapter is on operations management in manufacturing, but most aspects of the discussion are relevant to service operations as well.[8]

In most industries in most countries, it is becoming imperative to have a high-quality, low-cost product, regardless of the targeted market segment. Quality in manufacturing has become the price of entry in most industries.[9] Therefore, while this chapter introduces the basic concepts of operations management, it also offers insight into the changes that will be necessary if a firm is to compete in the future.

Operations Management in Manufacturing and Service Organizations[10]

Operations managers, whether they work in manufacturing or service organizations, are confronted with very similar problems. All organizations take inputs and transform them into outputs, as suggested by Figure 21.1. This is particularly clear in the manufacturing process, where a tangible product is produced; however, the same transformation occurs in service organizations. Labor is the principal input in service organizations, whereas raw materials, subcomponent parts, and labor are the major inputs in manufacturing operations. Put simply, a manufacturing organization transforms inputs into physical outputs, or products, and a service organization transforms inputs into nonphysical outputs, or services, that usually involve interaction with customers. Table 21.1 presents some other differences between the two types of organizations. Keep in mind, however, that some organizations produce both products and services; also, many jobs in a manufacturing organization are actually service jobs.

Operations management:
The planning, organizing, leading, and controlling of productive systems.

Operations managers:
Individuals responsible for producing the supply of goods or services in organizations.

Operations management is the planning, organizing, leading, and controlling of "all the activities of productive systems—those portions of organizations that transform inputs into products and services."[11] **Operations managers** are responsible for producing the supply of goods or services in organizations.[12] In most ways, operations managers practice the same functions of management as do other managers, but in very distinct ways. Operations management is changing rapidly and is strongly affected by such factors as the globalization of business, high-tech manufacturing, the impact of Japanese productivity and product quality, international financial conditions, workers' attitudes toward factories and work, governmental regulations, scarcity of productive resources, and changing societal attitudes toward competition.

Many of the forerunners of modern management discussed in Chapter 2, such as Frederick Taylor, Frank and Lillian Gilbreth, Henry Gantt, and others, were involved in manufacturing, and their management theories and principles reflect this background. Today, however, less than 25 percent of jobs in the United States are in manufacturing.[13] Service operations have increased in importance, but they have not yet been analyzed in the same detail as manufacturing operations.

FIGURE 21.1 OPERATIONS DECISIONS

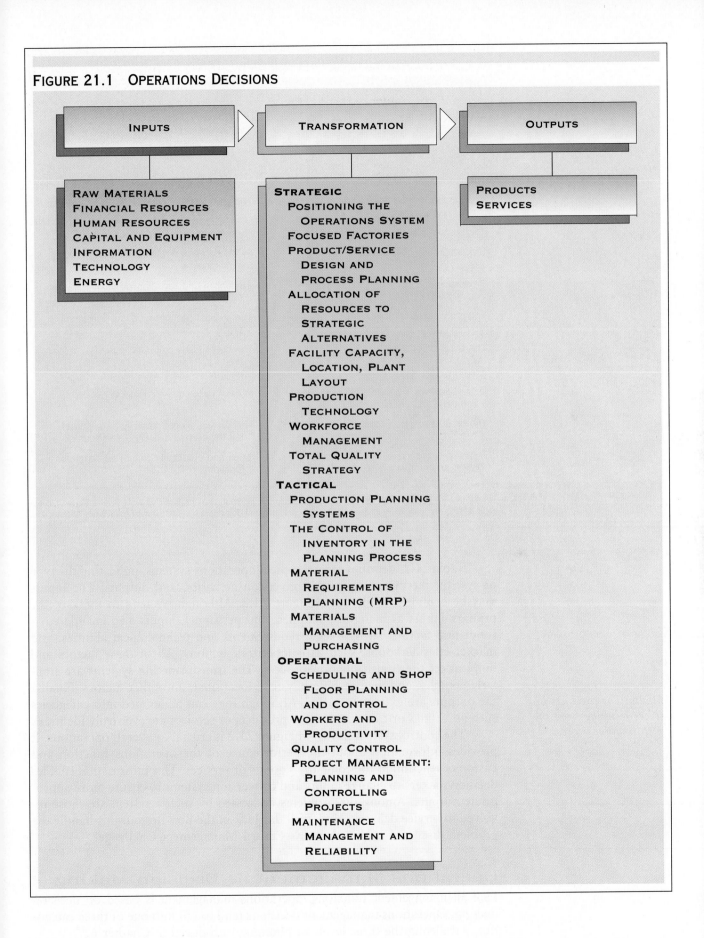

INPUTS

RAW MATERIALS
FINANCIAL RESOURCES
HUMAN RESOURCES
CAPITAL AND EQUIPMENT
INFORMATION
TECHNOLOGY
ENERGY

TRANSFORMATION

STRATEGIC
 POSITIONING THE
  OPERATIONS SYSTEM
 FOCUSED FACTORIES
 PRODUCT/SERVICE
  DESIGN AND
  PROCESS PLANNING
 ALLOCATION OF
  RESOURCES TO
  STRATEGIC
  ALTERNATIVES
 FACILITY CAPACITY,
  LOCATION, PLANT
  LAYOUT
 PRODUCTION
  TECHNOLOGY
 WORKFORCE
  MANAGEMENT
 TOTAL QUALITY
  STRATEGY
TACTICAL
 PRODUCTION PLANNING
  SYSTEMS
 THE CONTROL OF
  INVENTORY IN THE
  PLANNING PROCESS
 MATERIAL
  REQUIREMENTS
  PLANNING (MRP)
 MATERIALS
  MANAGEMENT AND
  PURCHASING
OPERATIONAL
 SCHEDULING AND SHOP
  FLOOR PLANNING
  AND CONTROL
 WORKERS AND
  PRODUCTIVITY
 QUALITY CONTROL
 PROJECT MANAGEMENT:
  PLANNING AND
  CONTROLLING
  PROJECTS
 MAINTENANCE
  MANAGEMENT AND
  RELIABILITY

OUTPUTS

PRODUCTS
SERVICES

TABLE 21.1 Differences Between Manufacturing and Service	
Manufacturing	**Service**
The product is tangible	The service is intangible
Ownership is transferred at the time of purchase	Ownership is generally not transferred
The product can be resold	No resale is possible
The product can be demonstrated before purchase	The product does not exist before purchase
The product can be stored in inventory	The product cannot be stored
Production precedes consumption	Production and consumption are simultaneous
Production and consumption can be spatially separated	Production and consumption must occur at the same location
The product can be transported	The product cannot be transported (though producers can be)
The seller produces	The buyer takes part directly in the production process and can indeed perform part of the production
Indirect contact is possible between the company and the customer	In most cases direct contact is needed
The product can be exported	The service cannot normally be exported, but the service delivery system can be
Business is organized by functions, with sales and production separated	Sales and production cannot be separated functionally

SOURCE: Adapted from Richard Normann, *Service Management: Strategy and Leadership in the Service Business,* copyright © 1984 by John Wiley & Sons Ltd., Chichester, England. Reprinted by permission of John Wiley & Sons, Ltd.

Outputs: The products or services resulting from the transformation process.

Table 21.2 identifies several typical operations systems, indicating the type of system, the primary inputs, conversion activities, and outputs. The inputs may be complex, as shown in Figure 21.2. Although we tend to think of the primary inputs as materials, supplies, and personnel, inputs also include environmental factors, such as legal requirements and technological abilities, and market considerations, such as competitors' actions. All of these factors and more affect the transformation process. The transformation systems are similarly complex and may include physical, locational, and other factors. Finally, the **outputs** are extremely varied. Although they can be lumped into categories such as airlines or cameras, no two products or services are ever truly identical.

The control system shown in Figure 21.2 is crucial to overall operations. It provides information about the performance of the operations function and customer reaction to the company's goods or services. This information enables decision makers to change inputs and conversion systems to ensure more appropriate outputs. Among the problems addressed by such a system are those involved in service delivery. How well did Jack in the Box Restaurants handle the problem discussed in this chapter's Ethical Management Challenge?

Operations Management as Decision Making

Like all management functions, operations management is based on decision making. Operations management decisions tend to fall into one of three categories, paralleling the three levels of planning introduced in Chapter 6.[14]

TABLE 21.2 Some Typical Operations Systems			
Operations System	Primary Inputs	Transformation Subsystem	Outputs
1. Pet food factory	Grain, water, fish meal, personnel, tools, machines, paper bags, cans, buildings, utilities	Converts raw materials into finished goods (physical)	Pet food products
2. Trucking firm	Trucks, personnel, buildings, fuel, goods to be shipped, packaging supplies, truck parts, utilities	Packages and transports goods from sources to destinations (location)	Delivered goods
3. Department store	Buildings, displays, shopping carts, machines, stock goods, personnel, supplies, utilities	Attracts customers, stores goods, sells products (exchange)	Marketed goods
4. College or university	Students, books, supplies, personnel, buildings, utilities	Transmits information and develops skills and knowledge (private/public service)	Educated persons
5. Mini warehouse	Facilities, personnel	Takes space and converts it into storage space for personal goods	Rental space

SOURCE: Adapted from *Production and Operations Management: A Problem Solving and Decision Making Approach,* Third Edition by Norman Gaither, copyright © 1987 by The Dryden Press, Inc., a division of Harcourt Brace, reprinted by permission of the publisher.

STRATEGIC DECISIONS

Strategic decisions involve deciding what products to make, selecting production processes, and expanding or locating facilities. These decisions have long-term (three to five years) significance.

TACTICAL DECISIONS

Tactical decisions about planning and production are made to meet annual demand. These decisions involve such issues as building inventory before the selling season. They are necessary for the ongoing production of goods and services to satisfy the seasonal demands of the market and provide profits for the company.

OPERATIONAL DECISIONS

Operational decisions are made daily for the purpose of planning and controlling ongoing operations. They concern such matters as assigning workers to jobs, ensuring the quality of products and services, scheduling production overhead costs, and maintaining machinery.

The Strategic Importance of Operations

Operations strategies are derived from business strategies aimed at achieving corporate objectives. In that regard, they are similar to the strategies employed in other functional areas—for example, marketing, finance, human resources, and information. Operations strategies must support the other strategies, principally the marketing strategy.

FIGURE 21.2 AN OPERATIONS SYSTEM MODEL

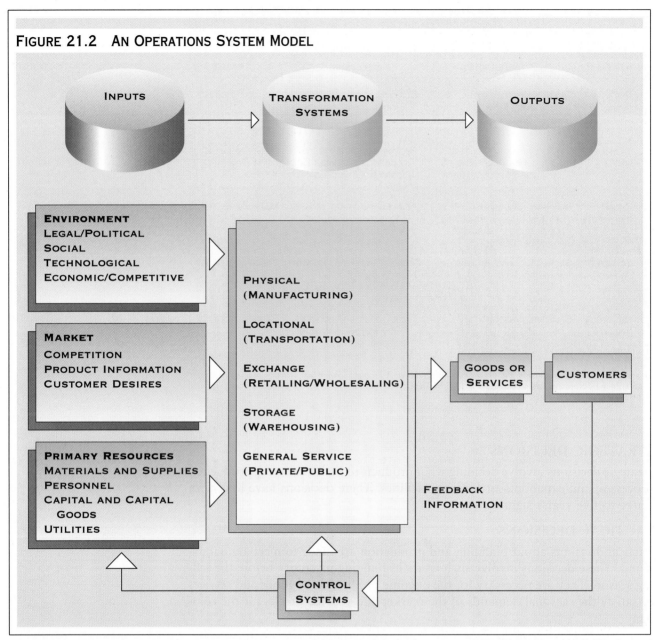

SOURCE: ADAPTED FROM NORMAN GAITHER, PRODUCTION AND OPERATIONS MANAGEMENT: A PROBLEM SOLVING AND DECISION MAKING APPROACH (CHICAGO: DRYDEN, 1987), P. 19.

As indicated in Chapter 7, there are two "generic" competitive strategies: relative differentiation and relative low cost. One of the major differentiation factors of the 1980s was high quality. Product flexibility/customization (and hence manufacturing flexibility) will be a major competitive weapon in the 1990s.[15] Low cost has also been critical to capturing market share and will continue to be in the 1990s. Manufacturing is obviously instrumental in achieving both differentiation and low cost.[16] Moreover, as the twenty-first century approaches, manufacturing and marketing strategies will be determined simultaneously; indeed, this is already occurring in the most successful firms.

Table 21.3 shows some of the major relationships between operations strategies and these two marketing strategies. As you can see, the marketing strategy affects the design of the manufacturing operation. For example, a low-

TABLE 21.3 Strategic Alternatives

Business Strategy	Strategy A Low-Cost Producer	Strategy B Product Innovator
Market conditions	Price-sensitive Mature market High volume Standardization	Product-features sensitive Emerging market Low volume Customized products
Operations mission	Emphasize low cost while maintaining acceptable quality and delivery	Emphasize flexibility while maintaining reasonable cost, quality, and delivery
Distinctive competence operations	Low cost through superior process technology and vertical integration	Fast and reliable new-product introduction through product teams and flexible automation
Operations policies	Superior processes Statistical process control Central location Economy of scale Tight inventory control Low-skill work force Highly automated	Superior products Flexible automation Fast reaction to changes Economies of scope Use of product teams Skilled workers Low automation
Marketing strategies	Mass distribution Repeat sales Maximizing of sales opportunities National sales force Low-cost advertising	Selective distribution New-market development Product design Sales made through agents High-cost advertising
Finance strategies	High capital needed Low risk Low profit margins	Low capital needed Higher risks Higher profit margins

SOURCE: Roger G. Schroeder, *Operations Management: Decision Making in the Operations Function,* 3rd ed. (New York: McGraw-Hill, 1989), p. 33. Reprinted with permission of McGraw-Hill.

cost strategy leads to manufacturing that emphasizes technology, processes, statistical process control, tight control over inventory, and mass distribution. Conversely, a product-innovation (differentiation) marketing strategy favors flexibility, new-product teams, fast reaction to changes, and selective distribution. Firms seeking both low cost and product innovation—such as Hewlett-Packard, Mazda, and Philips—face an extremely difficult task integrating what appear to be conflicting manufacturing systems requirements. Special efforts, such as cross-functional teams of marketers, manufacturers, human resources staff, and often customers, are necessary to achieve both goals simultaneously.[17]

The contribution of operations to business strategy varies with the firm and its situation; it can range from no involvement at all to initiating actions that yield a competitive advantage.[18] For example, many traditional firms view manufacturing as simply the making of products, but firms like Briggs & Stratten, Allen-Bradley, and Ford Motor Company expect the manufacturing department to prepare strategies, assist in designing products, and solve problems.

AT ALLEN-BRADLEY: AB realized that it had to improve operations. It had to cut costs and improve quality in order to be competitive. Operations became strategically important.

Strategic Operations Decisions

Strategic operations decisions concern products, processes, and facilities and their interrelationships. These decisions include positioning the operations system; focusing the factories; product/service design and process planning; allocating resources to strategic alternatives; determining facility capacity, location, and layout; production technology; and quality.[19]

Positioning the Operations System

Positioning the operations system involves making the following choices for each major product line in the business plan:

1. Type of product design
2. Type of production process
3. Finished-goods inventory policy[20]

Firms in service industries must also make strategic decisions related to positioning the operations system, but because manufacturing is not involved, the issues are different. In service industries, distribution as well as transformation may play an important part in operations. Much of the conversion process in a service industry is a result of interaction between the customer and the service provider. It thus becomes a human resource management function. Distribution channels may also have to be altered.

It took Jack in the Box nearly a week to publicly admit its responsibility for food poisonings suffered by customers at some of its outlets. Even then, it attempted to deflect the blame to state health officials and meat suppliers.

Foodmaker waited two weeks to offer to pay the victims' hospital costs. And it waited too long to counteract damaging—and often inaccurate—rumors. In San Diego, for example, the death of a child was linked to the fast-food chain by the local newspapers without conclusive evidence that she had eaten there.

SOURCE: Ronald Grover, "Boxed In at Jack in the Box," *Business Week* (February 15, 1993), p. 40.

Focused Factories

Many experts believe that factories perform more efficiently and effectively if they are focused on a particular product or market niche.[21] Outboard Marine, for example, has dedicated each of its factories to specific tasks in the manufacturing process. Its Spruce Pine, North Carolina, plant casts engine blocks using the rare "lost-form" technique that yields more powerful, yet less expensive, engines than conventional methods. Other plants add pistons, fuel systems, and other parts to the engine.[22] Many firms using focused factories emphasize that success depends on empowering employees, cross training them, and using the right motivational tools.[23] Conversely, marketing-oriented experts such as Thomas J. Peters believe that the factories of the future will have to be more flexible, less focused, and capable of turning out products for what are known as "mass-customized" markets.[24] The organization must be able to serve small, yet significant market niches that need particular products unique to their segment of the market. This means that the corporation's manufacturing or service operations must offer flexibility in producing the product or service.[25] Such flexibility is the primary thrust of Japanese manufacturing strategy in the 1990s.[26]

Many experts believe that factories perform better if they are focused on a particular product or market niche. The Spruce Pine, North Carolina, plant of Outboard Marine casts engine blocks; other plants add pistons, fuel system, and other parts.

Integrator: An individual who works with designers, serving as a liaison with manufacturing.

Cross-functional team: A team consisting of design, manufacturing, and marketing personnel who jointly design a product.

Concurrent engineering (CE): An approach to engineering in which a product and the process for making it are designed concurrently.

Design for manufacturing: An approach to product design that focuses on designing products that are simple enough so that manufacturing can be efficient and the product will have high quality.

Product/Service Design and Process Planning

Other important operations strategy decisions are related to the design of products and services and the operations processes chosen to produce them. Product design is important to competitiveness—for example, in creating features that attract customers and differentiate an organization's product from those of its competitors. In addition, product designs that can be produced cheaply will be more competitive with those of low-cost producers, such as firms in Japan and other Pacific Rim countries. Historically, design engineers have translated new technology into product innovation with little input from marketing managers. More recently, firms have begun to involve marketing personnel actively in the design process, using integrators, cross-functional teams, or product/process design departments to determine design.[27] The **integrator** works with designers, serving as a liaison with manufacturing. For example, if the marketing department seeks a product whose manufacturing cost is extremely low, the integrator might work with engineering personnel to design a very simple product with few parts. A **cross-functional team** consists of design, manufacturing, and marketing personnel who jointly design the product. Motorola, Inc., the electronics manufacturer, uses cross-functional teams to improve quality and cut costs. Its Austin, Texas, microprocessor plant uses cross-functional problem-solving teams to reduce cost and manufacturing time and improve the quality of the product.[28] Milliken, the textile giant, also uses such teams, often including customers, to improve not only manufacturing processes, but customer satisfaction as well.[29] The product/process design department oversees both areas.

Recently, U.S. firms have also begun using **concurrent engineering** (CE), in which the product and the process for making it are designed concurrently. Used by Japanese firms for a number of years, CE has proven effective in cutting costs and speeding products to market.[30]

As cost and quality have become more critical, the manufacturing process has had to meet these demands, often by simplifying product design. Using what its conceptualizer, Genichi Taguchi, refers to as "robust design," often called **design for manufacturing,** many firms are becoming more efficient.[31] Design for

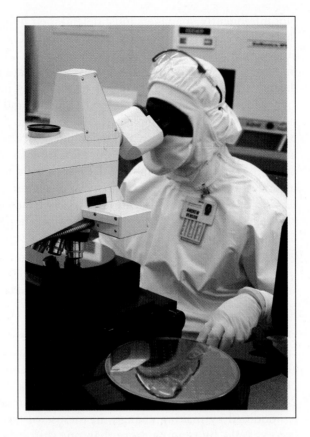

This Motorola technician is processing an 8-inch silicon wafer at the wafer fabrication plant. Motorola's microprocessor plant uses cross-functional problem-solving teams to reduce costs and manufacturing time and improve the quality of the product.

manufacturing means designing products that are simple enough so that manufacturing can be efficient and the product will have high quality. Black & Decker, for example, chose to simplify the design of its new coffeemaker in order to compete more effectively.[32]

Services and the jobs involved in providing them can also be simplified. Most retail stores have redefined the service process, reducing the number of clerks, allowing customers to roam at will, and placing clerks only in specialty areas such as perfumes, expensive clothing, or sporting goods. Larger universities have reduced the number of course preparations for professors, thereby simplifying their jobs.

Process planning is also a critical strategic choice. It determines how a product or service will be produced at the desired quality, in the required quantity, and at the budgeted cost. It is highly interdependent with other operations management activities—product design, facility layout, capital plant and equipment acquisitions, human resources utilization, facility capacity, job design, building design, quality control, forecasted demand for the product, and the allocation of operations management resources.[33]

Process planning: Planning that determines how a product or service will be produced at the desired quality, in the required quantity, and at the budgeted cost.

Allocation of Resources to Strategic Alternatives

Giant firms such as GE, Hitachi, and Siemens seem to have almost infinite capital resources. Most firms, however, have limited strategic resources that must be divided among several businesses, products, or functions. Consequently, those resources must be allocated in a way that will achieve the overall business strategy—and, in this case, the operations strategy. Most organizations have complex capital budgeting programs with stages of review for each major proposed capital purchase. The budgeting process is also used to allocate resources.

Not infrequently, managers must defend their budget requests in the presence of their peers. This technique is used at Dana Corporation, a manufacturer of automobile subassemblies. In what as known as "Hell Week," each division manager is required to make a brief presentation on his or her budget and defend it in front of two hundred or more key managers.[34]

Much of the financial, material, human, and information resource allocation process can be accomplished, at least in the preliminary stages, using some of the quantitative methods and techniques discussed in Chapter 8. For example, linear programming can be used in allocating fixed resources over a number of operating divisions, determining the mix of products that best satisfies operating objectives, or drawing up a production plan stating the number of products and services to be produced by various operating facilities. Linear programming can also be used for less strategic and more operational decisions—such as the mix of ingredients for a particular product or the assignment of personnel, overhead, or labor to various operations divisions.[35]

Facility Capacity, Location, and Plant Layout

FACILITY CAPACITY

Deciding how much production or service capacity is needed to meet demand is critical to any organization. Enormous amounts of capital investment are usually required to increase production capacity. Land, plant, and equipment must be purchased or built and related technologies developed. As shown in Table 21.4, there are several ways of changing long-range capacity. Capacity may also be modified by making changes in the use of technology or human resources. For example, by running more than one shift in a plant, thereby using existing facilities perhaps 16 or 24 hours a day as opposed to 8, a company may be able to avoid building another plant. To reduce capacity, workers can work fewer than 8 hours a day or 5 days a week; sometimes, however, organizations have little choice but to sell plants or equipment.

In the 1980s and 1990s, all three major U.S. automakers decided to reduce their long-range plant capacity—Chrysler and Ford first, between 1979 and 1983, and General Motors from 1987 to 1994. Billions of dollars were involved in these reductions.[36] The automakers' actions were extremely significant be-

---

TABLE 21.4 Ways of Changing Long-Range Capacity

Type of Capacity Change	Ways of Accommodating Long-Range Capacity Changes
Expansion	1. Subcontract with other companies to become suppliers of the expanding firm's components or entire products. 2. Acquire other companies, facilities, or resources. 3. Develop sites, build buildings, buy equipment. 4. Expand, update, or modify existing facilities. 5. Reactivate facilities on standby status.
Reduction	1. Sell off existing facilities, sell inventories, and lay off or transfer employees. 2. Mothball facilities and place on standby status, sell inventories, and lay off or transfer employees. 3. Develop and phase in new products as other products decline.

source: Adapted from *Production and Operations Management: A Problem Solving and Decision Making Approach,* Third Edition by Norman Gaither, copyright © 1987 by The Dryden Press, Inc., a division of Harcourt Brace, reprinted by permission of the publisher.

cause they amounted to conceding their lost market share to foreign competition. General Motors' plant closings came after the company had spent about $77 billion, from 1979 to 1990, building six new assembly plants and modernizing twelve others, only to emerge with an overcapacity of an estimated one million cars and trucks a year.[37] Chrysler reduced its capacity in the early 1980s and then acquired American Motors in 1987 in order to increase it again.[38] When its sales boomed in the late 1980s, Ford, too, faced the agonizing decision of how to expand its capacity, which it had reduced just a few years earlier.[39] Ironically, in 1993, while GM, most European firms, and some Japanese firms were reducing their plant capacity, Toyota was adding new plants.[40]

LOCATION OF FACILITIES

Decisions about the location of facilities are very important for firms in industries in which nearness to customers or raw materials or in which production factors such as utility costs are critical to the firm's operations and vary significantly with location. Location decisions begin with the selection of a country. Decisions on region, community, and site follow. The principal factors involved in each of these decisions are indicated in Figure 21.3.

Locational factors vary in importance in different industries. In a warehousing or retailing business, for example, it would be important to be near customers. A location near customers is not so important in heavy manufacturing. On the other hand, it might be extremely important for a firm in heavy manufacturing to be near its supply of raw materials; this is less important in retailing and warehousing.

The globalization of business has increased the complexity of decisions about facility location. Events like those unfolding in relation to the Europe 1992 initiative change how the game is played. For example, Avery International, a $1.5 billion office supply firm, reduced the number of its European warehouses from one for each country (fourteen) to five regional warehouses as the European market became more unified.[41] Many U.S. firms have located manufacturing plants outside the country to take advantage of significantly lower wage rates. Some have found that manufacturing "offshore"—that is, outside the United States—has definite limitations; as noted earlier, for example, the labor cost advantage may be offset by other costs. As a result, many firms have returned to manufacturing in the United States.[42]

FACILITY LAYOUT

Facility layout involves "planning for the location of all machines, utilities, employee work stations, customer service areas, materials, aisles, restrooms, lunchrooms, drinking fountains, internal walls, offices, and computer rooms, and for the flow patterns of materials and people around, into, and within buildings."[43] Facilities layout is an extremely complex problem, consisting of a large number of interrelated decisions that have been made easier by computer simulations and related plant layout software.[44] In manufacturing, focal issues include plant capacity for a specified period; the size and number of machines needed; the technology required to achieve desired production levels; the requirements for keeping workers motivated, safe, and healthy; building and site constraints; the organization's growth trends; and finally the size, strength, and characteristics of the materials involved.[45]

There are four basic types of layouts for manufacturing facilities: process, product, group technology, and fixed position. A **process layout** is designed to accommodate a large number of product designs and processing steps. It is often associated with job shops that manufacture a variety of products. A **product layout** accommodates only a few product and process designs and is associated

Process layout: A facilities layout designed to accommodate a large number of product designs and processing steps.

Product layout: A facilities layout designed to accommodate only a few product and process designs; it is associated with assembly lines that make a product in a fixed sequence of steps.

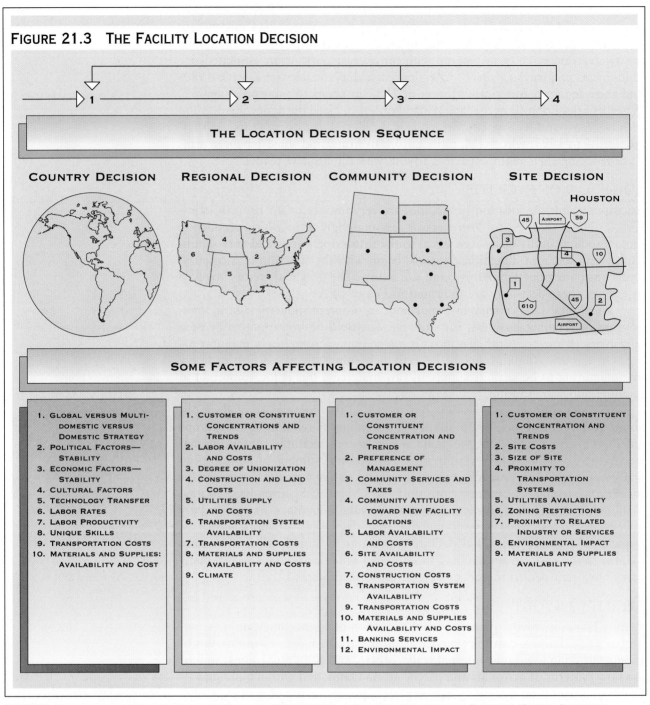

FIGURE 21.3   THE FACILITY LOCATION DECISION

THE LOCATION DECISION SEQUENCE

| COUNTRY DECISION | REGIONAL DECISION | COMMUNITY DECISION | SITE DECISION |

SOME FACTORS AFFECTING LOCATION DECISIONS

COUNTRY DECISION
1. GLOBAL VERSUS MULTI-DOMESTIC VERSUS DOMESTIC STRATEGY
2. POLITICAL FACTORS—STABILITY
3. ECONOMIC FACTORS—STABILITY
4. CULTURAL FACTORS
5. TECHNOLOGY TRANSFER
6. LABOR RATES
7. LABOR PRODUCTIVITY
8. UNIQUE SKILLS
9. TRANSPORTATION COSTS
10. MATERIALS AND SUPPLIES: AVAILABILITY AND COST

REGIONAL DECISION
1. CUSTOMER OR CONSTITUENT CONCENTRATIONS AND TRENDS
2. LABOR AVAILABILITY AND COSTS
3. DEGREE OF UNIONIZATION
4. CONSTRUCTION AND LAND COSTS
5. UTILITIES SUPPLY AND COSTS
6. TRANSPORTATION SYSTEM AVAILABILITY
7. TRANSPORTATION COSTS
8. MATERIALS AND SUPPLIES AVAILABILITY AND COSTS
9. CLIMATE

COMMUNITY DECISION
1. CUSTOMER OR CONSTITUENT CONCENTRATION AND TRENDS
2. PREFERENCE OF MANAGEMENT
3. COMMUNITY SERVICES AND TAXES
4. COMMUNITY ATTITUDES TOWARD NEW FACILITY LOCATIONS
5. LABOR AVAILABILITY AND COSTS
6. SITE AVAILABILITY AND COSTS
7. CONSTRUCTION COSTS
8. TRANSPORTATION SYSTEM AVAILABILITY
9. TRANSPORTATION COSTS
10. MATERIALS AND SUPPLIES AVAILABILITY AND COSTS
11. BANKING SERVICES
12. ENVIRONMENTAL IMPACT

SITE DECISION
1. CUSTOMER OR CONSTITUENT CONCENTRATION AND TRENDS
2. SITE COSTS
3. SIZE OF SITE
4. PROXIMITY TO TRANSPORTATION SYSTEMS
5. UTILITIES AVAILABILITY
6. ZONING RESTRICTIONS
7. PROXIMITY TO RELATED INDUSTRY OR SERVICES
8. ENVIRONMENTAL IMPACT
9. MATERIALS AND SUPPLIES AVAILABILITY

SOURCE: FIGURE FROM PRODUCTION AND OPERATIONS MANAGEMENT: A PROBLEM SOLVING AND DECISION MAKING APPROACH, THIRD EDITION BY NORMAN GAITHER, COPYRIGHT © 1987 BY THE DRYDEN PRESS, INC., A DIVISION OF HOLT, RINEHART AND WINSTON, INC., REPRINTED BY PERMISSION OF THE PUBLISHER.

Group technology: An approach to production in which a group of machines acts like a product layout for a family of similar products within a larger processing layout design.

with assembly lines that make a product in a fixed sequence of steps. In a **group technology** process, a group of machines acts like a product layout for a family of similar products within a larger processing layout design. Group technology will probably be used more in the future because it allows for more flexible manufacturing. In a **fixed-position layout,** the product remains in a fixed position and workers, parts, and machines move to and from the product. This type of layout is typical in aircraft assembly, bridge building, and ship construction.

In a fixed-position layout, the product remains in a fixed position and workers, parts, and machines move to and from the product. This type of facility layout is typical of aircraft assembly plants.

Fixed-position layout: A facilities layout in which the product remains in a fixed position and workers, parts, and machines move to and from the product.

Richard Schonberger, who has studied Japanese production techniques, suggests that there are two basic reasons for the success of Japanese manufacturing firms: productivity and quality. Productivity has been dramatically increased by the "just-in-time inventory" (JIT) approach; commitment to total quality control procedures has resulted in high levels of quality.[46] U.S. firms are taking these lessons to heart; there is a trend toward the Japanese model of production. There is greater emphasis on efficiency and quality, and to the extent that facility layouts can help this process, they are being changed. For example, layouts are being redesigned so that workers can see the entire layout and move quickly between work stations. Open work areas with fewer walls and partitions are becoming more common. Factories are getting smaller, with distances between machines decreasing as efficiency objectives become more critical. Less space is provided for inventories as organizations move to JIT manufacturing. Layouts are becoming increasingly flexible and group technology more prominent as shorter production runs are anticipated. In addition, workers are being trained at more than one job. Schonberger urges that companies focus on simplicity—in product design and in the production process. He believes that Japanese manufacturing management and systems can be transferred to the United States and other countries.[47]

Researchers Jit Seng Chan, Danny A. Samson, and Amrik S. Sobal suggest that the Japanese approach is more holistic than the approach characteristic of U.S. firms.[48] They agree, however, that the model can be applied in other cultures.

SERVICE FACILITY LAYOUTS

Unlike manufacturing facility layouts, service facility layouts are designed to bring large numbers of customers into the organization. Their purpose is either to meet customer service requirements or to facilitate technological, materials handling, or production efficiency.[49] A grocery store is very customer oriented; its layout is designed to keep checkout lines as short as possible, moving clerks in and out as the number of customers increases or decreases. Conversely, a discount merchandiser, whose customers order from inventory after selecting items

Computer-integrated manufacturing (CIM): *A broad label applied to the use of computers in design and manufacturing processes.*

Computer-aided design (CAD): *The use of specialized hardware and software to enable engineers to design products, components, electronic systems, and the like.*

Computer-aided manufacturing (CAM): *The use of specialized computer systems to translate the information in a CAD-generated design into instructions for automated manufacturing.*

Flexible manufacturing systems (FMS): *Clusters of automated machinery controlled by computers that have the flexibility to produce a wide variety of products efficiently.*

Automated storage and retrieval systems (ASRS): *Computer-controlled automated warehouses that include automatic placement and retrieval of parts.*

Robotics: *The use of robots to perform a manufacturing or service function.*

Automation: *The replacement of human workers with machines.*

from a showroom, has a layout designed more for efficiency than for service. Firms often use a mix of these layouts—for example, fast-food restaurant layouts emphasize technology, whereas the layout of a gourmet restaurant will emphasize customer service.

Most service facilities are designed to facilitate customer access. In a bank, for example, there are few walls or partitions, so that customers can see when a loan officer or a clerk is available. There are large, well-lit parking areas, as well as wide sidewalks, so that customers are able to move easily to and from the service area. In hospitals, the emphasis is on locating equipment and bringing the patient to it. Thus, elevators are large and aisles are wide so that patients can be moved easily.

Production Technology

Organizations must determine the amount and type of technology they want to employ. The trend in both manufacturing and services is toward increased use of technology. Among the most important technologies used today are automation, computer-aided design, computer-aided manufacturing, flexible manufacturing, automatic storage and retrieval systems, and robotics. Many of these applications of technology are included in computer integrated manufacturing.

Computer integrated manufacturing (CIM) is a broad label applied to the use of computers in design and manufacturing processes, including JIT (in which the firm keeps zero, or near zero, inventories), flexible manufacturing, robotics, high levels of automation, and automatic storage and retrieval systems.[50]

Computer-aided design (CAD) uses specialized hardware and software to enable engineers to design products, components, electronic systems, and the like on a computer terminal instead of a drawing board. General Electric, Texas Instruments, Exxon, Eastman Kodak, Boeing, and Caterpillar Inc. are just a few of the firms making use of this capability.[51]

Computer-aided manufacturing (CAM) encompasses specialized computer systems that translate the information in a CAD-generated design into instructions for automated manufacturing. The hardware for CAM is readily available, but the software is still limited in many industries.

Flexible manufacturing systems (FMS) are clusters of automated machinery controlled by computers that have the flexibility to produce a wide variety of products efficiently regardless of the size of the production run. GE and Westinghouse, among others, have plants with flexible manufacturing systems. A significant strategic advantage can be gained by using such systems.[52]

Automated storage and retrieval systems (ASRS) are computer-controlled automated warehouses that include automatic placement and retrieval of parts. Parts are ordered and retrieved as needed and transported automatically on self-guided carts.

Robotics involves the use of robots to perform a manufacturing or service function.

Within the broad categories of product, process, group technology, or fixed-position factory layouts, a critical strategic decision is the amount of **automation**—the replacement of human workers with machines—that must take place. There are four major stages of automation, based on the complexity of the tasks performed by the machines: mechanized aids, numerically controlled machines, robots, and CIM.[53]

Automation, particularly the use of robots and CIM, has had mixed results. At one time it was predicted that robotization and CIM would occur throughout American industry. Automation, robotization, and CIM have been shown to be very effective in improving productivity, even when only a few units

IN BOTH MANUFACTURING AND SERVICES, THERE IS A TREND TOWARD INCREASED USE OF TECHNOLOGY. COMPUTER-AIDED DESIGN HAS REVOLUTIONIZED THE DESIGN OF PRODUCTS, COMPONENTS, AND ELECTRONIC SYSTEMS AND HAS MADE TRADITIONAL DRAFTING EQUIPMENT OBSOLETE. COMPUTER INTEGRATED MANUFACTURING MAKES USE OF HIGH LEVELS OF AUTOMATION LIKE THE MAZAK AUTOMATED MACHINERY SHOWN HERE. THIS MACHINERY WORKS CONTINUOUSLY, VIRTUALLY UNATTENDED EXCEPT BY A DAYTIME MAINTENANCE CREW. ROBOTS HAVE ALSO COME INTO WIDESPREAD USE. EXPERIENCE HAS SHOWN THAT THE HIGHEST LEVELS OF PRODUCTIVITY RESULT FROM THE USE OF HUMAN RESOURCES IN COMBINATION WITH MODERATE AMOUNTS OF AUTOMATION.

are produced at a time.[54] However, the often-cited experience of General Motors at its NUMMI plant in Fremont, California, has revealed that proper use of human resources, in combination with moderate amounts of automation, but not necessarily robotization and CIM, often results in even higher productivity.[55]

Work Force Management

Organizations are increasingly recognizing that proper management of the work force is a key to productive manufacturing.[56] Organizations are changing their structures to provide workers with more challenging jobs, and those jobs are being designed to include more decision making. Labor unions are increasingly viewed as partners rather than as antagonists. One of the key ingredients in the success of Japanese manufacturing firms has been the way they manage people. Table 21.5 indicates the more humanistic approach of Japanese firms (Type J) compared to American firms (Type A).

The work-group orientation of Japanese management, when combined with the participative aspects of allowing workers to solve problems as they arise, has enabled Japanese firms to create very effective operating systems. This approach has a major impact on their ability to reduce costs and increase quality compared to most American firms.

Some American firms closely resemble Japanese firms. William G. Ouchi has labeled these Type Z firms.[57] Many U.S. firms are moving more in the direction of Theory Z management, which results in Type Z firms. General Motors' NUMMI plant has been one of the most successful of these efforts. The introduction of Theory Z management into the plant changed it from one of GM's worst plants into its best, in terms of productivity.[58]

Outsourcing and Offshore Production

Outsourcing: Subcontracting a function to another organization.

Offshore: Located outside the country of origin.

One of the major strategic operations decisions a firm must make is whether to outsource operations or not. **Outsourcing**—subcontracting a function to another organization—is a popular technique among manufacturers. In addition to operations, functions that are frequently outsourced include human resource management, information systems, and accounting.[59] A related decision is whether to go **offshore**—that is, outside the country—for manufacturing or

The introduction of Theory Z management into General Motors' NUMMI plant changed it from one of GM's worst plants into its best, in terms of productivity.

TABLE 21.5 Theory A, J, and Z Management

Type J Firms (Japanese Firms)	Type A Firms (American Firms)	Theory Z Firms (American Firms Operating Similarly to Japanese Firms)
Lifetime employment (for men)	Short-term employment	Long-term employment
Slow process of evaluation and promotion	Rapid evaluation and promotion	Slow evaluation and promotion
Nonspecialized career	Specialized career planning	Moderate career planning
Consensual decision making	Individual decision making	Consensual decision making
Collective responsibility	Individual responsibility	Individual responsibility
Implicit/subtle control	Explicit/formal control	Informal, implicit control with explicit measures available
Holistic concern for employees	Segmented concern for employees	Holistic concern for employees

SOURCE: William J. Ouchi, *Theory Z,* © 1981 by Addison-Wesley Publishing Company, Inc. Reprinted with permission of the publisher.

other functions. For example, many U.S. firms are building plants in Mexico to take advantage of lower labor costs.[60] (Some might question the ethics of such offshore operations. Not only are foreign workers paid extremely low wages, but large numbers of jobs in U.S. firms are eliminated.)

Total Quality Management (TQM)

Quality is a major strategic imperative of the 1990s. A commitment to quality should lead to a concerted effort on the part of all employees to be error-free in their activities, to seek ways to improve quality, and to strive constantly for quality. On the other hand, quality is what you say it is—a level of quality that is apppropriate to a particular market can be designed into a product or service.[61] In reality, however, most people want "high-quality" products and services. Japanese firms have emphasized quality through total quality management (TQM) programs. This has enabled them to capture large market shares in major industries such as autos, steel, and electronics. Most American firms are fighting back with their own TQM approaches. TQM is so important to management today that much of Chapter 23 is devoted to it.[62]

Tactical Operations Decisions

Tactical operations decisions are intermediate-range decisions; they occupy a middle level between strategic decisions about products, processes, and facilities and operating decisions having to do with planning and controlling day-to-day operations. They include decisions about production planning systems, independent demand inventory systems, resource requirement planning systems, and materials management and purchasing.

Production Planning Systems

While determining capacity is a strategic decision, meeting anticipated demand is a tactical, often short-term decision. There must be a master production schedule indicating what will be produced and when—within the next operating period or in subsequent periods. There must be sufficient capacity to satisfy market demand and keep production at desired levels.

Figure 21.4 provides an in-depth look at the relationships among strategic (long-range), tactical (intermediate-range), and operational (short-range) plans

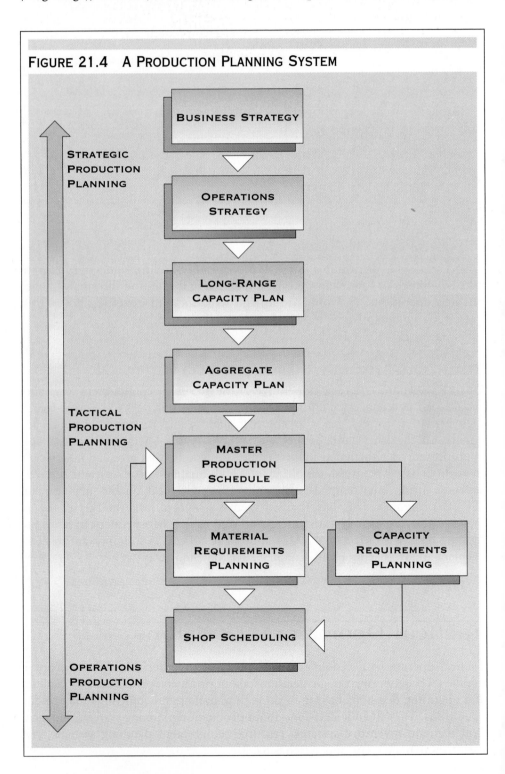

FIGURE 21.4   A PRODUCTION PLANNING SYSTEM

STRATEGIC PRODUCTION PLANNING

BUSINESS STRATEGY

OPERATIONS STRATEGY

LONG-RANGE CAPACITY PLAN

AGGREGATE CAPACITY PLAN

TACTICAL PRODUCTION PLANNING

MASTER PRODUCTION SCHEDULE

MATERIAL REQUIREMENTS PLANNING

CAPACITY REQUIREMENTS PLANNING

SHOP SCHEDULING

OPERATIONS PRODUCTION PLANNING

in the production planning system. The first step is to develop a long-range capacity plan based on sales forecasts for each product for each production period—either weeks, months, quarters, or years. These are then totaled until aggregate demand has been translated into requirements for workers, materials, machines, inventory, and facilities. Shorter-term resource allocation plans are then developed; the result is a master production schedule. Materials requirements planning, capacity requirements planning, and shop scheduling will follow. Linear programming is an excellent tool for production planning. A number of simulations are also available to assist in this planning process.

This chapter's Global Management Challenge discusses how a Spanish steel firm uses computers to control its entire manufacturing process, linking it to marketing.

Inventory Control

Inventory management has taken on new importance in recent years as manufacturing strategy has become an increasingly important part of business strategy.[63] **Inventory** is the supply of goods kept on hand for use in production or as a result of it. There are three principal types of inventory: finished goods, work-in-process, and raw materials. Supplies are a fourth type of inventory, which is found throughout the organization. Each type has its own purpose, and each represents a financial investment on the part of the company. Table 21.6 indicates why each type of inventory is necessary.

Inventory: The supply of goods kept on hand for use in production or as a result of it. The three principal types are finished goods, work-in-process, and raw materials.

TABLE 21.6 Why Are Inventories Necessary?

Type of Inventory	Reasons
Finished goods	1. Variation in customer demand from period to period rules out planning flows of products in to exactly match flows of products out.
	2. It is more economical to hold inventory than constantly to place emergency orders to meet customers' demands.
	3. It is physically impossible to instantaneously produce or acquire products when demanded by customers.
	4. Backlogging of customers' orders may be unacceptable.
	5. Allows efficient scheduling of production. This refers both to economic production runs and to stable production levels that may not match seasonal or other erratic demand patterns.
	6. Allows the display of products to customers.
In-process	1. Production rates of processing steps are uneven.
	2. Allows the uncoupling of operations. Each operation is then somewhat independent of other operations. This allows flexibility in planning each operation.
	3. Allows large batches of materials to be moved at one time between operations, particularly with process layouts. This reduces materials-handling costs.
Raw materials	1. It is physically impossible and economically infeasible to instantaneously supply raw materials and supplies when demanded by operations.
	2. Variation in demand for raw materials by operations from period to period and variation in delivery times of materials rule out planning flows of materials in that exactly match flows of materials out.
	3. Allows favorable unit prices through volume buying.
	4. Allows reduction of incoming unit freight costs through larger shipments.
	5. Allows more efficient materials handling through larger loads.

source: Norman Gaither, *Production and Operations Management: A Problem Solving and Decision Making Approach* (Fort Worth, Tex.: Dryden, 1987), p. 444.

ENSIDESA Integrates Computers into Manufacturing

When the Spanish steelmaker ENSIDESA built a $640 million steel plant at Aviles, Spain, in 1988, it wanted a state-of-the-art facility in which all production factors, from receipt of an order to computing the amount of oxygen to use in production, would be carefully calibrated. It wanted control of the various production sections to be automatic, and it wanted process computers to receive continuous and complete information about the status quo throughout production.

To put this information to good use, it designed an automatic coordinating system for each facility in the plant. This system consists of a complete and systematic schedule for each heat, or batch, of molten steel in process. The new system takes into account every possible event or delay in the process.

To make steel, molten pig iron is transferred from blast furnaces to the steel plant in special railroad cars. At the plant, it is fed into a 250-ton converter that blows in oxygen, thereby transforming it into steel. The process occurs in 250-ton heats. The molten steel is then tapped into ladles that carry it through one of several refining routes to give it its required chemical composition. The Aviles plant has three such areas: composition adjustment, reheating and oxygen blowing, and injection of desulphuring agents. Most heats end up at a continuous casting machine, where ladles are in one of two positions: waiting or casting. When a heat is

ECONOMIC ORDER QUANTITY (EOQ)

Economic order quantity (EOQ): The amount of inventory to be ordered that will minimize holding and ordering costs.

The **economic order quantity (EOQ)** is the amount of inventory to be ordered that will minimize holding and ordering costs. To determine the EOQ, the storage, management, and financing costs associated with holding inventory are balanced against the possible loss of sales to customers, plus the cost of lost production time, plus the costs of ordering. Formulas can be developed to determine the EOQ. These depend on product supply and demand and the associated cost of holding and ordering inventory. In most cases companies do not know the actual demand for their products, so forecasts must be made.

Numerous mathematical models and computer simulations have been developed to help maintain inventories at optimal levels. Figure 21.5 portrays a typical EOQ model. The EOQ always occurs at the point at which total inventory cost is minimized, the lowest point on the curve in Figure 21.5. It corresponds, in this case, to the intersection of the ordering cost and holding cost curves. Ordering costs decrease as the lot size of inventory ordered increases because fewer orders are placed during the period; holding costs increase as lot size increases.

LARGE VERSUS SMALL INVENTORIES

AT ALLEN-BRADLEY: One of the cornerstones of AB's success has been the use of JIT.

There are advantages to both large and small inventories. Factors favoring large inventories include fear of running out of stock; anticipation of possible jumps in demand; desire to keep ordering, shipping, and production costs low; desire to take advantage of favorable prices and quantity discounts; desire to have a hedge against inflation; and fear of unexpected events, such as strikes, embargoes, and natural disasters. Factors favoring small inventories include the desire

ready for casting, it is poured into a mold as a continuous moving slab, to be rolled and cut into smaller slabs—the final product.

To produce steel efficiently, the trick is to sequence heats without interruption, so that while one is inside the casting machine, the next has arrived and is in the waiting position; as one finishes, the next starts pouring. The technique, called continuous-continuous casting, increases machine yield while reducing maintenance costs. Compared with some American steel plants, the Spanish plant uses comparatively short sequences, so it's even more important to schedule the process to avoid idle time in the converter.

The star of the show at Aviles is a complex computer system designed by the process control department that automates control of the whole plant. It receives production orders from the business computer and generates the setpoints to control the processing—factors such as the amount of oxygen to use in the converter to produce a heat or the length at which to cut the slabs. The system also tracks materials throughout the plant, traps data, and generates information.

Under the new system, sceduling of orders can be optimized as well. The production orders generated by the business computer contain all the data required for each heat: scheduling guides, priorities, and steel grades, for example. The orders are organized in the most efficient sequence for one to three days in advance of their production. On the basis of information from the business computer and the state of affairs on the plant floor itself, the plant production staff can reorder sequences, if they choose, to maximize yields.

SOURCE: Adensio Díaz et al., "A Dynamic Scheduling and Control System in an ENSIDESA Steel Plant," *Interfaces* (September–October 1991), pp. 53–62.

to minimize working capital tied up in inventory; the desire to minimize storage costs; limitations on storage capacity; the desire to minimize insurance and tax expenses; fear of obsolescence; and the danger of spoilage.[64]

JUST-IN-TIME (JIT) INVENTORY SYSTEMS

Today, firms are trying to avoid holding large inventories of raw materials and finished goods. **Just-in-time** (JIT) is a system in which the firm maintains almost no inventory. Suppliers are required to provide just enough inventory for operations for a day or other specified period.[65] The JIT system, which American firms learned from the Japanese, has several benefits. First, it reduces inventory carrying costs and financing and management costs, but this is possible only with a reduction in ordering or setup costs. Second, it supports the company's efforts to be flexible and responsive to customer demand. Third, it helps improve quality. In the typical American inventory control system, workers simply throw away scrap pieces and defective parts; these are written off as part of the manufacturing process. The JIT system requires high-quality inputs.

A key aspect of JIT is **kanban**, a low-cost method of controlling inventory and product movement. The *kanban* (Japanese for "card") is used to signal that a worker's inventory is depleted; only then can the worker trade the *kanban* for additional inventory.[66] The next individual cannot complete his or her job until the previous worker has given him or her a perfect part. Thus, quality is built into the JIT system.

By using JIT, organizations not only improve quality, but also reduce their costs and improve productivity. JIT thus can be viewed as a forced system of

Just-in-time (JIT): *A system in which the firm maintains almost no inventory and suppliers are required to provide just enough inventory for operations for a day or other specified period.*

Kanban: *A low-cost method of controlling inventory and product movement.*

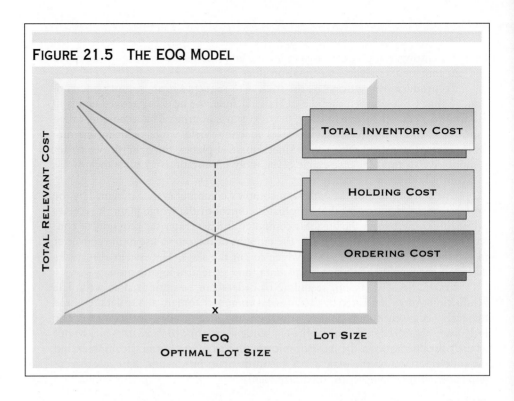

FIGURE 21.5 THE EOQ MODEL

- TOTAL INVENTORY COST
- HOLDING COST
- ORDERING COST

TOTAL RELEVANT COST

EOQ
OPTIMAL LOT SIZE

LOT SIZE

problem solving. Problems in the production process cannot be hidden by inventory buffers, but must be solved as they arise.[67]

In a JIT system, the company develops long-term relationships with a few suppliers that are willing to provide just-in-time inventory deliveries. Suppliers for major corporations, which can offer large contracts, are motivated to make changes in their delivery practices. Suppliers for smaller companies may not be so inclined. Even with large firms, some suppliers resist JIT because of the effort required; they may use warehouses or intermediaries to make JIT deliveries.

JIT systems are not easy to manage. Often, not only must raw materials or component inventories arrive just in time, but numerous parts must be shipped or stored in exactly the proper order. While some companies treat JIT as simply a way of getting suppliers to hold their inventories and cut costs, others work with their suppliers to make the process smoother, treating JIT as a philosophy of productivity improvement. They help their suppliers by giving them plenty of advance notice about what is due, when, and in what order.

The problems and benefits of JIT are illustrated by the case of Xerox. Xerox experienced major problems when it began using a JIT system. It attempted to transfer its inventory holding requirements to its suppliers. It cut the number of suppliers from more than 5,000 to just 300 and rewarded them with two- and three-year contracts. But management failed to recognize that suppliers were not able to make the system work by themselves. Xerox examined the situation and decided that it should make an effort not only to improve relationships with suppliers, but to help them manage the JIT process. Order schedules were firmed up so that suppliers could plan better. Classes were held for suppliers so that they could train their employees in the JIT process. Production planning was improved to help suppliers meet the company's demands.[68]

Materials Requirements Planning

Materials requirements planning (MRP) is a computer-based inventory planning and control system that examines the master planning schedule for required

Chrysler's just-in-time inventory system helps reduce inventory carrying costs and financing and management costs.

Materials requirements planning (MRP): *A computer-based inventory planning and control system that examines the master planning schedule for required input resources for each period covered by the plan.*

input resources—raw materials, parts, subassemblies, and assemblies—for each period covered by the plan. It then examines existing inventory levels and materials requirements and develops a schedule for ordering the necessary materials for arrival as needed.[69]

MRP systems have been used to manage extremely complex assembly processes involving large numbers of components, assemblies, and subassemblies, such as weapons systems. Martin Marietta has spent millions of dollars and thousands of worker-hours in developing its MRP II (an advanced MRP software program) to help manage its defense contracts.[70] Polaroid Corporation has used MRP to improve its on-time delivery performance in its industrial-electronic imaging division.[71] Harper Inc., a large furniture manufacturer, has used MRP II to reduce the time it takes to manufacture its products and to speed new products to market.[72]

Planning and Controlling Day-to-Day Operations

Day-to-day operations management involves the following issues: scheduling and shop floor planning and control, worker productivity, implementation of quality control, planning and control for each project, and maintenance management. In this section, we will discuss each of these issues briefly.

Scheduling and Shop Floor Planning and Control

Scheduling and shop floor planning involve tactical and short-range decisions regarding what to produce and when to produce it for each work area. How these problems are resolved depends partly on whether a product or a process layout is used. Scheduling is much easier in product layouts than in process layouts. In either situation, day-to-day scheduling requires that the operations manager move from the master production schedule to the capacity requirement plan to the MRP or other resources plan. Gantt charts, assembly charts, work process charts, and other scheduling devices are utilized. Labor must be assigned, dispatching orders must be given, and inventory must be withdrawn or made available. Priorities and sequencing must be determined. In process layouts, it is also necessary to decide which machine and which worker will carry out each order. Also, efforts must be coordinated among the various work areas.

Scheduling and shop floor planning are important in service industries as well as in manufacturing, as this chapter's Management Challenge reveals.

Worker Productivity

Like managers at other levels of the organization, operations managers must determine the most appropriate way to lead employees. This often includes decisions about job design as well as leadership style. Teamwork is a focal point as quality circles and similar concepts are used by increasing numbers of major manufacturers in the United States.[73] The effects of these techniques on productivity have been generally positive.[74]

Quality circles have also been used successfully in service industries. Other team-oriented approaches developed in Japan for such "individualistic" actions as computer programming have further demonstrated that teamwork can be effective in service industries.

MANAGEMENT CHALLENGE

Fixing Broken Schedules at American Airlines

Robert S. Norman manages current schedules for American Airlines. He and his team of six analysts not only develop new schedules aimed at implementing ambitious expansion plans, but they also fix broken schedules. That is where the real challenge lies. A typical day begins at 8:00 A.M. with a briefing by operations analysts. Thunderstorms diverted fifteen flights from American's Chicago hub and delayed others. Mechanical difficulties, a change of planes, and a delay waiting for a new crew resulted in a three-hour delay for a flight from Chicago to Manchester, England. A passenger on a plane on its way to Norfolk, Virginia, locked herself in the lavatory, took off all her clothes, and crammed them in the toilet. These are the kinds of incidents that upset passengers and drive Norman crazy.

Norman believes that you have to figure out what needs to be fixed and then decide whether it is fixable. Passenger "misconduct," such as that which occurred on the Norfolk flight, can't be corrected and can cause reverberations throughout the system. According to Norman, the goal is to "reduce delays to the point where any delays are beyond our control." Because the federal government publishes monthly statistics on flight arrival times and on-time percentages, being on time is important, but it must be done safely. Every change has an impact on at least one, and usually many, flight schedules.

Walter J. Aue, Norman's boss, comments that "scheduling aircraft is like working a jigsaw puzzle, except that every day you come in, someone has changed the shape of the pieces."

Norman and his staff must analyze reams of data every day, much of it supplied internally. For example, American publishes a four hundred-page monthly report that dissects every American flight, comparing all aspects of performance. But often one must depend on information from the outside. For example, when the Los Angeles airport closed one of its runways, American's schedulers knew about it in advance and were able to schedule flights around the change. However, in the summer of 1987, a runway at O'Hare Airport in Chicago was closed for repairs without advance notice. As a result, some American flights were delayed.

Quality Control

Achieving quality requires the commitment of the entire organization. Total quality control means that everyone is responsible for quality. It involves establishing policies, standards, and procedures; providing training in quality control; designing quality into products or services; eliciting the assistance of suppliers; controlling the production process; and controlling purchasing, logistics, and distribution.

Employees must participate in quality control if it is to be fully effective. Thus, at Ford Motor Company each worker is authorized to stop the assembly line if a quality problem arises. Some say that Henry Ford would turn over in his grave if he knew about this change in policy.[75]

The use of statistical sampling procedures to ensure quality has increased in most firms. Some firms, however, no longer sample items coming off the production line; instead, they inspect every single item. Computers are being

American Airlines has five major hubs and serves 150 airports with 420 planes and 2,140 daily flights. Scheduling its flights has been compared to working a jigsaw puzzle whose pieces change their shape each day.

American Airlines has five major hubs and serves 150 airports with 420 planes and 2,140 daily flights; yet, for seven straight months in 1988, it was number 1 on the government's on-time statistics list. As other airlines learn some of the tricks American has used, such as adding an average of eight minutes to every flight, American's advantage will depend even more on Robert Norman and his staff.

SOURCE: Robert L. Rose, "American Airlines' Fixer of Broken Schedules," *Wall Street Journal,* June 28, 1988, p. 35.

This engineer is reviewing operating conditions at Occidental Chemical Corporation's Lake Charles facility.

used extensively in quality control. Errors are reduced through computer-guided manufacturing systems. Computers also monitor parts and final products for acceptable levels of tolerance.

Kaizen: "Continuous Improvement," an important part of the quality control process at Japanese firms.

Kaizen, or "continuous improvement," is an important part of the quality control process at Japanese firms. They strive to improve products and processes continually and incrementally. This enables them to stay ahead of their competitors, especially U.S. firms, which make fewer improvements.[76] Many U.S. firms are adopting the *kaizen* concept. Chapter 23 discusses these issues in more detail.

This chapter's Quality Management Challenge shows how Samsung constantly seeks to improve quality.

Project Management

Project management: The planning and control of projects.

In addition to the ongoing planning and control of operations, operations managers are concerned with **project management,** the planning and control of projects. PERT and CPM, discussed in Chapter 8, are usually used to plan and control projects. Computerized versions of these and similar program planners are available. Major projects such as the construction of an office building or an airplane typically use PERT or CPM.

Maintenance Management

Maintenance management is extremely important. Malfunctions in manufacturing and service operations can lead to several problems: loss of production capacity, increased costs, decreased product or service quality, danger to employees, dissatisfied customers. There are two basic approaches to maintenance: repairs and preventive maintenance.

Preventive maintenance is critical to manufacturing operations using JIT inventory systems. No downtime can be allowed because there are no inventories to provide buffers between the company's various segments. As soon as one work area is idle, the rest of the plant will be idle as well. This is, of course, a danger with JIT inventory systems, and one reason why buffer inventories have historically been part of the manufacturing process.

AT ALLEN-BRADLEY: Quality is critical at AB. The company believes that it can compete successfully by listening to customers and by providing high levels of service and quality.

Samsung's Quest for Quality

There are four giant *chaebol,* or "business groups," in Korea—Hyundai, Daewoo, Lucky-Goldstar, and Samsung—and Samsung appears to be the one most likely to move Korea from a cheap-labor, manufacturing nation into one involved in the global arena of advanced technology.

Samsung was founded by a hard-driving patriarchal figure, Lee Byung-Chull, who was determined to narrow Korea's technological gap with Japan. Producing semiconductors was one of the company's highest priorities. Samsung has always felt the pressure of competing against the world leaders in memory chip manufacture, but because it has fewer financial and technological resources, it has always considered sheer determination to be a major weapon in its arsenal. Not a bad weapon: Samsung is currently the fifth-largest memory chip maker, with $1.2 billion in sales.

Now under the leadership of Lee Kun-Hee, son of the founder, Samsung is emerging as Korea's premier technological powerhouse, with its characteristic competitive drive now extending to telecommunications, aerospace, chemicals, and other fields. But the move toward technological preeminence is being accompanied by a dramatic paring down of the number and scope of businesses that Samsung operates.

In 1991, Samsung owned about thirty companies in fields as diverse as yarns and films, hotels and department stores, baseball, advertising, and credit cards. Its core businesses—machinery, electronics, and textiles—accounted for only 26 percent of its $49.3 billion in sales. By the year 2000, Samsung hopes to reduce the number of companies it operates—and to reach $200 billion in sales. Its core businesses are expected to account for 75 percent of sales by then.

Lee constantly emphasizes that the days of stressing growth and size over quality are gone. "We must specialize," he says. "If we don't move into more capital- and technology-intensive industries, our very survival will be at stake."

Although Samsung's R&D budget is still tiny compared with those of its major Japanese and U.S. competitors, such as Sony Corp. and General Electric Co., it is large by Korean standards. Samsung's commitment to quality over quantity is further evidenced by its multibillion-dollar, state-of-the-art microchip plant at Ki Heung, in which the company will have invested $3.2 billion by 1993.

Samsung's quality is well respected by companies like Hewlett-Packard (HP), with which it now works in the joint design and development of sophisticated reduced instruction-set computing (RISC) microprocessors for HP's well-regarded workstations.

SOURCE: Laxmi Nakarmi, "Samsung: Korea's Great Hope for High Tech," *Business Week* (February 3, 1992), pp. 44–45.

The Factory of the Future

The so-called factory of the future is almost upon us, and in many cases is already here. The principal characteristics of the **factory of the future** include automated machinery and all the aspects of CIM just discussed.

Most such factories will include fewer workers, but the workers who remain will be more highly skilled. Most will be involved in quality control, distri-

Factory of the future: A factory characterized by automated machinery and computer-integrated manufacturing.

bution, troubleshooting, and maintenance, as opposed to the actual manufacture of the product—which, for the most part, will be accomplished by computer-controlled machines. This complex interaction of people, machines, and ideas requires a new type of organizational structure and philosophy. For example, organizations will need to make greater use of cross-functional teams and develop more strategically oriented capital budgeting and accounting procedures.[77]

Foreign competition is providing the impetus for such factories.[78] U.S. firms cannot compete effectively against the lower wage rates and superior manufacturing processes of firms in many foreign countries. The factory of the future must be able to provide perfect quality at very, very low cost, with little inventory and virtually no waste.[79] It must be able to do so in response to global demand through global networks of suppliers.[80] Chapter 23 discusses these issues in more detail.

Productivity Management

Productivity is the organization's output of goods and services divided by its inputs. If the resulting ratio is large, productivity is high; productivity is low if the ratio is small.[81] One reason that concern for productivity has been so strong recently is that in the last few years the United States, while still leading the major industrialized nations in productivity, has seen its rate of productivity *growth* fall behind—often far behind—that of other major industrialized countries, especially Japan. In coming years, productivity levels in those countries may not only equal but surpass that of the United States if U.S. firms do not take action to increase their productivity.[82]

People and Productivity

Productivity can best be improved by either increasing the use of technology or making better use of human resources. Related means of increasing productivity include greater investment in R&D, investing in better equipment, and restructuring. In the mid-1980s, firms took action in all of these areas; as a result, productivity increased in goods-producing industries. It has not increased significantly in service industries but is beginning to show signs of progress.[83] Despite this progress, the United States still lags behind Japan, Britain, and France in productivity growth.[84]

Some experts question whether there are upper limits to productivity. People and machines have physical limits; therefore, significantly higher rates of productivity growth may not be possible. One of the major trends of the 1990s will be **re-engineering**, redesigning jobs to eliminate unnecessary tasks. Firms are already embracing this strategy, which often leads to workforce reductions.[85]

Re-engineering: Redesigning jobs to eliminate unnecessary tasks.

Technology and Productivity

One of the major strategies of U.S. firms for increasing productivity levels is to automate, to become more technologically advanced.[86] However, while technology offers a great deal of promise for manufacturing, significantly increasing output per hour, it does not appear to have the same impact on services.[87] All measures of productivity show clearly that productivity in service industries has not increased appreciably since 1980. Although there are some indications that technologies such as office automation can pay off for services, the gains have not been impressive.

The acquisition of technology must be aimed at a very specific goal; under such conditions, and when results are constantly monitored, productivity may increase.[88] For example, as mentioned earlier, Japanese firms have begun automating software development, and this has produced positive results.[89]

Operations Management as a Problem-Solving Process

Operations management is problem solving. The stages of the problem-solving process can be applied to any of the problems faced by operations managers. Because those problems are so varied, the process is not presented in detail here. Texts on operations management discuss issues such as recognizing and identifying problems and generating alternatives for specific types of operations problems.

Summary

(Before reading this summary, look again at the objectives listed at the beginning of the chapter.)

1. Operations management in manufacturing and service industries involves essentially the same three processes: inputs, transformation, and outputs. One of the primary differences between the two is that in service organizations the primary input is labor, whereas in manufacturing there may also be raw materials and subcomponent parts.

2. Operations management has become more critical in recent years because of foreign competition, principally from firms in Pacific Rim countries. U.S. and Canadian firms have had to improve their operations management skills and processes to remain competitive. As the business environment has become more global, the ability to compete globally has become more critical.

3. Strategic operations decisions focus on products, processes, and facilities. They are concerned with such issues as positioning the operations system; product/service design and process planning; allocating resources to strategic alternatives; and determining facility capacity, location, and plant layout. Tactical operations decisions include decisions about production planning systems, inventory control, and materials requirements planning. Day-to-day operations management decisions are related to scheduling and shop floor planning, worker productivity, quality control, project management, and maintenance management.

4. Operations is a strategic weapon because it can be used to produce products with characteristics that will make them competitive in the marketplace. Recently, operations management has focused on low cost and high quality.

5. The globalization of business has significantly affected operations management, especially in the United States and Canada. The penetration of U.S. markets by foreign competitors has focused attention on the operations function.

6. Operations management in Japanese firms focuses on high quality and low cost, worker participation in decisions, flexibility, simplification, JIT inventory systems, and quality circles.

7. Inventory has traditionally been used as a buffer against problems in the manufacturing process—when a problem occurred, inventory could be used to continue manufacturing while the problem was being fixed. Just-in-time (JIT) inventory systems do not provide such buffers. The manufacturing process must be perfect. The result is increased quality and lower costs.

8. By providing high-quality products, Japanese firms were able to penetrate American markets rapidly and take a significant amount of business away from many U.S. and Canadian firms.

9. The factory of the future will be based on CIM, incorporating computer-aided design, computer-aided manufacturing, flexible manufacturing systems, and automated storage and retrieval systems.

10. There are two basic ways to improve productivity: by using more technology and by using human resources more effectively.

General Questions

1. Research a major U.S. manufacturing company to discover what actions it has taken to become more competitive globally.

2. Discuss how quality can be improved in manufacturing and service companies.

3. Describe the factors contributing to the success of Japanese manufacturing firms.

4. Give examples to show how operations differ for various types of service and manufacturing firms.

5. Discuss the interrelationships among strategic, tactical, and operational-level operations management decisions.

6. Describe the relationships between marketing strategies and operations strategies.

7. Describe the importance of product simplification to competitiveness.

8. Review the major factors in determining facility location.

9. How does management of human resources affect operations?

10. How is a total quality strategy related to day-to-day quality management?

Questions on the Management Challenge Features

ETHICAL MANAGEMENT CHALLENGE

1. What did Jack in the Box do about its problem?

2. How could the company have handled the problem more ethically?

GLOBAL MANAGEMENT CHALLENGE

1. Describe how ENSIDESA uses computers in manufacturing.

2. Why is the use of computers critical to the company's global competitiveness?

MANAGEMENT CHALLENGE

1. How does this service operation resemble manufacturing?

2. How does it differ from manufacturing?

QUALITY MANAGEMENT CHALLENGE

1. How does Samsung's focus on quality contribute to its success?

2. How does quality fit into Samsung's overall strategy?

Allen-Bradley's Drive for 21st-Century Manufacturing

Allen-Bradley's CIM plant must be understood in terms of the company's overall strategy. When Allen-Bradley examined its situation in the mid-1980s, it recognized that it faced serious problems. After deciding how to cope with those problems, it realized that its actions would be part of a global strategy. It intended to increase sales throughout the world, and it would do so by increasing not only quality but also flexibility and speed. Thus, the CIM plant had to be capable of producing lots of any size; it had to be able to produce a single unit as quickly as if it were part of a batch of ten thousand. And it had to produce products of un-paralleled quality. It did both, and as a result Allen-Bradley's global sales have increased from 3 percent of total revenues to 30 percent in ten years.

Part of Allen-Bradley's strategy involved getting close to customers to learn their needs and to satisfy them so completely that they would not wish to switch to other suppliers. This strategy also was successful. When forecasts indicated a potential growth rate of 1700 percent for the 1988–1992 period, the firm went ahead and invested in the latest CIM technology in order to meet that demand.

DISCUSSION QUESTIONS

1. Explain how Allen-Bradley's CIM plant fits into its globalization strategy.
2. Discuss the company's actions in terms of the low-cost and differentiation generic strategies (see Chapter 7).
3. What might be the logical next step in Allen-Bradley's manufacturing strategy?

Smythe, Klein, Carstairs, Miller, and Ping, P.A.

Matthew Klein reviewed the financial statements in front of him. The firm had lost a little over $50,000 for the year. Smythe, Klein had three senior partners (each owning 30 percent of the firm), two junior partners (one owning 10 percent, one not active), five associate attorneys, and a staff of twenty. The staff consisted of one receptionist, one telephone answerer, seven people in data processing and related support services, two paralegals, two half-time clerical personnel, four partner secretaries, four floating secretaries, and one floating clerical person. The firm had grown rapidly in recent years, and Klein felt that the organization was getting out of hand.

He decided to call in a consultant to confirm his evaluation of the situation. After three days of intensive interviews with everyone in the firm, and after administering two questionnaires on organizational climate and work duties, the consultant identified the following major issues:

1. Morale was low because of a major rift between Jack Carstairs and Chuck Miller, the other two senior partners. Klein knew about this but hesitated to take action. He felt that Carstairs was out of line and behaving childishly, but he was needed for major litigation cases. He was really good in that area, and none of the junior partners could assume his duties for at least two more years.

2. Morale was also low because Miller was extremely authoritarian and tactless in carrying out his responsibilities as office manager.

3. Morale and productivity were correlated. People spent a tremendous amount of time backbiting, complaining, and playing psychological games.

4. There was a total absence of personnel management—there were no job descriptions, no performance appraisals, no employee handbook, and no clear compensation program, even for the attorneys.

5. The firm had no strategy.

6. Bookkeeping, recordkeeping, and even billing were disorganized.

DISCUSSION QUESTIONS

1. What problems of operations management do you see in this firm?

2. Discuss the concept of operations management in a service firm.

3. What solutions would you offer for the problems described in this case?

A few universities and colleges are conducting quality audits covering such issues as classroom instruction methods and professors' behaviors, placement activities, hours of operation, facilities, and institutional support such as libraries and computers. Usually, the core element of the audit is a questionnaire administered to students. Your instructor will divide the class into small groups. Each group is to list twenty to twenty-five questions that should be included in a quality audit questionnaire for your school. When all the groups have completed their lists, they can share them with the rest of the class. The class can then select the most critical questions to create the questionnaire.

"The reasonable man adapts himself to the world: the unreasonable one persists in trying to adapt the world to himself, therefore, all progress depends on the unreasonable man."

—George Bernard Shaw

"The entrepreneurs sustain the world. In their careers there is little of optimizing calculation, nothing of delicate balance in markets. They overthrow establishments rather than establish equilibria. They are the heroes of economic life."

—George Gilder
The Spirit of Enterprise

Entrepreneurship and Small-Business Management

CHAPTER OBJECTIVES

When you have read this chapter you should be able to:

1. Define entrepreneurship and distinguish it from small-business management.

2. Discuss several reasons why entrepreneurship is currently of major interest in the United States and Canada.

3. Discuss the stages of growth and how growth affects entrepreneurship and small-business management.

4. Discuss the transition from an entrepreneurship to a larger firm and the changes in management it demands.

5. Review current trends in entrepreneurship.

6. Discuss the relationships among competitiveness, innovation, and entrepreneurship.

7. Discuss the management of innovation.

M ANAGEMENT CHALLENGES DISCUSSED IN THIS CHAPTER:

 Accelerating rates of change.

 Increasing globalization of business.

 Quality and innovation as managerial imperatives.

Sam Walton, Entrepreneur and Manager

Perhaps no one better exemplified the entrepreneur who made the transition to professional manager than the late Sam M. Walton, founder of Wal-Mart, Sam's Wholesale Clubs, and Hypermart USA stores. Walton, the son of a Depression-era mortgage banker, graduated in 1940 from the University of Missouri with a degree in economics and immediately went to work for J. C. Penney as a trainee. Soon thereafter the entrepreneurial spirit struck him. He opened a Ben Franklin discount store in Newport, Arkansas, in 1945. At about the same time, his brother, Bud, opened a Ben Franklin store in rural Missouri. By the 1950s, Sam and his brother had opened sixteen Ben Franklin stores, and their stores had become the largest Ben Franklin franchises in the country. Most of their stores were located in rural areas where there was no competition. Walton believed that larger stores would do well in those areas. He took his idea to Ben Franklin's management, but they feared that such a move would lower their profit margins. Walton therefore decided to start his own chain of discount stores. In 1962, he opened the first Wal-Mart store in Rogers, Arkansas, not far from the company's current main office in Bentonville. His stores offered low prices with comparatively high levels of service. At first Wal-Mart focused on rural America, but as it grew it began to compete directly with Kmart and others.

By the end of 1992, Walton's empire had grown to 1180 Wal-Mart stores, 256 Sam's Wholesale Clubs, and 4 Hypermart USA stores in 45 states. Sales of over $55.5 billion were recorded for 1992. These sales allowed Wal-Mart to surpass Sears and Kmart and become the number 1 retailer in the United States.

Sam Walton had a strategic intent and made it work. What is unusual about his story is that he kept the entrepreneurial spirit alive in Wal-Mart as it was growing to a colossal size. His management style is well known. He was particularly demanding while at the same time highly relationship oriented. Until the number of stores became so great that the task was impossible, he could name all the store managers and many of their employees. And until the number of stores became so high, he used to visit every store at least once a year. He was well-known for antics such as jumping onto the boardroom table during Saturday morning management meetings and shouting "Who's number 1!" to which all present responded "Wal-Mart . . . Wal-Mart . . . Wal-Mart." When he asked the same question in the stores, the employees shouted back "The customer . . . The customer . . . The customer." He and his staff were meticulous about details and concerned about product and service quality. Walton learned early to delegate, and surrounded himself with an excellent staff. A spirit of entrepreneurial innovation permeated the firm. High-quality service and low prices enabled the firm to compete effectively.

Walton invigorated his company. He thought doing business should be fun. He had six abiding principles for managing the business: Think one store at a time; communicate, communicate, communicate; keep your ear to the ground; push responsibility—and authority—down; force ideas to bubble up; and stay lean, fight bureaucracy.

SOURCES: John Huey, "America's Most Successful Merchant," *Fortune* (September 23, 1991), pp. 46–59; Van Johnston and Herff Moore, "Pride Drives Wal-Mart to Service Excellence," *HRM Magazine* (October 1991), pp. 76–82; Bill Saporitos, "Is Wal-Mart Unstoppable?" *Fortune* (May 6, 1991), pp. 50–59; and Sam Walton, "Sam Walton in His Own Words," *Fortune* (June 29, 1992), pp. 98–106.

S am Walton of Wal-Mart, Steven Jobs and Stephen Wozniak of Apple Computer, Mary Kay Ash of Mary Kay Cosmetics, Ray Kroc of McDonald's, Debbi and Randy Fields of Mrs. Fields' Cookies, H. Ross Perot of Electronic Data Systems, and Massaru Ibuka and Akio Morita of Sony share a very important characteristic: They are successful entrepreneurs. Walton was perhaps America's most successful entrepreneur. He knew how to manage people. He learned how to delegate, control, and plan. He developed strategies and the related organizational structures that proved to be just right for his company. He worked very hard; he paid attention to detail; and he inspired his employees.

Many people believe that entrepreneurship makes America great. Much of this reverence for the phenomenon of entrepreneurship arises from the realization that small entrepreneurial firms contribute significantly to the well-being of the national economy. This was especially true in the ten-year period from 1977 to 1987. Most of the new jobs created in that period were generated not by the activities of major corporations, but by the start-up operations of small businesses. From 1977 to 1987, 17 million new jobs were created in small businesses, compared to a net loss of 3.1 million jobs among the Fortune 500 companies.[1] The number of new corporations formed per year reached 780,000 for the first time in 1990. Although many experts believe that this pace of growth cannot be continued, small businesses are expected to remain an important source of new jobs.[2]

David Birch of the Massachusetts Institute of Technology suggests that while the impact of entrepreneurship on the national economy is significant, entrepreneurship can have an even greater impact on a regional economy. In California, for example, 70 percent of the state's employment in the late 1980s resulted from the activities of small-scale entrepreneurs.[3] In the "rustbelt" of the Northeast and Midwest, where heavy industry has declined, many entrepreneur-

Debbi Fields and her husband Randy, owners of Mrs. Fields' Cookies, are among America's most successful entrepreneurs. The success of their company is due in part to a sophisticated information system that allows them to control internal operations as they occur.

ships emerged in the mid- to late 1980s as blue-collar workers, laid off by manufacturing firms, founded their own businesses.[4]

Entrepreneurship and small businesses are not unique to the U.S. economy. Entrepreneurship is becoming a global phenomenon as former socialist and communist countries embrace capitalism and as individuals in other capitalist countries see entrepreneurship as a way of improving their economic situation. Thus, for example, there are growing numbers of entrepreneurs in China, France, Poland, Hungary, Argentina, Ireland, Hong Kong, Korea, and Japan.

In the United States, where entrepreneurship is not new, its nature is changing. More women and members of minority groups are becoming entrepreneurs, and joint ventures, alliances, and network firms are becoming more common.[5]

This chapter explores entrepreneurship and small business, beginning by defining them and distinguishing between them. It then discusses the management of a small business or entrepreneurship, viewing each of the management functions from that perspective. Ways of preserving entrepreneurship are reviewed, and major trends in entrepreneurship are noted.

Defining Entrepreneurship

It is difficult to pinpoint exactly what entrepreneurship is.[6] Historically, entrepreneurship has been conceptualized partially as an economic function. In the early eighteenth century, Richard Cantillon observed that an entrepreneur was one who bore the risk of buying and selling.[7] Economists Adam Smith and Jean Baptiste Say suggested that an entrepreneur was someone who brought together the factors of production.[8] Austrian economist Joseph Schumpeter (1883–1950) later added innovation and the exploiting of opportunities to the activities of the entrepreneur.[9] Some management theorists have suggested that entrepreneurship is the creation of new enterprises.[10] Howard H. Stevenson and William H. Sahlman point out, however, that it is possible to identify entrepreneurs who did not purchase or sell, did not bring together the factors of production, were not innovators but followers, and did not create businesses but managed the work of others.[11] Thus, there are several differing schools of thought about entrepreneurship, and it is important to recognize the contribution of each.[12]

Today, entrepreneurship is considered to be as much an attitude as a role practiced in small and large organizations.[13] Stevenson and José Carlos Jarillo-Mossi define an **entrepreneur** as "a person who perceives opportunity; finds the pursuit of opportunity desirable in the context of his [or her] life situation; and believes that success is possible."[14] To this we add that an entrepreneur is someone who initiates changes.

Entrepreneur: A person who perceives opportunity; finds the pursuit of opportunity desirable in the context of his or her life situation; and believes that success is possible.

The key difference between entrepreneurs and other managers lies in their approach to problem solving. Entrepreneurs do not merely solve problems or react to problems; they look for opportunities. They are risk takers. This view of entrepreneurship was noted in 1964 by Peter Drucker, who indicated that "resources, to produce results, must be allocated to opportunities, rather than to problems. . . . Maximization of opportunities is a meaningful, indeed a precise definition of the entrepreneurial job."[15] In 1974, Drucker repeated this theme: "An entrepreneur . . . has to redirect resources from areas of low or diminishing results to areas of high or increasing results. He [or she] has to slough off yesterday and to render obsolete what already exists and is already known. He [or she] has to create tomorrow."[16]

Entrepreneurs also initiate change.[17] They may initiate changes in all aspects of organizational functioning—marketing, finance, operations, human resources, and information. Drucker has integrated this aspect of entrepreneur-

Flea market vendors may be considered urban entrepreneurs. They take risks and redirect resources from areas of low or diminishing results to areas of high or increasing results.

ship into his view of the opportunistic nature of entrepreneurs: "The entrepreneur always searches for change, responds to it, and exploits it as an opportunity."[18]

Other writers on entrepreneurship have attempted to identify the personal characteristics of entrepreneurs. Among the characteristics that have been widely attributed to entrepreneurs are the need for achievement, the need for control, an intuitive orientation, and a propensity to take risks. Other frequently discussed, but not universally accepted, characteristics are childhood deprivation, minority group membership, and work experiences during adolescence.[19] It also seems clear that a major reason for becoming an entrepreneur is to attain autonomy.[20]

Many people claim that the innovativeness associated with entrepreneurship is one of the major ways in which U.S. firms are able to compete with foreign firms.[21] Not all observers agree, however. George Gilder suggests that entrepreneurs often sell out to foreign competitors, with the result that American technology is transferred to foreign firms.[22] He also points out that only large firms have the staying power necessary to compete in many industries. Nevertheless, most management experts would agree that entrepreneurs help the United States compete successfully in international markets because they introduce and export new products, thereby helping to reduce the U.S. trade deficit.[23]

The Entrepreneurial Mystique

There is something exciting about being an entrepreneur.[24] It offers several psychological payoffs: the chance to be your own boss, initiate change, do it your way, take advantage of opportunities, and be at the forefront of change. There are also disadvantages—long hours, hard work, and risk. Most small businesses end in failure.[25]

Entrepreneurs have several characteristics that are very different from those of other managers.[26] A *Wall Street Journal*/Gallup survey suggested that entrepreneurs tend to be mavericks, dreamers, and loners. They have rough edges, are uncompromising, and need to do things their own way. They are not particularly good students, are more likely than other students to be expelled from school, and are less likely to graduate from college. They also are likely to take charge at an early age, are fired more frequently, and jump from job to job more often. (See Figures 22.1 and 22.2.)

The same survey found that Fortune 500 executives, entrepreneurs, and small-business executives share certain characteristics. All showed an inclination

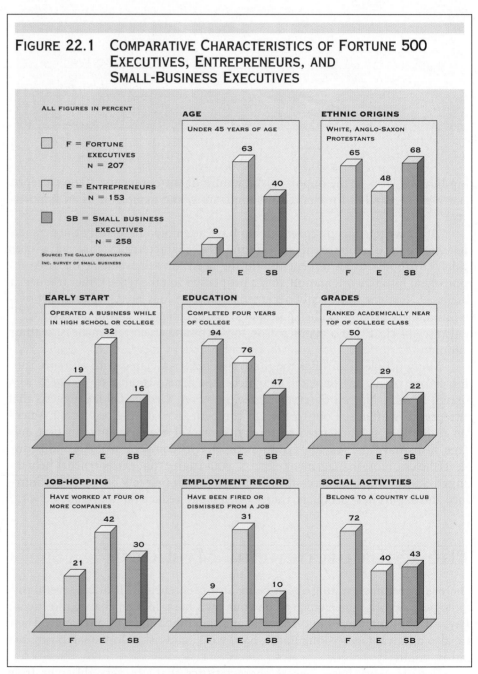

FIGURE 22.1   COMPARATIVE CHARACTERISTICS OF FORTUNE 500 EXECUTIVES, ENTREPRENEURS, AND SMALL-BUSINESS EXECUTIVES

ALL FIGURES IN PERCENT

F = FORTUNE EXECUTIVES N = 207

E = ENTREPRENEURS N = 153

SB = SMALL BUSINESS EXECUTIVES N = 258

SOURCE: THE GALLUP ORGANIZATION INC. SURVEY OF SMALL BUSINESS

AGE — UNDER 45 YEARS OF AGE: F 9, E 63, SB 40

ETHNIC ORIGINS — WHITE, ANGLO-SAXON PROTESTANTS: F 65, E 48, SB 68

EARLY START — OPERATED A BUSINESS WHILE IN HIGH SCHOOL OR COLLEGE: F 19, E 32, SB 16

EDUCATION — COMPLETED FOUR YEARS OF COLLEGE: F 94, E 76, SB 47

GRADES — RANKED ACADEMICALLY NEAR TOP OF COLLEGE CLASS: F 50, E 29, SB 22

JOB-HOPPING — HAVE WORKED AT FOUR OR MORE COMPANIES: F 21, E 42, SB 30

EMPLOYMENT RECORD — HAVE BEEN FIRED OR DISMISSED FROM A JOB: F 9, E 31, SB 10

SOCIAL ACTIVITIES — BELONG TO A COUNTRY CLUB: F 72, E 40, SB 43

SOURCE: ELLEN GRAHAM, "THE ENTREPRENEURIAL MYSTIQUE," WALL STREET JOURNAL, SPECIAL REPORT ON SMALL BUSINESS, MAY 30, 1985, SECTION 3, PP. 1,4,6–7.

FIGURE 22.2 ADDITIONAL COMPARATIVE CHARACTERISTICS OF FORTUNE 500 EXECUTIVES, ENTREPRENEURS, AND SMALL-BUSINESS EXECUTIVES

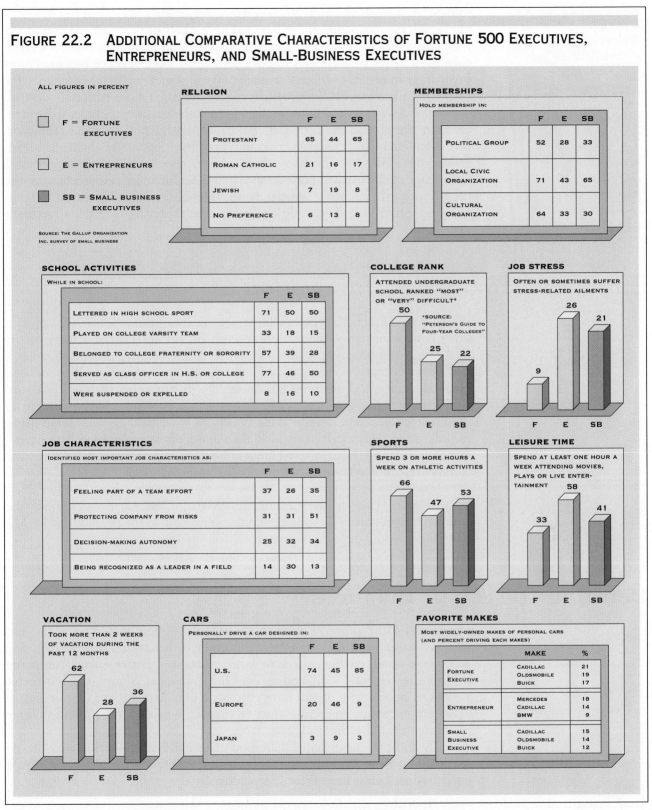

ALL FIGURES IN PERCENT

F = FORTUNE EXECUTIVES

E = ENTREPRENEURS

SB = SMALL BUSINESS EXECUTIVES

SOURCE: THE GALLUP ORGANIZATION INC. SURVEY OF SMALL BUSINESS

RELIGION

	F	E	SB
PROTESTANT	65	44	65
ROMAN CATHOLIC	21	16	17
JEWISH	7	19	8
NO PREFERENCE	6	13	8

MEMBERSHIPS

HOLD MEMBERSHIP IN:

	F	E	SB
POLITICAL GROUP	52	28	33
LOCAL CIVIC ORGANIZATION	71	43	65
CULTURAL ORGANIZATION	64	33	30

SCHOOL ACTIVITIES

WHILE IN SCHOOL:

	F	E	SB
LETTERED IN HIGH SCHOOL SPORT	71	50	50
PLAYED ON COLLEGE VARSITY TEAM	33	18	15
BELONGED TO COLLEGE FRATERNITY OR SORORITY	57	39	28
SERVED AS CLASS OFFICER IN H.S. OR COLLEGE	77	46	50
WERE SUSPENDED OR EXPELLED	8	16	10

COLLEGE RANK

ATTENDED UNDERGRADUATE SCHOOL RANKED "MOST" OR "VERY" DIFFICULT*

*SOURCE: "PETERSON'S GUIDE TO FOUR-YEAR COLLEGES"

50 25 22
F   E   SB

JOB STRESS

OFTEN OR SOMETIMES SUFFER STRESS-RELATED AILMENTS

9 26 21
F E   SB

JOB CHARACTERISTICS

IDENTIFIED MOST IMPORTANT JOB CHARACTERISTICS AS:

	F	E	SB
FEELING PART OF A TEAM EFFORT	37	26	35
PROTECTING COMPANY FROM RISKS	31	31	51
DECISION-MAKING AUTONOMY	25	32	34
BEING RECOGNIZED AS A LEADER IN A FIELD	14	30	13

SPORTS

SPEND 3 OR MORE HOURS A WEEK ON ATHLETIC ACTIVITIES

66 47 53
F   E   SB

LEISURE TIME

SPEND AT LEAST ONE HOUR A WEEK ATTENDING MOVIES, PLAYS OR LIVE ENTERTAINMENT

33 58 41
F   E   SB

VACATION

TOOK MORE THAN 2 WEEKS OF VACATION DURING THE PAST 12 MONTHS

62 28 36
F   E   SB

CARS

PERSONALLY DRIVE A CAR DESIGNED IN:

	F	E	SB
U.S.	74	45	85
EUROPE	20	46	9
JAPAN	3	9	3

FAVORITE MAKES

MOST WIDELY-OWNED MAKES OF PERSONAL CARS (AND PERCENT DRIVING EACH MAKES)

	MAKE	%
FORTUNE EXECUTIVE	CADILLAC OLDSMOBILE BUICK	21 19 17
ENTREPRENEUR	MERCEDES CADILLAC BMW	18 14 9
SMALL BUSINESS EXECUTIVE	CADILLAC OLDSMOBILE BUICK	15 14 12

SOURCE: ELLEN GRAHAM, "THE ENTREPRENEURIAL MYSTIQUE," WALL STREET JOURNAL, SPECIAL REPORT ON SMALL BUSINESS, MAY 30, 1985, SECTION 3, PP. 1,4,6–7.

AT WAL-MART: Sam Walton exemplified the mystique associated with entrepreneurs. Starting with nothing, he struggled to make Wal-Mart succeed. He had many of the personality characteristics associated with entrepreneurs.

toward hard work and high achievement from an early age. Most began working before the age of fifteen and earned about half of their college tuition. At least two-thirds work sixty or more hours per week. Corporate officers tend to have been better students and to have completed more years of college. Entrepreneurs tend not to be joiners or team players, something that is necessary for corporate management. Entrepreneurs also tend to be more ethnically diverse.

In reviewing several other studies, John A. Hornaday concludes that entrepreneurs are characterized by self-confidence, energy and diligence, ability to take calculated risks, creativity, flexibility, positive response to challenges, leadership, the ability to get along with people, responsiveness to suggestions, knowledge of the market, perseverance and determination, resourcefulness, the need to achieve, initiative, independence, foresight, profit orientation, perceptiveness, optimism, and versatility of knowledge, especially as related to technology.[27]

Entrepreneurship and Innovation

Whether it is practiced within a large organization (*intrapreneurship*) or in a small entrepreneurship, innovation depends on entrepreneurial activity for its existence. An innovation is any outgrowth of the creative process that has a significant impact on an organization, an industry, or a society.[28] Innovation involves change and therefore is associated with entrepreneurship.[29] Not surprisingly, two studies of innovation suggest that it is more likely to occur in small companies than in large ones.[30] On the other hand, several large firms, including 3M, Hewlett-Packard, Milliken and Company, Johnson & Johnson, and Dow-Corning, have fostered innovation, largely by adopting structures and cultures resembling those found in small entrepreneurships.[31]

Innovation is so critical to business success that much of Chapter 23 is devoted to it. This chapter's Innovation Management Challenge reviews the innovative approaches to selling computers brought to the PC industry by Michael Dell. Note how simple, yet successful, his innovations were.

Defining the Small Business[32]

The term *small business* is used to describe a business according to its size, whereas *entrepreneurship* describes an attitude or behavioral process that may occur in a small, medium-sized, or large business.[33] Entrepreneurs run many small businesses but not all, and perhaps not even most. Many small businesses are run by people who do not have entrepreneurial leanings and do not engage in the entrepreneurial process. Moreover, entrepreneurs can be found in large businesses as well as in small ones.

The most frequently cited definition of a **small business** is that provided by the Small Business Administration (SBA). To qualify for a loan from the SBA, a small business must have three characteristics:

Small business: As defined by the SBA, a small business does not dominate its industry, has less than $10 million in annual sales, and has fewer than one thousand employees.

1. It does not dominate its industry.
2. It has less than $10 million in annual sales.
3. It has fewer than one thousand employees.[34]

However, there are some additional qualifications:

1. The business must be independently owned and operated.

2. If in manufacturing, it should employ no more than 250 employees or be relatively small for its industry. In certain industries 1,500 employees is considered small.

3. If in wholesaling, it can have annual sales no greater than $9.5 million to $22 million, depending on the industry.

4. If in retailing or service, its annual sales are no greater than $2 million to $8 million, depending on the industry.

5. If in construction, its annual receipts cannot exceed $9.5 million for the three most recently completed fiscal years for general construction. In special trade construction, its annual receipts cannot exceed $1 million to $2 million for the same time frame, depending on the industry.

6. If in agriculture, its annual receipts cannot be greater than $1 million.

The SBA uses these characteristics as guidelines; they are not hard-and-fast rules.

There are numerous other definitions of a small business. For example, a business may be considered "small" if it is family-owned, if it is owned and operated by a small group of investors, if it is a franchise, if it operates locally, or if it has fewer than one hundred employees. Regardless of the criteria chosen, it is clear that small businesses are far more numerous than large ones. More than 99 percent of U.S. businesses have fewer than five hundred employees.[35]

Managing the Entrepreneurship/ Small Business

In Chapter 10 we examined some models that suggested that as organizations grow, they pass through a series of stages. The first stage might be called growth through creation. However, it is often followed by a crisis of leadership. In this crisis, the entrepreneur or small-business manager arrives at a point at which he or she can no longer run the business properly. It may be necessary to obtain

Bill and Adele Malley own and operate Malley's Chocolates, a family business that they started in 1935 with one small store. Since then the company has grown to thirteen stores and has annual sales of $6.5 million.

Michael Dell, Innovator and Entrepreneur

The idea that launched Dell Computer Corp. in 1984 was startling in its simplicity: Why not sell computers over the phone? Launched by then-nineteen-year-old Michael S. Dell from his college apartment in Austin, Texas, the idea grew into a $2 billion-a-year business—and the status of fourth-largest PC maker in the United States. Only IBM, Apple, and Compaq are bigger.

Dell now has a staff of well over 4,000 and hires more than 100 new employees a month. The company sells 42 PC designs and a full line of software and accessories, such as fax modems. It sells PCs in 18 countries, including Japan.

Dell's success has been compared with the triumph of David over Goliath. His formula was straightforward: Cut out dealers and distributors; design and assemble most PCs from off-the-shelf components; and run a no-frills operation, with the main emphasis on customer service. According to one software maker, Dell is the "most innovative guy for marketing computers in this decade . . . the quintessential American entrepreneur that does something everyone says is impossible."

The rewards for doing the impossible? A stunning 126 percent gain in sales for the fiscal year ending January 31, 1993, to $2 billion. Despite component shortages that created shipping delays, fourth-quarter revenues rose 117 percent, the fourth quarter in a row of triple-digit increases.

These numbers will constitute a hard act to follow, however, owing to several recent challenges now affecting the company all at once. For one, Dell will face formidable new competition in its own backyard: Its archrival Compaq will market PCs directly. Dell will also have to restrain its cutthroat—but not necessarily accurate—advertising policy. Compaq has sued and won an undisclosed sum over ads in several countries suggesting that comparable models were cheaper at Dell; a London court ruled that the ads contained "malicious falsehoods."

Perhaps more serious are quality and service problems. Some large-volume buyers estimate that Dell meets its promised six-day delivery schedule only about half the time. And its portable computers and notebooks have been plagued by glitches.

Dell hopes to remedy the problems by relying less on subcontractors in the future. Michael Dell may also have to revise some of the watchwords of his faith. Formerly, he held that the assemble-to-order, direct-response nature of his opera-

additional management training or to hire a professional manager. It may also be necessary to structure the organization on an economic basis, dividing tasks among several people. The entrepreneur can no longer manage alone. Nevertheless, the style and intentions of the entrepreneur will remain and will significantly affect the firm's future. Some entrepreneurs find it impossible to let go.[36]

Problem solving in the areas of planning, organizing, leading, and controlling occurs in entrepreneurships and small businesses much as it does in large organizations, with the exception that these processes tend to be less formalized and are often implied. A transition to formalized professional management is usually necessary to preserve an entrepreneurship in the long term.

Shown here are some of Dell Computer Corporation's products, which are designed and assembled from off-the-shelf components and sold directly to customers.

tion was more likely to meet his customers' needs. He reckoned that if parts could be purchased easily, it was foolish to incur the responsibility and expense of building them in-house. Instead of accumulating inventories of finished PCs, the Austin and Ireland plants would finish the machines only when customers specified their desires.

But the two major advantages of direct sales, price and convenience, are now being matched by low-priced electronics superstores—and Dell has started selling in them. "We're constantly reinventing ourselves," Dell says.

Even more reinvention may be necessary to keep pace with the rapidly changing PC business. Dell has assured investors that the company can still grow by 70 percent in 1993. But with cost already trimmed after a 1992 austerity program (which included a temporary 5 percent pay cut for top employees) and PC prices still plummeting, expansion is critical—and may need a lot more reinvention to achieve.

SOURCE: Stephanie Anderson Forest and Catherine Arnst, "The Education of Michael Dell," *Business Week* (March 22, 1993), pp. 82–87.

Planning

Perhaps the most important aspect of managing a small business is learning how to plan. Even in the start-up stages of an entrepreneurship, a business plan is critical. A business plan typically contains specific objectives, along with plans for reaching those objectives, for each of the organization's major economic functions. Special attention is paid to target markets; product development, pricing, distribution, and promotion strategies; and the organization's ability to finance marketing and operations.

A business plan includes at least the following information:

> AT WAL-MART: *It was Sam Walton's ability to learn to manage, to try different management systems, and to surround himself with professional managers that enabled Wal-Mart to make the transition from a small entrepreneurship to the number 1 retailer in the United States.*

1. An overview of the business, which helps define the organization's mission.
2. A specific set of objectives against which performance can be measured, both for the organization and for its employees.
3. A plan by which capital may be raised. Most banks, for example, require a detailed business plan before they will lend money to a new enterprise or an ongoing smaller one.
4. A marketing plan by which to run the organization.
5. A plan by which personnel may be recruited, an operations plan, and a materials purchasing plan.[37]

About 85 percent of all new businesses will fail within ten years of their start-up, 67 percent within four years. To avoid such failure, planning is critical.[38] Businesses fail for many reasons besides poor planning—including lack of capital and lack of understanding of marketing—but failing to set objectives and develop plans and budgets inevitably leads to failure. Performing a SWOT analysis (strengths, weaknesses, opportunities, and threats) enables the manager to prepare better strategic and operating plans. A budget enables the manager to predict potential cash shortages and to take necessary offsetting actions. Now that simulation models are available for PCs, virtually any small business can calculate pro forma financial statements (income statement, balance sheets, and cash flow) and understand its internal operations better as a result.[39]

Like managers in any organization, entrepreneurs and small-business managers need to ask themselves these questions:

1. Where are we now?
2. Where do we want to be?
3. How do we get there?

It is never easy to start a business. But American entrepreneurs may be interested to learn that it can be harder still in other countries. This chapter's Global Management Challenge describes the obstacles that faced a particularly gifted entrepreneur in a country that is much less receptive to the idea of entrepreneurship. How might entrepreneurship differ in the United States and Japan? What similarities might there be?

Curtis Bull is CEO of Atlanta-based Sentry Plastics and Packaging, Inc. His business plan focuses on a specific target market.

Organizing

Most of the organizational problems faced by a new business are growth-related and structural. For example, once an organization has a functional structure, a crisis of authority is likely to occur because managers of economic functions have not been delegated sufficient authority. Once such authority has been delegated, the question of control arises. New structures may be necessary to solve this problem.[40] We have also seen that as organizations grow, they typically change from a functional to a product to an SBU structure.

A major means of making organizations more efficient is to delegate more authority to lower-level positions. Middle-level management and staff positions are eliminated as much as possible. However, entrepreneurs typically have a high need for achievement and a high need for power.[41] It is often difficult for them to delegate, especially to front-line employees. Unfortunately, many entrepreneurs and small-business owners are unable to make this transition. Mary Lou Fox, founder and CEO of Westhaven Services Company, an institutional pharmacy based in Perrysburg, Ohio, has tried on four separate occasions to "let go" of her company and allow others to help her manage it. Each time, she has been unable to find the "right" people—people who would make the same decisions she would. "No one can do it the same way you can," she says.[42]

Leading

Entrepreneurs and small-business managers must become leaders as well as managers of their organizations. They must provide vision, mission, goals, and objectives. Most entrepreneurs must learn how to lead, although a few may be natural leaders. Some are visionaries and some are dynamic group leaders, but most are not.

About 90 percent of all registered business organizations have fewer than twenty employees.[43] Leadership of such an organization tends to be extremely personal. The entrepreneur or small-business manager must instill shared values in subordinates and be responsive to their needs. In other words, the entrepreneur or manager must act as a coach. It is often difficult for a person with a high need for achievement to fill this role.[44]

Controlling

Planning, organizing, and leading are not fully effective without control. Many entrepreneurs and small-business managers have difficulty learning how to control. Part of that deficiency is the result of poor planning: They do not set sufficiently detailed objectives with appropriate time frames. In addition, many entrepreneurs start with some technical knowledge—in engineering, medicine, computer programming, or sales—but have little understanding of proper management techniques. Sometimes entrepreneurs are not concerned about control because they are interested in ideas rather than in the day-to-day tasks of managing. Once an idea is launched, they are bored by the details of implementation.

Proper control depends on information. With the advent of PCs, there is no excuse for most small organizations not to have the information they need for effective control. An old saying about planning is, "If you don't know where you are going, any road will get you there." A similar one for control might be, "If you don't know where you have gotten to, you are not likely to get there again." Perhaps the most critical component of control for the small business is the budget. It helps establish not only objectives, but also a standard against which performance can be compared.

As discussed in Chapter 7, organizations tend to compete on the basis of their ability to differentiate or to produce at a relatively low cost.[45] Therefore, from a competitive viewpoint, cost control is absolutely mandatory.

Problem Solving

Entrepreneurs focus on opportunities. Therefore, they may not be adept at discerning problems or solving them. They may not even be interested in solving mundane, everyday problems. Although some small-business managers may be more management oriented than the typical entrepreneur, they too may need assistance in learning how to solve problems rationally as well as intuitively.

Table 22.1 provides an overview of the major differences between entrepreneurs and professional managers (or administrators).

Preserving Entrepreneurship

As entrepreneurs and small-business managers learn how to manage, their entrepreneurial orientation may be lost. Howard H. Stevenson and José Carlos Jarrillo-Mossi suggest that several actions must be taken to maintain an entrepreneurial outlook.[46] The entrepreneur or small-business manager must increase the perception of opportunities, build the desire to pursue those opportunities, and make people believe they can succeed.

As companies grow, their managers should ask themselves certain questions:

1. What is the appropriate concept of control?

month later, he got another 50 percent increase. The same the following month. In one year, monthly revenues went from about $10,000 to $2.3 million.

Son could have set up a business in the United States, where he had already set up a microcomputer company. (Son invented the prototype of what is now the Sharp Wizard, a calculator-sized computer that can do translations in several languages and can plug into telephone directories, scientific calculations, and business applications.) In addition, the business climate in the United States is more responsive to start-up firms. "There's more capital," Son says. "In the United States, there's not the negative perception of the entrepreneur that there is in Japan. . . . Japanese banks will not loan money to you because they are more conservative. And because of the culture, it's harder to attract the best employees. They like to work for the big companies or for the government because Japan is a lifetime employment country."

Why did Son return to Japan instead? Because he had a long-term vision. "I didn't have any evidence, but I believed in myself. I believed that someday I would have a very big company, a global business, and a very successful company. If I were able to do that, my headquarters should be in Japan. It's more difficult to start a business in Japan, but once I started it . . . it would be easier to keep the loyalty of the employees. . . . Japanese workers work harder, they have a stronger loyalty to the company, and they tend to stay in the company for a very long time. They don't often have bright creativity, but they work very hard to make continuous improvements."

SOURCE: Alan M. Webber, "Japanese-Style Entrepreneurship: An Interview with SOFTBANK's CEO, Masayoshi Son," *Harvard Business Review* (January–February 1992), pp. 93–103.

2. How does one emphasize the individual sense of responsibility, not authority?

3. What kind of failures is the company willing to accept?

4. How can teams be created and nurtured?

5. How does the company promote functional excellence in all positions?

6. How can the company assure continuous adaptive change?

Trends in Entrepreneurship

Several trends in entrepreneurship have been identified. In this section we will discuss some of the most significant of them, beginning with the phenomenon of the campus capitalist.

Campus Capitalists

In the mid-1980s, a major "craze" on college campuses was starting one's own business. There were only six entrepreneurial clubs on campuses in 1983, but by 1985 there were 250.[47] In these clubs, nineteen- and twenty-year-olds learn from successful entrepreneurs, many of whom are just a few years older than themselves. The businesses they engage in range from printing calendars and writing software to running pizza parlors. Undergraduate courses in entrepreneurship are full, and conventional business schools are offering more such courses.

Entrepreneurial contests are currently popular on many campuses. Typical is the contest sponsored by the University of Texas at Austin. Student teams are

AT WAL-MART: *Sam Walton was careful to make sure that Wal-Mart kept its opportunistic perspective. He encouraged people to seek out opportunities and rewarded them for doing so.*

TABLE 22.1 The Entrepreneurial Culture vs. The Administrative Culture

	Entrepreneurial Focus		Administrative Focus	
	Characteristics	Pressures	Characteristics	Pressures
A Strategic orientation	Driven by perception of opportunity	Diminishing opportunities Rapidly changing technology, consumer economics, social values, and political rules	Driven by controlled resources	Social contracts Performance measurement criteria Planning systems and cycles
B Commitment to seize opportunities	Revolutionary, with short duration	Action orientation Narrow decision windows Acceptance of reasonable risks Few decision constituencies	Evolutionary, with long duration	Acknowledgment of multiple constituencies Negotiation about strategic course Risk reduction Coordination with existing resource base
C Commitment of resources	Many stages, with minimal exposure at each stage	Lack of predictable resource needs Lack of control over the environment Social demands for appropriate use of resources Foreign competition Demands for more efficient resource use	A single stage, with complete commitment out of decision	Need to reduce risk Incentive compensation Turnover in managers Capital budgeting systems Formal planning systems
D Control of resources	Episodic use or rent of required resources	Increased resource specialization Long resource life compared with need Risk of obsolescence Risk inherent in the identified opportunity Inflexibility of permanent commitment to resources	Ownership or employment of required resources	Power, status, and financial rewards Coordination of activity Efficiency measures Inertia and cost of change Industry structures
E Management structure	Flat, with multiple informal networks	Coordination of key noncontrolled resources Challenge to hierarchy Employees' desire for independence	Hierarchy	Need for clearly defined authority and responsibility Organizational culture Reward systems Management theory

SOURCE: Howard H. Stevenson and David E. Gumpert, "The Heart of Entrepreneurship," *Harvard Business Review* (March–April 1985). Copyright © 1985 by the President and Fellows of Harvard College, all rights reserved.

invited to compete by submitting business plans. Judges select the most viable one.[48]

Upon graduation, many students are going into business for themselves rather than working for other firms. Typical is Thomas Madonna, who could not find a good job after graduation. With a partner, he founded Atlanta Multigraphics, which offers computer graphics to local businesses.[49]

Staying in the Family Business

Until fairly recently, the sons and daughters of entrepreneurs tended to seek jobs in large corporations rather than remain in the family business. However, that is changing, for a number of reasons.[50] Even though the children of entrepreneurs did not found the family business, it still offers them an opportunity to be an entrepreneur. Because small businesses are growing rapidly, the family business often provides opportunities for success and advancement that are lacking in

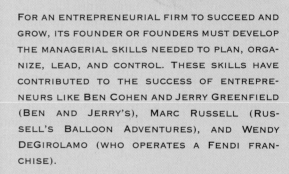

FOR AN ENTREPRENEURIAL FIRM TO SUCCEED AND GROW, ITS FOUNDER OR FOUNDERS MUST DEVELOP THE MANAGERIAL SKILLS NEEDED TO PLAN, ORGANIZE, LEAD, AND CONTROL. THESE SKILLS HAVE CONTRIBUTED TO THE SUCCESS OF ENTREPRENEURS LIKE BEN COHEN AND JERRY GREENFIELD (BEN AND JERRY'S), MARC RUSSELL (RUSSELL'S BALLOON ADVENTURES), AND WENDY DEGIROLAMO (WHO OPERATES A FENDI FRANCHISE).

Entrepreneurial contests are currently popular on many campuses. One such contest is run by Gary Cadenhead, director of the Moot Corp., shown here congratulating members of the 1993 winning team from the Kellogg School at Northwestern University.

large firms. In a small company, decisions can be made quickly, with a minimum of red tape. In addition, many members of the baby-boom generation are uncomfortable in the highly competitive environment of a large corporation. The family business can offer a gentler life-style and the security and pleasure of working with people you have known all your life.

Young people who stay with the family business seem to have a sense of responsibility along with the desire for freedom. Carole F. Bitter, president and CEO of Friedman's Supermarkets, a seven-unit chain with headquarters in Butler, Pennsylvania, comments, "I don't have a life of my own, but I'm my own boss." Most of these people would rather work hard to attain their own goals than strive to achieve the objectives of a large company.

Carole F. Bitter is president and CEO of Friedman's Supermarkets, a seven-unit chain with headquarters in Butler, Pennsylvania.

Leaving Large Corporations for Small Businesses

Increasingly, executives are leaving large corporations and going into business for themselves.[51] Typical is Gary Gandle, who left his position as an executive with Sonoco Products, a big South Carolina packing firm, to open a SpeeDee Oil Change & Tune Up outlet. He now owns three. Leaving the safety of a big corporation was "a little frightening," he recalls. "But it's also exciting."[52]

John Styles was a senior vice-president of operations for LifeMark, a Houston-based hospital management firm. He could see that the firm was unlikely to grow. With the aid of venture capital, he started his own company, Ambulatory Hospitals, which he expected to break even in a year. As is typical of entrepreneurs, he became bored by the day-to-day tasks of management, so he hired a CEO. Now he spends his time charting the company's future course.[53]

A frequent theme expressed by entrepreneurially oriented executives is the desire to be independent and to be able to take risks. But these needs are not the only ones reflected by people who are leaving big companies for what they see as greener pastures. As part of the restructuring of major corporations, many firms are selling subsidiaries to their managers. For example, a leveraged buyout by then president Joel E. Smilow helped turn Playtex around after its sales floundered under two different conglomerate owners in less than two years. Similarly, another former Beatrice subsidiary, Meadow Gold, prospered when it was bought by Borden, which renewed its focus on dairy products.[54]

Women and Minorities as Entrepreneurs

A record number of women are becoming entrepreneurs.[55] *Inc.* magazine's entrepreneur of the year for 1987 was a woman, Betsy Tabac, who runs a policy research and writing firm from her Cleveland home.[56] One reason suggested for the increase in women entrepreneurs is that many women feel that they are prevented from entering top management in large corporations.[57] The "typical" female entrepreneur is the first-born child of middle-class parents. Her father was often self-employed. She has a degree in liberal arts, is married, and has children. She begins her business venture when she is between the ages of thirty-

B. Smith is the owner of the successful New York restaurant that bears her name. Recent surveys indicate strong growth in entrepreneurship among members of minority groups, especially blacks and Hispanics.

five and forty-five.[58] Recent surveys also indicate a strong growth in entrepreneurship among members of minority groups, especially blacks and Hispanics. Being a minority entrepreneur is seldom easy, however, as this chapter's Diversity Management Challenge reveals.

International Entrepreneurship

All over the world, especially in Europe (including Eastern Europe and Russia) and the Pacific Rim, entrepreneurship is gaining in popularity. In Russia, entrepreneurs are helping to create a new economic system.[59] In France, many people are going into business for themselves and the government is reducing its role as an owner and operator of businesses.[60] This is true in Great Britain as well.[61] In Poland, entrepreneurs have launched western-style wholesale clubs.[62] In Japan, where entrepreneurship has been discouraged by the loss of face incurred by leaving a company, entrepreneurship is increasing significantly.[63] Even in the People's Republic of China, entrepreneurship and capitalism are on the rise and are being encouraged by the government despite its history of opposition to free enterprise.[64]

Intrapreneurseship

Intrapreneur: A company employee who is allowed to act like an entrepreneur on behalf of the company, rather than on his or her own behalf.

An **intrapreneur** is a company employee who is allowed to act like an entrepreneur on behalf of the company, rather than on his or her own behalf. The company subsidizes and encourages intrapreneurs to develop and implement their ideas. Gordon Pinchot developed the concept of intrapreneurship after recognizing the frustration and discontent shared by many managers and employees in large organizations. Pinchot comments that "the problem is that organizations hire people for their intelligence and imagination and then tell them what to imagine." He continues, "Entrepreneurs are people driven by a need to see their visions become real; intrapreneurs share that need. Intrapreneurs are people with entrepreneurial personalities. Intrapreneurs, like entrepreneurs, are always self-starting and both cannot be primarily motivated by money. Instead they are motivated by visions. To them, money is just a way of keeping score."[65] Intrapreneurs are best rewarded by the organization through programs in which results lead to compensation, much as an entrepreneur would be rewarded by the financial rewards of the marketplace.

Companies buy books like *In Search of Excellence* and *Intrapreneuring* for their managers because they want them to emulate the characteristics described in those books.[66] Recognizing that success depends on innovation and the seizing of opportunity, more and more corporations are attempting to incorporate entrepreneurship into their cultures. This trend could not come at a better time for major U.S. corporations, as they see many of their best employees leaving to become entrepreneurs, often to develop new products that compete directly with those of the firm they have left.

United Airlines, IBM, 3M, Texas Instruments, Northwestern Bell, and Kodak all have extensive intrapreneurship programs.[67] The 3-M Company has been especially good at fostering intrapreneurship.

INTRAPRENEURSHIP AND RESTRUCTURING

Much of the restructuring discussed in Chapters 9 and 10 is aimed at increasing the independence of managers of new products or SBUs, enabling them to act as if they were entrepreneurs. As intrapreneurs, corporate employees are allowed to take risks, their projects are funded, and they are allowed to turn their creations and inventions into innovations.

Black Entrepreneurs Overcome Obstacles

Otis Warren finally realized his dream. In the spring of 1992, he obtained the $38 million in financing he needed to fund his planned City Crescent office, apartment, and retail complex in downtown Baltimore. Obtaining the money should have been a lot easier than it was. After all, the U.S. General Services Administration (GSA) had agreed to lease up to 95 percent of the space for the first ten years. But the economy was slow, and this, along with the savings and loan debacle, caused lenders to cut back sharply on real estate loans.

Even though he faced all of these problems, Warren might also have been the victim of racial discrimination—if not blatantly, at least because he wasn't part of the "old boy" business network. "I did this (project) in spite of racism," the fifty-year-old developer comments. "To have confidence in the system, you have to prove racism can't stop you. But whatever the lenders' reasons were for not financing my project, what really excites me is to prove they were wrong."

Warren recognizes that the economy and the tougher lending laws imposed after the savings and loan bailout undoubtedly contributed to his difficulty. And although he had experience with smaller projects, he lacked experience with larger ones. Still, he feels that certain signs point to other causes. For example, a private funding group withdrew its support at the eleventh hour despite a guarantee of a fifteen-year lease by the City of Baltimore if the GSA did not renew its lease after ten years. More than one hundred lenders turned him down.

Eventually, after several near-misses and near-terminations of the project, Warren was able to obtain financing for City Crescent through taxable bonds issued by Maryland's Industrial Development Financing Authority. This did not happen without great personal distress, including a midnight rush to the hospital with chest pains.

Warren feels that discrimination played a role in his struggle. He isn't alone. Eighty-five percent of black entrepreneurs feel that they do not have the same chances of obtaining financing as their white counterparts.

SOURCES: Eugene Carlson, "Turned Down: A WSJ Survey Finds a Widespread Perception of Lending Bias," *Wall Street Journal*, February 19, 1993, pp. R1, R5; and Jeanne Saddler, "Obstacle Course," *Wall Street Journal*, February 19, 1993, p. R4.

Thomas J. Peters argues in *Thriving on Chaos* that the future faced by most organizations will be one of constantly accelerating rates of change, with each change more significant than the previous one.[68] This prediction is echoed by a number of authorities, including Alvin Toffler in *Future Shock*[69] and Michael Naylor, executive in charge of strategic planning at General Motors.[70] Peters argues that because of these changes and their increasing magnitude, organizations must be restructured into smaller units that can be more responsive to the demands of the changing marketplace. Responsiveness usually requires innovation. Peters sees pursuing fast-paced innovation as one of the five key steps for surviving in a chaotic environment, and an intrapreneurial orientation as one way to achieve innovation.[71]

Succession

One of the major problems entrepreneurs face is the issue of succession: Who will follow them as head of the organization? The entrepreneur must choose an appropriate successor if he or she expects the organization to be run well in the future. If investors are involved, their needs must also be recognized. Typically they seek a smooth transition from one top manager to another. The entrepreneur must establish criteria for his or her successor. Thus, when he decided to become less active in Wal-Mart, Sam Walton picked someone much like himself. The new CEO, David D. Glass, appears to be cut from the same cloth as Walton. Both are workaholics; both are dedicated to the company; and both have the same kind of good-natured humor. Since Walton's death, CEO Glass has carried on the Walton style.[72]

Summary

1. An entrepreneur is someone who perceives and pursues an opportunity, believes that success is possible, and initiates change. His or her business is an entrepreneurship. A small business is defined by its financial or other operating characteristics; some small businesses are entrepreneurial and others are not.

2. Entrepreneurship is currently of great interest because in recent years most new jobs have been created by small businesses. Moreover, small businesses have a higher return on investment than larger businesses, and they tend to be more innovative. Finally, entrepreneurship is associated with a high level of psychological satisfaction.

3. As organizations grow, preserving the entrepreneurial spirit becomes more difficult. The organization must increase the perception of opportunity, build the desire to pursue opportunity, and make people believe they can succeed.

4. One of the key responsibilities of an entrepreneur as the organization grows is to learn how to manage. This involves learning how to plan, organize, lead, and control.

5. Current trends in entrepreneurship include campus capitalists, young people staying in the family business, individuals leaving large corporations to start their own business, an increase in the number of women and minority entrepreneurs, and an increase in the level of entrepreneurship (intrapreneurship) in large corporations.

6. Organizations face more chaotic environments than ever before. Many experts perceive intrapreneurial arrangements as critical to future success for large organizations. Competitiveness and innovation have both been increased by such arrangements.

THINKING ABOUT MANAGEMENT

General Questions

1. Discuss why you would or would not want to be an entrepreneur.
2. Describe the major reasons that entrepreneurship has been important in recent U.S. economic history.
3. Review the topics of entrepreneurship and intrapreneurship and their relationship to competitiveness and innovation.
4. Indicate how an entrepreneur would plan, organize, lead, control, and make decisions.
5. Discuss current trends in entrepreneurship.

Questions on the Management Challenge Features

INNOVATION MANAGEMENT CHALLENGE

1. What innovations did Michael Dell bring to the computer industry?

2. What lessons has he learned about management?

GLOBAL MANAGEMENT CHALLENGE

1. Why did Son return to Japan to become an entrepreneur?

2. In Son's view, how does entrepreneurship differ in Japan and in the United States?

DIVERSITY MANAGEMENT CHALLENGE

1. Describe the obstacles Otis Warren faced in trying to obtain financing.

2. How does Warren's experience differ from that of a typical white entrepreneur?

E P I L O G U E

Sam Walton, Entrepreneur and Manager

Walton's management philosophy lives on. Typical of those who carry it on is Andy Wilson, one of 15 regional vice presidents, who spends 200 days a year in the air and on the road finding out what's happening in the stores in his region, which includes much of the western United States. During his visits to more than 125 stores, he compares Wal-Mart's prices with those of competitors through comparison shopping. He also analyzes problems within the stores, making quick decisions as to how to solve them or telling managers to do whatever it takes to solve them. The road trips provide excellent information for top management, as well as problems to be discussed at the Saturday morning meeetings in Bentonville. Typical is a session led by CEO David Glass focusing on empty shelves in several stores. A special department was formed to solve that problem, immediately.

DISCUSSION QUESTIONS

1. How does Walton's legacy live on?

2. Discuss how the Wal-Mart case reveals how organizational culture enables a firm to survive after the death of its founder.

Why Work for Someone Else?

Jack Hanrahan and his two partners had slowly but surely built their real estate business into a successful one. In the eleven years that they had worked together, their individual profits had risen from $25,000 per year to just over $100,000 per year. This did not include the appreciation of properties they owned, including the building in which their offices were located.

In early 1989, they had been approached by a national real estate group that was interested in purchasing their firm. Eventually the offer became too good to turn down. Hanrahan and his partners retained ownership of their building and received a five-year lease from the national firm. They each received handsome salaries but were asked to sign a noncompetitive contract for one year.

At first, Hanrahan loved the arrangement. He did not have to work as hard as he had in the past; he had no responsibility and could take it easy. But as the year went by, he began to think about going into business for himself again. He missed the excitement, the challenge, the rewards of seeing his business grow. He thought that when the year was up, he would start anew.

DISCUSSION QUESTIONS

1. Why would Hanrahan want to give up an easy job that paid him so well?
2. How does Hanrahan fit the profile of the entrepreneur?
3. What rewards will Hanrahan receive from his decision?

MANAGE
YOURSELF

The Entrepreneurial Profile

This Entrepreneurial Profile was created by the Center for Entrepreneurial Management, a 2,500-member private organization whose purpose is to provide educational and informational services. The profile focuses on twenty-six characteristics that seem to differentiate entrepreneurs from others. Read each question and select the answer that best seems to describe you or what you would do. After you have completed it, your instructor will tell you how to score it and will help you interpret the results.

1. How were your parents employed?
    a. Both worked and were self-employed for most of their working lives.
    b. Both worked and were self-employed for some part of their working lives.
    c. One parent was self-employed for most of his or her working life.
    d. One parent was self-employed at some point in his or her working life.
    e. Neither parent was ever self-employed.
2. Have you ever been fired from a job?
    a. Yes, more than once.
    b. Yes, once.
    c. No.

3. Are you an immigrant, or were your parents or grandparents immigrants?
   a. I was born outside of the United States.
   b. One or both of my parents were born outside of the United States.
   c. At least one of my grandparents was born outside of the United States.
   d. Does not apply.

4. Your work career has been:
   a. Primarily in small business (under 100 employees).
   b. Primarily in medium-sized business (100 to 500 employees).
   c. Primarily in big business (over 500 employees).

5. Did you operate any business before you were twenty?
   a. Many.
   b. A few.
   c. None.

6. What is your present age?
   a. 21–30.
   b. 31–40.
   c. 41–50.
   d. 51 or over.

7. You are the _____ child in the family.
   a. Oldest.
   b. Middle.
   c. Youngest.
   d. Other.

8. You are:
   a. Married.
   b. Divorced.
   c. Single.

9. Your highest level of formal education is:
   a. Some high school.
   b. High school diploma.
   c. Bachelor's degree.
   d. Master's degree.
   e. Doctor's degree.

10. What is your primary motivation in starting a business?
    a. To make money.
    b. I don't like working for someone else.
    c. To be famous.
    d. As an outlet for excess energy.

11. Your relationship to the parent who provided most of the family's income was:
    a. Strained.
    b. Comfortable.
    c. Competitive.
    d. Nonexistent.

12. If you could choose between working hard and working smart, you would:
    a. Work hard.
    b. Work smart.
    c. Both.

13. On whom do you rely for critical management advice?
    a. Internal management teams.
    b. External management professionals.
    c. External financial professionals.
    d. No one except myself.

14. If you were at the racetrack, which of these would you bet on?
    a. The daily double—a chance to make a killing.
    b. A 10-to-1 shot.
    c. A 3-to-1 shot.
    d. The 2-to-1 favorite.

15. The only ingredient that is both necessary and sufficient for starting a business is:
    a. Money.
    b. Customers.
    c. An idea or product.
    d. Motivation and hard work.

16. If you were an advanced tennis player and had a chance to play Boris Becker, you would:
    a. Turn it down because he could easily beat you.
    b. Accept the challenge, but not bet any money on it.
    c. Bet a week's pay that you would win.
    d. Get odds, bet a fortune, and try for an upset.

17. You tend to "fall in love" too quickly with:
    a. New product ideas.
    b. New employees.
    c. New manufacturing ideas.
    d. New financial plans.
    e. All of the above.

18. Which of the following personality types is best suited to be your right-hand person?
    a. Bright and energetic.
    b. Bright and lazy.
    c. Dumb and energetic.

19. You accomplish tasks better because:
    a. You are always on time.
    b. You are superorganized.
    c. You keep good records.

20. You hate to discuss:
    a. Problems involving employees.
    b. Signing expense accounts.
    c. New management practices.
    d. The future of the business.

21. Given a choice, you would prefer:
    a. Rolling dice with a 1-in-3 chance of winning.
    b. Working on a problem with a 1-in-3 chance of solving it in the allocated time.

22. If you could choose between the following competitive professions, it would be:
    a. Professional golf.
    b. Sales.

    c. Personnel counseling.

    d. Teaching.

23. If you had to choose between working with a partner who is a close friend and working with a stranger who is an expert in your field, you would choose:

    a. The close friend.

    b. The expert.

24. You enjoy being with people:

    a. When you have something meaningful to do.

    b. When you can do something new and different.

    c. Even when you have nothing planned.

25. In business situations that demand action, clarifying who is in charge will help produce results.

    a. Agree.

    b. Agree, with reservations.

    c. Disagree.

26. In playing a competitive game, you are concerned with:

    a. How well you play.

    b. Winning or losing.

    c. Both of the above.

    d. Neither of the above.

source: J. R. Mancuso, "The Entrepreneur's Quiz" (New York, Center for Entrepreneurial Management).

"Quality may be the biggest competitive issue of the late 20th and early 21st centuries."

—Stephen B. Shepard
Editor-in-Chief
Business Week

"The goal is . . . competitive innovation . . . . Firms that succeed will invent new products and markets that don't already exist."

—Gary Hamel and C. K. Prahalad

Managing Quality and Innovation

CHAPTER OBJECTIVES

When you have read this chapter you should be able to:

1. Describe the importance of TQM to competitiveness.
2. Indicate the contributions of W. Edwards Deming, J. M. Juran, and Philip Crosby to the TQM movement.
3. Describe the eight dimensions of quality.
4. Discuss zero defects as the next major approach to quality management.
5. Indicate how quality management in services differs from quality management in manufacturing.
6. Review whether TQM has been successful in the United States.
7. Discuss the relationships among creativity, organizational culture, and innovation.
8. Define the four P's of innovation.
9. Describe the four types of innovation.
0. Discuss the key features of innovation strategy.

MANAGEMENT CHALLENGES DISCUSSED IN THIS CHAPTER:

Accelerating rates of change.

Increasing levels of competition.

Quality and innovation as managerial imperatives.

Improving Innovation at Steelcase

The pyramids of Egypt symbolize a culture that was inert and set in its ways long before its eventual demise. In Grand Rapids, Michigan, there is a pyramid that symbolizes innovation and change. It is the new seven-story corporate development center of Steelcase Company, an office furniture manufacturer with annual sales of $1.6 billion.

Like many large, long-established American corporations, Steelcase was making a stodgy and boring, though high-quality, product. Its closest competitor, Herman Miller, Inc., posed a significant competitive threat because of its innovative spirit. Miller is credited with creating the "open office" by using "systems furniture" based on movable panels and furniture modules, and with leading in the design of the "ergonomic" chair, which constantly adjusts to changes in the user's position. In the 1970s, Steelcase was just a follower in these innovations.

Seeking to increase its dominance of the market, Steelcase has acquired a number of small, high-profile design companies. It now has a line of wooden office furniture and the rights to furniture designed by architects Frank Lloyd Wright and Le Corbusier. It has also rebuilt its physical facilities and reorganized its operations. The $111 million, 128-foot-tall pyramidal office building, the most visible change, clearly demonstrates the company's new commitment to innovation and style as well as quality.

Previously, the company's designers, engineers, and marketing personnel were housed in separate buildings. Now they are grouped together to facilitate employee interaction, a necessary requirement if new and creative products are to be developed. However, physical closeness alone does not generate cooperation and innovation. The showpiece building is more than just a flashy shape. Steelcase's idea is that everything that happens there is work, from coffee breaks to board meetings. Every inch of the building is designed to inspire creativity. Its center is dominated by a light and airy central atrium, called the town square. There are exterior terraces where people can work or eat. Coffee-break stations have marker boards to promote open exchange of ideas, and there are "caves" where individuals can go for solitude.

The new building is already inspiring its employees. The company has introduced a sleek new line of furniture, the Context line. In the words of James C. Soule, vice-president of the international division, "The bottom line for us is whether we produce better products." Steelcase is improving its already high quality and cutting costs by adopting autonomous work teams, investing heavily in plant and equipment, and performing work re-engineering. A 71-foot pendulum, computerized to follow the sun, has been installed as a symbol of the company's commitment to continuing change.

SOURCES: Jana Schilder, "Work Teams Boost Productivity," *Personnel Journal* (February 1992), pp. 67–71; Michael A. Verespej, "America's Best Plants: Steelcase," *Industry Week* (October 21, 1992), pp. 53–54; John A. Sheridan, "Frank Merlotti: A Master of Empowerment," *Industry Week* (January 7, 1991), pp. 24–27; Allen E. Alter, "The Corporate Make-Over," *CIO* (December 1990), pp. 32–42; John H. Sheridan, "World-Class Manufacturing (Part 1)," *Industry Week* (July 2, 1990), pp. 36–46; and Gregory Witcher, "Steelcase Hopes Innovation Flourishes Under Pyramid," *Wall Street Journal* (May 26, 1989), pp. B1, B8.

S teelcase's move into its new pyramid-shaped building was aimed at increasing innovation. The radical change in physical environment was accompanied by a similar change in job structure, with the two reinforcing each other to enhance innovation. The placement of a symbol of change, a pendulum, in the central atrium reminds employees of the company's goals of innovation and quality in a time of rapid change. All these actions helped modify the firm's culture to make it more innovative. Most companies are undergoing significant changes because of the management challenges discussed throughout this book; yet, at the same time, they must strive to focus on quality and innovation. These vital processes are so critical to business success that this chapter is devoted to examining them.

Total Quality Management and Beyond

Total quality management (TQM) is the creative problem-solving process of managing quality throughout the organization in order to improve its products and services. It includes the processes used to produce those products and services.[1] Successful TQM is an absolute must for competing in the 1990s and in the twenty-first century.[2] Indeed, TQM has been a significant managerial issue longer than any other such issue in the last forty years.[3] It has had a profound impact on the management of organizations throughout the world, but especially on U.S., Japanese, Canadian, and European firms.

The primary focus of TQM is the customer. TQM is aimed at satisfying customer needs.[4] This perspective is consistent with that of many management experts. For example, Peter Drucker long ago argued that the business of business is not to make a profit but to respond to customer needs. If this is done, everything else, including profits, will fall into place.[5]

Once the customer's needs have been determined, TQM focuses on planning for quality, using statistical quality control techniques, promoting team

Total quality management: The creative problem-solving process of managing quality throughout the organization in order to improve its products and services and the processes by which those products and services are made or take place.

Total quality management is vital in the automobile industry. At this Nissan plant, emphasis is placed on team problem solving.

problem solving, creating a culture for quality improvement, making quality a part of the entire organization, and integrating quality into supplier requirements.

Three experts have led the movement to improve quality: W. Edwards Deming, J. M. Juran, and Phil Crosby. In Japan, they are held in such high regard that quality awards named for them are given to firms that excel in managing quality. Many people credit Deming and Juran with teaching Japanese firms the quality-control skills that have made them such successful competitors. Deming focused on statistical quality-control approaches, whereas Juran advised on overall quality management. Although both Deming and Juran offered advice to U.S. firms in the 1950s, they were disregarded because at that time U.S. firms' manufacturing capabilities were the best in the world. By the 1980s, however, U.S. manufacturing practices had taken second place to those of the Japanese, and Deming and Juran were warmly embraced as champions of quality management.

In the 1980s, Phil Crosby also became a leading proponent of quality management. Under the banner of "zero defects," he launched a successful consulting practice that eventually opened offices throughout the world. The following paragraphs explore the contributions of Deming, Juran, and Crosby to the quality management movement while explaining some of the major tenets of TQM. Note that the three experts do not always agree on exactly how to proceed with TQM.

W. Edwards Deming and TQM

W. Edwards Deming was trained as a statistician. He began training Japanese managers in statistical quality control in 1950. His principal approaches to TQM include using statistics for quality control, continuously improving the design of a product and the processes used to create it, and changing management style to assist employees.[6] Probably more than any other person, Deming created the global quality movement.

Much of Deming's philosophy for improving quality is captured in his "fourteen points," which are presented in Figure 23.1. Notice the emphasis on continuous improvement and on improving management style. Deming's early work tended to focus more narrowly on manufacturing than that of Juran, who called for the application of TQM to the entire organization.[7] Notice, however, that in his fourteen points Deming has broadened his approach to include the entire organization.

J. M. Juran and Quality Planning

Some believe that J. M. Juran was more instrumental in teaching TQM to Japanese managers because his approach was broader than Deming's.[8] Juran believes that *quality* has two distinct, but related definitions: multiple product features and freedom from deficiencies. From the customer's perspective, the more product features, the higher the quality; and the fewer the deficiencies, the higher the quality.[9]

Juran's approach to quality management involves three primary functions, which he calls the **Juran trilogy**: quality planning, quality control, and quality improvement. **Quality planning** "is the activity of (a) establishing quality goals . . . and (b) developing the products and processes required to meet those goals."[10] It refers not only to external goods and services, but also to internal goods and services—for example, purchase orders, reports, and subassemblies.

Quality planning consists of several steps: "Establish quality goals, identify the customers (those who will be impacted by the efforts to meet the goals),

---

AT STEELCASE:
Steelcase already had high-quality products. It had invested in most of the latest technologies and management systems to improve quality.

Juran trilogy: Quality planning, quality control, and quality improvement.

Quality planning: The activity of establishing quality goals and developing the products and processes required to meet those goals.

FIGURE 23.1 DR. DEMING'S FOURTEEN POINTS

1. CREATE AND PUBLISH TO ALL EMPLOYEES A STATEMENT OF THE AIMS AND PURPOSES OF THE COMPANY OR OTHER ORGANIZATION. THE MANAGEMENT MUST DEMONSTRATE CONSTANTLY THEIR COMMITMENT TO THIS STATEMENT.

2. LEARN THE NEW PHILOSOPHY, TOP MANAGEMENT AND EVERYBODY.

3. UNDERSTAND THE PURPOSE OF INSPECTION, FOR IMPROVEMENT OF PROCESSES AND REDUCTION OF COST.

4. END THE PRACTICE OF AWARDING BUSINESS ON THE BASIS OF PRICE TAG ALONE.

5. IMPROVE CONSTANTLY AND FOREVER THE SYSTEM OF PRODUCTION AND SERVICE.

6. INSTITUTE TRAINING.

7. TEACH AND INSTITUTE LEADERSHIP.

8. DRIVE OUT FEAR. CREATE TRUST. CREATE A CLIMATE FOR INNOVATION.

9. OPTIMIZE TOWARD THE AIMS AND PURPOSES OF THE COMPANY THE EFFORTS OF TEAMS, GROUPS, STAFF AREAS.

10. ELIMINATE EXHORTATIONS FOR THE WORK FORCE.

11A. ELIMINATE NUMERICAL QUOTAS FOR PRODUCTION. INSTEAD, LEARN AND INSTITUTE METHODS FOR IMPROVEMENT.
   B. ELIMINATE M.B.O. INSTEAD, LEARN THE CAPABILITIES OF PROCESSES, AND HOW TO IMPROVE THEM.

12. REMOVE BARRIERS THAT ROB PEOPLE OF PRIDE AND WORKMANSHIP.

13. ENCOURAGE EDUCATION AND SELF-IMPROVEMENT FOR EVERYONE.

14. TAKE ACTION TO ACCOMPLISH THE TRANSFORMATION.

SOURCE: REPRINTED FROM OUT OF CRISIS BY W. EDWARDS DEMING BY PERMISSION OF MIT AND W. EDWARDS DEMING. PUBLISHED BY MIT, CENTER FOR ADVANCED ENGINEERING STUDY, CAMBRIDGE, MA 02139. COPYRIGHT 1986 BY W. EDWARDS DEMING.

determine the customer's needs, develop product features that respond to the customer's needs, develop processes that are able to produce those product features, establish process controls, and transfer the resulting plans to the operating forces."[11] According to Juran, quality planning is the key ingredient in achieving quality. Juran observes that product features and failure rates are largely determined during planning for quality. Recently U.S. companies have become increasingly aware that they have been absorbing high, unnecessary costs because they have not planned quality into their products. About one-third of the work done in these firms consists of redoing work that was not done right the first time.[12] Thus, quality planning is receiving more attention than it has in the past.

In Juran's analysis, **quality control** follows the basic steps of the control model presented in Chapter 18: "Evaluate actual quality performance, compare actual performance to quality goals, act on the differences."[13] **Quality improvement** is defined as the process that raises quality performance to unprecedented levels—in other words, breakthroughs. It has several steps: "Establish the infrastructure needed to secure annual quality improvement; identify the specific needs for improvement—the improvement *projects;* for each project, establish a project team with clear responsibility for bringing the product to a successful conclusion; provide the resources, motivation, and training needed by the teams to diagnose the causes, stimulate establishment of remedies, and establish controls to hold the gains."[14] Table 23.1 summarizes these three processes. Figure 23.2 shows the expected outputs from the quality planning process for each of its activities.

Although many quality consultants believe that quality starts with the customer's needs, Juran's approach begins with the establishment of strategic quality goals, such as Ford's "Quality is job one." These goals set the tone for what will follow. In other respects, Juran's approach is essentially the same as those of

Quality control: Follows the basic steps of the control model: Evaluate actual quality performance, compare actual performance to quality goals, and act on the differences.

Quality improvement: The process that raises quality performance to unprecedented levels.

TABLE 23.1 The Three Universal Processes of Managing for Quality

Quality Planning	Quality Control	Quality Improvement
Establish quality goals	Evaluate actual performance	Prove the need
Identify who are the customers	Compare actual performance to quality goals	Establish the infrastructure
Determine the needs of the customers	Act on the difference	Identify the improvement projects
Develop product features which respond to customers' needs		Establish project teams
Develop processes able to produce the product features		Provide the teams with resources, training, and motivation to: Diagnose the causes Stimulate remedies
Establish process controls; transfer the plans to the operating forces		Establish controls to hold the gains

SOURCE: J. M. Juran, *Juran on Quality by Design* (New York: Free Press, 1992), Fig. 1-6, p. 16.

Quality control involves evaluating performance, comparing actual performance to quality goals, and taking action to remedy any deficiencies.

other quality experts because the next step in his process is to identify customer needs.[15]

Phil Crosby and Zero Defects

Zero defects means exactly what it says—there will be no defects: The rate of conformance with standards will be 100 percent. Phil Crosby first started zero-defects programs at Martin Marietta and later as vice-president for quality at

Zero defects: No defects—100 percent compliance with standards.

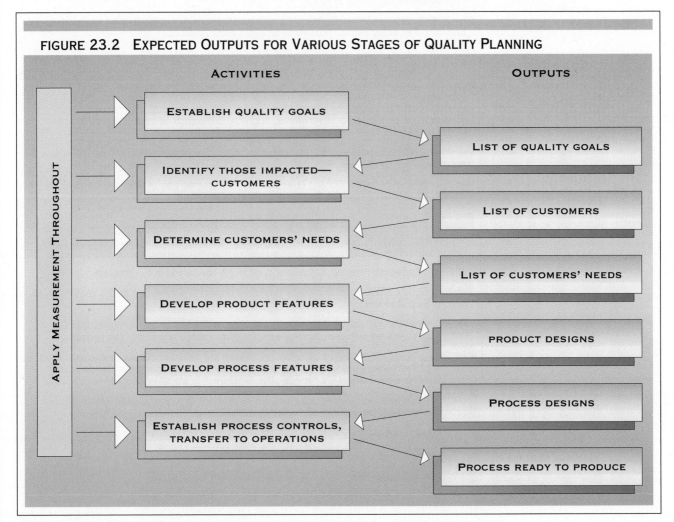

FIGURE 23.2   EXPECTED OUTPUTS FOR VARIOUS STAGES OF QUALITY PLANNING

ACTIVITIES — OUTPUTS

APPLY MEASUREMENT THROUGHOUT

- ESTABLISH QUALITY GOALS → LIST OF QUALITY GOALS
- IDENTIFY THOSE IMPACTED—CUSTOMERS → LIST OF CUSTOMERS
- DETERMINE CUSTOMERS' NEEDS → LIST OF CUSTOMERS' NEEDS
- DEVELOP PRODUCT FEATURES → PRODUCT DESIGNS
- DEVELOP PROCESS FEATURES → PROCESS DESIGNS
- ESTABLISH PROCESS CONTROLS, TRANSFER TO OPERATIONS → PROCESS READY TO PRODUCE

SOURCE: J. M. JURAN, JURAN ON QUALITY BY DESIGN (NEW YORK: FREE PRESS, 1992), FIGURE 1-9, P. 20.

ITT. Recognizing the potential for quality management throughout the world, he launched Phil Crosby & Associates in Winter Park, Florida, in 1979. The firm grew rapidly in the United States and eventually opened offices in Europe and in Pacific Rim countries.

Among Crosby's key contributions was the definition of what constitutes an appropriate quality improvement program. His principal beliefs about quality start from the idea that "quality is free"—that is, it should be part of the organization's ongoing processes and can be designed into them at little significant cost. In his view, costs result when things are not done right the first time and have to be redone. Crosby believes that quality is designed into products or services at the level desired (in terms of defects and features). Thus, high quality is defined as conformance with requirements. He also believes that for a quality improvement program to succeed, management must support it and participate in it.[16]

Table 23.2 summarizes Crosby's views on quality improvement programs.

TABLE 23.2 Crosby's Fourteen Steps to Quality Improvement

Step One: Management Commitment. Communicate with management about quality; get management committed to quality. Enable management to understand its responsibility for the success of the quality program.

Step Two: Quality Improvement Team. Form a quality improvement team using representatives from all major departments. Train them and give them authority.

Step Three: Quality Measurement. Develop a quantitative measurement system for all parts of the company.

Step Four: Cost of Quality Evaluation. The comptroller establishes the cost of quality, an indication of where corrective action will be profitable. The higher the cost, the more corrective actions need to be taken. As defined by Crosby, the cost of quality includes prevention costs such as design reviews, appraisal costs such as inspection costs, and failure costs such as rework costs.

Step Five: Quality Awareness. Now the measurements of what nonquality is costing the firm are shared with employees. Supervisors are trained to orient employees.

Step Six: Corrective Action. Solving quality problems becomes part of the organization's routine. It becomes part of the regular departmental meetings.

Step Seven: Establish an Ad Hoc Committee for the Zero-Defects Program. Three or four members of the quality improvement team are selected to investigate the possibilities of a zero-defects program. The idea is to begin to have people thinking in terms of doing things right the first time.

Step Eight: Supervisor Training. Managers at all levels are trained in the program.

Step Nine: Zero-Defects Day. In a single day, zero defects is established as the company's performance standard.

Step Ten: Goal Setting. During their regular meetings, managers should establish specific and obtainable objectives with their subordinates for thirty-, sixty-, and ninety-day periods.

Step Eleven: Removal of Causes of Errors. Individuals are asked to identify problems in their work area that prevent them from doing error-free work. This is done on a one-page form that identifies the functional area responsible for correcting the situation.

Step Twelve: Recognition. Award programs are established to reward quality performance— people who meet their goals or do something outstanding.

Step Thirteen: Quality Councils. Quality professionals and team chairpeople should be brought together to determine improvements in the quality program.

Step Fourteen: Do It Over Again. It takes about eighteen months, on average, to implement a quality program; by then it will be necessary to refresh the program.

SOURCE: Based on Philip B. Crosby, *Quality Is Free* (New York: Mentor/Penguin, 1980), Chapter 8.

The Eight Dimensions of Quality

As TQM has evolved, the definition of quality has broadened. David A. Garvin, author of *Managing Quality,* identifies eight dimensions of quality;[17,18] these are shown in Table 23.3. Competing on the basis of quality means competing on these eight dimensions. The two most traditional dimensions, conformance and reliability, are now included in a broader strategic framework. Note that there are trade-offs among the various dimensions and it is not always possible to achieve all of them.

Continuous Improvement

At many points in this book we have discussed *continuous improvement.* The concept of continuously improving both products and processes is a critical component of competitiveness in the 1990s and will remain so into the twenty-first century. As mentioned in Chapters 1 and 7, it is one of the five strategic imperatives for the 1990s.[19] With respect to TQM, continuous improvement is one of the major factors in a successful TQM program.

Continuous improvement is a two-part philosophy consisting of (1) designing and redesigning a product or service to make it easy to manufacture or deliver while satisfying customer needs, and (2) continuously improving the processes by which that product or service is manufactured or delivered in order to cut costs and/or add value to the product or service. *Kaizen,* as this philosophy is known in Japan, significantly affects organizational structure at both the micro and macro levels. It is an important element of strategy and affects leadership styles.[20,21]

Benchmarking and TQM

Benchmarking is critical to competition in the 1990s. It has always been perceived as an integral part of TQM. Benchmarking provides the firm with standards against which it can measure itself. It appears to be especially relevant to already successful firms that are trying to raise their level of performance.[22,23]

TABLE 23.3 Quality Defined

1. *Performance:* A product's primary operating characteristics—for example, acceleration for an automobile or sound and picture quality for a television set.

2. *Features:* Characteristics of a product that supplement its basic functioning—for example, free drinks on an airplane or the permanent-press cycle on a washing machine.

3. *Reliability:* The probability of a product malfunctioning or failing within a specified period.

4. *Conformance:* The degree to which a product's design and operating characteristics meet established standards.

5. *Durability:* Durability has two aspects: technical, in terms of the amount of use obtained from a product before it deteriorates, and economical, weighing the cost of additional repairs to an existing product versus buying a newer, more reliable one.

6. *Serviceability:* Speed, courtesy, competence, and ease of repair.

7. *Esthetics:* How a product looks, feels, sounds, tastes, or smells.

8. *Perceived Quality:* Because consumers usually do not have complete information, they rely on what they know to judge the quality of a product or service. Reputation is critical to this dimension.

SOURCE: Based on David A. Garvin, "Competing on the Eight Dimensions of Quality," *Harvard Business Review* (November–December 1987), pp. 101–108.

Zero Defects

TQM is based on the statistical management of defects. A certain level of defects is generally considered tolerable. The Greek letter *sigma* is used as a unit of measurement. One sigma means that 68 percent of products are acceptable. Three sigmas mean that 99.7 percent are acceptable. A highly publicized, often sought level of quality known as **six sigma quality** means that 99.999997 percent of products are perfect; in other words, only 3.4 defects for every million parts are allowed. However, that may not be good enough. To compete effectively, it may be necessary to achieve zero defects.

Six sigma quality: A highly sought-after level of quality— 99.999997 percent perfect, or no more than 3.4 defects for every million parts.

While some U.S. firms have subscribed to the zero-defects approach, most have not. In contrast, Japanese firms are making this approach one of their primary thrusts for competing in the next decade.[24] A leading Japanese industrialist says that while American firms are catching up in TQM, Japanese firms will still be ahead by ten to fifteen years because they are already moving beyond TQM to zero defects. A top executive of Toyota Corporation, for example, says that allowing 10 percent defects translates into four hundred thousand unhappy Toyota car owners a year. He wants to reduce that number to zero. Thus, it seems apparent that if U.S., Canadian, and European firms are to compete with Japanese and other Pacific Rim manufacturers, they must adopt a zero-defects rather than a TQM approach.

Some experts question whether it is possible to achieve zero defects. For example, after five years of concerted effort Motorola failed to reach six sigma quality, although it came close.[25] Even Toyota has not reached this goal. Only time will tell whether it is possible.

Teams

Teams have traditionally been considered the backbone of TQM programs. Quality circles and autonomous work teams were discussed in Chapter 15. These special types of teams are both applicable to TQM, but they must be instituted in stages. Team members must be trained in problem-solving techniques, preferably methods used in creative problem solving.[26]

AT STEELCASE:
Steelcase recently moved to autonomous work teams as a means of improving quality and productivity.

Teams have traditionally been considered the backbone of total quality management. Team members must be trained in problem-solving techniques.

Total Quality Management in Services

Quality is very tangible in manufacturing but much less so in services. Service quality encompasses all the elements involved in delivering or servicing a product. It is the context within which a product or service exists.[27]

TQM is often much more difficult to implement in services than in manufacturing, yet it can mean the difference between success and failure. Although it may not be difficult to control quality in some service organizations, such as McDonald's restaurants (which are almost manufacturing operations), it is difficult in others, such as health care, banking, airlines, and grocery stores. It can also be difficult in the support areas of manufacturing firms.

Surveys of customer satisfaction are often used to determine service quality, but other measures of quality need to be utilized as well. For example, perhaps physicians, nurses, and health-care facilities should be rated on the basis of such criteria as the number of operations performed by particular physicians and their success and failure rates. Service quality can apply to numerous aspects of services, as this chapter's Ethical Management Challenge indicates.

Successes and Failures of TQM

Is TQM worth the time and investment? Many firms have begun to ask themselves this question. In contrast to successful TQM programs in firms such as Xerox, Motorola, Cadillac, Buick, Saturn, Ford, Chrysler, Hewlett-Packard, and Federal Express, many firms report disappointing results with TQM. In a $2 million study conducted by Ernst & Young in conjunction with the American Quality Foundation, 554 firms in the auto, computer, banking, and health-care industries in the United States, Canada, Germany, and Japan were surveyed. The results demonstrated that, compared to German and Japanese firms, U.S. firms were slower and less successful in implementing TQM.[28] In a survey by McKinsey & Company of TQM programs in effect for more than two years, two-thirds of the firms surveyed reported poor results.[29] A survey of five hundred U.S. firms by Arthur D. Little found that only 36 percent felt that TQM was having a "significant impact" on competitiveness.[30] Finally, a survey by Rath & Strong of Lexington, Massachusetts, graded companies on TQM efforts to improve market share, rein in costs, and make customers happy. Most companies rated D's or F's.[31]

Most often, the problem appears to lie in how TQM is implemented.[32] Quality efforts work best when companies start with a strong focus on a few areas and expand from that base rather than install an across-the-board TQM program. The Ernst & Young study suggests that firms experiencing problems with TQM should form teams across and within departments and increase the level of training of all kinds. Firms with moderate levels of success should simplify processes, such as design, and focus on problem solving. The study also suggests that suppliers should be chosen by competitive bidding rather than reputation and that suppliers' quality efforts should be considered. For firms that have successfully implemented TQM, benchmarking is useful in identifying new products and services. There should be companywide quality meetings. Departmental teams should not be increased because they might hamper cross-functional coordination. Table 23.4 shows the TQM actions recommended by Ernst & Young for firms at all three performance levels.

Overall, the study cautions against empowerment except in high-performing organizations that have the right kind of culture. Low-performing companies usually lack "the training or strategy in place to make empowerment work."[33] The study does identify some "universal truths": "explaining the corporate strategic plan to employees, customers, and suppliers; improving and simplifying production and development processes; and scrutinizing and shortening 'half-cycle time' (how long it takes to get something done—from the design to the delivery of a product)."[34] The McKinsey & Company study blames the current wave of TQM failures on inexperience and disregard for the basic concepts of the quality process. Active commitment by top management is believed to be essential to TQM and was lacking in many of the reported cases of failure. Also critical to successful TQM programs is making quality improvement part of the performance appraisal process, beginning at the top of the organization and continuing down the hierarchy.[35]

Another important reason for failure of TQM is lack of understanding of TQM as a philosophy rather than as a set of practices. The entire concept must be understood and integrated throughout the organization. TQM is more than just reducing defects, or quality circles, or empowerment. In Japan, TQM is viewed as a philosophy, but in the United States it is often viewed as a quick fix and is expected to produce immediate results. U.S. firms need to have more patience and understanding to make this process more effective.[36]

A study of twenty U.S. firms conducted by the Government Accounting Office clearly shows that *if properly designed and implemented,* TQM effectively improves company performance in four areas: employee relations, operat-

TABLE 23.4 A Guide to TQM

	NOVICE Getting Started	JOURNEYMAN Honing New Skills	MASTER Staying on Top
		Measures	
Profitability	Less than 2% return on assets (ROA)	2% to 6.9% ROA	ROA of 7% and higher
Productivity	Less than $47,000 value added per employee (VAE)	$47,000 to $73,999 VAE	VAE of $74,000 and up
		Techniques	
Employee Involvement	$ Train heavily. Promote teamwork, but forget self-managed teams, which take heavy preparation. Limit employee empowerment to resolving customer complaints.	$ Encourage employees at every level to find ways to do their jobs better—and to simplify core operations. Set up a separate quality-assurance staff.	$ Use self-managed, multiskilled teams that focus on horizontal processes such as logistics and product development. Limit training, mainly to new hires.
Benchmarking	Emulate competitors, not world-class companies	Imitate market leaders and selected world-class companies	$ Gauge product development, distribution, customer service vs. the world's best
New Products	Rely mainly on customer input for ideas	Use customer input, formal market research, and internal ideas	Base on customer input, benchmarking, and internal R&D
Supply Management	Choose suppliers mainly for price and reliability	Select suppliers by quality certification, then price	Choose suppliers mainly for their technology and quality
New Technology	Focus on its cost-reduction potential. Don't develop it—buy it	Find ways to use facilities more flexibly to turn out a wider variety of products or services	Use strategic partnerships to diversify manufacturing
Manager and Employee Evaluation	Reward frontline workers for teamwork and quality	Base compensation for both workers and middle managers on contributions to teamwork and quality	Include senior managers in compensation schemes pegged to teamwork and quality
Quality Progress	$ Concentrate on fundamentals. Identify processes that add value, simplify them, and move faster in response to customer and market demands. Don't bother using formal gauges of progress—gains will be apparent	$ Meticulously document gains and further refine practices to improve value added per employee, time to market, and customer satisfaction	Keep documenting gains and further refine practices to improve value added per employee, time to market, and customer satisfaction

$ Activities that should reap the highest paybacks.

SOURCE: "Quality," *Business Week* (November 30, 1992), pp. 66, 67.

ing procedures, customer satisfaction, and financial performance. For example, the companies showed an average annual improvement in market share of 13.7 percent, an 11.6 percent drop in customer complaints, a 12 percent reduction in order-processing time, and a 10.3 percent decline in defects.[37]

In sum, both successes and failures of TQM have been reported. Research findings make it very clear that it is the design and implementation of the program that matter. If TQM is viewed as a philosophy, given sufficient time, and implemented in stages, it apparently works—and works well.

Global Perspectives

Japanese firms have initiated a worldwide quality competition. In response to the high quality of products of Japanese and other Pacific Rim firms, many U.S., Canadian, and European competitors initiated TQM programs. European firms

Most major U.S. companies are attempting to become world-class competitors. Coca-Cola dominates the Japanese soft-drink market.

World-class competitor: A firm that is capable of competing anywhere on the globe with any firm from any country.

are stretching their resources and capabilities to match Japanese product quality in light of the fact that the Europe 1992 initiative will give Japanese firms access to more European markets, especially in key areas such as autos. Becoming a **world-class competitor** means becoming capable of competing anywhere in the world with any firm from any country. Most major U.S. firms are attempting to become world-class competitors able to compete successfully in Europe, Japan, and other Pacific Rim countries. Apple Computer, for example, has significantly increased its sales of PCs in Japan. Coca-Cola dominates the Japanese soft-drink market, and until recently IBM did very well in Japan as well.

ISO 9000

ISO 9000: The International Standards Organization's standards of quality. In order to compete in European countries, foreign firms must meet these standards.

ISO 9000 refers to the quality standards established by the International Standards Organization (ISO). The standards are generic and can be applied in all industries. In order to compete in European countries, foreign firms must meet these standards.[38] European governments will certify firms for public bids on the basis of compliance with the twenty criteria spelled out in ISO 9000. Without certification, firms cannot bid on government contracts. As of mid-1992, fifty European firms, but only twelve U.S.-based firms, had achieved such certification. Compliance requires most U.S. firms to make adjustments in their quality programs; in particular, they have to strengthen their documentation and their policies and procedures. One of the first steps toward gaining certification is to conduct an internal quality audit.

Foxboro Corporation, a manufacturer of control systems based in Foxboro, Massachusetts, recognized in 1989 that it could not compete satisfactorily in Europe without modifying its quality program. John Rabbit, director of corporate business quality for Foxboro, acknowledges, "We were seeing signs that we were suffering the great American quality disease. Productivity wasn't up. Customer satisfaction was slipping away. We needed to do something."[39] Foxboro embarked on a major quality program, aiming to be certified and to become a global competitor. The program began in manufacturing and spread from there to the rest of the company. The change was not easy, but the head of manufacturing persisted. Eventually, after a year of hard work, the firm was internationally certified.

European Firms Face a Quality Crisis

Once upon a time, European craftsmanship was synonymous with fine quality. Today, however, that golden age is over for many European industries. European firms are trying to catch up with their foreign competitors, which are producing products of equal or higher quality at much lower prices.

Consider the case of the Swiss chemical giant Ciba-Geigy Ltd. In 1982 one of its top U.S. textile-dye customers, Milliken & Co., warned Ciba that if it wanted to keep its business it should adopt TQM practices fast. "We didn't know what they were talking about," says Bernardo De Sousa, Ciba's corporate quality officer. With a two-hundred-year tradition of precision engineering, Ciba believed it had "good Swiss quality" and made some of the purest dyes in the industry.

Once the company began investigating the complaints, however, it discovered that its manufacturing process was extremely inefficient and that errors were costing it an amount equivalent to 20 percent of sales. More ominous still, the company had never asked its customers to specify their product and service needs; as a result, competitors from India and Taiwan were able to garner sales with dyes of lower but acceptable purity—and much lower prices. Ciba realized that it had to change. "We needed new tools to increase productivity, improve our processes, and change our attitudes," De Sousa says.

Early in the 1990s, similar alarms sounded throughout Europe: Manufacturers found that they had fallen far behind U.S. and Japanese firms in using efficient quality-management techniques as a strategic weapon. A study of auto manufacturers showed that European automakers had not learned how to simultaneously raise quality and reduce costs. European plants took twice as long as Japanese plants to build a car but produced 97 defects per 100 vehicles—62 percent more than Japanese plants.

Ironically, European firms have traditionally emphasized quality. However, its time-honored methods of assuring quality have become costly and outdated. *Preventive* TQM is comprehensive and efficient—and saves money. "Europeans always worried about the quality delivered to the customer," explains an American quality consultant, "but not the efficiency to create it."

SOURCE: Jonathan B. Levine, "It's an Old World in More Ways Than One," *Business Week* (*The Quality Imperative*, Special Issue, October 25, 1991), pp. 26–28.

As a consequence of the quality program, Foxboro changed the way it made decisions. Before the program, decisions had been made in an impromptu fashion; problems were patched over until they could no longer be ignored. Now there is a structure for solving problems, and employees have been trained in problem-solving techniques. Everyone at Foxboro is committed to quality and feels responsible for it. Foxboro reports positive results from the certification program. Ninety-eight percent of deliveries are on time, compared to 85 percent before the program. Cost reductions totaling $1 million have been achieved as a result of seventeen quality-improvement team projects, at least partly because redundant work was eliminated. Team performance has improved, and cooperation has increased. The firm has won contracts in Europe that it would not have been able to obtain without changing its approach to quality.[40]

Many European firms also have quality problems, as this chapter's Global Management Challenge reveals. Ciba-Geigy let quality slip from its grasp.

The Baldrige Award

The Malcolm Baldrige National Quality Award is the United States' highest award for quality management and achievement. It was proposed by the U.S. Department of Commerce, signed into law in 1987, and first awarded in 1988. Given annually to two firms in each of three categories—manufacturing, service, and small business—the award helps U.S. firms focus on excellence. The Baldrige Award has three objectives: to increase awareness of quality as an important element in competitiveness, to share information on successful quality strategies and on the benefits derived from their implementation, and to promote understanding of the requirements for quality. Firms that seek the award must make a lengthy application and undergo a rigorous examination process.[41]

The Baldrige Award has helped many firms improve their product or service quality—even when they have not won the award. Simply undergoing the application and examination process has improved the performance of such firms as L. L. Bean, Goodyear Tire and Rubber Company, and the United States Automobile Association. Many firms use the Baldrige Award criteria as quality guidelines.[42]

In determining which firms will win the Baldrige Award, the examiners and judges look for "a plan to keep improving all operations continuously; a system for measuring these improvements accurately; a strategic plan based on benchmarks that compare the company's performance with the world's best; a close partnership with suppliers and customers that feeds improvements back into the operation; a deep understanding of the customers so that their wants can be translated into products; a long-lasting relationship with customers, going beyond the delivery of the product to include sales, service, and ease of maintenance; a focus on preventing mistakes rather than merely correcting them; and a commitment to improving quality that runs from the top of the organization to the bottom."[43]

The Management of Innovation

Today every facet of business, from strategy to daily operations, is full of new problems and opportunities. And the task of just "doing business" remains. This in itself is difficult enough without additional challenges. So how does a business, or any part of it, survive and prosper? *It innovates.* Virtually every leading authority on business, including Fortune 500 CEOs, researchers, and consultants, agrees that there is only one way that firms can cope with all the challenges confronting them in the 1990s, not to mention those they will face in the twenty-first century. They must be innovative.[44]

Innovation and Creativity

Origination: The process of generating something new.

Original: Describes something that did not exist previously.

Creativity: The process of originating something new that has value.

Creation: Something original that has value.

Origination is the process of generating something new. Something **original** is something new, something that did not exist before. **Creativity** is the process of originating something new that has value. There are many original ideas and concepts, but some may not have value and thus may not be considered creative. A **creation** is something original that has value.

Innovation is the process of creating something new that has a significant value to an individual, a group, an organization, an industry, or a society. The result of the innovation process is **an innovation**—a creation that has significant value. There are many creative ideas and concepts that have value but may not

The mobile robot group work room at Massachusetts Institute of Technology provides space and equipment for students who wish to create robotic devices. Some of their ideas may develop into money-making innovations.

have significant value in their application. Thus, they may not be innovations.[45] Innovation is how a firm or an individual makes money from creativity.

While the distinctions being made between these terms may seem somewhat superficial and academic, they are not. Why? Because to be innovative, you have to go beyond just being creative. You need to know whether the ideas you generate have the potential for significant value, the potential to become innovations. (And you must work in an environment that supports innnovation.)

Although U.S. firms and their employees are not nearly as creative as they should be, their performance record is even worse when it comes to turning creations into innovations. Hence, the global competitive positions of many U.S. firms have eroded significantly in recent years and will continue to erode significantly unless their rate of innovation increases. Firms as well as individuals must learn how to turn creation into innovation.

Finally, in solving the strategic challenges, in "doing business" every day, firms will not be as effective or as efficient as they should be if they cannot be innovative. Solving problems and pursuing opportunities require solutions, many of which are unique to the specific situation.

What organizations, their managers, and other employees seek is to create original ideas and concepts that end up as innovations, such as new or enhanced products or services, improvements in efficiency, highly competitive marketing campaigns, or superior management that leads to greater organizational success. These innovations are what business will be all about in the future. From now through the beginning of the twenty-first century, innovations are needed to help businesses survive and prosper while coping with the many challenges facing them.

Innovation: The process of creating something new that has significant value to an individual, group, organization, industry, or society.

An innovation: The result of the innovation process, a creation that has significant value.

Creativity—The Springboard to Innovation

Before we can have innovation, we must have creativity. The term *creativity* is derived from the Latin *creare*, "to make," and the Greek *krainein*, "to fulfill." *Creativity*, then (to expand on the original definition), is the skill to originate, invent, and conceptualize the new and to make the new valuable.[46] The key word here is *skill*. Creativity is a skill. It is not something mystical, available only to a few gifted individuals. It can be learned by anyone. Everyone possesses creativity. However, it has, for the most part, been socialized out of people by their parents, friends, teachers, and bosses.

Creativity can be incremental in the sense of small, progressive steps—such as the lengthy, painstaking research that led to the development of a polio vaccine. Conversely, creativity can involve giant leaps of progress whereby many points in the evolutionary chain of concepts are hurdled by a single effort. The main workings of Apple Computers' Macintosh personal computer, a highly advanced system, were a giant leap in technology when they were introduced in 1983.

The Four P's of Creativity and Innovation

Important to raising levels of individual, group, and organizational innovation is an understanding of the **four p's of creativity and innovation:** the *product*, the *possibilities*, the *processes*, and *personal* creativity. The first of the four P's, the product, is the result of creativity and innovation; it will not occur unless the other three P's are present.[47]

THE PRODUCT

The **product** can be a physical product, a service, or an enhancement to either; a process improvement; or a marketing or management improvement. To be a creative product, it must have value and not merely be original. To be an innovation, it must have *significant* value. Determining what has potentially significant value and what does not is difficult. Value is relative—relative to the values of the evaluator and to the time when the creation occurs. For example, twelve Hollywood studios turned down the "Star Wars" movie concept. Finally, Twentieth Century Fox agreed to take the risk; the result was the most financially successful movie of all time. Similarly, a group of inventors and investors offered to sell a new idea to IBM, General Motors, Du Pont, and several other major firms and were turned down by all of them. Finally, they decided to build and market the product themselves. The process was photocopying. They became multimillionaires. The company became Xerox.[48]

Even a successful entrepreneur may misjudge the value of a creation and, hence, the possibility of its becoming an innovation. Victor Kiam, of Remington Razor fame, was once offered the patent to Velcro for $25,000 and turned it down, believing it had no future. Total worldwide sales of Velcro products to date have been estimated at more than $6 billion.[49]

Turning out new products is what competitiveness is all about, as this chapter's Innovation Management Challenge reveals. Notice how Sharp Corporation's future depends on its ability to innovate.

THE POSSIBILITIES

Regardless of your creative talents, despite your knowledge or skill in creativity and use of creative processes, you will not be able to create many innovations if you are not functioning in a favorable situation—that is, if the **possibilities** for creativity and innovation do not exist. In particular, if the organization's culture does not encourage and even require creativity and the translation of creativity into innovation, neither of these processes will occur.

THE PROCESSES

A wide variety of creativity techniques—**processes**—can be used to increase the number and quality of solutions to problems. It takes time and effort to learn these, but it can be done. These techniques are directed at increasing creativity at several stages of the problem-solving process. Chapter 4 reviewed three of these techniques: brainstorming, storyboarding, and the lotus blossom technique. Many other processes can be used to improve creativity in both individuals and groups.[50]

The four p's of creativity and innovation: The product, the possibilities, the processes, and personal creativity.

The product: The result of the creation/innovation process; can be a physical product or service or an enhancement to either a process improvement or a marketing or management improvement.

Possibilities: Aspects of organizational culture that support innovation, that create the possibility for it to occur.

Processes: Techniques for increasing creativity.

Sharp's Flair for Innovation

Sharp, a diversified electronics company, has several rivals four or five times its size: Toshiba, Hitachi, Matsushita, and Sony. But it is not afraid. It has a not-so-secret weapon that it hopes will quadruple its sales by the year 2000. That weapon is a well-established penchant for innovation.

Sharp has introduced an impressive array of optoelectronics—devices that combine optics and electronics. Among its innovations are lightweight, energy-efficient liquid-crystal displays (LCDs) on laptop computers, semiconductor lasers that "read" compact disks, and the electroluminiscent computer screens on the space shuttle. The company now hopes to apply its optoelectronic savvy in such areas as filing systems based on erasable optical disks and high-definition video products.

Sharp's early gamble on LCDs (in 1970) put it in position for its current dominance of that market, now a $1.6 billion industry that is growing at a rate of 37 percent per year. LCDs are likely to replace bulky cathode-ray tubes in many TVs and computer systems as screen quality improves and prices come down. The latest technology, active-matrix LCDs, achieves color and clarity nearly equal to that of picture tubes—and Sharp makes 40 percent of the world's supply. The company will have spent $740 million on new LCD facilities by 1994, more than any other company.

Laser diodes are another optoelectronic gamble that has paid off for Sharp. Long before Sony and Philips developed the compact disk player, Sharp developed and commercialized technology to create laser diodes—tiny semiconductor crystals that release a beam of laser light when stimulated by an electric current. Sharp now makes nearly 50 percent of these diodes, which are used in optical disk drives for computers, laser printers, CD players, and videodisk players. Its engineers hope to leapfrog rivals like Canon, which dominates the laser printer market, with new products that combine the functions of laser printers, fax machines, and optical recording systems.

SOURCE: Neil Gross, "Sharp's Long-Range Gamble on Its Innovation Machine," *Business Week* (April 29, 1991), pp. 84–85.

PERSONAL CREATIVITY

Increasing your level of **personal creativity** involves not only learning creativity techniques, but also increasing the use of the right brain (which is linked to intuition) and freeing yourself from the restraints on creativity that are the result of early socialization. The latter task includes overcoming barriers to creativity and learning habits that enhance creativity. (These are described in more specialized books on creativity and innovation.)

Personal creativity: The individual's creative skills, which can be increased through training and resocialization.

In sum, creativity can be increased by learning processes (techniques) and improving personal creativity. If these occur within the right organizational setting (possibilities), the result is innovation, as shown in Figure 23.3.

The Four Types of Innovation

What the firm ultimately seeks is innovation. There are four principal types of innovation: product, process, marketing, and management.[51] **Product innovation** results in new products or services or enhancements to old products or

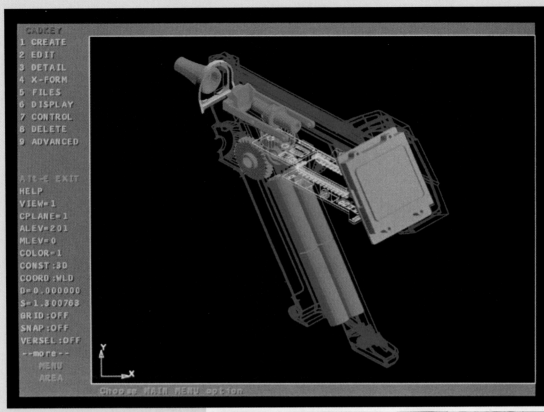

Four factors come into play in raising the level of individual, group, or organizational innovation. Known as the "four P's" of creativity and innovation, they are the *product*, the *possibilities*, the *processes*, and *personal* creativity. The product can be a physical product or service or a process, marketing, or management improvement. Technological aids like the **CADKEY 5** computer-assisted design program enhance the possibilities for creating innovations like Dlatek Inc.'s infrared clinical thermometer, shown here in a three-dimensional model. A variety of processes can be used to increase personal creativity, but these require a favorable situation. In particular, they require an organizational culture that encourages creativity and innovation.

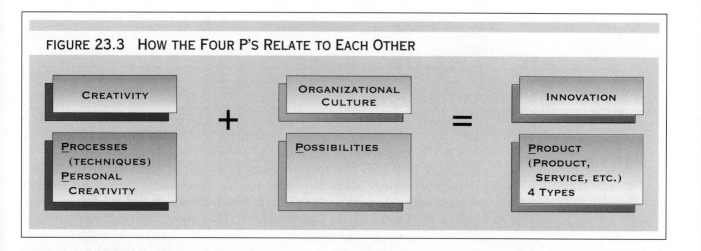

FIGURE 23.3 HOW THE FOUR P'S RELATE TO EACH OTHER

CREATIVITY

PROCESSES
  (TECHNIQUES)
PERSONAL
  CREATIVITY

+

ORGANIZATIONAL
CULTURE

POSSIBILITIES

=

INNOVATION

PRODUCT
(PRODUCT,
  SERVICE, ETC.)
4 TYPES

services. **Process innovation** is that which results in improved processes in the organization—for example, in operations, HRM, or finance. It focuses primarily on improving the efficiency with which resources are used, but it may also include improvements in the product. **Marketing innovation** is related to the marketing functions of promotion, pricing, and distribution, as well as to product functions other than product development (for example, packaging or advertising). **Management innovation** improves the management of the organization.

Studies of successful organizations suggest that they design more new products and concepts, utilize their resources more creatively (effectively and efficiently), market their products more creatively, and manage more effectively and efficiently than less successful organizations.[52] It is innovation in managing all the organization's economic functions—marketing, operations, finance, human resources, R&D, and information management—that separates truly successful companies from the others.

Product innovation: Innovation resulting in new products or services or in enhancements to old products or services.

Process innovation: Innovation resulting in improved processes in the organization.

Marketing innovation: Innovation related to the marketing functions of promotion, pricing, and distribution.

Management innovation: Innovation that improves the organization's management.

The Innovation Strategy

Firms have many choices with respect to their innovation strategy: to innovate or imitate, to pursue R&D or search and development (S&D), to focus on product or process innovation, to invest in the old or the new, to use "big bang" or continuous innovation, to be driven by market forces or by technology, to have selected (division) or total commitment, and to do basic research or applied research. Finally, in today's environment, firms have no choice but to pursue speed strategies. In the next few pages, we review each of these choices in more detail.

Innovate or Imitate

The initial choice is between innovation and imitation. Imitation is a choice that usually leads to financial suicide if no product or process innovations are forthcoming. Simply imitating someone else's products without improving them or producing them more cheaply will not result in a competitive advantage. If this choice is taken to mean product imitation, with process innovation leading to relatively low production costs, then imitation can be a viable strategy. This has long been the thrust of Japanese firms' innovation strategies. They have gained access to the technologies and product and service ideas of firms in other countries and used process innovation to convert these into low-cost products.

If a firm chooses innovation, product innovation alone will not sustain a competitive advantage.[53] Ultimately, both product and process innovations must occur in a coordinated fashion if a sustainable competitive advantage is to be obtained.

R&D or S&D

A firm also needs to determine how it will achieve innovation. For product innovations, the choice is between internal R&D and S&D.[54] S&D normally leads to the acquisition of firms for the purpose of obtaining their products or services. It may also lead to joint ventures or to the licensing of other firms' products or services. Major Japanese firms have followed an acquisition strategy in recent years, showing a voracious appetite for research and technology developed in the United States and elsewhere. They have also invested heavily in start-up companies, joint ventures, and licensing arrangements, and have sponsored U.S. research laboratories.[55] Two-thirds of all of the high-technology firms that have changed hands in the United States in recent years were bought by Japanese firms.[56]

The major question for R&D-based firms is how much to spend, measured as a percentage of sales. The U.S. industrial average is about 2 percent, compared to 2.9 percent for Japanese firms.[57] Firms spend widely varying amounts on R&D. Cypress Semiconductor, for example, spent an amount equal to 24.7 percent of sales on R&D in 1990; R&D spending by Merck, a leading drug manufacturer, equaled 11.2 percent of sales.[58] Investment in R&D as a percent of sales by U.S. firms has dropped in real terms in recent years for several reasons, including the short-term focus of performance measurements, the negative effects of mergers and acquisitions on R&D expenditures, the impact of leveraged buyouts, and the lack of available capital.[59]

Product or Process Innovation

U.S. and other North American firms are just beginning to fully appreciate the necessity for process innovation.[60] Product R&D funding has long been understood to contribute to competitive advantage. R&D investment levels are stated

Cypress Semiconductor spent an amount equal to 24.7 percent of sales on research and development in 1990.

in terms of product R&D. In contrast, process R&D has received little attention in the United States.[61] It is difficult to manage process R&D because of the nebulousness of the concept. Process creativity is a function of the efforts of individual employees, work groups, and managers improving their everyday efforts. Although it is sometimes difficult to prove the benefits of product R&D, funds for product R&D are at least identifiable in the budget. Process R&D depends on expenditures in such hard-to-pin-down areas as training and development, empowerment, and decentralization. Nevertheless, research clearly reveals that both process and product innovation are necessary for long-term competitive advantage. As noted earlier, product innovation alone is unlikely to create a sustainable advantage.[62] Sufficient funds must be allocated to process R&D.

To Invest in the Old or the New

Richard N. Foster, senior partner in McKinsey & Company, believes that "Innovation is the attacker's advantage." His many years of experience as a consultant have taught him that, in the long run, successful firms "recognize that they must be close to ruthless in cannibalizing their current products and processes just when they are most lucrative, and begin the search again, over and over."[63]

Foster observes that products and processes, which he sees as being based on technology (broadly interpreted as including how things are done), follow an S-curve relationship between effort (investment) and performance, as shown in Figure 23.4. In the beginning, at the bottom of the curve, there must be a relatively large investment before performance, defined as technological progress, occurs. Then, as breakthroughs happen, technological progress is great and investment is relatively small in the middle of the curve. Eventually, the cost of achieving more progress increases again, but the rate of progress decreases.

It is at the top of the curve that firms must choose when to stop investing in "new and improved Tide" and when to create a whole new product or process. It is at this point that they must choose whether to invest in the old or the new. But it is not just the flattening of the curve that poses a problem. The existence of other curves, representing newer technologies that displace the old ones on

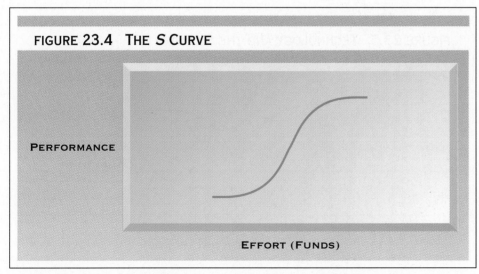

FIGURE 23.4 THE *S* CURVE

PERFORMANCE

EFFORT (FUNDS)

SOURCE: RICHARD N. FOSTER, <u>INNOVATION: THE ATTACKER'S ADVANTAGE</u> (NEW YORK: SUMMIT BOOKS, 1986) P. 31. COPYRIGHT © 1986 BY MCKINSEY & CO., INC. REPRINTED BY PERMISSION OF SUMMIT, A DIVISION OF SIMON & SCHUSTER.

which the firm has come to depend, poses a major problem in today's fast-changing world. As shown in Figure 23.5, firms may face *technological discontinuity*—that is, a gap between a firm's technology and those of its competitors.

Such gaps existed when steamships replaced sailing ships, when the ballpoint pen replaced the fountain pen, and when PCs began to replace minicomputers for many functions. Technological discontinuity also exists between Japanese and North American and European manufacturing processes in many industries, and between Japanese and North American and European management styles in many firms. In both cases, the Japanese firms have replaced old technologies (broadly interpreted) with new ones that have left their competitors in the dust.

There are strategies that can be used to extend the life of old technologies, such as adding more sails to sailing ships to try to make them faster and, hence, more competitive with steamships. Inevitably, however, and often quickly, the new technology will supplant the old one.[64] One study of U.S. and Japanese firms suggests that U.S. firms too often invest in research in the latter stages of the S-curve, whereas Japanese firms are quick to move on to new products and processes.[65]

"Big Bang" or Continuous Improvement

U.S., Canadian, and European firms have generally followed a strategy of going for the "big bang"—the major innovation on which new products and processes can be based. Such innovations are introduced periodically—say, every three or four years. This strategy has left those firms vulnerable to competition from Japanese firms, which continuously improve existing products and combine those product improvements with continuous improvements in processes. Because they are constantly improving products and processes, the Japanese firms do not have to make the quantum leaps that their competitors must make. As a result, they can bring new products to market faster; in a time of accelerating change in markets, economies, and competitors, this is a tremendous advantage.[66]

In Japan, as soon as a product is launched, the firm begins developing its replacement.[67] Ironically, like statistical quality control, continuous improve-

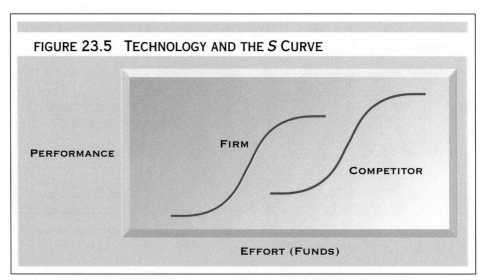

FIGURE 23.5 TECHNOLOGY AND THE *S* CURVE

SOURCE: RICHARD N. FOSTER, INNOVATION: THE ATTACKER'S ADVANTAGE (NEW YORK: SUMMIT BOOKS, 1986) P. 33. COPYRIGHT © 1986 BY MCKINSEY & CO., INC. REPRINTED BY PERMISSION OF SUMMIT, A DIVISION OF SIMON & SCHUSTER.

ment programs were introduced into Japan by U.S. consulting firms after World War II.[68] Now firms throughout the world must adopt this approach. The future of most firms lies in continuous improvement.[69]

Market-Driven Versus Technology-Driven Strategy

In the last twenty years, marketing courses have taught that new products begin with the customer. However, many U.S. organizations have not paid much attention to that dictum. General Motors, for example, made the cars that fit its high-technology, low-cost strategy, regardless of whether customers wanted them, in the belief that mass-marketing techniques could sell them. That strategy proved incorrect.[70] Ford Motor Company, on the other hand, surveyed thousands of consumers and incorporated the four hundred most desired features in its highly successful Taurus and Sable models.[71]

Thomas J. Peters and Robert H. Waterman, Jr., co-authors of *In Search of Excellence*, stated that "Getting close to the customer" is critical to success.[72] While that may have seemed obvious, their words came as a revelation to many American managers. Fortunately, many firms have sought to get closer to their customers—for example, by including customers in product and process design teams.

Experience has shown, however, that being close to the customer is not enough. Numerous products are invented that people never knew they wanted. For example, from 1980 to 1987, twelve of the thirteen best-selling consumer products were invented without market research; customers were convinced of their need for those products through advertising. Sony's Walkman is a classic example.[73] Later, TVman and Discman provided similar successes.

As *Fortune* magazine writer Brian Dumaine noted after examining rates of innovation in the United States and Japan, "An essential part of a creative culture is teaching people to lead the consumer, not follow him [or her]." Sony's Data Discman was developed after a Sony executive reasoned that executives would like to be able to carry large amounts of data with them. Robert Hall, senior vice-president of GVO, an industrial design firm in Palo Alto, California, states that "needs analysis" is necessary. Hall says, "To invent products out of thin air, you don't ask people what they want—after all, who would have told you ten years ago that they needed a CD player? You ask them what problems they have when they get up in the morning."[74]

Thus, a firm must be driven by *both* market and technology.[75] The approach of Japanese firms in bringing a product to market in "small starts" and performing market research on the target market with a real product, as opposed to a questionnaire about a proposed product, enables them to combine both approaches.[76]

Selected Versus Total Commitment

Firms can choose to depend on R&D, or on the R&D and operations units, for innovation, or they can involve everyone in the company in improving products and processes. By now, the appropriate choice should be obvious. In most industries, the firm that obtains a sustainable competitive advantage involves everyone in improving products and/or processes. For example, in a single year, employees at Toyota submitted 860,000 suggestions for improvement. Some 94 percent of those ideas were implemented. In Japan, about 66 percent of employees regularly submit suggestions, compared to only 8 percent in the United States.[77] Similarly, at the Cadillac Division of General Motors, employees redesign work, make suggestions, solve problems in teams, and participate in new-

Engineers at Chrysler use plastic scale models in automated tests that simulate actual road conditions. The results of the tests provide information for use in improving the durability and comfort of Chrysler cars.

product design. As a result, Cadillac has brought out highly successful new models and achieved substantial profitability, something that has eluded the rest of GM.[78]

Basic Research Versus Applied Research

U.S. firms have always believed in basic research. The "PhD syndrome" glorifies research for its own sake. From this perspective, something useful may flow from basic research, but what matters is the knowledge itself. Much basic research therefore does not have practical applications. In Japan, basic research was not emphasized before the late 1980s; instead, applied research was encouraged.[79] Japanese managers always think in terms of how to use what they have learned or acquired. Their focus is on applications, and this is a major reason for the success of their firms.[80] Research by strategic consultant and author Michael E. Porter showed that generic technology rarely improves competitiveness, but applied technology does.[81]

Japanese firms are currently reorganizing their R&D efforts so that teams of engineers, scientists, marketers, and manufacturers work simultaneously on three levels of innovation. At the lowest level, they seek incremental improvements of existing products. At the intermediate level, they try for a significant jump in product design and capabilities, as when Sony jumped from the micro tape recorder to the Walkman. At the highest level, the teams seek entirely new advances in product design and capability. For them, this is basic research. "The idea is to produce three new products to replace each present product, with the same investment of time and money—with one of the three then becoming the new market leader and producing the innovator's profit."[82] The message is clear: Firms need to pursue both basic and applied research.

Speed Strategies

Product covering: The strategy of producing instant product imitations to remain competitive in the face of rapid technological change.

Product churning: Rushing new products to market without market research.

Speed in product and process development has become a major focus of competitive strategy, especially in industries characterized by rapid technological change. Japanese firms are especially adept at creating instant imitations of other firms' products through a process known as **product covering.** They are also excellent at **product churning,** or rushing new products to market without conducting market research. They let the results of the first production run indicate what they should do to improve the product. According to a McKinsey

& Company study, compared to U.S. firms, Japanese firms develop new products in one-third to one-half the time and for one-tenth to one-quarter of the cost.[83] Improved speed of product development is enhanced by cross-functional design teams.

Conclusion

The concept of innovation has historically been limited largely to developing new products or services or creating improvements in old ones. More recently, Japanese firms have demonstrated the importance of process innovation. Today, U.S. managers recognize that marketing and management innovation are also critical to business success. And they have begun to recognize that to achieve these four types of innovation, they must make certain choices. They must decide whether to imitate or innovate, whether to invest in R&D or S&D, how much emphasis to place on product and process innovation, and whether to invest in old products or new ones. They also need to choose between the "big bang" and continuous improvement approaches, determine the extent to which their strategy will be driven by the market or by technology, determine the extent to which all members of the organization will be involved in improving products and processes, and balance basic and applied research. Finally, it is imperative to get new products to market quickly.

Summary

(Before reading this summary, look again at the objectives listed at the beginning of the chapter.)

1. TQM is absolutely critical to competitiveness. High quality is the price of entry in most industries today.

2. W. Edwards Deming contributed to TQM by teaching statistical quality control procedures and creating a quality philosophy, as expressed in his fourteen points. J. M. Juran broadened the scope of quality to include the entire firm; his perspectives on quality planning have been especially important. Philip Crosby introduced many U.S. firms to quality and to the concept of zero defects; he showed how to create a quality improvement program with his fourteen steps.

3. There are eight dimensions of quality: performance, features, reliability, conformance, durability, serviceability, esthetics, and perceived quality.

4. Because Japanese firms are moving toward zero defects as a quality standard, it is likely that firms throughout the world will be forced to do so as well.

5. Quality management is more difficult to quantify in services than in manufacturing. In services, HRM and operations are essentially the same thing. Thus, behaviors, as well as results, must be measured.

6. By and large, where it has been implemented appropriately, TQM has been successful—although not in the majority of cases. Failures seem to be due to improper implementation, lack of commitment, and lack of understanding of the TQM philosophy.

7. Creativity plus the right organizational culture will lead to innovation.

8. The four P's of innovation are product (the outcome of innovation), possibilities (organizational culture), processes, and personal creativity.

9. There are four types of innovation: product, process, marketing, and management.

10. The innovation strategy is based on decisions in these areas: innovate or imitate, R&D or S&D, product or process innovation, invest in the new or the old, "big bang" or continuous improvement, market-driven versus technology-driven strategy, selected versus total commitment, basic research versus applied research, and speed strategies.

General Questions

1. Why are both quality and innovation necessary to compete in the 1990s and beyond?

2. What role have Japanese firms played in making quality and innovation so critical to business success?

3. Is it possible to achieve zero defects? Why or why not?

4. Discuss the roles of continuous improvement, teams, and benchmarking to TQM.

5. Discuss the findings of various studies on the effectiveness of TQM and their impact on companies that are initiating or reviving TQM programs.

6. Discuss why organizational culture is so important to successful innovation.

7. Reread the Innovation Management Challenge in Chapter 4. What can you conclude about the culture of an innovative firm?

8. Review the innovation strategy of a firm with which you are familiar in terms of the strategic imperatives discussed in the chapter.

Questions on the Management Challenge Features

ETHICAL MANAGEMENT CHALLENGE

1. Evaluate the concept of treating ethics as an issue of conformance with standards.

2. What must happen for any ethics program to be successful?

GLOBAL MANAGEMENT CHALLENGE

1. In what ways is Ciba-Geigy typical of European firms with regard to quality and the Europe 1992 initiative?

2. What can Ciba-Geigy and the other firms discussed in this feature do to improve quality?

INNOVATION MANAGEMENT CHALLENGE

1. What is Sharp's strategy regarding innovation?

2. Will it succeed or fail? Why?

Improving Innovation at Steelcase

Steelcase has done more to change its ways than build some new buildings. To many managers, workplace flexibility means accommodating working mothers, but Steelcase has had striking success with a much broader interpretation. It has developed guidelines instead of rules and rewarded employees who interpret them creatively. It has also defined flexibility as a business requirement. Employee turnover has dropped to 3 percent, compared to the national average of 10 percent.

Coupled with the move into the pyramid was a companywide change in job structure, with eight hundred new self-managed work teams cutting across the traditional departments. In Steelcase's new state-of-the-art plant, built to make the Con-

text line of office furniture, forty-seven distinct teams control the work in response to customer demand. Up to 15 percent of the products are "specials," nonstandard in some way per a customer's request.

With so many changes, it is inevitable that some layoffs will occur. Layoffs adversely affect not only the individuals who are laid off, but the survivors as well. Wary and fearful of losing their jobs too, the survivors must be able to discuss changes with their managers. Steelcase made sure that job performance was not linked to job elimination; as a result, the psychological suffering of those who were let go was reduced and the morale of those who survived was improved.

DISCUSSION QUESTIONS

1. Discuss how you know that Steelcase's management was exceptionally sensitive to the effects of organizational culture on innovation.

2. Why was it necessary to build a new office building at Steelcase, instead of housing teams in the existing workplaces?

Quality to the Rescue

John Dobisky's electrical contracting firm, Quad-Cities Electric, which contracted only for commercial work, had increased its sales from $5 million to $30 million in less than five years. Dobisky attributed much of the growth to marketing strategies he had implemented after attending a series of management and marketing seminars at the Harvard Business School. But now the firm was meeting with some resistance in the marketplace. Some of his friends in the business community suggested that he needed to improve the quality of the firm's services. Apparently, because the firm had grown so rapidly, his guiding philosophies had gotten lost in the shuffle. And, to be truthful, he had never really viewed quality as part of service. Now, however, quality and, perhaps more important, proof of quality had become factors in winning contracts. Dobisky had read about quality improvement programs and had hired a consultant to advise him. But now he had to begin a TQM program in earnest.

DISCUSSION QUESTIONS

1. What are some of the major issues Dobisky should address as he begins his TQM program? (Consider, for example, Deming's fourteen points and Juran's quality planning.)

2. How would you go about setting up a TQM program? (Consider, for example, Crosby's fourteen steps.)

Deming's Fourteen Points

Test your understanding of Deming's fourteen points by using the college educational process as an illustration. The raw materials are entering students, knowledge, dissemination of knowledge, and technology. The operative employees are professors. The end product is the student who has completed an educational process, such as a course. For example, Deming's third point deals with building quality into the product, as opposed to testing at the end of the process. How could this be accomplished in the educational setting? Is this a matter of education or motivation? Perform a similar analysis of all fourteen points, either on your own or in a small group, as assigned by your instructor. This exercise will help you see how to apply the fourteen points, not just in manufacturing, but in service industries as well.

Glossary

Acceptance theory of authority: A manager's authority is measured by the subordinate's degree of acceptance of that authority.

Accommodative response: A response indicating that the company has accepted its economic, legal, and ethical responsibilities, though sometimes under pressure.

Achievement need theory: Individuals with a high need for achievement (nAch) also usually have a need for power (nPower)—control over others—and a relatively low need for affiliation (nAff)—social interaction.

Achievement-oriented leadership: A leadership style in which the leader emphasizes the achievement of difficult tasks and the importance of excellent performance and simultaneously shows confidence that subordinates will perform well.

Action research: Research in which an OD consultant diagnoses a situation and makes recommendations for acting on it.

Active listening: A program designed to teach individuals to listen not only to the content of what is being said but also to its emotional aspects, to provide feedback to the other person, or both.

Activity-based costing (ABC): A focus on identifying the real costs of a product by making more accurate alloca-

tions of overhead costs, identifying and reducing cost drivers, and identifying the activities that lead to value for the customer and eliminating those that do not.

Adhocracy control: A control strategy that relies on individual self-control, empowerment, and flexibility.

Administration and organization: An approach to management that focused on formulating principles for administering and structuring organizations.

Administrative model: A model of decision making that suggests that decision makers experience "bounded rationality" and must settle for something less than an ideal solution.

Affirmative-action program: A set of actions undertaken by an organization to fulfill its EEO obligations in a systematic way.

Annual operating plan: The one-year plan of action that states how a strategy will be implemented.

Artificial intelligence (AI): Attempts to enable a computer to simulate human reasoning by working with qualitative as well as quantitative information.

Assertiveness training: A program designed to teach individuals to communicate in a way that satisfies their needs while respecting the rights of others.

Assessment center: A two- or three-day program consisting of simulation exercises, tests, interviews, and problem-solving assignments used to measure an individual's potential for promotion or assignment to a specific job.

Attribution theory: Individuals tend to attribute success to themselves and failure to outside variables.

Authority: Legitimate power.

Automated storage and retrieval systems (ASRS): Computer-controlled automated warehouses that include automatic placement and retrieval of parts.

Automation: The replacement of human workers with machines.

Autonomous work team: A relatively small, highly trained, autonomous work group that takes responsibility for a product, project, service, or process.

Balance sheet: A financial statement that reveals the condition of the company at a given point in time.

Balanced scorecard: A combination of four sets of measures, or perspectives: financial, internal business, customer, and innovation and learning; used to evaluate organizational performance.

Basic action strategies: The fundamental strategies open to a single-business organization.

BCG matrix: A technique developed by the Boston Consulting Group in which each business's relative competitive position, as expressed by relative market share, is plotted against its growth rate.

Behavioral approach: A management approach concerned with increasing productivity by focusing on understanding the human element in an organization—individuals and groups and how they can be effectively and efficiently combined in a larger organization.

Behaviorally anchored rating scale (BARS): A series of behavioral activities that should be undertaken in a particular job, accompanied by verbal descriptions of several levels of performance for each activity.

Bet-your-company culture: An organizational culture that develops where feedback on decisions is slow but the risks are high.

Body language: A form of nonverbal communication that has four major components: facial expressions, eye contact, gestures, and body postures.

Brainstorming: A group creative problem-solving process in which no negative feedback is allowed on any suggested alternative until all alternatives have been generated.

Break-even analysis: An analysis whose purpose is to determine the point at which revenues equal costs, along with other relevant information.

Break-even point: A point at which the revenue generated from a project, product, or service equals the cost of generating that revenue.

Budgets: Quantitative statements that allocate resources to various units of the organization, usually for a period of one year or eighteen months.

Building and maintenance roles: Roles devoted to building and maintaining the group, such as encouraging members, mediating differences, compromising, communicating, and setting standards.

Bureaucracy: A form of organization characterized by division of labor, hierarchy of authority, members selected on the basis of their qualifications, and strict rules and procedures.

Bureaucratic control: A control strategy based on authority and carried out through rules, regulations, and policies.

Business strategy: Strategy that focuses on how the firm will obtain a strategic advantage and how it should use that advantage to beat the competition.

Capabilities: Collective, cross-functional, value-adding organizational processes that create competitive advantages.

Capital expenditure budgets: Statements of expenditures for major capital purchases, such as plant and equipment, inventories, and development costs, among others.

Cash budget: A forecast of cash receipts and disbursements.

Cash flow statement: A statement of the sources and uses of cash, used in controlling operations and finances.

Catalyst: Any event that triggers recognition of the need for an OD program.

Causal techniques: Techniques that can be used to suggest causes of the behavior of dependent variables and to predict events.

Centralized organization: An organization in which authority is not widely delegated and virtually all important decisions are made by top management.

Certainty: A condition in which a decision maker can predict the results of implementing each alternative 100 percent of the time.

Change agent: A consultant, sometimes internal but usually external to the organization, who helps initiate an OD program and then guides it.

Channel richness: The degree to which a communication channel can handle multiple cues simultaneously, facilitate rapid feedback, and establish a personal focus for communication.

Chief information officer (CIO): The manager who is responsible for managing the use of information and systems from a strategic viewpoint.

Chronemics: The study of the use of time.

Clan control: A control strategy that relies on social needs and is established largely through cultural artifacts.

Classical approaches: Approaches to management developed in the early twentieth century; include scientific management and the administration and organization approach.

Classical, or economic, model: A model of decision making that describes how decisions are made from a conceptual, analytical viewpoint.

Cohesiveness: The tendency

Command group: The structure of a formal group along the lines of authority within the organization.

Communication: The transfer of information from one communicator to another through the use of symbols.

Company strategy, structure, and rivalry: The conditions governing business in a nation, especially competition.

Comparable worth: Compensation on the basis of the job's worth to the organization regardless of the sex of the job holder.

Competitive advantage: Any factor that enables a firm to outdo its competitors in the marketplace.

Competitive environment: All the elements that affect the organization's competitive situation.

Competitiveness model: A model developed by William K. Hall that an organization can use to determine the optimal combination of two strategies—high differentiation relative to competitors and low cost relative to competitors.

Competitor analysis: A SWOT analysis of competitors for the purpose of understanding their strategies and determining where they are vulnerable.

Competitors: Organizations that market similar products or services to the same set of customers.

Complexity: The number of different jobs and departments in an organization and the interrelationships among them.

Compressed work week: An approach to work scheduling in which the total number of hours worked during a week is scheduled to be completed in fewer than the traditional five days.

Computer conferencing: A multiparty extension of electronic mail.

Computer integrated business: A firm whose main functions exchange information constantly and quickly via computers.

Computer-aided design (CAD): The use of specialized hardware and software to enable engineers to design products, components, electronic systems, and the like.

Computer-aided manufacturing (CAM): The use of specialized computer systems to translate the information in a CAD-generated design into instructions for automated manufacturing.

Computer-integrated manufacturing (CIM): A broad label applied to the use of computers in design and manufacturing processes.

Concurrent authority: A system in which all decisions by the line must be concurred with by the staff.

Concurrent controls: Control systems designed to detect variances from standards and undertake corrective action before a series of actions has been completed.

Concurrent engineering (CE): An approach to engineering in which a product and the process for making it are designed concurrently.

Conflict management: The choice of appropriate techniques for keeping conflict at a reasonable level.

Consideration: Behavior that indicates friendship, mutual trust, respect, and warmth.

Constituents: Major groups affected by an organization's decisions.

Contemporary management: A synthesis of traditional and contemporary approaches to management.

Content theories: Theories concerned with the internal factors that motivate people—needs and how they can be satisfied.

Contextual dimensions: Dimensions that help define a job; they include interpersonal relations, authority and responsibility for goal setting, and communication patterns.

Contingency approach: A management approach in which the manager's actions are dependent on the conditions of various key elements in a given situation.

Contingency plan: An alternative plan that may be put into effect if the chosen plan becomes inappropriate.

Contingency theories: Leadership theories suggesting that for any given situation there is a best way to manage.

Continuous improvement: Programs designed to produce continuous improvement in products and/or services.

Continuous reinforcement schedules: Reinforcement follows every occurrence of the desired behavior.

Control: The systematic process by which managers ensure that the organization is achieving its objectives and carrying out the associated plans effectively and efficiently.

Coordination: The process of integrating the efforts of individuals and departments to achieve the organization's purpose.

Core competencies: The organization's collective learning, especially as related to the technology and manufacturing processes that make it competitive.

Core job dimensions: The key dimensions identified by Hackman and Oldham: skill variety, task identity, task significance, autonomy, and feedback.

Corporate strategy: A strategic plan that identifies the business (or businesses) an organization will engage in and how it will fundamentally conduct that business.

Cost (expense) centers: Responsibility centers controlled on the basis of costs or expenses generated. Their budget is based on the cost of the inputs utilized in operations.

Creation: Something original that has value.

Creative problem solving: The process of practicing ongoing environmental analysis, recognizing and identifying a problem, making assumptions about the decision environment, generating creative alternatives to solve the identified problem, deciding among those alternatives, acting to implement the chosen alternative(s), and controlling for results.

Creativity: The process of originating something new that has value; the skill to originate, invent, and conceptualize the new and to make the new valuable.

Creativity circles: Groups of employees who meet to use creative techniques to solve problems facing the work group.

Critical path: In a large-scale project, the sequence of activities that requires the most time for completion.

Cross-functional team: A team consisting of design, manufacturing, and marketing personnel who jointly design a product.

Cultural diversity: The existence of different cultures within an organization or society; includes the emergence of women, older workers, and ethnic minorities as major components of the work force, as well as people from different countries working together.

Current ratio: A measure of the firm's liquidity—that is, its ability to handle short-term debts and liabilities. It is found by dividing current assets by current liabilities.

Customers: Individuals and organizations that consume an organization's products or services.

Data: Raw, unanalyzed facts.

Database: A set of data consisting of text, numbers, voice, and/or images.

Debt-to-total-assets ratio: A leverage ratio that indicates the firm's ability to handle its debts. It is found by dividing total debt by total assets.

Decentralized organization: An organization in which authority is widely delegated to subordinates.

Decision: A choice among alternatives.

Decision support system: A computer-based MIS that provides information and models that support decision making in an interactive manner.

Decoding: The process of interpreting a message.

Defensive response: A response to societal demands in which the organization admits its mistakes but claims that they are due to circumstances beyond its control.

Delegation of authority: The distribution of authority among subordinates so that they can make decisions and engage in activities designed to achieve the organization's objectives.

Delphi group: A decision-making technique utilizing a series of questionnaires administered by a central individual to experts who never meet face-to-face.

Demand conditions: The number and sophistication of domestic customers for an industry's product or service.

Departmental plan: Typically, a department's annual operating plan; it may include longer- or shorter-term plans that apply to the whole department.

Departmentation: The grouping of jobs under the authority of (usually) a single manager, according to some rational basis, for the purposes of planning, coordination, and control.

Depth: The amount of decision-making authority available to the job holder.

Descriptive statistics: Statistics that describe a situation as it currently exists.

Design for manufacturing: An approach to product design that focuses on designing products that are simple enough so that manufacturing can be efficient and the product will have high quality.

Development: The process of helping an employee grow, principally in his or her career but perhaps also as a human being.

Differentiation: The process through which each organization and department adapts its subcomponents to meet the constraints of its specific environment; the tendency of organizational subunits to become structurally different as a result of the need to adapt to different environments.

Directive autocrat: A leader who makes decisions unilaterally and closely supervises the activities of subordinates.

Directive democrat: A leader who wants full participation but closely supervises subordinates' activities.

Directive leadership: A leadership style in which the leader explains the performance goal and provides specific rules and regulations to guide subordinates toward achieving it.

Distribution models: Models that help a manager determine where products are to go and how they are to be shipped.

Division of labor: The subdivision of objectives and plans into smaller and smaller units until they reach the task level.

Divisional plans: Plans for an organization's major divisions—for example, the marketing plan for the year.

Downsizing: A restructuring process through which the organization becomes smaller; it may involve eliminating individual positions, groups, departments, and even whole business units.

Econometric models: Models that use a complex series of interdependent regression equations, combining both theory and applied research, to predict the performance of some dependent variable, often the national economy.

Economic order quantity (EOQ): The amount of inventory to be ordered that will minimize holding and ordering costs.

Economy: The general economic condition of a country (or countries) or region (or regions) in which an organization operates, represented by inflation rates, interest rates, currency values, and numerous other factors.

Effectiveness: The ability to set appropriate objectives and achieve them.

Efficiency: The relative amount of resources used to obtain effectiveness.

Electronic bulletin board: A computerized system for distributing memos throughout an organization.

Electronic data interchange (EDI): The exchange of data across organizational boundaries using information technology.

Electronic (E-) mail: The use of electronic circuitry to transmit written messages instantaneously.

Employee (labor) relations: The concerns of managing a unionized work force.

Employee orientation: A leadership style in which employees are viewed as human beings with individual, personal needs.

Empowerment: The process of giving employees the maximum amount of power necessary to do their jobs as they see fit.

Encoding: The process of transforming ideas into symbols that others will understand.

Entrepreneur: A person who perceives opportunity; finds the pursuit of opportunity desirable in the context of his or her life situation; and believes that success is possible.

Equal employment opportunity (EEO): A set of regulations barring employers from basing HRM decisions on race, sex, color, religion, national origin, physical or mental handicap (disability), pregnancy, age, or veteran status.

Equity theory: People will seek rewards only if they perceive that the rewards will be distributed equitably.

Ethical behavior: Behavior that is considered acceptable and appropriate by a society, organization, profession, group, or individual.

Ethical dilemma: A situation in which there is a conflict between the firm's economic goals and its social responsibility.

Ethical responsibility: The responsibility to act within the norms of a particular reference group, whether or not those norms have been transformed into laws or rules.

Europe 1992 initiative: The movement to form an integrated market for the twelve countries of the EEC.

Excellence approach to management: An approach in which characteristics of excellent firms are used as models for other firms.

Executive information system: An information system tailored to the specific needs of executives.

Expectancy: The expected probability that an action will result in a certain consequence.

Expectancy-instrumentality theory:

Individuals contemplate the consequences of their actions in choosing alternatives to satisfy their needs.

Expert system: An MIS that actually provides guidance to managers.

External audit: An audit conducted by individuals or firms outside the organization, typically by certified public accountants (CPAs).

External environment: All elements outside the boundaries of the organization that have the potential to affect the organization.

External environmental factors: Forces external to the organization—economic/competitive, technological, political/legal, and societal.

Extinction: Ignoring (not reinforcing) undesired behavior in the hope that it will not be repeated.

Factor conditions: Conditions that enable a nation to turn basic factors—natural resources, education, and infrastructure—into a specialized advantage.

Factory of the future: A factory characterized by automated machinery and computer-integrated manufacturing.

Fax machine: A machine that uses electronic circuitry and telephone cabling to transmit visual images.

Feedback: A message sent by the receiver to the sender during a communication.

Feedforward control: Control systems that anticipate changes rather than merely react to them.

Financial analysis: An examination of the organization's financial statements and the various ratios derived from information on its balance sheet and income statement.

Fixed costs: Costs that tend to remain constant regardless of the volume of output; they include such factors as depreciation of plant and equipment, overhead items, and insurance costs.

Fixed-position layout: A facilities layout in which the product remains in a fixed position and workers, parts, and machines move to and from the product.

Flexible manufacturing systems (FMS): Clusters of automated machinery controlled by computers that have the flexibility to produce a wide variety of products efficiently.

Flexi-time: A system in which a worker is allowed to set his or her own hours within common ranges, provided that the total number of hours worked during the week remains the same.

Force-field analysis: A view of change as resulting from the relative strength of driving and restraining forces.

Formal conmmunication: Communication that occurs through official channels and is sanctioned by the organization.

Formal group: A group created by the organization; its specific tasks are aimed at achieving the organization's objectives.

Formal structure: An organizational structure sanctioned by the organization and designed to achieve its objectives.

Formalization: The extent to which written documentation occurs within an organization.

Four p's of creativity and innovation: The product, the possibilities, the processes, and personal creativity.

Friendship groups: Groups that arise to satisfy social needs; the natural result of interactions among people working near each other.

Functional authority: A system in which a person, work group, or department is given line authority over decisions in other departments related to their area of expertise.

Functional manager: A manager who is responsible for a particular economic function of the organization or some part of it.

Functional strategy: A strategic plan that states how an organization can use its resources most effectively and efficiently to carry out corporate and business strategies.

Gantt chart: A simple chart that allows managers to schedule work forces across a series of tasks.

GE portfolio matrix: A technique developed by General Electric Co. to enable top management to determine which SBUs to retain in its portfolio, which to divest, and how to treat those it retains.

General environment: Elements—such as society, technology, the economy, and political/legal factors—that occasionally influence the organization or can be significantly influenced by it.

General manager: A manager whose responsibilties cover more than one function and often deal with all of them. General managers are normally CEOs or product or division managers.

Generic competitive strategies: According to Michael E. Porter, the three strategies among which organizations should choose in order to compete successfully are cost leadership, differentiation, and focus on a particular market or product.

Global management: The performance of management activities on a truly global basis, requiring a degree of coordination among activities that is not experienced in multidomestic/international operations.

Goals: Refinements of an organization's mission that address key issues within the organization.

Graicunas's theory: The theory that as the number of subordinates increases arithmetically there is an exponential increase in the number of possible relationships among them.

Grand strategy: The fundamental strategy from which all of the organization's other strategies and plans are derived.

Grapevine: The path of communication within an organization that exists outside the organization's formal communication channels.

Grievance procedures: Formal ways for employees to present grievances against the organization and its managers.

Grievance system: Policies, rules, and procedures for use in appraising performance, disciplining, and handling grievances.

Group: Two or more people who come into contact for a purpose and are dependent on one another to obtain their objectives.

Group decision process: A decision-making procedure in which each member of a group makes a large number of inputs on which other members build.

Group ethics: Behaviors prescribed by a particular group, such as the work group.

Group plan: A plan developed for a particular group—typically, but not necessarily, the actions it will pursue in carrying out its part of the annual operating plan.

Group technology: An approach to production in which a group of machines acts like a product layout for a family of similar products within a larger processing layout design.

Group think: A condition that exists when the tendency of members of a cohesive group to seek concurrence becomes so strong that it overrides realistic appraisal and alternative courses of action.

Groupware: Software that enables work groups and teams to tackle problems together through networked PCs.

Hawthorne effect: An effect produced by a secondary factor in an experiment, such as the attention given to the subjects, rather than by the factor under study.

Hawthorne studies: A set of experiments that examined the effects of workers' physical environment on their productivity.

Hersey-Blanchard contingency (life-cycle) theory: A leadership theory based on task and relationship behaviors, representing each of these dimensions of leadership behavior on an axis of a two-dimensional grid.

Horizontal organization: An approach to organizational design based on the belief that there are a certain number of key processes in any organization and that its structure should be based on those processes rather than on functions.

Human resource management (HRM): The process of first placing employees in jobs and then managing those employees; putting the right people with the right skills in the right place at the right time with the right motivation in order to accomplish the organization's strategy.

Human resource planning: The process of determining the staffing requirements necessary to carry out an organization's strategy, also referred to as personnel planning.

Hygiene factors: Need satisfiers extrinsic to the job; they are often referred to as dissatisfiers, meaning that if these items are absent, employees will be dissatisfied and may not perform as well as they would if the factors were present.

Ideation: The conception of an idea or thought; the first step in the communication process.

Implementation: Actions taken to carry out a selected problem solution.

Income statement: A financial statement that shows the condition of the company for a specified period.

Individual plan: A plan developed by an individual to contribute to accomplishing the organization's objectives.

Individual roles: Roles played by some group members to satisfy their own needs rather than the group's.

Individualism versus collectivism: The degree to which a culture is oriented toward the individual or the group.

Industry analysis: Analysis of the five factors that form an industry's structure: the strength and nature of the existing competition; potential entrants; the threat of substitutes; the bargaining power of suppliers; and the bargaining power of buyers.

Inferential, or predictive, statistics: Statistics used to predict what will happen in a given situation in the future.

Informal communication: Communication that occurs outside formal channels.

Informal group: Any group that is not part of the formal organizational structure and does not have a formal purpose related to performance.

Informal structure: Any structure within an organization that has not been formally prescribed by it.

Information: Data that have been put into a meaningful and useful context and communicated to a recipient who uses it to make decisions.

Information overload: An excess of information, resulting from excessive communication.

Initiating structure: Behavior that organizes and defines relationships or roles and establishes well-defined patterns of organization, channels of communication, and ways of getting jobs done.

Innovation: An outcome of the creative process that has a significant impact on an organization, a society, or an industry; it can be a product, a process, or an approach to marketing or management.

Innovation: The process of creating something new that has significant value to an individual, group, organization, industry, or society.

Inputs: All the data, text, voice, and images entering the information system and the methods and media by which they are captured and entered.

Integration: The direction of differentiated subunits' efforts toward the fulfillment of an organization's central purpose or mission.

Integrator: An individual who works with designers, serving as a liaison with manufacturing.

Intellectual capital: A term often used to decribe the firm's intellectual assets.

Interacting group: A group whose members meet face-to-face with open interchange.

Interest groups: Groups formed on the basis of common interests.

Intermediate plans: Plans that help translate strategy into operations.

Intermittent reinforcement schedules: Reinforcement follows some occurrences of the desired behavior but not others.

Internal audit: An examination of the organization's financial records and accounting systems performed by members of the organization.

Internal environment: All the elements that are contained within the organization's boundaries.

Internal environmental factors: Forces internal to the organization, including people (owners, board members, general management, organized labor, nonorganized workers, informal leaders) and all other factors within the organization's boundaries (corporate culture, leadership style, organizational structure, and similar factors).

Interpreting: The process of comparing new stimuli with similar ones stored in our perceptual set.

Intrapreneur: A company employee who is allowed to act like an entrepreneur on behalf of the company, rather than on his or her own behalf.

Intuitive thinkers: People who approach a problem more intuitively than logically.

Inventory: The supply of goods kept on hand for use in production or as a result of it. The three principal types are finished goods, work-in-process, and raw materials.

Inventory models: Models that provide guidance in managing inventory, most often in determining how much inventory to maintain at a particular point in time.

Inventory turnover ratio: An activity ratio that shows how well assets are being utilized. It is found by dividing sales by inventory.

Investment centers: Responsibility centers controlled on the basis of profit together with the amount of capital investment made to produce the profit.

ISO 9000: The International Standards Organization's standards of quality. In order to compete in European countries, foreign firms must meet these standards.

Japanese management practices: A set of management practices developed by Japanese firms, focusing primarily on increasing productivity through group decision making, cooperation, and harmony.

Job: A collection of tasks assigned to one individual.

Job analysis: The process in which existing and potential jobs are analyzed or reanalyzed, designed or redesigned, to ensure that they help fulfill the company's mission.

Job description: A description of the responsibilities and duties of a job.

Job design: The process of determining the content of a job or group of jobs, including the degree of authority associated with the job.

Job enlargement: An approach to job design that focuses on task variety, a meaningful work module, performance feedback, ability utilization, and worker-paced control.

Job enrichment: An approach to job design that encompasses employee participation, goal internalization, autonomy, and group management.

Job evaluation: The systematic determination of the relative worth of a job in an organization.

Job rotation: A system in which an employee moves from one job to another.

Job specification: A description of the kind of person needed to perform a job, in terms of skills, knowledge, and abilities; used as the basis of recruitment and selection.

Joint venture: A partnership between corporations.

Juran trilogy: Quality planning, quality control, and quality improvement.

Just-in-time (JIT): A system in which the firm maintains almost no inventory and suppliers are required to provide just enough inventory for operations for a day or other specified period.

Kaizen: "Continuous Improvement," an important part of the quality control process at Japanese firms.

Kanban: A low-cost method of controlling inventory and product movement.

Knowledge workers: Workers concerned with procuring, storing, organizing, maintaining, reading, analyzing, presenting, distributing, and employing knowledge in order to meet an organization's goals.

Language: The manipulation of recognizable symbols.

Law of effect: Of several responses to the same situation, those that are accompanied or closely followed by satisfaction will be more likely to recur; those that are accompanied or closely

followed by discomfort will be less likely to occur.

Leadership: The process of making choices about how to treat people in order to influence them and then translating those choices into actions.

Leadership Grid: A model of leadership consisting of a 9-x-9 grid that shows how a manager's concerns for people (relationships) and production (tasks) can be combined.

Leading: The process of making decisions about how to influence people's behavior and then carrying out those decisions.

Legal/political element: Laws and regulations at the local, state, national, and international levels, as well as individuals and organizations that attempt to influence the legal environment, such as lobbyists and protest groups.

Levels of responsibility: A model of social responsibility consisting of four principal components: economic, legal, ethical, and philanthropic responsibility.

Leveraging resources: Focusing on strategic intent and the future actions needed to achieve that intent.

Line: All functions that the organization cannot do without.

Line and staff concept: An approach to organization based on the distinction between line and staff officers, in which line officers make decisions directly related to the organization's objectives and staff officers provide advice and support.

Line authority: Authority within a given unit's chain of command.

Line managers: Managers who are directly concerned with accomplishing the objectives of a particular organization.

Linear programming: A technique in which a sequence of steps leads to the optimum solution of a problem characterized by a single goal and objective, a number of constraints, a number of variables, and a linear relationship among the variables.

Linking pin: The idea that the manager of each work unit serves as a linking pin among at least three groups: the group that he or she leads and manages, the group of managers at the same level of which he or she is a member, and the group of managers higher in the organizational hierarchy, of which the manager's boss is a member.

Litigation audit: An audit designed to determine an organization's potential exposure to litigation.

Long-range financial plan: A one- to five-year forecast of the organization's anticipated financial performance if the strategy is followed and succeeds to the degree believed necessary.

Lotus blossom: A creative problem-solving technique that uses a core thought as the basis for the expansion of ideas into an ever-widening series of surrounding windows (or "petals").

Lower-level managers: Managers who supervise front-line or operating employees.

Management: The creative problem-solving process of planning, organizing, leading, and controlling an organization's resources to achieve its mission and objectives.

Management audit: An examination of all facets of organizational activity.

Management by objectives (MBO): A process in which objectives are determined and distributed to succeeding levels of management; managers at each level participate in the formulation of action plans; and the plans are implemented.

Management by objectives, results, and rewards (MBORR): Broadening MBO to include checking for results and rewarding performance.

Management challenge: The task of changing the management process in the right direction at the right time to meet the demands of present and future situations.

Management challenges: Forces that change the nature of the management process and the functions, roles, and skills required of managers.

Management information system (MIS): A formal system for gathering and analyzing information.

Management innovation: Innovation

that improves the organization's management.

Management, or tactical, control: Control that focuses on carrying out the subplans included in a given strategy.

Management science: A broad term that encompasses virtually all rational approaches to managerial problem solving that are based on scientific methods.

Management science approach: Often called operations research or quantitative analysis; it employs mathematical techniques to solve problems.

Managerial span of control: The number of people a manager directs.

Managing change: A process in which the individual and the organization develop plans to influence change, implement it, and control its effects, as opposed to simply letting change happen.

Market control: A control strategy in which market mechanisms are allowed to establish the standards of the control system.

Marketing innovation: Innovation related to the marketing functions of promotion, pricing, and distribution, as well as to product functions other than product development.

Masculinity: A set of characteristics that many cultures would attribute to men, including acquisition of money and possessions, pursuit of advancement, and assertiveness.

Maslow's hierarchy: Human needs are ordered in a hierarchy such that lower-level needs must be satisfied before a higher-level need can be a primary motivator.

Mass production: Production in large quantities on assembly lines, with standardized parts and high specialization of labor.

Master budget: A summary statement of the organization's budgets, portraying sales, revenues, expenses, profits, capital employment, ROI, and the relationships among these and other items.

Materials requirements planning (MRP): A computer-based inventory planning and control system that ex-

amines the master planning schedule for required input resources for each period covered by the plan.

Matrix structure: A structure characterized by the simultaneous authority of project and functional managers over line and/or staff.

Mechanistic organization: An organization that focuses on hierarchical relationships and tends to be bureaucratic.

Middle managers: Managers who occupy the second layer—and often additional layers—of management in a large organization.

Mission: A broad statement of business scope and operations that distinguishes an organization from other, similar organizations.

Mission functions: Activities directly associated with accomplishing an organization's mission. These include planning, organizing, leading, and controlling.

Models: The component of an MIS that consists of a combination of procedural, logical, and mathematical models that manipulate input and store data.

Motivation: An internal drive to satisfy an unsatisfied need.

Motivation cycle: A sequence of events that begins with unsatisfied needs and ends after the individual has assessed the consequences of attempting to satisfy those needs or when the process is interrupted for some reason.

Motivation/performance cycle (MPC): A ten-stage model showing how managers can influence the motivation of subordinates.

Motivators: Need satisfiers intrinsic to the job; often referred to as satisfiers.

Multidomestic firm: An organization that operates across national boundaries but treats each country as a separate market, developing products solely for that market.

Multinational corporation: A firm that has significant operations in more than one country.

Need: Something we must have or want to have.

Need for achievement: A motivating

drive that causes an individual to seek high levels of achievement, defined primarily in economic terms.

Need to contribute to society: A motivating drive stemming from the desire to give something to society through one's occupation.

Negative reinforcement: The removal or lack of occurrence of a negative condition when the desired behavior occurs.

Network organization: A cluster of firms or specialized subunits coordinated by market mechanisms rather than by traditional chains of command; a form of organization in which coordination occurs horizontally rather than vertically.

New entrants: Organizations that may enter markets served by an existing organization.

New management: An evolving set of new approaches to management.

Noise: Any factor that interferes with communication.

Nominal group: A decision-making technique in which much of an interacting group's interpersonal exchange is eliminated in order to preclude the influence of a dominant personality.

Nonmonetary resource input budget: A nonfinancial budget including employee hours, units of product, and units of raw material.

Nonverbal communication: Body language and the use of time, space, touch, appearance, and aesthetic elements to convey a message.

Norms: Standards of performance or other behavior established by a group.

Objectives: Specific statements of anticipated results that further define the organization's goals.

Offshore: Located outside the country of origin.

Ombudsman: A position or department created to handle employee questions, complaints, and problems.

Operating budget: A financial statement for the forthcoming year, matching revenues and expenses and calculating anticipated profits or losses.

Operating plans: Plans that deal with day-to-day operations, typically for a period of less than one year.

Operational control: Control designed to ensure that operational actions are consistent with plans and objectives.

Operations management: The planning, organizing, leading, and controlling of productive systems.

Operations managers: Individuals responsible for producing the supply of goods or services in organizations.

Opportunity: A chance to improve the organization's situation significantly.

Oral communication: Speaking and listening.

Organic organization: An organization characterized by openness, responsiveness, and a lack of hierarchy.

Organization: A group of people working together to achieve a common purpose.

Organization chart: A pictorial representation of an organization's formal structure.

Organizational behavior modification (OBM): Application of the law of effect to motivate members of an organization to behave in specific ways.

Organizational climate: The desirability of the work and social environment within an organization.

Organizational culture: The pattern of shared values and norms that distinguishes an organization from all others.

Organizational design: The process of determining the best overall, macro structure for the organization and its major components, as well as the characteristics of structural elements such as spans of control and departmentation.

Organizational development (OD): In its broadest sense, any planned program for managing change; it is usually construed as the management of change in organizational cultures.

Organizational ethics: A code of ethics defining behaviors considered ethical within an organization.

Organizational learning: The process through which organizations learn.

Organizational structure: The result of the organizing process; consists of relationships among tasks and authority, reporting relationships, groupings of jobs, and systems of coordination.

Organizing: The process of determining how resources are allocated and prepared in order to accomplish an organization's mission.

Orientation: The introduction of a new employee to the organization—the requirements of the job, the social situation in which he or she will be working, and the organization's culture.

Original: Describes something that did not exist previously.

Origination: The process of generating something new.

Output: The product of the information system.

Outputs: The products or services resulting from the transformation process.

Outsourcing: Subcontracting a function to another organization.

Paralanguage: Tone of voice, inflection, speed, volume, and silence.

Parity principle: Anyone who is assigned the responsibility for achieving an objective should also be given the authority to achieve it.

Participative leadership: A leadership style in which the leader consults with subordinates about work, task goals, and paths to resource goals.

Path-goal theory: A leadership theory that focuses on the need for leaders to make rewards contingent on the accomplishment of objectives and to aid group members in attaining rewards by clarifying the paths to goals and removing obstacles to performance.

Perception: The process of organizing and interpreting incoming sensory information in order to define ourselves and our surroundings.

Perceptual set: An individual's existing information base.

Performance: Achievement of objectives in an effective and efficient way.

Performance appraisal: A formal evaluation of an employee's performance.

Permissive autocrat: A leader who makes decisions unilaterally but allows subordinates a great deal of latitude in execution.

Permissive democrat: A leader who allows high participation in both decision making and execution.

Personal creativity: The individual's creative skills, which can be increased through training and resocialization.

Personal ethics: Behaviors that an individual considers appropriate.

Philanthropic responsibilities: Responsibilities for which there are no societal laws, rules, or ethical statements, but for which expectations may exist nonetheless.

Plan: A set of actions designed to achieve an objective, goal, mission, or vision.

Planning: The process of setting objectives and determining how those objectives are to be achieved in an uncertain future; problem solving for the future in a changing environment.

Policies: Plans that provide general guidance.

Political action committees (PACs): Committees organized by companies to support political candidates who favor particular policies.

Portfolio matrix: A technique in which characteristics of the market and industry are plotted against the characteristics of the firm, forming a matrix.

Positive reinforcement: Giving a reward after the desired behavior occurs.

Possibilities: Aspects of organizational culture that support innovation, that create the possibility for it to occur.

Postaction controls: Control systems that determine whether an objective has been reached.

Power: The ability to influence others to carry out orders, or to do something they would not have done otherwise, in order to achieve desired outcomes; the ability to control others by influencing the strength and direction of their motivation.

Power distance: The degree to which the culture accepts any variance in power in organizational relationships, specifically those between superiors and subordinates.

Preaction controls: Control systems used to ensure that the necessary human, material, and financial resources are in place before the transformation process begins.

Premises: Assumptions about a situation and the future condition of factors in that situation that must be made as part of the planning process but should not be made without thorough consideration.

Proactive firm: A firm that goes beyond what is legally and ethically required.

Procedures: Plans that describe the exact series of actions to be taken in a given situation; a set of specific steps for performing a job.

Process culture: An organizational culture that evolves from situations in which feedback on decisions is slow and risk is low.

Process innovation: Innovation resulting in improved processes in the organization.

Process layout: A facilities layout designed to accommodate a large number of product designs and processing steps.

Process planning: Planning that determines how a product or service will be produced at the desired quality, in the required quantity, and at the budgeted cost.

Process production: The production of materials or goods in a continuous flow.

Process theories: Theories concerned with how people are motivated—specifically, with how they choose need satisfiers and how external factors affect that process.

Processes: Techniques for increasing creativity.

Product: The result of the creation/innovation process; can be a physical product or service or an enhancement to either a process improvement or a marketing or management improvement.

Product churning: Rushing new products to market without market research.

Product covering: The strategy of producing instant product imitations to remain competitive in the face of rapid technological change.

Product innovation: Innovation resulting in new products or services or in enhancements to old products or services.

Product layout: A facilities layout designed to accommodate only a few product and process designs; it is associated with assembly lines that make a product in a fixed sequence of steps.

Product plans: Plans that cover the activities related to a project for a set period, often a year.

Production orientation: A leadership style that stresses production and the technical aspects of the job, with employees viewed as the means of getting the work done.

Productivity: The relationship between a firm's output of goods and services and its inputs.

Professional ethics: Behaviors prescribed by a professional association as appropriate to members of that profession.

Profit centers: Responsibility centers controlled on the basis of the difference between revenues and expenses—that is, profit.

Profit concept: The belief that the primary responsibility of business is to make a profit.

Program: An intermediate plan that covers a broad set of activities.

Program evaluation and review technique (PERT) *and* ***critical path method (CPM):*** Network models used to plan and coordinate large-scale projects.

Project: Usually a subset of a program; the term is sometimes used as a substitute for program.

Project management: The planning and control of projects.

Project structure: A temporary function-based structure that is designed to carry out a specific project and is disassembled as each stage of the project is completed.

Proxemics: The study of interpersonal space.

Punishment: Reinforcement in which an undesired behavior is followed by an unpleasant consequence.

Purpose: The first step in planning—deciding what is to be accomplished.

Qualitative forecasting: An approach to forecasting that involves the use of judgments and opinions.

Quality circle: A group-based job design program in which a formal group of employees meets periodically during working hours to solve problems.

Quality circles: Specially formed groups consisting of three to twelve employees who meet on a regular basis to apply specific techniques and tools to problems affecting their work and work area; they subsequently present solutions and recommendations to their management for authorization.

Quality control: Follows the basic steps of the control model: Evaluate actual quality performance, compare actual performance to quality goals, and act on the differences.

Quality improvement: The process that raises quality performance to unprecedented levels.

Quality of work life (QWL): The extent to which individuals' needs in the workplace are satisfied.

Quality planning: The activity of establishing quality goals and developing the products and processes required to meet those goals.

Quantitative methods: A group of techniques that can improve problem solving by making it a more rational, analytical process.

Queueing models: Models that help a manager make choices about waiting-line problems.

Range: The variety and number of tasks in a job.

Reactive response: A response to societal demands in which the organization "fights all the way" against taking responsibility for its actions.

Receiving: The process in which various senses work in combination to detect a message and report it to the brain.

Recruitment: A series of activities intended to attract a qualified pool of job applicants.

Reengineering: Completely redesigning work to eliminate inefficiences.

Regression analysis: A statistical technique that determines the relationships between two or more variables, a dependent variable and one or more independent variables.

Reinforcement theories: Behavior that produces rewarding consequences is likely to be repeated, whereas behavior that produces no rewards or has punishing consequences is less likely to be repeated.

Related and supporting industries: The infrastructure of firms that support firms in a particular industry.

Reliability: The requirement that a test must produce the same results when taken by the same person more than once or when various forms of the same test are taken by the same person.

Resource bases: Collections of resources, including intangible assets such as employee skills and organizational knowledge, that serve as a basis for competition.

Resource-based strategy: Strategy based on the accumulation of resource bases.

Responsibility centers: Subunits of the organization to which resources are allocated for use in attaining specific objectives.

Restructuring: Redesigning the organization, often downsizing in an effort to make it more competitive.

Return on investment (ROI): A ratio that indicates the organization's income after taxes relative to its total assets. ROA = ROI

Return on total assets: A profitability ratio that indicates the success of the firm in earning profits. It is found by dividing net profits after taxes by total assets.

Revenue and expense budgets: Statements used by revenue and expense responsibility centers.

Revenue centers: Responsibility centers controlled on the basis of sales of products or services.

Rightsizing: Taking a long-term strategic perspective when examining the organization's human resource requirements. The focus is on creating not merely a lean organization, but one that provides high value to the customer.

Risk: A condition in which problem solvers lack complete certainty about the outcomes of their actions.

Risk propensity: Willingness to undertake risk for possible gain.

Robotics: The use of robots to perform a manufacturing or service function.

Role motivation: A drive stemming from enjoyment of the managerial role itself.

Rules and regulations: Plans that describe exactly how a particular situation is to be handled.

Sales forecasting: The process of predicting future sales.

Scalar chain of command: The formal distribution of organizational authority in a hierarchical fashion; defines authority relationships among individuals at different levels of the organization.

Scenario: A predicted or imagined sequence of events.

Scientific management: An approach to management that sought to find "the best way" to do the job. Scientific management had four underlying principles: the development of a true science of management; the scientific selection of the individual to fill each job; the scientific education and development of each employee so that he or she would be able to do the job properly; and cooperation between management and workers.

Selection: A process occurring before employment in which the organization determines the candidate best qualified to fill a particular position.

Selectivity: A process in which the brain sorts out what it believes to be the key stimuli from the thousands being received.

Self-efficacy: An individual's estimate of his or her capacity to affect performance on a specific task.

Shareholder value: The belief that a company's performance should be measured in terms of how much shareholders gain from what the business does.

Simulation: A model of a real-world situation that can be altered to show how changes in its various components would affect other parts of the model.

Single-use plans: Plans that are used once and discarded.

Situational approaches: Leadership theories suggesting that all factors must be considered when leadership decisions are to be made.

Situational management: A review of the key factors

Six sigma quality: A highly sought-after level of quality—99.999997 percent perfect, or no more than 3.4 defects for every million parts.

Small business: As defined by the Small Business Administration, a small business does not dominate its industry, has less than $10 million in annual sales, and has fewer than one thousand employees.

Social audit: An audit of an organization's social performance.

Social power: The power to influence various constituents.

Social power/social responsibility concept: The belief that business has a certain social responsibility because of the power it wields. If it fails to carry out that responsibility, society is likely to constrain its operations.

Social responsibility: An organization's obligation to solve problems and take actions that further both its and society's interests.

Societal ethics: A code of ethics defining behaviors that are acceptable and ethical within a society.

Societal/cultural element: The social, cultural, and demographic characteristics of the society or societies in which the organization operates.

Sociometry: An approach to the study of group structure that identifies four components of groups: a leader, a primary group, a fringe group, and an out-group.

Specialization of labor: The division of a task into smaller and smaller subunits until it can be repeated easily and successfully by an individual or group.

Stable environments: Environments that change very little.

Staff: All functions that are not desig-nated as line functions; they generally involve providing advice or assistance to the line functions.

Staff authority: Advisory authority that comes from outside a given unit's chain of command.

Staff managers: Managers who are in charge of units that provide support to the line units.

Staffing: The individual manager's role in the HRM process.

Stakeholder concept: The belief that management must account for the impact of the organization's activities on its stakeholders and take their interests into account in making decisions.

Stakeholders: Individuals and groups with a vested interest in an organization's actions.

Statistical reports: Information used to manage both the transformation process and the interrelationships among units of the organization.

Statistics: Data that have been assembled and clarified in some meaningful way.

Status symbols: Rewards used by an organization to enhance members' self-esteem and the esteem in which others hold them.

Storyboarding: A structured but flexible brainstorming process that focuses on identifying major issues and then brainstorming each of them.

Strategic alliance: An agreement by two corporations to cooperate.

Strategic audit: A detailed examination of the external environment and the organization's interface with it.

Strategic business unit (SBU): A major division within a multibusiness organization that operates much like an independent company and offers a set of distinct products to a distinct market.

Strategic control: Control concerned with the evaluation of strategy once it has been formulated or implemented.

Strategic fit: Trimming ambitions and matching strategy according to the corporation's current SWOT analysis.

Strategic intent: Ambition out of pro-portion to resources and capabilities; an obsession with winning.

Strategic management: The process of managing the pursuit of an organization's mission while managing its relationship to its environment.

Strategic plan: As used here, a business unit's principal competitive or business strategy.

Strategic planning: The process of establishing strategic objectives and formulating plans to accomplish those objectives.

Strategic thinking: Thinking through a strategy in order to provide direction.

Strategies: Major plans that commit large amounts of the organization's resources to proposed actions designed to achieve its major goals and objectives.

Strategy formulation: The process by which a corporation, business unit, or functional department determines its overall strategy.

Strengths: Internal situations that will help an organization achieve its objectives, overcome threats, overcome weaknesses, and take advantage of opportunities.

Structured problems: Routinely occurring problems that have readily identifiable attributes—the factors involved and their interrelationships. They have standard, almost automatic solutions, often referred to as programmed decisions.

Structuring by process: An approach to organizational design in which the organization examines its basic customer-related needs and structures itself to satisfy those needs.

Substitutes: Products or services whose function is similar to that of the product or service produced by the organization.

Substitutes for leadership: Systems that help define behavior and preclude the need for direct managerial actions.

Suppliers: Organizations and individuals that provide the materials an organization uses to produce outputs (including raw materials, subassemblies, labor, computer programs, energy, and others).

Supportive leadership: A leadership style in which the leader displays personal concern for subordinates.

Synergy: A condition in which the combined and coordinated actions of the parts (subsystems) of a system achieve more than all the parts could have achieved acting independently.

Systematic thinkers: People who approach a problem in a logical and rational manner.

Systems approach: A management approach that views the organization as interdependent with other systems in its environment.

Task force: A special type of group that comes together to solve a specific problem or series of problems.

Task group: A group that comes together to solve a specific problem or type of problem.

Task roles: Roles related to the task that has been assigned to a formal group or that an informal group has determined to undertake, such as offering new ideas, gathering information, and giving opinions.

Team: A group of people with shared authority, normally within the same department, who work together to identify and solve work-related problems.

Team building: A planned series of steps that begins with an examination of a group's functioning and ends with the implementation of changes to improve effectiveness.

Technology: The equipment, knowledge, materials, and experience employed in performing tasks within an organization; the organization of knowledge to achieve practical purposes. Also refers to the technicians, hardware, and software that make up the "toolbox" of an information system.

Telecommunications: A series of technologically based communication techniques and processes that assist in the management decision process.

Threat: An external environmental situation that may keep an organization from achieving its objectives.

Time series analysis: A technique in which the variable under analysis is plotted against time.

Top managers: Managers who direct their attention to the major issues affecting the organization, such as setting goals and objectives and devising strategies to meet them.

Total quality management: The creative problem-solving process of managing quality throughout the organization in order to improve its products and services and the processes by which those products and services are made or take place.

Tough-guy/macho culture: An organizational culture that develops when strategic problem solvers commit large sums of money in highly competitive situations.

Training: Programs designed to help employees gain specific job-related skills that will ensure effective performance.

Trait theories: Leadership theories that attempt to identify the common traits possessed by successful leaders.

Transactional leadership: A type of leadership in which the leader exchanges something he or she values for something valued by followers.

Transformational leadership: A type of leadership that involves changing the beliefs, needs, and values of followers.

Triad of key global markets: North America, Europe (EEC), and Japan.

TRRAP model of leadership: A model of leadership showing that leaders face five major sets of choices having to do with how much and/or what kind of task, relationship, reward, attitude, and participative behaviors to employ or emphasize.

Uncertainty: A condition in which managers cannot assign even a probability to the outcomes of the various alternatives that the problem-solving process generates.

Uncertainty avoidance: The degree to which a culture dislikes uncertainty or risk and therefore tries to reduce or avoid it.

Unethical behavior: Behavior that is outside the norms of a particular reference group.

Unit (small batch) production: The manufacture of a product or small number of products according to specific and unique customer requirements.

Unity of command: A principle stating that an individual should have only one boss.

Universality of management: The belief that management practices are applicable to all organizations.

Unstable environments: Environments that change constantly.

Unstructured problems: Nonroutine, complex problems with difficult-to-identify attributes. They normally have not been faced before and lead to unprogrammed decisions.

Valence: The value attached to a particular outcome by a particular individual.

Validity: The requirement that a test must be able to distinguish between candidates who will be successful in a job and those who will not.

Variable costs: Costs that vary with the volume of output; they normally include direct labor and material costs.

Verbal communication: Communication consisting of either speech (oral communication) or writing.

Video conferencing: The use of live television in a conference format.

Virtual corporation: A temporary network of independent companies that unite to exploit a specific opportunity.

Virus: A small unit of computer code that can attach itself to other programs, alter them, or destroy data kept on a disk.

Vision: Nonspecific directional and motivational guidance for the entire organization.

Voice mail: A system in which a computer acts as an answering machine, taking messages from callers.

Weaknesses: Internal situations that might keep the firm from achieving its objectives.

Whistleblowing: Disclosure of an illegal, immoral, or unethical action by members of the organization performing the action.

Work group: A group charged with transforming materials and other resources into products or services.

Work hard/play hard culture: An organizational culture that emerges in situations characterized by fast feedback and low risk.

Work simplification: An approach to job design in which the job is reduced to a very narrow set of tasks involving standardized procedures with little or no latitude for making decisions.

World-class competitor: A firm that is capable of competing anywhere on the globe with any firm from any country.

Written communication: The transmission of symbols in writing.

Yes/no control: A control system that consists of a specific action or series of actions that must be accomplished before the overall process can continue.

Zero defects: No defects—100 percent compliance with standards.

Zero-based budgeting: An approach to budgeting in which the budget starts at zero and all funding must be justified.

References

CHAPTER 1

1. John Byrne, "Management's New Gurus," *Business Week* (August 31, 1992), pp. 44–52, describes some of the latest approaches and their creators; also see Joann S. Lublin, "Trying to Increase Worker Productivity, More Employers Alter Management Style," *Wall Street Journal* (February 13, 1992), pp. B1, B3, for a discussion of how firms and managers are changing.
2. For a discussion of some of the benefits of several such changes, see John J. Sherwood, "Creating Work Cultures with Competitive Advantages," *Organizational Dynamics* (Winter 1988), pp. 5–26.
3. Rosabeth Moss Kanter, "The New Managerial Work," *Harvard Business Review* (November–December 1989), p. 85, for revolutionary changes, see John Byrne, loc. cit.
4. Ray Stata, "Organizational Learning—The Key to Management Innovation," *The Sloan Management Review* (Spring 1989), pp. 63–74.
5. Robert M. Fulmer first described the concept of the new management in *The New Management* (New York: Macmillan, 1976). His concept was concerned then, as mine is now, with the changes in the practice of management. He focused principally, but not exclusively, on the prescription for solving management's problems by becoming more participative. The changes occurring today are more sweeping than those in the 1970s.
6. Other themes of how managers work do exist. For example, see William Whitely, "Managerial Work Behavior: An Integration of Results from Two Major Approaches," *Academy of Management Journal* (June 1985), pp. 344–362; "How RPI Helps Locate Talent," *Business Week* (September 18, 1978), pp. 129–131.
7. For a review of their applicability to management and management education, see Stephen J. Carroll and Dennis J. Gillen, "Are the Classical Management Functions Useful in Describing Managerial Work?" *Academy of Management Review* (January 1985), pp. 38–51. Their conclusion was that the functional approach is still the best way to represent management work in educational situations.
8. I wish to thank Leon A. Dale for the addition of the phrase "uncertain future" to my original definition.

9. Author's conversation with Betty Mizzell.
10. Frank C. Barnes, "Nucor," in James M. Higgins and Julian W. Vincze, *Strategic Management: Text and Cases,* 5th ed. (Ft. Worth, Tex: Dryden 1993).
11. Frederick Rose and Pauline Yoshihashi, "Once Again, Chevron Restructures Its Vast Operations," *Wall Street Journal* (January 16, 1992), p. B4.
12. Anonymous, "Professional Profile: Ken Newton, Jr., of Hewlett-Packard," *Purchasing* (March 5, 1992), p. 45.
13. Ron Winslow, "Firms Perform Own Bypass Operations, Purchasing Health Care from the Source," *Wall Street Journal* (August 19, 1992), p. B1.
14. Lois Therrien, "Thomson Needs a Hit, and It's Up to Nizier to Go Fetch," *Business Week* (July 6, 1992), p. 80.
15. Alex Taylor, III, "A U.S. Style Shakeup at Honda," *Fortune* (December 30, 1991), pp. 115–120.
16. For example, see Barbara Ettorre, "Corporate Accountability '90s Style: The Buck Had Better Stop Here," *Management Review* (April 1992), pp. 16–21; John A. Byrne, "Can Ethics be Taught? Harvard Gives It the Old College Try," *Business Week* (April 6, 1992), p. 34; Richard P. Nielson, "Changing Unethical Behavior," *Academy of Management Executive* (May 1989), pp. 123–130; Laura L. Nash, "Ethics Without the Sermon," *Harvard Business Review* (November–December 1981), pp. 79–90; and "Businesses Are Signing Up for Ethics 101," *Business Week* (February 15, 1988), pp. 56–57.
17. T. A. Mahoney, T. H. Jerdee, and S. J. Carroll, "The Job(s) of Management," *International Relations* (February 1965), pp. 102–110.
18. Henry Mintzberg, "The Manager's Job: Folklore and Fact," *Harvard Business Review* (July–August 1975), pp. 49–61; and Lance B. Kurke and Howard E. Aldrich, "Mintzberg Was Right!: A Replication and Extension of the Nature of Managerial Work," *Management Science* (August 1983), pp. 975–984.
19. Mintzberg, ibid., p. 50.
20. Developed from "Skills of an Effective Administrator," by Robert L. Katz, *Harvard Business Review* (September–October 1974), vol. 52, p. 94. Research on two thousand managers by David McClelland and Richard Goyotzis un-

covered four primary sets of skills: goal and action management, directing subordinates, human resources management, and leadership, as reported in Mark B. Roman, "Know Thyself," *Success* (May 1987), pp. 46–52.
21. Patrick Fox, "Exploring Managers' Jobs," *International Journal of Manpower* (1991), no. 7, pp. 20–30; Charles Darwent, "The Shape of the Future," *Management Today (Anniversary Issue,* 1991), pp. 20–24; and John Sinclair and David Collins, "The Skills Time Bomb Part 3: Developing New Skills Mix," *Leadership and Organizational Development Journal* (1991), no. 5, pp. 17–20.
22. Andrew Kupfer, "Apple's Plan to Survive and Grow," *Fortune* (May 1, 1992), pp. 68–72.
23. For a review of the first-line manager's situation, see George S. Odiorne, "The New Breed of Supervisor: Leaders in Self-Managed Work Team," *Supervisor* (August 1991), pp. 14–17; Steven Kerr, Kenneth D. Hill, and Laurie Broedling. "The First-Level Supervisor: Phasing Out or Here to Stay?" *Academy of Management Review* (1986), pp. 103–117; and Leonard A. Schlesinger and Janice A. Klein, "The First-Line Supervisor: Past, Present, and Future," in Jay W. Lorsch, ed., *Handbook of Organizational Behavior* (Englewood Cliffs, N.J.: Prentice-Hall, 1987), pp. 370–382.
24. For a lengthy discussion of how the management process differs by level, see Jack Duncan, *Management* (New York: Random House, 1983).
25. Mahoney, Jerdee, and Carroll, op. cit., p. 109; Virginia R. Boehm, "What Do Managers Really Do?" Paper presented at the annual meeting of the AACSB Graduate Admissions Council, Toronto, June 15, 1981; J. P. Kolter, "What Effective General Managers Really Do," *Harvard Business Review* (November–December 1982), pp. 156–167; and G. David Hughes and Charles H. Singler, *Strategic Sales Management* (Reading, Mass.: Addison-Wesley, 1984), pp. 43–45.
26. Mintzberg, op. cit., p. 50; Kurke and Aldrich, loc. cit.
27. M. W. McCall and C. A. Sequist, "In Pursuit of the Manager's Job: Building on Mintzberg" (Greensboro, N.C.: Center for Creative Development, 1980); A. W. Lau, A. R. Newman, and L. A. Broedling, "The Nature of Managerial Work in the Public Sector," *Public Manage-*

ment Forum (1980), pp. 513–521; and Cynthia M. Parrett and Alan N. Lau, "Managerial Work: The Influence of Hierarchical Level and Functional Specialty," *Academy of Management Journal* (March 1983), pp. 170–177.

28. Boehm, loc. cit.

29. Joel Dreyfuss, "John Sculley Rises in the West," *Fortune* (July 9, 1984), pp. 180–183.

30. "The Strike That Rained on Archie McCardell's Parade," *Fortune* (May 19, 1980), pp. 90–99.

31. Author's discussion with a city official.

32. Myron D. Fottler, "Is Management Really Generic?" *Academy of Management Review* (January 1981), pp. 1–12.

33. Ibid.

34. Ibid.

35. "HRM Update," *Personnel Administrator* (February 1985), p. 12.

36. Anonymous, "Museum Gets Artsy with POS," *Chain Store Age Executive* (June 1991), pp. 44–45; Joshua Levine, "Art Chic," *Forbes* (August 21, 1989), pp. 94, 96.

37. Robert Doktor, Rosalie L. Tung, and Mary Ann Von Glinow, "Incorporating International Dimensions in Management Theory Building," *Academy of Management Review* (April 1991), pp. 259–261.

38. Michael E. Porter, *Competitive Strategy* (New York: Free Press, 1980).

39. For a discussion of both perspectives, see Henry W. Boettinger, "Is Management Really an Art?" *Harvard Business Review* (January–February 1975), pp. 54–64; and Ronald Gibbons and Shelly Hunt, "Is Management a Science?" *Academy of Management Review* (January 1978), pp. 139–144.

40. Thomas M. Mulligan, "The Two Cultures in Business Education," *Academy of Management Review* (October 1987), p. 593.

41. Amal Kumar Naj, "Allied Signal Streamlines into a Startling Turnaround," *Wall Street Journal* (May 20, 1992), p. 134.

42. For a discussion of management's challenges, some the same, some different, see Peter F. Drucker, *Managing for the Future: The 1990s and Beyond* (New York: Truman Talley Books/ Dutton, 1992), pp. 1–56; Robert B. Tucker, *Managing the Future: 10 Driving Forces of Change for the 90s* (New York: Putnam's, 1991); Editors of Research Alert, *Future Vision: The 189 Most Important Trends of the 1990s* (Naperville, Ill.: Sourcebooks Trade, 1991); John Naisbitt and Patricia Aburdene, *Megatrends 2000* (New York: Morrow, 1990); Frank Feather, *G Forces: The 35 Global Forces Restructuring Our Future* (New York: Morrow, 1989); Fred G. Steingraber, "Managing in the 1990s," *Business Horizons* (January–February 1990), pp. 50–61; Ronald Henkoff, "How to Plan for 1995," *Fortune* (December 31, 1990), pp. 70–78. For a discussion of how management may be impacted by these challenges, see Drucker, loc. cit.; Higgins and Vincze, loc. cit.; Brian Dumaine, "What the Leaders of Tomorrow See," *Fortune* (July 3, 1989), pp. 48–62; "What the Future Holds," *Centennial Edition, Wall Street Journal* (June 23, 1989); "The 21st Century Executive," *U.S. News & World Report* (March 7, 1988), pp. 48–51; Peter Nulty, "How Managers Will Manage," *Fortune* (February 2, 1987), pp. 47–50; Andrew Kupfer, "Managing Now for the 1990s," *Fortune* (September 26, 1988), pp. 44–47; and "Management for the 1990s," *Newsweek* (April 25, 1988), pp. 47–48.

43. Alvin Toffler, *Future Shock* (New York: Bantam, 1970), chap. 1.

44. Michael E. Naylor, then Executive in Charge of Strategic Planning for General Motors, speech to the Academy of Management, Chicago, August 14, 1986.

45. Steingraber, op. cit., p. 50.

46. Thomas J. Peters, *Thriving on Chaos: Hand-*

book for a Management Revolution (New York: Knopf, 1987).

47. Theodore Levitt, "Editorial," *Harvard Business Review* (January–February, 1988), p. 4.

48. Steingraber, op. cit., p. 50.

49. "Help Wanted: America Faces an Era of Worker-Scarcity That May Last to the Year 2000," *Business Week* (August 10, 1987), pp. 48–54.

50. Adapted from Michael Porter, *Competitive Strategy* (New York: Free Press, 1980), and William K. Hall, "Survival Strategies in a Hostile Environment," *Harvard Business Review* (September–October 1980), pp. 73–86.

51. Brian Dumaine, "Closing the Innovation Gap," *Fortune* (December 2, 1991), pp. 56–62; Tom Peters, "Get Innovative or Get Dead," *California Management Review* (Fall 1990), pp. 9–26; (Winter 1991), pp. 9–23.

52. Susan B. Garland, "Those Aging Boomers," *Business Week* (May 20, 1991), pp. 106–112. For a review of the demographics, see "Needed: Human Capital," *Business Week* (September 19, 1988), pp. 102–103; and William B. Johnston and Arnold H. Packer, *Workforce 2000: Work and Workers for the 21st Century* (Indianapolis, Ind.: Hudson Institute, 1987).

53. Nancy J. Perry, "The Workers of the Future," *Fortune Special Issue: The New American Century* (1991), pp. 68–72.

54. Arie de Geus, "Planning as Learning," *Harvard Business Review,* (March–April 1988), pp. 70–74.

55. Ikujiro Novaka, "The Knowledge Creating Company," *Harvard Business Review* (November–December 1991), pp. 96–109; Thomas A. Stewart, "Brainpower," *Fortune* (June 3, 1991), pp. 44–57.

56. Edward H. Gramlich, "U.S. Federal Budget Deficits and Gramm-Rudman-Hollings," *American Economic Review* (May 1990), pp. 75–80.

57. Charles W. L. Hill, Michael A. Hitt, and Robert E. Hoskisson, "Declining U.S. Competitiveness: Reflections on a Crisis," *Academy of Management Executive* (January 1988), pp. 51–60.

58. Robert T. Green and Trina A. Larson, "Only Retaliation Will Open Up Japan," *Harvard Business Review* (November–December 1987), pp. 22–28.

59. *Business Week Special Issue: The Quality Imperative* (June 1991); Barry K. Spiker, "Total Quality Management: The Mind-Set for Competitiveness in the 1990s," *Manufacturing Systems* (September 1991), pp. 40–45.

60. For example, see William P. Hewlett (chairman and co-founder of Hewlett-Packard), "Graduation Speech" as reported in Helen Pike, "Hewlett Sounds Call for Engineering Creativity in MIT Graduate Speech," *Electronic Engineering Times* (June 23, 1986), p. 78; John Sculley (CEO and chairman of Apple Computer), "Speech to MacWorld," February 1988, in which he indicated that only the innovative firm would survive in the future; Jack Welch (CEO and chairman of GE), who sees innovation driving productivity, which drives competition, as quoted in Thomas A. Stewart, "GE Keeps Those Ideas Coming," *Fortune* (August 12, 1991), pp. 41–49; Michael E. Porter (researcher and consultant), *The Competitive Advantage of Nations* (New York: Free Press, 1990), pp. 578–579, in which he observes that innovation, continuous improvement, and change are the cornerstones of global competitiveness; Michael E. Porter, *Competitive Strategy* (New York: Free Press, 1980), pp. 177–179, in which he discusses the criticality of innovation to competitiveness; Richard N. Foster (consultant), *Innovation: The Attacker's Advantage* (New York: Summit Books, 1986), p. 21, in which he indicates that in his thirty years at McKinsey & Company, every success-

ful firm he saw was innovative; Thomas J. Peters (consultant and researcher), op. cit., pp. 191–280, in which he indicates that innovation is one of five prescriptions for chaos (accelerating change, complex environment, global competition, and other challenges); and *Business Week* which considered the topic of innovation so critical to U.S. competitiveness, it devoted two special issues to it, in June 1989 and June 1990.

61. James M. Higgins, *101 Creative Problem Solving Techniques: Handbook of New Ideas* (Winter Park, Fla: New Management, 1993), p. 5.

62. M. Scott Myers, *Every Employee a Manager,* 3rd ed. (San Diego, Calif.: Pfeiffer, 1991).

C H A P T E R   2

1. Much of the discussion in these paragraphs is taken from Alan M. Kantrow, "Why History Matters to Managers," *Harvard Business Review* (January–February 1986), pp. 81–88.

2. These are condensed from the six approaches reported in Harold Koontz, "The Management Theory Jungle," *Journal of the Academy of Management* (December 1961), pp. 174–188; and the eleven reported in Harold Koontz, "The Management Theory Jungle Revisited," *Academy of Management Review* (April 1980), pp. 175–187.

3. Much of the discussion that follows on the evolution of management theory is derived from Daniel A. Wren, *The Evolution of Management Thought,* 2nd ed. (New York: Wiley, 1979), and Claude S. George, Jr., *The History of Management Thought,* 2nd ed. (Englewood Cliffs, N.J.: Prentice-Hall, 1972)

4. Wren, ibid., p. 3.

5. Ibid., chap. 22.

6. James D. Mooney and Alan C. Reiley, *The Principles of Organization* (New York: Harper & Row, 1947), pp. 1–34.

7. 1865 is a somewhat arbitrary year, but official statistics report agriculture as providing only 48 percent of the jobs in that year, apparently the first time since records were kept that it accounted for less than half. The statistics are cited in Stanley M. Davis, *Future Perfect* (Reading, Mass.: Addison-Wesley, 1987), p. 97. Davis discussed this point in a paper presented to the Strategic Management Society, Boston, October 14, 1987.

8. G. R. Butler, "Frederick Winslow Taylor: The Father of Scientific Management and His Philosophy Revisited," *Industrial Management* (May–June 1991), pp. 22–25, 27; Frederick W. Taylor, *The Principles of Scientific Management* (New York: Harper & Row, 1911), reissued as part of Frederick W. Taylor, *Scientific Management* (New York: Harper & Row, 1947). Both books share the same pagination.

9. Taylor, ibid.

10. Taylor, op. cit., p. 140.

11. Taylor, op. cit., pp. 40–50.

12. Anthony Corbo and Brian H. Keimer, "How to Effectively Link Compensation to Performance," *Industrial Management* (May–June 1991), pp. 21–22.

13. Butler, loc. cit.

14. Wallace Clark, *The Gantt Chart: Working Tool of Management* (New York, Ronald Press, 1922).

15. Mike Heck, "The Critical Path," *Infoworld* (November 26, 1990), pp. 67–90; Lamont Wood, "A Manager's Guide to Computerized Project Management," *Manufacturing Systems* (August 1989), pp. 18–24.

16. Henry L. Gantt, *Organizing for Work* (New York: Harcourt, 1919), p. 15.

17. Frank B. Gilbreth, Jr., and Ernestine Gilbreth Carrie, *Cheaper by the Dozen* (New York: Crowell, 1948).

18. See William R. Spriegel and Clark E. Meyers,

The Writings of the Gilbreths (Homewood, Ill.: Irwin, 1953).

19. See Lillian M. Gilbreth, *The Psychology of Management* (New York: Sturgis and Walton, 1914).

20. Earnest R. Archer, "Toward a Revival of the Principles of Management," *Industrial Management* (January–February 1990), pp. 19–22.

21. Max Weber, *The Theory of Social and Economic Organization*, ed. and trans. by A. M. Henderson and Talcott Parsons (New York: Free Press, 1947), pp. 329–333, adapted. Note that Weber was concerned with public organizations, whereas our discussion focuses on business organizations.

22. Ibid.

23. Henry C. Metcalf and Lyndall Urwick, eds., *Dynamic Administration: The Collected Papers of Mary Parker Follett* (New York: Harper & Row, 1940); and Mary Parker Follett, *Creative Experience* (London: Longmans, Green, 1924), chap. 5.

24. James F. Wolf, "The Legacy of Mary Parker Follett," *Bureaucrat* (Winter 1988–1989), pp. 53–57.

25. Mary Parker Follett, "The Process of Control," in L. Gulick and Lyndall Urwick, eds., *Papers on the Science of Administration* (New York: Institute of Public Administration, Columbia University Press, 1937), p. 161.

26. Metcalf and Urwick, op. cit., p. 262.

27. Chester I. Barnard, *The Functions of the Executive* (Cambridge, Mass.: Harvard University Press, 1938), p. 6.

28. Ibid., p. 4.

29. Ibid., p. 72.

30. Ibid., p. 115.

31. Ibid., p. 163.

32. Ibid., pp. 217–230.

33. Elton Mayo, *The Human Problems of an Industrial Civilization* (New York: Macmillan, 1933), pp. 71–72; also see Fritz J. Roethlisberger and W. J. Dickson, *Management and the Worker* (Cambridge, Mass.: Harvard University Press, 1939).

34. Ibid., p. 78.

35. Wren, op. cit., p. 290.

36. James R. Miller and Howard Feldman, "Management Science—Theory, Relevance, and Practice in the 1980s," *Interfaces* (October 1983), pp. 56–60.

37. Robert A. Gordon and James E. Howe, *Higher Education for Business* (New York: Columbia University Press, 1959).

38. Herbert A. Simon, *The New Science of Management Decisions* (New York: Harper & Row, 1960).

39. Fremont E. Kast and James E. Rosenzweig, "General Systems Theory: Applications for Organization and Management," *Academy of Management Journal* (December 1972), pp. 447–465.

40. See Ludwig von Bertalanffy, Carl G. Hempel, Robert E. Bass, and Hans Jones, "General Systems Theory: A New Approach to Unity of Science," *Human Biology* (December 1951), pp. 302–361; Ludwig von Bertalanffy, "General Systems Theory—A Critical Review," Walter Buckley, ed. *Modern Systems Research for the Behavioral Scientists* (Chicago: Aldine, 1968), p. 13; Ludwig von Bertalanffy, *General Systems Theory: Foundations, Development, Applications* (New York: Braziller, 1968); and Ludwig von Bertalanffy, *Organismic Psychology and Systems Theory* (Barre, Mass.: Clark University Press, 1968).

41. Kast and Rosenzweig, loc. cit.

42. Thomas A. Stewart, "The Search for the Organization of Tomorrow," *Fortune* (May 18, 1992), pp. 92–98.

43. Fred E. Fiedler, *A Theory of Leadership Effectiveness* (New York: McGraw-Hill, 1967), p. 147.

44. Paul Hersey and Kenneth H. Blanchard, *Management of Organizational Behavior: Utilizing Human Resources* (Englewood Cliffs, N.J.: Prentice-Hall, 1977). (First published in 1969 with earlier published material preceding the book.)

45. Fred Luthans, "The Contingency Theory of Management: A Path Out of the Jungle," *Business Horizons* (June 1973), pp. 62–72.

46. Charles Hofer, *Academy of Management Journal* (December 1975), pp. 784–810.

47. Koontz, "Management Theory Jungle Revisited," op. cit., p. 175.

48. William G. Ouchi, *Theory Z: How American Business Can Meet the Japanese Challenge* (Reading, Mass.: Addison-Wesley, 1981); Richard T. Pascale and Anthony G. Athos, *The Art of Japanese Management* (New York: Simon & Schuster, 1981).

49. "The Difference Japanese Management Makes," *Business Week* (July 14, 1986), pp. 47–50.

50. Dean M. Schroeder and Alan G. Robinson, "America's Most Successful Export to Japan: Continuous Improvement Programs," *Sloan Management Review* (Spring 1991), pp. 67–81.

51. Jeremiah J. Sullivan, "A Critique of Theory Z," *Academy of Management Review* (January 1983), pp. 132–142; J. Bernard Keys and Thomas R. Miller, "The Japanese Management Theory Jungle," *Academy of Management Review* (April 1984), pp. 345–356; S. Prakash Sethi, Nobuaki Namiki, and Carl L. Swanson, *The Attack on Theory Z: The False Promise of the Japanese Miracle* (Marshfield, Mass.: Pitman, 1984); and Peter F. Drucker, "'Behind Japan's Successes," *Harvard Business Review* (January–February 1981), pp. 83–90.

52. Thomas J. Peters and Robert H. Waterman, Jr., *In Search of Excellence* (New York: Harper & Row, 1982).

53. For example, see Barbara Levin, "Chevron's HR Conference: Strategic Planning to Meet Corporate Goals," *HR Focus* (May 1992), p. 9.

54. Ibid., chap. 3.

55. Thomas J. Peters, *Thriving on Chaos: Handbook for a Management Revolution* (New York: Knopf, 1987).

56. R. Duane Ireland and Michael A. Hitt, "Peters and Waterman Revisited: The Unended Quest for Excellence," *Academy of Management Executive* (May 1987), pp. 91–99; "Who's Excellent Now," *Business Week* (November 5, 1984), pp. 76–77; Daniel T. Carroll, "A Disappointing Search for Excellence," *Harvard Business Review* (November–December 1983), pp. 78–80; and Kenneth E. Aupperle, William Acar, David E. Booth, "An Empirical Critique of *In Search of Excellence*: How Excellent Are the Excellent Companies?" *Journal of Management* (December 1986), pp. 499–512.

57. John Byrne, "Management's New Gurus," *Business Week* (August 31, 1992), pp. 44–52.

58. Beth Enslow, "The Benchmarking Bonanza," *Across the Board* (April 1992), pp. 16–22; Steven Sillyman, "Guide to Benchmarking Resources," *Quality* (March 1992), pp. 17–18.

59. Edward R. Zilbert, proposes Theory E management, E for eclectic, in "Management in the 1990s," *Journal of Management Development* (1991), no. 2, pp. 7–14; and Gordon A. Pierce, in "Management Philosophies: What Comes After Theory Z?" *Journal of Systems Management* (June 1991), pp. 9–12, proposes Theory A, which would extract features from theories Y and Z. See also Lewis E. Schultz, "The Rings of Management: The New Management Theory," *Human Systems Management* (1991), no. 1., pp. 11–17.

60. Peters, loc. cit.; Robert H. Waterman, Jr., *The Renewal Factor* (New York: Bantam, 1987); Thomas J. Peters and Nancy K. Austin, *Passion for Excellence* (New York: Random House, 1986); Thomas J. Peters and Robert H. Waterman, Jr., *In Search of Excellence*, a television program aired on the Public Broadcasting System in 1985; and Peters and Waterman, loc. cit.

61. John Byrne, loc. cit.; George S. Odiorne, "Chaos in Management," *Manage* (August 1991), pp. 4–7; Robert Doktor, Rosalie L. Tung, and MaryAnn Von Glvinow, "Future Directions for Management Theory Development," *Academy of Management Review* (April 1991), pp. 362–365; Zilbert, loc. cit.; and Schultz, loc. cit.

CHAPTER 3

1. Paul Ingrassia and Timothy Aeppel, "Gearing Up: Worried by Japanese, Thriving GM Europe Vows to Get Leaner," *Wall Street Journal* (July 7, 1992), p. A1.

2. Stewart Toy, "Europe's Shakeout," *Business Week* (September 14, 1992), pp. 44–51.

3. "Ford Annual Report," (Detroit Michigan: Ford Motor Company, 1992).

4. "Business Without Borders," *U.S. News & World Report* (June 20, 1988), p. 48.

5. For example, Robert B. Tucker, *Managing the Future: 10 Driving Forces of Change for the '90s* (New York: Putnam, 1991); Editors of Research Alert, *Future Vision: The 189 Most Important Trends of the 1990s* (Naperville, Ill., Sourcebooks–Trade, 1991); Thomas J. Peters, *Thriving on Chaos: Handbook for a Management Revolution* (New York: Knopf, 1987); and John Naisbitt, *Megatrends* (New York: Warner, 1982).

6. Amanda Bennett, "Going Global: The Chief Executives in the Year 2000 Will Be Experienced Abroad," *Wall Street Journal* (February 27, 1989), pp. A1, A9.

7. Joann S. Lublin, "Younger Managers Learn Global Skills," *Wall Street Journal* (March 31, 1992), p. B1.

8. "The Fortune Directory of the 50 Largest Commercial-Banking Companies Outside the United States," *Fortune* (August 10, 1981), p. 220; "The Largest Commercial Banking Companies," *Fortune* (July 31, 1981), p. 117.

9. "Will We Ever Close the Trade Gap? *Business Week* (February 27, 1989), pp. 86, 92.

10. "Fitting into a Global Economy," *U.S. News & World Report* (December 26, 1988), p. 80.

11. R. Taggart Murphy, "Power Without Purpose: The Crisis of Japan's Global Financial Dominance," *Harvard Business Review* (March–April, 1989), pp. 71–94. This article describes the tremendous influence the Japanese have financially in the world.

12. John Meehan, "Now the Third World May Do Banks a World of Good," *Business Week* (June 8, 1992), pp. 94, 96; Norman Peagam, "The New Era in U.S. Banking: After the Bloodbath," *Euromoney* (March 1992), pp. S1–S2; Peter Truell, "Third World Debt Proposal Should Benefit Some Banks," *Wall Street Journal* (March 16, 1989), p. A9; and Charles F. McCoy and Peter Truell, "Lending Imbroglio: Worries Deepen Again on Third World Debt as Brazil Stops Paying," *Wall Street Journal* (March 3, 1987), pp. 1, 24.

13. Karen Elliot House, "The 90s & Beyond: As Power Is Disbursed Among Nations the Need for Leadership Grows," *Wall Street Journal* (February 21, 1989), pp. A1, A10.

14. Karen Elliot House, "The 90s & Beyond: For All Its Difficulties, the U.S. Stands to Retain Its Global Leadership," *Wall Street Journal* (January 23, 1989), pp. A1, A8; plus the events in Eastern Europe in November 1989, the opening of the Berlin Wall, and political and economic reforms in virtually all of Eastern Europe.

15. Robert B. Reich, "Who Is Them?" *Harvard Business Review* (March–April, 1991), pp. 77–88.

16. Kenichi Ohmae, *Triad Power* (New York: Free Press, 1985).
17. William G. Ouchi, *Theory Z: How American Business Can Meet the Japanese Challenge* (Reading, Mass.: Addison-Wesley, 1981).
18. Norman Coates, "Determinants of Japan's Business Success: Some Japanese Executives' Views, *Academy of Management Executive* (January 1988); pp. 69–72.
19. Edmund Faltermayer, "Does Japan Play Fair?" *Fortune* (September 7, 1992), pp. 38–52; Robert T. Green and Trina L. Larsen, "Only Retaliation Will Open Up Japan," *Harvard Business Review* (November–December 1987), pp. 22–28.
20. James C. Abegglen and George Stalk, Jr., "The Japanese Corporation As Competitor," *California Management Review* (Spring 1986), pp. 9–27.
21. Clay Chandler, Jacob M. Schleisinger, and John Bussey, "Gearing Down: Japan Economy, Built on Rapid Expansion, Forces Wrenching Shift," *Wall Street Journal* (December 7, 1992), pp. A1, A9; Bill Powell, "How Badly Is Japan Hurting?" *Newsweek* (August 31, 1992), p. 73.
22. Unless otherwise indicated, this list of factors is principally derived from "Labor Letter, Japan at Work," *Wall Street Journal* (March 3, 1993), p. A1, describes several recent trends in Japanese labor markets including reduced overtime, an aging workforce, and affluent and less-willing-to-work younger citizens; "Japan in the 1990s," *Tokyo Business Today* (January 1990), pp. 4–18; Carla Rappaport, "How the Japanese Are Changing," *Fortune* (Fall 1990), no. 8; pp. 15–22; "How Japan Is Changing," *Europe* (May 1990), pp. 10–12; "Hour of Power?" *Newsweek* (February 27, 1989), pp. 14–20; Lee Smith, "Divisive Forces in an Inbred Nation," *Fortune* (March 30, 1987), pp. 24–28; Joel Dreyfuss, "Fear and Trembling in the Colossus," *Fortune* (March 30, 1987), pp. 30–38; and Gene Bylinsky, "Trying to Transcend Copycat Science," *Fortune* (March 30, 1987), pp. 42–46. Where the sources are substantiated by other facts, additional footnotes will be indicated.
23. "Labor Letter: Japan at Work," op. cit.; Masayoshi Kanabayashi, "Bucking Tradition: In Japan, Employees Are Switching Firms for Better Work, Pay," *Wall Street Journal* (October 11, 1990), pp. A1, A19.
24. Ted Holden, "Revenge of the 'Office Ladies,'" *Business Week* (July, 13, 1992), pp. 42–43; Djehane A. Hosni, "Women in the Japanese Labour Market," *Equal Opportunities International* (1990), vol. 9, no. 6, pp. 11–14.
25. Karen Lowry Miller, "Now Japan Admits it: Work Kills Executives," *Business Week* (August 3, 1992), p. 35; "The High Price Japanese Pay for Success," *Business Week* (April 7, 1988), pp. 52–54; and Kathryn Graven, "The Home Front: Japanese Housewives Grow More Resentful of Executive Spouses," *Wall Street Journal* (September 30, 1987), pp. A1, A25.
26. "The Graying of Japan," *U.S. News & World Report* (September 30, 1991), pp. 65–73.
27. John J. Curran, "Why Japan Will Emerge Stronger," *Fortune* (May 18, 1992), pp. 45–56; and Richard I. Kirkland, Jr., "What If Japan Triumphs?" *Fortune* (May 18, 1992), pp. 60–67.
28. "Japan Builds a New Power Base," *Business Week* (April 10, 1989), pp. 42–45.
29. Stewart B. Toy, Jonathan B. Levine, Mark Maremont, and Karen Lowry Miller, "The Battle for Europe: Japan Muscles in on the West—and a Shakeout Begins," *Business Week* (June 3, 1991), pp. 44–52.
30. "Battle for the Future," *Time* (January 16, 1989), pp. 42–43.
31. Jacob M. Schlesinger, Clay Chandler, and John Bussey, "About Face: Era of Slower Growth Brings a Strange Sight—Japan Restructuring," *Wall Street Journal* (December 8, 1992), pp. A1, A10.
32. Tim Impoco, Nick Cumming, and Hannah Moore, "Where Growth is Job One," *U.S. News & World Report,* (December 21, 1992), pp. 70–75; Richard Miller, "Profiting in the Pacific Rim," *Target Marketing* (July 1990), pp. 26, 28; "Can Asia's Four Tigers Be Tamed?" *Business Week* (February 15, 1988), pp. 46–50.
33. Mark M. Nelson, "EEC Is Swamped by Would-Be Members," *Wall Street Journal* (May 13, 1992), p. A10; Shawn Tully, "Now the New New Europe," *Fortune* (December 2, 1991), pp. 136, 142.
34. Shawn Tully, "Europe 1992: More Unity Than You Think," *Fortune* (August 10, 1992), pp. 136–142; Stewart Toy, "Europe's Shakeout: The Race to Restructure Is Getting Frantic," *Business Week* (September 14, 1992), pp. 44–51.
35. Shawn Tully, "Europe Gets Ready for 1992," *Fortune* (February 1988), p. 81.
36. Richard A. Melcher, "Continental Drift: Now, A Two-Tiered Economy May Evolve," *Business Week* (October 5, 1992), pp. 34–38.
37. Toy, op. cit., p. 44.
38. Joe Radigan, "E Pluribus Europe," *Bank Systems & Technology* (December 1991), pp. 50–54.
39. G. J. van der Akken, presentation to the Strategic Management Society, Amsterdam, The Netherlands, October 18, 1988.
40. Shawn Tully, "Europe 1992: More Unity Than You Think," op. cit.
41. Kenneth H. Bacon, "Quick Reaction: Trade Pact Is Likely to Step Up Business Even Before Approval," *Wall Street Journal* (August 13, 1992), pp. A1, A4.
42. Robert H. Hayes and William J. Abernathy, "Managing Our Way to Economic Decline," *Harvard Business Review* (July–August 1980), pp. 67–77.
43. Charles W. L. Hill, Michael A. Hitt, and Robert E. Hoskisson, "Declining U.S. Competitiveness: Reflections on a Crisis," *Academy of Management Executive* (1988), no. 1, pp. 51–60.
44. Ibid., p. 53.
45. Kevin Kelly, "Maybe Caterpillar Can Pick Up Where it Left Off," *Business Week* (April 27, 1992); Ronald Henkoff, "The Cat Is Acting Like a Tiger," *Fortune* (December 19, 1988), pp. 70–76.
46. China is showing a surprise move to capitalism. See Ford S. Worthy, "Where Capitalism Thrives in China," *Fortune* (March 9, 1992), pp. 71–75, and James McGregor, "Reality is Overtaking Ideology in China," *Wall Street Journal* (March 2, 1992), p. A9. The CIS is having its problems. See Douglas Stanglin and Victoria Pope, "The Wreck of Russia," *U.S. News & World Report* (December 7, 1992), pp. 40–49.
47. Stephen Baker and Elizabeth Weiner, "Latin America: The Big Move to Free Markets," *Business Week* (June 15, 1992), pp. 50–55; Geri Smith and John Pearson, "The New World's Newest Trade Bloc," *Business Week* (May 4, 1992), pp. 50–51.
48. Michael E. Porter, "Changing Patterns of International Competition," *California Management Review* (Winter 1986), pp. 9–40.
49. Michael E. Porter, *The Competitive Advantage of Nations and Their Firms* (New York: Free Press, 1989). For a discussion of the more technical parameters of the definition of global strategy, see Gary Hamel and C. K. Prahalad, "Do You Really Have a Global Strategy?" *Harvard Business Review* (July–August 1985), pp. 139–148.
50. Stefan H. Robock and Kenneth Simmonds, *International Business and Multi-National Enterprises,* 3rd ed. (Homewood, Ill.: Irwin, 1983), p. 7.
51. Christopher M. Korth, *International Business, Environment of Management,* 2nd ed. (Englewood Cliffs, N.J.: Prentice-Hall, 1985), p. 7; Neil H. Jacoby, "The Multinational Corporation," *The Center Magazine* (May 1970), pp. 37–55.
52. *Wall Street Journal* (April 25, 1988), p. 26.
53. R. Hall Mason, "Conflicts Between Host Countries and a Multi-National Enterprise," *California Management Review* (Fall 1974), pp. 5–14.
54. Robock and Simmonds, op. cit., pp. 243–249.
55. Author's personal observations based on extensive research. The Japanese admit the need to bolster their R&D efforts in basic research.
56. For a study of differences between Japanese and U.K. companies, see Toyohiro Kono, "Long Range Planning of U.K. and Japanese Corporations—A Comparative Study," *Long Range Planning* (1984), no. 2, pp. 58–76.
57. Donald A. Ball and Wendell H. McCulloch, Jr., *International Business: Introduction in Essentials,* 2nd ed. (Plano, Tex.: Business Publications, 1985), pp. 39–48.
58. Alex Taylor, III, "Who's Ahead in the World Auto War?" *Fortune* (November 9, 1987), pp. 74–88.
59. James B. Treece, "Can Ford Stay on Top?" *Business Week* (September 28, 1987), pp. 78–86.
60. Lois Therrien, "McRisky," *Business Week* (October 21, 1991), pp. 114–122.
61. Kenichi Ohmae, "The Global Logic Strategic Alliances," *Harvard Business Review* (March–April 1989), pp. 143–154; Howard Perlmutter and David Heenan, "Cooperate to Compete Globally," *Harvard Business Review* (March–April 1986), pp. 136–152. Perlmutter and Heenan designate these alliances as global strategic partnerships (GSPs).
62. For a lengthy discussion of factors involved in making this choice, see Derek F. Channon, with Michael Jalland, *Multi-National Strategic Planning* (New York: Amacom, 1978), pp. 193–194.
63. Michael Porter, "Why National Triumph," *Fortune* (March 12, 1990), pp. 94–95, excerpted from Michael Porter, *The Competitive Advantage of Nations* (New York: Macmillan, 1990).
64. Geert Hofstede, "Motivation, Leadership, and Organization: Do American Theories Apply Abroad?" *Organizational Dynamics* (Summer 1980), pp. 42–63.
65. Geert Hofstede, *Culture's Consequences,* abridged ed. (Beverly Hills: Sage, 1984), pp. 72, 92, 132–133, 166–167.
66. See H. Landis Gabel and Anthony E. Hall, "Ford of Europe and Local Content Regulations," in James M. Higgins and Julian W. Vincze, eds., *Strategic Management: Text and Cases,* 4th ed. (Ft. Worth, Tex.: Dryden, 1987), pp. 944–972.
67. Mozamo P. Magaliso, "The Corporate Social Challenge for the Multinational Corporation," *Journal of Business Ethics* (July 1992), pp. 491–500; Brian Bremner, "Doing the Right Thing in South Africa?" *Business Week* (April 27, 1992), pp. 60, 64; "Pull Out Parade," *Time* (November 3, 1986), pp. 32, 34; "All Roads Lead Out of South Africa," *Business Week* (November 3, 1986), pp. 24–25; and "Fighting Apartheid, American Style," *U.S. News & World Report* (October 22, 1986), pp. 45–46.

C H A P T E R   4

1. James R. Evans, "Quality Improvement and Creative Problem Solving," *Production & Inventory Management* (Fourth Quarter 1990), pp. 29–32.
2. For a discussion of the importance of problem solving, see E. Frank Harrison, *The Managerial Decision-Making Process* (Boston: Houghton Mifflin, 1987), pp. 1–3. Note that he defines the terms *decision making* and *problem solving* somewhat differently than is done in this text.

For a perspective on CPS that was way ahead of its time, see Carl E. Gregory, *The Management of Intelligence* (New York: McGraw-Hill, 1962).

3. Marc Hequet, "Creativity Training Gets Creative," *Training* (February 1992), p. 44.

4. Based on George T. Huber, *Managerial Decision Making* (Chicago: Scott, Foresman, 1980), p. 8.

5. For a thorough discussion, see David A. Cowan, "Developing a Process Model of Problem Recognition," *Academy of Management Review* (October 1986), pp. 763–776.

6. W. F. Pounds, "The Process of Problem Finding," *Industrial Management Review* (Fall 1969), pp. 1–19; support for Pounds's research was found by C. E. Watson, "The Problem of Problem Finding," *Business Horizons* (August 1976), pp. 94–99.

7. W. F. Pounds, op. cit., p. 95.

8. Marjorie A. Lyles and Ian I. Mitroff, "Organizational Problem Formulation: An Empirical Study," *Administrative Science Quarterly* (March 1980), pp. 102–119.

9. Herbert Simon, *Administrative Behavior* (New York: Free Press, 1957).

10. Mark Brown, "Doubts: Some Thoughts on the Practice of Creative Problem Solving," *Leadership & Organization Development Journal* (1991), no. 6, pp. 15–17.

11. Annetta Miller, "Blindsided by the Future," *Newsweek* (August 31, 1992), p. 72.

12. Randall D. Brandt and Kevin L. Reffett, "Focusing on Customer Problems to Improve Quality," *Journal of Service Marketing* (Fall 1989), pp. 5–14.

13. Peter F. Drucker, *Innovation and Entrepreneurship: The Practice and Principles* (New York: Harper & Row, 1985).

14. Howard H. Stevenson, "Defining Corporate Strengths and Weaknesses," *Sloan Management Review* (Spring 1976), pp. 51–66.

15. N. Mohan Reddy, "Market Opportunity Analysis for Emerging Technologies," *Management Decision* (1990), no. 8, pp. 10–19.

16. For a discussion of the multiple purposes of the problem statement, see Roger J. Volkema, "Problem Formulation as Purposeful Activity," *Strategic Management Journal* (May–June 1986), pp. 267–279.

17. Allan R. Cohen, Stephen L. Rink, Herman Gadon, and Robin D. Willits, *Effective Behavior in Organizations*, 4th ed. (Homewood, Ill.: Irwin, 1988), pp. 24–29.

18. Sara Kiesler and Lee Sproull, "Managerial Response to Changing Environments: Perspectives on Problem Sensing from Social Cognition," *Administrative Science Quarterly* (December 1982), pp. 548–570; and Hillel J. Einhorn and Robin M. Hogarth, "Decision Making in Reverse," *Harvard Business Review* (January–February 1987), pp. 66–70. Einhorn and Hogarth also report problems with linking events—that is, misinterpreting causal relationships. Managers think they see relationships that do not exist, partly because they do not look long and hard enough for other relationships. Factors such as ego, prior attributions, and group processes can affect an individual's view of the cause of a problem. It may distort it. See Jeffrey D. Ford, "The Effects of Causal Attributions on Decision Makers' Responses to Performance Downturns," *Academy of Management Review* (October 1985), pp. 770–786.

19. Michael Simpson, "Opportunities for Innovation in the Metal Industry," *Journal of Business Strategy* (Summer 1986), pp. 84–87.

20. James M. Higgins, "The Leadership TRRAP," *Human Relations: Behavior at Work* (New York: Random House, 1987), pp. 206–210.

21. "Eureka: New Ideas for Boosting Creativity," *Success* (December 1985), p. 27.

22. Danny Miller, "Towards a Contingency Theory of Strategy Formulation," *Proceedings* (Academy of Management, 1975), pp. 64–66. National Meeting, August 10–13, 1975, New Orleans.

23. "Getting a Clearer View of Smog," *Business Week: Special Issue on Innovation in America* (June 1989), p. 73.

24. John Byrne, "Management's New Gurus," *Business Week* (August 31, 1992), p. 50.

25. Karen Lowry Miller, "55 Miles Per Gallon: How Honda Did It," *Business Week* (September 23, 1991), pp. 82–83.

26. Mike Vance, "Storyboarding" from "Creative Thinking," a series of audio cassette tapes on creativity, taken from the accompanying booklet to the tape series (Chicago: Nightingale-Conant, 1982); Jerry McNellis, "An Experience in Creative Thinking" (New Brighton, Pa.: McNellis Company, n.d.; and Lawrence F. Lottier, Jr., "Storyboarding Your Way to Successful Training, *Public Personnel Management* (Winter 1986), pp. 421–427.

27. Sheridan M. Tatsuno, "Breakthroughs: The Japanese Way," *R&D Magazine* (February 1990), pp. 136–142.

28. Andrew L. Delbecq and Andrew H. Van de Ven, "A Group Process Model for Problem Identification and Program Planning," *Journal of Applied Behavioral Science* (1971), pp. 466–492.

29. Christian N. Madu, Chu-Hua Kuei, and Assumpta N. Madu, "Setting Priorities for the I7 Industry in Taiwan—A Delphi Study," *Long Range Planning* (October 1991), pp. 105–118; Anonymous, "The Industry Executive: Making it in Europe 1992, *Canadian Insurance* (June 1991), p. 16; Yeong Wee Yong, Kau Ah Keng, and Tan Leng Leng, "A Delphi Forecast for the Singapore Tourism Industry: Future Scenario and Marketing Implications," *International Marketing Review* (1989), no. 3, pp. 35–46.

30. Based on, but not limited to, Lyle Sussman and Samuel D. Deep, *Comex: The Communication Experience in Human Relations* (Cincinnati: South-Western, 1980), p. 120; Norman R. F. Maier, "Assets and Liabilities in Group Problem Solving," *Psychological Review* (1967), pp. 239–249; and Gayle W. Hill, "Group Versus Individual Performance: Are N + 1 Heads Better Than One?" *Psychological Bulletin* (1982), pp. 517–539.

31. Maier, ibid.; Hill, ibid.

32. James A. F. Stoner, "Risky and Cautious Shifts in Group Decisions: The Influence of Widely Held Values," *Journal of Experimental Social Psychology* (1988), no., 4, pp. 442–459.

33. Simon, loc. cit.; James G. March and Herbert A. Simon, *Organizations* (New York: Wiley, 1958); D. W. Taylor, "Decision Making and Problem Solving," *Handbook of Organizations*, James G. March, ed. (Chicago: Rand McNally, 1965), pp. 48–68; Peer Sollberg, "Unprogrammed Decision Making," in *Research Toward Development and the Management Thought*, Proceedings, Academy of Management, H. P. Hotenstein and R. W. Williams, eds. (1967), pp. 3–16; Marcus Alexis and Charles Z. Wilson, eds., *Organizational Decision Making* (Englewood Cliffs, N.J.: Prentice-Hall, 1967), pp. 76–78; C. E. Lindblom, "The Science of Muddling Through," *Public Administration Review* (Spring 1959), pp. 79–88; J. V. Baldridge, *Power and Conflict in the University* (New York: Wiley, 1971); E. E. Carter, "The Behavioral Theory of the Firm and the Top Level of Corporate Decision," *Administrative Science Quarterly* (December 1971), pp. 414–429; and H. Mintzberg, D. Raisinghani, and A. Theoret, "The Structure of 'Unstructured' Decision Processes," *Administrative Science Quarterly* (June 1976), p. 58.

34. Simon, loc. cit.

35. Anna Grandori, "A Prescriptive Contingency View of Organizational Decision Making," *Administrative Science Quarterly* (1984), pp. 192–209.

36. Pounds, loc. cit.; Drucker, loc. cit.

37. Ian I. Mitroff, "On Helping a Large Governmental Organization to Do Research and Planning on Itself: A Case Study," unpublished working paper, University of Pittsburgh, undated, but in the 1973–1974 time frame; Ian I. Mitroff and Tom R. Featherington, "On Systemic Problem Solving and the Error of the Third Kind," *Behavioral Science* (September 1974), pp. 383–393.

38. Einhorn and Hogarth, loc. cit.; John McCormick, "The Wisdom of Solomon," *Newsweek* (August 17, 1987), pp. 62–63.

39. Simon, loc. cit.

40. John R. Schermerhorn, Jr., *Management for Productivity*, 2nd ed. (New York: Wiley, 1986), pp. 65–66.

41. "How IBM Made 'Junior' and Underachiever," *Business Week* (June 25, 1984), p. 106; "The Computer War's Casualties Pile Up," *U.S. News & World Report* (August 20, 1984), pp. 37–38; and John Marcous, Jr., "IBM's PCjr Computer is Fulfilling Its Promise After a Faltering Start," *Wall Street Journal* (December 13, 1984), p. 33.

42. Paul J. H. Scholmaker and Cornelius A. T. M. vander Heyden, "Integrating Scenarios into Strategic Planning at Royal Dutch Shell," *Planning Review* (May–June 1992), pp. 41–46; Christopher Knowlton, "Shell Gets Rich by Beating Risk," *Fortune* (August 26, 1991), pp. 79–82; Adrienne Lisenmeyer, "Shell's Crystal Ball," *Financial World* (April 16, 1991), pp. 58–63.

43. James L. McKenney and Peter G. W. Keen, "How Managers' Minds Work," *Harvard Business Review* (July–August 1974), pp. 79–90.

44. Isabel Briggs Myers, *An Introduction to Type* (Palo Alto, Calif.: Consulting Psychologists Press, 1980).

45. McKenney and Keen, op. cit.; pp. 79–90.

46. Ibid.

47. Victor H. Vroom and P. W. Yetton, *Leadership and Decision Making* (Pittsburgh: University of Pittsburgh Press, 1973).

48. Victor H. Vroom and Arthur G. Yago, *The New Leadership: Management Participation in Organizations* (Englewood Cliffs, N.J.: Prentice-Hall, 1988).

49. James M. Higgins, *The Profile of the Innovative Organization* (Winter Park, Fla.: New Management Publishing Company, Inc., 1994).

50. For example, see Ray Stata, "Management Innovation," *Executive Excellence* (June 1992), pp. 8–9.

51. For example, see Byrne, loc. cit.; and Thomas A. Stewart, "The Search for the Organization of Tomorrow," *Fortune* (May 18, 1992), pp. 92–98.

52. James M. Higgins, *Increasing Personal Creativity Potential* (Winter Park, Fla.: New Management Publishing Company, Inc., 1994); Dina Ingber, "Inside the Executive Mind," *Success* (January 1984), pp. 33–37; Daniel Coleman, "Successful Executives Rely on Unkind of Intelligence," *New York Times* (July 13, 1984), pp. C1, C2; Henry Mintzberg, "Planning on the Left Side, Managing on the Right," *Harvard Business Review* (July–August 1976), pp. 49–58; and Weston Agor, "The Logic of Intuition: How Top Executives Make Important Decisions," *Organizational Dynamics* (Winter 1986), pp. 5–18.

53. James M. Higgins, *101 Creative Problem Solving Techniques* (Winter Park, Fla.: New Management Publishing Company, Inc., 1993).

54. Higgins, *The Profile of the Innovative Organization*, loc. cit.; "Masters of Innovation," *Business Week* (April 10, 1989), pp. 58–63.

55. *Milliken: Quality Leadership Through Research* (Spartanburg, S.C.: Milliken, 1986), p. 5.

56. For a discussion of processes, see Roger Von Oech, *A Whack on the Side of the Head* (New York: Warner, 1985).
57. Ibid.; Betty Edwards, *Drawing on the Right Side of the Brain* (Los Angeles: J. P. Tarcher, 1979), distributed by St. Martin's Press, New York.
58. Agor, loc. cit.
59. Mintzberg, loc. cit.; Mintzberg, Raisinghani, and Theoret, op. cit., pp. 246–275; and Coleman, loc. cit. The latter reports on the research of Dr. Siegfred Streufert of the Pennsylvania State College of Medicine on the decision techniques of executives.

CHAPTER 5

1. For a review of the major issues, see Don L. Boroughs, "Cleaning Up the Environment," *U.S. News & World Report* (March 25, 1991), pp. 45–56.
2. "The Future Is Here," *Newsweek* (June 12, 1992), pp. 18–42; Lester R. Brown, Christopher Flowrin, and Sandra Postel, "A Planet in Jeopardy," *The Futurist* (May–June 1992), pp. 10–14; "What on Earth Are We Doing?" *Time* (January 2, 1989), pp. 22–39.
3. "The Global Greenhouse Finally Has Leaders Sweating," *Business Week* (August 1988), pp. 74–76; "Heatwaves," *Newsweek* (July 11, 1988), pp. 16–20; and Jerry E. Bishop, "Global Threat: New Culprit Is Indicated in Greenhouse Effect—Rising Methane Level," *Wall Street Journal* (October 24, 1988), pp. A1, A7.
4. Sharon Begley, "Was Andrew a Freak—Or a Preview of Things to Come?" *Newsweek* (September 7, 1992); Paul Handley, "Before the Flood," *Far Eastern Economic Review* (April 16, 1992), pp. 65–66.
5. Paul Hoverstein and Jack Williams, "Scientists Sound Ozone Alarm," *USA Today* (February 4, 1992), p. 3A; "A Gaping Hole in the Sky," *Newsweek* (July 11, 1988), pp. 21–24.
6. William G. Rosenberg, "The New Clean Air Act of 1990: Winds of Environmental Change," *Business Horizons* (March–April 1992), pp. 34–36; Michael H. Brown, "Toxic Wind," *Discover* (November 1987), pp. 42–49; and Douglas Staglin, "Seizing the Politics of Pollution," *U.S. News & World Report* (December 8, 1986), p. 45.
7. "The Rape of the Oceans," *U.S. News & World Report* (June 22, 1992), pp. 64–76.
8. Lawrence Ingrassia, "Dead in the Water: Overfishing Threatens to Wipe Out Species and Crush Industry," *Wall Street Journal* (August 16, 1991), pp. A1, A8.
9. ABC News, September 7, 1988; "Suddenly a Deathwatch on the Rhine," *Business Week* (November 24, 1986), p. 52.
10. Amal Kumar Naj, "Back to the Lab: Big Chemical Concerns Hasten to Develop Biodegradable Plastics," *Wall Street Journal* (July 21, 1988), pp. 1, 6.
11. Tom Waters, "Fall of the Rain Forest," *Discover* (January 1989), p. 40; "The Global Greenhouse Finally Has Leaders Sweating," loc. cit.
12. "Toxic Wasteland," *U.S. News & World Report* (April 13, 1992), pp. 40–51.
13. Robert Johnson, John Koten, and Charles F. McCoy, "State of Shock: Anheuser-Busch Company is Shaken by Its Probe of Improper Payments," *Wall Street Journal* (March 21, 1987), pp. 1, 31.
14. Eileen White, "In the Spotlight: Rash of Investigations Is Damaging Image of Northrop Corporation," *Wall Street Journal* (June 22, 1987), pp. 1, 23.
15. Edward T. Pound, "On the Take: Investigators Detect Pattern of Kickbacks for Defense Business," *Wall Street Journal* (November 14, 1985), pp. 1, 25.

16. Charles P. Alexander, "Crime in the Suites," *Time* (June 10, 1985), p. 56.
17. Charles P. Alexander, "General Dynamics Under Fire," *Time* (April 8, 1985), pp. 23–26.
18. Robert Guenther and Joanne Lipman, "Building Distrust: Construction Industry in New York Is Hotbed of Extortion and Bribery," *Wall Street Journal* (May 7, 1986), pp. 1, 22.
19. Andy Pasztor and Cathy Trost, "Bad Buys: Fraud Frequently Mars Government Contracts to Acquire Computers," *Wall Street Journal* (July 7, 1986), pp. 1, 9.
20. Sonja Steptoe and Francine Schwadel, "Ex-Manager at Shearson Firm, Six Others Indicted for Laundering Gambling Funds," *Wall Street Journal* (June 27, 1986), p. 5.
21. Rob Norton, "Lessons from BCCI," *Fortune* (September 9, 1991), pp. 153–156; Mark Maremont, "The Long and Winding Road to BCCI's Dead End," *Business Week* (July 22, 1991), pp. 54–55.
22. Robert Neff, "Debacle at Dow-Corning: How Bad Will It Get?" *Business Week* (March 2, 1992), pp. 36–37.
23. Theodore Levitt, "Editorial," *Harvard Business Review* (January–February 1988), p. 4.
24. "The Future is Here," loc. cit.
25. Richard L. Daft, *Organization: Theory and Design*, 2nd ed. (St. Paul, Minn.: West, 1986), pp. 18, 49.
26. Adapted from L. J. Bourgeois, "Strategy and Environment: A Conceptual Integration," *Academy of Management Review* (January 1980), pp. 25–39. His term *task environment* has been changed in this text to *competitive environment*.
27. Michael E. Porter, *Competitive Strategy* (New York: Free Press, 1980).
28. Ibid.
29. Thomas J. Peters and Robert H. Waterman, Jr., *In Search of Excellence* (New York: Harper & Row, 1982); Thomas J. Peters and Nancy K. Austin, *A Passion for Excellence* (New York: Random House, 1985); and Thomas J. Peters, *Thriving on Chaos* (New York: Knopf, 1987).
30. Richard N. Foster, *Innovation: The Attacker's Advantage* (New York: Summit Books, 1986); A. C. Cooper et al., "Strategic Responses to Technological Threats," *Proceedings,* Academy of Management (1974).
31. Brian Dumaine, "How Managers Can Succeed Through Speed," *Fortune* (February 13, 1987), pp. 54–59.
32. "The Future is Here," loc. cit.; Jeremy Main, "Here Comes the Big New Cleanup," *Fortune* (November 21, 1988), pp. 102–118.
33. Frances Cairncross, "How Europe's Companies Reposition to Recycle," *Harvard Business Review* (March–April 1992), pp. 34–45.
34. Brian O'Reilly, "Your New Global Workforce," *Fortune* (December 14, 1992), pp. 52–66; Laura Zinn, "Move Over Boomers, The Busters are Here—and They're Angry," *Business Week* (December 14, 1992), pp. 74–82; Sharon Nelton, "Winning With Diversity," *Nation's Business* (September 1992), pp. 18–23; Patricia W. Hamilton, "What a Changing Workforce Means for Business," *D&B Report* (January–February 1992), pp. 20–23; Diane Filipowski, "Perspectives—Do White Males Still Dominate the Work Force?" *Personnel Journal* (November 1991), p. 40; Nancy J. Perry, "The Workers of the Future," The New American Century, *Fortune* (Special Issue, 1991), pp. 68–72; William B. Johnston, "Global Work Force 2000: The New World Labor Market," *Harvard Business Review* (March–April 1991), pp. 115–127.
35. David Wessel, "Global Cooling," *Wall Street Journal* (September 17, 1992), pp. A1, A12.
36. Karen Springer and Annette Miller, "Doing the Right Thing," *Newsweek* (January 7, 1992), pp. 42–43.

37. Tom Burns and G. M. Stalker, *The Management of Innovation* (London: Tavistock, 1961).
38. Ibid.
39. Author's observation.
40. Robert B. Duncan, "Characteristics of Perceived Environments and Perceived Environmental Uncertainty," *Administrative Science Quarterly* (September, 1972), no. 3, pp. 313–327.
41. Sue Greenfield, Robert C. Winder, and Gregory Williams, "The CEO and the External Environment," *Business Horizons* (November–December 1988), pp. 20–26.
42. Laurie Hays, "Fighting Back: Chemical Firms Press Campaigns to Dispel Their 'Bad Guy' Image," *Wall Street Journal* (September 20, 1988), pp. 1, 30.
43. David Warner, "Making PACs Work for Business," *Nation's Business* (January 1992), pp. 55–56; "Small Companies Show Muscle in Efforts to Influence Congress" *Wall Street Journal* (October 3, 1988), pp. B1, B2.
44. Guenther and Lipman, loc. cit.
45. For a complete and recent review of social responsibility issues, see the special issue of *Business Horizons: Creating the Great Society: To Whom Is the Business Corporation Responsible?* (July–August 1991).
46. Neil H. Jacoby, *Corporate Power and Social Responsibility* (New York: Macmillan, 1973).
47. Jerry W. Anderson, Jr., "Social Responsibility and the Corporation," *Business Horizons* (July–August 1986), pp. 22–27; Keith Davis and William C. Frederick, *Business and Society: Management, Public Policy, and Ethics,* 5th ed. (New York: McGraw-Hill, 1984).
48. David J. Fritzche and Helmet Becker, "Linking Management Behavior to Ethical Philosophy—An Empirical Investigation," *Academy of Management Journal* (March 1984), pp. 156–175.
49. Archie Carroll, "A Three-Dimensional Conceptual Model of Corporate Performance," *Academy of Management Review* (October 1979), p. 499.
50. Milton Friedman, *Capitalism and Freedom* (Chicago: University of Chicago Press, 1962), p. 133; and Milton Friedman and Rose Friedman, *Free to Choose* (New York: Harcourt, 1979).
51. R. Edward Freeman and David L. Reed, "Stockholders and Stakeholders: A New Perspective on Corporate Government," *California Management Review* (Spring 1983), pp. 88–106; R. Edward Freeman, *Strategic Management: Stakeholder Approach* (Boston: Pitman, 1984).
52. William C. Frederick, Keith Davis, and James E. Post, *Business and Society: Corporate Strategy, Public Policy, Ethics,* 6th ed. (New York: McGraw-Hill, 1988), p. 36.
53. Archie B. Carroll, "The Pyramid of Corporate Social Responsibility: Toward the Moral Management of Organizational Stakeholders," *Business Horizons* (July–August 1991), pp. 39–48; Carroll, "A Three-Dimensional Conceptual Model of Corporate Performance," op. cit., p. 499; for an empirical test of a similar, but three-stage model, see Kimberly B. Boal and Newman Perry, "The Cognitive Structure of Corporate Social Responsibility," *Journal of Management* (Fall–Winter 1985), pp. 71–82.
54. Carroll, "A Three-Dimensional Conceptual Model of Corporate Performance," p. 500.
55. Frederick, Davis, and Post, op. cit., p. 52.
56. Carroll, "A Three-Dimensional Conceptual Model of Corporate Performance," p. 500.
57. "W. R. Grace, Massachusetts Water District Settle Suit," *Wall Street Journal* (January 12, 1987), p. 33; "U.S. Jury Fines Grace $100 Million in Trial Involving Bank Loan," *Wall Street Journal* (October 21, 1987), p. 4; and CBS television, "60 Minutes," Fall 1987. Also see "Why

Business Is Watching This Pollution Case," *Business Week* (March 28, 1986), p. 39.

58. Jeffrey A. Fadiman, "A Traveler's Guide to Gifts and Bribes," *Harvard Business Review* (July–August 1986), pp. 122–136.

59. Presentation by Donald Peterson, CEO and chairman of the board, Ford Motor Company, to the Academy of Management, Washington, D.C., August 14, 1989.

60. Jerry W. Anderson, Jr., "Social Responsibility in the Corporation," *Business Horizons* (July–August 1986), pp. 22–27.

61. Art Kleiner, "What Does It Mean to Be Green?" *Harvard Business Review* (July–August 1991), p. 38; "Business's Green Revolution," *U.S. News & World Report* (February 19, 1990), pp. 45–47.

62. Carroll, op. cit., pp. 501–502; Carroll uses the terms first employed by Ian Wilson in "What One Company Is Doing About Today's Demands on Business," in George A. Steiner, ed., *Changing Business Society into Relationships* (Los Angeles: Graduate School of Management, UCLA, 1975). He also references related strategies to each of the philosophical positions presented by Terry W. McAdams in "How to Put Corporate Responsibility into Practice," *Business and Society Review/Innovation* (Summer 1973), pp. 8–16.

63. Ian Wilson actually uses the term *reactive*, but I have used Terry McAdams's description of this same stage. Both are authors cited by Carroll, loc. cit., as developers of responsiveness continuums. See ibid.

64. "General Dynamics Under Fire," *Business Week* (March 25, 1985), p. 7.

65. Barry Meier, "Citizen Suits Become a Popular Weapon in the Fight Against Industrial Polluters," *Wall Street Journal* (April 17, 1987), p. 19.

66. David Kirkpatrick, "Environmentalism: The New Crusade," *Fortune* (February 12, 1990), pp. 44–52.

67. *American Express: Public Responsibility—A Report of Recent Activities* (New York: American Express, 1988).

68. Ibid.

69. For a review of the topic of corporate social performance, see Donna Wood, "Corporate Social Performance Revisited," *Academy of Management Review* (October 1991), pp. 691–718.

70. Edwin M. Epstein, "The Corporate Social Policy Process: Beyond Business Ethics, Corporate Social Responsibility, and Corporate Social Responsiveness," *California Management Review* (Spring 1987), pp. 99–114. A similar, earlier version of this process is described by Steven L. Wortex and Phyllis R. Cochrane, "The Evolution in the Corporate Social Performance Model," *Academy of Management Review* (October 1985), no. 4, pp. 758–769. In this model they described social corporate policy as a field examining social issues in management, including issue identification, issue analysis, and response developing. It is directed at minimizing surprises and determining effective corporate social policies.

71. Kathleen Black, address to the Academy of Management, Washington, D.C., August 14, 1989.

72. Theodore J. Kreps, "Measurement of the Social Performance of Businesses," in *An Investigation of Concentration of Economic Power for the Temporary National Economic Committee*, monograph no. 7 (Washington, D.C.: U.S. Government Printing Office, 1940).

73. Archie B. Carroll and George W. Beilier, "Landmarks in the Evolution of the Social Audit," *Academy of Management Journal* (September 1975), pp. 589–599.

74. James M. Higgins, "A Social Audit of Equal Opportunity Programs," *Human Resource Management* (Fall 1977), pp. 2–7.

75. Roger Gray, "Social Audit: Responding to Change?" *Management Accounting* (UK) (December 1989), pp. 8–9, discusses the use of the social audit in Great Britain.

76. David Silverstein, "The Litigation Audit: Preventative Legal Maintenance for Management," *Business Horizons* (November–December 1988), pp. 34–42.

77. Jean B. McGuire, Alison Sundgren, and Thomas Schneeweis, "Corporate Social Responsibility and Firm Financial Performance," *Academy of Management Journal* (December 1988), pp. 854–872. This article cites relevant authors from each of the three referenced perspectives.

78. Kenneth Aupperle, Archie P. Carroll, and John D. Hatfield, "An Empirical Examination of American Corporate Social Responsibility and Profitability," *Academy of Management Journal* (1985), no. 2, pp. 446–463; Philip L. Cochrane and Robert A. Wood, "Corporate Social Responsibility and Financial Performance," *Academy of Management Journal* (March 1984), pp. 42–56; and A. Ullman, "Data in Search of a Theory: Critical Examination of the Relationships Among Social Performance, Social Disclosure, and Economic Performance," *Academy of Management Journal* (July 1985), pp. 540–577.

79. McGuire, Sundgren, and Schneeweis, loc. cit.

80. Thomas M. Jones, "An Integrative Framework for Research in Business and Society: A Stop Towards an Elusive Paradigm," *Academy of Management Journal* (1983), no. 4, pp. 559–564.

81. LaRue Tone Hoemer, *The Ethics of Management* (Homewood, Ill.: Irwin, 1987), pp. 3–12.

82. Derek Bok, "Ethics, The University, and Society," *Harvard Magazine* (May–June 1988), pp. 39–50, contains an excellent discussion of what a university can do, how its curriculum can help, and what a professor can do philosophically to challenge students to think about ethical behavior.

83. Adrianne Cadbury, "Ethical Managers Make Their Own Rules," *Harvard Business Review* (September–October 1987), pp. 69–73.

84. Rick Wartzman, "Nature or Nurture? Study Blames Ethical Lapses on Corporate Goals," *Wall Street Journal* (October 9, 1987), sect. 2, p. 1.

85. Laura L. Nash, "Ethics Without the Sermon," *Harvard Business Review* (November–December 1981), pp. 79–90.

86. Arthur Bedeian, *Management*, 1st ed. (Hinsdale, Ill.: Dryden, 1986), p. 623.

87. John Paul Fraedich, "Signs and Signals of Unethical Behavior," *Business Forum* (Spring 1992), pp. 13–17, reviews several of these in more detail.

88. Preston Townley, "Business Ethics—An Oxymoron?" *Canadian Business Review* (Spring 1992), pp. 35–37.

89. "Businesses Are Signing Up for Ethics 101," *Business Week* (February 15, 1988), pp. 56–67.

90. Donald Robin, Michael Grallomakis, Fred R. David, and Thomas E. Moritz, "A Different Look at Codes of Ethics," *Business Horizons* (January–February 1989), pp. 66–73.

91. "Hertz Is Doing Some Body Work—On Itself," *Business Week* (February 15, 1988), p. 57.

92. Gerald Vinten, "Whistle Blowing: Corporate Help or Hindrance?" *Management Decision* (1992), no. 1, pp. 44–48; Janet P. Near, "Whistle-Blowing: Encourage It!" *Business Horizons* (January–February 1989), pp. 2–6.

93. Marcia Parmalree Miceli and Janet P. Near, "The Relationship Among Beliefs, Organizational Positions, and Whistle-Blowing Status: A Discriminant Analysis," *Academy of Management Journal* (December 1984), pp. 687–705.

They use the term *illegitimate;* I use the term *unethical.*

94. Joseph A. Raelin, "The Professional as the Executive's Aide-de-Camp," *Academy of Management Executive* (August 1987), pp. 171–182.

95. John A. Byrne, "The Best-Laid Ethics Program," *Business Week* (March 9, 1992), pp. 67–69.

96. John W. Hill, Michael B. Metzger, and Dan R. Dalton, "How Ethical Is Your Company?" *Management Accounting* (July 1992), pp. 59–61.

CHAPTER 6

1. For a discussion, see Henry Mintzberg, "What Is Planning Anyway?" *Strategic Management Journal* (July–September 1981), pp. 319–324; and Neil H. Snyder, "What Is Planning Anyway?: A Rejoinder," *Strategic Management Journal* (July–September 1982), pp. 265–267.

2. Gerry Johnson, "Managing Strategic Change—Strategy, Culture, and Action," *Long Range Planning* (February 1992), pp. 28–36.

3. Leon Rinehart, H. Jack Shapiro, and Ernest A. Callman, *Practice of Planning: Strategic, Administrative, and Operational* (New York: Van Nostrand Reinhold, 1981).

4. Donald R. Schmincke, "Strategic Thinking: A Perspective for Success," *Management Review* (August 1990), pp. 16–19; Arie P. DeGeus, "Planning as Learning," *Harvard Business Review* (March–April 1988), pp. 70–74; and William A. Bossidy, address to the Strategic Management Society, Boston, October 13, 1987.

5. Charles Hofer and Dan Schendel, *Strategy Formulation: Analytical Concepts* (St. Paul, Minn.: West, 1978).

6. Jim Bartimo, "Pushing Ahead: Compaq Plots Strategy to Widen Its Horizons Beyond a Niche in PCs," *Wall Street Journal* (April 10, 1991), pp. A1, A8.

7. "Georgia-Pacific Turns Paper into Gold," *Business Week* (August 15, 1988), pp. 71–72.

8. Sam Walton, "Sam Walton in His Own Words," *Fortune* (June 29, 1991), pp. 98–106.

9. For a discussion of programs/project plans and how to prioritize them, see Steven C. Wheelwright and Kim B. Clark, "Creating Project Plans to Focus," *Harvard Business Review* (March–April 1992), pp. 70–82.

10. Kenneth Labick, "The Big Comeback of British Airways," *Fortune* (December 5, 1988), pp. 163–174.

11. Pauline Yoshihashi, "Caesar's World's Strategy Is Bringing Back Past Glory," *Wall Street Journal* (February 20, 1992), p. B4.

12. Tom Richman, "Mrs. Fields' Secret Ingredient," *Inc.* (October 1987), pp. 65–72.

13. "Numbers Don't Tell the Story," *Business Week* (June 6, 1988), p. 105.

14. Marc Bassin, "Teamwork at General Foods: New & Improved," *Personnel Journal* (May 1988), pp. 62–70.

15. Steven Kaufman, "Going for the Buck," *Success* (January–February 1988), pp. 38–41.

16. James M. Higgins, "The Challenges Facing General Motors in 1992," in James M. Higgins and Julian W. Vincze, eds., *Strategic Management: Text and Cases*, 5th ed. (Ft. Worth, Tex.: Dryden 1993), pp. 29–56.

17. Marj Charlier, "Adolph Coors Is Looking Beyond Beer for the Future," *Wall Street Journal* (December 30, 1991), p. B2.

18. Ronald Grover, "Coors Is Thinking Suds 'R' Us," *Business Week* (June 8, 1992), p. 34.

19. Chuck Hawkins, "Hugh McColl's Masterwork," *Business Week* (April 27, 1992), pp. 94–95.

20. "A Software Whiz-Kid Goes Retail," *Business Week* (May 9, 1983), p. 111.

21. Gail DeGeorge, "Harris Is Looking Sharp in

Civvies," *Business Week* (January 20, 1992), p. 31.

22. IBM, *Annual Report, 1983* (Armonk, N.Y.), p. 3.

23. Author's discussion with IBM personnel.

24. William G. Ouchi, *Theory Z: How American Business Can Meet the Japanese Challenge* (Reading, Mass.: Addison-Wesley 1981).

25. John Sculley, with John A. Vern, "Sculley's Lessons from Inside Apple," *Fortune* (September 14, 1987), p. 120. Excerpted from John Sculley with John A. Vern, *Odyssey: Pepsi to Apple* (New York: Harper & Row, 1987).

26. For a discussion of planning under changing conditions, see Dale D. McConkey, "Planning in a Changing Environment," *Business Horizons* (September–October 1988), pp. 64–72.

27. Kenneth Labich, "Airbus Takes Off," *Fortune* (June 1, 1992), pp. 102–108.

28. Lawrence A. Bossidy, "Some Thoughts on Strategic Thinking," address to the Strategic Management Society, Boston, August 14, 1987.

29. Neil C. Churchill, "Budget Choice: Planning vs. Control," *Harvard Business Review* (July–August 1984), pp. 150–164.

30. Peter Lorange and Declan Murphy, "Considerations in Implementing Strategic Control," *Journal of Business Strategy* (Spring 1984), pp. 27–35.

31. For a more detailed review of this process, see Higgins and Vincze, op. cit., chaps. 3 and 4.

32. George A. Steiner, *Top Management Planning* (New York: Macmillan, 1969), pp. 81–82.

33. The author's personal experience as a consultant to this organization.

34. For example, see James C. Collins and Jerry F. Porras, "Organizational Vision and Visionary Organizations," *California Management Review* (Fall 1991), pp. 30–52; Thomas J. Peters, *Thriving on Chaos: Handbook for Management Revolution* (New York: Knopf, 1987), pp. 398–408; Noel M. Tichy and Mary Anne DeVanna, *The Transformational Leader* (New York: Wiley, 1986), pp. viii, ix, and chaps. 1 and 5; and Robert H. Waterman, Jr., *The Renewal Factor* (New York: Bantam, 1987), pp. 222–225.

35. Tichy and DeVanna, op. cit., p. 130.

36. Peters, op. cit., pp. 401–404.

37. Collins and Porras, loc. cit.

38. Colin Carlson-Thomas, "Strategic Vision or Strategic Con?: Rhetoric or Reality?" *Long Range Planning* (February 1992), pp. 81–89.

39. Philip Kotler, *Marketing Management: Analysis, Planning, Control*, 6th ed. (Englewood Cliffs, N.J.: Prentice-Hall, 1988), pp. 37–43; John A. Pearce, II, "The Company Mission as a Strategic Tool," *Sloan Management Review* (Spring 1982), p. 15.

40. John A. Pearce, II, and Fred David, "Corporate Mission Statements: The Bottom Line," *Academy of Management Executive* (May 1987), pp. 109–116.

41. Andrew Campbell and Sally Yeung, "Creating a Sense of Mission," *Long Range Planning* (August 1991), pp. 10–20.

42. Pearce, op. cit., p. 14.

43. David Coussey, "Pfeiffer Shifts Compaq's Focus to Saving Customers," *Info World* (June 22, 1992), p. 18.

44. Peter F. Drucker, *The Practice of Management* (New York: Harper & Row, 1954).

45. Charles W. Hofer and Dan Schendel, *Strategy Formulation Analytical Concepts* (St. Paul: West, 1979).

46. Max Richards, *Setting Strategic Goals and Objectives* (St. Paul: West, 1986), p. 22.

47. Adapted from and added to Edwin A. Locke and Gary P. Latham, *Goal Setting for Individuals, Groups, and Organizations* (Chicago: Science Research Associates, 1984).

48. Robert N. Anthony, John Dearden, and Norton M. Bedford, *Management Control Systems*, 5th ed. (Homewood, Ill.: Irwin, 1984), pp. 1–15.

49. Hofer and Schendel, loc. cit.

50. Drucker, loc. cit.

51. George S. Odiorne, *Management by Objectives* (New York: Pitman, 1965; *MBO II: A System of Managerial Leadership for the '80s* (Belmont, Calif.: Pitman, 1979).

52. For example, see Robert C. Ford, Frank S. McLaughlin, and James Nixdorf, "Ten Questions About MBO," *California Management Review* (Winter 1980), pp. 84–94; and Fred E. Schuster and Alva F. Kindall, "Management by Objectives—Where We Stand—A Survey of the Fortune 500," *Human Resource Management* (Spring 1974), pp. 8–11.

53. Heinz Weihrich, *Management Excellence: Productivity Through MBO* (New York: McGraw-Hill 1985)

54. Gary P. Latham and Gary A. Yukl, "A Review of the Research on Application of Goal Setting in Organizations," *Academy of Management Journal* (December 1975), pp. 824–845.

55. For a review of the various aspects of goal setting, see ibid.

56. For a lengthy review of the effects of participation, see Edwin A. Locke and E. M. Schwerger, "Participation Is Decision Making: One More Look," in Barry M. Stone, ed., *Research in Organizational Behavior*, vol. 1 (Greenwich, Conn.: JAI, 1979), pp. 265–339. For a description of the two main types of participation-setting objectives and formulating plans, see Jan P. Muczyk and Bernard C. Reimann, "The Case for Directive Leadership," *Academy of Management Executive* (November 1987), pp. 301–311.

57. For example, see Jack N. Kondrasuk, "Studies in MBO Effectiveness," *Academy of Management Review* (July 1981), pp. 419–430, for a review of 185 studies of MBO; also see Jan P. Muczyk, "Dynamics and Hazards of MBO Applications," *Personnel Administrator* (May 1979), p. 52; and Ford, McLaughlin, and Nixdorf, loc. cit.

58. Robert Rogers and John E. Hunter, "Impact of Management by Objectives on Organizational Productivity," *Journal of Applied Psychology* (April 1991), pp. 302–336.

59. Kondrasuk, loc. cit.; Ford, McLaughlin, and Nixdorf, loc. cit.

60. Rogers and Hunter, loc. cit.

61. James M. Higgins, *Human Relations: Behavior at Work*, 2nd ed. (New York: Random House, 1987), p. 288.

62. For example, see Robert L. Nydick and Ronald Paul Hill, "Using the Analytic Hierarchy Process to Structure the Supplier Selection Procedure," *International Journal of Purchasing and Materials Management* (Spring 1992), pp. 31–36.

63. William J. Kearney, "Behaviorally Anchored Rating Scales—MBO's Missing Ingredient," *Personnel Journal* (January 1979), pp. 20–25.

64. Jim M. Graber, Robert E. Briesch, and Walter E. Breisch, "Performance Appraisals and Deming: A Misunderstanding?" *Quality Progress* (June 1992), pp. 59–62.

65. Odiorne, *MBO II*, op. cit., pp. 127–140, for example, argues that managers should set three types of objectives: routine, creative, and personal development.

CHAPTER 7

1. For reviews of the relationship between strategy and financial performance, see Deepak K. Sinha, "The Contributions of Formal Planning to Decisions," *Strategic Management Journal* (September–October 1990), pp. 479–492; David M. Reid, "Where Planning Fails in Practice," *Long Range Planning* (April 1990), pp. 85–93; Charles B. Shrader, Charles Muford, and Virginia L. Blackburn, "Strategic and Operational Planning," *Journal of Small Business Management* (October 1989), pp. 45–60; John A. Pearce, II, Elizabeth R. Freeman, and Richard B. Robinson, Jr., "The Tenuous Link Between Formal Strategic Planning and Financial Performance," *Academy of Management Review* (October 1987), pp. 658–695; and John A. Pearce, II, D. Keith Robbins, and Richard B. Robinson, Jr., "The Impact of Grand Strategy and Planning Formality on Financial Performance," *Strategic Management Journal* (March–April 1987), pp. 125–134.

2. Charles Hofer and Dan Schendel, *Strategy Formulation: Analytical Concepts* (St. Paul, Minn.: West, 1978).

3. See John A. Pearce, II, "Selecting Among Alternative Grand Strategies," *California Management Review* (Spring 1982), pp. 23–31.

4. For a discussion, see Daniel Gilber, Edwin Hartman, John Mauriel, and Edward Freeman, *A Logic for Strategy* (Boston: Ballinger, 1988).

5. Based largely on James M. Higgins and Julian W. Vincze, *Strategic Management: Text and Cases*, 5th ed. (Ft. Worth, Tex.: Dryden, 1993).

6. Ibid., p. 5.

7. Ibid., p. 190.

8. Michael E. Naylor, a speech delivered to the Academy of Management, Chicago, August 14, 1986.

9. Author's discussion with Disney managers.

10. For reviews of recent research, see "Strategy Process Research," *Strategic Management Journal*, Special Issue (Summer 1992); "Strategy Content Research," a special issue of *Strategic Management Journal*, edited by Cynthia Montgomery (Summer 1988), Anne S. Huff and Rhonda Kay Rezer, "A Review of Strategic Process Research," in James G. Hunt and John D. Blair, eds., *Yearly Review of Management of the Journal of Management* (Summer 1987), pp. 211–236; and Liam Fahey and H. Kurt Christensen, "Evaluating the Research in Strategy Content," in James C. Hunt and John D. Blair, eds., *Yearly Review of Management of the Journal of Management* (Summer 1986).

11. Donald R. Schmincke, "Strategic Thinking: A Perspective for Success," *Management Review* (August 1990), pp. 16–19; Arie de Geus, "Planning as Learning," *Harvard Business Review* (March–April 1988), pp. 70–74; Lawrence G. Bossidy, speech to the Strategic Management Society, Boston, Massachusetts, October 13, 1987.

12. Paul J. H. Schoemaker and Cornelius A. J. M. van der Heyden, "Integrating Scenarios into Strategic Planning at Royal Dutch/Shell," *Planning Review* (May–June 1992), pp. 41–46; Ian Wilson, "Teaching Decision Makers to Learn from Scenarios: A Blueprint for Implementation," *Planning Review* (May–June 1992), pp. 18–22; DeGeus, op. cit.; Pierre Wacke, "Scenarios: Uncharted Waters Ahead," *Harvard Business Review* (September–October 1985), pp. 73–89; and Pierre Wacke, "Scenarios: Shooting the Rapids," *Harvard Business Review* (November–December 1985), pp. 139–150.

13. P. R. Stokke, W. K. Ralston, T. A. Boyce, and I. H. Wilson, "Scenario Planning for Norwegian Oil and Gas," *Long Range Planning* (1990), no. 2, April, pp. 17–26.

14. Michael E. McGill, John W. Slocum, Jr., and David Lei, "Management Practices in Learning Organizations," *Organizational Dynamics* (Summer 1992), pp. 5–17.

15. Ray Stata, "Organizational Learning—The Key to Management Innovation," *Sloan Management Review* (Spring 1989), pp. 63–74.

16. For a look at differences in perception relative to SWOT at a strategic level, see R. Duane Ireland, Michael A. Hitt, Richard A. Bettis, and Deborah Auld DePorees, "Strategy Formulation Processes: Differences in Perception of Strength and Weakness Indicators and Environmental Uncertainty by Management Level," *Strategic Management Journal* (September–

October 1987), pp. 18–20, 122–148. For a discussion of SWOT, see Nigel Piercy and William Giles, "Making SWOT Analysis Work," *Marketing Intelligence and Planning* (1989), nos. 5, 6, pp. 5–7.

17. C. K. Prahalad and Gary Hamel, "The Core Competence of the Corporation," *Harvard Business Review* (May–June 1990), pp. 79–91.

18. George Stalk, Philip Evans, and Lawrence E. Shulman, "Competing on Capabilities: The New Rules of Corporate Strategy," *Harvard Business Review* (March–April 1992), pp. 57–69.

19. For a review, see Joseph T. Mahoney and J. Rajendran Pandian, "The Resource-Based View Within the Conversation of Strategic Management," *Strategic Management Journal* (June 1992), pp. 363–380; also see, "Special Theory Forum: The Resource-Based Model of the Firm," *Journal of Management* (March 1991), pp. 97–212.

20. George Steiner addresses this issue more fully than anyone else I've read. See George A. Steiner, *Strategic Planning: What Every Management Must Know* (New York: Free Press, 1979), pp. 18–20, 122–148.

21. Gary Hamel and C. K. Prahalad, "Strategic Intent," *Harvard Business Review* (May–June 1989), pp. 63–76.

22. Gary Hamel and C. K. Prahalad, "Strategy as Stretch and Leverage," *Harvard Business Review* (March–April, 1993), pp. 75–84.

23. Higgins and Vincze, op. cit., p. 21.

24. Stanley M. Cherkosky, "Total Quality for a Sustainable Competitive Advantage," *Quality* (August 1992), pp. Q4, Q6–Q7.

25. Joseph T. Versey, "The New Competitors: They Think in Terms of Speed-to-Market," *Academy of Management Executive* (April 1991), pp. 23–33.

26. Sir Colin Marshall, speech entitled "From Bloody Awful to Bloody Awesome," to the Strategic Management Society, London (October 16, 1992).

27. Michael E. Porter, "From Competitive Advantage to Corporate Strategy," *Harvard Business Review* (May–June 1987), pp. 53–56.

28. Adapted from Peter Lorange, "Divisional Planning: Setting Effective Direction," *Sloan Management Review* (Fall 1975), pp. 85–87.

29. Agis Salpukas, "Greyhound Selling Its Bus Operations," *New York Times* (December 24, 1986), p. 29

30. For a recent discussion, see R. A. Proctor and P. J. Kitchen, "Strategic Planning: An Overview of Product Portfolio Models," *Marketing Intelligence & Planning* (1990), no. 7, pp. 4–10.

31. For a discussion of the matrix, see Barry Hedley, "A Fundamental Approach to Strategy Development," *Long Range Planning* (December 1976), pp. 2–11.

32. Amy Barrett, "The Loved One," *Financial World* (February 18, 1992), pp. 26–27.

33. Donald C. Hambrick, Ian C. MacMillan, and Diane L. Day, "Strategic Attributes and Performance on the BCG Matrix—A PIMS Based Analysis of Industrial Product Business," *Academy of Management Journal* (September 1982), pp. 510–531.

34. Porter, loc. cit.

35. Higgins and Vincze, op. cit., pp. 278–279.

36. Robert M. Tucker, "Quality Consulting Services: East Meets West in New Global Economy," *Quality* (August 1992), pp. Q23–Q24.

37. Michael E. Porter, *Competitive Strategy* (New York: Free Press, 1980).

38. William E. Fulmer and Jack Goodwin argue that low cost is just one form of differentiation in "Differentiation: Begin with the Consumer," *Business Horizons* (September–October 1988), pp. 55–63.

39. Brian Dumaine, "How Managers Succeed Through Speed," *Fortune* (February 13, 1989), pp. 54–59.

40. Michael E. Porter, *Competitive Advantage* (New York: Free Press, 1985), p. 12

41. For a brief review, see Higgins and Vincze, op. cit., p. 176.

42. William K. Hall, "Survival Strategies in a Hostile Environment," *Harvard Business Review* (September–October 1980), pp. 73–86.

43. Some additional research efforts support Hall's view; for example, see Alan I. Murray, "A Contingency View of Porter's Generic Strategies," *Academy of Management Review* (July 1988), no. 3, pp. 390–400; and Charles W. L. Hill, "Differentiation Versus Low Cost or Differentiation and Low Cost: A Contingency Framework," *Academy of Management Review* (July 1988), no. 3, pp. 401–412.

44. Murray, loc. cit., Hill, loc. cit,; and Peter Wright, et al., "Strategic Portfolio, Market Share and Performance," *Industrial Management* (May–June 1990), pp. 23–28.

45. Raymond E. Miles and Charles C. Snow, *Organizational Strategy, Structure and Process* (New York: McGraw-Hill, 1978).

46. S. Schoeffler, R. D. Buzzell, and D. F. Heany, "The Impact of Strategic Planning on Profit Performance," *Harvard Business Review* (March–April 1974), pp. 137–145.

47. For a review, see Higgins and Vincze, op. cit., pp. 121–122.

48. Michael E. Porter, *Competitive Advantage*, op. cit.

49. Kevin P. Cogne, "Sustainable Competitive Advantage—What It Is, What It Isn't," *Business Horizons* (January–February 1986), pp. 54–61.

50. Charles W. L. Hill, Michael A. Hitt, and Robert E. Hoskisson, "Declining U.S. Competitiveness: Reflections on a Crisis," *Academy of Management Journal* (January 1988), pp. 51–60.

51. Robert Grosse, "Competitive Advantages and Multinational Enterprises in Latin America," *Journal of Business Research* (August 1992), pp. 27–42.

52. For a discussion, see Jeffrey R. Williams, "How Sustainable Is Your Competitive Advantage?" *California Management Review* (Spring 1992), pp. 29–51.

53. For example, see Harold W. Fox, "A Framework for Functional Coordination," *Atlanta Economic Review* (November–December 1973), pp. 6–15.

54. James M. Higgins, "The Personal Computer Industry," in James M. Higgins and Julian W. Vincze, *Strategic Management: Text and Cases*, 4th ed. (Hinsdale, Ill.: Dryden Press, 1989), pp. 790–792.

55. For discussions of the coalition, see James Bryan Quinn, *Strategies for Change: Logical Incrementalism* (Homewood, Ill.: Irwin, 1980); L. J. Bourgeois, III, and J. V. Singh, "Organizational Slack and Political Behavior Among Top Management Teams," *Academy of Management Proceedings* (August 1983), pp. 43–47; and Henry A. Mintzberg, Duru Raisinghani, and André Theoret, "The Structure of Unstructured Decision Processes," *Administrative Science Quarterly* (June 1976), p. 258.

56. "The New Breed of Strategic Planners," *Business Week* (September 17, 1984), pp. 62–68.

57. Y. N. Cheng and F. Campos-Flores, *Business Policy and Strategy* (Santa Monica, Calif.: Goodyear, 1980), chap. 17; Yves L. Doz, "Strategic Management and Multinational Companies," *Sloan Management Review* (Winter 1980), pp. 27–46.

58. For a fuller discussion, see Jay R. Galbraith and Robert K. Kazanjian, *Strategy Implementation: Structure, Systems, and Process* (St. Paul, Minn.: West, 1986).

59. Higgins and Vincze, 5th ed., op. cit., chap. 9.

60. A. D. Chandler, *Strategy and Structure* (Cambridge, Mass.: MIT Press, 1962).

61. See Donald C. Hambrick and Albert A. Channella, Jr., "Strategy Implementation as Substance and Selling," *Academy of Management Executive* (November 1989), pp. 278–289.

62. Robert H. Waterman, Jr., "The Seven Elements of Strategic Fit, " *Journal of Business Strategy* (Winter 1982); also see Thomas J. Peters and Robert H. Waterman, Jr., *In Search of Excellence* (New York: Harper & Row, 1982).

63. Peter Benton, "Riding the Whirlwind," *Management Japan* (Autumn 1991), pp. 3–11; Henry H. Bean, "Strategic Discontinuities: When Being Good May Not Be Good Enough," *Business Horizons* (July–August 1990), pp. 10–14; David Ulrich and Margarethe F. Wiersema, "Gaining Strategic and Organizational Capability in a Turbulent Business Environment," *Academy of Management Executive* (May 1989), pp. 115–122; and Dale D. McConkey, "Planning in a Changing Environment," *Business Horizons* (September–October 1988), pp. 64–72.

CHAPTER 8

1. For a discussion of how quantitative methods can help managers better understand the problem, see Rick Hesse, "Management Science or Management/Science," *Interfaces* (February 1980), pp. 104–109; and Allen F. Grum and Rick Hesse, "It's the Process Not the Product (Most of the Time)," *Interfaces* (October 1983), pp. 89–93.

2. For a typical, more in-depth discussion of these problems, see K. Roscoe Davis, Patrick G. McKeown, and Terry Rakes, *Management Science*, 2nd ed. (Reading, Mass.: Addison-Wesley 1986), chap. 1; and David R. Anderson, Dennis J. Sweeney, and Thomas A. Williams, *An Introduction to Management Science: Quantitative Approaches to Decision Making*, 4th ed. (St. Paul, Minn.: West, 1986), chap. 1.

3. For example, see James Minno, "Firm Offers True Mainframe Statistical Power for PCs," *Marketing News* (January 7, 1991), pp. 51–52.

4. Based on the discussion by Ricky W. Griffin, *Management*, 2nd ed. (Boston: Houghton Mifflin, 1984), pp. 253–284; and the discussion by Louis E. Boone and David L. Kurtz, *Principles of Management* (New York: Random House, 1984), pp. 180–182. Also see M. J. Lawrence, "An Exploration of Some Practical Issues in the Use of Quantitative Forecasting Models," *Journal of Forecasting* (April–June 1983), pp. 169–179.

5. James S. Moore and Alan K. Reichert, "A Multivariate Study of Firm Performance and the Use of Modern Analytical Tools and Financial Techniques," *Interfaces* (May–June 1989), pp. 79–87.

6. The three organizations willing to sell their models of the U.S. economy to others are Chase Econometrics, Wharton Econometrics, and the Michael Evans Group.

7. For example, see Weston H. Agor ed., *Intuition in Organizations: Leading and Managing Proactively* (Newbury Park, Calif.: Sage Publications 1989), pp. 145–170.

8. James R. Evans, "Creativity in MS/OR: Improving Problem Solving Through Creative Thinking," *Interfaces* (March–April 1992), pp. 87–91.

9. For a more detailed review, see Jay Heizer and Barry Render, *Productions and Operations Management: Strategy and Tactics*, 3rd ed. (Boston: Allyn and Bacon, 1993).

10. G. Thomas and J. DaCosta, "A Sample Survey of Corporate Operations Research," *Interfaces* (1979), no. 4, pp. 102–111.

11. Norman Gaither, "The Adoption of Operations Research Techniques by Manufacturing Organizations," *Decision Sciences* (1975), vol. 6, no. 4, pp. 797–813.

12. W. Ledbetter and J. Cox, "Are OR Techniques Being Used?" *Industrial Engineering*, vol. 9, no. 2, pp. 1921–1977.

13. Jerry Wind, Paul E. Green, Douglas Shifflett, and Marsha Scarbrough, "Courtyard by Marriott: Designing a Hotel Facility with Consumer-Based Marketing Models," *Interfaces* (January–February 1989), pp. 29–47.

14. Jairo Munoz and Chase Nielsen, "SPC: What Data Should I Collect? What Charts Should I Use?" *Quality Progress* (January 1991), pp. 50–52.

15. Girish H. Subramanian, John Norek, Sankaran P. Raghunathan, Santash S. Kamitkar, "A Comparison of the Decision Table and Tree," *Communications of the ACM* (January 1992), pp. 89–94; James M. Neil, "Decision Analysis," *AACE Transactions* (1991), pp. SK4 (1–6).

16. Jacob W. Ulvila and Rex V. Brown, "Decision Analysis Comes of Age," *Harvard Business Review* (September–October 1982), pp. 130–141.

17. David Cohen, Stephen M. Haas, David L. Radloff, and Richard F. Yarrick, "Using Fire in Forest Management: Decision Making Under Uncertainty," *Interfaces* (September–October 1984), pp. 8–19.

18. Robert E. Luna and Richard A. Reid, "Mortgage Selection Using a Decision Tree Approach," *Interfaces* (May–June 1986), pp. 73–81; Jinoos Hosseini, "Decision Analysis and Its Application in the Choice Between Wild Cat Oil Ventures," *Interfaces* (March–April 1986), pp. 75–85.

19. Thomas J. Peters, "The Home-Team Advantage," *U.S. News & World Report* (March 31, 1986), p. 49.

20. Timothy L. Urban, "Deterministic Inventory Models Incorporating Marketing Decisions," *Computers & Industrial Engineering* (January 1992), pp. 85–93.

21. Quantitative methods have even been used to help reduce the airline overbooking problem. See Marvin Rothstein, "OR and the Airline Overbooking Problem," *Operations Research* (March–April 1985), pp. 237–248.

22. Richard C. Larson and Thomas F. Rich, "Travel Time Analysis of New York City Policy Patrol Cars," *Interfaces* (March–April 1987), pp. 15–26.

23. Phil Quinn, Bruce Andrews, and Henry Parsons, "Allocating Telecommunications Resources at L. L. Bean Inc.," *Interfaces* (January–February 1991), pp. 75–91.

24. Discussion of transportation procedures with a high-level executive in this firm.

25. David P. Carlisle, Kenneth S. Nickerson, Steven B. Probst, Denise Rudolph, Yosef Scheffi, and Warren B. Pal, "A Turnkey Computer Based Logistics Planning System," *Interfaces* (July–August 1987), pp. 16–23.

26. For a discussion of various types, see Peter Holmes, "Business Outlook '86," *Nation's Business* (January 1986), pp. 22–28; Spyros Makridakas and Steven C. Wheelwright, eds., *The Handbook of Forecasting* (New York: Wiley, 1982).

27. Ronald M. Weinberg, "Understanding Trends Is the Key to Using Them," *Marketing News* (July 6, 1992), p. 17.

28. Author's discussion with park officials.

29. For a discussion of the assumptions issue and the difficulty of modeling econometrically, see "The Art of Crunching Numbers," *The Economist* (May 9, 1987), pp. 68–69; and "Where the Big Econometric Models Go Wrong," *Business Week* (March 30, 198), pp. 70–73.

30. Nada R. Sanders and Larry P. Ritzman, "On Knowing When to Switch from Quantitative to Judgmental Forecasts," *Interfaces International Journal of Operations and Production Management* (1991), no. 6, pp. 27–37.

31. Barbara R. Michel, "Improving the Forecasting Process at L'Eggs Products," *Journal of Business Forecasting* (Winter 1991–1992), pp. 26, 30.

32. William J. Stevenson, *Production/Operations Management,* 2nd ed. (Homewood, Ill.: Irwin, 1986), p. 107.

33. Ibid., p. 108.

34. Debra M. Schramm, "How to Sell Forecasts to Management," *Journal of Business Forecasting* (Winter 1991–1992), p. 22.

35. David M. Georgeoff and Robert G. Murdick, "Manager's Guide to Forecasting," *Harvard Business Review* (January–February 1986), pp. 110–120.

36. "Leaner and Meaner," *The Economist* (July 11, 1992), pp. 66, 68.

37. A one-unit change in the independent variable results in either an exact proportional or multiplicative change greater than one in the dependent variable.

38. Robert J. Lambrix and Surendra S. Singhavi, "How to Set Volume-Sensitive ROI Targets," *Harvard Business Review* (March–April 1981), pp. 174–179.

39. Stevenson, op. cit., p. 190.

40. For a lengthy discussion of the technique, see Edward Markowski and Carol Markowski, "Some Difficulties and Improvements in Applying Linear Programming Formulations to the Discriminant Problem," *Decisions Sciences* (Summer 1985), pp. 233–247.

41. Ajay K. Rathi, Richard L. Church, and Rajendra S. Solanki, "A Macro Level Analysis of the Airlift Deployment Problem," *Computers & Operations Research* (November 1992), pp. 731–742.

42. Thomas J. Holloran and Jensen E. Bryn, "United Airlines Station Manpower Planning System," *Interfaces* (January–February 1986), pp. 39–50.

43. Jean Aubin, "Scheduling Ambulances," *Interfaces* (March–April 1992), pp. 1–10; Robert E. Marklin, *Topics in Management Science,* 2nd ed. (New York: Wiley, 1983).

44. James Gleick, "Breakthrough in Problem Solving," *New York Times* (November 15, 1984), p. A1.

45. For a recent review, see John R. Vacca, "Project Management Techniques," *Systems 3x/400* (September 1991), pp. 56–63.

46. Bajis Dodin, "Bounding the Project Completion Time in PERT Networks," *Operations Research* (July 1985), pp. 1–33.

47. Stevenson, op. cit., p. 630.

48. Gaither, op. cit., p. 653.

49. Mark B. Rowan, "The Critical Path," *Success* (September 1987), pp. 56–57.

50. For a discussion, see Dodin, loc. cit.

51. Stevenson, op. cit., p. 653.

52. Author's conversation with Blount Construction managers.

53. For example, see T. K. Littlefield and P. H. Randolph, "PERT Duration Times: Mathematics or MBO," *Interfaces* (November–December 1991), pp. 92–95.

54. Gerard I. Nierenberg, "Idea Generator," Experience Software Inc., Berkeley, Calif., 1985.

55. Bayard W. Wynne, "A Domination Sequence—MSLOR, DSS, and the Fifth Generation," *Interfaces* (May–June 1984), pp. 51–58.

56. Stephen Rosenberg, "Flexibility in Installing a Larger Scale HRIS: New York City's Experience," *Personnel Administrator* (December 1985), pp. 39–46.

57. William G. Wild, Jr., and Otis Port, "This Video Game Is Saving Manufacturers Millions," *Business Week* (August 17, 1987), pp. 82–84.

58. Ibid.

59. Ibid.

60. Mark R. Lembersky and Uli H. Chi, "Weyerhaeuser Decision Simulator Improves Timber Profits," *Interfaces* (January–February 1986), pp. 6–15.

61. Julie Wenderlich, Martin Collette, Laurence Levy and Lawrence Bodin, "Scheduling Meter Readers for Southern California Gas Company," *Interfaces* (May–June 1992), pp. 22–30.

62. Gordon L. Baker, Williams A. Clark, Jr., Jonathan J. Frund, and Richard E. Wendell, "Production Planning and Cost Analysis on a Micro Computer," *Interfaces* (July–August 1987), pp. 53–60.

63. Peter M. Senge, "Systems Thinking and Organizational Learning: Acting Locally and Thinking Globally in the Organization of the Future," *European Journal of Operational Research* (May 26, 1992), pp. 137–150; John D. W. Morecroft, "Executive Knowledge, Models and Learning," *European Journal of Operational Research* (May 26, 1992), pp. 9–27.

64. For a discussion of this latter point, see John C. Anderson and Thomas R. Hofman, "A Perspective on the Implementation of Management Science," *Academy of Management Review* (July 1978), pp. 563–571.

CHAPTER 9

1. Thomas A. Stewart, "The Search for the Organization of Tomorrow," *Fortune* (May 18, 1992), pp. 91–98; Charles C. Snow, Raymond E. Miles, and Henry J. Coleman, Jr., "Managing 21st Century Network Organizations," *Organizational Dynamics* (Winter 1992), pp. 5–20.

2. Stewart, loc. cit.

3. For a discussion of coordination, see John R. Schermerhorn, Jr., James G. Hunt, and Richard N. Osborn, *Managing Organizational Behavior* (New York: Wiley, 1988), pp. 328–330.

4. For a discussion, see Richard L. Daft, *Organization Theory and Design,* 2nd ed. (St. Paul, Minn.: West, 1986), p. 9. Daft more formally defines an organization as "a readily identifiable goal-directed social system working together in deliberately structured activity systems."

5. For example, see Mohammed M. Habib and Bart Victor, "Strategy, Structure, and Performance of U.S. Manufacturing and Service MNCs: A Comparative Analysis," *Strategic Management Journal* (November 1991), pp. 589–606; Roderick E. White, "Generic Business Strategies, Organizational Context and Performance: An Empirical Investigation," *Strategic Management Journal* (March–April 1986), pp. 217–231. For a review of the literature and synthesis of the two fields, see James W. Frederickson, "The Strategic Decision Process and Organizational Structure," *Academy of Management Review* (April 1986), pp. 280–297.

6. Based on Ernest Dale, *Organization* (New York: American Management Association, 1967), pp. 8–10.

7. Stewart, loc. cit.; George S. Odiorne, "The New Breed of Supervisor: Leaders in Self-Managed Work Teams," *Supervisor* (August 1991), pp. 14–17.

8. Thomas A. Stewart, "The Search for the Organization of Tomorrow," *Fortune* (May 18, 1992), pp. 91–98.

9. Kevin Parker, "Putting Back Together What Adam Smith Took Apart," *Manufacturing Systems* (August 1992), pp. 16–20.

10. Paul R. Lawrence and John W. Lorsch, *Organization and Environment* (Boston, Mass.: Division of Research, Harvard Business School, 1967).

11. Geary A. Rummler and Alan P. Brache, "Managing the White Space on the Organization Chart," *Supervisor* (May 1991), pp. 6–12.

12. Daft, op. cit., p. 385; Robert A. Dahl, "The Concept of Power," *Behavioral Science* (1957), pp. 201–215; W. Graham Astley and Paramijt S. Sachdeva, "Structural Sources of Intraorganizational Power: A Theoretical Synthesis," *Academy of Management Review* (January 1984), pp. 104–113.

13. Chester I. Barnard, *Functions of An Executive* (Cambridge, Mass.: Harvard University Press, 1938), pp. 163–174.

14. For a more recent discussion of the Lordstown experience, see Simon Caulkin, "The Human Factor in IT: Man and Machine," *Multinational Business* (Spring 1989), pp. 1–9; for an earlier discussion, see "Spread of GM's Lordstown Syndrome," *Business Week* (October 7, 1972), p. 72; "GM Efficiency Move That Backfired," *Business Week* (March 25, 1972), pp. 46–47; and D. N. Williams and R. A. Wilson, "Lordstown Shootout: Cost-Cutters vs. New Labor," *Iron Age* (February 3, 1972), pp. 38–39.

15. Based on this writer's experience as leader of the USAF Resources Audit Team that audited this colonel's operation.

16. Gary McWilliams, Punching in a Whole New Set of Commands at DEC, *Business Week* (October 12, 1992), p. 160; Gary McWilliams, "Crunch Time at DEC," *Business Week* (May 4, 1992), pp. 30–33.

17. Waino Soujanen, *The Dynamics of Management* (New York: Holt, 1966).

18. Charles C. Manz, "Self-Leadership . . . The Heart of Empowerment," *Journal for Quality & Participation* (July–August 1992), pp. 80–85.

19. For recent information on specific issues, see Robert D. Russell, "Innovation in Organizations: Toward an Integrated Model," *Review of Business* (Fall 1990), pp. 19–26; and Jeffrey Corrin and Dennis P. Slevin, "Strategic Management of Small Firms in Hostile and Benign Environments," *Strategic Management Journal* (January–February 1989), pp. 75–87. The class study is found in Tom Burns and G. M. Stalker, *The Management of Innovation* (London: Tavistock, 1961).

20. Carrie Dolan, "Hewlett-Packard Corporate Revamping Seen: Adding of Operating Chief Expected," *Wall Street Journal* (July 16, 1984), p. 2; "Who's Excellent Now?" *Business Week* (November 5, 1984), pp. 76–88; and Bro Utal, "Delays and Defection at Hewlett-Packard," *Fortune* (October 29, 1984), p. 62.

21. Stephen Kreider Yoder, "Quick Change: A 1990 Reorganization at Hewlett-Packard Already Is Paying Off," *Wall Street Journal* (July 22, 1991), pp. A1, A4.

22. Andrew D. Szilagyi, Jr., and Marc J. Wallace, Jr., *Organizational Behavior and Performance*, 4th ed. (Glenview, Ill.: Scott, Foresman, 1987), p. 557.

23. Stewart, loc. cit.; and Frank Ostroff and Douglas Smith, "Redesigning the Corporation: The Horizontal Organization," *The McKinsey Quarterly* (1992), no. 1, pp. 148–168.

24. Ibid.

25. Brenton R. Schlender, "Apple Sets Plan to Reorganize into 4 Divisions," *Wall Street Journal* (August 23, 1988, p. 2; Katherine M. Hafner, "The World According to John Sculley," *Business Week* (September 28, 1987), pp. 71–73; Peter Dworkin, "After a Long Diet, Apple Bites Back," *U.S. News & World Report* (January 26, 1987), pp. 47–48; and Joel Dreyfuss, "John Sculley Rises in the West," *Fortune* (July 9, 1987), pp. 180–183.

26. Gregory Bovasso, "A Structural Analysis of the Formation of a Network Organization," *Group & Organization Management* (March 1992), pp. 86–106; Charles C. Snow, Raymond E. Miles, and Henry J. Coleman, Jr., "Managing 21st Century Network Organizations," *Organization Dynamics* (Winter 1992), pp. 5–20.

27. Observations based on this writer's experience as an accountant for Lockheed, Georgia.

28. Douglas R. Sease, "Getting Smart: How U.S. Companies Devise Ways to Meet Challenge from Japan," *Wall Street Journal* (September 16, 1986), p. 1.

29. Thomas J. Peters and Robert H. Waterman, Jr., *In Search of Excellence* (New York: Harper & Row, 1982).

30. Ian MacMillan and Patricia E. Jones, "Designing Organizations to Compete," *Journal of Business Strategy* (Spring, 1984), pp. 22–26.

31. Observations based on this writer's experience.

32. This is a rule of thumb only. The contingency factors determine appropriate spans of control. However, if the manager is to perform all the desired leadership behaviors (see Chapter 16), the number of subordinates cannot become too large.

33. Based on this writer's experiences as a consultant.

34. For a lengthy discussion of the span of control, see David D. VanFleet and Arthur G. Bedeian, "A History of the Span of Management," *Academy of Management Review* (July 1977), pp. 356–372; and David D. VanFleet, "Span of Management Research and Issues," *Academy of Management Review* (September 1983), pp. 546–552.

35. C. W. Barkdall, "Span of Control—A Method of Evaluation," *Michigan Business Review* (May 1963), pp. 27–29.

36. John S. McClenahen, "Managing More People in the 90's," *Industry Week* (March 20, 1989), pp. 30–38.

37. Joseph B. White, "GM Aims to Break Even by Next Year," *Wall Street Journal* (November 13, 1992), p. A3; Jolie Solomon, "Can GM Fix Itself?" *Newsweek* (November 9, 1992), pp. 54–59; William J. Hampton and James R. Norman, "General Motors: What Went Wrong?" *Business Week* (March 16, 1987), pp. 102–110; and Jack A. Seamonds and Kenneth R. Sheets, "GM's November Massacre," *U.S. News & World Report* (November 17, 1987), p. 56.

38. Based on James D. Mooeny, *The Principles of Organization*, rev. ed. (New York: Hamber, 1947), p. 5; and on Daft, op. cit., chap. 6.

39. Author's discussion with Phil Crosby, Jr., and other staff in the firm.

40. Russell Mitchell, "GM Hasn't Bought Much Peace," *Business Week* (December 15, 1986), pp. 24–28; William J. Cook, "Perot's War with GM Ends in $743 Million Goodbye," *U.S. News & World Report* (December 15, 1986), pp. 52–54.

41. Peter G. W. Keen, "Redesigning the Organization Through Information Technology," *Planning Review* (May–June 1991), pp. 4–9.

42. Paul R. Lawrence and Jay W. Lorsch, *Organization and Environment: Managing Differentiation and Integration* (Homewood, Ill.: Irwin 1967), pp. 8–10.

43. Lawrence and Lorsch, loc. cit.

44. Rensis Likert, *New Patterns of Management* (New York: McGraw-Hill, 1961), pp. 113–115.

45. Charles Margerison and Dick McCann, "How to Improve Your Linking Skills," *Journal of European Industrial Training* (1992), no. 2, pp. i–iii.

46. Daft, loc. cit.

47. Kenneth L. Bettenhausen, "Five Years of Group Research: What We Have Learned and What Needs to be Addressed," *Journal of Management* (June 1991) reviews recent group research on pp. 345–381 and reviews recent research on teams on pp. 366–372. See also Anna Versteeg, "Self-Directed Work Teams Yield Long-Term Benefits," *The Journal of Business Strategy* (November–December 1990), pp. 9–12; Ed Musselwhite and Linda Moran, "On the Road to Self-Direction," *Journal for Quality & Participation* (June 1990), pp. 58–63; and Edgar F. Huse and Thomas G. Cummings, *Organizational Development and Change,* 3rd ed. (St. Paul, Minn.: West, 1985), pp. 5, 84.

48. Based on this writer's knowledge of a consultant's efforts to place team management in a dairy in Georgia.

49. Michael Rigg, "Vision and Valve: Keys to Initiating Organizational Change," *Industrial Engineering* (June 1992), pp. 12–13.

50. Stanley M. Davis and Paul L. Lawrence, *Matrix* (Reading, Mass.: Addison-Wesley, 1977), pp. 11–24.

51. Several of these are common problems as related to me by many of my students who work for Martin Marietta, which uses the matrix system. For a thorough review, see Eric W. Larson and David H. Gobeil, "Matrix Management: Contradictions and Insights," *California Management Review* (Summer 1987), pp. 126–138.

52. For a discussion of the possibilities, see Robert C. Ford and Randolph W. Alan, "Cross-Functional Structures: A Review and Integration of Matrix Organization and Project Management," *Journal of Management* (June 1992), pp. 267–294.

53. Carol Kennedy, "How Nokia Is Going High Tech," *Long Range Planning* (April 1992), pp. 16–25.

54. "Prodigy Now Credible as DM Medium," *Target Marketing* (March 1992), p. 18; Bill Saporito, "Are IBM and Sears Crazy?" *Fortune* (September 28, 1987), pp. 74–80.

55. Raymond E. Miles and Charles C. Snow, "Causes of Failures in Network Organizations," *California Management Review* (Summer 1992), pp. 53–72.

56. For example, see ibid.

57. James L. Gibson, John M. Ivancevich, and James H. Donnelly, Jr., *Organizations: Behavior, Structure, Processes,* 6th ed. (Plano, Tex.: Business Publications, 1988), p. 279.

58. For a theoretical research review of structuring as a decision process, see H. Randolph Bobbitt, Jr., and Jeffrey D. Ford, "Decision-Maker Choice as a Determinant of Organizational Structure," *Academy of Management Review* (January 1980), pp. 13–23.

59. Robert D. Hof, "Suddenly, Hewlett-Packard is Doing Everything Right," *Business Week* (March 22, 1992), pp. 88, 89; Barbara Buell and Robert D. Hof, "Hewlett-Packard Rethinks Itself," *Business Week* (April 1, 1991), pp. 76–79.

CHAPTER 10

1. Paul Sweeney, "Cut Costs, Make Money. Sometimes," *Global Finance* (April 1992), pp. 101–105.

2. Homa Bahrami, "The Emerging Flexible Organization: Perspectives from Silicon Valley," *California Management Review* (Summer 1992), pp. 33–52.

3. Alfred D. Chandler, Jr., *Strategy and Structure* (Cambridge, Mass.: MIT Press, 1962).

4. For example, see Thomas C. Powell, "Organizational Alignment as Competitive Advantage," *Strategic Management Journal* (November 1991), pp. 589–606.

5. For a review of these three, see J. C. Ford and John W. Slocum, "Size, Technology, Environment, and the Structure of Organizations," *Academy of Management Review* (October 1977), pp. 561–575.

6. A number of books make this point. Two very early books to do so were William G. Ouchi, *Theory Z: How American Business Can Meet the Japanese Challenge* (Reading, Mass.: Addison-Wesley, 1981); and Robert T. Pascale and Anthony G. Arthos, *The Art of Japanese Management: Applications for American Executives* (New York: Simon & Schuster, 1981).

7. John J. Morse and J. W. Lorsch, "Beyond Theory Y," *Harvard Business Review* (May–June 1970), pp. 61–68.

8. "The Next Paradigm?" *Chief Executive* (June 1992), pp. 61–65. The specific issue was flattening the pyramid.

9. For a discussion of contingency views on structure and on fitting structure to key situational factors, see W. Alan Randolph and Gregory G.

Dess, "The Congruence Perspective of Organizational Design: A Conceptual Model and Multivariate Approach," *Academy of Management Review* (January 1984), pp. 114–127; Andrew Van de Ven and R. Drazin, "The Concept of Fit in Contingency Theory," in Larry Cummings and Barry Stavo, eds., *Research in Organizational Behavior* (Greenwich, Conn.: JAI Press, 1983), pp. 333–365; and Raymond E. Miles and Charles C. Snow, "Fit, Failure, and the Hall of Fame," *California Management Review* (Spring 1984), pp. 10–28.

10. David J. Hall and Maurice A. Saias, "Strategy Follows Structure," *Strategic Management Journal* (April–June 1980), pp. 149–165.

11. Michael Tushman and David Nadler, "Organizing for Innovation," *California Management Review* (Spring 1986), pp. 74–92, discuss the theoretical and research perspective. See also "Masters of Innovation," *Business Week* (April 10, 1989), pp. 58–63, which discusses specific examples, principally 3M.

12. An advertisement in the *Wall Street Journal* (September 23, 1987), p. 39.

13. Danny Miller, "Configurations of Strategy and Structure: Towards a Synthesis," *Strategic Management Journal* (May–June 1986), pp. 233–249.

14. Henry A. Mintzberg, "Patterns in Strategy Formation," *Management Science* (May 1978), pp. 934–948.

15. Tom Burns and G. M. Stalker, *The Management of Innovation* (London: Tavistock, 1961).

16. For example, see Oskar G. Mink, "Creating New Organizational Paradigms for Change," *International Journal of Quality and Reliability Management* (1992), no. 3, pp. 21–35.

17. Kenneth Jennings, "Eastern's Final Days: Labor Relations Lessons for Managers in Other Organizations," *Transportation Journal* (Spring 1992), pp. 27–38; Aaron Bernstein, Michael O'Neal, and Gail DeGeorge, "Eastern: The Wings of Greed," *Business Week* (November 11, 1991), pp. 34–36; Gary Cohn, "Classic Mistake: Eastern Air's Borman Badly Underestimated Obduracy of Old Foe," *Wall Street Journal* (February 25, 1986), pp. 1, 27; Leslie Wayne, "Frank Bowman's Most Difficult Days," *New York Times* (February 17, 1985); and Gary Cohn, "Eastern Airlines Blasts Union Request for Revenue Share, Will Reinstate Cut," *Wall Street Journal* (February 6, 1985), p. 6.

18. Robert B. Duncan, "Characteristics of Perceived Environments and Perceived Environmental Uncertainty," *Administrative Science Quarterly* (September 1972), pp. 313–327.

19. Robert Howard, "The Designer Organization: Italy's GFT Goes Global," *Harvard Business Review* (September–October 1991), pp. 28–44.

20. Thomas A. Stewart, "The Search for the Organization of Tomorrow," *Fortune* (May 18, 1992), pp. 92–98; Frank Ostroff and Douglas Smith, "Redesigning the Corporation: The Horizontal Organization," *The McKinsey Quarterly* (1992), no. 1, pp. 148–168. In a related but different discussion of the horizontal organization, see Thomas A. Poynter and Roderick E. White, "Making the Horizontal Organization Work," *Business Quarterly* (Winter 1990), pp. 73–77; Roderick E. White and Thomas A. Poynter, "Achieving Worldwide Advantage with the Horizontal Organization" *Business Quarterly* (Autumn 1989), pp. 55–60; and Roderick E. White and Thomas A. Poynter, "Organizing for Worldwide Advantage," *Business Quarterly* (Summer 1989), pp. 84–89. White and Poynter do not use the term *process*, as does McKinsey & Company. Rather, they use the words *value adding activities* to describe the basic unit of structure. The two approaches are very similar. Poynter and White have researched how firms compete successfully on a global basis while staying close to local markets. They do this through horizontal organization structure.

21. Stewart, loc. cit.

22. Raymond E. Miles and Charles C. Snow, "Causes of Failure in Network Organizations," *California Management Review* (Summer 1992), pp. 53–57; Roderick E. White and Thomas A. Poynter, "Organizing for Worldwide Advantage, loc. cit.; Fred V. Guterl, "Goodbye Old Matrix," *Business Month* (February 1989), pp. 32–38; and Raymond E. Miles and Charles C. Snow, "Organizations: New Concept for New Forms," *California Management Review* (Spring 1986), pp. 62–73.

23. Charles C. Snow, Raymond E. Miles, and Henry J. Coleman, Jr., "Managing 21st Century Network Organizations," *Organizational Dynamics* (Winter 1992), pp. 5–20.

24. James Brian Quinn and Penny C. Paquette, "Technology in Services: Creating Organizational Revolutions," *Sloan Management Review* (Winter 1990), pp. 67–78.

25. Christopher Barnett and Pauline Wong, "Acquisition Activity and Organizational Structure," *Journal of Global Management* (Spring 1992), pp. 1–15.

26. James Brian Quinn, Thomas L. Doorley, and Penny C. Paquette, "Technology in Services: Rethinking Strategic Focus," *Sloan Management Review* (Winter 1990), pp. 79–87.

27. For a discussion of hollow manufacturing corporations, see Sak Onkvisit and John J. Shaw, "Myopic Management: The Hollow Strength of American Competitiveness," *Business Horizons* (January–February 1991), PP. 13–19. For a discussion of outsourcing information systems, see David Kirkpatrick, "Why Not Farm Out Your Computer?" *Fortune* (September 23, 1991), pp. 103–112.

28. John A. Byrne, "The Virtual Corporation," *Business Week* (February 8, 1993), pp. 98–103.

29. Paul R. Lawrence and J. W. Lorsch, "Differentiation and Integration in Complex Organizations," *Administrative Science Quarterly* (June 1967), pp. 1–47; and Paul R. Lawrence and J. W. Lorsch, *Organization and Environment* (Homewood, Ill.: Irwin, 1969).

30. Ibid., "Differentiation and Integration in Complex Organizations," p. 16.

31. Lawrence and Lorsch, "Differentiation and Integration in Complex Organizations," op. cit., pp. 3–4.

32. Ibid., p. 4.

33. Bahrami, loc. cit.

34. Ray Stata, "Organizational Learning—The Key to Management Innovation," *Sloan Management Review* (Spring 1989), pp. 63–74.

35. Gordon L. Lippitt and Warren H. Schmidt, "Crises of a Developing Organization," *Harvard Business Review* (November–December 1967), pp. 101–109; Bruce R. Scott, "The Industrial State: Oldness and New Realities," *Harvard Business Review* (March–April 1973), pp. 133–149; Donald H. Thain, "Stages of Corporate Development," *Business Quarterly* (Summer 1969), pp. 32–45; and J. R. Kimberly, "Organization Size and the Structurephile Perspective: A Review, Critique and Proposal," *Administrative Science Quarterly* (December 1976), pp. 591–597.

36. In addition, Ian McMillan and Patricia E. Jones have identified several combinations of first-level and second-level groupings that further complicate the design problem: function to function; function to product; function to customer; product to product; product to function; product to customer; geographic area to customer; customer to function; and customer to product. See "Designing Organizations to Compete," *Journal of Business Strategy* (Spring 1984), pp. 22–26.

37. John R. Kimberly, Robert H. Miles, and Associates, *The Organizational Life Cycle* (San Francisco: Jossey-Bass, 1980).

38. Thomas J. Peters, "Rethinking Scale," *California Management Review* (Fall 1992), pp. 7–28; Thomas J. Peters, "Doubting Thomas," *Inc.* (April 1989), pp. 82–92; "Is Your Company Too Big?" *Business Week* (March 27, 1989), pp. 84–94; Peters and Waterman loc. cit.; and "Getting Smart," *Wall Street Journal* (September 16, 1986), p. 1.

39. John Child, "Managerial and Organizational Factors Associated with Company Performance—Part II: A Contingency Analysis," *Journal of Management Studies* (February 1975), pp. 12–27.

40. Jacqueline Graves, "Leaders of Corporate Change," *Fortune* (December 14, 1992), pp. 104–114.

41. Amanda Bennett, "Downsizing Doesn't Necessarily Bring an Upswing in Corporate Profitability," *Wall Street Journal* (June 6, 1991), pp. B1, B8.

42. Sweeney, loc. cit.

43. Jewell G. Westerman and William A. Sherden, "Moving Beyond Lean and Mean," *Journal of Business Strategy* (September–October 1991), pp. 12–16.

44. Max Messmer, "Rightsizing, Not Downsizing," *Industry Week* (August 3, 1992), pp. 23–26; Bruce R. Pittenger, "Upside to Downsizing," *Executive Excellence* (October 1991), pp. 15–16.

45. For a review of the research, see C. Chet Miller, William H. Glick, Yau-De Wang and George P. Huber, "Understanding Technology-Structure Relationships: Theory Development and Meta-Analytic Theory Testing," *Academy of Management Journal* (June 1992), pp. 370–399; and Louis W. Fry, "Technology-Structure Research: Three Critical Issues," *Academy of Management Journal* (September 1982), pp. 532–552.

46. David E. Gillespie and Dennis S. Mileti, "Technology and the Study of Organizations: An Overview and Appraisal," *Academy of Management Review* (January 1977), p. 8.

47. For example, see Gareth Jones, "Task Visibility, Free Riding and Shirking: Explaining the Effect of Structure and Technology on Employee Behavior," *Academy of Management Journal* (June 1984), pp. 247–270.

48. For a theory of the impact of information technology on organizational design, see George P. Huber, "A Theory of the Effects of Advanced Information Technology on Organizational Design, Intelligence and Decision Making," *Academy of Management Review* (January 1990), pp. 47–71. See also Charles Perrow, *Complex Organizations: A Critical Essay*, 2nd ed. (Glenview, Ill.: Scott, Foresman, 1979).

49. Peter G. W. Keen, "Redesigning the Organization Through Information Technology," *Planning Review* (May–June 1991), pp. 4–9.

50. Joan Woodward, *Industrial Organization: Theory and Practice* (London: Oxford University Press, 1965).

51. Ibid., p. 35.

52. For a review of the literature on technology and its methodological problems, see Lewis W. Fry, "Technology—Structure Research: Three Critical Issues," *Academy of Management Journal* (September 1982), pp. 532–552.

53. Lyman W. Porter, Edward E. Lawler, III, and Jay Richard Hackman, *Behavior in Organizations* (New York: McGraw-Hill, 1975), pp. 232–243.

54. For example, see D. S. Pugh, D. J. Hickson, C. R. Hinings, K. M. MacDonald, C. Turner, and T. Lupton, "A Conceptual Scheme for Organizational Analysis," *Administrative Science Quarterly* (June 1963), pp. 291–315; and D. S. Pugh, D. J. Hickson, C. R. Hinings, and C. Turner, "The Context of Organizational

Structures," *Administrative Science Quarterly* (1969), pp. 91–113.

55. Jayant V. Saraph, "Human Resource Strategies for Effective Introduction of Advanced Manufacturing Technologies," *Production & Inventory Management Journal* (First Quarter 1992), pp. 64–70.

56. Peter Drucker, "New Templates for Today's Organization," *Harvard Business Review* (January–February 1974), p. 51.

57. Thomas A. Stewart, "Westinghouse Gets Respect at Last," *Fortune* (July 3, 1989), pp. 92–98.

58. For a review of the literature, see Robert I. Sutton and Thomas D'Aunno, "Decreasing Organizational Size: Untangling the Effects of Money and People," *Academy of Management Review* (April 1989), pp. 192–212.

59. Peter F. Drucker, "The Coming of the New Organization," *Harvard Business Review* (January–February 1988), pp. 45–53.

60. Stanley Davis, presentation to the Strategic Management Society, Boston, October 15, 1987.

61. Sang M. Lee, Fred Luthans, and Davis L. Olson, "A Management Science Approach to Contingency Models of Organizational Structure," *Academy of Management Journal* (September 1982), pp. 553–566; W. Alan Randolph and Gregory C. Dess, "The Congruence Perspective of Organization Design: A Conceptual Model and Multivariate Research Approach," *Academy of Management Review* (January 1984), pp. 114–127.

CHAPTER 11

1. Michael Hammer, "Reengineering Work: Don't Automate, Obliterate," *Harvard Business Review* (July–August 1990), pp. 104–112.

2. Stewart Toy, "Europe's Shakeout," *Business Week* (September 14, 1992), pp. 44–51.

3. David F. Smith, "The Functions of Work," *Omega* (1975), no. 4. pp. 383–393.

4. For example, see Thomas A. Stewart, "The Search for the Organization of Tomorrow," *Fortune* (May 18, 1992), pp. 91–98; James Graham, "Quality of Working Life and Total Quality Management," *International Journal of Manpower* (1992), no. 1, pp. 41–58.

5. James M. Higgins, *Human Relations: Behavior at Work* (New York: Random House 1987), pp. 298–299.

6. J. Richard Hackman and Greg R. Oldham, *Work Redesigned* (Reading, Mass.: Addison-Wesley, 1980), pp. 77–80.

7. See for example, Henry P. Sims, Jr., Andrew D. Szilagyi, and Robert T. Keller, "The Measurement of Job Characteristics," *Academy of Management Journal* (June 1976), p. 197; and Higgins, op. cit., Chapter 12, for a review.

8. Douglas R. Sease, "Getting Smart: How U. S. Companies Devise Ways to Meet Challenge from Japan," *Wall Street Journal* (September 16, 1986), pp. 1, 25.

9. Some feel that performance leads to satisfaction. Others feel that rewards lead to satisfaction and performance. Still others believe that satisfaction and performance are reciprocally causal. For a review of the literature, see the collection of studies reported in Frederick W. Herzberg, *The Managerial Choice: To Be Efficient and to Be Human* (Homewood, Ill.: Dow Jones-Irwin, 1976). For criticisms, see Robert J. House and Lawrence A. Wigdor, "Herzberg's Dual-Factor Theory of Job Satisfaction and Motivation: A Review of the Evidence and a Criticism," *Personnel Psychology* (Winter 1967), pp. 369–389; Steven Kerr, Anne Harlan, and Ralph Stogdill, "Preference for Motivator and Hygiene Factors in a Hypothetical Interview Situation," *Personnel Psychology* (Winter 1974), pp. 109–124; Benedict

Grigaliunas and Yoash Wiener, "Has the Research Challenge to Motivation-Hygiene Theory Been Conclusive?" An Analysis of Critical Studies," *Human Relations* (1974), vol. 27, pp. 839–871; Charles N. Greene, "The Satisfaction-Performance Controversy," *Business Horizons* (October 1972), pp. 31–41; Charles N. Greene and Robert E. Craft, Jr., "The Satisfaction-Performance Controversy Revisited," in Kirk Downey, Don Hellriegel, and John Slocum, eds., *Organizational Behavior: A Reader* (St. Paul, Minn.: West, 1977), pp. 187–201; Arthur H. Brayfield and Walter H. Crockett, "Employee Attitudes and Employee Performance," *Psychological Bulletin* (1955), vol. 52, pp. 415–422; Donald P. Schwab and Larry L. Cummings, "Theories of Performance and Satisfaction," *Industrial Relations* (1970), no. 4, pp. 408–430; Victor H. Vroom, *Work and Motivation* (New York: Wiley, 1964); and Enid Mumford, "Job Satisfaction: A Method of Analysis," *Personnel Review* (1991), no. 3, pp. 11–19.

10. Hammer, loc. cit.

11. For example, see Julie Cohen Mason, "IBM at the Crossroads," *Management Review* (September 1991), pp. 10–14; Linda Berg, Rich Blackwell, Jeanette Lewis, Gordon Phillips, Joe Pilch, and Geoff Potter, "New Wave QWL," *Journal for Quality and Participation* (January–February 1990), pp. 32–34.

12. Richard E. Kopelman, "Job Redesign and Productivity: A Review of the Evidence," *National Productivity Review* (Summer 1985), p. 239.

13. Richard E. Walton, "Quality of Work Life: What Is It?" *Sloan Management Review* (Fall 1973), pp. 11–21.

14. Graham James, "Quality of Working Life and Total Quality Management," *International Journal of Manpower* (1992), no. 1, pp. 41–58.

15. For a review, see J. Barton Cunningham and Ted Eberle, "A Guide to Job Enrichment and Redesign," *Personnel* (February 1990), pp. 56–61.

16. Vida Scarpello and John P. Campbell, "Job Satisfaction and the Fit Between Individual Needs and Organizational Rewards," *Journal of Occupational Psychology* (1983), pp. 315–328.

17. Chris Argyris, *Personality and Organization* (New York: Harper, 1957).

18. Douglas McGregor, *The Human Side of Enterprise* (New York: McGraw-Hill, 1960).

19. Frederick W. Herzberg, *Work and the Nature of Man* (New York: World, 1971).

20. Gene Bylinsky, "America's Best-Managed Factories," *Fortune* (May 28, 1984), pp. 16–27.

21. Carl Bozeman, "The Vough Approach at Granville-Phillips," *Journal for Quality & Participation* (March 1989), pp. 43–45.

22. Zandy B. Leibowitz, Beverly L. Kaye and Caela Farren, "What to Do About Career Gridlock," *Training & Development Journal* (April 1992), pp. 28–35.

23. "Job Rotation Keeps Swissair Flying High," *Management Review* (August 1985), p. 10.

24. Lance Hazzard, Joe Mautz, and Denver Wrightsman, "Job Rotation Cuts Cumulative Trauma Cases," *Personnel Journal* (February 1992), pp. 29–32.

25. For a review of what makes quality circles successful, see Bruno Fabi, "Contingency Factors in Quality Circles: A Review of Empirical Evidence," *International Journal of Quality & Reliability Management* (1992), no. 2, pp. 18–33.

26. Lori Fitzgerald and Joseph Murphy, *Installing Quality Circles: A Strategic Approach* (San Diego: University Associates 1982), p. 3.

27. Robert Wood, Frank Hoe, and Koya Azuni, "Evaluating Quality Circles: The American Application," *California Management Review* (Fall 1983), p. 43.

28. Michael J. Showalter and Judith A. Mulholland, "Continuous Improvement for Service

Organizations," *Business Horizons* (July–August 1992), pp. 82–87.

29. For a recent review, see Mahmoud Salem, Harold Lazarus, and Joseph Cullen, "Developing Self-managing Teams: Structure and Performance," *Journal of Management Development* (1992), no. 3, pp. 24–32.

30. Harry C. Katz, Thomas A. Kochan, and Mark R. Weber, "Assessing the Effects of Industrial Relations Systems and Efforts to Improve the Quality of Working Life on Organizational Effectiveness," *Academy of Management Journal* (September 1985), pp. 514–515; Lawrence Miller, "The Impact of Unity: Tearing Down the Barriers Between Management and Labor Leads to Increased Productivity and Greater Profits," *Management Review* (May 1984), pp. 8–15.

31. Gary S. Vasilash, "Teams Are Working Hard at Chrysler," *Production* (October 1991), pp. 50–52; Martha T. Moore, "Sorting Out a Mess," *USA Today* (April 10, 1992), p. 5B.

32. Stewart, loc. cit.

33. Kae H. Chung and Monica F. Ross, "Differences in Motivational Properties Between Job Enlargement and Job Enrichment," *Academy of Management Review* (January 1977), pp. 113–122.

34. Ibid.

35. Ibid.

36. Richard M. Roderick, "Redesigning an Accounting Department for Corporate and Personal Goals," *Management Accounting* (February 1984), pp. 56–60.

37. David C. McClelland, *Human Motivation* (Glenview, Ill.: Scott, Foresman, 1989), *The Achieving Society* (Princeton, N.J.: Van Nostrand, 1961).

38. For a discussion, see Robert B. Leventhal, "Union Involvement in New Work Systems," *Journal for Quality & Participation* (June 1991), pp. 36–39; Chan Choon Hian and Walter O. Einstein, "Quality of Work Life (QWL): What Can Unions Do?" *Advanced Management Journal* (Spring 1990), pp. 17–22.

39. See J. K. White, "Individual Differences and the Job Quality—Worker Response Relationships: Review, Integration, Comments," *Academy of Management Review* (July 1978), pp. 267–280; Milton R. Blood and Charles L. Hulin, "Alienation, Environmental Characteristics and Worker Responses," *Journal of Applied Psychology* (1967), pp. 284–290; William T. Rutherford and James M. Higgins, "Democracy at Work or Only Away from Work?" *Atlanta Economic Review* (November–December 1974), p. 8; and William E. Reif and Fred Luthans, "Does Job Enrichment Really Pay Off?" *California Management Review* (Fall 1972), pp. 30–37.

40. Bernard J. White, "The Criteria for Job Satisfaction: Is Interesting Work Most Important?" *Monthly Labor Review* (May 1977), pp. 30–35.

41. William J. Hampton and James R. Norman, "General Motors: What Went Wrong," *Business Review* (March 16, 1987), pp. 106–107.

42. Adapted from Robert N. Ford, "Job Enrichment Lessons from AT&T," *Harvard Business Review* (January–February 1973), pp. 96–106.

43. Pradip M. Khandwalla, "Mass Output Orientation of Operations Technology and Organizational Structure," *Administrative Science Quarterly* (March 1974), p. 74.

44. E. Mesthene, *Technological Change: Its Impact on Man in Society* (Cambridge: Harvard University Press, 1970); also see David F. Gillespie and Dennis F. Galletti, "Technology and Study of Organizations: An Overview and Appraisal," *Academy of Management Review* (January 1977, p. 8.

45. "High Tech: Blessing Occurs," *U.S. News & World Report* (January 16, 1984), p. 38.

46. "Factory Toils into Night Without People," *Orlando Sentinel* (December 22, 1985), p. F10.
47. Hampton and Norman, op. cit., p. 107.
48. "High Tech," op. cit., p. 43.
49. Nancy J. Perry, "The Workers of the Future," *Fortune, The New American Century,* Special Issue (1991), pp. 68–72.
50. Victor Lazzaro, "The Automated Apple Orchard," *Discover* (September 1985), pp. 80–81.
51. David Kirkpatrick, "Here Comes the Payoff from PCs," *Fortune* (March 23, 1992), pp. 93–102; Deidre A. Depke and Neil Gross, "Laptops Take Off," *Business Week* (March 18, 1991), pp. 118–124.
52. Peter Coy, "The New Realism in Office Systems," *Business Week* (June 15, 1992), pp. 128–133.
53. Ibid.
54. "Office Automation Restructures Business," *Business Week* (October 8, 1984), pp. 118–125.
55. Hammer, loc. cit.
56. Phil Patton, "The Best Year for Your Home Office," *Money* (July 1991), pp. 106–114.
57. Timothy K. Smith, "Electronic Control of Households Arrives with Advantages," *Wall Street Journal* (November 11, 1985), p. 27; Robert Johnson, "Rush to Cottage Computer Work Falters Despite Advent of New Technology," *Wall Street Journal* (June 29, 1983), pp. 37, 42.
58. Bob Filipczak, "Telecommuting: A Better Way to Work?" *Training* (May 1992), pp. 53–61.
59. Lura K. Romei, "Telecommuting: A Workstyle Revolution," *Modern Office Technology* (May 1992), pp. 38–40.
60. Alan Deutschman, "The Upbeat Generation," *Fortune* (July 13, 1992), pp. 41–48, 52–54.
61. Ibid., and for example, see Michael Brody, "Meet Today's Young American Worker," *Fortune* (November 11, 1985), pp. 90–98; "The New-Collar Blues," *U.S. News & World Report* (September 16, 1985), pp. 59–65.
62. Robert W. Goddard, "Work Force 2000," *Personnel Journal* (February 1989), pp. 64–71.
63. For example, see Patricia Brans, "What Workers Want," *American Demographics* (August 1992), pp. 30–37.
64. L. B. Russell, *The Baby Boom Generation and the Economy* (Washington, D.C.: Brookings Institution, 1982).
65. Daniel Yankelovich and Jay Immerwahr, *Putting the New Work Ethics to Work* (New York: Public Agenda Foundation, September 1983); Daniel Yankelovich, "Work, Values, and the New Breed," in C. Kerr and J. M. Roson eds., *Work in America: The Decade Ahead* (New York: Van Nostrand, 1979), pp. 3–26.
66. As quoted by John Naisbitt, *Megatrends* (New York: Warner, 1982), p. 184.
67. Simcha Ronen, *Flexible Working Hours: An Innovation in the Quality of Work Life* (New York: McGraw-Hill, 1981); Allan R. Cohen and Herman A. Gadon, *Alternative Work Schedules: Integrating Individual and Organizational Needs* (Reading, Mass.: Addison-Wesley, 1978).
68. Beth Rogers, "Companies Develop Benefits for Part-Timers," *HR Magazine* (May 1992), pp. 89–90.
69. Chris Tilly, "Dualism in Part-Time Employment," *Industrial Relations* (Spring 1992), pp. 330–347.
70. Michael A. Pollock and Erin Bernstein, "The Disposable Employee Is Becoming a Fact of Corporate Life," *Business Week* (December 15, 1986), pp. 52–56.
71. Simcha Ronen and Sophia B. Primps, "The Compressed Work Week as Organizational Change: Behavioral and Attitudinal Outcomes," *Academy of Management Review* (January 1981), pp. 61–74.
72. John M. Ivancevich and Herbert C. Lyons, "The Shortened Work Week: A Field Experiment," *Journal of Applied Psychology* (February 1977), pp. 34–37.
73. David Clutterbuck, "Why a Job Shared Is Not a Job Halved," *International Management* (October 1979), pp. 45–47; Michael Frease and Robert A. Zawacki, "Job Sharing: An Answer to Productivity Problems," *The Personnel Administrator* (October 1979), pp. 35–38.
74. For representative discussions of some of these issues, see James W. Dean, Jr., and Scott H. Snell, "Integrated Manufacturing and Job Design: Moderating Effects of Organization Inertia," *Academy of Management Journal* (December 1991), pp. 776–804; and Janice A. Klein, "A Reexamination of Autonomy in Light of New Manufacturing Practices," *Human Relations* (January 1991), pp. 21–30.

CHAPTER 12

1. Randall S. Schuler, "Strategic Human Resource Management: Linking the People with the Strategic Needs of the Business," *Organizational Dynamics* (Summer 1992), pp. 18–32; J. E. Butler, G. R. Ferris, and N. K. Napier, *Strategy and Human Resource Management* (Cincinnati: Southwestern, 1991); and Max Messmer, "Strategic Staffing for the '90s," *Personnel Journal* (October 1990), pp. 92–97.
2. "The Human Equation," *Business Week, Reinventing America,* Special Issue (Fall 1992), pp. 75–106.
3. Randall S. Schuler, Steven P. Galiente, and Susan E. Jackson, "Matching Effective Human Resource Practices with Competitive Strategy," *Personnel* (September 1987), pp. 18–27.
4. For a review of this issue, see Cynthia A. Lengneck-Hall and mark L. Lengneck-Hall, "Strategic Human Resources Management: A Review of the Literature and a Proposed Typology," *Academy of Management Review* (July 1988), pp. 454–470.
5. Schuler, loc. cit.; Messmer, loc. cit.; Butler, Ferris, and Napier, loc. cit.; Thomas A. Mahoney and John R. Deckop, "Evolution of Concept and Practice in Personnel Administration/Human Resource Management (PA/HRM)," in James G. Hunt and John D. Blair, eds., *Yearly Review of Management of the Journal of Management* (Summer 1986), pp. 223–242.
6. For example, see Rebecca A. Thacker, "Affirmative Action After the Supreme Court's 1988–1989 Terms," *Employment Relations Today* (Summer 1990), pp. 139–144; and Stephen Wermeil, "High Court's Affirmative Action Milestones," *Wall Street Journal* (March 26, 1987), p. 3.
7. Alvin C. Hill, Jr., and James Scott, "Ten Strategies for Managers in a Multicultural Work Force," *HR Focus* (August 1992), p. 6; Barbara B. Kalish, "Women at Work: Dismantling the Glass Ceiling," *Management Review* (March 1992), pp. 64; and Anthony J. Buonocore, "Older and Wiser: Senior Employees Offer Untapped Capabilities," *Management Review* (July 1992), pp. 44–52.
8. Laura Zinn, "Move Over, Boomers: The Busters Are Here—And They're Angry," *Business Week* (December 14, 1992), pp. 74–82; Robert Barker, "A Shortage of Basic Skills," *Business Week* (January 13, 1992), p. 39; Nancy J. Perry, "The Workers of the Future," *Fortune, The New American Century,* Special Issue (Spring–Summer 1991), pp. 68–72; Gary W. Loveman and John J. Gabarro, "The Managerial Implications of Changing Work Force Demographics: A Scoping Study," *Human Resource Management* (Spring 1991), pp. 7–29.
9. For example, see Daniel C. Feldman and Helen I. Doepinghaus, "Missing Persons No Longer: Managing Part-Time Workers in the 90s," *Organizational Dynamics* (Summer 1992), pp. 59–72.
10. William B. Johnston, "Global Work Force 2000: The New World Labor Market," *Harvard Business Review* (March–April 1991), pp. 115–127.
11. Ibid.
12. *Dictionary of Occupational Titles,* 4th ed. (Washington D.C.: U.S. Department of Labor, 1977).
13. Nicholas C. Byrne, "Successful Hiring Starts with a Complete Job Description," *Human Resources Professional* (Summer 1991), pp. 38–41; Mark A. Jones, "Job Descriptions Made Easy," *Personnel Journal* (May 1984), pp. 31–34.
14. J. Richard Hackman and R. G. Oldham, "Motivation Through Design of Work: Test of a Theory," *Organizational Behavior and Human Performance* (August 1976), pp. 250–279.
15. For a discussion, see Barbara Rarden, "A Practical Approach to Staff Forecasting," *Human Resources Professional* (Summer 1991), pp. 5–12.
16. Robert W. Goddhard, "Work Force 2000," *Personnel Journal* (February 1989), pp. 64–71; Martha E. Ingleshoff, "Managing the New Work Force," *Inc.* (January 1990), pp. 78–83.
17. Morton E. Grossman, in "The Growing Dependence on HRIS," *Personnel Journal* (September 1988), pp. 53–58, states that 40 percent of those who subscribe to *Personnel Journal* reported using such systems, and their use is growing.
18. For example, see Paul Y. Huo and Jack Kearns, "Optimizing the Job-Person Match with Computerized Human Resource Information Systems," *Personnel Review* (1992), no. 2, pp. 3–18.
19. Karen Matthes, "Companies Can Make It Their Business to Care," *HR Focus* (February 1992), pp. 4–5; William B. Johnston, "The Coming Labor Shortage," *Journal of Labor Research* (Winter 1992), pp. 5–10.
20. Karen Matthes, "Attracting and Retaining Hispanic Employees," *HR Focus* (August 1992), p. 7.
21. Ann Coil, "Job Matching Brings Out the Best in Employees," *Personnel Journal* (January 1984), pp. 61–64.
22. Donna L. Dennis, "Are Recruitment Efforts Designed to Fail?" *Personnel Journal* (September 1984), pp. 61–64.
23. Catherine D. Fyock, "Resourceful Recruiting," *Small Business Reports* (April 1992), vol. 17, no. 4, pp. 49–58.
24. Anthony M. Micols, "High-Tech Recruiting at Low Cost," *HR Magazine* (August 1991), pp. 49–52.
25. For a review, see William L. Donoghy, *The Interview: Skills and Applications* (Glenview, Ill.: Scott, Foresman, 1984).
26. Suggested by Mark S. Van Clisaf, "In Search of Competence: Structured Employee Interviews," *Business Horizons* (March–April 1991), pp. 51–55. See also *ASPA Handbook of Personnel and Industrial Relations,* vol. 1, Dale Yoder and Herbert G. Henneman, eds. (Washington, D.C., Bureau of National Affairs, 1974), pp. 152–154.
27. For a review of the process from a conceptual viewpoint, see Scott L. Martin and Karen B. Slora, "Employee Selection by Testing," *HR Magazine* (June 1991), pp. 68–70.
28. *Principles for the Validation and Use of Personnel Selection Procedures* (Berkeley, Calif.: Division of Industrial Psychology, American Psychological Association, 1986).
29. Robert M. Guion, *Personnel Testing* (New York: McGraw-Hill, 1965), PP. 29–31.
30. Larry Reibstein, "More Firms Use Personality Tests for Entry-Level, Blue-Collar Jobs," *Wall Street Journal* (January 16, 1986), p. 31; Thomas Moore, "Personality Tests Are Back," *Fortune* (March 30, 1987), pp. 74–82.
31. Reibstein, loc. cit.

32. Robert P. Tett, Douglas N. Jackson, and Mitchell Rothstein, "Personality Measures as Predictors of Job Performance: A Meta-Analytic Review," *Personnel Psychology* (Winter 1991), pp. 703–742.

33. "Privacy," *Business Week* (March 28, 1988), pp. 61–68.

34. "A Special News Report on People and Their Jobs and Offices, Field and Factories Reference Checking," *Wall Street Journal* (May 5, 1987), p. 1.

35. Joann S. Lublin, "Disabilities Act Will Compel Businesses to Change Many Employment Practices," *Wall Street Journal* (July 7, 1992), pp. B1, B5.

36. Ibid.

37. Author's conversation with a former personnel director for a large paper manufacturer; ibid.

38. Harvey MacKay, "Swim with the Sharks," *Success* (April 1988), p. 62.

39. John P. Wanous, "Installing a Realistic Job Preview: Ten Tough Choices," *Personnel Psychology* (Spring 1989), pp. 117–134; S. L. Premack and J. P. Wanous, "A Meta-Analysis of Realistic Job Preview Experiments," *Journal of Applied Psychology* (1985), pp. 706–718.

40. Jeff Brechlin and Allison Rossett, "Orienting New Employees," *Training* (April 1991), pp. 45–51. Also see Richard F. Federico, "Six Ways to Solve the Orientation Blues," *HR Magazine* (May 1991), pp. 69–70; and W. D. St. John, "The Complete Employee Orientation Program," *Personnel Journal* (May 1980), pp. 376–377.

41. See Harry B. Bernhard and Cynthia A. Ingols, "Six Lessons for the Corporate Classroom," *Harvard Business Review* (September–October 1988), pp. 40–48.

42. Shari Caudron, "Training Helps United Go Global," *Personnel Journal* (February 1992), pp. 103–105.

43. Kitty Pilgrim, CNN Business News, September 2, 1992.

44. Amanda Bennett, "Company School: As Pool of Skilled Help Tightens, Firms Move to Broaden Their Role," *Wall Street Journal* (May 8, 1989), pp. A1, A4; Janice C. Simpson, "Firm Steps: A Shallow Labor Pool Spurs Businesses to Act to Bolster Education," *Wall Street Journal* (September 28, 1987), pp. 1, 26.

45. Roger Ricklefs, "Faced with Shortages of Unskilled Labor, Employers Hire More Retired Workers," *Wall Street Journal* (October 21, 1986), p. 39.

46. Constance Mitchell, "Corporate Classes: Firms Broaden Scope of Their Education Programs," *Wall Street Journal* (September 28, 1987), p. 37.

47. Randy Ross, "Technology Tackles the Training Dilemma," *High Technology Business* (September 1988), pp. 18–23.

48. Tom Kramlinger, "Training's Role in a Learning Organization," *Training* (July 1992), pp. 46–51.

49. For a review of management development trends, see Bernard Keys and Joseph Wolfe, "Management Education and Development: Current Issues and Emerging Trends," *Journal of Management* (1988), no. 2, pp. 205–229.

50. Schuler, Galiente, and Jackson, loc. cit.; Douglas T. Hall, "Human Resource Development and Organizational Effectiveness," ed. in Charles J. Fombrum, Noel M. Tichy, and Mary Ann Devanna, *Strategic Human Resource Management* (New York: Wiley, 1984), chap. 11.

51. "Schooling for Survival," *Time* (February 11, 1985), pp. 74–75.

52. Thomas A. Stewart, "Brainpower," *Fortune* (June 3, 1991), pp. 44–57; Ikujiro Nonaka, "The Knowledge Creating Company," *Harvard Business Review* (November–December 1991), pp. 96–104.

53. Morton E. Grossman and Margaret Magnus, "The Boom in Benefits," *Personnel Journal* (November 1988), pp. 50–55.

54. Ibid.

55. Ron Winslow, "Strong Medicine: How Local Businesses Got Together to Cut Memphis Health Costs," *Wall Street Journal* (February 4, 1992), pp. A1, A7; Ronald Henkoff, "Yes, Companies Can Cut Health Costs," *Fortune* (July 1, 1991), pp. 52–56.

56. Douglas C. Harper, "Control Health Care Costs," *Personnel Journal* (October 1988), pp. 65–70; "Benefits Shock," *U.S. News & World Report* (March 28, 1988), pp. 57–74.

57. Richard E. Johnson and Susan J. Velleman, "Section 89: Close the New Pandora's Box," *Personnel Journal* (November 1988), pp. 70–76.

58. Michael Graham and Albert Hydey, "Comparable Worth in the United States: Legal and Administrative Developments in the 1980s," *International Journal of Public Administration* (September 1991), pp. 799–821; Aaron Bernstein, "Comparable Worth: It's Already Happening," *Business Week* (April 28, 1986), pp. 52–54; and Cathy Trost, "Pay Equity, Born in Public Sector, Emerges as an Issue in Private Firms," *Wall Street Journal* (July 8, 1985), p. 15.

59. Bernstein, op. cit., p. 52.

60. D. J. Fellner and B. Sulzer-Azaroff, "Increasing Industrial Safety Practices and Conditions Through Personal Feedback," *Journal of Safety Research* (January 1984), pp. 7–21; R. S. Haynes, R. C. Pine, and H. G. Fitch, "Reducing Accident Rates with Organizational Behavior Modification," *Academy of Management Journal* (1982), vol. 25, pp. 407–416; R. A. Weber, J. A. Wallin, and J. S. Chokar, "Reducing Industrial Accidents: A Behavioral Experiment," *Industry Relations* (1984), vol. 23, pp. 119–125; J. Komaki, K. D. Farwick, and L. R. Scott, "The Behavioral Approach to Occupational Safety: Pinpointing and Reinforcing the Safe Performance in Food Manufacturing Plants," *Journal of Applied Psychology* (1978), vol. 63, pp. 434–435.

61. Clare Ansberry, "Risky Business: Workplace Injuries Proliferate as Concerns Push People to Produce," *Wall Street Journal* (June 16, 1989), pp. A1, A8.

62. Jonathan Lee, "Sonoco Stresses Employee Involvement to Alter Company's Safety Performance," *Pulp & Paper* (March 1992), pp. 198–200.

63. John M. Ivancevich, Michael T. Matteson, and Edward Richards, III, "Who's Liable for Stress on the Job?" *Harvard Business Review* (March–April 1989); "Stress Claims Are Making Business Jumpy," *Business Week* (October 14, 1985), pp. 152–153.

64. William K. Coors, "Wellness Programs are the Right Prescription," *Business Forum* (Winter 1992), pp. 13–15; A. J. Brennan, "Worksite Health Promotion Can Be Cost Effective," *Personnel Administrator* (1983), vol. 28, no. 4, pp. 39–46; and J. J. Hoffman, Jr., and C. J. Hobson, "Physical Fitness and Employee Effectiveness," *Personnel Administrator* (1984), vol. 29, no. 4, pp. 101–114.

65. "Coors Ends Lie-Detector Tests for Job Seekers, But Added Drug Testing," Labor Letter, *Wall Street Journal* (September 16, 1986), p. 1; Ted Gest, "Using Drugs? You May Not Get Hired," *U.S. News & World Report* (December 23, 1985), p. 38.

66. Patricia S. Wall, "Drug Testing in the Workplace: An Update," *Journal of Applied Business Research* (Spring 1992), pp. 127–132.

67. Jeffrey A. Mello, "Educating Employees About AIDS: Meeting the Challenges," *HR Focus* (April 1992), p. 11.

68. Michael H. LeRoy, "State of the Unions: Assessment by Elite American Labor Leaders," *Journal of Labor Research* (Fall 1992), pp. 371–379; Julian W. Kiem, "America's Changing Unions," *Pulp & Paper* (June 1992), p. 132; Andrea Stone, "The Future of Labor Unions Under Severe Strain," *USA Today* (April 14, 1992), pp. 1B–2B; James M. Schlesinger, "Going Local: Plant-Level Talks Rise Quickly in Importance; Big Issue: Work Rules," *Wall Street Journal* (March 16, 1987), pp. 1, 15.

69. For a recent review, see Robert D. Bretz, Jr., George T. Milkovich, and Walter Read, "The Current State of Performance Appraisal Research and Practice: Concerns, Directions, and Implications," *Journal of Management* (June 1992), pp. 321–352.

70. Karen Matthes, "Will Your Performance Appraisal System Stand Up in Court?" *HR Focus* (August 1992), p. 5; Robert J. Nobile, "The Law of Performance Appraisals," *Personnel* (January 1991), p. 7.

71. "White People, Black People, Not Wanted Here?" *Business Week* (July 10, 1989), p. 31.

72. Sarah Lubman, "Hughes Aircraft Tries to Ease Pain of 12,000 Layoffs," *Wall Street Journal* (July 24, 1992), p. B6.

73. Schuler, loc. cit.

74. Discussion with a Disney manager.

75. Richard T. Pascale, "Fitting New Employees into the Company's Culture," *Fortune* (May 28, 1984), pp. 28–42.

76. Wendell L. French and Cecil H. Bell, Jr., *Organizational Development: Behavioral Science Interventions for Organizational Improvement* (Englewood Cliffs, N.J.: Prentice-Hall, 1973), p. 15.

77. Author's conversation with Barry Morris, a member of Anheuser-Busch's internal organizational development consulting group.

CHAPTER 13

1. A number of definitions of *culture* exist. This one seems to represent the principal elements in most of them. For example, see Ralph H. Kilmann, Mary J. Saxton, and Roy Serpa, "Issues in Understanding and Changing Culture," *California Management Review* (Winter 1986), pp. 87–94; and Robert H. Waterman, Jr., "The Seven Elements of Strategic Fit," *Journal of Business Strategy* (Winter 1982), pp. 69–73.

2. For example, see Brian Dumaine, "Creating a New Company Culture," *Fortune* (January 15, 1990), pp. 127–131; William G. Ouchi, *Theory Z: How American Business Can Meet the Japanese Challenge* (Reading, Mass.: Addison-Wesley, 1981); and Richard T. Pascale and Anthony Athos, *The Art of Japanese Management* (New York: Warner Books, 1981).

3. For a review of the progress toward 1992, see Shawn Tully, "Europe 1992: More Unity Than You Think," *Fortune* (August 24, 1992), pp. 136–142; Chris Brewster and Frank Bournois, "Human Resource Management: A European Perspective," *Personnel Review* (1991), no. 6, pp. 4–13; and Barry Louis Rubin, "Europeans Value Diversity," *HR Magazine* (January 1991), pp. 38–41, 78.

4. Paul Shrivastava, "Integrating Strategy Formulation with Organizational Culture," *Journal of Business Strategy* (Winter 1985), pp. 103–111.

5. James M. Cole, "Put On a Happy Face You Managers," *Wall Street Journal* (October 15, 1984), p. 471; Mary Kay Ash, *Mary Kay on People Management* (New York: Warner Books, 1984).

6. Russell Mitchell, "Jack Welch: How Good a Manager," *Business Week* (December 14, 1987), pp. 92–103; Jack Eagen, "The GE Record," *U.S. News & World Report* (November 23, 1987), pp. 48–49; and Peter Petre, "What Welch Has Wrought at GE," *Fortune* (July 7, 1986), pp. 43–48.

7. Thomas A. Stewart, "GE Keeps Those Ideas Coming," *Fortune* (August 12, 1991), pp. 41–49.

8. Terrence E. Deal and Allan A. Kennedy, *Corporate Cultures: Rites and Rituals of Corporate Life* (Reading, Mass.: Addison-Wesley, 1982); and P. M. Hirsch and Jay Andrews, "Ambush and Shoot-Outs of Knights of the Round Table: The Language of Corporate Takeovers," in L. R. Pondy, P. J. Fost, G. Morgan, and T. C. Dandridge, eds. *Organizational Symbolism* (Greenwich, Conn.,: JAI Press), pp. 145–146.

9. For a recent study of the various kinds of organizational rituals, see Christian Lange, "Ritual in Business: Building a Corporate Culture Through Symbolic Management," *Industrial Management* (July–August 1991), pp. 21–23.

10. Walter Kiechel, III, "Celebrating a Corporate Triumph," *Fortune* (August 20, 1984), p. 259.

11. Robert Hershey, "Corporate Mottos: What They Are, What They Do," *Personnel* (February 1987), pp. 52–56.

12. Ibid., p. 55.

13. For a discussion of how to compete on the basis of quality, see David A. Garvin, "Competing on the Eight Dimensions of Quality," *Harvard Business Review* (November–December, 1987), pp. 101–109.

14. Kathy Seal, "Western Kauai Values Values," *Hotel & Motel Management* (April 8, 1991), pp. 2, 68, 82.

15. *Eaton Corporation: 1985 Annual Report,* Cleveland, Ohio, p. 25.

16. J. B. Barney, "Organizational Culture: Can It Be a Source of Sustained Competitive Advantage?" *Academy of Management Review* (July 1986), pp. 656–665; "Corporate Culture: The Hard to Change Values That Spell Success or Failure," *Business Week* (October 27, 1980), pp. 148–160; Thomas J. Peters and Robert H. Waterman, Jr., *In Search of Excellence* (New York: Harper & Row, 1982); Deal and Kennedy, loc. cit; and Noel Tischy, *Managing Strategic Change: Technical, Political, and Cultural Dynamics* (New York: Wiley, 1983).

17. Ralph H. Kilmann, "Corporate Culture," *Psychology Today* (April 1985), pp. 62–65.

18. Deal and Kennedy, op. cit., pp. 107–108. For additional typologies, see Bernard C. Reimann and Yoash Wiener, "Corporate Culture: Avoiding the Elitist Trap," *Business Horizons* (March–April 1988), pp. 36–44; and Carol Hymowitz, "Which Corporate Culture Fits You?" *Wall Street Journal* (July 17, 1989), p. B1.

19. Jeremy Main, "Betting on the 21st Century Jet," *Fortune* (April 20, 1992), pp. 102–117; Kenneth Labich, "Boeing Battles to Stay on Top," *Fortune* (September 28, 1987), pp. 64–72.

20. Joan O. C. Hamilton, "Biotech's First Superstar," *Business Week* (April 14, 1986), pp. 68–72.

21. IBM internal documents.

22. Richard I. Osborne, "Core Value Statements: The Corporate Compass," *Business Horizons* (September–October 1991), pp. 28–34.

23. Company documents. Louis Kraar, "Roy Ash Is Having Fun at Addressogrief/Multigrief," *Fortune* (February 27, 1978), pp. 47–52; Thomas J. Peters, "Symbols, Patterns, and Settings: Optimistic Case for Getting Things Done," *Organizational Dynamics* (Autumn 1978), pp. 3–23.

24. Richard T. Pascale, "Fitting New Employees into the Company Culture," *Fortune* (May 20, 1984), pp. 28–42; Richard T. Pascale, "The Paradox of Corporate Culture: Reconciling Ourselves to Socialization," *California Management Review* (Winter 1985), pp. 26–41.

25. Reported to the author by a recent recruit.

26. Janet Guyon, "Culture Class: GE's Management School Aims to Foster Unified Corporate Roles," *Wall Street Journal* (August 10, 1987), p. 29; Judith H. Dobrzynski, "GE's Training Camp: An Outward Bound for Managers," *Business Week* (December 14, 1987), p. 98.

27. Pascale, "Fitting New Employees into the Company Culture," op. cit.

28. Dr. David Boles, senior vice-president, the Hay Group, Los Angeles. Quoted in "Tailoring Culture to Fit the Times," *Electric World* (February 1987), p. 29.

29. W. Jack Duncan, "Organizational Culture: 'Getting a Fix' On an Elusive Concept," *Academy of Management Executive* (August 1989), pp. 229–236; K. L. Gregory, "Native-View Paradigms: Multiple Cultures and Culture Conflicts in Organizations," *Administrative Science Quarterly* (September 1983), pp. 359–376.

30. Gregory, loc. cit.

31. William J. Cook, "Perot's War with GM Ends in $743 Million Goodbye," *U.S. News & World Report* (December 15, 1986), pp. 52–53; "How Ross Perot's Shock Troops Ran into Flack at GM," *Business Week* (February 11, 1985), pp. 118–119.

32. Alex Taylor, III, "What's Ahead for GM's New Team?" *Fortune* (November 30, 1992), pp. 58–61.

33. Joseph B. White, "Rays of Hope: Metamorphosis at GM, In Style and Substance, May Be Taking Hold," *Wall Street Journal* (February 13, 1993), pp. A1, A11.

34. Robert C. Maddox and Douglas Short, "The Cultural Integrator," *Business Horizons* (November–December 1988), pp. 57–59.

35. Julie Solomon, "Firms Address Workers' Cultural Variety: The Differences Celebrated, Not Suppressed," *Wall Street Journal* (February 10, 1989), p. B1.

36. Robert W. Goddard, "Work Force 2000," *Personnel Journal* (February 1989), pp. 64–71; Stephen L. Guinn, "The Changing Work Force," *Training & Development Journal* (December 1989), pp. 36–39.

37. Barbara Walker, DEC's director of its cultural diversity program, presentation to the Academy of Management, Washington, D.C., August 13, 1989.

38. R. Roosevelt Thomas, Jr., "From Affirmative Action to Affirming Diversity," *Harvard Business Review* (March–April 1990), pp. 107–117.

39. Alvin C. Hill, Jr., and James Scott, "The Strategies for Managers in a Multicultural Work Force," *HR Focus* (August 1992), p. 6.; ibid.

40. Taylor H. Cox, Jr., and Stacy Blake, "Managing Cultural Diversity: Implications for Organizational Competitiveness," *Academy of Management Executive* (August 1991), pp. 45–56.

41. Thomas, op. cit., pp. 112–117.

42. Ibid., p. 108.

43. Bob Filipczak, "25 Years of Diversity at UPS," *Training* (August 1992), pp. 42–46.

44. For a further discussion, see James M. Higgins, *Human Relations: Behavior at Work,* 2nd ed. (New York: Random House, 1987), pp. 332–334.

45. Thomas E. Moran and Frederick J. Wolkheim, "The Cultural Approach to the Formation of Organizational Climate," *Human Relations* (January 1992), pp. 19–47.

46. Rensis Likert, *New Patterns of Management* (New York: McGraw-Hill, 1961); Keith Davis, *Human Behavior at Work,* 5th ed. (New York: McGraw-Hill, 1977); George H. Litwin and Robert A. Stringer, Jr., *Motivation and Organizational Climate* (Boston: Division of Research, Graduate School of Business Administration, Harvard University, 1968); Garlie A. Forehand and B. Von Haller Gilmer, "Environmental Variation and Studies of Organizational Behavior," *Psychological Bulletin* (December 1964), pp. 361–382; and Andrew W. Halpin and D. B. Crofts, *The Organizational Climate of Schools* (Washington, D.C.: U.S. Department of Health, Education, and Welfare, July 1962).

47. William K. Dowling, "System Four Builds Performance and Products," *Organizational Dynamics* (Winter 1975), pp. 23–38.

48. Alvin Toffler, *Future Shock* (New York: Random House, 1970).

49. John Naisbitt and Patricia Auberdene, *Megatrends 2000* (New York: Morrow, 1990).

50. Thomas J. Peters, *Thriving on Chaos: Handbook for a Management Revolution* (New York: Knopf, 1987).

51. For example, see Marvon Cetron and Owen Davies, "50 Trends Shaping the World," *The Futurist* (September–October 1991), pp. 11–21; Robert B. Tucker, *Managing the Future* (New York: Putnam's, 1991); Editors of *Research Alert, Future Vision—the 189 Most Important Trends of the 1990s* (Naperville, Ill.: Sourcebooks Trade, 1991; Michael A. Hitt, Robert E. Hoskisson, and Jeffrey S. Harrison, "Strategic Competitiveness in the 1990s: Challenges and Opportunities for U.S. Executives," *Academy of Management Executive* (May 1991), pp. 7–22; Spyros Makridakis, "Management in the 21st Century," *Long Range Planning* (April 1991), pp. 37–53; Dietger Hahn, "Strategic Management—Tasks and Challenges in the 1990s," *Long Range Planning* (February 1991), pp. 26–39; Naisbitt and Auberdene, loc. cit.; *The 1990s and Beyond,* Edward Cornish, ed. (Bethesda, Md.: World Future Society, 1990); Fred G. Steingraber, "Managing in the 1990s," *Business Horizons* (January–February 1990), pp. 50–61; Thomas J. Peters, *Thriving on Chaos* (New York: Knopf, 1987); and John Naisbitt, *Megatrends* (New York: Warner Books, 1982).

52. For a lengthy review of definitions and related conceptual issues, see Donald F. Harvey and Donald R. Brown, *An Experiential Approach to Organizational Development,* 2nd ed. (Englewood Cliffs, N.J.: Prentice-Hall, 1982), pp. 72–73; and Wendell L. French, Cecil H. Bell, Jr., and Robert A. Zowacki, *Organizational Development: Theory, Practice, and Research* (Polano, Tex.: BPI, 1983), pp. 6–9.

53. Wendell L. French and Cecil H. Bell, Jr., *Organizational Development: Behavioral Science Interventions for Organization Improvement* (Englewood Cliffs, N.J.: Prentice-Hall, 1973), p. 15.

54. Author's conversation with one of the internal OD consultants at Anheuser-Busch.

55. Theodore Levitt, "In This Issue," *Harvard Business Review* (January–February 1988), p. 3.

56. Ronald W. Clements, "The Changing Fire of Organizational Development: Views of a Manager-Turned Academic," *Business Horizons* (May–June 1992), pp. 6–12.

57. Dumaine, loc. cit., contains a representative discussion. In addition, see Charles O'Reilly, "Corporations, Culture, and Commitment: Motivation and Social Control in Organizations," *California Management Review* (Summer 1989), pp. 9–25; and articles cited in Chapter 15 on autonomous work groups.

58. James Brian Quinn, "The Intelligent Enterprise: A New Paradigm," *Academy of Management Executive* (November 1992), pp. 48–63; Daniel Quinn Miles and Bruce Fresen, "The Learning Organization," *European Management Journal* (June 1992), pp. 146–156; and Ray Stata, "Organizational Learning—The Key to Management Innovation," *Sloan Management Review* (Spring 1989), pp. 63–74.

59. Kurt Lewin, *Field, Theory, and Social Science: Selected Theoretical Papers* (New York: Harper & Row, 1951).

60. Author's consultation with managers in this division.

61. Kurt Lewin, "Frontiers in Group Dynamics: Concept, Method, and Reality in Social Science," *Human Relations* (1947), pp. 5–41; Edgar H. Schein, *Organizational Psychology,* 3rd ed. (Englewood Cliffs, N.J.: Prentice-Hall, 1980), pp. 243–247; and Edgar F. Huse and Thomas G. Cummings, *Organizational Devel-*

opment and Change, 3rd ed. (St. Paul, Minn.: West, 1985), p. 20.

62. Paul R. Lawrence and L. R. Greiner, "How to Deal With Resistance to Change," in G. W. Dalton, Paul R. Lawrence, and L. R. Greiner, *Organizational Change and Development* (Homewood, Ill.: Irwin, 1970), pp. 189–197.

63. Lester Coch and John R. P. French, Jr., "Overcoming Resistance to Change," *Human Relations* (1948), pp. 512–532.

CHAPTER 14

1. Terence R. Mitchell, "Motivation: New Directions for Theory, Research and Practice," *Academy of Management Review* (January 1982), pp. 80–88.

2. Lyman W. Porter and Edward E. Lawler, III, *Managerial Attitudes and Performance* (Homewood, Ill.: Irwin, 1968); for a recent new, but similar perspective, see Edwin A. Locke, "The Motivation Sequence, the Motivation Hub, and the Motivation Core," *Organizational Behavior and Human Performance* (December 1991), pp. 288–299.

3. Based loosely on the integrative efforts discussed in Richard M. Steers and Lyman W. Porter, eds., *Motivation and Work Behavior,* 3rd ed. (New York: McGraw-Hill, 1983); John P. Campbell, Marvin D. Durnette, Edward E. Lawler, III, and Karl E. Weick, *Managerial Behavior, Performance and Effectiveness,* (New York: McGraw-Hill, 1970); Martin G. Evans, "Organizational Behavior: The Central Role of Motivation," *1986 Yearly Review of Management, The Journal of Management* (Summer 1986), pp. 203–222; the review in John B. Miner and H. Peter Dachler, "Personnel Attitudes and Motivation," *Annual Review of Psychology* (1970), vol. 54, no. 1, pp. 31–41; and those cited subsequently, but especially Abraham Maslow, Victor H. Vroom, Terence R. Mitchell, J. Stacy Adams, E. L. Thorndike, B. F. Skinner, Edwin A. Locke, and A. Bandura. For a theoretical model based on control theory, see Howard J. Klein, "An Integrated Control Theory Model of Work Motivation," *Academy of Management Review* (April 1989), pp. 150–172. Also see Locke, loc. cit.

4. Abraham H. Maslow, *Motivation and Personality,* 2nd ed. (New York: Harper & Row, 1970), p. 38.

5. Mahmoud A. Wahba and Lawrence G. Bidwell, "Maslow Reconsidered: A Review of the Research on the Need Hierarchy Theory," *Organizational Behavior and Human Performance* (1976), vol. 15, pp. 212–240.

6. Edwin C. Nevis, "Cultural Assumptions and Productivity: The United States and China," *Sloan Management Review* (Spring 1983), pp. 20–28.

7. Clayton P. Alderfer, *Existence, Relatedness, and Growth* (New York: Free Press, 1972); Clayton P. Alderfer and Richard Grizzo, "Life Expectancies and Adults' Enduring Strengths of Desires in Organizations," *Administrative Science Quarterly* (September 1979), pp. 347–361; John P. Wanovs and Abram Zwanis, "A Cross-Sectional Test of Need Hierarchy Theory," *Organizational Behavior and Human Performance* (February 1977), pp. 78–97.

8. For example, see Craig Miller, "Motivating Middle Managers," *Training* (August–September 1991), pp. 8–9; David R. Bywaters, "Motivating Management," *Executive Excellence* (November 1991), p. 18; Mindy Zeltin, "Older and Wiser: Tips to Motivate the 50s Crowd," *Management Review* (August 1992), pp. 30–33; and Sue Shellenbarger, "More Job-Seekers Put Family Needs First," *Wall Street Journal* (August 5, 1991), p. B1.

9. For example, see Laura Zinn, "Move Over Boomers: The Busters Are Here—And They're Angry," *Business Week* (December 14, 1992),

pp. 74–82; James W. Sheehy, "New Work Ethic Is Frightening," *Personnel Journal* (June 1990, pp. 28–36; and Barbara Whitaker Shimko, "New Breed Workers Need New Yardsticks," *Business Horizons* (December 1990), pp. 34–38.

10. Barbara Whitaker Shimko, "Pre-Hire Assessment of the New Work Force: Finding Wheat (and Work Ethic) Among the Chaff," *Business Horizons* (May–June 1992), pp. 60–65.

11. "Motivation 101 at Merrill Lynch," *Wall Street Journal* (June 14, 1984), p. 33.

12. Edward J. Ost, "Team Based Pay: New Wave Strategic Incentives," *Sloan Management Review* (Spring 1990), pp. 19–27.

13. David C. McClelland, *Human Motivation* (Glenview, Ill.: Scott, Foresman, 1985); David C. McClelland, *The Achieving Society* (Princeton, N.J.: Van Nostrand, 1961).

14. David C. McClelland, "Power Is a Great Motivator," *Harvard Business Review* (March–April 1976), pp. 100–110.

15. Richard Trubo, "Peak Performance," *Success* (April 1983), pp. 30–33, 56.

16. "For Gorbachev, Perestroika II May Mean Survival," *Business Week* (September 25, 1989), pp. 60–62; "The Risks of a New Revolution," *U.S. News & World Report* (October 19, 1987), pp. 31–58.

17. Charles Garfield, "World Leader in Teamwork," *Executive Excellence* (February 1990), pp. 9–10.

18. Cheryl McCurtie, "Mentoring Young Achievers," *Black Enterprise* (June 1991), pp. 336–338.

19. John B. Miner, *Studies in Management Education* (Atlanta: Organizational Management Systems Press, 1975).

20. For a review of the impacts of goal setting on performance, see Edwin A. Locke and Gary P. Latham, "Self-Regulation Through Goal Setting," *Organizational Behavior & Human Decision Processes* (December 1991), pp. 212–247.

21. Maslow, op. cit., p. 51.

22. For example, see Robert Waterman, Jr., "The Pygmalion Effect," *Success* (October 1988), p. 8; Dov Eden, "Self-Fulfilling Prophecy as a Management Tool: Harnessing Pygmalion," *Academy of Management Review* (January 1984), pp. 67–73; and J. Sterling Livingston, "Pygmalion in Management," *Harvard Business Review* (July–August 1969).

23. For a review of how setting objectives is motivating, see Edwin A. Locke and Gary P. Latham, *Goal Setting: A Motivational Technique That Works* (Englewood Cliffs, N.J.: Prentice-Hall, 1984).

24. Maslow, op. cit., p. 51.

25. Patricia Braus, "What Workers Want," *American Demographics* (August 1992), pp. 30–37.

26. Walter Kiechel, III, "How To Manage Salespeople," *Fortune* (March 14, 1988), pp. 179–180.

27. Kenneth A. Kovach, "What Motivates Employees? Workers and Supervisors Give Different Answers," *Business Horizons* (September/October 1987), pp. 58–65.

28. "Home Is Where the Heart Is," *Time* (October 3, 1988), pp. 46–53.

29. Frederick Herzberg, *Work and the Nature of Man* (New York: World, 1971); Frederick Herzberg, Bernard Mausner, and Barbara Snyderman, *The Motivation to Work* (New York: Wiley, 1959); and Frederick Herzberg, "One More Time: How Do You Motivate Employees?" *Harvard Business Review* (January–February 1968), pp. 53–62.

30. Ebrahim A. Maidani, "Comparative Study of Herzberg's Two-Factor Theory of Job Satisfaction Among Public and Private Sectors," *Public Personnel Management* (Winter 1991), pp. 441–448.

31. Robert J. House and Lawrence A. Wigdor, "Herzberg's Dual Factors of Theory of Job Sat-

isfaction, Motivation: A Review of the Evidence and a Criticism,"*Personnel Psychology* (September 20, 1967), pp. 369–389; and Joseph Schneider and Edwin Locke, "A Critique of Herzberg's Classification System and a Suggested Revision," *Organizational Behavior and Human Performance* (July 1971), pp. 441–458.

32. Victor H. Vroom, *Work and Motivation* (New York: Wiley, 1965); Terence R. Mitchell, "Expectancy Models of Job Satisfaction, Occupational Preference, and Its Effort: The Theoretical Methodological, and Empirical Appraisal," *Psychological Bulletin,* no. 79 (1974), pp. 1053–1075.

33. David A. Nadler and Edward E. Lawler, III, "Motivation: A Diagnostic Approach," in J. Richard Hackman, Edward E. Lawler, and Lyman W. Porter, eds. *Perspectives on Behavior in Organizations,* 2nd ed. (New York: McGraw-Hill, 1983), pp. 67–78.

34. For a review of how expectancy can be used with goal setting and Pygmalion, see Dov Eden, "Pygmalion, Goal Setting, and Expectancy: Compatible Ways to Boost Productivity," *Academy of Management Review* (October 1988), pp. 639–652.

35. Joseph R. Mancuso, "Go for the Goals," *Success* (February 1986), p. 14.

36. Ibid.

37. For a discussion of how to use the expectancy theory in a management system, see Thomas L. Quick, "Expectancy Theory in Five Single Steps," *Training and Development Journal* (July 1988), pp. 30–32.

38. Jeffrey A. Bradt, "Pay for Impact," *Personnel Journal* (May 1991), pp. 76–79.

39. J. Stacy Adams, "Toward an Understanding of Inequity," *Journal of Abnormal and Social Psychology* (November 1963), pp. 422–436; Paul S. Goodman and A. Freedman, "An Examination of Adams' Theory of Inequity," *Administrative Science Quarterly* (December 1971), pp. 271–288; Michael R. Carroll and J. E. Dettrich, "Equity Theory: The Recent Literature, Methodological Considerations in New Directions," *Academy of Management Review* (April 1978), pp. 202–210; and Robert P. Vecchio, "Models of Psychological Inequity," *Organizational Behavior and Human Performance* (October 1984), pp. 266–282.

40. Jerold Greenberg, "Employee Theft as a Reaction to Underpayment Inequity: The Hidden Costs of Pay Cuts," *Journal of Applied Psychology* (October 1990), pp. 561–568.

41. Richard C. Huseman, John D. Hatfield, and Edward W. Miles, "A New Perspective on Equity Theory: The Equity Sensitivity Construct," *Academy of Management Review* (April 1987), pp. 222–234.

42. Marilyn E. Gist, "Self-efficacy: A Theoretical Analysis of Its Determinants and Malleability," *Academy of Management Review* (April 1992), pp. 183–211.

43. Edwin A. Locke, "Toward a Theory of Task Motivation and Incentives," *Organizational Behavior and Performance* (May 1968), pp. 157–189; Edwin A. Locke, Karyll N. Shaw, Lise M. Saari, and Gary P. Latham, "Goal Setting and Task Performance: 1969–1980," *Psychological Bulletin* (July 1981).

44. Locke and Latham, loc. cit.

45. James L. Gibson, John M. Ivancevich, and James H. Donnelly, Jr., *Organizations: Behavior, Structure, Process,* 5th ed. (Plano, Tex.: BPI, 1985), p. 164.

46. Ibid., pp. 164–169; James M. Higgins, *Human Relations: Behavior at Work,* 2nd ed. (New York: Random House, 1987), p. 164.

47. Edwin A. Locke, Gary P. Latham, and Miriam Erez, "The Determinants of Goal Commitment," *Academy of Management Review* (January 1988), pp. 23–39.

48. Edward L. Thorndike, *Animal Intelligence:*

Experimental Studies (New York: Hafner, 1965 [1911]), p. 244.

49. B. F. Skinner, *Beyond Freedom and Dignity* (New York: Knopf, 1971); see also, Fred Luthans and Robert Kreitner, "A Social Learning Approach to Behavioral Management: Radical Behavioralists' Mellowing Out,'" *Organizational Dynamics* (August 1984), pp. 47–63.

50. For a recent discussion, see Maurice F. Villere and Sandra S. Hartman, "Reinforcement Theory: A Practical Tool," *Leadership & Organizational Development Journal* (1991), no. 2, pp. 27–31.

51. For a lengthy discussion, see Fred Luthans and Robert Kreitner, *Organizational Behavior Modification and Beyond* (Glenview, Ill.: Scott, Foresman, 1985).

52. Fran Tarkenton with Tad Tuleja, *How to Motivate People* (New York: Harper & Row, 1986).

53. Edward J. Feeney, "Modifying Employee Behavior: Making Rewards Pay Off," *Supervisory Management* (December 1985), pp. 25–27.

54. Kirk O'Hara, C. Merle Johnson, and Jerry A. Beehr, "Organizational Behavior Management in the Private Sector: A Review of Empirical Research and Recommendation for Further Investigation," *Academy of Management Review* (October 1985), pp. 848–865.

55. Gary P. Latham and Vandra L. Huber, "Schedules of Reinforcement: Lessons From the Past and Issues for the Future," *Journal of Organizational Behavior Management* (1992), no. 1, pp. 125–149.

56. For a recent discussion as applied to quality improvement, see Thomas K. Connellan, "Interpersonal Feedback," *Quality Progress* (June 1991), pp. 20–22.

57. Regina Eisman, "Remaking a Corporate Grant," *Incentive* (May 1992), pp. 57–63.

58. "Grading Merit Pay," *Newsweek* (November 14, 1988), pp. 45–46.

59. James P. Gutherie and Edward P. Cunningham, "Pay for Performance for Hourly Workers: The Quaker Oats Alternative," *Compensation & Benefits Review* (March–April 1992), pp. 18–23.

60. "Labor Letter," *Wall Street Journal* (October 25, 1988), p. 1.

61. See, for example, Dennis W. Organ, "A Restatement of the Satisfaction-Performance Hypothesis," *Journal of Management* (December 1988), pp. 547–557; Dennis W. Organ, "A Reappraisal and Reinterpretation of the Satisfaction-Causes-Performance Hypothesis," *Academy of Management Review* (April 1977), pp. 46–53; and A. H. Brayfield and W. H. Crockett, "Employee Attitudes and Employee Performance," *Psychological Bulletin* (1955), pp. 396–424.

62. Richard DeCharms, *Personal Causation* (Reading, Mass.: Addison-Wesley, 1968); Abraham Korman, "Toward an Hypothesis of Work Behavior," *Journal of Applied Psychology* (1970), vol. 54, no. 1, pp. 31–41; Maxwell Maltz, *Psycho-Cybernetics: The New Way to a Successful Life* (Englewood Cliffs, N.J.: Prentice-Hall, 1960); Robert A. Sutermeister, "The Employed Performance of Employee Need Satisfaction: Which Comes First?" *California Management Review* (1971), vol. 13, no. 4, pp. 43–47; and a host of articles in the educational and psychological literature.

63. P. Tharenon, "Employee Self-esteem: A Review of the Literature," *Journal of Vocational Behavior* (1979), pp. 316–349.

64. Ibid.

65. A. Bandura, *Social Learning Theory* (Englewood Cliffs, N.J.: Prentice-Hall, 1977); Harold H. Kelly and John L. Michael, "Attribution Theory and Research," *The Annual Review of Psychology* (1980), pp. 457–501. Also see Mark J. Martinko and William L. Gardner, "The Leader/Member Attribution Process," *Academy of Management Review* (April 1987),

pp. 235–249, for a discussion of a dyadic model of leader-subordinate attributional behavior; and Daniel Sandowsky, "A Psychoanalytic Attributional Model for Subordinate Poor Performance," *Human Resource Management* (Spring 1989), pp. 125–139, for a series of recommended actions for managers to take to overcome problems with attribution.

66. Alan J. Dubinsky, Steven J. Skinner and Tommy E. Whitler, "Evaluation of Sales Personnel: An Attribution Theory Perspective," *Journal of Personal Selling & Sales Management* (Spring 1989), pp. 9–21.

67. Donald B. Fedor and Kendrith M. Rowland, "Investigating Supervisor Attributions of Subordinate Performance," *Journal of Management* (September 1989), pp. 409–416.

CHAPTER 15

1. Warren Watson, Larry K. Michaelson, and Walt Sharp, "Member Competence, Group Interaction and Group Decision Making: A Longitudinal Study," *Journal of Applied Psychology* (December 1991), pp. 803–809; Marvin E. Shaw, *Group Dynamics: The Psychology of Small Group Behavior,* 3rd ed. (New York: McGraw-Hill, 1981).

2. Kenneth N. Wexley and Gary A. Yukl, *Organizational Behavior and Personnel Psychology* (Homewood, Ill.: Irwin, 1977).

3. For a recent discussion of the linking pin function of managers, see Cory A. Jones and William R. Crandall, "Determining the Sources of Voluntary Employee Turnover," *SAM Advanced Management Journal* (Spring 1991), pp. 16–20; for the original discussion, see Rensis Likert, *New Patterns of Management* (New York: McGraw-Hill, 1961), pp. 114–115.

4. Deborah L. Gladstein, "Groups in Context: A Model of Task Group Effectiveness," *Administrative Science Quarterly* (December 1984), pp. 499–517.

5. See Edgar H. Schein, *Organizational Psychology*, 3rd ed., (Englewood Cliffs, N.J.: Prentice-Hall, 1980), pp. 146–153.

6. James L. Gibson, John M. Ivancevich, and James H. Donnelly identify two types of task groups: the problem-solving group and the training group. The latter seems to be a special case of a task group—that is, a problem-solving group—and no such distinction is made here. The reader should be alert to the fact that some differences do exist. See James L. Gibson, John M. Ivancevich, and James H. Donnelly, *Organizations: Behavior, Structure, and Processes*, 7th ed. (Homewood, Ill.: Irwin, 1991), pp. 269–273.

7. David M. Herold, "The Effectiveness of Work Groups," in Steven Kerr, ed., *Organizational Behavior* (New York: Wiley, 1979), p. 95.

8. George Homans, *The Human Group* (New York: Harcourt, 1950).

9. For a representative discussion, see Raef T. Hussein, "Understanding and Managing Informal Groups," *Management Decision* (1990), Issue no. 8, pp. 36–41; and Dave Day, "New Supervisors and the Informal Group," *Supervisory Management* (May 1989), pp. 31–33.

10. John A. Seeger, in "No Innate Phases in Group Problem Solving," *Academy of Management Review* (October 1983), demonstrates that such stages occur primarily only when subject groups have never met before.

11. For example, see Kenneth L. Bettenhausen, "Five Years of Group Research: What We Have Learned and What Needs to Be Addressed," *Journal of Management* (June 1991), pp. 351–352; Bernard Bass, *Organizational Psychology* (Boston: Allyn & Bacon, 1965), pp. 197–198; J. Steven Heinen and Eugene Jackson, "A Model of Task Group Development in Complex Organizations and a Strategy of Implementation," *Academy of Management Review* (Oc-

tober 1976), pp. 98–111; and Connie J. G. Gersuh, "Time and Transition in Work Teams: Toward a New Model of Group Development," *Academy of Management Journal* (March 1988), pp. 9–41.

12. Not everyone agrees that problem-solving groups go through stages. For example, see Seeger, loc. cit.

13. Kenneth D. Benne and Paul Sheats, "Functional Roles of Group Members," *Journal of Social Issues* (1948), vol. 4, no. 2, p. 43.

14. Beverly Geber, "Saturn's Grand Experiment," *Training* (June 1992), pp. 27–35; David Woodruff, "At Saturn, What Workers Want Is . . . Fewer Defects," *Business Week* (December 2, 1991), pp. 117–118.

15. Benne and Sheats, op. cit., pp. 44–49.

16. Ibid.

17. J. L. Moreno, *Foundations of Sociometry*, Sociometry Monographs, no. 4 (Boston: Beacon, 1943).

18. Keith Davis, "Cut Those Rumors Down to Size," *Supervisory Management* (June 1975), pp. 2–6; "The Care and Cultivation of the Corporate Grapevine," *Dun's Review* (July 1973), pp. 44–47; and "Management Communication and the Grapevine," *Harvard Business Review* (September–October 1953), pp. 43–49.

19. Keith Davis, "Management Communication and the Grapevine," op. cit., p. 44.

20. Keith Davis, "The Care and Cultivation of the Corporate Grapevine," op. cit. p. 44.

21. Stanley J. Modic, "Grapevine Rated Most Reliable," *Industry Week* (May 15, 1989), pp. 11, 14.

22. Dianna Booker, "Link Between Corporate Communication and Quality," *Executive Excellence* (June 1990), pp. 17–18.

23. Bettenhausen, op. cit., pp. 354–356; E. J. Thomas and C. F. Fink, "Effects of Group Size," in Larry L. Cummings and William E. Scott, eds., *Readings in Organizational and Human Performance* (Homewood, Ill., Irwin, 1969), pp. 394–408.

24. R. Z. Gooding and J. A. Wagner, III, "A Meta-Analytical Review of the Relationship Between Size and Efficiency of Organizations and Their Subunits," *Administrative Science Quarterly* (December 1985), pp. 462–481.

25. Geber, loc. cit.; Woodruff, loc. cit.

26. Gooding and Wagner, loc. cit.

27. For a discussion of groups and size, see Rodney W. Napier and Matti K. Gershenfeld, *Groups: Theory and Experience*, 4th ed. (Boston: Houghton Mifflin, 1987), pp. 38–39, 87.

28. J. R. Hackman, "Group Influence on Individuals," in *Handbook of Industrial and Organizational Psychology*, M. D. Dunnetts, ed. (Chicago: Rand McNally, 1976), pp. 1455–1525.

29. Daniel C. Feldman, "The Development and Enforcement of Group Norms," *Academy of Management Review* (January 1984), pp. 47–53.

30. Daniel C. Feldman and Hugh J. Arnold, *Managing Individual and Group Behavior in Organizations* (New York: McGraw-Hill, 1983), pp. 447–448.

31. Irving Janis, *Victims of Group Think,* 2nd ed. (Boston: Houghton Mifflin, 1982). See also Carrie R. Leana, "A Partial Test of Janis's Group Think Model: Effects of Group Cohesiveness and Leader Behavior on Defective Decision Making," *Journal of Management* (1985), no. 1, pp. 5–17, for a research study that partially supports Janis's theory. See also Barbara Tuchman, *The March of Folly* (New York: Knopf, 1984).

32. Janis, loc. cit.

33. Ronald R. Sims, "Linking Group Think to Unethical Behavior in Organizations," *Journal of Business Ethics* (September 1992), pp. 651–652.

34. Michael J. Woodruff, "Understanding—and Combatting—Group Think," *Supervisory*

Management (October 1991), p. 8; Sami M. Abbasi and Kenneth W. Hollman, "Dissent: An Important But Neglected Factor in Decision Making," *Management Decision* (1992), no. 8, pp. 7–11.

35. For a review of the research on cohesiveness, see Marvin E. Shaw, *Group Dynamics* (New York: McGraw-Hill, 1981), pp. 110–112, 192.

36. Bettenhausen, op. cit., pp. 361–364.

37. Dorwin Cartwright, "The Nature of Group Cohesiveness," in *Group Dynamics: Research and Theory*, 3rd ed. (New York: Harper & Row, 1968), pp. 98–103.

38. Clay Carr, "Managing Self-managed Workers," *Training & Development Journal* (September 1991), pp. 36–42; Harlan R. Jessups, "New Roles in Leadership," *Training & Development Journal* (November 1990), pp. 79–83.

39. Frank Shipper, "Quality Circles Using Small Group Formation," *Training & Development Journal* (May 1983), p. 82.

40. Gayle W. Hill, "Group Versus Individual Performance: Are N + 1 Heads Better Than One?" *Psychological Bulletin* (1982), pp. 517–539.

41. For a review, see Bettenhausen, op. cit., pp. 354–356. Another recent research study details some of the complexities of problem solving in culturally diverse groups: See Taylor H. Cox, Sharon A. Lobel, and Poppy Lauretta McLeod, "Effects of Ethnic Group Cultural Differences on Cooperative and Competitive Behavior on a Group Task," *Academy of Management Journal* (December 1991), pp. 827–847.

42. One of the purposes of self-managed groups is to increase the quality of employee work life. See, for example, Henry Sims and Charles C. Manz, "Conversations Within Self-managed Work Groups," *National Productivity Review* (1982), pp. 261–269.

43. For a discussion, see J. Richard Hackman, "The Design of Work Teams," in Jay W. Lorsch, ed., *Handbook of Organizational Behavior* (Englewood Cliffs, N.J.: Prentice-Hall, 1987), pp. 343–357.

44. Barry M. Straw, "Organizational Psychology and the Pursuit of the Happy/Productive Worker," *California Management Review* (Spring 1987), p. 25.

45. Gregory P. Shea and Richard A. Guzzo, "Group Effectiveness: What Really Matters?" *Sloan Management Review* (Spring 1987), p. 25.

46. For a lengthy discussion of groups, see Marilyn E. Gist, Edwin A. Locke, and M. Susan Taylor, "Organizational Behavior: Group Structures, Process and Effectiveness," in J. D. Blair and J. G. Hunt, eds., *Yearly Review of Management of the Journal of Management* (1987), pp. 237–257.

47. For example, see Stephen Worchel, Wendy Wood, and Jeffrey A. Simpson, eds., *Group Process and Productivity* (Newbury Park, Calif.: Sage, 1992). Also see Taylor H. Cox, Sharon A. Lobel and Poppy Lauretta McLeod, "Effects of Ethnic Group Cultural Differences on Cooperative and Competitive Behavior on a Group Task," *Academy of Management Journal* (December 1991), pp. 827–847.

48. Shirley A. Hopkins and Willie E. Hopkins, "Organizational Productivity 2000: A Work Force Perspective," *SAM Advanced Management Journal* (Autumn 1991), pp. 44–48.

49. Rosemary Neale and Richard Mindel, "Rigging Up Multicultural Teamworking," *Personnel Management* (January 1992), pp. 36–39.

50. Bettenhausen, op. cit., p. 356.

51. David Kirkpatrick, "Here Comes the Payoff from PCs," *Fortune* (March 23, 1992), pp. 93–102; Robert J. Mockler and D. G. Dologite, "Using Computer Software to Improve Group Decision-Making," *Long Range Planning* (August 1991), pp. 44–57.

52. Rosemary Hamilton, "Andersen Makes Big Notes Buy," *Computerworld* (April 6, 1992), p. 4.

53. "New Software Helps PC Users Work as Groups," *Wall Street Journal* (February 24, 1988), p. 25; Louis S. Richman, "Software Catches the Team Spirit," *Fortune* (June 8, 1987), pp. 125–136; a demonstration by Wilson Learning Corporation to ASTD members in Orlando, Fl. displaying their group software.

54. Stephen Kreider Yoder, "Microsoft to Sell 'Windows' for Groups," *Wall Street Journal* (October 1, 1992), p. B10.

55. Emma Zevik, "Getting a Grip on Groupware," *Computerworld* (March 30, 1992), p. 60.

56. Darlene W. Caplan, Darrell Givens, Greg Luff, Edward P. Kowel, James L. Sturrock, and Diane D. Worden, "A Practical Roadmap for High Performing Natural Teams," *Journal for Quality & Participation* (June 1992), pp. 60–65; Mahmoud Salem, Harold Lazarus, and Joseph Cullen, "Developing Self-managing Teams: Structure and Performance," *Journal of Management Development* (1992), no. 3, pp. 24–32; Ed Musselwhite and Linda Moran, "On the Road to Self-direction," *Journal for Quality & Participation* (June 1990), pp. 58–63.

57. Thomas P. Mullen, "Integrating Self-directed Teams into the Management Development Curriculum," *Journal of Management Development* (1992), pp. 43–54.

58. Tom Brown, "Why Teams Go 'Bust,'" *Industry Week* (March 2, 1992), p. 20.

59. W. W. George, "Task Teams for Rapid Growth," *Harvard Business Review* (January–February 1981), pp. 103–116.

60. M. Michael Markowich, "Using Task Forces to Increase Efficiency and Reduce Stress," *Personnel* (August 1987), pp. 34–38.

61. Thomas J. Peters, *Thriving on Chaos: A Management Revolution* (New York: Knopf, 1987), p. 297.

62. Toby D. Wall, Nigel J. Kemp, Paul R. Jackson, and Chris W. Clegg, "Outcomes of Autonomous Work Groups: A Long-Term Field Experiment," *Academy of Management Journal* (June 1986), pp. 280–304.

63. See William D. Dyer, *Team Building* (Reading, Mass.: Addison-Wesley, 1977).

64. Robert L. Rose and Alex Kotlowitz, "Back to Bickering: Strife Between UAW and Caterpillar Blights Promising Labor Idea," *Wall Street Journal* (November 23, 1992), pp. A1, A8.

65. Shipper, loc. cit.

66. Bruno Fabi, "Contingency Factors in Quality Circles: A Review of Empirical Evidence," *International Journal of Quality & Reliability Management* (1992), no. 2, pp. 18–33; Walt Thompson, "Getting the Organization Ready for Quality Circles," *Training and Development Journal* (December 1982), p. 116.

67. Robert Wood, Frank Hall, and Koya Azumi, "Evaluating Quality Circles: The American Application," *California Management Review* (Fall 1982), p. 43.

68. Laurie Fitzgerald and Joseph Murphy, *Installing Quality Circles: A Strategic Approach* (San Diego, Calif.: University Associates, 1982), p. 3.

69. Allan Halcrow, "Portfolio," *Personnel Journal* (January 1988), pp. 10–11.

70. Dan Lippe, "Quality Circles Roll into Hospitals," *Modern Health Care* (August 1982).

71. Edward E. Lawler, III, and Susan A. Mohrman, "Quality Circles After the Honeymoon," *Organizational Dynamics* (Spring 1987), pp. 42–54.

72. Robert P. Steel et al., "Factors Influencing the Success and Failure of Two Quality Circles Programs," *Journal of Management* (Spring 1985), pp. 99–119.

73. Francoise Chevalier, "From Quality Circles to Total Quality," *International Journal of Quality & Reliability Management* (1991), no. 4, pp. 9–24; Rickey W. Griffin, "Consequences of Quality Circles in an Industrial Setting: A Lon-

gitudinal Assessment," *Academy of Management Journal* (June 1988), pp. 338–358.

74. Wood, Hall, and Azumi, op. cit., p. 40.

75. Alexander C. Philip, "A Hidden Benefit of Quality Circles," *Personnel Journal* (February 1984), p. 54.

76. David N. Landon and Steven Moulton, "Quality Circles: What's in Them for Employees?" *Personnel Journal* (June 1986), pp. 23–25.

77. Note, however, that group failure cold lead to lessened self-esteem. See Joel Brocker and Ted Less, "Self-esteem and Task Performance in Quality Circles," *Academy of Management Journal* (September 1986), pp. 617–623.

78. Simon Majaro, *The Creative Marketer* (Oxford, England: Butterworth-Heinemann, 1991), pp. 64–65; Sheridan M. Tatsumo, "Creating Breakthroughs, The Japanese Way," *R&D* (February 1990), pp. 136–142; Simon Majaro, *The Creative Gap: Managing Ideas for Profit* (London: Longman, 1988), pp. 106–119.

79. Kenneth Thomas, "Overview of Conflict and Conflict Management: Reflections and Update," *Journal of Organizational Behavior* (May 1992), pp. 263–274.

80. Richard Tanner Pascale, *Managing on the Edge: How the Smartest Companies Use Conflict to Stay Ahead* (New York: Simon & Schuster, 1990).

81. Kenneth Thomas, loc. cit.

82. For a decision-choice model helping the manager select which conflict resolution technique to use, see Danny Ertel, "How to Design a Conflict Management Procedure That Fits Your Dispute," *Sloan Management Review* (Summer 1991), pp. 29–42.

CHAPTER 16

1. Gary M. Yukl, *Leadership in Organizations*, 2nd ed. (Englewood Cliffs, N.J.: Prentice-Hall, 1989), pp. 1–5.

2. For additional definitions, see ibid., pp. 2–3.

3. Abraham Zaleznik, "Managers and Leaders: Are They Different?" *Harvard Business Review* (March–April 1990), pp. 126–135, and (May–June 1977), pp. 67–78; Ted Levitt, "Command and Consent," *Harvard Business Review* (July–August 1988), p. 5.; and John P. Kotter, *The Leadership Factor* (New York: Free Press, 1987).

4. Jack Falvey, "Before Spending $3 Million on Leadership, Read This," *Wall Street Journal* (October 3, 1988), p. A26.

5. For example, see Beverly Geber, "From Manager into Coach," *Training* (February 1992), pp. 25–31.

6. Zaleznik, loc. cit.

7. Ibid.

8. Noel M. Tichy and Mary Anne Devanna, *The Transformational Leader* (New York: Wiley, 1987).

9. James M. Korzes and Barry Z. Posner, *The Leadership Challenge* (San Francisco: Jossey-Bass, 1987). Kenneth Labich provides a similar list in "The Seven Keys to Business Leadership," *Fortune* (October 24, 1988), pp. 58–66: 1. Trust your subordinates; 2. Develop a vision; 3. Keep your cool; 4. Encourage risk; 5. Be an expert; 6. Invite dissent; 7. Simplify.

10. Chester I. Barnard, *The Functions of the Executive* (Cambridge, Mass.: Harvard University Press, 1938), pp. 160–175.

11. Chris Lee, "Followership: The Essence of Leadership," *Training* (June 1991), pp. 27–35.

12. Jeffrey A. Barrow, "The Variables of Leadership: A Review and Conceptual Framework," *Academy of Management Review* (April 1977), pp. 233–234.

13. John R. P. French and Bertram H. Raven, "The Bases of Social Power," in Dorwin Cartwright, ed., *Studies in Social Power* (Ann Arbor: University of Michigan Press, 1959). For a discussion of the uses of these powers, see Thomas A.

Stewart, "New Ways to Exercise Power," *Fortune* (November 6, 1989), pp. 52–64.

14. Daniel C. Pelz, "Influence: Key to Effective Leadership on the First-Line Supervisor," *Personnel* (1952), pp. 209–217.

15. Dennis Waitley, *The Psychology of Winning* (Chicago: Nightingale-Connant Corp., 1978), cassette tape.

16. This is also a familiar case in business, where the expert builds relationships and has power based on favors.

17. Yukl, op. cit., pp. 68–69, 90.

18. Shelley A. Kirkpatrick and Edwin A. Locke, "Leadership: Do Traits Really Matter?" *Academy of Management Executive* (May 1991), pp. 48–60. The references to this article provide a list of trait studies.

19. Yukl, op. cit., p. 70.

20. For an interesting view of certain personalities and leadership styles, see Seth Allcorn, "Leadership Styles: The Psychological Picture," *Personnel* (April 1988), pp. 46–54.

21. Douglas T. McGregor, *The Human Side of Enterprise* (New York: McGraw-Hill, 1960), pp. 33–34, 47–48.

22. J. C. Taylor, "An Empirical Examination of a Four-Factor Theory of Leadership Using Smallest Space Analysis," *Organizational Behavior and Human Performance* (1971), 6, pp. 249–266.

23. Yukl, op. cit., pp. 129–130.

24. Robert R. Blake and Jane S. Mouton, *The New Managerial Grid* (Houston: Gulf, 1978); also see Robert R. Blake and Jane S. Mouton, "How to Choose a Leadership Style," *Training & Development Journal* (February 1982), pp. 38–47.

25. Ibid., chap. 7.

26. One study with an extremely large sample size (sixteen thousand) found that high-achieving executives, about 13 percent of the total, cared about both people and profits. Average achievers were concerned only about profits, and low achievers were obsessed only with their own security. Low achievers displayed a basic distrust of their subordinates' abilities; high achievers viewed them optimistically. High achievers sought advice from underlings; low achievers did not. High achievers were listeners; and low achievers avoided communication, relying on policy manuals. ("Nice Guys in High Corporate Positions Get the Best Results from Subordinates," *Wall Street Journal* (August 22, 1978), p. 1.

27. Robert Tannenbaum and Warren H. Schmidt, "How to Choose a Leadership Pattern," *Harvard Business Review* (March–April 1958), pp. 95–101.

28. Jerome L. Franklin, "Down the Organization: Influence Processes Across Levels of Hierarchy," *Administrative Science Quarterly* (June 1975), pp. 153–165.

29. Fred E. Fiedler, *A Theory of Leadership Effectiveness* (New York: Mcgraw-Hill, 1967), pp. 10–37.

30. Robert P. Vecchio, "An Empirical Examination of Fiedler's Model," *Organizational Behavior and Human Performance* (June 1977), pp. 180–206; Fred E. Fiedler, "The Contribution of Cognitive Resources and Behavior to Leadership Performance," paper presented to the Academy of Management, Boston, August 12, 1984.

31. Robert J. House and Terrence R. Mitchell, "Path-Goal Theory of Leadership" *Journal of Contemporary Business* (Autumn 1974), pp. 81–97.

32. Ibid.

33. Robert T. Keller, "A Test of the Path-Goal Theory of Leadership with Need for Clarity as a Moderator in Research and Development Organizations," *Journal of Applied Psychology* (April 1989), pp. 208–212; Steven Kerr and John Jermier, "Substitutes for Leadership: Their Meaning and Measurement," *Organizational Behavior and Human Performance* (1978), pp. 375–403; Jon P. Howell and Peter W. Dorfman, "Leadership and Substitutes for Leadership Among Professional and Nonprofessional Workers," *Journal of Applied Behavioral Sciences* (November 1, 1986), pp. 29–46.

34. Ken Blanchard, "Situational View of Leadership," *Executive Excellence* (June 1991), pp. 22–23; Paul Hersey and Kenneth R. Blanchard, *Management of Organizational Behavior: Utilizing Human Resources* (Englewood Cliffs, N.J.: Prentice-Hall, 1977).

35. For example, see William R. Norris and Robert P. Vecchio, "Situational Leadership Theory: A Replication," *Group and Organization Management* (September 1992), pp. 331–342; John K. Butler and Richard M. Reese, "Leadership Style and Sales Performance: A Test of the Situational Leadership Model," *Journal of Personal Selling & Sales Management* (Summer 1991), pp. 37–46; Warren Blank, John R. Weitzel, and Stephen G. Green, "A Test of the Situational Leadership Theory," *Personnel Psychology* (Autumn 1990), pp. 579–597; and Jane R. Goodson, Gail W. McGee, and James F. Cashman, "Situational Leadership Theory: A Test of Leadership Prescriptions," *Group & Organization Studies* (December 1989), pp. 446–461.

36. Victor Vroom and Arthur G. Yago, *The New Leadership: Managing Participation in Organizations* (Englewood Cliffs, N.J.: Prentice-Hall, 1988); Victor Vroom and P. W. Yetton, *Leadership and Decision Making* (Pittsburgh: University of Pittsburgh Press, 1973).

37. Jan P. Muczyk and Bernard C. Reimann, "The Case for Directive Leadership," *Academy of Management Executive* (August 1987), pp. 301–311.

38. For example, see Larry E. Penley, Elmore R. Alexander, T. Edward Jernigan, and Catherine T. Henwood, "Communication Abilities of Managers: The Relationship to Performance," *Journal of Management* (March 1991), pp. 57–76, provides a lengthy review of the topic. See also Jay A. Conger, "Inspiring Others: The Language of Leadership," *Academy of Management Executive* (February 1991), pp. 31–45 for a review of the communication of organizational vision.

39. Penley et al., loc. cit.; Mark J. Martinko and William L. Gardner, "The Leader/Member Attribution Process," *Academy of Management Review* (April 1987), pp. 235–249; also see Larry E. Penley and Brian Hawkins, "Studying Interpersonal Communication in Organizations: A Leadership Application," *Academy of Management Journal* (June 1985), pp. 309–326.

40. James M. Higgins, "The TRRAP Model," *Human Relations: Behavior at Work*, 2nd ed. (New York: Random House, 1987), pp. 200–209.

41. For a lengthy discussion, see F. M. Jablin, "Superior-Subordinate Communication: The State of the Art," *Psychological Bulletin* (1979), pp. 1201–1222; and for a review of related research and a study of this aspect of communication, see Penley and Hawkins, loc. cit.

42. Warren Bennis and Burt Nanus, *Leaders* (New York: Harper & Row, 1985); William V. Haney, *Communication and Interpersonal Relations: Text and Cases* (Homewood, Ill.: Irwin-Dorsey, 1979), pp. 12–15.

43. For a review of the research, see Karl W. Kuhnert and Philip Lewis, "Transactional and Transformational Leadership: A Constructive/Developmental Analysis," *Academy of Management Review* (October 1987), pp. 648–657.

44. James McGregor Burns, *Leadership* (New York: Harper & Row, 1978).

45. Ibid., p. 4.

46. Bernard M. Bass, "From Transactional to Transformational Leadership: Learning to Share the Vision," *Organizational Dynamics* (Winter 1990), pp. 19–31; Bernard M. Bass, *Leadership and Performance Beyond Expectations* (New York: Free Press, 1985); and Bernard M. Bass, J. Avolio, and Laurie Goodheim, "Biography and the Assessment of Transformational Leadership at the World Class Level," *Journal of Management* (Spring 1987), pp. 7–19.

47. Bass, "From Transactional to Transformational Leadership: Learning to Share the Vision," op. cit., p. 27.

48. Ibid., p. 17.

49. Bernard M. Bass, "Leadership: Good, Better, Best," *Organizational Dynamics* (Winter 1985), pp. 26–40.

50. David Kirkpatrick, "The Revolution at Compaq Computer," *Fortune* (December 14, 1992), pp. 80–88; Catherine Arnst and Stephanie Anderson Forest, "Compaq: How It Made Its Impressive Move Out of the Doldrums," *Business Week* (November 2, 1992), pp. 146–151.

51. Noel M. Tichy and David O. Ulrich, "The Leadership Challenge: A Call for Transformational Leaders," *Sloan Management Review* (Fall 1984), pp. 59–68; also see Guran Ekvall, "Change Centered Leaders: Empirical Evidence of a Third Dimension of Leadership," *Leadership & Organizational Development Journal* (1991), no. 6, pp. 18–23.

52. Tichy and Devanna, loc. cit.

53. Darlene Caplan, Darrell Givens, Greg Luff, Edward P. Kowel, James Sturrock, and Diane D. Worden, "A Practical Roadmap for High Performing Natural Teams," *Journal for Quality and Participation* (June 1992), pp. 60–65; Harlan R. Jessup, "New Roles in Team Leadership," *Training & Development Journal* (November 1990), pp. 79–83.

54. Mark R. Edwards, "Symbiotic Leadership: A Creative Partnership for Managing Organizational Effectiveness," *Business Horizons* (May–June 1992), pp. 28–33.

55. Clay Carr, Managing Self-managed Workers," *Training & Development Journal* (September 1991), pp. 36–42; David Barry, "Managing the Bossless Team: Lessons in Distributed Leadership," *Organizational Dynamics* (Summer 1991), pp. 31–47.

56. Chris Lee, "Can Leadership Be Taught?" *Training* (July 1989), pp. 19–26.

57. "Trends in Leadership Training," *Leadership & Organizational Development Journal* (1991), no. 4, pp. vi–vii.

58. Marshall Whitmire and Philip R. Nienstedt, "Lead Leaders into the '90s," *Personnel Journal* (May 1991), pp. 80–85.

59. Joann S. Lublin, "Younger Managers Learn Global Skills," *Wall Street Journal* (March 31, 1992), p. B1; Jennifer J. Laabs, "The Global Talent Search," *Personnel Journal* (August 1991), pp. 38–42, 44.

60. Jay A. Conger, "Leadership: The Art of Empowering Others," *Academy of Management Executive* (February 1989), pp. 17–24.

61. Ibid.

62. Steven B. Kaufman, "Empowerment at Pacific Gas & Electric," *Training* (August 1991), pp. 46–48.

63. Frederick W. Smith, "Empowering Employees," *Small Business Reports* (January 1991), pp. 15–20.

64. Gary N. Powell, "One More Time: Do Female and Male Managers Differ?" *Academy of Management Executive* (August 1990), pp. 68–78.

65. Judy B. Rosener, "Ways Women Lead," *Harvard Business Review* (November–December, 1990), pp. 119–125.

66. W. Warner Burke and Peter Jackson, "Making the SmithKline Beecham Merger Work," *Human Resource Management* (Spring 1991), pp. 69–87.

67. Frederic William Swierczek, "Leadership and Culture: Comparing Asian Managers," *Leader-*

ship & Organization Development Journal (1991), no. 7, pp. 3–10.

68. Peter M. Senge, "The Leader's New Work: Building Learning Organizations," *Sloan Management Review* (Fall 1990), pp. 7–22.

69. Ibid., p. 9.

70. Ikujiro Nonaka, "The Knowledge-Creating Company," *Harvard Business Review* (November–December 1991), pp. 96–104.

71. Thomas A. Stewart, "Brainpower," *Fortune* (June 3, 1991),, pp. 44–57.

72. Michael E. McGill, John W. Slocum, Jr., and David Lei, "Management Practices in Learning Organizations," *Organizational Dynamics* (Summer 1992), pp. 5–17.

C H A P T E R   1 7

1. For a recent review of the latest research on trends in communication, see Janet Falk and Brian Boyd, "Emerging Theories of Communication in Organizations," *Journal of Management* (June 1991), pp. 407–446. This article reviews trends in four key areas: communication, media choice; computer-supported group decision making; communications technology and organization design; and communications networks.

2. Fred Luthans and Janet K. Larsen, "How Managers Really Communicate," *Human Relations* (1986), vol. 39, pp. 161–178.

3. Larry E. Penley and Brian Hawkins, "Studying Interpersonal Communication in Organizations," *Academy of Management Journal* (June 1985), pp. 309–326.

4. Daniel H. Boyd, Stephen D. Lewis, and Grady L. Butler, "Getting Your Message Across," *Management Review* (July–August 1988), pp. 7–10.

5. William V. Haney, *Communication and Interpersonal Relations* (Homewood, Ill.: Irwin, 1979), p. 3.

6. For an update on Wal-Mart, see John Huey, "America's Most Successful Merchant," *Fortune* (September 23, 1991), pp. 46–59; Bill Saporito, "Is Wal-Mart Unstoppable?" *Fortune* (May 6, 1991), pp. 50–59. The original anecdote is from Thomas J. Peters and Robert H. Waterman, Jr., *In Search of Excellence* (New York: Harper & Row, 9182), pp. 246–247.

7. Faye Rice, "Champions of Communication," *Fortune* (June 3, 1991), pp. 111–120.

8. William G. Scott and Terrence R. Mitchell, *Organization Theory: A Structural Behavioral Analysis* (Homewood, Ill.: Irwin, 1979), p. 3.

9. S. L. Smith, "Occidental Chemical: Making Changes for the Better," *Occupational Hazards* (May 1992), pp. 65–68.

10. Nancy Marx Better, "The Secret of Liz Claiborne's Success," *Working Woman* (April 1992), pp. 68–71, 96–97.

11. Tom Varian, "Communicating Total Quality Inside the Organization," *Quality Progress* (June 1991), pp. 30–31.

12. This model is based on a number of similar sources. For example, see Norman B. Sigband and Arthur H. Bell, *Communication for Management and Business*, 3rd ed. (Glenview, Ill.: Scott, Foresman, 1986); and Couillard L. Bovee and John V. Thill, *Business Communications Today* (New York: Random House, 1986).

13. Lyman W. Porter and Karlene H. Roberts, "Communication in Organizations," in Marvin D. Dunnette, ed., *Handbook of Industrial and Occupational Psychology*, 2nd ed. (New York: Wiley, 1983), pp. 1553–1589.

14. Jolie Solomon, "Business Communications in the Fax Age," *Wall Street Journal* (October 27, 1988), p. B1.

15. Laurey Berk and Phillip G. Clampitt, "Finding the Right Path in the Communication Maze," *Communication World* (October 1991), pp. 28–32.

16. Richard L. Daft and Robert H. Lengel, "Orga-

nizational Information Requirements, Media Richness and Structural Design," *Management Science* (March 1986), pp. 554–572; Richard L. Daft and Robert H. Lengel, "Information Richness: A New Approach to Managerial Behavior and Organizational Design," in *Research and Organizational Behavior,* vol. 6, Barry Stoll and Larry L. Cummings, eds. (Greenwich, Conn.: JAI Press, 1984), pp. 191–233.

17. Richard L. Daft, Robert H. Lengel, and Linda Klebe Trevino, "The Relationship Among Message Equivocality, Media Selection, and Manager Performance: Implications for Information Support Systems," *MIS Quarterly* (September 1987), pp. 355–366.

18. Walter St. John, "In-House Communications Guidelines," *Personnel Journal* (November 1981), pp. 872–878.

19. Larry R. Smeltzer and John L. Waltman, *Managerial Communication: A Strategic Approach* (New York: Wiley, 1984), p. 4.

20. Sandra G. Garside and Brian H. Kleiner, "Effective One-to-One Communication Skills," *Industrial & Commercial Training* (1991), no. 2, pp. 24–28.

21. Bruce K. Blaylock, "Cognitive Styles and the Usefulness of Information," *Decision Sciences* (Winter 1984), pp. 74–91.

22. Ray W. Darrel, "Overcoming Conflict with Structured Feedback," *Journal for Quality & Participation* (December 1991), pp. 64–68.

23. Linda L. Davidoff, *Introduction to Psychology,* 2nd ed. (New York: McGraw-Hill, 1980), p. 172.

24. As reported in Maxwell Maltz, *Psychocybernetics* (New York: Pocket Books, 1960), p. 22.

25. Elizabeth A. Smith, "Training Supervisors to Work Effectively with a Changing Workforce," *Industrial Management* (July–August 1992), pp. 30–32; Sondra Thiederman, "Breaking Through to Foreign-Born Employees," *Management World* (May–June 1988), pp. 22–23.

26. "Tradition Plays an Important Role in the Business Culture of France," *Business America* (May 6, 1991), pp. 22–23.

27. Nancy Heckel, "Transcending Boundaries," *Training and Development Journal* (July 1987), pp. 72–73.

28. For example, see Christine Mary Baytosh and Brian H. Kleiner, "Effective Business Communication for Women," *Equal Opportunities International* (1989), no. 4, pp. 16–19.

29. "Your Personal Listening Profile," Sperry Corporation, 1980, pp. 4–5.

30. Mark McCormack, *What They Don't Teach You at the Harvard Business School* (New York: Bantam, 1984), p. 13.

31. For a recent discussion of how to be a better listener, see Frank K. Sonnenberg, "Marketing: Barriers to Communication," *Journal of Business Strategy* (July–August 1990), pp. 56–59.

32. Patricia Buhler, "Managing in the 90s: Are You Saying What You Mean?" *Supervision* (September 1991), pp. 18–20.

33. For a discussion, see C. Barnum and N. Wolniansky, "Taking Cues from Body Language," *Management Review* (June 1989), pp. 59–60; and David Givens, "What Body Language Can Tell You That Words Cannot," *U.S. News & World Report* (November 19, 1984), p. 100.

34. As told to the author by a Holiday Inns' franchisee.

35. Norman B. Sigband, *Communication for Management and Business* (Glenview, Ill.: Scott, Foresman, 1969), p. 19.

36. Edward T. Hall, *The Hidden Dimension* (New York: Doubleday, 1968).

37. Discussion with a senior vice-president for that division.

38. Timothy K. Smith, "Open Offices, the Idea of the 70s, Are Up Against the Wall in the 80s," *Wall Street Journal* (September 26, 1985), p. 38.

39. Michelle Neely Martinez, "Work Space: In Search of a Productive Design," *HR Magazine* (February 1990), pp. 36–39.

40. Abner M. Eisenberg, *Understanding Communication in Business and the Professions* (New York: Macmillan, 1978), p. 392.

41. Sigband, op. cit., p. 354.

42. The information was related to this writer by a vice-president of the American firm. This seems to be a version of the clever Japanese habit of making Americans wait until the last moment to talk business on a business trip.

43. John T. Molloy, *Dress for Success* (New York: Wyden, 1975).

44. "Labor Letter: Dialogues with Workers Gained Increased Employer Attention," *Wall Street Journal* (January 3, 1989), p. A1.

45. Walter Kiechell, III, "No Word from Up High," *Fortune* (January 6, 1986), pp. 125–126.

46. Robert Tucker and Milan Maravec, "How BPX Fights Bureaucracy with Upward Feedback," *Human Resources Professional* (Spring 1992), pp. 30–32.

47. For a discussion, see Alan Zaremba, "Working with the Organizational Grapevine," *Personnel Journal* (July 1988), pp. 38–42.

48. For a classic discussion, see Carl R. Rogers and F. J. Roethlisberger, "Barriers and Gateways to Communication," *Harvard Business Review* (November–December 1991), pp. 105–111.

49. Chris Lee, "Training at Loew's Corp.: If It's Not Broken . . . ," *Training* (April 1985), p. 43.

50. Mark Hall, "Purging Information Overload," *Computerworld* (February 11, 1991), p. 25; David Ludlum, "10 Tips for IS Survival in the 1990s," *Computer World* (December 25, 1989–January 1, 1990), pp. 14–15; and Robert M. Losee, Jr., "Minimizing Information Overload: The Ranking of Electronic Messages," *Journal of Information Sciences: Principle and Practices* (1989), no. 3, pp. 179–189.

51. Thomas Gordon, *Leadership Effectiveness Training* (New York: Wyden, 1977), pp. 27–48, 193.

52. Patricia Jakubowski and Arthur J. Lange, *The Assertiveness Option* (Champaign, Ill.: Research Press, 1977); Manual J. Smith, *When I Say No I Feel Guilty* (New York: Dial, 1975).

53. For a review of the frequency of usage of several of these approaches, see Paul L. Blocklyn, "Employee Communications," *Personnel* (May 1987), pp. 62–66.

54. These are also called listening posts. See John R. Hundley, "Listening Posts," *Personnel* (July–August 1976), pp. 39–43.

55. "Casino Hits It Big with Employee Hot-Line," *Success* (June 1986), p. 26.

56. Gregory C. Parliman and Erica L. Edwards, "Employee Assistance Programs: An Employers' Guide to Emerging Liability Issues," *Employee Relations Law Journal* (Spring 1992), pp. 593–601.

57. Frederick A. Starke and Thomas W. Ferratt, "Behavioral Information Systems," *Journal of Systems Management* (March 1976), pp. 26–30.

58. Walter H. Reed, "Gathering Opinion On-Line," *HR Magazine* (January 1991), pp. 51, 53.

59. Susan G. Strother, "Workers Speak Up," 'Central Florida Business', *Orlando Sentinel* (October 3, 1988), p. 5.

60. J. J. Yore, "Dealing with Complaints," *Venture* (July 1985), pp. 25–26.

61. Steven E. Groffman, "American Airlines' Employee Suggestion Program Takes Off," *Human Resources Professional* (Summer 1992), pp. 13–17.

62. Louanne Klein, "PG&E Awards $2 Million for Employees' Bright Ideas," *Human Resources Professional* (Spring 1991), pp. 20–25, 60.

63. David Drennan, "Can You Hear Me Down There?" *Divestor* (July 1992), pp. 44–46.

64. Fred T. Allen, "Winning and Holding Employee

Loyalty," *Nation's Business* (April 1977), pp. 40–44.

65. "Business' New Communication Tools," *Dun's Review* (February 1981), pp. 80–82.

66. "Broadcast News Inc.," *Newsweek* (January 4, 1988), pp. 34–35.

67. Blocklyn, loc. cit.

68. Bruce G. Posner, "The Best Little Handbook in Texas," *Inc.* (February 1989), pp. 84–87.

69. Roger Nall, "How to Use Electronic Mail Successfully," *Supervisory Management* (January 1992), p. 11; Phillip G. Clampitt, "Voice Mail: Pros & Cons," *Communication World* (March 1992), pp. 12–15; and "The Portable Executive," *Business Week* (October 10, 1988), pp. 102–112.

70. Gregory L. Miles, "At Westinghouse E-Mail Makes the World Go Around," *Business Week* (October 10, 1988), p. 110.

CHAPTER 18

1. Gabriella Stern and Clare Ansberry, "Fouling Out: A Founder Embezzled Millions for Basketball, Phar-Mor Chain Says," *Wall Street Journal* (September 5, 1992), pp. A1, A5.

2. Robert G. Eccles and Philip J. Pyburn, "Creating a Comprehensive System to Measure Performance," *Management Accounting* (October 1992), pp. 41–44.

3. For example, see Ford W. Worthy, "Japan's Smart Secrete Weapon," *Fortune* (August 12, 1991), pp. 72–75?

4. For example, see Robert L. Simmons, "The Strategy of Control," *CA Magazine* (March 1992), pp. 44–50; and Jack Schember, "Mrs. Fields' Secret Weapon," *Personnel* (September 1991), pp. 56–58.

5. Raymond R. Reilly and Brian Campbell, "How Corporate Performance Measurement Systems Inhibit Globalization," *Human Resource Management* (Spring 1990), pp. 63–68.

6. Kenneth A. Merchant, *Control in Business Organizations* (Marshfield, Mass.: Pittman, 1985).

7. Robert J. Mockler, *The Management Control Process* (Englewood Cliffs, N.J.: Prentice-Hall, 1972), p. 2.

8. Frank B. Copley, *Frederick W. Taylor, Father of Scientific Management*, vol. 2 (New York: Harper & Row, 1923), p. 358.

9. Giovanni Giglioni and Arthur G. Bedeian, "A Conspectus of Management Control Theory: 1900–1972, *Academy of Management Journal* (June 1974), pp. 292–305; and Mockler, loc. cit.

10. For example, see Ralph E. Drtina and Theodore T. Herbert, "Strategic Control Systems: Definition and Identification of Significant Parameters in Business Usage," paper presented to the Strategic Management Society, Amsterdam, October 1988.

11. For example, see Harold Sirkin and George Stalk, Jr., "Fix the Process, Not the Problem," *Harvard Business Review* (July–August 1990), pp. 26–33.

12. Bob Davis, "Costly Bugs: As Complexity Rises, Tiny Flaws in Software Pose a Growing Threat," *Wall Street Journal* (January 27, 1987), pp. 1, 18.

13. "The Quality Imperative," *Business Week* (Special Issue, October 25, 1991); J. M. Juran, "Strategies for World Class Quality," *Quality Progress* (March 1991), pp. 81–85.

14. Mockler, loc. cit.

15. Davis, loc. cit.

16. For example, see John A. Miller, "Benchmarking Performance," *CMA Magazine* (June 1992), p. 23; Alex Markin, "How to Implement Competitive Cost Benchmarking," *Journal of Business Strategy* (May–June 1992), pp. 14–20; and Thomas A. Stewart, "GE Keeps Those Ideas Coming," *Fortune* (August 12, 1991), pp. 41–49.

17. Robert S. Kaplan, "One Cost System Isn't Enough," *Harvard Business Review* (January–February 1988), pp. 61–66.

18. Eccles and Pyburn, loc. cit.; Worthy, loc. cit.

19. Alex Taylor, III, "The Road Ahead at General Motors," *Fortune* (May 4, 1992), pp. 94–95; Jams B. Treece, "The Board Revolt," *Business Week* (April 20, 1992), p. 31.

20. Alex Taylor, III, "What's Ahead for GM's New Team," *Fortune* (November 30, 1992), pp. 58–61.

21. William T. Greenwood, *Management and Organizational Behavior Theories* (Cincinnati: Southwestern, 1965).

22. W. H. Koontz and R. W. Bradspies, "Managing Through Feedforward Control," *Business Horizons* (June 1972), pp. 25–36.

23. Rajaram Veliyath, "Strategic Planning: Balancing Short-Run Performance and Longer-Term Prospects," *Long Range Planning* (June 1992), pp. 86–97.

24. Harold Koontz and Heinz Weihrich, *Management*, 9th ed. (New York: McGraw-Hill, 1988), p. 492.

25. For a review of the different types of control, such as control results, control personnel, control specific actions, or avoiding control problems, see Kenneth A. Merchant, "Control Function in Management," in Max D. Richards, ed., *Readings in Management*, 7th ed. (Cincinnati: Southwestern, 1986), pp. 285–301.

26. Jack Gray and Diane Matson, "Early Warning Systems," *Management Accounting* (August 1987), pp. 50–55.

27. Rita Cruise O'Brien, "Brief Case: EIS and Strategic Control," *Long Range Planning* (October 1991), pp. 125–127; "Systems Review—Commander EIS: Providing Strategic Information to Bank Executives," *Banking Software Review* (Spring 1990), pp. 8, 11.

28. Michael E. Porter, *Competitive Strategy* (New York: Free Press, 1980).

29. "The Quality Imperative," loc. cit.

30. William G. Ouchi, "A Conceptual Framework for the Design of Organizational Control Mechanisms," *Management Science* (August 1979), pp. 833–838.

31. William G. Ouchi, "Markets, Bureaucracies, and Clans," *Administrative Science Quarterly* (March 1980), vol. 25, no. 1, p. 130, and "The Overview," pp. 129–141.

32. Richard L. Daft, *Organization Theory and Design*, 2nd ed. (St. Paul: West, 1986), p. 318.

33. Ouchi, "Markets, Bureaucracies, and Clans," op. cit., p. 136.

34. Alfred M. Jaeger and B. R. Baliga, "Control Systems and Strategic Adaptations: Lessons from the Japanese," *Strategic Management Journal* (December 1985), pp. 115–134.

35. Ibid., p. 128.

36. Frank Petrock, "Corporate Culture Enhances Projects," *HR Magazine* (November 1990), pp. 64–66.

37. Ouchi, "Markets, Bureaucracies, and Clans," loc. cit.; plus my interpretation of Petrock's work.

38. Cortlandt Cammann and David A. Nadler, "Fit Control Systems to Your Management Style," *Harvard Business Review* (January–February 1976), pp. 65–72.

39. Other control styles have been identified. For example, Gareth R. Jones identifies four dimensions of leader control behavior at the supervisory level: obtrusive vs. inobtrusive, situational vs. personal, professional vs. paternalistic, and process vs. output. See his "Forms of Control and Leader Behavior," *Journal of Management* (1983), vol. 9, no. 2, pp. 159–172.

40. Cammann and Nadler, op. cit., p. 71.

41. William H. Newman, *Constructive Control* (Englewood Cliffs, N.J.: Prentice-Hall, 1975); Earl P. Strong and Robert D. Smith, *Management Control Models* (New York: Holt, 1968); Peter Lorange and Declan Murphy, "Consider-

ations in Implementing Strategic Control," *Journal of Business Strategy* (Spring 1984), pp. 27–35; and Peter F. Drucker, *Management: Tasks, Responsibilities, Practices* (New York: Harper & Row, 1974), pp. 490–502.

42. Richard E. Walton, "From Control to Commitment in the Workplace," *Harvard Business Review* (March–April 1985), pp. 76–84.

43. Walt Bogdanovich, "Lax Laboratories: The PAP Test Misses Much Cervical Cancer Through Lab's Errors," *Wall Street Journal* (November 2, 1987), p. 1.

44. David A. Garbin, "Quality on the Line," *Harvard Business Review* (September–October 1983), pp. 65–75.

45. R. L. Dunbar, "Designs for Organizational Control," in P. C. Nystrom and W. H. Starbuch, eds. *Handbook of Organizational Design II* (London: Oxford University Press, 1981).

46. W. H. Read, "Upward Communication in Industrial Hierarchies," *Human Relations* (February 1962), pp. 3–15.

47. Garbin, loc. cit.

48. Lee Berton, "Convenient Fiction: Inventory Chicanery Tempts More Firms, Fools More Auditors," *Wall Street Journal* (December 14, 1992), pp. A1, A4.

49. Martha Brannigan and Laurie M. Grossman, "Comptronix Fires Its CEO But Keeps Two Other Aides," *Wall Street Journal* (December 14, 1992), p. B4.

50. This discussion is based partly on Newman, loc. cit., and Koontz and Bradspies, loc. cit.

51. "The Quality Imperative," loc. cit.; Keki R. Bhote, "Improving Supply Management," *Management Review* (August 1987), pp. 50–53.

52. Richard Koenig, "Exacting Employer: Toyota Takes Pains and Time, Filling Jobs at Its Kentucky Plant," *Wall Street Journal* (December 1, 1987), pp. 1, 31.

53. Robert W. Goddard, "Work Force 2000," *Personnel Journal* (February 1989), pp. 64–71.

54. John F. Preble, "Towards a Comprehensive System of Strategic Control," *Journal of Management Studies* (July 1992), pp. 391–409; Veliyath, loc. cit.; Malcolm J. Morgan, "Feedforward Control for Competitive Advantage: The Japanese Approach," *Journal of General Management* (Summer 1992), pp. 41–52.

55. Newman, op. cit., pp. 12–25.

56. Bank of America *Annual Report*, 1987.

57. James R. Hagy, "Running Scared at Winn-Dixie," *Florida Trend* (August 1992), pp. 44–49.

58. Peter Lorange, Michael F. Scott Morton, and Sumantra Ghosaki, *Strategic Control* (St., Paul: West, 1986), chap. 1.

59. James M. Higgins and Julian W. Vincze, *Strategic Management: Text and Cases,* 5th ed., (Ft. Worth, Tex.: Dryden, 1993), chap. 10.

60. Richard J. Schonberger, *Japanese Manufacturing Techniques: Nine Hidden Lessons in Simplicity* (New York: Free Press, 1982), contains an excellent discussion of operations management, including vital control issues.

61. Lynda M. Applegate, James I. Cash, Jr., and D. Quinn Mills, "Information Technology and Tomorrow's Manager," *Harvard Business Review* (November–December 1988), pp. 128–136.

CHAPTER 19

1. Richard L. Daft and Norman D. MacIntosh, "The Nature and Use of Formal Control Systems for Management Control and Strategy Implementation," *Journal of Management* (Spring 1984), vol. 10, no. 1, p. 57. While I use their basic framework, I have adapted the financial resource allocation process to their model in a slightly different way than they describe it. I have also added terms to clarify and broaden some of the definitions they have used

and added financial analysis to the strategic plan element because such analysis occurs at the strategic level.

2. Ibid., p. 61.

3. William G. Ouchi and Mary Ann Maguire, "Organizational Control: Two Functions," *Administrative Science Quarterly* (December 1975), vol. 20, pp. 559–569.

4. Robert G. Eccles and Philip J. Pyburn, "Creating a Comprehensive System to Measure Performance," *Management Accounting* (October 1992), pp. 41–44; John A. Miller, "The New Activity Performance Measure," *CMA Magazine* (April 1992), p. 34; Joel C. Polakoff, "How to Design a Performance Measurement Program," *Corporate Controller* (January–February 1992), pp. 49–53.

5. For a philosophical underpinning, plus a suggested model, see Robert S. Kaplan and David P. Norton, "The Balanced Score Card—Measures That Drive Performance," *Harvard Business Review* (January–February 1992), pp. 71–79; for another philosophical view, see Robert G. Eccles, "The Performance Measurement Manifesto," *Harvard Business Review* (January–February 1991), pp. 131–137.

6. For example, see Joseph M. Sieger, "Manage Your Numbers to Match Your Strategy," *Management Review* (February 1992), pp. 46–48.

7. Richard L. Daft, *Management* (Hinsdale, Ill.: Dryden, 1988), p. 588.

8. Daft and MacIntosh, op. cit., p. 59.

9. Michael E. Porter, *Competitive Strategy* (New York: Free Press, 1980).

10. Ford S. Worthy, "Japan's Smart Secret Weapon," *Fortune* (August 12, 1991), pp. 71–75; Toshiro Hiromoto, "Another Hidden Edge—Japanese Management Accounting," *Harvard Business Review* (July–August 1988), pp. 22–26.

11. Alfred M. Jaego and B. R. Baliga, "Control Systems and Strategic Adaptations: Lessons from the Japanese Experience," *Strategic Management Journal* (April–June 1985), pp. 115–134.

12. Steven B. Seilheiner, "Current State of Decision Support Systems and Expert Systems Technology," *Journal of Systems Management* (August 1988), pp. 14–18.

13. "The Computer Age Dawns in the Corner Office," *Business Week* (June 27, 1988), pp. 84–85.

14. Eugene Brigham, *Fundamentals of Financial Management*, 4th ed. (Hinsdale, Ill.: Dryden, 1986), chap. 7. Also see, Lloyd Brandt, Jr., Joseph R. Danos, and J. Herman Brasseaux, "Financial Statement Analysis: Benefits and Pitfalls," *Practical Accountant* (May 1989), vol. 22, no. 5, pp. 34–47; and Lloyd Brandt, Jr., Joseph R. Danos, and J. Herman Brasseaux, "Financial Statement Analysis: Benefits and Pitfalls (Part 2)," *Practical Accountant* (June 1989), pp. 68–78.

15. Paula Doe, "What's Buried Inside Japanese Annual Reports?" *Electronic Business* (February 10, 1992), pp. 28–34.

16. For an in-depth analysis of a current ratio, see Mary M. K. Fleming, "Current Ratio Revisited," *Business Horizons* (May–June 1986), pp. 74–77.

17. Roger K. Dovat, "ROI Revisited," *CPA Journal* (February 1992), pp. 61–62.

18. For a discussion, see Bernard C. Reimann, "Achieving Management Consensus Around Value-Creating Strategies," *Planning Review* (September–October 1989), pp. 38–46; and David L. Wenner and Richard W. LeBer, "Managing for Shareholder Value—From Top to Bottom," *Harvard Business Review* (November–December 1989), pp. 52–66.

19. Francis V. McCrory and Peter G. Gerstberger, "The New Math of Performance Measurement," *Journal of Business Strategy* (March–April 1992), pp. 33–38.

20. Robert S. Kaplan, "One Cost System Isn't Enough," *Harvard Business Review* (January–February 1988), p. 66.

21. Ibid.

22. "The Productivity Paradox," *Business Week* (June 6, 1988), p. 101. See the additional discussion on pp. 100–114.

23. Ibid., pp. 105, 112; John P. Campi, "Total Cost Management at Parker-Hannifin," *Management Accounting* (January 1989), pp. 51–53.

24. Ralph L. Benke, Jr., "Teaching Activity-Based Costing," *Management Accounting* (August 1992), pp. 61–62; Peter B. B. Turner, "Activity-Based Management," *Management Accounting* (January 1992), pp. 20–25.

25. Mike Walker, "Attribute Based Costing," *Australian Accountant* (March 1992), pp. 42–45.

26. Worthy, loc. cit.; Hiromoto, loc. cit.

27. Belverd E. Needles, Jr., Henry P. Anderson, and James C. Caldwell, *Principles of Accounting*, 4th ed. (Boston: Houghton Mifflin, 1990), pp. 30–31.

28. Ibid., pp. 31, 329–334.

29. Eccles and Pyburn, loc. cit.; Eccles, loc. cit.; Joseph M. Sieger, "Manage Your Numbers to Match Your Strategy," *Management Review* (February 1992), pp. 46–48; Linda J. Blessing, "New Opportunities: A CPA's Primer on Performance Auditing," *Journal of Accountancy* (May 1991), pp. 58–68.

30. Kaplan and Norto, op. cit., pp. 71–79.

31. Ibid.

32. For a recent discussion, see James M. Higgins and Julian W. Vincze, *Strategic Management: Text and Cases*, 5th ed. (Ft. Worth, Tex.: Dryden, 1993), pp. 367–397.

33. Alex Markin, "How to Implement Competitive-Cost Benchmarking," *Journal of Business Strategy* (May–June 1992), pp. 14–20.

34. Robert N. Anthony, John Dearden, and Norton M. Bedford, *Management Control Systems*, 5th ed. (Homewood, Ill.: Irwin, 1984), pp. 443–444.

35. Gordon Pinchot, III, *Intrapreneuring* (New York: Harper & Row, 1985).

36. Peter Gwynne, "The Pentagon's War on Costs," *High Technology* (March 1987), pp. 31–35.

37. Peter Pyhrr, "Zero-Based Budgeting," *Harvard Business Review* (November–December 1970), pp. 11–12.

38. "What It Means to Build a Budget from Zero," *Business Week* (April 19, 1976), p. 160.

39. Mark Dirsmith and Steven Jablonsky, "Zero-Based Budgeting . . . and Political Strategy," *Academy of Management Review* (October 1979), pp. 555–565.

40. For a review of zero-based budgeting, see Michael F. Duffy, "ZBB, MBO, PPB and Their Effectiveness Within the Planning/Marketing Process," *Strategic Management Journal* (January–February 1989), pp. 163–173.

41. Henry L. Tosi, Jr., "The Human Effects Budgeting Systems on Management," *MSU Business Topics* (Autumn 1974), pp. 56–57.

42. Raymond K. Suutari, "Rethinking Budgeting," *CA Magazine*, (October 1991), pp. 53–55.

43. Fred A. Shelton and Jack C. Bartes, "How to Create an Electronic Spreadsheet Budget," *Management Accounting* (July 1986), pp. 40–47.

44. Keith C. Gourley and Thomas R. Blecki, "Computerized Budgeting at Lord Corporation," *Management Accounting* (August 1986), pp. 37–40.

45. Srinivasan Umapathy, "How Successful Firms Budget," *Management Accounting* (February 1987), pp. 25–27.

46. John E. Rehfeld, "What Working for a Japanese Firm Taught Me," *Harvard Business Review* (November–December 1990), pp. 167–176.

47. Ronald G. Wells, "Guidelines for Effective and Defensible Performance Appraisal System," *Personnel Journal* (October 1982), p. 781.

48. John M. Ivancevich and William F. Glueck, *Foundations of Personnel/Human Resource Management*, 3rd ed. (Plano, Tex.: Business Publications, 1986), p. 280; Cristina G. Banks and Loriann Roberson, "Performance Appraisers as Test Developers," *Academy of Management Review* (January 1985), no. 1, pp. 128–142.

49. See the discussion in Chapter 13.

50. Karen Matthes, "Will Your Performance Appraisal System Stand Up in Court?" *HR Focus* (August 1992), p. 5.

51. Ivancevich and Glueck, op. cit., pp. 565–570.

52. "The Enemy Within," *U.S. News & World Report* (July 4, 1988), pp. 16–22.

53. J. Kendall Middaught, II, "Management Control in the Financial Services Industry," *Business Horizons* (May–June 1988), pp. 79–86.

54. Alan Murray and Paulette Thomas, "Dinosaur Industry: Bush's New Solution for Problem of S&L's Could Kill Them Off," *Wall Street Journal* (February 7, 1989), pp. A1, A4; Jeff Bailey and Charles F. McCoy, "Tricky Ledgers: To Hide Huge Losses, Financial Officials Use Accounting Gimmicks," *Wall Street Journal* (January 12, 1987), pp. 1, 19.

CHAPTER 20

1. Myron Magnet, "Who's Winning the Information Revolution?" *Fortune* (November 30, 1992), pp. 110–118; Michael Porter and Victor Miller, "How Information Gives You Competitive Advantage," *Harvard Business Review* (July–August 1985), pp. 149–160; Louis Fried and Richard Johnson, "Planning for the Competitive Use of Information Technology," *Information Strategy: The Executives Journal* (Summer 1992), pp. 5–14.

2. Magnet, op. cit., pp. 112–113.

3. Bridget O'Brian, "Course Correction: Tired of Airline Losses, AMR Pushes Its Bid to Diversify Business," *Wall Street Journal* (February 1993), pp. A1, 8; Connie Winkler, "AMR Hones Sabre to Sharpen Competitive Edge," *Computer World*, Section 2 (October 8, 1990), pp. 36–37.

4. David Wessel, "Marketing Tool: Computer Finds a Role in Buying and Selling, Reshaping Businesses," *Wall Street Journal* (March 18, 1987), pp. 1, 22.

5. Magnet, op. cit., pp. 110–111.

6. "Scramble for Global Networks," *Business Week* (March 21, 1988), pp. 140–148.

7. John G. Burch and Gary Grudnitski, *Information Systems: Theory and Practice*, 4th ed. (New York: Wiley, 1986), p. 3; see also, James L. Cash, Jr., F. I. McFarlan, James L. McKenney, and Michael Arthur Titale, *Corporate Information Systems Management: Text and Cases*, 2nd ed. (Homewood, Ill.: Irwin, 1988), chap. 1, for a discussion of information systems; and Jerome Kanter, *Management Information Systems*, 3rd ed. (Englewood Cliffs, N.J.: Prentice-Hall, 1984), pp. 9–13.

8. Steven L. Mandell, *Computers and Data Processing* (St. Paul: West, 1985).

9. Burch and Grudnitski, op. cit., pp. 5–6.

10. Thomas W. Malone, JoAnne Yates, and Robert L. Benjamin, "The Logic of Electronic Markets," *Harvard Business Review* (May–June 1989), pp. 166–170.

11. Ikujiro Nonaka, "The Knowledge Creating Company," *Harvard Business Review* (November–December 1991), pp. 96–109.

12. Ibid.

13. Kanter, op. cit., p. 6.

14. Ibid., p. 1; John P. Murray, *Managing Information Systems as a Corporate Resource* (Homewood, Ill.: Dow Jones-Irwin, 1984), chap. 1.

15. Henry C. Lucas, Jr., "Utilizing Information Technology: Guidelines for Managers," *Sloan Management Review* (Fall 1986), p. 39.

16. For a review of the concept, see Paul H. Chaney

and Norman R. Lyons, "MIS Update," *Data Management* (October 1980), pp. 26–32.

17. Guisseppi A. Forgionne, "Building Effective Decision Support Systems," *Business* (January–March 1988), p. 19.
18. Burch and Grudnitski, op. cit., pp. 37–41.
19. Ibid., pp. 37–38.
20. "Computers of the '90s: A Brave New World," *Newsweek* (October 24, 1988), pp. 52–53.
21. Burch and Grudnitski, op. cit., p. 39.
22. Ibid.
23. Ibid., p. 40.
24. Ibid., p. 41. Much of this discussion is based on this reference.
25. Scott Ambler, "Encouraging User Participation," *Computing Canada* (June 22, 1992), p. 23; Kate Kaiser and Ananth Srinivasan, "User-Analyst Differences: An Empirical Investigation of Attitudes Related to Systems Development," *Academy of Management Journal* (September 1982), pp. 630–646.
26. Tor Guimaraes, Magid Igbaria, and Ming-Te Lu, "The Determinants of DSS Success: An Integrated Model," *Decision Sciences* (March–April 1992), pp. 409–430; Blake Ives and Margrethe H. Olson, "User Involvement and MIS Success: A Review of Research," *Management Science* (May 1984), pp. 586–603.
27. "Information Power," *Business Week* (October 14, 1985), pp. 108–114.
28. Michael E. Porter and Victor E. Miller, "How Information Gives You a Competitive Advantage," *Harvard Business Review* (July–August 1985), pp. 149–160.
29. Paul Strassmann, "Computers and Software That Are Supposed to Tell Managers What Is Going on in Their Companies and Help Them Coordinate Activities," *Inc.* (March 1988), pp. 25–40.
30. Mary Kathleen Flynn, "Business Focus Is Key to Success," *Datamation* (July 15, 1987), p. 48.
31. Ido Millet and Charles H. Mawhinney, "Executive Information Systems," *Information & Management* (August 1992), pp. 83–92; C. Joseph Sass and Teresa A. Keefe, "MIS for Strategic Planning and the Competitive Edge," *Journal of Systems Management* (June 1988), p. 14.
32. Arnold E. Keller, *Info Systems* (June 1987), p. 22.
33. Sass and Keefe, op. cit., p. 15.
34. James E. Douglas, "The Executive Information System: A Power Drill for HR Data," *Human Resources Professional* (Summer 1992), pp. 45–48.
35. Sumantra Ghoshal and D. Eleanor Westney, "Organizing Competitor Analysis Systems," *Strategic Management Journal* (January 1991), pp. 17–31; Michael E. Porter, *Competitive Strategy* (New York: Free Press, 1980).
36. For a recent discussion, see Robert J. Mockler, "Strategic Intelligence Systems: Competitive Intelligence Systems to Support Strategic Management Decision Making," *SAM Advanced Management Journal* (Winter 1992), pp. 4–9.
37. Connie Winkler, "Battling for New Roles," *Datamation* (October 15, 1986), pp. 82–88.
38. "Technology Investment Measurements Fuel Barnett's Quality Service Initiative," *Bank Marketing* (May 1992), pp. 41–42.
39. Alice LaFlante, "Global Information Officers Entering IT Picture," *Computerworld* (August 19, 1991), p. 70.
40. Robert Knight, "DBMS-Facing 90s Obstacles," *Software Magazine* (December 1991), pp. 27–28; Lucas, loc. cit.
41. William J. Cook, "Improving on the Mainframe," *U.S. News & World Report* (June 8, 1992), pp. 52–54.
42. Ibid.
43. Russell Mitchell, "Where No Computer Has Gone Before," *Business Week* (November 25, 1991), pp. 80–88.
44. Lucas, op. cit., p. 41.

45. "The Portable Executive," *Business Week* (October 10, 1988), p. 103.
46. Erik Martensen, "E-Mail: Its Impact on Communications," *Office* (September 1992), pp. 60–61.
47. Ronald G. Childs and Walter K. Sheets, "How LTV Mail Enabled Its Applications," *Datamation* (July 1, 1992), pp. 33–35.
48. "The Portable Executive," loc. cit.
49. William J. Cook, "Dialing the Future," *U.S. News & World Report* (February 3, 1992), pp. 49–51.
50. "The Portable Executive," loc. cit.
51. Kathy Meier, "Voice/Fax Integration: Two Technologies Form a Powerful Combination," *Telemarketing Magazine* (September 1992), pp. 39–40.
52. Markus B. Zimmer, "A Practical Guide to Video Conferencing," *Training and Development Journal* (May 1988), p. 84. This article offers a series of questions and answers for people preparing to do their first video conference.
53. Eric J. Adams, "Video Conferencing Comes of Age," *World Trade* (November 1991), pp. 74–78.
54. Chris Holland, Geoff Lockett, and Ian Blackman, "Planning for Electronic Data Interchange," *Strategic Management Journal* (December 1992), pp. 539–550.
55. "An Electronic Pipeline Is Changing the Way America Does Business," *Business Week* (August 3, 1987), p. 8.
56. Theodore Justin Gage, "EDI Goes Global as Citi, Motorola Blaze the Trail," *Corporate Cashflow* (March 1992), pp. 8–10.
57. Much of the opening commentary in this section is based on an article by Steven B. Seilheiner, "Current State of Decision Support Systems and Expert Systems Technology," *Journal of Systems Management* (August 1988), pp. 14–19.
58. Ibid.
59. Peter G. W. Keen and Michael S. Scott Morton, *Decision Support Systems: An Organizational Perspective* (Reading, Mass.: Addison-Wesley, 1978), p. 1.
60. Pascale Zarate, "The Process of Designing a DSS: A Case Study in Planning," *European Journal of Operational Research* (December 16, 1991), pp. 394–402.
61. T. H. Winston, *Artificial Intelligence,* 2nd ed. (Reading, Mass.: Addison-Wesley, 1984), p. 1.
62. Daniel G. Schwartz and George J. Klir, "Fuzzy Logic Flowers in Japan," *IEEE Spectrum* (July 1992), pp. 32–35.
63. Ibid.
64. Ibid.
65. William Larry Gordon and Jeffrey R. Key, "Artificial Intelligence in Support of Small Business Information Needs," *Journal of Systems Management* (January 1987), p. 26.
66. Robert Michaelsen and Donald Michie, "Prudent Expert Systems Applications Are Providing Competitive Weapon," *Data Management* (July 1986), p. 31.
67. E. Robert Keller, "Expert Systems for Business Applications: Potentials and Limitations," *Journal of Systems Management* (June 1988), p. 10.
68. Engining Lin, "Expert Systems for Business Applications: Potentials and Limitations," *Journal of Systems Management* (July 1986), p. 19.
69. David H. Freedman, "AI Meets the Corporate Mainframe," *Info Systems* (February 1987), p. 32.
70. Jae K. Shim and Jeffrey S. Rice, "Expert Systems Applications to Managerial Accounting," *Journal of Systems Management* (June 1988), p. 10.
71. Freedman, op. cit., p. 36.
72. Jody L. Ryan, "Expert Systems in the Future:

The Redistribution of Power," *Journal of Systems Management* (April 1988), pp. 18–21.
73. Jeremy Main, "Computers of the World Unite," *Fortune* (September 24, 1990), pp. 115–122.
74. Ibid.
75. "Is Your Computer Secure?" *Business Week* (August 1988), pp. 64–72.
76. Ibid.
77. Ibid.
78. Lynda M. Applegate, James I. Cash, Jr., and D. Quinn Mills, "Information Technology and Tomorrow's Manager," *Harvard Business Review* (November–December 1988), pp. 128–136.
79. Paul B. Carroll, "Computers Bringing Changes to Basic Business Documents," *Wall Street Journal* (March 6, 1987), p. 33.
80. Much of the discussion in the organization section is taken from Nonaka, loc. cit. and C. W. Holsapple and A. B. Whinston, *Business Expert Systems* (New York: Irwin, 1987), chap. 13.
81. Ibid., p. 301.
82. Nonaka, loc. cit.
83. Ibid.
84. Michael E. McGill, John W. Slocum, Jr., and David Lei, "Management Practices in Learning Organizations," *Organizational Dynamics* (Summer 1992), pp. 5–17; Kathryn Rudie Harrigan, "Knowledge Workers: The Last Bastion of Competitive Advantage," *Planning Review* (November–December 1991), pp. 4–9, 48.

CHAPTER 21

1. For a discussion, see Aleda V. Roth and Jeffrey G. Miller, "Success Factors in Manufacturing," *Business Horizons* (July–August 1992), pp. 73–81; "The Quality Imperative," Special Issue of *Business Week* (October 25, 1991); and Stephen S. Cohen and John Zysman, "Why Manufacturing Matters: The Myth of the Post-Industrial Economy," *California Management Review* (Spring 1987), pp. 9–26.
2. "The Quality Imperative," loc. cit.; Jeremy Main, "Manufacturing the Right Way," *Fortune* (May 21, 1990), pp. 54–64; Joel Dreyfuss, "Victories in the Quality Crusade," *Fortune* (October 10, 1988), pp. 80–88; and "America's Leanest and Meanest," *Business Week* (October 5, 1987), pp. 78–88.
3. Andrew Kupfer, "How American Industry Stacks Up," *Fortune* (March 9, 1992), pp. 30–46.
4. J. C. Collier, "A Competitive Edge Through TQM," *Quality* (August 1992), pp. 12–13; Kerry Rottenberger and Richard Kern, "The Upside-Down Deming Principle," *Sales & Marketing Management* (June 1992), pp. 38–44; "The Quality Imperative," loc. cit.; W. Edwards Deming, "Roots and Quality Control," *Pacific Basin Quarterly* (Spring–Summer 1985), pp. 1–4. For a brief history of quality issues, see Jeremy Main, "Under the Spell of the Quality Gurus," *Fortune* (August 18, 1986), pp. 30–34, who discusses the efforts of W. Edwards Deming, Joseph M. Juran, and Phillip Crosby, among others.
5. Phil Crosby, *Quality Is Free* (New York: Mentor/Penguin, 1980).
6. Douglas McGregor, *The Human Side of Enterprise* (New York: McGraw-Hill, 1960).
7. Damon Darlin, "Trade Switch: Japan Is Getting a Dose of What It Gave U.S.: Low-Priced Imports," *Wall Street Journal* (July 20, 1988), pp. 1, 6.
8. For discussions of managing in services, see Ron Zemke, "The Emerging Art of Service Management," *Training* (January 1992), pp. 37–42; Richard B. Chase and Robert H. Hayes, "Beefing Up Operations in Service Firms," *Sloan Management Review* (Fall 1991), pp. 15–26; and Roger W. Schmenner, "How Can Ser-

vice Business Prosper and Survive?" *Sloan Management Review* (Spring 1986), pp. 21–32.

9. "The Quality Imperative," loc. cit.

10. Much of this chapter is designed around the strategic, tactical, and operational segmentation of the process approach found in Norman Gaither, *Productions and Operations Management: A Problem Solving and Decision Making Approach* (Chicago: Dryden, 1987), combined with the five key issues approach used by Roger G. Schroeder, *Operations Management: Decision Making in the Operations Function*, 3rd ed. (New York: McGraw-Hill, 1989).

11. Gaither, op. cit., p. 3.

12. Schroeder, op. cit., p. 4.

13. "Productivity: The U.S. Remains Leader of the Pack . . . ," *Business Week* (December 21, 1992), p. 18.

14. Adapted from Gaither, op. cit., p. 30.

15. Thomas A. Stewart, "Brace for Japan's Hot New Strategy," *Fortune* (September 21, 1992), pp. 62–74; Susan Moffat, "Japan's New Personalized Production," *Fortune* (October 22, 1990), pp. 132–135.

16. For a discussion of manufacturing strategy, see Steven C. Wheelwright, "Manufacturing Strategy: Defining the Missing Link," *Strategic Management Journal* (1984), pp. 77–91.

17. For a discussion, see Robert R. Bell and John M. Burnham, "The Paradox of Manufacturing Strategy: Defining the Missing Link," *Strategic Management Journal* (1984), pp. 77–91.

18. Robert H. Hayes and Steven C. Wheelwright, *Restoring Our Competitive Edge: Competing Through Manufacturing* (New York: Wiley, 1984).

19. Gaither, op. cit., p. 128.

20. Ibid., p. 129.

21. Wickam Skinner, "The Focused Factory," *Harvard Business Review* (May–June 1974), p. 113.

22. Douglas R. Sease, "Getting Smart: How U.S. Companies Devise Ways to Meet the Challenge from Japan," *Wall Street Journal* (September 16, 1986), pp 1, 25.

23. Clyde E. Witt, "Partnerships Drive Allison's Focused Factory," *Material Handling Engineering* (January 1992), pp. 36–40; Art Sneen, "Employee Empowerment Gives Focus to Focused Factories," *Manufacturing Systems* (February 1991), pp. 54, 56.

24. Thomas J. Peters, *Thriving on Chaos: Handbook for a Management Revolution* (New York: Knopf, 1988), pp. 16–34 and 47–190, with the discussion of flexible manufacturing on pp. 161, 163, and 203.

25. Stewart, loc. cit.

26. Ibid.; Moffat, loc. cit.

27. James W. Dean, Jr., and Gerald I. Susman, "Organizing for Manufacturable Design," *Harvard Business Review* (January–February 1989), pp. 28–36.

28. Sanjoy Kumar and Yash P. Gupta, "Cross Functional Teams Improve Manufacturing at Motorola's Austin Plant," *Industrial Engineering* (May 1991), pp. 32–36.

29. Thomas J. Peters, "The Home-Team Advantage," *U.S. News & World Report* (March 31, 1986), p. 49.

30. For a discussion of the importance of innovation to competitiveness, see, Joseph T. Vesey, "The New Competitors: They Think in Terms of 'Speed-to-Market,'" *Academy of Management Executive* (May 1991), pp. 23–33.

31. "The Best-Engineered Part Is No Part at All," *Business Week* (May 8, 1989), p. 150; and "How to Make It Right the First Time," *Business Week* (June 8, 1987), pp. 142–143.

32. Richard J. Babyak, "DFM Team Brews Cost-Cutting Coffeemaker," *Appliance Manufacturer* (November 1991), pp. 55–57.

33. Gaiter, op. cit., p. 143.

34. Dana Corporation, internal documents.

35. Gaither, op. cit., pp. 197–200.

36. James M. Higgins and Julian W. Vincze, "Integrative Case: The Strategic Challenges Facing GM in 1992," and "Industry Note: A Global Perspective on the U.S. Automobile Industry, February 1992," in *Strategic Management: Text and Cases*, 5th ed. (Ft. Worth, Tex.: Dryden, 1993), pp. 166–180.

37. Ibid.; Paul Ingrassia, "Losing Control: Auto Industry in U.S. Is Sliding Relentlessly into Japanese Hands," *Wall Street Journal* (February 16, 1990), pp. A1, A5; Paul Ingrassia and Joseph B. White, "Losing the Race: With Its Market Share Sliding, GM Scrambles to Avoid a Calamity," *Wall Street Journal* (December 14, 1989), pp. A1, A10.

38. Jacob M. Schlesinger and Amal Kuman Naj, "Chrysler to Buy Renault's Stake in AMC: Seeks Rest of Company," *Wall Street Journal* (March 10, 1987), p. 3.

39. Paul Ingrassia and Bradley A. Stertz, "Problems of Success: Ford's Strong Sales Raise Agonizing Issue of Additional Plants," *Wall Street Journal* (October 26, 1988), pp. A1, 16.

40. Alex Taylor, III, "How Toyota Copes with Hard Times," *Fortune* (January 25, 1993), pp. 78–81.

41. G. J. VandenAkker, CEO, Avery International Europe, presentation to the Strategic Management Society, Amsterdam, The Netherlands, October 18, 1988.

42. Edmund Faltermayer, "U.S. Companies Come Back Home," *Fortune* (December 30, 1991), pp. 106–112; Constantine C. Markides and Norman Berg, "Manufacturing Offshore Is Bad Business," *Harvard Business Review* (September–October 1988), pp. 113–120.

43. Gaither, op. cit., p. 327.

44. Thomas J. Russo, Jr., and Angelo J. Tortorella, "Plant Layout—Part 3: The Contribution of CAD," *Chemical Engineering* (April 1992), pp. 97–101.

45. For a discussion, see Gerald Najarian, "Plant Layout: Capital Improvement Without Capital Expenditure," *Manufacturing Systems* (September 1992), pp. 62–64.

46. Richard J. Schonberger, *Japanese Manufacturing Techniques* (New York: Free Press, 1982), p. viii.

47. Gaither, op. cit., p. 335.

48. For a recent review of this, see Jit Seng Chan, Danny A. Samson, and Amrik S. Sobal, "An Integrative Model of Japanese Manufacturing Techniques," *International Journal of Operations and Production Management* (1990), no. 9, pp. 37–56.

49. Ibid., p. 338.

50. Frederick C. Weston, Jr., "Computer Integrated Manufacturing Systems: Fact or Fantasy," *Business Horizons* (July–August 1988), pp. 64–68.

51. Gaither, op. cit., p. 13, is used for this discussion of CAD, CAM, FMS, and ASRS.

52. Patricia L. Nemetz and Louis W. Fry, "Flexible Manufacturing Organizations: Implications for Strategy Formulation and Organizational Design," *Academy of Management Review* (October 1988), pp. 627–638. For a review of usage of flexible systems in Europe, Japan, and North America, see Arnoud DeMeyer, Jinichiro Nakane, Jeffrey G. Miller, and Kasra Ferdows, "Flexibility: The Next Competitive Battle, The Manufacturing Futures Survey," *Strategic Management Journal* (1989), pp. 135–144.

53. Ibid., p. 149.

54. Cynthia A. Lengnick-Hall, "Technology Advances in Batch Production and Improved Competitive Position," *Journal of Management* (Spring 1986), pp. 75–90. James E. Ashton and Frank X. Cook, Jr., suggest that much more remains to be done, however. See James E. Ashton and Frank X. Cook, Jr., "Time to Reform

Job Shop Manufacturing," *Harvard Business Review* (March–April, 1989), p. 107.

55. William J. Hampton and James R. Norman, "General Motors, What Went Wrong," *Business Week* (March 16, 1987), p. 107.

56. Witt, loc. cit.; Art Sneen, "Employee Empowerment Gives Focus to Focused Factories," *Manufacturing Systems* (February 1991), pp. 54, 56.

57. William G. Ouchi, *Theory Z: How American Business Can Meet the Japanese Challenge* (Reading, Mass.: Addison-Wesley, 1981).

58. Richard J. Schonberger, "Is Strategy Strategic? Impact of Total Quality Management on Strategy," *Academy of Management Executive* (August 1992), pp. 80–87; Leopold S. Vansina, "Total Quality Control: An Overall Organizational Improvement Strategy," *National Productivity Review* (Winter 1989–1990), pp. 59–73.

59. Dana Dubbs, "Balancing Benefits of Outsourcing vs. In-House," *Facilities Design & Management* (August 1992), pp. 42–44; Edward W. Davis, "Global Outsourcing: Have U.S. Managers Thrown the Baby Out with the Water?" *Business Horizons* (July–August 1992), pp. 58–65.

60. Mart Moffett, "Southern Strategies: U.S. Manufacturers Already Are Adapting to Mexico's Free Trade," *Wall Street Journal* (October 29, 1992), pp. A1, A7.

61. Crosby, loc. cit.

62. For more detailed information on quality, see "The Quality Imperative," loc. cit.

63. As firms understand it better, the concept has broadened to include new issues such as its links with other logistical areas. See R. Natarajan, "Inventory Management—The Big Picture," *Production & Inventory Management Journal* (Fourth Quarter 1991), pp. 29–31.

64. Robert Kreitner, *Management*, 3rd ed. (Boston: Houghton-Mifflin, 1986), p. 627.

65. For a recent description, see James D. Schneider and Mark A. Leatherman, "Integrated Just-in-Time: A Total Business Approach," *Production & Inventory Management Journal* (First Quarter 1992), pp. 78–82; for another view, see Robert J. Schonberger, "The Transfer of Japanese Manufacturing Management Techniques to U.S. Industry," *Academy of Management Review* (October 1982), pp. 479–487.

66. There are actually two cards involved, but the essence of the system is as described.

67. Schonberger, *Japanese Manufacturing Techniques*, op. cit., pp. 1–3.

68. Dexter Hutchins, "Having a Hard Time with Just-in-Time," *Fortune* (June 9, 1986), pp. 64–66.

69. Gaither, loc. cit.

70. Author's discussion with Martin Marietta officials. For a detailed analysis, see Joseph Orlicky, *Materials Requirement Planning* (New York: McGraw-Hill, 1975).

71. "Polaroid Division Posts Quantum On-Time Progress," *Purchasing* (March 5, 1992), pp. 31–32.

72. Robert M. Knight, "Furniture Maker Uses MRP II to Cut Lead Time," *Computerworld* (June 8, 1992), p. 80.

73. Thomas R. Miller, "The Quality Circle Phenomenon: A Review and Appraisal," *Advanced Management Journal* (Winter 1989), pp. 4–7, 12.

74. Ibid.; and "Quality Circles: Do They Work?" *Incentive* (May 1989), pp. 71–77.

75. "What's Creating an Industrial Miracle at Ford?" *Business Week* (July 30, 1984), pp. 80–81.

76. Harold L. Gilmore, "Continuous Incremental Improvement: An Operations Strategy for Higher Quality, Lower Costs, and Global Competitiveness," *Advanced Management Journal* (Winter 1990), pp. 21–25.

77. Robert H. Hayes and Ramchandran Jakumar,

"Manufacturing's Crisis: New Technologies, Obsolete Organizations," *Harvard Business Review* (September–October 1988), pp. 77–85.

78. Elizabeth A. Haas, "Breakthrough Manufacturing," *Harvard Business Review* (March–April 1987), pp. 75–81.

79. For more information, see Stephen R. Rosenthal, "Progress Toward the Factory of the Future," *Journal of Operations Management* (May 1984), pp. 203–229; and Jack R. Meredith, "The Strategic Advantages of the Factory of the Future," *California Management Review* (Spring 1987), pp. 27–41.

80. Joel D. Goldhar and David Lei, "The Shape of Twenty-first Century Global Manufacturing," *Journal of Business Strategy* (March–April 1991), pp. 37–41.

81. John W. Kenrick, *Understanding Productivity: An Introduction to the Dynamics of Productivity Change* (Baltimore: Johns Hopkins, 1977), p. 114.

82. For a discussion, see Peter F. Drucker, "The New Productivity Challenge," *Harvard Business Review* (November–December 1991), pp. 69–79.

83. Myron Magnet, "Good News for the Service Economy," *Fortune* (May 3, 1993), pp. 46–52.

84. "Productivity: The U.S. Remains Leader of the Pack," *Business Week* (December 21, 1992), p. 18; "The Productivity Paradox," *Business Week* (June 6, 1988), p. 100.

85. Al Ehrbar, "Price of Progress: Re-engineering Gives Firms New Efficiency, Workers Pink Slips," *Wall Street Journal* (March 16, 1993), pp. A1, A11.

86. "The Productivity Paradox," loc. cit.; pp. 100–114; Catherine L. Harris et al., "Office Automation: Making It Pay Off," *Business Week* (October 12, 1987), pp. 134–146; Norman Jonas, "Can America Compete? Its Options Are a Surge in Productivity, or a Lasting Decline," *Business Week* (April 20, 1987), pp. 45–69.

87. Maureen F. Allyn, "Rising Factory Productivity Is Giving the Expansion Room to Run," *Fortune* (August 1, 1988), p. 25; and Joan Berger, "Productivity: Why It Is the Number One Underachiever," *Business Week* (April 20, 1987), p. 55.

88. "Office Automation: Making It Pay Off," loc. cit.; Dan Guttman, "The Automation Edge," *Success* (October 1987), pp. 30–38.

89. Otis Port et al., "The Software Trap: Automate—Or Else," *Business Week* (May 9, 1988), pp. 142–154.

CHAPTER 22

1. David L. Birch, "The Hidden Economy," *Wall Street Journal,* special section, (June 10, 1988), p. R23.

2. Jeanne Saddler, "Fears Mount That Small-Business Sector Is In a State of Permanent Retrenchment," *Wall Street Journal* (February 14, 1992), p. B1.

3. David L. Birch, loc. cit.

4. Bill Richards, "Starting Up: Blue-Collar Worker Laborers Laid Off in Rustbelt Try to Run Own Firms," *Wall Street Journal* (September 8, 1986), p. 1.

5. Anne Murphy, "The Start-Up of the Nineties," *Inc.* (March 1992), pp. 33–40; John B. Hinge, "Small Business: Big Numbers," *Wall Street Journal,* special section, (November 22, 1991), p. R18.

6. For recent reviews of the relevant research, see Murray B. Lou and Ian C. Macmillan, "Entrepreneurship: Past Research and Future Challenges," *Journal of Management* (June 1988), pp. 139–161; and Max S. Wortman, Jr., "Entrepreneurship: An Integrating Typology and Evaluation of the Empirical Research in the Field," *Journal of Management* (June 1987), no. 2, pp. 259–279.

7. For a review of Richard Cantillon's theory, see Joseph A. Schumpeter, *History of Economic Analysis* (New York: Oxford, 1954), pp. 215–223.

8. Robert C. Ronstadt, *Entrepreneurship: Text, Cases and Notes* (Dover, Mass.: Lord, 1984), p. 8.

9. Joseph A. Schumpeter, *The Theory of Economic Development* (Cambridge, Mass.: Harvard, 1934).

10. Low and Macmillan, op. cit., p. 141.

11. Howard H. Stevenson and William A. Sahlman, "Entrepreneurship: A Process, Not a Person," working paper, Division of Research, Harvard Business School, 1987, pp. 15–17.

12. J. Barton Cunningham and Joe Lischeron, loc. cit.

13. Ronstadt, op. cit., pp. 21–22; and Stevenson and Sahlman, loc. cit.

14. Howard H. Stevenson and José Carlos Jarillo-Mossi, "Preserving Entrepreneurship as Companies Grow," *Journal of Business Strategy* (Summer 1986), p. 12.

15. Peter F. Drucker, *Managing for Results* (New York: Harper & Row, 1974), p. 45.

16. Peter F. Drucker, *Management, Tasks, Responsibilities, Practices* (New York: Harper & Row, 1974), p. 45.

17. Paul H. Wilken, *Entrepreneurship: A Comparative and Historical Study* (Norwood, N.J.: Ablex, 1979), p. 60.

18. Peter F. Drucker, *Innovation and Entrepreneurship* (New York: Harper & Row, 1986), p. 28.

19. Stevenson and Sahlman, loc. cit.

20. Brent Bowers and Jeffrey A. Tannenbaum, "More Important Than Money," *Wall Street Journal,* special section, (November 27, 1991), p. R6.

21. Birch, loc. cit.

22. George Gilder, "The Revitalization of Everything: The Law of the Microcosm," *Harvard Business Review* (March–April 1988), pp. 49–61; see also "Big vs. Small," *Time* (September 5, 1988), pp. 48–49.

23. "The Long Arm of Small Business," *Business Week* (February 29, 1988), pp. 62–66; and Christopher Knowlton, "The New Export Entrepreneur," *Fortune* (June 6, 1988), pp. 87–102.

24. Peter F. Drucker, "The Entrepreneurial Mystique," *Inc.* (October 1985), pp. 34–44. Peter Drucker indicates that the whole concept of an entrepreneurial mystique is largely a mistake. He views entrepreneurship as any other discipline, such as management, with no particular formula. In his opinion, it requires very hard work but it can be learned.

25. See John B. Hinge, loc. cit.; and Brent Bowers and Jeffrey A. Tannenbaum, loc. cit., for related statistics.

26. Ellen Graham, "The Entrepreneurial Mystique," *Wall Street Journal,* Special Report on Small Business (May 30, 1985), Section 3, pp. 1, 4, 6–7. Small businesses consist of 250 businesses with 20 or more employees and less than $50 million in sales. The entrepreneurs were 153 chief executives of companies identified by *Inc.,* as among the 500 fastest growing companies in America. The Fortune executive group consisted of 207 CEOs from the Fortune 500 list. Almost all respondents were male.

27. John A. Hornaday, "Research About Living Entrepreneurs," in Calvin A. Kent, Donald L. Sexton, and Karl H. Vesper, eds., *Encyclopedia of Entrepreneurship* (Englewood Cliffs, N.J.: Prentice-Hall, 1982), p. 28.

28. The traditional view holds that an innovation is simply the application of an invention. See, for example, Edward B. Roberts, "Managing Invention and Innovation," *Research Technology Management* (January–February 1988), pp. 1–19; and Jay R. Galbraith, "Designing the Innovative Organization," *Organizational Dynamics* (Winter 1982), pp. 5–15. I have added the requirement of significance.

29. For a discussion of this issue, see Rosabeth Moss Kanter, *The Change Masters* (New York: Simon & Schuster-Touchstone, 1983).

30. David Birth, *Job Creation Process* (Cambridge, Mass.: MIT Press, 1978); and Karl H. Vesper, *Entrepreneurship and National Policy* (Chicago: Heller Institute, 1983).

31. "Masters of Innovation," *Business Week* (April 10, 1989), pp. 58–63. This observation is based on the descriptions of characteristics of these firms contained in the article.

32. For a discussion of the relationship of these two topics, see Max Wortman, Jr., "A Unified Framework, Research Typologies, and Research Prospectuses for the Interface Between Entrepreneurship and Small Business," in Donald L. Saxton and Raymond M. Smilor, eds., *The Art and Science of Entrepreneurship* (Cambridge, Mass.: Ballinger, 1986), pp. 273–332.

33. For a discussion of the process, see William D. Bygrave and Charles W. Hofer, "Theorizing About Entrepreneurship," *Entrepreneurship: Theory & Practice* (Winter 1991), pp. 13–22.

34. U.S. Government Printing Office, "The State of Small Business: A Report to the President," Washington, D.C., 1985.

35. Ibid., based on a population of 14 million business firms; Ellen Graham, "The Entrepreneurial Mystique," *Wall Street Journal,* Special Report on Small Business (May 30, 1985), section 3, pp. 1, 4, 6–7.

36. Barbara Bird, "Implementing Entrepreneurial Ideas: The Case for Intention," *Academy of Management Review,* (July 1988), pp. 442–453. This first stage, as described, here takes its terminology from Larry Greiner, "Evolution and Revolution as Organizations Grow," *Harvard Business Review* (July–August 1972), pp. 37–46.

37. A number of software packages provide excellent guidance in creating business plans.

38. "Matters of Fact," *Inc.* (April 1985), p. 32.

39. William M. Bulkeley, "With New Planning Software, Entrepreneurs Act Like MBAs," *Wall Street Journal* (June 2, 1992), p. B1.

40. Greiner, loc. cit.

41. David C. McClelland, *The Achieving Society* (Princeton, N.J.: Van Nostrand, 1961); and J. W. Atkinson, *An Introduction to Motivation* (New York: American Book, 1964).

42. Joshua Hyatt, "No Way Out," *Inc.* (November 1991), pp. 78–92.

43. "Fact Sheet: The State of Small Business: A Report to the President," *SBA News,* (Washington, D.C.: U.S. Small Business Administration, 1984).

44. This is my conclusion after reading McClelland, loc. cit.; and Atkinson, loc. cit.

45. Michael E. Porter, *Competitive Strategy* (New York: Free Press, 1980); and William K. Hall, "Survival Strategies in a Hostile Environment," *Harvard Business Review* (September–October 1980), pp. 73–86.

46. Stevenson and Jarillo-Mossi, loc. cit.

47. William Tucker, "Campus Capitalists," *Success* (October 1985), pp. 42–49.

48. Barbara Marsh, "Contests Pit Student Entrepreneurs Against Each Other," *Wall Street Journal* (April 28, 1992), p. B2.

49. Paul Lim, "Some New Grads Turn Entrepreneur, Not Employee," *Wall Street Journal* (June 25, 1992), p. B7.

50. Irene Pave, "A Lot of Enterprises Are Staying in the Family These Days," *Business Week* (July 1, 1985), pp. 62–63.

51. Kenneth Labich, "The New Low-Risk Entrepreneurs," *Fortune* (July 27, 1992), pp. 84–92; Gale Bronson, "Hitting It Big by Going Out on Your Own," *U.S. News and World Report* (October 21, 1985), pp. 50–51.

52. Ibid.

53. Gale Bronson, loc. cit.

54. Ibid.
55. Tom Richman, "The Hottest Entrepreneur in America," *Inc.* (February 1987), p. 54; and Steven P. Galante, "Composition of Delegates Reveals Rise of Women in Small Business," *Wall Street Journal* (August 8, 1986), p. 25.
56. Ibid.
57. Sarah Harderty and Nehama Jacobs, *Success & Betrayal: The Crisis of Women in Corporate America* (New York: Touchstone Books, 1987).
58. "What Do Women Want? A Company They Can Call Their Own," *Business Week* (December 22, 1986), p. 61.
59. John H. Sheridan, "Russia's Entrepreneurs: Pioneering the New Economy," *Industry Week* (August 17, 1992), pp. 36–43.
60. "America's Hottest New Export," *U.S. News & World Report* (July 27, 1987), pp. 39–41; and "France Gets Set for a Capitalist Comeback," *Business Week* (March 31, 1986), pp. 42–43.
61. Jay Finnegan, "Britain's New Generation of Company Builders," *Inc.* (November 1988), pp. 93–100; and Victoria Schofield, "Leading the Change," *Success* (January–February 1989), p. 8.
62. Sophy Fearnby-Whittingstall, "Enterprising Entrepreneurs," *International Business* (July 1992), p. 24.
63. "America's Hottest New Export," op. cit., p. 41.
64. Brenton Schlender, "China Really Is on the Move," *Fortune* (October 5, 1992), pp. 114–123.
65. Gordon Pinchot, III, *Intrapreneuring* (New York: Perennial Library/Harper & Row, 1985), p. 67.
66. Thomas J. Peters and Robert H. Waterman, Jr., *In Search of Excellence* (New York: Harper & Row, 1982); and Gordon Pinchot, *Intrapreneuring* (New York: Harper & Row, 1985).
67. Richard J. Ferris, "Capturing Corporate Creativity," *United* (January 1987), p. 7; John Naisbitt, "Helping Companies Hatch Offspring," *Success* (May 1987), p. 14; and Colby H. Chyandler, "Eastman Kodak Opens Windows of Opportunity," *Journal of Business Strategy* (Summer 1986), pp. 5–8.
68. Thomas J. Peters, *Thriving on Chaos: Handbook for Management Evolution* (New York: Knopf, 1987), chap. 1.
69. Alvin Toffler, *Future Shock* (New York: Random House, 1970).
70. Michael Naylor, "General Motors: A 21st Century Corporation," presentation to the Academy of Management, August 14, 1986, Chicago, Ill.
71. Peters, op. cit., chaps. 1 and 5, section 3, pp. 191–280.
72. Kevin Kelly and Amy Duncan, "Sam Walton Chooses Chip Off the Old CEO," *Business Week* (February 15, 1988), p. 29.

CHAPTER 23

1. Stanley M. Cherkasky, "Total Quality for a Sustainable Competitive Advantage," *Quality* (August 1992), pp. Q4, Q6–Q7. (Contains a representative discussion.)
2. Stephen B. Shepard, editor-in-chief, *Business Week* "Defining the Q-Word," *The Quality Imperative, Business Week,* Special Issue (October 25, 1991), p. 4.
3. Richard Tanner Pascale, presentation to the Strategic Management Society, London, October 15, 1992.
4. Virtually all of the leading quality experts agree. This is the position taken by experts W. Edwards Deming, J. M. Juran, and Phil Crosby. Their efforts are explained in the next few paragraphs.
5. Peter F. Drucker, *The Practice of Management* (New York: Harper & Row, 1954).
6. Andrea Gabor, "The Leading Light of Qual-

ity," *U.S. News & World Report* (November 28, 1988), pp. 53–56.
7. Jeremy Main, "Under the Spell of the Quality Gurus," *Fortune* (August 18, 1986), pp. 30–34.
8. For example, see Otis Port, "Dueling Pioneers," *The Quality Imperative, Business Week,* Special Issue (October 25, 1991), p. 17.
9. J. M. Juran, *Juran on Quality by Design: The New Steps for Planning Quality into Goods and Services* (New York: Free Press, 1992), pp. 8, 9.
10. Ibid., p. 13.
11. Ibid., p. 15.
12. Ibid., p. 2.
13. Ibid., p. 15.
14. Ibid., p. 15.
15. Ibid., pp. 27–34.
16. Phil Crosby, *Quality Is Free* (New York: Mentor/Penguin, 1980), chaps. 1–2.
17. David A. Garvin, *Managing Quality* (New York: Free Press, 1988).
18. David A. Garvin, "Competing on Eight Dimensions of Quality," *Harvard Business Review* (November–December 1987), pp. 101–108.
19. Nicholas R. Aquino, "Constant Improvement: A Strategic Imperative," *Business & Economic Review* (July–September 1991), pp. 18–21.
20. Masaaki Imai, "Kaizen Wave Circles the Globe," *Tokyo Business Today* (May 1990), pp. 44–48.
21. For a recent book on the subject, see George D. Robson, *Continuous Process Improvement: Simplifying Work Flow Systems* (New York: Free Press, 1991).
22. Gilbert Fuchsberg, "Quality Programs Show Shoddy Results," *Wall Street Journal* (May 14, 1992), pp. B1, B7.
23. For a recent book on the subject, see Kathleen H. J. Leibfried and C. J. McNair, *Benchmarking: A Tool for Continuous Improvement* (New York: Harper Business, 1992).
24. Peter Drucker, "Japan: New Strategies for a New Reality," *Wall Street Journal* (October 2, 1991), p. A12.
25. "Management Focus: Future Perfect," *Economist* (January 4, 1992), p. 61.
26. Edward de Bono, "Quality Is No Longer Enough," *Journal for Quality and Participation* (September 1991), pp. 12–17.
27. William A. Sherdeen, "Gaining the Service Quality Advantage," *The Journal of Business Strategy* (March–April 1988), pp. 45–48.
28. Fuchsberg, "Total Quality Is Termed Only Partial Success," loc. cit.; Fuchsberg, "Quality Programs Show Shoddy Results," loc. cit.
29. Kevin Doyle, "Who's Killing Total Quality?" *Incentive* (August 1992), pp. 12–19.
30. Jay Mathews, "The Cost of Quality," *Newsweek* (September 7, 1992), p. 49.
31. Ibid.
32. Fuchsberg, both citations; Ibid., pp. 48–49; Doyle, loc. cit.
33. Fuchsberg, "Total Quality Is Termed Only Partial Success," op. cit., p. B7.
34. Ibid.
35. Doyle, loc. cit.; Kathleen A. Quinn, "Successfully Integrating Total Quality and Performance Appraisal," *Human Resources Professional* (Spring 1992), pp. 19–25.
36. Fuchsberg, both citations; Doyle, loc. cit.; Cherkasky, loc. cit.
37. Brian Usilaner and Michael Dulworth, "What's the Bottom Line: Payback for TQM," *Journal for Quality and Participation* (March 1992), pp. 82–90.
38. Gary M. Stern, "Quality Time: ISO 9000," *Sky* (May 1992), pp. 22–26; Beate Halligan, "ISO 9000 Standards Prepare You to Compete," *Industrial Distribution* (May 1992), p. 100.
39. Stern, op. cit., p. 23.
40. Stern, loc. cit.; J. C. Collier, "A Competitive Edge Through TQM," *Quality* (August 1992), pp. Q12–Q13.
41. David A. Collier, "Service Please: The Malcolm

Baldrige National Quality Award," *Business Horizons* (July–August 1992), pp. 88–95.
42. Regina Eisman, "Why It Pays to Lose the Baldrige Competition," *Incentive* (April 1991), pp. 33–42, 98; Jeremy Main, "How to Win the Baldrige Award," *Fortune* (April 23, 1990), pp. 101–116.
43. Main, op. cit., p. 108.
44. For example, see William P. Hewlett (chairman and co-founder of Hewlett-Packard), "Graduation Speech," as reported in Helen Pike, "Hewlett Sounds Call for Engineering Creativity in MIT Graduate Speech," *Electronic Engineering Times* (June 23, 1986), p. 78; John Sculley (CEO and chairman of Apple Computer), "Speech to MacWorld," February 1988, in which he indicated that only the innovative firm would survive in the future; Jack Welch (CEO and chairman of GE), who sees innovation driving productivity, which drives competition, as quoted in Thomas A. Stewart, "GE Keeps Those Ideas Coming," *Fortune* (August 12, 1991), pp. 41–49; Michael E. Porter (researcher and consultant), *The Competitive Advantage of Nations* (New York: Free Press, 1990), pp. 578–579, in which he observes that innovation, continuous improvement, and change management are the cornerstones of global competitiveness; Michael E. Porter, *Competitive Strategy* (New York: Free Press, 1980), pp. 177–179, in which he discusses the criticality of innovation to competitiveness; Richard N. Foster (consultant), *Innovation: The Attacker's Advantage* (New York: Summit, 1986), p. 21, in which he indicates that in his thirty years at McKinsey & Company, every successful firm he saw was innovative; and Thomas J. Peters (consultant and researcher), *Thriving on Chaos: Handbook for a Management Revolution* (New York: Knopf, 1987), pp. 191–280, in which he indicates that innovation is one of five prescriptions for chaos (accelerating change, complex environment, global competition, and other challenges). *Business Week* considered the topic of innovation so critical to U.S. competitiveness, it devoted two special issues to it, in June 1989 and 1990.
45. For a different, but similar discussion, see Simon Majaro, *The Creative Gap* (London: Longman, 1988), pp. 2–11.
46. John G. Young, "What Is Creativity?" *The Journal of Creative Behavior,* vol. 19, no. 2, 2nd Quarter, pp. 77–87.
47. James M. Higgins, *101 Creative Problem Solving Techniques: The Handbook of New Ideas* (Winter Park, Fla: The New Management Publishing Company, 1993), chap. 1.
48. "Chester Carlson—Xerography," Xerox Internal Documents; "A Profile in Entrepreneurship," a special advertising session, *Inc.* (July 1988), pp. 109–110.
49. Victor Kiam, speech to the Roy E. Crummer Graduate School of Business, Rollins College, Winter Park, Florida, October 1985; Judith Stone, "Velcro: The Final Frontier," *Discover* (May 1988), pp. 82–84.
50. Higgins, loc. cit.
51. Ray Statta, "Organizational Learning—The Key to Management Innovation," *Sloan Management Review* (Spring 1989), pp. 63–74; Michael Porter, *Competitive Strategy* (New York: Free Press, 1980), pp. 177–178.
52. Richard Foster, *Innovation: The Attacker's Advantage* (New York: Summit, 1986); Thomas J. Peters, loc. cit.
53. Kornelius Kraft, "Are Product and Process Innovation Independent of Each Other?" *Applied Economics* (August 1990), pp. 1029–1038.
54. Marilyn L. Taylor and Kenneth Beck, "Marion Laboratories, Inc.," in James M. Higgins and Julian W. Vincze, eds., *Strategic Management: Text and Cases,* 4th ed. (Hinsdale, Ill.: Dryden, 1989), p. 522.

55. Barbara Buell, "Japan: A Shopping Spree in the U.S." *Business Week* (June 15, 1990), pp. 86–87; Otis Port, "The Global Race: Why the U.S. Is Losing Its Lead," *Business Week* (June 15, 1990), pp. 32–39.

56. Carla Rapoport, "Why Japan Keeps on Winning," *Fortune* (July 15, 1991), p. 76.

57. Robert Buderi, "The Brakes Go On in R&D," *Business Week* (July 1, 1991), pp. 24–26; Frederick Shaw Myers, "Japan Pushes the 'R' in R&D," *Chemical Engineering* (February 1990), pp. 30–33; Bruce C. P. Rayner, "The Rising Price of Technological Leadership," *Electronic Business* (March 18, 1991), pp. 52–56; Fumiaki Kitamura, "Japan's R&D Budget Second Largest in World," *Business Japan* (November 1990), pp. 35–47.

58. Buderi, op. cit., table, p. 26, for Cypress Semiconductors; and Merck Corporation, *Annual Report, 1990* (Rahway, N.J.: Merck Corporation, 1990), for Merck percentages.

59. Charles W. L. Hill, Michael A. Hitt, and Robert E. Hoskisson, "Declining U.S. Competitiveness: Reflections on a Crisis," *Academy of Management Executive* (January 1988), pp. 51–60; Robert H. Hayes and William J. Abernathy, "Managing Our Way to Economic Decline," *Harvard Business Review* (July–August 1980), pp. 67–77.

60. For a discussion of these issues, including relative amounts spent on the two types of R&D, see Ralph E. Gomory, "For the 'Ladder of Science' to the Product Development Cycle," *Harvard Business Review* (November–December 1989), pp. 99–105.

61. Marie-Louise Carawatti, "Why the United States Must Do More Process R&D," *Research-Technology Management* (September–October 1992), pp. 8–9.

62. Kraft, loc. cit.

63. Foster, op. cit., p. 21.

64. See ibid., chaps. 6 and 8.

65. Michael K. Badawy, "Technology and Strategic Advantage: Managing Corporate Technology Transfer in the USA and Japan," *International Journal of Technology Management* (1991), pp. 205–215.

66. Michael Czinkota and Masaaki Kotabe, "Product Development the Japanese Way," *Journal of Business Strategy* (November–December 1990), pp. 31–36.

67. Drucker, loc. cit.

68. Dean M. Schroeder and Alan G. Robinson, "America's Most Successful Export to Japan: Continuous Improvement Programs," *Sloan Management Review* (Spring 1991), pp. 67–81.

69. Roy Amara, "New Directions for Innovation," *Futures* (March 1990), pp. 142–152.

70. For a discussion, see James M. Higgins and Julian Vincze, "The Challenges Facing General Motors in 1992," *Strategic Management Text and Cases*, 5th ed., (Ft. Worth, Tex.: Dryden, 1993), pp. 30–54.

71. James B. Treece, "Can Ford Stay on Top?" *Business Week* (September 28, 1987), pp. 78–86.

72. Thomas J. Peters and Robert H. Waterman Jr., *In Search of Excellence* (New York: Harper & Row, 1982), p. 14.

73. P. Ranganath Nayok and John M. Ketteringham, *Breakthroughs* (New York: Rawson Associates, distributed by Scribner's, 1986).

74. Briane Dumaine, "Closing the Innovation Gap," *Fortune* (December 2, 1991), p. 58.

75. C. Merle Crawford, "The Dual-Drive Concept of Product Innovation," *Business Horizons* (May–June 1991), pp. 32–38.

76. Peters, op. cit., pp. 195–208; "What Makes Yoshio Invent?" *Economist* (January 12, 1991), p. 61.

77. Rolf C. Smith, Jr., and Raymond A. Slesinski, "Continuous Innovation," *Executive Excellence* (May 1991), pp. 13–14.

78. Robert S. Roy, "A Winning Approach," *Executive Excellence* (May 1992), pp. 16–17; John Teresko, "America's Best Plants: Cadillac," *Industry Week* (October 21, 1991), pp. 29, 32.

79. Neil Gross, "Japan: Hustling to Catch Up in Science, The R&D Elite," *Business Week* (June 15, 1990), pp. 72–82, 114–115.

80. Edwin Mansfield, "Technological Creativity: Japan and the United States," *Business Horizons* (March–April 1989), pp. 48–53.

81. Port, loc. cit.

82. Dumaine, loc. cit.

83. "What Makes Yoshio Invent," loc. cit.

Organization Index

Wells Fargo, 203
Wendy's, 229, 313, 545
Western Electric Company, 54–57
Westhaven Services Company, 797
Westin Kauai, 464

Westinghouse, 254, 375, 390, 395, 632–633, 643, 698
Weyerhaeuser, 297
Whirlpool, 514, 515, 772
Whole Foods Market, 643

Winn-Dixie, 670

Xerox Corporation, 22, 182, 254, 361, 445, 461, 463, 470, 581, 595, 597, 633, 662, 701, 772, 821, 823, 830

Name Index

Subject Index

and systems approach, 60
and technology, 407
see also Exxon Valdez oil spill
Natural work units, 402
Nature of Managerial Work, The
    (Mintzberg), 11, 12
Needs, 502–503, 505–512
    achievement, 509–511
    Alderfer's theory, 506–507, 512, 515
    expectancy-instrumentality theory, 517–
        520
    and groups, 546
    Maslow's hierarchy, 503, 505–506, 512,
        515, 516, 584–585
    motivation/hygiene model, 514–516
    satisfying, 512–514
    survey, 537
Negative reinforcement, 525
Negotiation, 10, 488, 630
Netherlands, 98, 103, 396
Network organizations, 341, 361–362
New entrants, 159
New management, 70
New Zealand, 103
Noise, 623–624
Nominal groups, 132
Nonmonetary resource unit budget, 701
Nonverbal communication, 627, 629–634
Norms, 464, 555–556
North American Free Trade Agreement, 92
Not-for-profit organizations, 16, 22–23
Notebook computers, 734

Objectives, 211–214, 512, 522, 545–546
    see also Management by objectives
OBM. *See* Organizational behavior
    modification
Occupational Health and Safety Act
    (OSHA), 446
OD. *See* Organizational development
Office automation, 406
    see also Automation; Information
        processing; Technology
Offshore moves, 79, 174–175, 228, 355,
    434, 748, 766–767
Ohio State studies, 585
Ombudsmen, 182, 639
Open-door policies, 639
Operating budget, 685
Operating plans, 200–201
Operational controls, 672–673, 706
Operations management, 748–779
    case studies, 748, 781
    day-to-day, 773–776
    and decision making, 752–753
    definition of, 750–752
    facilities, 760–764
    and factory of the future, 777–778
    focused factories, 757
    inventory control, 769–772
    materials requirement planning, 772–773
    offshore moves, 766–767
    outsourcing, 766
    and problem solving, 771–772, 779
    product/service design, 758–759
    production planning systems, 768–769
    production technology, 764–766
    productivity management, 778–779
    resource allocation, 759–760
    strategic decisions, 755–767
    strategic importance of, 753–755
    system positioning, 756
    tactical decisions, 767–773
    and total quality management, 767
    work force management, 766

Operations managers, 750
Operations research (OR), 57, 267
    see also Management science
Opportunities, 204
    see also SWOT analysis
Optimization analysis, 297–298
OR. *See* Operations research
Oral communication, 625, 627–629
Organic structure, 163, 358–359, 372
Organization chart, 314–316
Organizational behavior modification
    (OBM), 523–529
Organizational climate, 477–480
Organizational culture, 4, 192, 461–473
    artifacts of, 462–464, 465, 662
    case studies, 460, 492
    and control, 743–744
    and creative problem solving, 188, 467
    definition of, 461–462
    and groups, 547
    and human resource management, 453
    and innovation, 143
    and management levels, 17
    multiple, 472–473
    organizational climate, 477–480
    and planning, 208
    and problem solving, 489, 490
    and shared values, 468–473
    socialization, 469–472
    and strategic management, 245, 255–
        256, 464, 466–468
    training in, 40
    see also Cultural diversity; Environment
Organizational design, 352–378
    case studies, 352, 380
    choice of structure, 375, 377
    definition of, 354
    differentiation, 366–367
    and geographic dispersion, 374–375
    and global environment, 356–357, 362,
        374–375
    and growth, 367–369
    hollow corporation, 362, 364
    and management philosophy, 369–372
    mechanistic vs. organic, 357–359
    and problem solving, 376–378
    and strategic management, 355–367, 375
    and technology, 372–374, 375
    vertical vs. horizontal, 359–362, 363
    virtual corporations, 364, 366
    see also Organizational structure;
        Organizing
Organizational development (OD), 453,
    483–485, 588–589
Organizational ethics, 169
Organizational learning, 233, 607–608
Organizational purpose, 209–214
Organizational structure, 310–346
    administration and organization
        approach, 50
    case studies, 310, 348
    contingency approach, 62
    coordination, 312, 332–337
    definitions of, 311–312
    delegation of authority, 312, 316–322
    departmentation, 322–332
    division of labor, 312–316
    and employee participation, 318–320
    and entrepreneurship, 797
    flat vs. tall, 332
    and groups, 547
    informal structures, 312, 343
    Japanese management practices, 96
    and joint ventures, 340–341
    matrix structures, 339–340, 341

multidomestic organizations, 356–357
network organizations, 341
and problem solving, 342–346
project structure, 337
and strategic management, 254, 255, 354
systems approach, 62
and technology, 406
    see also Authority; Organizational
        design; Organizing
Organizations
    definitions of, 5, 312
    for-profit vs. not-for-profit, 16, 22–23
    informal, 52
    and information processing, 738
    mechanistic vs. organic, 163
    Weber's theories, 51
    see also specific topics
Organizing, 8, 33
    definition of, 311
    and entrepreneurship, 797
    future assumptions, 124
    and global environment, 100
    and management levels, 20–21
    see also Organizational structure
Orientation, 443
Origination, 828
OSHA. *See* Occupational Health and Safety
    Act
Outputs, 722, 752
Outsourcing, 766

Pacific Rim countries, 82, 85, 106, 804
    operations management, 749–750, 758
    total quality management, 825
    see also specific countries
PACs. *See* Political action committees
Pakistan, 103
Palmtop computers, 734
Paralanguage, 625
Parallel processing, 729–730
Parallel teams. *See* Cross-functional work
    groups
Parity principle, 318
Part-time employees, 410, 428
Participative leadership, 592, 593
Participative management. *See* Employee
    participation
Passion for Excellence (Peters & Austin),
    67
Passive recruitment, 432–433
Path-goal theory of leadership, 591–593
PCs. *See* Computer software; Information
    processing
People of color. *See* Minorities
Perception, 624–625
Perceptual set, 624
Performance, 502
    appraisals, 448–449, 471, 528, 685, 703–
        704
    measurement, 656, 743
    standards, 655–656, 659
    see also Employee motivation/
        performance
Permissive autocrat, 596
Permissive democrat, 596
Personal appearance, 634
Personal creativity, 831, 832
Personal ethics, 169
Personality, 636
Personality tests, 439–440
PERT. *See* Program evaluation and review
    technique
Philanthropic responsibilities, 169, 171
Philippines, 103
Physical environment, 55

Photo Credits

CHAPTER 1

Page 2: Wayne Eastep/Stock Market; page 5: John Abbott/John Abbott; page 15: Michael L. Abramson/Woodfin Camp & Assoc.; page 18: Gabe Palmer/Stock Market (top), Janet Century (center), William Strode/Woodfin Camp & Assoc. (bottom); page 21: Andy Freeberg; page 23: Jimmy Rudnick/Stock Market; page 32: Alex Quesada/Matrix.

CHAPTER 2

Page 38: Brown Brothers; page 41: Courtesy of Met Life; page 43: Bill Armstrong/Gamma-Liaison; page 46: The Bettmann Archive (left), The Bettmann Archive (bottom), Culver Photos (right); page 46: Engraving by Kay/The Bettmann Archive; page 53: Courtesy of AT&T Archives; page 55: Brown Brothers; page 56: Courtesy of AT&T; page 59: Courtesy of Berlitz; page 65: SPIA Press/R. Wallis.

CHAPTER 3

Page 76: Courtesy of Joe Stewardson; page 79: Alexandra Avakian/Woodfin Camp & Assoc.; page 87: R. Wallis/SIPA Press; page 91: Bill Swersey/Gamma-Liaison; page 95: Greg Girard/Contact Press Images; page 99: Patrick Frilet/SIPA Press (top), Greg Davis/Courtesy of KFC (center), J.B. Diederich/Contact Press Images (bottom); page 105: J. Kuus/SIPA Press; page 108: Mark Richards/DOT Pictures.

CHAPTER 4

Page 112: Tom Lulevitch/Research Associate, R. D. Wolfe; page 118: John Madere/Stock Market; page 122: Ken Kerbs/DOT Pictur DOT Pictures; page 125: Courtesy GM Saturn (top), John Abbott (bottom), John Colletti/Stock Bd Stock Boston (center); page 131: Ken Krebs/DOT Pictures; page 138: Karen Kasmauski/Woodfin Camp & Associates; page 142: Mitch Kezar; page 144: Milliken Co./Courtesy of Milliken Co.

CHAPTER 5

Page 150: Jeffrey D. Smith; page 153: Impact Visuals; page 158: Ken Kerbs/DOT Pictures; page 162: Photo Researchers; page 167: Contact Press; page 172: Courtesy of Pacific Bell; page 177: Sygma (top left), Contact Press (top right), Sipa Press (bottom), Sipa Press (center left); page 180: Mark Rosenthal/Fortune.

CHAPTER 6

Page 190: Susan Lapides; page 193: Andy Freeberg; page 199: John Abbott; page 202: Peter Yates; page 203: John Abbott; page 207: Robert Holmgren; page 211: Courtesy of Lexmark Int'l.; page 213: Robert Holmgren; page 215: Brownie Harris/The Stock Market (top), Bruce Ayres/Tony Stone (center), Bruce Ayres/Tony Stone (bottom); page 218: Andy Freeberg/Andy Freeberg Photography.

CHAPTER 7

Page 226: Karen Kasmauski/Matrix; page 230: Courtesy of Baldor; page 232: Peter Yates; page 235: Jim Knowles/Picture Group; page 237: Karen Kasmauski/Matrix; page 241: Andy Freeberg (bottom), Photofest (center left), Kenneth Jarecke/Contact Press Images (top), Greg Davis/The Stock Market (center right); page 247: Courtesy of Anheuser-Busch (left), Courtesy of KFC (right); page 251: Robert Holmgren; page 255: Courtesy of Ford Motor Co.

CHAPTER 8

Page 264: Bruce Ayres/Tony Stone Worldwide; page 267: Robert Reichert; page 272: Courtesy of IBM; page 276: Karen Kasmauski/Matrix; page 279: Courtesy of U.S. Personnel Management; page 280: Courtesy of IBM; page 283: Courtesy of IBM (top), Ed Wheeler/The Stock Market (center), Jon Feingersh/The Stock Market (bottom); page 284: Sepp Seitz/Woodfin Camp & Assoc.; page 288: Guy Gillette/Photo Researchers; page 292: Michael L. Abramson/Woodfin Camp & Assoc.; page 294: Fred Ward/Black Star; page 296: Courtesy of Thompson Financial Services.

CHAPTER 9

Page 308: Ken Kerbs/DOT Pictures; page 311: Ronnie Kaufman/The Stock Market; page 313: Janice Rubin/Black Star; page 317: Donald Miller/Monkmeyer Press; page 321: Robert Holmgren; page 325: Gabe Palmer/The Stock Market (top), Sittler/SABA Press (center), Janet Century (bottom); page 331: Janet Century; page 334: H. Laing/Black Star; page 336: Courtesy of Herman Miller; page 338: Ken Kerbs/DOT Pictures; page 345: Peter Arnold, Inc.; page 346: P. Perrin/SYGMA.

CHAPTER 10

Page 350: Courtesy of IBM; page 353: John Abbott (left), John Abbott (right); page 356: Robert Reichert; page 361: Sibbald; page 365: Roy Inman/Roy Inman Photography (top), Glasheen Graphics (center), John Abbott (bottom); page 366: Courtesy of Corning; page 367: Michael Abramson/Courtesy of 3M, Inc.; page 370: James Schnepe/Gamma-Liaison (left), John Abbott (center), John Abbott (right); page 375: Courtesy of IBM; page 378: Robert Holmgren.

CHAPTER 11

Page 382: R. Bossu/SYGMA; page 385: Courtesy of Volvo; page 389: Janet Century; page 390: Robert Holmgren/Peter Arnold, Inc.; page 391: Kevin Cruff; page 394: Courtesy of Thompson Consumer Electronics; page 395: Dan Ford Connolly/Picture Group; page 399: Karen Kasmauski/Matrix (bottom), Ken Kerbs/DOT Pictures (center left), Gabe Palmer/The Stock Market (center right), Ken Kerbs (top); page 405: Courtesy of GMFanuc Robotics Corp.; page 407: Ken Kerbs.